British Rail

1974–97

From Integration to Privatisation

British Rail

1974–97

From Integration to Privatisation

Terry Gourvish

Research by
Mike Anson

This book has been printed digitally and produced in a standard specification
in order to ensure its continuing availability

OXFORD
UNIVERSITY PRESS

Great Clarendon Street, Oxford OX2 6DP

Oxford University Press is a department of the University of Oxford.
It furthers the University's objective of excellence in research, scholarship,
and education by publishing worldwide in

Oxford New York

Auckland Cape Town Dar es Salaam Hong Kong Karachi
Kuala Lumpur Madrid Melbourne Mexico City Nairobi
New Delhi Shanghai Taipei Toronto
With offices in
Argentina Austria Brazil Chile Czech Republic France Greece
Guatemala Hungary Italy Japan South Korea Poland Portugal
Singapore Switzerland Thailand Turkey Ukraine Vietnam

Oxford is a registered trade mark of Oxford University Press
in the UK and in certain other countries

Published in the United States
by Oxford University Press Inc., New York

ISBN 0-19-926909-2

Antony Rowe Ltd., Eastbourne

Contents

Part 1 *Railways under Labour, 1974–9*

Contents

Part 2 *The Thatcher Revolution?*
British Rail in the 1980s

Part 3 *On the Threshold of Privatisation:*
Running the Railways, 1990–4

Contents

Part 4 *Responding to Privatisation, 1981–97*

Appendices

List of Illustrations

Cartoons

Plates

Between pages 258–259 and 418–419

List of Illustrations

List of Figures

List of Tables

List of Tables

Appendix tables

Acknowledgements

The author and the publishers wish to thank the following for kind permission to reproduce material.

Cartoons

Steve Bell and the *Guardian* for cartoons 4, 12, and 13; the Editor of *Modern Railways* for cartoon 5; Nicholas Garland and the *Daily Telegraph* for cartoon 6; Kevin Kallaugher and Cartoonists & Writers Syndicate for cartoon 3; John Kent and News International for cartoon 10; Stan McMurtry (mac), the *Daily Mail*, and Atlantic Syndication for cartoons 1 and 11; Jane Newton and the Centre for the Study of Cartoons and Caricature at the University of Kent, for locating and providing prints for cartoons 1, 2, 3, and 6; *Private Eye* magazine for its covers, reproduced as cartoons 8 and 9; the Press Association for cartoon 8; Keith Waite and the *Daily Mirror* for cartoon 2; Richard Wilson and News International for cartoon 7.

Figures

Department of Transport, Local Government and the Regions for Figures 5.2, 5.3, 5.4, and 9.3.

Plates

British Railways Board (Residuary) for plates 1–3, 4a, 8–13, 16–19, 25–7, 37, 39a and 39b, 40, 46–50, 53, and 56–60; Ken Burrage for plate 54; Jim Collins for plate 14; English Welsh & Scottish Railway for plate 62; Roger Ford for plate 4b; Derrick Fullick for plate 20; John Glover for plates 5, 21, and 33; Milepost 92½ for plates 28, 30, 32, 36, and 42–3; Brian Morrison for plates 15, 23, 29, 31, 34–5, 38, 44–5, and 55; Les Nixon for plate 7; Leslie Smith for plate 22; John Tidmarsh for plate 41; John Vaughan for plate 6; Virgin Trains for plate 61; John Walton for plate 24; and Westinghouse Rail Systems for plates 51–2.

Tables

President and Fellows of Harvard College and *Business History Review* for Table 7.1.

List of Interviewees

1. 1987–92

David Allen
Sir Peter Baldwin (DTp)
Cyril Bleasdale
Gerry Burt
Michael Bosworth
Michael Casey
Robin Corbett
James Cornell
Robert Dashwood
Derek Fowler

John Holroyd
John Hooker
Peter Land
Len Merryweather
Geoffrey Myers
John Palette
Frank Paterson
John Palmer
Sir Peter Parker

Sir Robert Reid (Bob
    Reid I)
Sir David Serpell
Gavin Simpson
Malcolm Southgate
Dr Robert Sparrow
Roger Temple
Dr Alan Wickens
Glyn Williams

2. 1997–2001

Lew Adams (ASLEF)
David Blake
Lord Bradshaw
Ian Brown
Brian Burdsall
Ken Burrage
Will Camp
Jim Collins (Railtrack)
James Cornell
Stewart Currie
Ian Hay Davison
    (Charterail)
Colin Driver
Richard Edgely
John Edmonds
Roger Ford (MR)
Sir Norman Fowler
    (Sec of State)

Roger Freeman
    (Min of PT)
Derrick Fullick (ASLEF)
Alastair Gilchrist
Prof Stephen Glaister
    (Imperial College)
Richard Goldson
Chris Green
Laurie Harries (RMT)
Prof John Heath (London
    Business School)
Roger Hillard
Maurice Holmes
Richard Hope (RGI)
Gil Howarth
David Howell
    (Sec of State)
Simon Jenkins

James Jerram
Alan Jones (BTOG)
Stephen Joseph (T2000)
Kazia Kantor
Lord Kelvedon
    (Sec of State)
David Kirby
James Knapp (RMT)
Prudence Leith
Leslie Lloyd
Lord McCarthy (RSNT)
John MacGregor
    (Sec of State)
David McKenna
Alec McTavish
John Mayfield
Sir David Mitchell
    (Min of PT)

John Nelson
Alan Nichols
James O'Brien
Sir Peter Parker
Lord Parkinson
  (Sec of State)
Dr Andrew Pendleton
  (MMU)
Lord Peyton
  (Sec of State)
Dr John Prideaux

David Rayner
Sir Robert Reid (Bob
  Reid II)
Lord Rogers
  (Sec of State)
Richard Rosser (TSSA)
Henry Sanderson
Leslie Smith
Chris Stokes
Trevor Toolan
James Urquhart

Sir Alan Walters
Ivor Warburton
Paul Watkinson
Dr Peter Watson
John Welsby
Richard Wilcox
Philip Wood (DTp)
Christian Wolmar
  (journalist)
Sir George Young
  (Sec of State)

Note: All interviewees are BRB unless stated otherwise.

Abbreviations and Acronyms

AAD	Annual Assembly of Delegates [ASLEF]
ACAS	Advisory, Conciliation, and Arbitration Service
ACI	Allied Continental Intermodal
AEEU	Amalgamated Engineering and Electrical Union
ALARP	As Low As Reasonably Practicable
APEX	Advance Purchase Excursion
APT	Advanced Passenger Train
APTIS	All Purpose Ticket Issuing System
ARC	Automatic Revenue Collection
ARS	Automatic Route Setting
ASI	Adam Smith Institute
ASLEF	Associated Society of Locomotive Engineers and Firemen
ATP	Automatic Train Protection
AVI	Automatic Vehicle Identification
AWG	Access Working Group
AWS	Automatic Warning System
AXIS	Accounting and Expenditure Information System
BAA	British Airports Authority
BEG	Business Engineering Group
BL	British Leyland
BLPES	British Library of Political and Economic Science
BP	British Petroleum
BR	British Rail
BRB	British Railways Board
BREL	British Rail Engineering Ltd
BRG	Business Review Group
BRIL	British Rail Investments Ltd
BRIMS	British Rail Incident Monitoring System
BRIS	British Rail Infrastructure Services
BRJCC	British Railways Joint Consultative Council
BRMG	British Rail Maintenance Group
BRML	British Rail Maintenance Ltd
BRPB	British Rail Property Board
BRPS	British Rail Pension Scheme

BRT	BR Telecommunications
BSC	British Steel Corporation
BTA	British Transport Advertising
BTH	British Transport Hotels
BTOG	British Transport Officers' Guild
BTP	British Transport Police
BTR1	Boat Train Route (Folkestone–Chislehurst)
C&D	Collection and Delivery
C&W	Cable and Wireless
CAPRI	Computer Analysis of Passenger Revenue Information
CBI	Confederation of British Industry
CCA	Current Cost Accounting
CE	Civil Engineering
CEGB	Central Electricity Generating Board
CEM	Cost-effective Maintenance
CEO	Chief Executive Officer
CER	Community of European Railways
CIG	Charging Implementation Group
CIT	Chartered Institute of Transport
CM&EE	Chief Mechanical & Electrical Engineer
CPRS	Central Policy Review Staff
CPS	Centre for Policy Studies
CRUCC	Central Rail Users' Consultative Committee
CS&EU	Confederation of Shipbuilding and Engineering Unions
CSG	Chairmen's Special Group on Privatisation
CSR	Cab Secure Radio
CT	Channel Tunnel
CTCC	Central Transport Consultative Committee
CTHST	Channel Tunnel High Speed Train
CTIC	Channel Tunnel Investment Committee
CTJCC	Channel Tunnel Joint Consultative Committee
CTL	Combined Transport Limited
CWR	Continuous Welded Rail
DETR	Department of the Environment, Transport and the Regions
DIADS	Diagram Input and Distribution System
DMU	Diesel Multiple Unit
DOE	Department of the Environment
DOO	Driver-Only Operation
DTI	Department of Trade and Industry
DTp	Department of Transport
DTS	Dynamic Track Stabiliser
EC	European Community
ECML	East Coast Main Line

Abbreviations and Acronyms

ED	Executive Director
EDC	Executive Directors' Conference
EEC	European Economic Community
EFL	External Financing Limit
EMI	Electrical and Musical Industries
EMU	Electric Multiple Unit
EPS	European Passenger Services Ltd
ER	Eastern Region
ERDF	European Regional Development Fund
EWS	English, Welsh and Scottish Railway
F&P	Finance & Planning (BRB)
FABS	Freight Accounting Business System
FIG	Mr Freeman's Implementation Group
FORWARD	FORecasting With Accurate Reliable Data
FOU	Freight Operating Unit
FR	Finance Registry (BRB)
FRS	Financial Reporting Standard
FWG	Franchising Working Group
GDP	Gross Domestic Product
GEC	General Electric Company
GIC	Group Investment Controller
GLC	Greater London Council
GM	General Manager
GN	Great Northern
HC	House of Commons
HSE	Health and Safety Executive
HST	High-Speed Train
IC	InterCity/Inter-City
ICF	Intercontainer-Inter frigo
ICI	Imperial Chemical Industries
ICL	International Computers Ltd
ICOBS	InterCity On-board Services
IEA	Institute of Economic Affairs
IECC	Integrated Electronic Control Centre
IFR	Investment and Financing Review
ILSS	Interactive Lineside Safety System
ILWS	Inductive Loop Warning System
IMU	Infrastructure Maintenance Unit
IPG	International Project Group
IR	Industrial Relations
ISRS	International Safety Rating System
ISU	Infrastructure Service Unit
IT	Information Technology

JIS	Joint Industry Scheme
JMD	Joint Managing Director
L&SE	London & South-East
LMR	London Midland Region
LOVERS	LOcal VEhicle Records System
LRT	London Regional Transport
LSE	London School of Economics
LT	London Transport
LTS	London Tilbury & Southend
M&EE	Mechanical & Electrical Engineering
M&M	Manufacturing and Maintenance
MBO	Management Buyout
MD	Managing Director
MEAV	Modern Equivalent Asset Value
MEBO	Management and Employee Buyout
MGR	Merry-Go-Round
MISP	Management Information Period Staff Position
MMC	Monopolies and Mergers Commission
MMU	Manchester Metropolitan University
MR	Modern Railways
MRC	Modern Records Centre
NAAFI	Navy, Army and Air Force Institutes
NAO	National Audit Office
NBRG	New Build and Repair Group
NCB	National Coal Board
NEDC	National Economic Development Council
NERA	National Economic Research Associates
NFC	National Freight Corporation
NICG	Nationalised Industries Chairmen's Group
NPV	Net Present Value
NRN	National Radio Network
NSE	Network SouthEast
NSKT	No Signalman Key Token
NUM	National Union of Mineworkers
NUPE	National Union of Public Employees
NUR	National Union of Railwaymen
OCRE	Overhead Cost Review Exercise
OfQ	Organising for Quality
OFT	Office of Fair Trading
OGAS	Other Grant-Aided Services
OIG	Objectives, Instructions and Guidance
OPRAF	Office of Passenger Rail Franchising
OPS	Other Provincial Services

Abbreviations and Acronyms

OR	Operational Research
ORR	Office of the Rail Regulator
OTMR	On Train Monitoring Recorder
PARIS	Parcels Accounting and Revenue Information System
PBSS	Passenger Business Strategy Study
PHIS	Passenger Historic Information System
PIG	Privatisation Issues Group
PMG	Production Management Group
PMM	Peat Marwick Mitchell
P&MM	Procurement and Materials Management
PMS	Passenger Marketing Services
POIS	Passenger Operations Information System
PORTIS	Portable Ticket Issuing System
PP&CCA	Profit Planning and Cost Centre Analysis
PR&P	Public Relations and Publicity
PRI	Privatisation Papers (BRB)
PRO	Public Record Office
PSBR	Public Sector Borrowing Requirement
PSO	Public Service Obligation
PSR	Passenger Service Requirement
PT	Public Transport
PTA	Passenger Transport Authority
PTE	Passenger Transport Executive
PT&R	Promotion, Transfer, and Redundancy
PVC	Price Variation Clause
R&A	Report and Accounts
R&D	Research and Development
RAVERS	RAil Vehicle Records System
RAWG	Regulation and Access Working Group
RDG	Railway Directing Group
RE	Railway Executive
REG	Railway Executive Group
RER	Réseau Express Régional
RETB	Radio Electronic Token Block
RfD	Railfreight Distribution
RGI	Railway Gazette International
RMG	Railway Management Group
RMT	National Union of Rail, Maritime and Transport Workers
ROCE	Return on Capital Employed
ROSCO	Rolling Stock Leasing Company
RPI	Retail Price Index
RPS	Railways Pension Scheme
RR	Regional Railways

RRE	Renewals and Refurbishment Element
RRR	Required Rate of Return
RSJC	Railway Staff Joint Council
RSNC	Railway Staff National Council
RSNT	Railway Staff National Tribunal
RSWG	Rolling Stock Working Group
RUCC	Rail Users' Consultative Committee
S&T	Signal and Telecommunications
S&TE	Signal and Telecommunications Engineering
SAU	Self-Accounting Unit
SCNI	Select Committee on Nationalised Industries
ScR	Scottish Region
SD	Sector Director, Safety Directorate
SDA	Scottish Development Agency
SJC	Special Joint Committee
SNCF	Société Nationale des Chemins de Fer Français
SO	Senior Officer
SoS	Secretary of State
SPAD	Signal Passed At Danger
SPAMS	Sector Performance Accounting Monitoring System
SR	Southern Region
SRA	Strategic Rail Authority
SSI	Solid State Interlocking
TARDIS	TOPS Ancillary Retrospective Data Information System
TEA	Train crew Expenditure Analysis
TESCO	Train Engineeering Service Unit
TGV	Train à Grande Vitesse
TGWU	Transport and General Workers' Union
TMSTG	TransManche Super Train Group
TLF	Trainload Freight
TOC	Train Operating Company
TOPS	Total Operations Processing System
TOU	Train Operating Unit
TQM	Total Quality Management
TRU	Track Renewal Unit
TRUST	Train Running System TOPS
TSGB	Transport Statistics Great Britain
TSSA	Transport Salaried Staffs' Association
TUC	Trades Union Congress
TUCC	Transport Users' Consultative Committee
UCS	Upper Clyde Shipbuilders
WCML	West Coast Main Line
WR	Western Region

Preface

When, in 1986, I completed a book on the first 25 years of British Rail, I little suspected that I would be chained to the engine for the next 15 years. That volume, *British Railways 1948–73: A Business History*, was commissioned by the British Railways Board and published by Cambridge University Press. Dealing with the first 25 years of nationalisation, 1948–73, it contained some trenchant comments, both about the quality and effectiveness of railway management, and about the defects of the relationship with government. But as the then chairman of British Rail, Sir Robert Reid (Bob Reid I), told me, British Rail had been transformed since the mid-1970s. A combination of business-led 'sector management', cost control, and improved relations with government had seen the public subsidy to railways reduced substantially, while at the same time investment levels were rising substantially. At that time there was no talk of a 'golden age', a term widely used in the railway press to refer to Bob Reid I's period (1983–90). A little hindsight, five years of privatisation, and a series of unfortunate accidents have given the phrase its wider currency. However, I must point out that plans to write a companion volume were set in motion long before railway privatisation was put on the political agenda. It was in 1987 that Reid asked me to undertake a series of interviews in anticipation of a 'volume two', a second book which would take the business history of British Rail up to date. Oral history, a vital component of contemporary history, presents many challenges. One of the greatest is the tendency for managers' memories to fade once their daily preoccupation with a major task has ended. The interviews undertaken in 1987–92 (see List of Interviewees) provided valuable insights into British Rail's management challenges before the spectre of privatisation cast its shadow. In fact, it was that spectre, first the promises and preparations of successive Secretaries of State for Transport, Paul Channon, Cecil Parkinson, and Malcolm Rifkind, then the immense challenge for the British Railways Board (BRB) of responding to the government's timetable for privatisation following the White Paper of 1992, which drove out all thoughts of commissioning a history. It was not until 1997, when the privatisation process had been completed that John Welsby and Peter Trewin, respectively Chairman and Secretary of the British Railways Board, engaged me to write about the period from 1974 to 1997.

My broad remit was to provide an authoritative record of the period, emphasising the organisational, economic, and financial changes and reflecting the views taken by the Board and senior railway managers. I was given full access to the records of the Board and its subsidiary businesses. However, no such privileges were enjoyed in relation to the records of government, since access for the period 1974–97 was closed under the 30-year rule operated by the Public Record Office (PRO). Nor did I obtain access to the records of the Board's successor institutions, such as Railtrack. Readers familiar with the earlier book will note some changes to the approach. This time I was determined to do more justice to the engineering and subsidiary business functions of the Board, and I trust that I have managed to do so. In other ways, of course, the remit was *very* different from my earlier brief. This work deals with the near past, bringing all the challenges for a historian of near-contemporary events, where hindsight is at a premium. There was an additional challenge. The book was written at a time when, following the accidents at Southall, Ladbroke Grove, and Hatfield, railways have been very much under the microscope. The daily comment in the press and broadcast media about the 'crisis on the railways' has provided additional stimulus, though the aim has been to present as objective an assessment as possible in the light of the existing records. I also had the benefit of a second series of interviews, conducted between 1997 and 2001 (see List of Interviewees), in which major players—railway managers, politicians, civil servants, trade unionists, academics, and journalists—offered frank assessments of the railways and the part they played in their management and performance. The project benefited greatly from the advice given by a steering committee chaired by Professor Peter Mathias, former Master of Downing College, and consisting of Michael Posner and Kenneth Dixon, former Board members, representing the Board, and Sir Geoffrey Owen of the London School of Economics (LSE) and Dr Stefan Szymanski of Imperial College, nominated by my employers, the London School of Economics, who took responsibility for ensuring publication. My thanks to all of them for their encouragement, advice, and above all stamina in reading the numerous drafts. I owe a particular debt to Peter Mathias, whose wise counsel steered me away from numerous infelicities. Peter Trewin acted as godfather, facilitator and (on occasions) spin-doctor, his supportive good humour ensuring that the writing process was both a pleasant as well as a stimulating exercise. Sonia Copeland administered the activities of the steering committee with characteristic efficiency and enthusiasm. A number of railway executives offered valuable advice on specific issues, notably Richard Davies, Alan Nichols, Ralph Porter, and David Redfern. All responsibility for such errors as remain in the book is mine alone, of course.

I owe a great deal to many others. It was a pleasure to renew my acquaintance with the railway records centre at 66 Porchester Road, London W2, which has housed railway records since the foundation of the British Transport Historical Records Office in 1951, exactly half a century ago. I first visited 'Porchester Road' in 1964, and worked there on the earlier book in 1980–5. This, last(?) stint, from 1997 to 2001, introduced me to a lively group of people with an extensive knowledge of the railway industry. Their banter, especially that directed at me, the LSE, and Leicester City Football Club, helped to wipe away any academic pretension. Equally, their companionship was evidence of the persistence of the 'railway culture', a culture which survives despite the many assaults on it offered by privatisation and the splintering of a large, integrated industry into many fragments. My thanks, then, to the staff at Porchester Road, led first by Robin Linsley, then by Christine Bruce, and last (but by no means least) by Allan Leach. Allan's infectious enthusiasm and skills as a project manager, together with his possession of a black book outlining the peccadilloes of a generation of railway managers, ensured that my visits to the centre were both pleasant and productive. In one aspect history did repeat itself. As in the 1980s, the writing of this book has been both a prelude and an accompaniment to the records-gathering process. While I was conducting my research, the considerable backlog of records was licked into shape and assembled and sorted by a combined team of British Rail staff and professional archivists. Much of this material, which formed the foundation of my book, has now been listed in preparation for transfer to the Public Record Office, or in some instances to other repositories. I should like to thank among the BR team Eddie Andrew, Jacqueline Chodak, Nick Collins, Wayne Gilliard, Sean McLoughlin, Mark Pardoe, Ralph Porter, David Rose, and Maurice Tomsett, and among the archivists Ted Rogers, Vicky Parkinson, Gemma Bentley, Phil Oakman, and Simon Lock. Others also showed generosity. Neil Butters, Secretary of the Railway Heritage Committee, lent me information on the Total Operations Processing System (TOPS); Alastair Gilchrist and Chris Potts, former railwaymen, provided help with specific issues. Andrew Pendleton of Manchester Metropolitan University (MMU) shared his research materials on flexible rostering with me. Sir Peter Parker, John Heath, Ken Burrage, Ian Brown, Peter Land, Gordon Pettitt, John Prideaux, Henry Sanderson, and Jim Urquhart donated or lent documents from their private archives. Sir Bob Reid (Bob Reid II) allowed me to consult his unpublished manuscript covering his period as Chairman. Peter Snape gave me the benefit of his experience as a parliamentarian and railway supporter. Professional and academic audiences gave valuable advice, in London (thanks to the Retired Railway Officers Society), Worcester, Glasgow, Tokyo, and Miami. Nick Tiratsoo and Lawrence Black helped with research on technical and engineering matters. The three principal trade unions, the RMT, ASLEF, and TSSA, generously consented to provide access to records. The search for cartoons was greatly facilitated by Jane Newton and the Centre for the Study of Cartoons and Caricature at the University of Kent. Transcription of the interviews, a mammoth task, was undertaken with efficiency and good humour by Pip Austin, assisted by Anne Romain. Robin Linsley and Alan Marshall helped with the illustrations. I should also like to thank all at Oxford University Press and in particular my long-suffering editor, David Musson, Sarah Dobson,

Gwen Booth, Susan Faircloth, my copy editor, and at the LSE, Carol Hewlett, Mina Moshkeri, Beverley Friedgood, Neil Gregory, and Kerry Fyffe.

Last, but certainly not least, this book could not have been completed without the input of my research assistant and colleague Mike Anson. Mike, whose Ph.D. thesis examined the railway workshops at Swindon, brought an immense knowledge of railway operating and engineering to the project, though sometimes the logistics of canal navigation and the fate of Stafford Rangers took precedence. His wife Jo provided advice on accounting conventions while also proving to be an exemplary proofreader. My sincere thanks to them both. My family suffered as ever, as the house filled up with railway papers, and there is a strong possibility that they will never travel by train again. To Sue, my best and long-suffering critic, Peter, and Matthew: chuff, chuff!

T. G.

Bow E3
May 2001

Introduction

British Rail after 25 Years of Nationalisation

1.1 The long march from 1948

The year 1974 may seem a somewhat puzzling choice as a starting date for a modern history of British Rail. The choice was influenced in large measure by the fact that I had written an earlier volume dealing with the first 25 years, 1948–73.[1] However, there are other reasons for electing to start in that year. First, there was a change of government, with Edward Heath's Conservative administration giving way to Harold Wilson's third Labour government, though here the transition was somewhat shaky, since there were two elections, in February and October. More significant, perhaps, was the passing of legislation which straddled both administrations. Important modifications of the British Railways Board's obligations were introduced in the Railways Act of July 1974. Another critical element was the fact that relations with government for this key nationalised enterprise were about to be transformed by massive economic difficulties which faced Britain in the wake of the oil crisis of 1973, heralding a period of high inflation, cash limits, investment restrictions, and labour unrest. These difficulties provided a challenge for *all* British businesses; for a public sector business where the effort to match prices to costs was a much more visible phenomenon the challenge was all the greater.

How were railways regarded in the mid-1970s, after a quarter century in the public sector? Change has been so rapid and so comprehensive since then that it is necessary first of all to assess the record under nationalisation, then to review perceptions of rail transport in the public mind, and finally to assess the 'political'

Introduction

economy of the railways. Ever since the Transport Act of 1947, which created the British Transport Commission, there had been a vigorous debate about the role and future prospects of rail transport in a country which was dominated increasingly by road transport. The frequent tinkering with the organisation and management of railways, first with the Commission (1948–62), and then with the British Railways Board (BRB) (1963–) was designed to improve the financial health of the business, but in fact the annual results were characterised by everlarger deficits. The frequent interventions of government, notably in 1962 when the Commission was abolished by Ernest Marples, and after the Transport Act of 1968, when the Board was encouraged to function as a top-level planning body along the lines advocated by McKinsey, were a response to a firm belief in Whitehall that railway managers were inbred, inward-looking, and resistant to change. This belief was contentious, though there was some truth to it; but in any case, organisational change could never address the deep-seated confusion about what the railways were actually supposed to achieve in a mixed economy—whom they were supposed to serve, and which groups (if any) were to enjoy the benefits of state subsidisation. From the beginning the politicians attempted to produce an entity which could combine public service aspirations and commercial viability, but after 25 years' experience this search was clearly something of a Holy Grail. From the perspective of railway managers there was a distinct confusion about the goals of British Railways, compounded by the capricious and pervasive nature of government intervention, which took place not only in relation to broad policy but also on detailed matters surrounding pricing, investment, and pay settlements. Attempts by the Department of Transport (DTp) to inject new managerial blood into the industry, spectacularly with the appointment of Dr Richard Beeching in 1961, were rarely successful. It was not only that 'outsiders' were treated with suspicion by railway-trained 'insiders'; newcomers quickly came to realise that running the railways under the legislative cloak of successive Transport Acts was a greater challenge than managing Palmolive or Batchelors Peas. Furthermore, managing this rather special example of industrial enterprise had to take place under the full glare of the media spotlight, again something which outsiders found unfamiliar.

Fundamental to the relationship between the various tiers of government and the railway industry was the perpetual struggle between the interests of the several parties. First, there were the passengers and freight customers, represented by consumer councils and by lobby groups created in response to the better organised road lobby. Then there were the railway managers, enthusiastic and often dedicated people with a real commitment to rail transport and, among the engineers, to best practice standards. Third, there was the general railway workforce, historically experiencing relatively low wage rates and long hours, but supported by a vigorous union movement. Fourth, there was an ambivalent Department of Transport, which was responsible for all modes of transport but undertook executive functions in relation to road building. Finally, the hard-nosed Treasury had a crucial role. In addition to applying all the familiar spending restraints of such a department it had acquired almost a pathological dislike of large public sector projects. For railways this belief had some substance. It had been nurtured by the considerable problems which had arisen when a concerted attempt was made to revitalise the industry with the ill-fated Modernisation Plan of 1955.[2]

Railways were judged in several ways, first of all by their customers, and in particular the passengers who travelled by train. Often taken for granted in the past, they were beginning to be better valued by 1974. Greater attention was being paid to what would now be called 'customer care', characterised by Dr Beeching's famous warning to managers to remember that 'Our Face is Our Bottom'.[3] Significantly, the suggested theme for the railways' 1974 objectives under the Management By Objectives procedure was 'care, courtesy, cleanliness'.[4] Senior managers were equally mindful of the continual assessment being made in political circles of the extent to which the railways were fulfilling the objectives laid down in the successive Transport Acts of 1947, 1953, 1962, and 1968, and meeting other requirements produced via the formal and informal interventions of government. Statutory obligations had always been a source of confusion, mixing together as they did social and economic goals—the Transport Acts of 1947 and 1962 required the Board to have due regard to adequacy, efficiency, economy, and safety of rail services, and to ensure that revenues matched appropriate costs; but since the White Papers of 1961 and 1967, which produced the first financial targets for nationalised industries, the satisfaction of financial criteria had begun to dominate. By the early 1970s there was a distinct feeling inside British Rail (BR) that 'as time has passed, the difficulty of meeting the financial criteria has impelled more than one major recasting of the objectives to such a point that financial discipline may now appear to have become an end in itself, rather than a condition associated with a wider general duty to serve the community'.[5] Over the course of their existence in the public sector railways had not only contracted (see Table 1.1) but also experienced a number of major policy shifts: the British Transport Commission's abortive search for transport 'integration' before 1953; the faith in increased investment represented by the Modernisation Plan of 1955–65; the greater realism of Beeching, who pursued 'rationalisation' and 'reshaping' in the early 1960s; and finally, the 1968 Transport Act, which with its introduction of grants to cover the costs of unremunerative passenger services had made a clear distinction between the 'commercial' and the 'social' railway. Each change had produced great expectations, and ultimately disappointments. In this regard at least, the situation facing the railways in 1974, as they confronted another shift in public policy, was much as it had been in 1947, 1962, or even in 1921 when the amalgamation of the private railway companies was imposed.

Contemporary attitudes were often shaped by knowledge about the financial ill health and market positioning of the industry. Market share had been falling

'Oh come on man—the train is only five minutes late'

1. British Rail's customer care campaign: mac, *Daily Mail*, 11 August 1977

steadily for over two decades; in 1973 rail transport (excluding London Transport) made up only 7 per cent of passenger-miles travelled in the UK and 15 per cent of freight tonne-miles, compared with 15 and 42 per cent twenty years before (Table 1.1). If not exactly a joke, then the railways were certainly held in low esteem by that section of society which was car oriented and upwardly mobile, the proto-yuppy generation. The environmental and public transport lobby groups, such as the National Council on Inland Transport and Transport 2000, exerted some influence, for example on rail closures and the issue of increased lorry weights, but in general their voice was weak.[6] Of course, there was a great deal of affection for the railways *per se*, much of it nostalgic and directed at the great days of steam. But those people who declared their enthusiasm for railways were often roundly condemned as trainspotters or 'gricers' and they themselves frequently distinguished between the railways, which they loved, and rail managements, whom they loathed. Press treatment was sometimes dismissive, with railways characterised in the manner of the Revd W. H. Awdry's *Thomas the Tank Engine*, and their managers seen as 'Fat Controllers' or else portrayed in Pooterish terms in cartoons and articles referring to 'puffers' and 'chuffers'.[7]

Table 1.1 British Rail in 1973 compared with 1953 and 1993/4

Year	Network (route-miles)	'Output'		Market share		Workforce ('000s)			Turnover (constant 1993/4 prices) (£m.)
		Passenger-miles (m.)	Freight tonne-miles (net, m.)	Pass. (%)	Freight (%)	Rail	Other	Total	
1953	19,222	20.6	23.2	15	42	594	44	638	6,402
1973	11,326	18.5	14.3	7	15	223	27	250	4,917
1993/4	10,275	18.9	8.6	4	6	115	6	121	3,645

Source: BRB, R&A 1956, 1973, 1993/4; Gourvish, British Railways, pp. 615–16; DETR, Transport Statistics Great Britain 1999, pp. 179, 181; Office for National Statistics, Economic Trends Annual Supplement 1999 Edition (1999).

Introduction

Attitudes like these were carried over into senior management, and into government–industry relations. The Board often displayed a siege mentality in an environment in which the motor car and the roads-building programme enjoyed clear priority, a situation barely disguised by civil servants and a succession of transport ministers. For example, when Peter Parker succeeded Richard Marsh as Chairman of British Rail in September 1976, he quickly discovered that the former Minister of Transport, Dr John Gilbert, 'admitted to being a motorway man himself'.[8] This was no surprise, of course. The government's Green Paper on Transport Policy in April of the same year had noted the tremendous growth in road transport over the period 1964–74 but had discounted the need for a defined transport policy.[9] While in some circles in 1974 there was firm support for a channel tunnel incorporating rail transport, the emphasis in transport infrastructure investment was firmly on motorways such as the M6, M62, M4, and M5, and on larger, heavier lorries. In the period 1967–72 the total length of motorways had more than doubled from 473 to 1,037 miles, thereby exceeding the 1,000-mile target set in 1960. The permitted weight limits on lorries were raised to 32 tons for articulated 4-axle vehicles in 1964, and to 24 and 30 tons for 3- and 4-axle rigid vehicles in 1972.[10] The number of heavy lorries (that is, over 8 tons) in use increased substantially from 5,000 in 1955 to 96,000 twenty years later, while the average length of haul increased by 50 per cent, from 22 to 34 miles.[11] Planning documents both within the UK and in continental Europe anticipated further increases in road mileage and lorry dimensions.[12]

It should also be noted that this was a world in which industrial relations were approached with extreme caution, a deviation from established norms was greeted with alarm, and fears of adverse publicity were rife. The militancy of the early 1970s may have faded with time; but we should acknowledge that union power meant far more then than it has done since the mid-1980s. Harold Watkinson, President of the Confederation of British Industry (CBI), captured the employers' mood well in a paper entitled 'Do we fight or lie down?' in 1976: 'Ted Heath took on the Unions and lost; Harold Wilson gave too much to the left for the sake of holding the Labour Party together... The reputation of the entrepreneur is still at a low ebb in public esteem'.[13] The miners' strikes of January–February 1972 and February–March 1974, each of which prompted a reduced, three-day working week, were characteristic of the time. The number of working days lost through industrial action totalled 70.4 million in the quinquennium 1970–4 and 52.4 million in 1980–4, compared with only 19.7 million in 1985–9 and 4.1 million in 1990–4.[14] Over half of the workforce were in unions in 1974, a figure which rose to a peak of 56 per cent in 1978 before falling steadily to 46 per cent in 1987 and 35 per cent in 1992.[15] Railway trade unionists, historically part of the 'auld alliance' of coal, railways, and transport workers, played a full part in this labour assertiveness. Unsurprisingly, then, senior managements were nervous, and decisions were often coloured by the 'industrial relations implications'. The formal minutes of the British Railways Board for 1974 and 1975 make this clear. The 'industrial relations situation' dominated the first six meetings, in January–May 1974, and only five of the 26 meetings held over the two years failed to discuss the topic in some aspect, whether pay claims, worker participation, no-redundancy guarantees, or whatever. This obsession was not confined to the Board; industrial relations issues also dominated the deliberations of the Railway Management Group (RMG) and the Executive Directors' Conference lower down the management hierarchy. The contrast with 1988–91 is sharp. Here only 10 of the 51 Board meetings considered an explicit 'industrial relations' item, the number rising to 19 if matters such as employee involvement, equal opportunities, and 'Quality through People', which were raised on the Board's initiative, are included.[16] It is also significant that it was in 1974 that the Board decided to re-establish a top-level consultation body, the British Railways Joint Consultation Council (BRJCC), which had ceased to meet in 1964. The immediate context was the need to ensure trade union support for the Board's lobbying in connection with the Railways Act; however, it is also clear that the formalising of consultation was held to be important by both sides given the existing climate.[17]

Management anxiety about labour relations frequently affected decision making. The extreme caution, even furtiveness, with which both the Board and the Department handled an urgent order for 60 diesel locomotives in 1974 provides a good example. The best of the tenders came from Brush Electrical of Loughborough, which proposed to build the locomotives in Romania using Romanian mechanical parts in order to speed delivery and were also offering metric specifications. However, the Board expressed great concern about the possibility of union opposition, from the National Union of Railwaymen in particular, and in the end a compromise was reached, whereby half the locomotives were to be built in Romania, and half in the UK. The Departments of the Environment and Industry were fully involved in the decision, which appears over-hesitant given that the Romanian content of the full order would have been only 30 per cent (and in the event was no more than 15 per cent).[18] The published response of David Bowick, the Chief Executive (Railways), to allegations made by the economists Richard Pryke and John Dodgson that the railways were grossly overmanned, is also revealing. Writing in *Modern Railways* in 1976 he suggested that 'the authors appear to have brushed aside the realities of industrial relations in the country's present social and economic conditions ... it will take a long time for the necessary confidence to be built up between management and unions so that there is a mutual belief in the search for benefits common to the industry and the individual employee'.[19]

Finally, the railway industry, in common with coal, another problem area in the public sector, was clearly suffering from the legacy of 25 years of bleak financial results and their attendant disapprobation. The search for explanations often ended up at the door of top management and remedies all too often were sought in further organisational change coloured by politically charged abuse. After nearly three decades in this environment it is no surprise to find

anti-nationalised industry views being widely canvassed. While many economists spoke, rather vainly in the end, about the need for marginal cost pricing to
secure allocative efficiency, others were beginning to mount a monetarist challenge to Keynesian orthodoxy, following concerns about 'stop-go' macroeconomic management and indeed doubts as to whether governments should seek
to steer the economy. Thus, Robert Bacon and Walter Eltis warned of the
'crowding-out' effects of public expenditure in a well-publicised article in the
Sunday Times in November 1975, and Milton Friedman issued Cassandra-like
portents from his Chicago bolt-hole of the threat to a free society in a country
where public expenditure level had apparently soared to almost 60 per cent of
GDP.[20] The political response to this may be found on the right of the Conservative party, where it was argued that 'Over-government is Britain's greatest
burden'.[21] Among transport specialists, the railways themselves were under fire
from economists such as Stewart Joy, in *The Train that Ran Away* (1973) and
Pryke and Dodgson, in *The Rail Problem* (1975). Both were uncompromising
tracts. The latter highlighted British Rail's failure to contain its deficit and reduce
costs. It also cast doubt both on the Board's corporate planning and on its case for
larger government support, as contained in the Railway Policy Review of 1972
and the 'Interim Rail Strategy' agreed with government in the following year
(see below). British Rail was characterised, it was claimed, by a poor management
'prodigal and tolerant of inefficiency'. Since Beeching's departure in 1965 'old
attitudes [had] slowly reasserted themselves. It has once again come to be
believed that railways are a national necessity, that they deserve far more investment, and that their operating costs are of no great importance'.[22] Similar, if less
extreme, criticisms were offered by Christopher Foster, in his books on the
control of public expenditure and the 'transport problem', and in his contribution
to a transport study group which published its findings in the journal *Socialist
Commentary* in 1975 (see below).[23]

Criticisms were voiced by numerous non-experts too. Lord Hewlett, writing in
July 1976 about a delayed journey on the West Coast Main Line caused by a
freight derailment, complained forcibly about the 'miseries of nationalised
travel'. 'If this is the state of the railways after 30 years of nationalisation', he
wrote, 'one is appalled at the prospect for both the aircraft and shipbuilding
industries' (which were about to be nationalised). He reached the predictable
conclusion that 'free enterprise could have made a great deal more effective use of
the hundreds of millions of pounds poured into some of these nationalised
undertakings, and there would have been a better service and a profit at the end
of the day'.[24] The notion that the public sector was far from efficient was even
reflected in the work of cricket writers.[25] As Marsh observed in 1974, 'Together
with labour relations and singing in the bath, knowledge of how the railways
should be run is provided by the Almighty at the moment of birth. It is a well-
known fact that the nation is divided between 27 million railway experts and
190,000 of us who earn our living on the railways'.[26]

1.2 The British Railways Board

What was the composition of the Board that was charged with steering the railways at this difficult time? Table 1.2 indicates the membership for 1974. What is striking is how far the balance between railway and non-railway representation had swung in favour of the latter. Both the chairman and deputy-chairman were non-railwaymen. Richard Marsh, the flamboyant former Minister of Transport, had been at the helm since 1971, and his deputy, Michael Bosworth, was a former partner of Peat Marwick Mitchell who had joined the Board in 1968. Nor were the full-time executive directors in any sense dominated by career railwaymen. After the retirement of Arthur Barker in November 1974, only two of the executive Board members were professional railwaymen—Robert Lawrence and David McKenna. Of course, the composition reflected the strategy and purpose of the Board in the wake of the recommendations of the management consultants, McKinsey, in 1968–9.[27] The intention had been that BRB should operate as a planning board for both the rail and subsidiary businesses, with executive functions devolved to senior managers without board status. In fact, a more hybrid arrangement was followed, with some members assuming executive responsibilities, though at this time the Chief Executive for the railway business, David Bowick, remained outside the Board, and indeed behaved more like a hands-on 'chief operating officer' than a genuine CEO.

How effective was this team? From one perspective the blend of railwaymen, executive directors, and non-executives was welcome. Sir Frederick Hayday, Lord Taylor of Gryfe, Sir Alastair Pilkington, and Alan Walker were men with wide experience who were seeking, somewhat ahead of their time, to show how non-executives could act as catalysts by challenging the proven ways of doing things. In September 1974 they were joined by Sir David Serpell, an experienced civil servant who had been permanent secretary at the Ministry of Transport and Department of the Environment from 1968 to 1972. Pilkington, an acerbic and forceful personality who had masterminded the float glass technology which had transformed his company, was particularly anxious to make Board members think more imaginatively about their role. Furthermore, their contributions at meetings with the Ministry were frequently telling. At a meeting in November 1974, for example, their interventions ranged from complaints about short-termism and the restrictions on the Board's freedom to exploit its property assets, to observations on pricing and investment.[28]

However, the organisational gains were more apparent than real. The effective deployment of non-executives was a theme which had been raised on a number of occasions, notably by Taylor, who had expressed concern about their impotence in the post-1970 organisation, while the low level of remuneration for part-timers—£1,000, a sum fixed in 1946—served to restrict the field to those who felt some commitment to the railways but were able to offer only limited

Table 1.2 The British Railways Board in 1974

Name	Date of appointment	Age on 1.1.1974	Departed	Previous post	Experience
Chairman (salary £23,110)					
Richard Marsh	1971	45	Sep. 1976	Minister of Transport	Politics, trade unions (NUPE)
Deputy Chairman (salary £19,100)					
J. M. W. Bosworth	1968	52	Jun. 1983	Partner, Peat Marwick Mitchell	Accountancy (PMM)
Full-time members (salary £13,600)					
A. V. Barker*	1968	62	Nov. 1974	Assistant GM, LMR	Railways, NAAFI
H. L. Farrimond	1972	49	Jan. 1977	Dir of Personnel, Dunlop	Personnel management (ICI, UCS, Dunlop)
Dr Sydney Jones**	1965	62	Jun. 1976	Chief of Research, BRB	Scientic research (CEGB)
R. L. E. Lawrence	1971	58	Sep. 1983	GM, LMR	Railways
David McKenna	1968	62	Aug. 1978	GM, SR	Railways
Part-time members (salary £1,000)					
Sir Frederick Hayday	1962	61	Dec. 1975	—	Trade unions
Sir Alastair Pilkington	1973	54	Jun. 1976	—	Glass (Pilkington)
Sir David Serpell†	1974	62	May. 1982	—	Civil service
Lord Taylor of Gryfe	1968	61	Jun. 1980	—	Retailing (Co-op)
W. G. Thorpe*	1968	64	Oct. 1974	Deputy Chairman, BRB	Railways
H. Alan Walker	1969	63	Jan. 1978††	—	Brewing (Bass Charrington)

* Left in 1974   ** Became part-time in July 1974   † Joined in 1974   †† Died

amounts of time.[29] There were also clear organisational problems associated with a Board which operated as a conglomerate holding company, but where the businesses—railways, engineering, shipping, hotels, hovercraft, property, consultancy (Transmark), and advertising (jointly owned by the National Bus Company)—were dominated by the first and largest. These problems were certainly not enhanced by the proliferation of overlapping committees, which meant that a given item could be routed through three to six committees before it was ready for Board endorsement.[30] Thus, although there were some creative minds at Headquarters, notably Michael Bosworth, who were backed up by a knowledgeable and competent management team, the Railway Management Group (RMG), the organisational effectiveness of the Board was questionable. The experiment with a planning Board, as recommended by the consultants McKinsey, but one which also embraced some functional responsibilities, did not seem to be working very well, and with hindsight the separation of the Board from the professional railway managers of the RMG was a mistake. The rectification of these difficulties was a matter to which both the Board and the Ministry would return many times over the next decade. Organisational problems were also evident at the level of middle management. The McKinsey prescription rested on the notion that regional management would be strengthened by the introduction of the 'Field Organisation', a proposal to remove one of the management tiers and replace the five existing regions with eight 'territories'. By 1974 it was clear that this attempt to restructure middle management was meeting fierce resistance, much to the annoyance and embarrassment of the Chief Executive, David Bowick. In fact, the proposal had to be abandoned in January 1975.[31] The change, which had been announced to Parliament in the Board's report to the Minister for Transport Industries of April 1972,[32] was scuppered by union opposition, a slump in the housing market, and demands for compensation which destroyed the scheme's viability.[33]

1.3 The Railways Act 1974

The year 1974 was also notable for important changes to the Board's formal relationship with the government. The intervention was timely. British Rail had announced a loss of £51.6 million for 1973, notwithstanding government grants totalling £91.4 million, and the financial situation was set to deteriorate further since the deficit had to be met by additional borrowing at market interest rates.[34] The Railways Act of 1974 provided a combination, as is so often the case in government–industry relations, of assistance and restriction.[35] Section 1 reduced the Board's capital debt from £438.7 million to £250 million with effect from 1 January 1975, and section 2 increased the limit on the Board's borrowing powers from £550 to £600 million (and from £700 to £900 million with the agreement of the Secretary of State for the Environment). In addition, government funding for inherited pension liabilities was provided for in sections 5–7. The capital reconstruction reflected an important and (for the Board, welcome) change, in that future expenditure on the maintenance of infrastructure assets was to be charged to revenue instead of capital.[36]

Sections 3 and 4 of the Act modified the Minister's existing functions in relation to the Board, repealing sections of the Transport Acts of 1962 and 1968. The most important change was the abandonment of the cumbersome and time-consuming practice of providing specific grants for each unremunerative passenger rail service which the government wished to support as socially necessary, under section 39 of the 1968 Act. This was replaced by a block grant system covering the passenger network as a whole: 'The Secretary of State . . . may give directions to the Board imposing on them obligations of a general nature with respect to the operation of the whole or any part of their passenger railway system.'[37] The block grant scheme, which was similar to that applied in the Netherlands, was compatible with Britain's recently incurred responsibilities under EEC law, and specifically a regulation of 1969 which referred to obligations 'to ensure the provision of adequate transport services' and to the payment of compensation to cover any financial burdens arising from such obligations.[38] Of more importance from the Board's perspective was the fact that the change emerged from an interaction with government over its deteriorating financial position in 1971–3. Its Railway Policy Review, submitted to the Ministry in December 1972, had contrasted the notions of the 'Viable' and the 'Necessary' Railway. It had concluded that the Board had no prospect of becoming viable under the terms of the 1968 Transport Act, nor would financial viability be achieved by major cuts in services and system size. Instead it had argued for a 'necessary railway' which would satisfy economic, social, and environmental requirements as part of a national transport plan.[39] The then Minister for Transport Industries, John Peyton, had certainly been influenced by British Rail's surprising contention that significantly smaller rail networks, to be reached by the painful process of withdrawing large numbers of grant-aided services, would in fact be *less* profitable than the existing system and would thus provide less value for money from a government perspective.[40] Consequently, he had approved in principle the Board's 'interim rail strategy', which emerged from the 1972 Review, namely a commitment to a stable and 'developing railway system' with largely 'commercial' terms of reference, an assurance that there would be no 'draconian' cuts in the network, a more realistic and adequate form of support, and the promise of increased investment. These commitments were apparently accepted by the incoming Labour administration.[41] Future policy was clarified by a Ministerial direction of 19 December 1974, from Fred Mulley, Minister for Transport, which stipulated that the Board 'shall from 1 January 1975 operate their passenger railway system so as to provide a public service which is comparable generally with that provided by the Board at present.'[42] Payments to cover the net cost of passenger services, which became known as the Public Service Obligation or PSO, were limited initially to £900 million, with provision for an increase of up to £1,500 million with Commons approval.

At the same time, however, the opportunity was taken in section 4 of the Act to firm up the Ministry's supervision of the Board's corporate planning activity, thereby giving the government more scope for intervention. In 'formulating policies and plans for the general conduct of their undertaking and the businesses of their subsidiaries', the Board was to 'act on lines settled from time to time with the approval of the Secretary of State'. In addition, the existing requirement (Transport Act 1962) about disclosure of information was strengthened and a further clause added requiring that the annual report should 'include such information as the Secretary of State may from time to time specify'.[43] Finally, a new form of assistance, capital expenditure grants for freight customers contemplating shifting from road to rail transport, was introduced in section 8. The grants were designed to cover the capital costs of providing new rail infrastructure, that is, sidings, terminals, and loading and unloading equipment. While the idea was a good one in view of the growing financial problems facing rail freight operations, the obligation was on the customer to apply for such assistance and the success rate was modest. In the period 1974–6 only 15 grants were obtained with a total value of £2.0 million.[44] In fact, freight operations were to receive more direct, unanticipated support over the next three years as recession, high inflation, and pricing constraints took their toll.

1.4 Marsh and the frustrations of public sector management

Formal procedures were one thing; informal relationships quite another. It is clear that relations between the Board and the government were far from cordial at this time. Marsh did not get on well with Mulley, and the formal requirement about disclosing information to government in the Railways Act reflected an increasing dissatisfaction and frustration within the Department of the Environment about the quality of the information it was being given on railway matters.[45] On one side, then, there was suspicion about the withholding of information, on the other resentment at interference in the management of the business. This situation tested the temper of the most equable; but when personal animosities surfaced, things became much worse. For example, Marsh had been extremely irritated by Mulley's intervention in April 1974 in the Field Organisation negotiations, which had then reached a delicate stage. Rail staff at Sheffield were aggrieved by the news that the territorial headquarters were to be at York, with the financial accounting centre divided between York and Doncaster. Mulley had served as MP for Sheffield (Park) since 1950, and when representatives of the rail unions and local government enlisted his help, he disconcerted Marsh by pleading for organisational 'stability'.[46] The quality of information was to become more critical given the new funding structure, which required the Board to calculate and isolate the 'avoidable costs' of its commercial rail businesses, freight, and parcels. The determination of infrastructure use in particular was a challenging affair, encouraging British Rail on the one hand to develop more sophisticated procedures and on the other to pursue costing regimes which would maximise the element of government subsidy. Thus, the presentation of convincing and transparent methods of costing was another major and long-running issue to exercise both Board and Ministry over the next decade, part of a wider debate on the need for improved information to facilitate government monitoring of nationalised industry performance.[47]

The main difficulty, however, was that Marsh, who tended to be an impatient and impetuous leader, had become disillusioned with the failure of the government, whether Conservative or Labour, to accept the need for long-term transport planning, to provide defined targets (other than negative ones) for railway management to follow, and, above all, to endorse fully and consistently his arguments for a 'Necessary Railway' as formulated in the 1972 Rail Policy Review. Of course, the dialogue continued, and in September 1973 the Minister had encouraged British Rail to produce a range of studies in order to define and refine the concept in the context of national transport needs. The Board had hoped that these studies would be produced on the initiative of the Department of the Environment (DOE), but it quickly emerged that this support would not be forthcoming. Consequently, in February 1974 it was decided to pursue these studies 'unilaterally'.[48] The situation was scarcely surprising given the widening gulf between Board and Department. Both Marsh and Bosworth were plainly disappointed by the ensuing Railways Act, which fell far short of the Board's aspirations. In the 'interim rail strategy' British Rail had argued the case for a flexible and robust system of government support based on: provision and maintenance of the railway infrastructure as a whole; compensation for the adverse effects of government intervention in areas such as pricing; and additional support from grants to cover unremunerative but socially necessary passenger *and freight* services.[49] However, this had been rejected, apparently on the grounds that what Marsh wanted ran counter to the government's interpretation of EEC regulations.[50] The Board knew that a commercial objective for freight and parcels was at the very least fragile and in the short run unattainable, beset as these businesses were by inflation and the pricing constraints of 1972–4. At this point there was a firm belief that to break up British Rail into separate businesses would be 'artificial and to some extent meaningless'.[51] The government was very quickly forced to commission a special report on freight from British Rail, then in 1975 to provide emergency support for freight and parcels, postponing the pursuit of a commercial objective until 1978 (see Chapter 2).

Abandonment under force of circumstances of the investment plans envisaged in the 'interim rail strategy' was another source of contention. The strategy had involved an undertaking to double the rate of investment, providing for the development of the Inter-City business via electrification schemes and new High-Speed Trains, and much-needed investment in freight wagons. The government initially accepted the argument, although the Minister, Peyton, had warned in October 1973 that he would have 'considerable difficulty with his colleagues in agreeing a sensible level of investment for railways'.[52] Indeed, in November investment ceilings were fixed for a four-year cycle at a level which was some 20 per cent below British Rail's expectations.[53] Then, to the Board's dismay, external circumstances almost immediately prompted a further cut of 20 per cent for the first of the four years, a decision announced in December, only three weeks after the Minister had endorsed the plan. Marsh was moved to complain in the annual report that 'no organisation can cope efficiently with such abrupt and frequent changes of policy'.[54] Worse was to follow, however. In May 1974 the Department asked the Board to assess the effect of a cut of 15 per cent for 1975/6, and in July it asked the railways to work to cuts of 10 per cent in each of the following two years. The Board duly protested, but these figures soon became firm targets, although not without some ambiguity as to their precise coverage.[55] It was true that planned investment levels remained higher than actual spending in the years 1969–73. Nevertheless, Marsh, in the annual report for 1975, could only express his disappointment that investment had been pegged at some 30 per cent below the level promised two years earlier, a complaint he repeated many times over the rest of his period in office, notably in a lecture at the Chartered Institute of Transport in January 1976.[56]

There was further frustration in 1975 with the process for determining investment for 1976–8, which not only proved to be a long-drawn-out affair but contained a number of disappointments from a railway perspective. The severity of the 1976/7 cut in comparison with those imposed elsewhere in the public sector (British Rail was required to bear a quarter of the £100 million reduction), the Department's refusal to allow the Board to vire resources between maritime and other projects, the late announcement of the ceiling for 1976/7, and continuing uncertainty beyond that, were all bones of contention. In August and September Bosworth was moved to complain to the Department about the position.[57] He got short shrift, but continued to argue that 'it is quite inequitable and unreasonable, even taking into account our present financial position, that BRB should suffer such a disproportionate cut compared to other Nationalised Industries … It is well-nigh impossible to plan the optimum use of investment when the ceilings are completely fluid beyond 1976, the end of which is now only 15 months away'.[58] Meanwhile Marsh told Gilbert, 'This means of course that the interim strategy set out in the Railway Policy Review, and hitherto accepted by Government, is perforce totally abandoned'.[59] Clearly, investment policy was one of the most frustrating issues for BR managers, since there was no shortage of prospects for investment—in electrification of the East Coast and Midland main lines, new diesel traction—a fleet of High-Speed Trains, to be followed by the Advanced Passenger Train—and computer-aided control. On the other hand, the housing and roads programmes were also subjected to large cuts after 1974,[60] and whether all these rail projects were strictly necessary, from the perspective of a government which wanted to put commuters and freight before 'businessmen's trains', or justified, in the sense that they would pass conventional rate of return criteria, were also relevant considerations. There were critics, notably Pryke and Dodgson, and the Socialist Commentary Transport Study Group, led by Christopher Foster. Both teams challenged the assumptions on which the network size studies had been based and the latter argued that as much as 40 per cent of the investment sought would not produce a 10 per cent return. Moreover, the Group contended that very little of the anticipated investment was directed at encouraging freight on to the railways.[61] The debate on appropriate and justified investment was to continue, fed later on by the findings of a comparative assessment of support for European railway systems, where the UK came top of the league in its self-financing ratio (the extent to which revenue covered costs), but near the bottom in relation to financial support as a percentage of GDP, and bottom in relation to investment per train-kilometre.[62]

In reviewing the mid-1970s one should not overlook the enormity of the macroeconomic challenges faced by British governments and businesses. Governments had to cope with international instability, high inflation, and large public spending increases, and in the process the Keynesian responses of the Treasury were challenged as the monetarist alternative began to assert itself beyond the confines of university common rooms.[63] In the circumstances, the relationship between the government and the nationalised industries as a whole was bound to be problematic, a fact which was clearly recognised by the Cabinet Office when Lord Rothschild, the Director-General of the Central Policy Review Staff, was asked to undertake a review in 1972, and later, in 1976, when the National Economic Development Office produced a lengthy report on the subject.[64] This said, the agenda for British Rail was also set by a chairman whose initial enthusiasm for the job had faded in a welter of self-pity and recrimination, a situation exacerbated by the tragic death of his wife in a car crash in August 1975.[65] Marsh's cynicism about the political process and his irritation with ministers and government officials despite his past experience was frequently evident. His own account of a meeting with Peyton in September 1973 makes this clear. The NUR had requested a meeting with the minister to discuss ASLEF's response to the High-Speed Train project. According to Marsh, Peyton said that he had to see the unions anyway because he had promised to consult them about a planned White Paper, but was 'prepared to accept any advice on what he should or should not say to the Unions. I said that in any case I would like him to have a chat first with Mr Farrimond and he immediately agreed with protestations of delight at the prospect and wonderment of the originality of thought I display on these occasions'. Later he observed: 'It may be of significance that heavily watered whisky was provided rather than champagne though this could have been merely the result of inflation.'[66] There was a further clash with Mulley in May 1975 over appointments to the Board, which led Marsh to point out to the Minister that he was 'deeply concerned at the degree of misunderstanding which clearly exists within the Department over the working relationship between the Board and the Railway. The true position is so much at variance with the view you have formed that I really would welcome the opportunity to discuss it with you further sometime'.[67] Three months later, after the government had been forced to step in to cover the freight deficit, relations were so bad that Marsh wrote to Gilbert to point out the Board's 'considerable concern . . . at the tenor and implications of discussions and correspondence between the Board and the Department in recent weeks. The Board was particularly concerned with the contents of a letter from the Department to Derek Fowler dated 25th July [instructing the Board to produce a "convincing action programme for the freight business"], which indicated that the Board's standing with Ministers could be in question.'[68] Later, when the DOE had been broken up and the Ministry of Transport was re-formed, Peter Lazarus, the new Deputy Secretary, told BRB chief secretary Gerry Burt that he was 'quite disturbed at the severe deterioration in relationships with BRB since his previous experience several years ago'.[69]

However, the underlying impression in 1974 was that for all the talk, all the planning and strategy meetings, the rail business was suffering from drift, or what the management consultants might have called 'incumbent inertia'.[70] Part of this was undoubtedly shaped by the difficulty the Board faced in getting government to make up its mind about the future use of the railways. But it did seem as if the rail managers themselves were not clear about their strategy other than maintaining the status quo. An observation made by Alastair Pilkington in 1979, when the Board was making a more conscious effort to define aims and objectives, was with the benefit of hindsight, perceptive. 'It is the particular responsibility of a Board', he argued, 'to give direction to an enterprise and it is impossible to give direction if the Board does not know where it wants to go. It is so easy to work very hard at existing problems and convince oneself that one is doing a good job. People who think it is a waste of effort to clarify their aims have never done it.'[71]

In the pages that follow we chronicle the efforts made by the industry to clarify its aims, place the rail businesses on a firmer footing, and respond adequately and with clarity to the intentions of the railway shareholder, the government. In Part 1 we examine the experiences of railways under the Labour governments of 1974–9; in Part 2 we assess the extent and significance of the 'Thatcher Revolution' in public sector management, 1979–90; finally in Parts 3 and 4 we consider

Introduction

the processes leading up to railway privatisation, as well as giving due weight to the considerable efforts made by railway managers to maintain and improve the quality and safety of rail travel in the early 1990s.

Part 1

Railways under Labour,
1974–9

Operating the 1974 Railways Act

Financial Results, Organisational Responses, and Relations with Government

2.1 The financial record to 1979

Over the period of Labour government, 1974–9, British Rail, in common with all the enterprises in the public sector, suffered from pricing restraints, tighter investment controls, intervention in salary and wage levels, and from June 1975 cash limits. The outcome, unsurprisingly, was an initial deterioration in the published financial results, a more intrusive regime for monitoring by government, and additional pressure on the business and its management. The published results for the calendar years 1975–9, the first four years under the new financial regime introduced by the 1974 Railways Act, are presented in Table 2.1 in both current and constant 1979 prices, compared with the results for 1971–4. Of course, some complexities of interpretation arise in the process, not only owing to the change in the support mechanism and a £189 million reduction in the Board's capital debt (and fixed assets), but also due to inflation, and the introduction of special adjustments, notably extraordinary items.[1] The belief that the 1974 Act, with its Public Service Obligation (PSO) funding, would at last place the railways on a break-even footing, unlike the four Transport Acts which preceded it, was soon severely tested and was ultimately found to be wanting. As Table 2.1 shows, the poor business performance of 1973–4, which

Railways under Labour, 1974–9

Table 2.1 British Rail's financial results, 1975–9, compared with 1971–4 (£m., in current and constant 1979 prices)

Year	PSO grant central and local govt.[*]	Non-passenger grant	Group operating surplus/deficit before interest	Group Profit & Loss Before extraordinary items	After extraordinary items
Current prices					
1971			30	−15	−15
1972			25	−26	−26
1973			6	−52	−52
1974			−86	−158	−158
1975	324	66	−28	−61	5
1976	319	39	14	−30	5
1977	363	−3	68	30	27
1978	434	—	58	7	52
1979	522	—	54	1	12
Constant 1979 prices					
1971			86	−44	−44
1972			65	−69	−69
1973			14	−126	−126
1974			−183	−336	−336
1975	544	111	−48	−102	9
1976	464	51	20	−44	8
1977	465	−3	88	38	35
1978	497	—	62	7	60
1979	522	—	54	1	12

[*] Passenger Transport Executives (PTEs).

Source: Appendix A, Tables A.1 and A.2.

produced group deficits of £52 million in 1973 and £158 million in 1974, was rectified to a certain extent, but the initial years of the new funding system were still rather disappointing. In 1975 and 1976 the accounts revealed deficits of £61 and £30 million respectively, before 'extraordinary items'. These items were, in fact, government payments of £66 and £39 million in support of the non-passenger sector, viz. freight and parcels, which had not been envisaged by the 1974 Act, and which the auditors, Peat Marwick Mitchell, insisted should be identified separately since the grants were not backed by statute.[2] Indeed, the alarming slump in the profitability of freight and parcels was a matter of great concern, both for the Board and for the DOE, and it provoked a number of sharp exchanges between Marsh and DOE officials in 1975–6.[3]

The results for 1977 and 1978 appeared to be much improved, with surpluses, before extraordinary items, of £30 and £7 million respectively.[4] At the same time the PSO grant, including payments from the Passenger Transport Executives (PTEs) of local government authorities, increased by 61 per cent, from £324 million in 1975 to £522 million in 1979 (including a special asset replacement allowance begun in 1978—see below). The Board congratulated itself heartily on its 1977 results, with press advertisements trumpeting 'a year of advance for British Rail, the backbone of the nation' and pointing to a marked improvement in the operating surplus from £14 million in 1976 to £68 million (see Table 2.1). However, the picture is less rosy if full account is taken of inflation. At first sight, the position looks more optimistic. If we express the profit and loss figures in constant 1979 prices, then the scale of improvement appears greater still, moving from deficits of £126 and £336 million in 1973 and 1974 to surpluses ranging from £8 to £60 million in 1975–9. Furthermore, the level of government subsidy fell. The PSO payment actually fell by 15 per cent in real terms in 1976, from £544 to £464 million, and even with increased support thereafter was still 4 per cent lower in 1979. If we add the non-passenger sector grants to the statutory PSO support, the total level of support in real terms fell from £655 million in 1975 to £522 million four years later, a reduction of 20 per cent. Unfortunately, however, the effects of inflation on the Board's historically based accounts were more pervasive, influencing such elements as depreciation, amortisation, and stock usage. After applying the Accounting Standards Committee (Hyde) Guidelines of November 1977 on current cost accounting, the Board revealed that its surplus of £27 million in 1977 would have been transformed into a loss of £178 million, or £128 million after gearing adjustment.[5] One response to the challenge of inflation was the government's introduction from 1 January 1978 of a special replacement allowance for the renewal of rail passenger assets instead of loans. However, this failed to produce a dramatic effect on the calculation of profit/loss in current cost accounting terms. The auditors reported that on a current cost basis the losses in 1978 and 1979 were £147 and £184 million respectively, reduced to £121 and £152 million after a gearing adjustment.[6] Quite clearly, the PSO regime, in Peter Parker's words, gave the Board 'only temporary shelter on the barren mountain of inflation'.[7]

2.2 Peter Parker and the impetus for organisational reform

Privately railway managers were more gloomy about their position, matching the Department's disquiet over the claims for additional support in 1975 and 1976. The Board noted that the 1974 Act had produced a further blurring of the railways' statutory obligations. There was some confusion as to whether the break-even requirement in the 1947 and 1962 Acts took precedence over the obligation to maintain passenger services at their existing level, and whether the break-even requirement itself had been rendered meaningless by the government's acceptance that the present network was to be maintained. But whatever the Board's precise obligations, it was recognised that the existing organisation needed to be reshaped to bring it into line with the new requirements, and specifically the division of activities into the subsidised (passenger) and the commercial. The subsidiary businesses in particular were to be retained only if a net financial contribution could be derived from them.[8] This emphasis on commercial trading provided an impetus for reform of the planning Board organisation which had been introduced in 1970 after advice from the consultants, McKinsey.[9] The desire for change was also encouraged by the evident failure of the Field Organisation to transform regional management by the beginning of 1975 (see Chapter 1), and the consequent pressure to impose a firmer grip from the centre. The initiative did not seem to rest with Marsh, who resisted a number of suggestions from the Minister, Fred Mulley, designed to strengthen the Board (see below), and who was in any case approaching the end of his term of office (he made no attempt to seek an extension beyond the expiry date of 11 September 1976). Instead, the baton was seized by existing board members dissatisfied with the existing position, such as Bosworth, and by Marsh's successor, Peter Parker, whose appointment was announced in March 1976, and who became a part-time member with effect from 9 April 1976.

The composition of the Board had already shifted somewhat before Parker joined the Board. Two members left in 1974: Willie Thorpe, a career railwayman and former chief executive, in October, and Arthur Barker, a Beeching appointee from NAAFI, in November. The Department of the Environment had caused some irritation by pressing Marsh to make changes. In January Sir Idwal Pugh, the Second Permanent Secretary, expressed the view that the present group of part-time members 'looked like a "dog's breakfast" to an outsider' and suggested that recruits in the areas of finance and marketing be sought, together with a female Board member. Marsh not only poured cold water on these ideas but also declared that he was 'fundamentally opposed' to Mulley's view that Thorpe should be replaced by the Chief Executive (Railways), David Bowick.[10] Later in the year, an internal DOE inquiry into the procedures for public appointments provided an opportunity for the Board to point out some of the existing difficulties which inhibited recruitment: the insecurity of employment produced by five-year appointments, coupled with the absence of a Board pension scheme, which affected younger managers; and relatively low salaries, made worse by the non-implementation of the Boyle Committee's recommendations on top salaries in December 1974, which scuppered at least one proposal.[11]

Despite all this talk, the only immediate changes came in September 1974 when Sir David Serpell, the 62-year-old former Permanent Secretary at the DOE (1970–2), became a part-time member, and in April 1975, when Derek Fowler joined the Board as a replacement for Barker, with special responsibility for the finance function. Serpell brought an abundant knowledge of the workings of Whitehall and had been Marsh's Permanent Secretary at the Ministry of Transport (1968–70). Mulley obviously intended that he would both strengthen and improve the relationship between the Board and its sponsoring Department.[12] Fowler was another Beeching appointee who had experience of local authority finance. Since 1972 he had been Controller of Corporate Finance, where he had quickly demonstrated a good grasp of the railways' financial and accounting problems and their organisational implications. A relatively young man of 46, he not unnaturally had some qualms about accepting the standard five-year appointment with no guarantee of reappointment by the Ministry or of re-employment by the Board. But he was also aware that both Marsh and the DOE were finding it very difficult indeed to attract an external candidate at existing salary levels,[13] and the protracted negotiations with the Department over the issue had a positive outcome in that they helped to establish a precedent which made it easier for younger professional railwaymen to join the Board in future.[14] The final, and symbolic, change of 1975 was the expiry in December of Sir Frederick Hayday's appointment as a part-time member, after 13 years on the Board. He was the last link with the first British Railways Board of 1963.[15] Of these changes, the appointment of Fowler as Board member with responsibility for finance was the most significant. Notwithstanding his initial concerns about the impermanence of a five-year appointment, he not only went on to become one of the longest-serving Board members—15½ years to 30 October 1990—but quickly asserted his authority at Board level. For example, in the months before his appointment was ratified he was given the opportunity to express his views on the existing organisation, and at a meeting of the Chairman's Conference in March 1975 pressed the idea that the Board Member (Finance) should have a more proactive role, embracing an involvement in the current operations of each business, including policy formation on pricing, financial reporting, and object-ives. This was a clear departure from the McKinsey concept, which recommended that directors should concern themselves only with broad strategy.[16]

Of course, Fowler's appointment did not resolve the difficulty of working with an executive team which was rather thin on the ground. An early example of the tensions this produced was the DOE's anxiety to see a strengthening of railway expertise at Board level. In May 1975 Mulley proposed to put Bowick on the Board and appoint an existing member, Robert (Bobbie) Lawrence, the long-serving professional railwayman, to the post of Vice-Chairman. Marsh opposed this idea on the grounds that the simultaneous appointments would serve to undermine Bowick's authority as chief executive and produce 'a degree of confu-sion of responsibility' at Board level. He was happy to endorse Lawrence's promotion, but the move stalled when Mulley announced that he saw the appointment as a way of relieving Bowick of some of his heavy load. Marsh's reply was a tart one: 'You really cannot share out the executive authority of a Chief Executive'.[17] The matter was only resolved after Gilbert succeeded Mulley as Minister in June. Lawrence's role expanded further after the decision of Dr Sydney Jones to relinquish his committee responsibilities in the same month (see below), and he was eventually installed as Vice-Chairman in November.[18] However, the situation was far from being resolved, and Bosworth made his views patently clear when in February 1976 he referred Marsh to the 'problems that result from trying to run the present management system with a Chairman plus four Board members'.[19]

Further changes made during the interregnum of Marsh and Parker hastened the process of innovation. Two part-timers with a scientific background left on the termination of their contracts in June 1976, Sir Alastair Pilkington and Dr Sydney Jones, leaving the Board somewhat embarrassingly below its statutory minimum number.[20] The former had had less time to give to the railways since his appointment as a director of the Bank of England in 1974, and his three-year term was not renewed.[21] The latter, yet another Beeching appointee, was a research scientist with a distinguished career—he had developed the Firestreak weapon at the Royal Radar Establishment in the 1950s and had been a Board member since 1965. However, he had never quite come to terms with the realities of operating within the railway bureaucracy, and had become frustrated by the slow progress of innovation in general and the Advanced Passenger Train project in particular. His move in June 1974 from full-time to part-time status was occasioned in part by his appointment as chairman of the Department of Industry's Computer Systems Board, and more generally by an apparent need for 'some intellectual reinvigoration'. But his decision to hold on to the chairmanship of the railways' Technical and R&D committees had not worked out very well and he gave up these responsibilities to Lawrence, who became the Board member for Engineering, Technology, and Research in June 1975.[22] Jones's departure left the way open for the resolution of organisational issues surrounding the technical and research functions. In the post-McKinsey organisation, the engineering departments had reported through the Executive Director (Systems & Operations) to the Chief Executive, but the R&D Division remained a separate business, reporting to Sydney Jones. By the beginning of 1975 management problems surrounding the leadership of the research function were evident,[23] and in August, after Lawrence had assumed Jones's responsibilities, the R&D Board and the Technical Committee were merged to form the Research & Technical Committee with Lawrence as Chairman. The aim was to effect a closer relationship between the research function, which was now designated a department instead of a business, and the various technical departments.[24]

The key change at the top was the elevation to 'managing director' status of David Bowick, the 53-year-old Chief Executive (Railways), in July 1976. The idea that the chief executive should not be a Board member, a pillar of the McKinsey formula, was thus finally nailed with Bowick's appointment as a full-time member, and the 'railway' representation on the Board was strengthened accordingly. As we have seen, the move had been suggested on a number of occasions by the DOE in 1974–5. But there were also internal explanations arising from the Board changes, the management pressures experienced by Bowick, and the long-running debates over the management of the engineering, research and operating functions. Bowick himself had hastened the process in 1975 in his response to the R&D issue. He had proposed the separation of the operations and engineering functions of the relevant executive director, that for systems and operations, and later on suggested that two deputy chief executive posts might be created. The latter ideas prompted at least one Board member (Farrimond) to suggest that the way out of the difficulty would be to put Bowick on the Board and to replace Jones.[25] An additional consideration was the semi-retirement of David McKenna, who stepped down as a full-timer in June 1976, to be reappointed as a part-time member for two years from 1 September. His position had been under something of a cloud since 1974 and his move helped to clear the decks for the more substantial changes that were to follow.[26]

At the same time the Board secretariat was strengthened. Since 1973 Evan Harding, born in 1919, and a career railway solicitor who joined the London & North Eastern Railway in 1946, had combined the posts of chief secretary and legal adviser. In June 1976 he relinquished the post of secretary, which was taken up by Gerald (Gerry) Burt. Burt, born in 1926, was another career railwayman with a Great Western background (from 1942) and operating experience, though his most recent position was in corporate planning. With an interest in organisational change and a political instinct for government–industry relations, he added executive support for organisational change at Board level. The aim of the separation of posts was to improve communication especially with government, and to allow Harding to focus on parliamentary matters and dealings with the Select Committee on Nationalised Industries.[27] Burt was to take a particular interest in streamlining Board and committee procedures following the 1977 reorganisation.[28] The change also took account of a change at government level since on 10 September 1976, two days before Parker became full-time chairman, the DOE ceased to have responsibility for transport. A separate Department of Transport (DTp) was reconstituted with William Rodgers replacing Gilbert as Minister of Transport and Peter Baldwin as the Permanent Secretary. Departmental critics of the railways, such as Tom Beagley and Bill Sharp, gave way to more sympathetic officials, notably Peter Lazarus and John Palmer. Contacts were also improved by a series of monthly progress meetings begun in October and by agreement that staff be exchanged through a process of secondment.[29] But there was also a new team at '222' (222 Marylebone Road, BR Headquarters). The new Chairman, and the new Chief Secretary, had an important role to play in mending broken fences with the ministry and its senior civil servants.

The appointment of a new Chairman brought a unique and somewhat para-doxical figure to British Rail. Parker was a businessman with Labour Party sympathies. Born in 1924, he had been educated in France, China, at Bedford School in England, and the universities of London, Oxford, Cornell, and Harvard. He combined several attributes: a left-wing background with distinguished war service, first with the Royal West Kents, then as a major in the Intelligence Corps; a thorough knowledge of Japanese with an enthusiasm for sports, including tennis, swimming, and (earlier) rugby football; a passion for the stage with political aspirations and numerous outside interests—notably London Univer-sity, Political and Economic Planning, the British Institute of Management, and the Foundation for Management Education. He was above all someone who possessed both an abundant experience of how senior management worked in the private sector, with Booker McConnell, Associated British Maltsters, Curtis Brown, Rockware, Clarksons, and Dawnay Day, amongst others, and an experi-ence of the public sector via part-time appointments with the British Steel Corporation (1967–70), British Tourist Authority (1969–75), and British Airways Board (1971–81).[30] Unsurprisingly, his presence gave an impetus to organisational change in British Rail. Within months the Board was heralding a new top organisation, introduced in January 1977. Parker, then aged 52, had been chairman of the Rockware Group, the glass and plastic container company, with a salary of £65,000 a year, when he took the job. The decision to accept an appoint-ment at a third of his existing salary, that is £23,300 (subsequently raised during a period of pay restraint by a derisory £239 in 1977), while a higher rate than the £20,000 enjoyed by the Prime Minister, Jim Callaghan, could certainly be taken as evidence of a commitment to the railway cause. The move was also a contrast with Parker's attitude a decade earlier, when he had turned down Barbara Castle's offer of the chairmanship in 1967.[31] The significance of the change at the top was as much to do with personality as with capability and competences. Parker was an enthusiast, a motivator, and above all a crusader with an appreciation of the public relations role. In this he was ideally suited to this high-profile job. However, it remained to be seen whether he had the other necessary attributes to prosper in what he called 'the piranha fish bowl of the public sector'.[32]

2.3 The new functional organisation of 1977

The 1977 organisation, worked up and agreed by the Board in December 1976, was introduced on 10 January 1977. Essentially it involved unpicking the McKin-sey formula of planning board/executive divisions and returning to a Beeching type of centralised, railway function-dominated board, the purpose being to 'tighten lines of command and communication'.[33] Lawrence decided to go part-time for personal reasons, and consequently Bowick became a second Vice-Chairman, his brief, a difficult one, to provide more co-ordination of railway management at Board level. The team of Parker, Bosworth, and Bowick bore some resemblance to Beeching's in 1964–5, when the Chairman was supported by two Vice-Chairmen in Shirley and Raymond.[34] Out went the executive director tier of railway management. Three new full-time posts were established at Board level, with direct functional responsibility for: Engineering & Research; Marketing; and Operations. The appointees were all ex-LNER career railwaymen in their early fifties who had joined the industry after completing their education and/or war service: respectively Ian Campbell, Executive Director (Systems & Operations) since 1973; Robert Reid, General Manager of the Southern Region, 1974–6; and James Urquhart, General Manager of the London Midland, 1975–6. Furthermore, they were all 'shrewd', 'resilient', and 'determined' Scots, who with Bowick provided a substantial 'MacMafia' presence on the new Board.[35]

Campbell came from a Scottish railway family. Joining the LMS briefly in 1942 aged 20 he obtained a first-class honours degree in engineering at University College London and was then recruited as a draughtsman with the LNER in 1947. One of only two railway managers to spend a year in the United States as part of the American post-war management education programs,[36] he had previously held posts that included Chief Civil Engineer, Scottish Region (1965–8) and General Manager of the Eastern (1970–3). Reid, educated at Malvern College and Brasenose College, Oxford, joined the industry in 1947, after war service with the Royal Tank Regiment, when he became one of the LNER's last traffic apprentices. He had been Deputy General Manager of the Eastern (1972–4) before moving to the Southern. Urquhart joined the LNER at the age of 16, before serving in the RAF, and had been Assistant General Manager of the Western (1967–9) and Chief Operations Manager at HQ (1969–72).[37] At the same time Clifford Rose replaced Bert Farrimond as the member responsible for personnel, including industrial relations. Farrimond had nursed ambitions to be Vice-Chairman, and had expressed dissatisfaction with his position when his appointment came up for renewal in the course of 1976. When his request for improved terms was turned down by Parker and Rodgers he decided not to seek reappointment, though he did retain the part-time chairmanship of the British Transport Hotels subsidiary until February 1978.[38] Rose had been Farrimond's deputy as Executive Director (Personnel). Another career railwayman, this time with a Great Western background (he became a booking clerk at the age of 15 in 1944), he was at the age of 47 slightly younger than the others. Educated at the Royal Grammar School, High Wycombe, he had served with the Royal Engineers during the war before becoming a traffic apprentice in 1955.[39]

The four newcomers represented railways past as well as railways future. Tradition was clearly exhibited with their backgrounds—three of them were part of another 'mafia', the club of former LNER traffic apprentices, which had also produced Bowick and Lawrence as well as an earlier generation of notables, including Willie Thorpe, Henry Johnson, Gerry Fiennes, and Fred Margetts.[40] However, this was not a return to the Beeching type of functionalism staffed by appointees from outside the industry, but a move involving insiders, and relatively young ones at that. Indeed, because all except Reid were below the railways' minimum retirement age of 55, they required safeguards relating to future employment and pension arrangements of the kind raised when Fowler had been appointed in 1975.[41] The fifth and final change was certainly an innovation. Michael Posner, a public sector economist and a Reader in Economics at Cambridge, was appointed as a part-time member with effect from 1 January 1977. Aged 45, he had been Director of Economics at the Ministry of Power in 1966–7 and subsequently an adviser or consultant to the Treasury, the IMF, and NEDO. He had just left the Treasury as Deputy Chief Economic Adviser, and was recruited to British Rail on the suggestion of civil servants in the DOE. His inclusion in a team dominated by the railway professionals was more than merely a counterbalancing one. Parker fully concurred in the DOE's view that an independent economist would help to reduce the conflict between the Board and the Department over the economic case for railways.[42] Thus, five new recruits, in an expanded membership of 14, made their first appearance at the Board meeting on 13 January 1977 (see Table 2.2). The membership was now radically different from that three years earlier (Table 1.2). Two-thirds of the new Board had not been there then, and only Bosworth of the full-timers provided an element of continuity. Furthermore, two of the longer-serving part-timers, McKenna and Walker, departed in 1978.[43]

Were the changes positive? It might be argued that Parker's Board represented a return to the status quo ante 1970, with a strong element of retrogression. However, this would be misleading. When Parker joined the railways there was a strong whiff of disarray. He himself recalled that 'railway fortunes were at an achingly low ebb'.[44] Given the evident financial problems surrounding the obligation to maintain the existing network and the frustrations in attempting to modernise at a time of severe economic stringency, it made very good sense in managerial terms to seek to return to the railways' essential core competences. The attempt to re-establish a clear line management for the railway business served to cement established routines and knowledge inside the business and to bring such knowledge forward to policy making more effectively than before.[45] Under Marsh the planning board had become detached from the realities of railway management, and according to a senior civil servant Lawrence was left as 'the only connection between this tribe of people in the Board and the actual Railway'. Lower down Bowick and his executive team had been left to get on with running the operation.[46] Planning had been in some ways an artificial exercise. Starved of information from railway-based departments, it had to accept the decisions taken by engineers and operators and was therefore more concerned with forecasting outputs than controlling inputs, a situation which was reinforced

Table 2.2 The British Railways Board in January 1977

Name	Date of appointment	Age	Departed	Previous post	Experience
Chairman (salary £23,359)					
Peter Parker	1976	52	Sep. 1983	Chairman, Rockware	Industrial management (private plus public)
Deputy Chairman (salary £19,539)					
J. M. W. Bosworth	1968	55	Jun. 1983	Board Member, BRB; Partner, Peat Marwick Mitchell	Accountancy (PMM)
Vice-Chairman & Chief Executive (Railways) (salary £18,039)					
David Bowick*	1976	53	Jan. 1980	Board Member, BRB; Chief Executive (Railways), BRB	Railways
Vice-Chairman (part-time) (salary £7,609)					
R. L. E. Lawrence	1971	61	Sep. 1983	Board Member, BRB; GM, LMR	Railways
Full-time members (salary £14,809–£15,959)					
I. M. Campbell	1977	54	Jan. 1987	ED (Systems & Operations), BRB	Railways
Derek Fowler	1975	47	Oct. 1990	Controller, Corporate Finance, BRB	Railways, local government
R. B. Reid	1977	55	Mar. 1990	GM, SR	Railways
C. A. Rose	1977	47	Jul. 1983#	ED (Personnel), BRB	Railways
J. G. Urquhart	1977	51	Aug. 1985	GM, LMR	Railways
Part-time members (salary £1,000 plus committee pay; McKenna £6,015)					
David McKenna	1968	65	Aug. 1978	Board Member, BRB	Railways
Michael Posner	1977	45	Aug. 1984	—	Economist (public sector)
Sir David Serpell	1974	65	May 1982	—	Civil Service
Lord Taylor of Gryfe	1968	64	Jun. 1980	—	Retailing (Co-op)
Sir Alan Walker	1969	66	Jan. 1978#	—	Brewing (Bass Charrington)

* Became Vice-Chairman (Rail) # Died

by the obligation to maintain the level of passenger services under the 1974 Act. Finance was also largely a response to operating, rather than a genuine control mechanism.[47] The new Chairman saw immediately that something had to be done. His aim with the new organisation was to improve the Board's effectiveness in directing and managing its business. The Minister was reassured that there would be 'a better mix of policy and management at Board level ... [enabling] the Board to concentrate attention on certain key business areas'.[48] A railway-dominated team did of course carry with it the danger of a retreat to old attitudes best summarised as 'engineers and operators know best', an emphasis on providing a good public service which did not always square with either the bottom-line or the economic and political realities of the late 1970s. This viewpoint has been associated with some of the professional railwaymen on the Board, such as Lawrence and Rose.[49] Unsurprisingly, then, it took some time to get the organisation bedded down and the functions clarified.

Much work needed to be done to evaluate the implications of the new functionalism and turn it into durable changes below the board. Following the removal of the 'executive director' tier of management, new posts were created at Headquarters, reporting lines were modified, and adjustments were made to the way decisions were moved up and down the hierarchy to regional level, particularly in engineering, where the centre assumed new responsibilities (See Figure 2.1). Encouraged by Burt,[50] a new streamlined committee structure was drafted in the course of 1977, debated at Board level in December 1977 and January 1978, and put in place by March. The number of formal Board committees was reduced from ten to four, leaving the Board Executive, which replaced the more informal Chairman's Conference; Audit; Planning & Investment; and Supply. The following were abandoned: Finance; Management Development; Research & Technical; and the steering groups for Accommodation, Productivity and Computers. Some of these functions, and others, were handled by advisory groups or panels: Design; Environment; Senior Appointments; Remuneration & Conditions; Research & Technical; and Strategy. At the same time, the extent of delegated powers was more explicitly stated, and the 15 matters reserved to the Board were listed.[51]

One of the major nettles grasped was the merging of the planning and investment functions at Headquarters. After lengthy discussions in December 1977 and January 1978, a single committee was established to handle both investment and shorter-term planning (i.e. five-year business plans and corporate plans), with considerable delegated powers. Tom Barron was appointed Director of Planning & Investment, reporting to Fowler, who added planning to his portfolio. Bosworth, previously the member responsible for planning, was to concentrate on the subsidiary businesses.[52] Further development and clarification of these vital functions saw the speedy abandonment of the new post of Director of Planning & Investment—Barron became a part-time Board member in April 1978—and the bringing together of investment work in the several departments—planning and

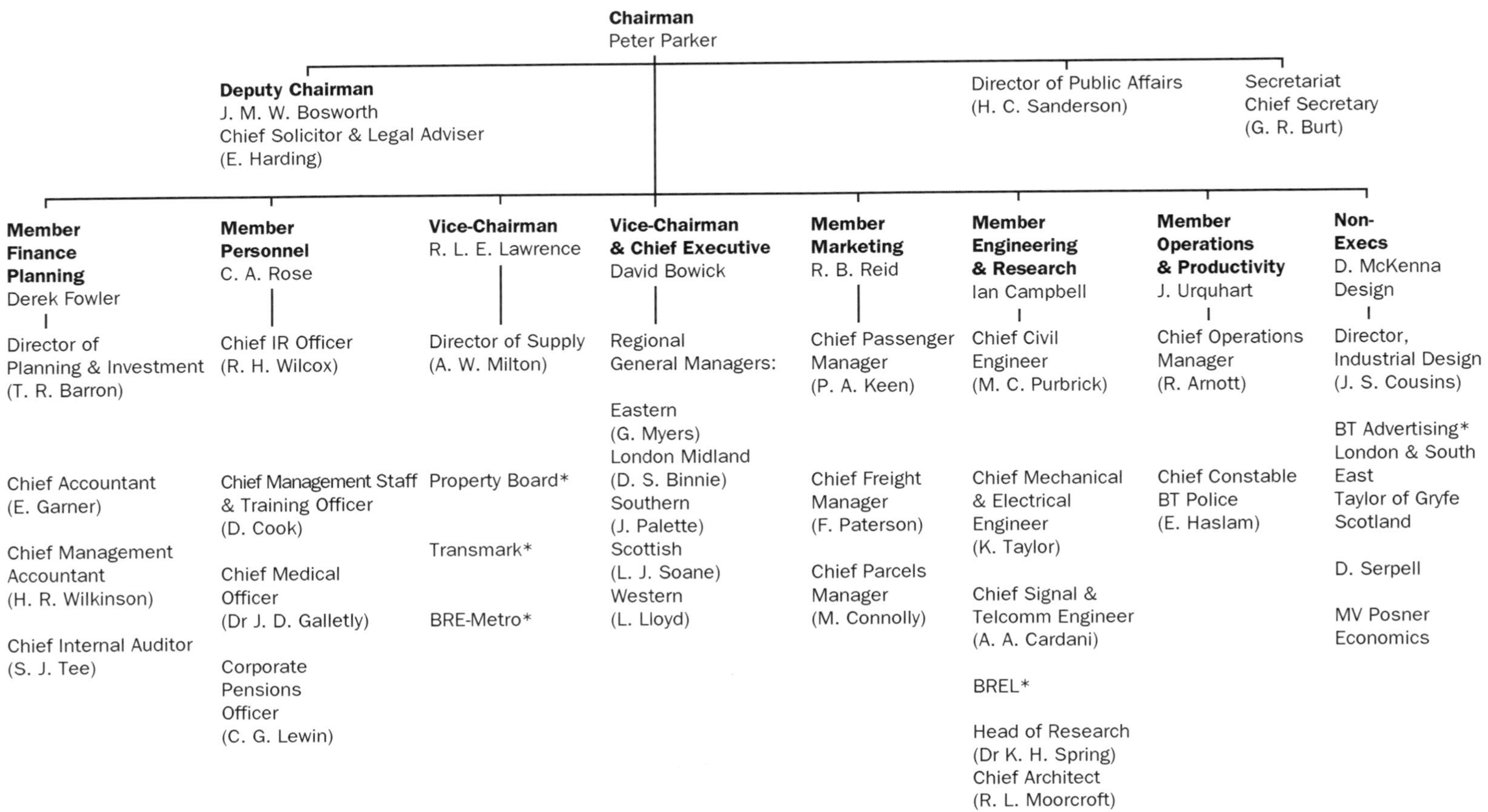

Chairman
Peter Parker

Deputy Chairman
J. M. W. Bosworth
Chief Solicitor & Legal Adviser
(E. Harding)

Director of Public Affairs
(H. C. Sanderson)

Secretariat
Chief Secretary
(G. R. Burt)

Member Finance Planning Derek Fowler	**Member Personnel** C. A. Rose	**Vice-Chairman** R. L. E. Lawrence	**Vice-Chairman & Chief Executive** David Bowick	**Member Marketing** R. B. Reid	**Member Engineering & Research** Ian Campbell	**Member Operations & Productivity** J. Urquhart	**Non-Execs** D. McKenna Design
Director of Planning & Investment (T. R. Barron)	Chief IR Officer (R. H. Wilcox)	Director of Supply (A. W. Milton)	Regional General Managers:	Chief Passenger Manager (P. A. Keen)	Chief Civil Engineer (M. C. Purbrick)	Chief Operations Manager (R. Arnott)	Director, Industrial Design (J. S. Cousins)
Chief Accountant (E. Garner)	Chief Management Staff & Training Officer (D. Cook)	Property Board*	Eastern (G. Myers) London Midland (D. S. Binnie)	Chief Freight Manager (F. Paterson)	Chief Mechanical & Electrical Engineer (K. Taylor)	Chief Constable BT Police (E. Haslam)	BT Advertising* London & South East Taylor of Gryfe Scotland
Chief Management Accountant (H. R. Wilkinson)	Chief Medical Officer (Dr J. D. Galletly)	Transmark*	Southern (J. Palette) Scottish (L. J. Soane)	Chief Parcels Manager (M. Connolly)	Chief Signal & Telcomm Engineer (A. A. Cardani)		D. Serpell
Chief Internal Auditor (S. J. Tee)		BRE-Metro*	Western (L. Lloyd)		BREL*		MV Posner Economics
	Corporate Pensions Officer (C. G. Lewin)				Head of Research (Dr K. H. Spring) Chief Architect (R. L. Moorcroft)		

*See Figure 2.2.

Figure 2.1 British Railways Board organisation, 1 March 1978

investment, corporate works, management accountant—under a single chief officer.[53] Of course, the changes brought with them some risks. Lord Taylor of Gryfe, the part-timer who had led a review of the post-McKinsey organisation in 1971,[54] expressed the fear that the new planning and investment committee was so important that it might supersede the Board, and argued that the latter should retain its right to examine options.[55] However, the changes were generally beneficial, producing more clarity, linking shorter-term planning with budgetary control under Fowler, and drawing a distinction between routine planning and the development of longer-term strategic thinking, a responsibility which was given to a new body, the Strategy Unit (see below). The new Board-level emphasis on marketing and public relations also demanded changes at senior officer level. Posts of Chief Passenger Manager (Peter Keen) and Chief Freight Manager (Frank Paterson) were established in January 1977, reporting to Reid, and a Director of Public Affairs was appointed, reporting to Parker: initially Henry Sanderson, then from August 1978 Grant Woodruff. Parker also employed Will Camp as a public relations adviser with a less formal brief. Camp was an accomplished 'spin-doctor' twenty years ahead of his time.[56] Other innovations included the following: the reorganisation in May 1977 of the regional railway advisory boards, with five instead of four to reflect the retention of the existing regional structure following the abandonment of 'Field', a smaller membership, and the inclusion of trade union representatives;[57] the restructuring of BR's management services from September 1977 with its division into two departments—computing and operational research, and productivity;[58] and the creation of an environmental panel in September 1977, with Bernard Kaukas as Director, Environment.[59]

At the same time the 'Railway Command Structure' was reorganised around a Railway Executive, in addition to the existing Railway Management Group (see Figure 2.2).[60] The Executive was made up of the functional board members plus the Directors of Planning & Investment (until April 1978) and Public Affairs. Given the job of translating Board policies into action, 'it was not to have specific powers as an Executive. All decisions will be taken by its members against the background of discussion and support in the Executive'. The Railway Management Group was a larger body which included the regional general managers and the Managing Director of British Rail Engineering Ltd (BREL). This was a forum for general railway management 'in which there shall be discussion about evolving policy and plans and exchange of views on the current conduct of the business'.[61] While there was some recognition at Headquarters that the railway business consisted of six 'principal business sectors'—four passenger (Inter-City, London & South East, Passenger Transport Executives, Other Provincial Services), Freight, and Parcels—the basic framework of rail management rested on five regions—Eastern, London Midland, Southern, Western, and Scottish, as it had done since nationalisation. Given the rather vague remits of the two 'horizontal' committees it is hard to see that the new 'command' structure was likely

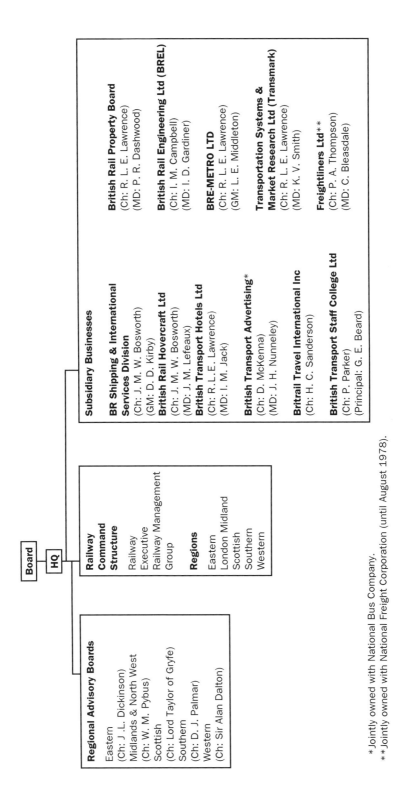

Board

HQ

Regional Advisory Boards

Eastern
(Ch: J. L. Dickinson)
Midlands & North West
(Ch: W. M. Pybus)
Scottish
(Ch: Lord Taylor of Gryfe)
Southern
(Ch: D. J. Palmar)
Western
(Ch: Sir Alan Dalton)

Railway Command Structure

Railway Executive
Railway Management Group

Regions

Eastern
London Midland
Scottish
Southern
Western

Subsidiary Businesses

BR Shipping & International Services Division
(Ch: J. M. W. Bosworth)
(GM: D. D. Kirby)

British Rail Hovercraft Ltd
(Ch: J. M. W. Bosworth)
(MD: J. M. Lefeaux)

British Transport Hotels Ltd
(Ch: R. L. E. Lawrence)
(MD: I. M. Jack)

British Transport Advertising*
(Ch: D. McKenna)
(MD: J. H. Nunneley)

Britrail Travel International Inc
(Ch: H. C. Sanderson)

British Transport Staff College Ltd
(Ch: P. Parker)
(Principal: G. E. Beard)

British Rail Property Board
(Ch: R. L. E. Lawrence)
(MD: P. R. Dashwood)

British Rail Engineering Ltd (BREL)
(Ch: I. M. Campbell)
(MD: I. D. Gardiner)

BRE-METRO LTD
(Ch: R. L. E. Lawrence)
(GM: L. E. Middleton)

Transportation Systems & Market Research Ltd (Transmark)
(Ch: R. L. E. Lawrence)
(MD: K. V. Smith)

Freightliners Ltd**
(Ch: P. A. Thompson)
(MD: C. Bleasdale)

*Jointly owned with National Bus Company.
**Jointly owned with National Freight Corporation (until August 1978).

Figure 2.2 The Board and its constituent businesses, 1 March 1978

to work very cohesively, and in a rather compartmentalised, consensual environment, the danger of overloading the chief executive was very real. The Board itself recognised some of the difficulties in striking an appropriate balance between the Centre and the Regions in a structure which was 'bound to be a continuing process of readjustment in BR or indeed in any enterprise of similar scale'.[62] However, the new structure of command did nothing to disturb the power of the regional general managers in determining much of the day-to-day decision making affecting railway operations. The wording of the remit makes this clear. The general managers now had three channels of communication with Headquarters—through the relevant chief officer, the relevant functional Board member, and the chief executive for matters of 'general management'. 'General Managers will choose the method of communication which is most direct and effective in the particular circumstances of each case, and using their knowledge of internal headquarters procedures'.[63] This was surely an opportunity to exercise divide and rule tactics at regional level. Moreover, the general managers were able to exploit the existence of personality clashes within the executive team, which served to undermine the effectiveness of the 1977–8 reorganisation. It is no surprise to learn that the newly installed functional Board members sometimes found it hard to discover where actual power lay. The answer was frequently to be found at the regional level.[64]

There were further modifications of the organisation in the summer and autumn of 1978. The proposals for planning were firmed up; and changes to the functional responsibilities of Board members were prompted by Bowick's serious illness in the first half of 1978 and Lawrence's appointment as Chairman of the National Freight Corporation with effect from January 1979. The establishment of a small Strategy Unit in July 1978 proved to be an important innovation. This was an in-house 'consultancy think tank', required to 'work with Headquarters departments and with Subsidiary Businesses to identify and develop areas of change necessary to the long-term success of the whole undertaking', to look at options, and 'turn these into meaningful business objectives'. Reporting to a Board-level Strategy Steering Group, it was to 'cover not only general forward planning and the identification of profitable growth areas for expansion, but also such matters as social and environmental analysis, diversification, long-term financial and personnel strategies, and research and development strategy'.[65] The Unit was headed by a 'high-flier' with a railway background, Geoffrey Myers, General Manager of the Eastern Region since October 1976, who became Director, Strategic Development. It consisted of a strong executive team which included David Cobbett, Arnold Kentridge, Dr John Prideaux, and Dr Kenneth Spring, and was further strengthened by the secondment of John Welsby from the DTp Railway Economics Unit in January 1979.[66] The Steering Group consisted of Bowick as chairman, Bosworth, Fowler, Barron, Posner, Myers, and Professor John Heath, a leading business strategy consultant from the London Business School.[67]

By this time Bowick had more time to devote to strategy. A serious illness, which caused his absence from the Board from December 1977 to April 1978, forced him to step down as Chief Executive in June 1978. His post was re-designated 'Vice-Chairman (Rail)', and he was asked to manage Strategy, Environment, European and International matters, and Industrial Design. He was succeeded as Chief Executive by Ian Campbell, who retained his functional responsibility for engineering and research. Yet more adjustment was required a few months later when Lawrence moved to the NFC, producing a further reallocation of duties. Lawrence's responsibilities as Chairman of the Supply Committee, British Transport Hotels, Transmark, BRE-Metro, and BREL were shared among Bowick, Bosworth, Campbell, and Urquhart (see Figure 2.3).[68] Functional though the Board now was, its rather complex configuration, with a full-time Chairman, Deputy Chairman, part-time Vice-Chairman, full-time Vice-Chairman (Rail), and a Chief Executive, tended to puzzle outsiders. When Gerry Burt sought reactions from colleagues outside BRB in November 1978, he received a revealing response from Robert Roseveare, Secretary of the British Steel Corporation. Roseveare confessed to a 'certain confusion about the respective roles of the "quorum Board", the Board Executive and the Railway Executive', and found 'it difficult to see clearly the relationship between two top rail posts—namely, the Vice-Chairman (Rail) and the Chief Executive (Railways)'.[69] The new organisation of 1977–8 had not solved all the issues relating to the corporate and railway command structures; and the Strategy Steering Group was to play an important role in promoting the more decisive changes which led to management by sector in 1982 (see Chapter 4). A further anxiety surrounded staffing at Headquarters. The centralisation process meant more work at 222 Marylebone Road, since responsibility for the engineering and architecture functions was taken from the railway regions, and some new departments were built up, for example in pension fund investment. Staff numbers increased by 14 per cent, from 6,100 at the end of 1973 to nearly 7,000 five years later. Fears of an overblown bureaucracy prompted a detailed report on the situation in March 1979 by Lewin, the Controller of Corporate Pensions,[70] while plans to move the core staff from the labyrinthine corridors of the old Great Central Hotel to slimmer, more modern premises in front of Euston Station, effected in November 1979, provided a further opportunity for the Board to pursue its desire to restrain staff costs.[71]

2.4 The subsidiary businesses

Another area of pressing concern was the Board's relationship with its subsidiary businesses. Their financial record was scarcely impressive, the 1976

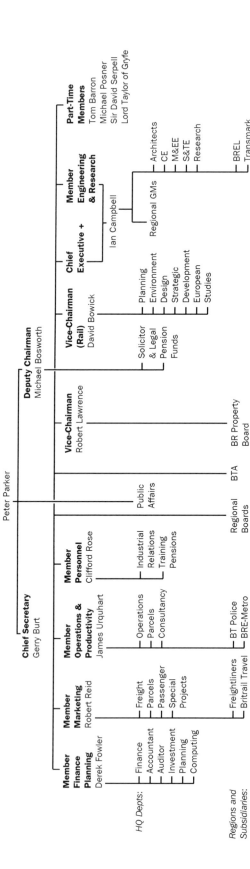

Figure 2.3 The revised Board organisation, 1 November 1978

accounts revealing an overall loss on operating account of £1.9 million for the rail workshops, rail catering, shipping, harbours, hovercraft, and hotels taken together.[72] The several organisations left much to be desired, the involvement of regional railway management hindered monitoring and control, and profit motivation was far from strong.[73] The Board faced mounting anxiety from the DTp about the financial implications of continuing to support these activities, while its earlier search for a definition of the 'Necessary Railway' (see Chapter 1), which had involved a division of activities into 'necessary' and 'optional', inevitably invited the suggestion that much of the periphery might indeed be 'optional'.[74] Parker began by asking some blunt questions himself about the subsidiaries' value to the undertaking: 'Are they regarded as providing positive development opportunities which through their contin-uing association with Railways, can be brought to the point where they can make a substantial contribution to the Board's finances? Or alternatively, are they seen as peripheral in relation to the Board's primary duty to provide railway services and likely to prove a distraction to top management...?'[75] Discussion in January 1977 came down firmly on the side of developing these businesses positively. The decision was taken to regard them as 'groups within the Group', and operate most of them as separate limited companies. To that end action was taken to seek wider powers from government and initiate other changes to give the subsidiaries greater commercial freedom. In the annual report for 1977 Parker emphasised that 'All of them need to be seen to be powerful businesses responding in their different markets in a competitive way. We expect them to perform at least as well as their private sector counterparts and we need to allow them to operate with the same degree of flexibility and oppor-tunity'.[76]

This laudable strategy faced several obstacles. Some matters lay outside the railways' direct control, requiring Ministerial or governmental consent to estab-lish more commercial freedom, for example, for BREL, the British Rail Property Board, and the Shipping and International Division.[77] However, reform was scarcely encouraged by the difficulty of attracting new managerial blood at existing (and constrained) salary levels into businesses starved of badly needed investment, and although the DTp expressed some sympathy for the idea of freeing up the subsidiaries, not least in the White Paper on *Transport Policy* of June 1977,[78] the government itself, in the White Paper on *The Nationalised Industries* of March 1978, advocated a tighter, rather than looser, control of public sector undertakings (see below).[79] The Board itself expressed some reser-vations about greater freedom, since it was recognised that the core business had many direct linkages with the subsidiaries, for example in engineering, train and station catering, and short-sea ferries.[80] Notwithstanding these difficulties, some positive and effective action was taken over the course of 1977–9. The reporting line was clarified for Managing Directors/Chief Executives by ending their joint responsibility to the subsidiary and main Boards.[81] This was followed by important changes to the organisation of the hotels, shipping, and freightliner businesses.

British Transport Hotels, responsible for both the hotels and railway catering, certainly presented as a sluggish business, short of investment and generally over-optimistic in its business plans.[82] The appointments of George Hill as Chairman and Managing Director (in 1974) and Bert Farrimond and Ian Jack as Chairman and Managing Director respectively (in 1976) did not produce dramatic improvement, though Farrimond reacted aggressively, if rather unrealistically, to the Board's resolution of January 1977 by advocating complete freedom for the business, including the power to review the hotels' portfolio and rationalise; acquire or build new hotels; remove statutory restrictions on station catering; and obtain access to private risk capital.[83] The company's Board was certainly strengthened with the appointment of Robert Reid in February 1977 and two outsiders, Sir Alexander Glen and Ms Prue Leith, in the following autumn.[84] Then, following a report commissioned from Coopers & Lybrand, major strategies for the two core businesses—hotels, and catering (the latter called 'Travellers Fare' from 1973)—were identified. A revised organisation, designed to provide the required impetus, was introduced from February 1978. This established separate divisional boards and managing directors for hotels and catering.[85] Then in August a Group Managing Director, Peter Land, was appointed to strengthen central direction.[86]

The performance of the Shipping and International Services Division, a heterogeneous collection of activities focused around the ferries and harbours, was undoubtedly affected by the strong competition offered by the private-sector shipping companies, which were unfettered by statutory or public obligations. In August 1977 the Board accepted the recommendations of an internal working party, which included the establishment of a limited company structure with profit-centre-based management, provision of greater levels of commercial freedom and delegated authority, and the hiving off of the international services function to a separate management unit.[87] The subsidiary was reconstituted as Sealink UK Ltd with effect from 1 January 1979, and the DTp responded by setting the new company a specific target, requiring it to achieve a real rate of return on net asset replacement cost of 5 per cent (before interest and tax) by 1982.[88] Finally, Freightliners Ltd, the ailing container business jointly owned with the National Freight Corporation, became a wholly owned subsidiary again in August 1978. This move, put to and accepted by the Select Committee on Nationalised Industries in 1977, was justified on the grounds that it would revitalise the business if it were more explicitly linked to the Railfreight activity.[89] However, the transfer was not an easy one given the subsidiary's sorry financial position. On its return to British Rail it had accumulated losses of £13.9 million on a capital of £26 million, necessitating a financial reconstruction and subsequent close attention to cash-flow and investment requirements.[90]

How successful was the refocusing exercise? Some progress was made in securing minor concessions from government in relation to commercial freedom.[91] For example, Ministerial consent was given in August 1978 to extended powers of manufacture, allowing BREL more latitude in using workshop capacity for outside work.[92] On the other hand, proposals requiring legislative change were more problematic. Thus, attempts to lift the restrictions on lease and leaseback transactions, which affected the British Rail Property Board, and to amend the statutory procedures affecting shipping routes made no headway.[93] The Board itself, while nervous of allowing its subsidiaries too much freedom in areas such as personnel and financial control,[94] did make progress in delegating greater powers, for example to the Property Board,[95] in pressing for more 'commercial' financial objectives,[96] and in encouraging a move away from highly geared capital accounts.[97] On the whole, however, the psychological impact of attempting to apply a more entrepreneurial strategy for the subsidiaries was probably more important than the immediate results, which were limited. The Board could take comfort from Transmark's Queen's Award for Exports in 1978,[98] but elsewhere there was much dissatisfaction, particularly with the financial performance of rail catering and British Rail Hovercraft, which suffered operating losses of £4.9 and £2.2 million respectively in 1978, and with the delivery record of BREL.[99] The short-term financial improvement was unspectacular. The difficulty of estimating and isolating asset value hinders calculation on a conventional ROCE basis, but the published accounts reveal that the loss on operating account for six subsidiary activities of £1.9 million in 1976 had been turned into a surplus of £9.2 million by 1978. This 'return' was modest when compared with the surpluses on operational and non-operational property, which amounted to £18.4 and £23.2 million respectively in 1976 and 1978.[100] Calculations of operating margins, and of the surplus expressed as a percentage of estimated capital employed, are given in Table 2.3. These again underline the fact that the subsidiaries, with the exception of land sales and letting, were contributing relatively little to group profits. Perhaps the main impact of the new 'entrepreneurial' emphasis lay in the contribution to the public policy debate. The Board's call for an injection of private capital to circumvent the investment straitjacket, while scarcely likely to capture the imagination of a Labour administration with its back to the wall in 1978–9, raised a fundamental issue in the corporate governance of the public sector, one which would be exploited by the incoming Conservative government after 1979 (see Chapter 4). Similarly, the perpetuation of a 'deficiency of assets position', that is, liabilities in excess of assets, for the hotels, shipping, hovercraft, and Transmark businesses, which necessitated regular Ministerial assent to a British Rail guarantee to creditors, was a constant reminder that it was difficult for these businesses to escape from the public sector with its control realities without a more radical approach.[101]

Table 2.3 BRB businesses: operating margins and estimated return on capital employed, 1976 and 1978

Activity	Operating margins (%)		Operating surplus as % of estimated capital employed, 1978
	1976	1978	
BR Workshops (external sales)	7.6	0.3	0.1
Ships/			8.8
harbours	−1.2	7.6	15.0
Hovercraft	0.0	−40.0	−14.1
Hotels	4.2	3.3	4.0
Retail and catering	2.5	2.4	—[a]
Property: operational	74.6	77.8	—[a]
non-operational	70.8	70.0	3.9
Transmark	8.0	13.0	—
Freightliners	1.7	2.0	9.2
Railways	0.01[a]	2.1[a]	6.1[a]

Source: BRB, *R&A 1979*, pp. 46–54, 75–6.

Note: Margins = 'Net profit & loss before interest as percentage of gross income'; for property = 'operating surplus before development land tax'. N.B. The figures differ from those which may be derived from the operating surplus/gross income data in the accounts, p. 79.
Estimated capital = net book values of ways and structures and vehicles, plant and equipment.

[a] 'Railways' includes rail and station catering, operational property, and commercial advertising (losses on rail catering were £4.9m. in 1978).

2.5 The strained relationship with government

The railways' new organisation, which seemed to some external observers to be rather backward looking, entrenched, and railwaymen dominated, put pressures on the relationship with government, which, as we have seen, was already badly strained. First, the new organisation was introduced at a time when much of the public policy debate was concerned with quite different objectives, expressed in the recommendations of the abortive Rothschild inquiry of 1972–3, the NEDO Report of November 1976, the Bullock Committee of Inquiry Report on *Industrial Democracy* of January 1977, the National Consumer Council's Report on *Consumers and the Nationalised Industries* of August 1976, the wide-ranging report from the Commons Select Committee on Nationalised Industries on the *Role of British Rail in Public Transport* of April 1977, and the White Paper on *Transport Policy* of June 1977. The NEDO Report had much in common with the internal report drafted by Lord Rothschild of the Central Policy Review Staff three years earlier. Both provided a damning indictment of the relationship between the public corporations and their sponsoring ministries, finding a lack of trust, uncertainty as to roles and responsibilities, and occasional open conflict. Both advocated a move away from the Morrisonian, 'arm's-length', public corporation, and both provoked a hostile reaction from the nationalised industries. For Rothschild, the solution lay in the 'membranes' concept, the idea of creating an agency interposed between the industries and the government—a Ministry of Nationalised Industries, a holding company, or an investment bank. None found favour with the chairmen of nationalised industries, however, and the report was quickly shelved.[102] NEDO, responding to the continuing interest of the Select Committee on Nationalised Industries, provided a more comprehensive, enduring, and public document. This time the organisational prescription was a two-tier board structure, consisting of a part-time policy council and a full-time corporation (executive) board. The councils were to be advisory, led by a government-appointed chairman and staffed by civil servants, industry executives, trade unionists, and consumers, and were to formulate consensual strategies designed to overcome existing conflicts.[103] The structure had additional attractions in that it resembled the industrial model successfully used in Germany and thought (by some at least) to be a factor in that country's impressive growth, international competitiveness, and superior governance systems.[104]

The fact that the 1977 organisation did not go in this direction clearly worried British Rail.[105] As Parker put it to his Minister, Rodgers, 'We prefer modified Morrison to more McKinsey…It is a pity that NEDO felt driven to the single solution of a Policy Council to cope with the Himalayan range of differences in the nationalised industries'.[106] Happily, the notion of two-tier boards was shelved following almost universal criticism from the Bullock Committee, the Nationalised Industries Chairmen's Group (NICG) and the individual corporations.[107] In any case, organisational questions were overshadowed by the Treasury-dominated response to the NEDO Report, which found eventual expression in the financial targeting and performance indicators of the 1978 White Paper on *The Nationalised Industries* (see below).[108] However, calls for a broader representation remained, supported by the Select Committee Report and White Paper of 1977.[109] British Rail, with its several layers of negotiation and consultation, was somewhat dismissive of further moves in the direction of industrial democracy. Marsh had made it clear that he regarded 'worker participation on Boards as somewhat akin to the virgin birth', noting that railway trade unionists were unlikely to be very enthusiastic. He claimed that Sidney Greene of the NUR had once told him: 'if you ever think that General Secretaries of my union are going to be treated on a par with Part-Time Board Members, you have got another think coming!'[110] However, a positive response to the issue was formally required by government following the endorsement of worker representation in the White Papers on *The Nationalised Industries* and *Industrial Democracy* in March and May 1978.[111] Steps were therefore taken from March 1978 to strengthen the consultation process by establishing a new top body—the British Rail Council—to deal with corporate policy matters, restructuring the BRJCC, which was to confine itself to consideration of day-to-day matters affecting the railways, and creating similar consultation bodies for each subsidiary business.[112] The unions had to be won over to the changes, of course, and ASLEF, which was in dispute with the Board over manning and pay relativity issues, conspicuously dragged its feet. Thus, the first meeting of the Rail Council was not held until July 1979.[113] This left the government's promise to strengthen consumer representation, which had been endorsed by the 1978 White Papers and included in the Queen's Speech in November. Proposals originating with the Consumer Council to give a reconstituted Central Transport Consultative Committee wider powers, notably an oversight of fares and charges, together with a seat on the Board, were advanced by the Select Committee on Nationalised Industries in April 1979, but progress was halted by the change of government.[114]

Second, the relationship with government highlighted the problems national-ised industry managers felt they had in running their businesses effectively. From the standpoint of the present day, when we have become accustomed to the debate about the need to establish sound 'corporate governance' in business, it must be remembered that for public sector managers the situation was very different. Rather than having to face shareholders' concern about high executive salaries, generous share option schemes, and weak monitoring systems, for railways and the other public corporations the problem was the reverse. The shareholder, the government, was felt to be too powerful, too interventionist. Managers operating through the NICG, which had begun to act more formally as a channel of communication with government in 1976, were lobbying for a kind of 'reverse governance' in which they hoped for more freedom not less, to fix salaries and incentives, fix investment levels, borrow more freely, and operate without so many statutory obligations and restraints.[115] In the early years of the Parker administration the British Railways Board and senior rail managers certainly felt themselves to be in a state of 'deep analysis' (1976 annual report), referring subsequently to an 'intense period of public accountability' (1977 annual report), and what Parker later famously called a state of 'perpetual audit' (1983).[116] Enquiries, audits, and policy reviews came thick and fast, consuming a vast amount of senior management time (see Table 2.4). Every conceivable area of managerial responsibility came under one of the several microscopes, and only the more persistent issues can be considered here.

As we have already observed, in the mid–late 1970s the dialogue with govern-ment was undoubtedly affected by dissatisfaction over low and unmodified levels of pay for Board members. This had the effect of holding down executive salaries lower down, producing a 'glass ceiling' on executive recruitment which was undoubtedly a factor in Parker's decision to promote railwaymen in 1977.[117] The issue was a concern for the chairmen of all the nationalised industries. The Boyle Committee on Top Salaries, reporting in 1974, noted that there had been no major review since 1969, and recommended substantial—30 per cent—in-creases for the higher judiciary, senior officers in the armed forces, senior civil

Table 2.4 British Rail's perpetual audit, 1976–8

Inquiry	Start date	End date	BR response
WP on Public Expenditure (Cmnd. 6393)	—	Feb. 1976	—
Transport Policy Consultation Document	—	Apr. 1976	BRB, *Opportunity for Change*, July 1976
WP on Cash Limits (Cmnd. 6440)	—	Apr. 1976	—
Nat Cons Council on Consumers & Nat Inds	Apr. 1975	Aug. 1976	—
NEDO on Nat Inds	June 1975	Nov. 1976	March 1977 SCNI 2nd Special Report, May 1977
Bullock Ctee on Ind Democracy (Cmnd. 6706)	Aug. 1975	Jan. 1977	—
WP on Govt Expenditure Plans (Cmnd. 6721)	—	Feb. 1977	—
WP on Cash Limits (Cmnd. 6767)	—	Mar. 1977	—
SCNI Role of BR (HC305-I)	May 1976	Apr. 1977	Sept. 1977 in Cmnd. 7038, pp. 31–41
WP on Transport Policy (Cmnd. 6836)	June 1976	June 1977	—
Govt Response to SCNI HC305 (Cmnd. 7038)	May 1977	Nov. 1977	—
WP on Public Expenditure (Cmnd. 7049)	—	Jan. 1978	—
Price Commission	Nov. 1977	Feb. 1978	—
WP on The Nat Inds (Cmnd. 7131)	Nov. 1976	Mar. 1978	Memo, July 1978; SCNI 6th Special Report, July 1978
WP on Cash Limits (Cmnd. 7151)	—	Apr. 1978	—
WP on Ind Democracy (Cmnd. 7231)	—	May 1978	—

servants, and public sector board members.[118] The government failed to enhance the pay of the latter group, however, and token increases in 1977—the £4 a week agreed in May in line with pay restraint, and Prime Minister Callaghan's announcement of a 5 per cent increase in December—merely served to heighten the sense of frustration.[119] Sir Denis Rooke, Chairman of the British Gas Corporation and of the NICG spoke for all when he trenchantly reminded Callaghan of the 'acute sense of injustice felt by all Board Members in the Nationalised industries at the blatant discrimination against them'.[120] For British Rail pay relativities were the main concern. Its submission to the Boyle Committee in October 1977 argued that the failure to advance Board members' salaries had created an impossible situation with regard to executive salaries, and from 1975 it had been forced to hold down its Senior Officer (SO) scale.[121] The alternative, rejected by British Rail but taken up by British Steel and Cable & Wireless, for example, was to pay executives more than board members.[122] There was no real move to advance Board members' salaries until after the Boyle Committee's Report of June 1978 had conceded that these were 'seriously out of date', and the government pledged to implement its recommendations in three stages ending in April 1980.[123] Even so, the situation remained far from satisfactory. Increases agreed in June and August 1978 and April 1979 took the Chairman's pay from £23,539 to £32,948 and that of the average Board member from about £15,000 to £19,000,[124] but clearly failed to correct pay levels for the ravages of inflation. The Chairman had been paid £23,100 in 1974, and ordinary Board members £13,600; these salaries were equivalent to £49,386 and £29,063 respectively in 1978 prices. The position of part-time members also demanded attention. Their £1,000 ceiling, unchanged for over 30 years, justified the NEDO Report's pithy comment that this reflected the 'comparatively limited contributions which they are in reality able or allowed to make in many corporations'.[125] British Rail had been able to circumvent the problem by paying additional sums for special responsibilities. Lord Taylor had been paid £3,000 since 1970, and Serpell received the same in 1978.[126] The Boyle Committee recommended that *all* part-timers' pay should be based *pro rata* on the full-time salary according to the time given, with a minimum of £1,500 (1974), then £2,000 (1978). However, all they received before the change of government was a share in the 10 per cent increase applied in August 1978, which took the basic rate to £1,100. This was the sum offered to Lord Caldecote, Chairman of Delta Metal and Legal & General, when he joined the Board in March 1979.[127] It was left to the Conservatives to make further adjustments to public sector pay after the election in May.[128]

The most serious problems arose over the attempts to identify the basic aims and responsibilities of the railway industry. The NEDO Report had concluded that British Rail often provided a rather extreme example of the difficulties inherent in the public corporations' relationship with the government. It noted that in spite of the 1974 Act there was particular haziness about the role of the railways in the economy, and that the intervention level in relation to investment projects and ceilings and pricing had been greater than was customary elsewhere in the public sector. Worse still, in the absence of agreement on overall strategy and related investment policy, such interventions tended to lack credibility. The blanket PSO grant, established without rational criteria for adjusting it, had inevitably invited a 'conflict between the department, which is unhappy at the level of subsidy required, and the corporation, which considers that it is particularly vulnerable to changing government priorities'.[129] The Board could point to its success in beating the PSO cash limit set by government from June 1975—by £35 million in 1976, £42 million in 1977, £56 million in 1978, and £14 million in 1979[130]—but at the same time gloomy prognostications were never far from the surface. Government directives requiring the PSO grant to be pegged at its 1975 level in real terms (June 1975, February 1976), then reduced by £20 million by the end of the decade (promised in the White Paper of June 1977), together with investment constraints, provided a financial straitjacket which stimulated ominous and ultimately regrettable public statements from the Board in successive annual reports. There were references to a 'concern with the crumbling edge of quality in some of our services because of shortage of investment' (1976), 'the danger of a crumbling edge of quality' (1977), and 'signs of cracks in quality of service' (1978), phrases which were to haunt Parker at the time of the Serpell inquiry in 1983 (see Chapter 5).[131] At the same time, the difficulties in getting freight and parcels businesses into the black, as required by the government, which persisted into 1979 greatly concerned both the DOE and its successor, the DTp. A break-even position for freight and parcels was reported for 1978, but the vulnerability of these businesses was evident to rail managers in 1978, and publicly demonstrated in combined losses of £3 million reported for 1979.[132]

The 'audit trail' of 1976–8 proceeded against this background of managerial frustration and government doubt. Earlier attempts to establish a national transport policy with a secure role for the railways had run into the buffers with the rather tame, laissez-faire consultation document on *Transport Policy* of April 1976, which rejected the need for a defined policy and provoked Marsh into publishing the *Opportunity for Change* riposte in July. The latter document, with its sections on planning, services, productivity, and investment, backed by several support papers and appendices, provided a more considered version of its arguments in the earlier Railway Policy Review (see Chapter 1). It argued vigorously that disinterested and professional long-term planning was required before the future role of the railways could be defined. It was sharply critical of many of the assumptions in the consultation document, notably the contention that too much public expenditure was being applied to transport in Britain, and challenged the idea that there was little to be gained from co-ordinated transport investment, rail electrification, the transfer of freight traffic from road to rail, or the holding down of passenger fares.[133] Both sides accepted the need for more co-ordination in transport policy, but British Rail was extremely critical of existing proposals, for a National Transport Authority to pronounce on investment and pricing, advanced by the *Socialist Commentary* think-tank and the TUC, or a more representative but weaker National Transport Council, suggested by the government. Above all, Marsh's Board challenged a basic premise which it felt had gained currency in Whitehall: 'The apparent expectation that the Board can uncover strategies that would drastically reduce the financial burdens on the community in the short and medium term, when our public expenditure problems are so acute, is basically unrealistic.'[134] British Rail's view was that major changes to rail provision would involve long lead times and high escape costs. While it accepted the need for specific financial objectives for the various sectors of the passenger business and promised a reduction in manpower of 40,000 by 1981, it emphasised that a more commercial approach to railway operation demanded radical adjustments to public sector 'governance'. Thus it suggested, for example, that the liabilities of businesses expected to be commercial, such as freight, be regarded as 'equity capital' rather than as interest-bearing debt.[135]

These arguments did nothing either to resolve the debate or to stem the tide of government-inspired investigation. In 1977 the role of the railways was examined twice in the space of three months, by the Select Committee on Nationalised Industries and in the White Paper which emerged from the Consultation Document, their lengthy reports running to 136 and 76 pages respectively. The Select Committee provided 54 specific recommendations in April. While many of these were limited in scope, the overall tenor of the inquiry may be judged by the fact that the majority of them dealt with targets and support mechanisms, improved disclosure of information, pricing and service levels, and investment.[136] The White Paper, published in June, covered much the same ground, though in more general terms.[137] Both documents expressed confidence in British Rail and support for a competitive railway industry in the future; Parker called it 'a general and positive reinforcement of the overall railway position'.[138] Thus, the Select Committee recommended that there should be no passenger rail closures and no general increases in passenger fares above inflation for five years, favoured electrification, and advocated additional investment above the existing ceiling where this could be shown to exceed the test discount rate. The White Paper also emphasised the need for investment, but made a positive gesture in the direction of giving the Board more freedom of action by promising to introduce a special replacement allowance for passenger asset renewal (which, as we have seen (p. 23) was introduced in the following year).[139] The documentation of 1977 could be seen as a vindication of Parker's more open, co-operative approach to the Department of Transport, which contrasted sharply with Marsh's whingeing.[140]

Nevertheless, there was bound to be uncertainty and debate about the future role of the railways given existing difficulties with freight, where two of the mainstay traffics, coal and steel, were in decline, and question marks had been raised about British Rail's ability to maintain competitiveness in the wagon-load business. At the same time, critics of government subsidies to the passenger business condemned the support given to middle-class London commuters and the relatively affluent who used inter-city services when they decided to leave their cars at home.[141] It is therefore no surprise to find that the two reports asked the Board to swallow some unpalatable suggestions, not least the Select Committee's view that its package of reforms would enable the PSO grant, which the Committee asked to have broken down on a regional basis, to be cut by £150 million in 1975 prices by 1981. Both Papers expressed the government's expectations of a higher level of efficiency, a commercial freight business, and a staged reduction in the support for the passenger businesses. As we have noted, the White Paper asked for a more modest reduction in the PSO of £20 million by the end of the decade, which was to be prefaced by a move to specific financial targets for the different sectors, notably for inter-city services.[142] After this, the government's own response to the Select Committee, published in November 1977, supported much of its argument. It promised a review of main-line electrification and provided a detailed forecast of the PSO grant for 1977 (though not on a full regional basis). However, the idea that the PSO could be cut by £150 million in four years was firmly rejected.[143] By this time, the emphasis in policy making lay with the move to tighter financial controls and firmer directives from government.

2.6 The 1978 White Paper and the search for railway objectives

The White Paper on *Nationalised Industries* of March 1978 was a famous landmark in the government's handling of the public sector. Here the government formally abandoned the contradictory signals of the 1967 White Paper, which had expected nationalised industries both to comply with financial disciplines, including minimum rates of return on investment projects, and to pursue marginal cost pricing in an environment where regulation, and price control in particular, became neither precise nor credible.[144] Ten years on, some of the political pressure had been eased in that the Public Sector Borrowing Requirement was redefined in 1976 to exclude investment financed from the internal resources of the public corporations. However, the government continued to emphasise the need to reduce the dependence on the narrower definition of government funding, and the strengthening of financial controls in the 1978 White Paper represented a return to the emphasis of an earlier White Paper in 1961, although this time there was the promise of more sophisticated targets and increased government monitoring and control.[145] The Treasury now aimed to give prominence in the government–nationalised industry relationship to the formulation of agreed corporate plans, financial targets, sectoral or social objectives where relevant, cash or 'external financing' limits, and performance and services indicators. There was also to be an adjustment to the investment rules, with the corporations now required to achieve a required rate of return for their overall programmes rather than for individual projects.[146] The White Paper also expressed the government's intention to take general powers to issue directions to boards in the form of statutory instruments, with provision for compensation for the additional costs which such interventions imposed.[147] In the event, the idea was subsequently abandoned by the Thatcher administration in 1980,[148] but the regime of financial targets, cash limits, and performance indicators represented a useful legacy from Labour, and one which the Conservatives exploited fully in the 1980s.

British Rail occupied a rather special place in the new thinking. It was then the only industry to have its social obligations identified and priced separately (in the PSO), and was more advanced than many parts of the public sector in its experience of corporate planning, financial disclosure (via the 1974 Act), and performance indicators. The new spirit of 'an open style of management and greater disclosure' was evident in the published reports and accounts for 1976 and 1977. In the former a modest breakdown of the PSO payments was offered for 1975 and 1976, together with five performance indicators for BR and an average of the major European railways. In the latter six efficiency indicators were provided for the first time;[149] there were also nine financial tables which gave, *inter alia*, detailed estimated breakdowns of the PSO funding in 1977, including revenue, direct costs, and contribution to indirect costs for four passenger sectors—Inter-City, London & South East, PTE services, and Other Provincial Services, a regional breakdown of indirect costs, and forecasts on the same basis for 1978.[150] The contrast with the British Steel Corporation was sharp. Here, both the Corporation and its sponsoring ministry, the Department of Energy, attracted the censure of the Select Committee for their failure to disclose the true financial position in 1976–7.[151]

In fact, British Rail's public debate with government was part of a more private debate with the DTp and the Treasury about the most appropriate way in which to cost the several parts of the railway business for funding and monitoring purposes. The impetus came from two directions: the costing requirements for rail freight, where British Rail opinion was that most track and signalling costs should be charged to the subsidised passenger business whose capacity, speed, and safety requirements were critical; and the need to develop more sophisticated methods of allocating the costs of movement and terminals to the various passenger 'sectors'. The intention of the government to establish financial targets for components of the PSO-supported railway was clearly important. As early as April 1976 the government's Consultation Document had floated the idea that by 1981 the outer-suburban services in London & the South East should be given the objective of covering their full allocated costs, the inner-suburban services that of maintaining their existing level of support, while the Inter-City services should at least meet their full allocated costs.[152] In 1977 the Select Committee endorsed the notion of a non-subsidised Inter-City sector, while the White Paper revealed that although the government had decided against imposing an immediate financial objective for the L&SE services, it fully endorsed the view that the Inter-City services should not be subsidised. Therefore its broad objective for the PSO—a £20 million reduction by the end of the decade (see above)—amounted in effect to a tough quasi-target for the commuter and cross-country services.[153] The process led on directly to the setting of interim targets in March 1980 for Inter-City, in the form of a precise monetary contribution to indirect costs after meeting current cost depreciation and amortisation, and for freight, where there was to be a contribution of two-thirds of current cost depreciation and amortisation, both targets to be achieved by 1982 (see Chapter 4).

There was also an internal dynamic for sector-based management accounting, in which British Rail itself sought improved methods of management control. This is clear from the way in which performance indicators were developed inside the business from 1977.[154] However, the most important change concerned costing. The management accounting system called PP&CCA—Profit Planning and Cost Centre Analysis—which had been introduced in 1971 to support budget forecasting and used to provide the basis for calculation of PSO support from 1974, was developed from 1977 on an actual basis to aid a move to contribution accounting for the passenger business. At the same time progress was made in separating joint costs using the 'avoidable costs' approach first highlighted in *Opportunity for Change*, then in the Annual Report for 1976, and later endorsed by the DTp, and by Price Waterhouse, the consultants engaged by the Price Commission to aid their investigation of British Rail pricing completed in February 1978.[155] The work undertaken by British Rail's finance department in the late 1970s began a process of management and financial accounting which was to have profound consequences for the way in which profitability was calculated and the railway businesses were financed and controlled in the future.[156]

In all this, one must be impressed with the co-operativeness and good humour of Parker and his team under the microscope of the public policy debate. They accepted the idea of sector-based targets, promised productivity improvements via a reduction in manpower, conceded that their fixed costs were not as inescapable as they had once argued, and submitted to the reality of a support mechanism which implied regular increases in real prices for customers. In the preparation of documents such as the 1977 White Paper their executives worked closely with the Department, while disclosure of information, both to the public and to the Department, was substantially improved.[157] This new spirit of co-operation, which was in marked contrast with the tensions which had preceded it, was intended to win the Minister and his civil servants round to a re-examination of the case for main-line electrification, increased investment, and a more stable, longer-term support system. However, the Board was unable to convince government of the desirability of a long-term policy for railways based on social cost–benefit criteria, and the move to sector-based evaluation was capable of being applied quite differently in other hands. Indeed, just as British Rail began to improve its management accounting techniques within a more rational but still clearly public sector framework, others, and notably economists such as Jack Wiseman and Stephen Littlechild, were arguing that the real challenge was to make nationalised industries more responsive to the disciplines of the market.[158] Of course, this debate gathered pace over the next decade.

Operations, Productivity, and Technological Change

3.1 The scale and complexity of railway operations

British Rail's activities were by any standards large and complex. Operations were both extensive and intensive. There were no fewer than 16,000 passenger trains a day serving 2,355 stations, and some 2,000 freight trains, working over a network of 11,289 miles. The density of operation in the London area was as great as anywhere in Europe.[1] Total staff numbered 256,000 in 1974, most of them (234,000) employed in the railway business, including maintenance, putting British Rail among the top five British companies in employment terms.[2] Furthermore, the several rail businesses varied greatly. If we assess them in relation to marketing and politics, for example, we find the passenger activities were retail businesses which were politically very sensitive. They were dominated in both volume and revenue terms by two large sectors, Inter-City and London and South East commuting (see Appendix D, Table D.1). Freight, in contrast, was company specific and industrial, with 3 per cent of its customers generating 89 per cent of freight tonnage in 1972–9—i.e. coal, steel, oil and aggregates (Appendix D, Table D.2). The business was also particularly sensitive to national economic fluctuations. Last, the smaller parcels business was both retail and industrial in nature.[3] The different businesses also varied in their revenue-generating capacity and contribution to the network's infrastructure costs, although as we have seen the allocation of joint costs to different businesses not only was problematic, but was to become as much a political as an accounting matter given the expectations of commercial viability for freight (from 1974) and Inter-City passenger services (from 1977).[4]

Charting operational trends is not straightforward. At the top, historic data were rarely discussed in detail. For example, when the Chief Executive (Railways) began his monthly reports to the Board in May 1977, the immediate reaction of the new part-timer, Michael Posner, was to ask that a statement be included showing the actual volume of business.[5] Senior managers in modern businesses spend most of their time planning, forecasting, estimating, and taking action against the budget, e.g. pricing action, cost reduction initiatives, and so on, in an environment set by 4-weekly and 12-weekly out-turns against budget. They rarely concern themselves with 'historical' results, the limited information on which is usually confined to the annual report and accounts, a matter for accountants and auditors to handle with one eye at least on commercial confidentiality. On the other hand, data analysis for marketing or operating purposes is frequently very detailed, and it can be difficult to see the larger picture for the minutiae of a particular traffic or set of contracts. Thus, there can be a disjunction between the budget managers and the operators, the latter presiding over a separate logic of their own based on a century and a half of operating custom and practice, underpinned by rule books, service scheduling, and train control techniques.

At the aggregate level, operating was relatively static in the mid–late 1970s. It is true that investment in new motive power, notably the introduction of Class 87 electric locomotives in 1973–5 and the Class 43 diesel-powered High-Speed Trains (HSTs) from 1976, provided opportunities for improvements to Inter-City services. Thus, British Rail's BR Public Relations Department's *Facts and Figures* booklets of 1978 and 1980 provided statistics indicating considerable advances in passenger service provision over the previous decade. For example, there were 28 trains a day between London and Birmingham in 1978, compared with only 15 in 1967, while the fastest journey time had improved by five minutes. The London–Bristol service had 24 trains instead of 14, with a 23-minute improvement in the fastest journey time. The number of London–Edinburgh trains had increased from 5 to 10 with an improvement of an hour for the fastest journey, while Glasgow enjoyed the greatest change, following electrification in 1974, the fastest train taking five hours in 1978 compared with six hours 40 minutes in 1967.[6] On the other hand, for many services comparatively little changed. For example, the electric commuter trains between London Liverpool St. and Gidea Park in Essex were operated at the same level of service over the two decades 1957–77,[7] while the provincial service between Norwich (Thorpe) and Sheringham, which consisted of nine trains on weekdays in 1922, was the same 55 years later.[8] The incentive to make radical changes was of course blunted by the requirements of the 1974 Act, which required a fixed level of passenger service, while the more urgent requirements of freight were tempered by the realisation that the simple shedding of traffic was certainly no panacea and in any case cut across the prevalent Board view that rail freight had beneficial environmental effects.[9]

Nevertheless, the several businesses were certainly not static, particularly those elements sensitive to economic fluctuations or those whose demand was relatively price elastic. This can be seen in data for the major sectors of traffic in the period 1972–9, derived from published material (see Tables 3.1 and 3.2). Passenger volumes increased by 6 per cent, 1972–4, fell by 8 per cent, 1974–6, then increased by 12 per cent to 1979, but remained lower than 1952 levels. A fuller assessment of the passenger business is hindered by the fact that in the mid-1970s the focus shifted in management accounting terms from analysis on a regional basis to one based on the major business sectors, and the database is consequently incomplete. What is interesting, however, is the differential experience of the sectors. Data attempting to allocate volumes and revenue to the three sectors on a consistent basis (i.e. correcting for the fact that services were moved from Inter-City in 1982) reveal that the Inter-City business exhibited strong growth in the late 1970s, 15 per cent up on 1972 volumes by 1979, while London and South East services were up by 10 per cent. However, the weakest sector, referred to somewhat marginally in management speak as either 'Other Grant-Aided Services' (OGAS) or 'PTE + OPS', only recovered its 1972 volume in 1979 (Table 3.1).[10] Revenue collected in constant prices failed to match volume changes in 1972–5, but some recovery was evident via pricing action in 1976–8. There was a 6 per cent increase in passenger-miles, 1972–8, but a 12 per cent increase in

Table 3.1 Passenger traffic volumes and revenue, 1952, 1972–9 (1972 = 100)

Year	Passenger volume Passenger-miles ('000 m.)				Passenger revenue 1979 prices (£m.)			
	IC	L&SE	PTE/OPS	TOT	IC	L&SE	PTE/OPS	TOT
1972	6.6	8.1	3.4	18.1	279	334	108	720
1952	—	—	—	113	—	—	—	93
1972	100	100	100	100	100	100	100	100
1974	109	106	100	106	99	98	91	97
1975	109	102	97	104	105	94	104	100
1976	94	105	88	98	111	92	109	102
1978	111	107	88	106	114	110	109	112
1979	115	110	100	110	114	108	114	111

Source: Appendix D, Table D.1.

Key: IC = Inter-City
PTE/OPS = Passenger Transport Executive and Other Provincial Services
L&SE = London & South East
TOT = Total

**Table 3.2 Freight traffic volumes and revenue, 1952, 1972–9
(1972 = 100)**

Year	Freight traffic Net tonne-miles ('000 m.)					Freight revenue 1979 prices (£m.)		
	Coal	Iron/Steel	Aggregates	Oil	Total	Coal	Iron/Steel	Total
1972	4.0	2.1	1.1	2.0	13.0	202	89	481
1952	—	—	—	—	175	—	—	311
1972	100	100	100	100	100	100	100	100
1974	102	105	136	95[a]	104	96	93	91
1975	112	90	118	75	100	99	78	85
1976	107	100	100	75	98	109	93	93
1978	105	81	118	85	95	109	75	91
1979	105	86	127	80	95	108	75	90

Source: Appendix D, Table D.2.

[a] new series.

revenue in real terms, though the impetus was lost in 1979 (Table 3.1). Average revenue per passenger-mile in constant 1979 prices fell from 4.00p in 1972 to 3.65p in 1974, increased to 4.20p by 1978, then fell back to 4.02p in 1979 (Appendix D, Table D.1). Freight tonnage was little changed, 1972–9, an improvement in 1973 being quickly followed by a deterioration, but tonne-mileage fell by 5 per cent, and both the iron and steel and oil/petroleum traffic fell quite sharply, traffic in 1978–9 being some 15–20 per cent down on that in 1972. The most visible trend was the fall in activity since the 1950s, and the shift in emphasis from wagon-load traffic to train-load traffic. In the 1970s coal tonnages were about half of that in 1952 (in 1979 46 per cent down on 1952), as was overall tonne-mileage (in 1979 also 46 per cent lower than in 1952) (Table 3.2). Traffic carried in train-loads increased substantially from 31 per cent in 1968 to 86 per cent in 1978.[11] In general revenue failed to match volume changes throughout the period 1972–9; but a fall in average real revenue per tonne-mile in 1972–5, from 3.70p to 3.16p, was followed by an improvement to 3.54p in 1978, though these earnings were well down on the 6.56p in 1952 (Appendix D, Table D.2).

3.2 Passenger pricing and marketing

No one should underestimate the challenge involved in pricing in the mid-late 1970s, when inflation was extremely high. For the railways there was the additional difficulty of satisfying political masters, some of whom spoke for the hard-headed Treasury, while others adopted a quite different stance by voicing the concerns of consumers and the trade unions. Pricing action took place within the government's general guidelines for the British economy but was also subject to the special restraints which the government was able to impose upon its public corporations, for example by intervening ahead of, and/or during, submissions to the Price Commission for increases under the successive stages of the statutory Counter Inflation Policy. From April 1973, when price restraint was lifted, pricing action was subject to the criteria established by Stages II and III of that policy. Applications for public sector price increases could be made if 'allowable costs' (labour, material, fuel, etc.) had risen, and/or if it was necessary for a loss-maker to contain its deficit.[12] Broadly, British Rail's objective for the passenger business was to maximise passenger-miles travelled within the financial constraints set by government, and notably the imposition of PSO and cash limits from 1975 (the stated intention of government from June 1975 was to peg the PSO grant at its 1975 level in real terms).[13] However, in the absence of firm government instructions it was in practice difficult, if not impossible, to determine the balance to be struck between deficit minimisation and traffic maximisation, between exploiting captive markets such as London commuting and pursuing a strategy based on equity for all social groups.[14] These constraints meant that rail managers, who following strong criticism from the National Board for Prices and Incomes in 1968 had moved from formula pricing on a rigid mileage basis to more flexible, market-based pricing,[15] had constantly to balance actions taken to trim costs against those designed to increase revenue in striving to meet the government's target for the rail subsidy. On top of this the marketing mix was complex. Although it could be reduced to a simple 3×3 grid comprising the three sectors and three types of fare—full, reduced, and season ticket (Table 3.3)—the market was highly segmented, particularly where journeys were leisure based.[16] In these circumstances, the difficulties involved in constructing new fare schedules and in estimating their impact on net revenue were considerable.

The complexities of passenger pricing should be borne in mind when considering Marsh's much publicised frustration with pricing restraints in 1972–4. The

Table 3.3 The passenger market matrix (1977 revenue data) (per cent)

Sector/Market	Inter-City	L&SE	PTE + OPS	TOTAL
Full (business)	26	11	5	42
Reduced (optional)	20	8	7	35
Seasons (work)	2	20	1	23
TOTAL	48	39	13	100

Source: BRB Passenger Department, Memo 30 November 1978, BRB 99-2-1 Pt. 8.

Railways under Labour, 1974–9

Chairman complained vigorously about his treatment in general and the delay in 1974 in particular. It took six months to process the initial application for a 12.5 per cent rise in fares. The increase, introduced in June, was reduced marginally following Mulley's insistence that London's commuters be treated less harshly. As a result, the planned rise for longer-distance season tickets of 12.5 per cent became the *maximum* not the *average* (Table 3.4).[17] Then in August Mulley intervened to prevent the Board from making further increases, of 5 per cent in October, and 7.5 per cent in December. This subsequently became an application for an increase of 12.5 per cent in December, which was further delayed by the Minister until late January 1975. The intervention cost £7.0 million in 1974, prompting the formal resolution that the government had 'completely negated the Board's pricing policy' and another blunt letter from Marsh to his Minister pointing out that the government had wrecked a delicately balanced approach. When three months later chancellor Healey took off the brakes the Board argued that 'the price base was so low the market could not take the increase needed'.[18] However, it is clear that the main difficulty was the failure to match escalating rail costs, which were rising much faster than the general inflation rate. According to British Rail's published estimates, costs had risen by about 55 per cent in 1972–4, 33 per cent in 1974 alone.[19] In fact, in relation to retail prices, the shortfall was less dramatic. While passenger fares rose by 33 per cent from 1971 to 1974, retail prices increased by 36 per cent, and passenger volumes actually improved by 6 per cent, 1972–4, as we have noted (Table 3.1).

Table 3.4 General fare increases, 1972–9

Date	Passenger fare increases (%)	Period	Average annual fare increase (%)	Annual RPI increase (%)
Apr. 1972	5	1971–2	12.9	7.5
Sep. 1972	7.5			
June 1973	5	1972–3	5.0	8.2
June 1974	12.5[a]	1973–4	12.5	15.9
Jan. 1975	12.5	1974–5	50.7	24.1
May 1975	16.5[b]			
Sep. 1975	15			
Mar. 1976	12	1975–6	12.0	16.6
Jan. 1977	12.5	1976–7	12.5	15.9
Jan. 1978	14.5	1977–8	14.5	8.2
Jan. 1979	9.4	1978–9	9.4	13.4

Source: Appendix J, Table J.1.

[a] Average reduced marginally following ministerial intervention (average 12.5% increase in long-distance L&SE season tickets became the maximum).

[b] 15.0% increase subsequently augmented as a result of 'additional pricing action'.

The pendulum swung the other way when British Rail took corrective action from 1974 (Table 3.4). The overall effect of the seven double-figure increases in 1974–8 was to raise standard fares by 145 per cent, while retail prices increased by about 110 per cent over the same period; the three increases in 1975 represented a rise of 51 per cent in a single year, double the rate of inflation, contributing to a fall in the volume of business of 7.5 per cent, 1974–6 (Table 3.1). Higher than average increases were introduced in both the London commuting areas and the provinces, the aim being to price high where demand was relatively inelastic in order to maximise the contribution of London's commuters to system costs, and for the loss-making provincial services to 'minimise the shortfall of receipts on direct expenses'.[20] The Chief Executive, Bowick, and his passenger managers were quick to express worries about the negative impact of the post-1974 price increases both on volumes and on earnings from key services, such as London–Scotland, which were already under pressure as a result of growing competition from the airlines. Managers also pointed to the marketing problems arising from the public's perception that rail fares were increasing more rapidly than the prices of other products. Thus, the effect of pricing policy on cost recovery was blunted not only by the delays inherent in the negotiations with the Ministry and the Commission, but by time-consuming internal management processes, and specifically qualms about the impact of large price hikes on the volume of business.[21] The latter caused the Board to postpone an increase planned for August 1976, provoked investigations into passenger 'downtrading', for example from first to second class, and stimulated a plethora of innovations to balance large increases in standard fares with selective reduced fares, notably the student (1974) and senior citizen (1975) railcards, and 'AwayDay' (1976), '17 Day Return' and 'Big City Saver' (1977) tickets, and special promotions linked to firms such as Kellogg's, which added greatly to the complexity of the fare structure.[22]

In contrast, the interventions of Ministers and the inquiries of the Price Commission had more limited effects. During the period of high inflation civil servants promoting the Treasury line pressed British Rail to make higher than planned price increases, notably in February 1975 when Bill Sharp, Under-Secretary (Railways) at the DOE, advocated greater increases for Inter-City and London & South East services.[23] However, the Board's perfectly reasonable response to this kind of intervention was to point out, first, that short-term objectives ought to square with longer-term objectives; and second, that it was proving difficult to get the Department to establish a precise aim for passenger pricing. There were currently at least three available options: to maximise net revenue; to maximise volume by increasing net revenue to the point where traffic was lost; and to maximise long-run revenue (by increasing net revenue with some traffic losses but without prejudicing future growth).[24] Attempts to push the railways to accelerate their pricing response so soon after prices had been artificially held down thus lacked credibility. Later on, the Ministry of Transport and the Price Commission took an entirely different stance in expressing qualms about the imposition of differentially high increases in the inelastic market of London commuting, where as Charles Williams, Chairman of the Commission (1977–9), pointed out to British Rail, 'you have them by the short and curlies'.[25] This view was expressed more publicly and more diplomatically when the Commission subjected the Board's proposals for January 1978 to a formal investigation. The intention had been to raise Inter-City fares by 14.1 per cent on average, and London & South East fares by 16.2 per cent, with some fares going up by up to 35 per cent (25 per cent in London). The Commission insisted on a ceiling of 20 per cent for any individual fare increase, but was compelled to accept the logic of price increases. Consequently, the overall impact of its intervention was negligible: the mean increase for the passenger sector was reduced from 14.6 to 14.5 per cent.[26]

Nevertheless, the Board was moved to abandon differentially higher fare increases in the London area, in favour of differential increases where service quality had been improved (e.g. Great Northern electrification), and to limit itself to one general increase per annum, following its voluntary decision to do so in 1976 and 1977, in accordance with the expressed wishes of both the Commission and the Minister, by this time William Rodgers.[27] In September 1978, during the planning stages for the 1979 round, a firmer prices and incomes policy reasserted itself. Rodgers asked Parker to follow a guideline limiting public sector price increases to 5 per cent. But British Rail's initial estimates of inflation indicated that a 10.5 per cent rise was necessary, and although this was later reduced to 9.5 per cent, no further ground was conceded. Notwithstanding departmental apprehensions British Rail proceeded with an average increase of 9.4 per cent in January 1979, and once again this rise was accepted by the Commission.[28] Thus, while there is some evidence that railway pricing behaviour in 1975–9 was moderated in detail by government intervention, the overwhelming conclusion is that railway managers set their own parameters in responding to overall financial constraints. In many ways the DOE and its successor, the Ministry of Transport, were caught in a trap of their own making. Since they were intent on keeping the PSO subsidy under strict control they could scarcely oppose the railways' 'hard pricing' to keep revenues in line with rising prices. Both sides were driven by an anxiety to keep within cash limits, and in the end this meant pricing up to market levels regardless of volume effects in order to improve the net revenue position.[29]

Of course, real price increases could be avoided if substantial cost reductions were made and productivity were increased. This will be dealt with in more detail below, but here it is necessary to refer to two elements: first, the case for fare reductions; and second, the approach to rail closures. Turning to the first, the leading rail union, the NUR, made itself the focus for efforts to oppose large fare increases. In 1976 it leaked plans for the 1977 increase to the press as part of a campaign to have rail pricing debated publicly.[30] At the same time, the union's general secretary, Sidney Weighell, a noted public transport campaigner and

2. Fare rises in the 1970s. Public concern expressed
by Keith Waite, *Daily Mirror*, 18 August 1976

founder member of the pressure group Transport 2000, advanced the argument
that a quite different strategy, viz. a trial *reduction* of 10 per cent in fares would
have a beneficial effect on net revenue.[31] However, this contention was rejected
firmly by both British Rail and the Price Commission. The Board, while prepared
to experiment with a pricing standstill as a gesture to the NUR,[32] was at the same
time in agreement that following tests of price elasticities a pricing *increase* for
London & South East of inflation plus 7.5 per cent over the period 1977–81 was
the best way to minimise future calls on the PSO.[33] As a regional passenger
manager observed, 'the real need today is not for reduced fares, we have too
many, but much greater staff productivity. We are not pricing ourselves out of
the business but *costing* ourselves out of it'.[34] The Commission, no doubt picking
up on data fed to them by British Rail via their consultants Price Waterhouse,

stated categorically that 'there is no prospect that general reductions might increase revenue'.[35] It noted that labour costs made up over 60 per cent of passenger costs, and exceeded passenger revenue. It suggested that a 1 per cent cut in such costs would have the same effect as a 1 per cent increase in net revenue via higher fares.[36] The alternative of pricing lower was thus firmly rejected.

The problem of loss-making passenger services was effectively shelved. Once again, the Price Commission highlighted the issue, revealing that the OPS sector had failed to cover its direct costs by an average £35 million per annum in 1974–7 (revenue £59 million, direct costs £94 million, at current prices), which contrasted with the average annual surpluses over direct costs of £87 and £37.5 million earned by Inter-City and London & South East.[37] However, any steps British Rail might have taken to secure substantial closures were blocked by the DOE. In January 1974, the Conservative Minister for Transport Industries, John Peyton, told the House of Commons that there would be no closures 'of substance' before 1975. Six months later, his Labour successor, Fred Mulley, endorsed this policy. He asked British Rail not to proceed with the closure of three significant lines where permission to close had already been obtained, viz. Ashford–Hastings, Kyle of Lochalsh–Inverness, and Bedford–Bletchley, while a further three proposals were refused: the Cambrian Coast line (Machynlleth–Pwllheli), Wimbledon–West Croydon, and Stockport–Stalybridge. Ministerial consent was given to only one proposal, Alston–Haltwhistle, which was eventually closed following road improvements in May 1976.[38] In 1975–7 approval was given to a mere handful of minor proposals, e.g. Maiden Newton–Bridport (May 1975), Morecambe–Heysham (October 1975, following withdrawal of the Belfast–Heysham ferry), East Brixton (January 1976), Mauchline Jnc.–Newton Jnc. and Dubbs Jnc.–Byrehill Jnc. (June 1977), and the station at Filey Holiday Camp (September 1977).[39]

Of course, bailing with teaspoons was clearly not the answer. The contention that marginal reductions in the passenger service made little difference to the bottom line seems to have been accepted by the DOE, and was invoked in 1976 when rejecting British Rail's proposal to close three passenger halts on the Cambrian Coast line.[40] This is not to say that no radical proposals existed. In 1974, for example, British Rail drew up a list of 24 possible candidates for closure, where the government grant had amounted to £6.2 million in 1973, but the scheme was shelved in the wake of the Railways Act and the new PSO regime.[41] Later in the same year, a more considered list of 82 services was drawn up 'just in case' the political climate changed. These were services where the operating ratio (operating costs/revenue) was 200 or worse and the average number of passengers per train was 20 or less; closure of 38 of these would trim the network by 939 miles and reduce the PSO by about £3.2 million.[42] In 1975, joint BRB/DOE reviews of specific service groups were initiated, but when Marsh proposed to the Minister, now John Gilbert, that he publicly identify a group of services with a limited future, supplying a list of 44 services, the offer was not taken up.[43] In the following year the government's Consultation Document suggested that feeder bus services might replace about 6 per cent of passenger-mileage, and later released an old list of 199 services which would be affected. British Rail responded positively to the idea, referring to it in its reply to the Consultation Document, *Opportunity for Change*. It then prepared an ambitious document on public transport integration which argued that 2,500 route-miles, 107 services, and 10 per cent of the passenger-mileage might be substituted by a combination of local authority-financed buses and special BR-controlled feeder services, building on the first of such schemes, the 'Corby Link' between Kettering and Corby, introduced in November 1976. Savings were estimated at £25 million per annum.[44] Again, union opposition was evident,[45] and given the fact that British Rail wanted the National Bus Company to withdraw from inter-city express routes as a quid pro quo, the proposal was something of a kite-flier and unsurprisingly the government dragged its feet. Further studies, for example those in Lincolnshire and Scotland, completed in 1978, provided additional proof of the hypothesis that substitute feeder bus services run as part of the railway network would provide a better and more cost-effective service than diesel multiple units (DMUs), but by this time hopes of a broader scheme had faded. British Rail's marketing director, Bob Reid, was now lamenting the fact that the government was showing little interest in more radical solutions to the local service problem.[46] By the beginning of February 1979, some progress was evident. An agreement had been reached with the major national bus companies, the National Bus Company and the Scottish Transport Group, on marketing co-operation, and a strategy for the 'Other Provincial Services' had been presented to the Board, where lines would be assessed in relation to four options: closure; bus substitution; retention; and quality improvement.[47] Much remained to be done, however. Passenger managers were left to exercise their discretion to rationalise services, as they did in 1975–6, but only within the existing base.[48]

3.3 Freight pricing and marketing

Freight pricing and marketing was a different matter. About half of the business was with large, regular customers offering train-load consignments, such as the National Coal Board (NCB) and the Central Electricity Generating Board (CEGB), and was therefore organised through fixed contracts with price variation clauses. These compensated British Rail for inflationary change by adjusting the rate every six months in response to movements in wage levels and retail and/ or wholesale prices.[49] After 1973 the practice was developed of adjusting the rates for the rest of freight traffic, including the ailing wagon-load business, in line with the contract business, that is, every six months. Much of the non-contract traffic was vulnerable to road competition, where quality was improving, and some managers were naturally anxious about pricing too high. However, ever mindful of the commercial directive for freight from 1974, the Board favoured a policy of pricing up to the market, and in general both the government and the Price Commission sympathised with this position. Nevertheless, freight applications during the counter-inflation stage of government policy (where applications could be made on either an allowable cost or a deficit basis) were not immune from intervention. In 1973, for example, applications to raise freight and parcels rates by 7.3 per cent in June were cut to 2 and nil per cent respectively, taking effect in July (Table 3.5).[50] The result was that over the two years to July 1974 freight rates rose by only 2 per cent but the inflation rate was over 30 per cent.[51]

The situation required a corrective pricing strategy for freight in 1974–5 that was every bit as tough as that adopted for the passenger business. It produced an increase in freight charges of 70 per cent from June 1974 to October 1975 (cf. Table 3.5), at a time when prices rose by about 28 per cent. The contrast with 1973 in government–railway relations was striking. In February 1975 the DOE's anxiety over a perceived failure to match escalating costs in freight operations prompted Sharp's request that British Rail double its proposed rate increase from 12.5 to 25 per cent. This was rejected, but it led to some rumbustious exchanges with DOE officials over 'elasticities', 'cost recovery', and 'blunt instruments', and subsequently to the DOE's expressed doubts about the freight strategy as a whole (see Chapter 2, p.22). In fact, accelerated inflation meant that the increase was subsequently measured as 14 per cent, and it was followed by a further rise of 15 per cent in October (Table 3.5). However, for British Rail the essential problem was that if freight pricing were pushed too far, volume would fall, and this would mean that the passenger sector would carry a larger infrastructure burden, with a knock-on effect on the PSO grant.[52] At the same time, new contracts with higher tariffs were negotiated as opportunities arose. The major achievement here was the renegotiation of the CEGB contract for the key traffic of power station coal. In March 1975 the Board gave notice to cancel the existing long-term agreements for carrying such coal of 1958 (all traffic) and 1963 (Merry-Go-Round (MGR) services) with the aim of securing a real price increase over the existing base of around 20 per cent. A new contract, operative for 15 years from 1 January 1976, established new rates tapering with distance for MGR and non-MGR traffics. Provision was made both for percentage increases in January for the years 1977–9 and for six-monthly price variations based on inflation. As a result the new contract delivered the desired increase while safeguarding the traffic for rail.[53] Other negotiations produced additional revenue from contracts for oil (Shell Mex and BP, Phillips Petroleum), lime (ICI, BSC), limestone (Foster Yeoman, Amalgamated Roadstone), Gypsum (APCM), and cement (APCM, Tunnel Cement). A new contract with APCM in 1977, for example, produced an increase in the real price of 22 per cent.[54] These contracts, and the CEGB one in particular, were very

Table 3.5 General freight and parcels rates increases, 1972–9

Date	Freight rate increases (%)	Date	Parcels rate increases (%)	Period	Annual rate increase—Freight	Annual rate increase—Parcels	Annual price increase—Producer prices
July 1972	5	July 1972	5	1971–2	5	5	5.2
July 1973	2	July 1973	0	1972–3	2	0	7.7
June 1974	18[a]	June 1974	12.5	1973–4	29.8	26.6	22.1
Oct. 1974	10	Dec. 1974	12.5				
Apr. 1975	14	July 1975	13	1974–5	31.1	13	23.5
Oct. 1975	15						
Apr. 1976	10	Jan. 1976	13	1975–6	18.8	13	16.3
Oct. 1976	8						
Apr. 1977	8	Mar. 1977	15	1976–7	16.6	15	18.7
Oct. 1977	8						
Apr. 1978	10	Jan. 1978	20	1977–8	18.8	32	9.1
Dec. 1978	8	Dec. 1978	10				
Sep. 1979	20	Sept. 1979	15	1978–9	20	15	11.7

Source: Schedule of 'Price Control 1971–75', 9 May 1975, BRB 99-2-50 Pt. 2; 'Outline of Rail Pricing Applications', 2 March 1976, BRB FR 246-2-134 Pt. 10; and other material in BRB 99-2-50 Pts. 2–4; BRB 99-6-2 Pts. 1–3; 99-2-1 Pts. 6–9; BRB FR 246-2-134 Pts. 6–10; Office for National Statistics, *Economic Trends Annual Supplement 1997*, p. 161.

Note: The percentages are approximations: applications for increases sometimes involved specific increases for the several types of business, e.g. for freight: contract with 6-monthly PVCs; contract with 12-monthly PVCs; negotiated rates; and national scales; and for parcels: negotiated rates; national scales; and contract.

[a] Originally '12–20%': 18% is given in S. W. Price, Memo 8 May 1975, BRB 99-2-50 Pt. 2.

profitable in that the base price per unit far exceeded the unit cost of operation. MGR services, which increased from 148 a day in 1972 to 255 in 1978 (230 serving the power stations), enjoyed operating ratios of only 40 per cent.[55] It is not too much to say that they provided a considerable measure of cross-subsidisation to the loss-making elements in freight.[56]

3.4 Operating costs and productivity

Operating costs were determined by operating practices, many of which were rooted in the distant past. Safety was a prime consideration, and in the late 1970s the record was good,[57] but certain elements were something of a relic and symptomatic of practices—often restrictive—which could and arguably should have been abandoned.[58] Modern equipment, and notably the replacement of the steam locomotive (which had disappeared completely by 1968), put further pressure on the necessity of retaining train crews consisting of driver, 'fireman', and guard. However, work routines and procedures relating to the maintenance of the infrastructure and rolling stock, as well as the operation of the trains themselves, were clearly influenced by the path-dependency or inertia inherent in all major technologies,[59] and once established were difficult to reform. In consequence, the major categories of expenditure did not change dramatically (Table 3.6). Employee costs made up over 60 per cent of operating costs, fuel and power 6–7 per cent, and materials, supplies, and services just over a quarter. Nevertheless, it is apparent that the proportion represented by employee costs did fall after 1975, for the railway activities from 67 to 61 per cent in 1978 and 1979, for the business as a whole from 64 to 57 per cent in 1979 (Table 3.6). While the data suggest that there was some success in restraining the labour cost element in British Rail activities, the shift in proportions may be merely a reflection of relative price movements during a period of high inflation, and the following decade was testimony to the fact that the scope for improvement was considerable.

Productivity measures and other indicators give some support to this contention, revealing the second half of the 1970s to be a period of modest progress. If we turn first to the staff statistics (Table 3.7 and Appendix G, Table G.1), we see that railway wage labour fell by 10,400 or 7.4 per cent from the end of 1973 to the end of 1979; for all rail staff the reduction was 13,200 or 6.8 per cent. The overall saving for all activities was under half of this, however, at 6,000, 1973–9, a fall of only 2.4 per cent. Some of the disparity was the result of changes affecting the subsidiaries. The hotels and shipping companies had 1,800 more staff in 1979 than in 1976, and Freightliners, employing 2,500, was returned to British Rail in 1978. But by far the most disturbing element was the absence of labour shedding

Table 3.6 Operating cost categories, 1963, 1974–9

Year	Employee costs	Fuel and power	Materials supplies, and services	Depreciation and amortisation
1. Railway				
1963	63	8	19	10
1974	65	7	22	6
1975	67	6	25	2
1976	67	7	24	2
1977	64	7	27	2
1978	61	6	28	5
1979	61	6	28	5
2. Railway and subsidiaries				
1963	61	8	21	10
1974	63	7	25	5
1975	64	6	28	2
1976	64	7	27	2
1977	61	7	30	2
1978	58	6	31	5
1979	57	6	32	5

Source: BRB, *R&A 1963, 1974–9*. For additional information on earlier years see Gourvish, *British Railways*, p. 466.

Table 3.7 British Railways Board staff numbers, 1973–9

Date 31 Dec.	Railway		Subsidiaries (all staff)	Group (all staff)
	Wages staff	All staff		
1973	139,800	195,200	54,900	250,100
1976	132,500	186,800	56,600	243,500
1979	129,400	182,100	62,000[a]	244,100[a]

Source: Appendix G, Table G.1 (data rounded to nearest hundred).

[a] Includes Freightliner.

in the British Rail workshops, where employment increased by 3,800 or 11.8 per cent (Appendix G, Table G.1). Here, the argument was that additional recruitment was necessary to handle the extra workload produced by servicing an ageing fleet of rolling stock, though this took no account of the abundant scope for higher productivity.[60] A loss of only 6,000 jobs was a far cry from the 41,000 reduction in railway labour achieved in 1969–73, or the cut of 40,000 promised by British

Railways under Labour, 1974–9

Rail in its *Interim Rail Strategy* of 1973 (and reaffirmed in its *Opportunity for Change* in 1976), to be delivered by 1981, or the larger figure of 67,000 which the economists Pryke and Dodgson felt was needed to bring employment down to *their* estimate of staffing requirements in 1981.[61]

With regard to operating productivity, it must be recognised that many problems exist in locating suitable measures for railway activities; and when performance is measured against that of other railway systems, the problems are multiplied. There is clearly a distinction to be made between the operating of trains, the filling of trains, and the financing of trains. Simple measures, for example, freight revenue per net tonne-mile, were found to be unsatisfactory measures of performance inside the rail business.[62] In assessing productivity change in British Rail over the period 1948–73 we resorted to rather crude measures of labour and total factor productivity, based on estimates of aggregate output, numbers employed, and net capital stock, using a Cobb–Douglas framework.[63] While this procedure may be acceptable in order to gain a rough idea of change over the longer term, it is less satisfactory for shorter-term assessments and when seeking to place British Rail's performance in a comparative setting. Here, judgements must be moderated by the knowledge that rail systems differ greatly in traffic density, traffic mix, conditions (note British Rail's low average freight length of haul), the types of asset used (note British Rail's low percentage of electrified route), competitive levels, regulatory and subsidy frameworks (the passenger service commitment was clearly important here), and the extent to which railway work is internalised or sub-contracted.[64]

Fortunately for our purposes the productivity debate became more public in the late 1970s, and this encouraged the release of much more information than was available previously. The DOE's Consultation Document of 1976 was a landmark here, disturbing British Rail with its indictment of domestic railway performance. Although the Department conceded that international comparisons could be misleading, it nevertheless placed British Rail bottom of a table of seven railway systems in 1973 in relation to both use of assets (measured by passenger-kilometres per carriage, and freight tonne-kilometres per tonne of wagon capacity) and use of staff (passenger-kilometres plus freight tonne-kilometres per employee).[65] The Board responded by providing more information in its annual report, beginning with the 1976 report, published in May 1977, and by commissioning research on comparative railway performance from the University of Leeds Institute of Transport Studies, which was published in December 1979, as the demand for public audit and performance indicators gathered pace.[66] A subsequent study of productivity performance was published by the Board in November 1982.[67] In Table 3.8 and Appendix C, Table C.1 we present some of the vast array of statistical material supplied by the Board for public consumption (12 performance indicators in 1978, 18 in 1979), and other data published subsequently, for example in the Serpell Report on *Railway Finances* in 1983. Output per employee experienced a decline in 1976–7 followed by a recovery in 1978–9,

Table 3.8 Productivity measures, 1974–9 (1974 = 100)

	Year					
	1974	1975	1976	1977	1978	1979
Passengers						
Passenger-miles per loaded pass train-mile (1974 = 103)	100	95	90	91	94	99
Passenger-miles per coaching traction-hour (1974 = 2,043)	100	96	93	96	101	107
Trains arriving on time or less than 5 mins late (percentage) (1974 = 91%)	100	100	102	102	100	96
Freight						
Net tonne-miles per loaded freight train-mile (1974 = 267)	100	107	115	121	124	128
Net tonne-miles per freight traction-hour (1974 = 1,723)	100	103	120	123	126	130
Average wagon-load (tonnes) (1974 = 20.55)	100	105	109	112	119	123
Revenue per wagon (1975 prices) (1974 = £1,012)	100	103	117	126	134	143
Global						
Loaded train-miles per train crew member (1974 = 6,230)	100	102	104	106	107	105
Revenue per £1,000 paybill costs (incl. workshops) (1974 = £1,083)	100	97	107	119	124	120

Source: Appendix C, Table C.1.

though this measure was undoubtedly affected by the reduction in freight volume (see Appendix D, Table D.2 and Table 3.2). The same phenomenon was at work in the passenger business, where passenger-miles per train-mile and per coaching traction-hour fell in the years when passenger-miles travelled fell, viz. 1974–6 (see Tables 3.8 and 3.1). On the other hand, some indicators exhibited steady progress. The number of train-miles run per train crew member increased from 6,230 miles in 1974 to 6,647 miles in 1978, an improvement of 6.7 per cent (although the 1979 results were disappointing). Most of the advance occurred in the freight business, where from 1974 to 1979 tonne-miles per train-mile improved by 28 per cent, tonne-miles per traction-hour increased by 30 per cent, and average wagon-load increased by 23 per cent (Table 3.8). Some of the financial measures were far from unsatisfactory. The PSO payments fell from 1.68p per passenger-mile in 1975 to 1.41p in 1978 in 1975 prices, an improvement of 16 per cent (Appendix C, Table C.1); real revenue per wagon increased steadily (by 43 per cent, 1974–9), and revenue per £1,000 paybill costs rose too, by 24 per cent, 1974–8). Quality measures such as passenger train punctuality are more difficult to interpret. The data for trains less than five minutes late reveal little or no improvement, and this holds true if comparisons are made with the 1950s and 1960s.[68]

Thus, progress in terms of productivity was rather unspectacular. Clearly, British Rail was being prodded by a concerned Treasury and Department to address the fundamental issues relating to its core businesses, especially freight. The Board recognised that working practices had to be reformed, and accepted that there was considerable scope for improving low operating productivity, but immediate changes, given existing industrial relations constraints, could be only limited. As Bob Reid and Derek Fowler recalled in 1980, 'It is accepted that operational performance during that time [1976–9] slipped', though this was ascribed to 'the effects of ageing equipment and under investment for the future'.[69] Lower down, percipient managers were beginning to appreciate that there was a critical need for productivity improvement. Financial problems, it was conceded, had followed on from the price restraints of 1972–4 and incomes policies which had produced real increases in rail staff costs of the order of 19 per cent, 1971–5 (24 per cent for all staff).[70] Inflation had had a larger than expected impact on rail costs because 'some "key" productivity levels have remained low' and there was a 'high degree of inertia in the Rail operational structure', particularly in relation to short-term fluctuations in traffic levels.[71] This was confirmed by the 1979 Leeds study, which showed that British Rail employed 87.3 train crew per million train-kilometres in 1977, a higher number than used elsewhere in Europe with the exception of Italy and Finland. Freight and parcels operating was particularly inefficient in this sense, with train crew employment amounting to 185.0; indeed, the Leeds study highlighted the fact that other railways had largely dispensed with drivers' assistants and guards in freight working.[72] While, as we shall see, some action was taken and a number of major initiatives were in the planning stage, radical policies would have to wait for a later period, after the Board's *Challenge of the 80's* document of 1979 and the 1981 Pay Agreement (see Chapter 5).[73]

Despite all the caveats, international comparisons could shed light on British Rail's problems, even where the results were apparently limited. Thus, an observation by the Select Committee on Nationalised Industries on the impressive train-loading statistics of Swedish Railways prompted the Board to send two regional operating managers to Sweden in October 1978. Their report was passed to Board members by Jim Urquhart, the member responsible for Operations and Productivity, in February 1979. He told his colleagues that 'there is little of significance in Swedish railway operational practice which we could beneficially adopt. It once again underlines the need for caution when making direct international performance comparisons'. However, the report itself highlighted a significant divergence in operating practices, including 'the almost total one-man operation of freight trains' in Sweden and 'high locomotive standards including maintenance'.[74] These were surely findings from which British Rail could learn. Lessons could also be drawn from the Leeds study's work on traction/ rolling stock maintenance in 1977. Although the researchers could not produce precise comparisons with other railways because they were unable to apportion workshop labour to particular businesses, they found it instructive that when British Rail Engineering Ltd (BREL) staff were excluded from the calculation British Rail's performance (number of maintenance staff per million train-kilo metres) looked good, but when they were included it looked poor.[75] British Rail paid lower wages and demanded longer hours from its staff, and there was considerable scope for more flexibility in the deployment of labour (especially in rostering).[76] On the other hand, some international indicators placed British Rail in a distinctly favourable light. Continental European railways had been no more successful than British Rail in shedding labour over the period 1971–6,[77] and in fact British Rail stood out as a high labour productivity system. It had experienced the greatest reduction in the number of wagons and the biggest improvement in tonne-kilometres per wagon, 1971–6, despite suffering the constraint of a low average length of haul. In relation to investment, a necessary accompaniment to labour shedding if quality of service were to be maintained, the handicap facing Britain's railways was all too evident. British Rail had the lowest level of investment per train-kilometre than any of the other nine rail ways studied. Financially, also, British Rail's 'performance' was far from poor. Measured by the extent to which revenue collected covered costs, it was only surpassed by Sweden (of course, comparatively high passenger prices were clearly important here). There was thus much food for thought from the 1979 study.[78]

The Pryke and Dodgson report on the 'rail problem' in 1975, which attracted considerable attention inside government, claimed that the basic malaise was caused not by under-investment but by over-manning. The two economists identified numerous opportunities to slim down the labour force, and, in particu lar: train crew (drivers, second and assistant drivers, and guards), where the 'archaic system' of hours and distance limits and inflexible practices relating to second drivers and route knowledge required reform; passenger guards and station staff, where there was scope for new methods of ticket inspection; train and permanent-way maintenance staff, where computer-aided control (TOPS), mechanisation (e.g. track tamping), and cuts in the wagon fleet and in marshal ling yards offered potential savings; and administration, where staffing levels appeared extremely high in comparison with those of other railways. Their overall calculations, which contained some rather optimistic expectations of the immediate possibilities,[79] compared railway labour in 1971 and 1981 and sug gested that there was room for labour shedding of the order of 87,500; by the beginning of 1974 this implied a reduction of about 67,000, 27,000 more than the cut promised by British Rail.[80] Of course, Pryke and Dodgson did not have the task of implementing such a policy with all its industrial relations implications. Politically such action was very difficult at this time. It cannot be said that managers were blind to the opportunities, but it required more than a report or a memorandum to shift the fundamentals in manpower utilisation.[81] As Urquhart later noted in relation to the lack of progress in addressing administrative costs, a particularly sticky issue, 'we don't lack ideas, but rather the will to make it all happen!'[82]

3.5 The unions, pay, and productivity

The position of the railway trade unions must be addressed here. Industrial relations bargaining was conducted in an environment shaped by long-standing sectional division. The largest union, the National Union of Railwaymen (NUR), had a membership of 170,000 which made it the sixteenth-largest in the country. It represented a diverse group of workers and consequently its priorities were to secure gains for all and to address in particular the problem of low pay (rates and earnings) at the bottom. On the other hand, the Associated Society of Locomotive Engineers & Firemen (ASLEF), the drivers' union, was a small, craft union with only 27,000 members. Often militant, it represented members who were anxious first and foremost to preserve their skill and responsibility differentials. White-collar interests were handled by the 71,000-strong Transport Salaried Staffs' Association (TSSA) and, to a lesser extent, by the British Transport Officers' Guild (BTOG).[83] A further complication was the fact that the manufacturing, maintenance, and engineering workers employed by BREL and the civil and mechanical & electrical engineering departments of British Rail were represented both by the NUR and by the Confederation of Shipbuilding & Engineering Unions, with disputes heard by the Railway Shopmen's National Council. In general, issues relating to pay and conditions, which proceeded through the enduring machinery of sectional councils, joint councils, the Railway Staff National Council (RSNC), and, finally, the Railway Staff National Tribunal (RSNT), involved complex negotiations with the triumvirate of NUR, ASLEF, and TSSA. Their rivalry was an irritant; indeed, many disputes had centred round the tendency of one of them to seek to 'leapfrog' over the others. The events of 1963–73 also established important precedents for our period. These years saw, first, a substantial growth in bonus schemes, which created pay inequalities both between and within grades of staff, followed by the freezing of such bonuses in the period 1968–73; and second, concerted efforts to involve the unions in pay and productivity arrangements, notably while Len Neal was at the Board (1967–71). The productivity initiatives, while changing some of the deep-rooted restrictive practices in the industry, had tended to bargain away most of the savings in improved pay and redundancy concessions.[84] British Rail managers thus not only required great skill and diplomacy in handling the labour force and its representatives, but also had much to do to advance the cause of productivity improvement and cost control. The position was intensified by the fact that NUR and ASLEF were both led by long-serving general secretaries of considerable ability and reputation in the British labour movement, in Sidney Weighell (1975–83) and Ray Buckton (1970–87).[85]

With regard, first, to formal bargaining activity, the later 1970s appear to be a rather contradictory period. The unions tended to accept government guidelines on incomes policy but engaged in numerous disputes over additional payments and working conditions. The record of unresolved disputes going to the final stage of the negotiating machinery for the majority of staff, the Railway Staff National Tribunal (RSNT), makes this clear. The RSNT decided no fewer than 25 disputed proposals or claims between July 1974 and August 1979, compared with only one in the preceding eight years. Only three of these referred to general pay claims; 22 were associated with various working practices and conditions, ranging from staff restructuring and rostering to allowances and Sunday work, and most (16) were decided in the eighteen months ending in June 1979.[86] The reasons for this are obvious. The ubiquity of pay restraint led the unions, and in particular, ASLEF, to seek concessions elsewhere. The miners strike of 1974 had been resolved by isolating payments for unsocial hours and conditions, which had circumvented the strict application of pay policies. Similar arguments could be made about railway jobs, as they had been earlier in the decade.[87] From the Board's perspective it was felt important to remove inequalities between staff receiving bonuses and those who were not, and to provide sufficiently attractive terms to attract recruits when labour markets were tight. The most important negotiations led to the first reference to the RSNT, which was reconvened with new members led by Dr William McCarthy of Oxford University, who was very much the unions' choice.[88] A lengthy review of the railways' pay structure, which had begun in 1972, resulted in stalemate in February 1974 and caused the Board to take the unusual step of itself requesting a reference to the RSNT. The latter's decision in July 1974, 'RSNT 42', incorporated most bonus payments into basic rates in a generous package of some £50 million in improvements which added about 15 per cent to paybill costs. The award did much to restore the differentials of the drivers. After the consolidation of mileage and additional responsibility payments, their basic rate of £35.50 was raised to £41.65, a gain of 17 per cent, which compared favourably with the 7 per cent received by railmen. On top of this, payments for irregular and unsocial houses were increased, and since the vast majority of drivers were classified in category 1, they received an additional 10 per cent, making £45.81 in all.[89] The settlement also acted as a template against which numerous subsequent disputes were judged.[90]

How antagonistic, then, was the union response to management initiatives in relation to restrictive practices? Naturally, the unions were intent on protecting income, employment, and conditions of working, including legitimate concerns over asbestos,[91] and were determined to resist both labour shedding without investment and an adverse shift in the 'effort bargain' to assist Treasury object-ives. They felt they had delivered much in productivity in the 1960s—as indeed they had—and were suspicious of having to respond radically again to 'political' exigencies at a time of high inflation. As we have seen, the Board's anxiety to defend British Rail's productivity performance in a comparative European con-text led to published material which reinforced union opinion that their record in co-operating with management over productivity-related change had been good. Furthermore, the long period of pay restraint, which hit public sector workers harder than those in the private sector, helped to fuel the notorious 'Winter of Discontent' in 1978–9. The rash of militant and highly visible strike actions in the British economy influenced British Rail's attempts to involve the rail unions in meaningful talks about further productivity deals.[92] One of the principal con-cepts, driver-only operation of passenger trains, was debated as early as 1975 when the Board was awaiting delivery of new electric suburban trains with automatic sliding doors (Class 313s). However, fears of provoking inter-union conflict (NUR versus ASLEF) tended to dominate management thinking, and consequently little progress was made.[93] In addition, a large number of issues affecting freight rationalisation were held up in the negotiating machinery due to union opposition. These included the restructuring of marshalling in the London area, rationalisation of Eastern Region services, computerised scheduling of train crew programming (the MGR 'Carousel' project), and single manning of Class 56 locomotives.[94] Instead of progress on such matters, the period saw a series of disputes about bonuses, special allowances, and 'extra responsibilities' which went to the RSNT. The majority of these involved claims from ASLEF, encour-aged by Ray Buckton and Bill Ronksley, seeking improved allowances (for lodging turns, signing on, and booking off), and limitations on HST rosters.[95] As one railway industrial relations manager recalled, 'they couldn't have the big ones so they flogged away at the small ones'.[96] However, a genuine attempt to introduce some incentives for delivering productivity did not work out as antici-pated. In 1978 the Board put forward a 'business performance' scheme which proposed to pay back to the unions half of the first 5 per cent of future gains secured in output per man-hour. This was not accepted, and was referred to the RSNT, which to the Board's dismay awarded 80 per cent of the first 5 per cent of savings to the unions and exempted 'vulnerable' commodity traffic such as coal and iron and steel. The Tribunal had tipped the balance in the unions' favour, and the Board, in settling, experienced government criticism, and made it clear that the scheme would only operate for a year. The payments, which amounted on average to a 2.6 per cent increase, were then consolidated into basic rates via a 2 per cent increase in April 1979.[97]

In relation to general rates of pay both British Rail and the rail unions adhered closely to the government's statutory and voluntary incomes policies. Thus, agreement was reached at the pre-arbitration stage of the negotiation machinery, the RSNC, for pay rises in line with the guidelines in 1973, 1974, and 1976–8 (see Appendix G, Table G.2). The only serious dispute arose in 1975 when the brakes came off the statutory incomes policy and the incoming Labour government adopted an (initially) sympathetic stance towards free collective bargaining. The unions rejected the Board's offers of first 20 per cent, then 21.2 per cent, and a referral of the dispute to the RSNT produced an award of 27.5 per cent (27.7 per cent with minimum earnings and equal pay elements) in May 1975. However, this decision was quickly overtaken by the precedents established by other public sector deals of over 30 per cent, and it took a strike threat by NUR and a 'beer and sandwiches' meeting with the prime minister, Harold Wilson, before a two-stage agreement providing 30 per cent plus additional concessions was reached at the RSNC in June. The victory was rather hollow, however, since the payment of the additional 2.5 per cent was caught up in the reintroduction of an incomes policy by Labour (Appendix G, Table G.2).[98] There was also some difficulty in 1979, in the wake of the 'Winter of Discontent'. Callaghan's attempt to hold pay rises to only 5 per cent badly misfired,[99] and the rail unions joined others in breaching the dam. There was some delay, which was exacerbated by the disputes arising from the Board's decision to introduce new bonuses by making additional payments to 'pay-train' guards in 1978. The unions eventually settled for 9 per cent, plus 2 per cent in consolidation of the 'business performance' scheme, plus part-payment of an interim award made under the Social Contract.[100]

Overall, the rail unions had some cause for disquiet. A loss-making industry was reducing its workforce and attempting to reform long-established working practices. Higher train speeds and an increase in vandalism were making operating jobs more stressful.[101] At the same time there were job vacancies in key areas at the wages being offered, and although interregional variations in labour markets were being exploited by the insistence of both NUR and ASLEF on national rates which reflected shortages in the more prosperous South-East,[102] it could hardly be argued that the rail unions had done well in the 1970s. At least the real value of the basic wage rate was maintained. It is difficult to be precise given all the various adjustments, but, for example, a railman's basic weekly wage of £17.20 in May 1971 became £25.65 after the implementation of RSNT 42 with effect from April 1974, and £48.95 in April 1979 (Appendix G, Table G.3). If the 1971 rate had been maintained in real terms using the RPI, the rates would have been about £23.40 and £48.15 respectively.[103] However, the comparative position of railway *take-home* pay in relation to the number of hours worked, and the purchasing power of average *earnings* as opposed to rates, were different matters, and they continued to concern the unions (Appendix G, Table G.4).

British Rail's senior managers had little cause for satisfaction. They had failed to make much progress with the unions on productivity, and each time new technologies were introduced, whether HSTs or ticket-issuing machines, the benefits seemed to be bargained away, as they had been in the 1960s. This was evident during the negotiations which followed the resolution of the dispute affecting pay-train guards in February 1978. The guards had settled for additional payments, in return for agreeing to examine all tickets. However, all this did was to provoke ASLEF and the TSSA into making claims for parallel improvements, which were considered by the RSNT. In Decision No. 60 of October 1978 the Tribunal again dismayed British Rail, this time by awarding drivers an additional payment of 25 per cent for each turn where the train was driven at speeds above 100 mph. In fact, none of the parties was prepared to accept the Decision. At the RSNC the Board suggested that any award be linked to the classification of drivers according to the type of work performed, a proposal which promised to save a considerable amount in training and route-learning costs. However, ASLEF strenuously opposed classification, favouring instead the earnings-sharing scheme enshrined in the long-standing Agreement of December 1939. The union were therefore not in favour of a special payment to HST drivers and asked instead for a 10 per cent increase across the board in recognition of 'additional responsibilities'. In RSNT Decision No. 62 of March 1979, the Tribunal recommended a 5 per cent increase in drivers' rates, an award which was resolved in detail at the RSNC, where the HST issue was also tackled by an agreement providing for the double-manning of such trains with a weekly mileage limitation. The drivers did have a case in relation to operating at much higher speeds, but British Rail's industrial relations managers could scarcely be proud of what they had achieved with ASLEF in 1978–9.[104]

Staff attitudes were critical to operating performance. Recruitment problems, the persistence of a rather inflexible approach to operations in which regional allegiances dominated, and numerous labour disputes, both official and unofficial, notably from drivers, had an impact on both productivity initiatives and the quality of service provided. This became evident during the 'Winter of Discontent', which led, for example, to protests from the National Coal Board (NCB) and the Private Wagon Federation about deterioration in the quality of the freight service. Sir Derek Ezra, the NCB Chairman, was moved to complain formally to Peter Parker in March 1979 about British Rail's failure to move coal stocks.

What gives me the greatest concern now [he wrote] is that, with the winter largely behind us and ASLEF for the moment at least quiescent, we are still suffering severe difficulties . . . because of the various unofficial actions which are being taken at railway establishments, particularly on the maintenance side and because of the shortage of guards.

By early April the shortfall in deliveries to power stations was about 3.5 million tonnes.[105] The wagon owners' complaints were potent enough to be passed to the Railway Management Group, where, in June 1979, they prompted a serious attempt to address the quality issue.[106]

However, all was not gloom and doom in management–union relations. Many managers, whether at the top or lower down, were beginning to appreciate that it was important to be frank with the trade unions and seek their support. A regional passenger manager told Parker a fortnight after his appointment: 'My recent experience/efforts have produced a "pay off" in that they have no real answer to my sincerity . . . I think this uncooperative attitude springs largely from the lack of knowledge on which they can base an understanding of the problems we face (this is especially so in marketing and pricing).'[107] A modest example of what could be achieved by a 'participative' approach was the action taken by the Southern Region in 1975–6 when Bob Reid was the general manager. In response to the short-term financial problems facing British Rail at that time, the Southern secured the co-operation of the trade unions at sectional council level in producing a package of measures designed to reduce passenger costs by trimming peak-hour and weekend services. Introduced from April 1976 the joint management-union initiatives made estimated savings of £1.7 million a year while optimising service levels and staff earnings.[108] This is an illuminating episode in view of the militant and uncooperative reputation of Southern Region trainmen at various times,[109] but was the exception rather than the rule.

3.6 The search for cost savings: limited success

How successful were British Rail's efforts to secure cost savings in the late 1970s? First of all, we should recognise that general approaches to cost accounting and control in British (and American) firms at this time were at something of a crossroads. *Financial* accounting clearly dominated and it was to take a considerable debate, furthered by writers on management such as Johnson and Kaplan, to correct the balance of emphasis.[110] Second, in the public sector, the successful implementation of cost-reducing strategies was influenced by the degree of urgency produced by government requirements. Consequently, there was a difference at this time in the response to freight and passenger costs, and also in the approach to operating costs as opposed to those of engineering, both civil and mechanical, the workshops, and administration. The system of surplus capacity grants provided under the 1968 Act was one such mechanism. This rewarded British Rail for shedding surplus infrastructure over the period 1969–73 with payments of up to £50 million. By 1971 a substantial shortfall in executing the promised rationalisation programme emerged, and it was quickly apparent to managers that given the resistance to passenger closures it was much easier to eliminate capacity which was surplus to *freight* requirements. In the circumstances the Department of Transport was forced to suspend grant payments, and eventually a reduced sum of £45.3 million was paid.[111] More important, of course, was the introduction of the PSO regime in 1974, which also focused attention on the freight business. The passenger railway was to be maintained at broadly its existing service level and subsidised, but freight was now required to cover its 'avoidable costs', that is, the costs which would be avoided if freight services were not operated. As we have noted (p. 22), the 1975 'crisis' in freight revenues produced insistent demands from Treasury and DOE officials for firmer responses from rail managers. This gave impetus to internally generated plans to effect economies in freight operations, which built upon the considerable rationalisation in the period 1962–73.[112] Although passenger operations had been subject to joint British Rail/DOE service reviews in 1974–5,[113] and its managers were also under pressure to deliver economies once the cash limits regime was in place in 1975, the general directive to maintain passenger service levels tended to inhibit the formulation of draconian remedies. In any case, rationalisation of passenger services was subject to more public scrutiny via the consumer consultation bodies, the CTCC and the TUCCs.[114] Finally, the organisation of the railways placed its own constraints on the process of cost control. Because initiatives were devised at the centre and were then passed down to the regional and divisional tiers of management, their success depended on the extent to which they were able to win the active support of the regional general managers and their staffs. Furthermore, any attempt to address mechanical engineering costs was constrained by the arm's-length yet cosy position of BREL, which in both operational and accounting terms was not the independent and free-standing subsidiary company it appeared to be (see p. 82). There were thus both institutional and political barriers to a determined assault on railway costs.

Action in relation to passenger costs was limited. That there was scope for a tougher response to loss-making services is not in doubt. In 1975 Bowick had some caustic things to say to his passenger managers about the viability of certain Inter-City services, for example the low loadings of trains from the West Midlands and North-West to Scotland and some trans-Pennine services, which with an operating ratio of 143 'must be failing to cover total costs substantially' and where 'the journey times are terrible'. Some seasonal services were far worse, prompting Bowick to note that 'there really are some horrific figures here and I really must have proposals which stop committing resources of all kinds for some of these operations'. These included Sheffield–Portsmouth (operating ratio: 565), Edinburgh–Fort William (ratio: 433), Crewe–Blackpool, and Manchester–Morecambe (ratio: 400), and the worst of all, Rhymney–Barry Island, where the ratio was 1,300—'in total I suppose £20 to earn £1'.[115] It is not clear how much headway was made. Although the worst examples were no doubt eliminated in the emergency service cuts of 1975/6, in general passenger costs escaped the kind of attention given to freight with its failure to break even in 1975–7.

Unsurprisingly, then, freight managers were more successful in effecting operational cost reductions than their colleagues in the passenger departments.

Their diagnosis of the problems in 1975 was soundly based. Low rates charged for bulk traffic remained profitable only because low unit movement costs in train-loads offset the poor productivity in terms of resource utilisation. The productive work of train crews was found to be only 3.7 hours per shift, and that of locomotives only 11 hours a day. The level of utilisation had become more critical because higher inflation had impacted on wage and wagon costs and the man-power content in freight costs was comparatively high. The problems were accentuated in the wagon-load traffic, a large, dispersed business crossing re-gional boundaries, where responsibility was fragmented and there was a high degree of operational inertia.[116] All this suggested possible solutions which, as we have seen, were difficult to implement without radical manpower strategies; but at least there was a desire to address costs in the problematic wagon-load sector, to withdraw lightly loaded services, to close under-utilised stations and depots, and prune the life-expired wagon fleet. Although the contraction of the once substantial wagon-load business was regretted by those who felt the railways should be carrying a higher volume of freight on environmental grounds, and who feared the implications for the covering of rail infrastructure costs, it made little sense either financially or environmentally to hang on to sporadic vacuum-braked wagon-load services, for example between Fakenham and Wymondham in Norfolk for domestic coal, grain, and fertiliser while Sainsbury's sent their traffic by road.[117]

What action was taken in the freight business? First, ongoing studies of lightly loaded freight services which had started before 1974 revealed opportunities for termination of service.[118] Then, strategic work conducted for British Rail's Fourth Corporate Plan gave impetus to a more determined policy, embracing an acceler-ation of the disengagement from wagon-load, a critical evaluation of freight-only lines, steps to improve low resource utilisation, and an attempt to confine freight working to weekdays.[119] Following an organisational change in 1976, which saw the appointment of a planning manager for wagon-load business in order to strengthen the business management of the sector, there was more determined action. This included reductions in train-mileage, rationalisation of rolling stock following the introduction of computerised monitoring via TOPS (see pp. 93–4), and a switch to potentially more profitable activity. The latter embraced the introduction of faster, scheduled services using air-braked vehicles introduced under the marketing name 'Speedlink' in 1977, and an emphasis on more effective collection and delivery via Freightliner, whose business grew by 11 per cent, 1974–8.[120] The assault on wagon-load may be seen in the rapid rundown of the wagon fleet. There were 437,400 freight vehicles at the end of 1968, 248,700 by the end of 1973, and only 137,600 at the end of 1979, 31 per cent of the 1968 fleet (Table 3.9). Over the period 1973–9 the number of marshalling yards also fell by 36 per cent, while the number of freight stations and depots fell by 18 per cent. Clearly, the rationalisation was not of the same scale as that of 1962–8 (see the percentage changes in Table 3.9), and the rail network available to

Table 3.9 Rationalisation of rail freight, 1962–79

Year	Freight stations and depots	Marshalling yards		Route-mileage open to freight	Freight vehicles	
		Major yards	All yards		Total	Of which air braked
1962	5,175	n.a.	602	17,481	862,640	n.a.
1968	912	n.a.	184	12,447	437,412	3,878 (1967)
1973	542	53	124	10,801	248,682	9,142 (1972)
1979	442	35	79	10,296	137,589	17,387
Percentage change						
1962–8	−82	—	−69	−29	−49	—
1968–73	−41	—	−33	−13	−43	+136
1973–9	−18	−34	−36	−5	−45	+90

Source: Gourvish, *British Railways*, p. 427; BRB, *R&A 1973–9*; BRB, *Facts and Figures* (1978/80); BRB Chief Executive's files, X23–38.

freight barely shrank, falling by only 505 miles (5 per cent of the 1973 network). Nevertheless, vehicle and marshalling yard cuts were comparable with those of 1968–73, and what was significant about the later 1970s was the attempt to focus both on cost reduction and on the marketing of more profitable segments of the business. The immediate impact of such changes was seen in the fact that from 1976 to 1979 freight unit receipts rose by 8 per cent while unit costs fell by a similar proportion, in spite of a 9 per cent fall in train-mileage. Consequently, the contribution of freight (the margin of receipts over direct expenditure) per train-mile increased by 70 per cent.[121]

The process was not without its problems, of course, particularly since rationalisation was pursued with assets which were old and unreliable. The Freight Committee minutes reveal the difficulties local managers had in maintaining quality of service in 1978–9. As we have seen, labour problems, and notably a shortage of guards, were a factor here. But the difficulties were also exacerbated by accelerated rationalisation exercises, and the low availability and high failure rate of locomotives, elements which were particularly evident in the Eastern and Scottish regions.[122] We must also be aware of the limitations of managers' actions. This was still a period when there could be a wide gap between planning at headquarters and action in the field, and it was not always the case that cost cutting went hand in hand with a firm idea of the 'bottom line'. One example must suffice. When Tom Barron, then Controller of Corporate Planning, was shown the draft marketing plan for steel traffic in 1975, he found it easy to point to deficiencies. There was, he pointed out, the lack of a clear message based on resource implications. Querying the reliance upon the simple operating ratio as a profit indicator and '"says it all" statistic',[123] he pointed out that the setting of contribution targets (i.e. contributions to freight avoidable costs) for each commodity group would be a much better procedure, the aim being to 'compel the marketeers to orientate their efforts to the worthy, though apparently ill-considered, aim of <u>maximising net revenue</u>'.[124]

Detailed plans to slim the administrative staff were drawn up but considerable 'slippage' was evident in the implementation stages. The intention had been to cut the salaried workforce by at least a third, or 8,000 jobs in a total of 24,000 staff at divisional level and above by 1981, though following a conference held in Peterborough in November 1976 the scheme was scaled down to 5,600 by excluding Professional and Technical staff. Progress was slow, however. At the end of the first year there were reported savings of 1,571, but little headway was made over the next two years. Salaried staff in rail functions (as defined in Table 3.7), who numbered 54,300 at the end of 1976, fell to about 52,600 in 1977, and totalled 52,700 in 1979.[125]

It is not easy to find evidence of substantial cost cutting in the vital areas of engineering (civil, signal and telecommunications, mechanical and electrical), which together made up a large and increasing proportion of total operating expenditure in the late 1970s. By 1979 they represented about 50 per cent of the total (Table 3.10). The 'culture of the railroad' encouraged the firm belief that safety and service reliability demanded adequate expenditure, a view perpetuated by Parker's references to the need for sufficient investment in infrastructure and the dangers, if this were not realised, of the 'crumbling edge of quality'. However, the measurement of what was adequate was a matter for debate, involving not only engineers, but operators, and civil servants from the Department of Transport and the Treasury, and, in 1982–3, the Serpell Committee. Furthermore, the

Table 3.10 Railways' engineering expenditure, 1974 and 1979—breakdown by major category (£m.)

Category	1974	1979
1 Infrastructure (track and signalling)	165.3 (19%)	473.4 (25%)
2 Locomotive and rolling stock maintenance and repair	183.8 (21%)	381.7 (20%)
3 Associated administrative costs (est.)[a]	25.0 (3%)	100.0 (5%)
4 Total railway operating costs	882.9	1,888.9
BREL's total expenditure[b]	149.3	385.6

Source: BRB, *R&A 1974, 1979*.

[a] Only the administrative costs associated with infrastructure are identified separately. Here, total administration costs for infrastructure and maintenance repair are estimated by doubling this figure.
[b] These figures are from BREL's operating account. The data for categories 2 and 3 include 'work done [for BRB] by Rail workshops'.

institutional arrangements for organising the work in the engineering departments served to obscure performance in a conventional management accounting sense. Much of the activity was organised at a regional level, making it more difficult to monitor and control from the centre. In the area of locomotive and rolling stock manufacture, maintenance, and repair, BREL, a subsidiary of the Board from 1970, supplied nearly all of British Rail's new-build and *heavy* repair and maintenance requirements, but on a cost-plus basis without competitive tendering. Its published operating accounts, which appeared in the Board's annual accounts, gave only the barest of information on the relationship between the subsidiary and its parent. BREL derived more than 90 per cent of its sales from British Rail. The unpublished accounts reveal an internal profit figure (before interest) of 2–3 per cent on these sales in 1974–6, but it is difficult, if not impossible, to determine whether quoted costs and prices were excessive or not. Interest charges, and adjustments thereto, reduced profits to something close to the required break-even point (there was a loss of £600,000 in 1976).[126] The financial information provided indicates that BREL was in fact a large and inadequately controlled department of British Rail rather than a genuine subsidiary. The enmeshment of revenues and finances was, however, accompanied by a degree of separation at management level, irritating the regional general managers and making it difficult for them to influence workshop performance.[127]

In October 1978, four years before the Serpell Report of 1983 found that there was considerable scope for savings in the engineering departments,[128] the Board was sufficiently anxious about the manufacturing and maintenance functions to give its newly formed Strategy Unit the task of examining them in some detail, focusing in particular on procurement and cost effectiveness. Two external consultants, Neville Abraham, of Resource Development International, and Michael Beesley, from London Business School, were engaged, reporting to a small but high-powered 'control group' consisting of two members of the Strategy Steering Group, Geoffrey Myers, head of the Unit, and Professor John Heath; Dr Ken Spring, one of the Directors of Strategic Studies; Ian Gardiner, Managing Director of BREL; and Ken Taylor, the Chief Mechanical & Electrical Engineer. The policy review produced by the consultants, completed in December 1979, revealed a catalogue of deficiencies. The planning and procurement of new equipment lacked 'tough commercial disciplines', and BREL's in-house design and R&D were 'unlikely to be in BR's long-term interests'. On the maintenance side, there were 'conflicting priorities', 'unclear accountability', 'system inertia', and standards which were not related to costs. At the time of the review BREL was failing to meet its output targets by considerable margins—for new construction 86 per cent for coaches and 63 per cent for EMUs, and in repairs 20 per cent for wagons and 13 per cent for locomotives (1978 data). Because the problems were found to be 'as much about the culture and the organisational style of the business as they are about processes and methods adopted', the review suggested that a completely new environment be created, with a competitive climate, clear accountability, and commercial disciplines. They recommended the establishment of a totally separate independent engineering company for 'new-build' manufacturing; and a rationalisation of the maintenance activity as between the workshops and the numerous (more than 150) BR depots, accompanied by the creation of a central task force to improve performance.[129] It was, of course, a different matter to translate accurate diagnosis into effective action, and there were institutional barriers to effecting speedy change, particularly on the maintenance side. There were also mitigating factors. If, as the consultants claimed, BREL suffered from the lack of a clear strategy and weak management accounting, then this is scarcely surprising given the difficulties it faced in responding satisfactorily to the uncertainties and vicissitudes of the railways' investment planning processes (see pp. 89–90), the short-term decisions taken to keep expenditure within the EFL, and the problems presented by a rapidly ageing asset-base. Nevertheless, it is quite clear from the events of 1978–80 that there was an internal determination to address the long-standing and thorny problem of mechanical engineering in British Rail. Another example of this was the preparation of a 'Manifesto' for BREL by its new chairman, Jim Urquhart, which advocated many of the same changes, notably its separation as a 'coherent fully accountable and profitable subsidiary business of BR, fulfilling as nearly as possible the financial and performance criteria expected of such a company in the private sector', and a contractual relationship with British Rail which provided for a 'profit element and sanctions'.[130] These initiatives were timely; but one had only prescriptions, not solutions, before the 1980s.

It was a pity that engineering costs could not be addressed with the same imagination and innovativeness that the Board used as Pension Fund Trustees in investing in works of art from 1974 as part of the strategy of protecting the real value of their investments. Notwithstanding the pressures provided by some adverse media reaction to the policy,[131] the pension funds invested £20 million in works of art in the period November 1974–December 1977, 3.6 per cent of their total external investment portfolio.[132] In September 1978, when £27 million had been invested, a limit of £40 million was set; by 31 May 1980 expenditure had reached £38.8 million, about 3 per cent of the investment portfolio.[133] It is difficult to be certain of the 'return' since no works were sold in our period. However, there is every indication that the investments compared favourably with more conventional assets.[134]

To conclude. The later 1970s were characterised by repeated concerns, both inside and outside the business, about rail operating cost levels, but it must be accepted that the immediate response was patchy. Much remained to be tackled in areas recognised to be problematic, notably the maintenance function, and train crew productivity. These themes would be addressed many times in the 1980s.

3.7 Railway investment: a disappointing record

Investment can be a complex subject to deal with, and railway investment is no exception. First, there were numerous difficulties of definition and coverage. Following the 1974 Railways Act spending on renewal of the basic infrastructure was transferred from capital to revenue account. Thus, from January 1975 government control extended to both new rolling stock and new infrastructure (charged to capital) and track and signalling renewal (charged to revenue).[135] Control was exercised by establishing spending limits or 'ceilings' for three separate categories: (1) railway investment; (2) investment in railway passenger facilities by Passenger Transport Executives; and (3) investment in British Railways Board subsidiaries, chiefly BREL and shipping. It is also important to distinguish between gross and net investment, although calculations of the latter usually give rise to numerous academic arguments about asset life and expiry rates. Furthermore, all calculations are bedevilled by the several ways of adjusting the data to take account of inflation. Second, investment, perhaps more than any single element in railway management, exposed the difficulties of the relationship with government. As was evident in the period 1948–73, and as noted in outline in Chapter 1, the long-running, time-consuming dialogue with government made it very difficult indeed to plan investment with confidence. There were several elements at work. First, the Board was dismayed by the government's speedy rejection of its plans, contained in the Rail Policy Review of 1972, for a higher level of spending, which was considered essential both to maintain the railway at its existing level of activity with an acceptable average asset life and to provide for technological improvements. Second, it was frequently exasperated by the imposition of budgetary cuts occasioned by the government's short-term economic policies. From 1975 these cuts intruded at both the capital level, via investment ceilings and controls on borrowing, and on revenue account spending, via control of the PSO and cash limits.[136] Third, there was continuing anxiety about the Board's failure to match expenditures or 'outturns' with the targets or 'ceilings' which were eventually agreed with government. The factors governing these shortfalls were both numerous and complex, but much of the problem stemmed from the way in which investment was planned and managed in such an environment. Fourth, the Board resented governmental intervention in matters of detail, which was apparent for example in the haggles with the DOE over individual projects such as the Advanced Passenger Train (APT), and the Department's refusal in 1975 to allow the virement of an investment allocation originally made to the shipping subsidiary.[137] Finally, British Rail faced considerable scepticism about the validity of its more ambitious investment plans, and notably, an accelerated rate of electrification, the Advanced Passenger Train, and the Channel Tunnel. The justification for such projects was challenged by sceptical Treasury officials, by transport economists employing conventional rate of return criteria (such as Pryke, Dodgson, and Foster), and by the anti-rail, pro-road lobby.[138] As we saw in Chapter 1, these opinions produced a situation in which British Rail was singled out for sterner treatment than the rest of the public sector (for example in the cuts announced in 1975). The Micawberish, play-safe tendencies of British civil servants, ministers, and their advisers, symbolised by the decision to abandon the Channel Tunnel project in January 1975, contrasted sharply with the more ambitious stance on investing in the future of the railways taken in countries such as France and Germany.[139]

Did anything dramatic occur in the period 1974–9? However we elect to measure investment, the answer appears to be no. Figure 3.1 and Table 3.11 provide an indication of what was happening to gross railway investment over both the long and short run. After the Modernisation Plan of 1955 had produced exceptionally high levels of railway investment in the decade 1956–65, investment fell sharply in real terms. There was a minor recovery from the low point in 1969 to 1975, much of it explained by the completion of the West Coast Main Line electrification, then a stabilisation over the years 1976–9 at around £335 million in 1979 prices, in line with government policy formulated in 1975–6, and confirmed in the 1977 White Paper.[140] This level of expenditure was clearly lower than in the period 1953–67 (Figure 3.1). In physical terms, the years 1974–9 saw the addition to the fleet of 230 locomotives and traction units, 687 EMUs, 1,072 passenger vehicles, and 8,570 freight vehicles; in addition, there were 3,160 more track-miles of Continuous Welded Rail (CWR) and 1,644 route-miles fitted with an Automatic Warning System (AWS). Permanent-way renewal and wagon building was comparable with previous years, but the rate of new construction for locomotives, EMUs, and passenger vehicles was well down on the average for 1963–73 (Table 3.12), and scrappings exceeded new acquisitions, including leasing. One might expect a lower rate of investment in some assets. For example, fewer new locomotives were needed with the reduction in freight traffic and the shift to passenger trainsets (HST, APT). The genesis of the diesel-powered HST may be found in an earlier period, when the Board submitted a £64 million scheme in 1972. However, the full introduction of the new trains, serving London, Bristol and South Wales (from 1976), and the East Coast Main Line (from 1978), was a significant development in our period. Indeed, the HSTs have proved to be one of the best investments made by Britain's nationalised railways. The operation of regular scheduled services at speeds of up to 125 mph—the fastest diesel services in the world—represented a major landmark in rail passenger travel.[141]

Nevertheless, this was but one example. In more general terms there was certainly a 'crumbling edge of quality',[142] which was evident in the 'cascading' of fairly elderly displaced rolling stock to less favoured parts of the system, and in the ramshackle state of the more peripheral parts of the network, where renewals had been postponed for some years. The stabilisation of investment at levels

'The Age of the Drain'

3. BR's investment programme, as seen by KAL (Kevin Kallaugher),
unpublished, 1982

which the Board considered inadequate caused it to rein itself in and make some tough choices about options. One consequence was the decision to embark upon major refurbishment programmes for rolling stock as an interim measure. The assets acquired during the early years of the Modernisation Plan of 1955 were approaching the end of their physical lives by the mid-1970s. Most of the 3,000-strong fleet of DMUs had been built in the period 1957–60, but the scaling down of the Board's investment plans in 1974 and the bleak prospects for substantial electrification prompted the decision to renovate the existing trains, rather than replace them with new. There were other influences, too. The OPS 'sector' was regarded as a cinderella activity with an uncertain future, a position reinforced by

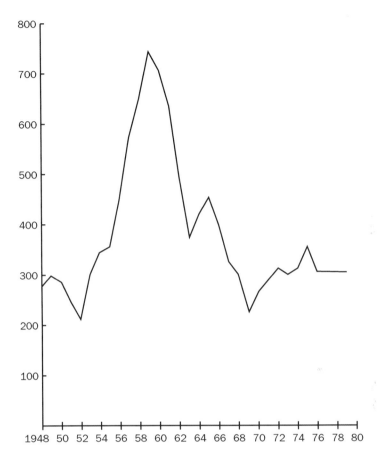

Note: Figures include CWR Programme.

Figure 3.1 Railway investment, 1948–79 (1979 prices)

then current plans for bus replacement. In 1975 the Board therefore authorised a major programme for DMU refurbishment over the period 1975–83. Altogether £13 million was spent in renovating 1,600 vehicles.[143] There was also an ageing fleet of EMUs, with an average age of 20 years. Here again, life extension was preferred to new investment. In 1977 authorisation was given to refurbish 500 vehicles as part of an ambitious programme to extend the life of some 5,000 Mark I EMUs to 40 years. This first scheme cost £43 million.[144] Infrastructure was also affected. On the one hand, British Rail embarked on major resignalling schemes, notably in the London area at Victoria and London Bridge. On the other, the decision to virtually postpone renewal of some 3,000 miles of less heavily used track was tantamount to a threat to close lines with considerable arrears, since

Table 3.11 Gross investment (railway and group), 1974–9 (£m., in current and constant 1979 prices)

Year	Railway[a]	Other[b]	Group[a]	Railway[a]	Other[b]	Group[a]
	(Current prices)			(Constant 1979 prices)		
1974	159	15	175	339	32	371
1975	211	21	232	354	36	389
1976	232	39	270	337	56	393
1977	265	32	296	338	41	379
1978	293	51	344	335	58	393
1979	331	70	401	331	70	401

Source: Appendix B, Tables 3.1 and 3.2 (totals may not sum due to rounding).

[a] Including expenditure on continuous welded rail (treated as investment until 1979), and track renewals.
[b] BREL, BTH, BRPB, Freightliner (1979 only), Sealink, Hovercraft, Corporate, and Research.

these would become unsafe over a three-year period, such as Appledore–Ore (Ashford–Hastings), Shrewsbury–Dovey Jnc., and Princes Risborough–Aynho Jnc.[145] In this situation it is obvious that net investment, which was found to be negative in the period 1963–73, remained negative over the rest of the decade.[146] Clearly, the difficulties in relation to investment, of which Marsh complained, were not resolved in the first part of Parker's term of office. The tension between British Rail's cries for more investment and the stance of sceptics in government, who could point to disappointing outcomes in comparison with estimated financial benefits, remained endemic.

The government's control mechanism in the 1970s was a mixture of stringency and leniency. Much of the dissatisfaction from British Rail's point of view centred on the instability of the five-year rolling programmes as an instrument for investment planning given the long lead times between the initiation of projects and their completion. The plans, which were firmed up into annual programmes in the year before spending was due to start, were subject to frequent modifications at short notice to square with Treasury expenditure plans, as we saw in Chapter 1. On the other hand, and ironically in view of the desire by government for tighter control of nationalised industry spending, the investigation of annual investment programmes in detail had been abandoned in 1970. Only those projects costing £1 million and over (from 1975 £2 million) required Departmental authorisation. Of course, the larger projects attracted particular scrutiny, adding to the delays, and there was the requirement (until the 1978 White Paper) that all projects should satisfy a test discount rate of 10 per cent, which was a tough hurdle for rail investments which were considered very worthy using broader criteria, such as network enhancement.[147] This said, there was in fact a

Table 3.12 Physical components of railway investment, 1974–9

Year	Rolling stock											Infrastructure	
	Locomotives		Power cars		Multiple units		Passenger coaching stock			Non-passenger coaching stock	Freight wagons	CWR track-miles	AWS route-miles
	Electric	Diesel	HST	APT	DMU	EMU	Loco-hauled	HST	APT				
1974	19	—	—	—	—	77	275	—	—	—	738	560	406
1975	1	—	—	—	—	76	173	143	—	1	1,504	571	387
1976	—	13	40	—	—	157	42	151	—	9	1,715	509	101
1977	—	22	34	—	—	131	24	120	6	16	1,344	512	300
1978	—	18	35	2	—	42	—	112	9	34	1,750	544	268
1979	—	16	27	3	—	204	17	526	15	3	1,519	464	182
Total	20	69	136	5	0	687	531			63	8,570	3,160	1,644
Annual average													
1974-9	3	11	23	1	0	114	89	88	2	10	1,428	527	27
1963-73	16	125	—	—	4	151	148	—	—	13	1,239	526	167

Source: BRB, *R&A 1974–9*; DOE/DTp, *Railway Accidents 1974–9*; Gourvish, *British Railways*, p. 511; Ian Campbell, Report on 'Renewal and Maintenance of Physical Assets: An Assessment of the Effect of Continued Restriction of Finance over a Ten-Year Period', 17 December 1980, BRB Minutes, 8 January 1981.

fair amount of freedom for the Board, its Investment Committee, and regional investment managers to determine what should be funded within the ceiling. In Whitehall there was a continuing suspicion that not everything was being handled with financial returns in mind, and the failure of officials to obtain regular and detailed back-checks on the actual financial returns accruing from previously authorised projects fuelled this. Progress in developing a satisfactory method of joint evaluation was slow.[148] We must have some sympathy with the Department of Transport on this score, since there is some internal evidence to support their qualms. For example, in 1974, Fowler, when Controller of Corporate Finance, pointed out to the Investment Committee that too many projects charged to revenue account were being presented with the impact on revenue being classified as 'non-monitorable'; the proportion was 88 per cent for railway projects compared with only 24 per cent for the subsidiaries.[149] Attempts were made to address this deficiency, but there were clearly problems with the monitoring process, as the Investment Committee noted in June 1976 and 1977,[150] and it must be conceded that it was difficult to estimate future revenue benefits given the way in which the business was organised in management accounting terms before the move to Sector Management. It is thus easy to see why civil servants and, indeed, politicians were persuaded by the view, presented for example by Christopher Foster in his evidence before the Select Committee on Nationalised Industries, that British Rail's investment programmes contained too many of the riskier projects, justified by expectations of increased revenue, and too few projects based on more secure estimates of cost savings.[151]

The railways' continuing inability to meet their spending targets provided ammunition for those in government who felt that higher levels of expenditure were neither necessary nor feasible. The investment shortfall was particularly high for railways in 1976–8, when it amounted to some 9–10 per cent of the government ceiling (see Appendix F, Table F.1). The time-consuming dialogue with the Department, and its procedural rules, did play their part here, not least the insistence that there could be no virement between the capital account ceiling and that for revenue account. However, this was only one element in the equation. British Rail's *group* investment performed much better, with an average shortfall of only 4 per cent in 1974–9. The contrast with railway investment was explained by the fact that it was much easier to adjust spending on bought-in items for the non-rail businesses, such as ships and road vehicles. Another device, but a rather blunt instrument as events proved, was to allocate investment expenditure above the ceiling (Appendix F, Table F.1). Nevertheless, under-spending still occurred, and it is clear that several internal factors were responsible for the lag, including inadequate appreciation by the railway regions of the time needed to develop projects, poor production scheduling within BREL, and industrial relations disputes in some of the workshops.[152]

3.8 The challenge of new technologies

When one turns to projects, one must have some sympathy for the government's concern, since railway R&D revealed problems in bringing new technologies such as the Advanced Passenger Train (APT) on stream, while the realised return on some of the more important new projects was either a matter shrouded in some secrecy or else very difficult to unravel sensibly, given a changing environment which had surfaced between a project's presentation and appraisal and its completion. Concerns about the actual return on investment were apparent in relation to the APT, electrification projects, the computerised wagon and train control system TOPS (Total Operations Processing System), and the new wagon-load train system 'Speedlink'.

The APT, a high-speed, tilting train, was a revolutionary technology which represented a distinct technological challenge. The idea of gas turbine propulsion having been abandoned, developmental investment on three electric prototypes was authorised in 1974. At this time, British Rail's strategy for Inter-City investment was to introduce electric APTs on the West Coast Main Line (Euston–North), deploy HSTs on other Inter-City routes starting with those on the Western Region, and electrify the East Coast Main Line (ECML, King's Cross–North) and/or the Midland Main Line (MML, St. Pancras–Leicester–Sheffield).[153] By 1979, however, doubts had surfaced about the prospects of this strategy. First, the Board encountered a considerable degree of government scepticism about the financial return on higher speeds (especially in comparison with the HST), which was evident when the DOE insisted that investment in the initial APT prototype be contained within the railways' overall capital investment ceiling.[154] Indeed, there was some anxiety internally about the Board's exposure to the charge of being production-led rather than business-led on both the APT and electrification plans.[155] Despite the fact that British Rail had already spent over 10 years in developing the train, 'painfully acquired through a period of fluctuating railway policy and financial status',[156] hopes to bring the prototype trainsets into service in 1978 were frustrated, and ultimately the project was abandoned (in 1986), with much embarrassment, made worse by the trumpeting it had received in the 1970s. Of course, departmental scepticism was a recurring problem, and there is evidence that the APT was not given the kind of resources which might have made a difference. It might be argued, and indeed it was, that it was misguided to develop a train designed to extract the best out of nineteenth-century infrastructure instead of pressing for completely new lines, as was achieved in France.[157] These arguments have some validity, but there were also engineering shortcomings, including a lack of full commitment within the railway, and with hindsight it can be seen that too much unproven technical wizardry was packed into the design. By the time the technical difficulties had been addressed, the goalposts had shifted and the momentum was lost.[158]

Railways under Labour, 1974–9

Equally problematic, and less excusable perhaps, was the failure to decide on a suitable successor to the worn-out DMUs and to bring a design into production before the end of the decade. In 1974 and 1976 authorisation was given to the construction of new prototype DMUs, the Class 210. This engineering-led venture produced an expensive (c.£1 million) and high-quality design. There was then a lurch in the opposite direction with the development of a low-cost (c.£140,000) light railbus, based on a Leyland bus body, the Class 140.[159] Ultimately neither proved to be a long-term solution. It was difficult in the circumstances for outsiders to sympathise with the Board. British Rail continued to bleat about the need for more investment, but it is clear that sometimes their internal R&D capabilities left something to be desired. Here, the contrast with the French railways was sharp. The ability of SNCF to successfully develop the TGV was a major factor in winning government support for it.[160]

Electrification came to the fore again following the highly visible improvement to London–Glasgow passenger performance following the completion of the electrified route in 1974.[161] British Rail, regarding the balance to have been tilted in favour of electrification by the 1973 oil crisis, then pressed for further development of a further 3,000 route-miles. Its Investment Committee put the ECML at the top of the list in July 1974, but replaced it with the MML by the end of December 1975, anticipating government authorisation of the first section as a self-contained suburban scheme, from St Pancras/Moorgate to Bedford (authorised in November 1976).[162] By this time there was internal pressure from corporate works managers such as Robin Johnson to work up a considered case of the major options,[163] and further impetus was given by the supportive comments in the report of the Select Committee on Nationalised Industries in April 1977 and the government's response to it in November. The latter argued that a joint review of the general case for main-line electrification be initiated on the basis of a preliminary update by the Board. This was duly worked up and presented to the Department of Transport in April 1978; it was distributed more widely as a discussion paper in the following month.[164] Both sides recognised that it had not been possible to make a straightforward financial case for electrifying either the ECML or the MML as individual projects, due to the very high initial costs of construction.[165] However, British Rail now took comfort in contemporary projections about the future relative prices of oil and electricity, together with the new rules for evaluating public sector investment projects contained in the White Paper on *The Nationalised Industries* of April 1978. This announced the abandonment of the 10 per cent Test Discount Rate and its replacement with a Required Rate of Return of only 5 per cent, which was to be applied to overall investment programmes, rather than to individual projects.[166] The Board made the additional argument that the existence of so many shared routes in the rail network meant that 'the combined net effect of electrification would exceed the sum of the quantifiable effects of electrifying individual lines'.[167] The Discussion Paper was thus able to conclude that a sound financial

92

case would be made for 'major enlargement of the electrified network'.[168] In the period under examination here, very limited progress was made with such ambitions. Only one major scheme was authorised—St. Pancras–Bedford, and only one was completed, the Great Northern suburban lines from King's Cross to Hertford/Welwyn (November 1976) and Royston (October 1977).[169] If one looked at the international league table of railway electrification, British Rail remained deep in the relegation zone.[170] When Labour gave way to the Conservatives in May 1979, the joint Department/BRB review had yet to provide a report.

When we turn to the actual returns to investment, we find that TOPS, the IBM-based computer system for monitoring and controlling freight movements, provides a good demonstration of the problems the Board often encountered in measuring benefits in a changing environment. The project was enthusiastically received by rail managers, but was quickly transformed by the changing nature of rail freight. As some of them have admitted, this was a very good idea which perhaps came too late for the wagon-load business.[171] The original submission of May 1971 envisaged an investment of £31.325 million and was quite explicit as to the high risks involved. Indeed, it identified three likely benefits—wagon fleet reduction, operating savings, and service improvement— and provided a series of estimated financial benefits (net present values at 10 per cent discount, with an eight-year project life), which ranged from £5.7 to £56.7 million. Its favoured estimate, however, which took no account of service improvements, was £19.3 million based on freight levels in the 1971 Freight Plan and £14.3 million based on a lower level of wagon-load business. When reassessed in March 1973 the NPV was given as £22.8 million to 1980, but this figure included a speculative estimate of the revenue retained from improved services.[172] Expenditure was reassessed downwards as the project proceeded, and by the time the system had been fully installed, in October 1975, the authorised outlay was a little over £26 million.[173] TOPS was much trumpeted, particularly by the then Chief Executive, David Bowick, and by Ian Campbell, the Executive Director (Systems & Operations), as transforming freight operations; it was defended by its supporters as fully justifying the investment and yielding more than the forecast benefits. Wagon availability improved by 25 per cent, enabling British Rail to scrap older wagons at an accelerated rate. An analysis of freight operating improvement since TOPS revealed that from 1975 to 1979 the payload per freight train increased by 17 per cent and the operating cost per train-mile fell by 11 per cent.[174] However, as we have seen, the re-evaluation of freight prospects had produced a firmer rationalisation policy for the wagon-load business, and by December 1978 the Chief Operations Manager, Bill Bradshaw, conceded that the estimated net benefits were much lower than forecast: £9.2 million in 1978 instead of the £24.9 million forecast four years earlier (£10.8 million converted from 1972 to 1978 prices). Most disturbing was the failure to distinguish *revenue* benefits— only £0.4 million had been identified compared with the £23.1 million claimed.

Railways under Labour, 1974–9

Bradshaw's calculation did not take account of several 'intangibles' or unquantifiable items, and he admitted that 'the extent to which BR has been better off . . . as a result of the introduction of TOPS is largely a matter for subjective estimation'.[175] There was a fair amount of truth in this. By the early 1980s TOPS became in effect the database for freight as a whole, embracing train monitoring, the billing of customers, and maintenance, and it was also linked to freight forecasting and off-line management information systems given the acronyms FORWARD and TARDIS. These enhancements, which took some time to show their worth,[176] were extended later on in the decade to embrace automatic vehicle identification for coal traffic, and control of the passenger business, with key information systems (POIS and PHIS) and automatic train reporting (TRUST). The developments were such that it could be argued that TOPS ultimately influenced 'almost every facet of railway life'.[177] It was thus almost impossible to assess the return on TOPS as against the original proposal. This was a general problem affecting rail investment. When in 1977 the Department put pressure on British Rail to provide them with back-checks, Fowler noted that 'we have not made much progress in resolving this problem' but defended inaction on the grounds that 'our experience . . . suggests that there is not a great deal to be gained by looking at projects several years after they have been implemented when, in many cases, circumstances have changed so much that at best it is difficult to identify causes of variation, success or failure, at worst, it is impossible to determine these causes'.[178]

'Speedlink' was another brave and innovative venture but here an ambitious first version was jettisoned in favour of a more realistic appraisal of the market opportunities in this amorphous, polyglot, and somewhat neglected area of rail working. The circumstances were as follows. In 1976 the R&D division at Derby completed work on an imaginative proposal for the wholesale improvement of the wagon-load business based on a containerised system to be operated by new trainsets (FMUs). This was quickly rejected as being too expensive: it envisaged over 200 new depots, 20 of them large, and 1,600 trainsets, at a cost of £2,074 million, a sum which was far in excess of the benefits to be gained from an estimated market of 50 million tonnes (the existing business amounted to 29 million).[179] Instead, Speedlink was relaunched in September 1977 as a more selective system based on existing high-speed freight trains using new air-braked wagons and serving major centres. By this time there were 29 services a day carrying 2.3 million tonnes, about 8 per cent of the wagon-load business, at speeds of up to 75 mph, and providing for traffic flows such as London–Glasgow, Manchester–Birmingham, and Birmingham–Newcastle. Two years later the number of services had increased to 38, and the traffic to three million tonnes. There was a fair amount of media speculation, fed by internal disquiet on the part of R&D gurus such as Ken Spring, that the 1976 cost figures had been inflated to facilitate rejection of the more ambitious proposal, but no one could deny that the modified scheme was a much better bet.[180]

3.9 Conclusion

The period 1974–9 was not short of progress in technical and operating terms. By the end of it High-Speed Trains had made a successful appearance, the prototype APTs were awaiting full trials, main-line electrification was firmly on the agenda again, and the Speedlink wagon-load service had been launched. But the belief inside British Rail, led by Parker's remarks at the top, was that so much more could be done with additional resources, and that the enterprise was running along a knife edge of potential difficulty due to postponed maintenance. The 'steady state' of British Rail investment left railway managers frustrated and with difficult choices to make over priorities, a situation which endured into the 1980s. A senior manager expressed it this way in 1982:

As each year passes, with investment pegged at its present inadequate level, the position worsens and becomes more critical. Average standards will continue to fall—at an accelerating rate as the average age of rolling stock and facilities increases—and there will be no alternative to reducing system size and the volume and quality of services. The peaking of renewals to be overcome eventually ... will increase and sharpen, and the opportunity to replace assets in a reasonably smooth, economic and orderly way will have been lost.[181]

On the other hand, from an external business perspective the problem of British Rail investment appeared more confused and unsatisfactory. In the Marsh and Parker years British Rail was seen to lurch alarmingly between ambitious optimism and stark realism, between euphoria and gloom. One moment there was excited talk of APTs and large-scale electrification; the next there were threats about 'crumbling edges' and having to close parts of the network because of maintenance arrears. To knowledgeable outsiders there was more than a hint of drift.[182] If the railways had been in the private sector the analysts would have had no hesitation in marking the shares down.

Part 2

The Thatcher Revolution?
British Rail in the 1980s

Sector Management and New Performance Targets

4.1 Margaret Thatcher's government and the railways

When the Conservatives were returned to office on 3 May 1979, there was little immediate impact on the way in which the nationalised industries in general, and railways in particular, were treated. It is easy to forget that talk of 'rolling back' the public sector and creating an 'enterprise culture' came a little later. In 1979, the Conservative party manifesto criticised Labour for enlarging the role of the State and spoke of 'restoring the balance': 'The State takes too much of the nation's income; its share must be steadily reduced'. Reference to privatisation was muted (the word itself was not used), with promised action being limited to returning aerospace and shipbuilding to the private sector and selling shares in the National Freight Corporation.[1] Exponents of 'supply-side' economics, such as Patrick Minford and Alan Walters, and right-wing critics of the public sector, such as John Redwood, tended at this stage to focus on the need for waste avoidance, value-for-money efficiency audits, and greater financial freedom rather than outright privatisation.[2] Furthermore, the dust had hardly settled on the 1978 White Paper on the relationship with the nationalised industries, which, as we have noted, had introduced a radical shake up in target setting and investment control,[3] the Transport Act of August 1978 had still to produce its desired outcomes in provincial public transport,[4] and, in any case, the government's first priority was to wrestle with what became one of the worst recessions in British economic history, 1979–81.[5] Thus, the years 1979–81 were in many ways a 'phoney war' period in the relations between right-wing conservatism and the nationalised industries; and the precise manner in which the public sector was to be 'rolled back' remained unclear for some time. In relation to transport, the policies of the Labour and Conservative parties appeared to be rather similar. A comparison of the 1977 White Paper on Transport with the riposte of the Shadow Minister of Transport, Norman Fowler, *The Right Track*, revealed consensus on the following: an emphasis on competition; fair competition between modes; no subsidies for inter-urban passenger transport; and no subsidies for freight transport. The difference between the two parties was initially 'one of degree rather than kind'.[6]

On the other hand, 1979 marked a very real turning point in the political economy of Britain, and with hindsight we may trace the origins of more radical policies. First of all, the government had a clear intention to change the direction of policy from demand management to control of the money supply, and to reduce the role of the state in economic activity.[7] In Whitehall it was appreciated that a change in attitudes was required between government officials and public sector managers, an aspiration which had found its way into the 1978 White Paper. With regard to railways, people had grown tired of the long-standing 'dialogue of the deaf' between the Board and the Department of Transport, in which 'the Department were essentially saying, "Look, we've got so much money, tell me what sort of railway I can get for it", whereas the Railway was saying, "tell me what railway you want, and I'll tell you how much it costs" '. By 1979 there was evidence, not least in the collaborative work on railway studies, the joint monthly progress meetings, exchanges of staff, and the secondment of the Department economist John Welsby to the Board's Strategy Unit, that a genuine effort was being made to transform the dialogue.[8] Indeed, those who cared to judge the balance of the debate could have perused the characteristically pithy comments of the newly-installed Chancellor of the Exchequer, Geoffrey Howe, in June 1979. Introducing his first budget Howe stated that 'we must make savings in public spending and roll back the boundaries of the public sector', and, more pointedly: 'finance must determine expenditure, not expenditure finance'. This statement surely indicated the future direction of the relationship between the Treasury and the public corporations.[9]

On top of this Britain now had a prime minister with a distinct antipathy towards the public sector in general and the railways in particular. Margaret Thatcher's first political contact with the industry had been made when she was for a very brief period (less than a year) Shadow Minister of Transport in 1968–9, just after the passage of Barbara Castle's substantial Transport Act. At the time, British Rail were introducing an innovation in their management training, a four-week course for senior managers. And when Frank Cook, the Principal of

the Woking Staff College, had the idea of inviting the two Conservative politicians thought likely to be responsible for transport in the future, Michael
Heseltine and Margaret Thatcher, to speak to the managers in the summer of
1969 he could have had no idea of the repercussions.[10] Mrs Thatcher's visit to
Woking on 9 May 1969 has been recalled by two of the members of the course,
James Urquhart and Leslie Lloyd. Urquhart, then Assistant General Manager of
the Eastern Region, had thoughtfully prepared a set of possible agenda questions
and put them on the blackboard in anticipation of the visit. However, when she
saw this she was plainly not impressed. 'Oh', she said, 'You people can't think on
your feet. You can't work out what you want, can you?' She went on to berate the
Board, including the Chairman, Henry Johnson: 'Anyway, there's only one
worthwhile member of your Board—Mr [Sydney] Jones.'[11] Lloyd's recollection
was that 'within three minutes she had lost the potential votes of every single
member . . . by her stridency and unreasonableness'. Urquhart said that when he
complained to the Chairman about Mrs Thatcher's treatment of the managers an
apology was extracted from her.[12] Her prejudices clearly persisted. A decade later,
when Opposition Leader, she had lunch with the Board, accompanied by Norman
Fowler. The date was 21 October 1977,[13] and the tone was censorious. Parker's
recollection is that 'she had talked to us about nationalisation with a hearty,
dismaying adamancy: to be nationalised, she explained, was an industry's admission of failure'. Fowler remembers a sharp response to being patronised: 'I
remember seeing a member of the British Rail board lectured for over an hour
after an approach of this kind in the course of which Margaret demonstrated that
she knew that particular industry only too well'.[14] Some of Parker's colleagues
recall their conversation with her, remarking that she was perfectly happy to
listen to one member and talk to another at the same time.[15] Then, when Bobbie
Lawrence was endeavouring to explain the complexities of the Property Board,
pointing out, 'why we even have a place with our own chip shop', she responded
acidly: 'Chip shop? That seems to be about the measure of some of you people in
Property Board'.[16] We must not make too much of all this, resting, as it does, on
internally generated mythology. In May 1983 Thatcher's humour was apparently quite different, when she paid an impromptu visit to Rail House after
naming a locomotive *Airey Neave*.[17] She got on better with Parker's successor,
Bob Reid, who was friendly with both Denis Thatcher and Nicholas Ridley, and
made a rare trip by train in 1987.[18] However, she continued to indicate her low
opinion of the quality of nationalised industry managers, and had no interest at
all in the railways. While it is not clear whether this had any influence on
the Ministers and civil servants concerned, it certainly cannot have helped the
Board.

From the perspective of senior railway management the change of government
offered opportunities as much as anxieties. British Rail managers concerned with
planning and strategy approached the change in a positive vein, seeing it as a
chance to recapture the broader vision for the industry lost in the 1970s with the

rejection of the Railway Policy Review of 1972. Behind the scenes documents were drawn up entitled 'Towards the next White Paper', which attempted to second-guess the future direction of transport policy and, having evaluated Norman Fowler's *The Right Track*, suggested that a basic continuity was the most likely outcome. When Fowler became the new Minister of Transport (Secretary of State from January 1981) he was quickly briefed by Parker on the 'major issues' affecting 'B. R. and Government'.[19] More visibly there were the key policy document *Challenge of the 80's*, which was offered to the trade unions in November 1979, the joint BRB/Department of Transport review of electrification in February 1981, and the statement on *Rail Policy*, published in March 1981. The first sought a positive response from the unions on productivity improvement. It set out British Rail's basic aims as follows: to develop the railways' market strengths with a distinct emphasis on business sectors; to restructure traditional business activities; to apply technological improvement in order to improve competitive position; to provide worthwhile jobs with improving conditions; and to meet the financial objectives set by government. The document argued for investment in 'equipment and technology and people', but laid particular stress on the need for reform of the operation and manning of trains, terminals, engineering, and so on, which 'will require some adjustment, redeployment and training of the workforce and will in some cases also impinge on the way jobs have traditionally been carried out'. Here British Rail expressed a determination to address the key issues in productivity improvement of flexible train rostering and Driver-Only Operation (DOO).[20] The early 1980s was to be preoccupied by the frustration with the unions' immediate reactions to such changes, and with ASLEF's resistance to DOO and flexible rostering in particular, which dominated Board agendas.

At the same time the continuing dearth of investment encouraged Parker and Bosworth to welcome the change of government as an opportunity to promote partnership with the private sector in order to inject capital into the various businesses, an idea advanced by Parker as early as 1977.[21] They took the initiative in offering to provide a paper for Norman Fowler on the scope for private-sector involvement in British Rail. Morgan Grenfell were engaged as consultants in July 1979 to advise on opportunities for the non-rail activities, and their advice was fed into a report sent to the Minister in October.[22] The joint review of the prospects for electrification, published in February 1981, also revealed the Board in a positive, policy-making mood. Here it was asserted that a substantial programme of electrification would return about 11 per cent in real terms.[23] In the following month, Parker led a further initiative with the publication of the Board's *Rail Policy* statement. This highlighted the need for additional railway investment, particularly in electrification, promised considerable improvements to 'customer service' in the 1980s, and advocated the adoption of an innovative approach to government funding of the 'social railway' based on the maximisation of passenger-miles (see below).[24]

Screening the Queen's Speech in May 1979 the Chief Secretary, Burt, observed that there was nothing of direct relevance, and no indication at this stage that privatising the Board's subsidiary businesses was in any way a priority.[25] There was reference to 'restricting the claims of the public sector on the nation's resources', but initial policy was all about ends rather than means. Thatcher, commenting on the Speech, promised to reduce the size of the public sector, but how this was to be done, and in which industries, was not spelt out.[26] The new Minister, Norman Fowler, was a relatively young man of 41 and very much a political rookie; this was his first ministerial post, and his previous experience was limited.[27] However, he had had three years in which to understudy the role, and was also a perceptive and likeable politician who responded to Parker's overtures by attending two of British Rail's pre-Board dinners.[28] The early references to railways in the new parliament were rather anodyne. In July 1979 backbencher Alan Clark asked Fowler whether he agreed 'that the chairman of British Rail's vanity is not matched by his competence', while Anthony Grant stated that British Rail had no business in running hotels.[29] The only substantive element was the announcement in October that as part of its competition initiative the government intended to refer the efficiency of London and South East commuter services to the Monopolies and Mergers Commission, which was to consider questions relating to the costs and efficiency of nationalised industries (see below).[30] Of course, there was a fair legacy to present to the incoming administration from the previous government—British Rail anxieties about its ability to live within cash limits as industrial activity slackened, its concerns about interference with its freedom to manage the passenger business (specifically the directive to maintain the passenger base of 1974 and a reluctance to agree to real pricing increases for London commuters), and the perennial issues of productivity and investment, including electrification, where a joint Department/BRB review of future prospects was in progress.[31] On the other hand, the government's planned reductions in the External Financing Limits for 1980/1, announced in November 1979, did not fall unduly heavily on the railways, a contrast with the treatment of the railways in 1975 (see Chapter 1) and in the circumstances a tribute to the persuasive powers of the new Minister and his Permanent Secretary, Peter Baldwin.[32]

4.2 The establishment of sector management, 1979–82

In organisational and business terms the major change in the 1980s was undoubtedly the move to establish business sectors and the associated changes which stemmed from this, including the setting of more specific financial targets for the rail and non-rail activities, and the first steps to privatise the Board's subsidiaries. In January 1982 the five business sectors, Freight, Parcels, and the three passenger service groups—Inter-City, Provincial, and London and South East—were given organisational emphasis in order to clarify bottom-line responsibility and accountability within the core business. The justification for the move was announced as early as the Board's annual report for 1979, published in April 1980:

British Rail is a mixed enterprise operating commercial and non-commercial services; the move towards setting financial targets for each sector underlines the distinctions between the sectors and presents a compelling case for an improved and refined approach towards financing their operations…by decentralising BR into clear accountable groups…[we] can create confidence in our stewardship of these national businesses and justify the case for investment.[33]

To that end five Sector Directors were appointed (see Table 4.1). Each Director, accountable to the Chief Executive (Railways), was given net revenue responsibility for the set of services in his sector and was charged with specifying to the regional general managers the standard of service required. He was also required to establish levels of affordable expenditure and investment and to conduct strategic planning exercises.[34]

Prior to 1982, as we have seen, the organisation was a four-tiered pyramidal structure of Board headquarters, region, functionally structured division (except in Scottish Region), and locally based area. The linchpin of the basic railway operation was the multi-functional region, led by a regional general manager. Since the merger of the Eastern and North Eastern regions in 1967, there had been five of these: the London Midland, Eastern, Western, Southern, and Scottish, though we should note that three had their headquarters within a two-mile radius of the Board in London, at Euston, Paddington, and Waterloo.[35] The regions consisted of functional departments concerned with marketing (passenger, freight, parcels), operations, engineering (civil, signal & telecoms, mechanical & electrical), finance, investment, and personnel, all of which were replicated at headquarters. The General Managers (see Appendix I, Table I.1) had complete control of nearly all the functions and activities within their geographical area, but because these boundaries did not coincide with the markets served, financial responsibility was very limited below Board level, engineering and 'traffic' managers were dominant, and the only person whose responsibilities embraced both costs and revenues was the Chief Executive (Railways). The situation followed on from the method of management accounting used. Although revenue and cost elements frequently crossed regional boundaries, an 'originating' basis was used whereby revenue was recorded and credited at the point of collection (irrespective of the final destination), and costs (e.g. train crew) were charged to the originating region.[36]

Table 4.1 British Rail's top-level organisation, 1 January 1982

Board		Age, salary, date appointed	Sector directors		Age, salary, date appointed
Chairman	Sir Peter Parker	(57, £60,000, Sep. 1976)	Inter-City	Cyril Bleasdale	(47, £27,350, Jan. 1982)
Deputy Chairman	Michael Bosworth	(60, £44,600, June 1968)	London & South East	David Kirby	(48, £34,800, Jan. 1982)
Vice-Chairman	Ian Campbell	(59, £35,045, Jan. 1977)	Provincial	John Welsby	(43, £27,000, Jan. 1982)
Vice-Chairman	Derek Fowler	(52, £35,045, Apr. 1975)	Freight	Henry Sanderson	(54, £31,400, Jan. 1982)
Chief Executive	Robert Reid	(60, £35,045, Jan. 1977)	Parcels	Michael Connolly	(55, £26,450, Jan. 1982)
Full-time:	Geoffrey Myers	(51, £32,000, Mar. 1980)	General managers		
	Clifford Rose	(52, £33,250, Jan. 1977)	Eastern	Frank Paterson	(51, £30,600, July 1978)
	James Urquhart	(56, £33,250, Jan. 1977)	London Midland	John O'Brien	(47, £27,900, Jan. 1981)
Part-time:	Viscount Caldecote	(64, £3,925, Mar. 1979)	Scottish	Leslie Soane	(55, £30,000, Jan. 1977)
	Simon Jenkins	(38, £3,925, Dec. 1979)	Southern	David Kirby	(48, £34,800, Jan. 1982)
	Sir Robert Lawrence	(66, £10,514, Feb. 1971)	Western	Leslie Lloyd	(57, £31,300, May 1976)
	Prudence Leith	(41, £6,287, Oct. 1980)			
	Roderick Macleod	(52, £6,287, June 1980)			
	Michael Posner	(50, £9,431, Jan. 1977)			
	Sir David Serpell	(70, £6,287, Sep. 1974)			

Source: BRB, *R&A 1982*; Misc. personnel information; Board members and managers' salaries as at 30.6.1982: BRB IR 82-11-21 Pt. 3.

Note: The following members in office in January 1977 (listed in Table 2.2) resigned prior to January 1982: Sir Alan Walker (died Jan. 1978), David McKenna (Aug. 1978), David Bowick (Jan. 1980), Lord Taylor of Gryfe (June 1980). In addition T. R. Barron served as a part-timer from Apr. 1978 to Apr. 1981.

The Thatcher Revolution

Dissatisfaction with the complex and lengthy hierarchical span of railway management had surfaced during the McKinsey exercise in the early 1970s but, as we have seen, the attempt to replace the regions with a 'Field Organisation' of eight territories had proved an embarrassing failure and was abandoned in 1975. The move to a more functional Board in 1977 did not ease pressures on the chief executive. These were evident in the debate about the virtues of combining the job with the position of Vice-Chairman,[37] in the duplication of functions provided by the twin pillars of the 'railway command structure', the Railway Executive and the RMG, and in the resignation of Bowick following his illness in June 1978 and his replacement by Ian Campbell. When Campbell was in turn replaced by Bob Reid in March 1980, the command structure was modified in order to sharpen up its effectiveness. The Railway Executive and the RMG were replaced by a Railway Directing Group (RDG) and a Railway Executive Group (REG). The regional general managers joined the chief executive and the functional Board members on the principal body, the RDG, and the nine major functional managers at Headquarters joined the regional general managers on the more executive REG. The move certainly indicated that the existing structure had been far from adequate.[38] We should not ignore the very real pressures on the chief executive and the difficulty he faced in pursuing the 'bottom line' for the several rail businesses with his managerial team. In a letter prepared as a response to a general manager sceptical of sector management in 1981, it was pointed out: 'You should not underestimate the penalties that any organisation suffers if the Chief Executive is so involved in co-ordinating the activities of his functional officers that he is denied time for reflection and forward thought. The only point at which the costs and revenues of the railway some [sic] together is on my desk and even then it is not in a form where I can readily assess the performance of major activities.'[39]

By 1982 the move to 'sector management' was heralded as placing managerial accountability for each sector clearly on one director without making significant changes to the organisation or increasing administrative costs. British Rail promised its managers that sector management would

introduce a sharper cutting edge in the battle to control costs [and] inject business criteria into a much wider range of decisions affecting rolling stock, infrastructure and administration. Business plans will line up with business responsibilities and there will be a much better understanding of where the railway business as a whole is making and where it is losing money. Specifying clear objectives...and appointing individuals responsible for making plans to reach these objectives and then to achieve them will mean, overall, better performance by the railway.[40]

At the same time a press release noted that the sector directors would carry 'a high measure of delegated net revenue responsibility' and would have a key role in planning targets and budgets and in monitoring performance. The point was made that the responsibilities of the regional general managers 'for day-to-day management' would remain unchanged, but this view was contradicted in part by the appointment of David Kirby to the combined post of Director, London and South East and General Manager, Southern Region, a response to the recommendations of the MMC (see below).[41]

4.3 'Business led' or 'government led'?

How had this change come about? How important was it? There is a temptation to see sector management as a government-led innovation, arising from a number of elements: the continuing financial problems experienced by the rail businesses after the 1974 Act; the growing irritation in Whitehall with the quality of railway planning, investment, and cost control mechanisms;[42] and the Treasury's insistence on imposing more sophisticated financial targets on the nationalised industries, which was enshrined in the White Paper of 1978. Certainly, the Department of Transport continued to press the Board to agree more specific objectives for their rail businesses, and as we have seen, the requirement that the freight business be 'commercial' was a constant concern in the late 1970s. Indeed, the earliest reference to six business sectors and three possible models for target setting—separate businesses, separate accounts, or separate revenue/cost accounts—appeared in a review of working relations between the Department and British Rail prepared by a study team led by Alan Simcock in December 1977. The review, which had been set up to help remedy existing tensions between the two bodies, concluded that improved planning and control procedures were needed to provide an agreed strategy for each of the sectors.[43] The strategy for the PSO grant, a reduction of £20 million by the end of the decade, which had been published in the White Paper on *Transport Policy* of June 1977, was modified after the change of government. Additional cuts of £9 million by 1980/1 and £15 million by 1982/3 were announced in November 1979 and March 1980 respectively.[44] More detailed targets for the 'sectors' expected to be 'self-supporting', i.e. Freight, Parcels, and Inter-City, to be achieved by 1982 (Table 4.2), were agreed in the autumn of 1979. The Board was not keen to see these published,[45] but departmental pressure led to the publication, in March 1980, of the targets for Freight and Inter-City, which were described as 'interim' since they fell short of a full commercial requirement. Freight was expected to cover two-thirds of its current cost depreciation, while Inter-City was to make an increased contribution to indirect costs of £28 million in 1979 prices, in line with intentions expressed in a strategy study of the passenger business that the sector's contribution to indirect passenger costs would be raised from about 17 per cent of the total to 25 per cent by 1991. The third target agreed with government, a commercial remit for Parcels, remained confidential.[46] In addition

Table 4.2 Government financial targets for the PSO and three 'sectors', 1979–88

PSO	Freight	Parcels	Inter-City
To reduce the PSO by an additional £9m. by 1980/1 (Nov. 1979)	*Interim target* To cover direct costs, an agreed contribution to indirect costs, and two-thirds of its depreciation, before interest, by 1982 (Mar. 1980)	To break even by 1982 before interest, but after current cost depreciation and agreed contribution to indirect costs (Mar. 1980)	*Interim target* To cover direct costs, current cost depreciation, interest, and train catering costs and make a contribution to joint indirect costs of £133 m. by 1982 (in 1979 prices, cf. £105 m. in 1978) (Mar. 1980)
To reduce the PSO by an additional £15 m. by 1982/3 (Mar. 1980)			
To accelerate reduction to £635 m. in 1983 prices by 1986 (Oct. 1983)	To achieve a current cost operating profit of 5% by 1988 (Oct. 1983)	To continue to earn a 'proper commercial return'* (Oct. 1983)	To achieve a 'full commercial objective' by 1985 (June 1981)
			To cease PSO support and achieve a current cost operating profit of 5% by 1988/9 (Aug. 1984)
To reduce the PSO to £555 m. in 1986/7 prices by 1989/90 (Oct. 1986)	Freight, Parcels, InterCity, Freightliner, and Travellers Fare to achieve an average 2.7% current cost operating profit on net assets before interest by 1989/90 (Oct. 1986)		
Modification to allow Inter-City and PTEs exemption from passenger directive in Transport Act 1974 (Mar. 1988)			

Source: BRB, *R&A 1979–88/9*; BRB Minutes, 1 November 1979.

* Internally agreed target in BRB Corporate Plan: profit before interest of £16 m. by 1986/7 (1984), £12 m. (1985).

to the stated targets, there was an expectation in government circles that the London commuter services (London and South East) would benefit if the Board were given a more specific target. This debate had begun with Crosland's Consultation Document of April 1976, which had suggested financial targets for the inner and outer suburban services. It was followed in 1977 by the recommendation of the Select Committee on Nationalised Industries that the PSO data be broken down on a regional basis (see Chapter 2, p. 49). The MMC inquiry instituted by the Conservatives, which reported in October 1980, took the issue a stage further. It made a number of swingeing criticisms of British Rail's management practices and performance, and although it opposed the idea of a separate region for L&SE, recommended that a senior manager be put in charge of the services. The Commission also indicated that the directive contained in the 1974 Act was inadequate and suggested that the financial objective for the services should be made clearer.[47] The Department was also involved in a review of the future of the provincial services in 1980–1, when financial difficulties were once again threatening to provoke a raft of closures.[48] At this time, the Minister, Fowler, declared that he was 'attracted by the notion of sectorization' for target-setting purposes.[49]

Broader issues also attracted the participation of civil servants and moved the debate towards sector management. First, the Department of Transport was fully involved with the Board in reassessing the PSO funding system in 1980, and in particular the extent to which it helped to set clear objectives for the 'non-commercial railway'. An alternative based on weighted passenger-miles maximisation was advanced but was not taken up (see Appendix K).[50] Second, there was the joint Department/British Rail review of the prospects for main-line electrification. In February 1981 this reported in favour of a large-scale programme, but produced the government response that it would consider schemes on a line by line basis against a 10-year plan, and then only if the Board demonstrated that it would achieve 'full commercial viability' for Inter-City by 1985. This was subsequently defined as a return of 5 per cent on assets employed, in line with the 1978 White Paper on *Nationalised Industries*.[51] Finally, in 1981 Thatcher had commissioned a report from the Central Policy Review Staff on ways to improve the relationship between government and the nationalised industries, a summary of which was made available to the Nationalised Industries Chairmen's Group in the late autumn.[52] The report encouraged the public sector to respond more to market disciplines, a view shared by the CBI, which felt that nationalised industries should 'follow commercial principles' and expressed disappointment at the failure of public policy to 'develop and maintain a control framework which acts as a reasonable but effective surrogate for the disciplines of the market'.[53]

There is, then, something in the argument that sector management was 'government led'. The term 'sector target management' was sometimes used by managers while working up the concept, and government requirements were often cited in memoranda supporting the change.[54] Particularly prominent was the assertion that the justification for further investment in the rail network depended to no small extent on demonstrating the delivery of performance based on sectorised accounts.[55] It might thus be argued that these 'directives' drove the planning and strategic mechanisms inside British Rail which led to sector management.[56] Furthermore, the deterioration in the Board's profit and loss account during the recession of 1979–82 made a nonsense of the interim targets and gave further ammunition to government critics of existing planning and budgeting systems, which found further expression in the report in early 1983 of the Serpell Committee, a body established by the Minister at Parker's invitation to examine the whole question of railway finances (see Chapter 5). The desire to get to grips with costs and revenues at a sectoral level must have been influenced by the Board's failure to contain the PSO. The central government portion of the total PSO grant (i.e. excluding PTE/local authority payments) rose by 20 per cent in real terms in 1979–82, while the PSO's share of total passenger income (fares plus central/local government payments) rose from 40 per cent in 1979 to 49 per cent in 1982 (see Table 4.9). At the same time the Board's group profit and loss position deteriorated sharply. In current prices a modest profit (after interest, but before extraordinary items) of £6.5 million in 1978 and £1.4 million in 1979 became a substantial deficit of £76.9 million in 1980, and although the 1981 results were better (a loss of £39.7 million), the 1982 results were poor, the rail strikes provoked by manning and rostering changes contributing to a loss of £175.0 million (Appendix A, Table A.2). The consequences of all this were the rejection of Parker's *Rail Policy* of 1981, with its high investment strategy and plans for substantial electrification, the unexpectedly hostile criticisms of the Serpell Committee, which roundly condemned the idea that there were no opportunities for substantial economies in railway operating, and the association of sector management with the tougher financial targets of October 1983, which specified an accelerated reduction in the PSO equivalent to a 25 per cent cut in real terms for the period 1983–6, a current cost operating profit for Freight of 5 per cent by 1988, and a 'commercial return' from Parcels (Table 4.2).

On the other hand, there is no evidence of direct pressure for organisational change by government. Indeed, all the documentation points in fact in the direction of a railway-led initiative. The Board and senior railway managers were well aware of the financial problems confronting their businesses, and determined to devise an improved organisation to help them tackle these problems. Drawing on the lessons derived from the 'Field Organisation' fiasco a small group centred on the Strategy Steering Group and Unit worked up the sector concept inside Headquarters without attracting unnecessary opposition and sold it to both government and potential opponents in the regions as a critical but limited restructuring of the chief executive's organisation at the top.[57] It bore all the marks of what the American social scientist Charles Lindblom has called the 'strategy of disjointed incrementalism', where a series of policy steps is taken to reach a radical position which would have been difficult if not impossible to attain in one move.[58]

The details are as follows. Studies of the business sectors had been started before the Strategy Unit was set up in the summer of 1978. A freight study had been completed, for example, and work on the passenger, parcels, and shipping businesses was 'in hand'.[59] However, the importance of this work was given greater emphasis with the establishment of the Unit, and the Strategy Steering Group. Over the next year two critical studies were undertaken, that of the London and South East commuter services, and of the passenger business as a whole—the Passenger Business Strategy Study (PBSS), both completed in October 1979. The aim of the latter was 'to throw light on the "value for money" relationships for the different sectors of the passenger business, and to provide a reasonable basis for Government decisions on future financial support'.[60] Section C of the study conducted a business sector appraisal using high and low fare options, and discussed *inter alia* the problem of sector boundaries in circumstances in which objectives were set for different sectors and when using an avoidable costs approach (see pp. 114–15).[61] At the top level, informal discussion of the idea of creating sectors took place at 'Springs' conferences of Executive Board members[62] in November 1978 and November 1979 which considered 'Managing Change', then more explicitly with pre-circulated papers at the next meeting in October 1980. In 1978 Bowick's characteristically florid paper on 'Change' had suggested that there was a need to produce defined strategies for each business sector.[63] More importantly, at the next conference in 1979 the idea of establishing accountable business managers for the sectors was raised, and the Strategy Unit was asked to work on it.[64] The main protagonists were: Reid, who succeeded Campbell as Chief Executive between the two Springs conferences; Derek Fowler, the Board member responsible for planning and finance, together with his Director of Finance, Philip Sellers; and Michael Posner, the part-timer responsible for the Strategy Unit. Inside the Strategy Unit the activists were Geoffrey Myers, the Director of Strategic Development, Bill Bradshaw, who succeeded Myers in March 1980,[65] John Prideaux, John Welsby, and Arnold Kentridge.[66] Last, and certainly not least, there was John Heath, Professor of Economics at the London Business School, whose lectures and Labour sympathies had attracted the attention of Peter Parker, leading to his appointment as a part-time consultant to advise the Strategy Steering Group on the development of business strategy.[67] At the 1980 Conference, the concept had been developed to the point where Heath was able to produce a paper on 'The Developing Rail Business—Towards Accountable Management', which stimulated an 'alternative view' from Fowler and Reid.[68] After the conference, which endorsed the idea of sector management, a working party was established to work up the proposal. This consisted of Reid and Sellers, who were assisted by a wider group which included Heath, Bradshaw, and Welsby. The RDG discussed the concept at its conference in Stratford-upon-Avon in November 1980, but it was not until August 1981 that the full Board formally approved the change. In the meantime, there had been much preparatory work, including a number of briefing sessions, notably a seminar for REG and part-time board members at the Great Eastern Hotel in July.[69]

Given the experience of the aborted Field Organisation, supporters of sector management were well aware that they should proceed quietly. While the need for change was emphasised to the general managers the favoured prescription in some circles at least was not revealed until later. Thus, as early as November 1979 a special meeting of the RMG, held at the Welcombe Hotel in Stratford-upon-Avon, chaired by Ian Campbell, had discussed the 'organisation and administration of the railway' and fully recognised that change was desirable. A *post-hoc* recollection of events, drawn up by David Pattisson in 1983, recalled that the managers had agreed that it was important to place responsibility for the 'bottom line' in the various rail businesses, and that 'there should be greater emphasis on sector (and even sub-sector) information'.[70] However, it was the Headquarters members of the RMG who had referred to the 'bottom line'. The paper prepared by Campbell for the meeting spoke only in terms of tinkering with the existing regional organisation, which he felt should remain firmly in place.[71] Indeed, Campbell was rather lukewarm about sectorisation. Shortly after he gave up the Chief Executive post to become Vice-Chairman, he expressed fears about the cost implications: 'I wonder whether we really have got the infinity of resources at a time of financial crisis to continue to seek perfection of inter-relationship between one section of our business and another'.[72] Later on, he thought that the sector management would 'confuse authorities and compound the difficulties', a view shared by Urquhart.[73] Scepticism like this ensured that supporters of change were careful not to arouse opposition by revealing their hand too early. In July 1980, for example, Rose and Posner reported to members of the Board Executive on the progress made with the initiatives begun at 'Springs 1979'. They noted that Reid and his colleagues had made considerable progress in identifying the changes needed to establish sector managers, which would mean that RGMs would be concerned only with production—'that is cost and quality'. However, this kind of thinking was not reported directly to forums including the RGMs. Furthermore, in the paper presented by Reid to the Board in August 1981 it was explicitly stated that the role of the general managers would be 'unchanged in concept'.[74] The Department was treated in the same way. Thus, when Myers prepared a somewhat explicit paper on 'Passenger Business Sectorisation' for a meeting with the Minister in October 1980 Posner quickly intervened to prevent its presentation.[75]

The Springs Conference in October 1980 revealed all the tensions evident in the process of innovation. First of all, the RGMs, having met informally in August, demanded an input into the meeting. Leslie Soane, General Manager of the Scottish Region, asked Reid if Executive Board members would consider a paper representing their views. Their memorandum, entitled 'Organising for

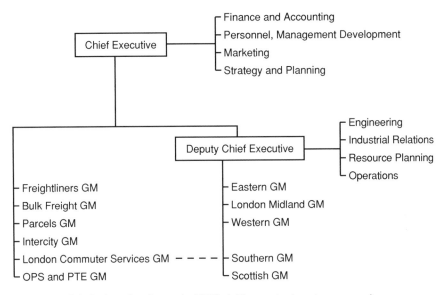

Figure 4.1 Options for change in 1980: 1. The product centre approach

Business Sector Targets', saw sectorisation as essentially a matter of responding to the government's financial targets, which, it was felt, could be achieved by 'an extension of existing procedures' involving Headquarters and the regions. The general managers also expressed fears about a new organisation, 'with its overtones of Field re-organisation, Trade Union and political re-action'.[76] Although there was some disquiet about allowing the general managers special access to Springs, this was conceded de facto by allowing the paper to be discussed at the RDG and by sending it to the Strategy Unit.[77] The key paper from Heath and others, a long and sometimes arcane document which bore all the marks of having been drafted by a committee,[78] also responded to the concerns of the RGMs. It offered the Springs delegates two options for change: Option 1—The Product Centre Approach, which involved the creation and development of 'profit-centred business units', turning the RGMs into production managers; and Option 2— The Regional Approach, which was to convert the regions into 'fully accountable profit centres' (see Figures 4.1. and 4.2). The latter was explicitly stated to be consistent with the ideas expressed in the Soane paper. Furthermore, there were soothing words for those worried about the prospect of radical change: 'the style of this Memorandum is that organisational development preferably should be incremental...What is being proposed...is not a major reorganisation of thousands of people in BR (as the Field study would have involved) but rather a re-definition of role among a relatively few people at the top'. On the other hand, the Heath paper caused offence elsewhere. The shift to accountable management was justified by reference not only to the separation of responsibility for

The Thatcher Revolution

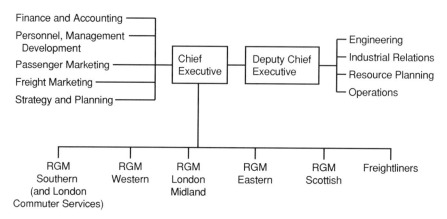

Figure 4.2 Options for change in 1980: 2. The regional approach

costs and revenue but also to BR's poor financial and operational performance, inadequate service delivery, faulty decision making, and notably 'the saga of miscalculations and misfortunes of the GN electrification and re-equipment scheme'.[79] This provoked Reid and Fowler, in their response to the paper, to refute most of these criticisms. Their memorandum clearly favoured a version of Option 1, noting that 'we do not need convincing it is the correct way to move'.[80]

The period from November 1980 to the end of 1981 was essentially one of working up the concept in detail. Much of the work was progressed by a Sector Management Steering Group established in April 1981.[81] There were many loose ends to tie: How many sectors were there to be? How were the boundaries between the passenger sectors to be drawn? Should there be sub-sectors and, if so, which ones? During 1981 it was decided to develop five sectors instead of six. Two proposals were abandoned. The first envisaged a separate sector for the services supported by the PTEs.[82] The second involved dividing the London commuting services, London and South East, into two, namely North of the Thames (essentially the Liverpool Street Division of Eastern Region) and South of the Thames (Southern Region). The idea of a separate Board for L&SE (cf. BREL and Sealink), was also rejected. It had been promoted by Norman Fowler, and was therefore given careful consideration by Reid and his colleagues.[83] But it provoked adverse reactions, notably from two of the new part-timers on the Board, the youthful journalist Simon Jenkins and Roderick MacLeod from Scotland, and was ultimately rejected.[84] The precise boundary between Inter-City and the two loss-making passenger sectors was a particular concern, given their very different remits. Early discussions pointed in the direction of confining Inter-City to the more profitable services, those 'carrying a high proportion of long distance traffic over medium/high density routes'. Thus, it was decided that the London–Bournemouth and London–Norwich services should be moved from Inter-City to

114

L&SE, while services in Scotland and the Trans-Pennine and Cardiff–Portsmouth trains were transferred from Inter-City to Provincial.[85]

A critical element in the process was the development of suitable management information systems to support the change, since sector directors were required to take responsibility not only for revenue streams but also for the cost of employing specific or 'dedicated' assets. The avoidable costs study, approved by the Railway Executive and Board Executive in April and May 1978 and completed in August 1980, was a first attempt to refine costing in order to produce meaningful management accounts for the change. Hitherto, the effort to allocate costs to sectors, derived from an accounting initiative called PP&CCA in the early 1970s,[86] had succeeded in attributing only 54 per cent of total costs; the new study produced an attribution level of 78 per cent, leaving only 22 per cent as 'residual costs'.[87] Further developments were required, of course; and these were addressed in 1981. First, 'pilot' financial statements were prepared for the Freight and Parcels sectors, involving 12- and 32-week out-turn estimates against budget. This was a relatively straightforward exercise, since for these sectors it was easier to determine total costs (including infrastructure costs).[88] Elsewhere, the treatment of joint indirect costs was more problematic. Cost analysis alone could not solve the problem of the rump of residual costs which remained unallocated. Under the arrangements for paying the PSO grant, such costs were charged to the passenger business, but this was clearly unsatisfactory given the existence of the government's interim financial targets. The search for a pragmatic solution was assisted by the debate about the shape and operation of the L&SE sector. Here it was argued that the infrastructure costs of the Southern Region and the Liverpool Street Division (representing 80 per cent of the commuter movements in the London area) should be deemed to exist primarily for L&SE as the 'prime user' and charged to that sector. Other users such as Freight would then have their avoidable costs 'charged out'. After this it was agreed that the 'prime user' approach should be applied to residual joint costs in all the passenger sectors on a hierarchical basis.[89]

At the same time there was a need to keep the lid on potential opposition, particularly from the RGMs. Frank Paterson of the Eastern Region was clearly a sceptic. In April 1981 he wrote to Reid, with 'blind' copies to the other RGMs, posing four questions about sector management: (1) How would the burden on the chief executive be lessened, given the fact that sector directors could not have complete responsibility for net revenue? (2) What was novel about the management tools to be applied? (3) How would sector management contribute to the 'massive changes needed over the next five years'? (4) Was British Rail encouraging the government to 'more complex and detailed interference with management?' These were 'Four obviously negative questions but unless you can answer them honestly in a way which will make sense to our managers and Trade Unions, then the Board will be seen to have the wrong priorities'. Paterson was 'fully committed to the need for improved management of sectors.

I question the theory that it is in the best interests of the Board to manage the railways by sectors'.[90] This kind of thinking was not confined to a few. As late as July 1981 there were seen to be doubters at both Board and senior management level.[91] Leslie Lloyd, General Manager of the Western Region, was a vocal critic at the seminar, articulating the view that to be accountable sector directors had to exercise authority, and the only way for them to do this would be to take it from the RGMs. This produced a soothing response from Heath, but he could not deny that the general managers would lose some functional authority.[92]

However, by mid-1981 Reid was clearly leading the charge and in no mood to compromise. This was demonstrated by his determination to drive the project home, by his choice of sector directors and by the manner in which the appointments were effected.[93] While it made little sense to disturb managerial continuity in Freight and Parcels, where Henry Sanderson and Michael Connolly, the chief managers, merely changed their titles, the appointees to the three 'new' sectors were bright young managers who had caught the eye in their existing posts, though they had limited experience of railways at the highest level. Significantly, two of them were managing subsidiaries which had corporate status and where as MDs they were responsible for both costs and revenues. Cyril Bleasdale, the Inter-City Director, had shown entrepreneurial drive and energy as managing director of Freightliners Ltd but his most senior railway post was at divisional manager level. David Kirby, the managing director of Sealink UK Ltd, was regarded highly enough to be given the difficult L&SE remit, but he had spent all of his career as a shipping manager.[94] For the problematic Provincial post, where the interface with government was critical, Reid turned to John Welsby, an economist who only three years before had arrived at British Rail on secondment from the Department of Transport. He had created a favourable impression in the Strategy Unit and had become Development Officer (Special Projects) in 1981.[95] Inevitably, these bold promotions meant disappointment, disruption, or early retirement for others. At Headquarters Peter Keen, the Chief Passenger Manager, was one of the casualties, Peter Corbishley another. Keen was concerned that the sector directors would usurp the role of Headquarters marketing; he became Director of International Marketing, while his former department was downgraded.[96] Corbishley, the Chief Planning Officer, also went as the sector initiative challenged the rationale for a separate central planning function.[97] General managers who were surplus to requirements or critical of the new direction were moved on or encouraged to retire. John Palette, having received somewhat peremptory treatment at the hands of Reid in Waterloo, was appointed General Manager (Administration) at Headquarters and asked to review the railways' administrative structure. However, soon afterwards he was given the more challenging job of deputising for Cliff Rose, the Board Member for Personnel, when the latter became seriously ill in August 1982 (he died in July 1983). He was subsequently appointed Managing Director (Personnel) in March 1983, reporting directly to Parker and with the status and authority of a Board member.[98] Leslie Soane was seconded to Headquarters for a brief period in 1981/2 to begin the work on administrative costs (Discretionary Cost Analysis).[99] In March 1983 he returned to Headquarters as Assistant Chief Executive (Reorganisation) to take rationalisation further under the banner of the Administration & Organisation initiative. Lloyd, General Manager of the Western Region, retired at the end of 1982.[100]

Thus, sector management was an organisational development which was essentially 'business led', that is, pursued by the Board itself in order to transform the way in which the business functioned and to improve the working relationship with government as paymaster. The new arrangements were consonant with government intentions in relation to monitoring of performance, and in fact the Board sold the idea to the Department of Transport as a minor modification of top management which did not require Ministerial consent under section 45 of the 1968 Transport Act.[101] The 'genealogy' of the change had been complex, involving many actors and different motives, and providing opportunities for the ambitious. On the other hand, the initial impact was limited. Five senior appointments were made, some reshuffling at Headquarters was evident, and some 'refocusing' was promised. The real significance of 'sector management' lay in the future.

4.4 The development of sector management, 1982–5

For sector management 1982 was only the beginning. That there was much to be done was quickly evident when delays occurred in bringing forth the management information necessary to establish the 'bottom line', especially for Provincial, the problematic sector of services spread throughout the network and subject to a contemporaneous joint Department of Transport/British Rail review.[102] The sector directors, based at 222 Marylebone Road (Kirby stayed at Waterloo), resembled Headquarters officers concerned with traffic functions, but their brief was much wider. Reid set them three tasks in April 1982: to develop business plans and gain the RGMs' full commitment to them; to review and challenge investment; and to focus on service cost reductions.[103] However, at the outset they lacked the dedicated staff to do much more than offer the Chief Executive support (see Table 4.3). They were expected to work through the RGMs, who in turn would instruct managers of sub-sectors falling within their geographical boundaries. The new appointees found their position uncomfortable at first. As one of them recalled, 'I remember going into an office which was completely

Table 4.3 Managers responsible to sector directors, 1982–9 (number)

Date	Freight	Parcels	L&SE	Provincial	InterCity
Jan. 1982	1	1	1	1	1
June 1983	31	9	3	3	8
Jan. 1985	49	13	3	4	8
June 1986	48	32	13	31	22
Aug. 1987	47	22	24	33	44
Nov. 1989	60	12	40	36	50

Source: British Rail Directories, 1981–9.

bare … and I shared an office with someone else's secretary for a while. It was really quite strange and then there was a feeling of being terribly lost.'[104]

Reid was determined to develop the system and maintain the impetus. His position was further strengthened when he took Campbell's place as a Vice-Chairman in January 1983. Campbell was effectively demoted, becoming a part-timer.[105] Reid was then appointed Chairman in the following September, combining the role with that of Chief Executive (see Table 4.4). Parker had agreed to a two-year extension of his contract in 1981 at the higher salary of £60,000, with the intention that he would complete some of the crucial tasks he had identified. But the Serpell inquiry proved unexpectedly hostile to the railways (see Chapter 5), the electrification programme was effectively shelved, and progress on productivity was hindered by union intransigence in relation to flexible rostering. Whatever the public relations statements may have said, he stepped down in rather bruised condition.[106] There was a delay before a successor was found, partly explained by the general election, and Reid's appointment was not universally welcomed.[107] The fact was that, as with the majority of such appointments since 1947, the department's preference was for a non-railwayman. After a number of unsuccessful efforts Tom King, during his brief tenure as Minister, approached Sir Richard Cave, Chairman of Thorn/EMI, but Cave was only willing to serve as part-time Deputy Chairman, in succession to Bosworth. As with Henry Johnson in 1967, Reid was very much a second choice, though he was more acceptable than most to a Conservative government which had been re-elected in June.[108] Reid and Parker differed in much more than their political sympathies. Parker, a great motivator of people, was more prepared to take on the government in intellectual debate than to confront opponents or weak links within the rail business. His appeal to consensus and convivial approach did not suit everyone, however, and his relations with Ministers Rodgers and Howell were not as warm as with Fowler, for example.[109] Reid, on the other hand, was a 'doer', intent on getting the job done within the guidelines established by a government whose politics he respected. If this meant taking on the mighty

4. The search for a successor to Peter Parker as Chairman, 1983:
Steve Bell, *Guardian*, 23 August 1983

barons in the railway regions, he was more than prepared to do so. Happy to see himself as a crusader battling against entrenched opposition, and often uncomfortably abrasive, his was a classic 'task-oriented' approach to management, quite the opposite of Parker's 'people-oriented' style.[110]

Under Reid's leadership the sector management concept encouraged a number of organisational responses from 1982. First, the committee structure underpinning the Chief Executive's role was modified once again. Reid had never been happy with the RDG and REG arrangement of April 1980 and in September 1982 the two bodies were replaced by a revamped 'Railway Executive' consisting of sector directors, regional general managers, and Headquarters officers.[111] The move was accompanied by more fundamental changes to the organisation at Board and Chief Executive level, where Reid was clearly influenced by Heath and the part-timer, Robin Caldecote.[112] The importance to be given to sector direction in the tripartite management 'matrix' of sector directors, functional officers at Headquarters, and regional managers (see Figure 4.3) was reflected in the appointment of two deputy chief executives at Board level, initially Myers, responsible for sectors and marketing, and Rose, responsible for resource utilisation (i.e. operations and engineering).[113] With this change, regarded by the Department as important enough to require formal Ministerial consent,[114] the other Board members ceased to be executive heads of railway functions. Although it was minuted that the proposals did 'not imply any fundamental change in the role of the Board itself', which was not to be 'distanced' from the railway business,[115] this was not so. The Board was being steered towards the planning role—Reid called it 'policy and audit'—which had been in use before 1977.[116] The new arrangements gave more authority in a functional sense to the new triumvirate of Chief Executive and deputies, working through the Railway Executive, and Reid expected the Board to operate more as a holding company in relation to the railway sectors.[117] Board committees were restructured in response to the change with effect from January 1983, giving the functional members Campbell

Table 4.4 The British Railways Board on 1 October 1983

Name	Date of first appointment	Age	Departed	Previous post	Experience
Chairman & Chief Executive (Railways) (salary: £63,600)					
Robert B. Reid	1977	62	Apr. 1990	Vice-Chairman & Chief Executive (Railways)	Railways
Deputy Chairman (part-time) (salary: £10,000)					
Sir Richard Cave	1983	63	Jan. 1986	—	Engineering, electrical, TV
Vice-Chairman (salary: £38,550)					
Derek Fowler	1975	54	Oct. 1990	Controller, Corp. Finance, BRB	Railways, Local Government
Deputy Chief Executive (Railways) (salary: £37,150)					
Geoffrey Myers	1980	53	Oct. 1987	Director, Strategic Devpmt, BRB	Railways
Full-time member (salary: £37,150)					
James G. Urquhart	1977	58	Aug. 1985	GM, LMR	Railways
Part-time members (salary: £4,160–£11,145)					
Lord Caldecote, DSC	1979	65	Feb. 1985	—	Elec. engineering, aviation
Ian M. Campbell, CVO	1977	61	Jan. 1987	ED (Systems & Operations), BRB	Railways
Simon Jenkins	1979	40	Apr. 1990	—	Journalism
Prudence Leith	1980	43	Sept. 1985	—	Catering
H. Roderick MacLeod	1980	54	June 1986	—	Shipping (Ben Line steamers)
Michael Posner	1977	52	Aug. 1984	—	Economist (public sector)

Note: James J. O'Brien was Assistant Chief Executive (Railways). He and Myers became 'Joint Managing Directors (Railways)' in February 1984, and O'Brien became a Board Member in April.

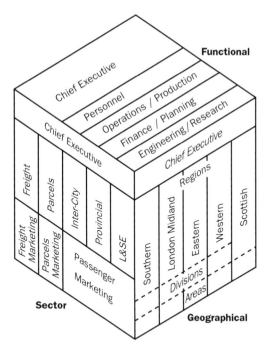

Figure 4.3 The management 'matrix', June 1982

and Urquhart new duties, and providing added emphasis on audit and review, technology, and safety.[118] Rose's illness led to a further change. Myers took charge of operations and engineering, while Jim O'Brien, General Manager of London Midland Region, succeeded him in the sectors and marketing portfolio (see Figure 4.4).[119] The posts were re-designated as 'joint managing directors' in February 1984, when Reid, while remaining head of the railway business, dropped the title of Chief Executive (Railways), and O'Brien joined the Board in April. At the same time the Board Executive, together with the more informal chairman's group (known by Parker as his 'dams'), were replaced by a new Chairman's Group consisting of Reid, Cave, Fowler, Myers, and O'Brien.[120]

Also in 1982, the finance and planning departments were reorganised to improve the budgeting-planning interface and to support the sector approach, following advice from Price Waterhouse and Peat Marwick Mitchell.[121] Planning was eliminated as a free-standing department, the senior planning and management accounting posts, held by Corbishley and Wilkinson, disappeared, and three directors were appointed, responsible for financial planning (Glyn Williams), budgetary control (Stanley Whittaker), and sector evaluation (David Allen), all reporting to Sellers as Director of Finance and Planning.[122] Allen's post was significant in providing the financial services for developing effective sector management. Management accounting was advanced, and a new sector-based

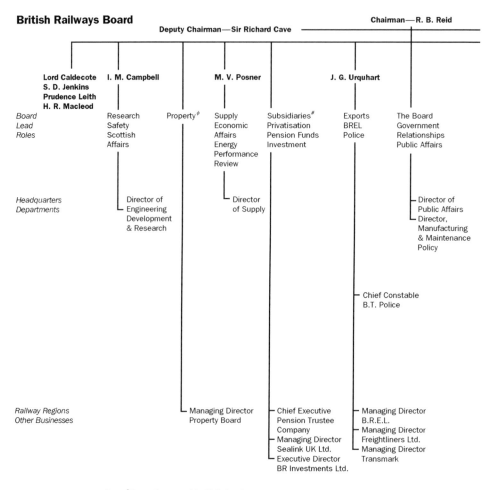

Figure 4.4 BRB organisation chart, February 1984

accounting system—SPAMS—was developed to replace PP&CCA.[123] Although the search for full cost attribution was sometimes obsessive and mechanistic, Allen was to make important contributions to sector definitions and evaluation, Inter-City strategy and costing conventions, and, in particular, the move from 'prime user' to 'sole user' (see below). The Strategy Unit was also reconstituted as a Policy Unit from June 1982. The new body, headed initially by Bradshaw, but more enduringly by John Prideaux, embraced economics, computing, and mathematical skills and serviced Board-level planning, combining the planning

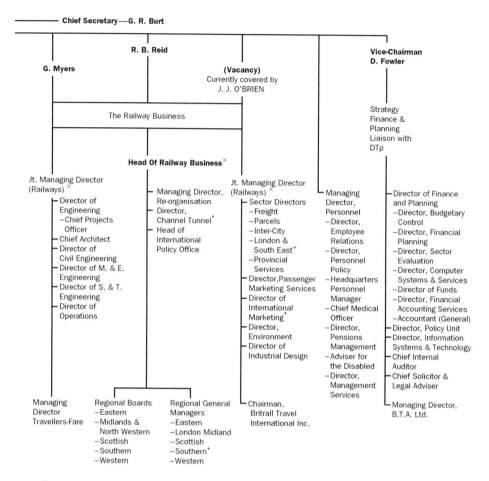

Chief Secretary—G. R. Burt

R. B. Reid

G. Myers

(Vacancy)
Currently covered by
J. J. O'BRIEN

Vice-Chairman
D. Fowler

The Railway Business

Strategy
Finance &
Planning
Liaison with
DTp

Head Of Railway Business×

Jt. Managing Director
(Railways) ×
- Director of
  Engineering
  - Chief Projects
    Officer
- Chief Architect
- Director of
  Civil Engineering
- Director of M. & E.
  Engineering
- Director of S. & T.
  Engineering
- Director of
  Operations

- Managing Director,
  Re-organisation
- Director,
  Channel Tunnel*
- Head of
  International
  Policy Office

Jt. Managing Director
(Railways) ×
- Sector Directors
  - Freight
  - Parcels
  - Inter-City
  - London &
    South East+
  - Provincial
    Services
- Director, Passenger
  Marketing Services
- Director of
  International
  Marketing*
- Director,
  Environment
- Director of
  Industrial Design

- Managing
  Director,
  Personnel
  - Director,
    Employee
    Relations
  - Director,
    Personnel
    Policy
  - Headquarters
    Personnel
    Manager
  - Chief Medical
    Officer
  - Director,
    Pensions
    Management
  - Adviser for
    the Disabled
  - Director,
    Management
    Services

- Director of Finance
  and Planning
  - Director, Budgetary
    Control
  - Director, Financial
    Planning
  - Director, Sector
    Evaluation
  - Director, Computer
    Systems & Services
  - Director of Funds
  - Director, Financial
    Accounting Services
  - Accountant (General)
- Director, Policy Unit
- Director, Information
  Systems & Technology
- Chief Internal
  Auditor
- Chief Solicitor &
  Legal Adviser

Managing
Director
Travellers-Fare

Regional Boards
- Eastern
- Midlands &
  North Western
- Scottish
- Southern
- Western

Regional General
Managers
- Eastern
- London Midland
- Scottish
- Southern+
- Western

- Chairman,
  Britrall Travel
  International Inc.

- Managing Director,
  B.T.A. Ltd.

×*Note:* The Railway Business is headed by a triumvirate comprising the
Head of the business and two Joint Managing Directors. Overall
control is exercised by the triumvirate operating flexibly, as the
need arises; but, normally, Report Lines are as shown above.

functions of the Board's Planning & Investment Committee (henceforth to be divided again) and the Strategy Steering Group.[124]

A full re-evaluation of embryonic sector management was carried out by consultants from Price Waterhouse, who were appointed in October 1982 to review the roles and responsibilities of sector directors, RGMs, and functional directors. They reported in May and August 1983, by which time the Board had also received the Serpell Committee's review. Both bodies expressed the view that further changes were needed to give sector directors adequate authority, in short to clarify and develop the relationships between the three types of manager in the matrix. The Serpell Report welcomed sector management, but doubted whether it would achieve its potential unless the sector directors had more authority. Because the three sets of managers enjoyed equal status in the managerial hierarchy, responsibility was seen to be diffuse and unclear. The report also recommended that the engineering function be fully integrated into sector arrangements. The minority report of Alfred Goldstein agreed with the majority view on this occasion, although it was characteristically more strident. The matrix, Goldstein argued, would not work; in its existing form it was 'a sure recipe for uncertainty, low morale and less efficiency'.[125] Price Waterhouse focused in particular on the relationship between sector directors and RGMs, and on the delegation of authority at sub-sector level. Two possibilities were rehearsed, the first proposing to make RGMs production managers providing services and marketing to the sector directors' specifications, the second giving the RGMs 'bottom-line' responsibility for sub-sectors falling wholly or mainly within regional boundaries. The issue was complicated by the fact that the sectors possessed different characteristics. The sub-sectors of Freight (now known as Railfreight) and Parcels were already well established. They were market based with interregional traffic flows. Building on the precedent set by the London Midland's freight management structure as early as the summer of 1982, national business managers had been appointed for the major train-load commodities (such as coal and petroleum) and parcels categories (e.g. Post Office, newspapers), and consequently the sector directors enjoyed a full measure of authority at sub-sector level (cf. Table 4.3).[126] On the other hand, the passenger sectors had sub-sectors which with one exception (Inter-City North-East/South-West) were geographically determined and located predominantly within a single region. The RGMs were being treated as sub-sector managers of the regionally based services of the London and South East and Provincial sectors, but the position on Inter-City had not yet been clarified. In consequence, in May 1983 Price Waterhouse recommended, and British Rail adopted, a mixed approach. For Freight, Parcels and Inter-City NE/SW, sub-sectors were placed under the command of the sector directors, who would establish 'cost and quality "contracts"' with the RGMs. However, for the vast bulk of passenger services the RGMs would act as sub-sector managers.[127] Thus, by the time the painful strikes over flexible rostering had been resolved (see Chapter 5), and British Rail was working to clearer directives from government in relation to its businesses, sector management had begun to take shape. In some areas of the rail business sector directors were beginning to override the authority of the RGMs; in others the relationship was more contractual. In August the role of the functional directors of Engineering, the Policy Unit, Finance & Planning, Civil Engineering, Mechanical & Electrical Engineering, S&TE, and Operations was clarified, underlining a shift of emphasis from 'direction' to 'consultation' and 'co-ordination', from day-to-day management to longer-term strategic planning.[128]

The process was taken a good deal further in the course of 1985. O'Brien, reporting to the Board in March, revealed that the sector directors were unhappy with the mixed approach. They complained in particular about the lack of a 'clear primacy in reporting lines', which had produced 'an ambiguous and confused matrix structure'. Their catalogue of additional concerns embraced the inability to control the Headquarters administrative costs charged to them, the lack of clarity in the definition of management units below sub-sector level (i.e. profit centres and cost centres), and the need to improve systems for inter-sectoral activities and infrastructure. Consequently, it was agreed that RGMs, who had already lost their divisions in 1984 (see below), would relinquish their personal roles as sub-sector directors and report only to Myers, the joint MD for operations and engineering.[129] The Board was concerned that the change 'might be perceived wrongly as a diminution of their status and importance',[130] but from this point the regional leaders were to be confined to production management. Price Waterhouse were asked to make a further review of sector management, and in July 1985 they produced a five-year programme for organisational development. Their recommendations included the move to a *two*-dimensional matrix of sector and region/area with a limitation of the executive role of Headquarters directors, and the development of 'bottom-line' responsibility at sub-sector level. The sub-sector managers were to make the interface with 'production' and build up brand identities, with consequent changes to planning and costing systems, and to contractual relationships between the elements in the matrix. Sector directors were expected to exercise more authority over engineering and personnel functions.[131] Considerable management time was devoted to promoting this organisational modification, including the deliberations of two working groups drawn from the Railway Executive, a two-day conference in Northampton, and the work of management assessment teams led by Bill Kent, the Director, Administrative Policy.[132] When Myers, who by this time was effectively the chief executive as Vice-Chairman (Railways),[133] reported on the 'evolving railway organisation' in November the new emphasis on sub-sector management was in place, and 26 sub-sectors had been established.[134] The new matrix, shown in Figure 4.5, distinguished clearly between sector directors as 'commanders', RGMs as 'contractors', and Headquarters functional directors as 'supporters', or, as later described, between 'specifiers', 'deliverers', and 'advisers'.[135]

The tightening up of managerial responsibility and reporting was assisted by important technical changes in the way the rail businesses were managed and controlled. These comprised a new method of allocating joint infrastructure costs—'sole user'—and adjustments to the boundaries between the passenger sectors. This work was clearly a response to the introduction of tougher and more precise objectives by government for the rail businesses in general, and for Inter-City in particular, and the Department of Transport was an important agent at all stages. The shift from 'prime user' to 'sole user' arose from the commercial

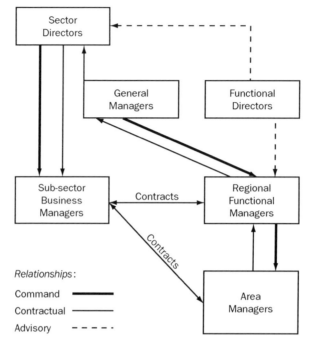

Figure 4.5 The new matrix, 1985

objective set for Inter-City in June 1981, which, as we have already seen, was in turn linked to government support for further electrification. When the first Inter-City prospectus was sent to the Secretary of State, now David Howell, in December 1981, promises of viability by 1985, defined as a Required Rate of Return of 5 per cent after current cost depreciation (or 3 per cent of the gross replacement cost on the assets employed), were based on the 'prime user' hierarchy of charging.[136] However, in the following year British Rail informed the Serpell Committee that the commercial objective was at risk with the prime user convention since a 'more refined estimate of costs properly chargeable to Inter-City' had transferred a higher level of infrastructure and administration costs to the sector. One suggestion offered was to adjust the costing criteria.[137] The Department of Transport's response to this news, passed by Tony Baker to Bradshaw, was that Inter-City should be charged only those infrastructure costs which would arise in the long term if it were the sole user.[138] Responding to this steer, British Rail began work on a revised prospectus and an alternative to the prime user approach.[139] The sole user approach charged sectors with the cost of those facilities which would be required if that sector were the only user of the line; the additional requirements of other sectors were then charged; unallocated costs, if any, were identified as 'surplus capacity' (see Figure 4.6).[140]

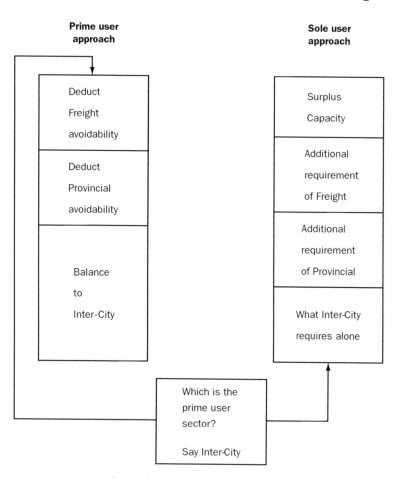

Figure 4.6 Prime user and sole user

Minds became concentrated after the presentation of a revised prospectus for Inter-City in March 1983. The Minister, David Howell, while unhappy to be told that even on a 'sole user' basis Inter-City would barely break even by 1986, was nevertheless attracted to the new costing concept as an incentive to remove surplus infrastructure.[141] Parker, in a parting shot to King in September 1983, designed to secure electrification of the East Coast Main Line (ECML), emphasised that Inter-City was essentially two businesses: the profitable ECML and West Coast Main Line (WCML); and the weaker routes. When taken together they might break even, but would not satisfy a 5 per cent profit objective.[142] There was little sympathy for this problem, however. Indeed, Nicholas Ridley's instructions to the Board to accelerate the planned reduction in the PSO grant without a major programme of rail closures, which were issued on 24 October, eight days after he had succeeded King as Secretary of State for Transport, did

127

little to increase the Board's room to manoeuvre.[143] At this stage both the Board and the Railway Executive were divided about how to confront the government on 'Inter-City commerciality'. Some, like Simon Jenkins, favoured taking an open stance and admitting that the sector was 'not wholly commercial on the present definition'. There was concern that actions taken on behalf of Inter-City should not prejudice the PSO outcome. Reid himself was unhappy about 'fudging the numbers'. Thus, when on Prideaux's initiative it was calculated that some £70–£145 million might be transferred from Inter-City by various manipulations involving route primacy, the allocation of terminal and administration costs, and boundaries, nervousness about approaching the government ensured that the work remained confidential.[144] However, there was the encouragement of a hint from the Department that a change in infrastructure cost allocation might be acceptable provided that it did not produce a raft of unallocated costs.[145] In these circumstances further work was undertaken.

The efforts of the sector evaluation team culminated in changes devised in 1983–4 and first introduced in the financial year 1985/6.[146] They were driven by new government requirements issued in August 1984. Following the preparation of an Inter-City strategy document in June 1984, Ridley informed Reid that the Inter-City target should be a 5 per cent operating profit by 1988/9, by which time the sector would cease to be eligible for PSO support. The directive was linked to government authorisation of the ECML electrification scheme, and, indeed to the promise of more generous support for investment in cost-reducing rolling stock (in fact, the investment authorised in the 15 months to March 1985 was greater than investment authorised in the previous six years). At this point the Secretary of State agreed that the sole user costing convention should be adopted, though in a modified form which provided for the charging of surplus capacity to sectors ('surplus add-back').[147] It is not clear how advantageous the change was. Publicly it was presented as a refinement more in tune with decision making and a 'powerful means of analysis for investment projects'.[148] However, in a note written for 'posterity' Posner noted that 'purer spirits' on the Board were dismayed by the move from prime to sole user as a means to secure government support for electrification, and felt 'dishonoured'. He also pointed out that sole user, by revealing a 'substantial slice' of surplus infrastructure had opened a 'new can of worms'. Howell's unsympathetic response to the Board's plight in May 1983, which was confirmed by Ridley's instruction in October, meant that the Board had been 'dishonoured to no avail'.[149] Others inside the business nursed qualms about the change in costing. Alec McTavish from the Policy Unit had been moved to write directly to Parker in November 1982 to point out that 'sole user' could not achieve the two policy objectives it was intended to satisfy—a break-even result for Inter-City and 'a sensible basis for managing infrastructure'.[150] Indeed, it is not certain how far the new accounting approach actually improved the prospects of Inter-City profitability. An estimate made in October 1983 reckoned that a gain of £62 million would come from the change to sole user (though £37 million of surplus capacity would be created). A later estimate in July 1984, which included 'surplus add-back', indicated that the improvement would be £44 million (in mid-1983 prices).[151] But it is not clear that these benefits were actually secured as Inter-City approached its apocalypse. Indeed, the financial gains anticipated in 1983 appear to have been cancelled out three years later by the introduction of more accuracy in costing methods, in particular location costing, aided by the refinement of computer models within the SPAMS framework undertaken in the name of the acronyms CAPRI, PARIS, FABS, LOVERS, and RAVERS.[152]

The boundaries issue was also driven by the anxiety to make Inter-City viable. As we have seen, major adjustments had been made in 1981 in order to strengthen the prospects of a commercial outcome. In 1982, in the more cautious forecast offered to the Serpell Committee, British Rail raised the possibility of adjusting the boundary between Inter-City and Provincial until a break-even target was reached, though it also argued that this course of action would make little managerial sense.[153] In any case, the Department had made it clear that further attempts to transfer a substantial number of routes out of the Inter-City 'core' would prompt a refusal to subsidise such routes.[154] The Inter-City strategy document of July 1983 returned to the boundaries issue, this time to see if the more profitable trains in the London and South East sector, for example Waterloo–Southampton/Bournemouth and Liverpool St.–Ipswich/Norwich, could be *added* to Inter-City.[155] Once again the Departmental view was negative, the Secretary of State, now Tom King, insisting that Inter-City viability should be assessed on the existing pattern of services. He was firmly opposed to deletions: 'I would be very reluctant to accept that the only way forward is a redefinition of the sector to exclude the more marginal services'.[156] After Ridley's instructions to the Board to accelerate the planned reduction in the PSO in October 1983, Prideaux's exercise calculated the benefits of moving some of the more profitable elements in London and South East to Inter-City at £29 million, later revised to £40 million. Although, as we have seen, no formal approach to government was made at this stage, managers were encouraged by some softening in the Department's stance. Apparently it would have no objection to boundary changes at the margin.[157]

Work continued on this basis over the first half of 1984, a year which was dominated by the damaging impact of a major coal strike. Proposals were included in the Inter-City prospectus in June, and these were accepted by the Secretary of State, Ridley, in August when he announced the new sector target, with the condition that no further changes were made.[158] The modifications involved the transfer from London and South East to Inter-City of Victoria–Gatwick and London–Ipswich/Harwich/Norwich trains, and the shedding of some North-East–South-West services to Provincial.[159] There was a logic to the idea that Inter-City should square operating with marketing characteristics and confine itself to high-speed, high-quality inter-urban and international (i.e. city

5. Cost attribution and sector management, 1984. Comic reflection on the prime user convention: *Modern Railways*, August 1984. Seated, left to right: Cyril Bleasdale (Sector Director, Inter-City), David Mitchell (Transport Minister, DTp), and Roger Ford (Contributing Technical Editor, *Modern Railways*).

centre–airport) transport. On the other hand, the exercise could also be seen as 'skimming off the cream and pouring away the sour milk', and it is evident that it generated considerable heat internally.[160] The original proposals had been much more ambitious, including the transfer to Inter-City of all boat trains, the London–Portsmouth, Brighton, and Bournemouth services, and some express trains in Scotland. The raid on London & South East was firmly resisted at sector and regional level,[161] where there was particular annoyance at the suggestion that London–Bournemouth services might be split between the two sectors. As one manager put it:

I must take the strongest exception to the distortions being built into the Bournemouth service evaluation in an attempt to produce some kind of benefit to the Inter-City Sector on transfer. It is absolute nonsense in marketing and managerial terms to talk of the Bournemouth service as two separate services... We are approaching the stage when you are saying 'Never mind the facts, let's put in some figures which happen to suit us'.[162]

In consequence, the limited adjustments agreed reduced the expected financial benefit of the boundary changes, but nevertheless these were expected to generate £25 million, nearly a quarter of the £103 million improvement promised in Inter-City's 'Into Profit' statement of December 1984.[163]

4.5 Further developments, 1986–9

After the intensive work on sector management in 1985, the developments of 1986–8 were concerned with the strengthening of both sector and sub-sector identities. 'Stage III' of the work on administration, which made a further assault on costs (see below), also focused on inculcating a team-based approach within the matrix in order to enhance organisational effectiveness. The latter was aided by organisational consultants from Bath University, Paul Bate and Alan Savage, who in studying British Rail's organisational culture exposed several weaknesses, notably a high degree of 'segmentalism' with poorly developed horizontal relationships, inadequate delegation, too much committee work, and a top-heavy headquarters. Inevitably, these problems could not be resolved speedily.[164] On the other hand, the promotion of sector identities progressed well. London and South East was relaunched as Network SouthEast (NSE) in June 1986, InterCity offered its swallow emblem in May 1987, and geographically based marketing was advanced with Scotrail, a Provincial sub-sector, and Cornish Railways, a short-lived initiative in 'localisation' in Western Region. Renaming of the subsectors in 1986 (Table 4.5) helped to associate these organisational units with specific assets. NSE and the Railfreight sub-sectors were given particular brand prominence with the introduction of new liveries on dedicated rolling stock and infrastructure. For the first time, customer awareness of sector-based activities was apparent.[165] Alongside these changes, the 'railway command' structure was once again modified to reflect the growing power of the sectors. A Business Review Group was established in 1985 as a subcommittee of Railway Executive.

Table 4.5 The sub-sectors in 1986

Railfreight	Parcels	InterCity	Network SouthEast	Provincial
Aggregates	Premium (Red Star)	East Coast Main Line	East	Eastern
Automotive	Newspapers	Anglia InterCity	North	Midland
Building Materials	Post Office	West Coast Main Line	Central	Scotrail
Coal, Distribution		Midland Mainline	SouthEast	Western
Coal, Electricity		Cross Country	SouthWest	
Coal, Other		Gatwick	West	
Distribution		Great Western		
Services		Mainline		
Metals		Charter Trains		
Petroleum				
Refuse				
Freightliner				

Source: Glyn Williams, 'Managing British Rail', October 1986, BRB.

It acted as a financial control mechanism, fixing control budgets and monitoring performance. Chaired by the Joint Managing Director responsible for businesses (sectors) and attended by the other JMD and the sector directors it quickly established primacy in a decision-making sense over the much larger and un-wieldy Railway Executive.[166] Lower down, the 160 or so area managers and engineers began to respond more and more to sub-sector manager directives.[167]

The process was given further impetus by the establishment of a new region for East Anglia, called Anglia Region, in April 1988. The intention here was two-fold. First, there was a need to strengthen the operating performance and enhance investment in the Liverpool St. and Fenchurch St. services, which were too remote from the Eastern Region's headquarters in York. Second, and equally important, the creation of the new region provided an opportunity to assess the effectiveness of a slimmed-down apparatus which might serve as a model for regional organisa-tions elsewhere. In Anglia Region production management embraced mainten-ance, area management was strengthened, and there was a single manager for infrastructure. John Edmonds was moved from Provincial to establish the new organisation as General Manager.[168] At the top there was also a reallocation of duties and change in reporting lines. O'Brien's duties as a Joint MD were signifi-cantly redefined. He was asked to progress the review of overhead costs (see p. 144), and prepare Travellers Fare, the station catering business, for privatisation. Kirby, the Vice-Chairman (Railways), assumed direct responsibility for the pas-senger businesses, leaving O'Brien with Freight, Parcels, and Freightliners. David Rayner, the other Joint MD, retained his responsibilities for engineering, produc-tion, and R&D (see Figure 4.7).[169] Effective direction was certainly needed. Having achieved the three-year objective of cutting the PSO grant by 25 per cent, British Rail was asked to repeat the dose. The objective set in October 1986 by the new Secretary of State, John Moore, was to reduce the PSO from £736 million in 1986/7 (later readjusted to £712.3 million) to only £555 million in 1989/90. At the same time, the unsupported sectors, Inter-City, Railfreight, and Parcels, together with Freightliners and Travellers Fare, were given the more flexible target of achieving a 2.7 per cent return on assets before interest by the same year (see Table 4.2).[170] Accompanying the new targets was Departmental concern, shared by the Treas-ury, that British Rail was meeting its PSO targets more by revenue increases as the economy boomed than by a more effective reduction of operating costs, a debate which reached a head in July 1987 over the results for 1986/7 (see pp. 148–9). Further examples of the relentless pressure on public sector efficiency encouraged by a bullish government were the detailed audits made of the supported passenger sectors, NSE and Provincial, by the MMC in 1987 and 1989 respectively, and the expectation, endorsed by the Department, that NSE would cease to be supported by 1992/3, which accompanied further, and tougher, three-year targets for InterCity, Railfreight, and Provincial set in December 1989.[171]

The Board reviewed the progress of sectorisation in September 1988, by which time the rail business had experienced considerable change. A rail-based Channel

Tunnel was being constructed, the subsidiaries (British Transport Hotels, Sea-link, etc.) had been sold, BREL had been split into 'new build' and maintenance businesses, several works had been closed, and the first stages of BREL's privat-isation had been completed with the disposal of the Doncaster Wagon Works and the Horwich foundry (the final sale of BREL was made in May 1989).[172] More important still, Paul Channon, Secretary of State for Transport, had raised the possibility of privatising the railway business itself, creating considerable uncer-tainty internally and, in some, a loss of morale (see Chapter 11). Richard Allan, Director of the Policy Unit, presented three organisational options: (A) to reduce the sectors' direct control over resources and production assets by emphasising contractual relationships; (B) to increase direct sector control to the extent that all resources and assets were owned; and (C) to pursue a middle course between the two extremes. Reid, supported by his Headquarters directors, was anxious to avoid the 'penalties of major organisational upheaval' and insisted that the Board should not prejudice options for privatisation. He therefore gave a strong steer towards Option C.[173] His was not the only voice on the Board, however. Two of the four part-time members appointed in 1985, Allen Sheppard, of GrandMet, and Oscar De Ville, of Meyer International,[174] expressed the view that more radical change was required. They favoured Option B as more likely to produce sharpened accountabilities and reductions in overheads. In the event, the Board endorsed the chairman's position. The evolutionary changes agreed and subse-quently implemented included the introduction of sector balance sheets for management accounting purposes only, and the division of Headquarters into a small corporate office, and a larger 'Group Services' organisation of self-account-ing units led by John Edmonds as MD. These were to sell services to the sectors from July 1989 on a full cost recovery basis. With O'Brien having retired in March 1989, Kirby, the Vice-Chairman (Railways) was supported by Edmonds and Rayner, the MD responsible for engineering and production (see Figure 4.8).[175] At the same time the railway management structure was altered once again to reflect the patent decline of the Railway Executive as a decision-making body. Criticised by the Bath University consultants as demonstrating many of the weaknesses in the railway culture (long routine meetings as substitutes for thinking, debating, and problem solving, lack of decisiveness, failure to expose or manage differences, etc.), it was wound up in July 1989 and instead the Business Review Group, expanded and renamed the Railway Management Group, became the principal railway committee.[176]

Despite these modifications, it is apparent that managerial tensions persisted within the matrix structure and that many sector accountabilities remained difficult to define (see pp. 142–3). This fact, together with the way in which British Rail approached the initial discussions on privatisation (see Chapter 11), encour-aged the Board to pursue organisational simplification as a matter of urgency. Sector management, Reid told successive ministers, Paul Channon and Cecil Parkinson, in June and September 1989, had 'run its course'. Earlier in the year

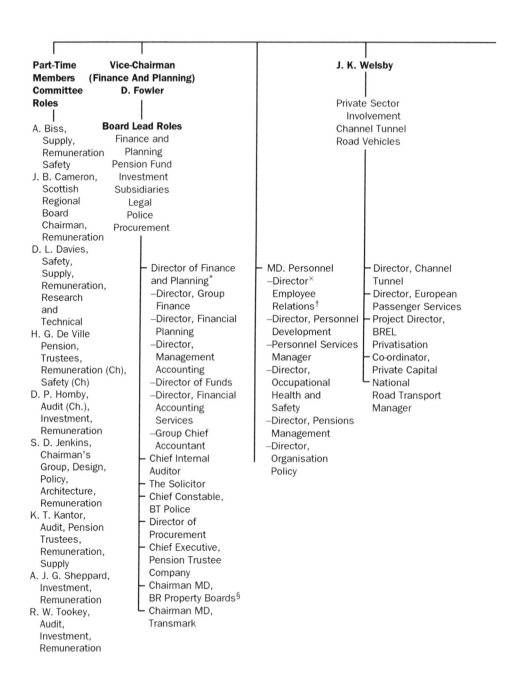

Part-Time Members Committee Roles

A. Biss,
 Supply,
 Remuneration
 Safety
J. B. Cameron,
 Scottish
 Regional
 Board
 Chairman,
 Remuneration
D. L. Davies,
 Safety,
 Supply,
 Remuneration,
 Research
 and
 Technical
H. G. De Ville
 Pension,
 Trustees,
 Remuneration (Ch),
 Safety (Ch)
D. P. Hornby,
 Audit (Ch.),
 Investment,
 Remuneration
S. D. Jenkins,
 Chairman's
 Group, Design,
 Policy,
 Architecture,
 Remuneration
K. T. Kantor,
 Audit, Pension
 Trustees,
 Remuneration,
 Supply
A. J. G. Sheppard,
 Investment,
 Remuneration
R. W. Tookey,
 Audit,
 Investment,
 Remuneration

Vice-Chairman (Finance And Planning)
D. Fowler

Board Lead Roles
Finance and
Planning
Pension Fund
Investment
Subsidiaries
Legal
Police
Procurement

— Director of Finance
 and Planning*
 —Director, Group
 Finance
 —Director, Financial
 Planning
 —Director,
 Management
 Accounting
 —Director of Funds
 —Director, Financial
 Accounting
 Services
 —Group Chief
 Accountant
— Chief Internal
 Auditor
— The Solicitor
— Chief Constable,
 BT Police
— Director of
 Procurement
— Chief Executive,
 Pension Trustee
 Company
— Chairman MD,
 BR Property Boards§
— Chairman MD,
 Transmark

— MD. Personnel
 —Director×
 Employee
 Relations†
 —Director, Personnel
 Development
 —Personnel Services
 Manager
 —Director,
 Occupational
 Health and
 Safety
 —Director, Pensions
 Management
 —Director,
 Organisation
 Policy

J. K. Welsby

Private Sector
 Involvement
Channel Tunnel
Road Vehicles

— Director, Channel
 Tunnel
— Director, European
 Passenger Services
— Project Director,
 BREL
 Privatisation
— Co-ordinator,
 Private Capital
— National
 Road Transport
 Manager

* Directly responsible to the Vice-Chairman (Railways) (D. D. Kirby) for Railway Financial issues.
× Responsible to the Vice-Chairman (Railways) (D. D. Kirby) for Railway Personnel issues.
† Responsible to the Joint Managing Director (Railways) (D. E. Rayner) for Railway Employee
 Relations issues.
§ In Operational Property matters, Managing Director, BR Property reports to J. K. Welsby through
 the Property Review Group.

Figure 4.7 BRB organisation chart, July 1988

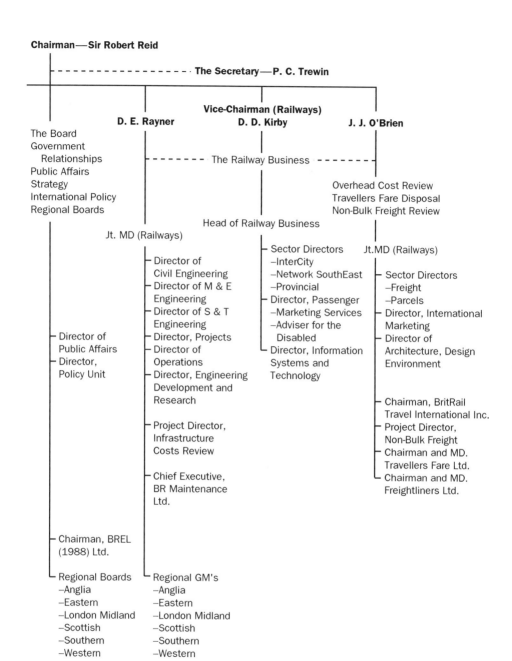

Chairman—Sir Robert Reid

- - - - - - - - - - - - - - - - **The Secretary—P. C. Trewin**

D. E. Rayner   **Vice-Chairman (Railways)**   **J. J. O'Brien**
                     D. D. Kirby

The Board
Government
  Relationships
Public Affairs
Strategy
International Policy
Regional Boards

- - - - - - - The Railway Business - - - - - - -

Overhead Cost Review
Travellers Fare Disposal
Non-Bulk Freight Review

Head of Railway Business

Jt. MD (Railways)

Sector Directors
  −InterCity
  −Network SouthEast
  −Provincial
Director, Passenger
  −Marketing Services
  −Adviser for the
    Disabled
Director, Information
Systems and
Technology

Director of
Civil Engineering
Director of M & E
Engineering
Director of S & T
Engineering
Director, Projects
Director of
Operations
Director, Engineering
Development and
Research

Project Director,
Infrastructure
Costs Review

Chief Executive,
BR Maintenance
Ltd.

Jt.MD (Railways)

Sector Directors
  −Freight
  −Parcels
Director, International
Marketing
Director of
Architecture, Design
Environment

Chairman, BritRail
Travel International Inc.
Project Director,
Non-Bulk Freight
Chairman and MD.
Travellers Fare Ltd.
Chairman and MD.
Freightliners Ltd.

Director of
Public Affairs
Director,
Policy Unit

Chairman, BREL
(1988) Ltd.

Regional Boards
  −Anglia
  −Eastern
  −London Midland
  −Scottish
  −Southern
  −Western

Regional GM's
  −Anglia
  −Eastern
  −London Midland
  −Scottish
  −Southern
  −Western

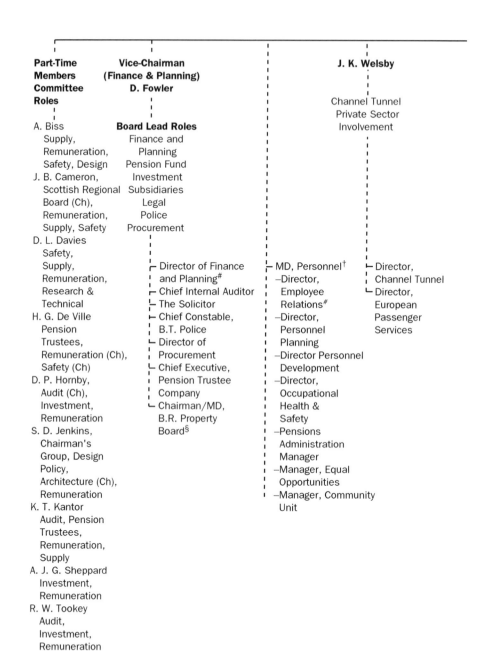

Vice-Chairman (Finance & Planning) D. Fowler

Board Lead Roles
Finance and
  Planning
Pension Fund
  Investment
Subsidiaries
Legal
Police
Procurement

- Director of Finance and Planning[#]
- Chief Internal Auditor
- The Solicitor
- Chief Constable, B.T. Police
- Director of Procurement
- Chief Executive, Pension Trustee Company
- Chairman/MD, B.R. Property Board[§]

- MD, Personnel[†]
- Director, Employee Relations[#]
- Director, Personnel Planning
- Director Personnel Development
- Director, Occupational Health & Safety
- Pensions Administration Manager
- Manager, Equal Opportunities
- Manager, Community Unit

J. K. Welsby

Channel Tunnel Private Sector Involvement

- Director, Channel Tunnel
- Director, European Passenger Services

* Directly responsible to the Vice-Chairman (Railways) (D. D. Kirby) for Railway Financial Issues.
† Responsible to the Vice-Chairman (Railways) (D. D. Kirby) for Railway Personnel Issues.
# Responsible to the Joint Managing Director, Operations and Engineering (D. E. Rayner) for Railway Employee Relations Issues.
§ In Operational Property matters, Managing Director, BR Property Board reports to J. K. Welsby through the Property Review Group.

Figure 4.8 BRB organisation chart, August 1989

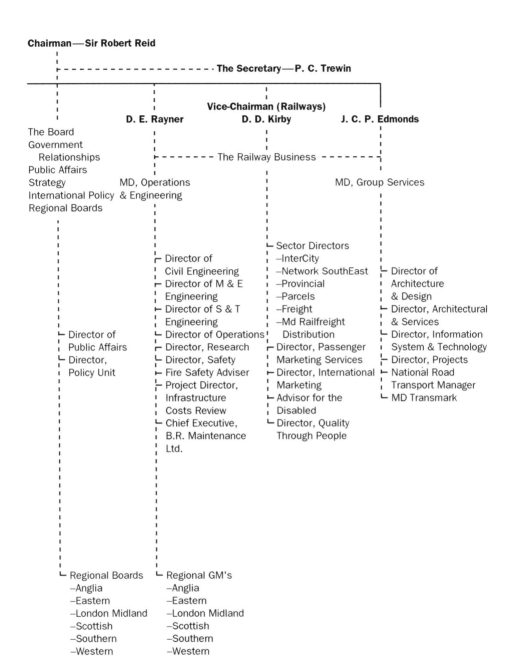

Chairman—Sir Robert Reid

The Secretary—P. C. Trewin

Vice-Chairman (Railways)

D. E. Rayner   **D. D. Kirby**   **J. C. P. Edmonds**

The Board
Government
   Relationships
Public Affairs
Strategy   MD, Operations   MD, Group Services
International Policy & Engineering
Regional Boards

                                           ⌐ Sector Directors
                          ⌐ Director of   –InterCity
                          | Civil Engineering –Network SouthEast   ⌐ Director of
                          ⌐ Director of M & E –Provincial | Architecture
                          | Engineering   –Parcels | & Design
                          ⌐ Director of S & T –Freight   ⌐ Director, Architectural
                          | Engineering   –Md Railfreight | & Services
⌐ Director of   ⌐ Director of Operations Distribution   ⌐ Director, Information
| Public Affairs   ⌐ Director, Research ⌐ Director, Passenger | System & Technology
⌐ Director,   ⌐ Director, Safety | Marketing Services ⌐ Director, Projects
| Policy Unit   ⌐ Fire Safety Adviser ⌐ Director, International ⌐ National Road
                          ⌐ Project Director, | Marketing | Transport Manager
                          | Infrastructure   ⌐ Advisor for the   ⌐ MD Transmark
                          | Costs Review | Disabled
                          ⌐ Chief Executive,   ⌐ Director, Quality
                          | B.R. Maintenance | Through People
                          | Ltd.

⌐ Regional Boards   ⌐ Regional GM's
  –Anglia   –Anglia
  –Eastern   –Eastern
  –London Midland   –London Midland
  –Scottish   –Scottish
  –Southern   –Southern
  –Western   –Western

The Railway Business

the Board had engaged Coopers & Lybrand to help formulate a further restructuring into decentralised, market-based companies under a small holding company.[177] This major task, progressed by Edmonds, produced the final development of sector management in 1991–2. Known as Organising for Quality or 'OfQ', it envisaged the establishment of self-contained businesses and the elimination of the regions, and thus ran counter to some of the models for privatisation being discussed at that time. It was also the responsibility of a new management team at the top. Reid's time at the Board had run its course too. In many ways his impact on both the organisation and its culture had been fundamental. He also did much to restore government confidence in the railways' financial performance (see pp. 146–50). Unfortunately, he could not shake off the bewilderment and loss of direction created by the government's early enthusiasm for rail privatisation. Battered by the adverse publicity which the major rail accidents at Clapham, Purley, and Bellgrove had created in 1988–9, the Plasser fraud inquiry (see Chapter 6), and by a particularly confrontational rail strike in the summer of 1989, he, like Parker before him, stepped down in bruised condition.[178] Uniquely he was replaced by a namesake: Bob Reid, Chairman and Chief Executive of Shell UK, who joined the Board on a part-time basis on 1 January 1990, became Executive Chairman in April, and full-time Chairman in October. The appointment on Parkinson's initiative of a leading industrialist, who had been particularly difficult to recruit given the existing circumstances,[179] did not come cheap; his starting salary was more than double that of his predecessor.[180] There was little prospect of a railwayman becoming chairman, particularly after the damage done by the 1989 strike. In any case, the obvious candidates, Myers, Kirby, and O'Brien, had all retired while still in their fifties. To a degree their departure reflected Reid's failure to develop a potential successor; certainly it left the Board short of experienced railwaymen.[181] On the other hand, John Welsby had caught the eye with his rationalisation of engineering and although a comparative newcomer on the Board he enjoyed support within the DTp. When he became Chief Executive, Railways on 1 January 1990, following Kirby's early retirement, the Board reverted to the more familiar form of external chairman and internal chief executive of the Parker and Marsh years. Once again the organisational merry-go-round had turned.[182]

4.6 The achievements of sector management

What did sector management accomplish? In organisational terms its most fundamental achievement was to emphasise segmentation and decentralisation of authority in place of the uniformity and standardisation which had long been characteristic of railway management.[183] Critical to this process was the breaking of the power of the regional barons in the rail business, whose ancestry could be traced back to the great general managers of the private companies in the nineteenth century, such as Mark Huish, Sir James Allport, and Sir Edward Watkin. The steps taken from 1982 represented a progressive erosion of the RGMs' authority and responsibilities. For example, when Maurice Holmes became Director of Operations at Headquarters in January 1983, he noted that the role of RGMs had begun to shift towards production delivery, and he interacted more and more with sector directors.[184] The erosion of power was evident in February 1986 when Cyril Bleasdale was replaced by John Prideaux as Director, InterCity and became General Manager, London Midland Region. The move was widely regarded inside the railways as a demotion for Bleasdale. Feelings that RGMs were now inferior beings in the railway hierarchy were such that Headquarters was moved to issue a management brief in October 1987 seeking to dispel the notion that sector directors had become senior to RGMs. But the plain truth of the matter was that they had.[185] Indeed, by this time the sector directors had begun to concern themselves with *production* management as well as the bottom line.[186]

The RGMs may have lost their direct responsibility for profitability, which in any case had been rather ill defined, but to what extent did the sector directors capture the 'bottom line'? How real was this responsibility? Press release after press release, statement after statement averred that clarity had been brought into reporting, that bottom-line responsibility was firmly in place, and there was a tendency in the secondary literature to assume that substantial and effective change was established in and from 1982.[187] However, as we have seen, early experience brought as much confusion as clarity. This was evident when O'Brien asked the sector directors to express their views in 1984.[188] The problems which surfaced here embraced dissatisfaction with both Headquarters (e.g. complaints about ambiguities in the relationship with Headquarters functions and numerous references to the continuing high costs of central services) and the regions (e.g. complaints about the difficulty in getting a grip on mechanical engineering costs). It was also evident that financial management systems were a long way from providing what sector directors needed to delegate to sub-sector level.[189] Even by 1989, 'AXIS II', a development which combined the expenditure and accounting system (AXIS) with SPAMS, had only just started to provide relevant management information at the sub-sector/area level.[190] With the exception of the freight sector, managerial staffs remained small until 1986 (cf. Table 4.3), and it took five years to produce a substantive change at the regional and area levels of management. We should also accept that the sectors varied considerably, not only in relation to their market characteristics but also in size, as Table 4.6 indicates.

Pretensions also differed. It had been a quite different matter to introduce new systems into, for example, InterCity and Freight. By 1986 the former tended to regard itself as a semi-autonomous division in a multi-divisional company, while the latter saw itself as a wholly owned subsidiary with internalised production

Table 4.6 British Rail's business sectors, 1982 and 1988/9 (£m., in constant 1982 prices)

Sector	Gross income		Operating surplus/Loss	
	1982	1988/9	1982	1988/9
InterCity	350	572	−196	41
LSE/NSE	448	636	−310	−98
Provincial	136	195	−489	−332
Railfreight	487	486	2	49
Parcels	93	89	8	−9
Total	1,514	1,978	−985	−349

Source: BRB, *R&A 1982, 1988/9*; GDP deflator (market prices, calendar years, Q1/1989 for 1988/9), from Office for National Statistics, *Economic Trends Annual Supplement 1999*.

resources. This distinction was strengthened when with the encouragement of the DTp to be more transparent about loss-making activities, the less successful elements of the non-passenger rail business, Freightliners Ltd and Speedlink (non-bulk freight), were re-established as Railfreight Distribution, a separate entity within Railfreight, in October 1988.[191] The Bath University 'culture' exercise (see pp. 131, 133) exposed the dangers of 'unrestricted sectorism', and it was clear that as late as 1987 Headquarters management were aware that there was still some confusion about responsibilities in relation to resource management and that, while the 'business-led' approach enjoyed wide currency among the staff, there was much to be done in 'communicating a clear, uncluttered message'.[192] Nor should one overestimate the immediate impact of sector management in addressing cost control and efficiency in the areas of civil and mechanical engineering and maintenance. Campbell apparently told Bleasdale when he became Director of InterCity that the APT was *his*, i.e. Campbell's, responsibility; only with its demise (see Chapter 6) was it made clear that APT fell within the InterCity remit.[193] This is not to deny that some initiatives were taken to contain engineering costs, notably the separation of the manufacturing and maintenance functions, the establishment of a separate maintenance company, BRML, and the review of infrastructure costs undertaken by James Cornell.[194] However, in 1989 the full benefits of the infrastructure exercise had yet to be realised, and contemporary reviews conceded that sectors had not made as much progress in managing engineering costs as they had with operating costs.[195]

Of course, there were gains, and substantial ones at that. First, more purpose, more realism, and above all, more participation was injected into rail planning and budgetary control, with the more conscious attempt to look at both the revenues and costs of services provided throughout the rail business. The transformation of the planning mechanisms in British Rail was important. It put an end to the number-plucking optimism of a series of five-year corporate plans, which attracted cynical responses inside the DTp and encouraged references to devices such as the 'angle of unreality'. Managers responsible for formulating plans were now expected to achieve the forecast results, and the plans themselves changed. Originally public relations documents designed to win government support, with the data frequently exhibiting a tendency to 'march to the right', they began to serve as a serious framework for internal action. It must be said that the combination of 'top-down' and 'bottom-up' planning of which the rail planners were so proud had the effect of reinforcing financial control from the centre and thus constraining the decentralising tendencies of the sectors.[196] Nevertheless, the provision of more realistic, deliverable rail plans in turn encouraged government to establish firm three-year objectives for the rail businesses.[197] The focus on the 'bottom line' was also sharpened by the privatisation of the subsidiary businesses, a process which gathered pace when a disposal instrument, British Rail Investments Ltd or BRIL was established in November 1980 as a wholly owned Board subsidiary. After British Transport Hotels and Sealink had been sold in March 1983 and July 1984 respectively, attention turned to surplus property and the engineering workshops, a process which helped the sectors to get to grips with the engineering components of their costs.[198] Second, the new posts of sector director and sub-sector manager offered opportunities for the gifted and less hidebound manager to come to the fore. In the 1980s InterCity was shaken up by the buccaneering Bleasdale and brought into profit by the more assiduous Prideaux, both of whom injected a more professional business strategy and sector-based loyalty into the business. More imaginative marketing embraced segmented pricing, improved on-board catering, and the introduction of standard class in place of second class in March 1987. Provincial, which had hitherto been a ragbag of services expected to be axed at any moment and lacking any definitive strategy, was transformed by the cost-reducing and quality-enhancing investment in motive power orchestrated by John Welsby and John Edmonds. In London and South East Kirby's competence and the flair of Chris Green, who succeeded him in 1986, plus the support of Richard Edgley and Gordon Pettitt, enabled the sector to reduce its burden on the PSO and generate an expansion in business, stimulated by marketing initiatives such as the introduction of the 'Capital Card' in January 1985 and 'Network Card' in September 1986 and quality-based actions such as 'Operation Pride', also in 1986.[199] Railfreight performed well under Sanderson and Colin Driver, returning a record operating surplus in 1988/9. The success of train-load traffic was the key factor, with 'new' businesses such as aggregates performing strongly in the late 1980s.[200] At the same time, resource allocation, which had been based on regional sponsorship, could be more effectively managed with business needs firmly in mind. The example which was much quoted by Reid concerned the transfer of HST sets from the Western Region to the London Midland's Midland Main Line in October 1982; unfortunately, the decision to redeploy the stock was made in 1981 before sector management was established.[201] However, later decisions were clearly attributable to firmer, 'bottom-line' management, including the provision of new trains such as the Class 321 'Networkers' for Network South-East from 1988, and new DMUs, notably the 'Sprinter' for the Provincial sector from 1985. There were also several cases of reduced investment costs following project reviews by sector directors—Reid's favourite was the substantial cut in the cost of a resignalling scheme at Leicester.[202] By the end of the decade, the dedication of rolling stock to particular sectors undoubtedly helped to improve cost control, notably in the freight business.[203]

But equally, tensions in the system persisted, affecting disillusioned RGMs and their dwindling staffs, functional managers in planning and marketing, and overburdened and bewildered Area managers. As we have seen, Headquarters' attempts to alter sector boundaries and accounting conventions, which involved attempts to pass burdens from one sector to another, inevitably produced some negative responses. In addition, sceptics could point to resource and investment squabbles where the value to the network was thrown out with the bath water of sector infighting. Investment decision making provides a good example of this. On the whole the associated changes in investment appraisal, authorisation, and control produced beneficial results, and the intervention of sector directors was positive in focusing minds on financial outcomes. However, elements likely to benefit the network as a whole sometimes foundered because no single sector was prepared to pick up the bill. The ECML electrification project, which was costed with the sole user convention, highlighted the problem. Because sector directors were obliged to ensure that their requirements were being met at minimum cost, they had a clear interest in seeking to minimise elements in the scheme. Thus, the electrification of the slow lines (two of four) between Peterborough and Stoke Summit (Lincs) and aspects of the Newcastle resignalling scheme generated a fierce argument between Bleasdale (InterCity) and Edmonds (Provincial) in 1985. Allen conceded that 'there will be occasions when the application of Sole User principles will not necessarily generate solutions to the corporate good'.[204] Disagreements could be and were resolved by arbitration, of course. The dispute over the Newcastle scheme was mediated by Myers and settled when InterCity agreed to make a compensatory payment to Provincial. On another occasion, in 1986, the reluctance of sectors to pay for *two* lines through the Calton Tunnels in Edinburgh produced an instruction from Myers to do so.[205] However, signalling schemes remained a bone of contention with the sectors. Apparently the methodology was stretching sole user concepts 'to breaking point'.[206] Lower down, the strict application of a sector approach could also lead to difficulties. In 1987, for example, some dust was raised when a member of the DTp's Railway Inspectorate complained to Holmes, the Director of Operations, that the Provincial Manager (Midlands) had refused to pay for safety improvements to a level crossing on the Cambrian Coast Line.[207]

Sector management was certainly in place; but it could scarcely be said that it had bedded down fully or transformed the middle managers' tendency to expect orders rather than assume responsibility. At the end of the decade, when the emphasis in sector operations had shifted from marketing and cost attribution to contracts and dedicated resources, there remained difficulties at Area level, where the operating managers felt a loss of status and consequently good recruits were scarce. Those in post complained of incompetent business managers, inadequate incentives to beat contracts, and poor support from finance (re information) and the technical functions (e.g. re maintenance and repair). There was an obvious need to establish a shared, 'team' approach as well as a purely contractual relationship. As long as RGMs survived, they regarded it as their responsibility to guard against the excesses of the sector approach, while their sector director colleagues continued to view them as custodians of the old, overblown bureaucracy wherein sector decisions were diluted and massaged.[208] A study of the business/production relationship by John Heath and Geoff Clarke (Policy Unit) in 1988, while noting that there was a considerable commitment to sector management among British Rail managers, identified numerous difficulties in the demanding environment of matrix management. Complexity was one element, with over 600 important one-to-one relationships. Conflicting requirements were another, these being evident in areas where no single sector predominated. In general, pressures were being created by the intrusion of sectors into the operating field, by the fact that both sectors and regions continued to consider themselves responsible for cost management, and by the clashes between the centralised, abrasive management style of the commercial passenger sector, InterCity, and the unsupported Provincial sector, caused by the fact that the former's route structure did not square with the Area unit of management.[209] This was evident in timetable planning problems on both the ECML and the WCML.[210] There were clearly implications for marketing and customer relations here. Passengers did not distinguish between sectors, and in fact their point of contact with staff was likely to be with someone who reported to the *regional* organisation.[211] None of this should be surprising. Railways remained a network business, and sector management involved breaking services into separate bits with the managers not owning all the assets. Some revenue streams and several elements of cost—notably terminals, infrastructure, and overheads—were determined to a considerable extent by the application of management accounting formulae. Refined as these were, they were no substitute for the disciplines of a free-standing business. In such circumstances, squabbles were bound to arise.[212]

The rationalisation of both regional and central administration costs was a major expectation from the development of sector management. British Rail had both a large Headquarters staff and an extensive regional bureaucracy, together amounting to about 52,000 salaried posts in 1979 and 1981, with 20 per cent located at Headquarters itself.[213] To what extent was this rationalisation achieved? We have already noted the launch in 1983 of an administration and organisation initiative, directed by Leslie Soane, which followed an undertaking made to the Serpell inquiry in 1982 that 8,000 jobs would be pruned by 1984 with estimated annual savings of £80 million. A major element in the programme was the elimination of the divisional tier in the regions. By March 1985 the axing of the 21 traffic divisions, together with other savings, including a cut in Headquarters posts of 1,100 or 11 per cent, had secured a net reduction of about 6,000 posts (of 6,322 identified), saving £71 million a year (£90 million if associated savings were included). The number of salaried staff had fallen to just under 40,000.[214] The removal of the divisions was accompanied by the transfer in 1984–5 of Western Region's headquarters from Paddington to Swindon, and of London Midland Region's Euston Headquarters to Birmingham, leaving a managerial hierarchy based on Headquarters (including sectors), regions, and areas. The relocation of London Midland prompted the Board to abandon 222 Marylebone Road and Rail House and move into the old regional Headquarters in Euston House at the end of 1986, which reduced administrative costs by about £20 million, and was made more glamorous by the fact that Claudine's, a massage parlour, continued to lease part of the ground floor.[215]

The Soane exercise was followed by further efforts. An administration and general expenses review, led by Welsby, the MD of Procurement & Special Projects, Kent, Director, Administrative Policy, and later by Peter Whittaker, Director, Organisation Policy, hoped to save £50 million a year by the end of 1986/7. Stage I involved an attempt to reduce non-staff costs, together with an additional offer of early retirement; stage II produced an analysis of procedures and activities in three production and two support departments at Headquarters and regional levels: namely operations, civil and S&T engineering, finance, and personnel. Altogether savings of about £22 million were identified in stages I and II. Stage III involved an in-depth analysis of the Western Region, accompanied by other initiatives (see above). It produced by the end of 1987/8 job losses of 2,616, with annual savings of the order of £35–50 million, and the prospect of a further cut of 1,000 in 1988/9. Staff at Regional Headquarters bore the brunt with a 20 per cent cut.[216] In assessing the overall savings, it must be conceded that it is difficult to obtain data on actual staff numbers in post on a consistent basis. Imperfect as the data may be, Table 4.7 shows that over the period 1982–8 salaried staff rationalisation produced a reduction in staff of 22 per cent (26 per cent in the regions). Notable as this achievement was, it still left BR with considerable administrative overheads. Sector directors such as Prideaux were quick to point out that since some of the regional cuts were simply transfers (see data for 1985–8 in Table 4.7), the burden of a large headquarters had not been resolved. Consequently, the issue remained a pressing one, and was taken up in renewed initiatives such as the Overhead Cost Review Exercise (OCRE), led by O'Brien, which sought to attribute overheads to the businesses and move to a competitive supply of headquarters services.[217]

Table 4.7 British Rail salaried staff, Headquarters and regions, 1982–8

Date	HQ	Regions	Total
Jan. 1982	10,770	39,147	49,917
Oct. 1983	10,361	35,272	45,633
Mar. 1985	9,240	30,550	39,790
Mar. 1988	9,974	28,914	38,888
Percentage change			
1982–5	−14	−22	−20
1985–8	+8	−5	−2
1982–8	−7	−26	−22

Source: BRB, Manpower Statistics 1980–4, O'Brien's Papers, Sec Box 2173; Soane, Memo to RE on 'Administrative Policy Review: Phase II', 17 December 1986; T. Toolan (MD, Personnel), Memos on 'Salaried Staff position', 25 May 1988, RE Minutes, 25 May 1988.

Generalisations are very difficult to make about an evolving and tension-ridden change, and the exercise for the business historian is particularly challenging since, as with all businesses, the surviving documentation inevitably tends to emphasise weaknesses and take achievements for granted. On the whole sector management produced a positive, internally generated response to an environment shaped by more precise obligations imposed on the large nationalised industries; and the more important aspect was that it began an assault on an entrenched rail culture based on engineering and production outcomes and values, which could be found elsewhere in the public sector such as in the Post Office, telecommunications, and electricity supply. When viewed in this context the railways' sector management was very much a product of its time, though the lessons learned on the railways were applied elsewhere. Thus, when Sellers moved to the Post Office as a Board member in 1984, he helped to orchestrate the reorganisation of postal operations into three separate businesses—Royal Mail Letters, Royal Mail Parcels (later Parcelforce), and Post Office Counters.[218] Sector management was also a product of broader management thinking in the 1970s and 1980s, which sought to attack bureaucratic ossification, encourage the decentralisation of decision-making power and accountability, and align managers with clearly defined financial responsibilities, trends which Bill Bradshaw noted when he reported specially to Reid on large-scale business organisation in 1988.[219] Of course, there are many ways to organise a large business enterprise, a fact reflected in the management literature, notably in Kanter's *When Giants Learn to Dance*.[220] British Rail's responses might be considered part of a more general prescription for large-scale enterprise exemplified by Peters and Waterman's advice, in their influential treatise *In Search of*

Excellence, to 'stick to the knitting', that is, concentrate on core activities. On the other hand, reconciliation of the liberating effects of decentralisation with the advantages of central strategic direction has always posed problems for management theorists, and it is interesting to note that the same authors were also insistent that 'matrix organisations' led to confusion and paralysis.[221] It must be conceded that the management challenge was particularly acute in the railway industry, and we should not expect the adjustment process to be smooth and uniform in a complex business which was operating '10,500 miles of multi-product plant'.[222]

Did the new system of management help British Rail to achieve its targets and improve its financial results? There is a classic historian's 'counterfactual' situation here, and no one would pretend that it is easy to unravel cause and effect in a complex trading environment, and where the numbers are influenced by the adjustments made in response to discussions with economists in the Treasury and Department of Transport. Having said this, we must recognise the strength of the improvement in operating and financial results in the 1980s, achieved while the railways were still in the public sector. First, four of the five sectors exhibited impressive gains in net operating, 1982–89/90, as Table 4.8 records. These businesses did well over the period 1982–88/9, with the position effectively held in the more difficult trading conditions of 1989/90. InterCity turned an

Table 4.8 Sector operating revenue, expenditure, and surplus/loss, 1982–89/90 (£m., in constant 1989/90 prices)

Year	Rev. 1982 = 100	Exp.	S/L £m.	Rev. 1982 = 100	Exp.	S/L £m.	Rev. 1982 = 100	Exp.	S/L £m.
	InterCity[a]			LSE/NSE			Provincial		
1982	100	100	−294	100	100	−465	100	100	−734
1985/6	147	112	−147	121	95	−270	129	96	−640
1988/9	163	97	61	142	97	−147	143	84	−498
1989/90	159	96	46	138	94	−138	135	84	−509
	Railfreight[b]			Parcels			Total[c]		
1982	100	100	3	100	100	12	100	100	−1,478
1985/6	95	97	−16	115	122	4	119	101	−1,069
1988/9	100	90	74	96	115	−13	131	93	−523
1989/90	95	87	60	86	106	−16	126	91	−557

Source: Appendix E, Table E.2 (subsidy excluded).
[a] Includes on-board catering from March 1986.
[b] Includes Freightliner from Oct. 1988 (when Freightliner was combined with wagon-load freight to form Railfreight Distribution, a division of Railfreight).
[c] Excludes Freightliner in 1982, 1985/6

operating loss of £294 million into a surplus of £61 million in 1988/9 (+121 per cent), and both NSE and Provincial made considerable inroads into their deficits. Freight's results were the most impressive statistically, a surplus of £3 million being turned into one of £74 million, this in spite of having to cover losses made by Speedlink, a fact highlighted when Railfreight Distribution was created in 1988. On the other hand, Parcels, which had turned in a surplus of £12 million in 1982, made an operating *loss* of £13 million (all in 1989/90 prices). Taken together, the sectors improved their net operating performance by some 65 per cent.

Accompanying these results, the PSO grant was cut substantially (Table 4.9). As we have seen, the government requirement was to cut the PSO by 25 per cent in real terms from 1983 to 1986/7, and by a further 25 per cent from 1986/7 to 1989/90. In fact, as Table 4.9 shows, the reduction over the three years to 1986/7 was 29 per cent, while that to 1989/90 was of the order of 43 per cent, although we should note that both reductions were affected in part by decisions taken on revenue-financed investment, charged to the PSO, and in the latter case, by a reduction in the interest paid on borrowings.[223] The central government portion of grant was reduced by 60 per cent in real terms, 1982–89/90, by which time it was over half the level paid in 1979. The proportion of passenger income represented by total grant, including PTE/local authority payments, fell from 49 per cent in 1982 to only 24 per cent in 1988/90. British Rail remained the least subsidised railway system in Europe, and the published data revealed that the gap between it and the other railways actually widened in the 1980s.[224] The Board could also point to other performance indicators which underlined the fact that British Rail had turned the rail businesses around. For example, passenger traffic volumes increased from 19.9 billion in 1979 and 16.9 billion in 1982 to 21.3 billion in 1988/9, a rise (on 1982) of 26 per cent and the highest level since 1960.

Table 4.9 PSO payments, 1979–89/90 (£m.)

Year	Central govt.		Central + Local govt		PSO (central + local govt) share of total passenger income (%)
	Constant 1989/90 prices	Index 1979 = 100	Constant 1989/90 prices	Index 1979 = 100	
1979	1,019	100	1,119	100	40
1982	1,226	120	1,331	119	49
1983	1,218	119	1,329	119	45
1986/7	863	85	957	85	36
1987/8	836	82	926	83	33
1988/9	567	56	648	58	25
1989/90	495	49	587	52	24

Source: Appendix A, Table A.1.

The Thatcher Revolution

Rail manpower was cut from 182,000 in 1979 to 161,400 in 1983 and 128,500 in 1989. Train-miles run per staff member increased from 1,521 in 1979 and 1,495 in 1982 to 2,123 in 1988/9. The improvement in these last two indicators since 1982 amounted to 20 and 42 per cent respectively.[225]

There was also an improvement in the Group's bottom line, though we must take note of extraordinary and exceptional factors which had an impact in particular years, not least the sale of assets, chiefly via an acceleration in the disposal of surplus property (see Chapter 7) and provision for restructuring and redundancy, for example for BREL. Table 4.10 reveals that the Board's overall operating surplus was particularly strong in the four years 1985/6–88/9, a period when the position after interest and tax was also sound.

We must express some clear reservations to set against this picture of substantial improvement. First, sector operating performance was affected in large measure by turnover growth in a period of economic boom: GDP increased by 26 per cent in real terms from 1982 to 1989. This was particularly evident in the passenger businesses. InterCity, Network SouthEast, and Provincial enjoyed a growth in real income of 67, 45, and 47 per cent respectively, 1982–88/9; the combined increase was 54 per cent (Table 4.8). Elsewhere, income growth was less evident. Freight experienced an increase of only 2 per cent, while for Parcels, which lost its lucrative News International and Mirror Group newspaper and Post Office parcels contracts in 1986–7, income fell by 1 per cent.[226] Indeed, increases in income, rather than an effective reduction in operating costs, helped the

Table 4.10 British Railways Board's profit & loss account, 1979–89/90 (£m., in constant 1989/90 prices)

Year	Operating Surplus/Loss before interest. &c.	Surplus/Loss after interest, tax & exceptional items[a]	Surplus/Loss after extraordinary items[b]
1979	116	3	27
1980	−33	−138	−107
1981	43	−64	−23
1982	−146	−262	−205
1983	114	16	96
1984/5[c]	−306	−380	−398
1985/6	71	−14	82
1986/7	84	3	−100
1987/8	125	54	335
1988/9	114	19	325
1989/90	−26	−46	270

Source: Appendix A, Table A.2.

[a] Exceptional items: 1988/9: overpayment of grant for 1987/8—£64.5 m.
[b] Extraordinary items: sale of assets, restructuring grants, &c.
[c] Fiscal year, 15 months.

passenger sectors to reduce their dependence on the PSO grant in the period to 1986/7, a fact which plainly dismayed officials in the Department of Transport and the Treasury. In March 1987 the Secretary of State, Moore, was moved to write to Reid to express his and the Treasury Chief Secretary's anxiety about the failure to address costs, which had necessitated an increase in EFL support and a higher than planned PSO ceiling. In consequence, he proposed to ring-fence revenue investment, track renewal, BREL transitional costs, and rail redundancy payments. This was followed in April by a letter from John Palmer, the Transport Deputy Secretary, to Reid spelling out the Department's worries based on a reworking of the figures supplied to it by the Board.[227] While the issue was in fact a complex one, embracing a host of cost components, including investment, depreciation, earnings, and fuel costs, the Board internally was forced to concede that there was much truth in the criticisms of the civil servants, particularly in relation to operations and overhead costs.[228]

Many of the effective gains in sector operating results were delayed until the end of the decade. InterCity, for example, experienced operating losses in all the years before the government withdrew the subsidy. Indeed, we should also raise an eyebrow at the sudden turnaround in InterCity results from one year (1987/8) to the next (1988/9). Here an operating 'loss' of £86 million became a 'profit' of £57 million (in constant 1989/90 prices, −£98 and +£61 million). It is clear that decisions made to increase revenue-financed investment while InterCity was still supported by the PSO, and to constrain it in the following year (when it was not so supported) were relevant mechanisms to take note of, before congratulating the Director, InterCity on an amazing result.[229] It should also be observed that operating surpluses were a far cry from the profit targets established by the Secretary of State for the 'commercial' businesses. As we have seen, these were modestly set at an average of 2.7 per cent before interest in October 1986. But as Table 4.11 reveals, even allowing for the flexibility inherent in the process, the actual results fell far short of the internal targets set by British Rail in the years 1987/8–89/90. In this sense, the hypothesis of rail 'viability' looks distinctly fragile.

We could say the same thing about the Group's 'bottom line'. The overall performance of British Rail in the 1980s was influenced to a considerable extent by the state of the economy and the absence or presence of major industrial disputes. Returning to Table 4.10, the operating losses in 1980, 1982, and 1989/90 may be attributed to recession (and in the last year to strikes), while the Board was adamant that the large losses in 1984/5 were caused in large measure by the militant coal strike of that year. The Board's overall profit in the late 1980s was certainly impressive; but it was enhanced by large sums derived from the disposal of surplus property, which were credited, quite rightly, as 'extraordinary items' (see Chapter 7). Sector management may have helped to focus railway managers in a more profit-conscious manner, but it would be stretching the definition to attribute such windfalls to a change in organisation. For all these reasons we

Table 4.11 Targets and outcomes for British Rail's commercial businesses, 1987/8–89/90 (£m., in current prices)

Business	Target 1987/8	Actual 1987/8	Target 1988/9	Actual 1988/9	Target 1989/90	Actual 1989/90
InterCity	14	−98	24	−26	20	21
Freight	39	−6	42	23	22	9
Parcels	5	−16	7	−17	−2	−20
Freightliner	1	−12	—	—	—	—
Contingencies/ Unallocated	−5	—	−16	—	21	—
Total	54	−120	57	−20	61	10

Source: BRB, *R&A 1987/8–89/90*.

should avoid making extravagant claims for the impact of the railways' managerial revolution.

4.7 Conclusion

In general terms, sector management represented a positive outcome helping British Rail to modernise its organisational responses and subordinate operating and engineering considerations to the fundamentals of income and expenditure. With all its tensions it was widely regarded inside the industry as a great improvement on previous forms of organisation.[230] Although it is easy to exaggerate the benefits of an ambitious process which was evolutionary and barely in place in full form before it was transformed again, the sector approach undoubtedly contributed to the improvement in rail finances in the 1980s and encouraged a sceptical, even indifferent Conservative government to provide investment for renewal. By responding in this way British Rail weathered the relatively hostile environment generated for nearly two decades by a government thrust towards market orientation and privatisation of the public sector. This is not to say that in the longer run it prevented government intervention, kept the business in the public sector, or won the industry more support than it deserved.[231] However, there was a very real possibility that the railways might have followed their fellow loss-maker, coal mining, into a programme of substantial rationalisation. Since this 'counterfactual' situation did not arise, it may be argued that the strategy adopted by railway managers was sound.

5

The Serpell Report

The Serpell Report, *Review of Railway Finances*, published in January 1983, was the most important policy document of the decade to affect the railway industry. Emerging from a public debate initiated by Peter Parker on the state of the railways and the need for a longer-term strategy, it produced controversy and even acrimony, leaving both Parker and David Serpell with a profound sense of disappointment and disillusionment. Yet there were also several positive outcomes from the policy review. Certainly, its ramifications spread far beyond a narrow definition of finance, to embrace planning and longer-term strategic objectives, government–railway relations, management structures, and costs, with special attention given to engineering costs. In this chapter we examine the antecedents to the appointment of the review committee in May 1982, the internal thinking behind its establishment, the way in which Peter Parker and his colleagues lost control of the review process following a change of Minister (Norman Fowler was succeeded by David Howell in September 1981), and the implications of the report for future railway management. In this latter context the following chapter will focus on the efforts to address train operating costs, together with the industrial relations problems these provoked, and on the steps taken to constrain and modernise the several engineering functions in British Rail, where operating was enmeshed with maintenance and manufacture. Finally, Chapter 6 will analyse the investment record of the 1980s, with particular emphasis on technological change—faster trains, improved signalling, and computerised applications such as ticketing. The implications for safety in the cost-cutting drive will also be examined.

5.1 The financial crisis of the early 1980s

To understand the circumstances surrounding the commissioning of the review we must first acknowledge the financial difficulties in which the Board was placed in the early 1980s, in large measure a consequence of a recession which depressed turnover and affected the financial performance of the public sector as a whole. The trading problems in 1979/80, compounded by a 13-week steel strike, were by and large circumvented,[1] but the following year was tougher. For the railways, there was considerable anxiety, reflected in Derek Fowler's monthly reports to the Board about the dangers of exceeding the EFL and PSO limits agreed with government.[2] The deteriorating position concentrated managers' minds in a number of areas. It caused considerable delay in the production of a five-year corporate plan, which was eventually published, for the first time, in December 1980. This included dire warnings about the effect of financial constraints, but retained optimistic assumptions about future investment, financial performance, and productivity gains.[3] It also stimulated an acceleration of asset sales, especially of surplus property, and a range of cost-cutting measures. Notable among the latter were the decisions to terminate the collection and delivery parcels service and to close a major Pennine route, the Manchester–Sheffield–Wath line, both with effect from July 1981. These were sensitive matters which provoked a considerable reaction from both the rail lobbies and the trade unions.[4] By September 1980 the situation was grave enough to prompt government concessions, including an increase of £40 million in the EFL for 1980/1.[5] British Rail managed to stay within the EFL at the higher figure, but the prospects for 1981/2 were certainly not regarded as being any brighter, and indeed in the event the limit was actually exceeded by some £40 million in that year, largely as a result of the strikes in early 1982 (see below).[6] This time the Corporate Plan had to be recycled four times, and, in the event, was neither formally presented to the Minister nor published.[7]

The short-term actions taken to stay within EFL limits inevitably embraced the postponement of expenditure, for example on infrastructure, which then raised question marks about marginal routes requiring large-scale renewal.[8] This state of affairs naturally revived anxieties about the low level of railway investment generally, a perennial theme which had been raised by Richard Marsh in the early 1970s. The debate about the implications for the rail network of constrained resources, encouraged by Parker and his public relations team, gathered pace over the course of 1980/1. At Board level the presentation of the five-year investment plan for 1980–4, in February 1980, the Corporate Plan for 1981–5 in November 1980, and the Board's Annual Report for 1980, in April 1981, provided opportunities for Parker to brief Norman Fowler on the implications of 'flat ceilings' of investment in the future (cf. Figure 5.1). The Minister was warned that 'service standards in general will inevitably fall at an accelerating rate', and that time was

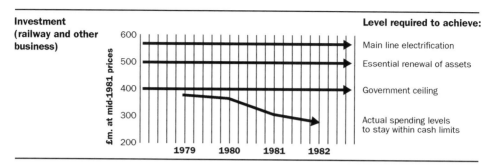

Figure 5.1 British Rail's investment challenge, 1981

'running out'. The existence of the 'crumbling edge of quality', which had 'been with us for some years', meant that it was confidently forecast that track mileage would have to be reduced from 22,000 to 19,000 by 1990, while the life-expiry of rolling stock assets acquired during the period of the Modernisation Plan in 1955–65 was revealed to be a further serious problem.[9]

The Board's position on infrastructure renewal was based on two reports from the then Chief Executive, Ian Campbell, assisted by the three chief engineers, Max Purbrick, Armand Cardani, and Ken Taylor.[10] These, dated March and December 1980, were welcomed at Board level as 'a major technical contribution to future strategy'.[11] They revealed Campbell to be a strong advocate of the view that the physical state of the railways was being threatened. Three scenarios for funding in the 1980s were examined: (1) an increase in investment to over-take the arrears in asset renewal; (2) continuing investment constraints with an increase in expenditure on repairs to extend asset life ('patching up'); and (3) continuing investment constraints with no additional patching up. Campbell concluded that the third—and worst—scenario was the most likely. The decade would therefore see 'either a rapid decline in standards of performance ... leading to widespread random closures ... or to the reduction of system size and business activity to that which can be maintained ... at an acceptable standard to both customer *and manager*' [my italics].[12] This pessimism, but not its conclusions, was inserted into the Corporate Plan for 1981–5 and in a letter to Fowler. The Minister was asked, in January 1981, to endorse scenario (2), i.e. a higher rate of asset renewal beginning in 1983, which, according to Campbell, would require a substantial increase in resources devoted to BREL and the railways' maintenance activity.[13]

Before the issue could be debated formally with the Department, it was fed into a more public campaign which sought to impress upon both the government and educated opinion that ambitious plans for electrification, a rail-based channel tunnel, and the 'developing railway' could not be reconciled with short-termist economies producing a run-down in facilities, and that a crisis point had been reached in public policy.[14] The origins of this position lay in discussion with Government Ministers on railway policy in 1980. A meeting which the Board had in March with Norman Fowler, Nigel Lawson, and Kenneth Clarke, among others, revealed the frustrations on both sides. The Board pointed out that the key problems were a deteriorating asset base, where 'the factor of safety was being eroded', and the inflexibilities of the EFL/PSO funding mechanisms. From the Ministers' perspective, it was essential that the Board addressed productivity improvement and avoided real pricing increases.[15] The temperature was raised when the Board decided to publish a policy document. Its statement on *Rail Policy* of March 1981, which was drafted and orchestrated by Michael Posner,[16] did not please the Department.[17] It began with the comment that 'a crucial decision has to be taken soon about the future of British Rail. BR must prepare to take either the path of progress by re-equipment and modernisation, or that of decline through a gradual but deliberate run-down of the system. We cannot continue as we have done in the past.'[18] At the same time Parker's penchant for consensus lobbying encouraged the production of a broader document, *Investment in Transport*. Published in February 1981 by the major transport organisations (BRB, British Roads Federation, Road Haulage Association, etc.) and five transport unions, it was intended to impress upon Fowler that there should be a substantial increase in transport investment generally.[19]

5.2 The 'balance sheet of change': electrification versus higher productivity

The gulf between the two sides polarised around two issues: electrification and the reform of working practices. Electrification, as we have already noted (in Chapter 3), had been on the agenda for some time. The long-awaited joint Board/Department review of main-line electrification, led by Michael Posner and John Palmer, was completed in December 1980, and finally published in February 1981. History reveals it to be a comprehensive and wide-ranging document. Its main conclusion, following extensive computer-based modelling, was that a substantial programme of electrification would be financially worthwhile, with an internal rate of return of about 11 per cent. In terms of scale, a number of options were examined and it was found that the larger ones, which envisaged the electrification of 2,300 and 3,400 route-miles, produced the highest returns. The largest, Option V, would see 83 per cent of passenger and 68 per cent of freight train-mileage electrically hauled.[20] The review was warmly welcomed by Parker as having a 'profitable logic which should make the case for more electrification irresistible'.[21] It also received favourable treatment in the press, an editorial in

Modern Railways praising its thoroughness and lucidity.[22] However, before Norman Fowler could present it to the Cabinet the waters were muddied by the intervention of the Central Policy Review Staff, and in particular, by Thatcher's request that the review be evaluated by her personal economic adviser, Alan Walters, who until 1976 was Cassel Professor of Economics at the LSE.[23] The involvement of Walters, who was apparently referred to the review by Alfred Sherman, Director of the right-wing Centre for Policy Studies,[24] was viewed with some trepidation by the Board. He was known to be hostile to nationalised industries in general and an advocate of a smaller railway network.[25] Unsurprisingly, he challenged the rationale for electrification. Posner noted that a meeting with him to discuss the assumptions underpinning the review in March 1981 had been 'rough'. There were arguments over journey-time and fare elasticities, traffic forecasts, and the future trends in fuel prices.[26] Walters was 'obviously determined to pick holes', and had challenged the size of the estimated return, stating that 'the World Bank [for whom he was an adviser] would not finance this sort of thing in an under-developed country'.[27] Subsequent ministerial discussions revealed the attitude to electrification to hinge upon the long-term prospects for InterCity and Freight, which were far from optimistic at this time. Nor was the Board's cause helped by the much publicised battle with the unions over its decision to close the Manchester–Wath line, which was an *electrified* route.[28] Thus, by the time Fowler was able to make a Commons statement on railway electrification in June 1981, the joint review had been subjected to considerable critical evaluation inside Whitehall. Whatever the Minister's personal view about the matter—he has since recalled that at the end of March he had 'circulated a paper which enthusiastically backed electrification', the case for which he believed to be 'overwhelming'[29]—he failed to support the plan as a single package. Instead he requested the submission of a 10-year programme of clearly profitable schemes on a line-by-line basis. In addition, as noted in Chapter 4, future electrification was to be linked to improvements in railway productivity and performance.[30] Despite Fowler's failure to endorse the electrification report Parker remained, to outsiders at least, characteristically optimistic, announcing that the statement 'amounts to a concrete declaration of faith in rail as a future industry'.[31] However, the large-scale electrification sought by the Board seemingly remained a distant prospect. Furthermore, the way in which the railways' affairs had been put under the microscope at Number Ten strengthened Parker's view that a more managed assessment of the railways' financial prospects was required.[32]

Higher productivity was the other pressing issue. This centred on the reform of working practices, which in turn required a more determined stance from railway management in its dealings with the trade unions. As we have seen (pp. 43–4), Parker's preference was for a consensual approach to industrial relations.[33] Nevertheless, there was also a determination to address the basic problems surrounding train operating productivity. This had been evident in the document

The Thatcher Revolution

Challenge of the '80's of November 1979, which declared that the unions should 'adopt a positive attitude towards change' and had identified the changes required—in the manning of trains, yards, and terminals; in engineering; and in administration. The document received a mixed response from the trade unions. ASLEF was particularly sceptical, with its president Bill Ronksley telling the 1980 conference, 'this is not productivity—it's slavery', and General Secretary Ray Buckton asking whether the Board was suggesting that the 'prosperity of the rail industry depend[ed] on a fourteen hour day and no meal breaks'.[34] The NUR, led by Sidney Weighell, expressed more willingness to co-operate on productivity, but only once the pay and conditions of railway workers had been improved.[35] This approach was encapsulated in the union's own policy document, *The Railwayman's Charter*, of 1979–80, which may be seen as an attempt to play Parker at his own game. The *Charter* identified a considerable quid pro quo, embracing improved basic rates, realistic payments for unsocial hours, a 35-hour working week, longer annual leave entitlement, and job security.[36] Unfortunately, the co-operation of ASLEF and the TSSA in this initiative was not forthcoming.[37]

Although the unions were happy to talk about taking productivity further, the gulf between expectation and action persisted over the course of 1980–1. The 1980 pay award (see below) was made conditional upon their commitment to 'speed up the timetable for change', and, in particular, to develop specific programmes in relation to freight, parcels, and administration, with precise deadlines for completion and implementation.[38] Little progress was made, however, and in July 1981 a special two-day meeting of the RSNC was convened in an attempt to make progress with the major areas of concern, namely, train manning (including Driver Only Operation (DOO) and the 'trainman' concept), variable ('flexible') rostering, and open station arrangements.[39] This initiative also failed to make an impact. For all Parker's activity, the unions could not be budged from their position that improved productivity had to be matched by additional rewards. The Chairman's efforts to secure a brighter future for the railways by means of consensus had limited success. A two-day meeting of the joint management–union British Rail Council in November 1980 developed the notion of a 'balance sheet of change', with determined action by the railways to improve productivity on the left-hand side of the account, and proposals to be put to the Minister, seeking support for electrification and other investments, on the right.[40] The idea was put to Norman Fowler at an enthusiastic meeting of the Council in January 1981. The Minister described the meeting as 'useful and constructive', while Parker was more upbeat in sensing an historic occasion: 'Everything points to a long-term faith in railways. We are a future industry.'[41] In fact, the consensual approach was beginning to break down. In June Cliff Rose, the Board member for Personnel, expressed anxiety about the lack of government response on the balance sheet. Without something positive, he warned Parker, 'there is a real danger of complete resistance to our initiatives which could lead to a major confrontation'.[42] The situation was not helped by Fowler's public statement on electrification, which demanded even more change on the left-hand side of the balance sheet, but offered little in return.

We must also recognise that the unions had genuine concerns about low pay and declining real incomes, which contributed to staff shortages and a high turnover rate. A report by the Low Pay Unit in 1980 found that the average earnings of British Rail manual workers in 1979 were lower relative to the national average than they had been in the late 1960s, with the decline particularly steep from 1975. When *hourly* earnings were examined the deterioration was even more marked. Furthermore, in 1979 there were 38,000 railwaymen with a gross basic pay of £54 a week or less, that is, insufficient without overtime to match the official poverty line for a family with two children.[43] The Board challenged several aspects of the report, but many of its findings were incontrovertible,[44] and it was scarcely surprising that the unions should claim a substantial increase in 1980 and that the Board should concede a settlement of 20 per cent, together with an undertaking to reduce the length of the working week from 40 to 39 hours. However, this was not the generous award it might seem. Retail prices had risen by 21.6 per cent since the last pay settlement in April 1979,[45] and as the NUR had pointed out, national rates (all industries and services) had increased by 94 per cent from April 1975 to February 1980, while those of railwaymen had risen by only 40–50 per cent.[46] Dissatisfaction therefore spilled over into the next pay round, in 1981, in the midst of the recession.

This time the Board offered only 7 per cent, conditional upon the resolution of the productivity talks, and claimed that it could ill afford even this.[47] A failure to agree resulted in the first reference of a general pay claim to the RSNT since 1975, and an appeal, also for the first time, to a relatively new body, the Advisory, Conciliation and Arbitration Service (ACAS).[48] In Decision No. 75 of July 1981 the Tribunal recommended an award of 8 per cent from 20 April 1981, with a further 3 per cent from 1 August, and a 15 per cent increase in minimum earnings. However, the Board did not accept the judgement. It offered the unions only the 8 per cent, expressing its determination that the additional 3 per cent would be paid at a later date provided that there was a 'firm realisation' of the outstanding productivity issues.[49] The Board's refusal to pay the 3 per cent incensed the unions, who were already irritated by the apparent failure of Parker's tripartite strategy and the 'balance sheet of change'. The NUR claimed that the government was the root cause, and the Board was 'petrified to risk anything', while ASLEF would not accept any linkage between the pay award and productivity. Both unions instructed their members not to report for work from 31 August.[50] There followed a hectic period of bargaining, accompanied by intense media coverage, and complicated by the unions' acceptance of a similar award for London Transport workers.[51] The dispute was then referred to ACAS, where, after three days of talks, 18–20 August, a compromise formula was reached and the strike was averted. Two separate undertakings on pay and productivity emerged. That on pay committed the Board to pay the 3 per cent and introduce the promised 39-hour week in January 1982; that on productivity committed the unions to complete discussions by given dates on the open station concept, flexible rostering, and easement of single manning (31 October 1981); freight train manning, and the trainman concept (1 January 1982); and the driver-only operation of commuter trains (May 1982).[52] By September 1981, then, there appeared some cause for congratulation, but matters were scarcely resolved. The Board had avoided a potentially disastrous national strike, and key productivity issues had been identified. However, delivering on the 'challenge' still had some distance to go.

5.3 The call for a review

Inevitably, the impasse affecting the Board, government, and the unions led to calls for a major reassessment of the railways' objectives, though we should note that a reappraisal was one thing; a full-scale independent review quite another. The circumstances were as follows. The notion of a major reassessment had been contained in several policy documents, notably in the Corporate Plan sent to Norman Fowler in November 1980, which 'suggest[ed] strongly the need for an early reappraisal of government policy towards the railways', and in *Rail Policy*, in 1981, which argued for 'a form of Contract for the Social Railway which will give us incentives, a clear sense of direction and a workable financing framework'.[53] Matters then reached a head. There were several complicating factors. For one thing, Parker's future had not been resolved. His negotiations with the Department, which eventually produced reappointment for a further two years, were not completed until the very last minute, in September 1981, after the idea of a review had been raised. Although he had agreed informally to stay on in July, his efforts to secure a re-evaluation of railway policy were conducted in circumstances in which there was some doubt, at least, about his own position. Indeed, at one stage (June 1981) he had told Fowler: 'if mine is not the right way . . . it would be wise to put in a new Chairman pronto'.[54] Second, Fowler's uncomfortable position between a rock (the Board) and a hard place (the Treasury and Number Ten) meant that all Parker's skills as a strategist and negotiator were required to move him in the required direction. On 27 July Parker wrote to Fowler at length exhorting him to meet the Board at an early date to discuss the salient issues: the railways' deteriorating profit and loss position and consequent difficulty in meeting the EFL target; the backlog of infrastructure renewal and maintenance; and the linkage of the delicate negotiations with the unions over pay and the reform of working practices with the promise of government support for electrification.[55] Four days later he met informally with Fowler and his Permanent Secretary Sir Peter Baldwin to discuss his own position. Some irritation was evident on both sides. The Department expressed its annoyance at the impact of the Board's corporate advertising campaign, though Fowler was more sympathetic to some of the elements in Parker's broader agenda, including the Commuter's Charter, rail access for the disabled, and greater awareness of environmental issues.[56] Parker, on the other hand, was disappointed that the government had failed to deliver anything in relation to electrification, when the Anglia scheme (Cambridge/Ipswich/Norwich/Harwich) had been with the Department for over three years.[57] He observed: 'There is no doubt in anybody's mind that we are going to have to sort out new financial arrangements for the industry. '81 to '82, subject to industrial relations, will be a struggle but we can come through in some order. '82–'83 is a wholly new circle of hell.' Parker left the meeting convinced that British Rail should prepare a set of proposals embracing modernisation, electrification, and the reform of working practices.[58]

Unfortunately, the Department's immediate response, delivered in Fowler's absence by the junior minister, Kenneth Clarke, was bleak. Clarke pointed out that the recession had severely restricted the government's room for manoeuvre, but his main thrust was that the Board's failure to contain railway costs had pre-empted the additional help given by the government, making it harder for the latter to justify more support.[59] Eventually, on 3 September, the idea of a review was articulated. A meeting of the Board and the Secretary of State held at Marsham Street was mainly concerned with the railways' immediate financial problems. However, on the Board's initiative asset renewal and the policy document *Rail Policy* were also discussed, and Parker suggested that a tripartite working party (BRB, DTp, Treasury) should conduct a financial review of the business, embracing long-term policy and business questions.[60] At this stage, BR thinking, contained in a note drafted by Bosworth, was for a working party or independent adviser to examine corporate plan projections, avoidable costing, business sector management, contracts for social sectors, asset renewal, and a financial reorganisation to provide stability for a 10-year period.[61] Fowler was not unsympathetic to the idea, but unfortunately he had no time to consider his response. Within a fortnight he was moved to Health and Social Services. His place at Transport was taken by David Howell, the 'languid, cerebral Old Etonian' whose record at Energy had been less than distinguished—he had presided over a surrender to the miners and had failed to obtain Cabinet endorsement of a major pipeline investment for British Gas.[62] As we shall see, by the time the review was finalised it had changed radically from the initial perceptions of Parker and his team.

The new Minister, as was often the case, had little or no experience of transport prior to appointment. Nor did he appear to warm to the task. Given a ride on the prototype APT, where railway managers thought the train ride 'very impressive', the new Secretary of State was reported to be 'completely unenthusiastic about what he had seen. His wet clammy handshake somehow summed up his attitude'.[63] On the other hand, he had firm ideas about the public sector, having written enthusiastically about privatisation as early as 1970. Furthermore, as his first meeting with the Board demonstrated, he picked up the essentials quickly in relation to finance, electrification, and industrial relations, and, offering a more strategic approach than his predecessor, was certainly not hostile to the idea of a review.[64] Unfortunately his position in Cabinet was not strong enough to ward off the determination of both the Treasury and Number Ten to contain railway expectations. British Rail embarked on preparatory efforts to anticipate the nature and shape of a review. Parker, aided and abetted by Baldwin, put it to Howell that a 'crisp review' of objectives was required, and thought the report should be kept confidential,[65] while in October Posner and Serpell worked on an 'Alternative Policy', essentially a strategic response to lower levels of financial support, conceived as a joint Department/BRB exercise.[66] However, in Whitehall attitudes were hardening. As early as 22 October Baldwin had 'talked mysteriously about who might carry out the review—and even left a faint air of something approaching a management audit', and in December Howell spoke of the review as a way of 'securing a more realistic and consistent monitoring of the industry'.[67] With the situation drifting and deteriorating, a review was seen by both Minister and Chairman as a useful holding operation until the Cabinet could be persuaded to adopt a more favourable stance.[68]

By the end of the year it was evident that the scale and scope of the review were being decided as much in Whitehall as in Rail House. The whole affair was rather messy. Howell and his team were extremely nervous of the possibility of Walters's intervention, and there was much talk of 'being in a tight box' and of 'keeping one's nerve'.[69] Press leaks scarcely helped. On 24 November *The Times* had suggested that there was a split between Parker, who wanted a joint BRB/DTp study, and the Central Policy Review Staff, which felt that a more rigorous scrutiny of the railways was required. The Department was particularly upset by a story in the *Financial Times* on 19 November that the Board was preparing for a 'funds fight' with the government, and Howell complained of a 'Berlin Wall' of criticism.[70] In such an environment it was difficult to arrange the appointments to the review, and more especially the post of chairman. Whitehall's preference was for an outsider, preferably a businessman. While it was reported that Ian Hay Davison, a prominent accountant with Arthur Andersen, was approached, apparently without success, more serious candidates included Derek Palmar of Bass, Sir Maurice Hodgson of ICI, and Sir David Orr of Unilever.[71] David Steel, Liberal Party leader, and Jeremy Hardie, the Social Democrat chairman of National Provident, were also considered.[72] However, no one could be found. Baldwin admitted that people were 'quite frightened of the job',[73] and, in the end Sir David Serpell, the 71-year-old former Permanent Secretary of the Department and a part-time Board member since 1974, was asked to lead the review. Serpell, who in consequence resigned from the Board on 5 May 1982, was regarded by both sides as a safe pair of hands.[74] Parker was enthusiastic about the choice, having remarked some months before, when arguing for a one-year extension to Serpell's appointment to the Board, 'he is about "the only man who could frighten us"'.[75]

The other members caused further complications, reflecting the tussles between the hawks in the Treasury and Number Ten, concerned officials in the Department of Transport, and the Board. In December 1981 both British Rail and Department officials had expected that there would be tripartite membership of the review, namely BRB, DTp, and Treasury—and the Board had indicated that Derek Fowler and Bob Reid would be its representatives.[76] However, any notion that the process would involve an arrangement similar to the electrification study, in which the civil servants would be 'led' to accept information provided by the railways, was dispelled in the five-month period between the decision to conduct a review (December 1981) and its establishment (May 1982).[77] The first sign of a change in the climate was the Minister's decision at the end of March to appoint an independent accountant to conduct a study of the 1982 Rail Budget. The appointment of P. J. (Jim) Butler, a senior partner of Peat Marwick Mitchell & Co., the Board's auditors, since 1965, was the result of growing concern inside the Treasury, reflected in the Department by Palmer and Lazarus, that the Board had not got a grip on its managers in relation to the bottom line. The Department had supplemented the PSO to the tune of £110 million for 1981, and expected 'firm action' on 'unit costs' in the 1982 round. However, the Board's original claim for 1982 amounted to £885 million, an increase above 1981 of about £60 million in real terms, which the Department considered to be the product of escalating costs rather than falling revenue. Howell therefore fixed the grant at only £804 million and dismissed the idea that the taxpayer should meet losses arising from the ASLEF dispute (see below). He asked Butler to examine the Rail Budget in the context of historic performance and the existing plans for improvement, and to advise on opportunities to improve the 'trading results by increased efficiency, cost reduction and improvements in financial control'.[78] Butler's work was seen as an important preparation for the review, but was intended to be independent, though there were clearly difficulties in that a rival firm, Price Waterhouse, was already advising the Board on its planning, budgeting, and accounting matters.[79] Shortly afterwards, the decision was taken to incorporate the Butler exercise into the fuller review, and to appoint him as one of its members.[80]

From this point the review became essentially a departmental initiative independent of the Board. The appointment of the other members made this clear. They were Leslie Bond, a director of the Rank Organisation and former Managing Director of Trusthouse Forte, whose appointment was endorsed by Serpell; and Alfred Goldstein, senior partner of the consulting engineers, R. Travers Morgan, whose appointment most certainly was not. Goldstein was a close friend of Walters; his appointment was visible proof that a direct channel to the Treasury/Number Ten interest had been established.[81] The terms of reference of this four-man team also indicated some shifting of the ground. The draft terms drawn up in December 1981 had referred, for example, to the 'Board's concern about the adequacy of expenditure on renewal of the assets'. However, this was omitted from the final remit, which was 'to examine the finances of the railway and associated operations . . . and to report [publically] on options for alternative policies, and their related objectives, designed to secure improved results in an efficiently run railway . . . over the next twenty years'.[82] And this exercise, now more focused on efficiency objectives than on the Board's long-term concerns, was entrusted to a group which, far from being, to borrow the nomenclature of the political scientists, 'captured' by railwaymen, gave every indication of having been captured by their opponents. As former chairman Richard Marsh noted with characteristic acerbity, appointing to the Committee two senior partners in the firms of consultants 'was rather like inviting the Kray family to pass judgement on the twins'.[83]

5.4 Squeezed by government, challenged by ASLEF

By the time the Serpell committee began its work the climate had changed in relation to the 'balance sheet of change'. In short, the balance had shifted in favour of a more hardline approach by government, seen in the Department's rejection of the Board's investment-based policy options for London commuter services, an emphasis on making better use of existing resources, and opposition to real fare increases.[84] On electrification, the Department adopted an obstructionist line. While the Anglia project was finally approved on 22 December 1981 during a debate led by Robin Cook,[85] the £41 million scheme was reduced to £30 million by rejection of its two Cambridge sections; British Rail had promised a 12 per cent return, but the calculation was considered to be 'insufficiently robust'.[86] The delay, and the withholding of part of the approval, were clear signs that the government was not prepared to offer more until sound plans had been produced to indicate commercial viability for Freight and Inter-City (see Chapter 4), and the unions had been brought to heel on productivity.[87] British Rail, which had identified the East Coast Main Line (ECML) as its first priority, took the initiative in October 1981 by asking Howell to give advance authority to proceed with the first part, a 27-mile section from Hitchin to Huntingdon. Parker pointed out that there was a real danger that Balfour Beatty's specialist construction team, which was about to complete the St. Pancras–Bedford electrification, would be disbanded due to lack of work. When this fell on deaf ears, the Board's frustrations finally boiled over. In November Parker attempted to force the government's hand by making the issue public, but the action only served to irritate the Minister and his colleagues.[88] Nor was the Board's cause helped by its taking much longer than expected to produce the requested 10-year programme of fully costed schemes—this did not materialise until August 1982.[89] Continuing scepticism in Whitehall was also encouraged by critical pieces such as that by the economist, Richard Pryke, a redoubtable opponent of the Board, who, writing in *New Society*, contended that electrification was 'a very borderline choice'.[90]

Undoubtedly, the biggest disappointment was the delay in obtaining approval for the ECML. This was a major scheme, amounting in all to 391 miles from Hitchin to Doncaster, Leeds, York, Newcastle, and Edinburgh. Stages I and II, to Leeds and Newcastle, estimated to cost about £212 million in 1982 (Q1) prices, were prepared for approval in principle, together with a further request for advance authority to proceed with the Hitchin–Huntingdon section (£13.89 million), which was submitted formally to the Department in March 1982, shortly after business plans for Inter-City and Freight had been produced.[91] However, Howell continued to adopt a stonewalling approach and the project stalled. By this time railway electrification had become a more visible political issue. The all-party Transport Committee of the House of Commons, chaired by Tom Bradley, the Social Democrat MP for Leicester (East), decided to re-examine the review. It published its findings in April 1982, just before the Serpell committee was convened. Engaging the services of Stephen Glaister, Cassel Reader in Economics at the LSE, the committee found the case for electrification to be persuasive, pressed for early approval of schemes and the ECML in particular, rejected the notion that the commercial viability of Inter-City and Freight was an overriding constraint, and condemned Number Ten for refusing to release the CPRS report which had criticised the original review.[92] The impact was limited. On this issue, as with others, the emerging right-wing thrust of a now more confident Conservative administration, strengthened by its experiences in pursuing the Falklands War, ensured that it was 'not for turning'.[93]

Continuing doubts about the state of British Rail's 'commercial' rail businesses made it difficult to secure agreement. There were also problems in providing adequate financial assessments, which is unsurprising given the doubts about the case for electrification in purely financial terms, something reflected in Glaister's evidence to the Transport Committee.[94] In September 1982 considerable anxiety was caused by the fact that the detailed appraisal of Stage I, Hitchin–Leeds, when assessed on its own, showed a return of only 3.7 per cent; an earlier calculation of 7 per cent had been revised downwards owing to sector-based operating decisions and departmental pressure to accept more realistic assumptions about the effects of 'cascading' redundant diesel HSTs to other routes. As a result the Board withheld formal submission.[95] Eventually, Stages I and II taken together were resubmitted in March 1983 and again in more detail in May, but without success, despite a forecast return of over 10 per cent. It was not until the end of July 1984 that the scheme was finally agreed, when a new Minister, Nicholas Ridley, approved a revised version of the entire scheme, costed at £306 million. This time a complete reappraisal, conducted with departmental help,[96] rehearsed numerous uncertainties, and concluded that the project only just passed the test discount rate of 7 per cent (see p. 88).[97]

The Thatcher Revolution

The other side of the balance sheet, industrial relations and productivity, plunged into a serious crisis, culminating in the costly strikes by ASLEF in January–February and July 1982.[98] The issue was clearly relevant to the Serpell deliberations, since such difficulties had a profound impact on the railways' planning and budgeting work, which was delayed, and also helped to focus attention on the industry's operating and engineering efficiencies. As we have seen, the Board had agreed with the unions in August 1981 that an outstanding pay award of 3 per cent would be met on the firm understanding that there would be progress in dealing with the remaining productivity issues. While something was achieved—by December 1981 the NUR had agreed to trials of the 'open station' concept and expressed an acceptance of flexible (variable) rostering—the overall prospects were bleak. The NUR was still refusing to accept DOO on the electrified St. Pancras–Bedford ('Bedpan') line, where trains had been ordered with sliding doors, and ASLEF remained militant. The drivers' union had threatened a one-day strike in October over passenger train cuts, continued to express its belief in the guaranteed eight-hour day established by the agreement of 1919, and refused to negotiate at all on flexible rostering, insisting that the introduction of the shorter working week should be decoupled from the rostering issue.[99] The Board, doubtless encouraged by the government's approach to invest-ment and electrification, was equally determined to make the change. Flexible rostering was seen as critical to the containment of costs, which were bound to rise with the shorter working week agreed in 1980 (see p. 157), and the Board made it clear that unless footplate staff negotiated on flexible rostering they would not be paid the outstanding 3 per cent nor enjoy the reduced (39-hour) working week, both due on 4 January 1982.[100]

ASLEF was unwilling to go to ACAS again and on 30 December Ray Buckton informed the Board that his union had banned voluntary overtime and rest-day working and would begin a two-day stoppage on 13 January 1982.[101] The dispute produced 17 strike days which cost the Board at least £60 million.[102] The episode also marked a new attitude by management in railway industrial relations.[103] New tactics included a strong public relations campaign, embracing national advertising, letters to employees, opinion polls of union members, and a tough stance which overrode internal doubts about the legality of withholding the pay award[104] and embraced a full examination of options to divide strikers and non-strikers, including a complete shutdown of the network as advocated by the '"Kill-em" School'.[105] Given the intransigence of both sides, it took a consider-able effort and some imaginative adjustments to the conventional negotiating machinery to produce a settlement, together with the intervention of non-com-batants such as the unaffected unions, members of the railways' arbitration body, the RSNT, Pat Lowry, Chairman of ACAS, and Len Murray, General Secretary of the TUC. The failure of talks at ACAS on 19, 22–23, and 26 January led the other rail unions, the NUR and TSSA, to suggest that ACAS should set up a special commission to try to break the deadlock.[106] Consequently, a Committee of Inquiry

Garland

THE WINNER

6. ASLEF's strike over flexible rostering, 1982. Equivocal outcome in the battle between
Sir Peter Parker (Chairman, BRB) and Ray Buckton (General Secretary, ASLEF)
as interpreted by Garland, *Daily Telegraph*, 17 February 1982.

was appointed on 2 February, comprising the same personnel as that of the
RSNT, viz. Lord McCarthy, Ted Choppen, and George Doughty, the famous
'three wise men walking down Regent Street', in McCarthy's phrase.[107]

ASLEF refused to either attend or submit evidence to this special committee,
which it regarded as a ploy to circumvent the existing machinery of negotiation.[108]
The atmosphere became very tense indeed in an industry not noted for adversarial
industrial relations. There were some extremely bitter exchanges between Parker
and Buckton, not least on the BBC's *Panorama* programme.[109] The numerous
press cartoons may have been amusing, but some of the political comments were
distinctly hostile. They included a *Daily Mail* 'exposure' of the political allegiances of the ASLEF executive and headlines branding the union as 'Wreckers',
an action undertaken, it seems, with British Rail help and one which still rankles
with the union.[110] Attitudes appear to have been more conciliatory at grass-roots
level. Some ASLEF drivers wrote to the special committee to express their dismay
with the intransigence of both sides. A long letter sent to McCarthy on 3 February
by Charles Swift, a driver with 37 years' service and leader of Peterborough City
Council, provides a good indication of existing attitudes. More even-handed than
the union leadership, he expressed frustration about the strike, pointed out that

many rosters involved considerable hardship in the form of unsociable hours, but conceded that there was much unproductive time in existing rostering and felt that there was considerable scope for productivity gains within the parameters of the eight-hour day.[111] In the event the committee leaned towards a spirit of compromise and respect for the existing machinery, recommending that ASLEF should negotiate positively and quickly on flexible rostering within the existing machinery of RSJC (Locomotive Section), RSNC, and, if necessary, RSNT, and that the 3 per cent should be paid. These recommendations, which greatly disappointed the Board, were accepted by both sides on 18 February, with Len Murray's help,[112] but the dispute did not end there. After a failure to agree at the RSJC and RSNC there was a further reference to the RSNT in March.[113] At this stage McCarthy took the unprecedented step of insisting on visits to depots in order to examine rostering in practice. The Tribunal went to four depots, in York, Glasgow (Polmadie), Bristol (Bath Road), and London (Euston), an innovation which clearly disconcerted the railway negotiators.[114] McCarthy had found it difficult to accept the assertions of the two sides at face value. He has since recalled: 'it's on visits that you decide what's possible, what they'll take. This is where you can talk to people, in pubs and in lavatories and at dinner, and you can talk to the lads on the railway, and talk to ordinary people. And slowly you get some idea of what is the margin within which you can work.'[115] But in spite of a worthy effort to tackle the labyrinthine ramifications of rostering, the RSNT had no luck with its Decision (No. 77) of 4 May, two days after the Serpell review had been announced. This vindicated the Board's stance by concluding that the parties should, subject to safeguards, agree on a system of flexible rostering, to be negotiated at local (depot) level, and at the same time modify existing national agreements relating to the guaranteed eight-hour day and double manning.[116] However, once again ASLEF was unwilling to accept the Tribunal's decision.[117]

Further bargaining was complicated by the 1982 pay round, a total stoppage by the NUR on 28–9 June, and an all-out strike by ASLEF on 4–18 July. Negotiations on pay, which began on 11 March, were conducted under the cloud of the productivity deadlock, and it is important to emphasise that while the spotlight was on ASLEF, *both* the non-salaried unions were involved, since the NUR were still resisting DOO on the St. Pancras–Bedford line, and there were *five* outstanding productivity issues to be settled.[118] Talks were interrupted by the RSNT's deliberations in March–April, and it was not until 28 May that the Board told the unions at the RSNC that it was prepared to pay 5 per cent with effect from 6 September 1982 subject to resolution of the remaining items in the 1981 productivity agreement by 30 July and a cessation of industrial action.[119] At this stage the NUR, where grass-roots militancy was fed by comparatively low wage levels, took the initiative. Ostensibly the union's grievance was about pay, with Weighell rightly regarding the Board's offer as 'dismal',[120] but there were other issues too. The NUR resented being subjected to threats aimed at ASLEF, and its Conference had already resolved to strike if the Board proceeded with a workshops rationalisation plan which involved the closure of the Shildon and Horwich workshops and the rundown of labour at Swindon, with total job losses of 5,000. It was also firmly opposed to DOO on the 'Bedpan' line, which BRB wanted to start in May 1982. When talks failed at the British Rail Council and RSNC on 17 and 22 June, where the unions insisted that pay and productivity should be considered separately, the NUR called an indefinite strike from 00.01 on 28 June, though it was quickly called off on 29 June. A combination of Weighell's tactics at the union's annual conference in Plymouth and the Board's climb-down on the workshops rationalisation, which was postponed as part of an attempt to isolate ASLEF, ensured that the strike, the first total stoppage since 1955, was a short one.[121]

No sooner had the NUR called off its action than ASLEF announced an indefinite withdrawal of labour from 4 July. This was a response to the Board's announcement on 25 June that since negotiations had failed it would impose new rosters without trade union agreement.[122] British Rail had maintained a tough line on the productivity issue, insisting on linking it to the pay round, and seeking assurances from government of its full support in the event of a prolonged dispute. At the RSNC on 28 May ASLEF had confirmed its total rejection of RNST 77, and it eventually became clear to the Board that tactics of isolation and persuasion alone would not work. Over 80 per cent of NUR guards were working flexibly for 50p for a turn by June 1982, and numerous attempts were made to encourage ASLEF to try new rosters on an experimental basis, but without success. The behaviour of Buckton was frequently disconcerting, his sentimental willingness to concede in negotiations being frequently 'corrected' after a return to his executive committee.[123] Parker and his Board, which had made every effort to convince the union to accept the rosters, including the sending of personal letters to drivers' homes, finally lost patience. Although the strike, which lasted a fortnight, was not total—about 8–10 per cent of services were run each day—the disruption could not be handled indefinitely. British Rail therefore took the unprecedented step of announcing, on 14 July, that it would close the railway down on 21 July and sack the strikers.[124] The impasse culminated in strong TUC pressure on ASLEF at renewed talks on 16–17 July, and a settlement on 18 July, three days before British Rail's threat to dismiss the strikers was due to take effect. ASLEF undertook to complete negotiations for the implementation of RNST 77 within six days.[125] Agreement was reached on 5 August, and by the end of the year 55 per cent of footplate staff were working on variable rosters.[126]

How significant was this victory for railway management? How tough had the Board been? To what extent was the outcome the product of pressure from the Thatcher government? Certainly, the victory was more symbolic than real. At least it demonstrated that railway management was prepared to confront some of its more traditional working practices in the interests of efficiency, and to take on the unions, which was very much in tune with the Thatcher government's stance. While the disputes of 1982 were frequently seen as indicative of government pressure on Parker and his Board,[127] the evidence indicates that the hard line emanated from the Board itself.[128] Hawks such as Reid, Urquhart, and Rose were patently frustrated with the intransigence of ASLEF, which had been given every opportunity to test new rosters in May and June 1982.[129] Yet they had retreated a considerable distance from their earlier plan to take on both unions in May, and the DOO issue remained unresolved.[130] Furthermore, the government took a close interest in the disputes. If, as both Thatcher and Howell have claimed, the government adopted a hands-off stance,[131] then it is puzzling that Howell should have attended so many BRB/DTp meetings to discuss the strikes, for example, on 22 and 30 June, 6, 7, 9, 12, and 16 July.[132] Earlier meetings had been attended not only by officials from the Department but also by members of the CPRS.[133] Indeed, there were a number of issues on which the views of 'government ministers', presented by Howell, Palmer, or Baldwin, were made known. For example, the government's preference in May had been to refrain from making a specific pay offer before securing agreement on productivity, which the Board failed to do, and to avoid industrial action in the autumn.[134] The government also fully endorsed the tactic of isolating ASLEF from the NUR, ignoring the unions' attempt to effect a closer co-operation via a Rail Federation of Unions.[135] Finally, while the ASLEF strike was in progress there were regular queries about the legality of closing down the railway.[136] Howell may have learned something from his uncomfortable period as Energy Minister when in early 1981 he had been forced, much to Thatcher's dismay, to retreat before the miners following the publication of a plan to introduce pit closures.[137] Of course, we can find examples of government rhetoric and some talk of invoking the Falklands spirit in the battle with ASLEF. The rail disputes may have been 'railway led', but they were also caught up in the government's broader agenda to confront the unions, fed on its experiences with steel, coal, and the NHS. Thus, the 1982 strikes had been 'virility symbols in the Cabinet's mind', said Parker.[138] He was also able to point to some remarks by Margaret Thatcher herself, for example at a Conservative rally in Cheltenham: 'The Nation was now confident enough to face the facts of life . . . [this was part of the] "Falklands Factor" . . . We are no longer prepared to jeopardise our future just to defend manning practices agreed in 1919 when steam engines plied the tracks of the Grand [sic] Central Railway and the motor car had not yet taken over from the horse'. She also told the Commons: 'there is no future unless working practices agreed in 1919 are updated'.[139] Simon Jenkins likened the victory thus: 'We have now captured South Georgia and landed at San Carlos. On to Port Stanley, bedpans in our packs and the guards left far behind!'[140]

   In contrast with all this gung-ho self-congratulation, it was more difficult to compute the economies generated by flexible rosters, since rostering was enmeshed in operating generally, which was difficult to transform quickly. The available evidence suggests that immediate savings were relatively modest, particularly when compared with the cost of the strikes (see Chapter 6).[141] What is unquestionable is that the dispute alienated much of the ASLEF union, a democratically based, disciplined institution, strongly wedded to the eight-hour day, and staunchly left-wing. Somewhat surprisingly, it co-operated fully with railway managers in seeking to resolve the complexities left by McCarthy's judgements on rostering.[142] However, there was still some obstructiveness at grass-roots level, notably at King's Cross. In May 1983, nine months after the agreement, 56 of the 256 depots had failed to adopt new rosters,[143] and the process of adjustment took years rather than months, characterised by numerous disputes about such things as 'padding' and 'balancing payments'.[144] Many felt it was time that this small, craft-based union, appealing to the past and anxious to hold on to a dwindling membership, should cease its blocking of necessary reforms in operating. In that sense the management's victory over the union had more significance for later (and more important) battles over manning. It certainly coloured thinking within the Serpell committee.

5.5 The Serpell reports

The Serpell committee thus began its deliberations in May 1982 during a period of considerable tension in the industry. Its work was long and hard. It examined 94 reports from British Rail and 69 from the Department of Transport, and considered evidence from no fewer than 172 bodies and individuals, including the trade unions, the CTCC and rail user groups (notably Transport 2000), the road lobby (British Road Federation, Road Haulage Association), 36 local authorities, and a number of transport specialists (such as Ken Gwilliam, John Heath, Peter White, and Tom Hart). In addition, a vast amount of detailed material was supplied to the consultants to the committee, Peat Marwick Mitchell & Co. and R. Travers Morgan & Partners.[145] It is evident that there was a fair amount of tension in the process. The team sat uneasily with itself. David Serpell took an essentially detached, academic approach to problems, and expected others to work in the same way. Goldstein, an awkward, intellectual right-winger fond of theoretical excursions and in favour of converting railways into roads, was quite the opposite. The others, Butler and Bond, appear to have made only limited contributions, though much analysis was carried out by Butler's team from Peat Marwick, which included Sheila Masters, a partner from 1983.[146] Their review was completed at the end of December, after much toing and froing. Its shape and content was undoubtedly affected by the direct interventions of the Minister, Howell, who in July had emphasised the need to focus on short-term (i.e. three–five years) issues, and in September, when he asked the chairman to try to complete the review 'by the end of November at the latest'. These requests were taken by Serpell to involve a modification of the committee's terms of reference.[147] The biggest blow to the chairman was the withdrawal from the main report of the maverick Goldstein, whom he had spent much time in seeking to placate. Encouraged by Alan Walters, Goldstein decided to produce his own minority report at the eleventh hour.[148] There were further difficulties when elements in the report were leaked to the newspapers by Will Camp in the period between Howell's announcement, on 23 December 1982, that a majority and minority report had been received, and publication by the HMSO four weeks later, on 20 January 1983.[149] With their doom and gloom references to another 'Beeching Axe' the newspaper articles distracted from the more positive aspects of the report, caused distress to Serpell, and did nothing to improve relations between the Board and the Department of Transport.[150]

The Report itself is difficult to summarise in brief. Essentially, there were two reports, the main 97-page document and Goldstein's shorter, 25-page declaration of dissent. Part I of the main document dealt with the finances of the railway, on the assumption that the existing network and funding framework (1974 Act) would be retained. The committee reviewed the principal businesses—passenger, freight and parcels, engineering, and BREL—then commented on investment, management and manpower, the relations between the Board and the Department, grant mechanisms, and the planning function. It offered several substantial criticisms of railway management. One of the most serious was directed at the planning function. Drawing on Butler's study for Howell, the committee identified numerous weaknesses in existing procedures, including over-optimism, inadequate linkage between plans and budgets in the first year of the planning cycle, and insufficient 'bottom-up' involvement. In reviewing the Inter-City business it was therefore unable to accept the forecasts contained in the prospectus of December 1981 and the subsequent Rail Plans of August and October 1982. The Report was particularly scathing about the Board's hasty attempts to make its Rail Plan more realistic. In consequence, a combination of gloomier revenue forecasts and adjustments to the 'prime user' costing convention had increased the sector's forecast deficit for 1985 by over £90 million 'in the space of less than 10 months'.[151] Substantial cost reduction, supported by improved selling, was the favoured prescription, as it was for the other businesses.[152] Pricing also came in for scrutiny, with the statement that the substantial discounts offered to season ticket holders should be re-examined.[153] Furthermore, although industrial relations and operational working practices were not discussed in any depth, they were implicitly addressed in the statements that railway cost levels were unnecessarily high and could be reduced in the period to 1986 by some £220 million.[154]

Of course, much of this would have been familiar to critics of the railways in the Department of Transport and in the Treasury. What was novel about Serpell was the scrutiny of British Rail's engineering functions, which made up about half of total rail costs amounting to £1,400 million (in 1981 out-turn prices). Here, there was a fundamental disagreement with the Board, which, as we have seen, had pressed the government for a substantial increase in expenditure to enable it to tackle the railways' 'crumbling edge'. The committee did not accept this prescription. On the contrary, with the aid of a report from Travers Morgan it argued that *substantial savings* on current spending were feasible. The committee identified ballpark savings of £220 million, about 40 per cent of which would come from civil engineering (Table 5.1). Better procurement, including the adoption of competitive tendering, was considered to be important, but by far the biggest slice of the savings (about 90 per cent) were to come from improved working practices and methods of project appraisal, including a leaner management structure, much tighter control of track maintenance, and rationalisation in the M&EE function (Table 5.1). The committee emphasised that the individual items should not be aggregated to produce a savings target, since it had not computed timescales, revenue effects, transitional costs, and consequent additional investment. Indeed, some increases in spending were fully expected, in particular for the additional maintenance required by the ageing fleet of rolling stock, an activity which was expected to cost about £20 million per annum more by 1986.[155] But the overall tenor of the Report was that far from requiring a substantial increase in investment, British Rail could function perfectly adequately with reduced amounts, and that engineering costs could be pruned by close to 20 per cent.[156]

Subsequent sections in the main report were critical of existing levels of government subsidy, British Rail's relationship with BREL, investment strategy, sector management, and the relationship with the Department of Transport. It was argued that a concerted attention to costs would enable British Rail to reduce its dependence on the PSO by 1986 and hold on to some of this improvement to 1992.[157] The committee noted that only Britain and India had railway organisations which manufactured their own rolling stock, questioned British Rail's relationship with its wholly owned subsidiary, BREL, and argued that the latter might be sold to the government, privatised, or reabsorbed by British Rail and drastically rationalised.[158] Turning to investment, the Report saw no justification for a 'high investment railway' and doubted whether main-line electrification would meet the government's requirements. Castigating British Rail for its over-optimism in investment appraisal, it suggested that the Board was neglecting opportunities for investing in projects with quicker payback, such as automated level crossings. The priority given to the 'high-risk' APT and the choice of DMU designs—the 141 and 210 (see p. 92)—were also criticised.[159] On sector management the committee adopted an equivocal stance. While a reduction in the PSO was seen to be partly dependent upon the effective development of the concept of businesses, it was felt that the new organisation was unlikely to deliver what was promised unless the sector directors were given much more authority.[160]

The relationship between British Rail and the Department of Transport was affected, the committee argued, by the failure of the former to achieve a financial performance consistent with its plans, though the Board's arguments that government policy was often inconsistent was also accepted. After advising both sides to improve their practices and procedures, Serpell could only conclude that the Department should direct its attention to longer-term policy making, a rather hollow pronouncement given Howell's interventions to steer the committee in

Table 5.1 British Rail's engineering functions: opportunities for annual cost savings identified by the Serpell Report, January 1983

Opportunity	Function	(i) Management structure	(ii) Civil Engineering	(iii) Signalling + Telecommunications	(iv) Mechanical + Electrical Engineering	(v) BREL maintenance	(vi) Total
Improved procurement			Rails/sleepers £4 m		Less sophisticated design + competitive tendering £20–25 m		£24–29 m
Improved practices	Leaner management £30 m	£30 m	Reduction in CWR renewal 1983–6[a] £23 m Weekday/single track possessions £25 m Lower maintenance standards £30 m	Standard installations £3 m Reduced technician cover £5 m Revised signal maintenance £5 m	Improved maintenance £20 m Depot rationalisation £25 m Inventory reductions £10 m	Rationalisation + efficiency gains £20 m	£196 m
Total		£30 m	£82 m	£13 m	£75–80 m	£20 m	£220–5 m

Source: Railway Finances, Chapter 6.

a The summary in para. 6.59 excluded the CWR savings of £92 m., 1983–6.

the opposite direction.[161] The committee also examined the funding mechanisms for the supported passenger railway, recommending that PSO Directions be issued for five-year periods, with a more comprehensive set of identified assumptions underpinning the grant, embracing service levels, closure policy, pricing, and quality objectives. The committee rejected the Board's idea of adopting a support system based on weighted passenger-miles maximisation, but thought alternatives such as direct support to consumers worthy of examination.[162]

Part II of the Serpell Report addressed the requirement to produce longer-term options for the railways, 'designed to secure improved financial results...over the next 20 years'. In fact, the committee only had time to consider a snapshot for 1992, a considerable retreat from its terms of reference. With the help of its consultants, Travers Morgan, it produced a broad range of network options, seven in all, in order to explore the implications of reducing or even eliminating the existing level of support. The options ranged from a fully commercial, unsubsidised railway of only 1,630 route-miles (Option A) to a 'high investment' option (H), retaining the existing network of 10,370 miles (less a planned reduction of 300 miles) (Table 5.2). The calculations were necessarily approximate and took no account of the very large transitional costs in pruning the network, or the

Table 5.2 The Serpell Report's network options and modelled results for railways in 1992 (1982 prices)

Network	Route-miles	Costs (£m.)	Revenue (£m.)	Passenger Deficit (£m.)	Total Surplus/ Deficit (£m.)
Existing	10,370	2,647	1,731	−933	−916
Reference 1	10,070	2,802	1,821	−987	−982
Reference 2	10,070	2,639	1,817	−854	−822
Option A	1,630	727	761	−32	34
Option B	2,220	954	935	−72	−19
Option C1	9,990	2,597	1,780	−807	−817
Option C2	8,310	2,391	1,724	−690	−667
Option C3	6,120	2,125	1,590	−564	−534
Option D	8,400	2,416	1,731	−707	−684
Option H	10,070	2,645	1,842	−848	−803

Source: Railway Finances, Pt. 2, Table 14.1.

Key: Reference 1 Existing network with cut of 300 miles.
　　　Reference 2 1 + higher level of efficiency assumed.
　　　Option A Unsubsidised, commercially viable railway—deleting all services where operating ratio > 0.85.
　　　Option B A + retention of London commuter services (resource costs minimisation).
　　　Option C1 Existing network less worst loss-makers = passenger deficit of £800 m.
　　　Option C2 Existing network with further cuts = passenger deficit of £700 m.
　　　Option C3 Existing network with further cuts = passenger deficit of £500 m.
　　　Option D Network serving all population centres over 25,000.
　　　Option H High investment railway.

costs of replacement bus services. However, the data indicated that the only way in which a *substantially* lower level of subsidy could be achieved would be to drastically reduce the network. As may be seen from Table 5.2, elimination of the PSO involved resorting to a skeletal network of only 1,600–2,200 miles. To cut the subsidy from £800 million to £500 million would mean a 40 per cent reduction in route-mileage (Option C3). The Reference Case Network, Option A, and Option C3 are shown in Figures 5.2, 5.3, and 5.4.

The presentation of a series of options without a strong steer in a particular direction was somewhat disconcerting. So too was the overall tone of the Report, which was equivocal, ambivalent, and approximate. There was much talk of having presented only preliminary and under-researched findings in the seven months available.[163] This may have been a factor in Goldstein's decision to produce his own report. Certainly, he felt unable to accept the emphasis on the short term to 1986. Criticising his colleagues for using the much-derided 1982 Rail Plan as the basis for their forecasting, he argued that revenue prospects had not been analysed adequately, and was much gloomier about the railways' short-term future, feeling that there was 'little or no likelihood' of containing the PSO at the 1975 level in real terms.[164] Parker was also attacked for promising additional savings in November 1982 after appearing before the committee: 'The Plan is not a Legokit to which arbitrary additions, taken from possible future plans, can be made'.[165]

This said, Goldstein spent much of his report in adding a more strident gloss on aspects of railway management which his colleagues had already criticised. Thus, he stated that BR's planning was 'in a state of severe disarray', was more pessimistic about sector management, and highlighted the contention that the freight business was not being charged its full infrastructure costs. He was keener to explore alternatives to the PSO funding mechanism, and more eager to price higher in London, abandon Provincial rail services to buses, and favoured Network Option C2 (8,310 miles), which he felt delivered substantial savings 'for a small degree of change'.[166] Unfortunately, he did not advance his position in a particularly direct way. It was clear that several sections of the main report had been redrafted to reflect his views, though without success. His additional comments did little to give the reader a strong steer. Nor did his conclusion, which required the government to broaden the debate and define 'with greater clarity the policy objectives'.[167]

5.6 Derailing Serpell

The outcome, from the Board's perspective, was completely unsatisfactory. Parker and his colleagues had co-operated fully with the Serpell committee and

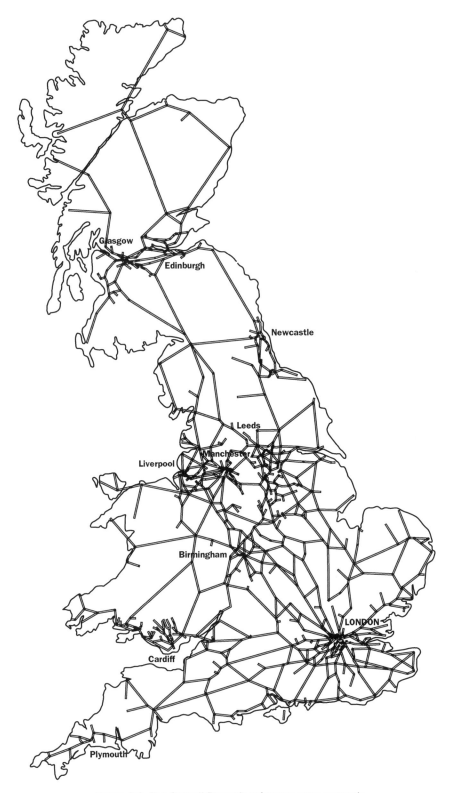

Figure 5.2 The Serpell Report's reference case network

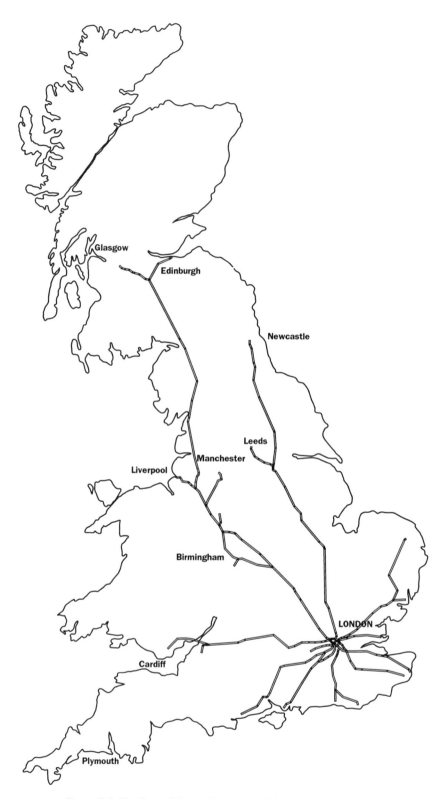

Figure 5.3 The Serpell Report's commercial network (Option A)

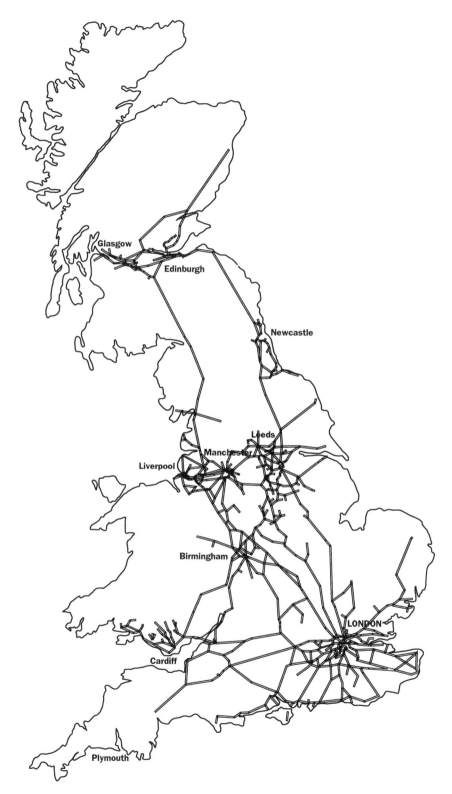

Figure 5.4 The Serpell Report's reduced support network (Option C3)

taken it into its confidence to such an extent that many of its criticisms had been first revealed by British Rail. Hoping for a supportive review advancing the cause of more support and more investment, they got a bleak document which, if anything, argued for the opposite. Worse still, the Report did little to help the government move to a clear-cut position on the railways. The Board's orchestrated leaks in January had focused media attention on the more draconian prescriptions offered for the network and the threat of large increases in commuter fares, and in so doing had diverted attention from some of the more damaging aspects of the Report, for example the indictment of rail planning.[168] On the other hand, Goldstein's scathing attack on the committee's methodology had undermined the government's wish to establish clear guidelines for the next three–five years.

The delay in publishing the Report gave the Board time to formulate a considered response, which was sent to Howell on 17 January and published with the Report three days later.[169] The process was as revealing about the inner workings of the Board as it was about the facts of the case. It is clear that the non-executive members had much to offer. Posner, for example, was adamant that a swift, aggressive reaction was required. He told Parker before Christmas: 'unless we respond quickly, firmly, extensively and (in some degree) aggressively, we shall be driven to resignation, Goldstein will join the Board (possibly as Chairman), the railways will be largely "Beechinged" again and the Parker era . . . will be seen merely as a penultimate act of a foredoomed tragedy—Wagnerian rather than Greek . . . if you (and we) sink, <u>this</u> Marsham St. team won't put to sea to save us'.[170] His colleagues also provided invaluable advice during the drafting stages. Prudence Leith condemned an initial draft as 'rather wet', cautioned against bleating at not being congratulated enough, and advocated a short, punchy response pointing to the dismissal of higher investment in a paragraph and the neglect of international comparisons. Simon Jenkins found the reports narrow, 'brusque and unsympathetic', with Goldstein's 'rather scrappy addendum' more tactful than the main report. He quickly exposed some of the problems with the network options and suggested that 'we should treat Serpell as a bit of a non-event. Much of its criticism is of aspects of the railway which have been built into rail policy since nationalisation and on which government must decide. Much of the rest is already in process of reform'. Robin Caldecote advised the Board to be 'coolly factual and not emotional nor offended', though he was later moved to write to Howell to express his disappointment with the Minister's post-publication response.[171] The professional railwaymen resented much of the criticism and were keener to refute it. Thus, Campbell, who found Goldstein's emphasis on the longer term more convincing than the main report, was scathing about the quality of Travers Morgan: 'the team demonstrated in part a complete ignorance of the most elementary fundamentals and in part a knowledge derived from minor overseas railways operating in completely different circumstances'. Philip Sellers refuted the attack on planning and investment appraisal.

He defended the October 1982 Rail Plan as the best plan ever produced by BR, and argued that much of the problem had been caused by Peats's refusal to accept either the work of Price Waterhouse for the Board or the latter's response to it.[172]

The Board's published response began with criticisms. British Rail was disappointed that the committee had: failed to agree on important issues; provided some unreliable information; made few specific recommendations; mixed policy and procedural issues; and failed to encourage 'the need to maintain momentum behind current initiatives'. This said, the Board fully accepted that improvements could be made to engineering, and that there should be agreement with government on new, specific objectives and monitoring procedures. It also endorsed the Report where it pointed out that a significant reduction in government support would lead inevitably to a smaller railway network, and where it noted that an acceleration in cost-reducing strategies would require additional supporting investment. On the other hand, it could not agree that there were no arrears of track maintenance and renewal or that standards of operating, maintenance, and renewal should be reduced (the superficiality of the analysis of signalling renewal was highlighted). The Board also defended its planning and investment procedures with some vigour, admonishing the committee for failing to recognise that planning was a continuous process. Areas of 'unreliability' were exposed: the potential for further cost reductions had been overstated; no account had been taken of the adverse impact on revenue and the customer of maintenance and operating economies; some of the results of the mathematical modelling were distinctly implausible; the testing of the high-investment alternative had been superficial; and the failure to provide international comparisons was 'an inexplicable absence'.[173]

In addition, there was a veritable torrent of media debate, which surprised and distressed Serpell, who was unaccustomed to so much public glare.[174] Newspapers with headlines such as 'Shoddy', 'Heading for buffers', and 'A really rotten report' provided a frenzy of initial protest.[175] Later on, the media fastened on to some of the more substantial criticisms. First, there was the manner in which the high-investment option had been assessed and dismissed.[176] Second, there were, in Richard Hope's phrase, 'bizarre anomalies' in the consultants' network maps, produced, it seems, by over-optimistic assumptions about the amount of 'contributory revenue' (the revenue earned on other services as a result of travel on a given service) that would be retained.[177] These criticisms were encouraged by contributions from Posner and Jenkins, which appeared in *The Times* and *The Observer* respectively.[178] There were also debates in both Houses of Parliament. In a lengthy Commons debate on 3 February Albert Booth pressed Howell strongly, Robert Adley condemned the Report 'as useless as a basis for decisions about the future of British Rail', and Robin Cook attacked the 'appalling incompetence of the technical work…One's reaction to its quality alternates between hilarity at the high comedy of some of the results and fury that they should be put forward as a firm basis for future policy decisions'.[179] The

7. 'Has British Rail shunted Serpell into a siding?'
Richard Wilson, *Sunday Times*, 9 January 1983

reaction in the Lords on 2 March was less shrill, but there were substantive criticisms from Marsh and Ezra, the former noting that the Report was 'of no value whatsoever in enabling us to make up our mind what we want of the railway'.[180] Last, but not least, there was another inquest by the House of Commons Transport Committee, which heard evidence from all the protagonists and delivered some fierce rebukes to Serpell and his team. Its report of 18 May reiterated many of the criticisms relating to costs, investment, and the emphasis on the shorter term. It thought the inclusion of the extreme network options had been 'positively unhelpful' and, given the Report's reception, 'an error of judgement', and reproached the committee for using Goldstein's and Butler's firms as consultants (their bills amounted to a not insignificant £627,000).[181] Finally, the committee, drawing on a remark by Peter Parker, regretted that so much of the Report had descended to the level 'where the professionals lock horns'.[182]

   In short, the Serpell Report, for all its sound and fury, was shunted into a siding (see cartoon in *Sunday Times*). Shelved pending a general election, and undermined by the Board's successful onslaught, it quickly lost credibility as a policy document. If anything, it created not stability but instability, particularly about the future size of the network, which greatly concerned local authorities such as Norfolk and Surrey.[183] Most disappointing of all was the focus on short-term needs and efficiency opportunities which moved the debate well away from a more imaginative perception of a modern railway and its investment requirements, which writing from today's standpoint might have spared us decades of worn-out passenger vehicles travelling over the south of England's outdated third-rail electrification. Howell paid the price for another mismanaged exercise as a minister. He tried to save his skin by first telling Parker of his dissatisfaction with the Board's initial response, and his desire to see the railways 'move further and faster', then by complaining to his Cabinet colleagues about the Board's 'monstrous incompetence'. But he did not survive the reshuffle which followed the general election of June 1983 and left the government.[184]

The aftermath of the Report was not entirely negative, of course. Before their departure, as we have seen, Fowler and Howell issued a set of path-breaking directions to the business sectors of British Rail which helped to give impetus to the development of sector management (see pp. 107–10). And although the Board had criticised the committee for neglecting the need to maintain momentum, it may be argued that the Report did encourage the Board to pursue efficiency measures in operating and engineering and to firm up its investment management. In the next chapter we examine each of these areas over the period c.1983–90.

Cost Control and Investment in the post-Serpell Railway

6.1 The operating cost problem: pay and productivity bargaining

This chapter is concerned with the efforts by British Rail to address some of the major problems identified by the Serpell Review of Railway Finances: operating costs; the size of the network; engineering costs; and investment. Turning first to operating costs, we have already observed that the attempts to improve the productivity of train staff was a major preoccupation in the 1980s, and drew railway managers into a labyrinthine process of bargaining with the rail unions. It is also clear from the internal documentation that the Board's failure to effect a speedy resolution of all the efficiency measures identified in 1981, and in particular, its failure to solve the dispute over Driver Only Operation (DOO) on the St. Pancras–Bedford ('Bedpan') line, had an impact upon both the Serpell committee's deliberations and the reception given to its findings by the interested government departments.[1] The Board's credibility was clearly challenged by the impasse over the Bedpan line, where new electric trains delivered in March 1982 were left idle in the depot for a year until the protracted dispute with the unions was resolved.[2] Indeed, the period 1983–90 saw a repeat of all the difficulties that had characterised railway industrial relations in 1980–2 and indeed, earlier, viz. attempts to link pay awards to productivity initiatives, which were often undermined by ambiguous rulings by the RSNT; a tendency for the employers to bargain away productivity gains by making additional payments to the staff; and British Rail's growing dissatisfaction with the RSNT, which encouraged it to contemplate modifying the 1956 negotiating machinery, in line with criticisms first made public by the MMC when examining the efficiency of London and South East services in 1980.

These elements were evident in the bargaining process of 1982–3. The RSNT's Decision No. 78 of September 1982 awarded 6 per cent for the 1982 pay round and combined its award with recommendations relating to specific areas of productivity, namely: DOO on the 'Bedpan' line, with guards retained experimentally for six months to collect revenue; agreement to three pilot schemes for DOO on freight services; serious discussions on 'easement', i.e. relaxation of single manning conditions; and an undertaking from the unions to submit proposals for the 'trainman' concept. The Board accepted that the RSNT had not 'explicitly linked' the pay award to achievement of the productivity items, but chose to take a tough line, insisting that it would not pay the increase until the productivity issues were settled.[3] The unions were not inclined to agree quickly. The NUR pressed for special driver-only payments, extracting an offer of £3.50 a 'turn' (shift) from the Board, which was later raised to £5 (a guard cost c.£12 a turn), but ASLEF used the machinery to hinder progress, and the dispute dragged on into 1983.[4] Attitudes within the NUR were hardened by a change at the top. Its right-wing general secretary Sidney Weighell was ousted after a failure to vote as instructed at the 1982 Labour Party conference, and he was replaced in March 1983 by Jimmy Knapp, a relatively inexperienced, rough diamond Scot with left-wing sympathies.[5] It was not until March 1983 that two further RSNT Decisions, Nos. 79 and 80, awarded £6 a turn for DOO on the Bedpan, in recognition of the 'isolation factor', and set out more specific proposals for speedy resolution of the other productivity items. A limited electrified service began in April, but the full service was not introduced until October 1983, 17 months later than originally intended.[6] British Rail negotiators had maintained a firm position, encouraged by Secretary of State David Howell and his officials, but it did appear that a fair proportion of the labour savings had been bargained away, perhaps an inevitable consequence of the low level of overall pay in the industry.[7]

Government interest in the disputes of 1982–3 had been keen,[8] and further progress with productivity was undoubtedly influenced by the battles between the union movement and the Thatcher government, which reached a head during the miners strike of 1984–5. The rail union leaders, Ray Buckton and Jimmy Knapp, presided over executives where the left wing became more dominant in the face of government hostility and public equivocation. It is also clear that attitudes on the management side hardened too. The death of Cliff Rose in July 1983 had not only left a big hole; it also severed much of the mutual respect of the industry's negotiators. His successors as Managing Director, Personnel, first John Palette (1983–6) and then Trevor Toolan, appointed from Land Rover in

December 1986, suffered by comparison, and since neither had a seat on the Board, they were not always able to moderate extreme views generated at that level.[9] That there was considerable scope for higher productivity was evident from the lack of progress in extending the DOO concept. Part of the problem lay with investment, since passenger operating required trains with sliding doors and additional equipment.[10] However, moves to extend the arrangement agreed for the 'Bedpan' to similar services where some investment was taking place, for example on the King's Cross (Great Northern) and Glasgow suburban lines,[11] were once again frustrated by months of tortuous negotiation at the several levels of the bargaining machinery. The introduction of DOO on freight services was also problematic. The issue, first raised in 1979, took a further two years to resolve, and by culminating in a bitter dispute in 1985 did nothing to improve the adversarial environment in bargaining.

RSNT Decision No. 78 had provided for trials with three freight services—Port Talbot–Llanwern and Immingham–Santon (iron ore), and Willesden–Garston (freightliner)—and these duly took place in the spring of 1983.[12] At the same time, the unions were informed of British Rail's intention to extend DOO (Passenger) working to Great Northern services.[13] Railway managers, led by Bob Reid and John Palette, became intensely frustrated by the slow progress made with these initiatives. Negotiations with the NUR were hindered by the union's insistence that the 'Bedpan' operations were no more than a trial, and at its annual conferences in 1983 and 1984 the membership voted to resist further productivity measures, including any extension of DOO.[14] The issue was further clouded by the unions' expressions of concern about safety implications, demands for radio communication,[15] and the reactions of both sides to the year-long miners strike of 1984–5. The rail unions supported the NUM by blacking the movement of coal, and shipments of oil and iron ore were also affected.[16] The strike was a lesson to both sides. British Rail lost an estimated £250 million in 1984/5, £70 million of which was the result of industrial action by railway staff,[17] and managers became more determined than ever to press on with DOO for freight, since the way in which its major customers, such as the CEGB and BSC, circumvented the stoppage using road transport jeopardised long-standing and lucrative agreements for the railways' core freight business. It then became imperative for British Rail to address freight costs and maintain competitiveness.[18] The recovery of lost business was not guaranteed. As Reid recalled when he met Knapp in August 1984: 'I rebutted his view that all the coal we lose could be retrieved to railways by NUM action after the dispute is over, on the basis that we do not live in a Marxist society where everything is regulated, and are not likely to.'[19] For the unions the coal strike revealed something of a credibility gap between the militant leadership at executive level and an anxious, more cautious rank and file, a phenomenon which was carried over into subsequent disputes. The atmosphere was scarcely helped by Board decisions which demonstrated a willingness to exploit the government's new trade union legislation. Thus, in May 1985 British Rail withdrew from the closed shop agreement of 1975, and in the following month threatened to sue NUR and ASLEF for £200,000 in lost revenue arising from a one-day strike in Derbyshire and Yorkshire on 17 January for which there had been no ballot.[20] At the same time the Board were also successful in applying for an injunction to prevent NUR members continuing their 'blacking' of the Class 143 diesel railbuses built by the private-sector firms Walter Alexander and Andrew Barclay.[21]

It was against this difficult background that the Board sought to introduce an extension of DOO. In April 1985 the unions were informed that notwithstanding the impasse in the machinery of negotiation the Great Northern and Glasgow passenger schemes were to go ahead beginning in the autumn; in the following month British Rail insisted that the trial freight services would be operated as driver only from July, while several more were identified for subsequent implementation.[22] Conflict was inevitable once Knapp had described these measures as 'pointing two fingers at agreed procedures'.[23] Guards at Glasgow walked out on 2 August when a colleague was suspended for refusing to work a train already converted for DOO, and while the NUR organised a strike ballot the dispute escalated, leading to a series of particularly acrimonious conflicts at the local level. Drivers refusing to work trains were sent home and 257 striking guards at Glasgow Central, Llanelli, Margam, and Immingham were dismissed for breach of contract.[24] Palette's public comments were notably antagonistic: for example, 'We are not going to accept a situation where the NUR Conference decides once a year how the railway operates' (9 August).[25] Critical to the resolution of the dispute was the ballot result, in which the NUR executive's recommendation to strike was narrowly defeated.[26] The union then resumed negotiations with British Rail and after an agreement reached in September, the guards were reinstated. This time, however, there was no weakening of the BR position. Full acceptance of DOO was required before the dismissed guards were taken back.[27] As Knapp put it, 'I felt I was in a position I had never been in before, where it appeared that some of my members had been taken prisoner, kidnapped or taken as hostages, and I was being handed a ransom note for their release'.[28] The freight services were then introduced, together with driver-only MGR trains from Worksop to Shirebrook and Foster Yeoman aggregates trains from Merehead Quarry. However, the results were neither startling nor instantaneous. By early October 1985 50 freight services were running under DOO conditions, a figure which had risen to 715 by September 1986.[29] Progress on the passenger side was much slower. A dispute over additional payments to signalmen hindered progress at King's Cross, while technical problems prevented the Glasgow scheme from starting until April 1986.[30] The limitations of the exercise were readily apparent. In September 1987, for example, the MMC report on Network SouthEast, which criticised the delay in progressing the initiative, revealed that

DOO had yet to be extended to the major commuter services south of the Thames, though plans to do so on a limited basis from autumn 1988 had been formulated.[31]

Easement of single manning conditions was another important area in operating productivity. The scope for gains may not have appeared dramatic, since 80 per cent of driving duties were already undertaken by one person under agreements of 1965 and 1968. However, the Board's aim in pressing for a further relaxation of the conditions was to secure a saving of 1,500 posts, 950 of them within two years.[32] The unions, led by ASLEF, took the view that the presence of two staff served to reduce the dangers arising from driver stress and fatigue; if single-manning were applied, particularly at high speeds, safety would be compromised. An additional concern was the rising tide of railway vandalism.[33] In an effort to resolve another issue which had been rumbling on since 1979 the Board had offered the staff a 50–50 share in productivity gains, estimated first at £1.50 a turn, then reduced to £1.25.[34] When the dispute was finally put to the RSNT in November 1985,[35] its chairman Bill McCarthy was plainly discomfited by the reference to safety and risk. His concern was reflected in Decision No. 92 of April 1986, which referred to the Tribunal's 'unique difficulties' and recorded its belief that 'issues of safety are not appropriate for determination by the RSNT'. McCarthy awarded drivers undertaking new single-manned duties £1.50 a turn and suggested that the two sides should refer the safety issue to the DTp Railway Inspectorate.[36] However, the Board, in introducing the agreed new arrangements in January 1987, which involved payments of £1.65 a turn, refused to abdicate its responsibility for safety under the 1962 Transport Act or to involve the inspectorate.[37] The MMC, which made a special study of the negotiating process, found the length of time taken 'wholly unacceptable'.[38] Finally, the last of the identified operating productivity issues, the 'trainman', later 'traincrew' concept, was eventually resolved in August 1988. This was in many ways the most important of the several measures to improve the flexibility of train staff. Proposals put to the unions in December 1986 contemplated a major restructuring by introducing the new wage grade of trainman/woman, which would replace the posts of driver's assistant, relief driver, and guard and provide a promotional route to both conductor and driver. The concept offered an opportunity to create flexibility in recruitment given the problems presented by an ageing cohort of drivers, to consolidate special payments into the basic rate, and to improve customer care on trains.[39] The principle had been conceded in 1983, but progress was affected by the difficulties with DOO and easement, and during the detailed negotiations in 1986–8 by inter-union disagreement about training and union membership. As a result, the idea of a single line of promotion for footplate staff and guards was abandoned. The implementation date of October 1988 came seven years after the idea was first raised with the unions. By this time Ray Buckton had been succeeded as General Secretary of ASLEF by the more conciliatory Neil Milligan.[40]

What, then, did British Rail gain from its protracted negotiations on operating productivity? Staff numbers certainly fell. The number of train staff fell by nearly 13,000 or 34 per cent and that of operating staff by over 28,000 or 37 per cent, 1979–90; after 1982 the reduction was 29 and 27 per cent respectively. Both groups experienced larger cuts than did railway employees as a whole, including salaried staff (Table 6.1).

What is clear is that the most disputed elements of management–union bargaining, viz. flexible rostering and DOO, produced uncertain returns in our period. Flexible rostering, for example, was very difficult to detach from other elements in the management of train staff,[41] but the surviving evidence indicates that the way in which it was introduced limited the effective gains. The change was operated through a myriad local practices in the depots, and much depended on the degree of co-operation provided by the staff on the ground. Devices such as 'padding' and 'balancing payments' (see p. 169) not only limited the extent of actual operational flexibility but also served to reduce the financial gains accruing to British Rail. The practice developed of paying staff for excess hours at overtime rates and writing off any shortfall in hours, procedures which were made permanent in 1985.[42] The only firm calculation to hand emerged in the same year, when the *Daily Express* alleged that there had been no gains at all; the same calculation was subsequently offered to the MMC when it undertook a second inquiry into the London commuter services (Network SouthEast) in 1987. Here, a 4 per cent annual saving in train crew costs was estimated for 1984, made up of 2.5 per cent achieved through not taking on extra staff as a result of the reduction in the working week to 39 hours, and 1.5 per cent in direct savings (improved scheduling, etc.). In financial terms, the saving was put at 1,400 posts or £9.7 million gross, £4.5 million net of additional and balancing payments.[43] However, we should also note managerial concern that some of the gains were lost in various ways—through additional overtime payments, recruitment of extra staff, disturbances to rostering at times of timetable change, and higher transaction costs.[44] Productivity was certainly not transformed quickly. The productive content (i.e. driving time, train preparation/disposal time) of turns worked rose only marginally in depots studied over the period May–October 1983, a phenomenon confirmed by public evidence on Southern Region drivers supplied to the MMC in 1980 and 1986.[45] Our view must be that if flexible rostering produced gains they were modest in relation to the cost of the strikes, and the change should rather be assessed in psychological terms in that it prepared the path for a range of other productivity developments. The same may be said of DOO, which by September 1986 had produced a net saving on the freight side of only 344 jobs, and where overall savings were hard to quantify.[46]

Nevertheless, we have already noted that significant job losses were achieved (Table 6.1), and overall savings were reflected in physical measures of productivity. Thus, train-miles run per train crew member rose from 7,099 in 1979 to 7,899 in 1983 and 10,727 in 1989/90. The improvement was a significant 51 per

Table 6.1 British Rail train and operating staff numbers, 1979–90

Year	Footplate staff		Train staff		Operating staff[a]		Conciliation staff		Railway staff[b]	
	No.	Index	No.	Index	No.	Index	No.	Index	No.	Index
1979	26,144	100	38,028	100	77,114	100	104,813	100	182,031	100
1982	23,922	91	35,480	93	66,182	86	95,093	91	161,402	89
1985	20,990	80	31,999	84	60,545	79	88,695	85	147,219	81
1988	18,184	70	27,746	73	52,520	68	77,176	74	133,567	73
1990	16,839	64	25,237	66	48,427	63	72,668	69	129,696	71
Change 1979–90	−9,305		−12,791		−28,657		−32,145		−52,335	

Source: Appendix G, Table G.1; BRB, *R&A 1979–89/90*.

[a] Footplate, train, station/yard, signalling, carriage/wagon examiners.
[b] Includes salaried staff and BT Police.

cent, 1979–89/90, 36 per cent over the period 1983–89/90.[47] Data on revenue per £1,000 of paybill costs provided more ambiguous results, however. The figure for 1979 was £1,537 and for 1983, £1,402; by 1989/90 the indicator had risen to £1,615, only 5 per cent higher than in 1979.[48] How successful, then, was British Rail in containing its operating costs? To what extent were job savings consumed by additional payments to the remaining staff and by provision for redundancy? The published data are difficult to interpret, since the calculation of operating costs per train-mile, for example, was adjusted on a number of occasions.[49] However, the accounts reveal that while two of the major components of railway costs, 'train operating expenditure' and its labour component 'train crew costs', both fell in real terms, 1979–90, the reduction was greater with the former (29 per cent, compared with 24 per cent). Consequently, the labour component increased from 64 to 69 per cent.[50] The internal data on paybill costs indicate that costs fell, but only modestly, the productivity initiatives of the 1980s tending to produce a smaller but more highly rewarded workforce (Table 6.2). Real paybill costs generally fell by 10 per cent, that in identifiable areas of operating, viz. footplate staff and train crew, by about 13 per cent (Table 6.2).

Undoubtedly, the scope for productivity was affected by the overall level of railway pay, which influenced union attitudes to alterations in working practices and necessitated additional payments. In general, as we have already seen (Chapter 3) railway pay rates were comparatively low, reasonable earnings were dependent on considerable hours of overtime, and for unions the maintenance of the real value of the rate was a matter of lengthy bargaining with the Board and de facto the Department of Transport and the Treasury. In the period 1979–90 pay awards in general did nothing to restore the comparatively modest position in the national pay ladder of British Rail rates, evoking some sympathy for the unions' position. Their leaders continued to complain in evidence that they had fallen behind other occupations. In 1990, for example, they pointed out that the basic pay of a 'railman', £33.35 in 1975, was £105.30 in 1989. Not only did this involve a reduction in real terms of over 6 per cent; it contrasted with the real gains made by other groups: 7 per cent by local authority manual workers, 9 per cent by agricultural workers, and 27 per cent by electricity supply workers.[51] After the problems of 1981–2 pay claims were settled fairly promptly in the period 1983–8 (with the exception of the claim in 1987), at levels ranging from 4.5 to 5.0 per cent (see Appendix G, Table G.2). Our evidence, derived from British Rail's Census of Earnings, suggests that in real terms the gain in earnings was comparable with national data for manufacturing and higher than a range of occupations customarily used for purposes of comparison (Table 6.3). For the railways' 'conciliation' (operating) staff, real average earnings in 1990 were 24 per cent higher than in 1979 (a gain of 2.0 per cent a year), though footplate staff did rather better, with a gain of 42 per cent (3.2 per cent p.a.). However, gains were modest before the mid-1980s, and basic rates did not increase to the same extent, which meant that hours worked remained comparatively high. For

Table 6.2 Paybill costs, 1979–89/90 (£m., in current and constant 1989/90 prices)

Year	Paybill costs—current prices				Paybill costs—constant 1989/90 prices			
	Footplate staff	Train crew	Conciliation grades[b]	Total railway	Footplate staff	Train crew	Conciliation grades[b]	Total railway
1979	134.1	191.3	496.8	870.5	287.2	409.7	1,064.1	1,864.6
1983	185.8	270.3	703.0	1,260.0	264.6	384.9	1,001.1	1,794.2
1985/6	199.9	293.4	745.4	1,369.3	252.5	370.6	941.4	1,729.4
1988/9	226.7	332.1	799.7	1,517.1	242.1	354.7	854.1	1,620.3
1989/90	249.9	358.6	877.8	1,670.0[a]	249.9	358.6	877.8	1,670.0[a]
Percentage change								
1979–89/90					−13.0	−12.5	−17.5	−10.4

Source: Appendix G, Table G.5.

[a] Including estimate for staff in self-accounting units.

[b] Railway operating workers whose conditions of service were determined by the first Railway Conciliation Boards after 1907.

Table 6.3 Average weekly earnings data, adult males, 1979–90

Year	British Rail				Construction	Gas and Electricity[a]	Manufacturing	Retail prices, all items, Q1 (1985 = 100)
	Footplate	Guards	General	Conciliation				
Earnings (current prices)								
1979	£94.56	£87.62	£81.06	£89.25	£91.2	£95.4	£97.9	56.0
1982	£148.49	£134.40	£126.25	£138.36	£131.4	£153.5	£138.1	83.5
1985	£195.35	£180.54	£163.59	£180.16	£156.8	£192.6	£172.6	102.0
1990	£305.14	£246.76	£236.82	£251.47	£245.7	£282.9	£250.0	127.1
Real earnings (1979 = 100)								
1979	100	100	100	100	100	100	100	
1982	105	103	104	104	102	108	95	
1985	119	120	116	116	103	121	106	
1990	142	125	129	124	121	133	115	

Source: Appendix G, Table G.4; comparative data for manual male workers on adult rates (pay not affected by absence), from *New Earnings Survey*, April 1979–90.
[a] Plus Water in 1979.

'conciliation' staff, hours worked rose considerably with increased business and recruitment problems in the late 1980s, averaging 52.1 hours a week in 1988–90 (cf. Table 6.4). In order to maintain comparability in earnings with the national average for manufacturing railwaymen had to work over seven hours a week more in 1990. Gas and electricity workers earned £30 a week more than conciliation staff but worked 10 hours less (Table 6.4). There was particular animus during the 1989 pay round, exacerbated by attempts by British Rail to reform the negotiating machinery (see below). Once again, British Rail's senior personnel manager privately conceded the argument. Echoing the views of Rose before him (see pp. 157). Toolan, writing in February 1989, noted that 'BR general pay settlements have been at the low end of the UK range for four successive years ... overall BR earnings have dropped back by about 6% compared with the UK average since 1985'. But in seeking a solution railway managers found themselves in a very tight box.[52]

The government encouraged employment reform while using its influence to keep the lid on pay settlements, subject to the broader strategy of weakening union power. While some writers have argued that the 'Thatcher revolution' involved a 'hands-off' approach to industrial relations bargaining in the public sector,[53] there is plenty of evidence of a 'hands on' approach. The more visible tactic of 'beer and sandwiches at No. 10', beloved of an earlier period,[54] may have disappeared, but the settlement of railway disputes continued to interest ministers closely. The 1984 claim, which was settled promptly by Reid with an offer raised from 4 to 5.2 per cent despite an internal wish to link it more firmly to productivity concessions, involved considerable encouragement from a government anxious to avoid a confrontation with both miners and railway staff, as was evident from documents leaked to the *Daily Mirror*.[55] The internal documentation confirms the position,[56] but in any case, government directives on sector profit targets and the PSO severely constrained British Rail's room for manoeuvre. Frustration on both sides was thus inevitable. From the management perspective, there was frustration with the delays inherent in the bargaining process, a desire to streamline the cumbersome, time-consuming, and expensive machinery of negotiation established in 1956, and irritation with the deliberations of McCarthy as chairman of the RSNT.

Reform of the five-level machinery[57] had been mooted several times, and was clearly in need of change, particularly since worker representation had not been reduced in line with cuts in the railway workforce. In 1987, for example, there was on average one representative for every 13 employees at regional level, and a four-representative LDC for as few as 35 employees.[58] The MMC's report of 1980 had highlighted the issue, and successive Secretaries of State, Howell (in 1981) and Ridley (in 1983), wrote to Parker to encourage reform.[59] In February 1983 Rose presented a detailed paper to the Board Executive which examined the possibilities, while Parker made the issue more public when, in the middle of the 'Bedpan' dispute, he complained that the procedures were 'too damned

Table 6.4 British Rail staff basic rates and hours worked, 1979–90

Year	Rates (Current prices)			Hours worked						
	British Rail			British Rail				Construction	Gas and Electricity[b]	Manufacturing
	Drivers	Guard/Conductor	Railman	Foot-plate	Guard	General	Conciliation			
1979	£74.20	£55.15	£44.95	45.2	50.5	53.8	51.8	46.5	44.7	46.0
1982	£110.40	£86.35	£69.10	44.7	48.0	51.8	49.2	44.6	43.0	43.8
1985	£126.85	£99.25	£82.60	45.3	49.7	53.2	50.7	44.4	41.0	44.6
1990	£184.30	£142.20[a]	£115.10	48.3	51.8	55.1	52.2	46.0	42.4	45.2
Real rates (1979 = 100)				**Index (1979 = 100)**						
1979	100	100	100	100	100	100	100	100	100	100
1982	100	105	103	99	95	96	95	96	96	95
1985	102	108	110	100	98	99	98	95	92	97
1990	112	116	115	107	103	102	101	99	95	98

Source: Appendix G, Table G.3.
[a] Conductor (grade change).
[b] Plus Water in 1979.

193

slow'.[60] Palette then made efforts to address the problem of the RSNT, whose 'pseudo-railway experts' were being over-used by unions with 'nothing to lose'.[61] In addition, pressure for a slimmer, more decentralised structure built up from the business itself, as a result of the restructuring of functions such as manufacturing and maintenance (see pp. 203–6) and the growing emphasis on areas within sector management (see pp. 131–2). The NUR was implacable in its opposition, however. There was much talk of reform at special joint committee meetings convened for the purpose between December 1983 and April 1986, but nothing was achieved, and the MMC's report of 1987 was particularly critical of this aspect of British Rail's performance.[62] At the same time, the refusal of the unions to agree to management's nomination of a successor to McCarthy as chairman of the RSNT was another unsatisfactory episode in the railways' industrial relations. British Rail had tried to replace McCarthy when his term of office expired in November 1983. While he agreed to continue on an ad hoc basis, Palette approached Ian Buchanan, an economist from Dundee University, whose experience as an ACAS arbitrator and chairman of the London Regional Transport Wages Board (since 1980) made him a sound candidate.[63] The TSSA eventually accepted Buchanan's nomination, but the NUR and ASLEF favoured John Hughes, Principal of Ruskin College, Oxford, and union nominee on the London Regional Transport Wages Board.[64] The impasse lasted three years before McCarthy finally stepped down in November 1986, and the unions, following an appeal to ACAS, withdrew their objection to Buchanan. He was appointed in May 1987.[65] There was also disappointment with the 'Worthing Agreement' reached with the unions in September 1984. For some time there had been dissatisfaction with a failure to resolve local disputes, particularly over changes in flexible rostering, and the unions pressed for an additional tier of negotiation. Management and union officials met at a hotel during the TUC Conference to discuss a number of issues raised by the 1984 Rail Plan, including line closures, depot and workshop rationalisation, and timetable changes. It was then agreed that an additional tier be inserted into the machinery above the level of sectional council in 'exceptional circumstances'. However, after a year of operation, Chris Green of Scotrail, reporting on behalf of the General Managers, informed the Railway Executive that there was plentiful evidence to show that the agreement had been 'used to cause procrastination in unpopular schemes', and had added to costs.[66] All this made railway managers willing collaborators in a tougher approach to the unions, which has been characterised by industrial relations expert Andrew Pendleton as 'hard human resource management'.[67]

These strands came together in a major dispute with the unions in 1989, which culminated in Trevor Toolan's resignation as MD Personnel and more indirectly in the retirement of David Kirby as Vice-Chairman. Toolan had been recruited by Bob Reid and Geoff Myers to undertake a range of necessary reforms in the personnel field, notably in training and development, managerial incentives and appraisal, graduate recruitment, and equal opportunities.[68] He joined British Rail after parting company with Land Rover following the failure of an MBO initiative, and was expected to continue the tougher line with the unions pursued for some time. He was well equipped to do so, ruffling feathers with the introduction of individual and performance-related contracts for 9,300 middle managers in 1988, which had the effect of removing their unions, TSSA and BTOG, from the pay bargaining process for managers.[69] Above all, it was expected that he would progress the necessary reform of the negotiating machinery. His efforts to do so coincided with the 1989 pay round, provoking the hostility of the NUR, which by this time had become more militant than ASLEF.

The events were as follows. In the autumn of 1987 British Rail developed radical proposals, contemplating a firmer focus on the Area tier of management (replacing the LDCs and sectional councils by local representatives and area councils), and a streamlining at national level (replacing the RSJC and RSNC). These reforms, which were in line with the MMC's recommendations, were seen as a prelude to the further decentralisation of bargaining.[70] When put to the unions in February 1988 they evoked a hostile response. The NUR leadership in particular was concerned about the perceived threat to its national power base. In addition, the general environment surrounding staff issues was being soured by an escalation in the number of local disputes as the empowered sector managers, now reaching down to area level, set about cost-cutting initiatives (see pp. 143–4).[71] Undaunted, on 1 November 1988 the Board gave the unions the necessary 12 months' notice of its intention to alter the machinery. By this time, the plans for decentralisation of bargaining had crystallised in favour of *functional* rather than *sectoral* change, building upon the existing separation of bargaining for staff in BREL, Freightliners, and the catering services (Travellers Fare, InterCity On-board services).[72] However, the NUR maintained an implacable hostility to any change.[73]

The unions' attitudes to change were scarcely mollified by the parallel negotiation over the pay claim for 1989/90. With inflation and pay awards rising sharply, Toolan recognised that British Rail ought to be relatively generous, particularly in the South-East where labour turnover had risen sharply.[74] However, the agreed strategy was to adopt a firm stance. In March and April 1989 the Board made offers of 6.7 and 7 per cent, then on 9 May elected to impose a 7 per cent increase on the unions pending a reference to the RSNT initiated by the TSSA.[75] The climate had been set by the uncompromising treatment of managers (see above), and the insistence on a revised pay and grading structure for signal and telecommunications staff in May 1988.[76] After a ballot the NUR embarked on a series of six one-day strikes over the period 21 June to 26 July; they were supported from 12 July by industrial action from ASLEF (a ban on overtime and rest-day working). The TSSA meanwhile went to the RSNT, where the recommendation on 7 July, influenced by new evidence of higher inflation, was an unconditional award of 8.8 per cent. The Board at first insisted on negotiating for a differential in favour of the TSSA, who had not gone on strike, and to offer 8.8

per cent 'with strings', in order to claw back the additional cost. However, it quickly caved in to offer 8.8 per cent 'without strings' on 15 July. ASLEF and the TSSA accepted this on 17 and 18 July, but the NUR took further industrial action and did not reach a settlement until 27 July.[77] The dispute attracted a particularly bad press. First of all, the handling of the dispute left much to be desired. It was conceded that Toolan and his colleagues had failed to anticipate the firmness of the unions' response, and that the NUR had 'out-manoeuvred' the Board.[78] Furthermore, Toolan was unused to the full glare of publicity a railway strike produced, and his televisual style was unappealing. With John Welsby sidelined in hospital, the interventions at critical stages of others, such as David Kirby and David Rayner, left much to be desired.[79] Second, tactical mistakes were clearly made. It was a major mistake to combine the pay and machinery issues simultaneously given the absence of an overriding organisational argument for reform and the hostile mood of the NUR.[80] Furthermore, the decision to approach the High Court for an injunction to halt the strike was with hindsight a disaster. British Rail had followed London Transport in going to court to seek an injunction,[81] but unlike their London colleagues had suffered an embarrassing defeat, both in the High Court and on appeal. The action, taken by Toolan after hasty consultation with Kirby and Derek Fowler, had the effect of completely undermining the authority of his Director, Employee Relations, Paul Watkinson, who was about to start negotiations with the unions at ACAS on 16 June when the instruction came to tell Knapp: 'see you in court'.[82] The episode also gravely affected the Board's authority. Toolan had taken the action on the assurance of counsel that there was an excellent chance of obtaining an injunction—insiders put it at 99.9 per cent. The defeats in the High Court and on appeal merely strengthened the resolve of the NUR hardliners.[83] Finally, the Board's position with the unions was weakened by the conjunction of rising inflation, the publication (on 5 July) of the railways' best ever financial results, the spectre of privatisation, and the distressing experience with accidents in 1988–9, of which Clapham (12 December 1988) was clearly the worst.[84]

After an internal inquest on what went wrong conducted by the personnel and public relations departments in the early autumn of 1989[85] Toolan was badly compromised. Reid had already told him that his position had become untenable, and in October steps were taken to obtain his resignation.[86] This took place with effect from July 1990, timed to follow Welsby's appointment as chief executive and a reorganisation of the personnel department.[87] We should have some sympathy with him. It may have been true that as an outsider he never enjoyed the full support of his senior colleagues; certainly, his approach often disconcerted, combining as it did an intractability with a remoteness bordering on academic detachment. However, the conduct of strikes is a collective responsibility, and it was his misfortune to experience interference at key moments both from the more hawkish members of the Board, such as Allen Sheppard, Richard Tookey, and Oscar De Ville, and from the government.[88] Once again, we should not ignore the influence of Whitehall in the conduct of the strike. As a senior railway manager has put it, there appear to have been 'political' motives on both sides, the NUR keen to make up ground lost during the miners strike, the government anxious not to lose its hold on the unions.[89] Thus, the Department gave full backing for imposing the 7 per cent offer, and was closely involved in the tricky and ultimately unsuccessful negotiating position taken after the RSNT decision.[90] The Board then softened its approach to industrial relations somewhat, particularly in the wake of the Clapham accident inquiry, and extended, first to January 1990, then indefinitely, its deadline for changing the negotiating machinery. For the time being, the issue was pursued in a more gentle fashion.[91] The difficulties coincided with signs that Reid was losing his grip, and took the edge off the good financial results of 1985/6–88/9. The legacy of Toolan's period was not entirely negative; he gave some impetus to the necessary reform of a traditional, male-dominated working environment, and the work on the bargaining structure bore fruit later at the time of the Organising for Quality (OfQ) reorganisation and privatisation (see p. 299).[92] But the events of 1989 demonstrated the limitations of adversarial labour relations and the difficulties the Board faced in trying to increase the pace of change. The perceived failures of bargaining in 1989, combined with the unlucky convergence of three major rail accidents, encouraged critics who had already begun to talk of privatisation.

6.2 Rationalising the network

When we turn to the rail network, we find that the scare stories about an extensive contraction, current at the time of the Serpell Review in 1983, proved to be completely wide of the mark. As Table 6.5 indicates, there was some reduction in the route-mileage available to the freight business, which is scarcely surprising given the decline in the wagon-load business, the reduction amounting to about 14 per cent, 1975–90, from 10,700 to 9,200 miles. There was also a 75 per cent reduction in the number of freight stations and a 50 per cent reduction in the track-mileage of sidings, a rationalisation comparable in scale with that in the decade after the Beeching Report (Table 6.5). But things were altogether different with passenger traffic. Although uncompromising managers such as Reid and Myers may have wanted to prune the loss-making, marginal routes, such intentions were moderated by the political opposition, both formal and informal, which rail closures invariably attracted. The result was that the network open to passenger traffic was only 70 miles less in 1990 than in 1975 (8,967; 8,897), in line with the directive in the 1974 Act, while the overall route-mileage fell by only 8 per cent (11,258; 10,307). While about 50 closures were effected in the

Table 6.5 Network size, passenger and freight facilities (stations), 1965–90

Date[a]	Route-mileage			Stations/depots		Track-mileage		
	Open to freight	Open to passengers	Total mileage	Freight (no.)	Passengers (no.)	Running	Sidings	All
1965	14,920	10,884	14,920	1,934	3,161	29,898	11,457	41,355
1973[b]	10,770	8,932	11,326	542	2,355	22,561	6,826	29,387
1975	10,723	8,967	11,258	497	2,358	22,401	6,471	28,872
1982	9,985	8,930	10,706	339	2,369	21,306	4,799	26,105
1985	9,563	8,888	10,441	145	2,376	20,676	4,022	24,698
1990	9,249	8,897	10,307	125	2,471	20,271	3,247	23,518
Percentage change								
1965–75	−28	−18	−25	−74	−25	−25	−44	−30
1975–90	−14	−1	−8	−75	+8	−10	−50	−19

Source: Gourvish, *British Railways*, pp. 427, 437; BRB, *R&A 1973–89/90*.
[a] 31 Dec., 1965–82; 31 March, 1985–90.
[b] As corrected 1974.

period 1980–9, most of them involved freight-only branches, minor stations, or station relocations. The only substantial closures were the Sheffield–Wath–Woodhead freight line in 1981 (discussed in Chapter 5), and a handful of passenger closures, Paisley–Kilmacolm, Sanderstead–Elmers End, and Huddersfield–Clayton (West) (1983), Tunbridge Wells–Eridge and Stratford–Tottenham Hale (1985).[93] The losses were more than made up by the gains, with the opening of over 160 new stations, producing a net increase of 113 or 5 per cent (Table 6.5).[94] Most of these were the product of initiatives and experiments funded by the local authority PTEs under section 20 of the Transport Act 1968. They were given impetus by a 1981 amendment to the Transport Act 1962 which exempted such 'experiments' from the extended closure procedures to which other lines and services were subject (the Speller Amendment), and by a joint British Rail/Association of County Councils *Review of Rural Railways* in 1984, which made 25 recommendations designed to encourage the retention and development of rural railways, including proposals for more flexible funding.[95] About 20 new routes or services were introduced or reintroduced. They included: the revival of Network SouthEast's North London line, boosted by the GLC-financed electrification of the Dalston–North Woolwich section in 1985, and further work in 1986–7 following the closure of Broad Street station; the Farringdon–Blackfriars section of the line to form London's north–south route, Thameslink, in May 1988; the Edinburgh–Livingston–Bathgate route in 1986, the first reintroduction of passenger services to a closed branch line outside the PTE areas since the time of Beeching; and Morecambe–Heysham, Coventry–Nuneaton, Coatbridge–Motherwell, Cardiff City (all in 1987), Aberdare (1988), and Hednesford–Walsall (1989).[96] The Bathgate initiative, funded from a variety of sources, was a particular success, making an operating profit of £224,000 in the second year of operation.[97]

This is not to say that British Rail faced no serious battles with the rail lobby. The most significant of these involved the Leeds–Settle–Carlisle line, a 72.5-mile north–south route which ran through underpopulated country, with the imposing but deteriorating Ribblehead Viaduct a potent symbol of the railways' 'crumbling edge'. Myers pressed for closure in 1983. A heavy maintenance liability, put at £10 million over five years, half of it to be spent on Ribblehead, was enough to produce 'a clear case for route closure'.[98] British Rail had done little to develop the service. Local trains had been withdrawn in 1970, freight trains were diverted, and when Inter-City services were re-routed in 1982 there were only two trains a day and only two intermediate stations, prompting suggestions that the service had been deliberately run down.[99] The Board's position, expressed by Reid in a letter to one of the local MPs in November 1988, remained firm that the line was 'no longer required by us'.[100] However, the proposal to close the route, together with the associated Hellifield–Blackburn line, published in December 1983, met protracted and highly politicised resistance, and a vigorous campaign was conducted by local authorities, tourist boards, and pressure groups, who had encouraged leisure interest in the line from 1975. British Rail's determination to press ahead was dented somewhat by the legal challenge of Brent Council to the proposed closure of Marylebone station in 1985, which raised the issue of disclosure of information and made the Board aware that the steps to be taken should be carefully considered and entirely constitutional.[101] In March 1986 the closure case for Leeds–Settle–Carlisle and Blackburn–Hellifield was considered by the TUCCs, which criticised BR for declining to release financial information and 'emphatically' recommended that consent be refused.[102] On top of this, the Settle line enjoyed a significant revival. The Board's anxiety to avoid charges of undermining the line led to improved marketing under a designated manager (Ron Cotton), while the local authorities decided to fund the reopening of eight intermediate stations in July 1986. As a result, passenger journeys trebled and revenue doubled from 1983 to 1986/7.[103] This created the danger of a judicial review on the grounds that the information underpinning the TUCCs' decision had become out of date, and there was pressure for BR to make its data publicly available.[104] The calculations, published in outline in December 1986, were that closure would save between £156,000 and £956,000 a year on operating account, while retention would involve expenditure of £3.5–£5.2 million on capital account (including £2.7–£4.3 million on Ribblehead Viaduct). On a net present value basis the cost of retention was between £4 and £14 million in 1986/7 prices.[105] In May 1988 a harassed Secretary of State, Paul Channon, and his Transport Minister, David Mitchell, declared that they were 'minded to give consent to closure' to both lines, but had decided to defer a final decision to allow new information to be assessed (British Rail was asked to undertake a trial repair of a Ribblehead arch), and to give an opportunity for the line to be offered to the private sector.[106] Meanwhile British Rail produced a revised financial case in October 1988. This, which was also made public, acknowledged that there had been a recent surge in passenger use, the estimate for 1988/9 of £1.7 million in revenue and 450,000 passengers being four and five times the 1983 figures respectively. Operating savings were now thought to lie within the range £69,000–£1.18 million, and the cost of maintaining Ribblehead to lie towards the lower bound at £2.75 million. Capital costs were reassessed at £2.4 million, only £0.9 million if contributions to the repair of Ribblehead promised by English Heritage and the local authorities were taken into account. The NPV cost of retention was put at £3–14 million in 1988/9 prices excluding these contributions.[107] An invitation to tender for the line was made in the autumn and by the end of the year had produced 12 bids. Of these nine were rejected, and two were regarded as serious, though their finances gave 'cause for unease'.[108] Transport Minister Michael Portillo suggested the idea of a joint BR/private-sector venture, but legal/PSO implications made this unacceptable.[109] The preferred bidder, Cumbrian Railways, found it difficult to complete the purchase, then amid the continued opposition of the TUCCs, strong protests from the local authorities, the intervention of English Heritage, and the threat of a judicial review, Channon intervened in April 1989 to tell Reid that he had refused his consent to closure.[110] The result was embarrassment for British Rail and Provincial in particular, and a considerable amount of wasted management time. With hindsight it might have been better to have developed the route within a cost-cutting policy.[111]

Bus substitution and road-rail conversion were also residual legacies of the Serpell Review. The substitution of bus services for rail, a recommendation of the Serpell Review, endorsed by the House of Commons Transport Committee, had, as we have seen, already engaged the attention of railway managers (see Chapter 3, pp. 62–3). In September 1982 and October 1983 Welsby, then Director, Provincial, produced two further reports. The first, which was submitted to the Serpell committee, was a detailed feasibility study which examined the financial effect on seven routes (Appendix J, Table J.2). It concluded that although in theory 40 or so services might be replaced at a lower cost, existing uncertainty about costs and quality were such as to raise question about the policy as a general prescription.[112] The second, part of a joint DTp/BRB response to Serpell, examined the legal, procedural, and financial implications of bus substitution.[113] At the same time the Department of Transport threw its weight behind the idea. In setting objectives in October 1983 Ridley pressed for the Board's early views on 'the practicality of introducing some guaranteed and subsidised bus services', and Reid accepted that 'suitable bus services have a useful part to play in giving greater value for money . . . for perhaps ultimately up to a quarter of provincial services'.[114] The joint review, *Rural Railways*, also supported the concept, producing seven recommendations emphasising the need for co-operation with local authorities. The Provincial Sector undertook further work on 10 cases, of which two were examined in detail (see Appendix J, Table J.2); the results, which were regarded as equivocal and deserving of further study, were sent to the Under-Secretary of State in December 1985. The 10 cases were estimated to produce savings of only £2–6 million per annum.[115] By this time legislation in the form of the Transport Act 1985 had been produced to give replacement bus services the same status as rail services in relation to subsidisation and closure mechanisms.[116]

However, despite the apparent consensus in favour of bus substitution, and a repeat of government intentions in 1986 and 1989, no progress was made. First, the strategy of the Provincial Sector had shifted to embrace positive investment in higher-quality, cost-reducing DMUs. Second, the Department, mindful of both financial and political considerations, was eventually persuaded by the argument in favour of rail investment. The Secretary of State's new objectives for British Rail in October 1986 made it clear that he wished to see a major review of lines with the potential for bus substitution before he would consider a reinvestment option for those lines.[117] In fact, the results of the review exercise were ambivalent. In the early part of 1987 a preliminary study of 33 routes/ services was conducted under Edmonds's direction, using criteria agreed with the

Department.[118] It concluded that services on the 1,200 route-miles involved made operating losses of about £17 million (£9 million of this in Scotland). Individual cases produced limited financial benefits, and only where a larger programme of substitutions was offered would such action be worthwhile. Even then DMU replacement needs would not be materially reduced (maximum savings were put at 125 vehicles). The calculation contrasted sharply with Treasury expectations that savings of £100 million a year might be achieved.[119] Of course, a large-scale programme was not on the cards, politically. Portillo made it clear that 'Scotland and Wales were no go areas for closure and bus substitution, at least at present'.[120] Attention was then focused on a smaller number of less controversial lines in England. Yet more detailed studies were undertaken (listed in Appendix J, Table J.2), but the conclusion was that investing in rail lines 'provided the same order of benefit' as closure and bus substitution. The 1987 review of the Barrow–Carlisle service, for example, had revealed operating losses of about £2.4 million a year, but in 1989 a more sophisticated assessment based on cost escapement/ revenue loss concluded that while the financial (NPV) benefit to Provincial of bus substitution amounted to £7.7 million over 10 years, the *corporate* benefit was *minus* £3.8 million (taking into account the intention to retain the line for freight).[121] The issue was dropped in 1989, but not before a great deal of management time had been consumed.[122]

The idea of converting railways into roads had been advocated in some quarters from the 1950s, notably by Brigadier Thomas Lloyd, founder of the Railway Conversion League.[123] The issue was revived in 1982 by Angus Dalgleish in a paper published by the Centre for Policy Studies which advocated conversion into toll roads. Supporters included Alfred Sherman, Director of the CPS (1974–84) and one of Thatcher's advisers, and leading planner Peter Hall, who suggested that the Woodhead line would be a suitable candidate for experimental conversion to private-sector operation.[124] There was also the more disconcerting support of retired railway executives such as Fred Margetts and Lance Ibbotson.[125] The Board decided to tackle the issue head-on. First, a short pamphlet provided a vigorous refutation.[126] Then Peter Parker and Michael Posner orchestrated a fuller and more independent examination of conversion in the London area, where some conversions had been suggested.[127] Commissioned by British Rail, this was undertaken by the consultants Coopers & Lybrand and G. Brian Parker, under the guidance of Posner, Sherman, and Professor Christopher Foster, a Coopers & Lybrand partner.[128] The report, published in 1984, concluded that road design standards made it uneconomic to convert. Of 10 routes studied only the Marylebone–Northolt route was sufficiently attractive to merit further study.[129] The idea was then effectively shelved. Thus, while the Serpell Review inspired a great deal of further work on network size, provincial rail services, bus substitution, and rail-road conversion, little was done to erode the railways' existing market-share, and the post-Serpell climate was much more positive than the critics in 1983 could have possibly imagined.

6.3 Engineering costs—M&EE

Engineering was the most innovative of the Serpell committee's areas of inquiry, since this critical element in integrated rail operations had rarely been the subject of visible public debate. As we have seen, the 'culture of the railroad' tended to produce an enclosed world of railway engineering, remote from, and sometimes hostile to, the world of the strategist and operator. This means that this world is often difficult for an outsider to penetrate, and there are hazards in attempting broad generalisations reinforced with a measure of hindsight. In the 1980s there was a genuine conflict between those who argued that Britain's railways were expensively 'over-engineered', managed cosily and wastefully with scant regard for competitive procurement, and those who expressed concerns about 'crumbling edges' and the operating and safety risks inherent in excessive cost-cutting in design, manufacture, and maintenance. Here we attempt to steer a course between these positions and focus on the achievements of British Rail in reforming the organisation of its engineering departments and addressing the issue of costs.

In Mechanical & Electrical Engineering (M&EE), which made up about 24 per cent of total railway costs and attracted the most attention from the Board and senior managers, the need for reform had been recognised internally in the late 1970s. Important investigations had taken place, notably under the auspices of the Strategy Steering Group in 1978–9 and with Urquhart's 'Manifesto' of April 1980 (see Chapter 3, pp. 82–3). This work revealed considerable dissatisfaction with the performance of BREL, the wholly owned subsidiary formed in 1970. The Manufacture and Maintenance Policy Review of November 1979 was a substantial document (100 pages plus appendices) which provided a scathing indictment of the subsidiary and its weaknesses, including serious production shortfalls, a lack of 'tough commercial disciplines' in manufacture (new build), and inadequate control of maintenance. The root of the problem was cultural and organisational; as Michael Casey, Director of M&EE, 1982–7, has recalled, 'it had been a very nice, close, cosy relationship which worked, but perhaps didn't work as effectively commercially'.[130] For that reason the Review recommended the separation of new build from maintenance with the establishment of an independent company for the former; and a radical rationalisation of both the major maintenance undertaken by BREL in its workshops and the routine maintenance carried out by British Rail in its depots (see p. 83). Accepting the diagnosis Urquhart, the newly installed Chairman of BREL, did not accept the prescription. His 'Manifesto' argued that BREL should have a clearer, more contractual relationship with the Board, while remaining its subsidiary (see p. 83). At the same time the Strategy Steering Group considered it impractical to separate BREL's new build from maintenance. There were some doubts about the limitations of this approach. Posner noted that the recommended action represented a considerable dilution of the proposals in the Review, while Burt observed percipiently that 'over the last 20 years, we have often tried to allocate specific works to new build and to maintenance respectively...Hitherto there have always been strong arguments put forward about the difficulties inherent in such a separation. However, I have always had a gut feeling that this was the right way to go'.[131] The Board's ideas were discussed with the Secretary of State and Department officials on a number of occasions over the next two years, and working parties were active, but once again progress was leisurely. Shortly before the Serpell Review Committee began its work, Urquhart produced another review of BREL, in January 1982. This examined the longer-term position: the halving of the number of workshops from 32 to 16 after 1963; the reduction in staff from 66,000 to 36,000; the closure of a further three workshops in the early 1970s; and the re-engagement of labour from the mid-1970s in line with BR forecasts of a greater workload and a shift of emphasis from freight to passenger work. Urquhart noted that in April 1981 the Board had endorsed the policy of giving its subsidiary a greater measure of freedom, and claimed that BREL had taken up the challenge of pursuing rationalisation, cost effectiveness, and a clear contractual relationship with the Board. Draft contracts for new equipment had been drafted; changes in accounting procedures had been introduced; design had been integrated within M&EE; there were firm plans for a further rationalisation of workshop capacity; and it had been agreed that the purchasing of materials should be transferred from BRB to BREL.[132] Thus, the Serpell review's criticisms of railway engineering were formulated in an environment of self-criticism within British Rail and a conscious drive for reform. As Parker told Howell, 'we firmly believe that our strategy makes sense post-Serpell as it did pre-Serpell'.[133]

The Serpell review was scathing about the engineering functions and argued forcefully that there was considerable scope for savings, or as Serpell has put it, 'there was gold in them thar hills'.[134] As regards ME&E the review felt that annual savings of c.£75–80 million might be produced by better procurement (less sophisticated design, competitive tendering), depot rationalisation, inventory reduction, and improved maintenance practices. It also argued that the position of BREL should be addressed, offering the options of reabsorption within BR, sale to the government, or privatisation. The Board's response was to concede that there was scope for reform of engineering, but to challenge the competence of Serpell's consultants, Travers Morgan (Chapter 5, pp. 178–9). It immediately commissioned its own consultants' studies, that on the M&EE function being undertaken by A. T. Kearney, that on civil engineering (CE) and signal and telecommunications engineering (S&TE) by Mott, Hay & Anderson (see pp. 209–10). The consultants reported in April 1983. While the principal aim was to provide an independent assessment of Travers Morgan's work—the scope for savings was found to be rather less than in the Serpell review—the brief went much further, embracing an independent evaluation of existing standards and practices. For M&EE, Kearney accepted much of the Serpell agenda for cost saving, but felt that the scope for savings was of the order of £55–70 million, 30 per cent less than shown by Travers Morgan. British Rail's engineers broadly accepted its recommendations. They included 'in-line management' for the engineering functions, the transfer of production design to BREL, centralised control of scheduled maintenance under the Director of M&EE, a reduction in the number of depots (from 75 to 30/40), and the need to increase the level of key spares for diesel locomotives. Other ideas, including the notion that 'little or no benefit would result from the purchase of American locomotives', required further evaluation. The recommendations were then incorporated into action plans for 1983.[135]

The Department of Transport's view on M&EE was made explicit in the objectives of October 1983. Ridley required the Board to complete the rationalisation of BREL as quickly as possible, and review the options for BREL, including privatisation, by mid-1984. Wherever possible rolling stock was to be procured by competitive tender.[136] The Board responded by first establishing procedures for competitive tendering in August 1983.[137] They then engaged Price Waterhouse to advise on the future role of BREL, and the consultants' views were fed into a further report from Urquhart and Myers in November. This again provided good diagnosis, but emphasised the uncertainty of the business environment facing BREL and the industrial relations and redundancy cost implications of radical restructuring. The report eschewed the more radical of six options for BREL in favouring the retention of the subsidiary 'as currently defined'. However, as the consultants noted, this option was an 'interim' measure which might well require review in the light of further work on the distribution of the repair and maintenance workload between BR's regional depots and the BREL workshops.[138] Reid, clearly doubting that the 'massive exercise' could be completed to such a tight timetable by the existing team of Urquhart, Ian Gardiner, and Philip Norman,[139] decided to establish a Board-level steering committee and a project manager to progress the reforms. This was endorsed by the Board at its meeting in December and in January 1984 John Welsby was moved from Provincial to the post of Director, Manufacturing & Maintenance Policy.

Welsby, a determined manager with no engineering baggage, proved a critical appointment in the successful restructuring of M&EE. His extensive report of June 1984 recognised that BREL's future had to be tackled within a comprehensive scheme for the entire manufacture and maintenance of traction and rolling stock, and laid the foundations for a programme of change embracing procurement, maintenance, and eventual privatisation over the period 1985–8. The pursuance of competitive sourcing for new construction clearly challenged the existing BRB/BREL relationship, and the Board followed Welsby's prescription. BREL would concentrate on new construction and heavy repair, assume responsibility for its production design work, and be re-established as a fully independent subsidiary. The nucleus of its new build workshops—Derby, Crewe, and York— would then be sold to the private sector.[140] Competitive tendering by BREL was encouraged by the establishment from April 1985 of separate trading accounts for competitive and single-sourced work as part of a financial restructuring.[141] At the same time, British Rail moved a fair distance from dependence upon its subsidiary. By 1987/8 the private sector had won 53 per cent of the post-1983 orders for locomotives and coaches and 45 per cent of those for wagons.[142] Equally, if not more important, maintenance had to be shaken up. Here, activity was based on traditional practice, where, for example, time and money were consumed in taking rolling stock to a parent depot to be fitted with new components, while emergency repair work was divided in an ad hoc manner between BREL's workshops and BR's depots. Welsby recommended a clear division between the two types of works. In order to reduce costs and increase asset availability, the concept of 'cost-effective maintenance', based on the speedy exchange of components, was introduced in April 1987. Worked up by the consultants H. J. Gorham & Associates and ratified by the Board in July 1985, CEM gave an enhanced role to BR's regional depots, and promised significant savings.[143] Thus, a considerable rationalisation of maintenance facilities was accompanied by an upgrading of depots, for example at Stratford (East London), Ilford, Bristol (Bath Road), Cardiff, Leeds (Neville Hill), and Plymouth (Laira), in order to handle major component changes for specific types of equipment.[144] These regional depots, together with others at Chart Leacon (Ashford), Selhurst, Slade Green, Birkenhead, and the four BRML workshops, were classified as the highest status, 'Level 5'. At the same time BR took over responsibility for the provision of spares, and a national spares (later 'supply') centre was established at Doncaster in April 1987.[145] The costs of the exercise were put at £47 million over the period 1986–91.[146]

The Board then moved to financially separate and break up BREL. Urquhart, who had never fully accepted the radical prescription,[147] stepped down as Chairman of BREL in April 1985 and then resigned from the Board.[148] A new BR-BREL Policy Group led by Reid assumed responsibility for progressing the changes, though Welsby, by this time MD (Procurement & Special Projects) and responsible for overall procurement activity, retained an executive interest in the BREL programme.[149] In April 1986, after considerable preparatory work, essential since this was a privatisation where BR required continuing access to the services provided, BREL was divided into a new build and repair group, NBRG, and a maintenance element, BRMG. A year later the latter, consisting of the workshops at Doncaster, Eastleigh, Springburn (Glasgow), and Wolverton, became British Rail Maintenance Ltd., a fully controlled BRB subsidiary, while the New Build Group—Crewe, Derby, York, Doncaster Wagon Works, and Horwich Foundry—was reconstituted as a series of companies in preparation for asset disposal. In September 1987 Doncaster Wagon Works was sold to a local management team, and in 1988–9 the remaining works, first Horwich Foundry, then the main works at Crewe, Derby, and York were sold (see Chapter 7, pp. 243–6).[150]

How far did these sweeping changes lead to the reduction of over-capacity and a reduction in costs? Further rationalisation of workshops capacity had been planned before the Serpell committee reported, producing the closure of Ashford in 1981, then Temple Mills and Horwich (except the Foundry) in 1983, with a substantial contraction at Swindon. Later on, the works at Shildon (1984) and Swindon (1986) met the same fate. Staff employed by BREL fell from 36,200 in December 1979 to 27,700 in December 1983 (a fall of 23 per cent), and to 18,500 in March 1987, about half the numbers in 1979. After privatisation the number was a mere 3,800 in March 1990. BR's own M&EE staff was also reduced. Accompanied by a rationalisation of depots and maintenance facilities, employment fell from 24,000 at the end of 1979 to 20,400 in 1983 (a fall of 15 per cent), and to 18,000 in 1990, 25 per cent lower than in 1979.[151] However, it should be observed that this substantial contraction in M&EE was not a costless exercise. Much time was consumed in explaining the changes to the trade unions, and at times considerable opposition was expressed.[152] This was generally deflected by redundancy packages, and the final bill for the restructuring of BREL was very high: around £200 million over the period 1985–9.[153]

The overall impact of management action on the financial and operational performance of M&EE is difficult to measure given the initial intermingling of functions with BREL and the later, radical restructuring. At the beginning of 1990 David Blake, Michael Casey's successor as Director, M&EE, informed the Board that since 1986/7 the M&EE function had achieved annual savings of some £90 million a year (15 per cent) in its basic costs.[154] Maintenance costs may be derived, and these certainly fell in real terms, by 21 per cent 1983 to 1988/9, and in relation to train-miles run by 26 per cent, though the figures for 1989/90 revealed a rise (Table 6.6). The external assessment of the MMC, in its audit of Network SouthEast and Provincial in 1987 and 1989, was that sector management had produced better articulated requirements from the rail businesses, helping to speed the process of reform and make for a better procured, more cost-effective railway. For Provincial, for example, it found that the sector's share of M&EE costs had fallen by 5 per cent in constant prices, 1985/6–87/8,

Table 6.6 Train maintenance costs, 1983–89/90 (in 1989/90 prices)

Year	Maintenance costs (£m.)	Index	Maintenance costs per train-mile (£)	Index
1983	£675.1	100	£2.70	100
1985/6	£618.4	92	£2.53	94
1988/9	£531.2	79	£2.01	74
1989/90	£543.3	81	£2.05	76

Source: BRB, *R&A 1983–89/90*.

notwithstanding transitional costs.[155] However, it was conceded that the factors influencing maintenance costs were many and varied, and visible improvement was not only a consequence of improved practices and better management. Thus, the real maintenance and overhaul costs of the DMU fleet fell from £102 to £44 million, from 1981 to 1987/8, an impressive reduction of 57 per cent, but much of this could be explained by the abandonment of older vehicles, a fleet reduction of 25 per cent, and investment in new Sprinters.[156] Productivity and reliability measures (for example, standard hour costs at depots and the casualty rate of vehicles) were also found to be difficult to interpret.[157] Nevertheless, internal assessments were that the new management of maintenance had produced an improvement of some 2–3 per cent in the availability of rolling stock. During the first year of operation, the average number of days on works per repair for a Class 47 locomotive fell dramatically from 70 to 32, while the figure for Mark II coaches was reduced from 22 to 6. The resultant financial savings were put at £25 million, 12 per cent of the heavy repair bill for traction and rolling stock.[158]

Procurement was also transformed, though to what effect is more difficult to ascertain. We may suggest that prices fell,[159] but there was no guarantee that the new equipment would be delivered on time or prove reliable and fault free, whoever supplied it. Thus, there were embarrassing delays in delivering the BREL-built Class 158 Sprinters for Provincial and the Class 319 EMUs for Network SouthEast, but the same was true of a private-sector order, that for Class 155 DMUs built for Provincial by British Leyland.[160] Furthermore, the competitive tendering process was not insulated from the political 'influence' which had so often bedevilled British Rail investment. Thus, in 1983 David Mitchell, then a DTp Parliamentary Under-Secretary, wrote to Reid referring him to GEC's plans for redundancies in Sheffield and suggested that he meet a joint deputation representing the management and workforce. Two years later Mitchell, in conveying the Department's formal approval of investment in Class 87/2 electric locomotives, which had received tenders from GEC, Brush (part of Hawker Siddeley), and BREL, noted that the specification indicated a preference for GEC motors and warned that 'it will be very important to demonstrate the [*sic*] Brush have been treated with complete fairness in competing either with GEC alone or with a combined bid from BREL and GEC. Second, it will be essential that BREL's bid should be proof against any accusation that it depends on hidden cross-subsidy'.[161] There was intervention of a more overt 'political' nature over the order for Class 91 electric locomotives in 1985. Tenders were received from GEC/BREL, Brush, and ASEA of Sweden. Matthew Durbar of Hawker Siddeley approached Myers during the negotiations to point out that 'if the order were to go abroad this would be a major blow to British industry in world markets and he would take every step possible to fight this situation'.[162] Jim Prior, the Conservative politician, made similar noises as chairman of GEC. After Brush had been told that its price was too high, and GEC that there was concern about the reliability of its transmission system, representatives of the two companies went to the Department in October 1985 to argue the case for a 'Buy British' policy. They emphasised the 'serious damage to their export potential in all types of railway equipment if they were seen to lose out in their home market to ASEA on technical grounds'. In the event the order went to GEC, with BREL carrying out the assembly.[163] The government also held a watching brief on the prospect of late delivery by BREL under competitive conditions. In November 1987 Paul Channon, the Secretary of State for Transport, told Reid that he was worried about placing the order for Class 158 Sprinters with BREL, given the 'potential financial risks which can be met ultimately only by the taxpayer'. He went on to state that it was 'essential for the credibility of the competitive process that these vehicles are delivered to time and within budget'.[164]

Clearly, we should be impressed with the progress made by Reid, Welsby, and their colleagues in the radical reform of the railways' M&EE, even if the immediate results were ambiguous in some areas, and notably as regards procurement. In addition, the initial impact of separate trading accounts exposed the gulf in 'performance' between the competitive and the non-competitive business undertaken by BREL. Over the two years from April 1985 to March 1987 single-sourced work for British Rail earned the subsidiary an operating surplus before interest of £46 million, while competitive contracts produced a *deficit* of £16 million.[165]

6.4 Engineering costs—CE and S&TE

Attention given to the civil engineering (CE) and signal and telecommunications engineering (S&TE) functions by the reformers was neither so determined nor so extensive, mirroring their comparative neglect by railway historians. CE accounted for about 20 per cent of railway costs; S&TE's share was much smaller at about 6 per cent. As with M&EE, the two departments had been production led; 'really what the engineers said, stood and went almost unchallenged'. The Serpell review was one of the first attempts to argue about what was being delivered in terms of value for money.[166] The recommendations of the consultants Mott, Hay & Anderson in 1983 may have given some comfort to the CE and S&TE engineers. For example, they confirmed the existence of a track renewal backlog, the consequence of the need to replace the extensive track relaying work carried out in the late 1950s and early 1960s. On the other hand, their long list of suggestions for improvement indicated that there was considerable scope for further effort. Thus, the consultants referred to the opportunities for streamlining the regional organisations, the urgent need for new cost-reducing technologies, and, in particular, a speedier development of computer systems for cost control. Other recommendations involved the need for greater flexibility in ganging practices and track possessions, the absence of a civil engineering manual covering the criteria and procedures for maintenance and renewal, and the uncovering of deficiencies in the management of signalling authorisations and work recording. All this underlined the Serpell review's diagnosis about the prospects for savings.[167]

In contrast, the 1980s was to prove a decade of development in both fields. Diagnosis of internal problems was certainly offered, though much of this was the result of prodding from the sectors. For example, successive Chief Civil Engineers, Max Purbrick and Stewart Currie, responded to the wide variations in regional cost profiles by encouraging the development of performance indicators for management control. The creation of a sophisticated matrix of first 16, then 36 track categories, based on speed, tonnage, and axle wear, helped the emerging sectors to assess their infrastructure requirements with more precision.[168] The engineers were also asked to react positively to the criticisms of the Serpell Committee's consultants, Travers Morgan, who had suggested that there were opportunities to make considerable savings by re-examining the procedures for track renewal and maintenance work, usually undertaken at weekends and at night.[169] On the initiative of Myers and the Business Engineering Group, the Policy Unit was asked in 1983 to examine the merits of weekday, daytime possessions. The review took some time, and the results were ambiguous. However, the momentum was maintained by the sector directors, who were responsible for infrastructure costs where they were 'prime users'. Here, John Prideaux, the Director of Inter-City, played a leading role in the two changes to emerge from the review: extended (30-hour) weekend possessions; and a 'big bang' approach, that is complete closure of the permanent way for long periods with major projects. The latter was adopted for example in a seven-week closure of Crewe Station in the summer of 1985, which saved at least £1 million, while extended weekend possessions became the norm with the help of new equipment, notably the Dynamic Track Stabiliser (see below).[170] The renewal of lines with low traffic densities was reassessed, and a number of techniques were applied, including 'patch' re-sleepering and the welding of jointed track.[171]

Considerable progress was made with the help of R&D and new investment. The work of the R&D Division at Derby encouraged the introduction of new machinery, some embodying microelectronics and laser and computer technology, to transform the efficiency of track monitoring, maintenance, and renewal. Thus, track monitoring was greatly improved with the work on the High Speed Track Recording Car, the Rail Flaw Detection Train incorporating ultrasonic testing, and the high-speed Structure Gauging Train.[172] Tamping machines were challenged, first by the Dynamic Track Stabiliser (DTS), which produced an immediate consolidation of the track after engineering work,[173] then by the Pneumatic Ballast Injection machine or Stoneblower, which was deployed in production prototype from 1984. There were also developments with automatic ballast cleaning, and the measurement by tamping machines of track align-ment.[174] All this represented a substantial enhancement of CE, though not all of these innovations were brought into significant production before 1990.[175] Sector requirements were critical to these innovations. InterCity's business plans rested on higher speeds, with the HSTs and new electric locomotives on the ECML, and Prideaux, the Sector Director, led the way in investing in nine DTS machines in 1987/8 following successful trials with two earlier machines. These reduced track-laying costs and permitted tracks used by the sector to be returned to higher-speed running immediately after engineering work. Savings were put at £18 million a year in 1988.[176]

In signalling, British Rail's development of Solid State Interlocking (SSI), in collaboration with GEC and Westinghouse, was critical to the effective signalling of high-density track. Based on control at central microcomputing signalling centres, it was first used at Leamington Spa in 1985, then at Inverness, Oxted, Dorchester–Weymouth, and on the ECML.[177] A further development was the Integrated Electronic Control Centre (IECC), the first of which opened at Liver-pool Street Station in March 1989. This was a super-signalling and train control centre, utilising SSI and ARS (Automatic Route Setting), the latter pioneered at Three Bridges, Sussex in 1983.[178] The Radio Electronic Token Block (RETB) and No Signalman Key Token (NSKT) were efficient, cost-reducing technologies for the less densely used rural railways. First used on the Dingwall–Kyle line in 1984, the systems had been applied to the Inverness–Wick/Thurso, East Suffolk, West Highland, and Cambrian lines by 1989.[179] The decade also saw the exploitation of British Rail's extensive telecommunications infrastructure, which was second only to BT. In 1983 access was sold to Mercury Communications in anticipation of the more competitive conditions provided by the Telecommunications Act of 1984. By 1989 the arrangement was producing a net income of over £6 million. In the following year BR Telecommunications Ltd was established as an independ-ent subsidiary.[180]

For all this activity, the containment of overall department costs was rather limited, at least before 1987. At the centre the initial thrust for reform had been blunted by the enormity of the task in rationalising the M&EE function. How-ever, the desire of sector managers to control not only the volume of engineering work but also its price led to revised terms of reference for the Business Engin-eering Group (BEG) and the commissioning by Jim O'Brien of reports on departmental cost strategies in 1987, giving impetus to cost-saving and quality-protecting changes.[181] Currie's report on CE revealed that there was much to be done; in particular, it provoked considerable criticism from Philip Wood, who as Director of the Policy Unit had been asked to comment on the responses. Wood noted that *total* CE costs, including investment, had fallen by only 9 per cent in real terms, 1979–85/6. Moreover, when corrected for system size, the perform-ance was even flatter. Expenditure per track-mile had fallen by only 2 per cent, while expenditure per 'equated track mile'[182] had *increased* by 6 per cent.[183] The improvement that had been made was attributed more to short-term budget cuts than to a determined assault on working practices. Wood was also worried by Currie's claim that it was difficult to reduce the unit costs of maintenance and by the fact that labour intensity, which had fallen in the early 1970s, had started to rise again despite further mechanisation. He was also exasperated by the argument that the CE workload was determined exogenously by the condition of the infrastructure. This he regarded as a 'counsel of despair', and when combined with the department's failure to produce output measures meant that the 'scope for coherent management action to reduce unit costs' was 'being severely restricted a priori'.[184] Wood was more sympathetic towards the S&TE report from William Whitehouse, but even here there was still much to concern the BEG. Expenditure on revenue account had fallen by about 10 per cent, 1979–86/7, but when the investment element was excluded a rise of 2 per cent was shown. Maintenance costs had been difficult to control. These had remained constant in real terms for a decade, despite a cut in staff, since manpower savings had been swallowed up by the higher wages and salaries needed to attract better qualified staff as the technology became more sophisticated. In fact, maintenance, renewal, and management control costs increased by 6 per cent in real terms from 1979 to 1986/7; over the same period maintenance and renewal costs (excluding investment) rose by 9 per cent in relation to both train- and track-miles. There was also a disturbing lack of relevant data for management control purposes. Spending on improved signalling clearly benefited the Operations function, but this could not be demonstrated adequately with existing data. Nor had unit cost reductions been monitored properly.[185] A further report by Holmes, the Director of Operations, provided a crude indicator of comparative departmental progress. The Operations and M&EE activities had cut their spending in real terms by 21 per cent over the period 1980–86/7, while the reductions achieved by CE and S&TE amounted to only 14 and 6 per cent respectively.[186] This contrast is also reflected in the manpower data. Staff numbers for CE and S&TE taken together fell by only 13 per cent, 1980–86/7, while for BREL/M&EE the reduction amounted to 38 per cent.[187]

The cost exercises exposed the pressing need for satisfactory measurement and control of unit costs.[188] The findings, coupled with DTp criticisms of a lack of progress in reducing costs (see Chapter 4, pp. 149–9) jolted Headquarters into more determined action. Reports commissioned from the consultants Kearney on CE and S&TE examined the scope for organisational savings, though they proved to be of limited value since they paid insufficient attention to the role of the sectors. A more vigorous internal response was then pursued, led first by Myers, then by David Rayner as JMD (Railways).[189] Cornell, an engineer with experience of general management (he was General Manager of Scottish Region), was seconded to Headquarters as Project Director of an Infrastructure Costs Review. This involved a review of the two engineering functions, in the context of sector requirements and procurement policy. The aim was to produce savings of £120 million a year or 20 per cent in three years. Once again, diagnosis was extensive, but as we noted in Chapter 4, the immediate impact was limited. Nevertheless, by 1990 savings of £36 million had been secured, mainly via the dedication of engineering locomotives, better management of plant and machinery, a reduction in ballast depth, and the rationalisation of manufacturing activities. The latter involved a withdrawal from non-core elements such as quarrying, foundry work (Redbridge), and concrete (York, Newton Heath), and a reduction in welded rails, switches, and crossings production; the establishment of self-accounting units to compete with external suppliers, some as the prelude to disposal (Meldon Quarry, Taunton Concrete Works); a move to competitive procurement of maintenance services, focusing on an examination of the relationship between engineering standards and business requirements; and the release of substantial amounts of land for sale. Acceleration of the programme promised to deliver further savings of £65 million in 1990/1. However, it is fair to say that there was still much to accomplish.[190]

What may be said about the impact of the 1980s and the post-Serpell environment on CE and S&TE? It is difficult to locate long-run data on a consistent basis. The rather limited published data on track, signalling, and telecommunications costs under the heading operating expenditure, 1983–89/90, shown in Table 6.7, reveal that overall costs did fall, by 19 per cent to 1988/9, with track and structures costs falling by 25 per cent. On the other hand, signalling costs were less successfully contained, while telecommunications proved a growth area with consequent higher costs. And as with train maintenance, there was a significant deterioration in 1989/90 (Table 6.7). When we express the data in relation to track-miles the gains seem less impressive: a fall of only 5 per cent, 1983–89/90 (Table 6.7).

The procurement of equipment was treated in the same way as for M&EE and with similar results, although progress was shaken by problems which developed with a near-monopolist supplier, Plasser Theurer of Austria, which distributed track maintenance machines from its West Ealing factory. The company provided much of the new equipment of the 1980s, some in competition with other firms, some single sourced.[191] Internal documentation indicates that Plasser, having won the contract to develop the prototype Stoneblower in 1983, proved slow in taking the project forward, principally because the new machine presented a threat to its market for tampers.[192] Furthermore, its cosy relationship with some of British Rail's engineers produced complaints from a competitor in 1983, then again five years later, culminating in the resignation of some senior managers in 1989 amid allegations that they had improperly accepted inducements. Publicity given to the unsuccessful prosecution of a corruption case in 1992 was indicative of the very real difficulty in establishing competitive procurement procedures in areas where there were very few suppliers.[193]

In railway engineering, then, the post-Serpell period saw considerable activity and much change, though this was more evident with M&EE than elsewhere.

Table 6.7 Track/structures, signalling and telecommunications costs, 1983–89/90 (in 1989/90 prices)

Year	Track/Structures		Signalling		Telecoms		Total[a]		Per track-mile			
	£m. (1)	Index	£m. (2)	Index	£m. (3)	Index	£m. (4)	Index	Index (1)	(2)	(3)	(4)
1983	£651.7	100	£156.2	100	£40.1	100	£819.6	100	100	100	100	100
1985/6	£566.7	87	£148.0	95	£52.2	130	£738.9	90	91	99	136	95
1988/9	£491.1	75	£147.6	94	£57.6	144	£662.1	81	82	103	157	88
1989/90	£530.1	81	£161.9	104	£66.6	166	£715.7	87	89	113	181	95

Source: BRB, *R&A 1983–89/90.*
a Deducting for level crossing grants (c.£20m.–£25m. p.a.), etc.

By 1990 considerable effort had been made to make engineers more 'business led', much of it driven by the requirements of the sector directors and their desire to take control of costs. The engineers themselves were more equivocal about the process. The publicity given to the three serious rail accidents of 1988–9 and to the Clapham accident in particular fed their anxieties about the dangers of excessive cost cutting and the risk of reducing quality as well as safety margins. In relation to the permanent way, for example, the picture was one of well-maintained major routes, symbolised by the state-of-the-art ECML, opened in July 1991, and a 27 per cent increase in the amount of continuous welded rail,[194] while elsewhere the number of temporary speed restrictions in operation was still a matter for concern, and on the periphery there was much 'postponed mainten-ance' and neglect, symbolised by the wrangling over the Ribblehead Viaduct on the Settle and Carlisle line. The available data are difficult to interpret. If the number of broken rails is taken as a proxy for the condition of the track, then there appears to have been an improvement in both welded and jointed track, 1985–90. On the other hand, the amount of track renewed fell in the later 1980s.[195] Nevertheless, by 1990 considerable strides had been taken to make engineering support for the railway more competitive, with privatisation of manufacturing and heavy maintenance leading the way.

6.5 The investment challenge

Investment, the subject of bitter arguments with the government throughout the 1970s, remained a pressing issue in the following decade. As we have noted, the recession of 1979–82 put a halt to any ambitious plans the Board may have had for enhanced investment, particularly in electrification (see pp. 109–10 and pp. 154–5). Although the continuing flat investment ceiling of $c.$£400 million per annum was felt to be demonstrably too low to maintain the assets of the business, such concerns became irrelevant given the increasingly tight con-straints of the External Financing Limit. In 1982 the Board placed an embargo on major new investment starts, and the five-year investment review forecast that spending over the period 1982–6 would be about 25 per cent (£478 million) below the ceiling ($c.$£2,000 million in mid-1981 prices). Since the Board was effectively using investment as a budgetary regulator, the government responded by ring-fencing certain elements of expenditure within the PSO grant. The introduction of a Renewals and Refurbishment Element (RRE) in 1982 was aimed principally at revenue investment in infrastructure. Shortfalls in spending against the RRE in the claim year were deducted from the PSO cash ceiling.[196]

The setting of business objectives by Ridley in October 1983 and the sanction-ing of the ECML electrification in July 1984—Reid called it 'the most important investment decision . . . in over 25 years'[197]—apparently heralded a period of higher investment endorsed by the government in return for a lower and redu-cing level of government subsidy. Further evidence of government support for rail transport was provided by the rather surprising collaboration of Thatcher's government with Mitterand's left-wing government in France over the Channel Tunnel project, which was maintained despite the distractions presented by the Falklands War. Here, then, it seems, was Parker's balance sheet of change, though it came in Reid's time, and rather late in the day at that. The Board's annual reports contain some bullish statements about the improvement in invest-ment levels, notably in 1984/5, when Reid observed that the authorised invest-ment in the 15 months to March 1985 was greater than that authorised in the previous six years, and again in 1989/90, when he noted that 'group investment was the highest in real terms for fifteen years'.[198] However, improved trading, together with cash windfalls from property sales, facilitated increased spending, making it possible for the government to reduce the EFL while raising the investment ceiling in 1987/8. In any case, the available data on British Rail's railway investment, including track renewals, indicate that it took some time to match the spending levels at the beginning of the decade. Gross investment, which averaged £719 million in 1979–80 in constant 1989/90 prices, fell sharply to only £554 million in 1982–3, a reduction of a quarter on 1979. It was only in 1987/8 that British Rail's investment exceeded the levels of 1979–80 (Table 6.8). The figure for 1989/90 was impressively high, 60 per cent higher than in 1982; if track renewals are excluded, the increase is closer to 100 per cent. But railway investment in the 1980s was not markedly higher than historical post-war levels. Indeed, it was little better than in the 1970s, and much lower than in the 1960s, while the average for 1981–90 was 8 per cent below the average for 1979–80 (Table 6.8).

Furthermore, for all the attention that investment in new rolling stock received and indeed, continues to receive, the data on components of investment show that rolling stock made up only 24 per cent of the total and had a particularly small share—16 per cent—in 1983–6 (Table 6.9). By far the largest component of railway investment was infrastructure investment (58 per cent overall, over 70 per cent in 1983–4), while 'other rail' investment consumed 18 per cent. Invest-ment in electrification made up only 7 per cent of the total (Appendix B, Table B.2). The data on physical asset investment tell the same story of limited asset acquisition (Table 6.10). Here, additions to stock were generally modest in comparison with the periods 1963–73 and 1974–8, except for multiple units, where there was a steady investment in EMUs, and a belated investment in DMUs from 1984 (see Table 6.11). It must be pointed out here that Provincial's Sprinters (Class 150), Super Sprinters (Class 155–6) and Express units (Class 158) were a great success. Their flexible and efficient running transformed not only the economics but also the speed and quality of journeys in the sector.[199] Equally, if not more important, the period 1979–82 saw the completion of the High-Speed

Table 6.8 Gross railway investment, 1979–89/90 (£m., in constant 1989/90 prices)

Year	Railway (excluding track renewals)	Railway (including track renewals)	Index 1979 = 100	
			(i)	(ii)
1979	493	709	100	100
1980	510	729	103	103
1981	423	636	86	90
1982	355	535	72	75
1983	344	572	70	81
1984	356	562	72	79
1985/6	489	663	99	93
1986/7	477	637	97	90
1987/8	597	770	121	109
1988/9	597	744	121	105
1989/90	693	845	141	119
Annual averages				
1979–80	501	718	102	101
1981–89/90	481	663	98	93
1960–9	755	1,060	153	149
1970–9	460	684	93	96
1980–89/90	484	669	98	94

Source: Appendix B, Table B.2; long-run investment data from BRB IA 20-8-5 Pt. 9.

Train programme, with the deployment of trains authorised for the West of England and North East/South West cross-country services, together with additional units for the ECML. The total investment in trainsets, maintenance, and associated infrastructure amounted to £272 million in 1981 prices.[200] While the HSTs have ultimately proved very successful, their introduction was not without difficulties. Production problems resulted in late deliveries from BREL, and there were also a number of protracted equipment defects which affected service reliability and contributed to unexpectedly high maintenance costs.[201] On top of this the trains were introduced in a difficult economic climate which hit predicted revenue growth. The early returns on the investment were thus disappointing, the contribution over train working and terminal expenses amounting to only £377 million in 1976–80 compared with the forecast of £667 million. Such results did nothing to ease the concerns surrounding investment in InterCity services. The DTp was already unsure about the viability of the HSTs. It had authorised lower numbers of sets in both of the Board's submissions for the ECML, and also requested an input into studies of HST deployment. In addition, as Derek Fowler reminded the Board, 'The results so far of investment in H.S.T.'s

Table 6.9 Components of railway investment, 1979–89/90 (£m., in constant 1989/90 prices)

Year	Components (percentage share in brackets)					
	Track renewals	Signalling and Track rationalisation	Total infrastructure	Traction and Rolling stock	Terminals and Depots	Total
1979	216 (30)	146 (21)	429 (60)	199 (28)	64 (9)	709
1983	228 (40)	122 (21)	419 (73)	93 (16)	47 (8)	572
1984	206 (37)	134 (24)	400 (71)	78 (14)	58 (10)	562
1988/9	147 (20)	109 (15)	356 (48)	221 (30)	168 (23)	744
1989/90	152 (18)	91 (11)	363 (43)	231 (27)	203 (24)	845
Totals						
1979–80	435 (30)	278 (19)	857 (60)	422 (29)	127 (9)	1,438
1983–6	608 (34)	355 (20)	1,209 (67)	284 (16)	221 (12)	1,797
1988–90	299 (19)	200 (13)	719 (45)	452 (28)	371 (23)	1,589
1979–90	2,068 (28)	1,256 (17)	4,268 (58)	1,763 (24)	1,139 (15)	7,402

Source: Appendix B, Table B.2.

must influence attitudes to investment in A.P.T.'s'.[202] This was a percipient comment. Progress with InterCity investment was clearly affected by the faith pinned in, and the difficulties experienced by, the Advanced Passenger Train (APT). This high-profile project, incorporating a tilting mechanism and hydro-kinetic braking, had its origins in the late 1960s. The new train was developed to permit faster speeds within the constraints of the existing infrastructure, a feature which distinguished it from the parallel development of the TGV by the French. Following successful tests with a gas-turbine unit in 1972–5 an investment of £26 million was authorised for three electric-powered prototype trainsets as the precursor to an entire fleet of trains for the WCML (see p. 91).[203] However, Ian Campbell's attempts to introduce the prototypes into service from 1978 suffered numerous delays (apparently 18 in all)[204] and ultimately proved unsuccessful. Although there were some successful runs, notably one for the press in October 1980, which attracted the enthusiasm and support of former BR engineer Roland Bond,[205] passengers generally found that the ride induced queasiness, while the train incorporated too many ambitious and untried elements of new technology.[206] The train's numerous failures, including a derailment in April 1980, and a disastrous attempt to run in service in December 1981, received less than sympathetic treatment in the media, and what should have been a technological celebration became something of a national joke, encouraged by the satirical magazine *Private Eye* (see cartoons 8 and 9). The difficulties highlighted the potential dangers in a business where 'technology push' could dominate 'market pull' in product development.[207]

Table 6.10 Physical components of railway investment, 1979–89/90

Year	Rolling stock											Infrastructure	
	Locomotives		Power cars		Multiple units		Passenger coaching stock			Non-passenger coaching stock	Freight wagons	CWR (track-miles)	AWS (route-miles)
	Electric	Diesel	HST	APT	DMU	EMU	Loco-hauled	HST	APT				
1979	16	—	27	3	—	204	17	112	9	3	1,519	416	182
1980	17	—	6	1	—	179	11	104	15	2	1,341	398	239
1981	17	—	39	1	—	210	8	34	—	—	1,217	227	130
1982	10	—	16	—	7	200	89	45	—	—	758	174	220
1983	24	—	—	—	2	188	108	—	—	—	307	194	177
1984/5	24	—	—	—	46	153	5	6	—	—	1	297	437
1985/6	15	—	—	—	237	115	38	13	—	—	7	603	377
1986/7	9	—	—	—	193	153	3	—	—	—	—	−21[a]	365
1987/8	1	—	—	—	146	44	—	—	—	—	124	187	146
1988/9	—	37	—	—	322	284	2	—	—	7	21	102	189
1989/90	—	10	—	—	58	210	60	6	—	47	13	127	n.a.
Annual average													
1979–89/90	12	4	8	0.4	92	176	31	29	3	5	483	246	224
1963–73	16	125	—	—	4	151	149	—	—	13	1,239	526	167
1974–8	4	7	14	0.4	—	103	103	83	1	12	1,384	539	292

Source: BRB, R&A 1963–89/90; Gourvish, British Railways, p. 511; DTp, Railway Accidents (from 1982 Railway Safety), 1979–89/90.

[a] Net reduction in CWR mileage shown.

Table 6.11 Major investment schemes authorised, 1979–88

Scheme	Authorisation	Authorised cost at base (£m.)
Traction and rolling stock		
Class 58 diesels, freight (15)[a]	1984	14
Class 60 diesels, freight (100)	1988	121
Class 90 IC (15), freight (30), parcels (5)	1984/7	44
Lightweight DMUs, Provincial (40)	1982	7
Lightweight DMUs, Provincial (150)	1983	25
Lightweight DMUs, Provincial (138)	1985	25
Sprinter DMUs, Provincial (100)	1984	25
Sprinter DMUs, Provincial (240)	1984	61
Sprinter DMUs, Provincial (228)	1985	65
Class 158 DMUs, Provincial (204)	1987	69
Class 158 DMUs, Provincial (423)[b]	1988	149
Class 317 EMUs, Strathclyde (60)	1984	11
Class 319 EMUs, NSE (56)	1987	18
Class 319/21 EMUs, NSE (324)	1988	127
Class 321 EMUs, NSE (184)	1987	59
Class 455 EMUs, NSE (505)	1977–83	119
Class 456 EMUs, NSE (48)	1988	21
Mark III sleeping cars (266)[c]	1979	43
Mark III coaches (180)[d]	1982	34
Driving van trailers IC WCML (57)	1986	17
Electrification[e]		
Anglia (Ipswich, Harwich, Norwich)	1980	57
Anglia (Bishop's Stortford–Cambridge)	1984	11
Anglia (Royston–Cambridge)	1987	2
Tonbridge–Hastings	1983	29
East Coast Main Line[e]	1984	306
North London line	1984	8
Bournemouth–Weymouth[e]	1985	53
South West Hampshire	1988	16
Resignalling		
Brighton line	1978	45
West of England	1980	28
Ayrshire Coast	1983	23
Leicester	1983	22
Waterloo	1984	31
Other[e]		
APTIS/PORTIS ticketing system	1982	17
Thameslink[e]	1984	59
Stansted Airport Link[e]	1985	40
Windsor rail link (Manchester)	1985	13

Source: BRB Investment Committee Minutes.

[a] A further 35 Class 58s were built under a 1977 authorisation for Class 56s.
[b] 128 vehicles subsequently transferred to Class 159 order in 1990.
[c] Order subsequently reduced to 210.
[d] Order subsequently reduced to 60.
[e] Including rolling stock.

'Welcome aboard the APT'

8. Reactions to the test runs of the Advanced Passenger Train,
Private Eye, 28 December 1981

The APT's continuing problems had a damaging impact on the investment strategy of Inter-City in general and the WCML in particular. In May 1980 an investment submission for 54 APT-S 'Squadron' trains had been produced, envisaging a total investment of some £250 million.[208] However, as further delays occurred and tensions rose, a fundamental reassessment of the project was necessitated. At first, the new strategy embraced the endorsement of a scaled-down, more conventional design for 20 units, abandoning elements of the original train,[209] but once the sector directors had been appointed in January 1982, responsibility gradually passed from Campbell to Reid as Chief Executive and Cyril Bleasdale, Director of the Inter-City sector. This was accompanied by a more commercial assessment of the returns to investment in higher speeds in the passenger markets served by the WCML, encouraged by sceptics on the Board such as Reid, Myers, and Posner, who were mindful of the need to achieve the viability for Inter-City required by government.[210] In 1983 the APT was effect-ively shelved, a personal defeat for Campbell, and motive power strategy shifted

'It's quicker by foot'

9. Peter Parker, Chairman of British Rail, experiencing the tilting mechanism of the Advanced Passenger Train, parodied by *Private Eye*, 2 July 1982. There are also references to ASLEF's strike over flexible rostering, and to the passenger marketing campaign led by disc jockey Jimmy Savile (pictured).

towards consideration of alternatives, including a new electric locomotive (the Class 89), an electric version of the HST, and the faster InterCity 225 (the Class 91).[211] The project continued *sotto voce* with 'development' status until it was finally abandoned, amid some embarrassment, in 1986.[212] It may be argued that the project was damaged by DTp anxieties and the spending cuts of the early 1980s,[213] by technical scepticism,[214] and finally by the more hard-headed evaluation of the commercial realities for Inter-City and the WCML, though it must have been galling for BR engineers to see the tilting train developed successfully in Sweden and Italy.[215] But the plain fact was that this bold example of R&D, which consumed at least £150 million in mid-1980s prices,[216] was neither developed well nor given the wholehearted internal support essential for success.[217] It distracted British Rail from commercially viable alternatives and, together with other disasters—the early experience with rail-bus replacements for the ageing DMU fleet (see p. 92, and service problems with the HSTs, and the Class 317 and 508 EMUs[218]—failed to reassure critics of railway management that higher levels of investment would pay dividends. The failure of the APT also had the effect of encouraging a 'downgrading' of the WCML in comparison with the ECML, the latter acquiring 'flagship' status with electric power, new locomotives (Class 91), and Mark IV coaches.[219]

Investment in freight was very limited in the 1980s. Spending on new BR wagons was about a third of historic levels, reflecting the desertion of the wagon-load business, and little was done about the locomotive fleet before 50 Class 58 diesels were introduced in 1983–7, and tenders were invited for the Class 60 in August 1987.[220] The developing crisis, and in particular the poor reliability of British Rail's Class 56, prompted Richard Painter of the aggregates firm, Foster Yeoman, to break the procurement mould by, first, insisting on a dedicated heavy haulage locomotive, and second, buying from the United States. The firm ordered four high-performance Class 59 diesel locomotives from General Motors in November 1984 and they were put into service in February 1986, the first foreign-built, privately owned engines to operate regularly on British Rail tracks. A fifth joined them in June 1989, by which time British Rail had responded to this prodding by acquiring the first of 100 Brush-built Class 60s.[221]

As we have already noted, expenditure on the infrastructure was dominated by the (not inconsiderable) task of renewal.[222] Following the rejection of its electrification plan the Board completed its promised 10-year programme in August 1982, though this had to be reassessed along with the Inter-City prospectus and was not completed until May 1983.[223] Thirteen schemes in all were prioritised, embracing electrification of the ECML, Paddington–West Country (Bristol/Cardiff/Plymouth), the Midland Mainline, and the York–Bristol cross-country route. All but three promised to satisfy the required 7 per cent return.[224] However, once again achievement fell far short of aspiration. A number of routes were electrified in addition to the ECML, notably the main lines in the Anglia Region (Cambridge/Ipswich/Harwich/Norwich), St. Pancras–Bedford, the Ayrshire Coast suburban and North London lines, and third-rail electrification of the lines to Bourne-mouth/Weymouth and the more controversial Tonbridge–Hastings line. A small but highly significant investment was the Thameslink project. The reopening of the Snow Hill tunnel between Farringdon and Blackfriars enabled Network SouthEast to provide through services between Bedfordshire, Hertfordshire, Kent, and Sussex. While relatively modest by the standards of French spending on RER lines in Paris, this £54 million investment (including trainsets) provided the first significant north–south services through London.[225] Just over 500 route-miles were electrified, 1979–90, taking the total to 2,800 miles; the proportion electrified was raised from 21 to 27 per cent. However, this was well down on continental European levels, and meant that only the three ECML schemes of the 13 listed in the 10-year plan were electrified. The others, notably the lines out of Paddington (except the Heathrow Express) and the Midland main line, remain diesel operated at the time of writing (2000). Essentially schemes had to be financed within the overall resources available to British Rail, which were increasingly subject to government constraint. One indication of the political environment in which this investment was conducted is provided by the debate over the Tonbridge–Hastings line, where a £24 million scheme to provide third-rail electrification was authorised in October 1983.[226] Traffic flows were far from high on a route which with its restrictive loading gauge presented operational problems, and in 1981 the Planning & Investment Committee recommended that the line be run down prior to eventual closure.[227] However, the proposal was caught up in the battle to increase the PSO grant, and the Board asked for an examination of alternatives. Campbell then produced a calculation which set the cost of electrifying this 'non-commercial' line against the savings to be obtained from closing lines in Scotland and Wales over a five-year period. Campbell concluded that the only way to 'finance' the electrification would be to close 'a number of politically very sensitive services'. The Board went on to submit a formal proposal for electrification, but its quality left much to be desired. Strong criticisms from the Department of Transport, expressed by Peter Lazarus and Robert Smith, led to the secondment of the latter to British Rail in 1983 to encourage improvements in investment appraisal (see pp. 226–8). The Tonbridge–Hastings case sheds illuminating light on the elements of scrutiny and justification in which electrification (and indeed other) projects operated.[228]

Elsewhere, some steady improvement was evident. A number of important resignalling schemes were completed, including the ECML schemes at Newcastle, York, and Leeds, and at Leicester and Waterloo. The Newcastle and Waterloo schemes, for example, both cost in excess of £30 million.[229] The diversion of the ECML at Selby to permit the exploitation of a large coalfield was funded by the NCB, but had a psychological impact in railway terms since it was the first stretch of new line built in Britain since the Manchester Sheffield and Lincolnshire Railway's extension to London Marylebone in 1899.[230] British Rail was also keen to exploit the potential offered by increased air travel by improving rail access to air terminals. The Gatwick Express, launched in May 1984, using existing rolling stock, enjoyed immediate success, encouraging the construction of a new line to serve London's third airport, Stansted. Authorised in July 1986, this £44 million project was opened in March 1991. Plans to provide rail links to Heathrow and Manchester airports were under discussion at the end of the decade.[231]

Undoubtedly, the main infrastructure project of the 1980s (and 1990s) was the Channel Tunnel. Plans for a tunnel had been shelved by the Labour administration in 1975, following a substantial rise in the cost of the associated rail link, and it was to Parker's credit that he was able to revive the idea during the potentially more hostile environment of the first Thatcher government and amid all the distractions of the Falklands conflict, and notably the sinking of the *HMS Sheffield* in May 1982. This he did by promoting a much cheaper alternative in the form of a single-bore railway tunnel known as the 'mousehole' or 'pea-shooter'. There was much lobbying behind the scenes with the aim of bringing Thatcher and Mitterand together.[232] However, Thatcher's preference was for a road link, and it was not until Reid's time that approval was given by the two governments for a twin-bore rail tunnel, in January 1986.[233] Preparatory work began shortly after the Channel Tunnel Act of July 1987, and tunnelling started at the beginning of 1988. Since the government had determined that the tunnel should be financed, constructed, and operated by a private-sector firm—Eurotunnel was the successful bidder—British Rail's interest was confined to associated infrastructure, stations, trains, depots, and proposals for a high-speed rail link to avoid crowded and outdated rail infrastructure in Kent. Nevertheless, all this amounted to a massive investment for the Board. The full story is told in Chapter 9 (pp. 319–40). Here we should note that by 1989/90 some £455 million had been committed and £57 million spent.[234]

As we have noted, rolling stock and major improvements to infrastructure caught the eye in the 1980s, but tended to obscure important investment in stations, computerised applications, and other investment. The most notable of a series of station developments was the Broadgate scheme, which involved closure of Broad Street station and the rebuilding of Liverpool Street while conserving its Victorian heritage. This impressive example of public-private partnership in investment—the property development by Rosehaugh Stanhope provided over £150 million for the rebuilding of Liverpool Street—started in July 1985 and was completed in 1991.[235] The work of the Railway Heritage Trust, established with the encouragement of part-time Board member Simon Jenkins in 1984, gave additional impetus to station refurbishment.[236] The development of a national computerised ticketing system was almost taken for granted by the public, though it brought immense benefits to the consumer in ticket issuing. The origins of the project lay in the search for Automatic Revenue Collection or ARC, which began in 1970 with an experiment in Scotland, proceeded in rather leisurely fashion, and embraced a pilot scheme in the London area by the end of the decade. By this time, the 'open stations' concept challenged the need for electronic ticket barriers, and the emphasis shifted to the urgent need to replace outdated ticket machines.[237] The All Purpose Ticket Issue System or APTIS, and its sister project, PORTIS—Portable Ticket Issue System—were authorised in 1983 at an estimated cost of £31 million, later raised to £38 million with provision for ticket encoding, acceptance of credit cards, etc.[238] Progress in taking the idea forward was rather slow. The initial project management was inadequate and there were also problems with cost escalation and technical elements associated with the software supplied by Thorn-EMI.[239] However, the benefits of the investment became immediately clear after the machines were introduced in 1986. The computers enabled speedy issue of a wide range of tickets on a national network basis, enhanced information available to booking clerks and conductors, and revolutionised the railways' management accounting information in the passenger businesses. The desk-top version, APTIS, was able to store national fare information and issue tickets to and from up to 2,500 destinations. The portable version could issue tickets for up to 99 locations. Schemes like these, including computerised seat reservation, took British Rail into the modern, computer age. APTIS and PORTIS necessitated the introduction of standardised tickets which spelled the end of the card tickets pioneered by Thomas Edmondson and in use since the beginning of the railway age.[240]

For all this activity net investment in the railways was negative in our period, as it had been since 1963.[241] Although precise calculations are difficult to make, the conclusion is not in doubt given the shedding of the subsidiary businesses, and the disposal of non-operational property (see Chapter 7). But even in the core business the overall stock of assets was not maintained over the period 1979–90 (Table 6.12). Scrapping exceeded acquisitions, and as a result the number of traction units fell by almost a half, freight assets were decimated, and there was a reduction of 15 per cent in track-miles. Of course, in some areas replacement assets and renewals provided higher quality and greater capacity. However, the overall picture was still one of disinvestment. For example, the number of passenger vehicles fell by 36 per cent, and while the new stock provided more seats, the overall number of seats available to passengers fell by a significant 21 per cent at a time of traffic growth.

The 1980s also saw a more determined effort to rectify deficiencies in investment programming, appraisal, and control, which had also been the subject of criticism in the Serpell committee. In 1984, Glyn Williams, the Director of Financial Planning, undertook an investigation into investment procedures, aided by Dr Robert Smith, seconded from DTp (he had already assisted with the ECML submission), and Dr Berry of the Manchester Business School. Wide-ranging proposals were advanced to alter existing practice, including: the use of the sole user principle of cost allocation in investment submissions; sponsorship of projects by sector directors; the separation of submission and appraisal for schemes costing over £250,000, with the appraisals to be conducted by independent

Table 6.12 Indicators of net disinvestment in railways, 1979–89/90

Year	Traction units		Coaching vehicles		Freight vehicles		Seats in passenger berths		Track open for traffic	
	No.	(Index)	No.	(Index)	No.	(Index)	No.	(Index)	No.	(Index)
1979	3,712	(100)	21,511	(100)	137,589	(100)	1,091,296	(100)	27,592	(100)
1983	3,053	(82)	16,963	(79)	54,510	(40)	971,097	(89)	25,664	(93)
1989/90	1,959	(53)	13,833	(64)	21,970	(16)	859,002	(79)	23,518	(85)

Source: BRB, *R&A 1979, 1983, 1989/90.*

227

analysts; and the creation of the new post of Investment Adviser. The intention was to provide back-checks both as a form of management audit and as a guide to future submission work.[242] The new procedures, together with an investment manual and a Passenger Demand Forecasting Handbook, were in place by June 1986, and were sufficiently robust to attract the endorsement of the MMC in 1987.[243] Nevertheless, some deficiencies remained, particularly in the appraisal of schemes,[244] and in 1987 a major review of investment authorisation procedures was undertaken following concerns expressed by the Board, and in particular the non-executive members Derek Hornby, Richard Tookey, and Allen Sheppard. As a result, simplified procedures and additional delegation to the businesses was injected into the process, including the introduction of a broader, strategic role for the Investment Committee.[245] The DTp, which had been won over by the improvement in the quality of investment submissions since 1985, expressed some scepticism about the extent of delegation to the sectors and asked for a review after about a year.[246] The Board asked for a review after six months, and further monitoring in March and July 1988 and February 1989 was sufficiently encouraging to produce a doubling of the delegation thresholds, with the limit for DTp consultation raised from £5 million (set in May 1983) to £10 million (from September 1989).[247] Project management, however, was an enduring area of anxiety. As we have seen, there were difficulties with all the major projects of the 1980s and the repeated shortcomings, including a 46 per cent escalation in Channel Tunnel Phase I costs in constant prices, and the continuing failure to match expenditure to budgets, prompted Kirby to commission a report from Touche Ross. Presented to the Business Review Group in August 1989, it resulted in the establishment of two task forces to strengthen project management and provide a further review of planning and programming, the results of which did not emerge until after the period covered by this chapter. It is difficult to say how far all this took British Rail. Expressions of concern should not be taken as an indicator of worst practice, and the repeated assessment of existing procedures should be seen more as a move towards higher-quality evaluation than the reverse. Nevertheless, there is something in the argument that project management was not of the same standard as the appraisal exercises which preceded them.[248] Group investment expenditure failed to match budgeted expenditure during the early 1980s, in 1982 by 10 per cent, and in 1983 by 16 per cent. The shortfall was lower, at 4–5 per cent, in 1984/5–86/7. However, in the latter year the data on railway investment revealed a worrying 15 per cent shortfall on revenue account and a deviation of more than 30 per cent in the *content* of the expenditure compared with budget, which led Stan Whittaker, the Director of Group Finance, to note that there was 'still inadequate consultation between Sectors, their Business Managers, Regions and Functional Officers as to actual requirements and the phasing of physical work and related expenditure at Budget preparation time'. In 1987/8 there was an overspend of 3 per cent, but a variation from budgeted intentions of £209 million or 43 per cent, and in the following year the shortfall was 7 per cent. For all the work of Touche Ross little immediate improvement was discernible: actual spending in 1989/90 was £124 million less than budget, a shortfall of no less than 16 per cent.[249]

Investment constraints, together with the pressure to meet ever-tighter government targets, inevitably raised issues of safety standards and the level of acceptable risk in rail operations. In fact, there was a steady extension of the network equipped with AWS (an additional 2,000 miles in the 1980s), and the safety record for much of the 1980s continued to be good, as it had been in the later 1970s (see p. 66). In 1980–3 only six passengers died in train accidents, and although the figure rose to 18 in 1984, chiefly as a result of the derailment at Polmont in July (in which 13 passengers died), in 1985 no passengers or staff were killed, an unprecedented achievement in British railway history.[250] However, any complacency about the issue that the data may have encouraged was shattered first by a fire in King's Cross underground station in November 1987, in which 31 people died, and then by two serious rail accidents. The first, at Lockington in July 1986, where eight passengers and a train driver died, involved the safety of automatic open level crossings and led to a review conducted by Professor Peter Stott. He concluded that while most of the crossing accidents had been caused by the failure of road users to obey traffic signals, at some locations train speeds and traffic movements made open crossings unsuitable. In consequence criteria were laid down for determining conversion to automatic half-barriers. As a result, 92 crossings had been converted by 1991.[251] The second, as we have already noted, jolted senior management. The Clapham Jnc. accident on 12 December 1988, in which 34 passengers and a driver died, raised a complex set of issues, embracing infrastructure and rolling stock standards, the management of infrastructure renewal, quality assurance, and the conditions experienced by railway labour. The crash, caused by the failure to cut back a redundant wire during renewals work, served as a shock to those who had assumed that British Rail's determined drive to reduce operating and infrastructure costs was a risk-free process. Clapham was followed by two more rail accidents in three days in March 1989 at Purley and Bellgrove (six passenger deaths). These were attributed to human error, namely the phenomenon known as SPAD or Signals Passed at Danger, steering the debate towards consideration of the desirability of large-scale investment in Automatic Train Protection or ATP, which unlike AWS would make it impossible for danger signals to be passed. The Board, concerned after the report on the King's Cross fire, had already taken steps to prioritise safety. In November 1988, Maurice Holmes, the experienced Director of Operations, was appointed Director of Safety. However, he had only been in the job for 11 days when the Clapham accident occurred.[252] His brief rapidly became an urgent one as the Board responded to a situation which took much of the gloss off the investment successes of the period.[253] It was to the Board's credit that it quickly accepted its responsibility to improve safety procedures following the report of the inquiry conducted by

Anthony Hidden, QC in November 1989.[254] That there was much still to be done was demonstrated by the concerns expressed by Rayner, the JMD (Railways) and others at a series of accidents in 1989, for example at Harrow, Warrington, Acton Grange, and West Ealing, which raised questions about standards and monitoring of maintenance. The raised temperature was demonstrated by the decision to withdraw the Class 90 locomotives in August when brake defects were discovered.[255] Safety became a prime consideration in the early 1990s.

6.6 Conclusion

The 1980s were an exacting decade for nationalised railways in Britain. Thorny and long-standing issues were raised, especially in industrial relations, and a determined effort, not always successful, was made to create a modern railway to compete with the more obviously spectacular and better-funded developments in France, Germany, and Japan, for example. Successes such as Sprinters and the ECML electrification, and the start of work on the Channel Tunnel, with the promise of a high-speed rail link to London, caught the eye, as did Liverpool Street station, flagship of a more determined response to property development which came with the emphasis on privatisation. On the other hand, we should not be carried away into thinking that Britain invested heavily in its railways. Much of the resources for continued maintenance and renewal came from rail revenues, the product of a relatively high pricing strategy which was maintained in the 1980s.[256] Total spending was not high in comparison with the 1960s, and was clearly insufficient to reverse a long-term record of net disinvestment. The Serpell review, for all the mud thrown at it in 1983, did give impetus to new management drives in the period, which saw a determined assault on the rather complacent, if not sloppy, management of costs in engineering and administration. When Bob Reid I handed over to his namesake in April 1990 there was a sound legacy of effective decentralised management, clearer objectives, and a shattering of the myth that railways could not achieve financial targets and 'break even'. Equally, there were difficulties, the safety issue being the most prominent, and below the surface there was evidence for those who cared to look that British Rail in general was far from being the modern railway system that more supportive countries were establishing for the twenty-first century. Above all, the spectre of privatisation heralded a new agenda which was to blow internal management responses off course and provide the biggest shake-up in the industry since 123 railway companies had been merged into the 'Big Four' by the Railways Act of 1921.

7

Selling the Subsidiary Businesses

7.1 The significance of disposal

The disposal of the British Railways Board's subsidiary businesses was significant for a number of reasons. First of all, there was the immediate context. The Thatcher governments were intent on reducing the public liability represented by the railways, and the Board was therefore encouraged to concentrate on its 'core' activities. At the same time, the sale of its hotels, ships, surplus property, and mechanical engineering works was expected to generate some much-needed cash for investment. Second, the public policy debate which accompanied the selling process revealed that though remaining in the public sector British Rail was in many ways in the vanguard of the debate about privatisation in the critical period of 1979–81, before the Conservatives had formulated a clear policy. As we shall see, the views of many managers, particularly those engaged in investment-starved subsidiary businesses, such as shipping and the hotels, were often more radical than those of the politicians. At several key moments they were closely involved in formulating policy with an inexperienced government whose appetite for political and economic dogma often exceeded its initial executive capacity. Third, the disposal of the subsidiaries together with large amounts of non-operational land in the period c.1980–8 was an important forerunner of what was to come. While it may be fanciful to suggest that there was a path-dependent process leading to railway privatisation, the earlier experience certainly raised all the issues and difficulties—the why, the how, and the debates about competitive tendering and sale proceeds—which came later.[1] Fourth, the sale of BREL and the engineering workshops had a profound psychological impact in breaking the mould of backward integration which had characterised Britain's railway industry since the 1840s. These sales were a very considerable step in the move to full privatisation. Finally, the early 1980s saw an early example of aspirations for private-public sector partnership, something which has been endorsed enthusiastically by the Blair government at the end of the 1990s. However, the lesson to be learned here, as will be evident below, was that the private element quickly drove out the public element, leaving the notion of partnership in tatters.

7.2 The search for private-public partnership

We turn first to the Board's initial reactions to the change of government in 1979, its response to 'privatisation', notably the establishment in November 1980 of British Rail Investments Ltd (BRIL), and events leading to the abandonment of the enthusiasm for private-public partnership in 1981. Following the Conservatives' election victory in May 1979 the climate inside British Rail, encouraged by Peter Parker, was to seize the initiative and seek to exploit potential opportunities. Nowhere was this more apparent than among the more entrepreneurial managers working for the Board's subsidiary businesses such as hotels and shipping, who had been victims of constrained investment for many years and were thus attracted to the idea of some form of public-private partnership. It is easy to be drawn by teleology into assuming that the disposal of the subsidiaries was a story of gradual and reluctant divestment, with the government slowly but inexorably turning the screw. In fact, as we have already noted (Chapter 4, pp. 99–103), the first Thatcher administration was more uncertain about privatisation than such a hypothesis implies. Initially, government policy was all about ends rather than means, with the urgent priority to curtail government spending. Thus, the Queen's Speech in May 1979 referred merely to the intention to 'restrict the claims of the public sector on the nation's resources', while Thatcher commented on it in very general terms, promising to reduce the size of the public sector and establish a larger 'healthy free enterprise sector'. How exactly this was to be done, and in which industries, was left unspecified. Her Chancellor, Geoffrey Howe, was equally determined to restrain public sector expenditure, emphasising with characteristic succinctness in June 1979 that 'finance must determine expenditure'. But the details remained to be worked out.[2]

On the railway side, British Rail seemed to be taking the lead in 1979. Hoping to capitalise on the change of government, the Board wanted privatisation to involve the attraction of private capital into its investment-starved businesses without loss of control. 'Hiving-off', with the industrial relations problems it would provoke, was to be avoided; so too was a forced sale of 'good assets', leaving the 'bad' in the public sector.[3] Unlike other enterprises at the turn of the decade, which were being encouraged to shed assets in order to concentrate on their 'core' business, in accordance with the recommendations of Peters and Waterman,[4] British Rail did not talk about dismemberment. Instead, it firmly endorsed Parker's Group of Groups concept of 1977, which made the case for joint venture capital, and the need for the subsidiaries to be allowed to 'operate with the same degree of flexibility and opportunity' as their private-sector counterparts.[5] Early evidence of this policy could be seen in the reorganisation of the hotels business and the reconstitution of the shipping services, as described in Chapter 2 (pp. 39–41). After the election Board members met informally with the new Minister of Transport, Norman Fowler, at the end of June 1979. Following the meeting British Rail volunteered to prepare a policy document on the opportunities for private-sector involvement in the Board's activities.[6] Parker and Bosworth then engaged the services of merchant bankers Morgan Grenfell, seeking advice on the best way to bring capital into the subsidiaries. There was a fertility of ideas at this time, embracing the notions of joint participation, the sale and lease-back of railway assets, and a holding company structure for the subsidiaries with a substantial placing of shares (49 or 51 per cent) with the private sector.[7] The consultants' report was incorporated in a 26-page document sent to Fowler in October. This examined the prospects for seven businesses (BREL, already the subject of internal review, was excluded). Ranked by turnover and employment, they were Sealink UK, British Transport Hotels (BTH), Freightliners, British Rail Property Board, British Transport Advertising (jointly owned with the National Bus Company), British Rail Hovercraft, and the rail consultancy business Transmark (see Table 7.1). The Board nailed its colours to the mast of 'partnership or joint undertaking'. It sought ministerial approval for action to find a company to acquire Hoverlloyd and then merge it with British Rail Hovercraft, undertake a public issue of shares in Sealink, and seek private-sector partners to develop the hotels business.[8]

The initiative, which caused some misgivings among part-time members such as David Serpell,[9] reveals the railways to be leading the way in policy making at this stage. The aim was to examine the scope for development and the opportunities for outside finance; the emphasis was clearly on partnership arrangements with the private sector and the retention of a sizeable public sector shareholding. Rejecting the idea of floating a holding company of subsidiary businesses, the Board's preferred policy was to develop special strategies for each business. The aim was, in Parker's words, to 'move our groups within the Group towards the same sort of dynamic and competitive environment, with the same flexibilities and constraints, as in the private sector'; the criteria to be employed included the long-term increase in net asset value and an improvement in group profitability. The Board did not think it appropriate to sell assets with potential unless the move could be seen to benefit the business in the long run. Synergy was the current watchword: the synergy of private and public investment and

Table 7.1 BRB subsidiaries, 1978

Business	Turnover (£m.)	Railway-related turnover (%)	Percentage of railway turnover	Employment end 1978
BREL	313.6	91	19	35,644
Sealink UK	159.3	34	10	10,565
British Transport Hotels[a]	83.4	60	5	10,783
Freightliners	51.0	100	3	2,423
British Rail Property Board	34.2	66	2	1,099
British Transport Advertising[b]	8.0	65	n.a.	n.a.
British Rail Hovercraft	5.6	21	0.3	495
Transmark	4.5	100	0.3	57

Source: BRB, R&A 1978; Gourvish, 'British Rail's Business-Led Organization', 142.
[a] Including station and train catering.
[b] x50% stake.

management. The injection of capital was to be varied to suit the defined needs of each business.[10] The government's reaction was mixed, however, and any suggestion that British Rail's subsidiaries should be developed and expanded within the public sector was regarded as unacceptable. Thus, in the negotiations that followed, the Board was forced to concede some ground. In February 1980 Norman Fowler demanded that the rail subsidiaries be transferred to a holding company 'free of statutory constraints that apply to the Board'. Only this, he said, would remove the existing disadvantages: a low priority for investment funds; the inhibitions of legal constraints; and insufficient management attention. He made it clear that these objectives would not be achieved 'by a merely piecemeal approach—still less by simply selling off assets, which is not my purpose'.[11] The departmental view was that the Minister should hold a majority of the shares in the holding company.[12] After much discussion, an examination of options by a joint DTp/BRB team, a Commons debate, and the further involvement of Morgan Grenfell, who had questioned the wisdom of a conglomerate of somewhat disparate assets,[13] the Board was able to persuade him to accept the idea of transferring the non-rail businesses to a wholly owned British Rail subsidiary—BRIL.[14] This was not without cost. The agreed package involved the more controversial step, in the opinion of some Board members, of transferring the railways' property assets, including some operational property, to the new holding company. This was apparently done in order to 'enable the Minister to win with colleagues and the headmistress'.[15] Nevertheless, at this point government intentions, as revealed by Norman Fowler and Kenneth Clarke in statements over the period March–July 1980, seemed to be at one with the Board's. Private-sector 'involvement', though with 'sufficient control' was advocated for four businesses: Sealink, BTH, Hovercraft, and the Board's 'property holdings'. This approach was preferred to a simple sell-off.[16]

However, Fowler was a minister with a particular appetite for privatisation. He had been instrumental in the inclusion in the 1979 Conservative Manifesto of the only clear pledges for such a course of action—relating to the National Freight Corporation and the British Transport Docks Board, plans for which were well advanced in early 1980. He was privately not persuaded by Parker's enthusiasm for a conglomerate BR, a kind of public sector Mitsubishi.[17] Reactions to his July 1980 statement in the press reflected this, with headlines such as 'Bridge over Muddied Waters' (*Guardian*), 'The Great Railway Bazaar' (*The Times*), and 'Great Train Robbery' (*Mirror*), plus a witty cartoon by John Kent in the *Sunday Times* (see Cartoon 10).[18] Unsurprisingly, then, over the ensuing months the climate changed, and the government was able to assert itself with a public corporation which had often shown itself to be unduly deferential to Whitehall's wishes.[19] In September 1980 Bosworth had asserted that the primary role of the holding company should be to encourage the subsidiaries to 'seek private capital where appropriate'.[20] However, he quickly changed his tune after his installation as Chairman of the newly incorporated BRIL in November,[21] and the emphasis shifted to embrace the sale of assets or equity. The seeking of capital became *primarily the initial role*, then the *principal initial role*, in subsequent drafts of BRIL's remit. Then, in December Bosworth reported to the Board that 'BRIL should ensure that the subsidiaries, where appropriate, seek external sources of capital through the sale of assets or the sale of equity, endeavouring to retain *as far as is reasonably practicable* [my italics] a shareholding'; he also reminded his colleagues that the government's aim was to ensure that 'the businesses in question pass as soon as is practicable—and certainly within the life of this Parliament—into majority private sector ownership and into effective private sector control'. It was this latter element which was clearly dominant by the spring of 1981.[22]

In this shift of policy the role of the Treasury was crucial. It was the Treasury that had insisted that 'escape from the public sector' should mean precisely that. It was soon made plain that a reduction in the Board's shareholding from 100 to 49 or even 30 per cent would not achieve this.[23] In fact, this disappointing news (for Parker and many of his colleagues) had been anticipated in the previous October, when Kenneth Clarke, then Parliamentary Secretary at the DTp, had told the Board informally that he 'was doubtful whether [it] . . . would be able to retain a major holding in any new developments with the private sector'.[24] BRIL, incorporated as a wholly owned subsidiary in November 1980, was given legal status by the Transport Act of 1981, which received the Royal Assent in July.[25] The Board transferred to it the assets of BTH (excluding Travellers Fare), Sealink, with its substantial harbour assets, Hovercraft, and the non-operational property of the Property Board, together with about £40 million of its operational property (including an office block at Euston Station). It clearly expected BRIL to function

10. Criticism of the proposed sale of British Rail's subsidiaries, 1980: Peter Parker, Keith Joseph, and Margaret Thatcher, as seen by 'Zelda', John Kent, *Sunday Times*, 20 July 1980.

as a free-standing holding company largely free of government interference and to confine its activities to privatisation advice and procedures, leaving day-to-day management in the hands of the Board.[26] However, the 1981 Act contained all the necessary powers for the Secretary of State to dictate the pace and content of a programme of disposal. This became imperative given the Board's serious cash-flow problems (see pp. 152–4) and the fact that policies for the hotels and shipping, which had a poor profits record, clearly implied an interventionist role for the new company. By the summer of 1981 senior managers conceded that the government would be able to use the new legislation to insist on the way in which privatisation was to be pursued, and that BRIL would be required by the government to act as a vehicle for the sale of assets to the private sector without the retention of a participatory stake.[27] Indeed, as early as February 1981 Jennie Page of the DTp had made it perfectly plain to Arthur Brooking, finance director of BRIL, that far from seeing the holding company as an advisory body, 'we saw BRIL as the driving force behind implementation of the policy'.[28] Government intentions became much clearer when Parker and the BRIL Board met the Secretary of State, now David Howell, in October 1981. Howell wished to 'set the pace of future privatisation'. His view, reinforced by his merchant bank advisers Samuel Montagu, was that 'given the severe financial problems facing the Railways Board, it was probably desirable for sales to take place as quickly as practicable'. All thoughts of partnership had evaporated.[29]

7.3 British Transport Hotels

The fate of the hotels was clearly affected by the change of direction. Successive managing directors, George Hill and Peter Land, frustrated by their inability to

respond to market opportunities, had wished to free British Transport Hotels, one of Britain's largest hotel chains, from some aspects of public sector constraint, notably those affecting investment. In 1979 Land had divided the estate of 29 hotels, golf courses, etc. into three categories—'leisure', 'city', and 'investment'—with the aim of identifying the best prospects for development. At first, joint venture activity was the aim, and there was a determination from the top down to develop existing assets.[30] The revitalisation of the Grosvenor Hotel in London in 1980 indicated what could be done with the right level of support. Thus, the initial policy on the hotels had been to invite commercial development by merging all or part of BTH with a suitable private sector partner. In 1980–1, before BRIL had been formed, the hotels management had had discussions with the De Vere Group about a sale and lease-back arrangement, but this idea, enthusiastically supported by BTH, did not find favour with the Treasury, since the deal was taken to involve a government guarantee of hotel rents.[31] In any case, British Rail's cash crisis was serious enough to force more radical possibilities to the surface, not least the idea in August 1980 that the entire hotels business should be sold.[32] In June 1981, in furtherance of the joint venture policy, three Scottish hotels, Gleneagles, and the Caledonian and North British in Edinburgh, were sold to a new company, Gleneagles Hotels plc, after attempts to develop them separately had failed.[33] With British Transport Hotels taking a third of the equity, a substantial shareholding was retained in the public sector, a procedure also followed in October when the ailing hovercraft business merged with Hoverlloyd.[34] Partnership was also the route taken to develop the hotels in Derby and Sheffield.[35] Unfortunately, the Gleneagles project was not conceived in a supportive environment. It was certainly consonant with the thinking of Parker and his Board,[36] but it had to run the gauntlet of criticism not only from the government, where both the DTp and Treasury expressed strong doubts that it really represented an escape from the public sector, but also from Morgan Grenfell, who attacked the substantial

237

discount of 23 per cent on the market valuation that the sale appeared to represent.[37]

BTH also took steps to address the problems of two of its subsidiaries: laundries, where the assets were in bad shape; and the wines division, where stocks were found to be particularly high. Prompted by BRIL the policy shifted over the course of 1979–81 from joint ventures to outright sale. There were three laundries, at Slateford (Edinburgh), Heworth (York), and Willesden (London). The latter required substantial investment, thereby inhibiting all ideas of a joint venture, and was closed; the others were sold to the St. George's Group in April 1982 for £1.1 million. The new owners then entered into three- and five-year agreements with BTH and British Rail for linen hire and laundry processing.[38] The wine business involved four activities: sales to BTH hotels; sales to Travellers Fare; a wholesale business; and a substantial mail order business operated as the Malmaison Wine Club.[39] The possibility of private-sector finance was explored in 1980, and talks took place with Les Amis du Vin and the Industrial and Commercial Finance Corporation. The negotiations were not successful, however,[40] and a further spur to privatisation came with an allegation of unfair competition, which became a policy matter when it was conveyed to Norman Fowler by Sir Ian Gilmour on behalf of a constituent. Fowler rejected the contention that the Malmaison Wine Club's connection with British Rail gave it an 'undue advantage' over private-sector competitors, but he did express the opinion that the Club was 'a prime candidate for early action'.[41] The hotels management tried to address the problem of high wine stocks. These were reduced by £2 million in 1980–1, but were still valued at a not inconsiderable £3.4 million at the end of 1981. In addition, BRIL's efforts to find an outright buyer did not prove successful.[42] Instead, an agreement was reached with a small independent company, Laytons Wine Merchants, in June 1982. Laytons agreed to take on the Malmaison business and to sell wine from stock on an agency basis over a two-year period.[43] Realised prices fell short of expectations, however, and there were particular difficulties with large stocks of 1978 Burgundy, which were disposed of at a loss. At the end of the year Laytons agreed to purchase the remaining wine plus goodwill for a disappointing £800,000.[44]

The future of a public-private partnership in British Rail's subsidiaries was effectively ended when the government insisted that there should be no 'symbiosis' between British Transport Hotels and the Gleneagles company. The Board's original stake in Gleneagles had been scaled down from 40 to 33.3 per cent to appease the Treasury, but it quickly emerged that even this stake was regarded as being too high.[45] When in 1983 the Gleneagles company proposed to fund a move into the London market by means of a rights issue, the Department of Transport ruled that BTH should not participate in it. Severance then became the only logical option, and 29.9 per cent was sold to the whisky firm Arthur Bell & Son for £6.07 million in December. Bells then launched a hostile (and ultimately successful) takeover bid for the company, and BTH sold its remaining 3.33 per cent stake for £826,000 in March 1984. The publicly held equity was thus disposed of for £6.9 million, more than double what it had been worth less than three years earlier. Here surely was a case for the retention of a public sector stake in preference to premature sale.[46]

By this time privatisation policy had already moved on to embrace outright sale of the remaining assets. In November 1982 tenders were invited for the rest of the hotel estate. The decision represented a major change of strategy. A BTH policy document of September 1981 had favoured development of the 'core' business of 19 hotels with the aim of placing shares on the market in 1984. However, BRIL, which had encouraged this approach, quickly moved to oppose it. In a memorandum to the main Board of 28 October 1981 Bosworth expressed doubts about the ability of the BTH management to improve its core in the time available, and threw BRIL's weight behind the immediate sale of 15 hotels, in addition to three others (Derby, Sheffield, and St. Andrews) where arrangements were already being made.[47] This provoked angry reactions from Sir Alexander Glen (the Deputy Chairman), James Forbes, and Peter Land at BTH, and for a time the atmosphere within the Board, BRIL, and BTH was extremely tense. The situation was certainly not helped by the dual position of Bosworth, British Rail's deputy chairman, who was chairman of both BRIL and BTH.[48] It is not clear how far BRIL's change of heart was influenced by the government. It may not be entirely coincidental that seven days before Bosworth's memorandum was sent Howell had asked BRIL to take early action in the disposal of its assets.[49] The subsidiary was certainly under pressure to produce appropriate cash flows through asset sales, and in March 1982 was set a target of realising £190 million net in current prices over the three years April 1982–March 1985.[50] Equally, Bosworth and his colleagues may have been convinced that the hotels company, whose far from lean organisation made operating losses in each of the years 1980–2,[51] would benefit from a change of management, while the government's advisers, Samuel Montagu, were reported to favour a sale by public tender.[52]

The Railways Board itself was in a rather delicate position. The evidence suggests that it tended to support the aspirations of BTH. Its response to the BRIL/BTH rift in October–November 1981 was to encourage BRIL to proceed with evaluation of the sale option while at the same time reaffirming its intention to maintain a stake in the ongoing hotels business.[53] It was certainly more supportive than either BRIL or the government of attempts made by Land, Group Managing Director of BTH, and his colleagues John Tee (Finance Director) and Derek Plant (Operations Director) to organise a management buyout of a number of the remaining hotels as an alternative to a sale by public tender.[54] There were obvious advantages to the Board in such a procedure, in the form of lower transaction costs and improved industrial relations. Between May and August 1982 considerable effort was put into a management bid of £29 million for 18 hotels, with the help of Kleinwort Benson and James Capel, but much to the disappointment of Peter Parker and his fellow Board members, the bid failed. The offer was apparently several millions below the market valuation, a fact which produced opposition from the cash-maximising BRIL and its advisers Morgan Grenfell.[55] Revised offers of £20.5 and £20.25 million for 12 hotels were made in October, the latter implying a discount of £3.47 million after allowing for certain benefits accruing to the Board. These also failed, though at the time of their abandonment the difference between the two sides appeared to be relatively small.[56] However, in the course of the haggling over the valuations the Secretary of State, Howell, stated categorically that he was concerned by the small equity involvement of the management team and could not defend a discounted purchase.[57] At this stage the government was extremely sensitive to the criticism that some of the early privatisation schemes, such as British Aerospace and Cable & Wireless (both in 1981), and Amersham International (February 1982), had involved offer prices which were low enough to provide city investors with immediate profits. Equally embarrassing was the sale by tender of Britoil in November 1982, which also provoked criticism when it left 70 per cent of the shares with the underwriters.[58]

British Rail was left with no option but to dispose of the hotels by public tender. In November 1982, 21 of the remaining 23 properties were offered for sale. The Board made every effort to keep the MBO concept alive, by announcing that bids for eight hotels or more would receive preferential treatment, and by offering to take 10 per cent of the equity in Land's company, Concorde Hotels.[59] However, Land's final attempt to keep the BTH management intact was doomed to failure, since it proved impossible to attract institutional support for only a right to bid. His presence also had the effect of deterring bidders, and only 10 of the hotels were sold by tender in March 1983. The others were disposed of subsequently by private treaty in small parcels in 1983–4 at a time when hotel profits and consequently hotel assets were depressed.[60] The BTH management were extremely disappointed by the turn of events.[61] They complained about the small number of tenders and the existence of some discounting against valuation, and Glen wrote angry letters to both Thatcher and Howell.[62] Land and Forbes also alleged that the success of the MBO offers had been prejudiced by an over-valuation of the hotels, caused by the assumption that the vendors, not the purchasers, would bear the costs of detaching the properties from BRB and of providing staff travel concessions. A revised valuation in 1982 would have closed the gap between the MBO and BRIL.[63]

This said, the sale of the hotels did not produce less for British Rail than a management buyout. While it is true that many of the hotels were subsequently re-sold at much higher prices,[64] the sum realised for the 10 hotels sold by tender was £25.6 million, 7 per cent above their valuation, and the total realisation for the 21 hotels was some £40 million, comfortably ahead of the valuation which Land and his colleagues had felt was generously high.[65] The total proceeds from the disposal of BTH assets, including profits on joint ventures, amounted to £60 million by September 1984.[66] Both BRIL and the government had resisted the temptation to sell the assets cheaply to the existing management, a situation which contrasted with that a decade later when railway assets were sold and re-sold. Two minor buyouts *were* achieved. In February 1983 Christopher Dunn and Gordon Miller bought BTH's Superbreak holiday business for a peppercorn, and in the following month Tee and Plant, operating as Compass Hotels, took a short lease and management contract on the two London hotels affected by development schemes, the Great Northern and Great Eastern.[67] Nevertheless, the aspirations of the Board and of the BTH management in 1979–80 had not been satisfied, and, as Glen put it to Thatcher, the result had been 'to annihilate a [sound] concern unnecessarily'. The trade unions were also staggered by the failure of the Board's approach. As an NUR document put it, 'the intention of gaining access to private finance to enable the subsidiaries to flourish, while still under the control of the Board, back-fired . . . the Board's desperate pragmatism gave the Government the opportunity to dress its ideological intentions in the convenient clothes of necessity'.[68]

7.4 Sealink and the harbours

There was less controversy with the disposal of Sealink and the harbours in 1984. Here again, the decisive element was the intervention of ministers and civil servants in the decision-making process. The Board's initial strategy for Sealink, as with the hotels, was to try to keep the business intact and move towards a public issue of a portion of the equity. But if this had been problematic with hotels, it was a distant prospect for shipping, which experienced considerable financial difficulties during the recession, with losses after interest of £11 million in 1981 and £6 million in 1982.[69] In consequence, the timetable for placing about 70 per cent of the share capital was a leisurely one: the issue was not expected to take place until the end of 1983 at the earliest. In fact, the government was more supportive of the Board's strategy than it had been with the hotels, for it did not dissent from the share issue policy until after the election of June 1983. First of all, it fully backed British Rail's opposition to European Ferries' opportunistic takeover bid for Sealink in December 1980. The predator, led by Keith Wickenden, the Tory MP for Dorking, was something of an embarrassment for the government, particularly since its unwelcome bid was referred to the MMC in March 1981, along with the Hovercraft/Hoverlloyd proposal. In December the MMC ruled that the proposed merger was against the public interest.[70] Nor did the government intervene in the offer of £30 million for a 51 per cent stake in Sealink made by Carnival Cruise Lines of Miami in January 1982. The owner, Ted Arison, a buccaneering entrepreneur of the Branson type, induced some qualms, but his offer was taken seriously enough, and the DTp asked for no more than to be fully informed. In the event the stumbling-block with BRIL was Arison's insistence on substantial deferred payments, and the negotiations were terminated in May 1982.[71] Finally, the decision to establish the harbours as a separate subsidiary of Sealink, provided for in the 1981 Transport Act, also worked in favour of a share issue option since it provided tangible assets for a company in which much of the asset value was in the form of leased ships.[72]

In this instance the change of emphasis came in 1983, by which time Sealink's results were improving.[73] The Conservatives had made privatisation a 'key element in the Government's economic strategy',[74] and the election victory in June gave the policy additional impetus. Thus Howell and his successors, Tom King and Nicholas Ridley, pressed British Rail to effect the early disposal of Sealink.[75] In November 1983 the Board and BRIL considered three options, drawn up and costed by Morgan Grenfell, namely: (1) the placing of 60 per cent of the equity in early 1984, followed by a subsequent offer for sale; (2) an immediate sale; and (3) an offer for sale in March 1985.[76] The Board, acting on advice from BRIL and Morgan Grenfell, threw its weight behind option (1). However, Ridley made it clear that notwithstanding the estimated yields from each option, which were £62–74, £65, and £80 million respectively, he could support only option (2), the immediate sale of the company by competitive tender. The 'need to test the market' was 'a key requirement'.[77] Ridley saw no reason why a Sealink consortium should not put in a bid. An MBO proposal was contemplated by Sealink's management but involved much complexity and in the event was not pressed. There was also agreement that the shipping business and the harbours should be sold as a single entity.[78] The Board duly offered the business to tender in the spring of 1984. The outcome was rather disappointing. The offer for sale presented numerous difficulties surrounding the relationship with British Rail, including its contracts with the several harbours and residual obligations affecting operations at Fishguard, Zeebrugge, etc. Only six companies expressed a serious interest, including a consortium assembled by the Sealink management. And of these, only one, British Ferries, a subsidiary of James Sherwood's company Sea Containers, proceeded to a formal offer.[79] Contrary to Ridley's statement in the House of Commons, Sealink was sold not to the highest bidder but to the *only* bidder. Labour spokesman John Prescott complained that Sealink had been sold 'at an unfavourable time at a knockdown price to a foreign company with an appalling record of operating under flags of convenience'.[80] The agreed price of £65.7 million in July 1984 may have been fair in the circumstances, given the difficulties which emerged after the sale, but it was a substantial discount on the estimated yield from option (3).[81] British Rail's stake in the hovercraft business also disappeared under depressing circumstances. The merger with Hoverlloyd in October 1981 failed to turn the business round. Losses amounted to £5.2 million in 1981/2, and £3.2 million in 1982/3, producing urgent requests for extended overdraft facilities and a guarantee from the Board of a portion of the overdraft, which required permission from an increasingly sceptical Department of Transport.[82] With receivership looming the entire business was sold to a management syndicate for a nominal sum in March 1984. The syndicate, led by Michael Keeling, bought seven tranches of assets for £1 each. Later, in June 1986, the reviving business was sold on to Sealink British Ferries for £5 million, a substantial profit, with the syndicate members making £600,000 each.[83] After the sale of Hoverspeed and Sealink the work of BRIL was regarded as completed and the subsidiary was reduced to 'dormant' status in November 1984.[84] The organisational device had certainly proved successful in pushing through the disposal of some of the more obvious but nonetheless integrated assets belonging to British Rail. However, there were sizeable 'non-railway' assets still to be dealt with, not least engineering and property. Decisions in relation to these after 1984 were made outside the BRIL framework.

7.5 The railway workshops

British Rail's substantial engineering activity was also caught up in the drive to release asset value. As we have seen (Chapter 6, pp. 203–9), the process began with a radical restructuring of the Mechanical & Electrical Engineering departments, and the introduction of competitive tendering for the railways' rolling stock requirements, initiated in 1983. Four years of such tendering saw the private sector obtaining orders worth £380 million for passenger vehicles (total: £720 million), and £45 million of the freight orders (total: £100 million). Another precedent was set by the aggregates firm, Foster Yeoman, when it introduced its own American diesel locomotives from General Motors in 1986. Foster Yeoman was also a large investor in its own wagons, which was part of an emerging trend. By 1987/8 31 per cent of the railway wagon fleet was privately owned, and a year later the proportion was close to 50 per cent. All this added up to privatisation in essence, even if no transfer of ownership was involved.[85] The sale of assets followed as the logical outcome of Welsby's 'Manufacturing and Maintenance' (M&M) initiative. This involved an extensive restructuring and rationalisation of the railway workshops, culminating in the separation of new build/major repairs from maintenance, the latter transferring to British Rail Maintenance Ltd, a wholly owned subsidiary, in April 1987. The sale of BREL's New Build and Repair Group was a natural sequel to this policy and indeed a government expectation since 1983. However, it was put on hold during the implementation stage of M&M.[86] However, by 1987 attention was directed towards options for the disposal of BREL's remaining works, at Crewe, Derby, York, Doncaster (wagon works), Horwich (foundry), and Swindon.

The Thatcher Revolution

The Swindon workshops had closed in 1986, and in the following year the site was sold for redevelopment to Tarmac Properties for just over £9 million. In this instance the decision to seek tenders produced a marked improvement over an earlier offer from Trafalgar House.[87] At Doncaster, 640 staff were employed on the new construction and repair of wagons. In October 1986 BREL's Board decided that these activities did not have a long-term future within the group, and in the following month the main Board agreed to the idea of selling the wagon works as a separate business. In May 1987 the assets were transferred to a new wholly owned subsidiary company, which was then offered for sale. Two bids were received, one from the Marmon Group, the American parent of the Procor companies, the other from an MBO trading as RFS Industries. After Marmon withdrew its bid, an improved offer from RFS was accepted, and in October 1987 Doncaster Wagon Works Ltd was sold to RFS for £4.75 million.[88] While the sale was being progressed the Board examined the options for the remainder of BREL. By this time BREL's top management had been strengthened. Philip Norman, the Chairman and Managing Director, gave up the latter function to an outsider, Peter Holdstock, in September 1986. Then the experienced businessman Sir David Nicolson, who had become a director in November 1986, succeeded him as non-executive chairman in April 1987. Their remit was to determine the optimal strategy for the engineering company.[89]

The Board's initial view, conveyed to the DTp in October 1986, was that 1988 was the earliest practicable date for disposal of BREL. It was accepted that the complexities involved in separating it from British Rail, with all the transitional costs of redundancy and restructuring, would be immense.[90] To make matters worse, the Board soon found itself in conflict with the subsidiary which it had encouraged to develop an arm's-length relationship. First, Holdstock made it clear that the restructuring of the group should take place *before* a sale; Welsby strongly disagreed.[91] Then there was a fundamental dispute about the BREL management's corporate plan. A three-year plan, produced in May 1987 following the separation of new build and maintenance, proposed to restructure the business into business groups and take determined action to reduce prices and costs. More controversially, however, the 'preferred path' to financial viability within the three-year timescale rested upon the Board's guaranteeing to place all of its repair work with BREL at set prices, to the detriment of the newly established BRML, and upon the extremely optimistic assumption that non-BR competitive sales would rise from £11 million in 1987/8 to £57 million in 1989/90 and £123 million by 1991/2. Not only did the document exhibit all the weaknesses of British Rail's old corporate plans, but it also ran counter to the Board's policy of competitive sourcing. Unsurprisingly, this preferred option, having been condemned by the Policy Unit, was rejected by the Board at a special meeting in June.[92] Relationships were clearly tense. They were not improved by the fact that the DTp had asked for an independent review of BREL's prospects as a quid pro quo for supporting the Board in its financial guarantees to its subsidiary. Price Waterhouse were commissioned to undertake the study.[93] At the same time, the Board was irritated by the fact that negotiations for orders which would involve parent company guarantees were taking place without its involvement and that Nicolson and Holdstock were pursuing the idea of an MBO consortium independently. There was particular anxiety about the revelation that Nicolson had discussed possibilities with Sir Peter Parker, now Chairman of Mitsubishi (UK), which compromised his position as Reid's man at BREL. He was thought to be 'sailing close to the wind'.[94]

In October 1987 BRB effectively ended 140 years of backward integration by deciding that ownership of BREL was not central to its core activities; continued ownership, it was argued, would inhibit the development of competitive sourcing, while a business strategy for BREL which embraced diversification of markets was best pursued in the private sector. Armed with the report from Price Waterhouse, which while scaling down BREL's sales projections confirmed that the business was potentially viable,[95] the Board decided that it should take responsibility for selling its subsidiary as quickly as possible by means of a trade sale, and that the business should be sold as a single unit. The only exception made to this was the decision to sell the Horwich Foundry separately. Once again, a wholly owned subsidiary was formed, in January 1988. After receiving three bids, including one from an MBO, the Foundry, which employed 330 staff, was sold to the Parkfield Group, a castings firm, for £3.125 million in August 1988.[96]

The decision to sell BREL itself was made public in November 1987 following its endorsement by the Secretary of State, Paul Channon.[97] There was a long and complex period of preparatory work, necessitating the appointment of Michael Casey, the Director of M&EE, as Project Director (BREL) in December.[98] The role of Nicolson and Holdstock remained delicate given their continued enthusiasm for a management and employee buyout (MEBO), and this ensured that Welsby and Casey, assisted by Lazards, who were employed to handle the sale, had to retain the initiative.[99] The assets were transferred to BREL (1988) Ltd, but the efforts to secure a quick sale were hampered by the fact that the lengthy prospectus and information documents were not issued until August 1988. In large measure the exercise was not a success. Railway vehicle and repair was an oligopolistic activity in the developed world, and in many countries virtually a monopolistic one. Furthermore, potential bidders were deterred by the belief that despite its turnover of some £300 million the business was not an attractive proposition and that, in any case, sale to a consortium involving an MEBO was likely.[100] Although canvassing extended to 50 companies in 11 countries, the Board received only 12 formal expressions of interest, and only two actual bids, one from GEC (in association with Alsthom), the other from an MEBO led by Holdstock, with hefty support from Trafalgar House, the British civil engineering, construction, property, and shipping conglomerate, and the Swedish-Swiss electrical engineering company Asea Brown Boveri.[101]

There was considerable anxiety in the period between the reporting of the two bids in October 1988, the decision to make the MEBO the preferred bidder in January 1989, and the completion of the sale in April. The two bids were quite different in their package of offers and assumptions, which raised numerous questions concerning existing orders and guarantees, notably for the Class 91 locomotives and Class 158 DMUs, warranty claims, restructuring and supplementary redundancy costs, directors' termination payments, tax losses, pension provisions, staff travel concessions, and the clawback of profits on future property development. Not least of the many complications was the need to verify net asset value. Negotiations with the bidders were also affected by the news of emerging difficulties— 'turmoil' according to Lazards—between the consortium partners, ASEA and Trafalgar House, and the BREL management team, after British Rail had demanded financial guarantees to cover warranty liabilities, which led to a modification of their respective stakes.[102] For a time there was a strong possibility that both bidders might withdraw, and the situation was not helped by the prospect of poor half-yearly results for BREL.[103] The process was prolonged because the sale to the MEBO attracted the attention of both the Office of Fair Trading and the European Commission. The latter, investigating a complaint that by writing off loan stock amounting to £64 million British Rail was effectively giving its preferred bidder the benefit of anti-competitive state aid, accepted the allegation but eventually approved the write-off.[104] It was not until April that BREL (1988) was sold to the consortium for £13.6 million. Managers and employees retained a stake of 20 per cent in the new business. Comment in the railway press was adverse, incredulity being shown that a business apparently worth about £80 million could be sold for under £14 million,[105] but internal papers and indeed post-sale experience make it clear that there were many outstanding and thorny problems involved in the purchase, not least a restructuring process estimated to cost £75 million. Both British Rail and the government were clearly relieved to see the sale of the four works proceed to a conclusion. However, competitive procurement did not improve with BREL in the private sector. Considerable difficulties were created by late delivery and product quality—notably with the Class 158s—and matters came to a head with a claim against British Rail of £150 million, which was eventually settled for £65 million when ABB bought out Trafalgar House in March 1992.[106]

7.6 The Property Board

The privatisation environment of the 1980s also affected British Rail's substantial property portfolio. In 1979 the estate amounted to a sizeable 200,000 acres, 85 per cent of which was designated as operational land. Since 1969 non-operational property had been managed by a wholly owned non-corporate subsidiary, the British Rail Property Board (BRPB).This body represented considerable expertise. Under the chairmanship of Bobbie Lawrence (1972–84) it attracted a strong non-executive team of property experts, including Jack Hughes, Ted Phillips, Frank Marshall, and Einion Holland.[107] Over the period 1975–9 rental income was clearly more important than sales, producing £31.2 million per annum gross and £22.3 million net after tax. The proceeds from sales amounted to £11.0 million per annum gross, and £9.2 million net (Table 7.2). Like the hotel managers the Managing Directors of the Property Board, Robert Dashwood (1974–80) and Gavin Simpson (1980–6) experienced all the traumas of the policy shifts inherent in the early period of privatisation. First there was a simple frustration with public sector constraints in the late 1970s. Then consideration was given to options for development, the managers favouring the retention of a sizeable estate coupled with a search for private-sector partnership. Finally, the government insisted on outright disposal, a policy which was pursued in such a manner as to attract criticism from the MMC when it examined British Rail's property activities in 1985. Dashwood's views provide a good example of the first phase. In 1980, shortly after his retirement, he complained to a friend, Cranley Onslow, the MP for Woking, that property was quite different from British Rail's other subsidiaries because it was essential to the core business. He therefore wanted the estate to be run properly, 'and not see more of the profits creamed off by the private sector'. The BRPB, he felt, should be free to take commercial risks using capital raised in the private sector. This was of course a vain hope. When Onslow passed Dashwood's letter to Norman Fowler, the reply, from Kenneth Clarke, was once again firm: however well managed the Property Board was, 'it cannot expect to behave as if it were a private sector property company whilst also enjoying public sector advantages'.[108]

The second phase was accompanied by a more determined sales effort driven by government demands and the Board's cash requirements. Before BRIL was established, the Department of Transport had already exerted strong pressure on the Property Board to dispose of a large proportion of the commercial property portfolio. This was consonant with the government's general policy, articulated as early as June 1979, of encouraging public authorities to dispose of land that was surplus to requirements. The intention was evident at a meeting in March 1980 where the civil servants also expressed doubts about the validity of British Rail's definition of 'operational' and 'non-operational'.[109] Under the banner of 'Sale-Speed' from 1980 the BRPB produced a gross income from sales averaging £40.6 million per annum in 1980–1, nearly four times the amount realised in 1975–9.[110] However, as with any property company, the immediate benefit to cash flow of sales had to be weighed against the loss of rents arising from long-term estate management. Unfortunately, *realpolitik* drove the decision-making process in

Table 7.2 British Rail Property Board: rental income and sales, 1975–89/90 (£m., in current and constant 1989/90 prices)

Year	(i) Rental income		(ii) Sales income		(iii) Gross cash contribution	(i) Rental income		(ii) Sales income		(iii) Gross cash contribution
	Gross	Net	Gross	Net		Gross	Net	Gross	Net	
1. Totals, current prices						Per annum				
1975–9	156.2	111.4	55.1	46.1	155.8	31.2	22.3	11.0	9.2	31.2
1980–84/5	318.1	225.5	339.7	293.3	508.5	60.6	43.0	64.7	55.9	96.9
1985/6–89/90	448.0	322.8	874.5	783.4	1,147.2	89.6	64.6	174.9	156.7	229.4
Total	922.3	659.7	1,269.3	1,122.8	1,811.5	59.5	42.6	81.9	72.4	116.9
2. Constant 1989/90 prices						Per annum				
1975–9	404.8	295.8	149.4	126.6	410.8	81.0	59.2	29.9	25.3	82.2
1980–84/5	468.3	331.0	484.0	417.8	732.2	89.2	63.0	92.2	79.6	139.5
1985/6–89/90	497.9	360.1	951.0	852.6	1,251.9	99.6	72.0	190.2	170.5	250.4
Total	1,371.0	986.9	1,584.4	1,536.2	2,394.9	88.5	63.7	102.2	99.1	154.5

Source: British Rail Property Board, *Directors' R&A 1974–89/90*.

Note: Some proceeds from the Liverpool St. station development are included in the gross cash contribution (iii).

the third phase, and given British Rail's cash crisis in the early 1980s, it was inevitable that the Property Board would be required to deliver more in cash than in rental income. When BRIL was established the intention was to transfer about £220 million worth of property—the non-operational estate (excluding closed branch lines) plus 10 designated operational properties—to a subsidiary of BRIL, British Rail Property Investments Ltd (1981). However, for both practical and policy reasons this was not considered necessary. In 1981 the Property Board evaluated four options: (1) to continue its 'optimum estate management policy'; (2) to continue with estate management, but make additional sales of £25 million a year, 1982–5; (3) to sell off the entire non-operational estate as soon as practicable; and (4) to offer for sale or issue shares in a new property company, with BRIL retaining a 30 per cent stake. Unsurprisingly, given the crystallisation of government policy, BRIL chose option (3) in December 1981, a decision endorsed by the main Board in February 1982. Once this was done, it was simpler to give BRIL authority to determine the timing and means of disposals. Thereafter, 1,400 of the most valuable properties, worth about £143 million, were earmarked for immediate attention with the aim of completing the selling process within three years.[111] However, this was not enough for the Department, who tried to persuade British Rail to complete the sales within two years.[112] Ridley's objectives for British Rail of October 1983 maintained the pressure by requiring the Board to 'continue to pursue a vigorous policy of property development and disposal'. Then, when most of the BRIL portfolio had been sold, Ridley turned his attention to the estate which remained 'operational'. His letter to Reid in September 1985 required the Board 'to make a commercial plan for identifying and divesting itself of all its underused or surplus property'.[113] The disposals may have produced a satisfactory outcome in terms of cash flow, as Table 7.2 indicates, but given the rising property market in the period 1984–9 were probably at the expense of long-term gains. Simpson, for example, was quite clear that accelerated sales had involved properties 'which, in the ordinary way, would have been retained as sound investments'.[114] He was supported by the MMC when the Department of Trade and Industry asked it to examine the operations of the Property Board. The resulting report in June 1985 highlighted some of the areas of concern in the process. The Commission's inquiry team, led by Deputy Chairman Sir Alan Neale, produced a rather daunting list of 43 recommendations for improvement, embracing organisation, valuation, discounting assumptions, and the assessment of development options. However, they were in general impressed by the effectiveness of the BRPB, and criticised the arbitrary nature of the sales timetable which had been imposed upon it. The MMC were quite clear that the lack of flexibility in the disposal strategy had worked against the optimisation of financial benefits.[115]

Nevertheless, the sales of railway property, undertaken as part of the government's general policy to encourage public authorities to dispose of land which was surplus to requirements, were remarkable in terms of cash flow, dwarfing the proceeds from the subsidiaries such as BTH and Sealink, where action had been more contentious (see Table 7.3). The gross income from property sales increased sharply, from £14 million in 1979 to £40 million in 1980, and £71 million in 1983; the property boom helped to swell the proceeds to £153 million in 1984/5 and £319 million in 1989/90. In 1983 the gross income from sales exceeded rental income for the first time, £71 million compared with £67 million, and the position was not reversed thereafter. In 1989/90 the ratio of sales to rental income was 2.7 : 1. The gross cash contribution of sales and rentals to Board finances increased in tandem, from £42 million in 1979 to £67 million in 1980, £101 million in 1983, £199 million in 1984/5, and £370 million in 1989/90 (see Appendix H, Table H.2). Table 7.2 highlights the change over successive quinquennia. From 1975–9 to 1985/6–89/90 net rental income trebled, and this was accompanied by a determined effort to exploit railway arches for small business use,[116] but net sales income increased 17-fold. The gross cash contribution increased by seven times. In *real terms*, the percentage increases were 22 573 and 205 per cent respectively.

The largest single income generator of all was the highly successful joint venture with Rosehaugh Stanhope to redevelop an *operational* property, the complex Liverpool Street/Broad Street site in London. Despite public sector constraints, some development work had been undertaken in the 1970s, notably the Blackfriars station site (£7 million, in association with the adjoining land-owners, King's College Cambridge), and at Euston Square (£31 million, in collaboration with the Norwich Union and Pension Fund Securities, following the failure of a private sector developer).[117] In the 1980s there were several developments in London, for example at Victoria, Charing Cross, and Fenchurch Street stations, using selective tenders, exclusive developer agreements, and the concept of the 'flying freehold' over operational sites. There were also successful schemes in the provinces, in Aberdeen, Preston, and Hull, for example.[118] However, the biggest achievement was the ambitious Liverpool Street scheme. Much thought about since discussions with local authorities in the early 1970s and a public inquiry in 1976–7, the scheme incurred expenditure of £1.4 million on consultants' fees in 1974–82, and a further £2.1 million to 1986.[119] The project encountered numerous problems in the early stages, not least a slump in the property market and the consequent termination of an exclusive agreement with the original developers, Taylor Woodrow and Wimpey in 1983.[120] A revised scheme was eventually undertaken in partnership with Godfrey Bradman of Rosehaugh, who had already made proposals for the development of Black-friars–Holborn Viaduct, and Stuart Lipton of Stanhope.[121] The development, begun in 1985 and progressed when Douglas Leslie was Managing Director (1986–92), was completed in December 1991. It added substantially to income, to the tune of £415 million by March 1993—£263 million net—while funding a much needed £152 million reconstruction of one of London's busiest commuter and main-line stations.[122]

7.7 Other businesses

Public sector managers also addressed other areas of what may be termed estate development, in relation to the Board's station catering and advertising businesses. Improvements tackled in the 1980s were in both cases followed by the introduction of competitive procurement, then by disposal to an MBO in 1987–8. Travellers Fare, British Rail's catering division, was detached from BTH in 1982, and then transformed, thanks to the efforts of full-time Board member Geoff Myers, part-timer Prue Leith, and a more focused management team led by Bill Currie.[123] Catering outlets were completely revamped, notably through the innovative and highly successful Casey Jones, Upper Crust, and Quicksnack brandings. Improved financial results followed. Station turnover increased by 61 per cent, from £46 million in 1982 to £74 million in 1987/8, and operating losses (all activities), which averaged £4 million a year, 1982–84/5 became surpluses from 1985/6, when the surplus was nearly £11 million. However, train catering remained a problem area, with losses averaging £5.8 million in 1982–85/6, after which the business was transferred to InterCity (in May 1986).[124] With government encouragement the Board introduced more competitive conditions into its catering from 1986.[125] The private sector was already operating some 85 station sites, and this presence was increased after eight open market tenders were undertaken for new units. These were followed by a more substantial programme of competitive tendering for the existing locations. Phase I embraced 96 sites which were offered to tender in 1987. Travellers Fare was successful in bids for 68 of these, with the result that further phases were abandoned in favour of outright sale.[126] After a tendering process the business with its 270 outlets and 3,200 employees was bought by a management consortium for £12.5 million in December 1988.[127]

British Transport Advertising Ltd was a poster advertising agency business jointly owned by BRB and the National Bus Company. Possessing virtually no assets, and non profit making, it produced no formal accounts: revenue was returned to, and expenses charged to, the two principals. British Rail benefited to the tune of £4.1 million a year in 'gross income', 1979–86/7, while internal calculations indicated that BTA made total net profits averaging £8.1 million a year, 1982–5, though the agency paid no site rentals to its principals.[128] As early as 1981 the Department of Transport received enquiries from the private sector about the possible acquisition of the business, even though it was not in the BRIL portfolio.[129] Interest continued, and David Howell raised the subject again in December 1982, but given the positive cash flows the Board was in no hurry to sell.[130] Eventually, the extension of competitive tendering principles to in-house services, developed by Derek Fowler, led the Board to develop an 'arm's-length' policy for BTA from 1985 with the intention of selling the business by competitive tender, preferably to the existing management. This course of action was hindered first by the withdrawal of the National Bus Company and the loss of valuable bus contracts following provision for its privatisation in the 1985 Transport Act, and then by the Secretary of State's insistence that BTA be subject to a full competitive tendering process.[131] It was not until August 1986 that the business was offered to tender. Six serious bidders emerged, and two, MAI (Mills & Allen), and a group of eight BTA managers led by the finance director Gordon Sykes, submitted attractive proposals. The balance was just in favour of the MBO, Ironlook Ltd, which bought the business, by this time wholly owned by British Rail, for £1.8 million in August 1987, and guaranteed the Board future revenues of about £10 million a year for five years.[132] To complete the list, the other sales were of the narrow-gauge Vale of Rheidol Railway, and Gold Star Holidays. The Vale of Rheidol Railway, a 12-mile, steam-operated line from Aberystwyth to Devils Bridge, was offered for sale in June 1988. Four bids were received, including one from an MBO of eight BR employees, but only one, from Brecon Mountain Railway Co., was considered to be satisfactory. The line was eventually sold to the preferred bidder for £306,500 in March 1989.[133] Gold Star Holidays, which began life as Golden Rail in 1970, was making losses in the region of £200,000 a year after interest in 1988 when the Board decided to dispose of it by means of a negotiated MBO. However, the DTp insisted on a sale by open tender and in the event the existing management did not submit a bid. In May 1989 the business was sold to Superbreak Mini-Holidays (formerly Dunn-Miller Associates), who had bought BTH's holiday business in 1983. The price paid was £212,000.[134]

7.8 Conclusion

What did all this achieve? The sale of assets obviously produced cash to address British Rail's financial problems, particularly in the recession of 1980–2. In the later 1980s disposals added substantially to cash resources, thereby assisting in the Board's efforts to reduce the PSO while enabling investment to be financed without additional borrowing. The gross proceeds from disposals amounted to about £1,390 million, 1980–89/90 (see Table 7.3), of which 87 per cent came from property sales. The net proceeds were lower, of course, but were still of the order of £1,080 million.[135] However, since investment was still controlled by government-imposed ceilings, and since British Rail continued to find it difficult to spend up to allocated levels (see Chapter 6) the impact upon investment activity was not dramatic. Rather it drew attention to the challenge to Treasury control of the industry via the EFL and cash limits which a substantial inflow of cash produced, and directed the Department's attention to the need to control British Rail in a more sophisticated way. Privatising the subsidiaries helped the government to reduce the level of railway subsidy, and there was *some* improvement in investment, but the net gain to public sector railways was rather negligible.[136] Furthermore, the *costs* of detaching the businesses must certainly not be ignored. The Board did not endeavour to compute the extent to which the gross take was eroded by associated costs—consultants' fees, selling commissions, and costs incurred in freeing the assets from BR control, especially in relation to staff.[137] Some of these continued to be incurred many years after the sale date. Indeed, as is evident from the more detailed accounts, the net gain to the business of sales was conspicuously less than the gross amounts, particularly in the case of BREL, where the loss on the sale was revealed to be £75.2 million in the annual accounts. A detailed back-check on Doncaster Wagon Works, for example, showed that the proceeds from sale—£4.75 million—had failed to match the book value of the assets by £4.5 million; with other costs the 'loss' was a not inconsiderable £7.25 million.[138] Similar calculations for Horwich Foundry and BTA produced losses after costs of £6.2 million and £412,500 respectively.[139] Even the sale of the relatively modest Vale of Rheidol Railway was no straightforward matter. The proceeds of £306,500 were offset by direct costs (Lazards: £140,000); undertakings to carry out 'separation' works, and contribute to bridge repairs at Llanbadarn and the repair of rolling stock (about £73,000); the cost of management time consumed in preparing a formal closure procedure, plus transfer of the company (incorporated in 1987) and its capital together with the light railway order; and, last but not least, dealing with the allegations of the MBO team of unfair practice, with the attendant threat of judicial review, which prodded the Board to pay £10,000 of the MBO's costs. Unsurprisingly, internal judgement was that the sale had been premature and had not produced a satisfactory amount.[140]

Should the subsidiaries have been sold? It was difficult to challenge the logic that these activities, while substantial in their own markets, were languishing in a public sector industry dominated by its core activity—railways. The hold of railway regional management on the hotels, shipping, and operational land had been conservative and rather negative for much of the period of nationalisation, and although Parker's Board had begun to address this problem at the end of the 1970s with the formation of Sealink UK and a stronger centralised hotels management, gains had not materialised when the Thatcher government began to press the idea of disposal. Managers such as Peter Land may have been disappointed with the break-up of the hotel estate but they did not seek to challenge the argument that escape from the investment and regulatory constraints of the public sector was desirable. On the other hand, the 'private sector good/public sector bad' hypothesis was not unassailable. For example, British Rail's on-train catering may have had its critics, but its full breakfasts enjoyed considerable support from consumers, and the efforts of Trust House Forte to provide a superior service with 'Cuisine 2000' on the WCML in 1987–8 proved to be little short of disastrous.[141] Furthermore, when the costs of pushing forward the sale of

Table 7.3 Asset disposals and cash flow, 1980–90

Business	Date of disposal	Method of disposal	Acquirer	Proceeds (£p, gross)
British Transport Hotels	1981–4	Various	Various	60.0m.
Gleneagles Hotels (3 hotels)	1981–4	Joint venture	Gleneagles Hotels	17.146m.
St. Andrews	March 1982	Private sale	Frank Sheridan	1.35m.
Midland Hotels (2 hotels)	April 1982	Joint venture	Midland Hotels	0.50m.
10 Hotels	March 1983	Competitive tender	Various	25.85m.
13 Hotels	March 1983–June 1984	Private sale, lease	Various	13.87m.
BR Hovercraft	Oct. 1981	Joint venture	Hoverspeed UK	14.3m.
Superbreak Holidays	Feb. 1983	MBO	Dunn Miller	—[a]
Hoverspeed UK	March 1984	MBO	Hoverspeed UK	(700p)
Sealink	July 1984	Comp. tender	British F/Sea Containers	65.7m.
British Transport Advertising	Aug. 1987	Comp. tender/MBO	Ironlook	1.8m.
Travellers Fare	Dec. 1988	Comp. tender/MBO	Evenmen	12.5m.
BREL	1987–9	Various		
Doncaster Wagon Works	Oct. 1987	Comp. tender/MBO	RFS	4.75m.
Horwich Foundry	Aug. 1988	Private sale	Parkfield Group	3.125m.
BREL main	April 1989	Comp. tender	Consortium (MBO, Trafalgar Hse, Asea)	13.6m.
Property				
Non-operational land	1980–90	Private sale	Various	1,214.2m.
Vale of Rheidol Railway	March 1989	Private sale	Brecon Mount. Rly	0.307m.
Golden Star Holidays	May 1989	Private sale	Superbreak	0.212m.
Total				1,390.5m.

Source: BRB.
[a] Peppercorn.

public assets in the 1980s are taken into account, the success of privatisation appears more fragile. We should also recognise that the process was not separate from the way in which privatisation of the core business was tackled. The move to competitive tendering, the increasing use of contracting out, and the divestment of the subsidiaries conditioned managers in British Rail to the process of privatisation, and the time-consuming work raised all the issues surrounding privatisation—of method, means, price, and political vicissitude—which reached a peak in the 1990s. When British Rail's managers were confronted with the prospect of railway privatisation—however remote it may have seemed in 1988—many of them were on familiar territory. If rail managers thought that the core business was sacrosanct they were in error; their actions in the 1980s had placed them on the slippery slope to full privatisation.

Part 3

On the Threshold of Privatisation: Running the Railways, 1990–4

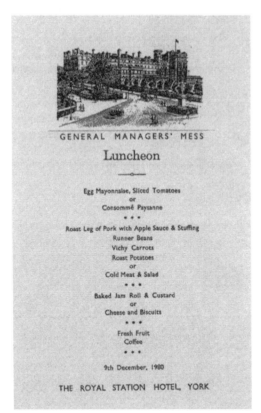

1. The railway culture 1: senior managers' course No. 1, Woking College, May 1969. Participants included Ian Campbell, Leslie Lloyd, Geoffrey Myers, Henry Sanderson and James Urquhart, and the group was addressed by shadow Minister of Transport Margaret Thatcher (see Chapter 4). (*BRB*)

GENERAL MANAGERS' MESS

Luncheon

———◇———

Egg Mayonnaise, Sliced Tomatoes
or
Consommé Payzanne
* * *
Roast Leg of Pork with Apple Sauce & Stuffing
Runner Beans
Vichy Carrots
Roast Potatoes
or
Cold Meat & Salad
* * *
Baked Jam Roll & Custard
or
Cheese and Biscuits
* * *
Fresh Fruit
Coffee
* * *

9th December, 1980

THE ROYAL STATION HOTEL, YORK

2. The railway culture 2: Menu from the General Manager's Mess, York, 9 December 1980. (*BRB*)

3. Sir Richard Marsh's Board, July 1976. Members from left to right: Derek Fowler, Lord Taylor of Gryfe, Sir Alan Walker, Michael Bosworth (Deputy Chairman), Herbert Farrimond, Sir Richard Marsh, Sir David Serpell, Robert Lawrence (Vice-Chairman), David Bowick, Peter Parker, Gerry Burt (Chief Secretary). (*BRB*)

4*a*. Sir Peter Parker's motivational management style: visit to Wolverton Carriage Works, *c.* 1980. (*BRB*)

4*b*. Sir Peter Parker's motivational management style: visit to Preston, March 1981. (*Roger Ford*)

5. Train operations, 1974–82: London commuter services, Victoria station, September 1975. (*John Glover*)

6. Train operations, 1974–82: lightly loaded freight: Willesden–Southampton freightliner service at Sonning, April 1976. (*John A. M. Vaughan*)

7. Train operations, 1974–82: vulnerable 'other provincial services':
Sheffield–Huddersfield DMU at Lockwood Viaduct, April 1976. (*L. A. Nixon*)

8. Investment, 1974–82: the High Speed Train, on the East Coast Main Line,
April 1978. (*BRB*)

9. Investment, 1974–82: the Advanced Passenger Train, undergoing trials, September 1980, near Beattock, on the northern section of the West Coast Main Line, electrified in 1974. (*BRB*)

10. Investment, 1974–82: the search for a new DMU: the prototype Class 140 Lightweight DMU, outside Bradford (Exchange) station, June 1981. (*BRB*)

11. Investment, 1974–82: Total Operations Processing System (TOPS), 1975. Intended to revolutionise wagon-loaded freight, the technology came to be applied more widely as a database and information system. (*BRB*)

12. Investment, 1974–82: air-braked freight wagon, 1976. (*BRB*)

13. Sir Robert B. Reid's Board, January 1987. Standing, left to right: Richard Tookey, David Kirby and Jim O'Brien (Joint Managing Directors, Railways), Oscar De Ville, Allen Sheppard, Simon Jenkins. Sitting, left to right: Grant Woodruff (Director of Public Affairs), Trevor Toolan (Managing Director, Personnel), Derek Fowler (Vice-Chairman), Sir Robert Reid (Bob Reid I), Geoffrey Myers (Vice-Chairman), Derek Hornby, Ian Campbell, John Batley (Secretary). There were no women on the Board at this time. Prudence Leith's appointment ended in September 1985, and the appointments of Kazimiera Kantor and Adele Biss were made in June and July 1987 respectively. (*BRB*)

14. Bob Reid I (centre) in the field: visit to Keith Jnc. signal box, April 1989. On right: John Ellis, General Manager, Scotrail. (*Jim Collins*)

15. Sector management: successive managing directors of InterCity at the naming of Class 43 No. 43154 *InterCity* at London Paddington Station, March 1994. Left to right: Chris Green, Cyril Bleasdale, and John Prideaux. (*Brian Morrison*)

16. British Rail marketing: the 'Age of the Train'. DJ and TV personality Jimmy Savile undertook a series of advertisements under this banner in the 1980s. (*BRB*)

Let the train take the rain
and the fog
and the ice
and the snow
and the risk
and the worry
and the time
and the hazards
and the stress
and the hold-ups
and the traffic
and......

This is the age of the train ⇌

17. British Rail marketing: the Network SouthEast/London Regional Transport Capitalcard, introduced in January 1985. (*BRB*)

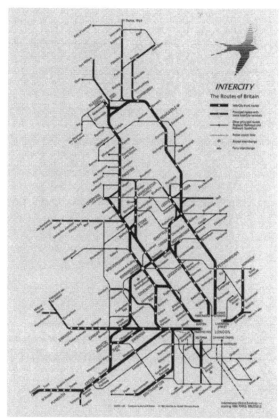

18. British Rail marketing: InterCity service map, 1993. (*BRB*)

19. Industrial relations: staff consultation meeting, Eastern Region, November 1978. Left to right: Cliff Rose (Board Member, Personnel), Frank Paterson (General Manager, Eastern Region), Maurice Holmes (Divisional Manager, Liverpool Street), Sir Peter Parker (Chairman). (*BRB/Maurice Holmes*)

20. Industrial relations: ASLEF's General Secretaries. Left to right: Derrick Fullick (1990–4), Ray Buckton (1972–87), and Neil Milligan (1987–9). (*Derrick Fullick*)

21. Industrial relations: the 'Bedpan' dispute: 1982–3 (see Chapter 5): idle Class 317 electric trains at Bedford, April 1982. (*John Glover*)

22. Industrial relations: Railfreight–trade unions liaison meeting, 1989. Left to right: Leslie Smith (MD, Trainload Freight), Jimmy Knapp (General Secretary, NUR), Colin Driver (Director, Freight), Neil Milligan (General Secretary, ASLEF), and Ian Brown (MD, Railfreight Distribution). (*Leslie Smith*)

23. British Rail's subsidiary businesses: BREL: Class 56 locomotive under construction, Doncaster Works, August 1980. (*Brian Morrison*)

24. British Rail's subsidiary businesses: BREL: Asbestos removal shop, Eastleigh. (*John Walton*)

25. British Rail's subsidiary businesses: Sealink: the *St. Anselm*, 1980. (*BRB*)

26. British Rail's subsidiary businesses: Hovercraft: the flightdeck of the *Princess Anne* (the *Princess Margaret* is visible through the windscreen), Dover, July 1978. (*BRB*)

27. British Rail's subsidiary businesses: Travellers Fare: Casey Jones outlet, Victoria Station. (*BRB*)

28. Train operations, 1983–93: The core business: East Coast Main Line. Class 91/ Mark IV coach train at Tallington, Summer 1993. (*Milepost 92½*)

29. Train operations, 1983–93: The core business: Merry-Go-Round coal train at Horbury, near Wakefield, April 1989. (*Brian Morrison*)

30. Train operations, 1983–93: aggregates train hauled by Foster Yeoman's Class 59 locomotive, built by General Motors, at Bedwyn, 1992. (*Milepost 92½*)

31. Train operations, 1983–93: Marginal operating: Speedlink train with only two wagons, hauled by Class 85 locomotive, at Carpenders park, November 1990.
(*Brian Morrison*)

32. Train operations, 1983–93: Marginal operating: DMU train at Fenny Stratford on the Bedford–Bletchley line, Summer 1990.
(*Milepost 92½*)

Business Performance, Pricing, and Productivity

8.1 A new chairman, a new board

When the privatisation of Britain's railways began to be actively debated in the early 1990s there were new players at the top, both within the industry and in Whitehall. The appointments of Bob Reid II, initially as a part-time member in January 1990, then as non-executive Chairman until April, and of John Welsby as Chief Executive, also in January 1990, produced another interregnum and a fair amount of change at the Board. Bob Reid's predecessor and namesake, Sir Robert, continued as Chairman until the end of March, and Derek Fowler, the long-serving Member for Finance, held the fort as Deputy Chairman until his retirement at the end of October, the month in which Reid became Executive Chairman. At the same time, four part-timers stepped down—Davies and Jenkins at the end of April, and Sheppard and Tookey at the end of July.[1] They were replaced in August 1990 by Kenneth Dixon, the former Chairman of Rowntree, who was Vice-Chairman of Legal & General and Deputy Chairman of Bass, and Professor Fred Holliday, former Vice-Chancellor of Durham University and a director of Shell UK. Eric Sanderson, Chief Executive of the British Linen Bank, followed in March 1991, by which time two new full-time members had been appointed and two more part-timers had stepped down. The new full-timers were both outsiders. James Jerram, who succeeded Fowler as the Member responsible for Finance and Planning, had left the accountants Arthur Andersen to take up the position of finance director at ICL (1984–7). He was subsequently finance director of the computer software companies SD-Scicon and SEMA. Dr Peter Watson, appointed to take charge of engineering and central services, was recruited from GKN, although in the 1970s he had been a scientific officer at the Railway Technical Centre at Derby.[2] The retiring part-timers were De Ville and Hornby. The consequent turnover was considerable—71 per cent in the two years March 1989–91 (see Table 8.1). Another part-time member was added in July 1991 when Peter Allen, the former Managing Director of British Steel's Strip Group, was appointed.[3] Nevertheless, there was continuity in the *process* of change. The search for new blood proved to be no easier than in Marsh's day when Fowler had been recruited. The starting salaries paid to Jerram and Watson, £85,000 and £100,000 respectively, reflected the disparity between the private and public sector in specialist board positions. They were paid 10 and 30 per cent more than Welsby, the Chief Executive, and 30 and 53 per cent more than the career railwaymen, Edmonds and Rayner.[4]

The political climate in which the Board operated was also profoundly changed. Although the same party was at the helm, the resignation of Mrs Thatcher in November 1990 and her replacement by John Major were significant changes. Major was a surprising choice as Prime Minister. Frequently underestimated and possessing remarkable resilience he had the task of steering the Conservatives through the murky waters of *fin de siècle* sleaze and policy uncertainties over Europe, to an unexpected victory in the General Election of April 1992.[5] When he was appointed, it was difficult to foresee that he would take the bold step of privatising the nation's railways, an industry usually regarded in Europe as rightfully belonging in the public sector. The late Thatcher administration had been keen on exploring the possibility of privatising British Rail, but it was scarcely a priority. Thus, at the Conservative Party Conference of October 1988 Paul Channon, then Secretary of State for Transport, had been relatively enthusiastic, announcing the commissioning of a series of studies on options for implementation. However, nine months later he was succeeded by Cecil Parkinson, who was certainly qualified for the job—he was a chartered accountant whose father had been a lengthman at Carnforth—but whose performance as a Minister was somewhat laid back following a difficult time as Minister of Energy. At the next party conference (in October 1989) he revealed that railway privatisation was not at the top of his agenda.[6] This was still the case in February 1990, when Reid I informed the Board that Parkinson had confirmed that privatisation was 'no longer a subject for urgent consideration', no further work on options should be done, and that the way was thus clear 'for the Board to get on, without distraction, with the task of managing the railway and improving performance'.[7] Within six months the policy wheel had turned again. After a meeting held at Chevening in September 1990 greater enthusiasm for privatisation emerged, though there was certainly no consensus on how to effect it.[8] Major's election

Table 8.1 The British Railways Board, 1 October 1990–1 March 1991

	Age[†]	Salary[‡]	Date of appt	Date of departure	Background
Chairman					
Sir Bob Reid	56	£200,000	Oct. 1990 (Jan. 1990)	Mar. 1995	Oil (Shell UK); Bank of Scotland
Deputy Chairman					
Derek Fowler, CBE[#]	61	£85,000	Apr. 1990 (Apr. 1975)	Oct. 1990	Local govt finance; railways
Chief Executive					
John Welsby, CBE	52	£77,000	Jan. 1990 (Nov. 1987)	Nov. 1992	Civil service; railways
Full-time members:					
John Edmonds	54	£65,300	July 1989	Mar. 1993	Railways
David Rayner	50	£65,300	Nov. 1987	Mar. 1994	Railways
James Jerram[*]	51	£85,000	Jan. 1991	—	Finance/computing (ICL, SEMA)
Dr Peter Watson, OBE[*]	46	£100,000	Feb. 1991	May 1994	Engineering (GKN)
Part-time members		£6,725			
Adele Biss	45		July 1987	June 1992	Public relations (Biss Lancaster/WCRS)
John Cameron, CBE	51		Aug. 1988	Sep. 1993	Farming (World Meats Group); Scotland
Sir Oscar De Ville, CBE[#]	65		Sep. 1985	Feb. 1991	Timber (Meyer Int.), engineering (BICC); CBI
Sir Derek Hornby[#]	60		Sep. 1985	Feb. 1991	Office systems (Xerox, Rank Xerox)
Kazia Kantor	41		June 1987	June 1999	Finance (Inchcape, HMV, Aegis, Grand Met)
Sir Allen Sheppard[#]	58		Aug. 1985	July 1990	Hotels/brewing (Grand Met)
Richard Tookey, CBE[#]	56		Aug. 1985	July 1990	Oil (Shell)
Kenneth Dixon	61		Aug. 1990	July 1997	Food manuf. (Rowntree); Bass, Legal & General
Prof Sir Fred Holliday, CBE	55		Aug. 1990	July 1993	Higher educ. (Durham Univ.); Shell UK; Lloyds Bank
Eric Sanderson[*]	39		Mar. 1991	Mar. 1994	Banking (British Linen Bank); Scotland

Key:
Those on BRB 1 Oct. 1990 but not 1 March 1991.
* Those on BRB 1 March 1991 but not 1 Oct. 1990.
† At 1 October 1990.
‡ For year 1 April 1990–31 March 1991, excluding bonus payments.

261

as leader gave further encouragement to the privatisers, and produced another Secretary of State for Transport in Malcolm Rifkind, a Scottish lawyer and former Secretary of State for Scotland, who became the third transport minister in 16 months. In May 1991 Rifkind expressed the intention to private British Rail within the lifetime of the next parliament, and asked Reid II to examine four 'structural options', together with the work of consultants engaged by the DTp.[9] Impetus was also provided by EC Directive 91/440 of July 1991, which stipulated that railway companies should be managerially independent of the State, required the separation of the rail infrastructure from service provision, at least in an accounting sense, and ordered competitive access to the networks of member states for international railway operators.[10] A White Paper on railway privatisation, expected by the end of the year, was delayed by in-fighting over options at Cabinet level,[11] but the Conservative manifesto for the 1992 election promised to 'end BR's state monopoly' and 'give the private sector the opportunity to operate . . . rail services' through franchising, and shortly after Major's victory, John MacGregor, a career politician who was appointed Secretary of State for Transport in the newly elected government, asked for the Board's reactions to ways of implementing the manifesto commitment in relation to liberalisation of access, passenger service franchising, and the disposal of railfreight. The government's White Paper *New Opportunities for the Railways* was duly published in July 1992.[12]

8.2 The challenge of the 1989–93 recession

During the 1980s organisational change had given increasing powers to the business sectors at the expense of the regions. In the early 1990s, the concept was taken further under the banner 'Organising for Quality' or OfQ. This major development, discussed more fully in Chapter 11, integrated the businesses and the engineering functions. The regions disappeared, and fully fledged decentralised businesses were created with full bottom-line responsibility and asset ownership. Given the trials and tribulations of privatisation and the introduction of OfQ, it was sometimes easy to forget that there was a national rail network to be run. And here too there were challenges. There were major investment projects to progress, notably the rail-based Channel Tunnel, a high-speed rail link connecting it with London and the North, and the Crossrail project, a new line to connect the railways east and west of London, in the manner of the rapid transit RER lines in Paris. None of this was straightforward. The legacy of the 1980s was positive in the sense that a public sector railway had demonstrated that it could improve its financial results while cutting its cost base and (for the most part) holding on to quality standards. But there were also negative elements. The

Clapham accident in 1988 had raised justifiable concerns about the railways' ability to deliver an acceptable level of safety throughout the organisation. The protracted strike of 1989 had provoked expressions of consumer disquiet, particularly among London commuters, whose demand was inelastic. Finally, the move to competitive procurement had been dented by reports of 'sleaze' in civil engineering and the much-publicised problems of late delivery and technical defects affecting some of the new equipment, notably the Class 158 DMUs and the Class 319 EMUs.[13] However, the major feature of the period 1990–4 was that while the performance of the rail businesses during Bob Reid I's time had been boosted by a sharp upturn in the economy and a strong property boom, the economic conditions facing his successor, Bob Reid II, were those of recession and a collapse of the property market. The recession of 1989–93 was not only one of the sharpest of the century, it was also the most protracted.[14] Rail traffic suffered correspondingly. Passenger-mileage fell by 12 per cent, from 21.3 billion miles in 1988/9 to 18.9 billion in 1993/4, while the reduction in freight traffic was more severe, with net tonne miles falling by 24 per cent, from 11.2 to 8.5 billion.[15] In this chapter we analyse the efforts of railway managers to meet government targets and operate railway services profitably and effectively. In the next chapter we examine their efforts to upgrade and safeguard the railway to meet the anticipated needs of the twenty-first century, notwithstanding the distractions of privatisation.

The overall 'performance' of British Rail in this period of transition may be gauged in financial terms from the profit and loss data in Table 8.2. Determination of long-term trends is hindered by numerous accounting changes, notably the decision to treat much infrastructure expenditure (notably track renewals) and the capital element of government grants as capital instead of revenue from 1992/3,[16] and compliance with Financial Reporting Standard No. 3 from 1993/4, which essentially required the Board to separate the profits or losses on the disposals of fixed assets, the costs of restructuring, and extraordinary items.[17] However, in spite of such adjustments, the basic trend is clear enough. Working with the post-FRS3 accounts in constant 1993/4 prices, group profits fell sharply from an estimated £40 million in 1988/9 and £30 million in 1989/90 to *minus* £194 million in 1991/2, and in the following year the deficit trebled—on the new basis from *minus* £65 to *minus* £189 million. There was some improvement in the following year, when the deficit was reduced to £108 million, but the unmistakable picture was one of substantial failure, demonstrating how vulnerable railway trading is to a downturn in the national economy.

How far were these results a matter of reduced government support? As we have seen, Treasury expectations at the end of the 1980s boom were of a much reduced dependence on subsidy, and a willingness to support only Provincial or Regional Railways over the longer term. In fact, PSO payments were cut by a half in real terms over the period 1979–89/90, while the proportion of total grant (PSO + PTE/local government) to passenger income and subsidy was half the

Table 8.2 British Railways Board's profit & loss account, 1988/9–93/4 (£m., in constant 1993/4 prices)

Year	Operating profit/ loss before other income, interest, tax, &c.	Operating profit/ loss before disposal of fixed assets but after exceptional items	Group profit/loss after exceptional items, interest, tax	Group profit/loss after disposal of fixed assets, interest, tax
	basis (i)[a]	basis (ii)[b]	basis (i)[a]	basis (ii)[b]
1988/9	138.5	—	393.8	40.0[e]
1989/90	−32.0	−26.2	326.7	29.5
1990/1	−48.3	−52.9	−12.4	−108.3
1991/2	−108.7	−104.7	−155.1	−194.1
1991/2[c]	20.0	24.0	−26.4	−65.4
1992/3	13.8	−96.9	−168.5	−188.5
1993/4	—	23.0	—	−108.4[d]

Source: Appendix A, Table A.2.
[a] Basis (i) pre-FRS3 reporting.
[b] Basis (ii) post-FRS3 reporting.
[c] Restated in line with 1992/3 accounting changes (capitalisation of revenue investment).
[d] Including restructuring costs of £48.3 m.
[e] Estimate.

Table 8.3 PSO payments, 1989/90–93/4 (£m., in constant 1993/4 prices)

Year	Central govt payments		Central + local govt payments		PSO share of total passenger income (%)
	£m.	Index 1989/90 = 100	£m.	Index 1989/90 = 100	
1989/90	600	100	711	100	24
1990/1	683	114	798	112	26
1991/2	956	159	1,080	152	32
1992/3	1,187	198	1,293	182	37
1993/4	930	155	1,035	146	32

Source: Appendix A, Table A.1.

1982 level by 1989/90 (Chapter 4, Table 4.9). To the extent that the improved results of the 1980s were the outcome of a boom, then the poor results after 1989/90 were influenced by government attempts to maintain the level of subsidy at late 1980s levels. In fact, this proved impossible to sustain. As Table 8.3 shows, PSO payments from central government, adjusted on a uniform basis, doubled in real terms in the four years from 1989/90 to 1992/3, with a reduction only in 1993/4; the share of grants in total passenger income rose from 24 per cent in 1989/90 to 37 per cent in 1992/3; in the following year the proportion was 32 per cent. Nevertheless, this increased level of support was still lower than that provided before 1986/7 (see Appendix A, Table A.1).

The problems of the recession were also reflected in the negotiations between the Board and the Department of Transport over the External Financing Limits (EFL) set by government (see Table 8.4). The Limit had been lowered progessively from the mid-1980s, as the Board's income exceeded budgetary estimates, a consequence of higher demand and buoyant property sales. At the height of the boom in 1988/9 the government had introduced a ring-fencing mechanism for property sales and grants from the European Regional Development Fund to facilitate reductions to the EFL.[18] The limit was then revised downwards to £641 million, but in the event the Board's requirement was only £375 million. Difficulties first arose in 1989/90, as the recession began to bite. The limit had been set at a historically low figure of £415 million, reflecting the benefits of healthy property sales and the boom (Appendix F, Table 2). After British Rail lobbying, it was increased to £635 million to take account of the cost of the railways' 'megaprojects' and the fare-capping requested by Parkinson, the Secretary of State. However, even with this increase the EFL was exceeded by £38 million.[19] The situation deteriorated in the following year, 1990/1. For the second year running the Board asked for additional support, this time to meet the higher costs associated with inflation and the safety requirements of the Fennell and Hidden reports on the King's Cross station fire and the Clapham rail accident. In response to a scaled-down request for £120 million, on top of the £598 million initially set, Parkinson agreed, somewhat reluctantly, to an increase of £102 million, making £700 million in all.[20] In fact, the Board exceeded the revised figure by some £316 million, an overshoot of 45 per cent, and both Reid and Welsby pressed Rifkind, now the Secretary of State, for an additional £740 million for 1991/2 on top of a figure which was already almost double the initial limit of the previous year (Table 8.4). With the favourite source of cash—property sales—having fallen sharply, the railways faced severe difficulties as a result of reduced demand, a position exacerbated by commitments to investment on the Channel Tunnel rail link, new trains, and safety.[21] The crisis led to a Treasury-imposed moratorium on further investment authorisations within the investment ceiling, and to a tripartite review of the railways' difficulties, with significant input from both the DTp and the Treasury.[22] The moratorium was bitterly resented by the Board. The point was put forcefully to the Minister that British Rail should not be 'held accountable for the sudden and recent deterioration in the performance of the wider economy . . . the use of investment as the cash regulator to offset short-term fluctuations in trading results is prejudicial . . . this policy has led to regular capital depletion in past years and has been a major factor in determining the age and condition of many of our assets'.[23] Rifkind expressed some sympathy for the

**Table 8.4 External financing limits and BRB expenditure,
1989/90–93/4 (£m., in current prices)**

Year	Initial EFL	Revised EFL	Actual requirement
1989/90	415	635	673
1990/1	598	700	1,016
1991/2	1,122	1,522	1,446
1992/3	2,041	2,096	2,064
1993/4	1,495	—	1,461

Source: Appendix F, Table F.2.

Board's plight, though he could not accept that its investment plans should be 'sheltered' from economic fluctuations. He added £400 million or a further 36 per cent to the limit, making £1,522 million, and agreed not to carry forward the overshoot in the previous year. His concessions were to be seen as 'an outstanding recognition by the Government of the importance of the railways and of their current financial difficulties'.[24] In fact, the protracted negotiations ensured that the Board's EFL requirement for 1991/2 was lower than that fixed by the government, to the extent of £76 million. By the end of 1991 relations with the Department had improved again, references to 'choppy water' having been replaced by talk of 'pulling together and no surprises'.[25] In 1992/3 the EFL was fixed at £2,096 million, including £803 million for investment in Channel Tunnel services, an increase of 230 per cent over that of 1989/90; in real terms the increase amounted to 180 per cent (Appendix F, Table F.2).

Despite these concessions British Rail found it difficult to meet the government's targets for its several businesses. In December 1989 Parkinson had produced a long list of stipulations for the three years to March 1993, embracing safety, quality, and finance, the most specific and wide ranging ever given to the industry, and intended to produce 'a safe, efficient and high quality railway' (Table 8.5).[26] They were supplemented in a follow-up, 'side' letter in January 1990 containing technical and commercially sensitive elements, notably a specific requirement for Railfreight Distribution.[27] The objectives for the businesses, produced with the help of British Rail forecasts and after some protracted negotiations, were, with the benefit of hindsight, optimistic: rates of return on assets, including infrastructure, of 4.75 and 4.5 per cent respectively for InterCity and Railfreight, a break-even objective for Railfreight Distribution, the removal of Network SouthEast from the PSO grant by 1992/3 (not in 1991/2 as the Department had wished), and a reduced subsidy for Provincial or Regional Railways of only £325–45 million (Table 8.5).[28] In fact, by the end of 1989 Kirby, Welsby, and Fowler were expressing anxiety at Board level about the prospects of meeting these 'tough' targets.[29] As Table 8.6 indicates, the business results

Table 8.5 Government objectives for the British Railways Board, 1990/1–93/4

1: December 1989, objectives for 1990/1–92/3

	Objective
Sector	
InterCity	£95 m. profit in 1992/3 or 4.75% on estimated asset values (incl. infrastructure)
Railfreight	£50 m. profit in 1992/3 or 4.5% on estimated asset values; performance of RfD to be improved[a]
Parcels	Endorsement of BRB profit target of £9 m.
Supported businesses	Investment to satisfy RRR (8%) Cost Benefit Analysis for other projects; market research to assess price/quality relationship; report on unit cost trends
Network SouthEast	Endorsement of BRB forecast of zero grant by 1992/3
Provincial (Regional Railways)	Endorsement of BRB forecast of reduction in subsidy from 65% costs in 1988/9 to 57% or £345 m. by 1992/3; request for a further £20 m.; bus substitution schemes to be pursued; review of marketing and fares; quality standards; BRB to produce proposals to charge PTEs full attributable costs
Broad objectives	
Safety	Implementation of Hidden inquiry recommendations; Safety plan by October 1990; joint BRB/DTp review of investment appraisal and funding of safety-related projects
Quality	IC punctuality to be monitored; NSE quality targets (1987) to be applied over daily peaks, and punctuality target to be increased from 90% to 92% by 1992 (88% for peaks); reliability and overcrowding to improve; charging for quality to be examined
Channel Tunnel services	BRB to invest in order to maximise commercial opportunities, including joint venture with Eurorail
Private sector involvement	To be taken further
Asset base of businesses	To include infrastructure
Public accountability	BRB to report in R&A on service quality, progress towards subsidy targets, profit before interest on CCA basis, etc.

Table 8.5 (continued)

2: March 1993, interim objectives for 1993/4

	Objective
Sector	
InterCity	Target of £12 m. profit
Network SouthEast	Target of £128m loss before PSO
Regional Railways	Target of £411 m. loss before PSO
Red Star Parcels	To be privatised during 1993
Transmark	To be privatised during 1993
Channel Tunnel Services	Infrastructure to be completed; freight services to begin on opening, passenger services in 1994
Broad objectives	
Safety	Further plan in 1993
Productivity and cost control	BRB to cut working expenses for the passenger businesses by at least 5% in real terms cf. 1992/3
Quality of service	Endorsement of Passenger's Charter and 1993 targets; special targets for train enquiry bureaux, ticket offices, and carriage cleaning; endorsement of surveys to gauge customer satisfaction; overcrowding objective: ratio of passengers to seats on individual trains not to exceed 135% on sliding-door trains and 100% on slam-door trains, standing not to exceed 20 minutes (criteria to be re-examined)

Source: BRB, *R&A 1989/90*, pp. 31–2; *1992/3*, pp. 37–8.

[a] Later defined as 'break-even by 1992/3' ('side' letter, January 1990).

slipped badly from 1991/2. We have already noted that rail traffic, measured in volume terms, suffered in the recession. Turnover fell markedly in real terms in the freight and parcels businesses, by 26, 34, and 51 per cent respectively for Railfreight Distribution, Trainload Freight, and Parcels over the six years to 1993/4 (Appendix E, Table E.2). Turnover held up better in the passenger businesses, but the InterCity objective was clearly threatened by a fall of 12 per cent in real revenue. In the passenger businesses as a whole, the problem seemed to be that it was difficult to prune operating costs before 1993/4, although judgement is obscured by the accounting changes. With Freight and Parcels, there appears to have been a more conscious effort to reduce costs in line with falling demand, an effect particularly noticeable with Parcels. Whatever the dynamics, the bold undertakings of December 1989 were exposed. It is difficult to assess performance against objectives precisely since the latter were set before infrastructure assets were included in the businesses' asset base, and

Table 8.6 Rail business turnover, expenditure, and surplus/loss, 1988/9–93/4 (£m., in constant 1993/4 prices)

1988/9 = 100

Year	InterCity Turn.	Exp.[a]	S/L £m.	NSE Turn.	Exp.[a]	S/L £m.	Total Turn.	Exp.[a]	S/L £m.	Trainload Freight Turn.	Exp.[a]	S/L £m.	Prov/RegRail Turn.	Exp.[a]	S/L £m.	Railfreight Distribution Turn.	Exp.[a]	S/L £m.	Parcels Turn.	Exp.[a]	S/L £m.
1988/9	100	100	73	100	100	−175	100	100	−622	100	100	170	100	100	−592	100	100	−82	100	100	−16
1989/90	97	97	67	98	96	−150	96	97	−616	95	95	158	94	97	−588	98	100	−87	89	90	−15
1990/1	96	98	55	97	93	−111	94	96	−688	87	95	109	96	94	−545	88	121	−169	80	90	−29
1991/2	92	99	2	96	98	−191	90	98	−892	82	96	71	94	100	−613	85	104	−125	67	82	−37

1991/2 = 100

Year	InterCity Turn.	Exp.[a]	S/L £m.	NSE Turn.	Exp.[a]	S/L £m.	Total Turn.	Exp.[a]	S/L £m.	Trainload Freight Turn.	Exp.[a]	S/L £m.	Prov/RegRail Turn.	Exp.[a]	S/L £m.	Railfreight Distribution Turn.	Exp.[a]	S/L £m.	Parcels Turn.	Exp.[a]	S/L £m.
1991/2	100	100	96	100	102	−20	100	100	−483	100	100	108	100	100	−520	100	100	−113	100	100	−34
1992/3	96	99	66	100	101	−47	98	99	−505	94	94	105	109	103	−514	96	90	−92	85	81	−23
1993/4	95	94	98	102	93	71	95	88	−265	81	82	85	109	94	−443	87	75	−62	73	66	−14

Source: Appendix E, Table E.2 (subsidy excluded).

[a] Revised data used for 1989/90 and 1990/1.

Data below line = revised accounting basis from 1992/3, with retrospective for 1991/2.

Table 8.7 Estimates of performance against objectives, 1992/3 (£m.)

Business	Target	Target in 1992/3 prices	Result
InterCity	95	112	65
Railfreight	50	89	13
Network SouthEast	Breakeven	Breakeven	−46
Regional Railways	−325 to −345	−383 to −406	−503

Source: Derived from Table 8.5 and Appendix E, Table E.1.

the Department and Board had different views in approaching this exercise, especially on the issue of asset valuation.[30] Nevertheless, we may suggest that the expectations for 1992/3 were not realised (Table 8.7).

The interim objectives for 1993/4, required by John MacGregor, Secretary of State from April 1992, and derived from British Rail's budget, were more realistic, though they were also shaped by the knowledge that much distracting work on privatisation was to be carried out. Set in March 1993, they required a modest £12 million profit from InterCity, expected Network SouthEast to lose no more than £128 million, and Regional Railways to lose £411 million before grant (Table 8.5). In fact, the results in that year were much improved. InterCity produced an operating profit of £98 million, Network SouthEast turned loss into profit with a surplus of £71 million, and the Regional Railways' loss of £443 million before subsidy was close to target. The Minister's request that the passenger businesses achieve a cost reduction of 5 per cent (originally 6 per cent) clearly produced a positive response (Table 8.6).[31]

8.3 Passenger services: the search for quality

Turning to the businesses, the achievements of the three passenger sectors during the 1980s—improved marketing, customer-orientated investment, and attention to costs—were put under pressure during the boom and ensuing recession. It was particularly difficult to maintain the improvements in the quality of service, which had been assisted by the establishment and publication of quality objectives. As early as 1979, when a cut in the PSO was threatened and commuting into London had become a matter of public debate, Peter Parker had inspired the publication of a Commuter's Charter discussion paper, which set out the Board's views about suitable performance indicators for London and the South East, including a 95 per cent punctuality and a 99 per cent reliability objective. These aspirations were taken up in the Monopolies and Mergers Commission's report of

1980, which made further recommendations about quality indicators, and in the Board's *Commuter's Charter*, published in June 1981.[32] Earlier still, in 1978, the official body representing rail users, the Central Transport Consultative Committee for Great Britain (CTCC), had begun to publish statistical information about the punctuality and reliability of train services supplied to it by British Rail on a regional basis. From 1981 information on carriage cleaning and the responsiveness of enquiry bureaux was also revealed to the CTCC, and British Rail began to publish information on service quality at stations and in its annual reports.[33] Initiatives to improve customer service were developed, notably Jim O'Brien's 'Customer First' Programme in 1983–4 and Chris Green's 'Operation Pride' on Network SouthEast (1986). In 1984 financial objectives for the London and SouthEast sector were tempered by quality objectives. The Board produced a detailed set of service standards for London's commuter services, embracing punctuality, cancellations, carriage cleaning, overcrowding, telephone enquiries, and ticket offices. These were agreed by both the DTp and the CTCC. Set out in an exhortatory letter from Nicholas Ridley to Bob Reid in July 1984, they were repeated, with some modification, in British Rail's 1984 Corporate Plan, published in October, which gave similar undertakings in relation to InterCity (see Appendix J, Table J.3). In the following year a *Code of Practice* booklet was published which confirmed the objectives in general terms, while the 1985 Corporate Plan contained internal targets for *all* the business sectors, including Freight and Parcels.[34] It was then a short step towards the setting of formal targets by the Department of Transport. These emerged after John Moore's objectives letter in October 1986 and were introduced in June 1987. Further specifications followed the MMC's Report on Network SouthEast in September, which recommended that the objectives be applied to individual routes, and Cecil Parkinson's Ministerial directive of December 1989 (Table 8.5, Appendix J, Table J.3).[35] The government's intention was to ensure that the sector met its financial objectives through genuine improvements in efficiency rather than by exploiting its monopoly position with commuters by reducing quality or raising fares.[36]

The published data on punctuality, reliability, and overcrowding are difficult to interpret, since they were not independently monitored (apart from the occasional MMC inquiries) until 1992, masked local variations and incomplete returns, and were also vulnerable to internal manipulation.[37] We should also note that the initial targets were more generous to British Rail than consumers had expected. As the CTCC observed, the punctuality targets, which required 90 per cent of InterCity trains to arrive within *10* (rather than five) minutes of the booked time, and Network SouthEast to ensure that 87.5 per cent (subsequently 90 per cent) of its trains arrived within five minutes, represented a dilution of the original benchmarks.[38] For the Board's part, there was increasing irritation with the use of the performance data by the CTCC and some of the TUCCs, which led to a decision to suspend the supply of information in 1986.[39] This said, it does seem that the efforts made to improve the punctuality and reliability of passenger services in response to consumer pressure suffered a setback in the early 1990s, and the overall record in satisfying the targets agreed with government was disappointing in several areas, for example, with InterCity punctuality, overcrowding on Network SouthEast, train reliability (cancellations), carriage cleaning, and the response rate of enquiry bureaux and ticket offices (see Appendix J, Table J.3).

The process was taken a step further with the introduction of a Passenger's Charter in May 1992. This arose from John Major's Citizen's Charter, a government initiative to strengthen the position of the customer in dealing with public services, which was launched with a White Paper in July 1991.[40] British Rail is generally seen as being lukewarm to the idea, resisting it along with the Department of Transport, the Treasury, and other departments.[41] However, this is misleading. In many ways, British Rail was ahead of the game. As we have seen, the setting of minimum standards for customers had a long pedigree; and with the encouragement of the CTCC, the National Consumer Council, and the Office of Fair Trading, managers were not only preparing a 'Fair Deal for Customers' leaflet but also working on a redrafting of the railways' conditions of carriage to square with modern circumstances, the requirements of the European Commission, and the decentralisation of rail businesses under OfQ.[42] There was also a well-established if ad hoc complaints procedure, under which £6.5 million had been paid out in various forms of compensation in 1990/1.[43] Much of this was included in the White Paper, and, unsurprisingly, one railway executive felt that the Major government was seeking to 'steal our clothes'.[44] Reid was also closely involved from the start. After a correspondence with Major over the standard of service from his Huntingdon constituency to London, he had been invited to attend the special Citizen's Charter seminar at Chequers in June 1991 which thrashed out principles.[45] Then, in August, the Board published its 'Fair Deal' leaflet which outlined passenger service objectives and a broad policy towards compensation.[46] The production of a Passenger's Charter, with its obvious financial implications, proved a considerable challenge and there was some delay. The Prime Minister and his advisers clearly thought that both the DTp and British Rail were being obstructive,[47] but this view is rather unfair. As Welsby noted, it was vital to ensure that managers were not diverted from the task of improving services, and equally important to 'ensure that unrealistic public expectations of compensation were not encouraged'.[48] Furthermore, with an election looming, it was scarcely surprising that senior BR managers should take their cue from Whitehall, where there was much opposition to Major's ideas, not least from the Treasury.[49] However, the principal explanation for the delay was the difficulty of producing a compensation scheme with so many interested parties external to the Board. It was therefore some months before an agreed document was launched publicly in March 1992.[50] This reaffirmed existing commitments to standards of quality for InterCity and Regional Railways, namely that 90 per cent of trains should arrive within 10 minutes of the booked time, and that 99 per cent of advertised trains should run. It then went further by setting specific punctuality and reliability targets for the 15 service groups in Network SouthEast (Appendix J, Table J.4), and establishing more precise provisions for compensation. A clear undertaking was made to give discounts to nearly 400,000 season-ticket holders if performance slipped 'by more than a small margin' (3 per cent for punctuality, 1 per cent for reliability). Other passengers could claim compensation, in the form of travel vouchers, if trains were delayed by more than an hour. The Board also committed itself to a considerable degree of transparency with the promise of regular, four-weekly reporting of actual performance against the targets.[51]

Of course, the whole exercise depended both on the nature of and realism in the target setting, and on the accuracy of the recording processes, and in relation to both there was some cause for concern, not least about the tendency to under-report late trains, a problem identified by independent auditors from Sheffield University appointed by British Rail.[52] We should also note that there was no immediate intention to bring the worst-performing lines up to the standard of the best. Understandably, business managers were keen to modify the targets to square with what they regarded as realistically achievable on certain routes. Thus, in the initial standards set in 1992, the Great Northern line was expected to achieve a 90 per cent punctuality rate, while for the London Tilbury & Southend line the target was only 80 per cent. Furthermore, behind the global figures for groups of services, individual services exhibited considerable deviation from the average, and the managing directors of the businesses were justifiably anxious to reduce some targets where performance was unlikely to improve in the short run, for example in relation to punctuality on InterCity's West Coast Main Line, Network SouthEast's Kent Link line, and Regional Railways' cross-country services.[53] Unfortunately, if equally understandably, the government was anxious that Charters be used to stimulate an improving level of public service. Thus, William Waldegrave, the Minister made responsible for the Office of Public Service and Science and its Charter Unit after the 1992 election, was adamant that targets should not be revised downwards in the light of experience, and indeed, for British Rail, the 1993 and 1994 targets were raised on 12 of the 15 Network SouthEast lines (Appendix J, Table J.4).[54] Nevertheless, the level of payments was lower than that made in 1990/1 under the old scheme: £1.9 million in 1992/3, and £4.7 million in 1993/4, effectively the first full year of the Charter's operation (together with a further £5.3 million arising from a two-day strike in April 1993). The greater proportion (63 per cent) was paid out in vouchers as compensation for delays, which arose mainly in the InterCity business. Season ticket discounts arose mainly on the problematic Kent Link and Kent Coast lines (95 per cent of Network SouthEast's £2.0 million pay-out in 1993/4).[55] Moreover, the operating record over the period April 1993 to March 1994 was deemed to be particularly satisfactory. No season ticket payments were being triggered over the whole of Network SouthEast, a situation which produced a congratulatory letter from the Secretary of State, John MacGregor, while

InterCity's Anglia service had been awarded a Charter Mark for its performance, a considerable contrast with the situation two years earlier, with the shoals of complaints from long-distance commuters.[56]

How far passengers or customers were impressed by this outwardly more sympathetic regime is difficult to gauge. The initial response from the media to the Passenger's Charter was mixed, in line with reactions to the charter initiatives as a whole. Particular scepticism was exhibited by the *Daily Mail*, which took its cue from the criticisms of the Consumers' Association, and from court actions taken by disgruntled commuters seeking to challenge British Rail's conditions of carriage.[57] Furthermore, an independent survey of consumer reactions to standards in a wide range of public services in 1993 placed British Rail near the bottom of the list.[58] Some commentators have maintained that whatever the reported performance, the punctuality and reliability standards were set at fairly low levels, understandable in an industry under pressure to improve safety and at the same time operate with reduced levels of government support.[59] Thus, MacGregor's congratulations were offered to Network SouthEast for achieving all its targets, but no fewer than seven of its lines were failing to achieve a punctuality rate of 90 per cent.[60] And whatever the statistics, there is no doubt that both the press and television were invariably attracted to specific, although less representative, examples of failure in railway performance, particularly those caused by the weather. Experiences in 1991–2, for example, were such that both the Department of Transport and the Commons were drawn into the debate, and phrases such as 'leaves on the line' and 'the wrong kind of snow' have now passed into Britain's folklore (see Cartoon 11). In February 1991 exceptionally heavy snowfall caused severe operating difficulties which were particularly evident in the area served by Network SouthEast,[61] and to the delight of the press, Terry Worrall, the Director of Operations, allegedly attributed the difficulties to the 'wrong kind of snow'.[62] The disruption to services, which lasted for over a week, raised several questions relating to engineering, operating and communications, and the Board immediately established an inquiry led by Malcolm Southgate (the Deputy Managing Director of European Passenger Services).[63] A number of operating and communication defects were revealed, but the overall finding was that the high incidence of traction motor failures was indeed caused by dry and powdery snow falling in considerable volume at abnormally low temperatures, while additional difficulties were created by snow which was packed into points and the sliding-door mechanisms of new EMU trains.[64] Dr Peter Watson, the newly appointed Member for Engineering, told the Board that an initial investment of £100–150 million would be required to mitigate the problems, and not surprisingly this solution did not impress Roger Freeman, the Minister for Public Transport.[65] British Rail also suffered as a result of its difficulties in maintaining operations with much lighter equipment during periods of leaf-fall in autumn. Modern, disc-braked rolling stock proved particularly susceptible to adhesion and signalling problems, and

**' 'Ello, 'ello–a vandal bent on disrutpting British Rail services
by dropping a leaf on the line, eh?'**

11. Leaves on the line: mac, *Daily Mail*, 5 November 1991

interruptions to services were common.[66] In 1991 Regional Railways was affected badly when leaf-fall prevented the new Class 158s from operating the track circuits, and Network SouthEast's Class 165s also encountered difficulties.[67] Again the issue reached Board level. Experiments with Swedish scrubbers were disappointing, and the best approach was found to lie in the application of Sandite together with the removal of vegetation, though the latter not only was costly but raised environmental issues.[68]

We must have some sympathy with British Rail in its attempt to respond to highly publicised examples of failure and performance indicators, which were influenced by factors outside managers' control. Weather problems were rarely set in context by the media, and indeed, such difficulties were common to all railway systems.[69] Furthermore, punctuality often varied in direct proportion to the age of the infrastructure and rolling stock used, as was evident with InterCity,[70] while reliability was affected by the supply of labour, with driver shortages contributing to the comparatively high level of train cancellations in Network SouthEast in 1989–91.[71] This said, there was much to applaud in the manner in which the three businesses performed under leading railway managers. At InterCity, the electrification of the East Coast Main Line was completed with a full service operating from May 1991, though it contrasted sharply with the deteriorating state of the West Coast, which had been the subject of a number of strategy studies, but aside from the electrification of the Carstairs–Edinburgh line, had attracted no substantial investment.[72] In 1992 Chris Green was appointed Director of InterCity and, characteristically, he continued the emphasis on marketing and quality initiatives which John Prideaux had started, though the influence of the two managers on operating costs was less pronounced (see Table 8.6, above). Green's legacy to John Nelson at Network SouthEast was a highly visible brand image and substantial investment in new rolling stock, including the 'Networker' trains (Class 465) introduced from 1992 (see p. 307). Service improvements included the opening of a direct link from Liverpool Street to Stansted airport in 1991, the progressive development of the once-threatened Chiltern line from London (Marylebone), and the improvement of Thameslink services, including the opening of a new station in the heart of London, City Thameslink.[73] The Provincial/Regional Railways business showed progressive improvement under the leadership of Sidney Newey (1987–90), Gordon Pettitt (1990–2), Jim Cornell (1992–3), and Paul King (1993–4). This sector also reaped the benefits of new trains, particularly once the Class 158s were finally delivered and the initial teething troubles resolved. These trains gave improved journey times and higher passenger comfort and enabled longer-distance services to be developed, such as Cardiff–Portsmouth, Norwich–Liverpool, and the Trans-Pennine route. Rural lines benefited from the conversion of the Class 155s to single-car units. The sector, invariably acting in partnership with local authorities and PTEs, continued to open new stations and introduce new services, such as Bridgend–Maesteg, Mansfield–Nottingham, and a further expansion of the Glasgow suburban network. Other notable projects included the Manchester Airport link and the Birmingham Cross City electrification schemes, operational from 1993 (see p. 310).[74] Furthermore, these developments were introduced at a time when the businesses were busily engaged on a fundamental reorganisation by incorporating infrastructure and its staff under the Organising for Quality initiative.

8.4 Passenger marketing and pricing

The marketing and pricing of passenger services were greatly transformed in the decade 1985–94, but here we must recognise that although the process reflected the growing importance of sector management in formulating initiatives, ultimate responsibility for the broad strategy of pricing remained with the Board, supported by centrally based managers in the passenger marketing department.[75] British Rail built upon many of the initiatives established in the 1970s: the abandonment of simple distance-based pricing in favour of more elaborate routines incorporating the amount of 'time away'; the use of selective pricing within an overall strategy of 'hard pricing', namely real price increases; differential increases by business, with higher than average rises for London commuters where operating costs were high and demand was relatively inelastic; and differential increases by service where the quality provided was higher (see Chapter 3, p. 60).[76] Table 8.8 provides a general assessment of the level of passenger fares. Increases were introduced every January from 1977 (with the exception of the November increases in 1980–2) until pricing strategies became more fragmented in the late 1980s. The Provincial sector, for example, tended to make pricing changes when service quality was enhanced by the introduction of new rolling stock, and such steps were taken not only in January but in May and September. The other businesses had followed suit by 1992.[77] In general, the Board priced forward for inflation, estimating the rate in the year to come; then, acting on the recommendations of the sectors, it added 'real' increases to this to determine the final price. Thus, in January 1989, when the estimated inflation rate was put at 5.8 per cent, InterCity added 4.5 per cent, Network SouthEast 3.4 per cent, and Provincial 2 per cent, to this figure (for full details see Appendix J, Table J.5). It is clear that the increases in rail fares outpaced the retail price index. Thus, from 1979 to 1984 average fares increased by 80 per cent, while retail prices rose by only 57 per cent; from 1984 to 1994 fares increased by another 102 per cent, while prices increased by 62 per cent. Over the period as a whole fares rose by 262 per

Table 8.8 British Rail's general fare increases, 1980–94

Date	Passenger fare increases (%)	Period	Average annual fare increase (%)	RPI change (%)
Jan. 1980	19.6			
Nov. 1980	18.8	1979–80	42.1	18.0
Nov. 1981	9.3	1980–1	9.3	11.9
		1981–2	0.0	8.6
Jan. 1983	7.8	1982–3	7.8	4.5
Jan. 1984	7.3	1983–4	7.3	5.0
Jan. 1985	6.6	1984–5	6.6	6.0
Jan. 1986	8.2	1985–6	8.2	3.4
Jan. 1987	5.0	1986–7	5.0	4.2
Jan. 1988	6.5	1987–8	6.5	4.9
Jan. 1989	9.4	1988–9	9.4	7.8
Jan. 1990	9.0[e]	1989–90	9.0[e]	9.4
Jan. 1991	9.5[e]	1990–1	9.5[e]	5.9
Jan. 1992	7.75[e]	1991–2	7.75[e]	3.8
Jan. 1993	6.0[e]	1992–3	6.0[e]	1.6
Jan. 1994	5.0[e]	1993–4	5.0[e]	2.5

Source: BRB, and see Appendix J, Table J.1; RPI from Office for National Statistics, *Economic Trends Annual Supplement* 1999.

[e] Estimated (pricing becomes more fragmented with businesses making changes outside the January round).

cent, but the retail price index went up by only 154 per cent, suggesting a real increase of 43 per cent (derived from Table 8.8). Individual fares provide a further illustration of this significant increase in the real cost of rail travel. Thus, from 1979 to 1994 the London–Winchester single fare rose by 315 per cent, the ordinary return by 343 per cent; London–Norwich fares increased by 289 and 319 per cent, and the more competitively priced London–Glasgow fares by 197 and 227 per cent. All these increases were significantly ahead of inflation.[78] Some of the discounted, pre-booked fares were cheaper in 1994 in real terms; others were not.[79]

Although the Department of Transport kept a close eye on British Rail pricing, there was comparatively little direct government intervention in the period. There was no room for a prices and incomes policy in Thatcher's Britain, and regular price hikes above the rate of inflation were clearly in line with Conservative thinking on objectives for the railway industry. Nevertheless, informal pressure was exerted at all times, much of this 'heavy breathing', as Peter Parker has called it, originating in the Treasury.[80] Sometimes, this informal influence took the form of specific requests, for example that there should be restraint in raising London commuter fares, or that fares should be raised differentially for services with a better quality.[81]

There were also instances of direct intervention to restrain or 'cap' fare increases, which were particularly evident during the recessions of 1979–82 and 1989–93. Thus, in response to pressure from the Department of Transport and the Treasury, a planned increase of 11.8 per cent from November 1982 (incorporating real increases of between 2.5 and 3.8 per cent in order to compensate for the 1982 dispute with ASLEF) was abandoned, and a much lower increase of 7.8 per cent was introduced in January 1983.[82] No doubt some of the government's anxiety was a response to the radical 'Fares Fair' policy of the Labour-controlled Greater London Council, led by Ken Livingstone and Dave Wetzel in 1981/3 (see below). Then, in 1989, as the next recession began to take hold, the Secretary of State asked the Board to 'cap' its increases for 1990,[83] a situation which persisted over the next four annual rounds (1991–4). In 1991, for example, the suggested 'cap' was 9.5 per cent for Network SouthEast and 15 per cent elsewhere, resulting in lost income estimated at £15 million.[84] The price rise of 1992 was 'scaled down' to 7.75 per cent on the Department's insistence, and for 1993 and 1994 there was further intervention in relation to Network SouthEast and, in particular, the size of the joint London Transport/British Rail Travelcard increases (see below). Pricing in the nationalised railway industry ended much as it had begun, with clear evidence of government intervention, and contradictory twists of policy. Thus, while the overall thrust of government policy was to encourage the raising of fares to improve financial performance, there were numerous examples of influence being exerted in the opposite direction.[85] The overall impact of this may have been to temper the pricing zeal of sector directors such as Prideaux and Green, but it did not affect the overall situation—evident to railway commentators—that British Rail fares, already high in a European context, had become even higher as the government demanded ever more economy from its railway industry. There were many references to the disparity. For example, it was asserted that the standard fare from London to Cardiff was equivalent to three days' unlimited travel on Netherlands Railways, while the 'Britrail' pass sold to tourists provided seven days' travel on Britain's network for the price of a London to Edinburgh ordinary return.[86]

Of course, average fare tables do not tell the full story from the passenger's perspective. As sector management developed, there was a considerable growth in discounted fares, and in the first half of the 1980s British Rail tested the market with a series of radical, imaginative strategies. Railcards offering concessionary tickets were extended to families and the disabled (in 1981) and to all young people (in 1984). A special offer of free national travel on 10 June 1978 to holders of Senior Citizen Railcards was followed by a number of successful promotions, including a £1 Day Return in November 1980, and similar offers in March and November 1982, and annually from November 1984. The London and South East sector offered similar deals, including Party-Size 'Awayday' tickets of £1 in July–September 1982, a 'Go Anywhere' £2 Day Return for Senior Citizens in November 1983, and special offers to Network Card holders from 1986. There were also numerous leisure packages promoted on a local basis, notably those promoted by Scotrail in 1983 and 1984. Cheap discounted travel was also offered to small groups using voucher promotions, for example in association with Lever Brothers (Persil) and Kellogg's.[87] Awareness of the strong competition offered by deregulated bus operators was the stimulus for much of this marketing effort, as it was in the provision of 'Saver' and 'Supersaver' tickets from 1985, followed by a range of advance purchase tickets (Apex, SuperApex, Advance Return, Superadvance, Leisure First, etc.), from 1987. There were also special 'two for one' offers by InterCity made in association with retailers such as Boots and Shell (1991–3).[88] The sales promotions of 1991–3 were estimated to have added £7.1 million to revenue.[89] Yet despite this heavy discounting, the average fare *paid*, measured by the data on average receipts per passenger-mile, also increased in real terms. The rise may not have been as sharp, but as Table 8.9 shows, there was a steady rise on this basis after a fall in 1982, when there was intervention from the Treasury and the Secretary of State. The average fare paid was 5 per cent higher than in 1979 by the end of the boom, 1988/9, and 14 per cent higher by 1993/4. This was lower than the 43 per cent real increase suggested by the data on average fare increases, but should not be dismissed.

British Rail, whose finances and strategy were firmly under the eye of the Treasury, could do nothing to equal the Greater London Council's London Transport fare cuts of 32 per cent in October 1981, and 25 per cent in May 1983 (following a politically charged legal judgement in the Lords and a 96 per cent *increase* in March 1982). These reductions, which also brought the public the popular zonal fare structure and the bi-modal Travelcard, were introduced

Table 8.9 Average receipt per passenger-mile, 1948–94 (1979 = 100)

Year	Average receipt per passenger-mile 1979 = 100 = 4.02 p	RPI[a]	Real average receipt per p-m Index 1979 = 100
1948	14	14	103
1963	21	24	85
1979	100	100	100
1982	136	143	95
1984/5	163	162	101
1988/9	206	197	105
1991/2	261	240	109
1993/4	286	251	114

Source: BRB, R&A 1979–93/4; Gourvish, British Railways, p. 470.
[a] Annual average, 1948–82; Q1, 1985–94.

to boost demand. They may have produced only short-term joy for London passengers before the Thatcher administration asserted central control over local government subsidisation (with the Transport Act of 1983), transferred responsibility for London Transport from the GLC to a new body, London Regional Transport, under DTp control in 1984, then abolished the GLC (in 1986). Nevertheless, it was a monument to a quite different approach to public transport provision and contrasted sharply with what British Rail managers were being asked to do.[90] British Rail, which competed with London Transport over many routes and provided a multiplicity of connections, was certainly affected by the battle for cheaper fares. First, co-operation with the GLC was swiftly ruled out. The latter's offer to compensate British Rail for any revenue losses arising from matching the fare reductions of October 1981 was rejected by the Secretary of State, Norman Fowler, who threatened to deduct the government's support to British Rail in response to any help from the GLC.[91] Second, the see-sawing of London Transport fares upset the equilibrium of fare levels between the two: the 32 per cent reduction of 1981 meant that LT fares, which had been 12 per cent higher overall than British Rail fares, fell to 72 per cent of BR (after November), then with the increase of 96 per cent in March 1982 became 39 per cent higher. The estimated revenue loss from the fare cuts was £15 million.[92] Thereafter the instruction to British Rail from government was to 'maintain a broadly consistent relationship with LRT fares'.[93] Passengers certainly welcomed the extension of the Travelcard concept to British Rail's London services with the tri-modal 'Capitalcard' and 'One Day Capitalcard' tickets in 1985–6. However, the defeat of the cheap fares policy had the effect of maintaining the rising real cost of travel in London, which had already seen the 'fare-box ratio', the proportion of operating costs met directly by passengers, increase from 61 per cent in 1975 to 78 per cent in 1980, making it one of the least supported systems in the developed world.[94] With British Rail under pressure to make Network SouthEast self-supporting by 1992/3, the popular Travelcard season ticket, from 1989 operated jointly with London Transport, came to be regarded as under-priced, and action was taken to increase the price of this 'premium' product from the early 1990s.[95]

As we have noted, the establishment of the business sectors from 1982 gave further impetus to more complex, segmented pricing activities based on the amount of time spent away, but there was always a tension between the desire to price for individual markets and the need to provide passengers with a simple, clear set of ticketing alternatives. Inevitably, pricing strategies moved back and forth between these two poles. By 1984 escalating complexity had not only begun to attract the disapproval of the CTCC but also fed internal anxieties.[96] One of the achievements of centralised passenger marketing was the return to a more simplified system in May 1985. In future, only four ticket types were to be used: ordinary (valid for three months), saver (one month), day return, and cheap day return. However, the reforms went beyond this, embracing a radical departure from earlier practice. Instead of setting prices according to the amount of time away, prices were to be related to the *time of travel*. Thus, peak-time travel was priced up, while discounts were offered for travel at off-peak times. The aim of the new fares, adopted after pressure from Cyril Bleasdale of InterCity for a system based on the train used rather than the time away, was to increase income, improve loadings, and relate prices more closely to costs.[97] It followed experimentation with 'Off Peak' (Saver) tickets in the Norwich Division in 1982.[98]

After this, there was a natural tendency to reintroduce more complexity again. By 1994 InterCity, for example, had produced a large number of discounted tickets aimed at market segments.[99] Sector requirements were also driven by the harsh realities of the 'bottom line', which made managers more aware of the revenue-cost ratios of specific traffics. The requirement that InterCity should return a profit had led the sector to make differential above-inflation increases for season tickets after 1983, notably in 1986.[100] As the pressure mounted to take the sector out of subsidy, Prideaux, in his Strategy Review of 1987, directed the Board's attention to the need for more aggressive pricing of long-distance season tickets, where fares barely covered marginal costs. An additional stimulus was the fact that the strong growth in demand for season tickets for journeys of over 50 miles—35 per cent in the two years to March 1988—had led to serious over-crowding on several trains during peak travel times.[101] InterCity's strategy encouraged the replacement of British Rail's national, mileage-related tariff for season tickets, where there were substantial discounts over longer distances, to a route-by-route policy, with higher fares for higher quality services. In the fare increases of January 1989 Prideaux clearly ruffled the feathers of consumer groups when he introduced increases of up to 21 per cent (15 per cent in real terms) in long-distance season ticket prices (e.g. standard class from Bristol, Kettering, and Grantham), a striking contrast with the much lower average 10.8 per cent increase for Network SouthEast tickets.[102] There was another hike in prices in the following January. A further 20 per cent was added to Bristol, Grantham, and Norwich fares, with higher increases for first-class season tickets (e.g. 24 per cent for Bristol, 25 per cent for Grantham, and 27 per cent for Newark). Thus, the Bristol–London standard class traveller experienced a 45 per cent increase in his season ticket from £2,900 a year in January 1988 to £4,200 in January 1990.[103] However, although at times sector strategies varied quite substantially and sometimes produced tensions between the respective managers, for example between InterCity and Network SouthEast re commuter season tickets,[104] there appears to have been relatively little to choose between them in terms of average increases over the longer run. Thus, in the period 1984–91 fares were lifted by 83 per cent in Network SouthEast, 76 per cent in InterCity, and 75 per cent by Provincial/Regional Railways (calculated from Appendix J, Table J.5).

A move to pricing based upon specifying the train to be taken gained ground in the 1990s. This radical approach for railways took the form of airline-type Apex fares, booked in advance for travel on designated trains. Developed with the help of the new computer-based ticketing and seat reservation technology, and extended with the introduction of SuperApex fares in May 1992, the move produced a considerable erosion of the universal 'walk-on' fare. Price discounting was high because the fares could be offered to fill up capacity train by train in a fully managed way. It was also a response to the very low fares introduced by some of the coach operators and to discounting by the airlines. The revenue from Apex tickets increased from £3 million in 1990/1 to £26 million in 1992/3, and about 40 per cent of the business came from new customers. Advance purchase discounting then became a major element of passenger pricing over the rest of the decade.[105]

In this and other ways the decade 1985–94 witnessed major changes in passenger pricing and marketing by British Rail. Building on the innovations of the late 1970s and early 1980s managers exhibited a considerable amount of imagination in fare setting, even if the resultant variety sometimes bewildered the consumer. Fares were targeted at particular segments of the market, and were increasingly related to the quality of the service offered and to the cost of providing it. The main criticism was that average fares were comparatively and historically high. From 1982 'real pricing' policies had significant, long-term effects on the average price of rail travel, notwithstanding the discounting element and the improvement in quality. The real average receipt per passenger-mile increased by 20 per cent from 1982 to 1993/4, at which point it was 34 per cent higher than in 1963 and 11 per cent higher than in 1948 (Table 8.9). Of course, the rising cost of travel owed as much to the strategies of central government for the public sector as to the internal preferences of railway managers.

8.5 Freight and parcels under pressure

The Freight and Parcels businesses faced more widespread pressures in our period, though neither attracted the media attention given to their passenger counterparts, and the general public's perception about them was somewhat limited.[106] As we have seen, from October 1988 it was possible to distinguish between the more profitable and the patently loss-making activities of Railfreight, namely Trainload Freight, the profitable bulk traffics such as coal, metals, and aggregates; and Railfreight Distribution (RfD), a separate division of Railfreight formed by a merger of Speedlink, the problematic wagon-load business, Freightliner, the equally problematic container business, and the international traffic handled by Railfreight International. The move clearly met the Department of Transport's intention that the distinction between loss-making and profit-making activities should be made transparent. On the other hand, there was clearly an internal rationale for merging the three elements. The operation of Freightliner as an independent, wholly owned subsidiary company was not working well, as was clear from the failure of its 1987 Plan, and the Board was determined to bring this business under more centralised control.[107] The RfD merger was intended to facilitate the unification of investment and train planning decisions for these bi-modal freight activities, in order to transform the financial and operational performance of each. There was also the incentive to exploit the opportunities which European deregulation and the opening of the Channel Tunnel were expected to bring. Subsequently, Trainload and RfD were constituted as separate business sectors as part of the OfQ reorganisation from 1990.[108] However, in the long recession of 1989–93 the pressures mounted in the trainload business also, following political intervention affecting British Rail's core customers. First, the steel industry was slimmed down, then privatised in 1988; the electricity generating industry, the major purchaser of domestic coal, followed in 1991; finally, in 1994 the coal industry itself was sold after a period of substantial rationalisation. As Table 8.6 indicates, the improved profit record of the late 1980s was difficult to maintain given the recession and these upheavals. Cost cutting continued to produce improvements, building on improved operating practices such as Driver Only Operation and the firmer control of dedicated assets, which began with the Railfreight Review of 1985 and the concept of the 'ideal operational freight railway'.[109] But there were distinct limits to the strategy given the comparatively low level of investment in freight assets during the 1980s and the increasing reliance on the private sector for new investment (see pp. 219–20 and p. 223).[110] As a result, Trainload Freight's impressive operating surplus of £136 million in 1989/90 was halved in 1991/2 (£68 million); further erosion in 1993/4 meant that over the recession the surplus fell by about two-thirds in real terms (see Table 8.6 and Appendix E, Tables E.1 and E.2). At the same time, RfD, far from covering its operating costs, as both railway managers and the Secretary of State had hoped, continued to make losses. The operating loss of £65 million in 1988/9 more than doubled, reaching £152 million in 1990/1, the first year of independent operation as a business. Thereafter, the withdrawal of the Speedlink network in July 1991 (see below) and other actions cut the losses to £119 million in the following year, and further action, including the rationalisation of Freightliner terminals and withdrawal from the train ferry service operated jointly with SNCF, saw the deficit fall by some 40 per cent to 1993/4.[111] In real terms the loss doubled to 1990/1, then fell by about 60 per cent to 1993/4 (Table 8.6 and Appendix E, Tables E.1 and E.2).

Undoubtedly, the period from 1988 to 1994 was dominated by arguments over the viability of the weaker business, RfD. The future of the loss-making Speedlink network had been debated vigorously for some time, the deliberations all the more poignant since there were expectations of new wagon-load and intermodal traffics from the Channel Tunnel. Indeed, British Rail faced the challenge of responding to its commitments to the operators of the Tunnel in relation to freight, which required some brave decisions on forward investment. In 1985 a major Freight Review had rejected the option of disengaging from Speedlink, together with the loss-making elements of train-load freight, for a policy of cost reduction. The intention was to ensure that Speedlink covered its direct and specific overhead costs by 1988/9. The policy was reaffirmed in 1987.[112] After RfD had been established with Ian Brown as Managing Director, the initial thinking, presented to the Board in May 1989, was still bullish after good overall results in 1988/9. Although RfD made operating 'losses' of £65 million, freight as a whole returned a record surplus of £69 million (Appendix E, Table E.1). Furthermore, the approach to the wagon-load business was undoubtedly influenced by the Board's commitments to the builders of the Channel Tunnel, Eurotunnel. Under the Usage Contract of July 1987 British Rail and SNCF were guaranteed half of the Tunnel's capacity in return for specified payments and undertakings, including a fixed annual charge. British Rail undertook to have available on the tunnel's opening (scheduled for 1993) the necessary infrastructure and rolling stock; the infrastructure was to be sufficient to permit the carriage of 5.2 million tonnes of non-bulk freight and 2.9 million tonnes of bulk freight per annum, a commitment backed by the Concession Agreement between the British and French governments and Eurotunnel. The two railways also undertook to cater for an agreed level of demand. Although this had not yet been translated into firm figures, Brown was working to an estimated RfD traffic of some 5.5 million tonnes a year by 1995/6.[113] Since wagon-load operations were commonly used in French freight working, it was difficult at this stage to contemplate a draconian policy for Speedlink, although railway managers had already raised question marks about both its future in the UK and the likely returns to RfD from the Channel Tunnel traffic given existing charging arrangements. Nevertheless, Brown felt that he could meet the Department's target of breaking even by 1992/3.[114] However, his financial projections, based on cost escapement and a 25 per cent reduction in the number of terminals, were quickly blown off-course by the onset of recession. By March 1990 it was clear that the nationwide Speedlink network would have to be abandoned. It lost £28 million on a turnover of £42 million in 1989/90, and £51 million on a turnover of only £39 million in the following year. Withdrawal was agreed by the Board in December and effected in July 1991.[115] The traffic itself was not large in volume terms (only 2 per cent of the total freight carried by British Rail). Nevertheless, the rationalisation focused attention on the need for a more cost-effective, higher quality service across the whole of the RfD sector. The review of Speedlink had revealed something which should have been obvious for some time, namely that if wagon-load was regarded as a stand-alone business, then the high cost of operating (marshalling and trip working accounted for 80 per cent of total costs) was uneconomic unless the length of haul was long, that is, over 500 miles, and traffic flows were sizeable, that is, at least 10 wagon-loads a day. Unsurprisingly in a country such as Britain, Speedlink operations had been some distance from this ideal.[116] The logical solution was to convert as much of the business as possible to trainload operating, where costs were lower. This policy was comparatively successful. Over 70 per cent of the former Speedlink business was retained in trunk-haul form or in contracted train-loads, for example the china clay traffic from Cornwall and the traffic from the Ministry of Defence ordnance depots.[117] Thereafter, the sector was engaged on a paradoxical mission to lobby aggressively for the investment necessary to retain and expand traffic while at the same time rationalising severely under the pressure to break even. Thus, RfD concentrated on: its longer UK hauls, and in particular the deep-sea freightliner traffic originating in Southampton, Felixstowe, and the new Thamesport terminal at Grain; the development of its international traffic flows; and its preparations for intermodal operations through the Channel Tunnel, using joint ventures with road hauliers and embracing the lighter, 'swap-body' technology for rail–road transfers.[118] The expectations of the latter turned out to be optimistic, however. Under half of the expected continental freight traffic had materialised by 1998.[119]

For Trainload Freight, confidence had been quickly restored after the shock of the miners' strike of 1984–5, when road haulage captured a surprising proportion of the core coal business. Indeed, in the late 1980s boom Railfreight made record profits, due entirely to the profitable flows of bulk freight provided by the handful of customers who had put up most of the £2.8 billion invested in railways by the private sector.[120] In 1989 the government had set Trainload the objective of making a profit of £50 million by 1992/3, equivalent to a return on assets of 6.1 per cent; it also expected an improvement to 8 per cent by 1994/5. In fact, its contemporary performance was comfortably above these targets, with returns of 10.3 per cent in 1988/9 and 9 per cent in 1989/90.[121] However, the conversion of the Trainload activity into a separate business sector under Leslie Smith as Managing Director coincided with the twin challenges of one of the century's worst recessions and the privatisation of the electricity industry. The latter ended the lucrative 1976 contract with the Central Electricity Generating Board (CEGB) for power-station coal from British pits. Since power-station coal was highly profitable and, indeed, the mainstay of the business, the radical reorganisation of electricity provided one of the biggest shocks ever experienced by the railways' freight business.[122] The performance of the sector was driven very substantially by the experience of the coal sub-sector, which accounted for some 60 per cent of total turnover (power-station coal accounting for over 45 per cent). While the tonne-mileage carried held up as a result of a shift to longer hauls (Appendix D, Table D.2), tonneage fell by 38 per cent between 1988/9 and 1993/4, and most significant of all, real income fell by 37 per cent. However, there were also problems elsewhere, notably in the construction and metals sub-sectors, which were hit by the slump in the building industry and the closure of the Ravenscraig steelworks in 1992. Here the tonneage carried fell by 30 and 23 per cent respectively, 1988/9 to 1993/4 (Appendix D, Table D.2).[123] In consequence, the objective of returning 8 per cent became increasingly elusive.[124]

Managerial effort focused on the preservation of the railways' power-station traffic. The close relationship between British Rail and its two key customers, the CEGB and the National Coal Board (from 1987 the British Coal Corporation), had persisted because the latter were to a degree locked into rail transport as a result of their extensive investment of £1 billion in railway and associated infrastructure.[125] However, a number of factors began to challenge the status quo. First, the termination of the CEGB's understanding with British Coal (with effect from January 1990) opened the way to a greater use of cheaper, imported coal, which disrupted existing traffic flows and encouraged new ones. Net imports, under 1.0 million tonnes a year in the 1970s, rose to 10.1 million in 1989 and 16.7 million a year in 1991–4, nearly a quarter of domestic production. Second, there was an increasing preference for alternative fuels, particularly gas. As a result UK coal production, which averaged 129 million tonnes a year in the 1970s, dipped sharply, from 94 million tonnes in 1991 to only 49 million in 1994, and the percentage of UK electricity generated by the major producers' coal-fired power stations fell from 60 per cent in 1991 to only 42 per cent in 1995. The resulting contraction of the British coal-mining industry was a considerable blow to the railways, whose infrastructure was fixed. In the four years after the miners' strike in 1985 the number of collieries fell from 169 to 86, and there were only 16 when the industry was sold to the private sector in 1994.[126]

The coal carriage contract of 1976, due to expire in 1991, had been revised in April 1986 following the second five-year review process. The CEGB agreed to continue with the existing pricing structure, but in return British Rail abandoned Clause 11, which guaranteed the railways all of the traffic. From this point the CEGB undertook to use rail for a minimum of 83 per cent of its domestic coal movements, and was thereby able to divert some traffic on to the roads.[127] As the plans for the privatisation of electricity were advanced, the contract was renegotiated in 1989/90 with the new, private-sector generators, National Power and

PowerGen. The new, four-year contracts, signed in March 1990, were less favourable to British Rail. Both sides had recognised that the 1976 agreement had been extremely profitable to British Rail. Average rates of £3.68 a tonne by 1988/9 produced large margins over costs (the return was about 45 per cent) and for a 25-mile haul rail rates were double the rates by road. The generators complained, with some justification, that prices were too high and that the profits were being used to cross-subsidise other areas of railway freight; British Rail, for its part, conceded that it could only maintain premium prices if new investment were provided to satisfy the new companies' demands for a high quality of service.[128] From March 1990 a fixed charge for 'capability' (manpower, track, signalling, etc.) and a variable charge for 'train movement' were drawn up for each of the supply points serving the 11 National Power and seven PowerGen power stations. These charges were in turn subject to an array of adjustments for performance, incentives, inflation, and so on. The train movement rate was subject to a tapered reduction designed to encourage the retention of the traffic, and there was an option to substitute imported for domestic supply (an amendment in 1991 provided for the future transport of imported coal from Avonmouth to National Power's Didcot power station). The contracts also stipulated minimum annual payments to British Rail, initially £175.6 million, over 30 per cent lower than the actual payment in 1989/90.[129] The forecast gross revenue from the new contracts was £209 million in the first year, 1990/1, falling to £194 million by 1993/4 (in 1990/1 prices).[130] The new generators proved more demanding than the CEGB had been. Both National Power and PowerGen expressed continuing dissatisfaction with Trainload Freight's charges, and invoked Rifkind's encouragement of open access to the rail network to seek to organise their own trains, a policy also pursued by British Nuclear Fuels.[131] When a new set of four-year contracts was negotiated in 1993–4 the companies drove harder bargains, and the political climate was fraught. The generators made frequent appeals to government to help them shape their relationships with British Coal and British Rail, since both were soon to be privatised. The government was anxious to see satisfactory and relatively long-term arrangements made between the electricity companies, the newly-formed Railtrack, the three, geographically based, freight divisions established prior to sale, and what was left of the coal industry. Negotiating in these circumstances was something of a trial.[132] The new contracts produced a considerable reduction in rates on falling traffic volumes, although there were some compensations in an increase in the average length of haul and in new traffics produced by environmental regulation.[133] However, the minimum charges, for example, were reduced to only £70 million, and thus the prospects for private owners of a coal business in decline and with reduced margins did not seem bright.[134]

After the new coal contracts were signed in 1990, Trainload managers undertook a comprehensive review of their business. This was a candid affair. Unusually in British Rail planning, which was so often characterised by false optimism,[135] the appraisal forecast gloomy results for the sector, with an expected return of only 3 per cent in the 'objective' years of 1992/3 and 1994/5. The business was divided into four constituent parts: the profitable 'core', dominated by power-station coal, aggregates, steel, and refuse; traffics which generated a significant cash margin; traffics which produced cash but used the 'non-core' infrastructure; and traffics which were 'cash neutral' (Figure 8.1). Smith then argued that it would be necessary to attack the two weaker segments, mainly domestic coal, finished steel, and most of the petroleum/oil traffic, and, on a geographical basis, most of the traffic in Northern Scotland, South-west England, and Central and North Wales. Only the core and significant cash-generating traffics using the core infrastructure were to be retained. The rest was to be made profitable or shed by a combination of stringent, discriminatory pricing, cost cutting, and the more intensive use of the assets which were to be retained. A further review in 1992, undertaken with the help of the consultants Mercer Associates, identified some 10 million tonnes of unprofitable traffic (the losses amounted to some £30 million on a turnover of £45 million). Seventy per cent of this, mainly steel products, was retained after repricing and revised operating methods, but three million tonnes were lost, notably much of the railways' cement business, though this was largely the result of a determined shift to road transport by the hard-pressed companies Blue Circle and Castle, actions which had the unusual effect of attracting adverse coverage by the media.[136] Over the period 1988/9–93/4 costs were pruned substantially. The locomotive fleet was halved, 40 per cent of the wagons were scrapped, a fifth of the workforce was cut, and operating costs were reduced by about 21 per cent in real terms.[137] Of course, as with RfD and Parcels, this work went on alongside firm if disconcerting plans to prepare the freight business for sale on a geographical basis.[138] While some of the decisions taken in the early 1990s served to move traffic from rail to road, thereby puzzling the environmentalists, the clear mandate from government, which was exploited on a number of occasions by Trainload Freight's major customers, was to cut out cross-subsidisation, withdraw from unprofitable traffics, and maximise the rate of return, while preparing the ground for a future in the private sector. On the eve of privatisation the railways' freight traffic had fallen to an all-time low of under 100 million tonnes, a mere 4.65 per cent of the market and half the share it enjoyed in 1974.[139] And even its most secure customers were looking to force rates down or run trains themselves. It is almost an understatement to conclude that British Rail's freight managers were being asked to maintain public sector operations in very trying circumstances.

Parcels remained very much the Cinderella business of British Rail, accounting for 4.5 per cent of railway turnover (excluding grant) in 1988/9 and only 2.5 per cent in 1993/4. Spared the publicity of an individual government objective in 1986, the sector was set the internal target of making a £7 million profit before interest by 1989/90, equivalent to a 5 per cent return on assets. In 1989 the Secretary of State endorsed a similar target for 1992/3, this time of

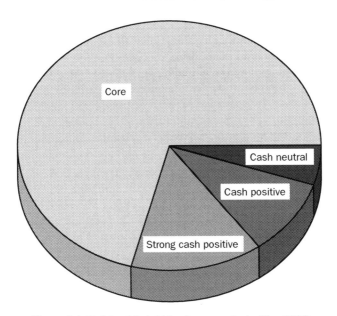

Figure 8.1 Trainload freight business analysis, May 1990

£9 million. Unfortunately, these objectives proved impossible to attain. Turnover fell from £125.5 million in 1988/9 to only £78 million in 1993/4, a reduction of over a half in real terms. The operating loss doubled in a year, from £13 million in 1989/90 to £26 million in 1990/1, and exceeded £30 million in the following year. Although cost cutting helped to bring the losses down to late 1980s levels by 1993/4, Parcels was clearly a loss-making activity (see Table 8.6 and Appendix E, Tables E.1 and E.2). Its difficulties had in fact built up over the 1980s as a result of strong competition from road transport and the changing nature of distribution, with the extension of the motorway network and an increasing emphasis on express delivery. While British Rail benefited from the impetus this gave to its own premium parcels business, Red Star, other parts of the business suffered. As we have seen (Chapter 5, p. 152), the general collection and delivery business had been abandoned in 1981 and five years later British Rail withdrew from the loss-making Royal Mail parcels business. At the same time its contracts with the newspaper industry, which were worth about £27 million a year, came under pressure as a result of the high cost of delivery to railheads, which was organised by the print unions, and by the more flexible response which road haulage could offer. In January 1986 Murdoch's News International suddenly withdrew from its 1985 contract, prompting a long legal battle which was eventually settled out of court in the Board's favour in 1989.[140] News International's withdrawal was followed in June 1987 by similar action from Robert Maxwell's Mirror Group Newspapers, and all newspaper traffic ceased in July 1988.[141] By the end of the decade, when a major strategic review of the sector was undertaken, British Rail's

Running the Railways, 1990–4

Parcels was essentially a two-sector business—Red Star, and Royal Mail Letters, subsequently re-branded as Rail Express Systems.[142]

Red Star, which had been established in the late 1960s and was constituted as a separate division in 1988, was profitable in the 1980s, and successive sector directors, Brian Burdsall and Adrian Shooter, were optimistic about its future prospects, not least from the growth of door-to-door services and from additional traffic promised by the Channel Tunnel. However, such hopes were quickly dashed by the recession. Operating surpluses—about £9 million a year in 1988/9 and 1989/90—dried up and subsequent years saw a rationalisation of activities accompanied by operating losses. These amounted to £9 million a year before redundancy costs in 1991/2 and 1992/3 on a turnover of £58 million and £47 million respectively.[143] Notwithstanding concern about its viability the business was an early candidate for privatisation, and in October 1992 John MacGregor announced his authorisation for British Rail to dispose of Red Star by a trade sale; he then made it one of his interim objectives for 1993. Offers were invited in June 1993, but the sale was aborted in December (see Chapter 12, pp. 418–19).[144] The Royal Mail Letters business, always more of a concern, made operating losses in the late 1980s—about £16 million in 1988/9. The prospect of breaking even appeared more remote when the Post Office adopted a more businesslike attitude to the relationship and demanded a better quality service at lower cost. A new contract operative from 1988 to 1993 gave British Rail higher rates—an increase of 20 per cent in real terms—and an estimated income of £46 million a year, but there was a price to pay. The Post Office secured the right to withdraw from individual contracted trains, while British Rail gave more specific undertakings on service quality—cancellations and late running (90 per cent of trains were to arrive within 10 minutes of the scheduled time)—with compensation payments for a failure to deliver. Since the available rolling stock was virtually life expired this was a brave commitment. The struggle to maintain quality added to costs and in the event there were failures to perform producing compensation payments to the Post Office of £1 million in 1989/90 and £0.5 million in the following year.[145] Reinvestment in postal service trains was prejudiced by the decision of the Post Office to withdraw from short-distance and weekend parts of the letters contract in 1990 at a cost to BR of some £4 million. A review of the sector's strategy for Royal Mail followed, encouraged by a supplementary or 'side' letter to the Secretary of State's 1989 objectives letter, which required British Rail to examine all options, including wholesale abandonment and major reinvestment.[146] The debate was also affected by broader issues relating to the calculation of Parcel's share of fixed costs and (for Red Star) the form of payments for use of passenger trains.[147] Attention to train performance produced improved results, and after 18 months of negotiation, a new contract promised a brighter future. The 13-year contract signed in December 1993 when Glyn Williams was Managing Director of Parcels allocated the railways a third of Royal Mail's letters traffic, and both sides promised to make the necessary investment. Indeed, the customer promised an initial investment of £101 million on 'Railnet', a new hub terminal facility for London at Willesden, together with a fleet of dedicated parcels trains.[148] By this time, of course, plans for privatisation were relatively advanced.

8.6 Productivity

How far was the managerial effort at a business level translated into productivity gains? Indications of the progress made are provided in Table 8.10. As we have noted, the recession presented a considerable challenge. The principal indicator of railway labour productivity—train-miles per member of staff—reveals a rather flat performance, following significant gains in the 1980s boom, but continued progress was made with productivity in train operating, where an improvement of 12 per cent was indicated for the period to 1992/3, and although the statistic slipped back in the following year, it remained 60 per cent above the 1979 figure (see pp. 187–8). Data on revenue per £1,000 of paybill costs also point up clearly the impact of the recession: in 1993/4 the revenue/cost ratio was 22 per cent down on the peak in 1989/90. Nevertheless, British Rail's performance remained strong in comparison with other European railways.[149] On the basis of train-kilometres run per member of staff, British Rail retained a healthy differential over the average performance—56 per cent in 1993/4.

While the introduction of new information technologies was by no means unimportant, the productivity record was largely determined, as in earlier periods, by the ability of British Rail managers to reduce the workforce while at the same time exercising restraint in increasing the rewards to those who remained, policies which were both complicated and given additional impetus by the onset of the long recession. As we have seen (Table 6.1), there had already been a considerable reduction of about 30 per cent in the numbers of railway staff in the 1980s. Pressures to take on extra staff for safety reasons in the wake of the Hidden report, coupled with a tendency to increase staffing as a consequence of the OfQ reorganisation in 1990–2, provided the catalyst for further 'downsizing'. As Table 8.11 indicates, there was a significant assault on staff numbers in the two years to 1993/4, in accordance with a policy articulated at Board Executive level and discussed with the unions in 1992–3. An initial scheme, which envisaged 7,000 redundancies, operated in the first year. A similar scheme with comparable target savings, was applied in 1993/4. Together they produced about 15,000 job losses, a reduction of 12 per cent. The rationalisation was particularly pronounced in the Freight and Parcels businesses (19–25 per cent), and in station and yard operating staff (22 per cent) (Table 8.11).[150] But overall paybill costs actually

Table 8.10 Railway productivity measures with European comparisons, 1989/90–93/4

Year	Train-miles per member of staff Rail business	Train-miles per train crew member Rail business	Revenue per £1,000 paybill costs
1989/90	2,113	10,727	£1,888
1990/1	2,115	10,961	£1,610
1991/2	2,061	11,218	£1,437/£1,517[b]
1992/3	1,927	11,994	£1,406
1993/4	2,029	11,568	£1,476

Percentage change

1989/90–93/4	–4%	+8%	–22%

European comparisons

Train-kms (loaded + empty) per member of staff

	British Rail	Average for 14 CER railways[a]	BR differential
1989/90	3,422	2,301	49%
1990/1	3,289	2,320	42%
1991/2	3,106	2,424	28%
1992/3	3,205	2,527	27%
1993/4	3,463	2,220	56%

Percentage change

1989/90–93/4	+1%	–4%	

Financial support to railways (real terms) 1975 = 100

	BR	SNCF France	DB Germany	FS Italy
1975	100	100	100	100
1979	79	122	131	96
1983	94	121	104	179
1989	44	131	95	243
1991	65	114	79	207

Source: BRB, *R&A* 1989/90–94/5; BRB, Data on State Financial Support, 1975–1991, AN170/20, PRO.
a Community of European Railways members, excluding Great Britain.
b Restated.

Table 8.11 Reductions in British Rail staff, by business and by category, 1989/90–93/4

Date: March/April	Staff (salaried and wage)								
	InterCity	Network SouthEast	Regional Railways	Trainload Freight	Railfreight Distribution	Parcels	HQ	Central Services	Total[a]
1990	—	—	—	—	—	—	—	—	128,439
1992	29,279	34,520	36,145	13,751	2,904	1,983	617	6,969	131,144
1994	26,094	30,519	31,574	10,284	2,330	1,599	512	6,190	115,509
Reduction 1992–4	11%	12%	12%	25%	20%	19%	17%	11%	12%

	Train + Operating Staff						
	Footplate	Other Train Staff	Signalmen	Traffic, Station/Yard	Traffic Staff (Conciliation)	Wages Staff	Salaried Staff
1990	16,839	8,398	4,904	16,839	47,838	86,903	39,594
1992	16,675	7,679	4,846	15,534	45,572	80,611	51,034
1994	14,445	6,688	4,760	12,150	38,554	64,241	51,120
Change:							
1990–4	−14%	−20%	−3%	−28%	−19%	−26%	+29%
1992–4	−13%	−13%	−2%	−22%	−15%	−20%	+0.2%

Source: Appendix G, Table G.1.

a Includes Railtrack (1994), BTP, Level 5 Maintenance Depots, BRPB, EPS, BRT, Union Rlys.

**Table 8.12 Index of railway staff paybill costs, 1989/90–93/4
(constant 1993/4 prices, 1989/90 = 100)**

Year	Footplate	Other train staff	Traincrew	Conciliation grades	Salaried	Total
1989/90	£297.6 m.	£129.6 m.	£427.1 m.	£1,045.5 m.	£735.3 m.[e]	£1,989.0 m.[e]
1989/90	100	100	100	100	100	100
1990/1	104	101	103	101	110	107
1991/2	105	97	103	95	131	110
1992/3	104	91	100	92	147	115
1993/4	97	83	93	82	144	107

Source: Appendix G, Table G.5.

[e] Includes estimated paybill figure for SAUs.

increased as the recession took hold, rising by 15 per cent in real terms from 1989/90 to 1992/3 as a result of higher expenditure on salaried staff, and only falling in 1993/4 when the staff cuts began to produce savings (Table 8.12). On the other hand, the paybill costs of wages staff fell steadily from 1990/1, with a reduction of 17 per cent in train staff (other than drivers) and 18 per cent in the conciliation grades. Some of the variation is explained by the restructuring of S&T, where some 9,000 engineers moved from wage to salary payments in 1992–3. However, it is also clear that while OfQ and safety initiatives produced upward pressures on salaried costs, the marked reduction in overall paybill costs in 1993/4 fell principally upon the wages staff. Here, rationalisation was particularly evident, and there was also a significant reduction in overtime payments (see Table 8.13).

8.7 Industrial relations in the early 1990s

The implications of the rationalisation for industrial relations were not insignificant. As was observed in Chapter 6, the temperature had become rather charged at the end of the 1980s, fuelled by the strike of 1989, the battle to introduce the traincrew concept, and the imposition of individual contracts for middle managers. The period had also seen the resignation (in 1990) of Trevor Toolan as Managing Director, Personnel. The drive to make staff cuts during what became a protracted recession and union anxieties over both the OfQ reorganisation and grade restructuring came together with the prospect of railway privatisation to produce a potent cocktail. This was particularly visible in 1993, when relations with the unions were extremely tense. Of course, levels of pay remained a central issue, and negotiations were especially difficult in 1991 and 1993. There were further problems in 1994 when the Board agreed a general pay settlement, but the newly constituted Railtrack company became involved in a protracted dispute with signalmen represented by the National Union of Rail, Maritime and Transport Workers or RMT (prior to 1991 the NUR).

The railway unions' approach to pay continued to involve the search for 'substantial' but unspecified increases. While the pay rounds of 1990 and 1992 were settled quickly at 9.3 and 4.5 per cent respectively,[151] that in 1991 was not. The Board's offers of 6.5 and then 7 per cent were rejected by the three unions following a rise in the retail price index of 8.9 per cent (to February 1991). The Associated Society of Locomotive Engineers & Firemen (ASLEF) and the Transport Salaried Staffs' Association (TSSA) elected to refer the case to the Railway Staff National Tribunal. However, the RMT, in more militant mood, decided to hold a ballot for strike action.[152] The Tribunal sat in May and after considerable internal disagreement produced a recommended award of 7.75 per cent. The unions accepted a revised offer on this basis and the RMT called off its ballot. There was much relief at the Board at the avoidance of the antagonism of 1989, though this feeling was tempered by continuing dissatisfaction with the operations of the RSNT. Only one of the three members of the Tribunal had been happy with the award. The judgement, number 97, proved to be its last general decision.[153]

The pay negotiations of 1993 were exacerbated by the wide-ranging problems produced by grade restructuring, further productivity initiatives and the unions' attempts to secure guarantees on conditions of work, including pensions, as the programme for privatisation developed (see Chapter 12). In the circumstances of prolonged recession the Board was able to offer only 1.5 per cent, in accordance with government guidelines for the public sector. This was accepted by ASLEF and the TSSA, but with Jimmy Knapp once again finding it difficult to restrain his left-wing colleagues, the RMT only accepted the deal in July after a ballot for strike action had been rejected by the union membership.[154] In 1994 the Board's offer of 2.5 per cent was accepted by the unions in May. However, Railtrack, the infrastructure company in the new regime, was unable to reach agreement with the signalling staff belonging to the RMT, where a ballot produced a four to one majority in favour of industrial action.[155] This early test of the new organisation's stance was not a success. Railtrack Chairman Robert Horton proved to be highly abrasive and there was much public sympathy for the signallers.[156] The failure to resolve the dispute resulted in serious industrial action in the form of a series of one- and two-day strikes over a four-month period in the summer. The railways suffered to the tune of £173 million in lost revenue, though the cost to the Board was reduced by a £140 million rebate on payments to Railtrack.[157] The Board's position was now a novel one. As Bob Reid acknowledged, 'it is, of course, not our dispute'.[158] Nevertheless, the origins of the dispute could be traced back to the Board's action in restructuring the S&T function over the period 1989–92, and it was in the Board's period of responsibility that the basic grievance took root—a fall in take-home pay of 11 per cent in real terms over the preceding five years which accompanied a fall in average working hours (see below). In addition, the Board retained a direct interest in that a generous settlement by Railtrack carried with it the danger of stimulating leap-frogging claims from British Rail staff. In the event, the signalling staff extracted a pay increase of 8.5 per cent, linked to productivity, significantly higher than the Board's 2.5 per cent. The dispute provided an early indication that a disaggregated railway industry offered only limited advantage in reducing the complexities of railway industrial relations over an integrated industry.[159] There were further problems in 1995, the last year to see bargaining on a national basis. An offer by the Board of 2.5 per cent was raised to 3 per cent following rejection by the unions. The revised offer was accepted by all but ASLEF which called two one-day strikes in July. The dispute was settled the following month after the Board made a commitment to progress the restructuring of drivers' pay on an individual operating company basis by August 1996 (see below). Thus, after four years of relative calm, railway industrial relations had become much more disturbed, with strikes called in each of the years 1993–5.[160]

Given this bargaining activity, what happened to railway pay levels in the period 1989–94? Basic rates, average earnings, and working hours are summarised in Table 8.13. Non-pensionable additions to pay had the effect of stabilising the basic rates in real terms over the period. But with hours worked for non-footplate grades falling by between 2.5 and 3.5 hours a week, some of this as a result of grade restructuring (see below), average weekly earnings actually fell in real terms for many railway staff even though the average for conciliation grades as a whole went up by 4 per cent. This experience was comparable with that in other parts of the economy. For example, average earnings in manufacturing fell by about 2 per cent in real terms in the period 1990–4, and while some workers did well (those in electricity and gas, for example) others did badly, with those in the construction industry suffering a reduction of 7 per cent. However, as in the previous decade, railway employees continued to work much longer hours to achieve comparable levels of take-home pay. Thus, the wages of footplate staff and workers in electricity and gas industries were similar, at £383 a week in 1994, but the railwaymen worked five hours more; general railway staff earned much the same as construction workers (c.£275 a week), but their hours averaged 51.6 a week compared with only 45.1.[161]

For the unions there were a number of other preoccupations besides pay. We have already referred to the reduction in the workforce over the period 1992–4. At a Rail Council meeting in November 1992 Chief Executive John Welsby indicated that 5,000 jobs needed to be cut. It was hoped that these losses would be achieved primarily through voluntary redundancy, and a special severance scheme, available until March 1993, was offered as an encouragement. Over 7,000 staff took advantage of the offer at a cost to the Board of some £155

Table 8.13 British Rail staff: basic rates, hours worked, and average weekly earnings, 1990–4

Year	Rates (current prices)			Hours worked				Average weekly earnings (current prices)			
	Footplate	Conductor	Railman	Footplate	Traincrew	General	Conciliation	Footplate	Conductor	General	Conciliation
1990	£184.30	£142.20	£115.10+12.65[a]	48.3	51.8	55.1	52.2	£305.14	£246.76	£236.82	£251.47
1992	£207.55	£160.10	£129.60+14.24[a]	48.1	49.3	52.8	50.6	£365.98	£278.08	£265.85	£291.06
1994	£215.90	£165.55	£134.85+14.80[a]	47.6	48.8	51.6	49.7	£382.70	£298.20	£275.44	£309.87
Real rates (1990 = 100)				*Hours index (1990 = 100)*				*Real earnings (1990 = 100)*			
1990	100	100	100	100	100	100	100	100	100	100	100
1992	99	99	99	100	95	96	97	106	99	99	102
1994	99	99	99	99	94	94	95	106	102	98	104

Source: Appendix G, Tables G.3 and G.4.

[a] Non-enhanceable supplement.

million.[162] Nevertheless, Knapp, together with Derrick Fullick, General Secretary of ASLEF, expressed considerable anger at the programme of job cuts, and both security and conditions of employment remained critical issues from the unions' perspective. At the start of 1993 relations remained extremely tense, and they were certainly not eased when Paul Watkinson, Group Personnel Director in succession to Trevor Toolan, was left to find out from the television news that the railway unions were considering strike ballots.[163] On the other hand, the management was not without fault. The unions were understandably indignant when they discovered that the proposed 'downsizing' had been announced to the media while the unions were in the process of being told about it.[164]

ASLEF's campaigning was focused on the need to safeguard the existing agreements relating to Promotion, Transfer, and Redundancy (PT&R) after privatisation. The Board attempted to convince Fullick that there was little to fear, but more specific assurances were sought on future arrangements, and the union elected to call a one-day strike on 16 April 1993.[165] The action was called off after further reassuring noises from Watkinson and the Board's agreement to discuss with the union the application of procedures to deploy train drivers in the new franchise companies.[166] The concerns of the RMT union were, however, more wide ranging, embracing demands for a guarantee of no compulsory redundancies and a commitment from British Rail to refrain from contracting out, particularly in relation to civil engineering maintenance work. Knapp made it clear that his union would take industrial action unless satisfactory undertakings were obtained, and ballots were held in March 1993. The Board was in no mood to concede, however, and the dispute rapidly became the most acrimonious since the strike of 1989, because the actions of the RMT and the CS&EU unions were co-ordinated with those of the coal miners.[167] Watkinson accused the RMT of seeking an excuse to take action in support of the National Union of Mineworkers (NUM), and called the action to ballot members 'irresponsible'. He continued, 'That you should try to justify it on the basis that BR has not given you categoric assurances on three unrealistic and unreasonable demands beggars belief'. Knapp's response was equally trenchant: 'I find much of your...letter to be offensive both to this Union and to me personally. To suggest that my actions have not been taken in my members' best interests but "to establish lawful grounds for what will essentially be sympathetic action in support of the N.U.M." is scandalous and untrue'.[168] Some of the difficulty was undoubtedly caused by the Board's anxiety to make savings under its voluntary severance schemes. It had therefore tended to downplay the strength of existing PT&R arrangements in its dealings with the unions. However, counsel's opinion was that these arrangements, strengthened by the European Acquired Rights Directive, gave a strong protection against compulsory redundancy.[169] National strikes called by RMT on 2 and 16 April 1993—the first since 1989—coincided with strikes by the miners. The response of the Board, in announcing the withdrawal of the facility for trade union subscriptions to be deducted at source, merely raised the temperature.[170] When the dispute came to an uneasy conclusion in May, following a more reassuring statement from the Board, it had merely served to lose the Board revenue.[171]

The dismantling of the existing Machinery of Negotiation, established in 1956, had been something of a holy grail for the Board. As Toolan had discovered, a tough line could prove costly, but in any case tackling the matter head-on became unnecessary, since the OfQ reorganisation offered a more subtle way of breaking down the traditional structure. Once the reorganisation was under way, a working party was established in 1991 to tackle bargaining issues. Working under the auspices of ACAS it produced a new machinery which came into effect in August 1992. This represented the most fundamental change in the collective bargaining arrangements since 1919–21. Bargaining founded on a classification of grades of work was replaced by a new procedure which created a more flexible and responsive structure, led by a new Railway Joint Council, an industry-wide body charged with the consideration of general pay and conditions affecting all railway staff. Issues affecting particular groups of employees were handled by councils for the several businesses and profit centres. The RSNT, much maligned by the Board, was finally abolished. Its last judgement was in September 1992.[172] However, this new machinery was to have a short life. It was amended in 1994 in response to the establishment of the shadow privatised companies. The business councils were replaced by divisional councils, and the Joint Council ceased to operate after the 1995 pay round.[173]

The work and grade restructuring initiatives of 1989–92 were deemed to be essential to the achievement of further productivity growth, through greater flexibility in the deployment of the workforce and improvements in recruitment and retention rates. This ambitious programme was intended to shape the pay and conditions of specific groups to fit the circumstances obtaining in the labour and skills markets in which these groups were placed.[174] It began with the restructuring of Signal & Telecommunications Engineering, where the concerns of the Hidden inquiry about excessive overtime following the Clapham accident produced the necessary impetus for change. Schemes for civil engineering workers, drivers, traffic grades (station and yard staff), senior conductors, signalling staff, carriage cleaners, and workshop staff followed. However, the efforts of British Rail managers, supported by a special productivity project team led by Sidney Newey, Welsby's assistant, met stiff resistance from the NUR/RMT, which was suspicious that there might be more losers than winners from the process, and preferred 'across-the-board' improvements. Some agreements were reached in a fairly straightforward manner, for example with civil engineering track supervisors (October 1991) and carriage cleaners (November 1991). Elsewhere, however, the path was littered with pitfalls. The negotiations relating to S&T staff were protracted, stretching over a 14-month period before they were finally introduced in April 1991 (though without full acceptance by RMT members). An offer to civil engineering's track grades was withdrawn after three years of formal bargaining. The restructuring of the senior conductor grade, an extension of the traincrew concept, was frustrated for over two years. A final proposal was rejected by the conductors by a very narrow margin in an RMT ballot in January 1992, in which the union recommended rejection; it then received only a luke-warm response in a ballot organised by the management in March. The problem was left for InterCity to resolve under the terms of the new machinery.[175] Driver restructuring, which involved ASLEF, of course, was regarded as a critical elem-ent. A package developed in January 1992, which sought to improve basic rates in return for productivity concessions, including single-manning as the norm and more flexible diagramming and rostering, fared no better than those relating to RMT staff. The union found the suggested basic rate, £13,300 for a 37-hour week (plus a £1,000 quality bonus), to be unattractive, but in any case many managers considered the proposals to be sub-optimal, since unlike the RMT proposals they sought to apply a generic solution across the range of busi-nesses.[176] An alternative strategy was followed after the 1995 pay round, when the privatisation process was more advanced. A number of company-specific proposals was negotiated separately with the passenger and freight operating companies, which spelt the end of the national agreement.[177] However, although some important adjustments to conditions of work in railways were effected on the eve of privatisation, progress was generally slow and a number of important initiatives foundered.

Grade restructuring was accompanied by more specific investments in prod-uctivity enhancement. Driver Only Operation (DOO), a major initiative of the 1980s, was the most important of these. As we have seen, implementation had been patchy, and the move had provoked considerable resistance on the part of the unions. Nevertheless, management efforts persisted, and by November 1991 Chris Green, then MD of Network SouthEast, was able to report that over half of the sector's inner suburban services were operating on this basis. Coverage had been extended to the Thameslink, Euston–Watford, Chiltern, South Central, West Anglia, and Great Eastern services, while extensions in the Strathclyde area of Scotland were also made.[178] Of course, the bargaining process remained keen. There were protracted negotiations over the grading of staff employed on revenue-protection duties and the rates of pay of signalmen. However, the greatest source of conflict arose from safety concerns about the ability of drivers to see the platform-monitoring equipment. Such considerations undoubtedly slowed down the rate of implementation, notably on the South Central and Northampton lines.[179] By the end of 1993/4 DOO was in place or in the process of being introduced on all NSE's suburban lines, with the notable exception of the South Western, where driver militancy ensured that no progress was made.[180] It is clear that single manning, when associated with the use of new trains with sliding doors, produced substantial gains in terms of improved reliability and lower costs, if it did not always reassure passengers worried about personal safety and vandalism.[181] Investment in DOO on the Great Eastern and West Anglia routes, for example, cost £10.6 million in 1989–92 but promised a reduction of 300 jobs with a net saving of £2.2 million a year. A more detailed back-check put the job losses at 259 but supported the contention that the scheme had produced a very satisfactory financial result, with a net present value of £3.3 million using a discount rate of 8 per cent.[182]

Over the first half of the 1990s then, the industrial relations strategy of the Board focused upon a drive to achieve higher levels of productivity through rationalisation and occupational restructuring coupled with a move to the decentralised bargaining arrangements deemed to be essential if the transition to a privatised railway were to be effected smoothly. However, it is clear that, in spite of the successful implementation of OfQ (see Chapter 11) and a new machinery of negotiation, the industry continued to suffer from the disturbances caused by the unions' battles on behalf of traditional, sectional interests. This was scarcely surprising. Government insisted on railway privatisation, and the government chose the formula adopted. The railway unions enjoyed a fair measure of public sympathy in their fight to preserve jobs and conditions of employment in the new environment.

Investment and
the Channel Tunnel

9.1 Promoting investment

Investment continued to be a critical element in the railways' experience prior to
privatisation. More than ever, the issue was bedevilled by debates about definitions and coverage. In the public arena, there were several inconsistencies
between the published data given in the Board's annual reports, the Department's
volume of transport statistics, and the series presented from time to time in
evidence before parliamentary committees or in response to Commons questions.
Sometimes, the differences were simply a matter of the accounting approach
adopted, although such decisions could, and often did, have a political dimension.
Thus, after years of debate the railways acceded to the Department's request that
all investment should be capitalised. From April 1992 infrastructure investments,
including track renewal costs, plus the capital element of government grants,
were charged to capital account, and from this point 'revenue investment' effectively ceased.[1] Nevertheless, it is clear that matters were not resolved by the
adjustment. There remained a lively internal debate between managers in British
Rail and civil servants from the Department about discrepancies in both the
historical record and the contemporary position on the eve of privatisation.[2] At
other times, the figures were presented in a bewildering fashion as part of a
political battle over the need for adequate support in furtherance of the Board's
investment aspirations. Thus, in the financial year 1993/4, when the Department
had set a published ceiling for the 'existing railway' (excluding investment in
connection with the Channel Tunnel) of £512 million (a sum increased subse-

quently to £616 million), it was disconcerting for British Rail's Public Affairs Department to find the Board working to a figure of some £841 million, an amount close to the £850 million Reid had declared to be essential to the good health of the passenger railway alone in the Annual Report for the previous year. In the Report for 1993/4, Reid stated that investment had in fact been maintained at £1,206.4 million, 'including £828.1m to renew and improve the assets of the existing railway'. However, later on, in evidence to the Commons Transport Committee in February 1995, he provided data showing that expenditure on the existing railway had been only £665 million.[3] The explanation lies in the fact that the first set of data was based on assets coming into use, the second set on expenditure actually incurred. For the purposes of this chapter, we refer to all expenditure incurred, with revenue investment included.[4]

In the six years to privatisation in 1994, the nature of the railways' investment activity changed radically. In the late 1980s the government had sanctioned higher levels of spending in return for lower levels of subsidy; investment in the 'new railway' had begun with the first expenditure in association with the Channel Tunnel, which opened in 1994; and this visible investment formed a contrast with the pressing needs of the 'old' or 'existing railway' in terms of infrastructure renewal and the replacement of rolling stock. Indeed, in the public mind the period from 1988 to 1994 was characterised by British Rail's investment in infrastructure and rolling stock to support rail services using the Channel Tunnel. In fact, the true picture is rather different. First, it is misleading to assume either that activity was dominated by spending in relation to the Channel Tunnel, or that there was an element of 'crowding-out'. It is true that investment on the 'New Railway' was a significant portion of rail spending in the six years to 1993/4: some £1,597 million, about a quarter of total expenditure. However, the 'Old Railway' continued to consume the lion's share of investment, as Table 9.1 indicates. After all, neither the infrastructure nor passenger service levels contracted substantially during the long recession. The length of route open to traffic, amounting to 16,599 km or 10,314 miles in 1988/9, was only marginally lower at 16,536 km or 10,275 miles in 1993/4. Although there was a contraction in freight activities, the passenger route-mileage was actually longer at 8,921 miles (14,357 km) compared with 8,891 (14,309), while the number of passenger stations increased too, from 2,470 to 2,493.[5] Second, we should note that *overall* spending was historically high, and in the early 1990s the government actually increased its commitment to railway investment even though subsidy levels were forced up sharply by the recession. Thus, total group investment, including that charged to revenue account, increased steadily from £926 million in 1988/9 to £1,508 million in 1992/3 in constant 1993/4 prices, with a four-year average of £1,278 million, 1989/90–92/3, higher than at any time since the mid-1960s. Even if we subtract all Channel Tunnel expenditure, British Rail invested to the extent of £996 million a year, 1989/90–92/3, again higher than the investment in any year after 1966 (Figure 9.1).

Table 9.1 Gross British Rail investment, 1988/9–93/4 (annual data, £m., in current and constant 1993/4 prices)

Year	Existing Railway (i)	New Railway (ii)	Group (iii)	(i)	(ii)	(iii)
	Current prices			Constant prices		
1988/9	722	6	728	919	7	926
1989/90	864	28	892	1,029	33	1,062
1990/1	869	178	1,047	962	197	1,159
1991/2	968	350	1,318	1,016	367	1,384
1992/3	955	521	1,476	976	532	1,508
1993/4	650	515	1,165	650	515	1,165
Total	5,029	1,597	6,626	5,553	1,652	7,205

Source: Appendix B, Tables B.1 and B.2. Columns may not sum due to rounding.

Understandably, perhaps, investment expenditure in the 'Old Railway' fell sharply with all the distractions of privatisation in 1993/4, to the extent of some 35 per cent. Nevertheless, in general the period was clearly buoyant in terms of investment support, representing a significant contra-cyclical element in the economy. Of course, given the comparative neglect of the railways over much of the 1970s and 1980s there was much still to be done to create a modern railway throughout the system.

What impact did this increased level of investment have? Taking a broad view the allocation of expenditure represented another break with the past. The proportion devoted to infrastructure fell steadily, from 73 per cent in 1983 to 48 per cent in 1988/9 and 33 per cent in 1992/3; the average for the six years to 1993/4 was 40 per cent. In real terms expenditure on infrastructure was maintained from 1983, although it is true that within this category spending on renewals fell from the relatively high level of 1983, while signalling and track rationalisation expenditure rose (Table 9.2). The principal reason for the comparative decline of infrastructure investment was that spending on the more visible and much publicised category of traction and rolling stock increased sharply in real terms, from £110 million in 1983 to £573 million in 1992/3 (in 1993/4 prices, excluding payments in advance). This category consumed a third of total group investment in the six years to 1993/4, double the proportion in the mid-1980s, and investment in terminals and depots also increased markedly, making up a fifth of total investment over the same period (Table 9.2).[6] Nor was the spending spread uniformly across the businesses. Data for 1985/6–92/3 reveal that the passenger business consumed 87 per cent, freight and parcels only 13 per cent; and within these broad categories, there were significant sectoral differences. The investment in the once neglected Network Southeast, at 43 per

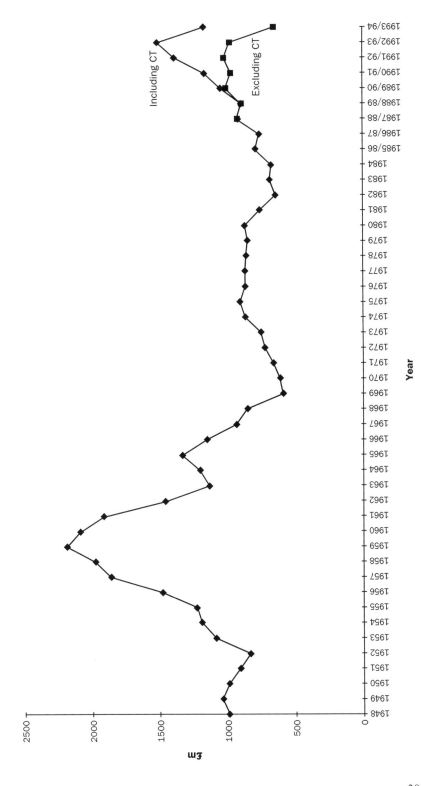

Figure 9.1 Railway investment, 1948–93/4 (£m., in constant 1993/4 prices)

305

Table 9.2 Components of total railway investment, 1983–93/4 (£m., in constant 1993/4 prices)

Year	Components (% share in brackets)					
	Track renewals	Signalling & track rationalisation	Total infrastructure	Traction & rolling stock	Terminals & depots	Total rail
1983	271 (40)	146 (21)	499 (73)	110 (16)	56 (8)	682
1988/9	175 (20)	130 (15)	430 (48)	263 (29)	200 (22)	893
1992/3	193 (13)	219 (15)	493 (33)	573 (38)	261 (17)	1,508
Annual average						
1988/9–1993/4	168 (14)	175 (15)	472 (40)	387 (32)	222 (19)	1,191

Source: Appendix B, Table B.2.

Total includes other items and deferred interest.

'New Railway' annual averages, 1988/9–93/4: Infrastructure, £57 m. (5%); Traction and rolling stock, £83 m. (7%); Terminals and depots, £57 m. (5%); Total, £275 m. (23%). See Appendix B for details.

cent of the total, was equal to that in InterCity and Regional Railways combined. Half the investment in traction and rolling stock in the period went to this sector in an effort to improve the reliability and comfort of commuting into London. Freight, on the other hand, fared less well, although, as we have seen, the private sector was expected to supply dedicated rolling stock and additional infrastructure along with its traffic.[7]

Physical investment, shown in Tables 9.3 and 9.4, bears out the analysis, indicating the scale of new purchases of rolling stock. Seventy-six electric locomotives were acquired, the Class 91 for the East Coast Main Line, and Class 90s shared by InterCity's West Coast Main Line, Railfreight Distribution, and Parcels. In addition, there were new diesel locomotives, the 100 Class 60s purchased for Trainload Freight. By far the most important element was the acquisition of nearly 2,300 multiple units by Network SouthEast and Regional Railways. Regional Railways benefited from the introduction of the Class 158s; once initial teething troubles had been resolved the new trains were deployed on a range of services in 1990–1, including Cardiff–Portsmouth, ScotRail, and TransPennine. The sector also ordered Class 323 EMUs for use in Birmingham and the North-West. However, most of the units went to Network SouthEast. The Thames and Chiltern lines were revitalised by a modernisation programme built around a £107 million investment in the Class 165/166 'Turbo' trains from 1991, while the unreliable Waterloo–Exeter service was improved substantially by new Class 159s. Delivery of the Class 319 and 321 EMUs for use north of the Thames was completed in 1990.[8] The most significant single investment was the £700 million 'Networker' programme, which was designed at last to improve quality and capacity on the heavily used South-Eastern suburban and Kent Coast lines south of the Thames. Sophisticated Class 465 and 466 EMUs were introduced here from October 1992, 190 trains in all with a final cost of £596 million, with supporting investment including longer station platforms, improved electricity supplies, and a new maintenance depot at Slade Green.[9] All this represented a considerable increase on levels of expenditure in the 1980s. Indeed, the investments made received the full backing of, and sometimes, a strong steer from, the Conservative government, though it continued to insist that schemes should pass conventional commercial tests.[10]

In comparison with Network SouthEast, InterCity and Freight were given less support in this period. InterCity's new investment was dominated by the East Coast Main Line, but in sharp contrast, the West Coast route languished despite numerous reviews and investment appraisals. The InterCity Strategy Review of 1987 had identified the upgrading of the WCML as a top priority, and in December 1989 a route strategy review was completed. Five options were evaluated, including the building of a new high-speed line from Crewe to London, but the favoured course of action, endorsed by the Board in January 1990, was to renew the existing infrastructure and reduce journey times by investing in new trains capable of speeds of up to 155 mph.[11] By June 1990 there were firm plans to acquire IC250 locomotives and Mark V coaches as part of a £750 million upgrade,

Table 9.3 Physical components of railway investment, 1988/9–93/4 (numbers)

Year	Additions to stock								
	Locomotives		Power cars	Multiple units		Passenger carriages		Non-	Freight
	Electric	Diesel	HST/APT	DMU	EMU	Loco-hauled	HST/APT	passenger	wagons
1988/9	37	0	0	322	284	2	0	7	21
1989/90	10	0	0	58	210	60	6	47	13
1990/1	29	20	0	160	262	182	10	1	193
1991/2	0	59	0	193	39	51	0	5	151
1992/3	0	14	0	37	78	0	0	25	487
1993/4	0	19	0	84	554	23	0	0	281
Total	76	112	0	854	1,427	318	16	85	1,146
Annual average									
1988/9–93/4	13	19	0	142	238	53	3	14	191
1979–87/8	14	5	9	68	156	30	34	0.5	570
1963–78	13	89	7	26	134	134	26	4	1,284
Stock at end									
Dec. 1978	312	3,268	109	3,293	7,341	5,967	412	4,430	150,371
Mar. 1988	230	2,040	197	2,382	7,022	2,891	712	1,635	28,884
Mar. 1994	260	1,428	197	1,820	6,570	1,790	712	910	13,871

Source: BRB, R&A 1963–93/4; Gourvish, British Railways, p. 511.

Table 9.4 Major investment schemes authorised, 'existing railway', 1988–94

Scheme	Date of authorisation	Estimated final cost at base price (£m.)
Traction and rolling stock		
Class 60 diesels, Trainload Freight (100)	1988	124
Class 158 DMUs, Provincial (499)	1987/8	127
Class 165/6 DMU 'Turbos', NSE (195)	1988/90	147
Class 159 DMUs, NSE: Waterloo–Exeter (66)	1990	33
Class 323 EMUs, Provincial (129)	1990	76
Class 456 EMUs NSE (24)	1988	21
Class 465/6 EMU 'Networkers', NSE (674)	1989/91/2	498
Container wagons, RfD (700)	1990	40
Electrification		
Edinburgh–Carstairs	1989	11
Cambridge–King's Lynn	1989	14
Birmingham Cross City	1989	29
Hooton–Chester/Ellesmere Port	1990	11
Leeds North West	1990	56
Southampton–Eastleigh–Portsmouth	1988	15
Manchester Airport Link	1989	25
Heathrow Express (Paddington)	1988	—[a]
Resignalling		
Great Eastern	1987/9/90	77
Merseyrail DC	1989	36
Paddington–West Drayton	1990	60
LTS	1992	87
Other		
Waterloo & City Line upgrade	1989	25
Track maintenance: Stoneblower	1992	17
Tribute Ticketing System	1992	17

Source: BRB Investment Committee.

[a] Joint venture with BAA; BRB disposed of its 30% stake in 1996.

and although the investment case was far from certain in commercial terms, approval was given in November, and in March 1991 tenders were sought for the construction of between 24 and 40 trainsets.[12] By December 1991 negotiations with the three parties prepared to bid had reached the stage where InterCity was able to produce a plan for 30 trains at a cost of £379 million.[13] Unfortunately, the recession put paid to the scheme, and in July 1992 the three contractors were suddenly told that the Board was unable to proceed.[14] This decision, together with a later unsuccessful bid to lease new rolling stock, left InterCity with no investment allocated to train renewals.[15] The outcome was an uncomfortable one inside the railway industry. Successive managing directors of InterCity felt rather sore about the project. John Prideaux had been disappointed by the scheme's somewhat lukewarm reception in some circles in 1990, while even Chris Green's Midas touch deserted him on this occasion. As Welsby recalled in 1998, refurbishment of the WCML had been announced every year since 1991 and sometimes twice, without any tangible results. Once again, the difficulty of progressing major projects during a recession was clearly demonstrated.[16]

The needs of freight were not entirely neglected; indeed, both sectors received new locomotives (Table 9.4). In comparison with earlier years, fewer wagons were purchased, the 1,100 vehicles acquired including only one major project—a £40 million investment in 700 container wagons for the Freightliner deep-sea business. Of course, we should note that the private sector was increasingly expected to supply its own needs. While the number of privately owned wagons remained stationary at about 13,700, the proportion of the wagon fleet privately owned rose from 35 per cent in March 1989 to 50 per cent in March 1994.[17] Spending on new infrastructure for the 'existing' railway was again limited. The total route-mileage of electrified line increased from 2,719 in March 1989 to 3,051 in 1994, and the percentage of electrified route increased from 26 to 30 per cent. New schemes included Edinburgh–Carstairs, Cambridge–King's Lynn, Birmingham Cross City, Hooton–Chester/Ellesmere Port, and Southampton–Eastleigh–Portsmouth, and Leeds North-West. Two new airport links were added: Network SouthEast's 3.5-mile link to Stansted Airport, a £43.5 million investment opened in March 1991, and Regional Railways' £25 million Manchester Airport line, opened in May 1993. Work on a third scheme, the Heathrow Express, a joint venture undertaken with the British Airports Authority, began in 1993, embracing electrification of the lines out of Paddington.[18] In addition, the Tonbridge–Redhill line was electrified in preparation for the Channel Tunnel freight services (see below). A number of major resignalling schemes were also undertaken. These included the Merseyrail (£36 million) and Paddington (£60 million) resignalling, completion of the Waterloo scheme (£44 million), and a start on the major upgrade of the London Tilbury & Southend line.[19] Many of the new investments were undertaken with the full support of, and indeed, sometimes on the initiative of, the local authorities' Passenger Transport Executives. New stations certainly came within the second category, notably with 20 stations opened in the Glasgow area thanks to the Strathclyde PTE, but the PTEs also invested substantially in the urban rail infrastructure, notably in the Birmingham area, with the Cross City electrification and the reopening of the Snow Hill–Smethwick line, both supported by the West Midlands PTE (Centro); the Manchester Airport link, partly financed by Greater Manchester, and the West

Yorkshire-sponsored Leeds North-West electrification.[20] Track maintenance was addressed with the order of 11 Stoneblower machines in April 1992, and the advances in ticketing represented by APTIS and PORTIS (see pp. 225–6) were developed further with the Tribute system. This £17 million investment introduced early in 1994 for InterCity and the fledgling European Passenger Services, combined timetable, fares, and seat reservation details in one ticket.[21]

9.2 Investment frustrated

This apparently impressive portfolio should not mask the fact that the severity of the recession, government interventions, and the uncertainties of privatisation all acted as distinct limits to the progress made. As we have seen, the Board's financial difficulties had resulted in Treasury restrictions on investment spending in 1990. The investment ceiling for 1991/2 was reduced from £1,378 million, the figure contained in the Investment and Financing Review settlement, to £1,070 million. During the early 1980s recession the ceiling had not been a critical factor because investment spending was so low. However, a decade later existing contractual commitments threatened to take the Board over the limit. As a consequence an investment moratorium was imposed by the Treasury in February 1991 and all new schemes required both the personal authority of John Welsby as Chief Executive and the formal sanction of the Department.[22] In order to cater for safety projects the limit was raised to £1,095 million, but the moratorium remained in force until the end of 1991, by which time government concerns about meeting the EFL had eased, and the limit was raised by a further £55 million. Expenditure of £300 million was then crowded into the final months of the year in order to spend up to the ceiling, but in spite of these efforts there was still a shortfall of £129 million.[23]

Given these circumstances it is no surprise to find that the leasing of rolling stock reappeared on the policy agenda, as it had in the early 1970s.[24] However, on this occasion the 'beauty contest' required from the three passenger businesses served only to frustrate rather than realise their ambitions. In his 1992 autumn statement the Chancellor, Norman Lamont, announced a change in the treatment of operating leasing. Henceforth only the lease rental payment would be charged against the EFL. He also set aside £150 million to be spent on the leasing of railway rolling stock in 1994–6. The government had three objectives: to provide work for hard-pressed domestic manufacturers; with privatisation imminent, to stimulate a market for second-hand rolling stock; and to transfer as much risk as possible to the private sector. In order to accelerate the investment by avoiding a full-scale procurement process under EC regulations, the projects needed to be follow-on orders rather than new builds.[25] The Board Executive considered three bids in April 1993: Regional Railways wished to lease Class 323 EMUs for use on its Leeds North-West lines, which were being electrified; Network SouthEast proposed the leasing of dual-voltage 'Networker' EMUs for the Great Northern and South-Eastern outer-suburban services; InterCity, in a late bid, asked for Class 91 locomotives and Mark IV coaches for the WCML. The Regional Railways' bid was quickly rejected. An earlier tranche of Class 323s, built by Hunslet TPL, had produced technical problems which were giving cause for concern and, in any case, the financial case was weak.[26] After closer examination a GEC Alsthom bid for the InterCity trains was also rejected. The scheme was found to fail on a number of grounds, with a poor NPV return given the quoted prices, a dependence on optimistic revenue gains, and a limited transfer of risk to the manufacturer.[27] This left the Network SouthEast scheme. Its handling provides a good example of the difficulty British Rail experienced in trying to progress investment with a government intent on privatisation. The manufacturers ABB offered three options: outright purchase; an operating lease; and a finance lease. Under the operating lease option the manufacturer would shoulder responsibility for all maintenance costs; a finance lease would provide for a limited warranty period, leaving British Rail with responsibility for maintenance and the carrying of spares. Here there arose a clash between the government's insistence on developing a test case for privatised conditions, and the Board's duty to adopt the most financially rewarding option. After a full examination of the proposals the Board was convinced that the transfer of risk under an operating lease involved a 'substantial additional cost', and Reid told Roger Freeman, the Minister for Public Transport, that given genuine uncertainties about the prospects of extracting premium pricing, the highest return was to be derived in fact from a finance lease (£56 million compared with £19 million). Indeed, if the revenue gains dependent on higher pricing were excluded, then the operating lease would produce no surplus at all. However, Freeman took the view that 'the operating and finance lease options are sufficiently finely balanced for it to be legitimate to take account of broader strategic considerations'. He therefore insisted that an operating lease be undertaken, and the order was placed on this basis in January 1994. Here, the Treasury's position had been critical; it was determined to use the scheme to see how much risk could be transferred to the private sector.[28]

Grand, but ultimately futile, investment aspirations were set out in the Board's visionary *Future Rail—The Next Decade*, published in July 1991. The document presented a 10-year agenda for new lines and the improvement of existing services. This was essentially a wish-list of schemes, with new trains and stations, the expansion of freight, the development of Channel Tunnel traffic, and the improvement of London's infrastructure with CrossRail and Thameslink 2000 (see below). The programme required expenditure of at least £1 billion a year for 10 years.[29] *Future Rail* expressed the strong and perhaps fanciful ambitions of leading managers, but these ambitions were frustrated by the failure to obtain higher levels of funding. Chris Green's vision for Network SouthEast was a clear one. He enthusiastically endorsed the concept of total route modernisation, which aimed to modernise *all* the assets of a particular line simultaneously, and incorporated the concept in an address to the Chartered Institute of Transport in May 1989 and in his upbeat 'Future Rail: London Agenda' of September 1991. However, at a time of financial constraint the bill was clearly too high. Deployed to good effect on the Great Northern, Northampton, and Chiltern lines, total route modernisation could not be extended further given existing investment controls. Consequently, the full benefits of the new 'Networker' trains were unrealised due to the abandonment of the signalling investment associated with the scheme. In addition, the lack of orders for further Networkers forced the sector to persist with ageing Mark I rolling stock.[30] Regional Railways and West Yorkshire PTE were also disappointed with the failure to obtain new rolling stock to match their investment in the Leeds North-West electrification. The failure of their leasing bid meant that when the scheme was completed in 1995, they had to make do with 'cascaded' Class 308 EMUs from Network SouthEast, vehicles which were older than the 'Pacer' DMUs they replaced.[31] At the same time, progress with electrification was extremely limited. The major schemes heading the list drawn up in 1981 in British Rail's *Review of Main Line Electrification* remained dormant: Paddington–Bristol/Swansea/Plymouth/Penzance, and the Midland Main Line from Bedford to Sheffield; while the West Coast Main Line was still in desperate need of attention. The economics of electric traction had changed dramatically since then, and even *Future Rail* limited its plans to 150 miles of route for Regional Railways. In the environment of the early 1990s there was also a possibility that the newly integrated, post-OfQ businesses might find it difficult to address the pressing needs of signalling infrastructure renewal.[32] In 1992 Welsby therefore commissioned a special report on the state of the existing infrastructure, together with recommendations for priority investment. Undertaken by Brian Hesketh, former Signalling Projects Director, it produced a priority list for future work. More worryingly, however, this painstaking report revealed substantial areas of apparent neglect.[33]

In London, there was a modest success with the modernisation of the Waterloo & City Line. Reopened in July 1993 after an expenditure of £25 million, it experienced teething problems and cost overruns before being transferred to London Transport nine months later.[34] However, more ambitious projects, such as Crossrail, and Thameslink 2000, failed to bear fruit. Cross-London schemes had long been regarded by planners as vital to the capital's public transport infrastructure; in Peter Parker's time, for example, the Board had produced a CrossRail Study, in November 1980, which envisaged a deep-level line linking Euston and Victoria.[35] In the 1970s and 1980s such schemes had little or no chance of attracting government support, but the impetus for more determined action came with a Central London Rail Study commissioned by the Secretary of State, Paul Channon, in March 1988, in response to the congestion created by a boom in London travel. Undertaken jointly by Network SouthEast, the Department of Transport, London Regional Transport, and London Underground, the study, published in January 1989, identified a number of serious options for development, including crossrail links from North to South and East to West, a Chelsea–Hackney underground, and capacity improvements to British Rail's new Thameslink services, which had commenced in May 1988 (see p. 224). The success of the RER network in Paris was a major stimulus.[36]

All these schemes required public funding, of course, and since the total bill was estimated to be in the region of £5–6 billion a degree of selectivity was required. In fact, the government was drawn to an extension of the Jubilee line to serve the ailing Docklands development at Canary Wharf, and it was prepared to support only one other scheme. The choice fell on an East-West Crossrail from Mile End to Royal Oak, linking Liverpool Street and Paddington, a project which was enthusiastically endorsed by Channon's successor, Cecil Parkinson, at the Conservative Party Conference in October 1990.[37] This £1.4 billion scheme, like the promise to improve safety with Automatic Train Protection or ATP (see pp. 355–9), foundered on the rock of financial realism. Work began on the joint British Rail-London Underground scheme with the intention of opening in 1999, but the investment authorisations were modest. By November 1991, when the estimated cost had escalated to £2.2 billion, the project was effectively put on a 'care and maintenance' basis. Nevertheless, British Rail had to go through several hoops, including a government cost audit, a request for greater involvement from the private sector, and detailed parliamentary scrutiny. Opposition to the route surfaced, while the local authorities expressed concern about the safety of deep tunnels. There were also problems in reconciling the differences in funding the joint scheme. London Underground's share was to be grant aided, while the British Rail portion was expected to produce a commercial return. The scheme effectively died in 1996.[38] There were similar difficulties with a second recommendation of the Central London Rail Study, namely that Thameslink services should be extended and improved. The success of the initial investment linking King's Cross and London Bridge via Blackfriars led to a £1 billion 'Thameslink 2000' project, extending services to the Great Northern lines from King's Cross, which was presented to the Board in September 1991.[39] Here again, there were difficulties in progressing the scheme. Despite a poorer cost–benefit rating, Crossrail was given preference. It was not until February 1996, after Crossrail had been shelved and opportunities arose to combine the Thameslink investment with the construction of the Channel Tunnel Rail Link terminus at St. Pancras, that a reconfigured scheme, costed at £650 million, was finally authorised by Sir George Young; by this time it was the responsibility of Railtrack. Even then, there were considerable delays in the implementation stage, and work has yet to start at the time of writing (2001). Thus, on the eve of privatisation, there was much project evaluation but precious little action.[40]

9.3 Project management and procurement

The need for effective project management and procurement remained as critical as ever. As we have seen (Chapter 6, p. 228), Kirby's concerns in 1989 had led to an investigation by Touche Ross of the management and forecasting of investment expenditure. Their report identified a number of shortcomings in overall project planning and control, and in investment programming and budgeting. In the light of these findings, two task forces were set up. The first, led by Glyn Williams, the Director, Financial Planning, was asked to tackle project planning and budgeting procedures. The second examined project management. It was led by Don Heath, the former project manager of the East Coast Electrification. Heath had been appointed Director, Projects in 1988 with an enhanced brief, that of improving the management of this activity by bringing together resources under an independent departmental head.[41] As a result of these initiatives, British Rail's project managers were given greater responsibilities, and additional staff were employed to strengthen regional investment management.[42] However, the regions were about to be dismantled with the OfQ reorganisation, and concerns were expressed that the implementation of the Touche Ross recommendations would be lost in the organisational transition.[43] One of the major areas of debate was the extent to which centralised investment appraisal and control, an enduring feature of nationalised railways in Britain, was required in a devolved, business-led organisation.[44] Under the post-OfQ structure the Board retained an overall monitoring of investment of larger projects (costing over £10 million) through the Business Review Group, supported by a small core staff at Headquarters. The Projects team became part of the Central Services organisation.[45] Taken together, these developments certainly appear to have improved the standard of project reporting in the early 1990s. One example was the inclusion of a 'lessons learned' section in the investment completion certificates submitted to the Business Review Group; subsequently, these lessons were collated for wider dissemination.[46] Of course, higher quality *reporting* did not necessarily stimulate satisfactory project outcomes. In the early 1990s much rested on the quality of investment management in the individual businesses.[47]

Scrutiny by the Department of Transport remained an important element in investment control. In 1993 it emerged that 25 railway projects required specific monitoring arrangements under the revised rules of September 1989 (Chapter 6, p. 228). In the past, the authorisation and subsequent control of investment expenditure had produced strained relations between the Board and the DTp (see Chapters 1, 2, 3, and 6). While, as we have seen, this tension persisted in the progressing of the immense investment required for the Channel Tunnel services, civil servants displayed greater confidence in the Board's processes in relation to the 'old' railway. Even so, pertinent questions could still be raised, as, for example, when the DTp queried the appraisal methodology used in the

1990 submission for the Network SouthEast Class 456 EMUs.[48] The main problem here was caused by changing the deployment of the new stock after authorisation by the Department, a situation which also occurred with the Cambridge–King's Lynn electrification scheme in the same year.[49] One area which continued to be accorded a low priority was that of investment back-checks. In 1992 the Department felt moved to remind the Board that it considered such checks to be an essential feedback to project appraisals.[50] However, the work was complex and time consuming, and business managers were reluctant to devote resources to historical exercises. A subsequent internal report confirmed that the whole process of *post-hoc* evaluation by British Rail had had a chequered history, something which will not surprise those familiar with the management of railway investment in the 1950s–70s.[51] In spite of the criticisms of the Serpell review (Chapter 5, p. 171), this area had not moved forward in line with other investment procedures.[52] Renewed pressure from both the Treasury and the Department increased the scope of project monitoring, to the extent that of the 25 large schemes earmarked for attention in 1993 the requirements for seven of them amounted to a full back-check (though not, rather surprisingly, the East Coast Main Line electrification).[53] In addition, investment managers at Headquarters elected to examine four projects in some depth—the 'Pacer' DMUs, Class 58 freight locomotives, Stansted Airport link, and Newcastle resignalling, in an effort to take post-implementation review more seriously. In fact, only one of these back-checks, that on the troubled 'Pacer' Railbuses, seems to have been carried out. This exercise, completed in September 1993, highlighted the difficulties caused by rushing hastily into acquiring vehicles without a clear business plan and a 'robust dmu replacement strategy'—though, in mitigation, there had been an urgent need in the late 1970s to replace units which contained asbestos. The maintenance and modification costs of the first and second builds exceeded forecast levels by 30 and 45 per cent respectively. In more general terms the back-check concluded that the whole-life cost of the new trains was scarcely lower than that of the first-generation DMUs they replaced, a finding which raised questions about the claims of modern, cost-saving technology.[54] A second monitoring exercise reached a more favourable finding, however. An evaluation of the investment in the Class 156 'Super Sprinter' DMUs was forwarded to the DTp in August 1991. Here the maintenance cost assumptions and utilisation levels included in the appraisal had actually been bettered by 40 and 43 per cent respectively. Furthermore, the revenue gains were impressive: a real increase of 37 per cent on the Anglia–Birmingham/North West routes from 1987/8 to 1990/1, with an estimated 6 per cent improvement attributed to the quality of the new vehicles.[55] Little more appears to have been attempted. It is therefore unfortunate that the absence of other studies makes it difficult to generalise about the real economic benefits of so many of the Board's significant investments.

Procurement policy, equally critical in the investment process, is another activity about which it is difficult to make satisfactory generalisations. As we have noted (Chapter 6), this had been a contentious subject in the 1980s, and in the early 1990s, encouraged by Watson's appointment to the Board, and by the requirements of the European Commission's Utilities Directives 90/351 and 92/13, further efforts were made to effect improvement.[56] One of the barriers to change was attitudinal—the 'supply' function was often regarded simply as 'buying', a routine clerical activity rather than a complex and interactive process. But its importance was demonstrated by the fact that some £1.5 billion was spent with external suppliers, a figure equivalent to 40 per cent of British Rail's operating costs. A review of railway procurement, undertaken by Roger Keeling, the Director of Procurement, in 1992, highlighted the extent of the challenge. Relations with suppliers were frequently adversarial, contractual relations were out of date, and there was a lack of integrated project management. The experience of the Class 158 project from 1987 highlighted the difficulties. The Project Manager had been appointed after the completion of the investment submission; he was also responsible for four other large projects. A measure of the effectiveness of project management discipline was provided by the level of post-contract-award variation orders, and here the number was comparatively high.[57]

Reform was advanced by a number of initiatives. A business optimisation study, endorsed by the Supply Committee in 1989, set a three-year savings target of £100 million, and put in place a devolved and professional organisation. In the first year, 1989/90, £39 million was saved, with further savings of £50 and £52.5 million in the next two years.[58] These savings, which exceeded the target by £41.5 million, were achieved primarily through the introduction of greater competition, post-tender negotiation, and the development of innovative procurement strategies. Over the three years to 1991/2, the proportion of competitively procured goods increased from 69 per cent to 89 per cent of expenditure, notable examples including concrete sleepers and steel rails.[59] Under OfQ procurement was combined with materials management (hitherto the responsibility of the engineers) to form a new Central Services profit centre called Procurement and Materials Management. In anticipation of the change a Procurement and Materials Management Strategy Review was produced in January 1992, providing the first comprehensive review of these activities across the whole of British Rail. While revealing a number of strengths the review also pinpointed some weaknesses. Operating costs were found to be comparatively high, planning was limited, the management of the supplier base was inadequate, and the administrative workload in processing large volumes of low-value orders was unnecessarily large.[60] Although some managerial tensions were produced by the organisational change, the results were generally positive. A new emphasis on partnership between the Headquarters function and its customers, the rail businesses, was endorsed, in the search for greater effectiveness, improved communication, and better value for money.[61]

A Supplier Accreditation Scheme, launched at the end of 1991, was perhaps the most critical innovation of the period. One of Watson's initiatives, it borrowed from the successful introduction of such schemes by Japanese and American companies, notably in electronics and the motor industry. For British Rail, the intention was to rectify the poor relationships with suppliers and reduce the massive supplier base, which embraced 25,000 different firms (though 280 of these accounted for 80 per cent of the annual spend).[62] A study was undertaken by the consultants Arthur D. Little, and was accompanied by two defining conferences with major suppliers at the Birmingham International Conference Centre in July 1992 and July 1993. Nearly 1,000 firms had qualified for accreditation by the time the consultants reported in 1994, and British Rail's annual expenditure fell from £1.5 billion in 1991/2 to £1.1 billion in 1993/4.[63] The reactions of the rail businesses varied, but it is clear that Network SouthEast, led by John Nelson, was an enthusiastic advocate of improving supplier relationships and of pursuing more innovative partnership deals with the private sector in the more straitened circumstances of the recession. Thus, the maintenance of the Chiltern line was put out to private competitive tender, the resignalling of the London Tilbury & Southend Line was managed via an innovative design and build contract, and more adventurous proposals surfaced, including private funding of the Third Rail infrastructure south of the Thames, which were only halted by the onset of privatisation and the creation of Railtrack as a government-owned company in April 1994.[64]

Of course, the acquisition of new traction and rolling stock remained the most visible aspect of railway procurement, and here the record remained patchy. For all the attempts to improve project management and foster more co-operative customer/supplier relationships, significant investments, such as the Class 60 and Class 92 locomotives, the Class 158 DMUs, the Class 323 and 'Networker' EMUs, and the Eurostar Class 373s, all experienced late delivery, cost over-runs and operational unreliability. Why was this? First, we must point out that British Rail was certainly not alone in its predicament, and indeed, may be regarded as a paragon of virtue alongside the record of, for example, the Ministry of Defence, the subject of a recent critical report by the National Audit Office.[65] Second, the enthusiasm of railway managers and engineers for improved technology also brought with it higher risks in the procurement process. New trains were technically much more complex than the equipment they replaced. For example, there were aluminium bodies, three-phase traction motors and regenerative braking, dual-voltage and sophisticated multiple signalling systems. We must contrast the way in which untried and technically complex equipment was ordered with the simpler and proven technology of, for example, the Class 321 EMUs, which thanks to long production runs were able to go directly into passenger service after leaving the works at York.[66] On the other hand, the needs of a modern railway, in terms of safety, speed, and comfort, demanded technological advance. Dependence on a relatively small number of suppliers for key equipment lay at the root of the problem. While of course British Rail's relationship with them could be made more 'interactive', it is clear that many of the problems stemmed from production problems inside the factory. Any notion that competitive rolling stock procurement from the private sector would be a happier experience than dealing with BREL in the cosier, 'bad old days' was unhappily misplaced.[67]

9.4 Investing in the Channel Tunnel

The most important single element of railway investment was undoubtedly the expenditure on Channel Tunnel services. Here, a considerable effort was directed at: first, the provision of the promised infrastructure and rolling stock to provide services on the opening of the tunnel; and second, the development of a high-speed link, intended to reduce journey times and match similar investments being progressed by the French and Belgian railways. The Board had no involvement in the construction of the tunnel itself, where work was started in December 1987 by the contractors, Transmanche Link, for the operators, Eurotunnel. Completed six years later after a series of financial difficulties, the Channel Tunnel was officially opened in May 1994. However, as we have seen, the eventual success of the project owed not a little to the earlier enthusiasm of British Rail for the idea. Peter Parker's determination to keep the tunnel alive after its abandonment by the Labour Government in January 1975, was significant. His efforts to interest both governments in a relatively cheap, single-bore rail tunnel in the earlier 1980s, though abortive, helped to keep the scheme on the policy agenda until it was taken up again in March 1985, when the British and French governments issued an invitation for promoters to submit plans for a fixed link.[68] At this stage neither the form the link would take (whether tunnel or bridge) nor the choice of transport modes to use it (whether rail or road or both) had been determined; and Margaret Thatcher's personal preference was for a road link.[69] However, all the bidding parties saw rail as an integral component in their designs, and in January 1986 a twin-bore *rail* tunnel was approved by the two governments. In February Thatcher and President Mitterrand signed the Franco-British Fixed Link Treaty, followed in March by the Concession Agreement with the Channel Tunnel Group and France-Manche, subsequently known as the Eurotunnel Group. By the time the Treaty had been ratified in July 1987, there was an exceptional degree of support for the project from Number Ten, although some railway managers clearly had reservations about the size of the overall commitment.[70]

Although the Board had no involvement in the construction of the tunnel itself there were extensive implications stemming from it. Under the Usage Contract with the tunnel concessionaires of July 1987, the Board and its partner SNCF took on substantial obligations to provide infrastructure and rolling stock, to plan rail services, and to pay specified tolls (both fixed and variable and subject to a guaranteed minimum usage charge), and a proportion of the tunnel's operating costs, in return for half of the tunnel's operating capacity. All this was necessary to provide Eurotunnel with the means to raise capital from the private sector. As already observed, the necessary infrastructure, to be in place by the 'target commencement date' of 15 May 1993, was to be sufficient to carry annually 17.4 million passengers and 8.1 million tonnes of freight. At the same time, the Channel Tunnel Act, also in July 1987, gave British Rail additional obligations. Section 40 of the Act required the Board to produce a plan (by the end of 1989) showing how it intended to secure the provision of international through-services to 'various parts of the United Kingdom', while section 42 specifically exempted the international rail services from any provision for government subsidy under existing legislation.[71] We should not underestimate the size of the obligation to Eurotunnel which, of course, influenced many of the investment decisions that followed. The fixed charge was seven million units of account, £21 million at 1992 exchange rates, the minimum guaranteed payment was 4.167 million units or £12.5 million *per month*, and at the beginning of 1991 the overall obligation, including damages, was estimated to lie between £403 and £1,454 million.[72]

The Channel Tunnel scheme, with its 48 infrastructure and 10 rolling stock projects the largest the Board had ever undertaken,[73] was such as to require the appointment of a number of key personnel. When the Fixed Link Treaty was signed in February 1986, Malcolm Southgate, the General Manager of London Midland Region, was appointed Director, Channel Tunnel, reporting to David Kirby as the responsible Board Member. However, the initial organisational support was rather limited for a job which encompassed project management, business direction, and extensive negotiations with external parties, and it was quickly realised that the management had to be strengthened to match the scale and complexity of the project and the accompanying financial risks. Kirby was succeeded in November 1987 by John Welsby, fresh from his success in rational-ising BREL, and in March 1988 his first project report emphasised the need for stronger management. There were three key elements in his approach. First, Southgate as Director, Channel Tunnel, was to be responsible for overall project management, and in particular the development of the high-speed rail link. Second, in order to plan and operate the passenger element, the Board established European Passenger Services (EPS) in May 1988, to be operated in effect as a sixth sector under the directorship of Richard Edgley, a passenger marketing and planning manager and from September 1986 the deputy director of Network SouthEast. Third, as we have already seen, the requirements of Channel Tunnel freight were met with the establishment of RfD as a separate entity under Ian Brown.[74] However, by the time Welsby was appointed Chief Executive in January 1990, there was clearly a need for further change, prompted by concern about cost over-runs and an examination of project management (see below). John

Palmer, a former Deputy Secretary with departmental experience of the tunnel project, became Managing Director, Channel Tunnel in December 1989 to oversee all elements of BR's involvement—the investment in infrastructure and rolling stock, the plans for passenger and freight services, and the high-speed rail link.[75] EPS then became a wholly owned subsidiary of the Board in November 1990, with Palmer as Chairman, Edgley as MD, and Southgate as Deputy MD, before passing directly into government hands in May 1994 as a prelude to privatisation. Finally, the new chairman, Bob Reid II, decided to provide a personal oversight of the Channel Tunnel project to allay Departmental anxieties, a role which was strengthened in the autumn of 1990 when he assumed direct responsibility for 'mega investment projects', producing a distinctly top-down approach.[76]

Allied to the division of responsibilities into project management, passenger traffic, and freight, was the separation of the project into three phases. Phase I embraced the investment necessary to operate services from May 1993 (substantially the investment listed in the usage agreement); Phase II covered the proposals for running international services north of London; and plans for further upgrading of the infrastructure, essentially the high-speed link, formed Phase III. This division was the product of an embarrassing escalation in costs, which prompted government concern in the summer of 1987 and again in the autumn of 1989. In January 1986 the then Secretary of State, Nicholas Ridley, had advised the Board to consider its estimate of £400 million as a maximum figure, and in March 1987 Bob Reid I had reassured Paul Channon that capital investment would be contained within this limit. However, within four months the Board was being asked to consider a 'minimum' figure of £700 million, the increase caused by a combination of underestimation and additional elements, including passenger services north of the Thames. In order to be seen to comply broadly with Ridley's intentions, the Board resolved to separate the 'core' project from additional items, and to seek to peg spending at £450 million for 'Phase I'. Phase I was then distinguished from Phase II (services north of the Thames, £250 million) and Phase III (£200 million for the route capacity improvements of a high-speed link).[77] In August Channon approved the expenditure of £550 million on Phase I, excluding an international station at Ashford (Kent), which he felt was not justified commercially, but warned Reid sharply that his authorisation was 'conditional upon the Board maintaining a stringent control over the costs of the project'. He also pointed out that he could give no commitment to Phase II. The Board responded by minuting, in October 1987, that an expenditure of £500 million was to be regarded as the absolute maximum.[78]

However, subsequent appraisals of Phase I raised the estimate to £707 million in February 1989, £885 million in July, and in October £905 million, or £1.1 billion allowing for all contingencies.[79] Before all this was fully revealed, Channon, writing to Reid in May 1989, shortly before he was replaced in a Cabinet reshuffle, expressed dismay that the investment was likely to cost 'considerably more' than the sum he had authorised.[80] The ensuing correspondence between Reid and the new ministerial team of Cecil Parkinson and Michael Portillo was even sharper when the new estimates were made known. Parkinson told Reid that 'the rate at which these estimates have increased cannot be acceptable to either of us', while Portillo, the Minister of State for Public Transport, was more forthright, complaining that 'the ceiling set has been ignored'. He demanded that those responsible for the projects should be 'motivated to achieve not only specification but also cost targets', and suggested that management consultants be jointly commissioned to examine cost control and project management arrangements for Phase I.[81] Reid concurred and suggested Touche Ross, who had already advised the Board on investment planning and control.[82] The consultants' report in December uncovered weaknesses in project definition and cost reporting, particularly in the period to May 1988, and recommended that a task force be established to strengthen project management. This was in place by January 1990. Touche Ross then produced a Master Plan setting out the necessary requirements to complete Phases I and II in time for the operation of services in 1993.[83] A second team of consultants, John Brown Engineers and Constructors, was also asked (in January 1990) to review the status of Phase I, and was subsequently engaged to provide project management support to British Rail staff. The reason for the approach to John Brown was two-fold: first, John Brown was a member of the Trafalgar House Group, a partner with British Rail and BICC (parent of Balfour Beatty) in Eurorail, the joint venture proposed for the high-speed rail link (Phase III). Clearly, Trafalgar House and BICC had an interest in the progress of Phase I, since it was envisaged that Eurorail would eventually acquire the passenger business. Second, further government authorisations, especially of revised cost estimates for the Waterloo Terminal and the North Pole Depot, were contingent on improved project management. In April 1990 John Brown were contracted at a cost of £11.8 million to provide overall project direction, drawing on the Touche Ross recommendations. A new monitoring and control system was introduced headed by David Chalkley of John Brown, an experienced project manager, notably in North Sea oil. Southgate then stepped down to take over the operational side of EPS.[84] In addition, a special Project Group and a separate Channel Tunnel Investment Committee were established under the chairmanship of Bob Reid II.[85]

John Brown's intervention certainly led to improved project management, but the revised estimate of costs amounted to a substantial £1.255 billion.[86] By this time concerns were beginning to surface in railway circles about the strength of the traffic estimates on which the case for investment was based. Both Welsby and Bob Reid I had been doubtful about the optimistic projections of the SNCF, and condemned the way the Channel Tunnel Bill had been 'Christmas-treed' at the committee stage, that is, laden with additional promises, particularly for tunnel services to the north, where the financial case appeared weak.[87] Even so, British Rail projections were subject to inflation too, the estimated revenue deriving from Phase I being upped by 26 per cent between the August 1987 and July 1990 appraisals. By January 1991 an appraisal document written by Roger Hillard, the Principal Investment Analyst, made it clear that the expected 8 per cent rate of return for Phase I was subject to considerable risks, while the likely return on Phase II, including Ashford International Station, was distinctly fragile, if not negative.[88] However, for all the huffing and puffing of ministers, the insistence of civil servants that individual projects whose costs had increased by more than 10 per cent should be reauthorised, and the efforts internally to improve project management, the plain fact of the matter was that the tunnel was a clear government commitment and binding contracts were in place. In such circumstances it was difficult to reject both increasing cost estimates and elements where the commercial return appeared at best to be marginal.[89]

The principal components of Phases I and II are shown in Table 9.5. Two of the most important elements of the passenger investment were the International Terminal at Waterloo and the North Pole maintenance depot in west London. Both were delayed amid Investment Committee concerns about rising costs and neither was submitted to the Secretary of State for approval until February 1990.[90] There was further delay as the DTp required assurances on project management, and the degree of frustration was such that Derek Fowler asked Edgley to begin preliminary work on the schemes before ministerial consent had been obtained.[91] The Waterloo Terminal, approved in May 1990, was originally envisaged as part of a joint venture with P&O, which came to nothing. A striking design by Nicholas Grimshaw & Partners was accepted for a facility which was part station, part airport-style terminal, and built alongside the existing station. Much was made of the fact that the terminal was handed over to EPS on time in May 1993 and within the budget, but, in fact, the final cost of £145 million (May 1994) was £48 million above Parkinson's original authorisation.[92] The North Pole depot, constructed on an awkward site near Old Oak Common, was also the subject of a failed bid from the private sector. This project was authorised at £74 million, then reauthorised at £84 million, but was completed in July 1993 at a final cost of £76 million, which was comfortably inside the revised budget.[93] There were also extensive infrastructure works in south and west London, including a new track layout between Waterloo and Stewart's Lane, and electrification of the West London line from Clapham to Willesden, to enable the new passenger trains to reach North Pole from Waterloo, and to allow electric locomotives to operate freight trains from the tunnel to a new operations centre at Wembley. In Kent a programme of resignalling, loading gauge clearances, and upgrading was undertaken, the most significant of which was the resignalling of the Boat Train Route between Folkestone and Chislehurst (BTR1). This project attracted the DTp's attention not only because of cost escalation—the scheme's estimated cost rose from £74.6 million in 1990 to £85.5 million in 1992—but because it highlighted the problem of British Rail investing on a commercial basis in a facility shared with a supported sector, Network SouthEast. The Board

Table 9.5 Phase I and Phase II components of Channel Tunnel investment, 1988–94 (£m., forecast out-turn costs in April 1994 at Q3/1989–90 prices)

Item	Estimated out-turn	Total
Infrastructure: Phase I		
Waterloo International Terminal	145.6	
Waterloo: associated work (Stewart's Lane, etc.)	77.3	
North Pole International Depot, etc.	79.6	
West London Line electrification, etc.	36.9	
Tonbridge–Redhill electrification, etc.	23.6	
Dollands Moor Freight Inspection Facility	35.8	
Wembley European Freight Operations Centre	16.8	
Other freight terminals	34.0	
Chislehurst–Folkestone resignalling	92.2	
Route upgrading, structural/clearance work, etc.	108.2	
Other (8 projects)	11.5	
		661.6
Infrastructure: Phase II		
Ashford International Station	37.6	
North London line electrification	16.4	
Other (17 projects)	36.5	
		90.5
Total infrastructure		752.0
Rolling stock: Phase I		
Class 373 trains	348.2	
Night service stock	68.6	
Class 92 locomotives	122.0	
Intermodal wagons	41.8	
Other (2 projects)	0.9	
		581.5
Rolling stock: Phase II		
North of London trainsets	113.0	
Class 92s—included in Phase I	0.0	
		113.0
Total rolling stock		694.5
Total		1,446.5

Source: BRB, 'Channel Tunnel (1993) Project Phases I and 2: Infrastructure and Rolling Stock Progress Reports No. 49, 27 February–2 April 1994', CTX MREP44, BRB.

sought to have the NSE expenditure which was triggered by the Tunnel charged to the PSO grant, but the Department refused, and the commercial sectors, EPS and RfD, would not pick up the bill. The solution was to charge NSE on an unsupported basis for renewals made in advance of requirements; its share of the total expenditure amounted to 38 per cent.[94]

The procurement of the international rolling stock was undertaken jointly by the British, French, and Belgian railways. British Rail was committed in December 1989 to purchase 14 of the 30 Class 373 trainsets, later called 'Eurostar' and modelled on the latest French TGV, to be built by TransManche Super Train Group, an international consortium of seven companies. The trains, for which an expenditure of £356 million was authorised by the Secretary of State, comprised two power cars and 18 coaches, and were designed to run at a maximum of 300 km per hour. Initial planning was based on up to 15 daily services each way between London and Paris and London and Brussels.[95] The order was to prove troublesome owing to the complexity of the trainsets, which were designed to function with diverse signalling and electrical power systems, and were sourced from 17 different factories. In consequence, not only was the cost much higher than first estimated—it rose from £230 million to £336 million in the first half of 1989— but suppliers also encountered problems in meeting the delivery and reliability specifications in the contract.[96] The Board was encouraged to believe that the companies' attention to project management had been less than optimal.[97] The trainsets arrived later, accompanied by a major dispute with TransManche and GEC Alsthom over the contract performance, exacerbated by the manufacturers' admission that their revised estimates of reliability were five and 22 times gloomier than those promised in the contract.[98]

Freight investment was also subject to some delay, since, as we have seen, the business had already experienced financial difficulties with both its Freightliner and Speedlink services, and a detailed strategy for RfD and its Channel Tunnel traffic was not endorsed by the Board until March 1990. At this point it was agreed that RfD should concentrate on trainload activities, particularly intermodal and automotive traffic. Demand forecasts suggested that the maximum level of 35 trains each way per day would be required by the end of the 1990s.[99] The core elements here were the electrification of the Tonbridge–Redhill line, the purchase of 30 Class 92 dual-voltage locomotives and 750 wagons (450 intermodal, 300 automotive). The Brush-built Class 92, according to Ian Brown 'the most complicated locomotive known to mankind',[100] was a powerful and particularly complex machine designed to haul heavy trains from France via the Tunnel to the north of England and Scotland. By December 1990 30 locomotives had been authorised, and a further seven were ordered by EPS and nine by SNCF, making a total build of 46. The authorised expenditure for the 37 British Rail locomotives was £102 million.[101] However, anxiety built up as the order was subject to escalating costs (£120 million by April 1992) and delayed delivery dates, the latter resulting in the spectre of RfD having no locomotives to use through the

Tunnel on opening. The frustration was such that Alan Nichols, the Director of Financial Planning, asked in 1993 for an estimate of the financial effect of British Rail's scaling down or withdrawing entirely from Channel Tunnel freight.[102] Moreover, when the engines were finally delivered in 1994–5, extensive problems were encountered when Railtrack refused them clearance because they were held to interfere with the functioning of domestic track circuits and signalling. Consequently, when first deployed in February 1995 they were confined to intra-tunnel running only, with diesel traction used north of the Tunnel. Class 92 working between the Tunnel and Wembley began in June 1996, but not via the Tonbridge–Redhill line, where the need to spend a further £30 million on track circuit work made the electrification virtually redundant. Clearance for running on the West Coast Main Line was not given until 1998.[103] The £87 million or so invested in freight terminals embraced the inspection facility at Dollands Moor, adjacent to the Tunnel, a freight operations centre at Wembley, the Willesden Euroterminal, and regional intermodal depots at Birmingham (Landor Street), Glasgow (Mossend), Liverpool, and Manchester (Trafford Park). In preparation for continental operations RfD also developed a number of joint ventures with rail capacity 'aggregators', namely Allied Continental Intermodal (ACI), Combined Transport Limited (CTL), Unilog, and Intercontainer-Interfrigo (ICF).[104] The impact of the freight investment was to prove disappointing, however. Sceptics were vindicated in 1995/6 when the Board set aside £500 million to write off the freight assets and meet the cost of the minimum usage charge payable to Eurotunnel.[105]

Most of the Phase I investment was completed by April 1994, in time for delayed international services to begin later in the year. The first through freight train ran in June 1994, and EPS services to Paris and Brussels commenced in November. In contrast, progress on Phase II, namely, construction of Ashford International Station (2A), and the provision of services north of London (2B), was more hesitant. The Ashford station, rejected by Channon in 1987, was reinstated in 1990 after political and local pressure. Despite a concerted re-appraisal the financial case for a project costed at £139 million (including works for the High-Speed Rail Link) remained weak, but expectations had been raised by the publicity given to the scheme.[106] British Rail's submission to Malcolm Rifkind in January 1991 did not produce a speedy response from the Department, which with the Treasury was concerned about the likelihood that the Board would exceed the EFL in 1991/2. In March and May Reid warned Rifkind that the station would not be ready in time for the commencement of passenger services and referred to a possible breach of the Usage Agreement, which listed the facility as part of the necessary infrastructure.[107] The eventual response, from Freeman, was equally forthright. 'The hard fact is', he wrote in November, 'that in present circumstances your proposed station cannot be afforded'.[108] The Board was asked to examine cheaper alternatives, including a temporary station of Portakabins proposed by Eurotunnel in an attempt to break the deadlock.[109] After a considerable amount of work British Rail produced further options in March 1992, the most serious of which was an expansion on the existing station site for £80 million, half the cost of the original scheme (£160 million in 1991/2 prices). However, the cheaper option would require further expenditure of £90 million if the Rail Link were built through Ashford, and inside British Rail there was some concern that neither scheme was financially robust.[110] Another year went by before MacGregor authorised expenditure on preparatory work, and the new station, built via a private financing arrangement with Laing, was not opened until January 1996.[111] Ashford provided a good example of the difficulties and delays which arose when local lobbying and political expediency were allowed to triumph over financial prudence.

Investment in the provision of daytime and night 'sleeper' services for destinations north of London proved equally problematic. Initial appraisal of the day services showed that the corporate case was marginal: the EPS business would gain, but only at the expense of InterCity. The extent of the 'significant risk' was then communicated to the Department.[112] Whatever the doubts, the political arguments for pursuing the scheme were 'powerful', since the Channel Tunnel Act committed the Board to make clear its plans for such services by the end of 1989. After extensive consultation, British Rail's booklet, entitled *International Rail Services for the United Kingdom*, expressed the intention to operate trains from Paris and Brussels to Wolverhampton and Manchester and to Leeds and Edinburgh. Eighteen-coach Class 373 formations would divide into two at Rugby and Peterborough respectively. Bob Reid I made it clear, in his introduction to the document, that 'Our duty is not to run a service because it is desirable: it is to run a service which will be profitable'.[113] Nevertheless, as with Ashford International, public expectations were high and investment submissions were prepared, even though they were somewhat marginal despite optimistic forecasts of traffic and pricing levels.[114] A proposal for seven trains was submitted to Parkinson, with the appropriate degree of caution, in October 1990. However, the prices quoted by the manufacturers were found to be too high, and a revised proposal, based on a shorter, non-splitting, 14-coach train and costing £108 million at Q2/1989 prices, was sent to Rifkind and approved in November 1991. The estimated return was 8 per cent for EPS but only 6 per cent to British Rail as a whole.[115] Matters became worse when the cost of the infrastructure improvements necessary to accommodate the trains—gauging and track circuit work on the East Coast and West Coast lines and a re-electrification of the North London line—rose alarmingly above the initial estimate of £31 million over the course of 1992 and 1993. This and internal doubts about the reliability of the traffic forecasts challenged the economics of the services. Richard Davies, British Rail's Financial Planning Manager (Privatisation), produced a sobering critique of the investment case for daytime services. He concluded that the choice lay 'between losing at least £10 per passenger by taking on the commercial risk of operating the ECML service and losing at most the same amount by gambling that the lawyers can come up with a good defence on our obligations to Eurotunnel'. By March 1994 the traffic forecasts were considered implausible, the corporate return had been revised downwards to only 4 per cent, and internal opinion clearly favoured limiting the services to the WCML.[116]

The plans for sleeper services involved four trains in each direction from France, the Netherlands, and Germany serving destinations in South Wales, the west of England, and Scotland. Although once again the appraisal was rather gloomy, a positive return was expected and Rifkind eventually endorsed the £130 million scheme (Q2/1990–1 prices) in July 1991.[117] Sleeper carriages, financed through a leasing agreement, were ordered in July 1992, and EPS purchased seven Class 92 locomotives to haul them. An international railway joint venture, European Night Services, was formed to operate the services.[118] However, despite the considerable investment, neither the day nor the night services has operated at the time of writing (2000). The responsibility for infrastructure investment passed to Railtrack in 1994 and, given the financial weakness of the case, was not prioritised. The stock delivered in 1995–6 has scarcely been utilised. The sleeper carriages were never made operational, and EPS (Eurostar UK) has put its Class 92 locomotives up for sale. Some of the seven Eurostar trains are currently being used on domestic services on the ECML.[119]

9.5 The High-Speed Rail Link: slow progress

The biggest disappointment was undoubtedly the delay in making progress with Phase III of the Channel Tunnel project. This involved the provision of a high-speed rail link and a second London terminal, with the aim of providing extra capacity and shorter journey times. British Rail was concerned in three periods of activity: the first, from 1988 to 1990, involved the initial identification of potential routes and the establishment of the joint venture with Eurorail that was scuppered by the government in the summer of 1990; the second, from 1990 to the autumn of 1991, saw further study, culminating in the production of a second proposal which the government also rejected; in the third, the Board's subsidiary, Union Railways, undertook further development work until the government announced its preferred route in 1994. In what was a most laborious and complex process, the Board often found itself sandwiched between the government's ambitions on the one hand, and the commercial interest of Eurotunnel and speculative investors from the private sector on the other. While the need for additional capacity was a matter for argument, Britain's procrastination certainly contrasted with the evident success of others in providing new infrastructure, first in France, and then in Belgium.

When the Channel Tunnel Act was passed in 1987, the Board's view was that additional capacity for international traffic would not be required in the foreseeable future. However, the Department's own *Kent Impact Study* took the opposite view, and consequently, the Board carried out a lengthy review of long-term route and terminal capacity, culminating in a report on *Channel Tunnel Train Services* published in July 1988. Its revised opinion, based upon the traffic forecasts of two sets of consultants, conceded that additional capacity might be required by the turn of the century. Four route corridors were identified, together with four locations for the second London terminal.[120] However, inside British Rail, enthusiasm was rather muted. There was a fair degree of cynicism about the strength of the forecasts, whether the more cautious estimate of 13.4 million passengers in 1993, prepared for British Rail by Martin Vorhees Associates and later updated by Coopers & Lybrand, or the more sanguine estimate of 16.5 million offered by the French consultants SETEC, employed by Eurotunnel.[121]

The options for the terminal were: King's Cross (Low Level), St. Pancras, Stratford (in east London), and White City (in west London), requiring a choice reminiscent of that made in the early 1970s and early 1980s.[122] At the beginning of 1989 the Board selected King's Cross. Feathers were ruffled in Newham Borough Council, which wished to regenerate Stratford. However, King's Cross was not only a most suitable site for a combination of international, commuter, and enhanced Thameslink traffic, but held to have a development value of £3 billion.[123] By March the Board had firmed up its ideas for the proposed route, from Cheriton via the centre of Ashford, then following the M20 motorway alignment to Detling, Upper Halling, Darenth, and Swanley, and thence in tunnels to King's Cross (Figure 9.2). Benefits were claimed for both international travellers and commuters. The London–Paris journey would be reduced to 2 hours 30 minutes, while the Ashford commuter would reach the capital in only 35 minutes.[124] The 68-mile route was accorded 'preferred' status after modifications, including additional tunnelling, by September 1989.[125] Unfortunately, from the start difficulties emerged, and the intention to deposit a private Bill in November 1989 was soon found to be premature. With the benefit of hindsight it can be seen that the way the project was handled left something to be desired. The Board had agreed with the Department that four routes should be evaluated and publicised, but this transparency merely widened the extent of an opposition which was often extremely vocal and articulate, and ranged from blatant 'nimbyism' to valid objections about noise and environmental impact.[126] Furthermore, the limited resources initially devoted to the scheme produced some unfortunate outcomes in public relations terms, particularly when maps of proposed routes were less than accurate.[127] British Rail's response was to strengthen the project management by appointing external personnel. Gil Howarth, from British Nuclear Fuels, was appointed Project Director of the Link in March 1989, and Alexander Gibb & Partners were engaged as the Engineering Design Managers.[128] At the same time, the Board's efforts to mollify the opposition to the

Running the Railways, 1990–4

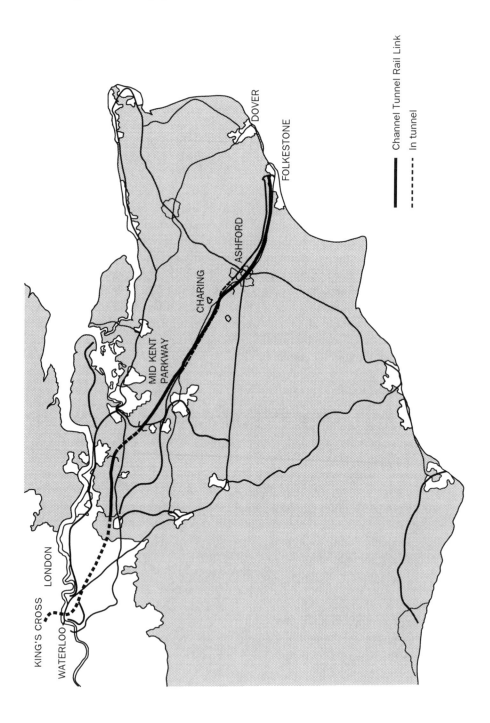

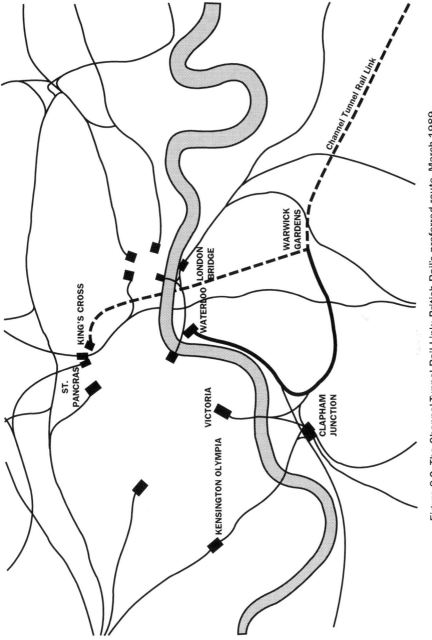

Figure 9.2 The Channel Tunnel Rail Link: British Rail's preferred route, March 1989

link had the effect of increasing its costs. The revised route was about £500 million more expensive than the nearest equivalent proposal of July 1988, and a generous compensation scheme for affected property-owners was introduced, the cost being put at £275 million in June 1989.[129]

If the selection of the route produced challenges, then the financing of it was to prove even more problematic. The government had made it very clear that there would be no public money for the link but, in any case, section 42 of the Channel Tunnel Act explicitly prevented the Secretary of State from providing grants in support of international rail services. The Board's logical response was to examine seriously the possibility of entering into a joint venture. Such a device would also have the advantage of enabling it to retain a measure of control, since there were understandable concerns that the government might attempt to transfer elements of the Channel Tunnel project to the private sector. In November 1988 the Board invited pre-qualifying bids to participate on a risk-sharing basis in the construction and operation of a rail link. Six consortia were then invited to tender, and serious discussions were held with two of them: Acer, comprising Acer Consultants, BAA, P&O, Canadian Pacific, and Hambros Bank; and Eurorail, made up of Trafalgar House and BICC. The initial talks revealed that the private-sector partners were clear that the scheme was not viable financially without government support, the estimated 'viability gap' ranging from £1.4 to £1.6 billion. Consequently, much of the debate centred on their view that the best prospect of securing a return lay in limiting the scheme to the above-ground section from Cheriton to Swanley.[130] In October 1989 the Board had decided that Eurorail was its preferred private-sector partner, a decision which was confirmed in the following month. However, the limited scheme option was rejected following legal advice while the King's Cross Bill was in committee stage, and the Board decided instead to defer the deposit of a private Bill for the link until November 1990.[131] Even so, this timetable remained tight—the final route had to be published by March 1990—and in consequence strenuous efforts were made to modify the 1989 route in order to reduce costs. A new alignment between Upper Halling and Hither Green in London promised to save £300 million in tunnelling costs. Even so, with this and other changes the estimated cost of the project in March 1990 was only reduced from £3 billion to £2.65 billion, and the rate of return of 3 per cent was some £1.2–£1.5 billion short of the commercial return expected by the private sector (using a discount rate of 12.5 per cent). Disagreements with Trafalgar House and BICC over the detailed management of the scheme also clouded the picture. British Rail made considerable efforts to save it by offering to make the scheme a public-sector project, and agreeing to transfer to the Joint Venture Phases I and II, together with substantial property development profits from the termini, and a payment for enhanced commuter service capacity. However, there was no escaping the fact that a government subsidy was still required. A submission from the joint venture to the Secretary of State at the end of March asked the government to provide generous long-term loan arrangements for its acquisition of the public investment of £1 billion in Phases I and II, and to put up £500 million as a grant in respect of the putative benefits to Network SouthEast commuters.[132] Unfortunately, the proposal did not prove acceptable to government. In June Parkinson agreed to safeguard the route from Detling to Cheriton, but found the project to be unviable, and was not prepared to provide a subsidy over and above the support required for Network SouthEast's investment in King's Cross/Thameslink. The scheme was therefore shelved and the joint venture wound up, a somewhat inauspicious start for the new chairman of British Rail, Bob Reid II.[133]

The second period saw further exhaustive work on potential routes, prodded by Parkinson's request that British Rail continue to explore the possibilities, with the aim of maximising the benefit to international travellers and commuters alike. Here the message was clearly one of containing investment costs by re-examining the line between the North Downs (Upper Halling) and London.[134] Other parties were also active. Two of the unsuccessful bidders for the joint venture proposal, Rail-Europe, a consortium of Laing, Mowlem, and GTM, subsequently joined by Manufacturers Hanover and Bechtel, promoted two routes known as RACHEL and TALIS, the first, originating in the 1970s, proposing an all-tunnel line from Dover to Rainham in Essex, the second adopting an easterly route through the Medway to Tilbury and Stratford. Both had been assessed and rejected by British Rail in 1989.[135] Consulting engineers, Ove Arup, promoters of KentRail, also pursued the idea of a more easterly route crossing the Thames north of Dartford and running via Stratford to King's Cross; they favoured a four-track line with provision for international freight. Finally, Newham Borough Council continued to lobby for the second terminal to be located at Stratford, proposing its connection to British Rail's southerly route.[136] The existence of these competing schemes required the Board to undertake a transparent evaluation process and carry out detailed work in consultation and in addressing environmental issues. The work must have been enormous. No fewer than 16 consulting firms were engaged to undertake a number of critical studies. Environmental concerns remained a stumbling block and in June 1990 Professor Fred Holliday, subsequently a part-time member of the Board, was asked to advise on procedures for an environmental impact assessment. The detailed work was overseen by Environmental Services Ltd, with socio-economic and development benefits examined by PIEDA and a study of traffic and revenue benefits produced by Coopers & Lybrand Deloitte. In November the consultants W. S. Atkins were appointed to carry out an independent strategic review and validate the Board's project methodology. In the light of changes to the project management of Phases I and II following the John Brown Report and the constitution of EPS as a separate subsidiary, the Rail Link Project became a separate business unit.[137]

After all this, the Board once again evaluated four route options, at meetings in April and May 1991: its own southerly route to King's Cross; Ove Arup's easterly route to King's Cross; Rail-Europe's easterly route to Stratford; and Newham's southerly route to Stratford. The main conclusion, reached at a special meeting on 2 May, was that if the Board's own route were taken as the base, all the other options were less attractive financially (see Table 9.6). Reid conveyed this view to Parkinson's successor, Rifkind, on the following day. The point was made that British Rail's southerly route to King's Cross, with an estimated financial return of 4.2 per cent, was the best, while Stratford was 'markedly less attractive for our customers even after the building of Crossrail and the Jubilee Line Extension'.[138] The government's decision was made public at the Conservative Party Conference in October 1991. Rumours were already circulating both inside and outside Whitehall that ministerial opinion was against the southerly line. After a leaked story in the *Independent* Reid wrote to Rifkind on 7 October expressing his concern 'at reading apparently well informed reports in the papers that the Government is not disposed to adopt the proposal which I put to you in my letter of 3rd May. I expect you would want to consult me before any such view became final'. No reply was received, however. Reid went 'hot-foot' up to Blackpool to lobby Rifkind at the Conference, but to no avail. On 9 October the Minister announced that King's Cross was confirmed as the second terminal, but to the Board's consternation, chose Ove Arup's easterly line as his preferred route. Political considerations had clearly been enmeshed with economic issues. Critical here was the fact that the Environment Secretary, Michael Heseltine, was an enthusiastic advocate of the regeneration possibilities offered by the easterly route, and his opinion, supported by Chris Patten, the Conservative Party chairman, and Peter Lilley, the Secretary of State for Trade and Industry, had clearly won the day in Cabinet. With an election looming, it must have been a relief to ensure that thousands of back gardens in Tory marginal constituencies in south-east London were reprieved.[139] Reid was furious. He publicly referred to a

Table 9.6 Channel Tunnel High Speed Rail Link: route evaluations, May 1991

Option	Capital (£m.)	Total cost (route & stations) (£m.)	Relative cost (£m.)	Relative benefits (£m.)	Cost/ benefit[a] (£m.)
BR south to King's Cross	3,425	3,565	Base	Base[b]	Base
Ove Arup east to King's Cross	3,905	4,245	−680	−205	−885
Newham south to Stratford	2,945	3,105	+460	−580	−120
Rail-Europe east to Stratford	3,570	3,940	−375	−760	−1,135

Source: BRB, Memorandum, June 1991, Appendix 1, Table 1, in BRB, *Rail Link*, June 1991.

[a] Discounted at 8% (discount at 4% also evaluated).
[b] Not published.

pantomime,[140] and condemned the Stratford route, arguing that it would 'take commuters where they don't want to go and add up to 20 minutes to their overall journeys'. In three replies to Rifkind he pointed out that some £175 million had already been spent on planning studies and the purchase of property in connection with the Board's route, and lamented that a 'golden opportunity has been missed'. He also expressed scepticism about the likelihood of private-sector success in funding the project alone, as had been proposed by the Secretary of State.[141] There was also annoyance about Rifkind's Commons statement on 14 October. This cited British Rail forecasts in arguing that the delay caused by the change of direction was inconsequential since the existing capacity would suffice until 2005, then claimed that the delay itself would be minimal. The notion that it would take only nine months for British Rail to provide information on the easterly route of the same quality as that for the southerly one was misleading, since the Minister had also taken up Arup's view that provision for freight traffic should be included in the assessment.[142] Rifkind's response was to ask British Rail to assist in safeguarding the government's favoured route, and to reject the Board's request for help with the losses incurred in promoting the southerly route.[143] It was subsequently agreed that British Rail should develop the project, working with Arup. This work was begun in tandem with consultants appointed by the Department of the Environment to re-examine the development potential of the East Thames Corridor.[144]

The final stage of the Board's interest in the Rail Link was undertaken by New Ventures and Union Railways. In January 1992 John Prideaux, the Managing Director of InterCity, was appointed Managing Director New Ventures, somewhat reluctantly. Succeeding Palmer, who had become Reid's special policy adviser, his main task was to translate the government's broad conceptual alignment into a fully developed scheme. He also assumed responsibility for the Heathrow Express scheme (see p. 310). Prideaux had made no secret of his view that InterCity should be privatised, and his change of job owed something to fears that with strong political ties with the Conservative government he might be pursuing his own agenda.[145] On the other hand, there was no doubting his ability to provide the necessary professionalism and impetus for a difficult brief. Arup joined the British Rail team in March, and on Prideaux's initiative New Ventures was then transformed into a subsidiary company, Union Railways, with effect from August 1992, with Prideaux as Chairman, and Howarth as Managing Director.[146] The change was intended to concentrate and ring-fence the existing project in the light of its possible privatisation, improve accountability, and help to boost morale which had been badly dented by Rifkind's decision.[147] Over 40 major consultants were engaged in the new round of development work, and determined steps were taken to ensure that the Treasury, DOE, and DTp were fully involved in the process.[148]

After an informal presentation by Union Railways in November 1992, the Board endorsed a document for the Secretary of State in January 1993; this was subsequently published with critical amendments as the *Union Railways Report* in March.[149] The background to these apparently straightforward events is a complex one, and interpretation is clouded by the numerous manoeuvres both inside and outside British Rail. First of all, it emerged in November that Prideaux had developed a potentially cheaper alternative route using the North London line, an existing surface railway, from Dalston to St. Pancras station, thereby avoiding expensive tunnelling and station works below ground. This had not been communicated to his colleagues. Prideaux's action threw into question the Board's existing commitments to the King's Cross Railways Bill, which was expected to receive its third reading in the Commons. Consequently, on legal advice the Board considered Prideaux's draft report in informal terms only.[150] Nevertheless, notwithstanding the Board's emotional attachment to King's Cross (Low Level), the St. Pancras alternative could not be ignored, particularly since it was clear in December 1992 that officials in both the Department of Transport and the Treasury were aware of its existence and keen to explore the idea of utilising the North London line, whatever terminal were chosen.[151] In January 1993 the Board discussed a further draft from Union Railways in which alternative approaches to London were *not* incorporated. This report was endorsed for submission to the Secretary of State, now John MacGregor. However, Reid told his colleagues that the Secretary of State required a comparative review of the London options to be taken forward, and this work was completed in February. Naturally, the conclusions were tentative. Reid observed that eight months' further work was required in order to determine whether the St. Pancras scheme was a viable and preferable alternative.[152]

The Union Railways line, in accordance with the government's remit a two-track railway with wide loading gauge to cater for international freight traffic, went from the Tunnel to Detling, north of Ashford, and thence to Swanscombe, Thurrock (where it crossed the Thames), Barking, Stratford, and King's Cross/ St. Pancras. An intensive assessment of alignment options embraced work on 1,000 kilometres for the 108-kilometre line, but there were few significant variations from Arup's 1991 route.[153] The North London/St. Pancras option was included at the end of the report.[154] Two business cases were presented: the Board Reference case; and the Board Policy case. The Reference case was designed to maximise financial performance before grant, while meeting accepted environmental standards. It allowed for the basic route and international terminal facilities at an estimated cost of £2.3 billion, plus £110 million for modifications to the infrastructure to accommodate domestic traffic. The figure of £2.4 billion was substantially less than the £4 billion estimate for the 1991 published route: this was achieved by adopting fewer tracks, steeper gradients (1 in 40 instead of 1 in 90), less tunnelling in central London, and lower terminal costs by detaching the Thameslink 2000 scheme. The Board Policy case was designed to maximise net economic benefits. It incorporated further options justified by a cost–benefit analysis of the impact on domestic services. These included additional trains and stations, a connection with CrossRail, and a link to Tilbury and Purfleet. For an additional £95 million, economic benefits of £355 million were forecast. A number of regeneration options was also presented, including a plan for 'Union Metro', linking the North London line to the North Kent line by means of a new tunnel under the Thames. A preliminary appraisal of the investment estimated the return on the Reference case at about 4 per cent and on the Policy case at 8 per cent. However, we should note that the calculations rested on a whole raft of assumptions, notably that the Jubilee Line Extension, CrossRail, and Thameslink 2000 would all be completed.[155]

The way the government chose to announce the route proved to be ill-judged. Somewhat surprisingly, the Chancellor of the Exchequer, Norman Lamont, in his budget speech on 16 March 1993, decided to make public the government's preference for the St. Pancras option. MacGregor had hoped to make his statement on the following day, but there was no parliamentary time, and his speech was delayed for almost a week. This hiatus provided the ideal circumstances for details of the report to be leaked, thus fuelling a further bout of opposition from interested parties in Kent. Eventually, on 22 March MacGregor announced that the government would adopt the Board's Reference case, but with a tunnel option in the Medway valley, and St. Pancras, which appeared to be less expensive, as the terminal. More importantly, MacGregor's statement represented a considerable shift of government policy. This time there was talk of public-private sector partnership, and the promise of substantial public sector support in recognition of the associated benefits to domestic rail services, quite the reverse of the view taken in 1990.[156]

Prideaux's ambush over the St. Pancras option resulted in tense relations with Bob Reid and his Board. Disagreements had surfaced when Prideaux presented his initial draft report of November 1992. British Rail officials were clearly discomfited by some of the more extravagant assumptions, notably the concentration on St. Pancras to the exclusion of both King's Cross and Waterloo, and by the size of the estimated returns (for example, 7.2 per cent for the Board Reference case, compared with the 4 per cent published later). One manager thought the ultimate financial case, with the return lifted to 12.5 per cent by making a free gift of EPS, 'worthy of Robert Maxwell', and the entire document 'worthy of Houdini'.[157] Leaks and newspapers speculations did not help. Following a story that Waterloo International might be obsolete in six years, Reid demanded a 'disciplined approach' of Prideaux when dealing with the press.[158] There were also disagreements about Prideaux's precise role and his intentions for Union Railways, where he favoured a speedy merger with EPS and a flotation.[159] MacGregor had already announced in March 1993 that Union Railways would be transferred to government ownership, and he made it clear to Reid that it was essential that Prideaux remained in charge. However, Reid increased the Board's representation on the Union Railways Board by adding Welsby, Horton, Edmonds, and himself.[160] Furthermore, Howarth, a critical figure in progressing the link, had accepted the job of Director, Major Projects at the embryonic Railtrack, initially on a part-time basis. The pressure upon him intensified, and he quickly asked to be released to join Railtrack on a full-time basis.[161] When Prideaux returned from leave in August, he found that Reid had taken his place as Chairman of Union Railways. After turning down the post of Managing Director, Central Services, he left the railway. The executive responsibilities exercised by Prideaux and Howarth were taken up by a new appointee, John Armitt, a former senior executive from the construction firm, John Laing, who was appointed Chief Executive.[162]

In March MacGregor had asked Union Railways to undertake yet further work and produce a report by October. There were three elements. First, another huge consultation exercise was undertaken as the route was refined further. Like the March report, the October 1993 report provided a number of options, mainly to lessen environmental impact. Second, the King's Cross/St. Pancras issue and the closely connected station for Thameslink 2000 services were addressed in greater detail. Modifications were made to the scheme, with international and Midland Main Line trains set to share the famous trainshed at St. Pancras (though the former would reach the station via a grade-separated junction). The studies now suggested that St. Pancras offered significant advantages in terms of cost, operations, environmental, and business impact. For Thameslink 2000 a new option was offered, a Midland Road station adjacent to St. Pancras and costed at £160 million (compared with £600 million under the original King's Cross (Low Level) scheme). Third, the options for intermediate stations were evaluated; the choice here lay between Stratford, Rainham, Ebbsfleet, and Nashenden (Rochester). A revised estimate of the cost of the basic scheme was provided: at £2.6 billion, excluding Thameslink 2000, it had risen by £200 million.[163]

As to financial viability, it remained the case that the scheme was highly uneconomic on conventional criteria. At British Rail Headquarters, Alan Nichols and Richard Davies expressed considerable scepticism about the October report, pointing out that the rate of return of 4–5 per cent was little changed from that estimated in March 1993. Using a discount rate of 12.5 per cent, the evaluation indicated that a large government grant of £1.5–£2.0 billion was required to make the project viable. Of course, by this time, such difficulties were a matter for the Department, which had effectively become the promoter of the scheme, rather than the Board.[164] After considering the report, MacGregor announced the detailed alignment of the Rail Link in January 1994. Two sections, at Ashford, and Pepper Hill (near Gravesend), were finalised in April. St. Pancras was confirmed as the London terminus and the planning safeguards at King's Cross were removed, thus finally killing off this cherished project. The original scheme for St. Pancras was amended incorporating a tunnel from Stratford to the terminus. An intermediate station at either Stratford, Rainham or Ebbsfleet was promised (see Figure 9.3). MacGregor confirmed that the private sector would assume full responsibility for the construction and operation of the link.

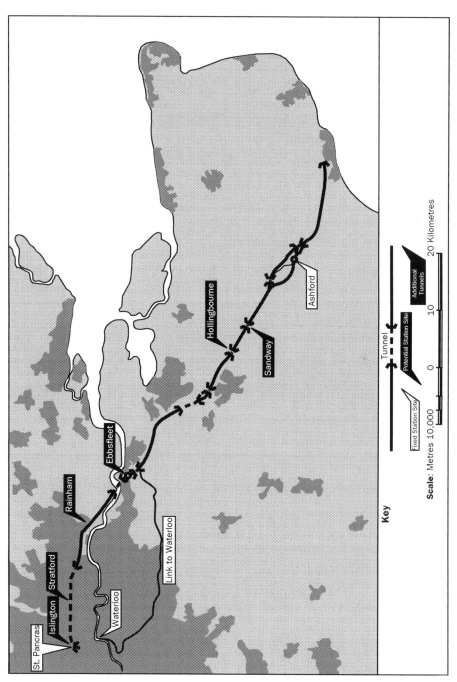

Figure 9.3 The Channel Tunnel Rail Link: the government's chosen route, January 1994

However, in a comment which appeared to modify the position established in the Channel Tunnel Act (see p. 332), he promised substantial government support 'in recognition not only of the significant domestic transport and regeneration benefits from the new line, *but also of some of the very large benefits to international passengers* [my italics]'.[165] A competition to find a private-sector promoter was announced in November 1993 and formally launched in March 1994. The successful bidder was to take over both Union Railways and EPS. In 1996 the concession was awarded to London & Continental Railways, a consortium of Arup, Bechtel, National Express, Virgin, and London Electricity, among others. However, as with other schemes before it, further problems were encountered and in January 1998 London & Continental announced that it could not raise the necessary finance, requiring a rescue operation organised by the Labour Secretary of State, John Prescott, in 1998–9.[166]

How are we to assess the Board's 'performance' in relation to the Channel Tunnel and the High-Speed Rail Link? It was clear from the outset that the Board was torn between attempting to introduce bold new railway investments and acting as the 'good steward' of the public sector by fulfilling its obligations to confine itself to schemes which were commercially sound. If there were sometimes criticisms of its response, for example by the Commons Transport Committee in 1992,[167] then it should be said that for once the traffic forecasting within the Board's investment department was more hard-headed than it was elsewhere. However the sums were done, whatever the assumptions made about related schemes, economic growth, and regeneration, and whatever the dogmatists inside government cared to believe, there was always going to be a need for a large subsidy for the High-Speed Link. This was something that many interested parties, including Sir Alastair Morton of Eurotunnel, fully recognised.[168] While some railway managers were dubious about the need for additional capacity for international services, the Board, ever obedient to its political masters, did its best to progress the scheme. It was all the more irksome, then, to find that the hoops through which it was forced to jump were more numerous than expected. Frequently disconcerted, and shunted around by the government as it wrestled with changes of route, vociferous protesters, and the complexities thrown up by armies of consultants, British Rail made a substantial commitment to the Channel Tunnel in terms of investment, resources, and management time. Some of its actions in the early stages of the process may be criticised, and a sizeable amount of public money was wasted. However, most of the blame rests with the government, where the perceived need to appease interests in Kent, South-east London, and the Regions produced the numerous vicissitudes, while the anxiety to open the way to private-sector ownership often flew in the face of the economic realities.

Safety

10.1 The Clapham accident and its aftermath

After the Clapham accident in December 1988 the issue of safety dominated the deliberations of the Board. Its actions in this area were conducted in a period which saw enhanced public scrutiny of railway safety, encouraged by the more proactive involvement of the Health and Safety Executive from 1990 (when it assumed responsibility for the Railway Inspectorate) and a more intrusive and legalistic inquiry process in the United Kingdom generally. The latter was a response to concern about a spate of other disasters: for example, the sinking of the *Herald of Free Enterprise* at Zeebrugge and the King's Cross Underground station fire in 1987, the *Piper Alpha* oil and gas rig disaster in 1988, and the M1 (Kegworth) air crash, the Hillsborough football stadium disaster, and the loss of the *Marchioness* on the Thames in 1989.[1] Furthermore, railway safety has remained a matter for public debate after privatisation, prompted by the serious accidents at Southall (September 1997), Ladbroke Grove (October 1999), and Hatfield (October 2000). Nor is the topic a simple one. Safety is a complex and wide-ranging concept, encompassing distinct elements of management action—in terms of organisation, investment, and business culture—and covering a wide range of incidents, attributable to equipment failure, organisational breakdown and human error, suicide, vandalism, and terrorism. All this means that a vast literature has been generated, quite apart from the documentation internal to the industry. In these circumstances, all we are able to do here is to sketch out the essential features of the action taken to improve safety from the perspective of the Board in the period 1989–94.[2]

On 12 December 1988, the day of the Clapham accident, the Secretary of State, Paul Channon, announced that there would be a public judicial inquiry into the

Channon the Useless Engine had come off the rails
again.
   "Ooer!" he said, "Here comes the Fat Controller!"
   "What a tirrible tregedy," said the Fat Controller,
"Where are the televison cameras? This is all your
fault," she told a passing stretcher case, "A person
could get killed on this clapped ite excuse for a
railway system!"
The passengers and crew all looked shamefaced.
   "That's why I'll be sticking to my Motor in
future!" she announced severely.

1

12. 'Channon the Useless Engine': safety concerns expressed by Steve Bell,
Guardian, 13 March 1989

causes and circumstances, under the provisions of the Regulation of Railways Act 1871. Anthony Hidden, QC agreed to undertake the investigation, the first to examine a collision between trains since 1876.[3] The Board also responded swiftly. Bob Reid I visited the site immediately, and less than 10 hours after the accident the Board accepted full responsibility and stated that it appeared to have been caused by a technical fault connected with preparations for the Waterloo resignalling scheme. An internal inquiry was then mounted and four days later British Rail announced publicly that the defective installation of signalling equipment was the probable cause.[4] The Clapham tragedy subjected railway safety to the full glare of public scrutiny for the first time since nationalisation, and the situation was aggravated by the subsequent accidents at Purley (Surrey) and Bellgrove (Glasgow) on 4 and 6 March 1989 respectively. It is quite clear that Reid and his Board experienced a profound sense of shock. Indeed, their counsel, Roger Henderson, QC, made it clear at the outset of the inquiry that 'British Rail wears a white sheet'.[5] Although the jury at the coroner's inquest in September 1990 reached a verdict of unlawful killing, the Director of Public Prosecutions had already decided not to pursue a prosecution for corporate manslaughter. However, charges under sections 2 and 3 of the 1974 Health and Safety at Work Act were brought by the Health & Safety Executive.[6] At the Central Criminal Court in June 1991 the Board pleaded guilty to two charges concerning its failure to ensure the health and safety of passengers and employees and was fined £250,000.[7]

The Hidden inquiry sat for 56 days from January to May 1989. Although primarily concerned with the events surrounding Clapham, Hidden was also asked to consider any common issues arising from the Purley and Bellgrove accidents. Over 13,000 pages of documentation were presented and the final report, published in November, extended to 230 pages and contained 93 recommendations, 78 of which concerned the Board and British Transport Police directly. The immediate cause of the accident was confirmed as a wiring error affecting signal WF138, the explanation already identified by the Board almost a year earlier. However, the ramifications of the Hidden inquiry went far beyond this single and simply identified error. The findings provided a comprehensive agenda for the improvement of railway safety, and were accepted unequivocally and in full by Bob Reid I and the Secretary of State, now Cecil Parkinson.[8] When the Board discussed the report in December 1989, David Rayner, who had become the Board Member responsible for safety in November 1987, a fortnight before the King's Cross fire,[9] highlighted three main areas of concern: systems and procedures affecting the S&T Department and Southern Region, which were implicated in the accident; the need to change the railways' overall culture and practice (safety management, quality assurance, training, etc.); and investment in safety-improving equipment and technologies, namely, Automatic Train Protection, train radios, data recorders (black boxes), and vehicle crashworthiness. The Board was required to produce within three months a report to the Secretary of State on its progress in implementing the recommendations, with further reports at six-monthly intervals. Three reports were produced, and by September 1990 52 of the 78 relevant recommendations had been tackled. The Clapham accident, then, was certainly a catalyst for change.[10] However, it was not the only influence. The reports of Fennell (King's Cross) and Taylor (Hillsborough) produced their own safety agendas, and these also required a response from British Rail. As the 1990s began it was evident that British Rail had much to do to establish a modern, best-practice health and safety organisation. As Rayner recognised, 'the challenge facing the Board that cannot be underestimated is that of achieving this vast cultural change given the ingrained attitudes of the industry'.[11]

The most urgent need was to address the primary causation identified by the report, which rested with the Southern Region's S&TE organisation. For some observers, the S&T function, which had always behaved in a rather detached way from the rest of BR, was made something of a scapegoat.[12] The Department was certainly in a state of shock after Clapham and its newly appointed Director, Ken Burrage, quickly saw the need to strengthen the management team and restore 'some steadiness and self-confidence'.[13] Yet Hidden uncovered a catalogue of weak management and failings in work preparation, supervision, inspection, testing, and checking. On top of this, training was found to be inadequate, and there were very real problems caused by staff shortages and excessive working hours. These facts could not be ignored. Of the Hidden recommendations, some 35 or so related specifically to S&T and the majority of them had been implemented before the Report was published in November 1989.[14] However, it was more difficult to resolve the underlying problems in signalling installation and maintenance—serious staff shortages, low basic pay, and long hours—problems which were particularly evident in London and the South-East. The out-going chairman, Bob Reid I, expressed his anxieties, after a visit to the regional S&T department at Wimbledon in February 1990. The region was being stretched by the response to Hidden, the substantial investment in the Channel Tunnel services and new 'Networker' trains, and the demands of the OfQ reorganisation. He reported: 'I do not believe we can cope with all the demands at present unless it is at the expense of diminishing quality and putting current operations and probably safety at risk'.[15] There was something in this view. While Chris Thompson, the regional S&T engineer, and his team worked tirelessly to improve audit procedures, effective communication, and monitoring, middle managers felt that the pace and scale of activity, and the 'plethora of instant decisions from above' were stretching them to the limit. The impending incorporation of the engineers into the rail businesses under OfQ was a further source of anxiety.[16] There were problems at management staff level, where promising junior engineers were often poached by telecommunications companies, and lower down, where niggardly pay levels encouraged excessive overtime. Efforts were made to improve recruitment with a major restructuring of S&T grades, a process begun in 1989 and which merged the wage and salaried staff and increased the basic rates by 25 per cent (see Chapter 8). Nevertheless, excessive overtime remained endemic. Particularly revealing is the fact that the response to high levels of overtime was a target stipulating a maximum working week of 72 hours, with no more than 13 shifts to be worked in any 14-day period. This was scarcely a draconian assault on the problem, and in any case the target was not achieved in full in 1992.[17] Although by this time considerable progress had been made in reforming the articulation of technical standards, installation procedures, design quality, and training, it was evident that some deep-seated and fundamental difficulties persisted.[18]

10.2 Transforming the safety culture

At one level, the Hidden Report was 'much ado about nothing'—after all, the primary cause of the Clapham accident had been identified by British Rail before the inquiry had started.[19] At another level, however, the Report exposed the weak and fragmented nature of the railways' entire safety management systems. Traditionally, safety had been based on semi-military lines and the primacy of the Rule Book, which laid paramount emphasis on absolute safety. In fact, it was found that 'the true position in relation to safety lagged frighteningly far behind the idealism of the words'.[20] Thus, when Bob Reid II, who had worked in oil, another safety-critical industry, arrived at the Board he found an organisation which had suffered a damaging blow to its safety culture.[21] In addition to Hidden and Fennell, further consultancy work, carried out for the Board by Du Pont, Arthur D. Little, and Bridget Hutter of Wolfson College Oxford, revealed numerous shortcomings in safety management. As John Welsby admitted, 'while we believed that all we were doing was driven by our preoccupation with safety, we were often deceiving ourselves'.[22] Against this background the transformation of perceptions about safety throughout the industry represented an immense task.

A prerequisite was strong leadership from the top. Bob Reid II made it clear from the beginning of his appointment that he was personally committed to change. Prior to Clapham, the reporting of safety matters, other than for serious incidents, seldom reached Board level, but at Reid's suggestion, from July 1990 the Chairman's Group devoted a monthly meeting to safety, where trends were monitored and all major accidents examined in depth. At the end of the year the long-standing Safety Committee, which met only four times a year, was disbanded and its responsibilities were taken up by the Chairman's Group, which was renamed Board Executive. Henceforth the Board Executive took on prime responsibility for safety, supported by a Safety Management Group (formerly the Production Management Group) and a Safety Panel, which had been established in May 1990 to authorise and monitor expenditure on safety initiatives.[23] In fact, the most fundamental change to the entire safety structure was brought about by the organisational requirements of Organising for Quality (OfQ). This involved the identification of clear lines of responsibility for safety, with each business unit validated by the Safety Standards Directorate (see Chapter 11, p. 382).

During the preparation of evidence for the Hidden inquiry it became clear that British Rail's management of safety practices had areas of significant weakness. Thus, in June 1989 the Board employed consultants to carry out an investigation of safety management on the West Coast Main Line, a move endorsed by the Hidden Report (Recommendation 38). The work was undertaken by the American firm Du Pont Safety Management Services and its charismatic executive Robert Webber.[24] A number of serious failings were identified, in particular the fact that safety was 'compartmentalised'—system safety being separated from the safety of staff—and its management more reactive than proactive. Du Pont made nine recommendations, identifying a range of measures designed to improve effective safety management. These included: a clear, written safety policy; an enhanced corporate safety organisation; a programme of safety audits; effective incident monitoring; and safety management training throughout the organisation.[25] In February 1990 a working group was established to take forward Du Pont's work and it was agreed that their proposals were sufficiently comprehensive to form the basis of a full Safety Management Programme. The Du Pont recommendations were disseminated widely to managers, and the Programme was launched by Welsby at a Chief Executive's Forum in July 1990, after which a revised BR Safety Policy Statement was distributed to every member of staff.[26]

A crucial component of the new approach was the development of an annual safety plan, as requested by Parkinson in his objectives letter of December 1989.[27] A first draft was considered by the Safety Committee in October 1990. Since the Plan was intended to be a public document, there was much debate about its precise wording. Reid II was keen for the Board to commit itself to 'absolute safety', but this apparently raised some concerns at the DTp over the implications for funding.[28] Nevertheless, the commitment was retained in the final, public document, which was published in February 1991. A glossy affair circulated to every railway employee, it enumerated policy aims and objectives and was designed to encourage continual improvements in safety awareness. Particular attention was paid to organisational issues, investment, and working methods.[29] Subsequent plans, in 1992–4, contained more specific and increasingly sophisticated targets covering employee and contractor safety, individual passenger and public safety, multiple-fatality risks, and safety management systems and procedures. The establishment of clearly articulated specific aims and objectives in relation to such elements as train doors, trespasses and suicides, and trackside operations, should have left no one in doubt that the Board was serious in its intent to encourage a widespread improvement in safety.[30]

The Safety Directorate established under Holmes in 1988 did not possess the resources to undertake more than reactive tasks, although its profile was certainly increased after the Fennell and Hidden reports. The consultants Du Pont recommended that British Rail adopt a more co-ordinated and integrated approach, and in August 1990 a strengthened corporate Safety Directorate was established to bring together existing functions such as fire safety and health and safety at work, and the new responsibilities such as safety audit and the proactive safety initiatives.[31] Subsequently, much progress was made, though it was only to be expected that a new broom would reveal a fair amount of dust. The value of safety auditing, for example, was identified by both Hidden (Recommendation 39) and Du Pont. Mike Siebert, a safety expert from United Biscuits, was recruited in July 1990 to head a new independent Headquarters Safety Audit department, and his proposals for its structure and scope were agreed in October. A widely accepted standard, the International Safety Rating System (ISRS), used in a recent audit of London Underground by the Railway Inspectorate, was adopted. ISRS produced a standardised numerical value which facilitated direct comparisons of management units and businesses and performance over time.[32] The programme, which envisaged no fewer than 128 formal audits a year, began in April 1992, and by June 1993 96 audits had been completed. However, these revealed only modest scores in several areas of safety, such as planned inspections, and personal protective equipment, highlighting the work still to be done at the level of the profit centre and business unit in applying group standards.[33] There was a similar experience with the establishment of a new database for accidents known as BRIMS (British Rail Incident Monitoring System) in 1990. Historically there had been no central collation of incident statistics, other than by the Railway Inspectorate. From this point it was clearly recognised that accurate monitoring by British Rail was essential in identifying hazards and providing data for risk-assessment exercises. However, the initial design did not function satisfactorily, and with the additional demands expected from the fragmentation of the industry under privatisation, the Board was forced to take further steps to improve the system in 1993. A new system had not been agreed when Railtrack assumed responsibility for BRIMS in April 1994.[34] There was more success with the pursuance of the Quality Through People initiative, encouraged by the Hidden Report (Recommendation 36), and the measures taken to improve training and the analysis of working practices. These all helped to foster in middle and lower management a better safety culture.

A good illustration of what could be achieved by specific targeting is provided by the issue of trackside safety. In June 1992 Reid appointed Graham Eccles, Network SouthEast's Director, Total Quality, to lead a fundamental review of the arrangements for protecting staff working on the track.[35] The report, completed in February 1993, found that in the decade 1982–91/2 experience had been disappointing, with 85 rail staff and contractors killed after being struck by trains. Over half of these deaths were attributable to a flawed safe system of work. Recommendations were made to heighten awareness and improve procedures, in particular by giving greater responsibility to the person in charge of work. The importance of automatic safeguards such as the Inductive Loop Warning System (ILWS) were examined, but were found to be both complex and expensive, though there was more enthusiasm for a computer-based Interactive Lineside Safety System (ILSS), which gave permanent way staff visual information about layouts, access points, and speed restrictions.[36] Nevertheless, the campaign had an instant impact. By the end of 1994 Welsby was able to tell the Board that no employee had been killed by a train for 16 months.[37]

Alcohol and drug abuse provided a further problem for safety managers. A concern of the railways from the industry's inception, drunkenness was prohibited by both company regulations and general legislation from the 1840s, the Regulation of Railways Act of 1842 making it one of the offences punishable by law. Unsurprisingly, then, drinking before or while on duty was prohibited in the British Rail Rule Book and liable to disciplinary action.[38] Nevertheless, it would be a mistake to deny that for much of the twentieth century something of a 'drinking culture' existed among all grades of railway staff, as was the case in many industries. But despite the general tenor of prohibition, safety policy in this area was generally reactive. It took a serious accident at Eltham in June 1972 before there was concerted action to examine signing-on procedures and the role of British Rail Staff Association Clubs in encouraging drinking, and to engage the unions in renewed vigilance. A subsequent survey in 1975 revealed that there were far too many cases of staff reporting for work under the influence of alcohol or of drinking while on duty. By 1980 a formal policy had been agreed with the trade unions,[39] and a further review in 1982 found that only 2–3 per cent of all disciplinary cases were alcohol related. However, this apparently reassuring picture was tempered by the knowledge that given what was known about alcohol abuse nationally, the true extent of the problem in British Rail was probably much higher than the existing statistics indicated.[40] The abuse of alcohol and/or drugs was clearly unacceptable in a safety-critical environment, and during the 1980s action was taken at the top by way of example to limit the amount of drinking undertaken as part of the 'mess culture' at management level.[41] Drug abuse received particular attention, prompting a revision of the Code of Practice agreed with the unions in October 1990, which included provision for drug testing.[42] However, further action was considered necessary in view of the publicity given to accidents where staff drinking or drug abuse was discovered, notably at Cannon Street in January 1991.[43] Pre-employment drug screening and post-accident drug testing were then introduced, measures which were strengthened by new regulations for public transport industries authorised by Roger Freeman, the Minister for Public Transport, incorporated in the Transport and Works Act of March 1992.[44] Nevertheless, there remained some uncertainty about the precise nature of the policy within management, and when Chris Green of InterCity sought to establish standards of behaviour for his own business he found several discrepancies between the various publications on the subject, prompting a plea for more consistency at the Railway Management Group in December 1992.[45] The Safety Directorate then turned its attention to formulating a more consistent set of rules, and the revised policy of October 1993 introduced, *inter alia*: clear guidelines for lunch breaks; a national scheme of testing for alcohol and drugs following safety-critical incidents or on suspicion of unfitness for duty; unannounced drugs screening for staff in safety-critical posts; and a fixed standard for alcohol/blood levels. As a result of such initiatives, the entire working environment inside British Rail was transformed.[46]

The objectives identified in British Rail's Safety Plans from 1991 also extended to factors beyond the Board's direct control. The physical interface between road and rail transport—level crossings, footpath crossings, etc.—continued to provide opportunities for accidents caused by human error or irresponsibility. The accident and casualty statistics were not insignificant. In 1990 there were 69 accidents and 23 deaths, in 1993/4 61 accidents and 14 deaths.[47] As noted in Chapter 6 (p. 229), the Board discharged its responsibility to improve the safety of half-barrier level crossings as required by the Stott Inquiry, its programme of modernisation being completed in 1991. But automatic crossings could not prevent indiscipline by road users, for example by driving around the half-barriers, and in 1993 a risk-assessment analysis was conducted on the existing designs.[48] In any case, in March 1994 over 7,000 of the 9,000 crossings in existence were unprotected, and of these, some 2,700 were footpaths.[49] The latter came under the spotlight after the deaths of a woman and two children at Carr Lane, Doncaster in June 1990.[50] The Board responded by obtaining powers to close certain crossings on safety grounds, for example on the East Coast Main Line. When the Board discussed the issue in November 1990 Terry Worrall, the Director of Operations, remarked that the ideal course of action would be to close all bridleway and footpath crossings, although this would have produced strenuous opposition from riders, ramblers, and the public generally. Yet there was no doubt that such footpaths represented a continuing anachronism when they crossed modern high-speed lines.[51] The phenomenon known as 'bridge-bashing', where road vehicles struck railway structures, was another perennial anxiety. From 1989 concerted efforts were made by the Railway Inspectorate to determine its true extent. Data were produced revealing 879 incidents involving under-bridges in 1990, 89 of which were classified as serious or potentially serious. The Board regarded the situation to be such as to warrant strong representations to both the DTp and local authorities.[52] Supportive noises were made by Parkinson in response, and attempts were made to raise awareness at local level. However, despite continuing anxieties, bridge-bashing incidents showed little sign of diminishing in either number or severity. In 1993/4 there were 816 reported incidents affecting under-bridges, 61 of them serious or potentially serious. In the circumstances all British Rail could do was to continue its lobbying of the relevant authorities.[53]

Trespass and vandalism were two extremely serious and growing problems. In the period 1990–93/4 there were over 16,000 reported incidents of trespass each year, with nearly 600 trespassers killed over the four-year period.[54] Safety campaigns were directed at schools in order to deter children from playing on the railway, but it is difficult to find evidence of substantial improvement.[55] Vandalism, a term embracing misdemeanours ranging from arson to graffiti, and stone throwing to more serious acts of sabotage, often endangered operational safety. Indeed, about a quarter of all train accidents were caused by malicious acts. The danger created by obstructions placed on railway lines was highlighted by a derailment at West Ealing in August 1988, and the deaths of a driver and passenger at Branchton, Strathclyde in June 1994. After the West Ealing incident, steps were taken to reduce the quantity of trackside materials and refuse, which were often used by vandals. An initiative called Operation 'Clean Sweep' resulted in the removal of 65,000 tonnes of material in the space of 18 months. By the time Railtrack was established as a Board division in April 1993, a new five-point trespass and vandalism policy had been developed.[56] Nor could the Board ignore the fact that the 600 deaths from trespass were matched by another 600 suicides.[57] A report from Strathclyde University commissioned by the Board in 1993 found that there was little the Board could do to reduce the incidence of suicide, but some practical measures were suggested, among them improved staff training and liaison with psychiatric hospitals.[58] The psychological impact of such incidents on drivers provided an additional challenge for the Board. Here it employed consultants to undertake a study of driver responses, and followed this up with stress management support and post-trauma counselling. These exogenous factors served to remind railway managers that safety could not be considered in a vacuum.[59] Terrorism was a serious dimension which attracted Bob Reid's personal involvement. The major incidents took place in February 1991, when bombs planted by the Provisional IRA exploded at Paddington and Victoria stations, with one person killed in the latter incident; a week later there was a lineside explosion at St. Albans. A further spate of bombing followed between December 1991 (Clapham Jnc.) and early 1992 (London Bridge, White Hart Lane, Wandsworth Common). In all some 40 explosive and incendiary devices were planted on or near railway property in the period to October 1994. In addition, there was also a large number of hoax calls—over 5,000 in 1991–4.[60] British Rail acted quickly to produce new guidelines for handling bomb threats. Litter-bins were removed, and closed circuit television was installed at the major London stations in 1993–4.[61] The most critical lesson of security alerts was not to relax vigilance, and with the encouragement of Reid and Welsby in particular, assiduous attention was paid to station and train inspections.[62]

What, then, was achieved in these efforts to transform the railways' safety culture? First, we must concede that the Board's intentions were viewed with some scepticism at lower levels of the organisation.[63] Webber of Du Pont found that prior to the introduction of the safety management programme, only 20 per cent of the staff he had met believed that the Board was serious in its commitment to safety.[64] Adele Biss, one of the Board's part-timers, passed on some of the complaints to Rayner after attending a safety management course in 1991. They included anxiety about resources, confusion about the precise responsibilities of individuals, and complaints about 'unstructured panic measures': managers 'felt they got too many urgent, "unprioritised, 'bridge to engine room' style instructions"' whenever a new danger was identified.[65] Similar worries were raised by Ken Burrage.[66] The need to gain the support of trade unions represented a further challenge. The unions were naturally anxious to ensure that their members' rights were protected, and had genuine fears about buck-passing and a growing 'culture of blame'.[67] Above all, the sheer scale of the dissemination process surprised many managers.[68] In its report for 1991/2 the Railway Inspectorate noted that the undoubted intentions of senior managers had not yet been applied throughout the industry. And when Reid asked the HSE to offer an opinion on British Rail's first Safety Plan (of 1991), he was told that the Board needed to adopt a higher profile if the safety drive were not to be regarded as a 'one-off' initiative. This message was also conveyed by Du Pont.[69] Of course, the Board had embarked on two ambitious ventures at the same time: to reform the safety culture; and to introduce a radical reorganisation of the business (OfQ). Indeed, it was felt that OfQ would be a key element in ensuring the effective implementation of the safety management programme. Nevertheless, it is clear that the widely publicised validation procedure was not without its weaknesses. Although the validations themselves were undoubtedly rigorous, a follow-up audit expressed concern that many had viewed the process as a hurdle to be jumped rather than as an ongoing process of improvement.[70] We must be careful not to overdo the criticism. We have focused, as the managers did, on the inadequacies of the programme and the elements remaining to be applied effectively. Such a radical shift in attitudes was always going to be a tough, demanding, and long-term affair. In the five years after Clapham Bob Reid and his Board achieved a considerable amount in raising awareness about safety, improving information systems, and providing the organisational base for a modern health and safety policy. Of course, no sooner had some stability been introduced than managerial attention was being diverted to the need to refashion the safety organisation to square with the needs of the more fragmented, post-privatisation period.

10.3 Additional spending on safety

In the wake of the Fennell and Hidden reports, the Board certainly increased its expenditure on safety. In broad terms some £750 million was spent on safety measures in the five years to March 1994.[71] Beyond this, it is difficult to be precise. The estimate is affected by three complicating factors. First, there were different classifications of safety expenditure. Spending on 'additional' or 'primary' safety arose directly from the Board's responses to the two judicial inquiries. Although including an element of investment, this was regarded as an operating cost charged to current account. 'Secondary' safety covered key projects outside the scope of Hidden and Fennell. Second, the basic figure of £750 million makes no allowance for the fact that capital investment in new rolling stock and new infrastructure also produced an enhancement of safety. Third, it is not easy to identify the areas to which the additional safety expenditure was directed, particularly during and after the OfQ reorganisation.[72]

The figures for the 1989 Corporate Plan were prepared before the publication of the Hidden Report, and although a commitment was made to spend an additional £200 million on safety over the quinquennium to 1993/4, it was clear that much more money would be needed to implement the recommendations. This position had the full support of government. Parkinson told the Commons when the Report appeared: 'I can assure the House that finance will not stand in the way of the implementation of the report'.[73] The Secretary of State then directed the Board to provide financial information with the first Hidden progress report. Forecasts were duly prepared showing the safety expenditure required *beyond* that included in the 1989 Plan. These provisional estimates, sent to Parkinson in February 1990, suggested that about £1,367 million (£273 million a year) was required to meet safety aspirations over the five years to 1994/5. Of this some 90 per cent was to be applied to satisfying the Hidden recommendations.[74] David Rayner noted that these high additional outlays had major financial and political implications. Moreover, it was difficult to equate the ambitions and resources of the businesses: in 1990, for example, some managers complained of their 'inability to spend money on more than a limited number of easily resourced projects'.[75] In a further calculation, Bob Reid II told Cecil Parkinson that £118 million was a more realistic figure for 1990/1, only 60 per cent of the intended figure in the five-year plan. In fact, the final figure was £140 million.[76]

Safety expenditure then became enmeshed in the protracted arguments over the EFL during 1991. Reid was certainly adamant about the importance of ring-fencing safety, telling Malcolm Rifkind: 'I cannot accept any reduction in the amount submitted for expenditure under this head'.[77] It is also clear that the Department urgently wanted more objective assessments of the value of safety expenditure.[78] The final figure for 1991/2 was £255 million. Spending in the following year, the last in which additional safety costs were identified separately, was £180 million. Thus, in total, there was some £545 million of ring-fenced safety expenditure in the three fiscal years from 1990/1 to 1992/3, a figure equivalent to 5 per cent of railway operating costs.[79]

Hidden raised wider implications concerning the valuation of railway safety, a debate which has intensified in the subsequent decade. Recommendation 48 called for a study of the 'appraisal procedure for safety elements of investment proposals', while No. 49 required the development of a system to prioritise safety projects. The ensuing work, on 'value of life' and safety benefit evaluation, was at the time both highly technical and highly emotive, especially when applied to the issue of Automatic Train Protection (see below). It was developed with the help of the consultants Coopers & Lybrand, and required delicate negotiations and close working with the Department of Transport, which was concerned about the cost implications and anxious to avoid treating the railways differently from other transport modes.[80] The subject was also incorporated into the Board Safety Plans. Objective 9 of the 1993 Plan promised that there would be 'full integration of safety benefit evaluation into formal project appraisal' during 1993/4, and that future funding discussions with the DTp would be supported by measures of the cost effectiveness of safety elements. This objective, which combined quantified risk assessment and value-for-money comparisons of projects with the notion of ALARP risk,[81] was met with effect from January 1994.[82]

Appraisal was one thing; satisfying the aspirations of the Hidden Report was another. The Board experienced much more difficulty in dealing with those elements which required capital investment in new safety technology. There were two particular hurdles: obtaining authorisation at a time of financial restraint; and the equally difficult challenge of resolving technological uncertainties. As we have seen, the Board was committed to regular, six-monthly reporting on its progress in implementing the Hidden recommendations. After February 1991 this reporting took the form of technical updates supplied to the Railway Inspectorate. By the time of the fifth such update, in October 1993, Mike Siebert, Holmes's successor as Director, Safety (from February 1992), suggested that they be discontinued since much of the programme had now been completed.[83] However, for a variety of financial and technical reasons, some of the recommendations had not been satisfied, and in particular those involving investment in train data recorders (recommendations 40 and 41), train cab radios (43), Automatic Train Protection (ATP) (46) and the replacement of Mark I stock (55).[84] A year later, these deficiencies were exposed tragically when five people were killed in a train collision at Cowden (Kent) on the Hurst Green–Uckfield line in October 1994. In the resultant inquiry Major C. B. Holden found himself repeating some of the views of the Clapham inquiry, and the Board was prompted to carry out a full review of the implementation process.[85]

The fitting of On Train Monitoring Recorders (OTMRs), also known as Train Data Recorders, the so-called black boxes, offered a number of benefits in accident inquiries and the monitoring of driver actions, although they could not of course save lives directly. Network SouthEast took the lead here, fitting data recorders to all of its new trains and about 15 per cent of its existing stock, for example the Class 319s and Class 442s, although the equipment chosen did not meet the standard specification set by the Board in 1993. Other businesses were much slower to respond. The principal reason for this was the high cost of fitting the devices retrospectively: about £20,000 per vehicle. On this basis it was estimated that it would cost Regional Railways £38 million to equip its fleet. Retro-fitting also presented some technical problems, for example on the Great Western with the old HST sets. Another source of delay was the fact that the installation of data recorders had much in common with elements of ATP (see below), and it was intended that the work would be concurrent. Even so, combining the two projects would make little difference to the cost of a national scheme, put at £160 million (without ATP) and £120 million (with). By 1994 internal opinion was that the project lacked a champion in operating circles and was virtually moribund.[86] The report of the Cowden inquiry was critical of the fact that the programme had 'fallen far behind schedule'. Major Holden observed that many of the uncertainties surrounding the Cowden crash would have been resolved by a black box recorder and he therefore recommended that a timed and costed programme be prepared for vehicles with a planned life of more than three years. After the Southall accident inquiry Professor Uff has made a similar recommendation.[87]

Radio communication was a complex field with several different systems in operation. The National Radio Network (NRN), known as 'Driver to Shore', was developed after the Polmont accident in 1984. It was cost effective and had wide coverage, but for a number of reasons—not least its dependence on British Rail's telephone network—was considered to be unsuitable for intensive use on suburban lines. Another possibility was offered by portable telephones, but these were found to have limited application. An alternative technology was offered by the Cab Secure Radio or CSR. Mandatory on lines with Driver Only Operation, it allowed direct, secure, and more reliable communication between driver and signalman and, more importantly, since it was linked to train describers it automatically identified the calling train. However, its high cost precluded its application on a universal basis. In addition, the NRN and CSR networks were neither compatible nor interchangeable. Thus, although about £50 million had been spent on radio communication since 1977, there was a fair amount of dissatis-faction with the performance of the existing equipment.[88] Hidden Recommenda-tion 43 called for a programme to install radio communication between driver and signalman on all traction units 'as a priority', though the system was not specified. It was expected that the programme would be completed in 1992. Four businesses—InterCity, Trainload Freight, Railfreight Distribution, and Regional Railways—made extensive use of the NRN 'Driver to Shore' technology. By early 1991 all InterCity and 60 per cent of freight locomotives were equipped, and a £9 million scheme to supply Regional Railways was due for completion at the end of 1992. In the event, the latter work was accorded a low priority and was not completed until 1994/5.[89] However, the greatest difficulty was experienced at Network SouthEast. Although supplied with NRN coverage, the business obtained authorisation in 1991 to spend about £46 million in fitting the superior CSR system to all cabs and all routes by 1996/7.[90] Unfortunately, the programme was curtailed in the severe financial constraints of the early 1990s and by 1993 only 55 per cent of the network had been enhanced. After several options had been evaluated, the decision was taken to install CSR but without train describers to 'high-risk' routes only, leaving the outer suburban areas with NRN. This left a rather unsatisfactory situation, evident in 1994. Most of Network SouthEast's trains had been fitted with CSR, but their operational effectiveness was limited because a large number of base stations had not been established. In these locations the NRN system was potentially available, but the trains had not been fitted with NRN radios.[91] Although the Cowden accident was caused by a signal passed at danger (SPAD), the inquiry found that the accident would have been prevented if CSR had been installed. Major Holden was not impressed by the fact that the decision to fit CSR on the Uckfield Line was announced by British Rail three days before the Cowden inquiry opened. The problem of establishing an effective radio system for Network SouthEast remained one for the privatised railway authorities to address.[92]

Another of the Hidden recommendations linked to new investment concerned the crashworthiness of the railways' old Mark I rolling stock (recommendations 54 and 55). The accidents at Clapham, Purley, Bellgrove, Newton, and Cannon Street had all raised concerns about the integrity of these vehicles, but when reporting to the Inspectorate ceased in October 1993 it was assumed that this requirement had been satisfied. The Board had been directed to complete its researches on the Mark I vehicles by April 1991, and then discuss the conclusions with the Railway Inspectorate in order to agree a programme of improvement to stock with a life-span of more than eight years. A report was completed in October 1990 and agreed with the Inspectorate over the course of 1991. By January 1992 both sides were agreed that the cost of the modifications was prohibitively high—over £200 million for the full programme, or about £34 million per life saved. But in any case, the Board fully expected to replace all but about 300 of the Mark I fleet within eight years. Thus, it was assumed that no further action was required.[93] Research on crashworthiness studies then turned to other rolling stock, and especially the new generation of aluminium-bodied trains.[94] The Cowden accident served to reopen the debate. Mark I vehicles were again found to offer poor protection in head-on collisions. More worrying was the fact that the intended investment in replacement rolling stock, for example additional Networkers, had been postponed. After concerns had been expressed by the Railway Inspectorate in 1995 the Board acknowledged that there still 2,700 Mark I vehicles in use, though it expected the number to fall to 1,400 by the year 2000. Given the investment difficulties and the lack of progress with ATP (see below) it became apparent that compliance with Recommendation 55 would have to be reassessed.[95] The Cowden report called for a new study and policy on the Mark I stock. At the time of writing (Summer 2000) there are still about 1,500 vehicles in service south of the Thames and the HSE has set the railways a final deadline for modification or replacement of 1 January 2003.[96]

10.4 Automatic Train Protection

The most important, and most publicised, element of potential investment in safety concerned the provision of a system of Automatic Train Protection (ATP), in order to prevent trains from passing red signals. Train protection has a long history. The Great Western introduced a rudimentary system as early as 1906, and extended it over its main routes in 1929–31. In the 1950s serious accidents at Harrow in 1952 and St. Johns (Lewisham) in 1957 prompted a commitment by the British Transport Commission to install an Automatic Warning System or AWS on British Railways.[97] This technology, developed for mechanical signals, gave the driver an advance warning, both visually and audibly, of each signal about 200 yards before it was reached. If the driver did not acknowledge caution (yellow) or stop (red) signals, the brakes were applied. Investment proceeded at a rather leisurely pace. Only 3,800 route-miles had been fitted with AWS before 1974,[98] and although the system was extended after 1972 to embrace compliance with speed restrictions, as late as July 1988 over 20 per cent of the passenger programme remained to be completed. At the end of the year 7,013 miles had been fitted.[99] The innovation served to reduce the number of accidents caused when signals were passed at danger (SPADs). However, AWS was in essence an advisory system which depended on the driver's response. Mistakes could occur if the driver was misled or took incorrect action after receiving the warning.[100] Improved versions, where signal aspects were shown in the cab, intended for the dense commuter network of the Southern Region, were tested from 1968, but not progressed after 1976.[101] In contrast to AWS, ATP is a more advanced technology which is both advisory and supervisory. Adopted by London Underground in simple form and by surface railways in many countries, it takes over control of the train if warnings are ignored, and brings it to a stop if a red signal is passed.[102] As we have seen (pp. 229–30), in November 1988, just before the Clapham accident, the Board had appointed Maurice Holmes as Director of Safety and resolved to proceed with an ATP system.[103] Holmes, part of a small team which had looked at ATP schemes in continental Europe earlier in the year, had already put it on record that the devolution to businesses of financial responsibility under sector management carried with it the danger of inhibiting safety investment proposals and thus eroding safety standards.[104] Concern had focused on the significant increase in the number of SPADs, which rose both in number—from 460 in 1979 to 653 in 1985 and 843 in 1988—and in relation to train-miles run. In 1986 Royal Holloway College had been asked to assist British Rail Research in conducting a three-year inquiry into causation.[105] Pressure was also exerted by the Chief Inspecting Officer of Railways, who while remaining in the DTp until 1990 became increasingly influenced by the concerns of the Health & Safety Executive, following the Act of 1974.[106] In his annual reports for 1985, 1986, and 1988 he had recommended that British Rail should introduce some form of ATP. By this time it was clear that the challenge of operating modern trains at higher speeds and in dense conurbations was stretching the capabilities of AWS.[107]

In October 1988 a joint proposal from Holmes, when Director of Operations, and Ken Hodgson (Director of S&TE), envisaged expenditure of about £140 million over 10 years on a selective system of ATP covering about 80 per cent of the passenger-miles run. With the encouragement of the Railway Executive, Chris Green of Network SouthEast then took this forward on behalf of the businesses. The intention was to embark on pilot studies to determine the system to be adopted, and consequently the initial investment appraisal for a national scheme was necessarily rudimentary. Green's outline appraisal in February 1989 referred to a figure of £250 million as the likely capital cost, although his colleague at InterCity, John Prideaux, felt that £400 million was a more realistic estimate,[108] and by December 1990 the estimate had risen to £660 million.[109] Later the Board readily admitted that capital costs had been underestimated and operating costs omitted.[110] There was a further problem. At the outset the Railway Executive had recognised that a national scheme would be unlikely to achieve the government's required rate of return for investment projects. An early (1988) attempt to calculate the financial benefit of ATP, measured by the cost of accidents caused by driver error, produced a relatively modest estimate of £6–10 million a year.[111]

In the more highly charged atmosphere which accompanied Hidden's judicial inquiry into Clapham, British Rail pressed ahead with the pilot schemes. Two contrasting locations were selected: Network SouthEast's Chiltern line from Marylebone to Aylesbury and Bicester, and InterCity's Great Western line from Paddington to Bristol. Together they extended to 450 track-miles. Ironically, the Investment Committee authorised the progressing of the schemes on 6

March 1989, the day of the Bellgrove accident and two days after the accident at Purley.[112] Both incidents were found to be 'ATP preventable'. Investments of £5.1 million (later £6.2 million) and £8.3 million (at Q4/1989 prices) were then authorised, with the aim of determining a BR standard specification for ATP by 1992, and progressing to national implementation over the period 1992–2001.[113] The work was supported by the findings of the Hidden inquiry, which heard evidence relating to both the Purley and Bellgrove accidents. Hidden's report in November 1989 endorsed British Rail intentions in relation to ATP, but expressed anxiety that the impetus for change might be lost. He therefore recommended that ATP should be fully installed five years after the completion of the pilot schemes, that is, by 1996/7.[114] This recommendation was endorsed by subsequent inquiries into accidents at Newton (near Glasgow) in July 1991 and at Cowden in October 1994, where SPADs occurred.[115] The findings of the Royal Holloway College exercise also maintained the pressure to introduce ATP. Although some questions were raised about the effectiveness of modern braking systems, equipment failures were rare. Human factors, notably misjudgement, accounted for 85 per cent of recorded SPADs.[116]

British Rail made a genuine attempt to pursue the publicised timetable for ATP, appointing a project director, Bob Walters, to progress the work. However, difficulties were soon encountered with the pilot schemes, and there was some debate at Board level about the prospects of upgrading AWS as an alternative, in which part-time members were prominent.[117] After competitive tendering, contracts were placed in February 1990 with two suppliers, GEC-GS for Chiltern and ACEC of Belgium for Great Western. In accordance with the Board's published safety plans limited trials began in 1991, though it was not until 1994 that the infrastructure installations extended to the Chiltern line and from Bristol (Parkway)–West Drayton, and there were a number of glitches, not least the difficulty in operating the system successfully on the Great Western with the HSTs.[118] From the start, however, British Rail had made it clear to Hidden that the timetable envisaged was a very tight one; after all, it had taken 30 years to install AWS. The Board also pointed out that it had been set two potentially conflicting requirements by the Inquiry: to develop ATP as a matter of urgency; and at the same time to undertake a thorough review of investment procedures. Here the Board was asked to put a financial value on safety, 'so that the cost effectiveness of safe operation on the railway occupies its proper place in a business-led operation'.[119]

By the time the pilot schemes were being implemented and a favoured system had been identified, the process of privatisation had begun and the prospects of introducing ATP on a national basis had faded. A veritable army of consultants had been engaged by British Rail to assist in producing a rigorous and sophisticated appraisal: Mott McDonald, Arthur D. Little, Sedgwick Wharf, AEA Technology, and the Environmental Risk Assessment Unit of the University of East Anglia. Independent risk assessment and safety benefit analyses were conducted.

Running the Railways, 1990–4

At the end of 1993 it emerged that there were very real doubts about the economics and operational advantages of both a national and a more limited, route-selective system. Lengthy debates at the Board in the first three months of 1994 rehearsed the arguments for and against ATP. Careful thought was also given to the political implications of revealing its conclusions given the imminent separation of Railtrack (in April 1994).[120] However, the findings were so unambiguous that there was no need to keep them confidential. As Rayner told the Board Executive in January 1994, the cost of ATP, some £500–£600 million, was extremely high in relation to the number of lives that would be saved, put at only 2.9 a year, plus injuries equivalent to 1.3 fatalities. The investment could not therefore be justified given the Board's safety criteria (which placed a value on a life of £3–£4 million for ATP-preventable accidents, judged to be potentially catastrophic). The net present cost per equivalent life saved for a national system amounted to £13.96 million, three times higher than the level considered to be acceptable; the cost of selective introduction was put at £7 million per life saved.[121] These findings were conveyed to the Secretary of State in an extensive report in March.[122] Here, opportunity costs were invoked: the proposed investment in ATP did not rank well against other safety investments, for example in signalling, structures and new rolling stock. Although the measurement of costs and benefits was clearly a complex art-form embracing a multiplicity of elements, there is no reason to believe that the Board had underestimated the benefits of ATP. Indeed, in some ways its calculations represented an overestimate.[123] The Board's change of heart, reached after some lively exchanges within its own ranks,[124] was then much debated, in discussions with the newly independent Railtrack, the DTp, and the HSE. There was further agonising about the appropriate methodology at a conference on 'Value for Money in Transport Safety', convened in July 1994 at the request of the Secretary of State, where risk managers, academics, transport specialists, and government officials exchanged views, and following an evaluation of the Board's Report by the HSE, once again produced at the request of the Secretary of State. In its Railway Safety Case of May 1994 Railtrack adopted a lower value of life than the Board (£2 million for catastrophic risks), and rejected the HSE's contention that there was a case for selective investment in ATP. The debate continued more publicly at the inquiry into the Cowden accident in 1994–5. The outcome was that both the Board and Railtrack committed themselves only to the completion of the pilot schemes, adoption of ATP or ATC (Automatic Train Control) for new, high-speed lines, and a search for cheaper alternatives for the rest of the network.[125] The abandonment of ATP was a disappointment to many, particularly in view of the government's earlier enthusiasm for safety investment. Parkinson had been particularly up-beat, assuring the Commons that 'investment in safety ... is not required to produce any sort of return: safety is justified as safety'. His junior minister, Michael Portillo, had made similar noises.[126] Behind the scenes, it may be that DTp qualms about the cost influenced the Board's deliberations. Certainly in early discussions about establishing the EFL figures for 1993/4 and 1994/5 BR were told that the Department could not support the planned expenditure for ATP in those years.[127] On the other hand, the case for such a large expenditure was a weak one, and there were other priorities for investment, many of which carried safety implications too. Improved risk assessment had revealed that the number of serious SPADs was low and falling, although the data collected also revealed a much higher than average incidence on certain lines, and, as the accidents at Southall and Ladbroke Grove have demonstrated, when they occur the consequences can be devastating.[128] Putting a cash value on the lives of individuals may appear callous, but the plain fact of the matter was that an investment of £600 million in ATP, in the words of one Board Member, was 'a pretty high price to pay to save a small number of lives': only three a year, a third of the *daily* death toll (10 persons) on the roads in 1994.[129]

There was better value for money to be had from action to prevent passengers falling from train doors, a problem not examined by the Hidden Inquiry. Although the problem of causation was complex, embracing the wayward actions of individuals, whether prompted by carelessness, suicide, or the misuse of alcohol and drugs, as well as detailed issues relating to the performance of train equipment (and especially the doors and door-locks), it was clear that the number of preventable deaths was comparatively large. A spate of incidents on InterCity trains running on the West Coast Main Line attracted media attention, where much was made of the dangers of the 'Tamworth Triangle'. Considerable publicity was provided by an ITV programme entitled 'Blood on the Tracks', broadcast in May 1992.[130] The Board had already expressed its concern, and consultants had been engaged, before an independent inquiry was begun by the Health and Safety Executive in May 1991. For example, a report by Knight Wendling in February 1991 had produced a series of recommendations to ensure improved safety, including a statistical investigation of incidents, improved maintenance, and an evaluation of full interlocking systems.[131] The report was passed to the HSE, which in May 1992 produced its own, interim report. This was critical of the Board in certain respects, recommending that British Rail formulate a plan to improve its monitoring and inspection systems and ensure that doors would not open inadvertently.[132] Its final report, published in May 1993, noted that in the period 1984–91 there had been 154 deaths, or 19 a year, a much larger figure than the 2.9 arising from accidents preventable by ATP.[133] British Rail responded by embarking on a determined assault on the problem. Action was undertaken on three fronts: maintenance improvements; procedures to prevent doors being partially opened on station platforms; the development of new primary locks and automatic central locking on InterCity trains; and proposals to modify the primary lock handles on the Mark I slam-door carriages of Network SouthEast and Regional Railways, pending the eventual withdrawal of these vehicles.[134] Here we are particularly interested in the InterCity initiative, authorised in June

1993, which represented the successful application of a relatively modest amount of investment—£17.5 million or £350,000 per life saved. The programme was completed in the course of 1995.[135] While the elimination of slam-door carriages on Network SouthEast presented a bigger challenge (see pp. 354–5) the InterCity programme showed what could be achieved to improve safety and reduce the number of fatalities without over-stretching the budget. Managers were encouraged by the fact that the number of fatalities halved in 1994/5.[136]

10.5 The safety record

To what extent was all this effort translated into an improved safety record? Table 10.1 provides an indication of the railways' record from the mid-1970s, though it should be noted that data for London Transport and other metropolitan railways are included. The number of train accidents, which had increased in the late 1980s, fell quite sharply in the three years to 1993/4, a 24 per cent improvement over the period 1988–90. A more significant measure, however, is the number of *significant* train accidents per million train-miles run. Here, the scale of the safety improvement is revealed clearly. Close to one accident per million miles in the mid-1970s, when the safety record was reckoned to be good (see p. 66), the incidence fell by over 50 per cent to 1993/4, and the improvement after Clapham was particularly striking (Table 10.1). In fact, there was a steady improvement in this statistic over time, the number of accidents falling by an average 3.9 per cent per annum from 1974. After Clapham the rate of decline was something like 9 per cent.[137] Of course, as at other times single accidents produced fatalities and caused public concern. As we have seen, the Cowden accident reopened the debate about investment in safety, while the earlier accident at Newton in 1991 produced a lively debate about responsibility. The Board focused on the fact that the accident had been caused by a train passing a red light; the drivers' union, ASLEF, campaigned vigorously for the elimination of single lead junctions.[138] On the whole, however, the safety record on the eve of privatisation was sound. If Clapham had been a traumatic shock, there was much for managers to take satisfaction in prior to the fragmentation and disposal of the nationalised rail industry. Of course, the record might have been better. There could have been less talk and more action in developing safety technologies, though we must bear in mind the severity and length of the recession which influenced the government in the early 1990s. Nevertheless, Welsby was able to reveal in his safety review for 1993/4 that while the industry should not be complacent—the incidence of SPADs continued to worry him, for example—no passenger had been killed in a train accident for the second successive year, and in 1993/4 no passenger or member of staff had been killed. Indeed, in the three and a quarter years between

Table 10.1 Railway accident statistics, British Rail and metropolitan railways, 1974–93/4 (annual averages)

Year	Train accidents	Significant train accidents[a]	Significant train accidents per million train-miles	Fatalities			
				Train accidents		Train + Movement accidents[b]	
				Passengers	Passengers + Staff	Passengers	Passengers + Staff
1974–7	1,205	270	0.98	12	17	37	85
1984–7	1,234	199	0.70	7	10	35	50
1988–90	1,349	188	0.61	13	16	45	60
1991/2–93/4	1,030	135	0.44	1	2	21	34

Source: DTp/HSE, *Railway Accidents* (from 1982 *Railway Safety*), *1974–93/4*.

a Accidents affecting passenger lines that are actually or potentially most dangerous to passengers, i.e. most collisions and all derailments.
b Train accidents + accidents involving train operations (level crossings, &c.). Excludes trespassers, suicides.

the Newton accident in July 1991 and the Cowden accident in October 1994 there were no passenger fatalities—an unprecedented achievement.[139]

The period to 1993/4 was a difficult one for the board of a nationalised industry about to be radically transformed on lines not of its choosing. If the chairmanship of Bob Reid I is seen as something of a 'golden age', for example by commentators such as Roger Ford, the consulting editor of *Modern Railways*, then it must also be noted that his last 15 months in office, 1989–90, tarnished his earlier achievements, with the three serious accidents of 1988–9 and a particularly acrimonious dispute with the unions. At the same time, his successor, Bob Reid II, had to endure a concerted press campaign mounted against him in 1991. In fact, as this and the previous chapters have shown, his period was difficult but by no means a dismal one. Given the recession, his was a heroic achievement in many ways: in the promotion of ambitious plans for public transport, particularly in London, the provision for Channel Tunnel traffic, a comparatively high level of investment, a reorganisation providing full decentralisation to the rail businesses, and the concerted attention to safety. This was all the more remarkable in view of the hostility shown by substantial elements in government—particularly during the EFL crisis of 1991—and the distractions of preparing for privatisation. History may well be much kinder to Bob Reid II.

Part 4

*Responding to Privatisation,
1981–97*

The Privatisation Debate and 'Organising for Quality'

The privatisation of the railways has a significance that extends far beyond the task of providing a narrative account of a long and complex process undertaken after the major targets of privatisation—telecommunications (1984), gas (1986), water (1989), and electricity (1990)—had been tackled.[1] These and other privatisations have been the subject of considerable attention, both academic and non-academic, and there is now an extensive literature dealing with the steps taken from the 1980s, not only by the Thatcher administrations but also by other developed countries, to privatise utilities and other businesses which were previously state owned. Nevertheless, railway privatisation deserves our consideration for several reasons. First, as we saw in Chapter 7, the sale of British Rail's subsidiary businesses was undertaken at a time when public policy was fluid, and in many ways the actions and opinions of railway managers helped to shape the debate. Second, the sale of the subsidiaries, together with large amounts of non-operational land, in the 1980s not only helped the government to reduce the size of its subsidy to railways but gave railway managers abundant experience of all the processes associated with privatisation, including public-private partnerships, tendering processes, and management buyouts. Third, British Rail, with the coal industry and to a lesser extent steel, were particularly noteworthy because here the government was selling off enterprises which had been patently loss making. Finally, the way in which privatisation was effected gave rise to vigorous debate and, indeed, continues to do so. The process led to an unprecedented fragmentation of what had been a highly integrated business; raised issues of safety versus profit; and created a change which remains by far the most unpopular measure of all the privatisations. The ramifications for public policy were particularly acute for an activity in which every delay, accident, price hike, or equipment failure attracts intense media attention. In this chapter we examine the initial approach to rail privatisation which developed in the 1980s; the Board's attempts to manage the railway in the face of considerable uncertainty, and, in particular, its efforts to enhance the railway organisation with OfQ from 1990; and the assault on that work represented by the decision to proceed with privatisation in the early 1990s.[2]

11.1 Origins, 1981–9

A great deal of academic attention has been focused on the origins of the privatisation thrust of the 1980s, with candidates for the distinction of being first including the steel industry in 1953, the Carlisle state brewery in 1974, or even the dissolution of the monasteries in the sixteenth century. At the same time, the search for intellectual origins has produced numerous candidates too, including Howell's work for the Conservative Policy Centre think-tank in the late 1960s, active right-wing policy groups such as the Institute of Economic Affairs (IEA) (1955), the Centre for Policy Studies (CPS) (1974), and the Adam Smith Institute (ASI) (1977), the work of British economists such as Eltis and Minford, and the influence of the Chicago School economists, and in particular, Milton Friedman.[3] Railway privatisation may have come late; but as we have argued, the industry was in the forefront of the Thatcher administrations' early experiences of the process, and we should not make the mistake of assuming that the core railway was something distinct from it, and something which was not really discussed until raised by Paul Channon as Secretary of State in 1988. First, privatisation was creeping, beginning with enterprises which were not readily identifiable as railway related, but moving closer to areas with which there was a distinct relationship, notably railway engineering, but also advertising and catering. Second, the first Bob Reid made much of the argument that the railway industry was being privatised from within by the greater participation of the private-sector through competitive tendering and outsourcing, and in the Railfreight business through the active investment in wagons and infrastructure. Indeed, in his annual statement for 1988/9, he referred proudly to the fact that the private-sector investment in railfreight—in terminals and rolling stock—amounted to a considerable £2.7 billion.[4] Third, we should note that at the time when the Board were discussing opportunities for attracting private capital into the subsidiaries, they were doing the same with their core business, rail services. This requires more detailed attention.[5]

Shortly after the Conservatives were elected in 1979 British Rail undertook an enthusiastic exploration of opportunities to bring private capital into the *railway* businesses on a partnership basis. Much of the work was undertaken in 1981–2, when the Board's financial position was particularly bleak. Proposals were advanced to sell the Merry-Go-Round wagon fleet to Tiger Railcar, embark on level crossing modernisation in association with Saturn Management, introduce 'Jumbo' ferries for Harwich freight, and build a rail/air terminal at London (Victoria) serving Gatwick Airport. There were also more speculative proposals, notably an extension of the relationship with Balfour Beatty to embrace private sector funding of specified electrification projects. However, like similar plans for the non-core subsidiaries, most of these projects, which envisaged leasing arrangements, came to grief. They foundered on the Treasury's insistence that a 'genuine' private-sector operation should be 'self-standing' and 'not overtly and covertly controlled, guaranteed or under-written by the nationalised industries', in accordance with guidelines for the injection of private-sector capital drawn up by an NEDC working party.[6] The idea of private-sector involvement in rail services was not allowed to drop, however, and in February 1982 Parker and Howell agreed that a tripartite working group of DTp, Treasury, and BRB should work up an outline scheme with the help of Morgan Grenfell. The group found it difficult to secure unanimity, but did agree that the most likely candidates for private financing were a dedicated Victoria–Gatwick service which might be isolated from the other railway operations, and the electrification of the East Coast Main Line. Each project would be owned and independently managed by a separate operating company. Separation was easier to contemplate in the case of Gatwick, though even here it was accepted that the NEDC guidelines would need to be relaxed, quite apart from industrial relations concerns which, as we have seen, were very real in 1982.[7] In October the Board agreed that the Victoria–Gatwick project should be developed, and Greycoats Investments began work on a rail/air terminal and office development at Victoria on a non-partnership basis. Investments in associated railway facilities and refurbished rolling stock were authorised in August 1982 and February 1983. A Victoria–Gatwick company was envisaged with assets of about £50 million; private investors were to be invited to subscribe up to £20 million to complete the work. However, by the time the Board next considered the proposal, in April 1983, the immediate pressure to progress it had subsided. The Serpell Committee had concluded that the prospects for introducing private capital into rail investment were not hopeful.[8] Some modest proposals did emerge as a result of external initiative. Three applications were made to British Rail by private parties expressing an interest in taking over particular branch lines. The most serious was by a group led by Simon Neave known as 'Rail Limited', which approached Howell in December 1982 with a proposal to lease and operate the loss-making Slough–Windsor line. Internal opinion was that serious proposals should be judged against agreed criteria, including guarantees on long-term service provision, infrastructure maintenance, contributory revenue safeguards, and provision for transitional costs. The Rail Limited proposition, which was to lease the line at a nominal rent in return for an undertaking to provide a specified service, did not meet the criteria, and the line was thought to be 'far from ideal as a "first" for privatisation'. Nevertheless, the proposal was taken seriously, and there was some support for the idea, notably from the Joint Managing Director (Railways), Jim O'Brien. It was not until December 1984 that the scheme was abandoned for financial and administrative reasons.[9]

The objectives set for British Rail in October 1983 by Ridley and in October 1986 by John Moore did not specify the involvement of the private sector in *rail* services. However, this option was not ruled out, either. In fact, Ridley said that he would welcome proposals for more private-sector finance and participation in the development of stations *and railway services* [my italics]. The overall thrust of the objectives was to increase private-sector involvement via 'specific programmes' provided that the aim of improving the Board's finances were met. This opened up the procurement, contracting, and sales elements discussed earlier, and it is clear that the boundaries of the 'core' activities were not necessarily easy to define.[10] Not only was there some radical thinking within senior management, beginning with Simon Jenkins's 'Radical Rail Policy' document of 1982 and O'Brien's work with the sector directors in 1985, and embracing such ideas as competitive tenders for the operation of terminals and ticket offices,[11] but the notion of contracting out lines or services did not disappear. The London Tilbury & Southend line from London (Fenchurch Street) was one possibility, pressed by the MP for Southend (East), Teddy Taylor; and, as we have seen, when British Rail sought to close the Settle–Carlisle line an attempt was made in 1988–9 to sell it by competitive tender to a private buyer.[12] Furthermore, as right-wing opinion gathered strength in the mid-1980s, political and academic attention focused on the notion of privatising British Rail *as a whole*. In 1984 Malcolm Gylee and David Starkie contributed short articles to the Chartered Institute of Transport's journal *Transport* and the IEA's *Economic Affairs* respectively, which advocated the creation of a separate rail track authority. Gylee felt that rail tracks should be managed and funded publicly in much the same way as Britain's roads, with rail services privatised and offered to franchisees; in Starkie's view the track authority might be a privately owned body which would supply paths for competing public and private operators of both commercial and 'socially necessary' services.[13] In the following year the Adam Smith Institute's *Omega Report* challenged the notion that public transport, including railway systems, inevitably required political control and government subsidy within the public sector environment. The report envisaged a progressive privatisation line by line, effected by a series of franchises. The assumption here was that the leaseholds would extend to a separable but integrated railway embracing track and terminals, rolling stock and services, together with non-operational land.

The contribution of the ASI was strengthened by the work of an ex-BR management trainee, Kenneth Irvine, who published *The Right Lines* in 1987 and *Track to the Future* in the following year. These more considered pamphlets set out the arrangements for segregating the rail infrastructure from operating. The new operators, some of whom might compete for the same traffic flows, would pay for the use of the network. The infrastructure/operating division was recommended because it was simple and straightforward, widened competition and consumer choice, and matched the existing organisational structure. It is also significant for our earlier argument that Irvine observed that much of the preparatory work for privatisation had already been undertaken by British Rail in selling off its subsidiary businesses and developing a closer relationship with the private sector in several areas of operation, and that the sale of BREL and the maintenance functions would be the prelude to full privatisation.[14] The work of Irvine and the ASI contrasted with that of the Centre for Policy Studies, which also contributed to the debate. In *Reviving the Railways: A Victorian Future?*, published in 1988, Andrew Gritten, a CPS researcher, condemned the legislative prescriptions both in 1921 and in 1947, and was critical of the government-led cost-cutting activities of the 1980s. Revival, he argued, demanded a managerial emphasis on growth instead of contraction and on more dynamic marketing. To effect the necessary change he envisaged turning the clock back still further by dividing British Rail into a dozen vertically integrated companies. Resembling pre-1923 railways such as the Midland and the London & North Western, these would enjoy reduced regulation and thus be able to exhibit enhanced entrepreneurship. An integrated form of privatisation was to be preferred to the establishment of an infrastructure monopoly, which would have little incentive either to improve efficiency and pass on savings to the customer, or to develop new routes. Furthermore, managerial accountability would be difficult to locate if the track and trains were divided.[15] Gritten and Irvine also rejected the idea of privatising either British Rail as a whole or the existing sectors. Thus when British Rail management's attention was drawn to the privatisation issue by Channon and Parkinson in 1988/9, all the options that were to surface over the next four years had been given an airing.[16] It is difficult to gauge DTp thinking at this stage (without access to the papers) but Channon tended to favour regional companies, a solution used in Japan in 1987,[17] while Parkinson's sympathies probably lay with the track authority option. Mary Parkinson, wife of the Secretary of State, whose family ran a major contracting business, presciently volunteered the opinion, on the footplate of the 15.50 King's Cross–Leeds train on 9 March 1989, that the best option for privatising British Rail would be to create a separate track company, with a number of businesses hiring space to run their services. This was taken to be a view shared by her husband.[18]

11.2 The Board's position: reluctant compliance

British Rail stayed outside the main debating arena, but this is not to say that railwaymen refrained from discussing the issue both among themselves and with the DTp. Many of the senior managers, including the Chairman, Bob Reid I, Derek Fowler, and Jim O'Brien, were enthusiastic about the process of involving the private sector in the industry's activities, though in relation to the 'core'— that is, rail services—they were more equivocal, or favoured a simple flotation as 'BR plc', building on sector management.[19] Furthermore, Channon's public statements in October 1988, at the party conference in Brighton and at a conference convened by the CPS, had to be taken seriously and demanded a considered response. Although the Minister accepted that rail privatisation could not be tackled before the next election, he confirmed that five options for doing so—BR plc, regional companies, track authority/operating companies, sector companies, and hybrid schemes—were being evaluated.[20] The origins of his pronouncements lay in discussions, and exchanges of working papers, involving the Department, British Rail, and the Policy Unit at Number Ten, over the period May–July 1988. Preliminary work on the Board's privatisation options organised by Richard Allan, a DTp Under-Secretary seconded to British Rail as Director of its Policy Unit, resulted in a '*tour d'horizon*' (Allan's phrase) of the possibilities, including the four principal options, together with evaluation of specific issues affecting them.[21] At this stage both the DTp and the new policy adviser at Number Ten, Greg Bourne, were very much dependent on the railways for ideas.[22] Consequently, the opportunity was taken to: question the competitive impact of a break-up of British Rail; challenge the Department's initial enthusiasm for a regional solution; criticise the ASI's track authority option; and push the 'BR plc' idea, though it was recognised that doing so might play into the hands of the ASI lobby since the sectors did not at that time manage their infrastructure.[23] There was a measure of agreement at this stage. Both Bourne and John Palmer (DTp) accepted that the track authority idea was flawed, as did a DTp paper of 10 June; and Bourne, keen to distinguish between the commercial and the subsidised railway and anxious that NSE should raise its prices to take itself out of grant, was equally persuaded against the regional alternative. On the other hand, there was some concern that the Department, which was hostile to the BR plc idea following initial criticisms of the privatised telecommunications and gas monopolies, might be persuaded to favour a hybrid, for example, a simple sell-off of a business or a region with a property 'dowry'. Reference was made both to Anglia and the Southern; in the latter case a proposal to float had emerged within the Southern Area Board as early as 1983, at a time when civil servants had made a confidential assessment of the prospects for rail privatisation.[24] In addition, Board members were far from unanimous on the course to take. At informal meetings in July Fowler was anxious to point out that 'no clear "winner" had emerged', and some of the non-executives, notably Simon Jenkins, expressed the view that it would not be wise to indicate a position, but Oscar De Ville, Derek Hornby, and the Board adviser, John Heath, took the opposite view. Jenkins then made it clear that he favoured the geographical option, while Allen Sheppard declared in favour of a sector-based solution. Sheppard also noted that the current enthusiasm in management circles for leaner, simplified management structures worked against the track authority model. All, however, were agreed that while the Board would 'conscientiously implement Government decisions on ownership'[25] and had nothing to fear from privatisation, the railways should be allowed to compete as an integrated whole within the inland transport market. They were also adamant that railway management should not be distracted from the 'vital task of running—and improving—today's railway', a view which was made clear when Reid met Channon.[26]

Unfortunately, distraction remained firmly on the agenda. Managers rightly feared the onset of another Serpell-type review, but they had no alternative but to join the DTp in a major study programme after the party conference. In November 1988 the Board agreed to participate in a full-scale assessment of the nature and financial viability of railway privatisation, embracing issues of structure, regulation, and subsidy. A special steering group consisting of Reid I, Fowler, and Welsby was created, supported by Allan, and Charles Brown as Policy Adviser, Privatisation; Lazards and Coopers & Lybrand were appointed as consultant advisers. The work was considerable, with British Rail's share of the consultants' fees amounting to £1.5 million.[27] Priority was given to a joint DTp/BRB study of the structural options for privatisation, and the work was given to the consultants Deloitte, Haskins & Sell. Despite its length Deloitte's report on six options in May 1989 was an inconclusive and somewhat disappointing document, leaving the two parties to work up their own joint report.[28] Here they drew upon evaluations of the financial viability of British Rail and the prospects of privatised models, conducted by Lazards and Coopers & Lybrand (for British Rail) and Samuel Montagu (for the Department).[29] Draft reports were completed in July and October. Remaining confidential—neither was discussed by the Board—they examined the case for each option and concluded that there was little to commend either the track authority option or the regional option. Both had the disadvantages of complexity and a failure to generate 'on-rail competition'. Consequently, a 'market-based' solution building on the existing businesses—a BR plc holding company, sector companies, or a hybrid structure—was favoured, and here it was noted that the commercial railway might achieve financial viability 'during the course of the 1990s'. However, this essential precondition for privatisation was founded on numerous optimistic and therefore 'fragile' assumptions, and the short run prospects were clearly less favourable.[30] In the wider arena political nervousness about further privatisation induced by difficulties with the electricity industry coincided with a downturn in the economy. Academic opinion centred on the fact that the railways' large and fixed sunk costs and their dependence on government subsidy worked against the introduction of effective competition and regulation, making privatisation 'a remote prospect'.[31] In October Parkinson announced at the party conference that privatisation 'may be the best way forward' but that this, with other decisions, 'are for the future'. When the Board dined with Parkinson and Portillo a few weeks later, it was accepted that rail privatisation was firmly on the back burner again.[32] European political developments also required close monitoring at the end of the 1980s. In 1988–90 the Board was concerned with an evaluation of the possible legislative accompaniments to the move to a single market by 1992, which raised such highly relevant issues (to the railway privatisation debate) as the desirability of injecting competition and access into the industry, and encouragement of a separate management of the infrastructure. Here, as with the broader involvement in privatisation, it was noted that what mattered was the *government*'s response to the 1992 initiative and the EC's railway policy document.[33]

In all this, the Board maintained that it was for government to take the initiative. In fact, policy towards privatisation could not be separated from an internal evaluation of the railways' sector-based organisation, and it is evident that while the Board sought to emphasise its 'neutral' position on individual options, the manner in which it progressed organisational change was very much driven by its preferred choice of post-privatisation structure. As we have seen, sector management had achieved much in terms of cost control and the nurture of 'bottom-line' responsibility. Furthermore, overhead costs had begun to be addressed by O'Brien's overhead cost review exercise (OCRE) and Cornell's infrastructure review, which prompted the recommendation that the provision of the railways' central services should be made more financially transparent by creating self-accounting units (SAUs), giving the sectors the opportunity to buy services in a competitive environment. In this way British Rail's headquarters would be divided into a 'group services' organisation and a small core of genuinely corporate activities. Over the period 1988–90 19 SAUs were established, covering areas such as BT Police, public affairs, research, architecture, and maintenance depots.[34] It was also recognised that the existing organisation, with its complex matrix of relationships between sectors, regions, and central functions, had to be simplified before any moves to privatise could be contemplated. There were examples where accountability had proved difficult to pin down, in relation to timetabling, cost overruns in M&EE budgets, and conflicts between sectors and regions over cost management. In the view of several railway executives the idea of a holding company with more developed sectors seemed to provide the best chance of preserving the business as a whole after a change of ownership, while it had some attractions in Whitehall because it offered the most promising way of improving viability before privatisation.[35]

In September 1988 the Board debated future organisational development, and, as we have noted (Chapter 4, pp. 32–3), agreed to adopt a gradual move towards enhanced sector control. However, the work with the DTp on privatisation options in 1988–9 called into question this evolutionary approach and gave impetus to the consideration of more radical proposals. When a special Board meeting was convened in April 1989 to discuss privatisation options in an informal way, 'radical decentralisation' was judged to be the best way forward regardless of future ownership. The matrix was to be simplified around a small 'holding company' headquarters, with devolved authority to sector-based subsidiary companies and profit centres, using 'line of route' principles, in which sectors would take responsibility for both the production and engineering resources of lines of route and rail service groups. The concept, which was developed by John Nelson, General Manager of Eastern Region, and Richard Bloomfield of the Policy Unit, was essentially that used in the reorganisation of the Anglia Region by Edmonds.[36] The proposal had the support of Sir Christopher Foster of Coopers & Lybrand, who identified considerable shortcomings in the idea of breaking up British Rail on either a regional or a sectoral basis. The only dissentient appeared to be Jenkins, who continued to press for a geographical break-up as 'a strong runner', saw merit in 'hybridity', and drafted a paper on a 'line of route company' for the East Coast Main Line.[37] His was very much the minority view, however. The consultants Coopers & Lybrand, in their paper entitled 'Future Structure for the Railways: A Decentralised Market-Based Structure', June 1989, reported clearly in favour of simplification and decentralisation on a business basis, a policy which was endorsed by the Board at a special meeting on 7 June.[38] In the following month John Edmonds was moved from Anglia Region to become a Board Member and Managing Director, Group Services. He was appointed to manage a Group Services organisation comprising six self-standing SAUs, which were to charge for their services on a break-even basis.[39] However, his main role was to develop and progress the notion of 'radical decentralisation'. A forceful, determined manager with little appetite for paperwork but with an impressive record of achievement at Provincial and Anglia, he had a clear concept of organisational change.[40] The decentralisation option was examined at a meeting of Executive Board members at the Britannia Hotel, Grosvenor Square, in September. The concepts developed by the consultants were taken further with the name 'organisational simplification', focusing on profit centre principles, with trading rules for inter-sector trading, and (following the Clapham accident) on a safety audit independent of line management. An ambitious starting date of April 1991 was set, though it was accepted that full implementation would not be possible until April 1992.[41] Government support for the strategy was sought from Channon in June, but there was another Cabinet reshuffle before it was endorsed by his successor, Parkinson, in November. The news was disseminated more widely in a letter to railway managers in a letter from the incoming Chief Executive, John Welsby, in December.[42] This, then, was the origin of the 'Organising for Quality' initiative, to which we now turn.

11.3 Organising for Quality

Emboldened by the government's apparent equivocation about privatisation, the Board decided to get on with the job of running the railways. It was strengthened by a new senior management team led by the second Bob Reid, who had been appointed by Cecil Parkinson in rather opportunistic fashion.[43] Outwardly a relaxed manager, he quickly surprised the Conservatives by adopting an enthusiastic, protective stance towards the railways and their operational functions. His task was not an easy one. In addition to the contemplation of major organisational change there was the requirement to progress the Channel Tunnel scheme with the high-speed rail link. British Rail also had to wrestle with the 'bottom-line' objectives for the sectors set in December 1989—improved profit targets for InterCity and Freight of 7.5 and 4.5 per cent respectively and a break-even requirement for Network SouthEast, by 1992/3, targets which were quickly threatened by the onset of a severe recession. Last, and certainly not least, there was the need to address the post-Clapham concern with rail safety. These elements were all critical to the prospects for railways whether the industry was private or public. However, organisational reform was central to the perceptions of the Board when privatisation was first studied with any seriousness. Described first as 'radical decentralisation', then rather optimistically as 'organisational simplification', it became by June 1990 'Organising for Quality'. The name had been coined by Ivor Warburton, the General Manager of the London Midland Region, and was subsequently known simply as 'OfQ'.[44] The change of name reflected the Board's existing emphasis on customer service and quality objectives, notably the Quality Through People programme, a Total Quality Management initiative developed by David Rayner in 1988 and progressed by Brian Burdsall as its Director.[45] Although OfQ had begun before Bob Reid II was installed as the new chairman, the former Shell executive quickly endorsed the change of direction.[46]

The concept was worked up by sector and regional teams reporting to a central project team led by Richard Goldson,[47] who, like Edmonds, had prior experience of something resembling an integrated railway when a manager of Merry-Go-Round coal traffic.[48] A raft of papers presented to the Board in January 1990 considered the development and current state of sector management, the central principles of devolutionary organisational change, the roles of a holding company and small Headquarters, business units and profit centres, and an implementation strategy. The initial intention was to replace the 'matrix' with seven business units: the three passenger sectors—InterCity, Network SouthEast, Provincial; Railfreight, divided into Trainload Freight and Railfreight Distribution; and two new businesses, British Rail Telecommunications, anticipating the commercial opportunities arising from deregulation, and European Passenger Services (EPS), anticipating the opening of the Channel Tunnel. Parcels was to become a trading division reporting to the passenger businesses. Each business would contain a group of profit centres. These would combine net revenue responsibility, all production functions, and marketing 'at a level much closer to the workface and the customer', and would therefore be expected to act as the principal focus of the new organisation. The critical change was that in this highly decentralised three-tier structure the business units would own all the assets, including infrastructure, and manage the production process. The holding company would confine itself to 'high-level' issues such as the corporate 'bottom line', long-term strategy, major investment decisions, and safety, the latter underpinned by a new organisation in line with the recommendations of the recently published Hidden Report on the Clapham accident.[49]

The first steps were agreed at a meeting of Executive Board Members at the Britannia Hotel in April 1990 and subsequently at a broader 'communication forum' in Croydon, convened in June by John Welsby. As with sector management, the decision was taken to progress the changes incrementally according to best Lindblomian principles.[50] Initially neither the Board, nor the unions, nor the Department were involved closely in the details, and despite the expressed reservations of some civil servants Edmonds clearly felt that a gradual approach would have the advantage of avoiding a lengthy reference of the new organisation to government under section 45(1) of the Transport Act 1968.[51] The first stage, to be completed by April 1991, involved the reorganisation of the Scottish, Anglia, and Southern regions. In January 1990 the posts of General Manager, ScotRail (Scottish Region) and Provincial Manager, ScotRail, had been combined under Cyril Bleasdale, and ScotRail was identified as a prospective profit centre of Provincial. In England, it was agreed that the general managers of the Southern and Anglia regions would report directly to Chris Green, the Director, NSE, and that six profit centres in Network SouthEast would be established to cover the routes in those regions.[52] After the Croydon meeting an OfQ Steering Group was created, consisting of Welsby (chairman), Edmonds, David Rayner, Board Member and MD for Operations and Engineering, Jim Cornell, the Director of Civil Engineering, and the business directors. The evolutionary approach envisaged further changes, first to the Eastern and Western regions, then to the most complex region, the London Midland, where changes were not expected before April 1992. The first profit centres for InterCity—the East Coast and Great Western main lines—and additional centres for Provincial—North East and South Wales & West—were determined, and the Provincial sector was renamed Regional Railways. A number of designate appointments—five InterCity route directors, nine NSE divisional managers, and 11 directors (Regional Railways, Trainload Freight, and Railfreight Distribution)—were then announced.[53] By June 1991 progress had been made in splitting the passenger functions in the Southern, Anglia, Western, and Eastern regions into 13 profit centres. The remaining functions in London Midland and Freight were tackled by April 1992 (see Table 11.1).[54]

Table 11.1 Railway businesses, profit centres, OfQ implementation dates, managers, and full-time staff numbers, 1991–2

Network SouthEast	Regional Railways	InterCity	Trainload Freight	Railfreight Distribution	Parcels
John Nelson Headquarters 22 June 1992 (2,060)	Gordon Pettitt Headquarters 22 June 1992 (1,373)	Chris Green Headquarters 22 June 1992 (1,103)	Leslie Smith Headquarters 6 April 1992 (1,618)	Ian Brown Headquarters 6 April 1992 (—)[a]	Glyn Williams Headquarters 6 April 1992 (48)
Thames & Chiltern 24 June 1991 Dick Fearn (2,159)	*Central* 6 April 1992 Mark Causebrook (6,134)	*Anglia & Gatwick Express* 27 May 1991 Andy Cooper (807)	*Coal* 6 April 1992 Kim Jordan (4,972)	*UK* 6 April 1992 Tim Hansford	*Red Star* 6 April 1992 (1,495)
North 6 April 1992 Euan Cameron (1,348)	*North East* 24 June 1991 Aidan Nelson (6,001)	*East Coast Mainline* 24 June 1991 Brian Burdsall (7,373)	*Construction* 6 April 1992 John Bates (1,777)	*Europe* 6 April 1992 Bill Shiplee	*Rail Express Systems* 6 April 1992 (402)
West Anglia/Great Northern 27 May 1991 Bob Breakwell (2,285)	*North West* 6 April 1992 Chris Leah (9,158)	*Great Western* 24 June 1991 Brian Scott (6,765)	*Metals* 6 April 1992 Julian Worth (4,539)		
Great Eastern 27 May 1991 Ian Dubbs (4,170)	*ScotRail* 27 May 1991 Cyril Bleasdale (9,325)	*Midland Cross Country* 6 April 1992 Richard Brown (3,575)	*Petroleum* 6 April 1992 Keith Hasted (722)		

London Tilbury & Southend
27 May 1991
Ken Bird
(1,280)

South East
29 April 1991
Geoff Harrison-Mee
(7,569)

South Central
29 April 1991
Chris Jago
(5,662)

South West
29 April 1991
Peter Field
(7,570)

Thameslink
6 April 1992
Jim Collins
(570)

South Wales & West
24 June 1991
Theo Steel
(4,358)

West Coast Mainline
6 April 1992
Ivor Warburton
(9,617)

Source: BRB, *R&A 1992/3*; OfQ project management reports; management information tapes, MISP level 9.

a HQ staff n.a. Total business = 2,873.

Responding to Privatisation, 1981–97

Internal opposition on this occasion was more muted than at the time of the field and sector management upheavals, but this is not to say that there was no opposition. First, there was some disquiet at Board level about the implications of OfQ for the Board's status and functions (see below). Second, at the senior and middle management level it soon became clear that OfQ was set to produce organisational changes which were both fragmented and far from simple. It was therefore necessary to embark on a series of lengthy briefing meetings and pay assiduous attention to consultation with the unions.[55] Unsurprisingly, there were complaints from the engineers. As organisational details were firmed up, David Blake, the Director of M&EE, told Edmonds that fragmentation was undesirable for staff in plant engineering and electrification, which should stay within central services at HQ. He warned 'that a number of issues are going by default to our cost at a later stage in terms of safety and adequate technical control of the railway'.[56] There was some justification for Blake's position. The way in which his engineers were stitched into the businesses created more, not fewer, posts— 327 added to a staff of 1,004—and by July 1991 George Buckley, the Managing Director, Central Services, was lamenting that the movement of specialist engineers into the businesses had gone too far. His view was that in the process M&EE had 'won both the battle and the war'.[57] A similar situation obtained in civil engineering.[58] Ken Burrage, the Director of Signal & Telecommunications Engineering, pressed his concerns even further throughout the implementation period, dragging his feet, insisting that profit centres should recruit technically qualified engineers, and warning about possible safety implications. In September 1989 he had told Edmonds that any reorganisation of his department should wait for at least two years. When Reid visited the S&T management at Wimbledon in February 1990 to examine the department's post-Clapham responses, Burrage complained that the OfQ working parties were driving ahead 'irrespective of the affect [sic] on current operations, the investment programme and the major initiatives on quality and safety'.[59] He maintained that the management of safety had to be improved *before* his engineering function could be passed into generalist hands, and as a result regional S&T engineers continued to function after the planned implementation dates. The Headquarters organisation was not entirely wound up until July 1992.[60]

More vocal, and more public, was the opposition that surfaced in the operating function around Peter Rayner, the swashbuckling if somewhat naive Regional Operations Manager of London Midland. First, a letter to area managers in the region in June 1990 found its way into the *Evening Standard* in August under the headline 'What a way to run a railway'. Rayner invoked Gerry Fiennes's warning in the 1960s that 'when you reorganise you bleed', and expressed the view that the OfQ proposals would produce immense and unnecessary complexity, higher staff costs, a deterioration in service to the customer, and a threat to railway safety. 'We are ditching an understood geographically logical organisation', he wrote, 'for a confused geographically extraordinary organisation solely to make ultimate privatisation easier and to enable subsequent asset stripping easier.... Safety is threatened, morale is destroyed, only blindly arrogant politically motivated, personally ambitious people can believe in it.'[61] After a reprimand he refused to lie down, and was joined in his 'rebellion' by Iain King, the Manchester Area Manager, who wrote to Bob Reid in February 1991,[62] and David McKeever, the Regional Quality and Performance Manager. A 34-page 'Yellow Book', assembled by Rayner as a compendium of managers' complaints, was sent to Reid in March. Their concerns centred on the claim that OfQ would not replace the matrix but merely move it lower down the managerial hierarchy. At the level of passenger services complexity would arise from the use of infrastructure with split owner-ship (for example station owned by one business, signalling by another), and from joint use. Recommendation 50 of the Hidden Report—'BR shall ensure that the organisational framework exists to prevent commercial considerations of a busi-ness-led railway from compromising safety'—was also invoked. Rayner's sug-gested alternative was a return to a 'network culture', with regional general managers responsible for production.[63] Predictably, this unsolicited and, in many ways unwarranted, expression of opposition, made worse by leaks to the press, led to the effective demotion of Rayner and his colleagues.[64] Having 'worked day and night at the ragged edge of current performance over the last five years', he had incorrectly ascribed operating problems to organisational prescriptions and had clearly acted foolishly.[65] For a few months the clamour over the opposition to OfQ was stoked up by media reactions, a protest from ASLEF, and an ill-attended adjournment debate in the Commons introduced by Nigel Spearing, Labour MP for Newham (South).[66] There was something in the argument that the London Midland Region required greater realignment under OfQ than the other regions, and that the establishment of coherent profit centres for Regional Railways presented something of a challenge. However, the majority of managers were encouraged to endorse the OfQ changes and many were given the opportunity to take up the challenge of combining responsibility for infrastructure, production, and marketing. Among this group there was a fair measure of enthusiasm.[67]

Aside from the businesses and profit centres, there remained a number of issues to be resolved, not least the details of the holding company and central services organisation. In December 1989 Coopers & Lybrand were asked to produce a report on the role, functions, structure, and style of the holding company. Their final report in May 1990 was rather adventurous. It recom-mended a 'strategic control' management style detached from the operational management of the business. The Executive Board members and a corporate office staff of about 120–50 would work as multi-disciplinary teams bridging functional boundaries; they would concern themselves with 'leadership and con-trol', standard setting, compliance, the monitoring of objectives, and relations with government. Emphasis was placed on the need to establish the company quickly, preferably at new offices distinct from the existing British Rail Headquar-ters.[68] Clearly, Coopers' advice raised important questions about the post-OfQ role of the main Board and its members. As Heath pointed out, the crucial issue was how Bob Reid II wished to operate. Was there enough to keep Executive Board members busy? What would Welsby, the new Chief Executive, do in the new structure? Would a 'network' type of organisation square with the control and monitoring aspects of the Board's responsibilities?[69] For a time there were some qualms at Executive Board level about losing control through a full transfer of power to the business directors and, in particular, to InterCity.[70]

Matters were resolved by the time the Executive Board members met again at the Britannia Hotel in October 1990. Reid's influence ensured that the Board would retain an executive role. The new chairman had decided that he would assume responsibility for 'mega' investment projects, essentially the 'new' railway—namely, the Channel Tunnel, the high-speed link to London, and the London Crossrail project—leaving Welsby to deal with the 'existing' railway. Jerram, Watson, Rayner, and Edmonds would preside over finance, technical standards, safety, and group services. A tripartite structure of Group Headquarters, Central Services, and the Businesses/Profit Centres was endorsed, though on Edmonds's recommendation the new Group Headquarters was to be introduced at a more measured pace than the consultants had suggested. It would embrace the functions of Group Finance, Employee Relations, Public Affairs, Policy Unit, and Secretariat, together with a new 'Group Standards' component, covering technical and operating standards, safety, and audit, which was intended to play a critical role in safety procedures (see above).[71] Adjustments were made to the Board's committee structure to reflect its changed role. A Board Executive replaced the Chairman's Group as the primary executive committee, taking on additional responsibilities for investment and safety. The Business Review Group was reconstituted with Executive Board members and the business directors to monitor the business performance of the railway. The other main committees were Channel Tunnel Investment, Research & Technical, Audit, and Procurement.[72]

The other key element in the new structure was the Central Services organisation. Developed by George Buckley, the Director of Research, who became Project Director in July 1990, Central Services were defined as those functions which the businesses were unwilling to provide for themselves, either because they were of a specialist nature, or because scale economies demanded provision centrally. The activities were far from peripheral. There were no fewer than 42 distinct departments employing a total of 14,000 staff and spending some £930 million a year. Buckley's proposals were also considered at the Britannia Hotel meeting in October. Most activities were placed within 12 profit centres and Buckley was put in overall charge of these as Managing Director, Central Services. The new centres, which were brought on line in a phased development along with the businesses and Headquarters changes by April 1992, were: Architecture & Design, British Rail Computing, Business Systems, Engineering R&D, Finance, Legal, Personnel, Procurement & Materials Management, Production, Project Management, Quality & Safety, and Transmark (see Figure 11.1).[73] They

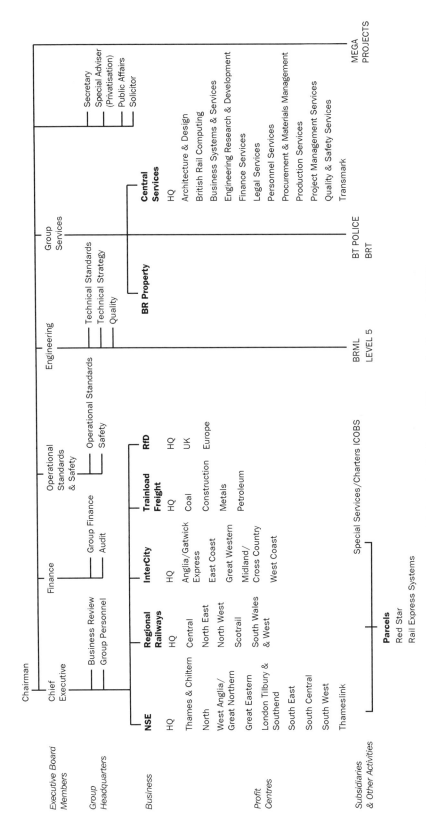

Figure 11.1 British Rail's post-OfQ organisation, April 1992

covered a diverse range from resignalling schemes to pensions management, and from safety consultancy to the production of wooden sleepers.[74]

Rail safety was an essential component of the OfQ initiative. After the Clapham accident there was a determination on all sides to review safety procedures, and Recommendation 34 of the Hidden Report stated unequivocally that 'BR shall require that any future reorganisation shall be properly planned, effectively resourced and implemented to an agreed timetable which takes account of all relevant problems'.[75] To meet this requirement a rigorous process of safety validation was established covering all elements of the new organisation. Responsibility for safety standards at Headquarters then passed to the Group Standards at Headquarters.[76] The new body comprised two elements: a Group Technical Standards Unit led by Jim Cornell, which dealt with engineering and technical standards and reported to Peter Watson; and a Group Operational Standards Unit led by Terry Worrall, which handled operating standards, including occupational health and safety, and reported to David Rayner.[77]

Property, parcels, telecommunications, and European Passenger Services also had to be fitted into the new organisation. The Property Board had been operating as a self-accounting unit since April 1990, providing agency services for the Board and its businesses. In May 1991 Edmonds set up a small working party under Colin Driver to review the position in the light of OfQ. His report, completed in November, identified two fundamental principles. First, each business would own and be responsible for its operational property, with property board directors and managers providing specialist support to businesses and profit centres, while a new 'business', BR Property, would own and be responsible for all non-operational or surplus property. Second, all the businesses would pay the full retention costs of the assets so as to focus attention on the opportunity costs of individual property holdings. These recommendations were accepted and the new organisation, with the restructured BR Property Board reporting to Edmonds, the Managing Director, Group Services, was in place by July 1992.[78] Parcels, as noted earlier, was retained as an independent entity. It had its own traction and rolling stock, but was relatively small and relied on the other rail businesses for infrastructure, terminals, access to passenger trains, and staffing. From April 1991 it therefore reported to the passenger businesses.[79] Both Telecommunications and European Passenger Services had been expected to become business units under OfQ, but instead the decision was taken to set them up as Board subsidiaries. British Rail Telecommunications Ltd was established in September 1990 to provide business telecommunications services on an arm's-length basis.[80] European Passenger Services Ltd, formed in November 1990, assumed responsibility for the control and development of the Board's Channel Tunnel services in association with French and Belgian railways.[81]

What, then, had OfQ achieved? When Edmonds presented his paper to the Board in January 1990, there were 101,000 staff in the regions, 3,000 in the sectors, and 17,000 at Headquarters.[82] By April 1992 the regions had been eliminated, some twenty years after this had been proposed by the 'Field Organisation',[83] and the functional staff had been divided among the sectors (119,000), and central services (7,000).[84] Initially, then, staffing did not fall, though subsequently there was a reduction to 109,000 (13 per cent) by 1994.[85] The essential organisation now consisted of five businesses and 27 profit centres (Figure 11.1). The British Rail Headquarters had shrunk in size, though with a staff of 640 it had a bigger presence than that initially envisaged by Coopers & Lybrand. For supporters, OfQ represented the full flowering of the business-led, sector management concept in British Rail first introduced on a modest scale in 1982. Edmonds went so far as to claim that it represented 'the biggest change in organisation ever undertaken on Britain's Railways'.[86] For the smaller number of sceptics this costly exercise—internal estimates put the implementation costs at £50–£70 million[87]—represented the fragmentation of the operating and engineering railway and introduced unnecessary complexity. And while the development of internal trading rules and track access charging familiarised managers with the kind of challenges they would face later with the privatised railway, on a significant portion of the network the process involved asset sharing on a basis which required goodwill as well as strictly commercial transactions.[88] From a broader perspective, the changes were very much in tune with the business gurus' preaching of the virtues of 'flexibility', leaner management, and a focus on 'core competences'. They also reflected an interest in learning some of the secrets of Japan's 'economic miracle', including her enthusiasm for *keiretsu* (loose but effective conglomerate holding companies), the obsession with quality first advanced by Edwards Deming, and the *kaizen* (continuous process) approach to management-led improvement.[89] However, the new organisation was not given the chance to prove itself fully. By April 1992, when the bulk of the changes had been put in place, Major had somewhat surprisingly won a general election with a clear promise to privatise the industry. From this point, the new organisation had to be reshaped radically once again to square with an approach to privatisation which was very much government led.

11.4 Privatisation re-emerges, 1990–2

In February 1990 Bob Reid and his senior managers had been assured that railway privatisation had been effectively shelved by the Conservative government. Only eight months later the issue became live once more. Parkinson had always been more enthusiastic than his public statements had implied, and in September a private, but much leaked, DTp-sponsored seminar at Chevening reopened the matter. This was followed by a much more bullish statement at the party conference than had been made the previous year, with Parkinson declaring that privatisation was no longer a matter of 'whether' but of 'how and when'.[90] In the autumn of 1990 the Department, this time working independently of the Board, commissioned further work from consultants. Putnam Hayes & Bartlett were asked to examine track access and charging assuming a 'business-led' and a 'track company' model, and a small ministerial committee comprising Roger Freeman, Minister for Public Transport, Francis Maude from the Treasury, and John Redwood from the DTI, examined the possibilities.[91] British Rail, informed that this work was proceeding, responded by asking National Economic Research Associates (NERA) to undertake work on 'Railway Infrastructure as a Common User Facility', with additional papers on franchising and 'competition in rail services'.[92] But there was no official indication of policy until May 1991, by which time Major had become Prime Minister, and Parkinson had been replaced by Malcolm Rifkind as Secretary of State for Transport. On 13 May Rifkind wrote to Reid, declaring: 'I have now reached the point at which I am clear about the definition of the main structural options for privatisation', namely: selling BR as a whole (unitary); selling by business sector; selling by region; and separating BR into track and operating companies. Regional Railways would continue to require government subsidy, but the solution here lay in franchising services to operators at the lowest cost. Pointing out that he wished to see 'all or most of BR privatised in the lifetime of the next Parliament', Rifkind asked for the Board's involvement in a new set of privatisation studies, which would review the work done in 1989 on financial viability and determine the 'practical implications and feasibility' of each option. Rifkind had 'reached no conclusions' about the choice of option, although his preference for encouraging 'innovation, diversity and competition' was held to rule out the unitary option (essentially BR after OfQ). He wished to make 'substantive progress in narrowing down the structural options by mid-July'.[93]

The agenda set by the Department embraced financial viability, safety, the regulation of and charging for track access, contractual arrangements for track owners and operators, the implications of a split BR for existing systems, and the timetable for implementation.[94] The additional work, undertaken by British Rail, the DTp, Lazards, Samuel Montagu, Putnam, NERA, and Leicester University,[95] and costing British Rail another £370,000 in consultants' fees,[96] was completed in July and fed into another report to the Secretary of State. The new document, drafted by the Department and, at Rifkind's request, given only limited circulation within British Rail, was, like its predecessor in 1989, rather inconclusive. The Department was in general in favour of splitting British Rail up, disposing of the freight businesses, and contracting out the loss-making Regional Railways services. InterCity and Network SouthEast were more problematic businesses, however, and in relation to the former it was difficult to choose between separation on an integrated basis and separation of track ownership from operating. The establishment of a track authority would ensure some on-rail competition and had marginal safety advantages in reducing the interfaces between track owners, but on the other hand, made it more difficult to plan major investments, added to transaction costs and carried the risk that such a body would not be as well motivated to contain infrastructure costs as a vertically integrated track owner. The report thus raised more doubts than positive recommendations by suggesting that the economic recession, together with additional spending on safety, had damaged the prospects of financial viability, and that the potential for 'on-rail competition', a concept taken up enthusiastically by both the Treasury and the Department of Trade & Industry, remained limited. Because the interdependence of the rail businesses produced operational complexity, transaction costs would rise. A 'relatively complex structure of contracts' and 'relatively detailed regulation' would be the inevitable consequence of privatisation, whatever form it took. The report concluded that a considerable amount of further work was needed before a White Paper could be produced.[97] The Board endorsed the opinion that privatisation of the railways would be a complex business. As Reid pointed out to Rifkind, 'the study has brought home to me the scale of the task we are undertaking'. He also expressed his concerns about the 'practical considerations of running a dependable, safe railway' and the need to safeguard current investment programmes. No judgement was offered on the various options other than to point out that the track authority solution 'distances responsibility for a very substantial part of railway operations from the direct pressure of the market place'.[98]

In September 1991 the Board Executive debated the subject at a special meeting held once again at the Britannia Hotel. The discussion of options was not as structured as some had hoped,[99] but the outcome was a reaffirmation of the 'unitary option', the argument for which was strengthened, in Board members' eyes, by emphasising the quality and cost-effectiveness objectives to be pursued under OfQ and specifically, taking the business structure and labour ownership down to profit centre level. However, given the gloomy financial projections and the stated preferences of government departments, support for this was scarcely likely.[100] Consequently, members devised a fifth option, not discussed previously with the Department. Emphasising the need to retain the operational integrity and safety of a national network, they floated the idea of a 'National Railway Authority', a hybrid concept which would enable the railways to embark on a 'progressive privatisation'—by contracting out services such as engineering, and franchising or selling selected lines and services to the private sector—all under the umbrella of an effective holding company which would not only own the track but also serve as the focus for strategic decision making.[101] This formed the substance of a key letter from Reid to Rifkind on 27 September. Reid sought to impress upon Rifkind that the government had not been clear about its objectives in pursuing privatisation, which made it difficult for British Rail to evaluate the several options. In any case, the joint studies had shown that none of the basic options passed the test of viability. The transfer of ownership seemed to have become an end in itself rather than the means to an end. Reid then turned to the Board's solution to this apparent impasse, one which would address the essential concerns, namely, the need to make the railways attractive to the investor, to run a safe, efficient, and reliable railway, and to facilitate a reduction in the industry's monolithic structure. Reid's 'way forward' embraced a strengthening of the new profit centres, a slimming down of the railway through a radical contracting-out process, and preparation for the franchising or sale of 'dedicated groups' of rail services.[102]

It is difficult to assess the political impact of the Reid–Rifkind exchange. From the current perspective it may be suggested that Reid was offering too much, and certainly his approach contrasted with that of Peter Parker, who had been less deferential to government and more prepared to argue his case in a public arena. Rifkind, on the other hand, was in something of a corner, like many a Secretary of State for Transport. Politically weak within the Cabinet and having irritated Major with his tendency, in common with others, to leak Cabinet conclusions, he had to an extent lost control of the privatisation initiative. Furthermore, his decision to endorse an *easterly* route for the Channel Tunnel Rail Link, instead of the southerly route chosen by the Board, which was announced at the party conference in Blackpool in October, infuriated Reid and was taken to indicate how far the Minister had lost the plot.[103] He was certainly not minded to run with Reid's rather unexciting policy of 'progressive privatisation', which was interpreted as a device for procrastination. The publication in July 1991 of EC Directive 91/440 gave him the opportunity to press for an approach more in tune with Treasury and DTI thinking. At the party conference he announced that he wished to go beyond the Directive, which called for the separation of infrastructure and operations and for open access to international services, to end British Rail's monopoly and open up access to the rail network to private operators of *domestic* freight and passenger services. His view was repeated in a letter to Reid sent on the same day.[104]

There then followed a 'phoney war' period before the publication of the government's intentions in its White Paper of July 1992. Inside the Department the preference was for a document which would not be unduly prescriptive, but right-wing ministers, notably Lilley, Maude, Redwood, and Mellor, pressed their view that the government should publish firm and specific commitments. The infighting served to delay the production of the White Paper, which had been confidently expected to appear in December 1991, by a further seven months.[105] During this period it was sometimes difficult to detach serious proposals from kite flying. Certainly, British Rail received a strong steer that Rifkind wanted to sell InterCity as an existing business, dispose of Freight, and proceed quickly with the franchising of services, such as London Tilbury & Southend and Chiltern (Marylebone). The proposal to sell InterCity, while having attractions to some, both inside and outside British Rail, was held to require a considerable public investment, while opinion remained divided on the infrastructure issue. Reid's personal view was that the 'cherry picking' of InterCity was the worst of all options.

However, in all his contacts with ministers he was keen to emphasise that his role was to carry out government intentions, whatever these were. In so doing he may have pushed policy in the direction of a track authority solution. Thus, his reply to Rifkind's suggestion that a commitment to sell InterCity, either as an operating company or as a vertically integrated concern, be included in the White Paper, was that 'achievement of these objectives is best met by a separation of the infrastructure from the operation ... More generally, I feel that the main thrust of the several strands of your policy on privatisation, access and franchising is to require a separation of the infrastructure from the operating companies'. Rifkind, however, retained a clear preference for selling InterCity as an integrated business.[106]

During the long wait for the anticipated White Paper, discreet lobbying continued and contingency planning took place on the communications strategy to be followed after publication. In November 1991 John Palmer, the Managing Director, Channel Tunnel and former DTp Deputy Secretary, was appointed as Reid's Special Policy Adviser, to lead the work needed to respond to privatisation and access issues, and an informal Chairman's Special Group on Privatisation was established to co-ordinate strategy.[107] Reid saw Rifkind in November and followed up the meeting with a negative comment on his proposals. The package of measures would make the protection of safety and the maintenance of service quality more difficult to achieve; InterCity's financial performance would not be such as to support a successful privatisation of an integrated business; and the period of transition would threaten necessary investment in rail services. Reid repeated his alternative proposal—the separation of responsibility for infrastructure and operations, with a gradual franchising of the latter.[108] However, the Board was unable to make an effective contribution given the delays and uncertainty surrounding policy formation in Whitehall.[109] Indeed, disagreements within the Cabinet proved such that Rifkind was forced to abandon his original plans. This became clear when Reid was asked for the Board's views on the previously discredited regional option, which had apparently attracted the personal support of Major.[110] In the event, no progress was made before the April 1992 election. Meanwhile, work was required on the associated issue of track access liberalisation, in accordance with EC Directive 91/440, which had legislative force and required a response from the UK government before January 1993 whatever it chose to do about ownership. In December 1991 the DTp commissioned Coopers & Lybrand Deloitte to undertake a study of access covering both the requirements necessary to meet EC 91/440 and the government's own plans for domestic liberalisation. The work was still proceeding when the White Paper was published.[111]

The government's access policy also required the Board to respond to concrete proposals from the private sector relating to rail service provision. As we have seen, Foster Yeoman, a leading aggregates firm, had already established a precedent in the Freight sector when it began to operate its own locomotives and rolling stock in 1986. Its example was followed by ARC four years later (see Chapter 6, p. 223). Charterail, formed in 1990, took private-sector involvement a stage further. A consortium of British Rail, GKN, and City institutions led by Robin Gisby as Managing Director, the company leased intermodal 'piggy-back' rolling stock from Tiphook and hired British Rail locomotives and drivers for the trunk rail element of a road-rail service. The first service, launched by Transport Minister Roger Freeman in July 1990, operated between Pedigree Petfoods at Melton Mowbray and London, Glasgow, and Manchester. It was followed by an Anglo-Scottish service from London (Cricklewood) in June 1992.[112] A similar operation was mounted without British Rail investment by Tiger Rail, which introduced wagonload services for china clay, calcium carbonate, and cider from Quidhampton to Port Elphinstone and St. Blazey to Mossend in 1991.[113] However, the much-vaunted Charterail joint venture soon ran into problems. Gisby and his colleagues were dissatisfied with the suitability and performance of the Class 47 locomotives provided for the services, and claimed that British Rail was charging inflated prices for haulage. That these points raised wider questions about the economics and pricing of Railfreight (see Chapter 8) was of little comfort to Charterail, which by 1992 had run into financial difficulties and was withholding a portion of the contracted price. The company ceased operations in August and went into liquidation, owing the Board £1 million. The venture did nothing to help the cause of either government or the Board. It scarcely trumpeted the virtues of private-sector involvement in railways, as the Department of Transport had hoped, but it also cast some doubt on the feasibility of Reid's alternative strategy of progressive privatisation.[114]

Whatever Charterail's problems, Reid agreed to undertake constructive discussions with other prospective operators, in accordance with Rifkind's commitment to open access of October 1991, though he was less sanguine about the conditions attached. Rifkind had asked Reid to charge 'fairly' for the use of BR facilities, and to allow private operators to use their own locomotives and train crews. Reid warned the Secretary of State that access charging involved complex issues, as indeed it did given the existing state of inter-business charging and the requirement that the Board pursue commercial objectives, while the deployment of drivers raised questions about safety and legal status.[115] By February 1992 expressions of interest had been received from three broad groups: small operators apparently wishing only to obtain information on British Rail's cost structure; larger concerns interested in joint ventures, including the Perth-based bus company Stagecoach run by Ann Gloag and Brian Souter, and Richard Branson's Virgin Atlantic; and large customers such as National Power, which wanted to reduce costs by running their own trains.[116] A major stumbling block emerged when counsel's opinion suggested that trains with privately employed drivers might not be authorised by statute. In addition, Welsby was understandably nervous about entering into arrangements which reduced railway turnover, something which emerged in the early negotiations with Virgin.[117] Consequently, only one proposal, that from Stagecoach, came to anything, though, like the Charterail venture, it ultimately proved to be a failure. Stagecoach first saw an opportunity in operating a low-cost EMU service between London and Glasgow, but it was encouraged to respond instead to InterCity's abandonment of seated (that is, non-sleeper) accommodation on its overnight London–Scotland services from May 1992. On 11/12 May, a few days after railway privatisation had been announced in the Queen's Speech, along with coal privatisation and a national lottery, Stagecoach introduced its own service from Aberdeen using six vehicles leased from British Rail, refurbished in Stagecoach livery and attached to InterCity trains. Like Charterail the project had been given some encouragement by the Conservatives; and as with Charterail, the economics of the contract (guaranteeing British Rail £860,000 a year for three years) were soon revealed to be disadvantageous. The effective abandonment of this first private-sector passenger rail service for 45 years took place after only five months.[118]

In the absence of a White Paper it was left to the election manifesto to reveal Conservative intentions for the industry. However, informal indications of a shift of policy emerged in February 1992. Philip Wood, now back in the Department following his secondment to the Board, revealed that Coopers, the access study consultants, had indicated in an interim report that a very complex and intrusive regulatory regime would be needed to secure access under Rifkind's late-1991 model; they were then asked to look at an 'additional model' assuming the separation of track and operating, the creation of a public sector infrastructure authority, the franchising of all passenger services, and the privatisation of freight and parcels.[119] It was this additional model that won the day and which was duly inserted into the Conservative Party manifesto in March. The proposals, to be achieved 'in the next Parliament', also promised to sell railway stations, while providing pledges on through-ticketing, service quality, and the continuance of subsidy 'where necessary'. Fair access to the track would be secured by a new Rail Regulator, who would award the franchises.[120] At this stage, of course, the Board, the Department, and most public opinion were at one in expecting a Labour victory to follow 'thirteen years of Tory (mis) rule', as had occurred in 1964. In January 1992 Labour's transport spokesman, John Prescott, had written to Reid promising that a Labour government would 'instruct BR to cease all activity presently involved in the preparation for privatisation and re-direct all resources to improving the quality of the rail service'. He also promised additional investment and a new financial framework which would put the railways on a 'comparable basis with other modes'. The election manifesto which followed was less explicit, however, pledging to 'invest in modern transport' but offering nothing about privatisation itself.[121]

The poor showing with the electorate of the Labour leader Neil Kinnock put paid to any lingering thoughts railway managers may have had of retaining the status quo. When Parliament reassembled in April 1992, Major chose as his Transport Secretary John MacGregor, latterly Minister of Agriculture, then

Leader of the House of Commons. He, like Margaret Thatcher before him, was not for turning. Determined to implement the manifesto proposals on transport as quickly as practicable, he wrote to Reid in April to seek the Board's response, suggesting that a day be set aside to discuss the key elements of implementation—access, passenger franchising, the disposal of Freight, and the timetable for change.[122] A fortnight later, on 28 April, he duly met with the railways' management team at a special meeting held at the St James's Court Hotel in London. Reid attended with Welsby, Jerram, Rayner, and Palmer, among others; the Secretary of State brought with him Roger Freeman and Steven Norris, his junior ministers, and a number of advisers, including Christopher Foster and former Board member Allen Sheppard. An introductory slide show did not prove a success, and the occasion quickly turned gloomy from the railway perspective, more 'infirmary' than 'hotel'. It was clear that MacGregor would entertain no deviations from government thinking, nor railway managers' complaints that his proposed timetable was too tight.[123] In private, however, he conceded that the policy carried considerable risks. Public expenditure could increase as a result of franchising, freight traffic might fall, new operators might not materialise, and the impact on the morale of British Rail staff was uncertain.[124] Work on the White Paper continued with minimal input from British Rail. Published eventually on 14 July 1992, *New Opportunities for the Railways* contained no surprises for readers of the manifesto. After all the numerous studies and policy briefings, the government, driven by the Treasury's insistence that no option would be accepted which retained a perpetual subsidy, concluded that 'no single solution is appropriate to all BR's businesses'. British Rail could not be sold *in toto* and there would be no substantial proceeds to the Exchequer. The chosen hybrid structure owed as much to political dogma and expediency as to theoretical niceties. The most fundamental element was the decision to break up the vertical integration of operations and infrastructure, which had been established by the Select Committee on Railways of 1839, and had just been reinforced by the OfQ restructuring of 1990–2. British Rail faced another painful reorganisation. There was to be no British Rail Track Authority, nor gradual privatisation via 'thin franchises'.[125] Instead, an independent track authority, Railtrack, would be established, together with separate operating companies. Passenger services were to be franchised, though the exact mechanisms were not specified, and the freight and parcels businesses sold. Two new regulatory bodies were to preside over the new structure: a Franchising Authority, to oversee the franchising process; and a Rail Regulator, to supervise access issues and protect the interests of passengers or consumers. Equally significant, the whole process was to be undertaken in the life of the next parliament. The railway managers, having marched to the top of the hill with OfQ, were being asked to march down again, and with some haste. The emphasis on on-rail competition had little support in either the economic or historical literature. The Japanese had privatised on the basis of *regional* passenger companies, in 1987, and although in Sweden operating and infrastructure had been separated in 1988, the objectives had been quite different, the two companies remained publicly controlled, and the amount of on-rail competition was minimal.[126] The work of economists also suggested that there would be considerable complexities in the transfer pricing and costing mechanisms required for a fragmented railway industry.[127] For once the headline writers were correct when they opined, 'What a way to run a railway'.[128]

12

Reorganising for Privatisation, 1992–4

12.1 From *New Opportunities* to the 1993 Railways Act

In the six months between the publication of the White Paper and the presentation of a Railways Bill in January 1993, there was something approaching frenetic activity both within the Board and in Whitehall. On the day of the White Paper's publication John MacGregor set out in a public letter to Bob Reid II the areas on which he required the Board's help and guidance. The list was a long one, embracing assistance in formulating policy on items such as restructuring, access, franchising, network benefits, and contracting out, together with work on more specific elements of privatisation, namely, safety, freight and parcels, and international services. Railway managers were no strangers to such exercises, of course, but this time the work had greater urgency and purpose. After all, *New Opportunities* had been extremely thin on detail, and the government had committed itself to complete the bulk of the rail privatisation within the life of the existing parliament. MacGregor recognised that the commitments he sought were taxing, and that the process would require 'joint continuous review' if it were to succeed. In a separate personal letter to Reid, the Secretary of State spelt out more explicit objectives. These were, *inter alia*, to make 'shadow' appointments to the track authority and operating companies as soon as possible; to settle the new structure by 31 December 1992; to identify the best structure for freight and parcels by 31 March 1993; and to effect the separation of British Rail's track and operating by April 1994 'at the latest'.[1]

Work proceeded by means of committees formed in the summer of 1992. At the top there was a Privatisation Steering Group to determine policy. Established in May 1992 it consisted of MacGregor and his team (Roger Freeman, Minister for Public Transport, Patrick Brown, the Permanent Secretary, Nick Montagu, Deputy Secretary, Philip Wood, and Roger Peal); Reid, Welsby, and Palmer of British Rail; Steve Robson, Under-Secretary at the Treasury; and Sir Christopher Foster, MacGregor's special adviser. Below this a Project Management Group, led by Montagu, and with Welsby, Jerram, and Palmer as BRB representatives, presided over 12 working groups handling the major components of the privatisation process.[2] A joint BRB/DTp seminar at Box Hill in September 1992, attended by advisers from KPMG Peat Marwick, Samuel Montagu, Lazards, and Linklaters, reviewed the progress made and agreed target dates for implementation to April 1994.[3] The fruits of this intensive effort were a series of consultation documents, published by the DTp over the period October 1992 to February 1993, which dealt with the franchising of passenger services, access to the network, rolling stock, safety, road/rail transport, pensions, and 'a voice for the passenger'.[4] At the same time work proceeded on a 'paving bill', an enabling measure introduced to facilitate the privatisation of both the coal and railway industries, by giving both boards the necessary powers to participate in the transfer of their activities to the private sector. First presented in May 1992, it received Royal Assent in January 1993.[5] While the Railways Bill was proceeding through its parliamentary stages, there were alterations to the way in which privatisation was managed at the top. Increasing concern that the degree of bureaucracy was hampering effective decision making led to the formation of a new group, Mr Freeman's Implementation Group or FIG, which first met in June 1993. Led by Roger Freeman and therefore having direct ministerial involvement, its other members were Reid, Welsby, Edmonds, and recent Board appointee Robert Horton, plus Montagu, Robson, Wood, and Roger Salmon, then the special adviser on franchising. Their main responsibility was to settle issues which other bodies had failed to resolve. Below FIG, the most important locus of joint decision making was the Restructuring Group, which replaced the Project Management Group in February 1993.[6]

In addition to all this internal activity, the House of Commons Transport Committee, led by the self-confessed rail enthusiast Robert Adley, Conservative MP for Christchurch, embarked on a lengthy and public review of the White Paper's proposals, taking oral evidence from no fewer than 138 individuals from 28 October 1992 to 10 February 1993, and receiving a plethora of written submissions (over 300 in all). Reid and MacGregor each made two appearances before the Committee, and former British Rail chairmen Marsh and Parker also gave evidence, as did British Rail's major customers, parties interested in privatisation, such as Jim Prior of GEC, Richard Branson of Virgin, James Sherwood of Sea Containers, and Sir Alastair Morton of Eurotunnel, the railway trade union leaders, lobby groups, and representatives of railways in Japan, Sweden, France,

Germany, and Argentina. The bones of British Rail were truly being picked over.[7]

The critical element to be determined was the shape and staffing of Railtrack. Here, as Montagu noted in September 1992, the government view was that Railtrack should be created 'as a lean and distinct company, at arm's length from the rest of BR'. By April 1994 it was to 'have complete control of its staff and other assets'. Montagu also saw 'attractions in removing what is at present an in-house capacity of civil engineers to another part of the BR organisation (with the private sector as their ultimate destination)'.[8] Senior appointments were clearly a major consideration at this early stage. In December 1992 MacGregor appointed Robert Horton, Archie Norman, and Jennifer Page to the Board as shadow Railtrack board members, with effect from 1 January 1993. They were joined in August by Christopher Jonas (Table 12.1). The new appointees were an eclectic group. Horton, appointed part-time Vice-Chairman of British Rail and Chairman designate of Railtrack, was a leading businessman. In common with his Chairman (Reid) and Secretary of State (MacGregor) he had been educated at St. Andrews University. As Chairman and Chief Executive of British Petroleum from 1990 he had acquired a reputation for managerial toughness and pig-headedness in almost equal measure. Certainly no diplomat, he had been ousted from BP in June 1992 after concerns about his aggressive, cost-cutting approach, in what the *Financial Times* had called a 'top-level coup in classic style'.[9] The others were less well known. Norman, aged 38, had worked for Citibank, McKinsey, and Woolworth's. As Chief Executive of Asda since 1991 he was an enthusiastic supporter of the Conservative Party and, indeed, a future shadow Secretary of State for Environment, Transport and the Regions. Page was Chief Executive of English Heritage, her reputation yet to be tarnished by association with the Millennium Dome; Jonas was a senior partner in Drivers Jonas, a leading firm of chartered surveyors and international real estate consultants. None had much practical experience of the railways, although Page, when a DTp Assistant Secretary, had been involved with the privatisation of the Board's subsidiary businesses (see Chapter 7). These appointments were followed by that of Edmonds, who stepped down from the Board to take the post of Chief Executive designate of Railtrack in March 1993.[10]

What was the mood inside British Rail at the move towards privatisation on government lines? One thing is clear. Whatever Bob Reid cared to say about obeying the shareholder, the majority of senior railway managers displayed implacable opposition to the proposed formula for privatisation. In circumstances similar to that of the earlier St. James's Court Hotel meeting, the managing directors and profit centre directors of the passenger businesses met the Secretary of State at Euston House in November 1992. They told him in no uncertain terms that their strong preference was for vertically integrated franchises and affirmed their continuing commitment to the gains represented by the 'Organising for Quality' reorganisation.[11] Shortly afterwards Chris Green of InterCity also raised his head above the parapet. Responding to the consultation document on

Table 12.1 The British Railways Board, 1 January 1993–31 March 1994

	Age[†]	Salary[‡]	Date of appt	Date of departure	Background
Chairman					
Sir Bob Reid	59	£216,195	Oct. 1990 (Jan. 1990)	Mar. 1995	Oil (Shell UK); Bank of Scotland
Deputy Chairman and Chairman designate of Railtrack					
Robert Horton	54	£120,000	Jan. 1993	Mar. 1994	Oil (BP)
Vice-Chairman					
Christopher Campbell	58	£81,200	Feb. 1994	Sep. 1997	Retailing (Debenhams), etc.
Full-time members					
John Edmonds, CBE	57	£70,593	July 1989	Mar. 1993	Railways
David Rayner, CBE	53	£70,593	Nov. 1987	Mar. 1994	Railways
James Jerram	54	£86,275	Jan. 1991	Dec. 2000	Finance/computing (ICL, SEMA)
Dr Peter Watson, OBE	49	£101,500	Feb. 1991	May 1994	Engineering (GKN)
Part-time members					
Peter Allen	64	£7,267	July 1991	June 1997	Steel (British Steel)
Javaid Aziz	41		Aug. 1993	Aug. 1996	Computing/IT (IBM)
James Butler, CBE	64		Mar. 1994	Nov. 1996	Accounting (KPMG Peat Marwick)
John Cameron, CBE	54		Aug. 1988	Sep. 1993	Farming (World Meats Group); Scotland
Kenneth Dixon	64		Aug. 1990	July 1997	Food manuf. (Rowntree); Bass, Legal & General
Prof Sir Fred Holliday, CBE	58		Aug. 1990	July 1993	Higher educ. (Durham Univ.); Shell UK; Lloyds

Table 12.1 (continued)

	Age[†]	Salary[‡]	Date of appt	Date of departure	Background
Christopher Jonas	52		Aug. 1993	Mar. 1994	Surveying (Drivers Jonas)
Kazia Kantor	44		June 1987	June 1999	Finance (Inchcape, HMV, Aegis, Grand Met)
Archie Norman	39		Jan. 1993	Mar. 1994	Food retailing (Asda)
Jennifer Page	49		Jan. 1993	Mar. 1994	Civil service, leisure (English Heritage)
Eric Sanderson	42		Mar. 1991	Mar. 1994	Banking (British Linen Bank); Scotland
Chief Executive (not on Board)					
John Welsby, CBE	55	£140,000	Nov. 1992	Mar. 1995[#]	Civil service; railways

Key:

† At 1 Jan. 1994.

Welsby was Chairman and Chief Executive from 1 April 1995.

‡ Without London Allowance (£1,415) and bonuses, for year 1992/3 (Campbell as at 1 Feb. 1994). Performance-related bonuses were: Reid £48,960; Rayner £16,220; Watson £23,155; Edmonds, £15,845; Welsby £11,740; Jerram £19,730.

franchising he wrote to Tony Baker at the DTp to express InterCity's 'firm commitment' to its future. His principal concern was with 'the levels of bureaucracy currently emerging...both in terms of the number and complexity of relationships and the degree of interference that a commercial operation can accept'. Vertical integration, he pointed out, had much to commend it. His proposal was to retain InterCity as a national holding company.[12] Such expressions of dissent fell on deaf ears, however.

For the Board, the first really tangible evidence that the balance of power had shifted in favour of Marsham Street was the way in which the Secretary of State took the initiative in making the new, high-level appointments to Railtrack. The choice of the shadow Board members was linked to the DTp's insistence that the new body should be independent of British Rail, the intention being to sell it to the private sector in the medium term.[13] Together the new appointees conveyed a strong message to Bob Reid and his colleagues that there was to be no backsliding on the commitment to execute the government's intentions, which now shifted to embrace the notion that Railtrack, to be established in shadow form in April 1993, was to become a quite separate, *government-owned* company within 12 months. While the press release noted that the appointments had been made 'after consultation with the Chairman, Sir Bob Reid', there is little doubt that he was far from comfortable with the circumstances surrounding the appointments. Horton was described as a man 'with extensive experience of running very large and complex organisations', but he was essentially a one-company man and a controversial one at that. The more disturbing feature was the fact that the letter in which Mac-Gregor informed Reid of the appointments contained the first intimation of the government's change of direction in relation to Railtrack.[14] There was also difficulty over the choice of the chief executive. Reid had first envisaged that he would chair Railtrack as a Board subsidiary, and thought that his engineering member Peter Watson would make an ideal chief executive. However, this idea did not find favour in Whitehall, and feathers were clearly ruffled when John Edmonds was approached informally by Christopher Foster in November 1992 before Horton had been formally appointed. Edmonds attracted suspicions of 'disloyalty' in Reid in much the same way as Prideaux had over the Channel Tunnel Rail Link, and was excluded from a meeting of Executive Board members on 24 November.[15]

Further disagreements were revealed by the protracted discussions over the need for an additional Board member to progress the privatisation policy and by Welsby's decision to leave the Board when his five-year term of office expired in October 1992. When the White Paper appeared Reid accepted the opinion that a new Board member was required to 'mastermind the commercial transactions and interfaces'. 'A person of considerable standing and weight', he or she would prepare the freight and parcels business for sale, direct the preparation of passenger franchises, and chair the Property Board. Although executive board members such as Welsby were worried about the impact of such an appointment on their respective roles in orchestrating the transfer of responsibilities to the new railway institutions, the Board prepared a job description for a 'Member, Private Sector Involvement'.[16] MacGregor's view, however, was that a *Vice-Chairman* was required to be the main adviser on privatisation.[17] In the event, however, he went on to give Horton that title, though without the wide-ranging functions envisaged. When it was time for Horton to step down MacGregor chose Christopher Campbell to be his successor as Vice-Chairman. This appointment, made with effect from February 1994, carried the specific brief to oversee the disposal of the non-passenger businesses. He was also asked to handle the embarrassing problem of Red Star Parcels, which had been offered for sale in June 1993 but withdrawn in December (see below).[18] More feathers were ruffled when the Secretary of State, who wanted Campbell to have a strong executive role, proposed that Welsby and Watson should report to him on day-to-day operations, although this idea was subsequently dropped. It is clear that MacGregor was anxious to ensure that the momentum for privatisation was maintained.[19] Welsby's decision to reject an offer of reappointment as Board Member and Chief Executive was mainly about money. Offered a further three-year term, he asked for a higher salary, and was reappointed for a further fortnight in November 1992 while negotiations continued. The Treasury refused to make a higher offer, however and Welsby stepped down from the Board in accordance with a re-engagement provision originating when Executive Board members were appointed in 1976 (see Chapter 2). In fact, little changed. Welsby, as Chief Executive (Railways), continued much as before; indeed, the Board accepted that he should have the 'status and authority' of a Board member. The only difference was his enhanced salary of £140,000, an increase of 70 per cent over the £82,000 he was paid to combine the two roles. The DTp were not entirely happy with the manoeuvre, which provided further evidence of the tensions produced by the uncertainties surrounding the privatisation process.[20]

The personal position of Bob Reid also presented something of a puzzle for the government. It was suspected that he and many of his colleagues were opposed to privatisation *per se*, but there is nothing in either the private or public record to indicate such a stance. What does emerge is that Reid's declarations of absolute loyalty to the government and its intentions were combined with strong criticisms of the central planks of the privatisation policy, namely, the separation of infrastructure, the complexities and confusions of franchising, regulation, and open access, the implications for future investment, and genuine doubts about the realism of the intended timetable. These surfaced, for example, in an interview on the Radio 4 Programme 'The World This Weekend' on 20 December 1992, and in numerous letters to MacGregor, some sent, others prudently held back.[21] In the circumstances it is scarcely surprising that the tone of some of the exchanges between Marsham Street and Euston House was distinctly snotty. For example, Montagu was unhappy with the wording of a BR Management Brief on Restructuring produced in October 1992. He reprimanded Welsby for failing to ensure that it reflected more closely 'the policy which Ministers have set'. There was particular annoyance with British Rail's failure to give the Department an opportunity to comment on the draft of a brief which gave the impression that no substantial changes would be made before April 1994.[22] In the following month Montagu complained in similar vein to Edmonds. The issue here was the DTp's desire to have five shadow passenger franchises up and running by April 1993, and British Rail's doubts about the practicalities of achieving this.[23] In Whitehall, by contrast, determination was the watchword. The reservations which some officials had about the willingness of the Board to carry through its programme led the DTp to ask Sheila Masters from KPMG to undertake a 'quick independent review' of British Rail's 'general assumptions and expectations' about the implementation of passenger franchising in March 1993. Acting as the government's special envoy and nicknamed the 'thought police' by BRB managers, Masters conducted a series of interviews with Board members and executives in order to ensure that the message was driven home: there was to be no resistance to the government's plans for the industry.[24]

If the Board's position was understandably equivocal, outside it the mood was more hostile. By the time the Railways Bill was published in January 1993, a considerable groundswell of criticism had built up, fed by the media and reflecting opposition from the railway trade unions, rail and public transport lobby groups, the Labour Party, and several Conservative backbenchers.[25] Adley, chairman of the all-party Transport Committee, was a leading critic. His committee's interim report, published on 20 January, the day before the publication of the Railways Bill, raised anxieties about the proposed formula, and posed 10 questions illustrating 'crucial areas of uncertainty'. Taking up Reid's theme these included: the potential conflict between the franchising of passenger services and the principle of open access; the wisdom of separating the management of the infrastructure from that of the trains; the value of building on existing geographical and product-based profit centres for operating purposes; and the risks of creating an 'orders gap' in the railway supply industry.[26] This was followed by a more considered Second Report in April, produced with the help of specialist advice and on-site visits.[27] The task had been complicated by the fact that the goalposts were moved considerably as the report was being drafted, but this did not prevent the Committee from advancing an impressive set of 87 wide-ranging conclusions and recommendations. The Committee's main intention had been to satisfy itself that the government's proposals would produce an improved railway system and were practicable. Here it reaffirmed all the doubts expressed in the interim report, and included some new ones. The observation was made that the form of privatisation adopted by the government was in international terms 'both novel and experimental'. It was also noted that the government's failure to link privatisation to explicit goals for the railways within an overall transport policy was a major weakness. This said, we should note once again that the committee's views represented an attack on means rather than ends. Adley, who died in May 1993, may have called the railway privatisation the 'poll tax on wheels', while old Tory heavyweights such as Nicholas Ridley, Lord Young, and Lord Whitelaw publicly cast doubt on the wisdom of proceeding with the policy.[28] There was, of course, a determined opposition from the political left. However, elsewhere the arguments were more about the structure chosen than the policy *per se*.[29]

The events of 1993, which culminated in the passing of the Railways Act on 5 November, generated a massive amount of documentation, not least in Hansard. The salient features have been outlined elsewhere, for example in Freeman and Shaw's recent monograph on railway privatisation, and although the chapters are sometimes rather self-serving, our account may thus be relatively concise.[30] It is true that the Bill was subject to a lengthy redrafting process as it proceeded through the two Houses; the Lords alone passed over 500 amendments. However, many of the debates were rather uninspiring. British Rail's Board Executive was informed that they were 'lacklustre and . . . poorly informed', and no truly radical changes were introduced.[31] In fact, this was to be expected in debating a bill which, for all its length (its 158 pages had expanded to 244 pages by the time it received the Royal Assent) was essentially an enabling measure. It did not deal with the new rail institutions in detail—there was no mention of Railtrack, for example—but confined itself to facilitating the necessary transfers from the public to the private sector. Thus, much of the meat of the privatised railway structure was determined outside Parliament.[32] In these circumstances one MP was moved to remark that 'It might have been preferable to have had a Bill of one clause which simply said, "The Secretary of State can do what he likes, how he likes, when he likes, and where he likes." It would have had more or less the same effect'.[33] This is not to say that some of the issues raised were unimportant. There was genuine anxiety, for example, about the prospects for railway pensioners, which inspired a lively opposition led by a former Minister of Transport, Lord Peyton, in the Lords. The protection of network benefits such as railcards and through-ticketing, and the ability of British Rail to participate in the bidding for franchises, were also the subject of appropriate clamour (see pp. 441, 426–7, 430–2). Nevertheless, in most of the key areas the government had its way.

12.2 The new railway structure

The new structure, which was established in April 1994, is well known. A summary of the main features—Railtrack, train operating units (TOUs) for the franchised passenger services, freight operating units (FOUs), rolling stock companies (ROSCOs), infrastructure maintenance units (BRIS), rolling stock maintenance (BRML), and ancillary businesses, together with the two regulators, the Office of the Rail Regulator (ORR), and the Office of Passenger Rail Franchising (OPRAF)—is given in Figure 12.1. However, since many of the details were

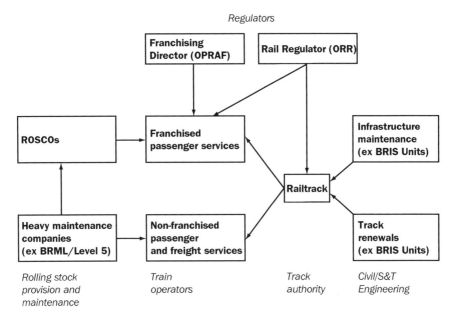

Regulators

Figure 12.1 Principal components of the privatised railway industry

determined outside the public arena, we must give some space to the contribution of the Board to finalising the structure, and to the impact on railway managers and staff of the process of disintegration.

12.2.1 *Railtrack*

We start with Railtrack. Here the Board was heavily involved in separating the fledgling organisation from the rest of the railway. MacGregor's insistence that Railtrack would be set up as a government-owned company, with Horton as Chairman, was made public during the second reading of the Railways Bill in the Commons in February 1993.[34] There was little time to effect the separation in shadow form by 1 April; indeed, matters were complicated by the fact that it was not clear whether such a major organisational change required the Secretary of State's formal consent under section 45 of the 1968 Transport Act (consent was eventually waived). In these circumstances the creation of Railtrack as a division of British Rail, rather than a subsidiary, was rather rushed through in March 1993, creating some anxieties among the non-executive Board members, such as Dixon and Holliday.[35]

In January 1993 Reid informed his colleagues that the initiative in designing the Railtrack organisation would rest with Horton as Chairman designate, and within six months Horton presented an outline structure for the Board's endorsement. He declared a preference for the classic decentralised, multi-divisional form, with a planning board and divisions. Railtrack Headquarters would handle corporate strategy and policy, leaving 10 geographically determined 'zones' to manage 'delivery and production'.[36] Anticipating government wishes, Horton also pressed for a public limited company structure for Railtrack, 'rather than a nationalised industry type of regime'.[37] However, on closer inspection it is clear that the organisation of Railtrack had been determined earlier, in the autumn of 1992, before appointments to the shadow Board had been made.[38] McKinsey & Co. were engaged as consultants to the Board, and presumably unaware of history—and specifically the same firm's promotion of the ill-fated Planning Board/Field Organisation in 1969—repeated this prescription for Railtrack some 23 years later. In a presentation which won some support inside British Rail, the consultants rejected the idea of building on the OfQ-style route groupings and suggested instead the precise formula—planning board and 10 zones—which Horton later took forward.[39]

What assets was Railtrack to own? The decision rested on the definition of Railtrack's precise role as a company. With the encouragement of Edmonds, the Chief Executive designate, the intention was to create what Richard Goldson has called 'an engineering-free corporation'. It was to own the track and signalling, but not the engineering activities. It was to function as an access, capacity management, and sales organisation, and it would buy in all its engineering requirements, not only the physical renewals and new construction, but also the detailed inspection and monitoring functions. With hindsight this appears to have weakened Railtrack's capability to manage the infrastructure properly. However, we should note that this prescription was fully supported within British Rail in 1992–4.[40] British Rail's property portfolio was then divided, with Railtrack taking the operational property, including the stations, which had just been assigned to the businesses under the OfQ reorganisation. Initially there was some disagreement about both the division and the responsibility for station management. Reid had pointed out that the existing definition of 'operational property' embraced a considerable amount of valuable land not essential for existing passenger and freight operations. Horton, on the other hand, took the opposite view, and also cast an eye on key non-operational properties, with an appeal to the need to 'retain value'.[41] MacGregor steered a path between these two positions. In general he accepted Reid's opinion that Railtrack should have only those properties that were truly operational, but in fact some non-operational property, worth £37 million, was transferred.[42] The issue of station management invited a conflict of interest between Railtrack and the train operators. This was resolved by requiring the new owners to lease the stations to the train operators using them, but an exception was made of 13 large stations, eight of them in London, where operating would involve several franchisees, and which also had property development potential. These stations were retained by Railtrack with a view to their eventual transfer to private-sector management. However, disagreement was recorded by Welsby, who felt that the policy agreed by MacGregor and Freeman, and in particular the notion that with the large stations three functions—concourse management, the exploitation of retail opportunities, and property development—should be handled separately, would increase operational complexity and encourage tensions between station operators and franchisees.[43]

Railtrack was officially 'launched' complete with its shadow executive in November 1993 and established as a government-owned company on the promised date of 1 April 1994.[44] The vesting mechanism, utilising the Railways Act, was a somewhat cumbersome, four-stage affair, consequent upon Railtrack's wish to function with a holding company/operating company structure. First, MacGregor directed the Board to form two companies, Railtrack Group plc, the holding company, and Railtrack plc, the operating company. Then the Board transferred the share capital of Railtrack Group to the Secretary of State. The third step involved the transfer of the operating company's share capital to the holding company. Finally, the assets and liabilities were transferred to the operating company.[45] There was a frantic rush to complete the work on time; it required the creation of a special transitional committee of the Board to approve and sign the necessary contracts, leases, and licences.[46] Whatever the private views of British Rail's Executive Board members and senior managers, the separation of Railtrack in such a short timescale must be regarded as a major achievement which could only have been carried out with their active support.[47]

Although Railtrack was to own the infrastructure, a critical feature of the new structure was the contracting in of maintenance and renewal work in civil, signal, and telecommunications engineering, electrical equipment, and fixed plant. The management of these functions in the existing organisation was integrated, and the labour force was large (some 37,000 in 1993). At the same time, it was clear that the activity contained substantial elements of inefficiency which had not been flushed out by sector management and OfQ, seen, for example, in the wide variation in productivity across the 26 civil engineering areas.[48] Consequently, it was recognised at an early stage that the necessary restructuring would require the unbundling of a very large number of individual posts.[49] Plans to create British Rail Infrastructure Services (BRIS) emerged in mid-1993, after work by Samuel Montagu and other advisers,[50] and in August organisational details were announced. Led by Jim Cornell, appointed Managing Director in July, BRIS was a large brief for a single engineering manager (annual turnover was put at £1 billion). A small headquarters team was responsible for establishing 14 largely self-standing infrastructure units or ISUs, based on the existing OfQ profit centres, together with seven design offices.[51] This structure, to operate from April 1994, was intended to be transitional, however, since the longer-term aim was to sell the activity to the private sector from April 1996. The consultants McKinsey were once again appointed by the Board to advise on a suitable form. They recommended in November 1993 that the ISUs should be paired and then split into seven maintenance units and seven track renewal units by April 1995. This option was accepted by all sides because it appeared to offer the best way of creating coherent and sustainable businesses in the private sector while at the same time maximising levels of competition for the benefit of Railtrack. The Department, in accepting the formula, urged the Board to make 'significant sales' as soon as possible.[52]

Another critical element in the process of change was the development of a contracting relationship between BRIS and Railtrack. This was also a sensitive area since it was necessary, in Freeman's words, to establish a 'balance between saleability of the companies and the early realisation of the benefits of competitive sourcing for Railtrack'.[53] Over a hundred individual draft contracts worth about £1.2 billion were hastily drawn up providing for maintenance and renewal within the Railtrack zones for periods of up to seven years. Modest profit levels, to be earned by real cost reductions and shared with the customer, were built into pricing.[54] Given their novel form and the speed with which they had to be negotiated, confidence in this new framework was rather fragile. As Cornell noted, 'From 1 April [1994] we face a brand new contracting regime, with a newly established customer who has high expectations and uncompromising demands. This customer will be supplied by a new contractor organisation who's [sic] key managers reflect only a small percentage of the previous organisation, and which has had to deal with imposed cuts on resources'.[55] On top of this BRIS was about to embark on a further round of restructuring and downsizing (the labour force, already reduced by 7,000 in under a year, shrank by a further 7,500 by the time the first units were sold in February 1996).[56] Cornell's fears were percipient. Consultants confirmed that BRIS's profit assumptions for the maintenance activity of 3.3 per cent would not attract private-sector purchasers, while Railtrack demanded progressive price reductions over the life of the contracts.[57] Difficult negotiations on pricing, benchmarking, performance, and other elements continued throughout 1994 and into 1995. Against this background of draconian reorganisation and transactional complexity, the management of the country's railway infrastructure entered uncharted terrain.[58]

12.2.2 Access

The development of a suitable access regime involved numerous critical issues. These ranged from broad principles (such as pricing, competition, and appeals to precedents elsewhere, notably electricity supply), to detailed aspects of contracts and licensing. However, two primary and interrelated themes may be identified: who should gain access to the rail network; and what would they pay? Such questions also had critical implications for the financial viability of Railtrack and the potential interest in franchising. Of course, access was already a contested area before the publication of *New Opportunities*, as we have seen (pp. 384–6). First, infrastructure charging arrangements were in place as part of the OfQ reorganisation. Second, work was in progress to meet the stipulations of EC Directive 91/ 440 of July 1991, which required member states to give international train operators access to their rail networks by 1 January 1993. Finally, there was also a history of domestic access, the private sector having been involved in domestic train operation since 1986, even if these activities were rather limited and often stumbling. Nevertheless, rapid progress in resolving the question of access, which lay at the heart of rail privatisation, was imperative since the DTp had set a target date for 'domestic liberalisation' of April 1994, a target which was clearly fundamental to the government's timetable.[59]

As we have noted (p. 387), Coopers & Lybrand were asked by the DTp at the end of 1991 to report on access issues. The results of their 'Stage I' work, which dealt with *international* access, in response to the EC Directive, were produced in June 1992. The Board expressed strong opposition to their proposals. The pricing formula suggested for both international and domestic access—a two-tier tariff based on detailed calculations of attributable and non-attributable costs—not only was thought to be unnecessarily complex for the relatively modest international traffic flows anticipated, but if applied to domestic access would threaten the commercial viability of much freight and InterCity traffic. The Board's first preference was to avoid making specific arrangements to meet the requirements of the Directive, a position which the German government had also taken.[60] While the DTp rejected this, all the parties had difficulties with the Coopers scheme. The pricing approach gave little scope for 'market economics and opportunity cost'. The Treasury was therefore anxious to avoid a situation where international access would set precedents for domestic access, while the DTp felt that the scheme appeared to conflict with the EC's requirement that access should be non-discriminatory. After considerable discussion British Rail accepted the Department's request to introduce interim arrangements for international access, based on existing, post-OfQ infrastructure costing conventions for EPS and RfD, and including a separation of infrastructure and operations in the 1993/4 accounts. And although the Board felt that the Coopers idea of an international access unit was unnecessarily bureaucratic, it agreed to set up such a body, in more modest form, in January 1993.[61] In fact, its reservations proved entirely justified, since in the period to April 1994 no serious bids were received.[62] However, the need to respond quickly to EC regulations certainly stimulated serious debate on the more important issue of *domestic* access via franchising.

The Access Working Group addressed policy towards domestic access and charging over the summer of 1992. Chaired by Philip Wood of the DTp, it consisted of representatives from the DTp, the Treasury, the DTI, and the Board. Debates were intense, with initial discussions centring on whether there should be an access hierarchy (compliant bidders coming first), and whether subsidised and unsubsidised operators should compete for train-paths. No one had a winning idea on the design, however, and the numerous discussion papers reveal the existence of serious disagreements at a senior level within Whitehall. At one stage Wood had to point out to Steve Robson that the railways presented a number of practical constraints which worked against the application of the Treasury's preference for theoretically elegant market formulae.[63] The main parties—the DTp, the Treasury, and British Railways Board—advanced three ways of tackling the access issue. The DTp's model envisaged a pivotal role for the Franchising Authority. The Authority would determine a preferred level and quality of service on a given line or route and then invite bids on a single franchise basis. The franchised train-paths would be 'exclusive' to the franchisee, but exclusivity would not apply to the routes themselves. Liberalisation would thus be established where other operators were able to secure access to run additional services for which paths could be found, though it was accepted that the degree of competition might need to be limited in order to make the franchises attractive to bidders. All operators would have to meet their attributable costs, together with an additional charge to cover unattributable costs. Under this scheme, bidders would be asked to bid for subsidy.[64] The Treasury, on the other hand, proposed a quite different process. Keen to maximise the opportunities for competition and private-sector entry, it suggested that Railtrack should first determine through market research the willingness of operators to run unsubsidised services, and then ascertain the Franchising Authority's willingness to subsidise specified standards of service. Railtrack would then take the lead, inviting all potential rail operators to bid simultaneously for track access rights in an auction. After this the new company would package up the timetable into several hundred bundles of access rights based on these market signals. Bids, which might be either positive or negative, would represent the amount an operator was willing to pay for a bundle of access rights, *excluding* any subsidy that the Franchising Authority might offer. Fundamental to the Treasury's position was its insistence that Railtrack should be financially viable. To that end the notion of a reserve price was advanced, that is, that which secured Railtrack full cost recovery plus an 8 per cent return on a current cost basis. Railtrack would set its charges at either the bid price or the reserve price, whichever was the higher. The Franchising Authority would specify service criteria and where necessary top up bids which were either negative or below the reserve price.[65]

In the initial discussions of these two models some difficulties with the Treasury's option emerged. First of all its model was rather complex. Second, the reserve price system, which would establish a 'visible hand' over the market and thus determine prices, might be undermined, for example, by deliberate underbidding. But above all there were serious objections from the DTp to the Treasury's easy assumption that the assets underpinning services for which the bids were too low to provide an 8 per cent return would not be replaced; the existing political opposition to rail closures effectively challenged this logic. Indeed, the level of return suggested for Railtrack flew in the face of the realities of BR's commercial performance, which despite marked improvement in the 1980s was still some way short of such a level. For these reasons the model, which appeared to be derived from experience of bus deregulation, carried with it a strong risk of what Wood termed a 'vicious downward spiral', where both the railways' traffic and financial performance would decline because marginal traffic was asked to pay too much while profitable traffic was asked to pay too little to support system costs. Charles Bridge of the DTI also expressed reservations, specifically about the regulatory and franchising complexities inherent in the Treasury's 'ingenious' proposal. And the Department's adviser, Christopher Foster, argued that setting an inflexible rate of return for Railtrack represented a 'perverse approach to pricing' and might be damaging.[66]

It was at this point that British Rail intervened. Welsby in particular had become frustrated by Whitehall's theoretical and technically complex academic discourse. He noted that the existing proposals were 'either impractical to operate or would have severely negative implications for the future of rail traffic'. The access regime, he contended, was the keystone on which the White Paper rested and thus a practical set of proposals had to be agreed quickly if the franchising timetable were not to be severely compromised. Resorting to 'clean-sheet of paper tactics', he favoured the introduction of a 'facility charge' to cover the fixed infrastructure costs of passenger lines. This would be paid by the Franchising Authority to Railtrack and would form the bulk of the latter's income. All access contracts for passenger train-paths would be agreed between the Authority and Railtrack. The idea was worked up into a considered scheme and submitted to the Department, together with a critique of the idea of reserve prices commissioned from N. M. Rothschild.[67]

In October 1992, then, the debate was still a live one, and in a further frantic round of discussion there was evidence of some convergence. The Treasury abandoned the reserve price system, and recognised that it might be necessary to treat the initial franchising differently from operations when the new system was fully developed. The implications for the freight businesses were also considered, and all parties readily accepted that it was important to avoid a situation where rail traffic was sacrificed to Railtrack's profitability target. Eventually it was agreed that Railtrack should be allowed to negotiate separately with freight operators for access.[68] After the DTp and the Treasury managed to resolve most of their differences in early November, two models were being actively discussed: Whitehall's simultaneous franchising/access auction; and British Rail's facility charge for non-variable costs. However, there remained the crunch issue of the apparent contradiction between successful franchising and open access. Whitehall's option continued to give a prominent place to open access and on-track competition; on the other hand it remained more complex and harder to introduce than the Board's option and significant financial risks were likely to remain with Railtrack. Thus MacGregor and the Conservative government were presented with a stark choice. Either priority was given to the maximisation of competition and the privatisation of Railtrack, or the emphasis should be on the successful franchising of passenger services by the Franchising Authority.[69] At this stage the uncertainties were clearly worrying. Simon Linnett of Rothschild, which had been involved in all the UK utility privatisations since 1985, warned: 'There is no sale which has reached this stage in the legislative process in anywhere near the same level of Government confusion as we perceive at present. If this current planning confusion is reflected finally in a confused structure for the industry, it will be a tragedy both for the railways and for the taxpayer'.[70]

There was further confusion when Ministers rejected the Whitehall option. The result was further compromise, and the presentation of a hybrid scheme, announced in the Commons in February 1993 and incorporated in the Department's Consultation Document *Gaining Access to Britain's Railway Network* published in the same month. The hybrid involved an administered Franchise Authority-led initial phase, taking as its starting point the 1994 timetable and existing freight contracts. For the first generation of franchises the Franchising Director was to negotiate access and charges with Railtrack. Operators would then make bids, with any shortfall made up in subsidy. A critical feature, designed to meet concerns that open access and franchising might be incompatible, was the notion that competition would be 'moderated' to make the early franchises more attractive. Railtrack would then negotiate access with freight and open access passenger operators (such as EPS) on a commercial basis, with these non-franchised services meeting at least their avoidable costs. The compromise was 'aimed at ensuring the successful transfer of British Rail's services to the private sector at the earliest opportunity'.[71]

These expressions of intent had to be translated into concrete access contracts, licensing agreements, and infrastructure charging mechanisms. Work on the last of these was overseen by a Charging Implementation Group (CIG), consisting of representatives from the DTp, BR/Railtrack, and the Treasury, which was established in March 1993 with a wide-ranging remit to implement the track access regime. A broad set of charging principles and methodology was drawn up. Railway managers concerned in the process were able to draw on their prior experience of the 'sole user' and OfQ infrastructure costing conventions to put flesh on the bones of the government's acceptance that charging should be 'market' based, that is, operators should meet their directly attributable avoidable costs plus a differential contribution to fixed costs. The favoured model of administered charges, developed by the newly installed Railtrack staff and supported by the DTp, was to work as follows. First, the avoidable infrastructure costs of the non-franchised (freight and international passenger) services would be identified; then the short run (use-related traction current and wear and tear) and long-run incremental costs of each passenger business unit (including electricity supply, track maintenance, and possibly peak-related elements) would be calculated on the assumption that it was 'last on the network'. The remaining common costs, where two or more passenger businesses used the same route, would be left as a sizeable rump to be allocated as part of the fixed-cost element of the access charge. This approach differed sharply from the OfQ approach regime, where a clear hierarchy of cost responsibility was established and all costs were exhausted and charged to specific businesses.[72]

There was heavy criticism inside BR of this shift in costing approach. Welsby, dismayed that his demand-driven 'facility charge' had been dropped, thought the new methodology 'wasn't worth a crock of shit'; it did nothing, he argued, to maximise either revenue or social welfare.[73] However, aside from the intellectual objections, the principal concern rested with the expense and complexity of applying the new principles. In a 'scoping report' produced by the consultants Coopers & Lybrand in May 1993 it was estimated that progressing the selected charging regime would consume a considerable workload—about 550 person-weeks to September 1993; a 'do minimum' alternative was also offered, requiring about 170 person-weeks, but this would involve identifying only the short run variable costs of each franchise, leaving the rest to be allocated as common costs. It was clear that to progress the Railtrack/DTp model in full would not only carry with it heavy and expensive administrative and consultancy burdens but also jeopardise the tight timetable for implementation. Jerram, in particular, was unhappy with the projected cost of consultancy and contracting—put at £3.0 million by Coopers—and he demanded that the work be put out to tender, but the more important aspect was the utility of the proposal relative to other, simpler approaches to costing.[74] There was something of an impasse until Coopers were asked to proceed with the work on the 'first cut' of cost allocation for some of the initial franchises, which was completed in August 1993. This applied the three-stage tariff, but revealed that there was still much to be done to resolve some of the detailed issues, notably peak charging, exclusivity, and quality of access premiums, station and depot charges, and short-cut costing methods.[75]

The work continued, amidst numerous anxieties, into 1994. Jerram, in particular, was pessimistic, telling Board Executive that the assumption that access agreements for all the Train Operating Units could be completed by April 1994 was 'wildly optimistic'. Board members were concerned about the Department's proposal (later abandoned) to exclude the Rail Regulator from participation in the initial agreements, and there was also a worrying gulf between British Rail and Railtrack over a range of access issues.[76] Both parties found the contracts too imprecise for comfort, and it is no surprise to find Edmonds, Railtrack's Chief Executive, recalling that the negotiation 'was a testing experience for all the parties involved'. The first set of access charges was not produced until February 1994, severely curtailing the opportunity for checking and further negotiation.[77] At the same time there was frenetic activity to produce the relevant access contracts for each of the 25 TOUs, together with 170 freight access contracts; altogether 198 contracts were required.[78] While all concerned performed heroics to produce these on time, the work was done in a state of considerable tension. When Welsby told Edmonds, in a letter of 21 March 1994, that there was still

much to resolve, not least the setting of quality standards for Railtrack's infrastructure and an agreement on prices, he suggested that the Board might pay
Railtrack a flat monthly fee 'to enable the trains to continue to run'. In response
Edmonds played down the extent of the difference between the two bodies, and
pointed out that most of Welsby's concerns, including the idea of a quality
standard, had not featured over the contract development process, and could
be included in future contracting. Wood also became involved, telling Welsby
that the flat fee proposal would 'drive a coach and horses through the approach
which the Government has throughout wanted' and asking that 'at the most
senior level the two organisations should knock heads together'. This produced
the desired effect, but it remained the case that when Railtrack gave British
Rail the revised figures on 30 March 1994 the Board had no time to discuss
them.[79]

What of the access charges themselves? Railtrack's 'first cut' of charges for
1994/5, made public in the Commons on 18 February, was based on the calculation that it required a revenue from franchises of £2,183 million to contribute to a
more realistic return of 5.6 per cent (though this was expected to reach 8 per cent
after three years) on assets valued according to Modern Equivalent Asset Value
(MEAV) principles. Of this sum, very little was avoidable: 80 per cent was in the
form of fixed costs (37 per cent specific to operators, 43 per cent apportioned).
After revisions, a 'second cut' in April trimmed the return to 5.1 per cent, and the
required revenue from franchises was put at £2,065 million, the charges ranging
from £162 million for InterCity's West Coast Main Line to £9 million for
Gatwick Express.[80] The process of revision produced some considerable swings
in fortune for individual TOUs—West Anglia Great Northern's charge was
reduced by 20 per cent, for example, while InterCity Anglia's charge increased
by 50 per cent.[81] However, the more important point was that in comparison with
the OfQ regime the new charging regime produced very different results. First,
the overall infrastructure charges were significantly higher because a commercial
Railtrack placed greater emphasis on capital charges which, with the required
return and a MEAV-based depreciation charge, made up around £1 billion or 40
per cent of the total (capital charges under OfQ on an historic cost basis were only
about 10–15 per cent of total 'costs'). Second, at the business unit level, since
there was no hierarchy of attribution, secondary and tertiary users had to pay
towards the fixed costs formerly borne by prime users. Thus, for example,
Gatwick Express was charged £9.0 million, three and a half times the £2.6 million
charged under OfQ conventions, and NSE's London Tilbury & Southend had to
pay £39.5 million, more than twice the OfQ rate of £19.1 million.[82] The new
charges, arrived at in considerable haste, formed a considerable portion of British
Rail's 1994/5 costs, and there was a strong suspicion that the calculation was
favourable to Railtrack. It was no surprise to find the new financial year beginning with demands from both the Board and the newly installed Rail Regulator,
John Swift, for an immediate review.[83]

12.2.3 *Franchising*

Franchising itself was an early subject for discussion, and indeed was the subject of DTp debates without British Rail present before the White Paper was published in July 1992.[84] After preliminary work, in which there was much agonising over the size, duration, and exclusivity (or otherwise) of franchises, the DTp tested the market through invited responses to its Consultation Document published in October 1992. Inevitably, the existing structure of 19 profit centres—five in InterCity (seven including two subdivisions), nine in Network SouthEast, and five in Regional Railways—made them ideal candidates for potential franchising, and these were listed with summary financial and technical information for 1991/2. The shape of future franchises and the vertical integration issue were left open. One of the few firm statements was that the British Railways Board would not be permitted to bid for franchises, but considerable encouragement was given to British Rail managers to initiate MBOs.[85] MacGregor also revealed, in evidence before the Commons Transport Committee in the same month (October 1992), that franchises would be of comparatively short duration, five–seven years, though longer where an encouragement to invest in rolling stock was required.[86] In the debates between the various parties and their advisers, there was little disagreement in principle, and British Rail undertook case studies for eight profit centres in the three passenger businesses to see how they could be prepared for franchising.[87] The main difference of opinion was over the timetable. Ministers wanted initial franchises to start in 'shadow' form in April 1993, with the first ones transferred a year later. British Rail, on the other hand, maintained forcefully that it was impossible to do this. Reid, Edmonds, and Welsby offered to progress a 'fast five'—London Tilbury & Southend, Chiltern, Gatwick Express, Thameslink, and Anglia, where the operations were more self-contained and the level of complexity was therefore reduced; later, work was limited to a 'fast three': Gatwick, Thameslink, and Anglia.[88] Even so, they argued that they could not establish shadow franchises in 'real' form, that is not only operationally, but with all the financial and contractual apparatus to satisfy potential bidders, until the end of 1994. This dispute, which produced considerable tensions between the two sides, revealed once again the gulf between the more academic theorising of the government departments and their advisers and the more practical approach of British Rail. Montagu may have castigated Edmonds for appearing to pull back from a commitment to progress franchises more quickly, but the fact of the matter was that the DTp and Samuel Montagu, their principal advisers, had to accept that there was a material difference between (a) indicating operational integrity and (b) running in full 'shadow' form, that is, establishing a track record to enable bidders to come forward.[89] On top of this, there were numerous barriers to a speedy response, not least matters of contract, systems, staffing, and industrial relations. Progress demanded that an adequate contracting regime be laid down with Railtrack and other partners. However, at a critical meeting in December 1992 Welsby pointed out that about 160 contractual elements were needed even for the simpler of the profit centres where no track was owned.[90] It was also necessary to ensure that railwaymen were appointed with the appropriate project management skills to establish shadow franchises. After MacGregor's announcement of the first seven of these in February 1993, it was clear that the workload in 1993–4 would be immense. Shortly afterwards Welsby therefore appointed special franchise development directors to work alongside the existing profit centre managers of five of the seven franchises.[91]

Another barrier to change was the disappointing response to the Department's Consultation Document of October 1992. This 'market testing' produced little serious interest, the only replies of substance arguing, like Green (see above), that franchises should be vertically integrated.[92] The poor response alarmed the DTp to the extent that it looked at splitting profit centres into a variety of chunks to attract more interest. Again, British Rail was forced to take a negative stance, pointing out with justification that splitting existing service groups would add materially to complexity.[93] In these circumstances and given the difficulties experienced elsewhere in the privatisation process, notably with access, progress had to be more leisurely than ministers wished. Only one shadow franchise was established before 1994, that of Gatwick Express in October 1993.[94] The agreed list of 25 franchises (see Figure 12.2) was made public in May 1993, and BR train operating units for these were established in April 1994 (see Table 12.2). However, franchising contracts for only three of them, South West Trains, Great Western, and London Tilbury & Southend, were signed before the end of 1995.[95]

12.2.4 *Freight and Parcels*

The 1992 White Paper promised to create, within the life of the Parliament, a competitive and privately owned Railfreight industry through the liberalisation of access and the privatisation of British Rail's freight operations. The existing businesses were to be divided into a new, but unspecified, structure, while the parcels activities, Red Star and Rail Express Systems, were to be sold.[96] Malcolm Rifkind had already encouraged British Rail to provide access to private-sector operators. However, the efforts of companies such as Charterail and Tigerail to run their own services did not prove successful (see p. 388), and the Railfreight businesses themselves were struggling to produce commercial results in the early 1990s recession. Outsiders expressed considerable dissatisfaction with the Board's strategy, which involved substantial rationalisation and the shedding of traffic, a position which was given prominence in evidence to the Commons Transport Committee in 1992–3.[97] At the end of 1992 Freeman referred Reid to 'mounting disquiet' about the approach railway managers were taking to unprofitable freight traffic. The point was made forcefully that private-sector operators with lower cost burdens might be able to operate successfully traffics which British Rail could not, and the Minister asked British Rail to launch a new access initiative

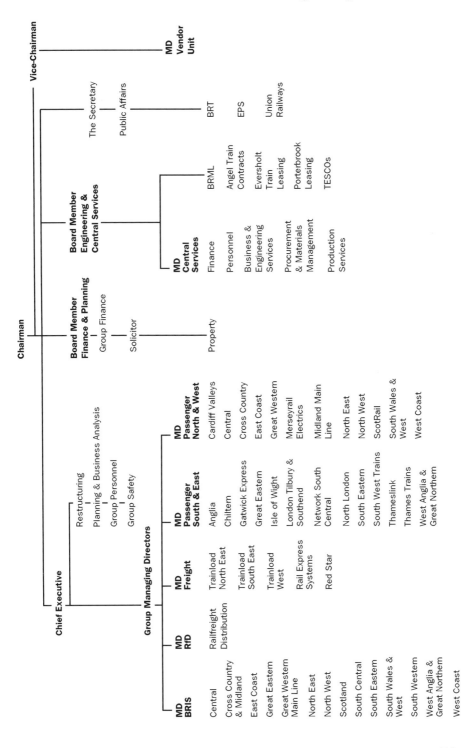

Figure 12.2 BRB organisation chart, 1 April 1994

413

Table 12.2 Train and freight operating companies, managers, and full-time staff numbers, April 1994

South & East	North & West	Freight	RfD
John Nelson (20,449)	Paul King (28,470)	Glyn Williams (9,762)	Ian Brown (3,025)
Anglia Andy Cooper (694)	*Cardiff Valleys* John Buxton (277)	*Trainload North East* Ian Braybrook (1,980)	
Chiltern Adrian Shooter (311)	*Central* Mark Causebrook (2,578)	*Trainload South East* Kim Jordan (2,643)	
Gatwick Express Rob Mason (308)	*Cross Country* Chris Tibbits (286)	*Trainload West* Julian Worth (3,562)	
Great Eastern Bob Breakwell (1,692)	*East Coast* Brian Burdsall (2,804)	*Rail Express Systems* Charles Belcher (474)	
Isle of Wight Dominic Booth (44)	*Great Western* Brian Scott (2,967)	*Red Star* Richard Eccles (1,103)	
London Tilbury & Southend Rail Chris Kinchin-Smith (758)	*Merseyrail Electrics* Richard Parkins (1,236)		
Network SouthCentral Graham Eccles (3,185)	*Midland Mainline* Richard Brown (1,192)		
North London David Watters (1,173)	*North East* Bob Urie (2,826)		
South Eastern Richard Fearn (4,537)	*North West* Bob Goundry (3,412)		
South West Trains Peter Field (3,914)	*ScotRail* Chris Green (4,183)		
Thameslink Jim Collins (444)	*South Wales & West* Theo Steel (1,460)		

Table 12.2 (continued)

South & East	North & West	Freight	RfD
Thames Trains Roger MacDonald (1,159)	*West Coast* Ivor Warburton (4,013)		
West Anglia & Great Northern Ken Bird (1,472)			

Source: BRB, *R&A 1993/4*; management information tapes, MISP level 9.

to halt the diversion of traffic from rail to road. Reid's response was cool. Private-sector operators had found 'the basic economics of the operation as portrayed by BR [to be] a close approximation to reality'. He saw little point in making new overtures while the debate on privatisation was under way. Freeman, however, remained unconvinced.[98] This exchange lay at the heart of all the arguments over freight privatisation. The challenge was to privatise the several activities in such a way that future viability was not jeopardised and traffic lost to road haulage. The discussions on access focused on the critical issue of the level of charges, and the merits or otherwise of encouraging 'own-account' operations by major custom-ers. And as with other components of the privatisation process, the restructuring timetable was challenging.

After British Rail, assisted by Lazards, conducted a Stage I evaluation of freight and parcels in the summer of 1992, consultants were engaged jointly by the DTp and Board to review structural options for the sale of the businesses. The contract was awarded to Mercer Management Consulting, which had already carried out work on freight for the Board revealing substantial areas of unprofitability (Chapter 8, p. 288).[99] Concurrent with this work the Department canvassed the views of major customers. The exercise revealed a worrying lack of under-standing about the realities of freight train economics and pricing, a marked reluctance to operate trains, and anxiety about charges and the continuity of contracts.[100] The contribution to policy making from Whitehall was provided principally by Brian Wadsworth from the DTp, chairman of the joint Freight Working Group, and Philip Rutnam from the Treasury. The latter noted that the freight businesses should be treated as price *takers* not price makers, and the industry should be reshaped to maximise competitive pressures, thereby creating incentives to reduce costs.[101] Wadsworth readily agreed with this view. However, the real challenge lay in determining how to break up the businesses into meaningful and viable bits without destroying them.[102] Mercer's Stage II report, completed in March 1993, underlined this fear by arguing that much of the traffic was not viable in the long run and thus a commodity-based reorganisation was undesirable. Only the core elements of Trainload Freight were really sustainable. A very large part of RfD's best component, contract services, was 'not reinvestable', Freightliner was 'significantly cash negative', Trainferry services offered 'no prospect of ever becoming cash positive', and prospective returns on the Channel Tunnel business were 'uncertain'. Concentrating on TLF and RfD Contract, the consultants recommended a restructuring into two or three geographically based haulage companies. On-rail competition would be established for the 'A' type flows—the profitable large-volume, short-haul traffic (30 per cent of the business)—but not for 'B' type flows—the low-volume, long-haul traffic (the latter further subdivided into 'B Core', the sustainable business (38 per cent), and 'B Tail' (32 per cent), to be abandoned to road). Mercer also advanced the idea of 'pawns', 'A' type, out-of-territory traffics which might be allocated across corporate boundaries to increase the element of competition. The overall strategy rested on the critical assumption that Railtrack would be allowed to set prices in line with market prices.[103] MacGregor largely endorsed the consultants' report. In April he informed Reid that TLF and the RfD contract business would be restructured into three new companies: West, North East, and South East. However, the notion of 'pawns' was abandoned, the Secretary of State feeling that it would be perceived as a gimmick. Other parts of Railfreight, principally the non-contract RfD traffics, could not be sustained and would be lost. The embryonic Channel Tunnel business would remain with British Rail 'for the time being'. The ailing Freightliner business provided the biggest headache. Here MacGregor was attracted to Mercer's suggestion that an 'inside-in' approach to privatisation might work, with the terminals sold, joint ventures encouraged, and the provision of a time-limited subsidy to domestic intermodal traffic. Rail Express Systems, on the other hand, would be detached from British Rail and sold as a single entity. The government was particularly concerned about the timetable for sale of the main freight businesses. Mercer had suggested that at best the process would stretch well into 1995; MacGregor found this 'far too long'. British Rail responded by appointing a Business Restructuring Director and three development directors, and the government's intentions, including a target date of April 1994 for the completion of the corporate restructuring, were then made public.[104]

What were the Board's reactions to the new freight structure? First of all, there was clearly a disagreement with the government over the extent of the reorganisation. Reid, Welsby, and Jerram were concerned by the radical nature of the proposal. In the early stages of policy making, British Rail had thought that at most two companies were needed—North and South. However, the reaction of the DTp, expressed by Wadsworth, was that two companies was 'pretty unambitious in terms of cutting the cake'.[105] The disagreement surfaced at several points in 1993/4. British Rail's argument was that the proposed West company would have a weaker traffic mix than the other companies and be vulnerable to competitive attack from them. At the same time North East would be open to attack from large players such as National Power, while South East would be heavily dependent on the volatile aggregates sector.[106] There were further problems with competition issues and the handling of surplus assets. Welsby was, as ever, characteristically blunt about the dangers inherent in the process of preparing Freight for sale, and was particularly perturbed by the financial implications for the Board of encouraging the three new businesses carved out of TLF and RfD to act in a competitive way from April 1994 while still in the public sector.[107] Viability was also threatened by the introduction of regulation. After a report by Mercer on Freight Access Regulatory Risk in August 1993 there were genuine fears that the Regulator might encourage Railtrack to price in such a way as to encourage the companies to shed traffic, or force the Department to provide subsidies.[108] The Board was also discomfited by the DTp's initiative in pressing for the detachment of surplus assets from the new companies. With the encouragement given to open access it was quite likely that a new entrant could acquire surplus rolling stock and drive prices down; Jerram felt that as much as 40 per cent of integrated freight revenues might be lost.[109] Access charges were another element in the debate. While there was a general understanding of the need to balance Railtrack's revenue requirement with the ability of freight companies to pay for access, there was still the matter of pitching the level. The aim of the initial agreements was to produce no losses for Railtrack while producing a minimum level of profit for the new companies. The Board argued that at least initially any surplus 'fat' should stay with the companies to encourage successful disposal.[110] However, it was clear as policy was worked out that if access charges were pitched at Railtrack's incremental costs, a great deal of marginal traffic would be lost.[111] All this prolonged the anxieties over viability. Ministers quite clearly favoured competition, diversity, and the encouragement of open access. The government, Freeman warned Welsby in September, 'should not tilt the playing field against new entrants by taking action to stifle any nascent market in second-hand equipment...I propose to tell inquirers that some equipment... will become available for purchase next year'.[112] Matters were not helped when Freeman made his position public at a freight conference on 5 October, nor when the note of a somewhat acrimonious meeting between Welsby and Freeman three days later was leaked to Hugh Bayley, Labour MP for York, and found its way into the newspapers. On this occasion Welsby reiterated his fears for the future of rail freight. The profitability of TLF rested on a very narrow customer base and was earned on a very small part of the freight network. The Board's objective of maximising freight volumes was clearly at risk from the 'twin threats' of open access and regulation. Internal competition between the three new companies and the sale of surplus assets would only aggravate the position. Welsby was unhappy at handing the newly appointed managing directors of the three companies a brief to handle restructuring and major downsizing as two unrelated issues. The prospects for a successful disposal of the freight businesses were remote: 'All you'll be left with is a car boot sale: I'm not joking . . . I don't see how there will be anything still to sell; certainly not the cake, just the cherries'.[113] Work produced by Lazards put flesh on the bones of the Board's arguments, estimating that on relatively optimistic assumptions, including confining charges to avoidable costs, and ignoring the impact of new entrants, as much as 28 per cent of freight tonne-mileage was at risk. In overall terms the economics of rail freight were distinctly fragile.[114] Nevertheless, the reorganisation went ahead to schedule. In April 1994 Glyn Williams, Managing Director of Parcels, was appointed MD of a newly constituted Freight Group, which comprised five companies, three for freight, and two for parcels.[115]

In these circumstances, it was scarcely surprising that the negotiation of the initial track access charges was a protracted affair. Signed at the last gasp on 31 March 1994 without the approval of the Rail Regulator, whose powers were not made operational until 2 April, the 200 contracts produced an aggregate figure of £190 million, of which the former Trainload Freight flows represented £153 million.[116] Wadsworth was highly complimentary about British Rail's efforts, congratulating Glyn Williams on completing 'a complex task, delivered to a timescale that many people thought virtually impossible'.[117] Nevertheless, this achievement could not hide the uncertainties surrounding the future of rail freight and the new companies. The negotiations with Railtrack had been difficult. As late as 25 March Williams had informed the Department that Railtrack's proposed charges were 'completely unacceptable and, combined with the uncertainties created by open access, would make it unlikely that we will be able to sell the three TLF companies'. RfD made a similar complaint about the proposed charge for its Channel Tunnel traffic.[118] The government did make some progress in extending the range of freight grants. The existing section 8 grants, introduced in 1974, had produced only modest subsidies: about £84 million over two decades.[119] The Railways Act 1993 provided not only contributions towards the cost of new freight facilities, extended to embrace rolling stock as well as infrastructure, but track charges grants of up to 100 per cent. In this way the uncertainties of the new charging regime were tempered by the promise of support for traffic which was vulnerable to a switch from rail to road.[120]

The sale of the several elements in the new structure created numerous headaches. There was considerable debate about the privatisation of RfD's Channel Tunnel and Freightliner operations, which continued under Ian Brown's management. In 1993–4 disposal of the parcels businesses was tackled as a first step. Rail Express Systems was to be separated from British Rail and sold as a separate business, though this had to wait for the renegotiation of the key contract with the Post Office, which was successfully completed in December 1993. However, the priority in 1993–4 was the privatisation of the loss-making Red Star. MacGregor was determined to make progress with an early sale, and he felt that Red Star offered the best prospects. Unfortunately, the initial attempts to dispose of it proved to be a protracted and embarrassing affair. Approved by the

33. Airport links: Stansted Airport station, April 1991. (*John Glover*)

34. Closure? The Settle & Carlisle line. Dundee–Plymouth train diverted due to engineering works on the West Coast Main Line, at Garsdale, March 1989. (*Brian Morrison*)

35. Bus substitution? Assessed for substitution by buses in 1987, the Llandudno Jnc.–Blaenau Ffestiniog service near Blaenau Ffestiniog, September 1998. (*Brian Morrison*)

36. Quality of service? London (Fenchurch Street)–Southend, the 'Misery Line'. Class 302 train at Fenchurch Street, Summer 1991: a time of pronounced dissatisfaction by passengers. (*Milepost 92½*)

37. Investment, 1983–9: Class 150 at Chester Road, near Birmingham,
August 1984. (*BRB*)

38. Investment, 1983–9: Class 158 at Reedham, April 1992.
(*Brian Morrison*)

39*a*. Investment, 1983–9: Liverpool Street/Broad Street development: before, 1982. (*BRB*)

39*b*. Investment, 1983–9: Liverpool Street/Broad Street development: under construction, March 1990. (*BRB/John W. Byrne*)

40. Investment, 1983–9: Computerised ticketing: the All Purpose
Ticket Issuing System (APTIS), in use in 1985. (*BRB*)

41. Investment in the early 1990s: Class 60 freight locomotives, showing four sub-sector
brandings (left to right: petroleum; coal; construction; and metals). (*John Tidmarsh*)

42. Investment in the early 1990s: Channel Tunnel services: Waterloo International Terminal, completed on time and within budget in May 1993, shown here in Summer 1995. (*Milepost 92½*)

43. Investment in the early 1990s: Eurostar train near the Tunnel's mouth at Dolland's Moor terminal, Summer 1995. (*Milepost 92½*)

44. Investment in the early 1990s: Network SouthEast's 'Networker':
special train for MPs and media representatives leaves Cannon Street,
11 August 1992. (*Brian Morrison*)

45. Investment in the early 1990s: 'Turbo' trains, London Marylebone station,
March 1992. (*Brian Morrison*)

46. Investment in the early 1990s: Infrastructure maintenance:
Network SouthEast's Dynamic Track Stabiliser, Mark's Tey,
October 1988. (*BRB/John W. Byrne*).

47. The 'wrong kind of snow': East Croydon station,
11 February 1991. (*BRB*)

48. Leadership contrasts 1: Sir Robert Basil Reid (Bob Reid I) and Sir Robert Paul Reid (Bob Reid II), 1990. (*BRB/Railnews*)

49. Leadership contrasts 2: John Welsby (Chairman of British Railways Board) (left) and Ed Burkhardt (President and Chief Executive, Wisconsin Central) (right), on the sale of British Rail's three trainload freight companies in February 1996. (*BRB/Phil Caley*)

50. British Rail's technological successes:
Solid State Interlocking Rack and Terminal,
Leamington Spa, 1985. (*BRB*)

51. British Rail's technological successes: The Electronic Control Centre (IECC). Desk
position at London Liverpool Street, 1992. (*Westinghouse Rail Systems*)

52. British Rail's technological successes: The Radio Electronic Token Block (RETB) equipment in a Class 37 locomotive, Dingwall, 1984. (*Westinghouse Rail Systems*)

53. Safety: the Clapham accident, 12 December 1988. (*BRB*)

54. Safety: The Chief Executive's visit to S&T design centre, Reading, September 1990. John Welsby, Chief Executive (seated, centre), and Ken Burrage, Director, S&T Engineering (standing, centre). (*Ken Burrage*)

55. The path to Privatisation 1: New entrants in Freight. Charterail service launched by John MacGregor, Secretary of State for Transport, Cricklewood, 11 June 1992. (*Brian Morrison*)

56. The path to Privatisation 2: New entrants in Passenger traffic. Stagecoach's Aberdeen–London service, May 1992. (*BRB*)

57. The path to Privatisation 3: the last British Rail service. Railfreight Distribution's Class 92 No.92003 *Beethoven* hauls the 23.15 from Dolland's Moor to Wembley at 23.59 on 21 November 1997, the last loaded train to start a main-line journey under British Rail ownership. (*BRB/Chris Wilson*)

58. Significant relationships? 1: Sir Peter Parker with Prime Minister Margaret Thatcher, and Baroness Airey of Abingdon, at the naming of Class 86 locomotive No.86311 *Airey Neave*, 14 May 1983. (*BRB*)

59. Significant relationships? 2: Bob Reid I and Nicholas Ridley, Secretary of State for Transport, *c.*1985. (*BRB*)

60. Significant relationships? 3: Bob Reid II and John MacGregor, Secretary of State for Transport, December 1992. (*BRB/John W. Byrne*)

61. The future? Virgin Trains's new tilting train, the Pendolino, at Old Dalby test track, June 2001. (*Virgin Trains*)

62. The future? EWS Class 66 locomotive at EWS's steel terminal, Wolverhampton, 2000. (*EWS*)

Board in October 1992 and offered for sale in the following June, Red Star attracted seven bids but of these only two, from an MBO and a consortium called Caledonian and London Enterprises, were serious.[121] There were problems with both bids, however, and in November 1993 the Board Executive recommended that the sale be abandoned. The Department accepted the decision with reluctance. Its inquest produced some acrimonious exchanges, with MacGregor demanding improvements in the financial prospects of the business so that it might be sold in 1994.[122] The newly appointed Vice-Chairman, Christopher Campbell, had no more luck with the sale than had his predecessors. It was not until September 1995 that Red Star was finally sold to an MBO team for a peppercorn.[123] As for the core TLF business, the new operating units, subsequently renamed Loadhaul (North East), Mainline (South East), and Transrail (West), were offered for sale in 1995. Ironically, given the disagreement between the Department and the Board, they were eventually acquired by a single purchaser, a consortium led by the American operator Wisconsin Central, which also bought RfD and Rail Express Systems.[124]

12.2.5 *ROSCOs*

The government's decision to establish rolling stock companies (ROSCOs) to lease equipment to the operating companies stemmed logically from: (1) its insistence that franchises should be of comparatively short duration, normally five–seven years, while new stock had an economic life of 25–40 years; (2) its anxiety to encourage franchise operators who might otherwise be deterred by the burden of capital investment in equipment; (3) an apparent commitment to continuing investment in railway rolling stock; and (4) an acceptance that with so much of the existing stock 'route specific' in nature, a market for second-hand equipment would not function effectively enough to remove the 'residual value risk' at the end of a franchise. After these issues were debated in November 1992 a consultation document published in January 1993 offered two options. Under Option 1, a piecemeal sale to private-sector lessors, British Rail would first lease stock to franchisees as each franchise was let, then sell the assets to private-sector lessors by competitive tender. Under Option 2, the entire fleet would be transferred to between three and five public sector leasing companies, which would then be privatised if a track record of successful leasing were established.[125]

While there was more agreement among the parties here than with other aspects of privatisation, some differences of emphasis did emerge. Both options had advantages and disadvantages. Option 1 would encourage market mechanisms to function, but might leave the older stock in British Rail's hands; Option 2 promised to create companies strong enough to take up a wider portfolio of stock but at the expense of a functioning market. Both British Rail and the Treasury were keen to transfer the assets to private-sector leasing companies without guarantees about the recovery of residual values. The DTp, on the other hand, felt that some kind of transitional guarantee would be necessary to stimulate interest, and suggested a number of ways of providing this.[126] The residual value question was also relevant to the thorny issue of encouraging the private sector to invest in *new* rolling stock, a matter which was also debated vigorously, with British Rail asked to undertake leasing of £150 million of new stock as a pilot project (see pp. 311–12).[127] The consultation stage revealed considerable interest from the private sector, but at the same time an unwillingness to take on the residual value risk and a fear of railway administration in the event of insolvency. Thus, Option 2—public sector companies—appeared to be the more attractive, and there was also an expressed preference for 'lean' companies, which were regarded as being easier to sell to the private sector in due course. Here the government accepted British Rail's view that *three* companies taking a mixed portfolio of stock would provide the necessary balance of competition for supply and economies of scale.[128] Thus, at the end of April 1993 Freeman announced that the Board would transfer its entire passenger fleet of 11,000 vehicles (book value: £2 billion at written-down historic cost) to three rolling stock companies by 1 April 1994.[129]

Although broad policy making was relatively straightforward, detailed aspects and the process of transfer itself were once again complex and time consuming. The lack of an existing market for stock and the comparative rarity of the leasing device in railways (though introduced for some Channel Tunnel stock in 1993), provided their own challenges. Another irritant was the fact that, in contrast to the aircraft industry, there were no legal requirements for maintenance, and thus the quality of the existing maintenance documentation was far from high. The nature of the leasing regime and the maintenance capability of the new companies were other matters requiring resolution.[130] In June 1993 Freeman made a further announcement. The ROSCOs would be set up as BRB subsidiaries in the first instance, offering operating leases (to revised, moderated guidelines for the public sector issued by the Treasury), and thereby bearing the residual value risks. At the same time, they would be lean companies with no in-house maintenance capability, although they would be responsible for ensuring that heavy maintenance was undertaken. In order to stimulate commercial behaviour and their subsequent transfer to the private sector they would operate with the aid of private-sector advisers to provide the necessary financial skills and leasing experience. In order to safeguard new investment an additional clause was inserted into the Railways Bill giving the Franchising Director powers to encourage such investment with guarantees about deployment and to act with the PTEs in relation to local government-supported services.[131] Hambros Bank were duly appointed as advisers to British Rail, working on matters such as the corporate structure, fleet allocation, the financing regime, valuation, and taxation.[132] The two latter items proved to be particularly difficult. Hambros's valuation of the passenger stock, which had an average age of 16 years, made on an equivalent cost basis, produced a figure of £4,341 million, 350 per cent higher than existing book value, and a consequential rental (assuming a return of 8 per cent) of £785 million. Although later scaled down to £3.5 billion, with an implied rental of £676 million, the valuation nevertheless produced an increase of some £400 million in the cost of railway rolling stock, a fact which caused considerable concern inside British Rail, particularly since it utilised a *finance*-lease model and yet produced no guarantee that new trains would be ordered.[133] On taxation, the Board feared that incorporation would prevent it from offsetting ROSCO profits against previous trading losses: about £100 million a year was at stake. This was only resolved when Freeman assured Reid in March 1994 that a clause would be inserted in the Finance Bill to permit losses to be transferred to the successor companies and set against taxable profits.[134] The passenger fleet was duly transferred on 1 April to the three leasing companies: Angel Train Contracts, Eversholt Leasing, and Porterbrook Leasing, and the master lease was signed, after extensive amendment, on 15 July.[135] However, much remained to be done. Leasing to TOUs and contracting for heavy maintenance consumed much of 1994/5. This activity was made more urgent with the government's determination to offer the ROSCOs for sale in 1995, an intention made public in July 1994. An information memorandum was issued in May 1995, and the sale agreements were signed in November.[136]

12.2.6 *Other elements*

How did the remaining elements of British Rail fit into the new structure of April 1994? We have already seen (pp. 321, 337) that in preparation for privatisation the Channel Tunnel ventures EPS and Union Railways were to become government-owned companies. The management of the transfer of EPS was made the responsibility of a new Board member, Jim Butler of KPMG Peat Marwick, a past member of the Serpell Committee in the early 1980s. Appointed in March 1994, he succeeded Palmer as Chairman of EPS in April, and the business passed into government hands in the following month. Union Railways followed somewhat later, in April 1995.[137] The Board's Central Services portfolio remained as a significant group of activities, acquiring some additional elements when the passenger businesses were dismantled, notably the Train Engineering Service Units (TESCOs). Here, too, the Secretary of State's preference was for an early transfer to the private-sector. An initial proposal, put up by George Buckley when Managing Director in November 1992, envisaged transfer of the core units as a single entity. However, the Board rejected this option. Given the heterogeneous nature and patchy performance of Central Services, the course of action likely to maximise sale proceeds was to embark on a programme of restructuring before disposing of the various components as individual businesses.[138] To facilitate the sale of these and other business, a Vendor Unit was established in April 1993, led by David Blake, former MD of the King's Cross Projects Group. Drawing on staff previously engaged on the stalled King's Cross redevelopment (see pp. 329–40), it was given the task of examining internal management bids for franchises and other elements of British Rail and progressing the sale of the non-core businesses. In its first year of operation it sold the Transmark consultancy business (to Sir William Halcrow & Partners), Meldon Quarry (to ECC Construction Materials), and the rolling stock of the Charter Train Unit (to Flying Scotsman Railways), and began work on sales elsewhere, notably of the BRML/Level 5 maintenance depots and BR Telecommunications.[139]

   The government had no plans to change the responsibility of the British Transport Police (BTP) for security and law and order on the railways. However, it was not immediately clear who would continue to employ and fund the force after privatisation. It was the Board's contention that the BTP should be employed by Railtrack and that the Police Committee should be appointed by either the Secretary of State for Transport or the Home Secretary. Of course, new arrangements would be needed if Railtrack were to be privatised. The government quickly accepted this view and attention was then directed towards the matter of funding, which proved more difficult to resolve.[140] Unfortunately, a lack of parliamentary time prevented the inclusion in the Railways Act of the necessary transfer arrangements, and so the Board continued to act as employer of the police.[141] This situation created a problem of jurisdiction from April 1994. The Railways Act involuntarily curtailed the jurisdictional powers of the BTP, and it was also necessary to establish agreements with Railtrack and the new operators concerning the employment of BTP services. The DTp hastily prepared a new scheme for the police, and the Transport Police (Jurisdiction) Act of 1994 passed through its main stages in both Commons and Lords in one day—21 and 24 March respectively, apparently the only measure to do so since the Official Secrets Act of 1911. The Act, with its attendant Order, provided the mechanism for licensed operators to contract for BTP services. However, the legislation did not apply to operators such as EPS and London Underground which did not require a licence, and although these operators reached agreement with the BTP there was clearly some inconsistency in the jurisdiction initially provided for the post-privatisation railway.[142]

12.2.7 *Regulation*

The regulatory regime provided numerous challenges. Britain's railways were certainly no stranger to the process; indeed the private-sector companies had been heavily regulated, with the 'visible hand' of the state affecting most areas of the business as early as 1900 and notably in the inter-war period.[143] However, the architects of the regulatory apparatus of the 1990s encountered all the perennial problems surrounding control of the railways, notably that of reconciling public service objectives, particularly for passengers, with commercial ones, a situation which surfaced in the 1900s, when the industry sought to restructure itself out of its financial difficulties, again in the 1930s, when the railway companies asked for a 'Square Deal', and once more after the War, when railway managers had to cope with the post-1947 framework. The lessons of all this railway history were that future regulation would not be a straightforward matter, particularly since policy makers were, like their predecessors in the 1960s and 1970s, anxious to preserve not only the commercial but also the loss-making elements of rail transport, a stance which contrasted sharply with the way in which the other major public sector loss-maker, British Coal, was handled. In consequence the new regime had to wrestle with the conflict between the reality of loss-making activities and the search for a genuinely competitive and therefore fragmented structure, which meant that it was necessarily enmeshed with access and franchising issues. At the same time, there were justifiable doubts as to whether the industry could be privatised *in toto*. Thus, the new regulatory regime was put in place *before* the industry was fully disposed of, and was expected to evolve with the privatisation process, a situation which contrasted with experience elsewhere in the British privatisation programme.[144]

In these circumstances, the scope of regulation was largely determined by the nature of railway privatisation itself. The new regime had to embrace the relationship between Railtrack and the rest of the industry (and access charging in particular), the franchising process for passenger services, and functions previously executed by the Board, such as the maintenance of network benefits. Prior to the White Paper, it was envisaged that there would be a single body responsible for the twin functions of industry regulation and franchising. However, both the Board and the Treasury expressed concerns about this proposal because of the dangers of creating serious conflicts of interest. When *New Opportunities* was published, the government stated that there would be *two* institutions: a franchising authority; and a rail regulator.[145] At this time the basic relationships between the key players had still to be determined, and discussions on regulation were dependent upon the progress made elsewhere, notably in the protracted debates on access and franchising.[146] Shadow regulators were appointed by the Secretary of State as 'special advisers' in January 1993, just before the Railways Bill was published. The newcomers were recruited from outside the railway industry. Roger Salmon, a merchant banker with Rothschild who had been involved in progressing a number of privatisations, notably gas and water, became the Franchising Director designate. John Swift, QC was a lawyer specialising in competition law who had advised on several high-profile takeover battles. A man with abundant experience of the railways as a long-distance commuter, he became Rail Regulator designate. Most utility regulators were appointed once the structure had crystallised; for Salmon and Swift there was still much to be decided about their precise roles, both with the disaggregated railway and with each other. Before their five-year appointments were confirmed, in November and December 1993 respectively following the passage of the Railways Bill, the regulators had to rely on staff seconded from British Rail, notably Chris Stokes, Charles Brown, and John Rhodes, and therefore ran some risks of regulatory capture.[147]

Responding to Privatisation, 1981–97

How did the Board view the issue of regulation? There is certainly evidence of disquiet at the scale and complexity of what was being proposed. In December 1992 Reid informed MacGregor that there was likely to be 'inherent tension between an independent regulator on the one hand and compliance with your own objectives ... on the other'. He suggested that Railtrack remain outside the regulatory arena until it was privatised, and that regulation be confined to the facility charges for the franchised network, that is, the 'point at which activities transfer to the private sector'. Jerram followed this up by writing to Swift in February 1993 to plead the case for simplification, pointing out the virtues of railway *deregulation* in the United States following the Staggers Railroad Act of 1976. The Board's fears were shared by the Commons Transport Committee, which recommended that Railtrack and the Franchising Authority be merged into a single Rail Authority. Such suggestions were firmly rejected by MacGregor, who told Reid that 'regulation could not conceivably be an optional extra'.[148]

After the appointment of Salmon and Swift there could be only a short period of planning and preparation before the new railway structure came into effect on 1 April 1994. The two regulatory authorities, established as statutory bodies and known as the Office of Passenger Rail Franchising (OPRAF) and the Office of the Rail Regulator (ORR), derived their powers both from the Railways Act and from guidance documents issued by the Secretary of State. The Act stipulated that both regulators be subject to departmental guidance. The Director of Passenger Rail Franchising was required to exercise his functions so as to fulfil the Secretary of State's objectives in relation to passenger rail services. This requirement took the form of a 39-paragraph document entitled 'Objectives, Instructions and Guidance' (OIG), issued in March 1994. The Rail Regulator was intended to function with more independence. Nevertheless, in the initial phase, to the end of 1996, he too was required to take into account guidance from the Minister. This was set out in a letter dated 31 March 1994.[149]

The basic roles and responsibilities of the two bodies were as follows. The Rail Regulator was given a wide range of duties, many of which were shared with the Secretary of State. They were reminiscent of the conflicting objectives of 'economy' and 'public interest' inserted into the 1947 Transport Act when the railways were first nationalised. Thus Swift was expected to protect the interests of users, promote the use of the railway network, and promote efficiency, economy, and competition in the provision of railway services, and at the same time 'to have regard' to the financial position of the Franchising Director and the financial requirements of operators. Specific functions were also identified. The first of these was the regulation of access to the track, stations, and depots. Although, as we have seen, the initial access agreements, signed prior to 2 April 1994, did not fall within the remit of the Regulator, it was the government's intention that they be replaced by renegotiated agreements approved by the Regulator during 1994/5. In addition, Swift was given responsibility as International Rail Regulator for international access rights. Second, the Regulator granted and enforced a range of licences, relating to the network as a whole, trains, stations, and depots. The licences laid out conditions of compliance and were a requirement for operating railway assets. Third, it was the Regulator's duty, alongside the Director-General of Fair Trading, to enforce domestic competition law, preventing monopoly abuse and anti-competitive behaviour. In addition, he was to review the provision of railway services and assess closure proposals. Swift also funded and sponsored new statutory consultative organisations, the existing watchdogs of CTCC and regional TUCCs having been replaced (on 1 April 1994) by a Central Rail Users' Consultative Committee (CRUCC) and regionally based Rail Users' Consultative Committees (RUCCs) with strengthened responsibilities, including the authority to consider fares and levels of service.[150] The main functions of the Franchising Director were to negotiate, award, and monitor passenger franchises. There was much to be decided here, since prior to April 1994 the efforts of Whitehall and British Rail had concentrated upon the establishment of Railtrack. Nevertheless, in the OIG document Salmon was set the objective of securing a franchising regime 'as soon as reasonably practicable'. He too was given '1947-type' objectives: to secure an 'overall improvement' in the railways' passenger services, encourage 'efficiency and economy' in the provision of such services, and 'promote the use and cost-effective development of the railway network'. Salmon's Office also assumed responsibility for making subsidy payments, previously paid as the PSO, and for receiving payments from any profitable franchises.[151]

It is clear from both commentators and the actors themselves that there were concerns about the nature of the regulatory apparatus which had been erected. The first related to the independence of the two bodies and their continuing relationship with the Secretary of State, who of course remained the banker for the subsidised railway. At the outset Swift expressed some qualms about the extent of his independence. He was constrained in two ways. First, the various licences were granted under the terms of a General Authority issued by the Secretary of State; second, he was subject to the latter's 'guidance' until 31 December 1996. Such elements were unprecedented in British privatisation. In fact, the precise wording of the guidance, with the Regulator required only 'to take into account' the Minister's views, gave Swift some room for manoeuvre. The Franchising Director's instructions were more explicit about how the work should be conducted, and in these circumstances it was scarcely surprising that he encountered more difficulty in his relations with Marsham Street, a situation exacerbated by Salmon's penchant for ignoring civil service etiquette.[152]

It was also evident that the two bodies were going to be very different animals. This emerged, for example, in a debate over the requirements for the provision of information in the licences for the new train operating companies (TOCs). In January 1994 Reid had told MacGregor that he could not accept that the Regulator should have *direct* access to the information systems of licence holders. The Franchising Director concurred with the Board and identified an underlying difference of perspective between the two officers. He noted that while the Regulator saw TOCs as regulated utilities, which should be subject to the same licence information provisions as a regional electricity company or British Gas, they were also to be commercial entities akin to Holiday Inns or Budget Rent-a-Car, working within a franchise agreement. If they made excess profits then that was their reward for risk taking. Salmon felt that prospective franchisees would be deterred by the prospect of exposure to regulation in the manner in which utilities were treated. He also pointed out that franchisees would also require reassurance on the dangers of 'double jeopardy', that is, that an agreement with the Franchising Director might be contradicted by the requirements of the Regulator. The Department steered a middle course between the views of the two regulators.[153] In fact, Swift was keenly aware, at an early stage of the debate, of the dangers of 'regulatory risk', and in particular the need to handle areas of dual responsibility with care.[154]

The inherent contradiction between the concept of franchising and that of open access has already been emphasised. Since one of the Regulator's functions was to promote competition, he was placed in potential conflict with his counterpart, whose primary task was to sell franchises. Swift has recalled that he raised the issue at his first meeting with the DTp, with the reply passed down through the hierarchy of uncomfortable civil servants.[155] The eventual solution was to moderate competition in the early stages of the process. The Regulator duly proposed that 'no significant' competitive new entry be allowed before 31 March 1999, and that 'substantial restrictions' should remain for a further three years.[156]

In some areas, the dual regime was overlapping, messy, and confusing. Shared and sometimes blurred responsibilities were evident in relation to the interests of passengers, for example with ticketing, station information, retailing, and complaints.[157] In the formative stages of policy making, it was unclear who the 'consumer's champion' would be. The arguments revolved around the crucial matter of the need to preserve network benefits—through-ticketing and inter-availability, discount cards, warrants and passes, and published timetable information.[158] The early view of the Department was that in broad terms the market should be allowed to determine provision, though there were elements (such as through-tickets and revenue allocation) where co-operation between operators would be expected.[159] However, the possible threat to the maintenance of such facilities provided the opponents of privatisation with a strong card. MacGregor was ostensibly forced to make appropriate concessions in the Bill, although these probably owed something at least to skilful parliamentary management. By the end of 1993 the Secretary of State had also announced that interavailability, and therefore common pricing, would normally be a requirement of the franchise agreements.[160] There were ramifications for wider policy in the impact of ticket availability on competition and the profitability of future franchises. An early indication of this occurred when Gatwick Express was launched as a shadow franchise in October 1993. Here the Board was instructed to introduce price competition between Gatwick Express and Network SouthEast, both of whom ran trains from Victoria to Gatwick, and differential pricing and marketing were applied.[161] The move created anxiety within both the CTCC and the media and provided a concrete example of the complexities which privatisation would bring along with the promised benefits. Furthermore, the assurances on common pricing excluded discounted fares, and thus did nothing to dispel consumer fears that the price and conditions attached to these popular tickets would change when private operators took over from British Rail.[162]

There were also some gaps in the regulatory arena. There was no strong central responsibility for strategic planning, Railfreight, the ROSCOs, and the BRIS/ Railtrack relationship. These elements were left for a subsequent, Labour government to address. As matters stood in April 1994, it remained to be seen how this hastily concocted edifice would function in the future.

12.2.8 *Safety*

The final component of the new structure was railway safety. As we have seen (pp. 344–5), the Board had responded to the Clapham accident by transforming its approach to safety management, and it was clearly essential that this new culture was assimilated within the privatised industry. The White Paper had stated that the government would establish a framework which would 'guarantee that the necessary safety performance is maintained and observed across the railway'. MacGregor asked the Health and Safety Commission to produce a report and the resulting document, *Ensuring Safety on Britain's Railways*, was published as a consultation document in January 1993. Initially the Board seemed far from happy with the proposals, which envisaged a hierarchy of responsibilities from the Health and Safety Executive (HSE) to Railtrack and the operators, and its concerns were presented forcefully during the drafting stages. In November 1992 Rayner, the Board member responsible for safety, expressed forthright views to both the HSE and the Department. In a letter entitled 'Ensuring Safety on Britain's Railways', he argued that responsibility should not be disaggregated in the new structure, nor should it rest with Railtrack in areas where it lacked the necessary authority. He was also unhappy with the proposal that safety validation be 'cascaded' from the HSE to Railtrack and then to the operators; in his view, it was best handled by an independent party. Rayner's criticisms were followed up by Reid, who told the Secretary of State that responsibility for safety should remain with the Board until the new organisations were firmly established; thereafter responsibility should pass to a single, industry-wide body, thus retaining the value of an overall 'directing mind'.[163] Nevertheless, *Ensuring Safety* laid the foundations for the new safety regime, and following reassurances about the need to equip Railtrack with the necessary powers to conduct validations effectively, the proposals were fully accepted by the government and endorsed by the Board in January 1993.[164] Rayner, giving evidence to the Commons Transport Committee, stated that there was no reason to believe that the new structure would be less safe. However, it was clear that it had not been modified in the way the Board had suggested, and he was therefore anxious to point out that it would require 'meticulous care and a lot of attention'.[165]

At the heart of the new arrangements was the concept of the safety case, a statement of the way in which safety would be handled. The procedure was enforced through the Railway (Safety Case) Regulations of 1994. All users of the railway were required to have a case validated by Railtrack in its role as infrastructure controller. Railtrack's own safety case was in turn to be validated by the HSE. A more controversial element was the location of Rayner's Group Standards and Safety Directorate, which had its origins in the OfQ reorganisation and had identified some 20,000 standards and procedures (4,000 of which were considered mandatory operational and engineering requirements). The consultation document rehearsed the possibilities, and appeared to favour the establishment of an independent standards body. However, the decision was quickly taken to transfer the Directorate to Railtrack as a ring-fenced activity. When this was effected in April 1994, Rayner fulfilled the same responsibilities as Director, Safety & Standards for Railtrack, which replaced the Board as the 'directing mind' for safety.[166]

Edmonds, Railtrack's first Chief Executive, has expressed the view that the new arrangements worked well, particularly the cascading system of validation. On the other hand, the subsequent series of accidents—Southall, Paddington, and Hatfield—have placed post-privatisation safety under the microscope. In this context we should point out that despite the Board's qualms about added complexity, it fully supported the mechanisms followed in 1993–4.

12.3 Managing change, 1992–4

Thus far, the new structure has been considered against the background of fluid policy formulation. However, equally important from the Board's perspective was the actual restructuring necessary to meet the government's policy directives and the impact this would have on British Rail staff at all levels. It was the most complex and politically charged reorganisation that the Board had ever undertaken. It was also carried out to an imposed timetable.

How was the process to April 1994 managed? On the bridge, the Board and Board Executive received regular reports on progress, and in addition a number of high-level groups were established. There were informal bodies such as the 1994 Group and special-purpose meetings such as those of the Transitional Committee, but the pivotal role was played by the BRB Committee on Restructuring, which met from January 1993 to March 1994. Its initial members—Reid, Horton, Welsby, Edmonds, Allen, Cameron, and Dixon—all had to declare that they had no interest in any franchise proposal or acquisition of any part of the Board's business. The committee took all the key restructuring decisions relating to Railtrack, the franchises, units to be sold, and units to be formed within BR. It also approved all senior appointments.[167] The work of the committee was underpinned by the appointment in March 1993 of Richard Goldson as Director, Restructuring. Goldson, who had cut his teeth on the management of the OfQ process, was essentially the project manager for privatisation. He was supported by a small team specialising in franchises, safety, contract development, IT systems, rolling stock, and infrastructure engineering.[168] A heavy burden also fell on BR's in-house lawyers, where Terence Jenner, the Assistant Solicitor, and a small team played a critical role in preparing the legal framework for the transfer schemes.[169]

A top priority was the staffing of the new Railtrack organisation. Total staff built up to 750 by March 1994, and on vesting day (1 April) the organisation expanded to nearly 11,000, 6,000 of whom were signalling and supervisory staff.[170] Of course, most senior managers had to be selected from among the existing Board personnel, although it was unclear which of them would be willing to join the new company. Nobody had any experience of running a track authority; operators were probably more interested in the possibility of MBOs; and BRIS appeared to be the natural future home for the engineers. However, for the more risk averse, a public sector corporation may have appeared to be a relatively safe haven, while it was clear that Railtrack would have major responsibilities in the privatising structure. The functional heads were found from a group of experienced managers, including David Allen (Controller, Finance), John Ellis (Production), Gil Howarth (Major Projects), Nigel Ogilvie (Civil Engineering), and Simon Osborne (Solicitor and Company Secretary).[171] Where there was a determination to recruit from outside the industry, difficulties emerged. Thus, at Board level it was some time before a finance director was found, the post remaining unfilled until July 1994 when Norman Broadhurst joined Railtrack from the engineering conglomerate VSEL. Outside the Board, it proved difficult to find an electrical engineer, and there was also a relative dearth of experienced engineers among the zonal directors. While all of them were found from within the railways, only five of the 10 managers had a civil engineering background.[172]

With the government's announcements on the shape of franchised services, the Board decided that all the train operating units, whether operating in shadow form or not, would be in place in April 1994. In consequence, at Headquarters passenger train operations were reorganised into two groupings, North & West, and South & East, each with an a Managing Director reporting to Welsby. This revised structure left the managing directors of the three existing passenger businesses without a role. The post of MD, North & West, was offered to Chris Green of InterCity, but he elected to go to Scotrail instead. Neither post presented the challenge of his former empire, and he left the industry in 1995 (though he has since returned as Chief Executive of Virgin Trains). Paul King, MD of Regional Railways, was then appointed to the North & West post, and John Nelson, MD of NSE, became MD of South & East.[173] At the same time applications were invited from senior executives for the posts of designate managing director of the shadow franchise and TOCs. Welsby made it clear that the appointees should have an aspiration to enter the private sector, either as an equity partner or as an employed director. Of course, there was a risk that neither would materialise and some encouragement was given to applicants by offering job-protection arrangements and promising staff development assistance, for example in the area of contract negotiation.[174] The 47 applicants for 24 posts were interviewed by Reid, Welsby, and Watkinson and the appointments were approved by the Committee on Restructuring in August 1993. All but one of the 19 existing passenger business unit directors moved to a Managing Director post in the new organisation (the exception being Cyril Bleasdale of Scotrail, who retired). This did not mean that there were no opportunities for others. The creation of additional operating companies allowed some younger managers to advance, for example Chris Tibbits (Cross-Country), Robert Mason (Gatwick), and Adrian Shooter (Chiltern).[175] With these people in post, the rest of the top management structure was developed for each company, including that for the freight businesses, led by Glyn Williams and Ian Brown.

The impending changes placed considerable strain upon the Board's personnel strategy. It was clear that there were potential conflicts in balancing the Board's need to retain knowledge in running the railways against allowing staff to explore possibilities within the private sector. While the government did not want the Board to bid for franchises, it was keen to encourage MBOs. There were challenges to the Board's continuing operations from both younger managers with ambition and experienced staff for whom the privatised railway held no attractions. In consequence, the Board needed to keep certain key people in post to manage the privatisation process, though in effect they would be working themselves out of a job. To overcome this a small number of senior executive staff were 'handcuffed' to the Board through special contracts with two-year notice periods and enhanced pension arrangements.[176] For the majority of railway staff the period was one of considerable uncertainty, compounded by the substantial reduction in jobs which accompanied the preparations for privatisation. In consultation with the trade unions, procedures based on managed placement rather than advertising were developed to manage the 'mass migration' of staff in April 1994 and limit the possibility of disenchanted staff leaving the industry and creating damaging shortages. However, the situation was very fluid in 1993–4, and Goldson expressed fears that recruitment from outside might be undertaken before the full extent of the remaining staff—'the lost tribe of Israel'—had been identified.[177]

Aside from job security, the protection of pensions and travel facilities was a major preoccupation of the Board and its staff. The White Paper had stated that the security of rights enjoyed by pensioners and members would not be undermined by privatisation.[178] This was a significant matter. There were over 341,000 members of the several pension funds, the largest of which was the British Rail Pension Scheme (BRPS), and the assets were valued, in December 1992, at £8.5 billion. Rumours and speculation did little to ease fears. In one instance, MacGregor was forced to write to newspapers to dispel stories that the fund was to be transferred to the Treasury.[179] Initial ideas were aired in the DTp's consultation document *Railway Pensions after Privatisation*, and the government's decisions on the issue were announced in May 1993. Contending with the technical nature of pensions provision was complicated by the fact that the industry was not to be privatised all at once and that the structure was to be so fragmentary. For employees, it was proposed that a joint industry scheme (JIS) would replace the current BRPS arrangements and offer benefits 'no less favourable than those in the existing scheme'. The consultation document had suggested two choices for railway pensioners: first, that a proportion of the BRPS assets be set aside as a closed fund, with pensioners dependent on the future performance of the fund for their security; second, that appropriate funds be transferred to a government-backed scheme, fully guaranteed to match changes in the Retail Price Index. When there was little support for the second option, MacGregor announced that a closed scheme would be set up.[180]

The Board remained deeply dissatisfied with the proposal. In July, Jerram reported that despite lengthy discussions, two important issues remained unresolved. The first related to the impact of moving to a closed fund for current pensioners. It was likely that with no new income coming in fund managers would necessarily become more cautious. In order to guard against this and other possible sources of deficiency, the split of the existing funds between employees and pensioners would have to be weighted in favour of the latter. The consequent reduction in the size of the initial JIS fund would therefore lead to increased contribution rates for both employer and employee. To resolve these problems, the Board wanted the government to provide a solvency guarantee for the closed fund.[181] The second sticking point concerned the 'indefeasible right'. The government had already conceded the Board's view that British Rail employees who were transferred involuntarily to the private sector should have the right to remain in the JIS for as long as they did not voluntarily leave the railway industry. This indefeasible right would hold if an employee was subsequently transferred to another employer, whether inside or outside the railway industry. MacGregor had apparently conceded the point in his May statement, but it subsequently emerged that the government's proposal applied only to employees who remained in the 'railway industry'. This clearly raised difficulties of definition, but there was also the possibility that employees might lose the right because their employer lost a railway contract.[182]

With pensions Reid was not willing to remain obedient to the directives of the government. In a letter to Patrick Brown he pointed out that while he had scrupulously maintained the position that issues of ownership, structure, and regulation were for government and Parliament to determine, the Board had a statutory duty to care for the interests of its employees and must have regard for the position of its pensioners. Its responsibilities in relation to pensioners were legally complex, but the view was taken that it was free to apply a 'properly exercised discretion', and this was interpreted as embracing intervention through parliamentary and public channels if satisfactory arrangements were not secured. The Pension Fund Trustees were also mobilised to lobby for improvements.[183] After a meeting between the government and Pension Trustees on 20 July 1993 agreement was reached in a Memorandum of Understanding, which promised that the government would provide an absolute solvency guarantee for RPI-linked payments from the fund, and that pensioners might benefit from up to 40 per cent of any actuarial surpluses generated. The timing allowed MacGregor to announce details of the agreement on the following day, when the House of Lords was due to debate pensions.[184] Discussion and amendments in the Lords, especially the support offered by Lords Peyton and Marsh, were a crucial element in maintaining pressure on the government and ensuring that the Railways Bill reflected the 'no less favourable' commitment given on pensions. Peyton, in particular, had been adamant that for the government to force an arrangement on pensioners which was 'uncertain and possibly prejudicial' was not acceptable.[185] Further debate, on the coverage of the 'indefeasible right' and the precise application of the Memorandum of Understanding, ensured that the issue remained a contested one until the Railways Act received the Royal Assent in November, and, indeed, beyond.[186]

Following the Royal Assent, a joint working party comprising representatives of the Pension Trustees, the Board, Railtrack, the Department, and professional advisers met to discuss the implementation of the new pension arrangements and agree the terms of the necessary Orders under the Act. Two statutory instruments came into force on 31 May 1994. The first established the joint industry scheme, known as the Railways Pension Scheme (RPS), and the second gave protection to those who were members and pensioners of the BRPS before the Railways Act came into force. The Orders contained a notable concession on the long-running debate on the indefeasible right. Ministers now agreed that employees could remain in the joint scheme even when changing jobs voluntarily.[187] A further Order transferred pension rights and assets to the new scheme on 1 October 1994; the pensioners' section was then closed to new members. Another complex and long-drawn-out element was thus resolved, with a much more favourable outcome than had been offered 18 months earlier.[188]

On the matter of concessionary travel, initial plans proposed to discriminate against staff of non-passenger operations, which attracted criticisms from British Rail. Reid warned MacGregor that all railway staff were expecting a 'cast iron safeguard', and asked the Secretary of State to 'look hard' at the issue, since the arrangements would be 'seen by staff as a signal of the Government's willingness to consider their real concerns'.[189] While appearing to many observers to be a perk, discounted travel was a vital component in the pay structure, particularly where commuting was required. Indeed, for many staff the economics of working in London would have been untenable without travel concessions.[190] The Department conceded the point, and promised a clause in the Railways Act empowering the Regulator to include 'appropriate conditions' in the passenger operating licences. On the other hand, Freeman, in replying to Reid, was by no means sure that all the new employees should obtain these facilities free.[191] The arguments dragged on for nearly a year, with Reid continuing to emphasise the importance of the issue and calling for statutory provision. Freeman deemed a statutory duty to be inappropriate, but the matter was finally resolved when the Franchising Director was given an explicit objective requiring him to secure the continuation of these facilities. For the non-passenger businesses the maintenance of the concessions involved the levying of a charge on the purchasers.[192]

12.4 Conclusion

What do the events of 1992–4 reveal? The Board and the majority of senior British Rail managers opposed the government's choice of model for railway privatisation. While some were hostile to privatisation *per se*, most would have been far happier to run with a private, but vertically integrated industry, since they believed that the final flowering of sector management under the OfQ reorganisation had produced the best organisational framework the Board had ever had. The period was consequently one of disequilibrium combined with frenetic activity. The appointments of Horton, Edmonds et al. symbolised the impending break-up of one of the world's most integrated railway systems, creating uncertainty and in some a sense of impending disaster. At the same time, privatisation itself was by no means certain. The strength of the opposition to the government's policies was apparent throughout the political spectrum (though momentum was lost with the sudden death of Robert Adley), and votes in both houses of Parliament were often uncomfortably close. Only with the introduction of the first passenger franchises in February 1996 did the die seem cast. On the whole the Board did not seek to exploit the political ambiguities around it. This was, as it had always been, a disciplined, obedient industry and, encouraged by the Chairman's numerous pronouncements, a group of key managers began a period of extremely hard work in an attempt to meet the series of imposed and tight deadlines. No one should underestimate the amount of midnight-oil burning that was undertaken.

It also emerged that here the government had embarked on a rather peculiar privatisation, distinct from that of BT, gas, water, or electricity. British Rail was a loss-making industry but unlike coal and steel one still regarded as strategically important. Consequently the government pursued a 'neutron bomb' policy, wishing to rid themselves of their responsibilities while leaving the financially fragile services intact. Unsurprisingly, then, there was a fair amount of confusion in the process. The difficulty of squaring the Treasury's desire to inject the disciplines of competition with the Department of Transport's determination to make the sell-off work bedevilled government policy making. This was of course but one example of the contradiction which often faced regulated utilities: that of achieving efficiency and profitability while satisfying public interest goals. For Britain's railways this tension was evident many times, for example in 1886–94, 1918–21, 1947, 1963, and 1968, but it was no less acute in the early 1990s. The demands of public policy making thus made it inevitable that privatisation would be at best partial, and that whether through regulation or subsidy the government would continue to play a major role in the railways' fortunes. At the same time the Board also exhibited its own contradictions. Reid, its Chairman, was torn between the desire to defend the integrity of the industry and the need to execute government policy. His statements often promised total obedience and yet were full of profound scepticism. Welsby, the Chief Executive, was another key player. It has been suggested that he was less than fully co-operative in assisting the government in its goals.[193] However, while he sometimes overdid the Cassandra-like prognostications, as policy making developed his reservations about many of the proposals were soundly based on a clear understanding of the economics of railway operating, something not always shared by the various government departments and their coterie of advisers and consultants. The facile prescriptions of many newcomers to the railway was bound to irritate. As John Swift has recalled, 'the structure that was prepared on the blackboard of Marsham Street . . . proved to be more complex, more difficult and more costly to implement than those textbook designers and blackboard designers thought in the first place'.[194] At the same time the new structure had its deficiencies, notably in relation to strategy and research.

It was clearly an achievement to set Railtrack up and prepare the ground for franchising and sales in little over a year and a half. The combination of determined ministers—MacGregor and Freeman in particular—and hard-working senior railway managers was critical to the process. While the achievements were considerable, the charged environment in which it all took place should not be ignored. A good indication of this can be found in the final exchanges between Reid and MacGregor as Vesting Day—1 April 1994—approached. On 31 March Reid wrote to his Secretary of State to review the work done and explain how the key activities were being handled under the new arrangements. He noted that the process of transfer had 'required remarkable commitment from managers throughout the industry' as they rose to the challenge of separating and validating the responsibilities for infrastructure and network operation from train operating. Division of the physical assets, he pointed out, had been 'a complex exercise of vast proportions'. MacGregor conceded that the effort had been 'enormous' and commended in particular the 'seamless transition to the new organisation and responsibilities'. However, it was almost two months before he saw fit to reply, on 27 May, a fact which did little to improve relations between the dispossessed and the new regime.[195]

Endgame

How well did Britain's nationalised railway industry perform over its last two decades? To what extent has our perspective shifted in the four years since the process of privatisation was completed in 1997? Judgements are inevitably influenced by recent events: the difficulties experienced by Railtrack after a series of accidents; concerns about continuing investment; consumer dissatisfaction with the fragmented nature of the industry; the intense spotlight of media attention; and a growing culture of blame when things go wrong. However, we must make our position clear. Too many critics of privatisation make the appeal to a somewhat hazy perception of the glorious or inglorious past of 'old British Rail', imprecise as to both time and place. Some look back with nostalgia; others, like Archie Norman, a former Board member, have no regrets at all, remembering the Board as symbolising 'all that was wrong with the railway'.[1] In this final chapter we summarise briefly the main steps in the privatisation of the railways after 1994, then evaluate the performance, warts and all, of public sector management over twenty years of significant change. Only then may we make a considered judgement of what was gained, and what was lost, in the years 1994–7.

13.1 The 'great railway bazaar'

From April 1994 British Rail effectively ceased to exist as an integrated public sector operator. All attention was focused upon the sale of the assets assembled for privatisation. The Board continued to provide railway services until each business was sold. With one exception, that of Railfreight Distribution (RfD), this was achieved by April 1997. The need to obtain clearance from the European

Commission for the sale of RfD meant that the last public sector service ran on 21 November 1997. During the period 1994–7 British Rail acted in essence as an agency for disposal to the franchisees and new owners. Prime responsibility for these tasks, which resembled those of a receiver, was given to a new chairman, John Welsby, who succeeded Bob Reid II in April 1995 (Table 13.1). Welsby combined the functions of Chairman and Chief Executive, as Bob Reid I had done less formally from 1983, but in very different circumstances. There was also a change of minister. John MacGregor, who had steered the privatisation frame-work through the parliamentary process, was replaced as Secretary of State for Transport by Dr Brian Mawhinney in July 1994. It fell to him, and his successor, Sir George Young, to preside over the politically delicate process of the sales themselves. The major element of policy making after MacGregor's departure was Mawhinney's decision to offer Railtrack to the private sector via a stock exchange flotation in May 1996.

Welsby's Board was at first a rather thin vehicle. The Chairman was supported by Christopher Campbell as Vice-Chairman, his particular brief being to sell off the non-passenger businesses. James Jerram stayed on as member for finance and planning. Paul Watkinson had joined the Board as member for personnel in 1994. Some strengthening was obviously required as the number of Board meetings increased. Tony Roche added engineering expertise from 1996—he had been Director of M&EE and subsequently Group Managing Director of Central Ser-vices. After Campbell reduced his commitment to two days a week in August 1996, Jerram became Vice-Chairman (from October). Two part-time members provided additional executive input. Kazia Kantor played a continuing role in the audit function, while Sir William Francis, a former President of the Institution of Civil Engineers, took a particular interest in the disposal of the infrastructure units.[2] Essentially the Board was required to fulfil the government's objectives for the sale of the several businesses. When this was completed, British Rail was left with only residual elements, chiefly non-operational property, the British Transport Police, and obligations under the Channel Tunnel's usage agreement.[3] It was left to the incoming Labour government of 1997 to breathe a residuary BRB into new life. John Prescott, Deputy Prime Minister and Secretary of State for the Environment, Transport and the Regions, was committed to 'an inte-grated transport policy contributing to environmental goals', but the privatisa-tion structure had created a planning void. In August 1997 he asked the Board to provide a formal advisory role within this remit, which also demanded 'more effective use of our railway system'. After Sir Alastair Morton had been ap-pointed Chairman in April 1999, the Board was effectively merged with the Office of Passenger Rail Franchising to form the Shadow Strategic Rail Author-ity. The new body was required to act as the principal regulator, taking responsi-bility for passenger franchises, freight and track access grants, and consumer protection, and to bring forward proposals for railway investment. Its full status was secured in February 2001, after the passage of the Transport Act 2000.[4]

Table 13.1 The British Railways Board, 1 April 1995–30 November 1997

	Age[†]	Salary[‡]	Date of appt	Date of resignation	Background
Chairman and Chief Executive					
John Welsby, CBE	56	£180,000	Apr. 1995 (Nov. 1987)	Mar. 1999	Civil service; railways
Vice-Chairman					
Christopher Campbell, CBE[*]	59	£85,725	Feb. 1994	Sep. 1997	Retailing (Debenhams); shipbuilding (British Shipbuilders)
Full-time members					
James Jerram[**]	55	£89,760	Jan. 1991	Dec. 2000	Finance/computing (ICL, SEMA)
Tony Roche	51	£142,140	Apr. 1996	Aug. 1998	Railways
Paul Watkinson	54	£125,000	Oct. 1994	Jan. 1999	Railways
Part-time members					
Peter Allen	64	£7,560	July 1991	June 1997	Steel (British Steel)
Javaid Aziz	42	£7,560	Aug. 1993	Aug. 1996	Computing/software (IBM UK; Silicon Graphics)
James Butler	66	£7,560	Mar. 1994	Nov. 1996	Accounting (Peat Marwick); Camelot
Kenneth Dixon	65	£7,560	Aug. 1990	July 1997	Food manuf. (Rowntree); Bass, Legal & General
Sir William Francis	68	£15,570	Mar. 1994	June 1997	Construction (Tarmac; Trafalgar House)
Kazia Kantor	45	£31,140	June 1987	June 1999	Finance (Inchcape, HMV, Aegis, Grand Met)
William Watson	57	£7,560	July 1994	June 1997	Insurance (Alexander & Alexander)

[†] At 1 April 1995.
[‡] For year 1 April 1995–31 March 1996 (Roche, 15 April 1996), excluding London Allowance and performance-related bonus payments.
[*] Part-time from 1 August 1996.
[**] Vice-Chairman from 17 October 1996.

The details of the disposal and early record of privatised railways, very much a contemporary obsession, lie outside the remit of this book. The activities of Railtrack, the operating companies, ROSCOs, and the regulators have been fully chronicled in both the national and railway press, and have attracted analysis from academics, transport professionals, and others engaged in the process.[5] The principal landmarks were as follows. In 1995 the first two passenger franchises, South West Trains and Great Western Trains, were awarded, and the major maintenance depots were sold, along with the parcels businesses Red Star and Rail Express Systems, British Rail Telecommunications, train catering, and a number of engineering and infrastructure support businesses (the most valuable being Signalling Control UK). In 1996, the busiest year, the BRIS maintenance and track renewal companies were sold, as were the ROSCOs, and the three core freight companies, which were acquired by Wisconsin Central's English Welsh & Scottish Railway (EWS). The first passenger franchises began operations (in February), 11 more franchises were awarded, and more service activities were disposed of, notably Interlogic and BR Research. All 25 passenger rail franchises had been awarded by March 1997, and the final part of the jigsaw, Railfreight Distribution, was sold to EWS in November. Altogether some 115 sales, franchises, and other disposals were effected. The Board realised £876 million in sales proceeds, producing a profit over asset value of £258 million. Government sales are excluded from this calculation (Appendix L, Tables L.1 and L.2).[6]

Of course, the process was not without delays, argument, and media complaints about errors of judgement, the latter fuelled by generous portions of hindsight. Many, if not all, are well known to aficionados of rail privatisation. However, we must make reference to specific areas of concern. First, the aspirations of the Treasury and Department of Transport for greater levels of on-rail competition did not always materialise. After all the agonising about the number of freight companies required (see pp. 416–18), Young was forced to accept the financial logic of selling the three core freight companies to a single purchaser, EWS, which also bought Rail Express Systems and RfD.[7] Second, the Board had always maintained that the timetable for privatisation was an extremely tight one. The failure to settle the passenger franchises within the agreed timescale was a very visible example of the difficulties. The objectives for the Franchising Director, set in April 1994, were to award the first six franchises by the end of 1995 and to ensure that at least 51 per cent of British Rail's passenger services were provided by new operators by 1 April 1996. However, the complexity of the contractual arrangements provided a considerable challenge, and the objectives were not met until April and October 1996 respectively.[8] There were also embarrassments. In February 1996, for example, the Franchising Director was forced to abandon the award of the London Tilbury & Southend franchise, after allegations of ticketing irregularities by the preferred bidder, an MBO.[9] The minimum level of train services required under the franchise agreements, specified in the Passenger Service Requirement (PSR), also caused a furore in 1995.

Endgame, 1994–7

The Highland Regional Council pursued legal action to save the Euston–Fort William sleeper service, and the union-supported lobby group 'Save Our Railways' won a judicial review of the conditions for the first franchises. The review found the initial PSRs to have been set too low, necessitating a change in the wording of the Franchising Director's objectives and narrowing the freedom of action of the new operators. Finally, there were some awkward negotiations with Strathclyde PTE which threatened to jeopardise the letting of the Scotrail franchise. Intended to be one of the first to be awarded, it was not completed until 31 March 1997.[10] This said, it was no mean achievement for the Franchising Director, first Roger Salmon, and following his resignation, John O'Brien, to complete the franchising process before the May 1997 election.

Considerable debate was stimulated by the allegation that some assets were sold off far too cheaply, a common complaint in Britain's experience of privatisation. Here, the ROSCOs attracted particular attention. Transferred to government ownership for nil consideration in 1995, they were sold in early 1996 for £1,743 million, at a time when there was much anxiety about future prospects. Within months the press were claiming that the price should have been higher after Porterbrook was sold again in December for £298 million more than its purchase price of £528 million. Writing in *Modern Railways*, Alan Williams found the sale 'shocking, disgraceful and scandalous':

Shocking, because the Government told us that the whole point of breaking up our railway system was to introduce competition and allow market forces to get to work, yet less than six months later, the re-integration has begun—at taxpayers' expense. Disgraceful, because Porterbrook has ordered no new trains... yet has been able to sell essentially exactly what it bought at a profit of £400 [*sic*] million... And scandalous, because that £400 million... could have bought an entire fleet of new TGV-style trains for the West Coast main line.[11]

By December 1997 all three businesses had been sold on for £2,652 million, indicating a 'loss' to the Treasury of some £900 million. The Commons Public Accounts Committee was heavily critical of the Department of Transport. It suggested that the Department, by failing to manage the sale satisfactorily, had enabled a number of BR managers to become millionaires and risked discrediting the entire privatisation process. The National Audit Office reckoned that the discounted value of the income streams forgone was some £760 million higher than the sale price.[12] Last, but certainly not least, the determination to float Railtrack in May 1996 came earlier than expected. The intention here was to prevent an opposition government from pursuing a U-turn with privatisation and at the same time to generate income for the Treasury.[13] It certainly narrowed the options available to the incoming Labour administration of 1997, since, as the Board pointed out in a brief to John Prescott in May 1997, it had been expected that government influence over the railway would be exercised through the ownership of Railtrack. As it stood, there were 'no powers for Ministers to determine the development of infrastructure in any direct sense'.[14] Here too, the market initially placed a much higher value on the shares than did the government. Floated at £3.90 a share, Railtrack was valued at £16.05 in October 1998, a four-fold increase in only 2½ years. The 'added value' was even greater with the BRIS companies, acquired by Jarvis, Balfour Beatty, and Amec, among others, and with BR Research, bought by AEA Technology. Labour threats of re-nationalisation may have played their part in discouraging initial interest. However, it seems likely that the value of privatised British Rail had increased by around £11 billion by the autumn of 1998.[15] Time will tell how far this enhanced value can be maintained. There are clearly many doubts. The adversarial stance adopted by Railtrack managers on their severance from 'old BR' dismayed many in the railway industry and made them gloomy about future prospects. The government's decision to establish the new company in the private sector, and to sell British Rail's infrastructure maintenance capability to separate private-sector firms, produced elements which have distinguished the British model from infrastructure separation undertaken in other countries (for example in Sweden), and have proved problematic. Railtrack operates rather like the absentee landlord of an office block, who collects rents but undertakes no property services directly; outside contractors are employed to undertake emergency repairs when tenants complain. This is a caricature of course, but there is more than a grain on truth in it.[16] Nor could it be argued that the move to 'privatisation' has had an immediate effect in reducing the level of government financial support. In fact, for various reasons—principally, the building in of profits for the various corporate players, leasing charges, and the move to current cost (MEAV) depreciation—the total support level jumped from about £1.1 billion in 1993/4 to nearly £2 billion in the following year.[17]

Less publicised perhaps were the financial arrangements which helped to ensure the success of some of the sales. For example, the handling of accumulating cash balances during the sale of the maintenance depots in 1994–5—these increased from £1 million to £17 million but were not reflected in sale prices—elicited criticism from the National Audit Office. In 1996, when Freightliner was bought by an MBO, the purchase of this problematic business was facilitated by the government's agreement to pay track access charges estimated at £75 million over five years.[18] The disposal of the last business, RfD, was even more generous. This was another substantial loss-maker. The Board had already made a provision in the 1995/6 accounts of £500 million, to write off the Channel Tunnel freight assets and meet the cost of the minimum usage charge payable to Eurotunnel for access to the Tunnel until November 2006. The sale of the business to EWS carried with it a Board commitment to make net payments of up to £242 million over eight years, the major element of which was the undertaking to pay up to £168 million in usage charges until April 2005.[19]

For the Franchising Director the challenge was to dispose of the operations at fair and realistic prices while building in a steady reduction in the level of subsidy.

Endgame, 1994–7

In the first four rounds of franchising the Board tried to bid, in accordance with the amendment inserted into the 1993 Act, but the Director ruled this out, feeling that 'there would be a very dodgy market if the dominant incumbent had been bidding'.[20] From the Board's perspective there was a distinct possibility that in the absence of satisfactory tenders from the private sector it would be left as an operator by default, and consequently it wished to bid on a commercial basis. However, the initial franchises were agreed on relatively generous terms, there was no shortage of interest from private parties, and the Board therefore decided not to bid for the remaining franchises. Nevertheless, anxieties remained. By November 1996 it was clear that some of the more recent tenders had been very aggressive, for example for Thames Trains and South Wales & West, and inside British Rail doubts were expressed as to the longer-term viability of some of the franchises given the very demanding targets they had been set, with built-in reductions in regulated fares ('RPI − X') and subsidy, and tighter service requirements.[21] Doubts of this kind remain a concern. Private operators have yet to experience depressed trading conditions, though recently traffic has been severely disrupted following the Hatfield accident of October 2000, and some of the franchises, for example Virgin Cross Country, Northern Spirit, Wales & West, and First North Western, have already encountered very real financial problems.[22]

Whatever the debates about the value of British Rail assets, the selling prices, and subsequent market values, there is no doubt that in 1994–7 railway operating performance was affected by the distractions created by privatisation and, in particular, by the government's decision to accelerate the flotation of Railtrack. Successive chairmen made this clear to the Department of Transport. In November 1994, for example, Bob Reid II wrote candidly to Brian Mawhinney:

Performance has declined since April. One of the main reasons has been that managers have not been free to concentrate on making the complex new organisational arrangements work…The finances of the industry are in disarray. After successful efforts over the years to strengthen financial discipline, it is utterly disconcerting that, over seven months into the year, we do not have a settled financial regime…If an early privatisation of Railtrack is contemplated then I have serious reservations about the practicality of achieving that in addition to the programme we are currently seeking to achieve.

Mawhinney conceded that the task confronting British Rail was 'massive', but could not accept Reid's view of Railtrack's privatisation. The company, he believed, had 'made a determined start to establish itself as a viable business, and I have no doubt that the objective of privatisation has acted as a spur on its management and staff'.[23] Welsby expressed similar concerns later on, stating publicly in his annual report for 1995/6 that the pressure on many key managers had been 'intense'. A deterioration in the quality of passenger service provided was certainly evident in 1994/5, compounded by the effects of the signal workers' strike, and tensions in the relationship with Railtrack. The punctuality and reliability statistics revealed that 63 of the 102 measures had exhibited a deterioration.[24] The results were also mixed in the following year, with 53 of 118 measures indicating a poorer performance than in 1994/5. Subsequent improvements were in large measure attributable to the acquired experience of managers in working with the new disaggregated structure, though the recovery proved to be short-lived.[25] Enthusiasts of privatisation who use the transitional period 1994–7 as the benchmark against which to judge the effectiveness of the new regime are clearly being unfair. Nor should we be influenced by more emotive appeals. British Rail had no difficulty in winning plaudits from its shareholder and banker. Thus, John MacGregor, having received the Board's report and accounts for 1993/4, made a particular note of the operating profit; the impressive reduction in operating costs; 'the very substantial improvement in the supported sectors, enabling investment to be maintained at high levels while reducing the need for grant'; and the continuation of an impressive safety record. He told Reid: 'You and your staff are to be congratulated on this excellent performance, especially as it has been achieved at a time of such major change'. In the more difficult year 1994/5 Mawhinney was more circumspect, but two years later Young, his attention drawn by John Welsby to a quotation critical of BR in a Sunday newspaper, was quick to point out that the railway 'was an industry full of talented and committed people'.[26]

13.2 A 'golden age'?

Given the almost universal dissatisfaction with Britain's privatised railway structure, several commentators view the period of Bob Reid I's chairmanship, 1983–90, as something of a 'golden age' in modern railway operating. Roger Ford of *Modern Railways*, and Chris Green, Chief Executive of Virgin Trains, are but two proponents of this view.[27] If the 1970s were rather dismal, and our opening chapters certainly document this, then the mid–late 1980s were much brighter. The Thatcher governments set the industry clear objectives, and the Board transmitted these to managers through the 'business-led' approach of sector management. InterCity met its objective of breaking even (though not without some accounting adjustments), and government support fell sharply to historically low levels, levels which were also much lower than those enjoyed by the railways of other European countries. Investment rose. For rail passengers the HSTs flourished, and the East Coast Main Line was electrified. The subsidised sectors, Provincial and Network SouthEast, experienced revived fortunes as identifiable brands, based on the acquisition of new rolling stock. Passenger traffic increased sharply, from 16.9 billion passenger-miles in 1982 to 21.3 billion in 1988/9, an increase of 26 per cent. This impressive growth, evidence that British

Endgame, 1994–7

Rail did not confine itself to managing decline, was in many ways the product of a long boom. However, the recent increase in traffic (up by about 33 per cent from 1993/4 to 1999/2000) may also be attributed to economic prosperity, and contemporary applause for the achievement of the private operators in this regard should clearly be placed in context.[28] Last, but not least, there was an authority and purpose in an integrated railway led by a strong manager. We need only contrast the way in which Bob Reid immediately accepted full responsibility for the Clapham accident in 1988 with the more contemporary panic, evasion, and hand-wringing.

On the other hand, there were clearly some negative elements in the 'golden age'. Railway charges for both passenger and freight services were comparatively high, again both historically and in comparison with continental European railways. While comparatively inelastic traffics were retained, the period saw much shedding of freight, something which has concerned environmentalists. Railway investment was not as high as some of the railways' more enthusiastic supporters claimed, a fact evident from Figure 9.1. And in any case, some of the increase in spending, for example on rolling stock, was made possible by once-and-for-all sales of surplus property. Nor were investing levels impressive when compared with those made in France and Japan, for example. A study of railway infrastructure investment over the period 1987–91 revealed spending in France to be five times higher.[29] Yet it can scarcely be argued that privatisation has had the immediate effect of rectifying these shortcomings. Reports continue to point to high and rising level of fares, despite the application of 'RPI − X' formulae, compounded by the restrictions placed on 'walk-on' saver tickets.[30] And investment fell sharply during the privatisation period, from 1992/3 to 1995/6, accompanied by Roger Ford's irritating (to ministers) reference to the number of days (eventually 1,064) without a new rolling stock order.[31] Although spending has risen since then, investment remains a pressing concern, as is evident in the current aspirations of the Strategic Rail Authority, expressed in its *Strategic Agenda*.[32] In one thing, however, Reid I's railway set a real benchmark. In 1989/90 the central government's PSO support to railway operations was only £495 million, £655 million in 1997/8 prices, a level much lower than that required by the 'privatised' railway after 1997 (the OPRAF grant alone was £1,425 million in 1997/8). The contrast with the last PSO grant in 1993/4, when economic conditions were less favourable, was also sharp. The payment then was £930 million, £1,033 in 1997/8 prices; OPRAF's first support to the privatised railways was 38 per cent higher than this.[33] Of course, radical reductions are built into the franchise contracts and the subsidy is set to reach the 'Bob Reid I' benchmark in 2003–4. Nevertheless, at the time of writing the government subsidy to the railways is significantly higher than it was under British Rail. And this is quite apart from the cost of privatising the railways (at least £600 million),[34] and the opportunity cost of selling off assets more cheaply than the market valued them shortly afterwards.

13.3 How entrepreneurial was British Rail?

Privatisation has often been heralded as a device to free up managers bound by public sector bureaucracy and restraints. This may be so, particularly at the middle and lower levels of the hierarchy. However, recent events have questioned the extent of the change brought about by the new railway operators, and the cost of establishing this new 'enterprise' needs assessment too. What this book has shown is that there was no shortage either of competent and charismatic managers, or of innovation, notwithstanding the restraints imposed by Treasury and DTp. Sector management and 'Organising for Quality' (OfQ) did much to release young talent within the railway organisation, talent which might have been stifled by the more bureaucratic structure of regional management. Furthermore, recruitment from the universities was strong in the 1960s, bringing in an impressive group. While in the old railway culture much store was set by the value of the traffic apprenticeship, which created important management cliques such as the 'men from Whitemoor [marshalling] yard', the 1980s and 1990s were dominated by a gifted Oxbridge group, in which managers such as Bob Reid I, John Prideaux, John Edmonds, David Kirby, Chris Green, and behind the scenes, Roger Hillard, were noteworthy. Leaders like these were as dynamic as any in the private sector. For example, Reid revolutionised the way in which middle management handled costs and revenues, Prideaux took InterCity into profit, and Edmonds transformed British Rail's cinderella business, Provincial. Chris Green created the important brands Scotrail and Network SouthEast; in the face of gloom and under-funding, he introduced marketing innovations and encouraged a greater sense of pride in service provision, elements which still endure in the public mind after privatisation. BR research and engineering skills produced an impressive series of innovations. References we make to obvious failures, such as the APT, the difficulties of procurement, and the relationship with BREL, should not be allowed to diminish the strength of the contribution elsewhere. British Rail led the world in signalling technology—solid state interlocking, integrated electronic control centres, and the use of fibre optics—and portable ticketing equipment.[35] Furthermore, many public sector managers have either led MBOs or participated successfully in private-sector operations. British Rail provided £2.2 million in support of 67 MBO teams; of these 17 were successful as bidders.[36] The greater freedom of action provided by the privatised railway encouraged former British Rail managers quite as much as managers from the bus and engineering companies who entered the industry. The contribution of John Prideaux of Angel Trains, Chris Green of Virgin, Richard Brown and Richard Goldson at National Express, and Adrian Shooter of Chiltern, for example— surely nails the Thatcher-led myth that public sector managers were inferior or lacked enterprise. If the intention of privatisation was to inject some *new* managers into train operating, there has been precious little evidence of it.[37]

13. Privatisation: 'Invasion of the Train Snatchers', by Steve Bell, *Guardian*, 7 February 1997

13.4 Transforming the cosy railway culture?

There was more to British Rail than the entrepreneurial spirit of some of its managers, and we are not attempting to sweep some of the less attractive features of this public sector industry under the carpet. As this book has shown, for much of our period there were persistent difficulties with industrial relations, restrictive practices, a cautious approach to cost control, particularly from the engineers, and a somewhat cosy approach to procurement, particularly where the Board's subsidiary, BREL, was involved. But here too there was radical change. If the flexible rostering dispute of the early 1980s appeared to bring few tangible results it certainly symbolised the wresting of the initiative from the unions. Productivity gains in operating were delivered subsequently by Driver Only Operation, the establishment of the traincrew concept, and by numerous restructurings. The reduction in the workforce was very sharp, corporate numbers falling by 52 per cent from 250,000 at the end of 1973 to only 121,000 in March 1994. The selling of the subsidiary businesses contributed to this fall, but the number of staff working for the core rail business fell by 39 per cent over the same period, from 190,000 to 115,000, helping to produce the improvements in productivity which were particularly evident in the 1980s. Where the need for restructuring was firmly identified the Board pursued it vigorously. However, as we have also noted, confrontational industrial relations strategies did not always succeed, and managers were well aware that the operation of a 24-hour railway system required the experience, dedication, and co-operation of railway men and women. For the staff the last two decades of nationalised railways were years of substantial change, and promotional opportunities were often increased. But in many areas of the railway, both in white- and blue-collar work, a culture of stability was replaced by one of uncertainty, compounded by technological change, job losses, organisational instability, and the persistence of comparatively low pay rates and long working hours.

At management level too there has been cultural and organisational change. The emphasis on business-like operations, customer care, and effective cost control was not an invention of the privatised railway; and the move away from the old military-style mess culture of senior management also began in the 1980s. The various engineering departments, mechanical and electrical, civil, and signal and telecommunications, had often presented themselves as something of a closed world even to railway managers at Headquarters and in operating. But they too embraced the sector management concept and the monitoring of costs which gathered pace in the 1980s, and under OfQ they were integrated into the businesses. Unfortunately, this substantial experiment in change had so little time to prove its worth. We have also seen how both procurement and project management were transformed, notably in the pressing circumstances produced by the Channel Tunnel investments. Difficulties persisted, of course, but the way in which investment appraisal and completion certification were handled, for example, reveals a considerable advance by the early 1990s over practice twenty years before. The extent of this 'revolution' should not be exaggerated, of course. As we have seen, the railways remained an overwhelmingly male preserve, and many functions retained a strong whiff of conservatism. Yet enduring elements have a value, too. Where privatisation has threatened to erode the long-held sense of loyalty, dedication, and responsiveness to operating crises characteristic of many British Rail staff it must be a matter for regret.

13.5 Can the public sector manage large-scale investment?

This history has referred many times to the difficulties British Rail experienced in planning investment, procuring equipment, and containing project costs, and it is clear that the Treasury held a most jaundiced view of the capability of nationalised industry to manage large-scale projects. There is of course a fair amount of support for the Treasury's view. In the railway industry the failures and escalating cost of the Modernisation Plan of 1955 set the tone; the APT perpetuated it; and the burgeoning commitments of the Channel Tunnel gave rise to concern in the 1990s. But we must point out that not all of this should be laid at the door of the railway managers. Civil servants were equivocal too, for example about the APT, and many of the difficulties created by the Channel Tunnel project stemmed from political machinations and from the overblown expectations of the British regions that direct services would be viable. It is also true that elsewhere in the public sector there were numerous cases of exceeded budgets and disappointments, as is revealed by an examination of nuclear power, the Thames Barrier, the Millennium Dome, and much defence procurement. But it is also evident to business historians that investment is inherently risky for all enterprises, and companies such as Ford, ICI, and BP are no strangers to faulty investment appraisal, poor project management, and cost overruns. Nor should Treasury scorn be always taken at face value. Ministers with experience of business were often equally dismissive of Treasury officials who sought to second-guess the professionals, and allowed their anti-public sector sentiments to surface. In the view of one Secretary of State the Department was 'stuffed full of economic backseat drivers. None of them could run a bloody whelk-stall'. It is a fact that large railway projects are challenging affairs; they are certainly not comparable to erecting a factory in a greenfield site. Many successful schemes were undertaken in our period, notably the electrification of the East Coast Main Line and the Channel Tunnel works. They were managed with minimal disruption to day-to-day services, something which would be envied by today's operators faced with the disruption produced by the Hatfield accident. And for those who may begin to despair of public-private partnerships, we may turn to the shining example of redevelopment of Liverpool Street and Broad Street stations in London in the late 1980s. The long-held view that public sector managers are inferior beings has little foundation. And as the old adage has it, managers who work for Pilkingtons should not throw stones.

13.6 The 'visible hand' of government?

We have noted at several points in this history that the relationship with government was a frustrating one for railway managers, as it often was for civil servants and ministers on the other side. In Britain regulation of the railways has fluctuated between a policy of profit maximisation with strong social welfare constraints, evident from the 1840s to nationalisation in 1947, and one of traffic maximisation with severe financial constraints, evident during the period of public ownership (1948–97).[38] In the latter period regulation became synonymous with parsimony, in terms of both investment and subsidy to the fare-paying passenger, a situation which, whatever the economic arguments, does not obtain in Europe as a whole. All the contradictions of the government's role as shareholder, banker, and customer were reflected in the multi-layered interventions which it made. Privatisation gained support when it promised to take the railways out of the Treasury's control of cash and investment, a process which was both tedious and frustrating, particularly in periods of recession. The relatively low priority accorded by Whitehall to rail transport, in comparison with other calls on the public purse, including road transport, encouraged an emphasis on extracting value for money from the industry. When this approach resulted in the reduction of waste and feather-bedding, then it was clearly beneficial. However, when it encouraged railway managers to cut rather than cure, it had a negative effect on the demand for rail transport. The government's insistence that Railfreight should return profits at a time of investment restraint prompted managers to abandon traffic in the first half of the 1990s, a process which was damaging in environmental terms. Freed from some of the shackles of the government-railway relationship, the American firm, EWS, led by Ed Burkhardt (until July 1999), has succeeded in increasing traffic by 46 per cent since 1995/6. Nevertheless, the government has done little to skew the economics of freight haulage, which still favour road by a considerable margin. Furthermore, despite the intentions of government to refrain from intervention in detail once precise objectives had been given to the Board, the evidence shows that this kind of intervention continued, whether in relation to the annual pay round, the handling of labour disputes, the authorisation of investment projects, or the capping of fare increases. Unfortunately, escaping from the public sector has not been the straightforward matter some enthusiasts of privatisation believed it to be. In the frustrating 1970s and 1980s public sector managers were required to pass through numerous government hoops. But is it any different today? The work of the private track authority and private operators has been hamstrung by the several layers of regulation and intervention in the charging regime. Recent events, and notably the deterioration of service after the Hatfield accident, have reduced the level of trust in private-sector undertakings and increased the clamour for state control. Government intervention is still with us; only the hoops are different. On top of this, privatisation has added greatly to transaction costs. If the academic analyses of Ronald Coase, Alfred D. Chandler, Jr., and Oliver Williamson have any validity, then it is likely that we shall see the 'visible hand' of more integrated businesses or the reassertion of more extensive government control emerge to exploit the transactional economies of scale and scope which remain after the privatisation process. On the other hand, as Dieter Helm has noted, utilities such as gas, water, and telecommunications are actively pursuing the separation of functions, and a greater level of contracting out, and if the Conservatives' railway privatisation model has failed, there are currently serious doubts about the prospects for Labour's policy of integration and railway reinvigoration.[39]

13.7 Conclusion

We have seen much to commend in the way railways operated in the years 1974–94. Once a rather unwieldy, monolithic structure, British Rail provided comparatively safe, improving services, began to revolutionise marketing, and showed greater attention to customer care. Symbols of this change are numerous. They include the InterCity HST, Network SouthEast's livery, Liverpool Street Station, and the catering revolution begun by Prue Leith and Travellers Fare. This is not to say everything was wonderful; it clearly was not. The difficulties were all too evident when Richard Marsh handed over the baton to Peter Parker in 1976. Then there were deep-seated problems with industrial relations, low staff morale, and in Whitehall an attitude to railways of at best neglect, at worst contempt. Parker's period (1976–83) was difficult. His infectious enthusiasm was stretched to the limit at times, and his attempts to raise the profile of railways in the public policy arena backfired with the embarrassments of the Serpell Report. On the other hand, many of the radical initiatives began during his chairmanship: sector management; public-private partnership, which surfaced as a solution to the capital-starved subsidiary businesses; the Channel Tunnel; and the reassertion of authority over the trade unions. The balance sheet of Bob Reid I's period (1983–90) has already been set out, and it was clearly positive. His successor, Bob Reid II (1990–5), had a rougher ride. If his enthusiasm for railways and in particular new projects sometimes disconcerted ministers and civil servants, there was no doubting his commitment to the industry. No lover of rationalisation, he was at his best as a hands-on project manager. And the encouragement he gave to the transformation of British Rail's handling of safety was a particular achievement, though one which privatisation has served to unpick. Furthermore, we should remember that it was in his time that sector management reached its full flowering. 'Organising for Quality' may have had its detractors, but it offered Britain the best prospects of a more streamlined, customer-oriented, empowered organisation in an integrated form.

As privatisation develops, what has been lost organisationally (and possibly financially) becomes clearer. The railway industry had begun in a disaggregated manner in the 1820s and 1830s, but quickly coalesced to demonstrate the advantages of a network industry. The provision of safe and high-quality services, evident in the mid–late 1980s, was based on the establishment of firm hierarchical control and the setting of clear objectives. Many of the criticisms made by British Rail of political solutions for the industry in 1988–94 (set out in Chapters 11 and 12) remain highly pertinent. In the new world of the Strategic Rail Authority, experts are busy looking for new prescriptions. One thing is clear. British Rail's managers worked long and hard to produce their own organisational solution for the industry. Having introduced OfQ in 1992, they were required to dismantle it in 1992–4. In both cases the timescales were short. Comparisons with Humpty Dumpty are relevant. An integrated railway could be put back together again, and with the engineering units and franchises there has been some evidence of coalescence: National Express, for example, currently operates nine franchises. However, the prospect of full integration seems rather remote. Instead the vexing and multifaceted relationship between government and the railways remains, as does the mix of profit-maximising and welfare-maximising objectives, and much of the 'risk' will continue to reside with the State if a given level of service is required by society. As two insiders, John Welsby and Alan Nichols, have pointed out: 'The fundamental problems of government having to choose how much it wishes to spend on supporting the passenger railway, and what are its priorities for the use of that support, have not been addressed by privatisation and will surely return'.[40] Was it really worth all the trouble and risk to dismantle what the two Bob Reids erected?

Appendices

Mike Anson

The constant price series are calculated using the GDP deflator at market prices contained in Office for National Statistics, *Economic Trends Annual Supplement 1999 edition* (1999). Unless otherwise indicated, '1984' refers to a 12-month calendar year and '1984/5' to a 12-month financial year commencing April 1984.

Appendix A Financial results

Table A.1 PSO payments, 1975–93/4
(£m., in current and constant prices)

Year	Central government	Local government (PTEs, etc.)	Central and local government	PSO share of total passenger income (%)
Current prices				
1975	303.7	20.4	324.1	
1976	294.1	25.0	319.1	
1977	330.5	33.0	363.5	
1978	394.4	39.7	434.1	
1979	475.9	46.6	522.5	
1980	577.1	56.5	633.6	
1981	748.9	61.3	810.2	
1982	817.3	69.9	887.2	
1983	855.6	77.8	933.4	
1984/5[a]	1,069.5	103.2	1,172.7	
1984/5	—	—	942.1	
1985/6	819.1	76.8	895.9	
1986/7	713.9	72.5	786.4	
1987/8	726.2	77.6	803.8	
1988/9	530.6	75.9	606.5	
1989/90	495.5	91.3	586.8	
1990/1	599.2	100.7	699.9	
1991/2	892.0	115.8	1,007.8	
1992/3	1,154.8	103.1	1,257.9	
1993/4	930.0	105.4	1,035.4	
Constant 1979 prices				
1975	509.6	34.2	543.8	43
1976	427.6	36.3	464.0	39
1977	422.7	42.2	464.9	38
1978	451.2	45.4	496.6	38
1979	475.9	46.6	522.5	40
Constant 1989/90 prices				
1979	1,019.4	99.8	1,119.2	40
1980	1,034.7	101.3	1,136.0	40
1981	1,208.0	98.9	1,306.9	44
1982	1,226.0	104.8	1,330.8	49

Appendix A

Table A.1 (continued)

Year	Central government	Local government (PTEs, etc.)	Central and local government	PSO share of total passenger income (%)
1983	1,218.4	110.8	1,329.2	45
1984/5[a]	1,411.7	136.2	1,547.9	43
1984/5	—	—	1,243.6	44
1985/6	1,034.5	97.0	1,131.5	40
1986/7	863.1	87.7	950.8	36
1987/8	836.6	89.4	926.0	33
1988/9	566.7	81.1	647.7	25
1989/90	495.5	91.3	586.8	24
Constant 1993/4 prices				
1989/90	600.1	110.6	710.6	24
1990/1	683.1	114.8	797.9	26
1991/2	956.2	124.1	1,080.4	32
1992/3	1,187.7	106.0	1,293.1	37
1993/4	930.0	105.4	1,035.4	32

Source: BRB, *R&A 1975–1993/4*; DTp, *Transport Statistics Great Britain*.

[a] 15 months.

Note: the data take account of adjustments for earlier years, and include the special replacement allowances (from 1987/8 capital renewal provision), i.e. 1978 £50.0 m., 1979 £56.9 m., 1980 £69.0 m., 1981 £80.3 m., 1982 £87.6 m., 1983 £93.0 m., 1984/5 (15 months) £125.0 m., 1985/6 £104.0 m., 1986/7 £109.0 m., 1987/8 £123.4 m., 1988/9 £74.5 m., 1989/90 £78.9 m., 1990/1 £95.0 m., 1991/2 £208.9 m. They exclude payments for maintenance of level crossings, which were credited to operating costs, viz., 1975 £9.0 m., 1976 £10.1 m., 1977 £10.5 m., 1978 £10.8 m., 1979 £12.9 m., 1980 £15.2 m., 1981 £17.4 m., 1982 £17.5 m., 1983 £20.4 m., 1984/5 (15 months) £24.9 m., 1985/6 £18.2 m., 1986/7 £18.6 m., 1987/8 £22.0 m., 1987/8 £20.9 m., 1988/9 £20.9 m., 1989/90 £22.3 m., 1990/1 £26.1 m., 1991/2 £27.2 m., 1992/3 £29.0 m., 1993/4 £32.1 m. In 1988/9 the method of calculating the PSO was changed, reducing the amount claimable by £33.0 m. The change took the form of a reduction in interest paid on borrowings. In addition, £64.5 m. was deducted to cover overpayment in 1987/8, but this is not shown here. Other charges as extraordinary items are also excluded.

From 1991/2 a change was made in the treatment of capital renewal provision (in earlier years this was included in turnover with an equivalent amount as depreciation charged to P&L account). On the new basis the grant was made up as follows:

	Grant included in turnover	Grant as exceptional item	Capital grant
1991/2	£406.5 m.	£1.3 m.	£484.2 m
1992/3	£504.5 m.	£96.4 m.[*]	£553.9 m.
1993/4	£439.6 m.	£43.9 m.	£446.5 m.

[*] A special voluntary severance grant, included in turnover when restated in following year.

From 1992/3 all capital grants were credited to deferred income. Sums were released to P&L account over the economic lives of the assets: 1992/3 £191.8 m., 1993/4 £172.0 m. EC grants, etc. are excluded. They amounted to: 1991/2 £40.9 m., 1992/3 £100.0 m., and 1993/4 £100.4 m.

Table A.2 Group operating surplus/loss and profit and loss, 1971–93/4 (£m., in current and constant prices)

Year	Group operating surplus/ loss before interest, &c.	Group profit and loss after interest, tax, and exceptional items	
		Before extraordinary items	After extraordinary items
Current prices			
1971	30.2	−15.4	−15.4
1972	24.9	−26.2	−26.2
1973	5.7	−51.6	−51.6
1974	−85.9	−157.8	−157.8
1975	−28.3	−60.8	5.5
1976	13.7	−29.9	5.3
1977	68.4	29.7	27.0
1978	54.0	6.5	52.2
1979	54.4	1.4	12.5
1980	−18.7	−76.9	−59.8
1981	26.6	−39.7	−14.5
1982	−97.5	−175.0	−136.8
1983	80.2	11.3	67.4
1984/5[a]	−261.8	−311.2	−317.8
1984/5	−231.6	−288.1	−301.3
1985/6	56.6	−11.5	65.3
1986/7	69.9	2.4	−82.6
1987/8	108.5	47.3	290.9
1988/9	107.0	18.2	304.3
1989/90	−26.4	−46.4	269.8
Constant 1979 prices			
1971	85.9	−43.8	−43.8
1972	65.4	−68.9	−68.9
1973	13.9	−126.0	−126.0
1974	−182.8	−335.8	−335.8
1975	−47.5	−102.0	9.2
1976	19.9	−43.5	7.7
1977	87.5	38.0	34.5
1978	61.8	7.4	59.7
1979	54.4	1.4	12.5
Constant 1989/90 prices			
1979	116.5	3.0	26.8
1980	−33.5	−137.9	−107.2
1981	42.9	−64.0	−23.4
1982	−146.2	−262.5	−205.2
1983	114.2	16.1	96.0

Table A.2 (continued)

Year	Group operating surplus/ loss before interest, &c.	Group profit and loss after interest, tax, and exceptional items	
		Before extraordinary items	After extraordinary items
1984/5[a]	−345.6	−410.8	−410.5
1984/5	−305.7	−380.3	−397.7
1985/6	71.5	−14.5	82.5
1986/7	84.5	2.9	−99.9
1987/8	125.0	54.5	335.1
1988/9	114.3	19.4	325.0
1989/90	−26.4	−46.4	269.8

Pre-Financial Reporting Standard No. 3 reporting

Year	Operating profit/ loss before other income, interest, tax, &c.	Operating profit/ loss after other income	Exceptional items	Group profit/loss after exceptional items, interest, tax, &c.
Current prices				
1988/9	107.0	113.6	221.6	304.3
1989/90	−26.4	−22.6	316.2	269.8
1990/1	−42.4	−38.7	82.2	−10.9
1991/2	−101.4	−94.8	31.4	−144.7
1991/2[b]	18.7	25.3	31.4	−24.6
1992/3[b]	13.4	18.4	−86.3	−163.9
Constant 1993/4 prices				
1988/9	138.5	147.0	286.8	393.8
1989/90	−32.0	−27.4	382.9	326.7
1990/1	−48.3	−44.1	93.7	−12.4
1991/2	−108.7	−101.6	33.7	−155.1
1991/2[b]	20.0	27.1	33.7	−26.4
1992/3[b]	13.8	18.9	−88.7	−168.5

Table A.2 (continued)

Post-Financial Reporting Standard No. 3 reporting

Year	Operating profit/loss before exceptional items	Exceptional items	Operating profit/loss after exceptional Items	Profit/loss on disposal of fixed assets	Group profit/ loss before interest, tax, &c.	Group profit/loss after interest, tax, &c.
Current prices						
1989/90	—	—	−21.6	69.8	48.2	24.4
1990/1	—	—	−46.4	5.8	−40.6	−95.0
1991/2	—	—	−97.7	−2.1	−99.8	−181.1
1991/2[b]	—	—	22.4	−2.1	20.3	−61.0
1992/3[b]	18.4	−112.7	−94.3	6.9	−87.4	−183.4
1993/4[b]	157.8	−134.8	23.0	37.8	12.5	−108.4
Constant 1993/4 prices						
1989/90	—	—	−26.2	84.5	58.4	29.5
1990/1	—	—	−52.9	6.6	−46.3	−108.3
1991/2	—	—	−104.7	−2.3	−107.0	−194.1
1991/2[b]	—	—	24.0	−2.3	21.8	−65.4
1992/3[b]	18.9	−115.8	−96.9	7.1	−89.8	−188.5
1993/4[b]	157.8	−134.8	23.0	37.8	12.5	−108.4[c]

Source: BRB, *R&A 1971–93/94*.

[a] 15 months.
[b] Restated in line with 1992/3 accounting changes (revenue investment capitalised, &c.).
[c] Including restructuring costs of £48.3 m.

Revised data used where available. Note, for example, the restatement of extraordinary surpluses which resulted from a revised method of treating non-operational property had the effect of improving the original surplus/loss figures for 1982–84/5: 1982 by £19.4 m., 1983 by £55.7 m., and 1984/5 by £118.6 m.

Appendix B Investment

Table B.1 Gross investment, 1970–93/4 (£m., in current prices)

Year	Track renewals	Signalling and track rationalisation	Electrification	Total infrastructure
1970	34	15	3	59
1971	37	23	9	72
1972	39	27	13	88
1973	42	27	12	96
1974	51	24	11	106
1975	61	43	11	121
1976	70	38	9	120
1977	82	47	7	153
1978	98	56	11	190
1979	101	68	14	200
1980	122	74	15	239
1981	132	78	15	243
1982	120	74	8	221
1983	160	86	14	294
1984	156	101	23	303
1985/6	138	78	64	309
1986/7	132	66	74	284
1987/8	150	92	76	361
1988/9	138	102	48	333
1989/90	152	91	56	363
1990/1	122	141	59	356
1991/2	162	189	60	437
1992/3	188	214	40	386
1993/4	151	242	30	382

Source: BRB IA 20-8-5.

Note: Figures may not sum due to rounding. Gross investment includes investment charged to capital and revenue account, pre-payments, and deferred interest. Track renewals includes continuous welded rail. Infrastructure includes telecommunications, and plant and equipment. Total rail includes 'other' rail. From 1990/1, 'Other non-rail' is included elsewhere (1990/1, £40 m.; 1991/2, £44 m.; 1992/3, £54 m.). Total 'group' investment is 'rail' plus subsidiaries (including investment in enterprises sold during the period). From 1988/9 Channel Tunnel = 'New' railway, Rail + Other non-rail = 'Existing' railway.

Traction and rolling stock	Terminals and depots	Total rail	Other non-rail	Channel Tunnel	Total group
16	7	84	11	—	96
18	8	99	9	—	108
18	7	115	12	—	127
21	7	128	17	—	145
28	12	159	15	—	175
60	22	211	21	—	232
87	22	232	39	—	270
86	21	265	32	—	296
75	20	293	51	—	344
93	30	331	70	—	401
125	35	406	52	—	459
109	35	395	46	—	441
102	25	357	33	—	389
65	33	402	33	—	435
59	44	426	36	—	462
89	92	525	25	—	550
83	124	527	16	—	543
154	153	668	25	—	693
207	157	697	26	6	728
231	203	845	19	28	892
303	191	869	0	178	1,047
353	152	968	0	350	1,318
407	122	955	0	521	1,476
161	52	650	0	515	1,165

Appendix B

Table B.2 Gross investment, 1974–93/4 (£m., in constant prices)

Year	Track renewals	Signalling and track rationalisation	Electrification	Total infrastructure
Constant 1979 prices				
1970	107	46	8	184
1971	104	66	24	204
1972	102	72	35	231
1973	104	65	30	233
1974	109	51	23	226
1975	102	71	19	204
1976	102	56	13	175
1977	105	60	9	196
1978	113	65	13	217
1979	101	68	14	200
Constant 1989/90 prices				
1979	216	146	30	429
1980	219	132	28	428
1981	213	126	24	392
1982	180	111	12	332
1983	228	122	20	419
1984	206	134	30	400
1985/6	174	99	81	390
1986/7	160	80	89	343
1987/8	173	106	88	416
1988/9	147	109	51	356
1989/90	152	91	56	363
Constant 1993/4 prices				
1988/89	175	130	61	424
1989/90	181	108	67	432
1990/1	135	156	65	394
1991/2	171	198	63	459
1992/3	193	219	41	394
1993/4	151	242	30	382

Traction and rolling stock	Terminals and depots	Total rail	Other non-rail	Channel Tunnel	Total group
49	21	261	35	—	296
52	22	282	26	—	308
47	20	303	32	—	334
52	17	313	41	—	354
59	26	339	32	—	371
101	36	354	36	—	389
127	31	337	56	—	393
110	27	338	41	—	379
86	23	335	58	—	393
93	30	331	70	—	401
199	64	709	151	—	860
223	63	729	94	—	823
176	57	636	75	—	711
152	37	535	49	—	584
93	47	572	47	—	619
78	58	562	48	—	610
113	116	663	32	—	695
100	150	637	19	—	656
177	176	770	29	—	799
221	168	744	28	6	778
231	203	845	19	28	891
263	200	887	33	7	926
275	242	1,007	23	33	1,062
335	211	962	0	197	1,159
371	160	1,016	0	367	1,384
416	125	976	0	532	1,508
161	52	650	0	515	1,165

Appendix B

Table B.3 Long-run group investment, 1970–93/4 (£m., in constant 1993/4 prices)

Year	Track renewals	Signalling and track rationalisation	Electrification	Total infrastructure
1970	269	119	24	466
1971	268	167	65	522
1972	261	181	87	590
1973	262	168	68	598
1974	277	130	59	576
1975	261	182	49	520
1976	260	143	32	447
1977	268	153	24	500
1978	287	165	33	555
1979	258	174	36	511
1980	261	158	33	509
1981	254	150	28	467
1982	214	132	14	395
1983	271	146	24	499
1984	245	159	36	477
1985/6	208	117	96	465
1986/7	190	95	107	409
1987/8	206	126	104	496
1988/9	175	130	61	430
1989/90	181	108	67	450
1990/1	135	156	65	438
1991/2	171	198	63	532
1992/3	193	219	41	493
1993/4	151	242	30	487

Source: BRB IA 20–8–5.

Note: Figures include expenditure on Channel Tunnel.

Traction and rolling stock	Terminals and depots	Total rail	Other non-rail	Total Group
126	55	664	87	751
131	58	718	65	783
121	47	771	80	851
131	44	798	106	904
150	67	863	83	946
257	92	904	91	995
324	80	861	144	1,005
282	69	864	104	968
219	58	855	148	1,003
237	76	844	180	1,024
266	75	867	112	979
209	68	759	89	848
182	44	638	59	697
110	56	682	56	738
93	70	670	57	727
134	138	790	38	828
119	179	759	23	782
211	210	917	34	952
263	200	887	33	926
275	242	1,039	23	1,062
389	246	1,159	0	1,159
480	261	1,385	0	1,384
573	261	1,509	0	1,508
340	123	1,165	0	1,165

Appendix C Productivity and performance indicators

Table C.1 British Rail productivity measures, 1974–93/4

Passenger

Year	Passenger-miles per loaded pass. train-mile			Passenger-miles per coaching traction-hour	Trains arriving on time less than 5 mins late (%)
1974	103	—	—	2,043	91
1975	98	—	—	1,958	91
1976	93	—	—	1,903	93
1977	94	—	—	1,957	93
1978	97	—	—	2,054	91
1979	102	—	—	2,187	87
1980	97	—	—	—	89
1981	95	—	—	—	90
1982	96	—	—	—	88
1983	97	95	—	—	90
1984/5	—	95	—	—	90
1985/6	—	98	—	—	89
1986/7	—	99	100	—	90
1987/8	—	—	102	—	90
1988/9	—	—	—	—	—
1989/90	—	—	—	—	—
1990/1	—	—	94	—	—
1991/2	—	—	91	—	—
1992/3	—	—	91	—	—
1993/4	—	—	87	—	—

Table C.1 (continued)

PSO payments per passenger-mile (pence)

	Price levels				
	1975	1983	1987/8	1991/2	1993/4
1975	1.68	—	—	—	—
1976	1.61	—	—	—	—
1977	1.56	—	—	—	—
1978	1.41	—	—	—	—
1979	1.51	3.89	—	—	—
1980	—	4.00	—	—	—
1981	—	4.80	—	—	—
1982	—	5.52	—	—	—
1983	—	4.98	6.03	—	—
1984/5	—	—	6.20	—	—
1985/6	—	—	5.02	—	—
1986/7	—	—	4.10	—	—
1987/8	—	—	4.08	4.56	—
1988/9	—	—	—	4.84	—
1989/90	—	—	—	4.25	—
1990/1	—	—	—	4.61	—
1991/2	—	—	—	5.83	3.61
1992/3	—	—	—	—	4.30
1993/4	—	—	—	—	3.36

Appendix C

Table C.1 (continued)

Freight

Year	Net tonne-miles per loaded freight train-mile			Net tonne-miles per freight traction-hour	Average wagon-load (tonnes)	Revenue per wagon (£, 1975 prices)
1974	267	—	—	1,723	20.55	1,012
1975	285	—	—	1,779	21.54	1,042
1976	307	—	—	2,064	22.47	1,181
1977	324	—	—	2,119	22.99	1,275
1978	331	—	—	2,178	24.52	1,357
1979	343	—	—	2,247	25.20	1,446
1980	338	—	—	—	25.83	—
1981	358	—	—	—	27.17	—
1982	366	—	—	—	30.31	—
1983	377	288	—	—	—	—
1984/5	—	267	301	—	—	—
1985/6	—	—	312	—	—	—
1986/7	—	—	331	—	—	—
1987/8	—	—	346	—	—	—

Table C.1 (continued)

Global

Year	Loaded[a] train-miles per traincrew member		Output per employee		Revenue per £1,000 paybill costs[b]				
					Including workshops		Excluding workshops		
1974	6,230	—	—	—	—	1,083	—	—	—
1975	6,377	—	100[c]	—	—	1,049	—	—	—
1976	6,471	—	99	—	—	1,163	—	—	—
1977	6,602	—	102	—	—	1,294	—	—	—
1978	6,647	—	105	—	—	1,346	—	—	—
1979	6,536	7,099	107	1,521[d]	—	1,297	1,537	—	—
1980	6,700	7,244	103	1,570	—	1,237	1,465	—	—
1981	6,914	7,478	106	1,597	—	1,200	1,398	—	—
1982	6,414[e]	6,947	114	1,495	—	1,085	1,262	—	—
1983	—	7,898	—	1,686	—	—	1,402	—	—
1984/5[f]	—	7,880[g]	—	1,713[h]	—	—	1,245	—	—
1985/6	—	8,252	—	1,797	—	—	1,484	—	—
1986/7	—	8,564	—	1,835	—	—	1,510	—	—
1987/8	—	9,568	—	1,987	1,888	—	1,594	—	—
1988/9	—	10,485	—	—	2,040	—	1,672	2,110	—
1989/90	—	10,727	—	—	2,113	—	1,615	1,888	—
1990/1	—	10,961	—	—	2,115	—	1,550	1,610	—
1991/2	—	11,218	—	—	2,061	—	1,382	1,437	1,517
1992/3	—	11,994	—	—	1,927	—	—	—	1,406
1993/4	—	11,568	—	—	2,029	—	—	—	1,476

Source: BRB, *R&A 1974–94/5*.

[a] 'Train-miles' from 1983.
[b] Data subject to numerous adjustments.
[c] Weighted index of passenger-miles + freight net tonne-miles (1975 = 100).
[d] Train-miles.
[e] 7,074 after adjustment for strike action.
[f] 15 months.
[g] 8,045 after adjustment for strike action.
[h] 1,749 after adjustment for strike action.

Appendix D Passenger and freight traffic volumes and revenue

Table D.1 Passenger traffic volumes and revenue, 1952–96/7

Passenger volume (estimated '000m. passenger-miles)

Year	IC	LSE/NSE	PTE+OPS PROV/RR	Total
1952	—	—	—	20.5
1953	—	—	—	20.6
1967	6.6	8.3	3.1	18.1
1972	6.6	8.1	3.4	18.1
1973	6.9	8.3	3.4	18.5
1974	7.2	8.6	3.4	19.2
1975	7.2	8.3	3.3	18.8
1976	6.2	8.5	3.0	17.7
1977	6.8	8.4	3.0	18.2
1978	7.3	8.7	3.0	19.1
1979	7.6	8.9	3.4	19.9
1980	7.5	8.1	3.2	18.8
1981	7.3	8.0	3.2	18.5
1982	7.1	7.0	2.9	16.9
1983	7.6	7.8	2.9	18.3
1984/5[a]	—	—	—	22.6
1984/5	7.9	7.5	3.0	18.5
1985/6	7.9	8.1	2.9	18.8
1986/7	7.8	8.5	3.0	19.2
1987/8	8.3	9.0	3.3	20.6
1988/9	8.3	9.4	3.6	21.3
1989/90	8.0	9.4	3.5	20.9
1990/1	7.9	9.2	3.5	20.6
1991/2	7.6	8.9	3.4	19.9
1992/3	7.6	8.4	3.7	19.7
1993/4	—	—	—	18.9
1994/5	—	—	—	17.8
1995/6	—	—	—	18.6
1996/7	—	—	—	19.9

Table D.1 (continued)

Passenger revenue (£m.)

Year	IC	LSE	PTE+OPS	Total	Revenue per mile (pence)
Current prices					
1952	—	—	—	112	—
1967	72	81	27	180	—
1972	106	127	41	274	—
1973	115	140	42	297	—
1974	130	153	46	329	—
1975	174	188	67	429	—
1976	190	234	81	505	—
1977	233	270	90	593	—
1978	279	320	103	702	—
1979	317	360	123	800	—
1980	376	433	145	954	—
1981	382	487	154	1,023	—
Constant 1979 prices					
1952	—	—	—	667	3.25
1967	264	297	99	659	3.64
1972	279	334	108	720	3.98
1973	281	342	103	725	3.92
1974	277	326	98	700	3.65
1975	292	315	112	720	3.83
1976	276	340	118	734	4.15
1977	298	345	115	758	4.16
1978	319	366	118	803	4.20
1979	317	360	123	800	4.02
1980	315	363	121	799	4.25
1981	288	367	116	770	4.16

Source: BRB, *R&A 1952–81*; DTp/DETR, *TSGB*; BRB, *Facts and Figures* (1st edn, 1978, 2nd edn, 1980).

[a] 15 months.

The data are not strictly comparable since numerous adjustments were made to the series to reflect boundary changes, etc. Where available, post-1983 extrapolations used. From 1982 see sector operating results (Appendix E).

Appendix D

Table D.2 Freight traffic volumes and revenue, 1952–96/7

Freight carried (m. tonnes)

Year	Coal	Iron/Steel	Aggregates[a]	Oil	Total
1952	172.7	—	—	—	289.0
1953	—	—	—	—	294.0
1967	124.0	36.0	10.0	12.0	204.0
1972	89.4	31.7	14.2	21.6	177.3
1973	101.0	35.5	17.0	21.0	196.0
1974	88.0	31.0	17.4	18.9	175.6
1975	97.2	25.7	15.1	17.1	174.6
1976	97.0	29.5	13.2	16.7	176.4
1977	93.8	26.0	14.1	17.6	170.8
1978	94.0	24.7	15.4	17.2	170.5
1979	93.5	25.1	15.2	16.4	169.3
1980[b]	94.1	13.0	15.9	13.7	153.5
1981	95.2	18.2	13.8	12.3	154.2
1982	88.4	14.2	13.9	11.6	141.9
1983	87.9	15.9	15.6	10.8	145.1
1984/5[c]	14.5	10.5	15.8	9.8	65.2
1985/6	81.9	16.0	16.7	9.2	139.7
1986/7	77.2	17.3	18.1	9.8	138.4
1987/8	78.8	19.6	19.5	10.1	144.4
1988/9	79.2	20.6	22.9	10.8	149.5
1989/90	75.8	18.9	23.5	10.2	143.1
1990/1	74.7	18.0	20.1	10.0	138.2
1991/2	75.1	17.8	17.7	10.0	135.8
1992/3	67.9	15.9	15.8	9.5	122.4
1993/4	48.9	15.8	16.1	9.0	103.2
1994/5	42.5	16.9	16.8	8.1	97.3
1995/6	45.2	15.1	11.5	6.3	100.7
1996/7	52.2	—	—	—	101.7

Table D.2 (continued)

Freight traffic ('000m. tonne-miles)

Year	Coal	Iron/Steel	Aggregates[a]	Oil	Total
1952	—	—	—	—	22.8
1953	—	—	—	—	23.6
1967	—	—	—	—	13.8
1972	4.0	2.1	1.1	2.0	13.0
1973	4.5	2.4	1.3	2.0	14.3
1974	4.1	2.2	1.5	1.9	13.5
1975	4.5	1.9	1.3	1.5	13.0
1976	4.3	2.1	1.1	1.5	12.7
1977	4.3	1.8	1.2	1.7	12.6
1978	4.2	1.7	1.3	1.7	12.4
1979	4.2	1.8	1.4	1.6	12.4
1980[b]	4.0	1.1	1.5	1.4	10.9
1981	4.0	1.4	1.3	1.4	10.9
1982	3.5	1.2	1.3	1.4	9.9
1983	3.7	1.3	1.5	1.4	10.6
1984/5[c]	0.5	1.18	1.55	1.37	7.33
1985/6	3.11	1.30	1.55	1.24	9.94
1986/7	3.11	1.55	1.80	1.30	10.31
1987/8	2.86	1.67	1.80	1.24	10.87
1988/9	2.98	1.74	2.05	1.37	11.25
1989/90	2.86	1.55	1.99	1.30	10.38
1990/1	3.11	1.43	1.68	1.24	9.94
1991/2	3.11	1.49	1.55	1.24	9.51
1992/3	3.36	1.43	1.55	1.24	9.63
1993/4	2.42	1.30	1.43	1.18	8.58
1994/5	2.05	1.06	1.55	1.12	8.08
1995/6	2.24	1.06	1.43	1.12	8.26
1996/7	2.36	—	—	—	9.38

Appendix D

Table D.2 (continued)

Freight revenue (£m.)

Year	Current prices			Constant 1979 prices		
	Coal	Iron/Steel	Total	Coal	Iron/Steel	Total
1952	—	—	251	—	—	1,495
1972	77	34	183	202	89	481
1973	87	39	198	212	95	483
1974	91	39	205	194	83	436
1975	120	41	245	201	69	411
1976	152	57	307	221	83	446
1977	178	56	348	228	72	445
1978	192	59	384	220	67	439
1979	218	67	432	218	67	432
1980	248	47	460	208	39	385
1981	274	65	504	206	49	379

Revenue per tonne-mile (pence, constant 1979 prices)

1952	—	—	6.56
1972	5.05	4.24	3.70
1973	4.71	3.96	3.38
1974	4.73	3.77	3.23
1975	4.47	3.63	3.16
1976	5.14	3.95	3.51
1977	5.30	4.00	3.53
1978	5.24	3.94	3.54
1979	5.19	3.72	3.48
1980	5.20	3.54	3.53
1981	5.15	3.50	3.48

Source: BRB, *R&A 1952–96/7*; DTp, *TSGB*; BRB, *Facts and Figures*, 1978/80.

[a] 'Earths & stones' to 1982, 'Construction' from 1983.
[b] Affected by steel strike.
[c] Affected by miners' strike.

From 1982 see sector operating results (Appendix E).

Table D.3 Parcels traffic and revenue, 1972–87/8

Year	Traffic (m. tonnes)	Revenue (£m.)
1972	—	68.6
1973	1.93	73.8
1974	1.83	75.3
1975	1.72	87.7
1976	1.45	98.2
1977	1.31	109.6
1978	1.25	119.4
1979	1.23	130.8
1980	1.18	141.2
1981	0.95	119.4
1982	0.70	—
1983	0.90	—
1984/5	0.90	—
1985/6	0.70	—
1986/7	0.70	—
1987/8	0.70	—

Source: BRB, R&A 1972–87/8.

From 1982 see sector operating results (Appendix E).

Appendix E Sector operating results

Table E.1 Sector operating results, 1982–93/4 (£m., in current prices)

Year	InterCity			London and South East/ Network SouthEast		
	Turnover	Expenditure	Surplus/loss	Turnover	Expenditure	Surplus/loss
1982	350	546	−196	448	758	−310
1983	439	598	−159	546	794	−248
1984/5[a]	577	810	−233	722	1,026	−304
1984/5[a]	685	857	−172	737	1,063	−326
1985/6	613	731	−117	644	867	−223
1985/6	613	729	−116	644	858	−214
1986/7	658	757	−99	710	872	−162
1987/8	733	819	−86	805	975	−170
1988/9	803	746	57	892	1,030	−138
1989/90	833	787	46	930	1,068	−138
1989/90	833	777	56	930	1,056	−126
1990/1	851	801	50	998	1,153	−155
1990/1	892	842	50	998	1,098	−100
1991/2	897	895	2	1,044	1,226	−182
1991/2	897	806	91	1,044	1,063	−19
1992/3	889	824	65	1,069	1,115	−46
1993/4	897	799	98	1,115	1,043	71

Source: BRB, *R&A 1982–93/4*.

[a] 15 months.
[b] Trainload Freight from 1988/9.

Provincial/Regional Railways			Parcels		
Turnover	Expenditure	Surplus/loss	Turnover	Expenditure	Surplus/loss
136	625	−489	93	85	8
164	653	−489	115	99	16
208	817	−609	149	130	19
230	891	−661	150	135	15
209	713	−504	127	121	6
209	716	−507	127	124	3
224	698	−474	119	116	3
247	720	−473	120	127	−7
274	740	−466	126	138	−12
276	785	−509	120	136	−16
276	770	−494	120	133	−13
304	807	−503	116	142	−26
304	796	−492	116	142	−26
313	897	−584	102	136	−35
313	808	−495	102	134	−32
349	852	−503	89	112	−23
359	801	−443	78	93	−14

Table E.1 (continued)

Year	Railfreight/Trainload Freight[b]			Railfreight Distribution		
	Turnover	Expenditure	Surplus/loss	Turnover	Expenditure	Surplus/loss
1982	487	485	2	—	—	—
1983	529	521	8	—	—	—
1984/5[a]	408	689	−281	—	—	—
1984/5[a]	431	695	−264	—	—	—
1985/6	547	564	−17	—	—	—
1985/6	547	560	−13	—	—	—
1986/7	557	532	25	—	—	—
1987/8	555	511	44	—	—	—
1988/9	511	377	134	170	235	−65
1989/90	517	384	133	177	250	−73
1989/90	517	381	136	177	250	−73
1990/1	510	411	99	173	325	−152
1990/1	510	411	99	173	325	−152
1991/2	505	438	68	175	294	−119
1991/2	505	403	103	175	282	−108
1992/3	490	387	103	172	262	−90
1993/4	432	347	85	160	222	−62

Freightliner			Total rail business		
Turnover	Expenditure	Surplus/loss	Turnover	Expenditure	Surplus/loss
70	74	−4	1,584	2,573	−989
98	96	2	1,891	2,761	−870
126	124	2	2,190	3,596	−1,406
126	124	2	2,359	3,765	−1,406
106	108	−2	2,246	3,104	−857
105	111	−6	2,245	3,098	−853
105	111	−6	2,373	3,086	−713
98	104	−6	2,558	3,256	−698
—	—	—	2,776	3,266	−490
—	—	—	2,853	3,410	−557
—	—	—	2,853	3,367	−514
—	—	—	2,951	3,639	−687
—	—	—	2,992	3,614	−621
—	—	—	3,036	3,886	−850
—	—	—	3,036	3,496	−460
—	—	—	3,058	3,552	−494
—	—	—	3,041	3,305	−265

Appendix E

Table E.2 Sector operating results, 1982–93/4 (£m. in constant prices)

Year	InterCity			London and South East/Network SouthEast		
	Turnover	Expenditure	Surplus/loss	Turnover	Expenditure	Surplus/loss
Constant 1989/90 prices						
1982	525	819	−294	672	1,137	−465
1983	625	852	−226	778	1,131	−353
1984/5[a]	762	1,069	−308	953	1,354	−401
1984/5[a]	904	1,131	−227	973	1,403	−430
1985/6	774	923	−148	813	1,095	−282
1985/6	774	921	−147	813	1,084	−270
1986/7	796	915	−120	858	1,054	−196
1987/8	844	943	−99	927	1,123	−196
1988/9	858	797	61	953	1,100	−147
1989/90	833	787	46	930	1,068	−138
Constant 1993/4 prices						
1988/89	1,022	949	73	1,135	1,310	−175
1989/90	992	925	67	1,108	1,258	−150
1990/1	942	887	55	1,105	1,276	−172
1990/1	987	932	55	1,105	1,215	−111
1991/2	942	940	2	1,096	1,287	−191
1991/2	942	846	96	1,096	1,116	−20
1992/3	909	842	66	1,093	1,140	−47
1993/4	897	799	98	1,115	1,043	71

Source: BRB, *R&A 1982–93/4*.

[a] 15 months.
[b] Trainload Freight from 1988/9.

Provincial/Regional Railways			Parcels		
Turnover	Expenditure	Surplus/loss	Turnover	Expenditure	Surplus/loss
204	938	−734	140	128	12
234	930	−696	164	141	23
275	1,078	−804	197	172	25
304	1,176	−873	198	178	20
264	901	−637	160	153	8
264	904	−640	160	157	4
271	844	−573	144	140	4
285	829	−545	138	146	−8
293	790	−498	135	147	−13
276	785	−509	120	136	−16
349	941	−592	160	175	−16
329	917	−588	143	158	−15
337	893	−557	128	157	−29
337	881	−545	128	157	−29
329	941	−613	107	143	−39
329	848	−520	107	141	−34
357	871	−514	91	114	−23
359	801	−443	78	93	−14

Table E.2 (continued)

Year	Railfreight/Trainload Freight[b]			Railfreight Distribution		
	Turnover	Expenditure	Surplus/loss	Turnover	Expenditure	Surplus/loss
Constant 1989/90 prices						
1982	731	728	3	—	—	—
1983	753	742	11	—	—	—
1984/5[a]	539	909	−371	—	—	—
1984/5[a]	569	917	−348	—	—	—
1985/6	691	712	−21	—	—	—
1985/6	691	707	−16	—	—	—
1986/7	673	643	30	—	—	—
1987/8	639	589	51	—	—	—
1988/9	546	403	143	182	251	−69
1989/90	517	384	133	177	251	−73
Constant 1993/4 prices						
1988/9	650	480	170	216	298	−82
1989/90	616	454	162	211	298	−87
1990/1	564	455	109	191	360	−169
1990/1	564	455	109	191	360	−169
1991/2	531	460	71	184	309	−125
1991/2	531	423	108	184	296	−113
1992/3	501	396	105	176	268	−92
1993/4	432	347	85	160	222	−62

Freightliner/Railfreight Distribution			Total rail business		
Turnover	Expenditure	Surplus/loss	Turnover	Expenditure	Surplus/loss
105	111	−6	2,376	3,860	−1,484
140	137	3	2,693	3,932	−1,239
166	164	3	2,891	4,747	−1,856
166	164	3	3,114	4,970	−1,856
134	136	−3	2,837	3,920	−1,082
133	140	−8	2,835	3,913	−1,077
127	134	−7	2,869	3,731	−862
113	120	−7	2,947	3,751	−804
—	—	—	2,965	3,488	−523
—	—	—	2,853	3,410	−557
—	—	—	3,532	4,153	−622
—	—	—	3,398	4,010	−612
—	—	—	3,267	4,028	−761
—	—	—	3,312	4,001	−688
—	—	—	3,187	4,080	−892
—	—	—	3,187	3,671	−483
—	—	—	3,126	3,631	−505
—	—	—	3,041	3,305	−265

Appendix F Government financial controls and out-turns

Table F.1 Investment ceilings, allocations, and out-turns, 1970–9 (£m., in constant 1979 prices)

Year	DTp ceiling	BRB allocation	Allocation over ceiling (%)	Out-turn	Variation (out-turn over ceiling)	Variation (%)
Railway						
1970	237.6	243.5	2	238.9	1.2	1
1971	263.8	277.8	5	258.1	−5.7	−2
1972	282.5	308.8	9	282.0	−0.5	0
1973	345.5	401.2	16	294.0	−51.5	15
1974	339.2	431.6	27	320.5	−18.7	−6
1975	331.1	402.7	22	353.1	22.0	7
1976	335.4	355.8	6	306.2	−29.2	−9
1977	342.8	348.5	2	308.4	−34.4	−10
1978	336.3	380.0	13	306.1	−30.2	−9
1979	308.0	361.9	18	302.3	−5.7	−2
Averages						
1970–3	282.4	307.8	9	268.3	−14.1	−5
1974–9	332.1	380.1	14	316.1	−16.0	−5
1970–9	312.2	351.2	12	297.0	−15.3	−5

Appendix F

Table F.1 (cont.)

Year	DTp ceiling	BRB allocation	Allocation over ceiling (%)	Out-turn	Variation (out-turn over ceiling)	Variation (%)
Group						
1970	268.3	278.5	4	273.9	5.6	2
1971	303.6	320.4	6	284.3	−19.3	−6
1972	328.5	356.4	8	313.5	−15.0	−5
1973	398.0	452.0	14	335.0	−63.0	−16
1974	378.8	473.1	25	352.8	−26.0	−7
1975	376.0	451.5	20	388.8	12.8	3
1976	376.0	400.0	6	362.7	−13.4	−4
1977	387.5	398.2	3	349.2	−38.4	−10
1978	381.0	430.1	13	364.0	−16.9	−4
1979	380.0	446.8	18	372.8	−7.2	−2
Averages						
1970–3	324.6	351.8	8	301.7	−22.9	−7
1974–9	379.9	433.3	14	365.0	−14.8	−4
1970–9	357.8	400.7	12	339.7	−18.1	−5

Source: BRB IA 20–8–5.

486

Table F.2 External financing limit, 1980/1–93/4 (£m., in current and constant 1993/4 prices)

Year	Current prices				Constant prices (1980/1 = 100)		
	Initial	Revised	Requirement	+/–	Initial	Revised	Requirement
1980/1	750	790	790	0	100	100	100
1981/2	867	920	960	40	107	108	112
1982/3	950	923	848	–75	110	102	93
1983/4	960	953	811	–142	108	102	87
1984/5	936	930	1,045	115	100	94	106
1985/6	918	910	910	0	93	88	88
1986/7	771	784	777	–7	75	72	72
1987/8	751	630	591	–39	70	56	52
1988/9	753	641	375	–266	65	52	31
1989/90	415	635	673	38	33	49	51
1990/1	598	700	1,016	316	45	50	72
1991/2	1,522	1,522	1,446	–76	108	103	97
1992/3	2,041	2,096	2,064	–32	141	137	135
1993/4	1,495	1,495	1,461	–34	101	96	94

Source: BRB, *R&A 1980–93/4*; MMC reports on *NSE* (1987) and *Provincial* (1989).

Note: 1987/8 revised figure is based on adjustments due to ring-fencing of property sales at £150m. and deduction of European Development Fund Grants.

Appendix G Staff, pay settlements, rates and earnings, paybill costs

Table G.1 Staff numbers, 1973–94

Year	Railway					
	Drivers	Footplate	Guards	Traincrew	Station/yard	Conciliation
1973	20,341	27,839	12,242	40,081	34,876	108,545
1974	20,433	27,762	12,214	39,976	36,857	109,199
1975	19,929	26,770	11,998	38,763	37,601	106,737
1976	20,360	27,565	12,528	40,093	34,640	110,720
1977	20,044	26,644	11,965	38,609	33,192	106,690
1978	19,856	26,176	11,737	37,913	33,460	104,457
1979	19,874	26,144	11,884	38,028	33,649	104,813
1980	19,972	25,991	11,849	37,840	29,056	102,531
1981	19,377	25,497	12,028	37,525	26,997	100,412
1982	18,452	23,922	11,558	35,480	24,520	95,093
1983	17,818	22,608	11,209	33,817	23,416	92,011
1984	17,093	21,526	10,892	32,418	22,237	88,847
1985	16,948	20,990	11,009	31,999	19,941	88,695
1986	16,801	20,349	10,738	31,087	19,256	85,006
1987	16,588	19,655	10,361	30,016	18,886	82,216
1988	15,981	18,184	9,562	27,746	18,033	77,176
1989	—	17,086	8,931	26,017	17,489	73,306
1990	—	16,839	8,398	25,237	17,038	72,668
1991	—	16,919	8,210	25,129	16,438	72,184
1992	—	16,675	7,679	24,354	15,534	65,542
1993	—	15,765	7,447	23,212	13,780	58,573
1994	—	14,455	6,688	21,143	12,150	51,974

Source: Grade totals from BRB census of earnings and IR tapes; aggregate figures for 1973–89 from BRB, *R&A 1973–89*, 1990–4 from IR tapes.

Note: Census of earnings data taken at Mar./Apr., except 1973 = Oct., 1982 = May. Calendar year to 1983, then financial year to March 1994.

Railway			Subsidiaries		Group total
Wages	Salaried	Total	BREL	Total	
139,809	55,396	195,205	32,420	54,878	250,083
142,656	56,812	199,468	33,746	56,434	255,902
138,347	56,231	194,578	35,268	57,049	251,627
132,543	54,290	186,833	35,459	56,644	243,477
129,726	52,563	182,289	35,677	57,784	240,073
129,876	52,322	182,198	35,644	61,066	243,264
129,394	52,637	182,031	36,236	62,053	244,084
126,110	51,949	178,059	36,567	61,621	239,680
120,408	49,989	170,397	34,648	56,855	227,252
115,378	46,024	161,402	31,098	51,320	212,722
111,132	44,291	155,423	27,661	45,366	200,789
—	—	—	—	—	—
107,366	39,853	147,219	25,377	33,450	180,669
103,162	39,595	142,757	22,816	31,003	173,760
100,303	39,766	140,069	18,517	26,920	166,989
94,679	38,888	133,567	13,116	21,181	154,748
91,810	38,651	130,461	3,896	4,782	135,243
90,102	39,594	129,696	3,809	4,665	134,361
87,554	42,713	130,267	3,908	4,847	135,114
80,611	51,034	131,645	3,895	4,941	136,586
72,193	51,993	124,186	3,413	5,199	129,385
64,241	51,120	115,361	3,119	5,506	120,867

Table G.2 BRB general pay settlements, conciliation and salaried staff, 1973–94

Due date	Offer	Settled	Details
Apr. 1973	£1 wk + 4%	As offer	Total deal worth 7–9%. In line with incomes policy.
Apr. 1974	7% + 1%	As offer	1% 'flexibility margin' related to annual leave and unsocial hours. RSNT 43 found against ASLEF. In line with incomes policy.
Apr. 1975	20%/21.2%	30.0%	RSNT 45 award of 27.5% was rejected by NUR. Settlement allowed for 27.5% from April and 2.5% from August 1975.
Apr. 1976	£6 wk	As offer	Basic rates reduced to April 1975 levels, + £6 per week non-enhanceable supplement. Rejected by ASLEF but RSNT 47 found in favour of Board. In line with TUC Social Contract.
Apr. 1977	5%	As offer	'Second earnings supplement'. Subject to £2.50 minimum/£4.00 maximum per week. In line with TUC Social Contract.
Apr. 1978	9.63%	16%	Restored August 1975 basic rates; £6 supplement non-enhanceable supplement retained but second earnings supplement withdrawn. In line with government guidelines (10% max.).
Apr. 1979	5%	9% + 2%	2% for consolidation of Business Performance Scheme. In addition, £2 of £6.00 non-enhanceable consolidated. RSNT 66 subsequently ruled that further £2.00 be consolidated in August 1979 and remaining £2.00 in January 1980. Breached government guidelines (5% max.).
Apr. 1980	13% + 4%	20%	Effective May 1980. Included clauses on productivity and restructuring initiatives.
Apr. 1981	7%	8% + 3%	RSNT 75 awarded 8% from April and a further 3% from August 1981. After discussions at ACAS, the 3% was linked to productivity initiatives (see Chapter 5, pp. 157–8).
Apr. 1982	5%	6%	RSNT 78 awarded 6%. Effective from September 1982.
Apr. 1983	4.0%	4.5%	Effective from June 1983.
Apr. 1984	4.0%	4.9%	
Apr. 1985	4.25%	4.85%	Rejected by TSSA but RSNT 90 found in favour of the Board.
Apr. 1986	4.5%	5.0%	
Apr. 1987	4.0%	4.5%	RSNT 95 found in favour of the Board.
Apr. 1988	4.5%	5.0%	Introduction of non-enhanceable allowance for lowest grades.
Apr. 1989	6.7%/7.0%	8.8%	RSNT 96 found in favour of TSSA and awarded 8.8%.
Apr. 1990	8.0%/8.5%	9.3%	Effective from May 1990.
Apr. 1991	6.5%/7.0%	7.75%	RSNT 97 awarded 7.75%.
Apr. 1992	4.0%	4.5%	
Apr. 1993	1.5%	As offer	
Apr. 1994	2.5%	As offer	

Source: Minutes of Railway Staff National Council (RSNC) and decisions of Railway Staff National Tribunal (RSNT).

Table G.3 BRB basic wage rates for driver, guard, and railman, 1973–94

Effective from	Driver/footplate £	Guard/conductor £	Railman £	Non-enhanceable £
Apr. 1973	33.00	25.25	21.80	—
Apr. 1974	35.50	27.30	23.85	—
Apr. 1974	41.65	31.75	25.65	—
Apr. 1975	53.10	40.50	32.70	—
Aug. 1975	54.15	41.30	33.35	—
Apr. 1976	53.10	40.50	32.70	6.00
Apr. 1977	53.10	40.50	32.70	6.00
Apr. 1978	62.80	47.90	38.70	6.00
Apr. 1979	74.20	55.15	44.95	4.00
Aug. 1979	76.20	57.15	46.95	2.00
May 1980	93.85	73.40	58.75	—
Apr. 1981	101.35	79.25	63.45	—
Aug. 1981	104.15	81.45	65.20	—
Sep. 1982	110.40	86.35	69.10	—
June 1983	115.35	90.25	72.20	—
Apr. 1984	121.00	94.65	76.25	—
Apr. 1985	126.85	99.25	82.60	—
Apr. 1986	133.20	104.20	87.75	—
Apr. 1987	139.20	108.90	92.20	—
Apr. 1988	146.15	114.35	96.80	10.65
Apr. 1989	168.60	130.10	105.30	11.60
May 1990	184.30	142.20	115.10	12.65
Apr. 1991	198.60	153.20	124.00	13.65
Apr. 1992	207.55	160.10	129.60	14.24
Apr. 1993	210.65	162.50	131.55	14.45
Apr. 1994	215.90	165.55	134.85	14.80

Source: BRB census of earnings and BRB Personnel Department pay circulars.

All grades received the non-enhanceable supplement 1976–9, from April 1988 supplement applied to railman only.

Appendix G

Table G.4 BRB average weekly earnings and average hours worked, 1974–94

Year	Average weekly earnings			
	Footplate £	Guards/Conductors £	General £	Conciliation £
Mar. 1974	43.37	40.05	37.84	41.27
Mar. 1975	62.43	58.04	52.04	57.76
Apr. 1976	73.66	66.19	63.01	68.52
Apr. 1977	78.56	71.92	67.55	73.80
Apr. 1978	82.86	76.34	71.94	78.72
Apr. 1979	94.56	87.62	81.06	89.25
Apr. 1980	109.08	102.48	94.91	103.57
May 1981	129.66	117.57	112.14	121.56
May 1982	148.49	134.40	126.25	138.36
Apr. 1983	157.52	146.10	136.09	148.39
Apr. 1984	169.06	154.08	143.46	158.48
Apr. 1985	195.35	180.54	163.59	180.16
Apr. 1986	206.35	187.60	171.92	187.19
Apr. 1987	211.16	187.42	172.18	190.51
Apr. 1988	238.67	200.88	185.56	207.80
June 1989	303.48	245.44	223.27	252.29
Feb. 1990	305.14	246.76	236.82	251.47
Feb. 1991	331.97	262.87	239.05	280.73
Apr. 1992	365.98	278.08	265.85	291.06
Apr. 1993	388.56	297.53	282.02	311.73
Apr. 1994	382.70	298.20	275.44	309.87

Source: BRB census of earnings.

Only includes staff who worked a full week.

Year	Average weekly hours worked			
	Footplate	Guards/Conductors	General	Conciliation
	£	£	£	£
Mar. 1974	44.6	50.1	52.2	50.5
Mar. 1975	45.1	50.1	52.2	50.9
Apr. 1976	44.0	47.8	52.1	49.8
Apr. 1977	44.1	48.8	52.5	50.3
Apr. 1978	44.5	49.6	53.3	51.2
Apr. 1979	45.2	50.5	53.8	51.8
Apr. 1980	44.9	50.1	54.0	51.4
May 1981	44.7	48.3	53.1	50.3
May 1982	44.7	48.0	51.8	49.2
Apr. 1983	44.5	47.7	52.2	49.4
Apr. 1984	44.3	48.0	52.4	49.9
Apr. 1985	45.3	49.7	53.2	50.7
Apr. 1986	45.4	49.5	53.1	50.2
Apr. 1987	45.3	48.9	52.7	50.0
Apr. 1988	46.3	49.6	53.8	51.3
June 1989	48.2	51.3	54.7	52.8
Feb. 1990	48.3	51.8	55.1	52.2
Feb. 1991	48.1	50.8	53.6	52.8
Apr. 1992	48.1	49.3	52.8	50.6
Apr. 1993	47.7	48.8	52.3	50.4
Apr. 1994	47.6	48.8	51.6	49.7

Table G.5 BRB paybill costs, 1979–93/4 (£m., in current prices)

Year	Footplate	Guards	Traincrew	Conciliation	Wages	Salaried	Total
1979	134.1	57.2	191.3	496.8	595.6	274.9	870.5
1980	157.9	68.4	226.2	581.3	708.3	325.9	1,034.1
1981	171.3	74.3	245.7	630.3	767.7	368.5	1,136.2
1982	162.5	78.1	240.6	637.8	779.9	387.7	1,167.6
1983	185.8	84.5	270.3	703.0	853.6	406.4	1,260.0
1984	186.1	85.6	271.8	713.5	865.6	413.1	1,278.7
1984/5[a]	232.6	107.0	339.6	892.0	1,082.4	513.5	1,595.9
1985/6	199.9	93.5	293.4	745.4	904.5	464.8	1,369.3
1986/7	207.7	96.4	304.2	760.6	926.3	484.0	1,410.2
1987/8	214.1	97.6	311.7	770.5	942.6	514.6	1,457.2
1988/9	226.7	105.5	332.1	799.7	976.6	540.6	1,517.1
1989/90	249.9	108.8	358.6	877.8	1,052.6	617.4	1,670.0
1990/1	279.0	118.7	397.7	958.4	1,197.5	730.7	1,928.2
1991/2	297.3	120.3	417.6	941.8	1,159.9	915.0	2,074.9
1992/3	304.2	115.5	419.7	944.1	1,172.9	1,058.7	2,231.6
1993/4	289.0	107.7	396.7	858.0	1,065.9	1,061.9	2,127.8

Source: BRB Personnel microfilms.

[a] 15 months.

Note: 1989/90 salaried figure adjusted to include Self Accounting Units. 1990/1–93/4 figures are predicted year-end costs on BRB national payroll system.

Appendix H Subsidiaries—hotel sales and property board income

Table H.1 Hotel disposals, 1981–4

Hotel	Built	Purchaser	Date of disposal	Price (£m.)
Gleneagles	1924	Gleneagles	June 1981	10.25
Caledonian, Edinburgh	1903	Gleneagles		
North British, Edinburgh	1902	Gleneagles		
St. Andrews	1968	Frank Sheridan	Mar. 1982	1.35
Midland, Derby	1840/1862[a]	Midland	Apr. 1982	0.50
Royal Victoria, Sheffield	1862	Midland		
Grosvenor, London	1861	MF North	Mar. 1983	11.00
Charing Cross, London	1865	MF North		4.00
Great Western, London	1854	MF North		2.50
Royal Station, York[b]	1853/1878	Batchshire (Sea Containers)		1.30
Turnberry	1906	Batchshire		3.00
Lochalsh, Kyle	1896[a]/1935	Batchshire	Mar. 1983	0.50
Tregenna, St. Ives	1774/1878[a]	Batchshire		0.70
Welcombe, Stratford-on-Avon	1869/1931[a]	Batchshire		1.70
Adelphi, Liverpool	1826/1892[a]	Oakleydene (Britannia)	Mar. 1983	0.90
Grand, Hartlepool	1901/1912[a]	Jifbarge (WHSN)	Mar. 1983	0.25

Table H.1 (continued)

Hotel	Built	Purchaser	Date of disposal	Price (£m.)
Royal Station, Newcastle	1854/1892	Virani Group		0.80
Royal Station, Hull	1851	Virani Group		0.63
Great Northern, Peterborough	1851	Virani Group		0.35
Manor House, Moretonhampstead	1907/1929[a]	Virani Group	Mar./Apr. 1983	0.81
Central, Glasgow	1885	Virani Group		0.45
Station, Inverness	1856	Virani Group		0.45
Station, Perth	1890	Virani Group		0.35
Station, Aberdeen	1870/1910[a]	Virani Group		0.80
Midland, Manchester	1903	Heathside Catering (GMC/CU)	Apr. 1983	4.10
North British, Glasgow	1870[a]/1905	Archyield	Jan. 1984	1.00
Queens, Leeds	1863/1937	Trusthouse Forte	June 1984	4.18
Great Eastern, London	1884	Compass	Mar. 1983	Contract
Great Northern, London	1854	Compass	Mar. 1983	0.30

Source: Oliver Carter, *An Illustrated History of British Railway Hotels, 1838–1983* (Garstang, 1990), pp. 120–4; BTH, 'Cash Proceeds from Sale of Assets', 19 December 1983, F. J. Leese–M. B. Potter, 8 October 1984, BTH Privatisation General Files (Potter), 13, 15.

[a] Purchased.
[b] Includes Friars Garden Hotel (1981).

Table H.2 BR Property Board lettings, sales, and gross cash contribution, 1974–89/90 (£'000, in current prices)

Revenue account lettings income

Year	Gross non-operational	Gross operational	Gross lettings	Net non-operational	Net operational	Net lettings	Net profit after tax
1974	7,488	11,303	18,791	5,281	9,559	15,651	15,651
1975	8,127	13,659	21,786	5,546	10,984	17,025	17,025
1976	9,187	16,469	25,656	6,330	12,165	19,515	19,468
1977	10,512	19,858	31,024	7,102	14,753	22,310	21,749
1978	11,748	23,237	34,985	8,051	17,351	25,402	24,092
1979	12,306	30,470	42,776	8,350	21,780	30,130	29,044
1980	13,752	36,759	50,511	10,092	25,616	35,708	34,638
1981	20,999	35,632	56,631	12,744	26,400	39,144	37,901
1982	21,882	39,740	61,622	13,393	30,385	43,778	40,792
1983	20,882	46,176	67,058	13,581	36,349	49,930	55,757
1984/5	20,995	61,272	82,267	12,021	46,395	58,416	56,376
1985/6	13,303	56,320	69,623	6,419	42,306	48,725	47,404
1986/7	12,406	62,702	75,108	6,683	49,183	55,866	54,873
1987/8	10,718	71,791	82,509	5,479	57,047	62,526	61,551
1988/9	11,511	89,220	100,731	5,897	70,326	76,223	71,939
1989/90	—	—	120,000	7,700	85,200	92,900	87,000

Appendix H

Table H.2 (continued)

Year	Capital account			All activities (revenue and capital accounts)		
	Gross sales	Net sales	Surplus	Turnover	Net surplus	Gross cash contribution
1974	14,100	13,300	—	32,891	—	—
1975	11,055	10,100	6,593	32,841	23,498	25,650
1976	14,683	13,376	6,762	40,339	25,840	32,080
1977	5,897	4,377	2,873	36,921	24,464	24,519
1978	9,834	7,431	4,236	44,819	28,180	31,157
1979	13,672	10,823	3,772	56,448	32,435	42,404
1980	40,184	32,820	9,868	90,695	44,940	66,834
1981	41,098	38,280	13,483	97,729	51,088	68,673
1982	34,484	28,943	9,499	96,106	49,520	73,173
1983	71,129	62,064	5,705	138,187	60,426	100,934
1984/5	152,788	131,242	12,147	235,055	68,518	198,861
1985/6	81,675	73,653	17,639	151,298	64,376	120,425
1986/7	102,034	88,210	11,050	177,142	65,118	128,990
1987/8	162,140	152,369	26,116	244,649	88,465	209,978
1988/9	209,667	191,676	45,127	310,398	119,327	317,374
1989/90	319,000	277,500	—	—	—	370,400

Source: BR Property Board Directors' Report and Accounts.

Net operational lettings includes other operational income. Gross cash contribution includes Broadgate development: 1988/9, £73.4 m.; 1989/90, £123.5 m. Net sales proceeds figure is gross sales less expenses and tax. Surplus is net sales less net book values.

Appendix I British Railways Board senior staff

Table I.1 BRB regional general managers and sector directors, 1974–94

Regional general managers

Eastern	London Midland	Scottish	Southern	Western	Anglia
Bill Reynolds (1973–6)	John Bonham-Carter (1971–5)	Alex Phillip (1971–4)	Bob Reid (1974–7)	Fred Wright (1972–6)	John Edmonds (1987–9)
David Cobbett (1976–7)	Jim Urquhart (1975–7)	David Cobbett (1974–6)	John Palette (1977–81)	Leslie Lloyd (1976–82)	David Burton (1989–92)
Geoffrey Myers (1977–8)	David Binnie (1977–80)	John Palette (1976–7)	David Kirby (1982–5)	Bill Bradshaw (1983–5)	
Frank Paterson (1978–85)	Jim O'Brien (1980–3)	Leslie Soane (1977–83)	Gordon Pettitt (1985–90)	Sydney Newey (1985–7)	
David Rayner (1986–7)	Malcolm Southgate (1983–6)	Gordon Mackie (1983–4)	John Ellis (1990–2)	Brian Scott (1987–92)	
John Nelson (1987–92)	Cyril Bleasdale (1986–90)	Chris Green (1984–6)			
	Ivor Warburton (1990–2)	Jim Cornell (1986–7)			
		John Ellis (1987–90)			
		Cyril Bleasdale (1990–2)			

Appendix I

Table I.1 (continued)
Sector directors

InterCity	LSE/NSE	Provincial/Regional Railways	Parcels	Railfreight
Cyril Bleasdale (1982–6)	David Kirby (1982–5)	John Welsby (1982–4)	Mike Connolly (1982–6)	Henry Sanderson (1982–5)
John Prideaux (1986–92)	Chris Green (1986–92)	John Edmonds (1984–7)	Brian Burdsall (1986–8)	Colin Driver (1985–91)
Chris Green (1992–4)	John Nelson (1992–4)	Sydney Newey (1987–90)	Adrian Shooter (1989–91)	*Trainload Freight*
		Gordon Pettitt (1990–2)	Glyn Williams (1991–4)	Leslie Smith (1991–4)
		Jim Cornell (1992–3)		*Railfreight Distribution*
		Paul King (1993–4)		Ian Brown (1988–96)

Source: BRB.

Appendix J Passenger pricing, bus substitution, quality objectives, and charter targets

Table J.1 British Rail's general fare increases, 1972–94

Period	Date	Passenger fare increases (%)	Average annual fare increase (%)	Annual RPI increase (%)
1971–2	Apr. 1972	5.0	—	—
	Sep. 1972	7.5	12.9	7.5
1972–3	June 1973	5.0	5.0	8.2
1973–4	June 1974	12.5[a]	12.5	15.9
1974–5	Jan. 1975	12.5	—	—
	May 1975	16.5[b]	—	—
	Sep. 1975	15.0	50.7	24.1
1975–6	Mar. 1976	12.0	12.0	16.6
1976–7	Jan. 1977	12.5	12.5	15.9
1977–8	Jan. 1978	14.5	14.5	8.2
1978–9	Jan. 1979	9.4	9.4	13.4
1979–80	Jan. 1980	19.6	—	—
	Nov. 1980	18.8	42.1	18.0
1980–1	Nov. 1981	9.3	9.3	11.9
1981–2	—	0.0	—	8.6
1982–3	Jan. 1983	7.8	7.8	4.5
1983–4	Jan. 1984	7.3	7.3	5.0
1984–5	Jan. 1985	6.6	6.6	6.0
1985–6	Jan. 1986	8.2	8.2	3.4
1986–7	Jan. 1987	5.0	5.0	4.2
1987–8	Jan. 1988	6.5	6.5	4.9
1988–9	Jan. 1989	9.4	9.4	7.8
1989–90	Jan. 1990	9.0e	9.0	9.4
1990–1	Jan. 1991	9.5e	9.5e	5.9
1991–2	Jan. 1992	7.75e	7.75e	3.8
1992–3	Jan. 1993	6.0e	6.0e	1.6
1993–4	Jan. 1994	5.0e	5.0e	2.5

Source: Gourvish, *British Railways*, pp. 482–3; BRB, *R&A 1972–9*; Schedule of 'Price Control 1971–75—Significant Events', 9 May 1975, BRB 99–2–50 Pt. 2; Jones, Memo, 1 August 1975, BRB 99–2–1 Pt. 6; Sanderson–Bowick, 21 October 1975, BRB 99–2–1 Pt. 7; BRB Minutes, 13 November 1975; RPI from Office for National Statistics, *Economic Trends Annual Supplement 1997*, p. 161.

[a] Average reduced marginally following ministerial intervention (average 12.5% increase in long-distance L&SE season tickets became the maximum).
[b] 15.0% increase subsequently augmented as a result of 'additional pricing action'.
e estimated (pricing more fragmented with businesses making changes outside the January round).

Appendix J

Table J.2 Routes considered in bus substitution studies, 1982–9

September 1982 (7)

Darlington–Bishop Auckland
March–Doncaster
Morpeth–Berwick
Newport–Gloucester
Norwich–Sheringham
Shrewsbury–Chester
Stratford-on-Avon–Leamington Spa

December 1985 (10)

Barton-on-Humberside–Cleethorpes
Darlington–Bishop Auckland
Dorchester–Yeovil/Castle Cary
Gainsborough–Barnetby (sent to Secretary of State, 6 December 1985)
Kirkcaldy–Perth (sent to Secretary of State, 6 December 1985)
Kyle of Lochalsh–Dingwall/Inverness
Nottingham–Newark
Rose Grove–Colne
Stranraer–Ayr
Thurso/Wick–Dingwall/Inverness

April 1987 (33)

Gainsborough–Barnetby
Barton-on-Humber–Cleethorpes
Gainsborough–Sleaford–Spalding–Peterborough
Norwich–Sheringham
Newark–Nottingham
Skipton–Carnforth–Morecambe
Darlington–Bishop Auckland
Knottingley–Goole
Middlesbrough–Whitby
Felixstowe–Ipswich
Stranraer–Ayr
Kilmarnock–Dumfries
Fort William–Mallaig
Ladybank–Perth
Inverness–Wick/Thurso
Inverness–Kyle of Lochalsh
Exeter–Barnstaple
Exeter–Exmouth
Liskeard–Looe
Par–Newquay
Plymouth–Gunnislake
Truro–Falmouth
St Erth–St Ives
Bristol–Severn Beach

Whitland–Pembroke Dock
Llanelli–Craven Arms
Shrewsbury–Pwllheli
Barrow-in-Furness–Carlisle
Rose Grove–Colne
Wrexham–Bidston
Blaenau Ffestiniog–Llandudno Junction
Matlock–Sinfin
Oxenholme–Windermere

March 1988 (3 + 2)

Ladybank–Perth
Gainsborough–Barnetby
Bristol–Severn Beach
Burnley–Colne
Derby–Sinfin

1989 (23—all sent to Department of Transport except Lincoln–Sleaford)

Barton–Habrough
Bishop Auckland–Darlington
Barrow–Carlisle
Church Fenton–Moorthorpe
Derby–Crewe
Doncaster–Gainsborough
Exeter–Barnstaple
Exeter–Exmouth
Falmouth–Truro
Knottingley–Goole
Lancaster–Barrow
Lincoln–Sleaford
Liskeard–Looe
Middlesbrough–Whitby
Norwich–Sheringham
Ormskirk–Preston
Par–Newquay
Plymouth–Gunnislake
St Erth–St Ives
Scarborough–Hull
Sunderland–Hartlepool
Westbury–Weymouth
York–Harrogate

Source: BRB Provincial, files on Bus Substitution, AN176/305–8, PRO.

Appendix J

Table J.3 Quality objectives and performance, 1984/5–93/4

Year	Punctuality: percentage of trains arriving within 5/10 mins of booked time						
	IC	NSE			Prov/RR		
		(All)	(Day)	(Peak)	(All)	(Express)	(Urban)
Objectives							
1984/5	—	87.5	—	—	—	—	—
1985/6	85.0	87.5	—	—	—	—	—
1986/7	87.0	90.0	—	—	85–97	—	—
1987/8	90.0	90.0	—	—	85–97	—	—
1988/9	90.0	90.0	—	—	85–97	—	—
1989/90	90.0	—	90.0	87.5	—	90.0	90.0
1990/1	90.0	—	92.0	88.0	—	90.0	90.0
1991/2	90.0	—	92.0	88.0	—	90.0	90.0
1992/3	90.0	—	92.0	88.0	—	90.0	90.0
1993/4	90.0	92.0	—	—	—	90.0	90.0
Performance							
1984/5	n.a.	90.0	—	—	91.0	—	—
1985/6	73.0	91.0	—	—	89.0	—	—
1986/7	77.0	91.0	—	—	98.0	—	—
1987/8	87.0	92.0	—	—	97.0	—	—
1988/9	87.0	92.0	—	—	91.0	—	—
1989/90	84.0	—	90.0	83.0	—	91.0	90.0
1990/1	85.0	—	90.0	85.0	—	90.0	90.0
1991/2	84.0	—	91.0	85.0	—	92.0	90.0
1992/3	87.0	—	n.a.	88.0	—	91.0	91.0
1993/4	91.0	92.0	—	—	—	92.0	90.0

Year	Reliability: percentage of trains run					Overcrowding: percentage compliance required		
	IC	NSE	Prov/RR			NSE	Prov/RR	
			All	Express	Urban		Slide	Slam
Objectives								
1984/5	—	98.5	—	—	—	100	—	—
1985/6	—	98.5	—	—	—	100	—	—
1986/7	99.5	98.5	98.5–100	—	—	100	—	—
1987/8	99.5	99.0	98.5	—	—	100	—	—
1988/9	99.5	99.0	98.5	—	—	100	—	—
1989/90	99.5	99.0	—	99.5	99.0	100	100	100
1990/1	99.5	99.0	—	99.5	99.0	100	100	100
1991/2	99.5	99.0	—	99.5	99.0	100	100	100
1992/3	99.0	99.0	—	99.5	99.0	100	100	100
1993/4	99.0	99.0	—	99.0	99.0	100	100	100
Performance						% in excess of requirement		
1984/5	n.a.	98.1	n.a.	—	—	n.a.	n.a.	n.a.
1985/6	n.a.	98.1	n.a.	—	—	4.2	n.a.	n.a.
1986/7	99.2	98.4	99.5	—	—	4.1	n.a.	n.a.
1987/8	99.5	98.8	99.1	—	—	4.2	n.a.	n.a.
1988/9	99.0	98.6	98.8	—	—	4.0	n.a.	n.a.
1989/90	98.0	96.0	—	97.0	96.0	3.5	0.0[a]	0.0[a]
1990/1	97.8	97.9	—	98.2	97.1	3.1	0.0[a]	0.0[a]
1991/2	97.8	98.7	—	98.8	98.1	2.8	1.0	0.8
1992/3	98.8	98.4	—	99.1	98.5	2.5	1.0	0.5
1993/4	99.2	98.9	—	98.7	98.4	2.5	0.7	1.1

Appendix J

Table J.3 (continued)

| Year | Standards: carriage cleaning | | | | | |
| | Daily interior clean | | | Daily exterior wash | | |
	IC	NSE	Prov/RR	IC	NSE	Prov/RR
Objectives						
1984/5	—	—	—	—	100	—
1985/6	—	100[b]	—	—	100	—
1986/7	—	100[b]	—	—	100	—
1987/8	100	100	95–100	95	100	75–100
1988/9	100	100	95–100	95	100	75–100
1989/90	100	100	100	95	100	100[c]
1990/1	100	100	100	95	100	100
1991/2	100	100	100	95	100	100
1992/3	100	100	100	95	100	100
1993/4	100	100	100	95	100	100
Performance						
1986/7	n.a.	87	n.a.	n.a.	87	n.a.
1987/8	97	94	91	94	94	93
1988/9	98	89	95	95	89	94
1989/90	98	77	88	95	77	81[c]
1990/1	98	81	91	95	81	92
1991/2	97	79	95	95	79	96
1992/3	96	85	93	95	85	97
1993/4	96	80	94	95	80	97

Source: BRB, *R&A 1986/7–93/4*; BRB, Corporate Plan, 1983, 1984, 1985.

[a] 'Targets generally not exceeded'.
[b] Heavy interior clean every four weeks.
[c] Every two days from 1989/90.

Note: Punctuality measured by trains arriving within 5 minutes. From 1986/7, InterCity moved to 10 minutes. From 1988/9, Provincial used 5 minutes for urban/short rural and 10 minutes for express/long rural. Overcrowding load factors not to exceed 135% on sliding door and 110% on slam door trains with no standing for longer than 20 minutes.

Year	Response rate: Enquiry bureaux (% calls answered in 30 sec.)			Ticket offices: maximum of 5 min. peak queuing time (% achieved)		
	IC	NSE	Prov/RR	IC	NSE	Prov/RR
Objectives						
1984/5	—	—	—	—	—	—
1985/6	—	95	—	—	100	—
1986/7	—	95	—	—	90	—
1987/8	95	95	95	100	100	100
1988/9	95	95	95	100	100	100
1989/90	95	95	95	100	100	100
1990/1	95	95	95	100	100	100
1991/2	95	95	95	100	100	100
1992/3	95	95	95	100	100	100
1993/4	95	95	95	100	100	100
Performance						
1986/7	n.a.	77	n.a.	n.a.	94	n.a.
1987/8	58	85	77	91	97	n.a.
1988/9	73	90	78	91	98	n.a.
1989/90	80	89	81	91	98	100
1990/1	77	88	79	91	97	100
1991/2	85	91	87	92	97	100
1992/3	79	86	86	86	92	100
1993/4	68	72	84	86	92	100

Appendix J

Table J.4 Passenger's Charter targets on Network SouthEast lines, 1992–4

Line	Peak Punctuality Target			Reliability Target		
	1992	1993	1994	1992	1993	1994
Great Northern	90.0	90.0	91.0	99.0	99.0	99.0
Northampton	90.0	90.0	90.0	99.0	99.0	99.0
Thameslink	89.0	89.0	89.0	99.0	99.0	99.0
Chiltern	88.0	90.0	92.0	99.0	99.0	99.0
South Western Lines	88.0	88.0	90.0	98.0	98.0	99.0
Kent Link	88.0	88.0	88.0	98.0	98.0	98.0
South London Lines	88.0	88.0	89.0	97.0	97.0	98.0
West Anglia	88.0	90.0	91.0	98.0	98.0	99.0
Solent & Wessex	86.0	86.0	87.0	98.0	98.0	98.5
North London Lines	85.0	87.0	87.0	97.0	97.0	97.0
Sussex Coast	83.0	83.0	85.0	99.0	99.0	99.0
Kent Coast	82.0	82.0	82.0	98.0	98.0	99.0
Thames	80.0	85.0	85.0	98.0	98.5	98.5
London Tilbury & Southend	80.0	85.0	88.0	97.0	97.0	98.0

Source: BRB, *R&A 1991/2–93/4*.

Note: Peak Punctuality Target is percentage of trains arriving within 5 minutes of scheduled time at London termini, Monday–Friday 0700–1000 and evening arrival time at final destination of trains leaving London between 1600 and 1900. Reliability Target is percentage of trains run on weekdays.

Table J.5 Sector pricing, 1984–92 (percentage increases)

Year	IC			NSE			PROV/RR			All passenger businesses		
	Inflation	Real	Total	Inflation	Real	Total	Inflation	Real	Total	Inflation	Real	Total
1984	6.5	0.4	6.9	6.5	1.1	7.6	6.5	0.2	6.7	6.5	0.8	7.3
1985	5.3	0.8	6.1	5.3	1.9	7.2	5.3	0.5	5.8	5.3	1.3	6.6
1986	5.6	3.7	9.3	5.6	1.7	7.3	5.6	1.9	7.5	5.6	2.6	8.2
1987	2.3	2.6	4.9	2.3	2.6	4.9	2.3	3.9	6.2	2.3	2.7	5.0
1988	3.7	3.5	7.2	3.7	2.4	6.2	3.7	2.5	6.2	3.7	2.8	6.5
1989	5.8	4.5	10.3	5.8	3.4	9.2	5.8	2.0	7.8	5.8	3.6	9.4
1990	6.0	3.4	9.4	6.0	5.2	11.2	6.0	0.8	6.8	6.0	3.0	9.0e
1991	8.0	2.2	10.2	7.0	2.5	9.5	8.0	3.0	11.0	—	—	9.5e
1992	—	—	7.5–9.5	5.0	3.5	8.5	—	—	—	—	—	7.75e

Source: Confidential memoranda to BRB, 1983–91.

Note: All increases effective from January. Price increases are a composite of an estimation of future inflation and a real increase.

e = estimated.

Appendix K Passenger-miles maximisation

Passenger-miles maximisation was developed as an alternative to the post-1974 PSO funding regime by BRB's Strategy Steering Group, assisted by Richard Edgley, then Passenger Manager (Policy), under the direction of Michael Posner, part-time member, BRB in 1980. The concept arose from a joint assessment of the PSO regime by BRB and the DTp, where the aim was to examine the extent to which the PSO provided clear objectives for the non-commercial railway. The imposition of cash limits on British Rail had highlighted the inconsistency between the specification by government of a fixed set of service requirements under the 1974 Act and the provision of a fixed amount of money for these service requirements. 'Passenger-miles maximisation' involved adding the objective of maximising 'weighted passenger-miles'. The Board would be set the objective of maximising the number of passenger-miles for a given level of grant. Weights would be set so that different types of passenger-mile were valued differently. For example, a mile travelled by a passenger on a rural service would be valued differently from that travelled by a London commuter. The aim was to obtain the maximum possible usage of the 'social railway' consistent with satisfying an overall financial constraint. A further advantage was the establishment of a benchmark against which to judge managerial decisions on passenger service provision. Another variant of the approach was to relate the grant paid directly to the number of passenger-miles or to the revenue collected. The greater the passenger-mileage or revenue the larger the grant. Unfortunately, this ingenious though somewhat complex idea did not find favour with either the DTp or the Serpell Committee. See Michael V. Posner, Memo on 'Alternatives to the PSO System', 17 September 1980, Board Exec. Minutes, 25 September 1980; DTp, *Railway Finances* (1983), paras. 11.9–11.

Appendix L British Rail sales and disposals

Table L.1 Businesses sold and transferred, 1993–7 (£m., current prices)

Business	Sale date	Sale price (at final completion)	Profit/loss	Buyer
BRIS Infrastructure Maintenance Companies				
Scotland	14 Feb. 1996	27.5	21.8	Track Action (MEBO)
Western	25 Mar. 1996	11.8	5.5	Amey Railways
Eastern	2 Apr. 1996	29.7	27.5	Balfour Beatty
South East	2 Apr. 1996	14.4	13.7	Balfour Beatty/MBO
South Western	18 Apr. 1996	11.0	14.4	AMEC
Central	19 Apr. 1996	18.8	17.9	GT Railway Maintenance (GEC Alsthom/Tarmac)
Northern	18 June 1996	9.0	9.4	Jarvis
BRIS Track Renewal Companies				
Scotland	8 Feb. 1996	10.6	8.2	Relayfast (MBO)
Central	29 Feb. 1996	2.9	2.8	Tarmac
Eastern	15 Mar. 1996	11.0	4.7	Fastline Group (MEBO)
Southern	2 Apr. 1996	5.9	0.7	Balfour Beatty
Northern	23 May 1996	4.5	5.0	Fastline Group
Western	23 July 1996	8.5	9.2	Relayfast

Table L.1 (continued)

Business	Sale date	Sale price (at final completion)	Profit/loss	Buyer
BRIS Infrastructure Design Units				
DCU Birmingham	25 July 1995	0.02	−1.7	Owen Williams
IDG Glasgow	18 Aug. 1995	1.0	−1.4	Scott Wilson Kirkpatrick
Mainline Swindon	18 Aug. 1995			
CEDG York	15 Sep. 1995	3.0	0.8	British Steel
BPE Mechanical & Electrical Engineering Consultancy	15 Sep. 1995	0.2	0.0	James Scott (AMEC)
CEDAC London	15 Dec. 1995	−1.4	−7.5	W. S. Atkins
PowerTrack Engineering	15 Dec. 1995			
Freight and Parcels				
Red Star Parcels	5 Sep. 1995	−0.3	−3.9	MBO
Rail Express Systems	9 Dec. 1995	11.2	21.9	English Welsh & Scottish Railway
Load Haul	24 Feb. 1996	237.2	−20.8	English Welsh & Scottish Railway
Mainline	24 Feb. 1996			
Transrail	24 Feb. 1996			
Freightliner	25 May 1996	−4.9	−13.0	MCB Ltd (MBO)
Railfreight Distribution	22 Nov. 1997	4.5	−118.4	English Welsh & Scottish Railway
Passenger				
OBS Services	3 Oct. 1995	11.6	10.7	European Rail Catering (MBO)
Heathrow Express	19 July 1996	19.8	19.8	BRB 30% share sold to BAA
BR International	24 Mar. 1997	7.7	6.7	Grand Lignes International

Rolling Stock Maintenance (Former BRML/Level 5 Depots)

Swindon Electronic Service Centre	31 Mar. 1995	0.4	0.3	ABB Customer Support Services
Chart Leacon	5 June 1995	19.4	−1.1	ABB Customer Support Services
Doncaster	5 June 1995			
Ilford	5 June 1995			
Glasgow	6 June 1995	5.7	−17.1	Railcare Ltd (Babcock International/Siemens)
Wolverton	6 June 1995			
Eastleigh	7 June 1995	7.1	−11.7	Wessex Traincare (MEBO)

Central Services

Train Engineering

The Engineering Link	18 Mar. 1996	1.0	0.1	MBO
Interfleet Technology	22 Mar. 1996	0.5	0.1	MBO
Network Train Engineering Services	1 Apr. 1996	0.9	−0.3	W. S. Atkins

Signalling and Telecommunications

Signalling Control (UK)	1 Dec. 1995	39.2	35.3	Westinghouse Signals
BRT	21 Dec. 1995	140.9	132.6	Racal Electronics
Interlogic Control Engineering	4 Jan. 1996	19.9	14.7	ABB Daimler-Benz Transportation (Signal)
Opal Engineering	14 Feb. 1997	8.5	7.9	W. S. Atkins

Other

Transmark	7 Apr. 1993	5.1	6.7	Sir William Halcrow and Partners
Meldon Quarry	4 Mar. 1994	5.0	5.0	ECC Construction Materials
Charter/Special Trains (asset sale)	31 Mar. 1995	1.2	—	Flying Scotsman Railways
Baileyfield Switch & Crossing Works	7 July 1995	1.3	0.9	VAE-Baileyfield (MBO joint venture)
Ditton Timber Treatment Works	1 Sep. 1995	0.5	0.1	Phoenix Timber Group
Quality & Safety Services	10 Nov. 1995	0.3	0.2	Ingeby 805 (MBO)

Appendix L

Table L.1 (continued)

Business	Sale date	Sale price (at final completion)	Profit/loss	Buyer
Railway Occupational Health	30 Nov. 1995	0.7	0.5	Occupational Health Care plc
Castleton Works	14 Mar. 1996	0.3	0.0	British Steel Track Products
College of Railway Technology	29 Mar. 1996	0.6	−1.3	Advicepart Ltd (MBO)
BR Projects	26 June 1996	0.6	−0.6	MBO
Scientifics	9 Dec. 1996	2.0	0.9	Atesta Group
BR Research	20 Dec. 1996	10.5	7.8	AEA Technology
Nationwide Fire Services	6 Jan. 1997	−0.001	−0.5	Serco Group
National Railway Supplies	31 Jan. 1997	43.5	21.5	MBO/Unipart (49%)
BR Business Systems	31 Jan. 1997	31.0	13.8	Sema Group
Rail Operational Research	4 Feb. 1997	1.7	1.4	BR Projects
Railtest	14 Feb. 1997	7.8	6.1	Serco
Raildata (RDDS) Railpart (UK) Ltd	6 Mar. 1997	64.1	0.7	Unipart Rail Holdings
Rail Direct	Apr./June 1997	1.6	0.4	—

(Rail Direct sold as three call centre companies: London, 1 Apr. 1997; Scotland, 7 June 1997; Northern, 7 June 1997)

Summary

	Sale Price	Profit/loss
BRIS Infrastructure Maintenance	122.2	110.2
BRIS Track Renewals	43.4	30.6
BRIS Infrastructure Design	2.8	−9.8
Freight & Parcels	247.7	−134.2
Passenger	39.1	37.2
Rolling Stock Maintenance	32.6	−29.6
TESCOs	2.4	−0.1
S&T	208.5	190.5
Central Services	177.2	63.6
GRAND TOTAL	875.9	258.4

Other closures/disposals:
Crewe Timber Works, 25 Mar. 1994; Crofton Track Works, 25 Mar. 1994; Newton Heath Concrete Works, 25 Mar. 1994; Architecture and Design Group, 31 Mar. 1994; Haulmark, 30 Sep. 1994; Brighton Fabrication Works, 25 Nov. 1994; Shettleston Fabrication Works, 23 Dec. 1994; BR Legal Services, Dec. 1994/Jan. 1995 (passed to Vizards and Kennedys Solicitors); Taunton Concrete Works, 2 Feb. 1995; The Grove Management Centre, 16 Feb. 1995; Materials Technology (Derby), 31 Mar. 1995; Materials Engineering Group, 31 Dec. 1995; Engineering Development Unit, 2 Aug. 1996; *Rail News*, 30 Sep. 1996 (title sold and subsequently relaunched); Railway Claims, 13 Oct. 1996; First Procurement, 31 Dec. 1996; Collectors Corner, 24 Jan. 1997 (included in sale of National Railway Supplies); BR Savings, 31 Jan. 1997.

Table L.1 (continued)

Transferred to government for nil consideration

Business	Transfer date	Effect on BR balance sheet	
Railtrack	1 Apr. 1994	142.7	Net assets transferred
(Railtrack was floated on 20 May 1996 with a valuation of £1.9 bn. and new equity and debt of £600 m.)			
Channel Tunnel			
EPS	9 May 1994	−798.0	Net assets transferred
Union Railways	1 Apr. 1995	−42.6	Net assets transferred
St Pancras station, and land and buildings at Kings Cross/Stratford	31 May 1996	−25.0	Net assets transferred
Rolling Stock Leasing Companies			
Angel Train Contracts	12 Aug. 1995	−619.4	Net assets transferred
Eversholt Leasing	12 Aug. 1995	−681.0	Net assets transferred
Porterbrook Leasing Company	12 Aug. 1995	−444.6	Net assets transferred
Sparesco	9 Oct. 1995	−14.8	Net assets transferred

(After allowing for deferred grant income not transferred, the net assets transferred on the four companies was −£599.3 m.)

Government sale of the leasing companies in 1996

Porterbrook Leasing	8 Jan. 1996	528.3	MBO
Angel Trains	16 Jan. 1996	696.3	GRS Holding Co (Prideaux & Associates, Babcock & Brown, Nomura)
Eversholt Leasing	2 Feb. 1996	518.3	MBO
Sparesco	2 Feb. 1996	—	Jointly owned by ROSCOs

Source: BRB, R&A 1993/4–97/8; BRB, Privatisation News; BRB, Completion Accounts and Analysis of Business Sales.

Note: The profit/loss figure is that given after the completion accounts process and takes account of net assets. The BRIS units were sold with a guaranteed minimum assets value and there was no completion accounts process.

Table L.2 Franchised passenger services, 1996–7

BR Train Operating Unit	Effective from	Franchisee
South West Trains	4 Feb. 1996	Stagecoach Holdings
Great Western	4 Feb. 1996	Great Western Holdings (MBO/First Bus/3i)
East Coast	28 Apr. 1996	Great North Eastern Railway (Sea Containers)
Gatwick Express	28 Apr. 1996	National Express Group
Midland Mainline	28 Apr. 1996	National Express Group
South Central	26 May 1996	Connex Rail (CGEA)
LTS Rail	26 May 1996	Prism Rail
Chiltern Railways	21 July 1996	M40 Trains (MBO/Laing)
South Eastern	13 Oct. 1996	Connex Rail (CGEA)
South Wales & West	13 Oct. 1996	Prism Rail
Cardiff Railway	13 Oct. 1996	Prism Rail
Thames Trains	13 Oct. 1996	Victory Railway Holdings (MBO/Go-Ahead Group)
Island Line	13 Oct. 1996	Stagecoach
Anglia Railways	5 Jan. 1997	GB Railways
CrossCountry	5 Jan. 1997	Virgin Railways
Great Eastern	5 Jan. 1997	First Bus
West Anglia Great Northern	5 Jan. 1997	Prism Rail
Merseyrail Electrics	19 Jan. 1997	MTL Trust Holdings
North West	2 Mar. 1997	GW Holdings
North London	2 Mar. 1997	National Express Group
North East	2 Mar. 1997	MTL Trust Holdings
Thameslink	2 Mar. 1997	GOVIA (Go-Ahead/VIA GTI)
Central	2 Mar. 1997	National Express Group
West Coast	9 Mar. 1997	Virgin Railways
ScotRail	31 Mar. 1997	National Express Group

Source: BRB, *R&A*; BRB, Privatisation News.

Note: each company was sold for £1. During the completion process payments were made and received to bring the net assets to zero.

Notes

Explanatory note

This book draws heavily on the records of the British Railways Board and its constituent parts. The survival of archival material has been affected by the numerous reorganisations and, above all, by the process of rail privatisation. Papers on some activities, for example the Board itself and its secretariat, have survived well; for others, notably, the passenger and freight businesses and the engineering functions, the records are patchy. The primary sources cited are those of the British Railways Board (BRB), unless stated otherwise. Many of the records relating to the first 15 years of nationalised railways were transferred to the Public Record Office some years ago. When work started on this book in 1997 the bulk of the post-1962 archive remained in a largely uncatalogued state in the Board's repository in Porchester Road, London W2. While the book was being written (1997–2001) a concerted effort was mounted to catalogue records and then transfer them to the PRO. In the notes that follow reference is made to the PRO number of records to be transferred where known. File references, e.g. BRB 23-4-1, are to the Board's secretariat unless otherwise specified. The place of publication of books is London unless stated otherwise.

Chapter 1

1 T. R. Gourvish, *British Railways 1948–73: A Business History* (Cambridge, 1986).
2 Ibid. pp. 256ff.; G. C. Peden, *The Treasury and British Public Policy 1906–1959* (Oxford, 2000), pp. 517, 523–4, 531.
3 Beeching, cited in P. A. Keen, Memo on 'Customer Care: Putting the Passenger First', 22 April 1977, BRB 95-1-5.
4 BRB Railway Management Group (RMG) Minutes, 21 August 1974.
5 BRB, Railway Policy Review, Report to Minister for Transport Industries, Draft, 19 October 1972, p. 1, AN121/331, (PRO). This comment, part of a long historical overview developed by Michael Bonavia, was omitted from the final version sent to the Minister in December. See BRB 21-12-92 Pts. 1 and 2.
6 Gourvish, *British Railways*, p. 456.
7 Cf. *Daily Mail*, 20 December 1974 (mac cartoon); *Sun*, 8 December 1975 (John Kent cartoon), reproduced on cover of Richard Marsh's autobiography, *On and Off the Rails: An Autobiography* (1978); *Sunday Express*, 17 November 1974 (Cummings cartoon); *Guardian*, 13 March 1989 (Steve Bell cartoon).
8 Peter Parker, 'Notes on Meeting with Dr John Gilbert—15th October 1976', 18 October 1976, BRB 20-100-3/1.
9 DOE, *Transport Policy: A Consultation Document*, vol. I (HMSO, April 1976).

10 *Annual Abstract of Statistics*, 1974–80; George Charlesworth, *A History of British Motorways* (1984), pp. 50, 74, 94–5; Theo Barker and Dorian Gerhold, *The Rise and Rise of Road Transport 1700–1990* (Basingstoke, 1993), p. 93.

11 Length of haul data for 1953–73: *Report of the Inquiry into Lorries, People and the Environment* [Armitage Report] (1980), pp. 5, 8.

12 The EEC recommendations of 1972 were for a 40-tonne gross weight and 11-tonne axle weight by 1980. David Starkie, *The Motorway Age: Roads and Traffic Policies in Post-war Britain* (Oxford, 1982), pp. 107–14.

13 Watkinson, 'Do we fight or lie down?', 25 May 1976, paper for CBI President's Committee Meeting, 3 June 1976, Modern Records Centre (MRC) MSS 200/C/1/1/PC/76.

14 *Annual Abstract of Statistics*, 1974–97.

15 Chris Wrigley, 'Trade unions, strikes and the government', in Richard Coopey and Nicholas Woodward (eds.), *Britain in the 1970s: the troubled economy* (1996), pp. 274–5; personal communication from Jeremy Waddington (Warwick University), 9 February 1998.

16 In contrast, safety was discussed at 37 of the 51 meetings, and the Channel Tunnel at 38. Minutes of BRB, RMG, and Executive Directors' Conference, 1974–5; BRB, 1988–91.

17 British Railways Joint Consultative Council (BRJCC) Minutes, 2 August 1974 (first meeting).

18 The locomotives were required to meet anticipated additional demand for coal traffic in the wake of the oil crisis. See D. Fowler, Memo to BRB Investment Committee on 'Construction of 60 Type 47 Diesel Locomotives', 31 May 1974; A. W. Milton, Memo to Supply and Investment Committees, 31 May 1974, Investment Committee Minutes, 4 June 1974; J. M. W. Bosworth, Memo on 'Construction of 60 Type 47 Diesel Locomotives', 4 June 1974, BRB Minutes, 14 March and 13 June 1974, Confidential BRB Minute, 27 June 1974. Only the point about metric specifications was put to the unions at the BRJCC, while *The Times* referred only to speed of delivery. BRJCC Minutes, 17 January 1975, *The Times*, 9 October 1974, p. 22.

19 David Bowick, 'Are the railways really grossly overmanned?', *Modern Railways*, March 1976, p. 87, a response to Richard Pryke and John Dodgson, *The Rail Problem* (1975). The argument received considerable coverage in the press. See *Sunday Times*, 23 November 1975, *Daily Express*, 27 November 1975, *The Times*, 12, 17, and 19 December 1975.

20 Robert W. Bacon and Walter A. Eltis, 'Too few producers: the drift Healey must stop', *Sunday Times*, 1975, and see their subsequent *Britain's Economic Problem: Too Few Producers* (1976) and also R. W. Bacon et al., *The Dilemma of Government Expenditure* (IEA, 1976); Milton Friedman, 'The Line We Dare Not Cross: the Fragility of Freedom at 60%', *Encounter*, November 1976, cited by Peter M. Jackson, 'Public Expenditure', in Michael Artis and David Cobham (eds.), *Labour's Economic Policies 1974–1979* (Manchester, 1991), p. 74. On the contribution to the 60% figure of generous methods of calculating public expenditure see Peter Browning, *The Treasury and Economic Policy 1964–85* (1986), pp. 232–3.

21 Cf. Kenneth Clarke, letter to *Daily Telegraph*, 4 August 1976, p. 12.

22 Pryke and Dodgson, *The Rail Problem*, p. 274.

23 Christopher Foster, *The Transport Problem* (1963, 2nd edn., 1975), and *Politics, Finance and the Role of Economics: an Essay on the Control of Public Enterprise* (1971); 'Transport Policy', *Socialist Commentary*, April 1975.

24 Lord Hewlett, 'Miseries of nationalised travel', letter to *Daily Telegraph*, 14 July 1976, later cited in the leader, 'No orchids for Lord Hewlett', in *Modern Railways*, September 1976, p. 333.

25 Frances Edmonds, *Another Bloody Tour* (1987), cited in Robert Millward, 'The nationalised industries', in Michael Artis and David Cobham (eds.), *Labour's Economic Policies*, p. 141.

26 Richard Marsh, STC Communications Lecture on 'The Economics of Indecision', 17 May 1974, cit. in *Modern Railways*, July 1974, p. 253.

27 Gourvish, *British Railways*, pp. 368–74.

28 A. J. Morgan (Minister's PS), Note of 'Meeting with British Railways Board, on 14 November 1974', BRB 20-100-30/1.

29 Gourvish, *British Railways*, pp. 373, 382.

30 G. R. Burt (Chief Secretary, BRB), Memos on 'Board Procedures', 5 November 1976 and 21 February 1977, BRB 30-2-7.

31 David Bowick, Memos on 'Railway Field Organisation', 2 January and 7 February 1975, BRB Chairman's Conference Minutes, 6 January and 27 February 1975, BRB Minutes, 13 February 1975; Gourvish, *British Railways*, pp. 384–7; Interview with Gordon Pettitt, 6 November 2000. For further details see BRB Review of the Railway Field Organisation Papers, AN124/184, PRO.

32 BRB, *Second Report of the Board on Organisation*, 21 April 1972, P.P. 1971–2, xxxix, HC223.

33 Demands made by TSSA representatives in negotiations in the London Midland Region indicated that the overall staff savings would fall from £9.5m. (£11.5m. in 1974 prices) to only £2.3m., while £14m. would be added to a redundancy/resettlement bill of £18m. Bowick, Memo, 2 January 1975, cit. Sunk costs in office accommodation were put at £4.2m. in 1976: Memo to Investment Committee, 20 May 1976, BRB 30-1-118. See also Malcolm Wallace, *Single or Return? The History of the Transport Salaried Staffs' Association* (1996), pp. 392–4.

34 BRB, *R&A 1973*, p. 12.

35 Railways Act 1974 c. 48.

36 Director, Policy Review, Memo on 'Railways Bill', 31 January 1974, BRB Chairman's Conference Minutes, 4 February 1974.

37 Transport Act 1968, s. 3(1).

38 EEC Regulation 1191/69, Article 1; Evan Harding, Memo on 'Railways Act 1974', 1 November 1974, Chairman's Conference Minutes, 4 November 1974; T. R. Barron, Memo on 'Financial Support System', 25 September 1975, BRB 23-1-6; Fowler, Memo on 'Payments by Government for Complying with a Public Service Obligation (PSO)', 5 January 1982, BRB 33-40-1.

39 BRB, Railway Policy Review: Report to the Minister for Transport Industries, December 1972, and see A. V. Barker, reported in Memo, 8 June 1972, BRB Minutes, same date. A summary of the Board's report was published with the title *Review of Railway Policy* in June 1973.

40 The Department had asked BRB to examine the implications of withdrawing 44, 73, and 123 grant-aided services by 1976, 1981, and 1985. The smallest cut was found to be

the most advantageous financially. BRB, Railway Policy Review: Support Paper B on 'The Passenger Business' and see also BRB Finance Dept. file, AN123/333, PRO. The network studies were referred to in Pryke and Dodgson, *The Rail Problem*, pp. 13–19, and in Marsh, *On and Off the Rails*, pp. 166–7.

41 Michael Bosworth, Memo on 'Rail Policy Review—Railways Bill', 5 July 1974, BRB Minutes, 11 July 1974; RMG Minutes, 26 June 1974; BRB, *Review of Railway Policy. Summary of Report to the Government*, July 1973; BRB, *R&A 1973*, p. 3.

42 The Direction was not made public until the publication of BRB's Report and Accounts, 1976, p. 24.

43 Railways Act 1974, s. 4(2), (3), (5a).

44 R. B. Reid–Board, 31 January 1979, BRB 147-1-1. By 1 January 1979 only four grants of over £1m. had been awarded, to Redland Roadstone, Duport Steel, Ford (UK), and NCB. Ibid.

45 Interview with Sir David Serpell, 12 March 1991, John Palmer, 4 August 1992, and John Welsby, 30 April 1998. Clearly, Marsh and Mulley were very different men. Marsh wrote of Mulley: 'Fred Mulley seemed to carry an enormous chip on his shoulder which made it impossible for us to develop a close working relationship', Richard Marsh, *On and Off the Rails*, p. 188. Barbara Castle's diary for 14 December 1975 noted: 'Poor Fred has such a whining voice and is so humourless that he merely succeeds in sounding comical', Barbara Castle, *The Castle Diaries, 1974–76* (1980), p. 596.

46 Mulley–Marsh, 26 April, Bosworth–Mulley, 1 May, and Mulley–Bosworth, 2 May 1974, Mulley–Ian Podmore (Chief Executive, Sheffield City Council), 22 January 1975, BRB 30-1-118 Pt. 4.

47 Gourvish, *British Railways*, p. 395; Bosworth, Memo, 5 July 1974, cit.; and cf. HC, *Seventh Report from the Committee of Public Accounts, 1983–4*, HC139, pp. vii–xiii.

48 Marsh–Peyton, 23 October 1973, Memo on 'Long Range Strategic Planning', 6 February 1974, BRB 23-1-6; BRB Press Release on 'Strategic Studies', 8 April 1976. BRB later established a chairman's 'Think Tank' in 1975 to define the railways' role in national transport policy, as part of a contribution to the government's green paper of 1976.

49 Bosworth, Memo, 5 July 1974, and see also his Memo of 31 January 1974, Chairman's Conference, 4 February 1974.

50 RMG Minutes, 26 June 1974. The idea that infrastructure support ran counter to EEC regulations was strenuously denied inside BRB. Cf. Barron, Memo, 25 September 1975, BRB 23-1-6.

51 BRB, 'A Report on the Rail Freight Business', p. 2, in Bosworth–Pugh, 4 June 1975, BRB 23-1-6.

52 Bosworth, 'Note of Meeting at the Department of the Environment 24th October 1973', BRB 20-100-3/1.

53 Cf. White Paper on *Public Expenditure to 1977–78*, December 1973, P.P. 1973–4, v, Cmnd. 5519.

54 Gourvish, *British Railways*, p. 510; Marsh, in BRB, *R&A 1973*, p. 3.

55 However, it was made clear that investment in the Advanced Passenger Train was to be contained within the overall allocation. See Investment Committee Minutes, 3 September 1974 and 1 July 1975; Executive Directors' Conference Minutes, 8 and 22 July 1974; Chairman's Conference Minutes, 29 July and 2 September 1974; Bosworth,

Memo on 'Investment', 1 August 1974, BRB Minutes, 8 August 1974; T. L. Beagley (Deputy Secretary, Transport Industries, DOE)–Bosworth, 24 July 1974, G. R. Burt, 'Salient Papers, 1975/6'.

56 BRB, *R&A 1975*, p. 4; *Railway Gazette International*, April 1975, pp. 149–51; White Paper on *Public Expenditure to 1979–80*, February 1976, P.P. 1975–6, xxv, Cmnd. 6393; Marsh, lecture, 'The Railway in the Transport Scene', 12 January 1976, reported in *Modern Railways*, March 1976, pp. 83–4 and see also Marsh, *On and Off the Rails*, pp. 196–7.

57 Bosworth–W. J. Sharp (Under-Secretary (Railways), DOE), 21 August and 26 September 1975, and replies, 9 September and 10 October 1975, Burt, 'Salient Papers, 1975/6'. See also Gilbert–Marsh, 5 September 1975, Burt, 'Salient Papers, 1975/6'.

58 Bosworth, Memo on 'Investment Cuts 1976–78', 2 October 1975, BRB Minutes, 9 October 1975; BRB Investment Committee Minutes, 1 July–22 December 1975.

59 Marsh–Gilbert, 10 October 1975, Burt, 'Salient Papers, 1975/6'.

60 Jackson, in Artis and Cobham, *Labour's Economic Policies*, p. 80.

61 'Transport Policy: the Report of a Study Group', *Socialist Commentary*, April 1975, pp. 35, 39–41. The Group was led by Les Huckfield, MP and Christopher Foster, and drew on the work of several transport economists, including Ken Gwilliam, John Dodgson, Kenneth Button, Mayer Hillman, and Stewart Joy.

62 BRB and University of Leeds, *A Comparative Study of European Rail Performance* (December 1979), pp. 42, 44, 46.

63 Cf. Browning, *The Treasury*, pp. 59ff., and Andrew Britton, *Macroeconomic Policy in Britain 1974–87* (Cambridge, 1991), pp. 23–4.

64 NEDO, *A Study of the UK Nationalised Industries: Their Role in the Economy and Control in the Future* (1976). The Rothschild study is referred to in BRB 20-3-50 and 21-3-50. See also T. G. Weyman-Jones, 'The Nationalised Industries: Changing Attitudes and Changing Roles', in W. P. J. Maunder (ed.), *The British Economy in the 1970s* (1980), pp. 198–9.

65 Marsh, *On and Off the Rails*, pp. 1–2, and cf. the 1974 and 1976 lectures, cit.; Chairman's Conference Minutes, 4 September 1975.

66 'Note of Meeting held at D.O.E. at 17.00 on 3.9.73', BRB 20-100-3/1.

67 Marsh–Mulley, 7 May 1975, BRB 48-2-1 Pt. 2.

68 Marsh–Gilbert, 14 August 1975, referring to Sharp–Derek Fowler, 25 July 1975, in Burt, 'Salient Papers, 1975/6'.

69 G. R. Burt, Memo to Parker and Bosworth on 'Discussion with Deputy Secretary, D.O.T.', 20 September 1976, BRB 20-100-3/1. Lazarus had been Under-Secretary (Railways and the Channel Tunnel) in the Ministry of Transport, 1968–70.

70 Cf. Marvin B. Lieberman and David B. Montgomery, 'First Mover Advantages', *Strategic Management Review*, 9 (1988), 41–58.

71 Pilkington–Bowick, 24 April 1979, BRB 30-1-4 Pt. 8.

Chapter 2

1 The problem of interpreting the change in the support mechanism was raised by Derek Fowler, Board member for Finance, at BRB Minutes, 11 March 1976, where it was argued that from 1974 to 1975 overall government support had changed by between £17m. and minus £17m. in real terms. An additional irritation was the fact that until

1984 the Board worked to calendar years while the government worked to fiscal years. Fowler, Memo on 'Proposed Change in Accounting Year from Calendar to Fiscal Year', 25 August 1983, BRB 241-62-1 Pt. 3.

2 BRB, *Report & Accounts 1975–6 (R&A)*, statement 1A, and BRB Minutes, 11 March 1976 and 10 March 1977. The auditors also insisted that government funding of superannuation liabilities, i.e. in 1976 interest on superannuation funding debts of £48.6 m. (1975) and £65.2 m. (1976) and interest on superannuation funds deposits of £13.9 m. (1975) and £8.4 m. (1976) (reimbursed by the Secretary of State) should be made more visible in the accounts: 'Note of points discussed at the meeting with Auditors on the 1976 Accounts 2nd March, 1977', BRB Finance Committee Minutes, 9 March 1977. The support mechanism also embraced special grants for maintaining level crossings, beginning with a payment of £9.0 m. in 1975 (see Appendix A, Table A.1). Adjustments for previous years further complicate the picture: payments made after 1974 under section 39 of the Transport Act 1968, of £3.3 m. (credited to 1975 accounts) and £0.8 m. (1976), were recovered by the Secretary of State in the 1976 accounts in a deduction of £4.1 m.

3 Cf. BRB Minutes, 14 August 1975, and correspondence with DOE, e.g. Sharp–Fowler, 25 July 1975 and reply, 6 August 1975, Marsh–Gilbert, 14 August and 5 December 1975, Gilbert–Marsh, 5 September 1975, Ken Marks (DOE)–Marsh, 31 December 1975, Anthony Crosland–Marsh, 6 April 1976, BRB Marsh correspondence, 1973–6.

4 The extraordinary items here involved a small *repayment* on the non-passenger support account in 1977, and £46 million of 'other items' in 1978.

5 E. Garner (Chief Accountant), Memo on 'Inflation Accounting', 2 October 1978, BRB 241–2–5; BRB Minutes, 4 November 1977; BRB, *R&A 1977*, p. 13, and cf. *Accountancy Age*, 12 May 1978, p. 11. Gearing adjustment allowed for the fact that part of the costs of inflation was carried by the Board's lenders.

6 BRB, *R&A 1978*, p. 64; *R&A 1979*, pp. 60–1.

7 BRB, *R&A 1977*, p. 7.

8 See G. R. Burt, Memo on 'Board and Business Objectives', 30 March 1976, BRB 30-1-4 Pt. 8.

9 British Rail's McKinsey-inspired organisation of 1970 is examined in Gourvish, *British Railways*, pp. 368–81.

10 I. V. Pugh–Marsh, 29 January 1974, and Marsh, 'Notes of Meeting with Sir Idwal Pugh—Wednesday, 30.1.74. Structure and Running of the Board', BRB 48-2-1 Pt. 2.

11 R. D. Poland (DOE)–Marsh, 27 September 1974; Marsh–Pugh, 4 March 1975; A. C. Farrow (Board Secretary, BRB), Note, 30 November 1976, BRB 48-2-1 Pt. 2. Marsh had proposed to appoint George Hill, Chairman and Chief Executive of British Transport Hotels, 1974–6, as a replacement for McKenna, but the DOE refused to vary the standard terms.

12 Mulley–Serpell, 30 August 1974, BRB 48-2-38; Interview with Sir David Serpell, 12 March 1991.

13 Interview with Derek Fowler, 16 February 1990; on recruitment problems see Marsh's comment in *The Times*, 11 October 1977, cit. in Gourvish, *British Railways*, p. 573.

14 Marsh–Sir Idwal Pugh (2nd Permanent Secretary, DOE), 24 September 1974, Marsh–Harding, 16 December 1974, BRB 48-2-39; Pugh–Marsh, 14 February 1975, BRB 48-2-1 Pt. 2; Confidential Memo on 'Board Membership', BRB Minutes, 13 February 1975, and also 10 April and 8 May 1975.

15 By this time Hayday was regarded by Marsh to be a 'declining asset'. See Marsh–Pugh, 21 March 1975, Harding–Marsh, 20 November 1975, BRB 48-2-16; BRB Minutes, 11 December 1975; Gourvish, *British Railways*, p. 331.

16 Marsh, Confidential Memo on 'Board Organisation', Chairman's Conference Minutes, 27 March 1975.

17 Marsh–Mulley, 7 and 19 May, Mulley–Marsh, 14 May and 4 June 1975, BRB 48-2-1 Pt. 2.

18 BRB Minutes, 12 September 1974, 13 November 1975; Gilbert–Marsh, 25 September 1975, BRB 48-2-34 Pt. 1; Gourvish, *British Railways*, p. 379.

19 Cf. Bosworth–Marsh, 11 February 1976, BRB 48-2-23.

20 Marsh–P. R. Baldwin (Second Permanent Secretary, DOE), 30 June 1976, BRB 48-2-1 Pt. 2. Marsh blamed the Department for this 'absurd and indefensible position'.

21 Marsh–Pugh, 21 March 1974, BRB 48-2-16.

22 Marsh, Note for Papers, 2 April 1974; Jones–Marsh, 28 June 1974, Marsh–Jones, 11 April 1975, BRB 48-2-23; BRB Minutes, 12 June 1975.

23 A lack of leadership was evident in the R&D management function under Dr K. H. Spring. Cf. 'Note of Meeting between Mr J. M. Bosworth, Dr. S. Jones and Dr K. H. Spring on Thursday, 19th September 1974', BRB 48-2-23, and interview with Dr Alan Wickens, 10 April 1989.

24 Evan Harding, Confidential Memo on 'Organisation of Research & Development', 20 January 1975, Chairman's Conference Minutes, and Confidential Discussion Note, 23 January 1975; Harding, Memo, 5 August 1975, BRB Minutes, 14 August 1975.

25 Marsh, Confidential Memo, 27 March 1975, cit.; BRB Minutes, 8 July 1976.

26 In 1974 the Minister had contemplated asking for McKenna's resignation: Marsh–Sir Robert Marshall (2nd Permanent Secretary, DOE), 16 December 1974 and reply, 20 December 1974, BRB 48-2-28.

27 Bosworth, Confidential Memo, 7 June 1976, BRB Minutes, 10 June 1976, and BRB 50-4-4 Pt. 2.

28 See Burt, Memos on 'Board Procedures', 5 November 1976 and 21 February 1977, BRB 30-2-7.

29 Cf. Minutes of 'Monthly Progress Meeting Between DTp and BRB: 2nd Meeting 19 November 1976', with Bosworth, Memo, 26 November 1976, Chairman's Conference Minutes, 2 December 1976; Bosworth–Cliff Rose, 14 January 1977, BRB 75-18-4 Pt. 2; Interviews with Sir Peter Baldwin, 19 June 1991 and John Welsby, 30 April 1998. Two key officials were seconded to British Rail in January 1979: Edward Osmotherley, who went to Planning, and John Welsby, who joined the Strategy Unit (see below). Osmotherley was quickly recalled, however. John F. H. Kearney (Management Development Officer, BRB)–Burt, 17 July 1979, Peter Baldwin (Permanent Secretary, DTp)–Parker, 8 October 1979, BRB 75-18-4 Pt. 2.

30 Sir Peter Parker, *For Starters: The Business of Life* (1989); profile in *Punch*, 3 November 1976, p. 778; BRB 50-4-4 Pt. 2. Parker was also director of Victoria Deep Water Terminal (Chairman, 1971–6) and the Renold Group.

31 The circumstances here were not only personal. Parker was perfectly aware that a low salary at the level of chairman placed ceilings on other managers below. This was a pressing theme in the nationalised industries in the 1970s. See Parker, *For Starters*, pp. 132–40; *Punch*, 1976, cit.; Gourvish, *British Railways*, pp. 360–1, 573–4. On press reaction to the salary see press cuttings for 8 April 1976 in BRB PR&P 302-5-6.

32 *Financial Times*, *Daily Telegraph*, *and Guardian*, 8 April 1976.

33 Parker–William Rodgers (SoS, DTp), formal letter, 26 November 1976, BRB 48-2-2 Pt. 1.

34 Parker–Rodgers, confidential note, 26 November 1976, BRB 48-2-2 Pt. 1; Gourvish, *British Railways*, pp. 338–9.

35 Parker, *For Starters*, p. 205. The adjectives are Parker's.

36 See T. R. Gourvish and N. Tiratsoo (eds.), *Missionaries and Managers: American Influences on European Management Education, 1945–60* (Manchester, 1998).

37 BRB 50-4-4 Pt. 2 and 48-2-42, 48-2-45.

38 Gilbert–Farrimond, 27 May 1976 and reply, 2 July 1976; Bosworth, 'Note of Meeting with Peter Baldwin, Friday, 1st October, 1976', and P. R. Baldwin–Farrimond, 8 October 1976, BRB 48-2-36 Pt. 1; Parker, 'Notes on discussion with HLF on 11th October 1976' and Parker–Farrimond, 22 October 1976, BRB 48-2-36 Pt. 2.

39 BRB 50-4-4 Pt. 2 and 48-2-44.

40 Cf. Gourvish, *British Railways*, pp. 329, 339, 364, 377.

41 It is clear that Campbell, Reid, Rose, and Urquhart obtained more favourable terms (an undertaking to re-employ at the maximum salary level of the comparable grade to that last filled, with continuation of corresponding pension rights) than Fowler had in 1975, the latter having to make substantial personal contributions to enhance his pension. See Parker, Confidential Memo on 'Board Organisation', BRB Minutes, 9 December 1976; Burt–Campbell et al., 10 December 1976, and Burt–J. Palmer (Under-Secretary (Railways), DOE), 13 December 1976; Farrow, Note, 30 November 1976; C. G. Lewin (Controller, Corporate Pensions)–Burt, 3 December 1976, BRB 48-2-1 Pt. 2.

42 M. V. Posner–Parker, 15 September 1976, BRB 48-2-46; *The Times*, 25 September 1976. On the DOE initiative see 'File Note of Meeting with Mr Beagley, Friday, 20/8/76', Bosworth, 'Note of Informal Lunch Meeting with Peter Lazarus Friday, 10th September 1976', BRB 20-100-3 Pt. 1.

43 McKenna departed at the end of his two-year contract on 31 August 1978, Walker died in office on 3 January 1978. BRB Minutes, 12 January and 12 August 1978.

44 Parker, *For Starters*, p. 184.

45 Interview with Derek Fowler, 16 February 1990, and cf. Richard R. Nelson and Sidney G. Winter, *An Evolutionary Theory of Economic Change* (Cambridge, MA, 1982); David Teece and Gary Pisano, 'The Dynamic Capabilities of Firms: an Introduction', *Industrial and Corporate Change*, 3(3) (1994), 537–56; Gary Hamel and C. K. Prahalad, *Competing for the Future* (Cambridge, MA, 1996).

46 Interview with Sir Peter Baldwin, 19 June 1991.

47 Interview with Derek Fowler, cit.

48 Parker–Rodgers, confidential note, 26 November 1976, cit.

49 The latter apparently was often fond of referring in somewhat reverential terms to the 'Mother Railway': Parker, *For Starters*, p. 206.

50 Cf. Burt, Memo on 'Board Procedures', 21 February 1977, BRB 30-2-7.

51 Burt, 'Board Headquarters Admin. Instructions No. 1 March 1978: Board Organisation and Procedures', and papers in BRB 30-2-1 Pt. 2 and 30-2-8 Pt. 3; BRB Minutes, 8 December 1977, 12 January 1978. The 15 reserved matters were: basic objectives; strategies via the annual Corporate Plan; business performance review; matters requiring Ministerial consent; basic relationship with government and parliament; matters with major strategic, commercial, or political sensitivity; major organisational changes;

major questions of personnel policy; senior posts; major questions of commercial policy and practice, including pricing; safety; overall control of finance and funding; R&D policy; significant public statements, including the annual *R&A*; standards of conduct.

52 See Burt, Memos on 'Board Organisation and Procedures', 5 and 22 December 1977, with Appendix D (Bosworth, Memo on 'The Role and Place of Planning', 5 December 1977), BRB Minutes, 8 December 1977, 12 January 1978.

53 Burt, Confidential Memo on 'Board Organisation and Procedures Planning and Investment', 2 February 1978, BRB Minutes, 9 February 1978. In September 1978 Dr B. J. Nield became Chief Investment Officer.

54 Report of the Committee of Enquiry on 'Conduct of the Board's Business', April 1971, BRB 30-2-30; Gourvish, *British Railways*, pp. 382–4.

55 Taylor–Burt, 20 December 1977, BRB Minutes, 12 January 1978.

56 Camp advised British Rail from February 1977 through his company Camden Communications for a reported £15,000 p.a. He had been a public relations adviser to Harold Wilson, and Director of Information Services at British Steel: *London Evening News*, 4 February 1977, 30 September 1980.

57 The boards were set up on a trial basis until 1979. Trade union representatives from NUR and TSSA were appointed, but ASLEF declined to participate: BRB Minutes, 14 October, 11 November, and 9 December 1976, 10 February 1977, 1 March and 17 May 1979; Bowick and Burt, Memo, 5 November 1976, Burt, Memos, 29 February and 10 May 1979; Chairman's Conference Minutes, 2 February 1978; TSSA file on 'Regional Railway Boards', G1/A1, TSSA.

58 The computing/OR officer was to report to Fowler, the productivity officer to Urquhart. The aim was to sharpen the response to a commitment to increased productivity. See Fowler and Urquhart, Memo on 'Role and Organisation of Management Services', 14 September 1977, Chairman's Conference Minutes, 22 September 1977. Hylton Craig, Director, Management Services since July 1976, became Director, Management Services (Data Processing & OR) in August 1977, but there was difficulty in filling the other post. It was not until October 1978 that Michael Ferrand of Cannon Assurance was appointed Director, Internal Consultancy Services, following a headhunting operation. See Rose, Confidential Memo, 5 September 1978, BRB Minutes, 14 September 1978.

59 BRB Minutes, 8 September 1977. The Panel included Sir Hugh Casson, President, Royal Academy, Sir Paul (from 1978 Lord) Reilly, Director of the Design Council, and Michael Middleton, Director of the Civic Trust.

60 Burt and Rose, Confidential Memo on 'Board Organisation', 6 December 1976, BRB Minutes, 9 December 1976.

61 Bowick, Memo on 'The Railway Command Structure', 5 December 1977, BRB Minutes, 8 December 1977.

62 BRB Minutes, 12 January 1978.

63 Bowick, Memo, 5 December 1977, cit., appended to BRB Admin. Instructions No. 1, March 1978, cit. For a General Manager's reaction see John Palette (GM, Scottish Region)–Bowick, 22 December 1976, BRB Chief Executive's files, AN156/59, PRO.

64 Interviews with Sir Robert Reid, 16 December 1987, and Gerry Burt, 21 September 1987.

65 BRB Strategy Steering Group Terms of Reference, 6 July 1978, BRB 22-24-85.

66 Their expertise embraced personnel (Kentridge), planning (Prideaux), R&D (Spring), and overseas projects (Cobbett).The others—P. G. Douglas, S. J. Gielnik, G. R. Papworth, and G. Watts—had experience in planning and finance. There was some irony in the conjunction of Myers and Cobbett: Myers had owed his elevation to the post of GM (Eastern) to an embarrassment experienced by Cobbett, which forced him to step down. See Burt and Rose, Confidential Memos, 31 March 1977, BRB Minutes, 14 April 1977; *Glasgow Herald*, 26 March 1977; Interview with Geoffrey Myers, 19 May 1992.

67 Parker was also a member ex officio. See Bowick, Memo on 'Strategy Unit', 5 September 1978, BRB 20-23-1.

68 Bowick became Chairman, Supply Committee; Bosworth Chairman, BT Hotels, Campbell Chairman, Transmark, and Urquhart Chairman, BRE-Metro, and BREL (in place of Campbell). BRB Minutes, 12 October 1978, and Board Headquarters Admin. Instructions No. 9, September 1978, BRB 30-2-1 Pt. 2.

69 Robert W. Roseveare (Secretary, British Steel Corporation)–Burt, 21 November 1978, BRB 30-2-8 Pt. 4.

70 C. G. Lewin, 'Headquarters Staff Report', March 1979, pp. 3, 6, 8, BRB Board Members General Papers, Secretariat [Sec] Box 2285.

71 The initial stimulus for the move to Euston, first raised in 1973, was the urgent need to refurbish '222'. See Burt and Rose, Memos, 4 April 1977, Chairman's Conference Minutes, 7 April 1977, 2 February 1978; BRB Minutes, 14 April and 9 June 1977, 9 February 1978. The first meetings held at Rail House, Euston, were Board Executive, 22 November 1979, and the Board, 6 December 1979. The block was part of a major development by the British Rail Property Board.

72 BRB, *R&A 1976*, pp. 35–8. These losses were more than made up by the surplus on non-operational property of £6.3 m.

73 Interview with Michael Bosworth, 22 March 1988.

74 Cf. Chairman's Conference Minutes, 22 April 1976.

75 Parker, reported in Bosworth, Memo on 'Board and Business Objectives: Subsidiaries', 12 January 1977, BRB Minutes, 13 January 1977.

76 BRB Minutes, 13 January 1977; BRB, *R&A 1977*, p. 8.

77 Since 1969 the Minister had imposed a constraint on the use of railway workshops, where only marginal surplus capacity at any one works was to be used for private party work. Property transactions, particularly those relating to lease and lease-back arrangements, were subject to Departmental approval, and shipping operations were fettered by numerous restrictions. See T. R. Barron (Controller of Corporate Planning), Confidential Memo on 'Board and Business Objectives: Subsidiaries', 6 January 1977, BRB Minutes, 13 January 1977, BREL Minutes, 9 November 1977; Burt, Memo on 'Board Subsidiaries—Powers of Manufacture', 24 August 1978, BRB Minutes, 14 September 1978.

78 Department of Transport, Scottish Development Department, and Welsh Office, *Transport Policy*, June 1977, P.P. 1976–7, xlviii, Cmnd. 6836, para. 213: 'If there are obstacles to a genuinely profitable future for them, the Government will consider with the Board what practicable means there are for overcoming or removing them.'

79 Treasury, *The Nationalised Industries*, March 1978 [published in April], P.P. 1977–8, xxxvii, Cmnd. 7131.

80 Cf. BRB Minutes, 12 May 1977; Bosworth, Memo on 'Board and Business Objectives: Subsidiaries', 31 March 1978, BRB Minutes, 13 April 1978.

81 Burt, Memo on 'Board Organisation and Procedures', BRB Minutes, 8 December 1977.

82 The hotels were seen as comfortable but rather shabby; the rail catering service was the subject of considerable criticism. Cf. Baroness Seear (LSE)–Parker, 3 August 1977, BRB PR&P 302-42-15.

83 Farrimond–Parker, 22 March 1977, BRB 367-22-1 Pt. 5.

84 BTH Ltd Minutes, 16 February and 14 September 1977; BRB Minutes, 12 May and 8 September 1977.

85 BTH Minutes, 18 May, 20 July, 16 November, and 14 December 1977; Lawrence, Confidential Memo on 'British Transport Hotels Ltd', 2 February 1978, BRB Minutes, 9 February 1978. The two MDs were Ian Jack and Bill Currie. Coopers & Lybrand had controversially advocated the transfer of the hotels to the National Enterprise Board.

86 Land, Director of Corporate Planning, National Freight Corporation, was a former chief accountant of BRB Western Region: Rose, Confidential Memo, 11 July 1978, BRB Minutes, 13 July 1978; Interview with Peter Land, 10 May 1978.

87 Bosworth, Memo on 'Report by Special Working Party on Shipping & International Services Division', 28 July 1977, BRB Minutes, 11 August 1977. On the setting up of the European Rail Traffic Manager's Organisation see P. Corbishley (Chief Planning Officer), Memo on 'Board and Business Objectives', 15 March 1978, BRB Minutes, 13 April 1978.

88 BRB Minutes, 10 August and 14 December 1978, 4 January 1979; BRB, *Third Report of the Board on Organisation*, November 1978, P.P. 1978–9, xxiv, HC2.

89 Freightliners had been 51% owned by the NFC since 1969; an earlier Select Committee, in 1973, had rejected the idea of a return to BRB ownership. Gourvish, *British Railways*, p. 365; BRB, *Transport Policy: An Opportunity for Change* (July 1976), p. 18; *Report of S.C. Nat. Ind. on The Role of British Rail in Public Transport*, vol. I, 5 April 1977, P.P. 1976–7, xxxiii, HC305–I, paras. 271–6; William Rodgers, *Parl. Deb. (Commons)*, 5th ser. (Session 1977–8), vol. 939, 21 November 1977, cols. 1189–90.

90 Fowler, Memos on 'Freightliners Ltd.—Annual Accounts 1977', 5 January 1978 and 'Freightliners Ltd. Financial Reconstruction', 3 August 1978, Bowick and Burt, Memo on 'Freightliners Ltd.', 2 June 1978, BRB Minutes, 12 January, 8 June, and 10 August 1978; BRB Board Executive Minutes, 2 March and 3 August 1978.

91 Notably at the Department/BRB monthly progress meetings, September–December 1977, referred to in Peter Corbishley, Memo, 15 March 1978, cit.

92 Burt, Memo on 'Board Subsidiaries—Powers of Manufacture', 24 August 1978, BRB Minutes, 14 September 1978.

93 Lawrence, Memo on 'Commercial Property Development—Lease and Leaseback Transactions', 3 August 1977, BRB Minutes, 11 August 1977; BR Property Board Minutes, 16 June and 18 August 1977; Corbishley, Memo, 15 March 1978, cit.

94 Cf. Bosworth and Burt, Memo on 'Relationship Between Board and Subsidiary Activities', 7 December 1978, BRB Minutes, 14 December 1978.

95 BRB Minutes, 9 March 1978.

96 Chairman's Conference Minutes, 23 June 1977. Minimum expectations were for subsidiaries to generate sufficient profit, after providing for depreciation at historic cost, to cover attributed interest and provide for asset replacement.

97 See Fowler's December 1978 proposals for an in-house financial reconstruction of the freightliners, hovercraft, and Sealink businesses, which involved the introduction of

more 'risk' capital, i.e. non-interest-bearing capital, into the balance sheets. Fowler, Memo on 'Financial Reconstruction of the Board's Divisions and Subsidiaries', 4 December 1978, BRB 29-1-10 Pt. 3; Board Executive Minutes, 7 December 1978.

98 BRB Minutes, 13 April 1978.

99 These activities were however affected by external constraints, not least the difficulties with hovercraft vessel procurement, losses on contract, and poor industrial relations, and the fact that BREL's main role was to service a customer—BRB—which was unable to give stable forecasts of requirement. See Corbishley, Memo, 15 March 1978 cit.; Interview with Ian Gardiner, MD, BREL in *Modern Railways*, February 1980, pp. 61–4; BRB, *R&A 1977*, p. 33, *1978*, p. 35; BRB Minutes, 9 March, 13 July, and 10 August 1978; Board Executive Minutes, 6 July 1978.

100 BRB, *R&A 1978*, p. 79. Gross income in the published BREL accounts included income from BRB after eliminating internal interest and profit. The operating surplus shown was thus on external sales only. Ibid. p. 51.

101 See Ministerial assents, 1979–82, in BRB 29-1-10 Pt. 3. The total deficiency guaranteed amounted to £20 m. by 1981, viz. Sealink £10 m., hovercraft £5 m., hotels £4 m., and Transmark £1 m. J. L. Walton (Director of Accounts)–Burt, 11 February 1981, BRB 29-1-10 Pt. 3.

102 'Note for File', 13 June 1972; 'Note of Discussion between Chairmen [of NIs] and Lord Rothschild', 29 October 1972; NICG, 'Relations between the Government and Nationalised Industries', 25 February 1974, BRB 21-3-50.

103 NEDO, *A Study of UK Nationalised Industries: Their Role in the Economy and Control in the Future* (1976), pp. 8–12 and see summary in BRB 373-33-12 Pt. 5. The study arose out of a recommendation in the *Report of the Select Committee on Nationalised Industries (S.C. Nat. Ind.) on Capital Investment Procedures*, December 1973, P.P. 1973–4, x, HC65, and the government's response in Treasury, *Capital Investment Procedures*, June 1975, P.P. 1974–5, xxvii, Cmnd. 6106.

104 Cf. the debate in *Modern Railways*, January 1977, pp. 1–2; Jonathan Charkham, *Keeping Good Company: A Study of Corporate Governance in Five Countries* (Oxford, 1994), pp. 6–58, 363–4. The Bullock Committee argued that it would be difficult to introduce the German system into British company law: *Report of the Committee of Inquiry on Industrial Democracy*, January 1977, P.P. 1976–7, xvi, Cmnd. 6706, pp. 72–7.

105 Confidential Memo on 'Board Organisation', 9 December 1976, BRB Minutes, 9 December 1976.

106 Parker–Rodgers, 6 January 1977, BRB 373-33-12 Pt. 5; NICG papers, 6/22, BLPES. British Rail's published response was on 31 March 1977, *Second Special Report of S.C. Nat. Ind. on Comments by Nationalised Industries on the National Economic Development Office Report*, P.P. 1976–7, xxxv, HC345, pp. xv–xvii.

107 *Report on Industrial Democracy*, 1977, p. 161; NICG Meeting, 21 June 1976, 'NICG Comments on NEDO Study of Nationalised Industry Relations', 15 June 1976; NICG papers, 6/21, BLPES; Jim Driscoll (British Steel Corporation), Note with 'NEDO Report: Initial Reactions', 5 November 1976, 6/22, BLPES; Note for Ministerial–NICG Liaison Meeting, 26 January 1977, BRB 373-33-12 Pt. 5. For background see John Vickers and George Yarrow, *Privatization: An Economic Analysis* (Cambridge, MA, 1988), pp. 128–9.

108 See Driscoll–NICG Members, 28 April 1977, enclosing 'Draft Report by Officials on Issues Raised, Other than Questions of Board Structure', in Burt and Fowler, Memo to Chairman's Committee, 3 May 1977, BRB 373-33-12 Pt. 5.

109 *S.C. Nat. Ind.*, *Role of British Rail*, 1977, paras. 427–32; DTp, *Transport Policy*, 1977, paras. 279–91.

110 Marsh–Colin Ambler (National Coal Board), 24 October 1975, BRB 80-1-40.

111 Treasury, *Nationalised Industries*, 1978, paras. 28–9; *Report on Industrial Democracy*, May 1978, P.P. 1977–8, xviii, Cmnd. 7231.

112 BRB Minutes, 9 March and 10 August 1978. In the event, no consultation bodies were established for the subsidiary businesses.

113 Ibid., 14 December 1978, 5 April and 6 September 1979.

114 Board Executive Minutes, 7 December 1978; Queen's Speech, 1 November 1978, *Parl. Deb. (Commons)*, 5th ser. (Session 1978–9), vol. 957, col. 6; *Second Report of S.C. Nat Ind. on Consumers and the Nationalised Industries: Pre-Legislative Hearings*, April 1979, P.P. 1978–9, xviii, HC334, paras. 39–45.

115 BRB Minutes, 11 November 1976, NICG papers, 6/21–2, BLPES and BRB 373-33-12 Pt. 5. Parker, who received a knighthood in June 1978, acted as chairman of NICG in that year.

116 BRB, *R&A 1976*, p. 5, *1977*, p. 5; Parker, Dimbleby Lecture, 1983, BRB.

117 Gourvish, *British Railways*, p. 573 and see above, fn. 29.

118 Review Body on Top Salaries, *Report No. 6: Report on Top Salaries* (December 1974), P.P. 1974–5, xxxii, Cmnd. 5846; NBPI, *Report No. 107 on Top Salaries in the Private Sector and Nationalised Industries* (March 1969), P.P. 1968–9, xlii, Cmnd. 3970.

119 The May 1977 increase was backdated to 1 January 1977, the December increase of 5% applied from 1 January 1978, though up to 10% could be paid to Board members earning under £13,000: see correspondence and papers in BRB 48-2-1 Pt. 2. Eventually, the government conceded the full 10%, in August 1978, as part of its staged acceptance of Report No. 10 (see below).

120 Rooke–Callaghan, 23 December 1977, BRB 48-2-1 Pt. 2.

121 BRB Memo, 18 October 1977, BRB 48-2-1 Pt. 2.

122 For BSC see NEDO, Report, 1976, p. 35; for C&W see *Financial Times*, 15 September 1977.

123 Review Body on Top Salaries, *Report No. 10: Second Report on Top Salaries* (June 1978), P.P. 1977–8, xlviii, Cmnd. 7253; Gourvish, *British Railways*, p. 573; Prime Minister's Written Answer, 4 July 1978, *Parl. Deb. (Commons)*, 5th ser. (Session 1977–8), vol. 953, 97–8. The Committee suggested a salary of £40,000 for the Chairman of BR, £21,000–£26,000 for BRB members.

124 Lazarus–Parker, 27 April and 10 August 1978, 12 April 1979, and supporting papers in BRB 48-2-40.

125 NEDO, Report, 1976, p. 35.

126 Lawrence and Barron were paid higher salaries for working three or four days a week. Posner, due to receive in 1978 a similar sum to that paid to Serpell and Taylor, was caught up in the Boyle implementation exercise, and not paid more until 1979. See BRB 48-2-29, 34, 38, 46, 47.

127 Review Body, *Report No. 10*, para. 88; Lazarus–Parker, 10 August 1978, BRB 48-2-40; Rodgers–Caldecote, 21 November and 27 December 1978, BRB 48-2-28.

128 An award in August 1979, backdated to April, took Parker's salary to £36,950 and the average Board member to £21,500. Posner and Serpell were paid £4,500 and Caldecote £2,330. See A. C. Farrow, Note, 7 August 1979, BRB 48-2-48.

129 NEDO Report, 1976, pp. 24, 30, 32, 36–8.

130 BRB, *R&A 1979*, p. 5. These figures refer to the extent to which the Board beat the PSO cash limit. Lower figures, of £17 m., £27 m., and £8 m. for 1976, 1977, and 1978 record the extent to which the Board beat the contracted price: *R&A 1978*, p. 5.

131 BRB, *R&A 1976*, p. 5; *1977*, p. 6, *1978*, p. 6; Interview with John Palmer, 4 August 1992.

132 Board Executive Minutes, 3 August 1978; BRB Minutes, 10 August 1978; BRB, *R&A 1978*, p. 24; *1979*, pp. 4, 23.

133 DOE, *Transport Policy: A Consultation Document* (2 vols., 1976), esp. I, paras. 7.10–11, 7.31–7, 7.39, and 7.63; BRB, *Opportunity for Change*, pp. 7–9, 14–15, 17, and see also *Modern Railways*, June 1976, pp. 215–20, September 1976, pp. 337–40.

134 BRB, *Opportunity for Change*, p. 10; TGWU Press Release, 13 April 1976, in TUC File on Transport Policy, 1976, MSS292/D/File 6537, MRC.

135 BRB, *Opportunity for Change*, pp. 13–15, 19, 36–7. The 1978 White Paper on *Nationalised Industries* stated that no further industries would be allowed to issue equity (public dividend) capital: paras. 86–8.

136 S.C. *Nat Ind., Role of British Rail*, 1977, pp. cxxv–cxxix. Of the 54 recommendations, 11 dealt with service levels, competition, and pricing (including the call for a London travelcard), 10 with targets and subsidy/support mechanisms, 9 with disclosure of information, 8 with investment, and 4 with productivity and staff cuts (including reductions in the number of second trainmen and guards).

137 DTp, *Transport Policy*, 1977, summary, pp. 67–70.

138 Parker, in BRB, *R&A 1977*, p. 5. The Board's published response to the Select Committee was in September 1977: DTp, *The Role of British Rail in Public Transport: The Government's Response to the First Report from the Select Committee on Nationalised Industries* (Session 1976–77), HC305, November 1977, P.P. 1977–8, xl, Cmnd. 7038, Annex, pp. 31–4.

139 S.C. *Nat Ind., Role of British Rail*, paras. 89, 359, 412, 426; White Paper on *Transport Policy*, paras. 218–20. The Select Committee also supported BRB on the equity capital concept, freightliner ownership, and tax constraints on heavy lorries, paras. 259, 276, 294.

140 Cf. 'When you've got it—flaunt it', editorial in *Modern Railways*, May 1977, p. 165. Here, Parker's stance was contrasted with the mass whingeing of the rail lobby and Maginot Line thinking in some BR circles.

141 This is reflected in the Consultation Document of 1976, paras. 2.27, 3.6, and Annex, pp. 20–1.

142 S.C. *Nat. Ind., Role of British Rail*, paras. 180, 253, 305, 468 (Table); *Transport Policy*, 1977, paras. 223–5, p. 61 (Table).

143 DTp, *Role of British Rail: Government's Response*, November 1977, Cmnd. 7038, paras. 6–7, pp. 21–2 (Tables).

144 Treasury, *Nationalised Industries: A Review of Economic and Financial Objectives*, November 1967, P.P. 1967–8, xxxix, Cmnd. 3437.

145 Treasury, *The Financial and Economic Obligations of the Nationalised Industries*, April 1961, P.P. 1960–1, xxvii, Cmnd. 1337; Jim Tomlinson, *Government and the*

Enterprise Since 1900 (Oxford, 1994), pp. 205–7; D. Heald, 'The Economic and Financial Control of U.K. Nationalised Industries', *Economic Journal*, XC (1980), 243–65; Vickers and Yarrow, *Privatization: An Economic Analysis*, pp. 130–4.

146 White Paper on *Nationalised Industries*, 1978, paras. 19, 44, 48–9.

147 Ibid., paras. 20–1. The new powers were based on provisions in the Electricity Industry Bill: Department of Energy, *Re-Organisation of the Electricity Supply Industry in England & Wales*, April 1978, P.P. 1977–8, xi, Cmnd. 7134, Annex B, ss. 9–11.

148 John Biffen (Chief Secretary to Treasury)–Sir William Barlow (Post Office and NICG), 3 April 1980; Biffen, Written Answer, 3 April 1980, *Parl. Deb. (Commons)*, 5th ser. (Session 1979–80), vol. 962, *325.*

149 Six performance indicators were given for 1967–77: passenger-miles and net tonne-miles per member of staff employed; passenger-miles per loaded passenger train-mile; net tonne-miles per wagon; loaded train-miles per total route-mile; and average wagon-load. Four international indicators were also provided.

150 BRB, *R&A 1977*, pp. 10–14. A promise to provide actual rather than estimated results by sector was not kept. See Terence R. Gourvish, 'British Rail's "Business-Led" Organization, 1977–1990: Government–Industry Relations in Britain's Public Sector', *Business History Review*, 64 (Spring 1990), 124 fn. 27.

151 See *Reports of S.C. Nat. Ind. on The British Steel Corporation*, November and December 1977, P.P. 1977–8, xxxvii, HC26–I, xxxviii, HC127–I.

152 DOE, *Transport Policy*, 1976, vol. I, paras. 7.46, 7.52–3.

153 DTp, *Transport Policy*, 1977, paras. 130–2, 168, 171, 276.

154 J. Urquhart, Memo to BRB Railway Executive on 'Performance Indicators', 13 February 1978.

155 BRB, *Opportunity for Change*, pp. 12–13; BRB, *R&A 1976*, pp. 14–15; Price Commission, *British Railways Board—Increases in Passenger Fares*, February 1978, P.P. 1977–8, xlvii, HC225, paras. 1.29–32, 5.2; Derek Fowler, 'Financial Analysis of Railway Operations', *Chartered Institute of Transport Journal*, May 1979, 281–8.

156 Chairman's Conference Minutes, 3 March 1977, BRB Minutes, 10 March 1977; Fowler, Memo to Railway Executive, 6 March 1978, BRB 248-757-1; Fowler, Memo on 'Development of Avoidable Cost Techniques for Rail Business Sectors', 12 May 1978, Board Executive Minutes, 25 May 1978; H. R. Wilkinson (Chief Management Accountant), Memo to Railway Executive on 'Profit Planning & Cost Centre Analysis; Sector Avoidable Costs Study', 8 February 1979, BRB 248-757-1; Gourvish, 'British Rail's "Business-Led" Organization', 118, 124; BRB, *Measuring Cost and Profitability in British Rail* (1978).

157 Cf. Bosworth, Confidential Memo, 3 February 1977, BRB Minutes, 10 February, 10 March, and 13 April 1977; Fowler, Memo on 'Disclosure of Financial and Associated Information to the Department of Transport', 6 September 1978, BRB Minutes, 8 June and 14 September 1978.

158 Jack Wiseman, 'The Political Economy of Nationalised Industry', in J. M. Buchanan et al. (eds.), *The Economics of Politics* (IEA Readings 18, 1978); Stephen C. Littlechild, *The Fallacy of the Mixed Economy* (IEA Hobart Paper 80, 1978) and 'Controlling the Nationalised Industries: Quis custodiet ipsos custodes?', *Birmingham University Faculty of Commerce & Social Sciences Discussion Paper*, Series B, no. 56 (August 1979).

Chapter 3

1 BRB, *R&A 1974*, p. 47; BRB, *Facts & Figures* (June 1978), pp. 18, 25. In 1972 442,000 people travelled daily into central London on BR trains during the 7–10 a.m. peak. *Facts & Figures*, p. 18.

2 BRB, *R&A 1974*, p. 49. *The Times 1000 1976–1977* (1976), pp. 26–7, 103, provides data for 1975. British Rail was ranked third in employment with 251,627, behind the Post Office and the National Coal Board. The largest employer in the private sector was GEC (206,000). In turnover terms British Rail was ranked seventeenth.

3 Reid, Memo on 'Marketing Initiatives 1977/78', 2 March 1978, BRB Minutes, 9 March 1978.

4 Interviews with Derek Fowler, 16 February 1990, and David Allen, 9 July 1990. A 'hypothetical' example provided by Fowler in February 1977 showed an infrastructure cost of £460m., and contributions of £80m. by freight, £140m. by Inter-City, and £70m. by London & South East. Fowler, Memo to Chairman's Conference on 'White Paper—Financial Matters: Contribution Accounting', 28 February 1977, Appendix A, Chairman's Conference Minutes, 3 March 1977.

5 Bowick–F. D. Pattisson, 13 May 1977, Chief Executive file on 'Monthly Reports to the Board', AN156/2, PRO.

6 BRB, *Facts and Figures* (2nd edn., 1980), p. 19. The Bristol data are for Temple Meads only (there were also 14 trains a day serving Bristol (Parkway): British Rail timetable, 2 May 1977–7 May 1978, RAIL915/11, PRO).

7 94 trains called at Gidea Park in both 1957 and 1977; in 1957 these were 74 terminating and 20 terminating at Brentwood or Shenfield, and in 1977 63 terminating and 31 terminating at Shenfield. British Railways (Eastern Region) timetable, 16 September 1956–16 June 1957 (Alterations, 6 May 1957), RAIL908/11; British Rail timetable, 1977–8, RAIL915/11, PRO.

8 There were changes in the intervening years, e.g. 10 trains on weekdays in 1936 and 1956, and 12 in 1966. See Great Eastern Railway timetable, 2 October 1922, RAIL 943/1; Bradshaw's Railway Guide, September 1936, RAIL903/270; British Railways (Eastern Region) timetable, September 1956–June 1957, 18 April 1966–5 March 1967, RAIL908/11, 29; British Rail timetable, 1977–8, RAIL915/11, PRO.

9 Cf. BRB, *Transport Policy: An Opportunity for Change* (July 1976), pp. 51–2.

10 OGAS = Other Grant-Aided Services, PTE + OPS = the services funded by the Passenger Transport Executives of local authorities plus 'Other Provincial Services'.

11 BRB, *Facts and Figures* (1980), p. 26. The Serpell Report of 1983 showed train-load traffic increasing from 55% in 1970 to 86% in 1979: *Railway Finances. Report of a Committee chaired by Sir David Serpell KCB KMG CBE* (1983), p. 21.

12 Cf. David H. Jones (Executive Director, Finance, BRB), Memo on 'Rail Pricing in 1973 and 1974', 1 August 1974, BRB 99-2-1 Pt. 6. The Minister could not refuse increases justified solely on 'allowable cost' grounds; the Price Commission could not refuse increases justified on a deficit basis, but was subject to ministerial direction on the amount to be approved.

13 BRB, *R&A 1976*, p. 4; Price Commission, Report on *British Railways Board—Increase in Passenger Fares*, 15 February 1978, P.P. 1977–8, xlvii, HC225, pp. 1, 3, 11.

14 Cf. Kenneth Westoby (Senior Economist, BRB Corporate Planning)–Tom Barron and Gerry Burt, 8 September 1974, BRB 99-2-1 Pt. 6; Alan Chamberlain (Chief Passenger

Manager, Western Region), Paper on 'Pricing—Possible Policies', December 1980, BRB 99-2-1 Pt. 9.

15 Gourvish, *British Railways*, pp. 479–82; Price Commission, *British Railways Board—Increases in Passenger Fares*, 1978, pp. 3, 12, 21–3.

16 A tabulation for 1978–9 divided full fares into four categories (1st single, 1st return, 2nd single, 2nd return), reduced fares into nine (AwayDay 1st, 2nd; weekend 1st, 2nd; monthly 1st, 2nd; economy; big city saver; other) and seasons into four (week, month, quarter, annual). Tabulation of 'B.R. Passenger Journeys and Receipts 1978–1979', 1980, BRB 99-2-1 Pt. 9. Further subdivisions were made on a sector basis. In London & South East, for example, there were three subdivisions—Inner, Outer, and Peripheral—and within each of these four segments—Peak Season, Peak Full Fare, Off-Peak Full Fare, and Off Peak Reduced Fare. H. C. Sanderson (Executive Director, BRB Passenger), Memo to Executive Directors' Conference on 'Passenger Business Objectives: London and South-East Area', 7 October 1976, BRB 99-2-1 Pt. 7.

17 BRB RMG Minutes, 27 February, 27 March, 19 April, and 22 May 1974; Notification to Price Commission, 28 February 1974, BRB 99-2-50 Pt. 1; Mulley–Marsh, 26 March 1974, Marsh–Mulley, 3 and 10 April 1974, BRB 99-2-1 Pt. 6; Jones, Memo, 1 August 1974. Part of the delay was caused by the Board itself, which tried to include the estimated costs of the 1974 pay round in an allowable costs application. When this was rejected the Board shifted to an application on a deficit basis.

18 BRB Minutes, 8 August 1974, Marsh–Mulley, 27 August 1974, BRB, *R&A 1974*, p. 3, cit. in Gourvish, *British Railways*, pp. 485–6; Anthony E. T. Griffiths (Executive Director, BRB Passenger), Report on 'The Passenger Business', March 1975, BRB Minutes, 8 May 1975; Schedule of 'Price Control 1971–75—Significant Events', 9 May 1975, BRB 99-2-50 Pt. 2; Paper on 'Outline of Railway Pricing Applications and Effect of Government Intervention', 2 March 1976, BRB FR 246-2-134 Pt. 10.

19 BRB, *R&A 1972–4*. The reported costs increases were: 10% (1972), 6% (1973), and 33% (1974).

20 Bowick, Confidential Memo on 'Passenger Pricing: 1976', 4 November 1975, BRB Minutes, 13 November 1975. Differential increases in 1977 were: Inter-City 10%, L&SE 16%, and OPS 13%. Robert B. Reid, Memo on 'Marketing Initiatives 1977/78', 2 March 1978, BRB Minutes, 9 March 1978.

21 Cf. BRB Minutes, 13 February, 9 October, and 13 November 1975; Griffiths, Report on 'The Passenger Business', March 1975, cit.; Bowick, Memo on 'Passenger Pricing: 1976', November 1975, cit., and Griffiths–Bosworth, 10 February 1975, BRB 99-2-1 Pt. 7; Bowick, Memos on 'Pricing: Passenger Business', 7 May and n.d. [September 1976], BRB Minutes, 8 January, 13 May, and 23 September 1976; Reid, Memo on 'Procedures and Timescale for Increasing Fares and Charges', 26 January 1979, BRB 99-2-1 Pt. 8. Of course, part of the complexity of the internal processes was caused by the need to prepare a range of pricing schemes in an attempt to anticipate government thinking: Griffiths, Report, 1975, cit.

22 BRB, *R&A 1975–7*; BRB Minutes, 13 May 1976; Bowick, Memo, September 1976, cit. The complexity of fares was tackled in 1979. See Reid, Confidential Memo on 'Revision of Reduced Fare Structure', 22 February 1979, BRB Minutes, 1 March 1979.

23 W. J. Sharp (DOE)–Bowick, 24 February 1975, BRB FR 246-2-134 Pt. 6; 'Rail Pricing in 1975: Note of a Meeting held at 222 Marylebone Road on Friday 28th February 1975', BRB 99-2-50 Pt. 1.

24 Cf. Marsh, 'Note of Meeting with Sir Idwal Pugh held on 6.2.75. at his request and in response to my letter to him dated 29.1.75.', 12 February 1975, BRB 99-2-1 Pt. 7; Bosworth–Pugh, 27 March 1975, Marsh's Papers, BRB. Marsh put it this way: 'On the one hand the Government were urging us to price to the limit and on the other hand the Minister was telling all and sundry that we were a social service now'. Marsh, 'Note'.

25 'Notes of Meeting with Price Commission 29th October 1977', BRB 99-2-50 Pt. 3.

26 Price Commission, *British Railways Board—Increases in Passenger Fares*, 1978, p. iv.

27 Ibid. pp. 28, 38; BRB Minutes, 13 May 1976; Peter Baldwin–Parker, 5 December 1977, BRB 99-6-2 Pt. 2; Rodgers–Parker, 19 September 1978, BRB 99-2-1 Pt. 8. In fact, a second increase in 1978 was found to be unnecessary on financial grounds: BRB Minutes, 11 May 1978.

28 Reid, Confidential Memo on 'Passenger Pricing 1979', n.d., BRB Minutes, 8 June 1978; Reid–Parker, 18 September 1978; Rodgers–Parker, 19 September 1978 and reply, 5 October 1978, BRB 99-2-1 Pt. 8; Williams (Price Commission)–Parker, 23 November 1978, BRB 99-2-50 Pt. 4; BRB Minutes, 10 August, 12 October, and 14 December 1978.

29 Cf. discussion in BRB Minutes, 8 January and 13 May 1976; Posner–Parker, 22 September 1978, Parker–Rodgers, 5 October 1978, BRB 99-2-1 Pt. 8.

30 Bowick, Confidential Memo on 'Passenger Pricing 1977', 7 October 1976, BRB Minutes, 14 October 1976.

31 Parker, Confidential Memo on 'Pricing: Passenger Business', 23 September 1976, BRB Minutes, 23 September and 14 October 1976; BRJCC Minutes, 15 September and 29 October 1976; *Modern Railways*, November 1976, pp. 417–18; Philip Bagwell, *The Railwaymen: The History of the National Union of Railwaymen. Volume 2: The Beeching Era and After* (1982), p. 337.

32 Cf. RMG Minutes, 15 December 1976.

33 Sanderson, Memo, 7 October 1976, cit. The calculation was of course extremely sensitive to assumptions about future real staff costs.

34 Bert Gemmell (Chief Passenger Manager, Eastern Region)–Parker, 23 September 1976, BRB 99-2-1 Pt. 9.

35 Price Commission, *British Railways Board—Increases in Passenger Fares*, 1978, p. 3.

36 Ibid., p. 1.

37 Ibid., p. 17.

38 DOE Press Notice, 28 January 1974, BRB 33-60-1 Pt. 5; Sharp–Harding, 30 July 1974, BRB 33-1-5 Pt. 8.

39 Sharp–Harding, 30 July 1974, K. Peter (DOE)–Harding, 30 April 1975, A. Flexman (DOE)–Burt, 26 October 1977, BRB 33-1-5 Pt. 8; BRB 33-65-13; BRB 33-64-22; BRB 33-62-115 Pt. 2; BRB PPO 4–7 and 4–10. A full list of minor closures, station resitings, etc., appears in Gerald Daniels and Les Dench, *Passengers No More* (3rd edn., Shepperton, 1980). The others were: Gloucester (Eastgate) (Dec. 1975), Gogarth (Jan. 1976), Cheltenham Spa (Racecourse) (March 1976), Canonbury–Finsbury Park (Nov. 1976), Backworth (June 1977), Blackhouse Jnc.–Hawkhill Jnc. (June 1977), and Bootle–Edge Hill (May 1978).

40 John Palmer (DOE)–Burt, 5 July 1976, BRB 33-1-5 Pt. 8.

41 Operating losses in 1973 ranged from 2.2p to 14.0p per passenger-mile. The lines/services involved included Glasgow–Oban, Glasgow–Fort William, Barking–Kentish Town, Manningtree–Harwich, Bournemouth–Weymouth, Rugby–Stafford,

Ipswich–Felixstowe, and Shrewsbury–Aberystwyth. See 'Review of Passenger Services', n.d. [*c.*1974], loose in BRB Guard Book 16 (1974–5).

42 Griffiths, enclosing 'Passenger Services Review', 15 November 1974, BRB Chief Executive's files, BRB X31–139. The total saving was put at £3.5–4.0m. (using historic data and assuming 70% of costs could be saved within two years). Group I (22 services, 689 route-miles, £3.0m. saving) included many lines which appeared in the earlier list of 1974 (n. 41 above).

43 Marsh–Gilbert, 11 August 1975, Marsh's Papers; Sharp–Barron, 5 May 1975, BRB X31–139. This list included Glasgow–Oban, Inverness–Wick/Thurso/Kyle, Fort William–Mallaig, Swansea–Shrewsbury–Aberystwyth, Lincoln–Skegness, Hull–Scarborough, Ipswich–Lowestoft, York–Harrogate, Kentish Town–Moorgate, Romford–Upminster, Bedford–Bletchley, and Ashford–Ore.

44 DOE, *Transport Policy*, Vol. I (1976), para. 7.59; BRB, *Opportunity for Change* (1976), para. 5.9; BRB, Memo to BRJCC on 'Public Transport Integration', November 1976, BRB PPO 1–7 Pt. 1; *Financial Times*, 29 January 1977; *Modern Railways*, January 1977, p. 3, April 1977, p. 155.

45 Cf. NUR, *Coming True?* (n.d. but 1976), pamphlet in BRB Provincial file on bus substitution, etc., AN176/45 Pt. 1, PRO; BRJCC Minutes, 10 December 1976, 16 November 1978, and 15 March 1979. See also Bagwell, *The Railwaymen*, Vol. 2, p. 337.

46 Reid, Confidential Memo on 'Local Rail Services', 2 May 1978, BRB Minutes, 11 May 1978.

47 Reid, Memo on '"Other Provincial" Services and Bus/Rail Integration And Co-ordination', 1 February 1979, Board Exec. Minutes, 8 February 1979; BRJCC Minutes, 15 March 1979.

48 Cf. Marsh–Gilbert, 11 August 1975, Marsh's Papers.

49 Reid, Memo on 'Pricing Strategy—Freight', May 1977, Chairman's Committee Minutes, 26 May 1977. Wages were given a minimum weighting of 60% in the formula.

50 The Minister, Peyton, considered applications for a 5% rise in fares and a 7.3% increase for freight and parcels. Agreeing to the 5% increase for passengers, he could only accept a 2% increase in freight rates (no increase for parcels) to keep the increase to the average dictated by the prices and incomes policy. The estimated cost was put at £6.3m in 1973, £13.5m in a full year. Paper on 'Outline of Railway Pricing Applications', March 1976, BRB FR 246-2-134 Pt. 10.

51 S. W. Price (Chief Freight Planning Manager, BRB), Memo on 'The Recent Financial Performance of the Freight Business', 8 May 1975, BRB 99-2-50 Pt. 2; Chairman's Conference Minutes, 23 October 1975; quarterly producer price index (home sales, unadjusted) from Office for National Statistics, *Economic Trends Annual Supplement 1997*, p. 161.

52 Sharp–Bowick, 24 February 1975, cit.; 'Rail Pricing in 1975. Note . . .', cit.; David S. Binnie (Executive Director, BRB Freight)–Sharp, 20 August 1975, BRB FR 246-2-134 Pt. 8. Inside the DOE John Rosenfeld was prominent as a pro-Treasury 'hawk'. See Bowick, File Note on 'Railway Pricing in 1975', 3 March 1975, BRB 99-2-50 Pt. 1.

53 Bowick, Memo to Chairman's Conference on 'Carriage Contract—B.R/Central Electricity Generating Board', 19 February 1975, and Binnie–Dr T. Broom (Director of Operations, CEGB), 11 March 1975, BRB 102-15-21 Pt. 3; Chairman's Conference Minutes, 4 March 1976; BRB and CEGB, 'Agreement—Carriage of Coal to Power

Stations', 5 November 1976, BRB Registered Doc. 38–1; *Modern Railways*, November 1989, pp. 579–87. The MGR rates ranged from 47.8p a ton for journeys of up to 4 miles or 11.95p per ton-mile to 2.79p a ton-mile for 60 miles, and 1.448p for 350 miles. The non-MGR rates ranged from 14.8p (to 4 miles) to 4.36p (60 miles), and 3.74p (350 miles). There were agreed percentage increases for 1977–9 of 6.53%, 4.66%, and 4.22%; the price variation clause provided for rates to be adjusted twice a year applying the formula: 0.9 (55% manual wage index plus 45% manufacturing wholesale price excluding food drink and tobacco). Clause 11 reserved the traffic to rail except in an emergency. The details were regarded as commercially sensitive and therefore reported only orally to the Chairman's Conference and the Board, Minutes 4 and 11 March 1976 respectively.

54 See Bowick, Memos on 'Major Freight Contracts', 19 November 1975, 25 October and 13 December 1976, Chairman's Conference Minutes, 4 December 1975, 4 November 1976, 27 January 1977.

55 Bowick, Memo, 19 February 1975, cit.; BRB, *Facts & Figures* (1978), p. 25, (1980), p. 27. On the earlier history of the MGR services see Gourvish, *British Railways*, pp. 489–91.

56 Interview with Leslie Smith, 27 July 1998.

57 There were no passenger fatalities in train accidents in 1976 and 1977 and the average for 1974–9 was 11.5 p.a. (BRB plus LT, 4.5 p.a. excluding the Moorgate accident of 1975), compared with 33 p.a. in the 1950s. Deaths in railway working averaged 101.2 p.a. 1974–9, compared with 292 in the 1950s. On the other hand the number of train accidents was little improved, 1,150.2 p.a. 1974–9 compared with 1,194 in the 1950s. DTp, *Railway Accidents, 1950–79*. One of the worst accidents was a sleeping car fire at Taunton in July 1978, when 12 people died. The incident occurred at a time when a project was being developed to replace the old sleepers with new stock: see Peter Keen, Memo, March 1978, BRB RPL24/7/2/2; Planning & Investment Committee Minutes, 16 May and 30 October 1978.

58 An example of 'ancient practices' is provided by route-learning procedures. On the Western Region an 'analysis of techniques' for the Paddington–Newport route in 1972 included 'counting the number of times reflections of a river are seen through trees'. J. C. Williams (Western Region), 'Interim Report on Route Learning', 20 October 1972, BRB MTN4/26.

59 The adaptation of major established technologies requires a critical mass of social, political, and institutional support. Cf. Paul David's work on the QWERTY key-board, e.g. 'Understanding the Economics of QWERTY: the necessity of history', in W. N. Parker (ed.), *Economic History and the Modern Economist* (Oxford, 1986), and also his 'The Hero and the Herd in Technological History: Reflections on Thomas Edison and the Battle of the Systems', in Patrice Higonnet et al. (eds.), *Favorites of Fortune: Technology, Growth and Economic Development since the Industrial Revolution* (Cambridge, MA, 1991). See also Wiebe E. Bijker, Thomas P. Hughes, and Trevor J. Pinch (eds.), *The Social Construction of Technological Systems: New Directions in the Sociology and History of Technology* (Cambridge, MA, 1987).

60 Cf. Ian D. Gardiner (MD, BREL), Memo on 'British Rail Engineering Ltd.—Capacity to meet BR load requirements', 24 July 1979, Campbell's Papers, BRB TRO21/1.

61 BRB, *Transport Policy: An Opportunity for Change* (July 1976), p. 19; Richard W. S. Pryke and John S. Dodgson, *The Rail Problem* (1975), p. 176. Pryke and Dodgson stated that the 1981 requirement was 152,920, compared with 240,560 at the end of Jan. 1971,

and 219,600 at the beginning of 1974. Their data differ from those in BRB, *R&A*, since they sought to exclude staff working on capital projects and non-rail staff.

62 Cf. BRB Freight Committee Minutes, 14 April 1978.

63 Gourvish, *British Railways 1948–73*, appendix C.

64 BRB and University of Leeds, *A Comparative Study of European Rail Performance* (December 1979), pp. 15–26. Britain had only 20.7% of its route-kms electrified, the lowest in Europe except for Denmark (5%); eight railways had at least 35% electrified (end-1976 data). British Rail's average length of haul (excluding Freightliner) was 119km in 1977, the lowest except for Norway (94km) and Belgium (111km).

65 DOE, *Transport Policy*, Vol. I, para. 7.29, p. 61 (table). The document noted: 'each railway has its own characteristics and markets . . . But it certainly appears that there is still room for a large improvement on the part of British Rail'.

66 Cf. Michael Power, *The Audit Society: Rituals of Verification* (Oxford, 1997).

67 BRB, *Productivity Performance: An Analysis by the British Railways Board of its Productivity Performance since 1977* (Nov. 1982).

68 Data from 'Passenger Train Punctuality: Summary of Results 1948–1977', appendix to Ian M. Campbell, Memo on 'Quality of Service—Customer Care', 3 April 1978, BRB 95-1-5 (adjusted for comparability with late 1970s data).

69 Reid and Fowler, Memo to BRB Springs Conference on 'The Developing Rail Business: An Alternative View', 28 October 1980, Posner's Papers, Sec Box 2258.

70 Taken from calculations of 'Railway Real Wages and Salaries per Employee' and 'BRB Real Staff Expenses per Employee', 1963–75, in Bosworth, Memo on 'Real Staff Cost and Planning Assumptions', 28 March 1977, Chairman's Conference Minutes, 31 March 1977.

71 Price, Memo on 'The Recent Financial Performance of the Freight Business', 8 May 1975, cit.

72 BRB/Leeds, *Comparative Study*, pp. 18–19. Again, only Italy and Finland employed more staff in freight and parcels operating. Passenger data were better: British Rail's 56.4 crew per million train-km was lower than in five European railway systems: West Germany, Italy, Netherlands, Belgium, and Finland.

73 BRB, 'Productivity Report September 1981', BRB 81-2-1; Interview with James Urquhart, 30 July 1998.

74 Urquhart–Bosworth et al. on 'Performance Indicators: International Comparisons', enclosing 'Report on Visit of A. M. Bath, Chief Operating Manager, Western Region, and R. J. Poynter, Divisional Operating Superintendent, Nottingham, London Midland Region, to Swedish Railways (SJ) 10th–12th October 1978', Posner's Papers, Sec Box 2259. The quotation is from p. 13.

75 BRB/Leeds, *Comparative Study*, pp. 20–1 (the table actually refers to train *miles*). Civil engineering, signalling, and telecommunications work was difficult to evaluate comparatively and the study could only reach very tentative conclusions. Ibid., p. 22.

76 BR staff worked *c.*25% more hours on average, while real railway earnings per hour were some 40–110% higher outside Britain. BR's standard week was Monday–Saturday with 5 × 8-hour turns of duty, cf. Monday–Sunday elsewhere, and variation in length of turn. Ibid., pp. 15–16, 40–1, 52–3.

77 Ibid., p. 24. BRB's staffing reduction was put at 8.11%. Only two of the nine railways had a better record (Sweden, Denmark), and the percentage change ranged from +12.39% (Italy) to −10.02% (Sweden).

78 Ibid., pp. 45–6, 52–3, 68, 90, 102, 106. With BRB staff per train-km at 100, only the Netherlands (55) and Sweden (85) were more economical. BRB investment was calculated as £0.264 per train-km, with the other railways investing £0.41–1.99. BRB recovered 71.2% of costs. While Sweden recovered more (83.1%), for the other eight railways the range was 32.0–61.2%.

79 Cf. Urquhart (Executive Director, BRB Personnel)–Bowick, 22 January 1975, BRB Board Members General Papers, Sec Box 2283. Urquhart questioned many of Pryke's assumptions, e.g. British Rail's ability to deliver new investment by 1981 (continuous braking throughout, elimination of short wheelbase wagons, introduction of new wagons to facilitate faster freight train working, etc.), and pointed out that no adjustment had been made for effecting change within the established machinery of negotiation, or for national changes in conditions of work.

80 Pryke and Dodgson, *The Rail Problem* (1975), pp. 136–84. The major savings compared with 1971 were to come from train crews: 28,820 (59%); train maintenance 21,510 (36%); management staff 11,000 (31%), and track maintenance: 8,840 (23%).

81 This view was forcefully expressed by Bowick in a published critique of Pryke and Dodgson, 'Are the railways really grossly overmanned?', *Modern Railways*, March 1976, pp. 86–7. Bowick argued that the real problems, aside from 'the realities of industrial relations', were inadequate investment and customer requirements, notably the insistence on 'a very high peak service provision'.

82 Urquhart, Memo to Parker on 'Productivity', 26 June 1981, and cf. also Urquhart–Parker et al., 17 March 1982, BRB 81-2-1 Pt. 2. The same picture—much diagnosis, less real progress—can be seen in the deliberations of the Productivity Steering Group headed by Bowick in the mid-1970s: see Bowick, Memo 30 July 1975, Chairman's Conference Minutes, 7 August 1975.

83 See Gourvish, *British Railways* (for an outline of industrial relations 1948–73); Bagwell, *The Railwaymen*, Vol. 2; Interviews with Richard Rosser, TSSA, 22 February 2000, and James Knapp, 31 October 2000. Data from *The Times 1000 1980–1*, p. 14; Bagwell, pp. 417–18; Brian Murphy, *ASLEF 1880–1980. A Hundred Years of the Locoman's Trade Union* (1980), p. 62; Malcolm Wallace, *Single or Return?*, p. 521.

84 Cf. Gourvish, *British Railways*, pp. 541–62; Bagwell, *The Railwaymen*, Vol. 2, pp. 183–4.

85 Weighell was a member of the TUC General Council 1975–83, Buckton in 1973–86 (Chairman, 1983–4). Both were active supporters of the public transport pressure group Transport 2000: (*Who's Who*).

86 RSNT, Decision No. 40, 14 June 1966; RSNT, No. 41, 6 June 1968; RSNT, No. 42, 24 July 1974–RSNT, No. 66, 22 August 1979, BRB Bound Volumes of RSNT Decisions.

87 Gourvish, *British Railways*, p. 559.

88 Cf. Farrimond, Confidential Memo to Chairman's Conference, n.d., BRB Minutes, 11 October 1973. Dr (from 1975 Lord) McCarthy was a lecturer in industrial relations and Fellow of Nuffield College Oxford. The other members were Hugh Clegg, Professor of Industrial Relations, University of Warwick (for NUR/ASLEF) and J. Grange Moore (for BRB). Clegg was replaced by George H. Doughty in 1975, Grange Moore by Edward Choppen in 1978.

89 I.e. £35.50 plus 10% for additional responsibilities (£3.55), £2.60 for consolidation of mileage bonuses below 200 miles, making £41.65, plus an additional 10% for unsocial hours (£4.16). The three categories of irregular and unsocial hours payments (IUP)

were raised by 10, 7.5, and 5%. RSNT, Decision No. 42, 24 July 1974, paras. 109, 129, 138–40, 156; ASLEF, *Locomotive Journal*, August 1974, p. 2.

90 Other 'conciliation' grades benefited from the consolidation of bonus/additional responsibility payments and increased payments for IUP. Salaried staff gained from grade restructuring. A future programme of work envisaged more job analysis, incentive schemes, and a situation where 'it is accepted that general settlements contain a substantive reform element'. RSNT, Decision No. 42, 24 July 1974, paras. 179–84; Interview with John Holroyd, 19 October 1990.

91 See BRB Industrial Relations Committee Minutes, 7 September 1976; Management brief for BRJCC Meeting, 18 February 1977; correspondence in BRB 21-8-7 Pt. 1.

92 Cf. Nick Tiratsoo, '"You've Never Had It So Bad": Britain in the 1970s', in Nick Tiratsoo (ed.), *From Blitz to Blair: A New History of Britain Since 1939* (1997), pp. 172–3.

93 Campbell and Urquhart, Memo on 'One-Man Operation of Trains', 13 June 1975, Chairman's Conference Minutes, 26 June 1975, 22 July 1976; BRJCC Minutes, 20 November 1975, 7 April 1976. There were safety considerations too, the accident on London Transport at Moorgate (28 February 1975, 43 killed) being fresh in the mind.

94 Statement by Ian Campbell, BRJCC Minutes, 25 July 1978, and file note on 'BRJCC: 16 November 1978—The Freight Business', 16 November 1978, BRB 99-1-100 Pt. 3. This is not to say that all these initiatives were sound: 'Carousel', for example, was a very complex project. Interview with Leslie Lloyd, 17 August 1998.

95 Note especially RSNT, Decisions Nos. 49, 51–2, 56–60 (all 1978). W. H. (Bill) Ronksley encouraged ASLEF to take claims rejected at the RSNC to the final stage. He was Vice-President of the union, 1960–72 and President, 1974–82.

96 Interview with Holroyd, cit.

97 The scheme involved a pay-back of £12.5m. to December 1978 on revenue gains of £18.5m. See RSNT, Decision No. 61 (30 October 1978); Palmer (DTp)–Cliff A. Rose (Member, Personnel, BRB), 21 November 1978, Rose, File Notes of Meetings with Secretary of State, 17 and 22 November 1978; Rose, Memo to Railway Executive on 'Railway Business Performance Scheme', 26 March 1979, BRB 81-17-13; Interview with Lawrie Harries (NUR), 5 August 1998.

98 The story is told in full in Bagwell, *The Railwaymen*, Vol. 2, pp. 219–23. See also RSNT, Decision No. 45, 29 May 1975.

99 Chancellor of the Exchequer, *Winning the Battle against Inflation*, July 1978, P.P. 1977–8, xlix, Cmnd. 7293, p. 4.

100 Bagwell, *The Railwaymen*, Vol. 2, pp. 228–30 and see RSNT, Decisions Nos. 60 (30 October 1978) and 62 (23 March 1979).

101 Cf. ASLEF's case re RSNT Decision No. 42, 1974; proceedings of ASLEF Special AAD, 10 August 1974, and Bill Ronksley, at ASLEF AAD, 3 June 1981, ASLEF.

102 Stewart Joy, 'Public and Private Railways', *Journal of Transport Economics and Policy*, 32(1) (January 1998), 31.

103 Data from RSNC Minutes, 1971–9: ONS, *Economic Trends Annual Supplement 1997*.

104 RSNT, Decisions Nos. 60 and 62, cit.; Management Paper to RSJC (Loco), 22 December 1978, BRB 81-17-13; Joint Agreement for the Manning of High-Speed Trains, May 1979, RSNC Minutes, 12 January, 12 and 19 April, 15 August 1979, 11 January 1980; Interviews with Urquhart and Lloyd, cit.

105 Sir Derek Ezra–Parker, 2 March 1979, BRB 99-2-1 Pt. 8; 'Note of a meeting between Sir Derek Ezra, Sir Peter Parker and Glyn England Thursday, 5 April 1979', BRB 102-15-21 Pt. 3. See also RMG Minutes, 23 May 1979, Freight Committee Minutes, 19 June 1979.

106 William P. Bradshaw (Chief Operations Manager) and Henry C. Sanderson (Chief Freight Manager), Memo to RMG on 'Current Freight Performance—Customer Dissatisfaction', 18 June 1979, BRB 95-1-5; RMG Minutes, 19/20 June 1979; Bradshaw and Sanderson, Memo to Regional General Managers on 'Quality of service: Private Wagon Federation', 16 July 1979, BRB RF18; Interview with Urquhart, cit.

107 Gemmell–Parker, 23 September 1976, cit.

108 BRB Southern Region, *A Participative Approach to Cost Reduction in British Railways* (December 1976). Malcolm Southgate led the management team, while the unions were led by H. Bagilhole and T. Rimmer.

109 Cf. unofficial action in 1964 and 1965, Gourvish, *British Railways*, pp. 538–40.

110 H. Thomas Johnson and Robert S. Kaplan, *Relevance Lost: The Rise and Fall of Management Accounting* (Boston, MA, 1987). For a critique see Anne Loft, 'The history of management accounting: relevance found', in David Ashton, Trevor Hopper, and Robert W. Scapens (eds.), *Issues in Management Accounting* (2nd edn., 1995), pp. 17–24.

111 Peter Scott-Malden (Deputy Secretary, DOE)–Bosworth, 25 October 1971, David H. Jones (ED, Finance) et al., Memo to BRB Railway Investment Panel, 15 February 1973, Bowick, Memo to Railway Investment Panel, 23 June 1975, BRB 21-2-90; RMG Minutes, 22 September 1971 and 26 January 1972. The grants covered the cost, pending removal, of track and signalling equipment. It is clear that when the elimination of surplus capacity involved the withdrawal of passenger services difficulties arose. However, the shortfall had more to do with restrictions on investment and revised operating requirements.

112 Gourvish, *British Railways*, pp. 426–8.

113 Bowick, File Note, 18 September 1974, BRB X31–139.

114 Gourvish, *British Railways*, pp. 428–9.

115 Bowick, File Note on 'Passenger Train Service Review: Inter City', 18 February 1975, BRB X31–139.

116 Price, Memo on 'The Recent Financial Performance of the Freight Business', 8 May 1975, cit.; 'Development of Air-Braked Wagon-Load Service. Notes of Meeting held on Monday, 19th January and Continued on Wednesday, 28th January, 1976', Chief Executive's file on 'Organisation: Freight Department', AN156/61, PRO.

117 See Stanley B. Hobbs (Chief Freight Manager, Eastern Region)–F. D. Pattison (Chief Administrative Officer, BRB), 1 March 1979, Chief Executive's file on 'Withdrawal of Freight Services', BRB X23–38.

118 In 1972/3, for example, a study of *c.*700 services had led to the withdrawal of 174 services, saving 1.75m. train-miles; the remainder were reassessed in 1973/4, saving 1.12m. train-miles. RMG Minutes, 26 June 1974.

119 Jones (ED, Finance)–Binnie and Griffiths (EDs, Freight and Passenger) on 'Action arising from Rail Plan 1976–81', 23 August 1974, and Binnie–Jones, 12 September 1974, BRB X31-139; Bowick, at BRJCC, Minutes, 21 May 1975; Bosworth, Memo on 'Freight & Parcels Paper', 17 October 1975, Chairman's Conference Minutes, 23 October 1975.

120 'Development of Air-Braked Wagon-Load Services . . .', 1976, and Binnie–Campbell, 6 September 1976, AN156/61, PRO; *Modern Railways*, June 1979, p. 238.

121 BRB Productivity Report, February 1982, p. 14, BRB 81-2-1.

122 BRB Freight Traffic Committee Minutes, 21 June and 14 July 1978, 22 May and 17 July 1979.

123 Bowick–McBeath, 6 March 1975, Chief Executive's file on 'Commodity Plans—1975–1981 Steel', AN156/556, PRO. The ratio was calculated using TOPS-based movement/terminal costs and budgeted gross receipts.

124 Barron–Bowick, 7 October 1975, AN156/556, PRO.

125 Urquhart, Memo, 16 May 1978, RMG Minutes 17–18 November 1976, 23 May 1978.

126 BREL, *R&A 1974–6*. The internal profit margin on external sales was 6–8%, 1974–6.

127 Interviews with Urquhart and Smith, cit.

128 *Railway Finances* (Serpell Report), chapters 6–7.

129 'Manufacturing and Maintenance Policy Stage I Report' (n.d.), enclosed in Myers–Parker et al., 12 November 1979, Myers, Memo to BRB Strategy Steering Group on 'Manufacturing and Maintenance Policy Review', 14 December 1979, BRB 81-1-1 Pt. 3.

130 Urquhart, 'A Manifesto for British Rail Engineering Ltd', 16 April 1980, BRB 81-1-1 Pt. 3. Urquhart had succeeded Campbell as Chairman of BREL in February 1979.

131 E.g. *Daily Express*, 25 November 1974, *The Times*, 15 April and 11 May 1978.

132 S. F. Cox (Chairman, Pension/Superannuation Fund Investment Committees) and C. G. Lewin (Controller, Corporate Pensions), Confidential Memo on 'Superannuation Fund: Investment in Works of Art', 30 May 1974, BRB Minutes, 11 July and 10 October 1974; Lewin, Confidential Memo on 'Investment in Works of Art', 3 April 1978, BRB 86-3-149 Pt. 2. British Rail worked in association with Sotheby's using the jointly owned shell company Lexbourne.

133 BRB Board as Trustees Minutes, 27 March and 3 July 1980; John Morgan (General Manager, BR Pension Funds), Memo to Trustees, 25 June 1980, BRB 86-3-149 Pt. 3.

134 At 29 February 1980 the book cost of the works of art was £37.2m. and their estimated current value was £48.6m., the net gain of 12% p.a. comparing well with an increase in the FT All-share index of 13.8%. J. A. Morgan, Report to Trustees, 19 March 1980, BRB 86-3-149 Pt. 3. The works of art were sold from 1987, and the return to March 1990 on two-thirds of the collection was 14.6% p.a., producing a real return of 6.4% p.a. By the time the bulk of the sales had been completed in November 1997 the return had slipped to 4.3% p.a. British Rail Pension Trustee Co. Ltd, Annual Report, 1990/1, 5 September 1991; Susan Adeane (Company Secretary, Railways Pension Trustee Co. Ltd), Circular, 28 November 1997, Jerram's Papers, B37/19/BM.

135 Jones, Memo on 'The Railways Act 1974—Its Consequence for Investment Control', 27 June 1975, Burt, 'Salient papers, 1975/6'.

136 See H. R. Wilkinson (Chief Finance Officer, BRB), Memo, 8 December 1975, BRB New Works 27-4-500 Pt. 2.

137 T. L. Beagley (Deputy Secretary, Transport Industries, DOE)–Bosworth, 24 July 1974, Sharp–Bosworth, 9 September and 10 October 1975, Burt, 'Salient Papers, 1975/6'.

138 Cf. Gourvish, *British Railways*, esp. pp. 507–29; Chapter 1, p. 16.

139 Cf. TEST [for Transport 2000], *Investing in British Rail* (June 1983); Steer Davies Gleave (for Bow Group et al.), *Promoting Rail Investment* (August 1994); Reg Harman et al., *Investing in Britain's Railways* (Reading, 1995); and E. Roxanne

Powell, 'The Frontiers of State Practice in Britain and France: Pioneering High Speed Technology and Infrastructure, 1965–1993', Ph.D. thesis, London School of Economics, 1996.

140 White Paper on *Public Expenditure*, P.P. 1975–6, xxv, Cmnd. 6393, February 1976; 'Consequences of a Stabilised Investment Ceiling for the Railways. Joint Memorandum by the Department of Transport and the British Railways Board' (n.d.), Posner's Papers, Sec Box 2257, BRB.

141 BRB, *R&A 1976*, p. 3; *Modern Railways*, May and October 1976, pp. 186–9, 383–4, June 1978, pp. 257–8, November 1986, pp. 571, 593–6; *Proc. ICE*, 64 (May 1978), 207–25.

142 BRB, *R&A 1976*, p. 7.

143 In second quarter 1982 prices. Bosworth, Memo on 'Diesel Multiple Unit Refurbishing', 26 March 1975, BRB Minutes, 10 April 1975; John Edmonds (Director, Provincial), Memo to Investment Committee on 'Diesel Multiple Unit Refurbishment Projection: WG60127: Completion Certificates', n.d. [1987], BRB PNW 24-5-4 Pt. 4. Asbestos removal was included in the programme in 1980. About 1,000 DMU vehicles were treated before refurbishment effectively ceased in 1984. By this time new lightweight trains had been developed offering better value than renovation/asbestos removal.

144 In second quarter 1983 prices. Peter A. Keen (Chief Passenger Manager) and Ken Taylor (CMEE), Memo on 'Life Extension and Refurbishment of Electric Multiple Units', n.d., Investment Committee Minutes, 15 November 1977, and see also 5 March 1984; MMC, *British Railways Board and London and South East Services. A Report on Rail Passenger Services Supplied by the Board in the South East of England*, October 1980, P.P. 1979–80, lxxviii, Cmnd. 8046, para. 11.31; MMC, *British Railways Board: Network SouthEast. A report on rail passenger services supplied by the Board in the south-east of England*, September 1987, P.P. 1987–8, l, Cm. 204, table 10.1.

145 'Consequences...', pp. 2–3. Other routes affected included Ipswich–Lowestoft, Shrewsbury–Aberystwyth, and Inverness–Kyle of Lochalsh. Keen–Regional General Managers, 24 June 1977, Campbell's Papers, IN1-1-1.

146 Gourvish, *British Railways*, p. 602.

147 Ibid., pp. 517–20; BRB Investment Committee Minutes, 4 November 1975; SCNI, *Role of British Rail*, 1977, paras. 380–1, 386. After the 1978 White Paper a real test discount rate of 7% was used (until 1989).

148 Cf. Palmer–Barron on 'Monitoring and Backchecks of Investment Projects', 17 May 1977, Campbell's Papers, IN1-1.

149 Fowler, Memo to Investment Committee on 'Effect of Investment on Revenue Account', 28 August 1974, BRB 23-4-23.

150 Investment Committee Minutes, 22 June 1976, 14 June 1977; Robin H. Johnson (Chief Corporate Works Officer, BRB), Memo to Investment Committee on 'Major Investment Projects: Monitoring of Revenue Benefits', 29 October 1976.

151 SCNI, *Role of British Rail*, 1977, para. 375. This view was repeated by the Serpell Report in 1983: *Railway Finances*, p. 44. Fowler admitted in 1977 that by failing to devise a satisfactory system for monitoring revenue benefits British Rail was 'very vulnerable to external criticism that while we are pressing for higher levels of investment, there are still significant areas in which we have invested in the past where we

are not certain whether the promised benefits have fructified'. Fowler–Barron, 24
May 1977, Campbell's Papers, IN1-1.

152 Cf. Hedley R. Wilkinson (Chief Management Accountant, BRB), Memo, 2 February
1978, Johnson, Memo on '1977 Investment Programme', and Dr Bernard J. Nield
(Chief Investment Officer, BRB), Memo to Planning & Investment Committee on
'Five-Year Investment Programme 1979 to 1983', 7 November 1978, BRB 23-4-2 Pt.
15. Naturally, the *group* performance was emphasised in submissions to the Serpell
Committee in 1982. See Roger Hillard–Edward Osmotherly (DTp), 26 July 1982,
BRB IA 20-8-5 Pt. 4.

153 Investment Committee Minutes, 16 July 1974; 29 June, 7 September, and 25 October
1976, 15 November 1977; I. M. Campbell (Chief Executive), Memo to Investment
Committee on 'Advanced Passenger Train: The Evolution of a Policy for a West Coast
Main Line Service Fleet', 11 January 1978, Investment Committee Minutes, 19
January 1978.

154 Beagley–Bosworth, 24 July 1974, Burt, 'Salient Papers'.

155 Cf. comments of Controller of Corporate Planning contained in Johnson, Memo to
Investment Committee on 'Inter-City Investment Policy', 23 August 1976, BRB
23-4-9; RE Committee Minutes, 19 December 1977.

156 Campbell, Memo 11 January 1978, cit.

157 Cf. Richard Cottrell (Conservative MEP for Bristol), 'East Coast electrification: a
mistake?', *Modern Railways*, November 1984, pp. 577–9.

158 Interview with Dr Alan Wickens, 10 April 1989; Stephen Potter, *On the right lines?:
the limits of technological innovation* (1987); L. H. Williams, *APT—A Promise
Unfulfilled* (Shepperton, 1985).

159 The two 210 prototypes cost £3.4m. Taylor and A. H. Wickens (Director of Labora-
tories), Memo to BRB Technical Management Group on 'Low Cost Diesel Multiple
Stock', 18 August 1978, and Keen, Memo to BRB Railway Executive Group on 'Class
210 Diesel Electric Multiple Units', 7 May 1980, Campbell's Papers, ME2-3.

160 Roger Ford, 'The dmu dilemma', *Modern Railways*, August 1981, pp. 345–9, and
'DMU replacement—can BR ever get it right?', ibid., March 1984, pp. 121–5; E. R.
Powell, 'The TGV project: a case of technico-economic dirigisme?', *Modern & Con-
temporary France*, 5(2) (1997), 199–214; Interview with John Welsby, 30 April 1998.

161 The final cost of the Weaver Jnc.–Glasgow scheme was £74.58m. in Sept. 1973 prices:
Investment Committee Minutes, 2 April 1974.

162 Investment Committee Minutes, 16 November 1976.

163 Cf. Johnson–Bosworth, 13 October 1976, enclosing Memo on 'Electrification Policy—
Summary of events since 1972', BRB New Works 182-2-1 Pt. 3.

164 SCNI, *Role of British Rail*, April 1977, P.P. 1976–7, xxxiii, vol. I, HC305; DTp, *Role
of British Rail in Public Transport. The Government's Response*, November 1977,
P.P. 1977–8, xl, Cmnd. 7038, para. 6; BRB, 'British Railways Traction Policy—The
Question of Electrification', April 1978, BRB Minutes, 13 April 1978; BRB, *Railway
Electrification: A British Railways Board Discussion Paper* (May 1978), BRB 182-1-1
Pt. 5.

165 DTp, *Role of British Rail*, para. 49; BRB, *Railway Electrification*, p. 2. BR's Investment Committee went further, noting that the conclusions of a separate 1978 study
were that 'even if all adjustments in favour of electrification were combined, it was by
no means certain that a robust case could be made for electrifying the ECML as an

individual project nor that the financial return could be adequate to meet the future criterion of Required Rate of Return': Investment Committee Minutes, 18 April 1978.

166 DTp, *Role of British Rail*, para. 51; BRB, *Railway Electrification*, p. 2; Treasury, *The Nationalised Industries*, April 1978, P.P. 1977–8, xxxvii, Cmnd. 7131, paras. 58–64.

167 BRB, *Railway Electrification*, 1978, p. 9.

168 Ibid., p. 15.

169 In addition, the Witham–Braintree branch was electrified in September 1977: *Modern Railways*, January 1977, pp. 9–10, November 1977, p. 450, February 1978, pp. 61–4.

170 In 1977 BRB was seventeenth in a table of 21 railways ranked by percentage of electrified route, ahead of only Czechoslovakia, Hungary, Portugal, and Romania: BRB, *Railway Electrification*, p. 16.

171 Robert Arnott, *TOPS: The Story of a British Railways Project* (n.d., c.1979); Interviews with Urquhart and Lloyd, cit. and Henry Sanderson, 7 September 1998.

172 The figure of £22.8m. represented a reduction from an earlier estimate of NPV, including revenue retention, of £37.0m.: Bowick, Memo to Investment Committee on 'Design, Development, Implementation and Maintenance of a Computer Centred Information and Transit Control System for Freight Traffic', May 1971, BRB Minutes, 10 June 1971; Fowler (Controller of Corporate Finance), Memo on 'T.O.P.S. Reassessment of Project', 27 March 1973, Investment Committee Minutes, 3 April 1973; Arnott, *TOPS*, pp. 3–4.

173 £26.18m. at December 1975: Investment Committee Minutes, 16 December 1975. Expenditure to 30 June 1975 amounted to £16.62m.: Robin H. Johnson (Principal Corporate Works Officer), Memo on 'TOPS Progress Report', 8 December 1975, Investment Committee Minutes, 16 December 1975.

174 Bowick, Memo on 'Tops Publicity', 19 June 1975, Bowick–Campbell, 13 October 1976; Johnson, Memo 8 December 1975, cit.; R. Arnott, R. J. Day, and W. K. H. Dyer, 'TOPS equipment', *Railway Engineering Journal*, September 1975, 109–11; Arnott, *TOPS*, p. 113.

175 William P. Bradshaw (Chief Operations Manager), Memo on 'TOPS—Overdue Remit to Planning & Investment Committee', 4 December 1978, Dr Bernard J. Nield (Chief Investment Officer), Memo on 'TOPS—Report on Emerging Benefits', 28 June 1979, BRB Planning & Investment Committee Minutes, 9 January and 24 September 1979.

176 BRB RMG Minutes, 21 September 1977. On contemporary doubts about the value of enhancements, including TARDIS and FORWARD, and complaints about implementation delays, see BRB Freight Committee Minutes, 13 February and 11 September 1976, 14 July and 17 February 1978; TOPS Steering Group Minutes, 13 May 1976; and Arnott, *TOPS*, p. 61.

177 The major extensions and upgrades were: real-time wagon destination data (authorised: 1976), direct customer access (1977), cripple wagon control and planned preventive maintenance (1977), parcels vehicle control (1978), locomotive maintenance and shopping control (1978), replacement of punched cards (1979), marshalling yard management (1979–83), TARDIS database application (1980), centralised power control (1981), consignment through TOPS (CTT, 1981–3), Passenger Operations Information System (POIS, 1984), Train Running System TOPS (TRUST, 1984), Passenger Historic Information System (PHIS, 1984), Automatic Vehicle Identification (AVI, 1985), and Diagram Input and Distribution System (DIADS,

1986). Bradshaw, Memo, cit.; Transmark, 'An Introduction to BR TOPS', June 1986, and 'BR TOPS and its development since 1975', November 1987 [my thanks to Neil Butters for these references]; Graham Sheldrake (Assistant Rail Investment Analyst), Memo on 'Investment Appraisal: TOPS Network Renewal', 3 July 1987, BRB SEV/ IA/70-5. Cf. also G. F. Allen, *British Railfreight Today and Tomorrow* (1984), pp. 21–2.

178 Fowler–Barron, 24 May 1977, responding to Palmer–Barron, May 1977, Campbell's Papers, cit.

179 BRB Research & Technical Committee Minutes, 6 October and 3 November 1976; Binnie, Memo to BRJCC, 8 November 1976, BRJCC Minutes, 18 February 1977.

180 Dr K. H. Spring, at BRB Research & Technical Committee, Minutes, 3 November 1976; Binnie–Bowick, 10 December 1976, BRB 147-6-1; *Railway Gazette International*, December 1976; *New Scientist*, 9 December 1976; *Modern Railways*, February 1977, p. 72. It was some time before the profitability of 'Speedlink' was properly assessed: cf. BRB Railway Executive Minutes, 31 March 1980.

181 Peter Corbishley (Chief Planning Officer, BRB)–John Palmer (Under-Secretary (Railways), DTp), BRB 23-4-2 Pt. 19.

182 Cf. Stewart Joy, 'Public and Private Railways', *Journal of Transport Economics and Policy*, 32(1) (January 1998), 33.

Chapter 4

1 *Conservative Party Manifesto 1979*, pp. 8, 15; James Foreman-Peck and Robert Millward, *Public and Private Ownership of British Industry 1820–1990* (Oxford, 1994), p. 333; John Vickers and George Yarrow, *Privatization: an Economic Analysis* (Cambridge, MA, 1988), p. 155.

2 Cf. Patrick Minford, 'Monetarism, Inflation and Economic Policy', in Arthur Seldon (ed.), *Is Monetarism Enough?* (IEA, 1980), pp. 1–23, and *The Supply Side Revolution in Britain* (1991); Alan Walters, Wincott Lecture, 1978; John Redwood, *Public Enterprise in Crisis: the Future of the Nationalised Industries* (Oxford, 1980); John Redwood and John Hatch, *Controlling Public Industries* (Oxford, 1982).

3 Chapter 2, pp. 49–50.

4 Transport Act, 1978, c. 55, 2 August 1978.

5 Tony Buxton et al. (eds.), *Britain's Economic Performance* (1994), p. 35; M. J. Artis (ed.), *Prest and Coppock's The UK Economy* (13th edn., 1992), p. 11.

6 Geoffrey Myers (Director of Strategic Development), Memos to BRB Strategy Steering Group on 'Towards the Next White Paper' and 'Supplement on Conservative Party's "The Right Track"', February 1979, Strategy Steering Group Minutes, 15 March 1979.

7 Cf. Jim Tomlinson, *Government and the Enterprise Since 1900* (Oxford, 1994), pp. 309–10.

8 Interview with John Welsby, 30 April 1998, and see Chapter 2.

9 Sir Geoffrey Howe, *Parl. Deb. (Commons)*, 5th ser. (Session 1979–80), vol. 968, 12 June 1979, col. 246; Gourvish, 'British Rail's "Business-Led" Organization', 148.

10 Eric Merrill (Chief Public Relations Officer, BRB)–Henry C. Johnson (Chairman, BRB), 31 January 1969, BRB 70-21-4 Pt. 4. See also Peter Bancroft, *The British Transport Staff College at Woking* (Alton, Hants, 1997), pp. 25–7, 53.

11 Thatcher was Shadow Minister of Transport, 14 November 1968–20 October 1969. In the autobiography covering this period she noted: 'Transport was not one of the more interesting portfolios, because Parliament had just passed a major Transport Bill reorganizing the railways...all in all, Transport proved a brief with limited possibilities.' Margaret Thatcher, *The Path to Power* (1995), p. 143. There is no mention of the Woking visit.

12 Interview with James Urquhart, 30 July 1998. The story is also told by Parker in *For Starters*, p. 277, and see interview with Peter Parker, 16 May 1991.

13 See Chairman's Conference Agenda, 6 October 1977; BRB Visitors' Book, 1973–89. There are suggestions elsewhere that the lunch was on the 19th: Bosworth, Memo to Parker et al. on 'Lunch in Mess with Mrs. Thatcher, Wednesday, 19th October 1977', 13 October 1977, Chief Executive's files, AN156/104, PRO.

14 Ibid.; Norman Fowler, *Ministers Decide. A Personal Memoir of the Thatcher Years* (1991), p. 90.

15 Urquhart's recollection is as follows: 'At the Board meeting she'd asked me a question but she was talking to Peter [Parker] and so I had stopped speaking. [She said] 'Speak up, Urquhart! I can do more than one thing at a time. Speak up!' Interview with Urquhart, 1998. The story is also told by Michael Bosworth, Interview, 22 March 1988.

16 Ibid. And cf. also interviews with Leslie Lloyd, 18 August 1998 and Parker, cit.

17 On 14 May 1983. BRB Public Affairs file on 'Naming of 86311 Airey Neave', BRB PA 171-16-4; Parker, *For Starters*, pp. 278–80.

18 Her return rail journey from London to York on 7 February 1987 was referred to in BRB, *R&A 1986/7*, p. 18, and see Reid–Thatcher, 11 February 1987, Reid I's Papers, Sec Box 2204. In September 1984 she attended a presentation in York on the electrification of the ECML: Thatcher–Reid, 27 September 1984, BRB 20-14-4 Pt. 2. In the following year she declined Reid's offer of a private Pullman coach to the Conservative party conference in Blackpool for security reasons, but the correspondence was warm: Reid–Thatcher, 12 July, Thatcher–Reid, 18 July 1985, BRB 20-100-7 Pt. 1. In January 1987 she made a point of writing to Reid to thank BR staff for coping with severe weather: Thatcher–Reid, 23 January 1987, Reid I's Papers, Box 2204. On Reid's relationship with Nicholas Ridley (appointed Secretary of State for Transport in 1983) and Denis Thatcher (they were both keen golfers) see *Economist*, 21 May 1988, p. 35; *Sunday Times*, 12 March 1989, p. B5; interview with David Kirby, 13 January 1999.

19 Burt, Memo on 'Major Issues—B.R. and Government', 11 May 1979, BRB Minutes, 17 May 1979.

20 *Challenge of the 80's*, appendix to RSNC minutes, November 1979, BRB; BRB, *R&A 1979*, p. 6.

21 Bosworth–Bowick and Fowler, 6 July 1979, BRB 29-12-1 Pt. 1. The 'Group of Groups' concept, referred to by Bowick as the Peter Parker Zaibatsu Syndrome, and the possibility of attracting joint venture capital were raised in BRB, *R&A 1977*, p. 8, and see also *1980*, p. 11; Bowick, Memo 18 September 1979, BRB 29-12-1 Pt. 1.

22 Morgan Grenfell reported on 14 September 1979, and the Minister was sent a report on 'Private Sector Involvement in the Activities of the British Railways Board' on 10 October. See Bosworth, Memo on 'Private Sector Involvement in the Activities of the Board', 26 July 1979, BRB Minutes, 2 August 1979; Bowick and Fowler, Memo on 'Private Sector Involvement in the Activities of the Board', 21 September 1979, Board

Executive Minutes, 27 September 1979, BRB Minutes, 4 October 1979; Parker–Fowler, 10 October 1979, BRB 29-12-1 Pt. 1.

23 BRB and DTp, *Review of Main Line Electrification: Final Report* (February 1981).

24 BRB, *Rail Policy. A Statement by the British Railways Board of its Policy and Potential for the 1980s* (March 1981).

25 Burt, Memo on 'Queen's Speech', 16 May 1979, BRB Minutes, 17 May 1979.

26 *Parl. Deb. (Commons)*, 5th ser. (Session 1979–80), vol. 967, 15 May 1979, cols. 48, 79; Gourvish, 'British Rail's "Business-Led" Organization', 140–1.

27 Fowler had been Shadow Minister of Transport, 1976–9, though noted subsequently that at the time of his appointment (January 1976) 'I knew nothing of transport'. Norman Fowler, *Ministers Decide*, pp. 81–6.

28 On 4 July and 3 October 1979: BRB 20-20-9 Pt. 1.

29 *Parl. Deb. (Commons)*, 5th ser. (Session 1979–80), vol. 970, 18 July 1979, col. 1752; vol. 971, 23 July 1979, col. 127.

30 Fowler–Parker, 2 October 1979, referring to clause 11 of the Competition Bill: BRB 21-3-34 Pt. 1. The announcement was made by Sally Oppenheim, the Minister for Consumer Affairs, on 3 October. *Financial Times*, 4 October 1979; *Parl. Deb. (Commons)*, Session 1979–80, vol. 973, 7 November 1979, Norman Fowler, Oral Answer, col. 392.

31 Burt, draft note on 'Major Issues B.R. and Government', 11 May 1979, BRB Minutes, 17 May 1979.

32 Parker, Note on 'Meeting with Norman Fowler—6.6.79.', and File Note on 'Meeting with Minister, Tuesday 31 July [1979]', 2 August 1979, BRB 20-100-3/1; Parker–Fowler, 16 August 1979, Parker's Papers, Sec Box 2215; Baldwin–Parker, 28 September 1979, BRB Minutes, 1 November 1979; Minutes of Monthly DTp/BRB Progress Meeting, November 1979 [11th meeting], AN156/104, PRO; Treasury, *The Government's Expenditure Plans 1980–81*, November 1979, P.P. 1979–80, lxv, Cmnd. 7746. A factor in the relatively lenient treatment of British Rail was undoubtedly the Board's track record in observing government financial controls: cf. BRB Minutes, 6 December 1979. There was further support for the railways in the following year: cf. Parker–Fowler, 18 December 1980, BRB 33-40-1.

33 BRB, *R&A 1979*, pp. 5–6.

34 Reid, Confidential Memo on 'Sector Management', 3 December 1981, BRB Minutes, 3 December 1981; BRB Management Brief, 10 December 1981.

35 The Eastern Region's HQ was at York, the Scottish Region's at Glasgow. The Scottish Region's divisions had been abolished in 1966: Gourvish, *British Railways*, p. 378.

36 Glyn Williams (Director, BRB Financial Planning), Paper on 'Managing British Rail', October 1986, BRB; J. C. P. Edmonds (Board Member), Support paper on 'Evolution of BR's Sector-led Organisation Structure', 23 January 1990, BRB Minutes, 23 January 1990; David Allen, 'Management Accounting Developments in British Rail', in Maurice W. Pendlebury (ed.), *Management Accounting in the Public Sector* (Oxford, 1989), pp. 80ff.

37 Bowick held both posts January 1977–June 1978, and Reid did so January–September 1983.

38 RMG Minutes, 19 March 1980; Campbell, Memo on 'The Railway Command Structure', 22 February 1980, BRB Chief Executive's files, AN156/778, PRO; Reid, Memo on 'Railway Command Structure', 17 June 1981, BRB Minutes, 2 July 1981.

39 Reid–Frank Paterson (GM, Eastern), 14 May 1981, drafted by Philip Sellers (Director of Finance—see Sellers–Reid, 11 May 1981), AN156/778, PRO.

40 BRB Management Brief, 10 December 1981.

41 BRB Press Release on 'The Railway Business—Sector Management', 7 December 1981. Kirby relinquished the post of General Manager (Southern) in April 1985. His deputy, Gordon Pettitt, succeeded him.

42 Cf. Peter Lazarus (Deputy Secretary, DTp), in DTp, 'Note of a meeting held at 2 Marsham Street, SW1 on Friday, 16 April 1982', 2 June 1982, BRB 20-100-3 Pt. 4.

43 DTp, 'Review of Working Relations between the Department of Transport and the British Railways Board', December 1977, BRB 20-51-4.

44 BRB, *R&A 1980*, p. 15.

45 BRB Minutes, 6 September 1979; Reid, Memo on 'Interim Financial Targets', 24 October 1979, BRB Minutes, 1 November 1979.

46 Norman Fowler, Written Answer, 17 March 1980, *Parl. Deb. (Commons)*, 5th ser. (Session 1979–80), vol. 981, 2–3; BRB Minutes, 6 March 1980, RMG Minutes, 19 March 1980; Myers, Memo on 'Passenger Business Strategy Study', 24 June 1980, BRB Minutes, 4 September 1980; Bradshaw–Parker, 5 November 1981, BRB 182-1-1 Pt. 5. The Inter-City target was based on a contribution of 21%: *Railway Finances* [Serpell Report], p. 14. It is not clear why the Parcels target remained unpublished. The implications for the NFC, and the decision to abandon C&D parcels, undertaken in October 1980, may have been factors. Cf. BRB Minutes, 25 September 1980.

47 MMC, *British Railways Board and London and South East Services. A Report on Rail Passenger Services Supplied by the Board in the South East of England*, October 1980, P.P. 1979–80, lxxviii, Cmnd. 8046, para. 12.19, recommendation 32.

48 Cf. Myers, Memo to RDG on 'Provincial Services', 8 July 1981, BRB 33-40-1.

49 'Note of a Meeting with the Minister to Discuss the "Non-Commercial Railway"', 29 October 1980', 3 November 1980, BRB 20-100-3/1.

50 See Board Exec. Minutes, 25 September 1980; BRB, *Rail Policy* (March 1981), Annex 1; Interview with Richard Edgley, 7 August 2000; papers in BRB 33-40-1, and Appendix K.

51 BRB and DTp, *Review of Main Line Electrification* (February 1981), Board Exec. Minutes, 12 February 1981; Norman Fowler, *Parl. Deb. (Commons)*, 6th ser. (Session 1980–1), 22 June 1981, vol. 7, cols. 21–2. Fowler did not define commercial viability, but the departmental view was that it should be taken to be 'a 5% return on net assets after current cost depreciation but before interest': A. T. Baker (DTp)–Edward B. C. Osmotherly (Secretary, Serpell Committee), 28 September 1982, Sector Evaluation Papers, BRB PFS/810; David Howell (Secretary of State for Transport)–Parker, 4 May 1983, BRB 20-3-2 Pt. 2.

52 Robert Marshall (Chairman, NICG)–Geoffrey Howe (Chancellor of the Exchequer), 20 January 1982, BRB 21-4-7; Burt, Memo on 'The Relationship between Government and Nationalised Industries', 16 February 1982, BRB Minutes, 1 April 1982.

53 CBI paper on 'The Will to Win', and Director-General's Note on 'Public Sector Industries', n.d., CBI President's Committee Minutes, 2 July 1981 and 10 May 1982, CBI archive, MSS200/C/1/1/PC/81, MRC.

54 Cf. Reid, Memo on 'November Conference 1980', 8 July 1980, RDG Minutes, 16 July 1980; Myers, Memo to RDG on 'Business Management—Parcels', 16 July 1980,

Campbell's Papers, TRO-11-2; Reid, Memo to RDG on 'Sector Target Management', 21 November 1980, and Minutes of Special RDG meeting at the Welcombe Hotel, Stratford-upon-Avon, 21 November 1980, BRB Chief Executive's files, AN156/778, PRO.

55 Cf. Kenneth Clarke (Parliamentary Under-Secretary, DTp)–Parker, 7 August 1981, BRB 20-100-3/1.

56 Cf. Derek Fowler–Campbell, Memo 11 April 1979, Chief Executive's files, AN156/104, PRO.

57 Interviews with Geoffrey Myers, 19 May 1992, John Prideaux, 14 December 1998, and David Kirby, 13 January 1999.

58 Charles E. Lindblom, *The Policy-Making Process* (Englewood Cliffs, NJ, 1968), pp. 26–7.

59 Strategy Steering Group Minutes, 10 July 1978.

60 Bowick, Memo on 'Passenger Business Strategy Study', Board Exec. Minutes, 22 February 1979.

61 'Strategic Study Report London & South East Services', 18 October 1979, Strategy Steering Group Study Team, 'Passenger Business Strategy Study', 31 October 1979, Strategy Steering Group Minutes, 18 and 31 October 1979. An updated version of the study was completed in June 1980: Myers, Memo 24 June 1980, cit.; Interview with Myers, 1992.

62 The 'Springs' meetings, two-day conferences held outside London, were devised by Parker as a way of encouraging more creative strategic thinking on Board issues, chiefly management succession, organisation, and planning. The first was held at the Bell Inn, Aston Clinton in October 1977; the term 'Springs' was used to refer to all the meetings, because the meetings in 1978, 1979, and 1980 were held at The Springs, North Stoke nr. Benson, Oxfordshire. See Burt, Note, September 1982, BRB20-20-13. Posner attended the conferences in 1980 and 1981.

63 Bowick, 'Some Thoughts on … "Change" the Essential Ingredient in "Surviving" Or "The Only Thing That is Constant is Change" ', 27 October 1978, BRB 20-20-13.

64 Cf. Rose and Posner, Memo to Board Exec. on 'Springs 1979', 1 July 1980, BRB 20-20-13.

65 Myers took Reid's place as Board Member, Marketing.

66 Also important was Philip Sellers, Director of Finance under Fowler. Interview with Bill Bradshaw, 15 November 1998, Myers et al. Note that Prideaux moved to LMR as Divisional Manager, Birmingham in October 1980.

67 Interview with Professor John Heath, 21 July 1998. Heath was first appointed in September 1978: draft appointment letter, 25 August 1978, Chief Executive's files, AN156/924, PRO.

68 Heath, paper for Springs Conference 1980 on 'The Developing Rail Business—Towards Accountable Management', 15 October 1980; Reid and Fowler, Memo on 'The Developing Rail Business—An Alternative View', 28 October 1980, Posner's Papers, Sec Box 2258. The Conference was held 30–1 October 1980.

69 In fact, the attendees were Reid, Caldecote, Jenkins, Leith, Macleod, and Urquhart from BRB, the five RGMs, Casey (BREL), Baker from DTp, and 20 officers from HQ. See Note on Seminar, July 1981; RDG papers, 21 November 1980; Reid, Remit to Working Party, 28 November 1980, enclosed with Reid, Memo, 3 December 1980, REG Minutes, 10 December 1980.

70 F. D. Pattisson, Memo on 'Sector Management', 26 January 1983, enclosing Pattisson and Heath, Memo on 'Sector Management', 13 January 1983, Chief Executive's files, AN156/779, PRO.

71 Campbell, Memo on 'The Organisation and Administration of the Railway', 15 October 1979, Campbell Papers, XD-1; Note of Discussion, RMG Meeting, 10 November 1979, Chief Executive's files, AN156/73, PRO.

72 Campbell–Posner, 19 May 1980, BRB Chief Executive's files, AN156/300, PRO.

73 Campbell, Memo to Springs 1981 Conference on 'Sector Management', 12 October 1981, AN156/778, PRO; Interview with Bob Reid (I), 16 December 1987.

74 Rose and Posner, Memo on 'Springs 1979', 1 July 1980, Board Exec. Minutes, 24 July 1980; Reid, Memo on 'Business Sector Management', 27 July 1981, Appendix A, BRB Minutes, 6 August 1981. On secrecy see also interviews with Reid (I), 1987, and Welsby, 1998.

75 Myers–Board Members on 'Ministerial Meeting on Non-Commercial Railway', 17 October 1980, enclosing paper on 'Passenger Business Sectorisation and Sector Financing', 16 October 1980; Posner–Myers and Burt, 20 October 1980, BRB 20-100-3/1.

76 'Organising for Business Sector Targets. Memorandum of a Discussion at General Managers' Informal Meeting: 19 August 1980', enclosed with Soane–Reid, 9 September 1980, BRB.

77 Bradshaw was particularly unhappy that the RGMs should have special access to Springs, but access was obtained via the RDG: see Pattisson–Rose, 12 September 1980, Rose–Reid (I), 18 September 1980, AN156/778, PRO; Soane, Memo on 'Organising for Business Sector Targets', 22 September 1980, RDG Minutes, 1 October 1980, 21 November 1980; Interview with Frank Paterson, 6 August 1987.

78 Heath–Parker, 17 October 1980, Parker's File on 'Springs 1980', PP3. My thanks to Sir Peter for providing access to his personal archive.

79 Heath et al., Memo on 'The Developing Rail Business', 15 October 1980, cit., pp. 1–4, 13–20, 24.

80 Reid and Fowler, Memo on 'The Developing Rail Business—An Alternative View', 28 October 1980, cit. This one-page memo was accompanied by a four-page appendix of refutations.

81 This consisted of Reid, Myers, Sellers, Fred Sykes (Principal Finance Officer (Strategies & Plans), BRB), Baker (DTp), and Pattisson.

82 Cf. Keen, Paper No. 4 on 'Sector Management and the Passenger Business', 7 July 1981, and Reid, Memo to BRB, 24 April 1981, AN156/778, PRO.

83 Reid, Memo for RDG, 21 November 1980, and Memo on 'Business Sector Management—Supplementary Paper', 11 February 1981, Board Exec. Minutes, 12 and 26 February 1981; Memo on 'Business Sector Management (London & South East Sector)', 29 May 1981, BRB Minutes, 4 June 1981.

84 Board Exec. Minutes, 26 February 1981; Simon Jenkins, Memo to Reid and Board Members on 'Sector Management for L&SE', 19 June 1981, Roderick MacLeod–Reid et al., 20 July 1981, Chief Executive's files, AN156/778, PRO. Peter Corbishley, the Chief Planning Officer, was also a sceptic: Corbishley–Reid, 26 August 1981, Bradshaw–Reid, 15 October 1981, AN156/778, PRO; Interview with D. Glyn Williams, 15 June 1990.

85 Cf. Keen, 'Sector Management and the Passenger Business', 7 July 1981, cit.; Reid–Board Members on 'Sector Management Seminar: 14 July 1981', 24 July 1981, BRB

361-194-7; Parker–Howell, 16 December 1981, enclosing 'InterCity Financial Pro-spects', 14 December 1981, BRB 20-23-2 Pt. 1; Cyril Bleasdale (Director, Inter-City), *InterCity Strategy. Vol. I: Business Analysis* (July 1983); Interview with Edgley, 2000.

86 PP&CCA—Profit Planning and Cost Centre Analysis—was introduced in 1971 as an aid to analysis of budget forecasts. It was then deployed to calculate financial support under the PSO regime. In 1976 analysis of actual results was undertaken to assist monitoring of PSO payments. Avoidable cost studies were developed to more clearly relate indirect costs to the business sectors and to help determine appropriate contri-butions. See H. R. Wilkinson (Chief Management Accountant, BRB), Memo on 'Profit Planning & Cost Centre Analysis—Sector Avoidable Costs Study', 8 February 1979, BRB Railway Executive (RE) Minutes, 12 February 1979.

87 Derek Fowler, Memo, 18 August 1980, BRB 260-79-1; RDG Minutes, 22 October 1979. The critical breakthrough was the addition of train crew expenditure analysis (TEA).

88 Myers, Memo to RDG, 16 July 1980; Reid, Memo on 'Business Sector Management', 4 February 1981, Board Exec. Minutes, 12 February 1981.

89 In essence this meant that Inter-City or L&SE would be regarded as of equal import-ance in the hierarchy, with Freight, Parcels, and Provincial charged their avoidable costs as marginal users. See Memo on 'Sector Management: A Summarised Presenta-tion of the Working Party's Proposals founded on Development of Management Accounting Principles', 23 January 1981, AN156/778, PRO; Board Exec. Minutes, 12 February 1981; Reid, Memo to Board Members, 24 April 1981, BRB 361-194-7; Sellers, Memo to Sector Management Seminar on 'Principles and Procedures of Management Information Provision', 25 June 1981, and Keen, Paper No. 4 on 'Sector Management and the Passenger Business', 7 July 1981, AN156/778, PRO.

90 Paterson–Reid, 30 April 1981, AN156/778, PRO. Paterson also expressed his doubts to Parker: Paterson–Parker, 5 November 1981, and reply, 10 November 1981, Parker's Papers, Sec Box 2215.

91 Cf. John Thackway (Director, Personnel Development, BRB), strictly private note to Pattisson on 'Sector Management Services (A note written as if for Bob Reid)', 16 July 1981, AN156/778, PRO.

92 MacLeod–Reid, 20 July 1981, Heath–Reid, 3 August 1981, enclosing Lloyd–Heath, 28 July 1981, and Heath–Lloyd, 7 August 1981, AN156/778, PRO.

93 Cf. Sellers–Reid, 8 January 1981, AN156/778, PRO.

94 Board Succession papers, 1983; Interviews with Cyril Bleasdale, 10 July 1987, and David Kirby, 13 January 1999. See also 'Meeting the Sector Directors', series in *Modern Railways*, starting in July 1982 with Kirby, p. 301ff. Bleasdale had been Divisional Manager, Doncaster, Eastern Region.

95 Thackway, 'Action note of Discussion with Board Executive Members: 10 March 1983', 15 March 1983, Posner's Papers, Sec Box 2258; Interview with Welsby, 1998.

96 Keen–Reid et al. on 'Sector Management', n.d., Chief Executive's files, X70–30; Heath–Reid on 'Sector Management: Marketing', 7 July 1981, AN156/778, PRO; Interview with Edgley, 2000. Peter Haydon, Keen's deputy, became Chief Passenger Marketing Manager in the downgraded department: Reid, Confidential Memo to BRB, 2 December 1981, cit.; BRB Press Release, 1 February 1982.

97 Cf. Bradshaw, Memo to Sector Management Steering Group, 17 September 1981, Corbishley, Memo on 'Planning Implications of Sector Management', 29 September

1981, AN156/778, PRO. Corbishley's post was eliminated when the finance and planning departments were reorganised in September 1982 (see below).

98 Burt, Memo, 29 January 1982; Reid, Confidential Memo, 3 August 1982, BRB Minutes, 5 August 1982; RE Minutes, 23 March 1983; Interviews with R. H. Wilcox, 28 October 1998, and Maurice Holmes, 11 November 1998. Parker's suggestion that Palette become a Board member was abandoned when Howell would only agree to a 12-month appointment: Parker–Howell, 4 November 1982 and reply 10 March 1983, Parker's Papers, PP21.

99 Discretionary Cost Analysis involved a review of staff whose work was considered 'discretionary' rather than necessary for running the business. See Special Board Exec. Meeting Minutes, 26 February 1982, BRB Finance & Planning FP/O/JC/114.

100 REG Minutes, 11 November 1981; RE Minutes, 23 March 1983; BRB Press Release, 17 December 1982. Paterson, GM Eastern Region, retained his post after pledging his allegiance to the new 'king'. Paterson–Reid, 14 July 1981, AN156/778, PRO.

101 John Palmer (DTp)–Burt, 6 November 1981; Memo of Meeting of Sector Management Steering Group and others (including Baker (DTp)), 27 November 1981, BRB.

102 Cf. Myers, Memos on 'Provincial Services', 29 June 1981 and 'Other Provincial Services', 20 October 1981, RDG Minutes, 8 July and 30 October 1981; Sellers–Reid, 29 October 1981, AN156/778, PRO.

103 Reid–Sector Directors, 6 April 1982, AN156/779, PRO.

104 Interview with Bleasdale, 1987.

105 See Parker–Campbell, 18 June 1982, Parker–Howell, 14 September 1982, Howell–Campbell, 29 October 1982, BRB 48-2-42; Parker–Howell, 5 October 1982, Parker's Papers, PP21.

106 Parker had apparently hoped for a salary of £70–80,000, plus freedom to enhance his earnings as a director of Rockware and Clarksons. A few public sector managers were earning more, e.g. Sir Michael Edwardes of BL. See David Howell (Secretary of State for Transport)–Parker, 23 October 1981, BRB 48-2-40; *The Times*, 11 September 1981; *Financial Times*, 18 and 30 September 1981.

107 BRB Minutes, 4 August, 1 September 1983. Reid's official letter of appointment was dated 2 September, only 10 days before he became Chairman. BRB Minutes, 6 October 1983. Reid clearly enjoyed Parker's support: see Parker–Howell, 5 October 1982, Parker's Papers, PP21. On press reactions see *Financial Times*, 18 May and 3 September 1983, and *Sunday Times*, 29 May and 17 July 1983; *New Statesman*, 5 August 1983. The appointment was also held up because Peter Lazarus, successor to Sir Peter Baldwin as Permanent Secretary, DTp, did not wish to see his former boss appointed as a part-time chairman. Other names canvassed included Lord King of British Airways, Norman Payne (BAA), and Alfred Goldstein, a member of the Serpell Committee.

108 Cave was appointed Deputy Chairman for three years from 1 October 1983. He was a Director of Tate & Lyle and Thames TV, and became Chairman of Vickers in January 1984. He resigned with effect from 1 January 1986 as a result of ill health and died on 5 December: BRB 48-2-53.

109 Note, for example, Parker's failure to persuade Rodgers to find a seat on the Board for Will Camp, who became his public relations guru, and John Bowman, President of the NUR. See Parker–Burt, 7 February 1977, BRB 361-81-1; Interview with Lord Rodgers, 19 October 1998.

110 Interviews with Myers, 1992, and Bill Bradshaw, 25 November 1998, and cf. Fred E. Fiedler, *A Theory of Leadership Effectiveness* (New York, 1967), pp. 13–14, and Gourvish, 'British Rail's "Business-Led" Organization', 126–7. Reid was described as ' "Neutron Bob" Reid—the one that takes out the people while leaving the buildings standing': *Modern Railways*, November 1983, p. 601.

111 Bradshaw, Memo, 17 September 1981, cit.; Reid, Second Draft Memo to BRB on 'The Railway Command Structure', 25 November 1981, and Memo to BRB on 'The Railway Command Structure (RDG/REG)', 28 November 1981; Reid–Heath, 13 May 1982, enclosing draft report to Board Exec. on 'The Railway Business', Reid, Memo for Board Dinner, 28 June 1982, AN156/779, PRO; BRB Minutes, 1 July 1982; Reid, Confidential Memo on 'The Railway Command Structure', 28 July 1982, BRB Minutes, 5 August 1982. The RE consisted of CE, deputy CEs, 5 Sector Dirs, 4 RGMs, and 4 HQ Dirs (Engineering, Finance & Planning, Operations, and Public Affairs).

112 Caldecote–Reid, 20 July 1981 and 5 July 1982; Reid–Heath, 13 May 1982, cit., AN156/778–9, PRO; Reid–Caldecote, 27 July 1982, BRB 20-20-13; Interview with Myers, 1992.

113 Director of Public Affairs, 'Talking points', 9 September 1982; Burt, Confidential Memo on 'Board Organisation & Procedures', 25 November 1982, BRB Minutes, 2 December 1982. For a time Reid considered the idea of having one deputy rather than two.

114 See Palmer–Burt, 5 November 1982, Parker–Howell, 23 December 1982 and reply, 13 January 1983, BRB 48-2-1 Pt. 3.

115 BRB Minutes, 1 July and 5 August 1982; Pattisson, 'Note of Discussion at pre-Board Dinner', 30 June 1982, 6 July 1982, BRB 30-2-1 Pt. 2.

116 Cf. Pattisson, Memo on 'Board and Railway Organisation', 28 June 1982, BRB 30-2-1 Pt. 2. Campbell expressed fears of a return to a post-McKinsey Board: Campbell–Pattisson, 21 June 1982, AN156/779, PRO.

117 Reid, draft report on 'The Railway Business' May 1982, and Memo for Board Dinner, 28 June 1982, cit. Reid rejected a more radical proposal advanced by the consultants Price Waterhouse, in June 1982. Under this model, the Chief Executive was to be supported by a smaller Railway Executive Group with RGMs excluded, the management line then extending to three committees representing sectors (SDs), operations (RGMs) and engineering, followed by a regional executive group at the bottom. Price Waterhouse, Report on 'Sector Management and the Future Organisation Structure of the Rail Business', 16 June 1982, AN156/779.

118 Burt, Confidential Memo 25 November 1982, cit.; Board HQ Admin. Instruction No. 28, December 1982. The Audit Committee became the Audit & Review Committee (Ch.: Parker) with enhanced powers, while the Research & Technical panel and the Safety Review Group were reconstituted as main board committees (Ch.: Campbell). Urquhart became chairman of Transmark and (from March 1983) of Freightliners. Posner's responsibilities were also increased. In addition to serving as a member of Board Executive and Chairman of the Supply Committee, he was given the task of co-ordinating review studies for the Audit & Review Committee. Campbell and Urquhart were effectively sidelined. Cf. Burt, 'File Note of Lunch Discussion with Peter Lazarus, Monday, August 9 1982', 9 August 1982, BRB 20-100-3 Pt. 4; Interview with Urquhart, 1998.

119 Reid, Confidential Memo, 8 June 1983, Board Exec. Minutes, 9 June 1983; Reid–O'Brien, 9 June 1983, BRB 48-2-54. Initially the status of Myers and O'Brien differed. Myers, as a Board member was *Deputy* Chief Executive, while O'Brien was *Assistant* Chief Executive.

120 Reid, Confidential Memo on 'Board Organisation', BRB Minutes, 5 January 1984; RE Minutes, 22 February 1984; BRB HQ Instruction No. 34, February 1984, Chief Executive's file on 'Board Meeting Procedures', AN156/1, PRO; Parker, *For Starters*, p. 215.

121 Price Waterhouse, Report on 'Progress regarding implementation of recommendations set out in our report dated 6 January 1982', 21 March 1983, BRB.

122 Derek Fowler, Memo on 'Reorganisation of Headquarters Finance & Planning Departments', 25 August 1982, BRB Minutes, 2 September 1982. On Corbishley's views see Corbishley–Reid, 26 August 1981 and Bradshaw–Reid, 15 October 1981, AN156/778, PRO.

123 Sector Performance Accounting and Monitoring Systems (SPAMS). See David Allen (Director, Sector Evaluation, BRB), presentation to BRB RE, 27 April 1983, RE Minutes, 27 April 1983; Sellers, Memo on 'Finance and Planning', 23 June 1983, BRB Minutes, 4 August 1983.

124 Bradshaw, Memo to Fowler on 'Policy Unit', n.d., Posner's Papers, Sec Box 2259; Pattisson, Memo enclosing BRB Admin. Instruction No. 25, 10 June 1982, BRB 30-2-1 Pt. 3; Interview with Bradshaw, 1998. Note that Bradshaw was replaced in January 1983 by Malcolm Southgate, who went to LMR as GM in July. He was in turn replaced by John Prideaux (September 1983–February 1986). The Computing Strategy Unit was moved to a new department—Information Systems & Technology—in August 1983: BRB HQ Admin. Instruction No. 31, August 1983, AN156/1, PRO.

125 *Railway Finances* [Serpell Report], 1983, pp. 47, 177. Goldstein, from the consultants Travers Morgan, was a committee member. His contention that inadequate sector direction might lead to responsibility reverting by default to the RGMs was strongly contested: cf. Pattisson and Heath, Memo, 13 January 1983, AN156/779, PRO.

126 *Modern Railways*, June 1983, pp. 307–9; Interview with Brian Burdsall, 19 June 2000.

127 Price Waterhouse, draft discussion paper on 'Role and Responsibilities of Sector Directors and Regional General Managers', May 1983; Report on 'Role and Responsibilities of Sector Directors, Regional General Managers and Functional Directors', August 1983; RE Minutes, 24 May, 8 August, and 21 September 1983; BRB Minutes, 6 October 1983. The Premium Parcels sub-sector was an exception: here, the business was handled by RGMs.

128 Price Waterhouse, Report, August 1983; RE Minutes, 8 August 1983; Myers, Memo, 4 October 1983, Chief Executive's files, AN156/837, PRO; Myers, Memo, 25 November 1983, BRB 30-2-600. There were some exceptions. Functional directors retained responsibility for such matters as co-ordination of workshop maintenance and repair programme, management of the telecommunications network, etc.

129 James J. O'Brien, Memo on 'Sector Management', February 1985; Myers and O'Brien, Report, 29 March 1985; BRB Minutes, 7 June 1984, 7 March, and 4 April 1985; RE Minutes, 20 March 1985.

130 BRB Minutes, 7 March 1985 (restricted circulation).

131 Price Waterhouse, Report on 'Proposal for an Organisational Development Strategy', July 1985, O'Brien's Papers, Sec Box 2173.

132 BRB RE Minutes, 24 July and 23 October 1985; Myers and O'Brien, Memo on 'Organisation Development', 24 September 1985, BRB Minutes, 3 October 1985; Myers, Memo to RE Members on 'The Evolving Railway Organisation', 21 November 1985, O'Brien's Papers, Box 2173.

133 Reid, Confidential Memo on 'Managing the Railway', 1 November 1985, BRB Minutes, 7 November 1985. Myers became Vice-Chairman (Railways) in April 1985, and Kirby (Director, L&SE) took his place as a joint managing director in December, retaining his responsibility for the Channel Tunnel. When Myers retired in Nov. 1987, Kirby became Vice-Chairman (Railways), David Rayner (GM, ER) became a joint managing director, and John Welsby joined the Board with executive responsibility for procurement, private-sector initiatives, and the Channel Tunnel. BRB HQ Admin. Instruction No. 128, September 1987; Reid–Ridley, 8 November 1985, BRB 48-2-54.

134 Myers, Memo 21 November 1985, cit. The Memo was used as the basis for a BR Management Brief on 'The Evolving Railway Organisation', 2 December 1985. At this stage there were 26 sub-sectors and 60 profit centres. The sub-sectors were:

> *InterCity*: ER, LMR, WR, SR, Services(HQ).
> *LSE*: ER, WR, London Suburban Services, SR-Central, SR-SE, SR-SW.
> *Provincial*: ER, MR, Scotrail, WR.
> *Railfreight*: Coal, Metals, Speedlink Chemicals, Petroleum, Construction, Speedlink Management Group, Freightliner Haulage.
> *Parcels*: Red Star, Newspapers, Post Office.

Ian Phillips (Director, Finance & Planning, BRB), Memo on 'Railway Organisation', 14 November 1985, RE Minutes, 20 November 1985.

135 Cf. MMC, *British Railways Board: Network SouthEast. A report on rail passenger services supplied by the Board in the south-east of England*, P.P. 1987–8, l, Cm. 204, September 1987, p. 23, cit. in Andrew Pendleton, 'Structural Reorganization and Labour Management in Public Enterprise: A Study of British Rail', *Journal of Management Studies*, 31 (January 1994), 39.

136 BRB, 'Inter-City Financial Prospects', 14 December 1981, with Parker–Howell, 16 December 1981, BRB 20-23-2 Pt. 1. The target was spelled out in Edward Osmotherley (DTp)–Sellers, 26 September 1983, BRB Financial Planning Files, RPM 8316/4.

137 BRB Memo to Serpell Committee on 'Financial Targets for Inter-City', n.d. [c.September 1982], BRB Director of Sector Evaluation files, BRB PFS/810 Pt. 1.

138 Bradshaw–Sellers et al., 1 October 1982, enclosing Baker (DTp)–Osmotherley (Secretary, Serpell Committee), 28 September 1982, and DTp, 'Inter City Financial Objectives: DTp Comments on Paper by BRB', September 1982, BRB PFS/810 Pt. 1.

139 Fowler, Memo, 10 November 1982, Board Exec. Minutes, 11 November 1982; Allen, Memo on 'Sole User Costing: An Overview', n.d., RE Minutes, 27 April 1983, and Memo on 'Infrastructure Costing and Sector Management', 17 November 1983, RE Minutes, 23 November 1983.

140 Sole user was also more liberal in the way it addressed the charging of secondary sectors, and more sophisticated in its approach to 'complexity' (points, crossings, etc.) and signal operations. See e.g. Alec D. McTavish (BRB Policy Unit)–Board Exec. Members, 25 November 1982, BRB 182-1-1 Pt. 6; Allen, Memo to RE, 27 April 1983, cit.; Allen, Memo on 'Infrastructure Costing and Sector Management—the Sole User

Regime', 23 July 1984, BRB Minutes, 2 August 1984; Gourvish, *British Railways*, p. 395.

141 Howell–Parker, 4 May 1983, BRB 20-23-2 Pt. 2.

142 BRB Minutes, 1 September 1983; Parker–King, 9 September 1983, Parker's Papers, Box 2215.

143 Nicholas Ridley–Reid, 24 October 1983, BRB 30-1-5. Ridley followed David Howell (14 September 1981–10 June 1983) and Tom King (11 June–15 October 1983) as Secretary of State for Transport.

144 Roger Hillard (Principal Finance Manager, Sector Evaluation, BRB)–Allen on 'Inter-City Targets', 3 November 1983; Allen–Prideaux (Director, Policy Unit), 3 November 1983, Prideaux–Fowler, 9 November 1983, Prideaux–Fowler and Allen, 21 December 1983, BRB PFS/812 Pt. 1.

145 Cf. Prideaux–Posner, 11 November 1983, BRB PFS/812 Pt. 1.

146 Phillips, Memo on 'Progress in Financial Management Information Systems for Sectors', 17 October 1985, RE Minutes, 23 October 1985.

147 Director, Inter-City, BRB, InterCity Strategy, June 1984, published more widely as *InterCity—Into Profit* (December 1984). See Bleasdale–Allen, 15 August 1984, BRB PFS/812 Pt. 2; Allen, Memo on 'Infrastructure Costing …', 23 July 1984, cit., BRB Minutes, 2 August 1984; Ridley–Reid, 10 August 1984 and reply, 20 August 1984, BRB PFS/812 Pt. 2; BRB, *R&A 1984/5*, p. 4. The electrification quid pro quo went back to the days of Parker and Howell and a statement by Howell on 25 November 1981: *Parl. Deb. (Commons)*, 6th ser., (Session 1981–2), vol. 13, *396*. See also John Moore (SoS for Transport)–Reid, 21 October 1986, BRB 30-1-5.

148 Allen, 'Management Accounting Developments', pp. 99–104.

149 Posner, Note for File on 'Electrification and the Viable Railway', 9 May 1983, Posner's Papers, Sec Box 2264.

150 McTavish–Parker, 25 November 1982, BRB 182-1-1 Pt. 6.

151 Allen–Sellers, 31 October 1983, BRB PFS/812 Pt. 1; Allen, Memo to BRB, 23 July 1984, cit.

152 Cf. Reid–David Mitchell (Parliamentary Under-Secretary, DTp), 14 October 1985, BRB 20-100-7 Pt. 1; BRB Confidential Memo, 22 January 1986, BRB Minutes, 27 January 1986. For SPAMS see fn. 123 above; CAPRI = system for passenger income budgeting and monitoring on a sector basis; PARIS = same for parcels, FABS for freight; LOVERS (LOcal Vehicle RecordS) and RAVERS (RAil VEhicle RecordS) provided disaggregated data on rolling-stock maintenance. See Phillips, Memo on 'Progress on Financial Management Information Systems for Sectors', 17 October 1985, RE Minutes, 23 October 1985; Phillips, Memo on 'Management Information Systems—Current Situation', 16 May 1986, RE Minutes, 20 May 1986; BR M&EE Maintenance Systems Group, 'Rail Vehicle Records System Overview', 15 May 1987, BRB F&P RPM 8711/10.

153 BRB Memo to Serpell Committee on 'Financial Targets for Inter-City', cit.

154 DTp, 'Inter-City Financial Objectives', September 1982, cit.

155 Cyril Bleasdale (Director, Inter-City), 'InterCity Strategy, Vol. 2: Examination of Options', July 1983, p. 33.

156 Tom King (SoS for Transport)–Reid, 4 October 1983, BRB PFS/812 Pt. 1.

157 Hillard–Allen, 3 November, Prideaux–Posner, 11 November, and Prideaux–Fowler and Allen, 11 December 1983, cit., BRB PFS/812 Pt. 1.

158 Allen–Sector Directors, 22 June 1984, BRB PFS/812 Pt. 2; Ridley–Reid, 10 August 1984, cit.

159 Here, there had been some encouragement from the DTp. Cf. Hillard–C. E. Simpson (DTp), 23 December 1983, BRB PFS/812 Pt. 1.

160 Cf. Allen, Memo to InterCity Strategy Conference on 'The Definition of the InterCity Sector', 18 January 1984, BRB PFS/812 Pt. 1.

161 Ronald C. Mitchell (Chief Finance Officer, Southern Region)–Hillard, 8 February 1984 and reply, 10 February 1984; Hillard–Bleasdale, 14 February 1984, BRB PFS/812 Pt. 1.

162 Mitchell–Allen, 9 May 1984, BRB PFS/812 Pt. 2.

163 InterCity, *InterCity—into Profit* (December 1984), pp. 12–13; BRB Press Release, 6 December 1984. £47m. was to come from cost reduction, and £31m. from income generation (figures at 1984/5 prices). The L&SE services were transferred on 1 April 1985. The only boundary change to be contemplated in the 1980s came in 1988, when the creation of a new Cross Country sector was proposed, but soon abandoned. BRB Minutes, 14 March and 2 June 1988.

164 John Barker (Director of Personnel Development)–Myers and O'Brien on 'BR Culture Study', 22 April 1985, and Barker–Myers et al. on 'Organisation Development on BR', 11 June 1986; Memo to Dr Paul Bate, 'Organisation Development in British Rail', March 1987, BRB; 'Note of a Meeting held at Britannia Hotel Thursday, 12th November 1987', Chairman's Group Minutes. On 'segmentation' see Rosabeth Moss Kanter, *The Change Masters: Corporate Entrepreneurs at Work* (1985), pp. 28–32. The Western Region was used as a guinea pig for the Stage III exercise, which was progressed by Welsby as MD, Procurement & Special Projects, and Stan Whittaker, Director, Organisation Policy: Welsby, Memo, n.d., RE Minutes, 17 September 1986; Toolan (MD, Personnel) and Welsby, Memo, n.d., RE Minutes, 18 March 1987.

165 BRB InterCity Press release, 30 April 1987; *Modern Railways*, June 1984, pp. 318–19, November 1987, pp. 575–8, and special report, November 1987; ibid., p. 628; BRB, Railfreight Design Guide, 1988; James Cousins, *British Rail Design* (Danish Design Council, Copenhagen, 1986); Interview with Bradshaw, 1998.

166 BRB Business Review Group (BRG) Minutes, 26 September 1985; John G. Batley (Secretary, BRB), Memo on 'Update of Financial Management Procedure for the Railway Business', 9 October 1985, RE Minutes, 23 October 1985; Allen, 'Management Accounting Developments', p. 83.

167 Cf. BRB Production Management Group Minutes, 23 July 1986; *Railway Gazette International*, November 1988, pp. 739–41.

168 Kirby, Memos, 9 and 14 July 1987, Chairman's Group Minutes, 16 July 1987; Memo, 30 July 1987, BRB Minutes, 6 August 1987; Progress Report, 5 October 1988, BRB Minutes, 13 October 1988; *Railway Gazette International*, November 1988, pp. 739–41. There was another organisational experiment in Scotrail, where the 10 area managers were cut to four.

169 BRB HQ Admin. Instruction No. 130, April 1988, BRB 30-2-1 Pt. 4; MMC, *British Railways Board: Provincial. A report on rail passenger services supplied by the Board in Great Britain for which the Board's Provincial business sector takes financial responsibility*, P.P. 1988–9, xlvii, Cm. 584, February 1989, pp. 23–4.

170 Moore–Reid, 21 October 1986, BRB 30-1-5, reproduced in BRB, *R&A 1986/7*, pp. 4–5.

171 MMC, reports, 1987 and 1989, cit.; Parkinson–Reid, 19 December 1989. InterCity was required to earn a $4\frac{3}{4}$% profit by 1992/3, Railfreight a profit of $4\frac{1}{2}$%, while Provincial was asked to reduce its subsidy from 65% of costs in 1988/9 to 57% by 1992/3.

172 BRB, *R&A 1983/4–89/90*.

173 Cf. Richard Allan (Director, BRB Policy Unit), Note on 'Organisational Development', 23 September 1988, BRB Strategy Meeting Minutes, 26 September 1988; David Allan (Director, Management Accounting), Memo on 'Next Steps in Sector Accountability', August 1988, BRB PO/DPA 24; and Allen, Memo to Britannia Hotel Meeting of Chairman's Group, 16 September 1988.

174 Sheppard (from 1990 Sir Allen) was Chief Executive of Grand Met 1986–93 and Chairman 1987–96; De Ville (from 1990 Sir Oscar) was Chairman of Meyer Int. 1987–91. The other appointees were Derek (from 1990 Sir Derek) Hornby of Rank Xerox and Richard Tookey of Shell. They replaced Cave, Leith, MacLeod, and Urquhart. Further appointments of part-timers included two women, Kazimiera Kantor, sector director of Grand Met and Adele Biss, director of Aegis Group, appointed in June and July 1987 respectively. The other recruits were David Davies, former deputy-MD of Racal Electronics, appointed in May 1987, and John B. Cameron, farmer (chairman of World Meats Group), and experienced engine-driver (owner of 60009 *Union of South Africa*), appointed in August 1988.

175 BRB Minutes, 26 September 1988; Peter Trewin (Secretary, BRB), Memo to Executive Board Members on 'The Board and the Corporate Office', 6 December 1989, BRB 30-2-1 Pt. 6.

176 Note on 'BR Culture: Issues and "Cultural Features"', n.d. [*c.*1987], BRB; David Rayner, Memo on 'Structure for Managing the Railway', 13 July 1989, RE Minutes, 19 July 1989; RMG Minutes, 30 August 1989, BRB Minutes, 7 September 1989.

177 Reid–Paul Channon, 8 June 1989, Derek Fowler's Papers, Sec Box 2250; Reid–Cecil Parkinson, 22 September 1989, Reid (I)'s Papers, Sec Box 2208. For a short summary of events to December 1989 see John Edmonds, 'Evolution of BR's Sector-Led Organisation Structure', 23 January 1990, cit. Channon was Secretary of State from 13 June 1987 to 23 July 1989, Parkinson from 24 July 1989 to 27 November 1990.

178 See BRB, *R&A 1988/9*, p. 8; *The Times*, 7 March 1989, *Financial Times*, 19 and 27 July 1989.

179 The list of 'refuseniks' apparently included Lord King and Colin Marshall of British Airways, Michael Bishop (British Midland Airways), David Simon (BP), Alastair Morton (Eurotunnel), Sir Peter Thompson (NFC), and Sir John Nott, former Defence Secretary: *The Times*, 1 and 13 November 1989, *Guardian*, 6 December 1989, and *Financial Times*, 7 December 1989; Cecil Parkinson, *Right at the Centre* (1992), p. 295.

180 Robert Paul Reid became Sir Bob Reid in June 1990. The two men were referred to inside the business as 'Bob Reid I' and 'Bob Reid II', or less reverentially as 'half-price Reid' and 'full-price Reid', since their salaries were very different: R. B. Reid's final salary was £90,950; R. P. Reid's starting salary was £200,000 plus a performance-related bonus: BRB 48-2-45 Pt. 2, BRB 48-2-67 Pt. 1.

181 For concern about the loss of this expertise see Roger Ford, 'BR—looking thin on top?', *Modern Railways*, November 1989, p. 566. Myers's early retirement was

apparently prompted by rows with Reid when the DTp criticised the Board for failing to address cost reduction when responding to the EFL for 1986/7.

182 BRB, *R&A 1989/90*, p. 2; Trewin, Memo, 6 December 1989, cit.; Interview with Philip Wood, 18 December 2000.

183 Cf. Andrew Pendleton, 'Structural Reorganization', 39–41.

184 Interview with Maurice Holmes, 11 November 1998.

185 BRB Management Brief on 'Sectors and Regions: Where They Stand', 8 October 1987; *Modern Railways*, July 1989, p. 353. The Brief reproduced extracts from Reid's presidential address to the Railway Study Association in the same month.

186 *Railway Gazette International*, November 1988, pp. 739–41.

187 Cf. Peter White, *Public Transport. Its Planning, Management and Operation* (3rd edn., 1995), p. 9; Nigel G. Harris and Ernest Godward, *The Privatisation of British Rail* (1997), pp. 40–1; Steven Knight and Howard Johnson (eds.), *The Comprehensive Guide to Britain's Railways* (Peterborough, 1998), pp. 6–7; Cyril Boocock, *Spotlight on BR* (Penryn, 1998), pp. 86–8. Boocock, an engineer, claims that sectorisation originated in the department of M&EE in 1979, but the appointment of 'sector' engineers for Inter-City, Suburban, and Freight was essentially for design purposes and had nothing to do with sector management as conventionally understood. Cf. *Modern Railways*, April 1984, p. 189.

188 O'Brien–SDs, 20 July 1984, BRB Policy Unit Papers, AN170/124, PRO.

189 Letters to O'Brien from Sanderson (24 July), Kirby (15 August), Bleasdale (17 August), Connolly (24 August), and Edmonds (29 August 1984), ibid.

190 'AXIS', *Finance in Focus* (finance journal of British Rail), 17 (January 1985); Stan Whittaker (Director, Finance & Planning, BRB), Memo on 'Report on Finance & Planning Department', 27 April 1989, BRB Minutes, 4 May 1989; *Railway Gazette International*, November 1988, p. 741.

191 Paul Channon (SoS for Transport)–Reid, 19 May 1988, BRB F&P RPM8815/3; Richard Allan, Memo, 16 September 1988, cit.; O'Brien, Memo, 25 November 1988, BRB Minutes, 31 March, 4 August, and 1 December 1988; BRB HQ Admin. Instruction No. 133, September 1988, BRB PA159; Interview with Jim O'Brien, 10 February 1999. Oxford Corporate Consultants (Hugh Davidson) were used.

192 Welsby, Memo, n.d., RE Minutes, 17 September 1986; P. J. Whittaker (Director, Organisation Policy), Memo to Myers, Kirby, et al., 12 November 1986, O'Brien's Papers, Sec Box 2173.

193 Interview with Bleasdale, 1987.

194 Cornell's review began in 1987: BRB Press Release, 5 June 1987. For the position in 1989 see Cornell, Memo on 'Infrastructure Costs Initiative—Review of Progress', n.d., BRB Minutes, 2 November 1989.

195 Cf. Philip Wood (Director, Policy Unit, BRB), Note on 'Relations between Sectors and Production', n.d., RE Minutes, 27 January 1988; Richard Allan, Memo, 16 September 1988, cit.; Bradshaw, Report to Reid on large-scale organisation, n.d. (c.1988). My thanks to Bill Bradshaw for this reference.

196 Allen, 'Management Accounting Developments'; Tony Prosser, *Nationalised Industry and Public Control: Legal, Constitutional and Political Issues* (Oxford, 1986), pp. 120–4; John Heath, 'Planning in Transport', in John Grieve Smith (ed.), *Strategic Planning in Nationalised Industries* (1984), pp. 220–1. The 'angle of unreality' (the angle between the trend of past traffics and the forecast of future growth) and the

'march to the right' (the tendency for organisations to forecast increases in revenue and when things go wrong to simply displace the line to the right) were two of a series of axioms associated with British Rail planning, coined by former DTp statistician Ken Glover in the late 1970s: Glover, 'Examining Railway Figures: Some Useful Concepts', n.d., enclosed in Charles Brown (Director, Privatisation Studies Group, BRB), Memo, 13 May 1993, BRB IA 20-08-05 Pt. 10.

197 Not all the post-sector management plans were realistic. Note, for example, the criticism of optimism in the 1984 Rail Plan: Prosser, *Public Control*, pp. 123–4.

198 Gourvish, 'British Rail's "Business-Led" Organization', 135–8.

199 A One-Day Capital Card was introduced in June 1986. BRB Management Brief, 2 March 1987; BRB Press release, 21 November 1984, Network SouthEast press releases, 10 June, 21 August 1986; *Modern Railways*, October 1987, p. 522, November 1987, pp. 575–8; Interviews with Chris Green, 1 March 2000, Richard Edgley, 2000, John Nelson, 22 August 2000, and Gordon Pettitt, 6 November 2000.

200 Sanderson was succeeded as Sector Director by Colin Driver in 1985. See *Modern Railways*, January 1989, pp. 13–15; Roger Ford, 'The Sector Builders', *Modern Railways*, January 1992, pp. 48–9.

201 Reid, Railway Business Situation Report, BRB Minutes, 4 November 1982, Reid, 'All Change for Railway Management—How British Rail is Facing the Challenge of Competition', Address to Institute of Administrative Management, 23 April 1985, but cf. BRB Passenger Committee Minutes, 14 April and 15 September 1981, REG Minutes, 16 September and 14 October 1981; Leslie Lloyd (GM, WR)–Keen, 27 August 1981, Keen, Memo 8 October 1981, and other material in BRB IC file, AN182/90, PRO. I am grateful to Roger Temple for drawing my attention to this. See also John Gough, *British Rail at Work: InterCity* (1988), p. 24, Mike Vincent and Chris Green (eds.), *The InterCity Story* (Sparkford, 1994), pp. 36–7, and *Modern Railways*, May 1982, pp. 210–12, December 1982, pp. 557–60.

202 BRB Press releases, 19 November 1984, 8 April 1986, 27 May 1987; Reid, 'All Change', p. 15. Reid put the saving on the Leicester project at 30%, but in fact it was about 50% (£22.2m. (Q1/1983 prices) cf. £43.7m. (Q4/1981 prices)). O'Brien (GM, LMR), Memo to P & I Ctee., 1 February 1982, BRB S&T 206-11-23 Pt. 1; P & I Ctee. Minutes, 6 June 1983; Investment Committee Minutes, 4 July and 3 October 1983; John V. Gough, 'Leicester Signalling Centre', *Modern Railways*, December 1987, pp. 635–6; *Modern Railways*, January 1992, p. 49.

203 Colin Driver (Director, Railfreight), Memo on 'Freight Review: Progress Report', 3 June 1985, BRB Minutes, 6 June 1985; Driver–David E. Rayner, 6 December 1988, BRB DMEE File P52; Allen, 'Management Accounting Developments in British Rail', p. 106; Clarke and Heath, paper, 1988 (see fn. 209); *Modern Railways*, October 1987, p. 522.

204 Allen–Dr B. J. Nield (Director, Projects), 31 January 1985, reply to Nield–Allen, 22 January 1985, Sector Evaluation file on 'Attribution of capital costs to sectors: resignalling—York working party', 3.5. See also Myers–Paterson, 14 January 1985, ibid.; Interview with Frank Paterson, 1987, and Heath, 1998.

205 Myers–Sector Directors (Freight, Parcels, InterCity, and Provincial), 29 October 1986, Myers's Papers, Sec Box 2236.

206 Allen, 'Report on the Application of Sole User Principles with particular reference to Infrastructure Investment Schemes', August 1987, BRB IC File on 'Sector

Infrastructure Location Costing', AN182/340, PRO. There were also continuing problems with contingency cover, engineering possession policies, and route primacies.

207 Major P. M. Olver (DTp Railway Inspectorate)–Holmes, 6 March 1987 (letter refers to 'Cumbrian Cost Line'), 6 March 1987, and reply, 23 April 1987, BRB Director of Operations Files, MM/S/16/8; RE Minutes, 22 April 1987.

208 Maurice Holmes (Director of Operations)–O'Brien, 12 March 1986, O'Brien's Papers, Box 2173; Whittaker, Memo to Myers et al., November 1986, cit.; Toolan and Welsby, Memo to RE, March 1987, cit.; *Railway Gazette International*, November 1988, p. 738. On the weaknesses in Area management see also MMC, *Network SouthEast*, 1987, pp. 22–3.

209 BRB PMG Minutes, 23 July 1986; RE Minutes, 17 February 1988; Wood, Note to RE on 'Relations between Sectors and Production', cit., enclosing Geoffrey Clarke and John Heath, Preliminary Report on 'Business/Production Relationship Study', n.d. (1988); Clarke and Heath, 'Business-Production Relationships Study', 3 July 1988, Heath's Papers. On complexity see Phillips, Memo to Northampton Conference, August 1985 on 'Managing the Rail Business', 16 August 1985, O'Brien's Papers, Box 2173.

210 Cf. Edmonds, Support paper, January 1990, cit.

211 Wood, Note, cit.

212 Richard Allan, Memo, 16 September 1988, cit. A staff attitude survey in 1990—entitled 'Open Line'—underlined some of the difficulties presented by sector management. Only 16% of the 8,773 respondents replied favourably to the suggestion that senior management was providing a clear sense of direction for the organisation, only 19% to the suggestion that BR as a whole was well managed. My thanks to Neil Butters for this reference.

213 HQ staff includes Finance Department staff 'out-based' in the regions. Folder of reports to BRB, Soane's Papers, Box 16.

214 Soane (Assistant Chief Executive (Reorganisation)), Memo, 18 May 1983, RE Minutes, 24/5 May 1983; Soane (MD (Re-Organisation)), 'Administration & Organisation Initiative Completion Report', 14 March 1985, RE Minutes, 20 March 1985. Voluntary redundancy/early retirement accounted for 4,250 posts.

215 Savings were reduced by an overspend on refurbishment of c.£7m. BRB Minutes, 4 October 1984; BRB, *R&A 1986/7*, p. 8; Derek Fowler, Memo to BRB on 'London Office Accommodation Strategy', n.d., BRB Minutes, 2 April 1987. On Claudine's see 'Sex-Press Service at BR's posh HQ', *News of the World*, 4 April 1993, p. 25.

216 Welsby, Memo on 'Admin. & General Expenses', July 1985, RE Minutes, 24 July 1985; Welsby, Memo on 'Administrative Policy Review: Stage 2', 14 July 1986, RE Minutes, 23 July 1986; Whittaker (Director, Organisation Policy), Memo on 'A&O Stage III—Final Report', n.d., RE Minutes, 23 May 1988.

217 O'Brien, Memo on 'Overhead Cost Review', 11 March 1988, BRB Minutes, 31 March 1988.

218 Post Office, *R&A 1985/6*, pp. 2, 7–8 and cf. Pendleton, 'Structural Reorganization and Labour Management', 1994, 33.

219 Cf. Trevor Colling and Anthony Ferner, 'The Limits of Autonomy: Devolution, Line Managers and Industrial Relations in Privatized Companies', *Journal of Management Studies*, 29 (March 1992), 209; C. Hill and J. Pickering, 'Divisionalization, Decentral-

izationand Performance of large United Kingdom companies', *Journal of Management Studies*, 23 (1986), 26–50; Bradshaw, Report, n.d. (*c*.1988). Bradshaw was seconded to Wolfson College, Oxford after leaving the post of General Manager, Western Region, in 1985.

220 Rosabeth Moss Kanter, *When Giants Learn to Dance. Mastering the Challenges of Strategy, Management, and Careers in the 1990s* (London and New York, 1992), pp. 11–13.

221 Thomas J. Peters and Robert H. Waterman, *In Search of Excellence* (New York, 1982), pp. 306–7, 314. Peters and Waterman's work was known to BRB Board Members when they considered the move to sector management. A copy of their article on 'Structure is not Organization' in *The McKinsey Quarterly* (Summer 1980), 2–20, is in Parker's file on 'Springs 1980', Parker's Papers, PP3.

222 Welsby, Memo, RE Minutes, 17 September 1986, cit.

223 Interview with Alan Nichols, BRB (ex-DTp), 21 January 1999, and BRB, *R&A 1988/9*, p. 42. The adjustment, a response to the knowledge that the Board was benefiting from large cash sums from property sales, but was charging the PSO with interest on borrowings, reduced the PSO by £33m. in 1988/9. In addition, £64.5m. was deducted as an exceptional item to meet the overpayment for 1987/8.

224 BRB, *R&A 1983*, p. 53, *1990/1*, p. 53. Support/GDP = 1982: BR 0.34% cf. 0.76% for eight European railways incl. BR); 1989/90: BR 0.12% cf. 0.70% for 14 European railways excl. BR.

225 BRB, *R&A 1983*, *1988/9* and cf. Gourvish, 'British Rail's "Business-Led" Organization', 130–2. Train-miles run per staff member in 1982 were affected by the strikes in that year: the figure for 1983 was 1,685.

226 On the loss of parcels contracts see *Modern Railways*, February 1987, pp. 10, 63.

227 Moore–Reid, 27 March 1987, BRB F&P RPM87/6/3; Palmer–Reid, 23 April 1987, RPM 87/6/1/1.

228 Malcolm Spiller (Senior Finance Manager, Revenue Budgets, BRB)–Allen, 13 May 1987, BRB RPM 87/6/1/1; BRB Railway Planning Conference Minutes, 20 May 1987; Phillips, Memo on 'Cost Trends in the Passenger Business', 27 June 1987, BRB Minutes, 4 June and 2 July 1987.

229 Interview with Alan Nichols, cit.

230 Cf. Heath and Clarke, 1988; Wood, Note, cit.

231 Cf. Bradshaw's argument that sector management offered the government *too much* of an opportunity for intervention: lecture to Railway Studies Association, reported in *Modern Railways*, January 1992, p. 29.

Chapter 5

1 BRB Minutes, 7 February–1 May 1980; Jean Hartley, John Kelly, and Nigel Nicholson, *Steel Strike: A Case Study in Industrial Relations* (1983), pp. 32–7; Paul Blyton, 'Steel', in Andrew Pendleton and Jonathan Winterton (eds.), *Public Enterprise in Transition: Industrial Relations in State and Privatized Companies* (1993), p. 175.

2 Reid, Memo on 'Financial Prospects—Railways—1980', 19 May 1980; Derek Fowler, reports on the financial position, BRB Minutes, 1 May–2 October 1980, and especially Memo on 'Financial Prospects for Fiscal Year 1980/81, Calendar Year 1980 and Results for 24 Weeks', July 1980, BRB Minutes, 7 August 1980.

3 BRB, *Corporate Plan 1981–85* (1980): the optimism included a steady rise in investment from £277 m. in 1980 to £461 m. in 1987, and a promise to convert the railways' operating loss after interest from −£68.7 m. in 1980 to +£135.4 m. in 1985: pp. 33, 57. See also Philip Bagwell, *End of the Line? The Fate of British Railways Under Thatcher* (1984), pp. 64–6.

4 BRB Minutes, 3 July, 7 August, 4 and 25 September, and 2 and 14 October 1980. C&D Parcels were costing *c.*£80 m. p.a. to operate and losing *c.*£38 m.: *Modern Railways*, December 1980, p. 530. Savings from closure of the Manchester–Sheffield–Wath line were put at £2.5 m. p.a.: Richard H. Wilcox (Director, Industrial Relations, BRB)–Sidney Weighell (General Secretary, NUR), 8 April 1981, BRB Chief Executive's files, AN156/340, PRO.

5 Norman Fowler–Parker, 18 September 1980, Chief Executive's files, AN156/104, PRO; Derek Fowler, BRB Minutes, 14 October 1980. Concessions included the freedom to carry over money not spent, and help with the transitional costs associated with termination of the C&D parcels business. BRB Minutes, 2 October 1980; Norman Fowler–Parker, 24 November 1980, AN156/104, PRO.

6 Derek Fowler's comments, BRB Minutes, 5 February–2 April 1981 and BRB, *R&A 1982*, p. 5.

7 Peter Corbishley (Chief Planning Officer, BRB), Note, 15 January 1982, and draft Memo on 'Rail Planning and the Price, Waterhouse Report' (n.d.), Chief Executive's files, AN156/332, PRO; BRB, *R&A 1981*, p. 7. Criticisms of British Rail's financial and business planning mechanisms by Price Waterhouse were a further factor: Price Waterhouse, 'Review of the Financial Planning and Control Criteria and Management Information Procedures', 6 January 1982, BRB 240-1-72 (folder).

8 Cf. BRB Minutes, 14 October 1980; Reid's comments, BRB Minutes, 4 December 1980; Philip Bagwell, *End of the Line?*, pp. 29–30.

9 Derek Fowler, Memo on 'Five-Year Investment Programme 1980 to 1984', 24 January 1980, BRB Minutes, 7 February 1980; BRB, *Corporate Plan 1981–85*, pp. 3, 13–14 and *R&A 1980*, pp. 8–10. See also Bagwell, *End of the Line?*, pp. 64–5.

10 Successively Chief Civil Engineer, Chief Signal & Telecommunications Engineer, and Chief Mechanical & Electrical Engineer.

11 Ian Campbell, Memo on 'Railway Investment—Strategies for Sustaining the System', March 1980, Board Exec. Minutes, 27 March 1980, BRB Minutes, 3 April 1980; Campbell, Report on 'Renewal and Maintenance of Physical Assets: An Assessment of the Effect of Continued Restriction of Finance over a Ten-Year Period', 17 December 1980, BRB Minutes, 8 January 1981.

12 Campbell, Report, December 1980, p. 2.

13 BRB, *Corporate Plan 1981–85*, p. 14; Campbell, Memo, March 1980, p. 9; Report, December 1980, p. 10; BRB Minutes, 8 January 1981; Parker–Norman Fowler, 26 January 1981, AN156/105, PRO.

14 On the corporate advertising campaign see BRB Management Brief, 7 July 1980; Grant Woodruff (Director of Public Affairs)–Reid, Urquhart, and Rose, 2 July 1981, BRB 182-1-1 Pt. 5.

15 DTp, 'Note of Ministers' Meeting with British Railways Board to Discuss Railway Policy, 19 March 1980', 20 March 1980, AN156/105, PRO. Lawson was Treasury Financial Secretary, Clarke was DTp Parliamentary Secretary. The meeting was also attended by James Lester, Parliamentary Secretary, Dept. of Employment.

16 Board Exec. Minutes, 14 October 1980. On the genesis of the document, in earlier drafts entitled 'The Point of Decision' and 'A Developing Contract', see Posner's Papers, Sec Box 2260. The final version was edited by David Serpell: BRB Minutes, 5 March 1981.

17 Cf. DTp, Note D on 'Rail Policy Statement', for Meeting with Secretary of State, 3 September 1981, Parker's Papers, PP20(A); Serpell–Parker, 14 October 1981, Posner's Papers, Box 2260.

18 BRB, *Rail Policy. A Statement by the British Railways Board of its Policies and Potential for the 1980s* (March 1981), p. 5.

19 *Investment in Transport* (24 February 1981). The document was signed by BRB, BRF, RHA, Freight Transport Association, National Freight Co., AUEW, ASLEF, NUR, TGWU, and TSSA. See also *Modern Railways*, April 1981, pp. 146–7; Bagwell, *End of the Line?*, p. 121.

20 Option III, the 'medium' programme, would extend electrification to 75% of passenger train-mileage and 54% of freight. DTp and BRB, *Review of Main Line Electrification: Final Report* (February 1981), pp. 1, 4.

21 BRB Press Release, 11 February 1981; Parker, *For Starters*, p. 221.

22 *Modern Railways*, April 1981, p. 145; *Railway Gazette International*, March 1981, p. 167.

23 Walters (Sir Alan from 1983), transport economist, *inter alia*, was Cassel Professor 1968–76. He was Professor of Economics at Johns Hopkins University, Baltimore, until 1991: *Who's Who*. He advised Thatcher from 1981 to 1984: Interviews with Sir Alan Walters, 22 March 1999, Sir Norman Fowler, 20 April 1999.

24 Interview with Walters, 1999. Sherman was a critic of nationalised industries and an advocate of the conversion of railways into roads. See Anthony Ferner, *Government, Managers and Industrial Relations: Public Enterprises and their Political Environment* (Oxford, 1988), p. 148; Nicholas Ridley, '*My Style of Government': The Thatcher Years* (1991), pp. 7–8.

25 Cf. Posner: 'In my judgement, it might be best for us to keep out of his way entirely …I repeat—these are dangerous fields in which to tread', Posner–Parker et al., 29 January 1981, and see also Posner–Parker, 24 March 1981, BRB 361-194-7. Parker–Posner, 7 October 1981 was in similar vein: 'Larry Tindale [ICFC]… told me that they had had Walters to lunch and he was simply staggering in his anti-nationalisation talk'. See also Ridley, '*My Style of Government*', p. 7.

26 The review's standard assumption was an increase of 1% p.a. in real fares and Inter City traffic. Its elasticity ranges were, e.g. for Inter City traffic: journey times −0.7 to −1.0; and fares −0.8 to −0.5. On fuel prices, it used Dept. of Energy forecasts in real terms (low, standard, high) for 1978–2010, e.g. for 1978–90: diesel oil +70–110%, electricity +10–40%, noting that the most likely combination was high oil + standard electricity, i.e. for 1978–90 +110% and +25%. DTp and BRB, *Review of Main Line Electrification*, pp. 2–3, 13, 27, 35, 39. In fact, the Dept. of Energy's forecasts were hastily revised with narrower initial differentials, cf. *The Times*, 30 April 1981. With the benefit of hindsight, we now know that Walters was correct in arguing that real energy costs would fall over the next 20 years. Over the period 1978–90 heavy fuel oil (industrial sector, excluding VAT) fell in real terms by 47%, electricity (excluding VAT) by 21%: DTI, *Digest of UK Energy Statistics 1999*, p. 244.

27 Posner–Parker and Board Exec. Members, 30 March 1981, BRB 361-194-7.

28 Posner–Burt, 14 May 1981, BRB 361-194-7; *The Times*, 30 April 1981, in BRB 182-1-1 Pt. 5.

29 Fowler, *Ministers Decide*, pp. 137–8, and cf. his reply to a Commons question on 20 June 1979, *Parl. Deb. (Commons)*, 5th ser. (Session 1979–80), vol. 968, cols. 1312–13, also cit. in Bagwell, *End of the Line?*, p. 31.

30 Fowler, statement, 22 June 1981, *Parl. Deb. (Commons)*, 6th ser. (Session 1980–1), vol. 8, cols. 21–7. The call for a revised programme was very much a compromise solution agreed with the Treasury: Interview with N. Fowler, 1999.

31 BRB Press Release, 22 June 1981 and cf. *Modern Railways*, August 1981, pp. 337–8.

32 Cf. Parker, 'Note on Talk with the Secretary of State and Peter Baldwin Friday, 31st July', 3 August 1981, BRB 20-100-3 Pt. 3; Parker–Posner, 7 October 1981, Posner–Parker, 2 November 1981, BRB 361-194-7.

33 Or what Pendleton has called a 'tacit alliance': Andrew Pendleton, 'Markets or Politics? The Determinants of Labour Relations in a Nationalized Industry', *Public Administration*, 66 (Autumn 1988), p. 289; Pendleton, 'Railways', in Pendleton and Winterton (eds.), *Public Enterprise in Transition*, pp. 53–6.

34 *Locomotive Journal*, July 1980, p. 9; December 1980, p. 6, ASLEF. Ronksley was Vice-President of ASLEF, 1960–72, and President, 1974–82.

35 NUR Executive Committee Minutes, 10–14 March 1980, min. 349, National Union of Rail, Maritime and Transport Workers (RMT).

36 The Charter was sent to Parker in September 1980: Weighell–Wilcox, 9 March 1981, BRB IR 81-17-14. See also *Transport Review*, 4 January 1980, p. 1; NUR Exec. Ctee. Minutes, 26 September 1980, min. 1757, RMT; Urquhart, statement to RSNT, cit. in BR Management Brief, 16 August 1982; Sidney Weighell, *On the Rails* (1983), p. 69; Bagwell, *End of the Line?*, pp. 69–72.

37 Bagwell, *End of the Line?*, p. 72; Weighell, *On the Rails*, p. 70.

38 Viz. 31 May 1980 (timetabling), April 1983 (implementation): RSNC Minutes, 28 April and 13 May 1980; BRB Management Brief, 29 April 1980.

39 BRB Minutes, 2 July 1981, RSNC Minutes, 14–15 July 1981. DOO = driver-only operation, applicable to both freight and suburban passenger operations; the 'trainman' = a grade to replace both 'driver's assistant' and 'guard', providing a promotional route to 'driver'; 'variable' rostering = flexibility around the fixed 8-hour day; the 'open station' concept involved the replacement of ticket barriers at stations with on-train ticket examination (mainly for Inter City).

40 BR Council Minutes, 19–20 November 1980. On the clear strategic linkage at Board level of pressure for higher productivity with demands for higher investment see BRB Special Minutes, 20 July 1981.

41 BRB Management Brief, 30 January 1981; Weighell, *On the Rails*, pp. 73–5; Bagwell, *End of the Line?*, pp. 73–4.

42 Rose–Parker, 4 June 1981, BRB 361-194-7.

43 BR manual earnings relative to nat. ave.: 1969–79 −5%, 1975–9 −11%; hourly earnings 1969–79 −9%, 1975–9 −12%; the poverty line was the point at which Family Income Supplement operated: for a two-child family this was £74, but BR's Minimum Earnings Level was only £66.60. Tim Owen, *Wrong Side of the Tracks—Low Pay in British Rail* (Low Pay Unit Pamphlet no. 14, 1980), pp. 5, 7–9, 14, and see also *Modern Railways*, January 1981, p. 7, and Bagwell, *End of the Line?*, p. 111.

44 Rose–Board Members, 19 November 1980, BRB 361-194-7, but see also private sympathy for the unions' position on low pay in Posner, Memo on 'British Rail's Strategy—August 1981', 20 August 1981, BRB 240-1-72 Pt. 1.

45 The RPI increased by 21.55% from 1979:Q2 to 1980:Q2: *Economic Trends Annual Supplement 1996/7*, p. 155. The speedy resolution of the 1980 pay round was also partly explained by the concurrence of the long steel strike. Cf. Bagwell, *The Railwaymen. Vol. 2*, p. 232.

46 RSNC Minutes, 25 March 1980, and see also Bagwell, *End of the Line?*, pp. 75, 111 and *The Railwaymen. Vol. 2*, p. 232.

47 RSNC Minutes, 13 April 1981; Rose, Memo on 'Pay', 7 April 1981, BRB 82-30-2 Pt. 4; Weighell, *On the Rails*, pp. 80–1.

48 RSNC Minutes, 28 April 1981, BRB Minutes, 7 May 1981. While the 1980 claim was the first railway claim to be heard by ACAS, it had considered disputes affecting LT workshop staff in 1976 and LT staff in 1979: Bagwell, *The Railwaymen. Vol. 2*, pp. 287–8.

49 Rose, Memo, 17 July 1981, BRB Special Board Minutes, 20 July 1981; RSNC Minutes, 21 July 1981; Reid, letter to railwaymen, August 1981, Chief Executive's files, X81-51.

50 BRB Minutes, 6 August 1981; Weighell, *On the Rails*, pp. 73–8, 81–2; Bagwell, *End of the Line?*, pp. 77–8.

51 Cf. BRB Management Briefs, 5, 13, and 18 August 1981; press cuttings in X81–51, including *Sunday Times* and *Observer*, 9 August 1981, *The Times* and *Financial Times*, 10 August 1981.

52 RSNC Minutes, 27 August 1981; BRB Minutes, 3 September 1981; BRB Management Brief, 21 August 1981; Bagwell, *End of the Line?*, pp. 78–9.

53 BRB, *Corporate Plan 1981–85*, p. 2; *Rail Policy*, p. 23, cit. in Bagwell, *End of the Line?*, p. 122. The latter advocated a revised PSO based on passenger-miles maximisation: see Appendix K.

54 Parker–Fowler, 15 June 1981, and see also 23 July and 6 August 1981; Fowler–Parker, 31 July 1981; Parker–Howell, 23 September 1981, and reply, 25 September 1981, Parker file on 'Pastures', Parker's Papers. See also Parker, *For Starters*, pp. 228–30; Interview with N. Fowler, 1999. The difficulties concerned pension arrangements.

55 Parker–Fowler, 27 July 1981, AN156/105, PRO.

56 On these issues, see BRB, *R&A 1980*, p. 10, *1981*, pp. 11–12; BRB Minutes, 7 August 1980. A sum of £6 m. was allocated to environmental improvement (mainly stations), 1978–80. In February 1981, William G. Buchanan, Vice-President in Europe, Canadian National Railways, was appointed Special Adviser for the Disabled.

57 Cf. Parker–Fowler, 23 July 1981, BRB 182-1-1 Pt. 5. On Anglia, an informal notification to DTp was made after approval in principle by BRB's Planning & Investment Committee in May 1978; the formal submission was in November 1980: P&I Committee Minutes, 16 May 1978, 11 November 1980; Philip Sellers (Director of Finance), Memo to P&I Ctee., 18 January 1982, BRB 182-1-1 Pt. 6; Parker–Fowler, 23 July 1981, BRB 182-1-1 Pt. 5.

58 Parker, 'Note on Talk with the Secretary of State and Peter Baldwin Friday, 31st July', 3 August 1981, BRB 20-100-3 Pt. 3.

59 Clarke–Parker, 7 August 1981 and cf. Fowler–Parker, 23 March 1981, AN156/105, PRO, and interview with John Palmer, 4 August 1992.

60 DTp, 'Note of a Meeting with the British Railways Board held on Thursday 3 September 1981', 8 September 1981, BRB 20-100-3 Pt. 3; David P. Knighton (Briefing

Officer, BRB Secretariat), 'Note of Meeting between the Secretary of State and the Board at the Department of Transport on Thursday 3rd September 1981', 8 September 1981, BRB 240-1-72 Pt. 1.

61 Bosworth, Note on 'Terms of Reference for a Working Party', 3 September 1981, Parker's Papers, file on 'Meetings with SoS', PP20(A).

62 *The Times*, 12 September 1981; Parker, *For Starters*, p. 237; Andy McSmith, *Kenneth Clarke: A Political Biography* (1994), p. 79; Margaret Thatcher, *The Downing Street Years* (1994), pp. 140–2, 307.

63 Pattison, File Note, 16 November 1981, AN156/105, PRO.

64 Knighton, 'Note of Initial Meeting between the new Secretary of State and Board Members at the Department of Transport on Wednesday, 20th October 1981', 21 October 1981, BRB 20-100-3 Pt. 3; Parker–Chairman's Group on 'Meeting with Sir Peter Baldwin Tuesday 20th October', 21 October 1981, BRB 240-1-72 Pt. 1; David Howell, *A New Style of Government* (Conservative Policy Centre, 1970), p. 8 (reform by a party believing in less government 'becomes ... a key instrument in the drive for public economy and in the process of transferring functions and activities back to the private sector'. A footnote referred to 'privatisation'); Richard Cockett, *Thinking the Unthinkable: Think-Tanks and the Economic Counter-Revolution, 1931–1983* (1994), pp. 200–1; Interview with Lord Howell, 11 May 1999.

65 According to Parker, Howell 'said it was bound to be a strain if it all went public and I reminded him that he might lose initiative if it became a public circus': Parker–Chairman's Group, 21 December 1981, Parker's Papers, PP20(A). See also interview with Sir Peter Baldwin, 19 June 1991.

66 Serpell–Parker, 8 October, BRB 240-1-72 Pt. 1; Serpell–Parker, 14 October, Parker–Posner, 19 October, and Posner–Parker and Burt, with enclosures on 'An Alternative Policy for BRB', 30 October 1981, Posner's Papers, Box 2260.

67 Burt, 'File Note of Discussion between Board Executive (Messrs Rose and Urquhart absent) and DTp officials (Peter Baldwin, Peter Lazarus, H. N. Rosenfeld, John Palmer) on Thursday, October 22, 1981', 27 October 1981, AN156/105, PRO; Peter C. Trewin (Parliamentary & Customer Liaison Manager, BRB), 'Note of Meeting with Secretary of State Wednesday, 2nd December 1981', 3 December 1981, AN156/105, PRO.

68 Cf. Parker, 'Note of Meeting with Secretary of State Wednesday 5th November 1981', n.d., AN156/105, PRO (note that the BRB 240-1-172 Pt. 1 version of the note is annotated 4th November) and Woodruff–Reid, 19 November 1981, AN156/105, PRO.

69 Parker, Note, cit.

70 *The Times*, 24 November 1981; *Financial Times*, 19 November 1981, enclosed with Baldwin–Parker, 20 November 1981, Parker's Papers, file on 'SOS/DtP', and see BRB 240-1-72 Pt. 1; Trewin, Note, cit.

71 Hay Davison, Managing Partner in Arthur Andersen, 1966–82, was approached by David Mitchell, Under-Secretary of State at the DTp, but declined the offer since he had been asked to become Deputy-Chairman and Chief Executive of Lloyd's of London: conversation with author, 1991. See also Trewin, Note, cit.; *Sunday Times*, 6 December, *The Times*, 7 December 1981.

72 John Heath–Parker, 26 February 1982, Parker's Papers, unref. file.

73 Parker, Note on 'Meeting with Sir Peter Baldwin: 18 March, 1982', Parker's Papers, PP14.

74 Serpell resigned from the Board because his appointment came from the DTp alone, and not jointly with BRB. He has recalled his surprise: 'I was staying at this country cottage in Dilwyn in Hertfordshire … I was absolutely flabbergasted because all the talk had been about getting a good neutral': Interview with Sir David Serpell, 12 March 1991.

75 Parker, Note, 3 August 1981, cit.; Interview with Sir Peter Parker, 2 August 1999.

76 DTp, 'BRB/DTp Monthly Progress Meeting. Note of a Meeting held at 2 Marsham Street, SW1 on Monday, 14 December 1981', 8 January 1982, AN156/104, PRO; Derek Fowler, Note, 26 January 1982, BRB 240-1-72 Pt. 2.

77 In fact, the first official notification that a review would be conducted was made in the White Paper on *Government Expenditure Plans 1982–83 to 1984–85*, P.P. 1981–2, li, Cmnd. 8494, 9 March 1982, Vol. II, para. 71. However, Parker had revealed the news in a statement at Doncaster on 8 December 1981: BRB Press Release, 8 December 1981, *Financial Times*, 9 December 1981.

78 Howell–Parker, 31 March 1982, BRB 240-1-72 Pt. 2 (leaked to the *Guardian*, 26 April 1982). Butler had been a Director of the Mersey Docks & Harbour Co. since 1971.

79 Cf. P. J. Butler (Peat Marwick Mitchell)–D. Holmes (DTp), 30 April 1982, and Bosworth–Derek Fowler, 6 April 1982, BRB 240-1-72 Pt. 2, and see Board Exec. Minutes, 26 November 1981, and fn.7 above.

80 Sellers–Parker, 27 May 1982, BRB 240-1-72 Pt. 1 (Lascelles files); Board Exec. Minutes, 12 August 1982.

81 Interviews with Serpell, Parker, and Baldwin, 1991; Palmer, 1992; Walters and Howell, 1999; DTp, Press Release, 5 May 1982, BRB 240-1-72 Pt. 1 (Lascelles files). Bond had spent nine years with BEA; Goldstein had been Chairman of the Planning & Transport Research Advisory Ctee., 1973–9 and a member of Baroness Sharp's Advisory Ctee. on Urban Transport, 1967–9. He and Walters had sat on the Roskill Commission on London's Third Airport, 1968–70.

82 Burt–Palmer, 10 December 1981, Baldwin–Parker, 27 April 1982, BRB 240-1-72 Pt. 1; *Railway Finances*, Introduction, p. 5.

83 Lord Marsh, *Parl. Deb. (Lords)*, 5th ser. (Session 1982–3), vol. 439, 2 March 1983, col. 1143.

84 BRB, Policy Options for London & South-East Rail Services (February 1981), put to Norman Fowler on 11 June 1981. The document was subsequently criticised by Howell after a consultation process in November. See Parker, 'Note on Meeting … 5th November 1981', cit.; Howell–Parker, 10 November 1981, Parker's Papers, PP21; Howell, reported in *Modern Railways*, January 1982, p. 5.

85 MP for Edinburgh (Central), at the time of writing Foreign Secretary. Cook found it curious that the government should after a two-year process ask a 'whole new series of fundamental questions' about railway electrification and thought a line-by-line approach a 'logical absurdity': Robin Cook, *Parl. Deb. (Commons)*, 6th ser. (Session 1981–2), vol. 15, 22 December 1981, cols. 962–3.

86 Kenneth Clarke, ibid. col. 967, and see also P&I Ctee. Minutes, 11 November 1980; Palmer–Derek Fowler, 23 December 1981, and Sellers, Memo to P&I Committee, 18 January 1982, BRB 182-1-1 Pt. 5; Derek Fowler–Board, 5 January 1982, BRB 182-1-1 Pt. 6. The two Cambridge elements, Cambridge–Bishop's Stortford and Royston–Shepreth Jnc., were not authorised until January 1984 and March 1987 respectively:

Ridley–Reid, 16 January 1984, David Mitchell (Minister for Public Transport)–Reid, 4 March 1987, BRB 182-1-1 Pt. 7.

87 Cf. DTp, 'Note of a Meeting between the Secretary of State and the Rail Council at 2 Marsham Street on 17 December 1981', 29 December 1981, Parker's Papers, PP20A; Howell, Written Answer, 30 November 1982, *Parl. Deb. (Commons)*, 6th ser. (Session 1982–3), vol. 33, *141*; Howell–Parker, 4 May 1983, cit. Fowler's statement of 22 June 1981, BRB 20-3-2 Pt. 2.

88 Parker–Fowler, 11 August 1981, Parker–Howell, 12 October 1981, BRB 182-1-1 Pt. 5; BRB Press Release, 20 November 1981; *Guardian*, *Daily Telegraph*, and *Financial Times*, 21 November 1981, *Sunday Times*, 22 November 1981; Interview with Howell, 1999.

89 Parker, writing to Norman Fowler, 11 August 1981, admitted that the exercise would take 'months' not 'weeks', BRB 182-1-1 Pt. 5; he told Howell much the same thing, Parker–Howell, 12 October 1981, ibid. The submission was made in Derek Fowler–Howell, 3 August 1982, Parker's Papers, PP21; BRB Minutes, 5 August 1982.

90 Richard Pryke, 'Should British Rail Go Electric?', *New Society*, 27 August 1981, pp. 347–8, cit. in Posner–Woodruff, 2 September 1981, BRB 182-1-1 Pt. 5. Pryke thought the traffic and train-mile projections were too high and argued that the case rested too heavily upon fuel price differentials.

91 P&I Ctee. Minutes, 9 March 1982; Derek Fowler, British Rail Council Minutes, 15 April 1982; Parker–Howell, 22 April 1982, BRB 182-1-1 Pt. 6.

92 The Committee also expressed regret that its request for oral evidence from the CPRS had been rejected: *HC Transport Committee, 2nd Report Session 1981–82 on Main Line Railway Electrification*, P.P. 1981–2, xxxi, HC317.I, para. 8.

93 Howell–Parker, 4 May 1983, cit. and cf. Thatcher's phrase at the 1980 party conference: Margaret Thatcher, *Speeches to the Conservative Party Conference 1975–1988* (1989), p. 64.

94 Glaister's report forms Appendix B of the HC Transport Committee report: 'Main Line Electrification: Assessment of key issues by the Committee's Specialist Adviser (Dr Stephen Glaister), April 1982, HC317.I, pp. xliv–lx. Because Glaister had doubts about the robustness of the energy price forecasts and was concerned by the fact that the financial benefits did not emerge until after 2000, he favoured the government's demand for a line-by-line justification of electrification projects: Interview with Prof. Glaister, 28 April 1999.

95 Dr Bernard J. Nield (Chief Investment Officer, BRB) and Derek Fowler, Memo, 22 September 1982, P&I Ctee. Minutes, 28 September 1982; Derek Fowler, Memo, 30 September 1982, BRB Minutes, 7 October 1982. The problem here was that modern HSTs were being used on the ECML. Returns from electrification were reduced: (1) when Inter-City decided to use HSTs on the Midland Main Line before waiting for cascaded sets from the ECML; and (2) by an acceptance that revenue betterment arising from cascading sets to the North-West/South-West routes could not be counted because the cost of 'like-for-like' replacement was very similar to the cost of building new HSTs for these routes. Cf. also Posner–Myers, 3 March 1983, and Alfred W. Boucher (Principal Investment Manager, BRB), Memo to BRB Investment Committee, 20 April 1983, BRB 182-1-1 Pt. 7.

96 Dr Richard Smith, who was seconded to BRB from the DTp for two years, conducted the reappraisal of the project: Myers's Papers, Sec Box 2240.

97 Investment Committee Minutes, 11 and 25 May and 6 June 1983; Howell–Parker, 4 May 1983; Reid, Memo 27 April 1983, BRB Minutes, 5 May 1983; Parker–Howell, 10 May 1983, Howell–Parker, 20 May 1983, Reid–Ridley, 23 May 1984, Ridley–Reid, 31 July 1984, BRB 182-1-1 Pt. 7.

98 There have been several accounts of the industrial relations difficulties of 1981–2, including Parker, *For Starters*, pp. 228–60; Weighell, *On the Rails*, pp. 80–98; Bagwell, *End of the Line?*, pp. 82–120; and Ferner, *Government, Managers*, pp. 96–100.

99 BRB Management Brief, 14 October 1981, Rose, Memo, 22 October 1981, BRB Minutes, 5 November 1981, and Memo to Railway Executive Group [REG], 4 November 1981, Chief Executive's files, X81-51; Wilcox–Reid and Urquhart, 16 November 1981, Chief Executive's files, X81-70; REG Minutes, 14 October, 11 and 25 November 1981; O'Brien (General Manager, LMR)–Reid, 16 November 1981, Rose–Reid and Urquhart, 3 December 1981, Rose, Memo, 23 December 1981, X81-70; Weighell–Wilcox, 23 December 1981, BRB IR 81-17-14 Pt. 2.

100 Cf. Wilcox–Rose, 13 November 1981, X81-70; Burt, 'File Note of Discussion Between Board Executive and DTp Officials...December 10, 1981', 15 December 1981, AN156/105, PRO; BRB Railway Directing Group Minutes, 16 December 1981; Wilcox–Weighell (NUR), Buckton (ASLEF), T. H. Jenkins (TSSA), A. Ferry (CSEU), and J. Dalgleish (BTOG), 23 December 1981; Rose, Note on 'ASLE&F Action', 5 January 1982, X81-70.

101 Buckton–Wilcox, 30 December 1981, X81-70.

102 Parker–Howell, 25 March 1982, enclosed in Derek Fowler, Confid. Memo, 30 March 1982, BRB Minutes, 1 April 1982. The Board's figure was the 'net trading loss'. Higher figures (presumably the revenue loss) were reported in *Modern Railways* (£90 m., April 1982, p. 146), and *Railnews* (£100 m., 22 Feb. 1982, p. 2).

103 Cf. Pendleton, 'Railways', pp. 54–5; Ferner, *Governments, Managers*, pp. 96, 99, 106, 128–9, 149.

104 Cf. BRB Minutes, 4 February 1982; Wilcox–Parker, Reid, et al., 5 January 1982, enclosing Frank Kitching (Principal Industrial Relations Officer, BRB)–Wilcox and Sydney Hoggart (Deputy Director, Industrial Relations, BRB) on 'A.C.A.S. [*sic*] Dispute', 5 January 1982, X81-70.

105 Cf. Reid, letters to staff on 'ASLE&F Dispute', January, 14 and 26 January 1982; BRB, advertisements on 'The ASLEF Dispute', placed in national newspapers, 15 and 19–20 January 1982; Parker–Howell, 8 January 1982; Woodruff–REG, 5 February 1982, X81-70; Opinion Research & Communication, 'A Survey of BR Employees', February 1982, X81-51; Reid, Restricted Circulation Memo on 'ASLE&F Dispute', n.d. [*c*.9 February 1982], X81-70. Contemplation by rail management of drastic responses to ASLEF was prompted by the union's escalation of the dispute by altering the days chosen for three one-day stoppages from Tuesday, Thursday, and Sunday to Wednesday, Thursday, and Sunday.

106 BRB Minutes, 22 and 26 January 1982; REG Special Minutes, 25 January and 1 February 1982.

107 Interview with Lord McCarthy, 24 September 1998.

108 ASLEF Circular, 3 February 1982, ASLEF.

109 Cf. 'Rail's Big Three Clash on TV', *Daily Mail*, 9 February 1982, p. 9. Bagwell makes the point that more days were lost through railway strikes in 1982 than in the whole of 1948–81: *End of the Line?*, p. 82.

110 List of 'ASLEF Officials and Executive Members', n.d. [June 1982], in BRB Employee Relations Dept. Confidential File on 'NUR/A.S.L.E.& F. Executive Committees & Other Trade Unions', BRB IR 20-1-3, and cf. *Daily Mail*, 3 February, p. 6 ('Stop Subsidising these Wreckers') and 9 February 1982, p. 9 ('The Shadowy Seven who keep strike going'); Interviews with Lew Adams, 29 July 1998, Derrick Fullick, 26 January 2001. See also *The Times*, 12 January 1982, and BRB IR 80-52-74 Pt. 2.

111 Charles W. Swift–Lord McCarthy, 3 February 1982, X81-70. The letter is worth quoting *in extenso*:

Dear Lord McCarthy

It is 4.46am and I lie here in my bed watching the minutes ticking by on the digital alarm clock at my bedside presented to me by the Area Manager of British Rail for 35 years service. I should have been at work this morning at 0001 . . . I lie here feeling very bitter and cross . . . I have let the cat in and it is looking at the canary, perhaps with the same feeling as I have towards British Railways Board and ASLEF at this moment in time . . . Those of us who have had connections with British Rail over the years could write a book on the corrupt practices that take place. This is not the main issue . . . I would like to quote as examples of what is wrong two of the four weeks I have worked since the Christmas period. One week I started duty at 1607. I then sat in the Mess Room playing cards and dominoes until 1937, some three hours thirty minutes before I actually started work. I worked the 1950 to Lincoln and back to Peterborough single manned. During the course of that week I had over 17 hours and 30 minutes totally unproductive time sitting doing nothing at all. The following week my turn of duty began at 1451 as a passenger to Nottingham to work the 1725 Nottingham to Peterborough—one hour of actual work and some five hours unproductive time . . . In that week I had over 30 hours of unproductive time. I could, given a sensible productivity agreement, easily have signed on and worked the 1451 to Nottingham, worked back to Peterborough arriving at 1830, have left Peterborough again at 1950, to Lincoln and arrived back at Peterborough at 2235, (a roster of 8 hours 5 minutes work) and have done both jobs comfortably.

Swift had written in similar vein to Parker, 10 August 1981, ibid. His views on unproductive time were echoed in Roger Ford, 'Variable-day rostering in practice', *Modern Railways*, May 1982, pp. 205–8.

112 ACAS, 'Committee of Inquiry Report and Recommendations on a Dispute between BRB and the ASLE and F' (16 February 1982); BRB Special Minutes, 16 February 1982; Wilcox, Memo on 'ASLE&F Dispute', 18 February 1982, enclosing agreed statement on 'Rail Dispute', signed by Rose, Buckton, Weighell, Jenkins, Lowry, and Murray, 17 February 1982, X81-51. The Committee's findings were widely seen as a defeat for Parker: cf. *Daily Mail*, 19 February 1982, p. 6.

113 RSJC (Loco.) Minutes, 25 February 1982; RSNC Minutes, 1 March 1982; RSNT, Decision No. 77, 4 May 1982, pp. 4–5, BRB.

114 RSNT Decision No. 77, p. 1; Note of RSNT Meeting with the Assessors, 19 March 1982, Posner's Papers, Sec Box 2267.

115 Interview with McCarthy, 1998.

116 RSNT Decision No. 77, pp. 41–4. The Tribunal rejected ASLEF's view that changes could be made without abandoning the eight-hour day, but noted that appropriate 'safeguards and criteria' should be agreed, covering working hours, unsocial hours, overtime, etc. It also regarded its decision to have been the most difficult since RSNT

42, ibid., p. 15. Parker, writing to Reid and Rose, observed: 'the McCarthy Report ... vindicates us triumphantly': Note, 11 May 1982, X81-51.

117 ASLEF, Executive Committee Minutes, 12 May 1982, ASLEF; *Locomotive Journal*, May 1982, pp. 1, 67.

118 In addition to flexible rostering and DOO on the 'Bedpan' line, there was DOO on non-passenger trains (NUR), easement of conditions for single manning of traction units (ASLEF), and the trainman concept (ASLEF). The NUR's view on DOO (passenger) was that guards should be retained as 'train superintendents' for revenue protection: Weighell–Wilcox, 15 February 1982, X81-51.

119 RSNC Minutes, 11 March and 28 May 1982; Rose–Parker, 20 May 1982, Rose–Parker, 8 June 1982, enclosing 'File Note on Discussions with Secretary of State, Junior Ministers and Officials, Chairman, Chief Executive, and C. A. Rose', X81-51.

120 RSNC Minutes, 28 May 1982, and cf. *Transport Review*, 18 June 1981, p. 1 and Weighell, *On the Rails*, p. 88. Cliff Rose privately conceded that BR staff were lagging behind other sectors and confessed that 'BR basic rates for the lower grades compare most unfavourably with those in some reasonably comparable occupations such as postmen and labourers in the fuel industries': Rose, Confidential Memo on '1982 Pay', 29 April 1982, BRB Minutes, 6 May 1982.

121 Brief for Chairman on '1982 Industrial Relations: Problems Analysis, 13 May 1982', and Reid–Parker, 17 May 1981, X81-51; RSNC Minutes, 17 June 1982; BRB Minutes, 3 and 24 June and 1 July 1982; P. C. Trewin, Note on 'Meeting with Secretary of State: 22nd June 1982', 24 June 1982, X81-51; Weighell, *On the Rails*, pp. 90–2.

122 'ASLEF Dispute Diary', *Modern Railways*, September 1982, pp. 386–8. The legality of the Board's stance was not strong. Cf. Michael Baker (Chief Solicitor & Legal Adviser, BRB), Memo on 'Legal Consequences of Imposing Flexible Rostering', 2 June 1982, and Wilcox, 'Note for File', 4 June 1982, BRB IR 81-17-14/3(b) Pt. 2.

123 Cf. conciliatory gestures at the RSNC, RSNC Minutes, 22 and 25 June 1982, and reaffirmation of 'total commitment to the retention of the eight-hour day' when announcing the strike, in Buckton, letter to ASLEF branches and LDCs, 30 June 1982, X81-51. See also BRB Minutes, 1 July 1981, Parker, *For Starters*, p. 234, and Weighell, *On the Rails*, pp. 86, 93–5.

124 BRB Minutes, 13 July 1982; BR Management Brief, 14 July 1982; Howell, *Parl. Deb. (Commons)*, 6th ser. (Session 1981–2), vol. 27, 14 July 1982, col. 1035; text of recorded freephone message for footplate staff, 15 July 1982, X81-51. See also papers in BRB LB/12/105/A5.

125 BR Management Brief, 19 July 1982.

126 Buckton–Wilcox, 5 August 1982, Holroyd–Kitching, 21 December 1982, BRB IR 81-17-14/3 (b) Pt. 2.

127 Cf. *The Times*, 22 February 1982 ('BR was told to settle with Aslef', p. 22, denied in Woodruff–Burt, BRB 80-52-3 Pt. 4).

128 Notes of Meetings with Secretary of State, 22 June and 26 July 1982, X81-51.

129 Cf. Reid–Parker, 17 May 1982, Rose–Parker, 20 May 1982, X81-51.

130 File Note, 24 May 1982, X81-51; BRB Minutes, 27 May 1982; Weighell, *On the Rails*, pp. 93–4; Bagwell, *End of the Line?*, pp. 90–1.

131 Thatcher, comments in House of Commons, e.g. *Parl. Deb.(Commons)*, 6th ser. (Session 1981–2), vol. 27, 8 July 1982, col. 456; Interview with Lord Howell, 11 May 1999.

132 Trewin, Notes on 'Meeting with Secretary of State: 22nd June 1982', 24 June 1982, '26th June 1982', '7th July 1982', n.d., '12 July 1982', 14 July 1982, '16th July 1982', 26 July 1982, '26th July 1982', 28 July 1982, X81-51; '30th June 1982', 2 July 1982, '9th July 1982', 12 July 1982, '16th July 1982', 26 July 1982, Parker Papers, file on 'SoS & DTp'.

133 Viz. Sparrow and McKenzie of the CPRS, who attended joint meetings on 24 and 27 May 1982: File Note, 24 May 1982, 'Notes of Meeting held at 15.30 on Thursday 27th May at the Department of Transport', n.d., and R. A. J. Mayer (PS to SoS), 'Note of a Meeting about British Rail Industrial Relations 27 May 1982', 9 June 1982, Rose–Parker, 8 June 1982, enclosing 'File Note on Discussions with Secretary of State, Junior Ministers and Officials, Chairman, Chief Executive and C. A. Rose', X81-51; BRB Minutes, 27 May 1982.

134 'Notes of Meeting with John Palmer at 10.15 on 27th May 1982', n.d., Mayer, Note, 9 June 1982, X81-51. Rose had readily agreed that 'If there was to be industrial action on the railways, then July and August was as good a time to have it as any'.

135 The Federation was established in September 1981, though the industrial disputes ensured that it did not meet until June 1983. Cf. *Transport Review*, 11 September 1981, p. 1, 12 February 1982, p. 1, 24 June 1983, p. 1. *Locomotive Journal*, September 1981, p. 1, October 1981, p. 3; Weighell, *On the Rails*, pp. 127–9; Bagwell, *End of the Line?*, p. 179.

136 Trewin, Notes on 'Meeting with Secretary of State: 12 July', '16th July', cit. There was also anxiety about a plan to recruit and train temporary drivers, Lazarus, the DTp Deputy Secretary, informing Reid that 'any such crash course [*sic*] would not turn out an effective driver': Lazarus–Reid, 6 July 1982, X81-51.

137 Margaret Thatcher, *The Downing Street Years* (1993), pp. 139–43.

138 Parker, Secret 'Note on Meeting with SoS—26th March 1982', 26 March 1982, X81-51.

139 Thatcher, 3 July 1982, reported in *Sunday Telegraph*, 4 July 1982, p. 1 and *The Times*, 5 July 1982, p. 1; 15 July 1982, *Parl. Deb. (Commons)*, 6th ser. (Session 1981–2), vol. 27, 15 July 1982, col. 1164.

140 Jenkins–Parker, 24 July 1982, X81-51, and cf. Parker–Reid and Rose, 11 May 1982 ('we were right, in August, in forcing the pace through the strikes, so that, as in the Falkland issue, somebody comes to the table to negotiate'). Jenkins's analogy was prompted by his role as adviser to the Commons Select Committee on Defence and its examination of the Falklands War. He thought BRB had conducted its 'war' with ASLEF in a model way, particularly at the public relations level.

141 Cf. Andrew Pendleton, 'The Barriers to Flexibility: Flexible Rostering on the Railways', *Work, Employment and Society*, 5 (2) (June 1991), 252–4; Ferner, *Government, Managers*, pp. 128–31; Interviews with John Palette, 9 November 1990, John Holroyd, 12 December 1990, and Paul Watkinson, 14 July 1999. On managers' doubts see O'Brien (GM, LMR)–Wilcox, 23 June 1982, BRB IR 81-17-14/3 Pt. 2; Holmes, Memo 13 March 1985, BRB IR 81-17-14/3 Pt. 5.

142 Interview with John Holroyd, 19 October 1990.

143 Hoggart (Director, Employee Relations, BRB), Memo to RE on 'Variable Rostering—Footplate Staff', 19 May 1983, BRB IR 81-17-14/3(b) Pt. 2; Hoggart–Buckton, 6 March 1984, BRB IR 81-17-14/3(b) Pt. 4.

144 Padding and balancing payments arose from the agreement that working hours would be reconciled over an eight-week, 312-hour cycle. Padding was the practice of making up drivers' hours, e.g. by adding hours to turns, or by including 'spare' (covering) turns. Balancing payments arose because rostering/timetable changes did not always coincide with an eight-week cycle. With both sides failing to reach agreement, the practice developed in 1983–6 of paying for time owing (i.e. above 312 hours) at the overtime rate, while writing off hours owed to British Rail. See, for example, Memo on 'Variable Day Roster: Balancing Payments', 7 February 1985, BRB IR 81-17-14/3(b) Pt. 5 and Interview with Andrew Pendleton, 6 July 1999. In November 1986 Buckton produced a list of 21 topics: Buckton–Paul Watkinson (Director, Employee Relations, BRB), 26 November 1986 and reply, 17 December 1986, BRB IR 81-17-14/3(b) Pt. 5.

145 *Railway Finances*, Annex A, pp. 87–9; Malcolm J. Southgate (Director, Policy Unit, BRB)–Derek Fowler, 12 January 1983, and list of papers, n.d. [January 1983], BRB Policy Unit file, AN170/343, PRO.

146 See Sellers–Parker, 27 May 1982, BRB 240-1-72 Pt. 1; and Bosworth–Parker, 25 August 1982, ibid. Pt. 3.

147 Howell–Serpell, 10 September 1982, Burt–Peter E. Lazarus (Permanent Secretary, DTp), 29 March 1983, and reply, 18 April 1983, in BRB 240-1-72 Pt. 2 (Lascelles files); Serpell, evidence, 1 March 1983, *House of Commons Transport Committee, 2nd Report Session 1982–83 on Serpell Committee Report on the Review of Railway Finances*, P.P. 1982–3, xxvii, HC240, QQ. 1, 6–8; Interview with Serpell, 1991.

148 On 9 December 1982. Serpell, Bond, Butler, and Osmotherley (Secretary to Serpell Committee)–Howell, 20 December 1982, *Railway Finances*, p. 1; Interview with Sir Alan Walters, cit. and cf. Parker, 'Note of Meeting with Sir Peter Baldwin, 29 July 1982', 29 July 1982, Parker's Papers, PP14, and Ron Lewis, M.P. (Carlisle) and NUR member, *Parl. Deb. (Commons)*, 6th ser. (Session 1982–3), vol. 36, 3 February 1983, cols. 456, 460.

149 Part of the delay was caused by discussion of whether sensitive commercial information should be excluded: see Parker–Howell, 6 January 1983, BRB Secretary's Papers. Note that data on freight revenue by commodity and on parcels costs and profits were withheld in the published report: *Railway Finances*, Pt. 1, Table 3.2 and para. 4.14. In addition, references to the Post Office letter mail contract were deleted, and some amendments were made by committee members. Howell also attributed the delay to the complications of printing the maps: evidence, 9 March 1983, *HC Transport Ctee Report on Serpell Committee*, Q. 238.

150 *Railway Finances*, preface, p. 12; Interviews with Serpell, 1991, Will Camp, 27 January 1999. The newspaper articles on 23 and 24 December 1982 speculated that the railways' investment plans had been rejected, then followed Howell's statement in identifying Goldstein as the author of the minority report, and revealing that the committee had presented a series of options, rather than firm recommendations: Howell–Parker, 22 December 1982; Howell, written answer, *Parl. Deb. (Commons)*, 6th ser. (Session 1982–3), vol. 34, *680*; *Guardian*, 23 and 24 December, *Financial Times*, 24 December, in BRB 240-1-72 Pt. 4. The *Daily Star* referred to 'a new Beeching Axe', 24 December 1982. The post-Christmas leaks were more substantial: see fn. 168 below. The leaking was raised by the HC Transport Committee when it interviewed Parker on 8 March 1983: *Report on Serpell Committee*, QQ. 166–72.

151 From −£17 m. to −£111 m. in 1982 prices: *Railway Finances*, Pt. 1, preface, p. 12; paras. 2.8–2.13 and Table 2.3; paras. 12.2, 12.6–7.

152 For Inter-City the scope for cost reduction was put at £39 m.: ibid. Pt. 1, para. 2.12. On the other businesses see Pt. 1, paras. 2.23, 2.30, 3.27, and 4.15 and chap. 5.

153 Ibid., Pt. 1, para. 2.18.

154 Ibid., Pt. 1, paras. 2.12, 2.30, 3.27, 12.17–24.

155 Ibid., Pt. 1, para. 6.52.

156 Ibid., Pt. 1, para. 6.52; conclusion, p. 85.

157 Ibid., Pt. 1, paras. 12.25–30. The reduction in PSO support was contingent upon assumptions about revenue, transitional costs, sector management, etc.

158 Ibid., Pt. 1, paras. 7.6, 7.27–30.

159 Ibid., Pt. 1, paras. 6.40–1, 8.12, 8.14, 8.18, 8.23–36.

160 Ibid., Pt. 1, paras. 9.3–5, 12.25.

161 Ibid., Pt. 1, paras. 10.3–6, 10.12–15.

162 Ibid., Pt. 1, paras. 11.8–11, 11.14–19 (there are no sections 11.12–13). The Report also recommended that the Board should move to financial instead of calendar years in its annual reporting: Pt. 1, para. 10.18.

163 Ibid., conclusion, p. 85.

164 *Committee on the Review of Railway Finances: Minority Report by Alfred Goldstein, CBE*, 22 December 1982, paras. 1.06, 2.05–14, 3.30. He stated that 'The search for a base position in projections of the near future, thus proved, as it nearly always must, to be the pursuit of a continually moving target': para. 2.07. He also criticised the committee's decision to assess PSO prospects in relation to a 1975 baseline, which was considered to be the 'wrong emphasis': paras. 3.13–15.

165 Goldstein, Minority Report, paras. 3.19, 4.10.

166 Ibid., paras. 3.01–9, 3.35–42, 3.48–54.

167 Ibid., paras. 6.03–7. Note a supplementary volume contained 13 diagrams of existing traffic flows, and a copy of Travers Morgan's engineering study: *Railway Finances: Supplementary Volume*, 1983.

168 Cf. *Financial Times*, 29 December, *Guardian*, 30 December 1982, 4 January 1983, *Observer*, 2, 9, and 16 January 1983, *The Times*, 5 January 1983, *Tribune*, 14 January 1983, *Sunday Times*, 9 January 1983.

169 Parker–Howell, 17 January 1983, BRB 240-1-72 Pt. 4; Parker–Serpell, 18 January 1983, Parker's Papers, file on 'Serpell Report'; BRB, *The Review of Railway Finances. The initial response by the British Railways Board to the report of the Committee on the Review of Railway Finances* (Jan. 1983); *Railnews*, February 1983, p. 1. Note that only the *Daily Telegraph* appears to have given BR's document serious attention: *Daily Telegraph*, 21 January 1983.

170 Posner–Parker, 23 December 1982, Parker's Papers, file on 'Serpell Report'.

171 Jenkins–Parker, 2 January, Caldecote, note, 5 January, and Prudence Leith–Derek Fowler, 14 January 1983, ibid.; Caldecote–Howell, 1 February 1983, BRB Secretary's Papers. See also Board Exec. Minutes, 3 January 1983; BRB Minutes, 6 January 1983.

172 Campell–Parker, 2 January 1983, Parker's Papers, file on 'Serpell Report'; Campbell, 'First Comments on Engineering Chapters', 3 January 1983, Sellers, 'First Comments on Planning & Investment Chapters', 3 January 1983, appendices to Derek Fowler, Memo to BRB, 4 January 1983, BRB Pre-Board Dinner, 5 January 1983. A vigorous defence of planning and investment was produced as BRB, *Finance in Focus. The*

Finance Journal of British Rail, special edn., Jan. 1983, in BRB 240-1-72 Pt. 5. See also Sellers–Parker, 28 July 1982, Derek Fowler–Board Members, 3 August 1982, BRB 240-1-72 Pt. 3.

173 BRB, *Initial Response*; see also Trewin, 'Parliamentary Briefing—Wednesday 2nd February, 1983', 31 January 1983, BRB 240-1-72 Pt. 5.

174 Interview with Serpell, 1991. Some of the comment was personal, e.g. 'What can you expect from this Serpell? He was just the boy taking down notes in the Stedeford Committee', attributed to 'a retired railway manager' in *Modern Railways*, March 1983, p. 124.

175 'A really rotten report', *Guardian*, 'Back to the engine shed', *Financial Times*, 'Heading for the buffers', *Daily Mail*, 'On the wrong track', *Daily Mirror*, 'You can bet this rail plan will be shunted into the siding', *Sun*, 'Shunted Aside', *Daily Express*, 'Shoddy verdict on Serpell rail report', *Standard*, 'The train now leaving Britain', *Daily Star*, 'Derail these rail wreckers', *Morning Star*, all 21 January 1983, cuttings in BRB 240-1-72 Pt. 5.

176 A high-investment option assuming *no efficiency gains* had been compared not with the base option but with the alternative base which *did* incorporate efficiency gains. The pressure group Transport 2000 commissioned the consultants TEST to produce revised options; its high-investment option showed a deficit of £738 m.: TEST, *Investing in British Rail* (1983), reported in *Modern Railways*, August 1983, p. 394.

177 E.g. 'A computer's comic cuts block the Serpell line', *New Scientist*, 27 January, and Richard Hope, editor, 'Serpell's Options: slow death or quick kill?', *Railway Gazette International*, March 1983, pp. 180–2. The 'anomalies' included western services terminating at Exeter (not Plymouth/Torbay) in network C3, the West Highland line terminating at Crianlarich (not Oban/Fort William) in C2, and the retention of Lewes–Uckfield but abandonment of north Kent services in B.

178 Posner, 'More pressure, more squeaks', *The Times*, 21 January; Jenkins, 'There is a better way to run a railway', *Observer*, 23 January 1983.

179 Albert Booth, Richard Adley, and Robin Cook, *Parl. Deb. (Commons)*, 6th ser. (Session 1982–3), vol. 36, 3 February 1982, cols. 432–6, 448, 477.

180 Lord Marsh and Lord Ezra, *Parl. Deb. (Lords)*, 5th ser. (Session 1982–3), vol. 439, 2 March 1983, cols. 1142, 1167–9.

181 £627,342 reported by Lord Lucas of Chilworth, ibid. cols. 1201–2.

182 *HC Transport Ctee, Report on Serpell Ctee*, paras. 10–17, 20, 22–3, 26; Parker, evidence to the Ctee., 8 March 1983, Q. 185.

183 County Secretary, Norfolk County Council–Secretary, BRB, 11 March 1983, and Clerk & CE, Surrey County Council–Secretary, BRB, 29 April 1983, BRB 240-1-72 Pt. 1 (Lascelles files).

184 Howell–Parker, 19 January 1983, BRB 240-1-72 Pt. 4; Woodruff–Parker and R. O. Faulkner–Woodruff, 24 January 1983, Parker's Papers, file on 'Serpell January 1983'; *Guardian*, 24 January 1983.

Chapter 6

1 Cf. Caldecote–Howell, 1 February 1983, BRB Secretary's Papers.

2 Cf. Lord Ferrier, *Parl. Deb. (Lords)*, 5th ser. (Session 1982–3), vol. 430, 3 March 1983, col. 1183; *The Times*, 21 January 1983; *Modern Railways*, April 1983, p. 170.

3 RSNT Decision No. 78, 10 September 1982; Urquhart, Confidential Memo to Board Exec. on 'Industrial Relations Situation Report', 23 September 1982, X81-51; RSNC Minutes, 20 October 1982. Urquhart deputised for Rose owing to the latter's absence through illness.

4 See Urquhart, reported in BRB Minutes, 4 November 1982; Reid–Palmer, 10 December 1982, enclosing brief for SoS, X81-51. By this time John Palette was the Managing Director, Personnel. He was acting Director from Aug. 1982, and Managing Director from March 1983. BRB Press Release, 21 March 1983.

5 Weighell declined to support NUM candidate Eric Clarke for election to Labour's National Executive Committee. He has recalled that he chose to resign giving three months' notice on 5 October 1982 rather than face suspension, in order to prevent a militant response to the RSNT's 6% offer, due to be debated at an NUR conference in Birmingham. It may be that he expected the conference to ask him to withdraw his resignation. See Weighell, *On the Rails*, pp. 158–69; Interviews with John Palette, 9 November 1990, and William McCarthy, 1998.

6 RSNT Decisions Nos. 79 and 80, 15 March 1983; *Modern Railways*, June 1983, p. 285; the first passenger service was operated on 30 March: *Modern Railways*, May 1983, p. 228.

7 Reid, File Note on 'R.S.N.T. 79/80', 16 March 1983, Myers's Papers, Sec Box 2246; Interview with Palette, 1990.

8 Cf. Trewin, 'Note of a Meeting with Secretary of State: 21.12.82', 5 January 1983, X81-51.

9 It is evident that Reid was often in favour of an uncompromising stance. Cf. Reid–Parker, 1 March 1983, Myers's Papers, Box 2246. Part-timers such as Allen Sheppard were of like mind: Interviews with Trevor Toolan, 10 June 1999, and Sir Peter Parker, 2 August 1999.

10 That is, cab radios and on-platform mirrors or CCTV. BRB, 'Paper presented at Watford 14/15 July 1981', BRB IR 81-17-14; BRB Management Brief on 'Driver Only Operation: Background', 13 August 1985.

11 Railway Executive (RE) Minutes, 24–5 May 1983.

12 March/April–May 1983. There were some problems with the Willesden–Garston trial and a retrial took place in July 1984. Drivers were paid £6 a turn as on the 'Bedpan' line. RSNC Minutes, 16 March 1983. Sidney Hoggart (Director, Employee Relations, BRB), Memo to RE on 'Productivity Initiatives, Progress Report', 20 September 1984, RE Minutes, 26 September 1984.

13 Hoggart–Buckton, Knapp, and Lyons, 4 May 1983, BRB IR 75-2-205 Pt. 1.

14 Knapp–Hoggart, 29 March 1984, BRB IR 81-17-14/DOO (non-passenger); RSJC (Traffic) Minutes, 15 June 1983; RSNC Minutes, 27 September and 9 November 1983; NUR, Conference Decisions, 1983 and 1984; Interview with Jimmy Knapp, 31 October 2000.

15 Cf. RSJC (Traffic) Minutes, 22 September 1983; Osmotherley (DTp)–Reid, 20 January 1984, and reply, 2 February 1984, and Frank Kitching (BRB Employee Relations Manager)–Palette, Hoggart, and Holmes, 31 January 1984, Myers's Papers, Sec Box 2244; Hoggart, Memo, 20 September 1984, cit.; Holmes, Memo on 'Radio for Driver Only Operation', n.d., RE Minutes, 26 September and 24 October 1984.

16 There is an extensive literature on the strike. See, for example, Peter Wilshire, Donald Macintyre, and Michael Jones, *Strike: Thatcher, Scargill and the Miners* (1985);

Geoffrey Goodman, *The Miners' Strike* (1985); Michael Crick, *Scargill and the Miners* (1985); Ian Macgregor, *The Enemy Within: The Story of the Miners' Strike 1984–5* (1986), esp. pp. 262–5; Thatcher, *Downing Street Years*, pp. 344–77.

17 In accounts for 15 months to 31 March 1985: BRB, *R&A 1984/5*, pp. 3, 15.

18 Cf. British Rail Council Minutes, 14 December 1984, 22 and 29 January and 26 February 1985; *Modern Railways*, November 1984, p. 562.

19 Reid, Confidential 'Note of Discussion with Mr. James Knapp, General Secretary, N.U.R.', 20 August 1984, BRB Secretary's Papers, Box 2111.

20 This claim, based on the Trade Union Act 1984, was subsequently withdrawn. BR Management Briefs on 'Trade Union Membership Agreement', 11 June 1985, and 'Legal Action Against NUR/ASLEF', 7 and 14 June 1985; Palette–Myers, 1 July 1985, Myers's Papers, Sec Box 2244.

21 In the event the NUR called off the blacking. BRB Minutes, 6 June 1985; Baker–Palette, 29 July 1985, O'Brien's Papers, Sec Box 2173; legal documentation in BRB Solicitor's Papers, file LB/AS/AR.

22 Hoggart–Buckton and Knapp, 30 April (2 letters), and 24 May 1985, BRB IR 81-17-14(c).

23 *Transport Review*, 21 June 1985, p. 1.

24 Memo on 'Driver Only Operation', 13 January 1986, BRB 81-17-14(c); Memo to BRB Special Meeting, 28 August 1985, Myers's Papers, Box 2244.

25 Cit. in 'DOO Dispute diary', *Modern Railways*, October 1985, p. 494.

26 For: 4,360; against: 4,815; turnout: 84%. BR Managing Directors Advisory Committee Minutes, 28 August 1985, BRB IR 81-17-14.

27 BRB Minutes, 5 September 1985, RSJC (Traffic and Loco.) Minutes, 17–19 September 1985, BR Management Brief, 20 September 1985. On the tough stance, see Palette–Knapp, 29 August 1985, BRB IR 81-17-14(c).

28 Knapp, reported in *Modern Railways*, October 1985, p. 495.

29 Myers, reported in BRB Minutes, 3 October 1985; Holmes, Memo on 'Driver Only Operation (Non-Passenger)', n.d. [September 1986], RE Minutes, 17 September 1986.

30 Hoggart, Memo to Reid on 'Chairman's Visit to the Secretary of State 17 October 1985', 16 October 1985, BRB IR 81-17-20 Pt. 2; Railway Personnel Group Minutes, 14 October 1985; *Modern Railways*, November 1985, p. 550, June 1986, p. 293.

31 MMC, *British Railways Board: Network SouthEast*, October 1987, paras. 8.13, 8.56, 9.11.

32 180 drivers and 1,320 driver's assistants. Kitching, Memo to RE on 'RSNT Decision No: 92', 20 May 1986, Hoggart–Members of RE on 'Railway Staff National Tribunal: Traction Manning Proposals', 3 February 1986, Myers's Papers, Box 2244; Gourvish, *British Railways*, pp. 541, 553–4.

33 On public concern about this issue in the late 1980s see *The Times*, 21 October 1988.

34 Hoggart, Memo 20 September 1984, cit.; RSNT, Decision No. 92, paras. 49, 54(b) and (c).

35 A year after there had been a failure to agree at RSNC: Minutes, 21 November 1984.

36 RSNT, Decision No. 92, April 1986, paras. 158–9, 169, 172(c); Interview with McCarthy, 1998. The Tribunal also recommended a joint review of driver error, stress, and strain, building on research carried out at Nottingham University. See Tom Cox

and Roger Haslam (University of Nottingham), Reports on 'Occupational Stress in Train Drivers', November 1984 and November 1985, BRB.

37 RSNC Minutes, 12 September and 25 November 1986; Watkinson–Myers, Palette, and Holmes, 19 May 1986, Watkinson–Knapp, Neil Milligan (ASLEF), and Charles Lyons (TSSA), 14 October 1986, Myers's Papers, Box 2244.

38 MMC, *Network SouthEast*, 1987, para. 8.55, Appendix 8.2.

39 BR Management Brief on 'The Traincrew Concept', 18 December 1986 and cf. MMC, *Network SouthEast*, 1987, paras. 9. 18–19, MMC, *British Railways Board: Provincial*, February 1989, paras. 6.10–13, 6.20.

40 BR Management Briefs on 'The Traincrew Proposals', 27 October 1987, and 'Final Deal Sought on Traincrew', 6 June 1988; Trevor Toolan (MD, Personnel), Memo on 'Traincrew Proposals', February 1988, BRB Minutes, 11 February 1988; RSNC Minutes, 16 August 1988; Interview with Paul Watkinson, 14 July 1999. Milligan succeeded Buckton in September 1987. He was welcomed by British Rail as a more moderate force: cf. Watkinson–Reid et al., 9 March 1987, BR IR 20-1-3. Milligan himself remarked: 'No, I am not, nor have I been, a part of the "loony left" ': Milligan–Watkinson, 11 March 1987, ibid.

41 Cf. for example Holmes, Memo on 'Variable Day Rostering', 13 March 1985, BRB IR 81-17-14/3(b) Pt. 5; John Holroyd (Personnel Planning and Systems Manager, BRB), Memo on 'Variable Day Rostering (VDR)', March 1986, Holroyd's Papers, BRB.

42 RSJC (Loco.) Minutes, 23 September 1985, and see Pendleton's research on flexible rostering, based on interviews with depot staff at Crewe, Euston, Nottingham, Swindon, Toton, etc. I am grateful to Dr Pendleton for access to this material.

43 Holmes, Memo, 13 March 1985, cit. This calculation assumed a saving of 4% or 1,392 posts at £7,000 p.a. in 1984 prices = £9.74 m., less £5.25 m. in additional costs (= 0.58 p a turn plus balancing payments of £0.5 m.). See also 'The great rail "bonus" farce', *Daily Express*, 14 March 1985, p. 1, which claimed overtime had risen substantially; and MMC, *Network SouthEast*, para. 9.22. BR's riposte to the *Daily Express* produced higher financial savings, viz. £14.1 m. gross, £8.0 m. net of special payments and overtime: Hoggart–Editor, *Daily Express*, 15 March 1985, BRB IR 81-17-14/3(b) Pt. 5.

44 Andrew Pendleton, 'The Barriers to Flexibility: Flexible Rostering on the Railways', *Work Employment & Society*, 5 (2) (June 1991), 241–57, and Pendleton, research notes. One example of the difficulties was the dispute at King's Cross depot over alterations to rosters in 1984: Kitching–Buckton, 6 March 1984, BRB IR 81-17-14/3 Pt. 4.

45 That is, Doncaster: 60.41%, May 1983, 61.74%, Sept. 1983; King's Cross, 64.47%, 64.75%: Appendix B of Memo to Railway Personnel Group on 'Flexible Rostering of Traincrew', 16 April 1984, BRB IR 8-17-14/3(b) Pt. 5. The MMC found driving time was 45% in 1980 and 47.5% in May 1986: MMC, *Network SouthEast*, 1987, para. 9.25.

46 Holmes, Memo, September 1986, cit.; Audit Manager (ER), Report, 16 October 1986.

47 BRB, *R&A 1979–89/90*. The calculation discounts an adjustment in 1989/90 which lowered the indicator by *c*.4%. If we take account of the change, the improvement would be 57% and 41% respectively.

48 The data are also affected by recalculations.

49 The strikes of 1982 and 1984/5 made interpretation of the raw data problematic.

50 BRB, *R&A 1979*, *1989/90*:

	Train operating expenditure	Train crew costs	Train crew/ operating	RPI (1985 = 100)
1979	£351.7 m.	£225.3 m.	64%	59.9
1989/90	£553.0 m.	£379.5 m.	69%	133.3

51 NUR and ASLEF, submission to RSNC, 22 February 1990: railman £33.35 (1975), £105.30 (1989); LA manual workers £31.90, £115.48; agricultural workers £30.50, £112.02, electricity supply workers £35.64, £152.56. Retail prices (all items) increased by 337% over the period: Office for Nat. Stats, *Economic Trends Annual Supplement 1997*, p. 161.

52 Toolan, Confidential Memo on '1989/90 Pay', February 1989, BRB Minutes, 9 February 1989.

53 E.g. Ferner, *Government*, *Managers*, p. 23.

54 Cf. Gourvish, *British Railways*, pp. 219–22, 242, 533–8, 547–8.

55 Andrew Turnbull (Private Secretary, PM Office)–Henry Derwent (DTp), 16 April 1984, reproduced in *Daily Mirror*, 6 June 1984, p. 1. The newspaper observed that Reid had been advised by Thatcher and Ridley on the tactics to be used in handling the pay claim, pp. 1, 4–5. The story was confirmed by Downing St. See *The Times*, 7 June 1984, pp. 1–2, which referred to the leaked correspondence, including Osmotherley–Ridley, 2 April 1984, John Gummer (Minister for Employment)–Ridley, and Ridley–Nigel Lawson (Chancellor of Exchequer), 13 April 1984. The attempt by John Prescott, Labour's transport spokesman, to force an emergency debate on the issue was unsuccessful, ibid., p. 4. See also Ferner, *Government*, *Managers*, pp. 118–19.

56 BRB Chairman's Group Minutes, 15 March 1984: 'Government's support for Board's position noted, so long as issues do not lead to association with NUM dispute'. BRB Minutes, 7 June 1984, formally recorded a denial of influence: 'at all times, contact with Government had been solely on the basis of the Chairman keeping the Secretary of State informed of developments'.

57 Viz. LDC (local), Sectional Council (regional), RSJC, RSNC, and RSNT. See MMC, *British Railways Board: London & South East services*, October 1980, paras. 6.1–28.

58 Toolan, Memo to BRB on 'Machinery of Negotiation', n.d. [September 1987], BRB 80-12-1; MMC, *Network SouthEast*, 1987, para. 8.53. Cf. Swift (ASLEF driver)–Parker, 10 August 1981, X81–51: 'here we have one of the most glaring examples of wasteful expenditure in the public sector that there ever was'.

59 MMC, *London & South East*, 1980, para. 6.54 ('The complex framework of negotiating and consultative procedures in BRB . . . is in need of simplification'); Howell–Parker, 21 December 1981, BRB 80-12-1 ('The questions are I think whether the present right of any of the parties to take issues to the Railway Staff National Tribunal ought to continue, and if not what steps you would think it right to take to secure changes'); Ridley–Parker, 24 October 1983, reproduced in BRB, *R&A 1983*, p. 4 ('The Government wants you to secure improvements to the railways' present industrial relations machinery, which has hampered good communications and slowed down the necessary pace of change').

60 Rose, Memo to Board Exec. on 'Machinery of Negotiation and Consultation', 9 February 1983, Board Exec. Minutes, 10 February 1983; Parker, reported in BR Press Release, 9 February 1983. Union objections were voiced at BR Council, Minutes, 17 February 1983.

61 Cf. Rose, Memo, cit.; Palette, Memo on 'Machinery of Negotiation', 24 June 1983, BRB Minutes, 7 July 1983, Board Exec. Minutes, 22 December 1983.

62 MMC, *Network SouthEast*, 1987, para. 8.49.

63 Hoggart–Knapp, Buckton, and Lyons, 13 December 1983, Palette–McCarthy, 27 September 1984, McCarthy–Palette, 15 November 1984, Palette–Ian Buchanan, 18 December 1984, Palette–Reid, 9 January 1985, BRB IR 80-06-03 Pt. 4; Palette, Memo to BRB Chairman's Group on 'Industrial Relations Report', February 1985; BRB/unions Special Joint Committee (SJC) Minutes, 5 February 1985.

64 SJC Minutes, 14 April 1986; Palette, Memo on 'RSNT', 30 April 1986, Chairman's Group Minutes, 8 May 1986.

65 Palette–Sir Pat Lowry (Chairman, ACAS), 31 July 1986, Toolan–Buchanan, 15 April 1987 and reply, 17 April 1987, BRB IR 80-06-03 Pt. 4; SJC Minutes, 21 November 1986; Toolan, Memo n.d., BRB Minutes, 5 March 1987.

66 SJC Minutes, 13 January and 15 December 1981, 12 December 1983, 10 December 1984; Memo on meeting between representatives of BRB, NUR, and ASLEF, at Worthing, 5 September 1984, BRB; Chris E. W. Green, Memo to BRB RE on 'Worthing Agreement', 16 September 1985, RE Minutes, 28 November 1984, 24 July and 18 September 1985.

67 Pendleton, 'Railways', 1993, p. 57.

68 Toolan, Employment Contract, 5 November 1986, BRB Secretary's Papers; BRB Press Release, 27 November 1986; Interviews with Toolan and Watkinson, 1999.

69 The process had been introduced for senior managers in 1987: 'On the Right Track to High Performance', *PM Plus*, August 1990, pp. 14–15, and IDS Top Pay Unit, July 1990, p. 15, in BRB IR 82-11-61/3; BRB Minutes, 8 September 1988; BRB Employee Relations Circular Letter, 31 August 1988, BRB IR 82-11-61 (PL); Interview with Watkinson, 1999; and note Ferner, *Government, Managers*, pp. 106–7. Letters from aggrieved managers underlined the dissatisfaction which the move caused, leading the unions to make an unsuccessful appeal to the chairman of the RSNT, Buchanan. Cf. letters to Watkinson from H. Mitchell, n.d. (*c*.13 June 1988), Dolores M. Peat, 12 June, R. Neil Johnson, 14 June, David N. C. Baily, 15 June, and P. J. Lawrence, 17 June 1988, and Buchanan, Decision, November 1988, BRB IR papers.

70 Toolan, Memo, n.d. [September 1987], and Memo on 'Development of Area Manager Role—Machinery of Negotiation', 30 October 1987, BRB Minutes, 1 October and 5 November 1987; MMC, paras. 8.52–60.

71 SJC Minutes, 3 February 1988; BRB Minutes, 11 February 1988; Pendleton, 'Management Strategy and Labour Relations on British Rail', University of Bath Ph.D. thesis, 1986, p. 151, cit. in Ferner, *Government, Managers*, p. 107; Interviews with Watkinson, 1999, Knapp, 2000.

72 Known as ICOBS. Toolan, Memo on 'Restructuring of Bargaining Arrangements', n.d. [October 1988], BRB Minutes, 8 and 13 October 1988.

73 BRB Minutes, 4 May 1989; Knapp–Toolan, 3 July 1989, BRB 82-2-55.

74 Toolan, Memo, February 1989, cit.

75 BRB Minutes, 9 February, 9 March, and 6 April 1989; Susan Hoyle (BRB Public Affairs), Confidential Report to Reid on 'To Investigate Media and Other Public Criticism of BR's Handling of the NUR/ASLEF Dispute and to Assess the Performance of BR's PA Function during the Strike Period', 23 August 1989, pp. 5–6, BRB Secretary's Papers. Note that only the TSSA had formally rejected the 7% offer before the imposition. The NUR rejected it on 10 May, ASLEF on 9 June.

76 Cf. BRB Minutes, 5 May and 7 July 1988; RSJC (Traffic) Minutes, 3 May 1988.

77 BRB Minutes, 6, 7, and 18 July 1989; RSNT Decision No. 96, 7 July 1989; Hoyle, Report, p. 7; A. J. Deboo (BRB Personnel Manager (Corporate & General)), Confidential Report on 'The 1989 Pay Negotiations and Dispute: An Assessment of the Performance of the Corporate Personnel Team', 6 October 1989, pp. 15–17, BRB Secretary's Papers.

78 Hoyle, Report, pp. 10, 21–2; Deboo, Report, pp. 5–7.

79 Cf. *Independent*, 13 July, *The Times*, 14 July 1989, cit. in Hoyle Report, pp. 1, 24, and cf. Deboo, Report, pp. 9–11; Interview with Watkinson, 1999. Welsby was absent from the Board meetings of 8 June to 3 August 1989. Particular criticism was directed at the handling of events after the Court defeat (q.v.), 21–4 June, and at the White House Hotel and ACAS meetings after the RSNT Decision, 10–12 July.

80 Knapp–Toolan, 3 July 1989, BRB IR 82-2-55. Toolan's judgement seems to have been faulty here. Cf. his argument in October 1987, that 'the time will never be better to streamline the IR system', Memo, Oct 1987, cit. See also Deboo, Report, pp. 5, 7, and Interviews with Toolan and Watkinson, 1999.

81 On LRT see *London Underground v. NUR*, Judgment, 4 May 1989, BRB Solicitor's Papers, LB/122/12; *The Times*, 5 May 1989; *Independent*, 11 May 1989.

82 Interviews with Watkinson, 1999, Lawrie Harries (NUR), 5 August 1998, Knapp, 2000. The action was taken to halt the strike on the grounds that some union members had not been balloted. The opinion of BR's counsel, Christopher Carr, QC, certainly contrasted with Justice Vinelott in the High Court, who offered the opinion that the evidence did not come 'anywhere near' justifying an injunction. See *The Times*, 19 June 1989, p. 2; 20 June, p. 1; 27 June, p. 1.

83 Deboo, Report, pp. 14–15; Hoyle, Report, p. 14.

84 BRB, *R&A 1988/9*.

85 The inquests were undertaken by Susan Hoyle (BRB Public Affairs) and A. J. Deboo (BRB Personnel Manager (Corporate & General)). See Hoyle, Report, 23 August 1989, cit. and addendum, 19 September 1989; Deboo, Report, 6 October 1989, cit.; BRB Minutes, 12 October 1989.

86 Support for Toolan fell away over the course of the summer. Thus, while he received the Board's full backing over a libel in the *Today* newspaper in July his request for a vote of confidence in October was rejected. BRB Minutes, 7 July 1989; Reid–Toolan, 17 July 1989, Reid, File Note, 22 October 1989; Note for File, 23 October 1989; Welsby, Note for File, 31 October 1989, BRB Secretary's Papers. His departure had already been leaked to the press: cf. *Guardian*, 19 October 1989.

87 Toolan's post was abolished and the function split between Watkinson as Director, Employee Relations, and Hugh Jenkins as Director, Human Resource Development. BRB Minutes, 5 July 1990.

88 BRB Pre-Board Dinner, 5 July, Minutes, 6 and 7 July 1989; Hoyle, Report (addendum, after interview with Fowler), pp. 31–2. Toolan believed that Knapp would have

accepted 7.5% if offered in May 1989; the attempt to extract a differential in favour of the TSSA and to offer 8.8% with strings was an 'untenable brief'. Cf. Deboo, *Report*, pp. 12, 15; Interview with Toolan, 1999. If Deboo is to be believed, executive members of the Board were in some disarray in July 1989: *Report*, p. 9.

89 Interview with David Kirby, 13 January 1999.

90 See 'Memo of Discussion held at Marsham Street on Wednesday 19 April 1989 with the Secretary of State', n.d., BRB Secretary's Papers. Reid also met the SoS on 11 July 1989.

91 BRB Minutes, 18 July, 3 August, 12 October, and 22 November 1989.

92 Toolan's resignation should not obscure the more positive aspects of his work in employee relations, e.g. in equal opportunities and combating racism. The participation of women was limited at all levels: 2% of staff in Jan. 1980, 3% in Feb. 1990. The number of senior managers increased from two to 36 (4%). They were located at HQ in the personnel, public affairs, finance & planning, and legal departments. Racism acted as a restraint on recruitment in some areas of the business. However, the percentage of non-white staff in British Rail was 6.4% in July 1990, which compared favourably with the 4% in GB employment. See BRB Minutes, 3 December 1987, 5 May and 1 December 1988, Minutes, 8 March 1990; BRB, 'Manpower Monthly', October 1990; equal opportunities statements in BR Management Brief, 10 November 1987, 11 and 26 July 1988.

93 List of 47 closures, 1980–9 in David St. John Thomas and Pat Whitehouse, *BR in the Eighties* (Newton Abbot, 1990), p. 138.

94 List of 159 stations, 1980–9 in Thomas and Whitehouse, *BR*, pp. 137–8. There were some transfers to local authority metro systems, notably the Tyne & Wear Metro (1980–3), and, later, the Manchester Metrolink tram network (1992).

95 Transport Act 1962 (Amendment) Act 1981, 2 July 1981, c. 32 ; BRB and Association of County Councils, *Review of Rural Railways* (1984), pp. 5–7; W. N. Stirling, 'Section 20: milestone or millstone?', *Modern Railways*, April 1983, pp. 185–8. Anthony Speller was Conservative MP for North Devon, 1979–92.

96 List of 18 re-openings in David Henshaw, *The Great Railway Conspiracy* (Hawes, 1991), pp. 240–1; *Modern Railways*, April 1986, p. 189; June 1986, pp. 324–5; June 1989, pp. 296–8; Thomas and Whitehouse, *BR*, p. 138. Other lines included Glasgow Low Level (1979), Burnley–Todmorden (1984), Trowbridge–Chippenham (1985), Kensington–Willesden and Addlestone Jnc.–Byfleet Jnc. (1986), Corby–Kettering (1987), and Oxford–Bicester (1988).

97 MMC, *Provincial*, p. 123. 1988/9 figure = £142,000. Funding of Bathgate by SDA, Lothian Regional Council, West Lothian District Council, Livingston District Council, and European Regional Dev. Fund. Small surpluses were earned by Morecambe–Heysham, Coventry–Nuneaton, and Cardiff.

98 Myers, Memo, 22 April 1983, Board Exec. Minutes, 28 April 1983.

99 Ron R. Cotton (BRB Project Manager, Settle & Carlisle)–Alec McTavish (Planning & Investment Manager, Provincial), 24 November 1986, enclosing 'Settle–Carlisle Closure Proposal: Key Points made by Objectors', BRB Prov 462-71 Pt. 5, and cf. Henshaw, *Railway Conspiracy*, p. 208 and Stan Abbott and Alan Whitehouse, *The Line that Refused to Die: The Story of the Successful Campaign to Save the Settle and Carlisle Railway* (Hawes, rev. edn., 1994), pp. 30, 57–8, 62–3. The closure proposal, which due to BR errors had to be issued three times in the period December

1983–August 1984, produced over 22,000 written objections: Joint Report of NW and NE England TUCCs, 17 December 1986, paras. 5.18–20, in BRB Prov 462-71 Pt. 6; Abbott and Whitehouse, *Line that Refused*, pp. 55, 71.

100 Reid–Michael Jopling, 10 November 1988, Welsby's Papers, Sec Box 2308.

101 BRB Minutes, 6 June and 4 July 1985. The challenge was unsuccessful: see Jim O'Brien, Memo to Chairman's Group, 22 April 1986, O'Brien's Papers, Sec Box 2180. The proposal to close Marylebone came in 1984 and was linked to the response to road-rail conversion (see below). It is difficult to understand in view of the revival in fortunes of the lines from Marylebone under the 'Chiltern Line' marketing initiative. See BRB Press Release, 15 March 1984, BRB Minutes, 4 April and 2 May 1985. The concern of London Transport about the capacity of the Metropolitan line to cope with the closure led to the abandonment of the idea: BRB Minutes, 3 April and 1 May 1986. *Modern Railways*, July 1986, p. 369.

102 NW and NE TUCCs, Report, cit. It was not a requirement for BR to release financial information, since TUCC hearings were concerned only with 'hardship'.

103 The stations were: Armathwaite, Lazonby, Langwathby, Kirkby Stephen, Garsdale, Dent, Ribblehead, and Horton-in-Ribblesdale. Data: pass. journeys 93,000 (1983), 280,000 (1986/7); revenue £474,000 (1983), £938,000 (1986/7), from Edmonds–Reid et al., 23 December 1986, enclosing 'The Financial Case for the Closure of the Settle–Carlisle Line', n.d. (December 1986), BRB Prov 462-71 Pt. 5. On Ron Cotton's work see Abbot and Whitehouse, *Line that Refused*, pp. 68–70, 93ff.

104 Cotton–McTavish, 24 November 1986, Mitchell–Councillor W. Cameron, 22 January 1987, BRB Prov 462-71 Pt. 5; Mitchell, *Parl. Deb. (Commons)*, 6th ser. (Session 1986–7), vol. 110, 11 February 1987, col. 438; Chairman's Group Minutes, 23 February 1989; BRB Minutes, 5 May 1988; David Mitchell–Reid, 16 May 1988, BRB Prov 462-71 Pt. 11; 'Notes of meeting between Department of Transport and British Railways Board on 10 September [1988] at Euston House', BRB Prov 461-5-1 Pt. 2.

105 The calculation included £0.79 m. for RETB/singling in the event of retention: 'The Financial Case', December 1986, cit. Ribblehead estimates: £2.7 m. based on the estimate of independent consultants, PEIDA, engaged by the local authorities; £4.3 m. from BRB. It appears that Ribblehead's problems arose from leaks in the decking rather than from more serious structural weaknesses. Abbot and Whitehouse, *Line that Refused*, pp. 10, 56, 73–4, 80.

106 Mitchell–Reid, 16 May 1988, cit. The idea of privatising the line seems to have originated in BR thinking: cf. Trewin, Note on 'Visit to Settle & Carlisle Line 25/26 June, 1985', n.d., BRB Prov 462-71 Pt. 4.

107 Director, Provincial, 'Financial case for the closure of the Settle–Carlisle railway line (updated)', October 1988, BRB Prov 462-71 App. I.

108 BRB Minutes, 1 December 1988, 12 January 1989. The serious bidders were: Cumbrian Railways (Michael Heathcote and Kenneth Ryder) and Tony Thomas. One of the bids came from a 15-year-old boy, who offered £3 m. and asked for a seat on the Board: Welsby, Memo to Chairman's Group, 24 November 1988, Welsby's Papers, Sec Box 2308.

109 Simon Osborne (BRB Solicitor)–Newey, 15 April 1988, Kirby's Papers, Sec Box 2148; Welsby–Osborne, 4 January 1989, Welsby's Papers, Box 2308; BRB Minutes, 12 January and 9 February 1989; Chairman's Group Minutes, 16 and 23 February 1989.

110 NW and NE England TUCCs, Second Joint Report, December 1988, BRB Prov 462-71 Pt. 13; J. D. Carr (for Joint Councils [Cumbria C.C., Lancs C.C., West Yorks PTA and PTE] Steering Group)–S. B. Newey (Director, Provincial), 14 December 1988, enclosing JCSG, 'Settle–Carlisle Railway The Case for Retention', 10 December 1988, BRB Provincial file on '1989/90 Study'; BRB Minutes, 6 April 1989; Channon–Reid, 10 April 1989, BRB Provincial Files: Settle & Carlisle, 462-71 Pt. 4.

111 Newey in particular was criticised and in the event replaced as Director, Provincial by Gordon Pettitt in April 1990. Embarrassing leaks about the Settle–Carlisle line, concern about equivocal presentations to the DTp, criticisms of proposals for the reorganisation of the Provincial sector, and the embarrassment of late delivery of the Class 158s and operational problems with the Class 155s contributed to his resignation. See Derek Fowler–Reid, 1 December 1987, BRB Prov 462-71 Pt. 11; Welsby–Newey, 25 September 1989, Kirby's Papers, Box 2148; Chairman's Group Minutes, 30 March and 27 April 1989; *Modern Railways*, February and July 1989, pp. 63, 341–2.

112 Welsby, 'Assessment of the Feasibility of Bus Substitution on Existing British Rail Services', 24 September 1982, BRB 33-40-5.

113 Welsby–Fowler et al., 28 October 1983, enclosing report on 'Bus Substitution', n.d., BRB 33-40-5.

114 Ridley–Reid, 24 October 1983, BRB 30-1-5 cit.; Reid–Ridley, 17 January 1984, BRB 33-40-5.

115 O'Brien–David Mitchell (Under-Sec. of State, DTp), 6 December 1985, enclosing Edmonds (Director, Provincial), Memo on 'Bus Substitution', 4 December 1985, BRB Prov 461-5-1 Pt. 1.

116 Of course, the main purpose of the Act was to deregulate local bus services. BRB/ACC, *Rural Railways*, pp. 3, 30–40; Transport Act 1985, 30 October 1985, c. 67.

117 'The new powers which Parliament has provided for you to subsidise guaranteed substitute bus services … give the opportunity to review those cases where attractive bus services could meet the needs of travellers … You will wish to conduct such reviews before proposing re-investment in rolling stock for lines of this character': Moore–Reid, 21 October 1986, reproduced in BRB, *R&A 1986/7*, p. 4.

118 See C. P. Poole (DTp), Note on 'Provincial Sector/DTp Progress Meeting Euston House—26 February 1987', 12 March 1987, BRB Prov 461-5-1 Pt. 2.

119 Edmonds, Memo on 'Bus Substitution and its Impact on the next DMU Submission', 27 April 1987, Chairman's Group Minutes, 30 April 1987; BRB Minutes, 5 November 1987; MMC, *Provincial*, 1989, paras. 10.54–63, 10.91. The over-estimation of the savings potential was an embarrassment for John Palmer (Dep-Secretary, DTp): Robert A. Cochrane (Planning & Investment Manager, Provincial)–Edmonds, 18 September 1987, BRB Prov 461-5-1 Pt. 2.

120 Quoted in Sidney Newey (Director, Provincial)–Reid, 16 September 1988, BRB Prov 461-5-1 Pt. 3.

121 Newey–J. R. Coates (DTp), 14 September 1989, enclosing Memo on 'Bus Substitution', 14 September 1989, BRB Prov 461-5-1 Pt. 3; Newey–Colin Driver (Director, Freight), 25 September 1989, 461-5-3 Pt. 5.

122 Chairman's Group Minutes, 28 September 1989; Newey–J. R. Coates (DTp), 12 October 1989, BRB Prov. 461-5-1 Pt. 3.

123 *Railway Gazette*, 29 April 1955, pp. 472–3; 28 October 1960, pp. 500–1.

124 Angus Dalgliesh, *The Truth about Transport* (CPS, March 1982); Bradshaw–Parker, 28 April 1983, Andrew Wybrow (DTp)–Pattison, 22 June 1982, BRB 283-3-11. Hall, Professor of Geography at Reading University, 1968–89, had examined the idea for a previous government: see Peter Hall and Edward Smith, 'Better use of Railways', University of Reading Discussion Paper, November 1975.

125 Lance Ibbotson, 'Reconstruction of British Railways', July 1981, published in November 1982, BRB 283-3-11 (folder); Fred Margetts–Parker, 4 December 1982, BRB 240-1-72 Pt. 3.

126 BRB, *Why our trains should stay on the rails* (October 1982).

127 E.g. Elmers End–Sanderstead, Wimbledon–Sutton, Wandsworth–Chiswick, Marylebone–High Wycombe. See Bradshaw (General Manager, Western Region)–Parker, 28 April 1983, BRB 283-3-11. Bradshaw had met Sherman on a train to Darlington.

128 Sherman (knighted in 1983) was a visiting fellow, LSE, 1983–5; Foster (knighted in 1986) was Professor of Urban Studies, LSE, 1976–8 and a visiting professor, 1978–86. Walters was also involved in the project: see Burt–Lazarus, 13 July 1983, BRB 283-3-11.

129 Posner, Sherman, and Foster (Steering Committee), *A Report on the Potential for the Conversion of Some Railway Routes in London into Roads* (1984), BRB 283-3-11 (folder); BRB Minutes, 1 March 1984.

130 Interview with Michael V. Casey, 29 June 1989.

131 Posner, Memo to BRB on 'Manufacturing & Maintenance Policy Review', 17 April 1980; Burt–Chairman and Secretary, SSG, 20 December 1979, BRB 81-1-1 Pt. 3.

132 Urquhart, 'British Rail Engineering Ltd: A Review', 28 January 1982, Campbell's Papers, TRO-21-1.

133 Parker–Howell, 15 April 1983, Myers's Papers, Sec Box 2238.

134 Interview with Serpell, 1991.

135 Ian D. Gardiner (Dir of Engineering)–Burt, 31 January 1983, BRB 240-1-72 Pt. 5; Gardiner, Memo, to Board Exec. on 'Engineering Consultants Reports', 25 April 1983; Myers, Memos, 29 April and n.d. [July] 1983, BRB Minutes, 5 May and 7 July 1983.

136 Ridley–Reid, 24 October 1983, BRB 30-1-5, reproduced in BRB, *R&A 1983*, p. 4.

137 See BRB Minutes, 4 August 1983.

138 Price Waterhouse, Report on 'BR/BREL Relationships and the Corporate Role of BREL', 10 November 1983 (draft in Welsby's Papers, Sec Box 2334); Urquhart and Myers, Memo to Board Exec. on 'The Role of British Rail Engineering Ltd', 18 November 1983, in Reid, Confidential Memo on 'Manufacturing and Maintenance—Policy Aims', 24 November 1983, BRB Minutes, 1 December 1983. The options were: Serpell I (separate BREL under direct government control); Serpell II (privatise); Serpell III (reabsorb into BRB); BREL I—current definition; BREL II (new build and refurbishing only); BREL III (new build, refurbishment, and heavy repairs only).

139 Successively Chairman BREL, Director of Engineering, and MD, BREL.

140 Welsby, Draft Report on 'Manufacturing and Maintenance Policy', 15 June 1984, Welsby Papers, Sec Box 2336; Welsby, Strictly Confidential Memo to BRB on 'Manufacturing and Maintenance Policy and Options for BREL', 2 July 1984, BRB Minutes, 5 July 1984; *Modern Railways*, April 1984, p. 169; Edgar J. Larkin and John G. Larkin, *The Railway Workshops of Britain, 1823–1986* (1988), pp. 121–5. The option of selling a nucleus was preferred to the alternative—the sale of individual works.

141 Fowler, Memo on 'Financial Separation of BR & BREL', 23 May 1985, BRB Minutes, 6 June 1985; BRB, *R&A 1985/6*, p. 43.

142 Gourvish, 'British Rail's "Business-Led" Organization', 137.

143 The concept involved fitting components as close to the rolling stock's home base as possible, and moving to 'component life extraction', i.e. replacing specific parts when life expired rather than at routine service intervals. See H. J. Gorham (Gorham & Associates) and C. P. Boocock (Assistant Regional M&EE (North), LMR), Report on 'Cost Effective Maintenance Study: Initial Report', 2 April 1985, BRB DMEE MM/ 30-3, and note subsequent reports in June and August 1985 and February 1986, Welsby's Papers, Sec Box 2330; BRB Minutes, 2 April and 4 July 1985; 3 April 1986; MMC, *Network SouthEast*, 1987, para. 10.11; Interview with Welsby, 1998.

144 Welsby, Memo on 'Manufacturing & Maintenance Policy—Progress Report', 27 March 1986, BRB Minutes, 3 April 1986; BRB, *R&A 1986/7*, p. 11; *Modern Railways*, May 1987, p. 233. Plymouth (Laira) provided the pilot scheme for CEM, by handling component exchange for the Class 50 locomotives. In fact, a component-exchange system had been introduced in the 1960s for diesel hydraulic locomotives by Western Region at its Swindon Works: Michael Anson, 'Management and Labour Relations at Swindon Railway Locomotive Works, 1947–67', Ph.D. thesis, University of Exeter, 1998, p. 125; Interview with Casey, 1989. A similar system was used at Chart Leacon depot, Ashford, in the early 1980s: *Modern Railways*, August 1982, pp. 365–8.

145 Welsby, Report, 1984, cit.; and Memo to BRB on 'Manufacturing & Maintenance Policy—Progress Report', 3 January 1986; BRB Production Management Group Minutes, 14 April 1987.

146 The investment element was £18 m. Robert A. Cochrane (Investment Adviser), Memo, 30 May 1986, Investment Committee Minutes, 2 June 1986.

147 In particular, he felt that the pre-privatisation 'nucleus' should contain a larger repair element. Cf. Urquhart and Norman, Private Memo to Reid et al. on 'The Future of BREL', 20 June 1984, Posner Papers, Sec Box 2268; and BRB Minutes, 5 July 1984.

148 BRB Minutes, 4 April and 2 May 1985; BREL Board Minutes, 18 April 1985. Norman became Chairman and MD of BREL from 1 May 1985. He joined BR as MD BREL from John Brown of Coventry in November 1981. BRB Press Release, 25 November 1981.

149 Welsby, Confid. Memo on 'Manufacturing and Maintenance Policy and Options for BREL', 26 April 1985, BRB Minutes, 4 April, 2 May, and 6 June 1985.

150 BRB Minutes, 4 July 1985; Gourvish, 'British Rail's "Business-Led" Organization', 137–8. The disposal companies were Doncaster Wagon Works Ltd, Horwich Foundry Ltd and BREL (1988) Ltd.

151 BRB, Manpower Statistics, 1980–4; BRB IR cassettes, MISP level 8, March 1990.

152 The trade unions promised to fight the Board's plans for workshop closures, competitive tendering, and M&M: cf. BR Council Minutes, 17 February 1983, 14 December 1984, and 21 January 1986. However, ballots for industrial action in 1986 did not receive members' support. An indication of grass-roots feeling was provided by the insensitive announcement of the closure of Swindon works at the time of the GWR 150th anniversary celebrations. A planned exhibition at the works had to be cancelled after the workforce withdrew its co-operation: *Modern Railways*, August 1985, p. 391; September 1986, p. 457.

153 A total of £288.1 m. was set aside for restructuring, 1984–7. Of this, £82.1 m. was paid back in 1988/9. In addition, there were losses on sale of £7.2 m. for Doncaster Wagon Works, £6.2 m. for Horwich Foundry, and £75.2 m. for BREL (1988): BRB, *R&A 1984/5–88/9*.

154 David Blake (Dir, M&EE), Memo, 8 January 1990, BRB Minutes, 11 January 1990.

155 MMC, *Network SouthEast*, 1987, para. 7.59.

156 MMC, *Provincial*, 1989, paras. 7.14–15, Table 7.3.

	1981	1987/8
Asbestos removal	£7.7 m.	—
Old vehicles—overhaul	£38.2 m.	£5.2 m.
—maintenance	£56.3 m.	£22.3 m.
New vehicles—overhaul	—	£0.1 m.
—maintenance	—	£16.1 m.
Total	£102.2 m.	£43.7 m.

157 MMC, *Network SouthEast*, paras. 10.15–22, 10.75–6, *Provincial*, paras. 7.25–7, 7.63–4.

158 J. P. (Phil) Crosby (Maintenance and Quality Assurance Engineer, BRB), Memo on 'New Maintenance Policy. Report on Performance during first year of operation, 1 April 1987 to 31 March 1988', 9 May 1988, BRB DMEE 170-144-1054 Pt. 2; Interview with Casey, 1989.

159 For example, Metro-Cammell's tender for Mark IV coaches was £7 m. lower than the BREL tender of £83.8 m. in 1986: Fowler, Memo 3 November 1986, BRB Minutes, 6 November 1986.

160 Peter S. Higham (Director of Supply, BRB)–Dr K. Lloyd (Sales & Marketing Director, Leyland Bus Ltd), 11 June 1986, Welsby's Papers, Sec Box 2313; Chris Green (Director, Network SouthEast)–Myers, Kirby, and Welsby, 24 August 1987, Welsby's Papers, Sec Box 2311; Chairman's Group Minutes, 8 December 1988.

161 Mitchell–Reid, 7 November 1983 and 7 February 1985, BRB 171-6-1 Pt. 2.

162 Myers–Fowler and Welsby, 4 October 1985, Welsby's Papers, Sec Box 2311.

163 G. D. Miles (DTp), 'Note of a Meeting with Representatives of Brush and GEC to discuss BR's procurement of the Class 91. 7 October 1985', 8 October 1985, Welsby's Papers, Box 2311; BRB Minutes, 13 February and 7 August 1986. On the initial problems with the Class 91 see Welsby, Production Reports, BRB Minutes, 6 September and 6 October 1990.

164 Channon–Reid, 17 November 1987, Welsby's Papers, Box 2311.

165 BRB, *R&A 1985–7*.

166 Interview with James Cornell, 22 September 1989.

167 Myers, Memo 29 April 1983, cit.

168 BRB Civil Engineering [CE] Committee Minutes, 3 June and 29 September 1989; MMC, *Provincial*, 1989, para. 7.38; Interview with Cornell, 1989.

169 *Railway Finances*, supplementary volume, pp. 28–9.

170 BRB Business Engineering Group [BEG] Minutes, 19 September 1983, 17 September 1984, 10 June and 11 November 1985; Prideaux, Memo on 'Engineering Possessions—Radical Alternatives', June 1986, BEG Minutes, 9 June 1986; Production

Management Group Minutes, 13 January 1987; BRB, *R&A 1985/6*, p. 10. The Settle and Carlisle line was closed for two weeks in October 1989: *Modern Railways*, December 1989, p. 659.

171 CE Committee Minutes, 29 September 1987; MMC, *Provincial*, 1989, paras. 7.39–40.

172 Dr Robert Sparrow (Director of Research, BRB)–Currie, 13 February 1986, BRB CE 195-40-51; BRB CE Committee Minutes, 27 September 1988; BRB, *R&A 1986/7*, p. 15; Interview with Dr Robert Sparrow, 9 May 1989, and Alastair Gilchrist, 6 September 1999; Mark Edworthy, 'Television Measurement for Railway Structure Gauging', *SPIE (Proceedings of the International Society for Optical Engineering)*, 654 (1986), 8ff. See also documents in BRB CE 195-2-90 Pt. 2.

173 Alastair Gilchrist (Group Manager, Dynamics, R&D Derby)–H. H. Jenkins (Permanent Way Engineer, BRB), 24 June 1976, BRB CE 185-217-601 Pt. 1; *Modern Railways*, April 1988, pp. 177–8, 184. *Railway Gazette International*, February 1988, p. 93; David Rayner (JMD (Railways)), *Railway Gazette International*, November 1989, pp. 747–8.

174 Papers in BRB CE 195-2-59; BRB Press Release, 29 March 1983; Investment Committee Minutes, 3 October 1983; Interview with Sparrow, 1989; Roger Butcher, *On-Track Plant on British Railways* (4th edn., 1991), p. 17, (5th edn., 1994), p. 39.

175 The first post-prototype Stoneblower was not delivered until 1995, following a contract with the American firm, Pandrol Jackson: Butcher, *On-Track Plant*, p. 39.

176 Currie and Prideaux, Memo, 30 September 1987, Investment Committee Minutes, 5 October 1987; *Modern Railways*, April 1984, p. 184. The trials were conducted by Bob Clarke, Leeds Area Assistant Engineer, Eastern Region.

177 Interviews with Sparrow, 1989, Ken Burrage, 2 November 2000. There were 24 installations by December 1990: *Modern Railways*, March 1991, p. 153.

178 BRB Research & Technical Committee Minutes, 4 July 1989; MMC, *Provincial*, 1989, Appendix 7.1; *Modern Railways*, October 1989, pp. 533–4.

179 The systems were also used on the Central Wales, Maiden Newton, Barnstaple, Whitland–Pembroke Dock, and Newquay lines. See *Modern Railways*, January and October 1985, pp. 28–30, 509; MMC, *Provincial*, Appendix. 7.1; Ken Burrage (Deputy Director, S&TE)–T. C. Reardon (Principal Assistant Solicitor, BRB), 29 February 1988, BRB S&TE 207-30-20 Pt. 8.

180 Burrage (Director, S&TE), Memo, 9 May 1989, Investment Committee Minutes, 5 June 1989; BRB, *R&A 1990/1*, p. 28; BRB Minutes, 6 May 1982; A. H. Wickens, 'Railway Technology in 2001—Promise and Reality', *Modern Railways*, October 1985, pp. 509–10.

181 O'Brien, Memo on 'Engineering Cost Strategies', n.d., BEG Minutes, 12 January 1987.

182 Equated track-miles = track-miles adjusted for maintenance workload.

183 Philip Wood, Memo on 'Civil Engineering Cost Strategies—Policy Unit Overview', 8 April 1987, BEG Minutes, 13 April 1987.

184 Wood, Memo cit. Paybill costs as a percentage of CE costs rose from 53.9% in 1979 to 57.1% in 1985/6.

185 W. H. Woodhouse (Director, S&TE), Report to BEG on 'S & T Engineering Cost Strategies', 23 October 1987, BRB; Wood, Memo to BEG on 'S & T Engineering Cost Strategies—Policy Unit Overview', n.d., BRB DMEE 22-24-75 Pt. 8; BEG Minutes, 9 November 1987.

186 Holmes (Director of Operations, BRB), Report to BEG on 'Cost Strategies—Operations Department', October 1987, BEG Minutes, 9 November 1987.

187 BRB, Manpower Statistics, 1980–4; BRB IR cassettes, CBTB level 8, Pt. 13-86/7-16, March 1987.

188 BEG Minutes, 13 July and 9 November 1987.

189 Kearney, Report on 'Signals and Telecommunications Engineering—Organisation and Systems Review', June 1987, Welsby's Papers, Sec Box 2338; BRB Production Management Group Minutes, 15 June, 14 July, and 11 August 1987, Kearney Civil Engineering Steering Group Minutes, 7 July 1987, Welsby's Papers, Sec Box 2355.

190 BRB Production Management Group Minutes, 17 May 1988; Cornell, Memo on 'Infrastructure Costs Initiative—Review of Progress', 17 August 1988, BRB Minutes, 8 September 1988, and Cornell, Memo on 'Infrastructure Costs Initiative—Review of Progress', n.d., BRB Minutes, 2 November 1989.

191 Investment Committee Minutes, 3 October 1983, 6 October and 1 December 1986, 5 October 1987.

192 PBI Working Group Minutes, 7 December 1987 and 11 January 1988, Currie–Rayner, 29 April 1988, Paul R. Strange (Project Engineer, Permanent Way, BRB)–M. G. Reynolds (Project Manager, PBI 84 Stoneblower), 1 December 1987, 19 April 1988, BRB 185-217-603 Pt. 5; Andrew Jukes (BRB Investment Adviser), Memo, 24 February 1989, and Cornell, Memo on 'Production Stoneblowers', February 1989; Investment Committee Minutes, 3 May 1988, 6 March and 5 June 1989, 30 April 1990.

193 The competitor in 1983 was NEI's subsidiary Cowans Sheldon. See S. M. Baker (MD, NEI Cranes)–J. M. Dowell (Purchasing Agent, BRB), 6 October 1983, Purbrick–Kirchen (Dept of Industry), 16 December 1983, BRB CE 195-2-90 Pt. 4; BRB Supply Committee Minutes, 10 March 1983; Posner–Trewin, 23 February 1984, Posner's Papers, Sec Box 2266. On the investigation of 1988–92 see, e.g., Dr Josef Theurer–Reid, 29 September 1988, Osborne–Reid, 10 October 1988, Kirby's Papers, Sec Box 2151; papers in BRB CE 195-2-90 Pts. 3–4; Toolan, 'Notes of Meeting between Messrs. D. E. Rayner, T. Toolan and T. J. Green . . . 26th September 1988', 27 September 1988; 'Notes of Meeting between Messrs. D. E. Rayner, R. Toolan and D. S. Currie . . . 21st September 1988', Currie's Papers, BRB. Currie was suspended, but elected to resign on the following day: Currie–Rayner, 23 September 1988, Currie's Papers, BRB; 'Note for File', 7 October 1988, BRB 48-2-45 Pt. 2; *Guardian*, 21 October 1988, p. 26; *The Times*, 9 March 1989, p. 3, 1 October 1992, p. 3, 2 October 1992, p. 9, 8 December 1992, p. 2, 15 December 1992, p. 3.

194 1979: 9,982 miles of CWR; 1989/90 12,644 miles. DTp, *Railway Accidents* (from 1982 *Railway Safety*), 1979, 1990.

195 Weld failures per 1,000 miles: 30.48, 1985; 15.82, 1990; plain line-joint breaks per 1,000 miles: 35.52, 1986; 27.15, 1990; track-mileage renewed: 811 p.a., 1976–8, 801, 1982–84/5; 673, 1985/6–86/7. Stewart Currie, Report to PMG on 'CE Cost Strategies Update', 13 September 1988, Appendix 5; Jim Cornell (Dir., CE), Memo to Board Exec., 16 April 1992.

196 Campbell, Memo on 'Renewal and Maintenance of Physical Assets', December 1980, cit.; Alfred W. Boucher (Principal Investment Manager, BRB), Memo on 'Investment Review 1982–86/92: 5-year Investment Programme 1982–1986', 22 October 1981, P&I Committee Minutes, 27 October 1981; BRB Minutes, 7 January 1982; Peter

Corbishley (Chief Planning Officer, BRB), Memo on 'Investment and Financing Review', 7 June 1982, BRB 23-4-2 Pt. 19A; Roger Hillard (BRB Policy Unit)–Osmotherly (DTp), 26 July 1982, BRB IA 20-8-5 Pt. 4; BRB, *R&A 1982*, p. 17. The RRE mechanism ceased in 1988/9: MMC, *Provincial*, para. 4.16.

197 BR Management Brief, 30 July 1984.

198 BRB, *R&A 1984/5*, p. 4; *1989/90*, p. 1.

199 *Modern Railways*, May 1987, pp. 254ff., January 1989, pp. 24–7.

200 Fowler, Memo, 22 September 1981, BRB Minutes, 1 October 1981.

201 REG Minutes, 27 May and 14 October 1981; 'Notes of Emergency Meeting held 20th July 1983 to Discuss HST Performance', n.d., David H. Ward (InterCity Services Manager), Brief, 6 September 1983, Reid (I)–J. Towler (Chairman North East TUCC), 31 July 1986, InterCity file 625. GEC agreed a £7 m. compensation package in relation to the Paxman Valenta engines: *Railnews*, February 1986.

202 Fowler, Memo, September 1981 cit. and see also Investment Committee Minutes, 1 October 1974, P&I Committee Minutes, 4 July 1978 and 12 February 1980.

203 Investment Committee Minutes, 15 January 1974 and 5 August 1975; BRB Minutes, 14 February 1974; Press Release, 27 January 1976; Campbell, Memo on 'Advanced Passenger Train: The Evolution of a Policy for a West Coast Main Line Service Fleet', n.d., RE Minutes, 19 December 1977. The story of the APT is also told in Stephen Potter, *On the Right Lines? The Limits of Technological Innovation* (New York, 1987), and see extract in *Modern Railways*, January 1987, pp. 30–3; L. H. Williams, *APT—A Promise Unfulfilled* (Shepperton, 1985).

204 *Modern Railways*, August 1984, p. 415.

205 Roland Bond–Campbell, 5 October 1980, BRB Chief Executive's files, AN156/700, PRO. Bond noted that 'the train is certainly a splendid achievement . . . taking curves 50% faster than one used to roll and lurch round them on Royal Scots and Stanier Pacifics'. On Bond see Gourvish, *British Railways*, pp. 146, 263.

206 BRB Press Release, 20 May 1980; Campbell–Parker, 22 August 1980, Reid–Dr J. Galletly (Chief Medical Officer, BRB), 8 October 1980, AN156/700, PRO, and see also papers in IC file, AN182/177, PRO; Campbell, Memo on 'The Advanced Passenger Train—A Progress Report', 29 January 1981, BRB Minutes, 5 February 1981; Interview with Dr Alan Wickens, 10 April 1989.

207 BRB Minutes, 1 May 1980; Campbell–APT Steering Group, 22 April 1980; *Modern Railways*, February 1982, pp. 62–3, July 1982, p. 291; *Private Eye*, 28 December 1981, 2 July 1982; Parker, *For Starters*, pp. 271–3. For BRB reactions see Press Releases, 23 February and 17 March 1981.

208 £150 m. on the trainsets (54 plus 6 prototypes), £100 m. on depots and infrastructure. Peter A. Keen (Chief Passenger Manager, BRB), Memo on 'Investment Submission for Advanced Passenger Trains (APT-S) on West Coast Main Line', 16 May 1980, P&I Committee Minutes, 11 June 1980; BRB Minutes, 19 June 1980.

209 E.g. *two* power cars, hydrokinetic brakes, and articulated bogies. On the change of course see BRB Minutes, 5 March and 5 November 1981; Campbell–Keen, 6 October 1981, Campbell–Reid, 11 January 1982, AN156/701, PRO; Campbell, Memo on 'The Advanced Passenger Train', 24 May 1982, BRB Minutes, 3 June 1982.

210 BRB Minutes, 1 July and 4 November 1982; BRB Research & Technical Committee Minutes, 2 March and 7 September 1983; Bleasdale and Don L. Heath (APT Project Manager), Memos on 'APT—Progress Report', 17 February and 14 June 1983, RE

Minutes, 23 February and 22 June 1983; Parker–Campbell, 9 March 1982, Posner–Myers, 3 May 1983, Posner's Papers, Sec Box 2257; *Modern Railways*, January 1983, pp. 13–14.

211 Myers, Memo on 'APT Progress', 1 August 1983, BRB Minutes, 8 August 1983; BRB Management Brief, 15 August 1983; Interview with Casey, 1989. Two electric HSTs were authorised in 1983 but abandoned in 1984; only one Class 89 locomotive was constructed.

212 BRB Strategy Committee Minutes, 18 October and 16 December 1983; Posner–P. S. Higham, 13 January 1984, Posner's Papers, Box 2257; BEG Minutes, 10 November 1986; *Modern Railways*, September 1986, pp. 458–9.

213 Cf. Campbell–Casey (CM&EE) et al., 3 October 1980, Derek Fowler–John Palmer (DTp), 7 November 1980, Campbell–Reid, 11 January 1982, AN156/700-1, PRO; Campbell, Memo, 24 May 1982, cit.; Sir Hugh Ford (Ford and Dain Partners Ltd), at BRB Research & Technical Panel Minutes, 29 January 1982.

214 Cf. *New Scientist*, 22 September 1982, p. 812; Nick Hamer, 'Who needs a train that tilts?', *New Scientist*, 22 September 1982, pp. 838–9.

215 Richard Branson's Virgin Trains have ordered tilting trains for WCML.

216 *Modern Railways*, September 1986, p. 459. The three prototype trains cost £36.3 m. in July 1984 prices: Prideaux, Memo to Investment Committee, January 1989, BRB Box K(I).

217 BRB R&TP Committee Minutes, 29 January 1982, and see Potter, *On the Right Lines*, pp. 117–50, 193–5. Wickens has argued that 'the project was under-resourced from the start'. He puts the turning point at 1973/4 when the DTp, which had helped to fund initial development, offered to pay 80% of the investment in 10 prototypes. The Board rejected this, however, and instead three prototypes were built. Interview with Wickens, 1989; Potter, *On the Right Lines*, pp. 117–19, 194.

218 *Modern Railways*, January 1982, p. 6, August 1984, pp. 398–9, 417. The Class 91s were designed with a detachable power-car for mixed traffic use: *Modern Railways*, August 1986, pp. 201–3.

219 InterCity Press Release, 28 June 1991; Mike Vincent and Chris Green (eds.), *The InterCity Story* (Sparkford, 1994), p. 32.

220 Investment Committee Minutes, 3 August 1987.

221 *Modern Railways*, January 1988, pp. 37–44, August 1989, p. 395, October 1995, pp. 616–21. ARC, another aggregates firm, bought four GM diesels; they entered service in October 1990.

222 Of infrastructure investment 48% was spent on track renewal, 29% on signalling and track rationalisation, 1979–89/90. Appendix B, Table B.2.

223 D. J. Cobbett (Director, Strategic Studies, BRB)–Reid et al., 10 May 1983, enclosing Cobbett–Osmotherley (DTp), 10 May 1983, BRB 182-1-1 Pt. 7.

224 These were: York–Healey Mills, Derby–Leeds, and Paddington–Coventry/Birmingham. Cobbett–Osmotherley, 10 May 1983, cit.

225 Network SouthEast Press Release, 25 April 1988.

226 Mitchell–Reid, 27 October 1983, BRB 182-1-1 Pt. 7.

227 Fowler, Memo on 'Investment Policy—Non-Commercial Railway', 26 August 1981, BRB Minutes, 3 September 1981.

228 Campbell, Memo on 'Investment Policy—Non Commercial Railways: Closure of Certain Routes to Finance Improvements on Others', 23 November 1981, BRB

Minutes, 3 December 1981, 4 November 1982. Posner–Parker, 16 February 1983, Posner's Papers, Sec Box 2261; Investment Committee Minutes, 11 November 1983.

229 Investment Committee Minutes, 1 October 1984, 6 May 1987.

230 P&I Committee Minutes, 25 February 1980; BRB, *R&A 1982*, p. 23; Jack Simmons and Gordon Biddle (eds.), *The Oxford Companion to British Railway History* (Oxford, 1997), p. 189. The £60 m. project was funded by the NCB.

231 Investment Committee Minutes, 7 August 1989.

232 Parker, *For Starters*, p. 223; Interview with Sir Peter Parker, 2 August 1999.

233 *Modern Railways*, March 1986, p. 122.

234 Malcolm Southgate (Director, Channel Tunnel), Memo, 22 May 1990, Investment Committee Minutes, 4 June 1990. On the Channel Tunnel see, e.g., Michael R. Bonavia, *The Channel Tunnel Story* (Newton Abbot, 1987), Ian Holliday, Gerard Marcou, and Roger Vickerman, *The Channel Tunnel: Public Policy, Regional Development and European Integration* (1991); Graham Anderson and Ben Roskrow, *The Channel Tunnel Story* (1994); Colin J. Kirkland (ed.), *Engineering the Channel Tunnel* (1995); Interview with Southgate, 30 September 1992.

235 O'Brien, Memo, 22 August 1984, BRB Minutes, 6 September 1984, 14 February 1985, 1 May 1986; Godfrey Bradman (Rosehaugh Stanhope)–Reid, 30 July 1985, Reid (I)'s Papers, Sec Box 2202; BRB, *R&A 1991/2*, p. 30.

236 BRB Minutes, 1 November 1984; BRB, *R&A 1984/5*, p. 11; Railway Heritage Trust, *Annual Report 1989/90*, p. 2. The Trust made grants totalling £5.3 m. and attracted external funds of £2.3 m. for 187 projects to March 1990.

237 The Scottish experiment involved 'stored ride' ticketing on the Glasgow–Gourock/ Wemyss Bay line. See documents in Chief Executive's files, AN156/449, PRO; RE Minutes, 12 February and 22 October 1979. Campbell was particularly sceptical about the ARC pilot scheme on Southern Region. He told Reid, 'this seems to be becoming a dodgier project almost every time I look at it': Campbell–Reid, 4 July 1979, AN156/ 449, PRO.

238 P&I Committee Minutes, 10 August 1982; Investment Committee Minutes, 6 December 1982, 4 July and 11 November 1983, 2 July 1984; BRB Minutes, 5 April 1984; *Railnews*, January 1983; *Railway Gazette International*, February 1983, p. 82; *Modern Railways*, May 1984, pp. 256–7; Interview with Ivor Warburton, 18 January 2000.

239 Cf. Campbell–Myers, 22 June 1980, Sellers–Campbell, 8 April 1981, AN156/450, PRO; 'Brief Synopsis of APTIS Development', n.d. [July 1983], David E. Rayner (Chief Passenger Manager, BRB), Memo to Investment Committee, 1 July 1983, D. J. Cobbett–Fowler, 9 November 1983, BRB PZ 22-0; Interviews with Roger Temple, John Hooker, and Robin Corbett, 28 November 1989. The initial authorisation had been for £21.5 m. The consultants, Nolan, Norton, were called in to assess the project in 1983, O'Brien was asked to assume personal responsibility for the project, and Roger Temple was appointed as full-time project manager in January 1984.

240 BRB Minutes, 13 February, 6 March, and 7 August 1986; RE Minutes, 23 July, 17 September, and 22 October 1986; BRB, *R&A 1986/7*, p. 12; *Railnews*, March 1985, April 1986; *Modern Railways*, June 1989, pp. 294–5; Simmons and Biddle, *Companion*, p. 141.

241 Gourvish, *British Railways*, p. 509.

242 Fowler, Memo on 'Proposals for Strengthening Investment Procedures within British Railways Board', 18 September 1984, Chairman's Group Minutes, 28 September 1984, BRB Minutes, 4 October 1984, D. Glyn Williams and Sidney B. Newey, Memo on 'Investment Programming, Appraisal and Control', 11 October 1984, Williams and R. J. Smith, Memo on 'Investment Programming, Appraisal and Control', 11 December 1984, RE Minutes, 24 October and 19 December 1984; Interview with Glyn Williams, 15 June 1990.

243 RE Minutes, 19–20 November 1985; Investment Committee Minutes, 7 January, 4 March, 2 September, and 2 December 1985; MMC, *Network SouthEast*, 1987, paras. 7.1–26, 7.52–3. The first Investment Adviser was R. A. Cochrane, recruited from Coopers & Lybrand: Investment Committee Minutes, 4 November 1985; Ian Phillips (Director of Finance & Planning, BRB), Memo 23 December 1986, BRB Minutes, 8 January 1987. The Passenger Demand Forecasting Handbook, prepared with the help of Dr Stephen Glaister of LSE, helped managers reach informed decisions on service planning and investment appraisal. Emerging from post-sector management pressure for a centralised response to forecasting, it was inspired by Geoffrey Myers, John Welsby, John Prideaux, and Charles Brown, and was progressed from 1984 by a Passenger Demand Analysis and Forecasting Group. See Welsby (Director, Provincial)–Malcolm Southgate, 2 March 1983, Philip Wood, Memo to Investment Committee on 'Passenger Demand Forecasting Handbook', 29 August 1986, BRB Policy Unit file on 'Passenger Demand Analysis', AN170/101, PRO; Investment Committee Minutes, 6 October 1986; BRB Policy Unit, 'Passenger Demand Forecasting Handbook', June 1986, and revised edition, June 1989; Interview with Prof. Stephen Glaister, 28 April 1999.

244 RE Minutes, 19 November and 17 December 1986, and cf. MMC, *Network South-East*, paras. 7.53–8.

245 The thresholds for delegated authority were raised from £0.25 m. to £1 m. for sector directors, while schemes from £1–5 m. were to be considered by the JMDs operating through a Railway Investment Sub-Committee: RE Minutes, 20 May 1987; Hornby and Tookey, Memo on 'Review of Investment Regulations and Procedures', 28 July 1987, Investment Committee Minutes, 3 August 1987; Fowler, Memo to Chairman's Group and Investment Committee, 26 October 1987, Chairman's Group Minutes, 29 October 1987; Glyn Williams, Memo, n.d., Investment Committee Minutes, 2 November 1987; BRB Minutes, 5 November 1987.

246 Alan Nichols (DTp)–Glyn Williams, 23 October 1987; Investment Committee Minutes, 2 November 1987; RE Minutes, 16 December 1987.

247 Andrew Jukes (Investment Adviser, BRB), Memo, 30 January 1989, Investment Committee Minutes, 6 February 1989 and see also 28 March 1988 and 4 September 1989; BRB Minutes, 12 October 1989.

248 Kirby–Stan Whittaker, 13 March 1989, Rayner–Don L. Heath on 'RIMs Project Management', 13 March 1989, Williams–Kirby, 28 April 1989, Kirby's Papers, Sec Box 2154; BRG Minutes, 17 March and 30 August 1989; Fowler, Memo, 6 February 1990, BRB Minutes, 15 February 1990; Investment Committee Minutes, 30 April and 2 July 1990.

249 Boucher, Memo on 'Out-turn for Year 1982', 14 February 1982 [*sic*: prob. 11 February 1983], BRB 23-4-2 Pt. 19A; Investment Committee Minutes, 2 April 1984, 3 June 1985; Memos to Investment Committee from Stan Whittaker (Director,

Budgetary Control) on 'Investment Spending for Year Ended 31st March 1986', 28 May 1986, and Whittaker (Director, Group Finance) on 'Actual Spending for Year to 31st March 1987', 28 May 1987, and on 'Actual Spending to 31 March 1988', 1 June 1988; and John Horton (Group Chief Accountant) on 'Actual Spending for 1988/9', 31 May 1989, and on 'Actual Spending for 1989/90', 29 May 1990.

250 The good record in 1985 was the fifth in a decade in which not a single passenger was killed. DTp, *Railway Safety: Report on the Safety Record of the Railways in Great Britain 1985*, p. 7. The Polmont accident was caused by a cow on the line. The average number of passenger fatalities 1980–90 was 6.8. DTp, *Railway Accidents* (from 1982 *Railway Safety*), *1980–90*. Not all commentators were impressed by the safety record. Stanley Hall pointed out that since freight activity had reduced considerably, improvement was to be expected. Yet the number of passenger collisions had not fallen. Hall, *Modern Railways*, July 1985, p. 364.

251 DTp, *Railway Safety 1987*, p. 21; BRB Minutes, 2 July 1987; BRB Safety Committee Minutes, 7 December 1989; BRB, *R&A 1990/1*, p. 7.

252 BRB Safety Committee Minutes, 1 December 1988; Stanley Hall, *Railway Accidents* (Shepperton, 1997), pp. 120–1.

253 Interview with Holmes, 1989; BRB Minutes, 12 January 1989.

254 Cf. BRB, *R&A 1988/9*, p. 8; *1989/90*, p. 7.

255 BRB Safety Committee Minutes, 7 September 1989; *Evening Standard*, 17 August 1989, p. 1; *Modern Railways*, October 1989, p. 507.

256 See Appendix J, Table J.1 and cf. the passenger pricing increases reported in DTp, *Transport Statistics Great Britain 1991*, Calendar of Events and also *Independent*, 14 July 1989, p. 2.

Chapter 7

1 Cf. Thatcher, *Downing Street Years*, p. 686.

2 Margaret Thatcher, *Parl. Deb. (Commons)*, 5th ser. (Session 1979–80), vol. 967, 15 May 1979; cols. 48, 79; Sir Geoffrey Howe, vol. 968, 12 June 1979, col. 246; Gourvish, 'British Rail's "Business-Led" Organization', 148.

3 Board Exec. Minutes, 9 August 1979, Harding–Bosworth, 11 July 1979, and Rose–George Watts (Director, Strategic Studies, BRB), 19 September 1979, BRB 29–12–1 Pt. 1, and cf. also *Financial Times*, 28 February 1980, *Modern Railways*, April 1980, p. 146. On union opposition see Peter Snape (NUR-nominated MP for West Bromwich East)–Parker, 5 July and 2 August 1979, BRB 29-12-1 Pt. 1.

4 Thomas J. Peters and Robert H. Waterman Jr., *In Search of Excellence: Lessons from America's Best-Run Companies* (New York, 1982), pp. 292ff.

5 BRB, *R&A 1977*, p. 8.

6 Meeting with Norman Fowler, 28 June 1979, referred to in File Note, 31 August 1979, BRB 20-100-3/1; Bosworth, Memo on 'Private Sector Involvement in the Activities of the Board', 26 July 1979, BRB Minutes, 2 August 1979; Board Exec. Minutes, 14 June and 27 September 1979; Parker–Norman Fowler, 10 October 1979, BRB 29-12-1 Pt. 1; Norman Fowler, *Parl. Deb. (Commons)*, 5th ser. (Session 1979–80), vol. 979, 20 February 1980, cols. 423–4.

7 Bosworth–Bowick and Derek Fowler, 6 July 1979, Hon. Patrick Spens (Morgan Grenfell)–Bosworth, 23 July 1979, BRB 29-12-1 Pt. 1; Bosworth, Confidential Memo

to BRB on 'Private Sector Involvement in the Activities of the Board', 26 July 1979, BRB Minutes, 2 August 1979, Board Exec. Minutes, 9 August 1979. Bosworth has recalled that he was attracted to the idea of a holding company when visiting the Canadian Pacific: Interview with Michael Bosworth, 22 March 1988.

8 Morgan Grenfell, Reports, 31 August and 14 September 1979, BRB 29-12-1 (folder); Bowick and Derek Fowler, Confidential Memo on 'Private Sector Involvement in the Activities of the Board', 21 September 1979, BRB Minutes, 6 September and 4 October 1979; Reid, File Note on 'Meeting with Minister 24th September 1979', 24 September 1979, BRB 20-100-3/1; Parker–Norman Fowler, 10 October 1979, enclosing Report to Minister of Transport on 'Private Sector Involvement in the Activities of the British Railways Board', October 1979, BRB 29-12-1 Pt. 1.

9 Cf. Serpell–Burt, 24 September 1979, BRB 29-12-1 Pt. 1, and see also Board Exec. Minutes, 27 September 1979.

10 Parker–Fowler, 10 October 1979, and Report, pp. 1-2, 7, 26, BRB 29-12-1 Pt. 1.

11 Norman Fowler–Parker, 14 February 1980, BRB 29-12-1 Pt. 1, and Fowler, Commons statement, 20 February 1980, cit.

12 Cf. J. Palmer (DTp)–Bosworth, 6 March 1980, BRB 29-12-1 Pt. 1.

13 Board Exec. Minutes, 28 February 1980; Parker–Norman Fowler, 19 February and 11 March 1980, Fowler–Parker, 4 March 1980, Spens–Bosworth, 12 March 1980, Jennie Page (Assistant Secretary, DTp)–Watts, 17 March 1980, BRB 29-12-1 Pt. 1; Debate on British Railways (Subsidiary Businesses), introduced by Robin Cook, *Parl. Deb. (Commons)*, 5th ser. (Session 1979–80), vol. 984, 9 May 1980, cols. 795–808. The DTp engaged the services of Philip Shelbourne of Samuel Montagu to advise them: Norman Fowler–Parker, 2 April 1980, BRB 29-12-1 Pt. 1; *Observer*, 25 May 1980.

14 BRB Minutes, 1 and 22 May 1980; Bosworth, Memo on 'Introduction of Private Capital', 31 July 1980, BRB Minutes, 7 August 1980; Report of Joint DTp/BRB Team on 'Introduction of Private Capital in the British Railways Board's Subsidiaries' (80pp.), 15 May 1980; Bosworth, 'Note of Meeting with Minister Monday 2 June 1980', 5 June 1980, Bosworth, 'File Note of Meeting at Department of Transport Thursday, 12 June 1980', 16 June 1980, BRB 29-12-1 Pt. 1. Baldwin, the DTp Permanent Secretary, noted that while Fowler had agreed to the holding company's being 100% BR owned, 'we still have the problem of silencing Nigel Lawson': Parker, 'Note on telephone conversation with Sir Peter Baldwin', 3 July 1980, BRB 29-12-1 Pt. 2.

15 Bosworth–Parker, 12 June 1980, BRB 29-12-1 Pt. 1 and cf. Bosworth, File Note, same date, cit.

16 Norman Fowler, *Parl. Deb. (Commons)*, 5th ser. (Session 1979–80), vol. 988, 14 July 1980, cols. 1054–5, and cf. his speech to the Railways Division of the Institute of Mechanical Engineers, reported in DTp, Press Notice, 7 March 1980, and press (*Guardian*, *The Times*, *Financial Times*), 8 March 1980, in BRB 29-12-1 Pt. 1; Kenneth Clarke (Parl. Sec. to Minister of Transport), *Parl. Deb. (Commons)*, 9 May 1980, cit., cols. 801–8; Burt, Memo on 'The Development of Privatisation', 22 March 1983, BRB 29-12-1 Pt. 4. However, Clarke's views on the meaning of 'hiving-off' were rather different from those of the Board: cf. Bosworth–Parker, 2 June 1980, and Bosworth, Note, 5 June 1980, cit., BRB 29-12-1 Pt. 1.

17 *Economist*, 8 March 1980, pp. 69–70; Interview with Sir Norman Fowler, 20 April 1999.

18 Press cuttings for 15 July 1980 (*Sunday Times*, 20 July) in BRB 29-12-1 Pt. 2.

19 Cf. Burt: 'BR worries too much about meeting the various restrictions placed on it by Government': Note on 'Special Eastern Region Board Dinner, April 1, 1980', 2 April 1980, BRB 29-12-1 Pt. 1; Interview with Lord Peyton, 1 November 1999.

20 Bosworth, Memo on 'BRB Subsidiaries—Introduction of Private Capital', 1 September 1980, BRB Minutes, 4 September 1980.

21 The BRIL Board consisted of Bosworth (Chairman; BRB, BTH, Sealink, Hovercraft), Urquhart (BRB, BREL); Arthur Brooking (Finance Dir. BR Property Board), Jeremy Cotton (Carr Sebag (stockbrokers)), James Forbes (Tate & Lyle and BTH), Sir Jack Hughes (Jones Lang Wooton (Property consultants) and BR Property Board), Philip Ling (Johnson & Firth Brown (steel)), and Eric Parker (Trafalgar House and Sealink). BRB Minutes, 4 December 1980. Ling and Cotton were proposed by Norman Fowler: Fowler–Parker, 23 October 1980, BRB 29-12-3 Pt. 1. Urquhart replaced Caldecote, an initial appointee, who declined the position owing to pressure of work: Caldecote–Fowler, 21 November 1980, BRB 29-12-3 Pt. 1. John Morgan, BR Pensions Fund Manager, joined the BRIL Board in June 1981: BRB Minutes, 2 July 1981.

22 Bosworth, Draft Memos on 'Introduction of Private Capital—Role of Holding Company', 10, 21, and 28 November 1980, BRB 29-12-1 Pt. 2 and BRB 29-12-3 Pt. 1, and BRB Minutes, 4 December 1980, and see also his Memo on 'The Role and Responsibilities of British Rail Investments Limited', 11 February 1981, BRB Minutes, 5 March 1981.

23 Note, for example, A. P. Brown (DTp)–Philip Sellers (Director of Finance, BRB), 15 January 1981, BRIL 100-78-1, and NUR concern over remarks made by Kenneth Clarke, Parliamentary Under-Secretary of State, DTp, in Standing Committee E, 10 February 1981, col. 162, BRJCC Minutes, 19 February 1981, and BRB Memo to BR Council, March 1981, BR Council Minutes, 19 March 1981; Bosworth–Norman Fowler, 1 April 1981, BRB 29-12-1 Pt. 3; Brooking–Bosworth, 16 March 1981, BRIL 100-78-1.

24 Burt, Note of 'Pre-Board Dinner 3 October 1979. Significant Points Emerging During the Discussion', 4 October 1979, BRB 20-100-3/1.

25 BRB Minutes, 4 December 1980; Transport Act, 1981, 31 July 1981, c. 56.

26 Cf. Board Exec. Minutes, 27 November 1980, 29 January 1981; BRB Minutes, 5 February 1981.

27 Transport Act, 1981, Pt. 1, ss. 1–3. Section 1(2) prevented BRB from selling any shares in a subsidiary without the SoS's consent; section 3(1) gave the SoS authority to 'give directions to the Board requiring them: (a) to exercise their powers (of disposal) in a specified manner and in relation to a specified subsidiary'. See also Bosworth, Memo on 'The Role and Responsibilities of British Rail Investments Ltd', 2 March 1981, BRB Minutes, 5 March 1981.

28 Page–Brooking, 26 February 1981, BRB 29-12-3 Pt. 1.

29 DTp, 'Note of a Meeting with the Board of British Rail Investments Ltd 21 October 1981', 29 October 1981, with BRIL Board Minutes, 19 November 1981. In August 1981 Bosworth even suggested that the government might buy a controlling stake in BRIL in order to derive financial benefits more quickly. This idea was quickly rejected. See BRIL Board Minutes, 18 August and 14 September 1981, Board Exec. Minutes, 20 August 1981, BRB Minutes, 9 September 1981; Interview with Michael Bosworth, 22 March 1988.

30 Cf. Parker–Sir Robert Clark (Chairman, Hill Samuel), 31 July 1979, BRB 29-12-1 Pt. 1; Sir Alexander Glen (BTH)–Parker, 9 June 1980, Parker's Papers, file on 'Privatisation'.

31 The idea of borrowing on the security of the hotel assets was rejected for the same reason. Memo on 'Business Potential', 2 February 1981, Land–Sir Alexander Glen, 27 March 1981, Bosworth–L. Jackson (De Vere), 10 July 1981, Peter Land's Papers; Interview with Peter Land, 10 May 1988.

32 BTH Board Minutes, 10 September 1980; Peter Land (MD, BTH), Manuscript History, subsequently published privately as *Sauce Supreme: the Annihilation of British Transport Hotels Ltd* (*c.*1989), p. 33; Interview with Land, 1988.

33 The scheme was developed with the help of the Bank of Scotland and its subsidiary, the British Linen Bank: BTH Minutes, 24 October 1980, BTH Working Party–BTH Board, 27 March 1981, Land's Papers; Land, History, pp. 30–1, 34. In 1980 there were plans to float Gleneagles as a separate company, and to do the same with the two Edinburgh hotels, the Caledonian and the run-down North British. The Gleneagles scheme foundered when the valuation put on it by Morgan Grenfell, based on offering a 50% stake, was, at £2.4m., considerably lower than Christie's valuation of £8m. based on outright sale. The Edinburgh proposition required the addition of Gleneagles to make the scheme attractive to the private sector. See Land–Bosworth, 16 January 1981, enclosing BTH, Note on 'Proposal to Introduce Private Sector Finance', 15 January 1981, AN109/1872, PRO; P. M. R. Spens (Morgan Grenfell)–Land, 1 October 1980, enclosing Spens–Bosworth, same date, Land's Papers.

34 British Rail Hovercraft Ltd, trading as Seaspeed, was merged with Hoverlloyd, owned by the Swedish company Brostroms Rederi, to form Hoverspeed UK. British Rail received £14.3m. in consideration and British Rail Hovercraft Ltd retained a 50% stake. Bosworth, Memo to BR Hovercraft Board, 15 October 1981, BRB 29-12-8 Pt. 3; BRB, *Railnews*, July 1981, pp. 2–3; BRB, *R&A 1981*, pp. 31, 33.

35 The arrangement was with the Harris family, owners of the Clarendon Hotel, Derby. The new company was called Midland Hotels, in which BTH retained a 40% stake (on which a put and call option was operative after three years). See BTH Minutes, 27 March 1981; Brooking–G. D. Miles (Asst. Secretary, DTp), 13 August 1981, BRB 29-12-12; BRB Minutes, 6 August 1981. Protracted negotiations prevented agreement until April 1982.

36 Cf. BRB, *R&A 1981*, p. 4: 'The Board has retained substantial shareholdings in both new companies [Gleneagles, Hoverspeed] which have now moved outside the controls of the public sector'.

37 Bosworth, Memo on 'Introduction of Private Capital—Gleneagles Hotels Limited', 30 April 1981, BRB Minutes, 7 May 1981. The discount of 19.5%, principally a reflection of arrears of repairs and maintenance, was recalculated as 23.4% after allowing for deferred payments. Both Bosworth and Land have claimed that Morgan Grenfell's criticisms were driven in part by disappointment at not getting hold of the hotels themselves: Interviews with Bosworth and Land, 1988.

38 Brooking, Memos to BRIL Board on 'Privatisation of the Laundries', 11 November 1981, BRIL Board Minutes, 11 November 1981, and to BRIL Executive Committee on 'Laundries: Summary of the Transaction with St George's Group plc', 1 April 1982, BRIL 300-86-4 Pt. 2; St. George's Group plc–Shareholders, 2 March 1982, BRIL 300-86-1; and see also papers in BRB 29-12-4. The Willesden plant was acquired by St. George's, which was subsequently taken over by Spring Grove. The sale of the

laundries followed an opportunistic offer from Sunlight in 1979, and the acceptance within BTH that given the state of Willesden outright sale was the best option: Land, Memo on 'Background to the Proposed Sale of BTH Laundries', 23 January 1981, BTH Board Minutes, 28 January and 27 February 1981.

39 C. G. Lewin (Co-ordinator, Private Capital, BRIL), Note for Papers, 3 April 1981, Lewin's Files, BRIL IPC21; Memo to BRIL, 22 May 1981. Turnover was BTH: £1.25m.; Wholesale: £0.75m.; Travellers Fare: £0.2m.; Malmaison: £1m.

40 BTH Board Minutes, 24 October 1980, 27 February 1981; Brooking, Memo on 'Wines', 21 May 1981, BRIL Board Minutes, 22 May 1981; Land–Neville Abraham (les Amis du Vin), 27 March 1981, Land–Brooking, 15 April 1981, BRIL IPC21. Allied Breweries also expressed an interest.

41 Gilmour was representing the complaint of a constituent, Philip Eyres. Rt. Hon. Sir Ian Gilmour–Norman Fowler, 18 June 1980 and reply, 25 July 1980, BRB 29-12-1 Pt. 2. The complaint opened a can of worms in relation to BTH's costs and the validity of its transfer pricing: cf. J. D. Orme (DTp)–S. J. Tee (Finance Director, BTH), 19 March 1981, and Lazarus–Sellers, 17 June 1981, BRIL 300-97-1.

42 Land, Memo on 'Wines Division', 1 February 1982, Brooking, Memo on 'Wine Division of British Transport Hotels Limited', 10 March 1982, BRIL 300-97-1. Stock was valued at £5.0m. in Jan. 1980, and £5.6m. in March 1980: S. J. Tee (Finance Director, BTH)–Clive Coates (Head of Wines & Spirits, BTH), 14 and 16 January 1980, R. Richardson, File Note on 'Wine Stock Levels', 3 March 1980, BTH File on 'Wines Division', AN109/1334, PRO.

43 Land, Memo to BTH Board on 'Wines Division', 1 February 1982, BRIL 300-97-1; BRIL Board Minutes, 16 March and 11 June 1982.

44 John Tee (Finance Director, BTH)–Bosworth, 20 January 1983, D. H. C. Sumner and C. A. G. Spiller, Report, 24 May 1983, BTH and Graham Chidgey (Laytons) Agreement, 29 December 1983, BTH file on 'Sale of Wines Business', AN109/1707, PRO.

45 Patrick Brown (DTp)–Philip Sellers, 15 January 1981, BRIL-G Papers, Box 6; Bosworth, Memo, 30 April 1981, cit.; Interviews with Bosworth and Land, 1988.

46 BRB Minutes, 1 December 1983, 5 January and 2 February 1984; BTH Minutes, 20 December 1983, 29 March 1984; BRIL Minutes, 10 January and 13 March 1984; David Mitchell (Parl. Under-SoS, DTp)–Bosworth, 5 and 13 December 1983, Bosworth–Parker, 7 December 1983, Bosworth–Mitchell, 16 January 1984, BRB 29-12-13; R. M. Gaunt (Co. Sec. GH plc)–Bosworth, 31 October 1983, Potter's BTH File on GH plc No. 8, AN109/1872, PRO. The evidence suggests some acrimony between the non-BRB directors and BRB directors in Gleneagles Hotels plc: cf. BRIL Minutes, 13 September and 10 November 1983.

47 BTH, 'Business Strategy 1981', 18 September 1981, Land's Papers; BTH Board Minutes, 15 September 1981; Bosworth, Memo on 'British Rail Investments Limited—Progress Report', 26 August 1981, and Confidential Memo on 'Introduction of Private Capital: B.T. Hotels Limited', 28 October 1981, BRB Minutes, 3 September and 5 November 1981. On Derby and Sheffield see n. 35; on St. Andrews, sold to Frank Sheridan in March 1982, see BTH Board Minutes, 23 February and 24 March 1982, and documents in Potter's BTH Files No. 2, AN109/1870, PRO.

48 Glen–Parker, 28 October 1981, Forbes–Parker, 30 October 1981, BRB 29-12-1 Pt. 3; BTH Board Minutes, 3 November 1981; BRB Minutes, 5 November 1981; Interview with Land, 1988.

49 Meeting of Secretary of State and BRIL Board, 21 October 1981, reported in BRB Minutes, 5 November 1981, and cf. Parker, Notes, 4 November 1981, BRB 240-1-72 Pt. 1.

50 BRB Minutes, 4 March 1982.

51 Operating losses before interest: 1980: £0.3m.; 1981: £2.4m.; 1982: £1.6m. BRB, *R&A 1980–2*.

52 Interview with Land, 1988.

53 BRB Minutes, 5 November 1981. The reaffirmation, missing from the draft minutes, was added to the finally agreed minutes: see BRB 29-12-1 Pt. 3.

54 BRB Minutes, 7 January 1982; Board Exec. Minutes, 8 July 1982; Bosworth, Memo on 'B.T. Hotels: Privatisation', 27 July 1982, BRB Minutes, 5 August 1982; Bosworth–Burt, 23 July 1982, Land–Parker, 9 August 1982, Parker's Papers, file on 'Privatisation'; Parker–Howell, 2 August 1982, Parker's Papers, PP20(B). On the growing popularity of the MBO from the late 1970s see David Clutterbuck and Marion Devine, *Management Buyouts: Success and Failure away from the Corporate Apron Strings* (1987), pp. 1–9.

55 Bosworth, Memo on 'Privatisation of Hotels', 24 May 1982, BRB Minutes, 3 June 1982; Brooking (BRIL), Memo on 'Proposed Offer by Management Consortium', 1 July 1982, BRIL Board Minutes, 8 July 1982; Bosworth–Palmer (Under-Secretary, Railways, DTp), 13 July 1982, enclosing Memo on 'Hotels—Proposed Offer by Management Consortium', 12 July 1982, Bosworth–Burt, 23 July 1982, Bosworth–Land, 13 August 1982, BRB 29-12-13. The 18 hotels were valued by Christies and Druce at £35m. The offer of £29m. amounted to £26.7m. allowing for deferred payments, a discount of £8.3m. However, taking into consideration the benefits to BRB of accepting the MBO the discount was reduced to £6.2m. Brooking, Memo 8 October 1982, Parker's Papers, PP20(B).

56 It appears that a discount of £2m. would have been acceptable. See Kleinwort Benson–Bosworth, 29 September 1982, David Ewart (Morgan Grenfell)–Bosworth, 6 October 1982, Parker's Papers, PP20(B); J. P. MacArthur (Kleinwort Benson)–Bosworth, 25 October 1982, BRB 29-1-2-1 Pt. 4. The £20.5m. offer (for seven freehold, three leased, and two management contract hotels) amounted to £18.6m. allowing for deferred payments, while the hotels were valued at £24.0m., implying a discount of £5.4m., reduced to £4.0m. allowing for MBO benefits (see n. 55). This offer was then altered to £20.25m., by excluding a lease on the Great Northern, producing a discount of £3.47m. against valuation: Bosworth, Memo, 5 October 1982, BRB Minutes, 7 October 1982; Brooking, Memo 8 October 1982, cit. The discount was only £1.47m. above the figure of £2m. which Morgan Grenfell would have supported: Board Exec. Minutes, 14 October 1982.

57 Trewin, Note on 'Meeting with Secretary of State: 3rd August 1982', 4 August 1982, Reginald Eyre (for SoS)–Parker, 4 August 1982, Parker's Papers, PP20(B); Palmer–Bosworth, 18 October 1982; Land, Tee, and Plant–Howell, 14 October 1982, R. Bird (Private Secretary, DTp), 22 October 1982, Land's Papers; Howell, *Parl. Deb. (Commons)*, 6th ser. (Session 1982–3), vol. 32, Written Answer, 23 November 1982, *467*.

58 *The Times*, 22 November 1982, 'BR—Howell's Hotel Howler?', *Guardian*, 26 November 1982, in BRB 29-12-13; Vickers and Yarrow, *Privatization*, pp. 160–2, 174–5. Amersham shares were offered for 142p; their price on the first day of trading (25 Feb. 1982) was 188p, and on 25 Feb. 1989, 537p.

59 BRIL, Invitation to Tender, 2 December 1982, AN109/1349, PRO; BRB Press Release, 19 November 1982; Board Exec. Minutes, 25 November 1982; Bosworth–Sir Peter Baldwin (Permanent Secretary, DTp), 29 October 1982, Bosworth–Land, 11 November 1982, Palmer–Bosworth, 17 November 1982, Bosworth–Palmer, 30 November 1982, G. D. Miles (DTp)–Bosworth, 7 January 1983, BRB 29-12-13.

60 Of 21 hotels sold, 10 went to four bidders in February 1983, nine by private treaty in March 1983. The remaining two were sold in 1984. This left two properties, the Great Eastern and Great Northern hotels, which were affected by development proposals and were therefore taken on short lease by two of Land's colleagues, Derek Plant and John Tee (Compass Hotels). For a full list of the disposals in 1983–4 see Appendix H, Table H.1.

61 Cf. Land–Bosworth, 16 November 1982, Bosworth Papers, File on 'Privatisation. Hotels MBO, Pt. 2': 'We have delivered everything that has been asked of us in our kamikaze role. We have now sawed so far through the branch on which we are sitting'.

62 Glen–Thatcher, 21 March and 19 April 1983, Thatcher–Glen and Howell–Glen, both 30 March 1983, Glen–Howell, 19 April 1983, BRB 29-12-13. BTH Board concerns about the tendering process were conveyed to the valuers and merchant bank advisers in Bosworth–Ewart (Morgan Grenfell), R. Shaw (Druce) and D. Rugg (Christie's), 25 February 1983, BRB 29-12-3.

63 BRIL Board Minutes, 22 March and 24 May 1983; Land, History, pp. 96–7, 122–3; Interview with Land, 1988, and see also David Rugg (Christie & Co.)–Bosworth, 1 March 1983, Land's Papers.

64 Cf. *Catering Times*, 29 April 1983, *Caterer and Hotelkeeper*, 19 April 1984, cutting in Bosworth's BRIL-G Papers, Boxes 16 and 17. Note that Virani sold the Moretonhampstead Hotel within 72 hours of buying it: *Exeter Express and Echo*, 19 April 1983, cutting in Bosworth's BRIL-G Papers, Box 17.

65 The 18 hotels in the first Land MBO proposal were sold for a total of £37m., 28% more than the offer of £29m. BRIL rejected a bid from M. F. North of £32.88m. for all 21 hotels: BRIL Board Minutes, 15 February 1983.

66 F. J. Leese–M. B. Potter, 8 October 1984, enclosing 'BRIL—Sale of B.T. Hotels', Potter's Files: Hotels Privatisation—General, AN109/1873, PRO. The figure included a total of £52.3m. for the hotels. Other elements: £1.2m. for the laundries (£0.9m. and £0.3m. for sale of Willesden site), £0.8m. for the wine stock, £5.4 in profit from sale of Gleneagles shares (net), £50,000 on sale of Midland shares, and £0.25m. from sale of interest in housing development with Bovis Homes (Scotland) at Gleneagles.

67 Compass Hotels leased the Great Northern for £300,000, and entered into a management contract to operate the Great Eastern for £30,000 p.a. plus a share of the profits. See AN109/1873, PRO.

68 NUR, 'Background Briefing Notes Prepared by NUR Research Group on British Rail Subsidiary Businesses', January 1981, AN109/1873, PRO.

69 Sealink UK, *R&A 1982*, p. 18. Figures are for Sealink Group and equate to the loss after interest and tax but before extraordinary items.

70 Keith Wickenden (European Ferries)–Parker, 8 December 1980 and reply, 9 December 1980, BRB 29-12-7 Pt. 1 and BRIL 100-87-5; Sealink UK Board Minutes, 15 December 1980; Norman Fowler–Wickenden, 15 January 1981, Bosworth Papers, Sec Box 2164; Parker–Fowler, 27 January 1981, BRB 29-12-7 Pt. 1; Palmer–Bosworth, 8 December 1981, BRIL 600-79-1; Interview with Michael Bosworth, 22 March 1988; MMC,

European Ferries Limited, Sealink Limited: A Report on the Proposed Merger, December 1981, P.P. 1981–2, xiv, HC65, pp. 97–8; *The Times*, 9 December 1980. The Hovercraft merger was not found to be against the public interest: MMC, *British Rail Hovercraft Limited and Hoverlloyd Limited: A Report on the Proposed Merger*, June 1981, P.P. 1980–1, xxxiv, HC374, p.48.

71 File Note on 'Meeting with Mr. Arison, Sir Frederick Bolton, D. D. Kirby, J. M. Bosworth on 12 November 1981', 16 November 1981, Richard Strang (BRIL), 'Note of a Meeting held at Rail House on 29th January, 1982', n.d., Strang (BRIL), Memo 8 March 1982, BRIL Board Minutes, 16 March 1982, BRIL 600-77-4; BRIL Board Minutes, 16 February and 20 April 1982; Sealink UK Board Minutes, 17 February 1982; Bosworth–Bill Parkhurst (Hamilton Corp.), 6 May 1982, BRIL 600-77-4; Bosworth, Memo on 'Privatisation of Sealink UK Limited', 12 May 1982, BRIL Board Minutes, 18 May 1982; Bosworth, Memo on 'Privatisation of Sealink U.K. Limited', 26 May 1982, BRB Minutes, 3 June 1982. As a way of meeting the problem with deferred payments the possibility of a consortium arrangement with Finance for Shipping Ltd was explored.

72 At the end of 1981 Sealink operated 45 ships, 10 of them leased. Net book value was £165.6m.: owned ships: £41.5m (25 %), leased ships £84.8m (51%). Sealink UK, *R&A 1981*, p. 11. The 14 harbours were: Folkestone, Harwich, Heysham, Holyhead, Newhaven, Parkeston Quay, Stranraer, Gravesend, Tilbury, Ryde, Lymington, Fishbourne, Portsmouth, and Fishguard.

73 Net profit after interest in 1983 was £4.0m.: Sealink UK, *R&A 1983*, p. 23.

74 John Moore (Financial Secretary to the Treasury), 'Why Privatise?' speech, 1 November 1983, reproduced in John Kay, Colin Mayer, and David Thompson (eds.), *Privatisation and Regulation: The UK Experience* (Oxford, 1986), p. 78.

75 G. D. Miles (DTp), Note on 'Meeting about Sealink Privatisation, 10th May 1983', 11 May 1983, Tom King (SoS, DTp)–Parker, 20 July 1983, BRB 29-12-15 Pt. 1; BRB Minutes, 6 October 1983.

76 Morgan Grenfell, Memos on 'Sealink (UK) Limited: Financial Comparisons of Options for Privatisation', 21 October 1983, and 'Sealink: Options for Privatisation', 10 November 1983, Bosworth, Confidential Memo on 'Sealink Privatisation—Progress Report', 28 October 1983, BRB Minutes, 6 October, 3 November, and 1 December 1983.

77 Ridley–Reid, 29 December 1983, BRB 29-12-15 Pt. 1.

78 In August 1983 Lord Inchcape of P&O wrote to the Secretary of State to demand that the harbours should be sold separately to independent, non-shipping operators, but nothing came of this idea. See Earl of Inchcape–King, 8 August 1983, BRIL 600-82-1. The option of disposing of the harbours separately was rejected by Morgan Grenfell: J. A. Morgan (Executive Director, BRIL), Memo, 30 September 1983, BRB Minutes, 6 October 1983.

79 The serious enquiries came from Sea Containers; Trafalgar House; Ellerman Lines; Common Brothers; the Charterhouse Japhet Consortium (Sealink management, NFC, Globe Investments), and R. E. Cardy. Derek Fowler, who succeeded Bosworth as Chairman of BRIL in March 1984, handled the tender: Fowler–Ridley, 18 July 1984, BRB 29-12-15 Pt. 2; Sealink UK Board Minutes, 11 April 1984; BRIL Board Minutes, 13 March and 9 July 1984; BRB Minutes, 10 July and 5 August 1984; L. C. Merryweather (MD, Sealink, 1982–5), Notes, 19 July 1988.

80 *Parl. Deb. (Commons)*, 6th ser. (Session 1983–4), vol. 64, 18 July 1984, Nicholas Ridley, and John Prescott, cols. 313–15. Ridley subsequently pointed out that the government had retained a 'golden share' in Sealink for strategic reasons, preventing the company from disposing of the whole or more than 25% of the fleet without the consent of the SoS: Ridley, Written Answer, 24 July 1984, ibid., *554–5*. The assets were sold on in a deal with Temple Holdings (including Stena) in 1990: Sea Containers News Release, 2 February 1990.

81 Cf. Ewart (Morgan Grenfell)–Derek Fowler, 18 July 1984, BRB 29-12-15 Pt. 2.

82 Bosworth–Howell, 5 November 1982, G. D. Miles (DTp)–Bosworth, n.d. [24 December 1982], and 16 February 1983, BRB 29-12-8 Pt. 3.; BRIL Board Minutes, 25 January 1983; BRB Minutes, 6 January 1983. Hoverspeed UK accounts for 1982/3 had not been agreed when the sale took place. See BRB 29-12-8 Pt. 4.

83 Bosworth, Memo to BRIL Board on 'Hoverspeed (UK) Limited', 15 February 1984, Terence Jenner (Assistant Solicitor, BRB)–Burt, 19 March 1984, BRB 29-12-8 Pt. 4; BRB Minutes, 5 January and 2 February 1984; *Financial Times*, 13 June 1989, p. 3; Interview with Bosworth.

84 Derek Fowler, Memo on 'British Rail Investments Ltd.', 27 September 1984, BRB Minutes, 4 October 1984; Fowler–Palmer (DTp), 4 October 1984, Osmotherley (DTp)–Fowler, 7 November 1984, BRB 29-12-3 Pt. 2.

85 BRB, *R&A 1987/8*, pp. 6–7; *1988/9*, p. 6.

86 Ridley–Reid, 24 October 1983, cit.: 'You should complete your review by the middle of next year [i.e. 1984] of the options for the future of BREL, including the options for privatisation.'

87 The actual sum was £9.067m., with provision for an additional 25% of any extra profit arising from enhanced planning consent [est. £1.36m.–£2.00m.]. The original developers were to be the Swindon-based White Horse Holdings, backed by Tarmac, but in the event Tarmac acquired the site. Douglas Leslie (MD, BRPB), Memo to BRPB, 18 December 1986, BRB Investment Committee Minutes, 1 December 1986, 7 January and 2 February 1987; BRB Minutes, 8 January 1987, BREL Board Minutes, 10 June 1987.

88 Welsby, Confidential Memos on 'Doncaster Wagon Works', 2 July and 23 September 1987, BRB Minutes, 2 July, 23 September, and 5 November 1987; Marmon, Memo, 12 June 1987, BRB GCA 53–009 Pt. 1.

89 BREL Board Minutes, 21 July 1986; BRB Press Release on 'Management Changes at BREL', 19 March 1987, Welsby's Papers, Sec Box 2295. Nicolson was Chairman of VSEL (Vickers Shipbuilding) and Northern Telecoms. He was the former chairman of Production-Engineering (1963–8), British Airways (1971–5), BTR (1969–84), and director of numerous companies, including Bank of Montreal, CIBA-Geigy (UK), Costain, Delta Metal, GKN, MEPC, and Rothmans: *Who's Who*. Holdstock joined BREL from the Emhart Corporation, where he had been Vice President, Operations—Europe & America. My thanks to Roger Ford for this information.

90 Reid–Sir Alan Bailey (Permanent Secretary, DTp), October 1986, enclosing draft letter to SoS, Welsby's Papers, Sec Box 2295. It is not clear whether the letter was actually sent.

91 BREL Board Minutes, 17 December 1986.

92 'BREL Plan 1987/8–1989/90', May 1987, Confidential Memo 4/87, BRB; Philip Wood (Director, Policy Unit, BRB)–Reid, 27 May 1987, Wood, Confidential Note for 'British

Railways Board: Strategy Meeting, 1 June 1987', 27 May 1987, Welsby, Brief for Board Members, 28 June [*sic*; actually May] 1987, Board meeting, 1 June 1987, referred to in BRB Minutes, 4 June 1987.

93 J. R. Coates (DTp)–Welsby, 23 March 1987, Coates and Welsby–C. Ames (Price Waterhouse), 30 March 1987, Welsby–Coates, 1 May 1987, enclosing H. J. Hyman (Price Waterhouse)–Welsby, 29 April 1987, Welsby's Papers, Sec Box 2320.

94 Michael J. Roberts (Lazard Bros & Co.), Note for File, 29 July 1987, Wood–Reid, 5 August 1987, 'Notes of the Meeting of BR-BREL Policy Group held on Friday, 7th August 1987', n.d., Welsby's Papers, Box 2295; Wood, 'Notes of the Meeting of the BR/BREL Policy Group held on Monday, 2nd November 1987', 3 November 1987, Welsby's Papers, Sec Box 2300.

95 Wood–Chairman's Group on 'BREL', 21 October 1987, enclosing draft Confidential Memo for BRB, 21 October 1987.

96 The agreed price was £2m. + £1.125m. for sub-leases. The three bids were from Dennis Castings, an MBO, and Parkfield. Welsby, Confidential Memo on 'Disposal of Horwich Foundry Ltd.', 7 July 1988, BRB Minutes, 26 October 1987, 7 July and 4 August 1988.

97 Reid–Channon, 28 September 1987 and reply, 1 October 1987; Reid–Channon, 24 November 1987, and reply, 30 November 1987, enclosing Paul Channon, *Parl. Deb. (Commons)*, 24 November 1987, cols. 141–8, Reid (I)'s Papers, Sec Box 2204; BR Management Brief, 24 November 1987; BRB Minutes, 3 December 1987.

98 BRB Press Release, 10 December 1987. Casey had been Director, M&EE prior to his appointment as Project Dir., BREL. He was succeeded as Dir., M&EE by David Blake.

99 Cf. Wood–Reid, 29 October 1987, Roberts, File Note, 17 December 1987, Welsby's Papers, Box 2295; Confidential 'Notes of the meeting of the BR/BREL Policy Group held on Monday, 2nd November 1987', Welsby's Papers, Sec Box 2300. Nicolson withdrew from the consortium, but joined it after the sale: see File Note for Reid, March 1989, Welsby's Papers, Sec Box 2294.

100 Cf. unfavourable press comment reported in Roberts–Welsby, 11 January 1988, Welsby's Papers, file on 'BREL General 1988', Sec Box 2295; Roberts–M. V. Casey (Project Director, BREL), 11 April 1988, Welsby's Papers, file on 'BREL PSG', Sec Box 2303.

101 Roberts, File Note, 17 December 1987, cit.; Roberts–S. K. Reeves (DTp), 6 July 1988, File Note on 'BREL Potential Purchasers State of Play', 2 September 1988, Welsby's Papers, Sec Box 2296; Chairman's Group Minutes, 13 October 1988.

102 The consortium stakes were changed from 20% TH, 20% ASEA, 60% MEBO to 40% TH, 40% ASEA, 20% MEBO. Confidential Note on 'Sale of BREL—Review Meeting Wednesday 4th January 1989 Euston House', n.d., Welsby's Papers, Box 2303; Welsby, Memo on 'Disposal of BREL (1988) Limited', n.d., Chairman's Group Minutes, 5 January 1989; Welsby, Confidential Memo on 'Disposal of BREL (1988) Limited', n.d., BRB Minutes, 12 January 1989. For financial details of the two bids see Welsby, Memos, January 1989, cit. and Roger Ford, 'Apples v oranges in BREL bidding', *Modern Railways*, January 1989, p. 9.

103 BRB Minutes, 3 November 1988; Roberts–Welsby, 17 November 1988, Welsby's Papers, Sec Box 2296.

104 Welsby, Memo on 'Sale of BREL—Submission to OFT', n.d., Chairman's Group Minutes, 8 December 1988, 23 February and 2 March 1989; BRB Minutes,

6 April 1989; Reeves–Casey, 23 January 1989, EC 65/64/85, Welsby's Papers, Sec Box 2294.

105 Cf. Roger Ford, 'BREL sale surprises', *Modern Railways*, June 1989, p. 285.

106 BRB Minutes, 4 May 1989; Jerram, Memo to BRB Board Executive, 24 March 1992, BRB Board Executive Minutes, 24 March 1992; Roger Ford, 'To BREL and back', *Director*, June 1992, pp. 57–9, 'British Rail Procurement—a decade of disillusion' and 'British Rail Procurement—from confrontation to partnership', *Modern Railways*, January 1993, pp. 22–6, April 1993, pp. 218–21.

107 Lawrence was succeeded as Chairman by Sir James Swaffield (1984–91). Interviews with John Mayfield (Finance Director, BRPB, 1983–93), 16 December 1999, and Gavin Simpson, 3 November 1988; Gordon Biddle, *The Railway Surveyors: The Story of Railway Property Management 1800–1990* (Shepperton, 1990), pp. 203ff. The BRPB also conducted transactions with third parties for the operational estate and maintained records. MMC, *British Railways Board: Property Activities. A Report on the Efficiency and Costs of the British Railways Board in its Property Activities*, P.P. 1984–5, lxix, Cmnd. 9532, June 1985, paras. 1.5–7, Appendix 4.3(d).

108 Robert Dashwood–Cranley Onslow, 17 June 1980, Clarke–Onslow, 1 September 1980, Dashwood's Papers.

109 Michael Heseltine (SoS for Environment), Commons statement, 13 June 1979, cited in MMC, *Property Activities*, 1985, p. 46 n. 2; 'Notes of Meeting with Department of Transport held on Monday, 31st March, 1980, 274/280 Bishopsgate', n.d., Brooking–Gavin Simpson (MD, BRPB), 10 April 1980, Brooking Files, BRIL ACB2.

110 Appendix H, Table H.2; BRPB Minutes, 19 July, 16 August, and 18 October 1979; 17 January and 15 May 1980; Myers–Dashwood, 6 August 1979, Brooking's files, BRIL ACB2. In constant 1989/90 prices the increase in 1980–1 over 1975–9 was × 2: £67.5m. cf. £30m.

111 BRIL Board Minutes, 16 December 1981, 22 April 1983; Brooking, Memo on 'Evaluation of the Alternative Strategies for Privatising the Property Portfolio', 8 September 1981, Lewin's Files, BRIL IPC3; Brooking, Memo, 10 December 1981, BRIL 500-88-4; BRIL Board Minutes, 16 December 1981; Bosworth Memo on 'Privatisation Strategy of the Non-Operational Portfolio', 2 February 1982, BRB Minutes, 4 February 1982; Simpson, Memo to BRPB on 'B.R.I.L.—Privatisation Strategy Property Disposals', 11 March 1982, BRB 29-12-3 Pt. 2; MMC, *BRB: Property Activities*, 1985, paras. 3.6, 3.10.

112 Brooking–Michael Baker (Chief Solicitor, BRB), 19 May 1982, Howell–Sir Robert Lawrence (Chairman, BRPB), 2 June 1982, BRB 500-88-1 Pt. 2. Bosworth enlisted Sir Peter Baldwin's help in convincing the Minister that a two-year timescale was sub-optimal: Bosworth, Memo on 'Timescale for Disposal of Non-Operational Property', 26 May 1982, BRB Minutes, 3 June 1982; Bosworth–Baldwin, 22 July and reply 29 July 1982; Bosworth–Howell, 24 August 1982, BRIL 500-88-1 Pt. 2.

113 Ridley–Reid, 24 October 1983, in BRB, *R&A 1983*, p. 4; Ridley–Reid, 3 September 1985, BRB 372-22-13 Pt. 2.

114 Simpson–Brooking, 26 November 1982, BRIL 500-88-1 Pt. 2; Interview with Mayfield, 1999.

115 MMC, *BRB: Property Activities*, 1985, paras. 1.21, 6.47; Biddle, *Railway Surveyors*, pp. 210–13.

116 The BRPB invested *c.*£42m. in arches, 1986/7–90/1. About 8,000 lettings, mainly in London, produced a gross income of £21m. in 1989/90. BRPB, Draft Report, 1990.

117 R. H. Johnson, Memo to BRB P&I Committee on 'Blackfriars Station Development', 4 July 1980, BRB 336-3-95; D. A. Barber (Director, Development, BRB), Memo to BRPB on 'Euston Square Development', 10 February 1981, BRB 336-3-54 Pt. 2; Robert Dashwood, cit. in *Estate Times*, 11 April 1980. The unsuccessful developer was Peachey Property Corporation.

118 Cf. BRB Minutes, 1 May 1986; BRB, *R&A 1985/6*, p. 26, *1987–8*, pp. 29–30, *1988–9*, p. 28; Biddle, *Railway Surveyors*, p. 218; Interview with Mayfield, 1999.

119 Memo to P&I Committee, 19 July 1982, BRB 336-2-101 Pt. 3; Simpson and Green, Memo to Investment Committee, 26 March 1986, Pt. 4.

120 Simpson and Kirby, Memo to Investment Committee, 6 December 1983, Investment Committee Minutes, 9 January 1984.

121 Derek Fowler, Memo on 'Liverpool Street/Broad Street Redevelopment', 19 June 1984, BRB Minutes, 5 July and 6 September 1984 and cf. Godfrey Bradman (Rosehaugh plc)–Reid, 10 May 1983, Chief Executive's files, X92-1.

122 Investment Committee Minutes, 7 January 1985; A. J. Dorman (Project Director, Property Development), Memo, 9 March 1983, BRPB Minutes, 17 March 1993; Nick Derbyshire, *Liverpool Street: A Station for the Twenty-First Century* (Cambridge, 1991), p. 11. Dorman's Memo estimated BRB income at £415.4m. (including capital payments on Phases 1–5 of £295.7m., and capital plus the capital value of rents on Phases 6–14 of £119.7m.), the cost of the station and railway works at £152.0m., and the net surplus at £263.4m.

123 The first Travellers Fare Board consisted of Geoffrey Myers (Chairman), Leith, Currie, and Philip Sellers. BRB Travellers Fare Board Minutes, 21 January 1982.

124 BRB, *R&A 1982–87/8*. It should be noted that real costs were underestimated, since Travellers Fare paid less than commercial rents to BRB: see Chairman's Group Minutes, 11 August 1988.

125 Ridley–Reid, 17 November 1983, BRB 29-12-6; BRB Minutes, 1 August and 5 September 1985, 9 January 1986.

126 BRB Minutes, 7 August 1986; J. J. O'Brien, Memo on 'Competition Policy: Travellers Fare', 3 October 1986, BRB Minutes, 6 November 1986; O'Brien, Memo on 'Travellers Fare: Competitive Tendering', 7 January 1988, BRB Minutes, 7 January; O'Brien, Confidential Memo on 'Travellers Fare Ltd: Options for Sale', 2 June 1988, BRB Minutes, 2 June 1988.

127 BRB Minutes, 8 September, 3 November, and 1 December 1988. There were 36 enquiries, but only four bids, of which only two—an MBO, and a Compass/Wagon Lits joint venture—made specific offers.

128 BRB, *R&A 1979–86/7*; Arthur Andersen & Co., 'British Transport Advertising Limited: Strategy Report on Corporate, Financial and Marketing Operations', August 1985, vol. II, p. 15, BRB GCA 512-2.

129 Enquiries from Poster Media and Multimark: S. C. Whiteley (DTp)–Lascelles (General Secretary, BRB), 7 October 1981, BRB 29-12-11.

130 Howell–Parker, 9 December 1982, and reply, 15 December 1982, BRB 29-12-11; BRB Minutes, 6 October 1983; Derek Fowler–Gordon Sykes (Finance Dir., BTA), 13 March 1985, Fowler's Papers, Sec Box 2256. Mills & Allen was the would-be purchaser in 1982–3.

131 Derek Fowler, Confidential Memos on 'Competition Policy: British Transport Advertising', 28 August 1985, 3 January 1986, BRB Minutes, 5 September 1985, 9 January 1986; Reid–John Moore (SoS, DTp), 5 June 1986, Mitchell–Reid, 23 June 1986, BRB 20-100-7 Pt. 1; Vickers and Yarrow, *Privatization*, pp. 382–3. Delay was also caused by the Board's anxiety to safeguard the position of the staff in the event of a sale, which necessitated the formation of another entity, BTA Division, in 1986.

132 Derek Fowler, Confidential Memos on 'Competition Policy: British Transport Advertising', 31 October 1986, 28 April and 27 July 1987, BRB Minutes, 6 November 1986, 4 June and 6 August 1987, and see also Minutes, 7 August 1986, 8 January, 5 March, and 7 May 1987.

133 Chairman's Group Minutes, 10 September 1987; Welsby, Confidential Memo on 'Disposal of Vale of Rheidol Railway', 4 August 1988, BRB Minutes, 4 August 1988; M. V. Casey (Project Director, Privatisation), Memo, 3 April 1989, Sharpe Pritchard (Solicitors)–Solicitors Department, BRB, 21 March 1990, BRB GCA S16-1 Pt. 5.

134 Kirby, Memos on 'Privatisation of Gold Star Holidays', 8 December 1988, 23 March 1989, Chairman's Group Minutes, 14 July and 8 December 1988, 23 March 1989; BRB Minutes, 9 March and 8 June 1989. In addition, there remained Meldon Quarry, which provided aggregates for ballast, etc. The SoS was keen to dispose of it: see Fowler–Mitchell, 19 January 1987, Fowler's Papers, Sec Box 2255. However, it was not sold until March 1994, when ECC Construction Materials acquired it for £5m.: Christopher Campbell (Board Member, BRB), Memo on 'Privatisation Report for March 1994', n.d., BRB Minutes, 14 April 1994.

135 Estimate based on net property proceeds (£1,077m.), plus net proceeds from BTH, Sealink, Travellers Fare and, BTA (£96m.), less losses on engineering disposals (£89m.).

136 Interviews with Derek Fowler, 1990, Alan Nichols, 29 November 1999.

137 Cf. J. B. Smith (Group Accountant, BRB)–Welsby, 27 October 1987, Welsby's Papers, Sec Box 2295.

138 This included £1.6m. in leasing liabilities, £619,000 for site separation, and £159,000 in merchant bank fees; the total of £7.245m. was treated as an extraordinary item in the Board's accounts, BRB, *R&A 1987/8*, p. 49, n. 13; John Cook (for John Horton, GCA, BRB)–Financial Accountant, Railways, 14 April 1988, Welsby's Papers, Sec Box 2309.

139 John Cook–Financial Accountant, Railways, 18 April 1988, ibid.; BRB, *R&A 1988/ 9*, p. 43.

140 Welsby, Memo, 4 August 1988, cit.; Welsby–Neil Howard (OVAL (424) [the MBO]), 22 September 1988, Welsby–J. R. Coates (Under-Secretary, Railways, DTp), 12 September 1988, and other material in Welsby's Papers, Sec Box 2309; papers in BRB 381-6-1, and BRB GCA S16-1. esp. J. M. Greenwood (Management Audits Group, BRB)–J. A. Horton (Group Chief Accountant, BRB), 27 July 1990; *Private Eye*, 14 October 1988.

141 Prideaux (Director, InterCity), Memo on 'InterCity On Board Services Report', 30 June 1988, BRB Minutes, 7 July 1988; Chairman's Group Minutes, 11 and 18 August, 1 September, 5 October, and 8 December 1988. As a result of the debacle heads rolled in InterCity: see Prideaux, 'On Board Services Strategy Review', April 1989, BRB; *Modern Railways*, July 1990, p. 346.

Chapter 8

1 Jenkins resigned on taking the post of Editor of *The Times* (1990–2).

2 See BRB 48-2-200 Pt. 3; *Who's Who*.

3 Allen was appointed for his Welsh connections: see Allen Bailey (DTp)–Reid, 16 November 1990, P. D. Allen file, BRB 48-2-73.

4 BRB 48-2-63, 67, 68, and BRB Secretary's Papers, Box 2052. The differential narrowed a little in April 1991 when Welsby's salary was increased to £82,000 and those of Edmonds and Rayner were increased to £69,500. Jerram was found by the headhunters, Odgers, who also produced other candidates, notably Michael Sheasby of Squibb, Eddie Weiss (Racal Chubb), Barrie Stevenson (DRG), Brian Currie (Arthur Andersen), Peter Edwards (Ernst & Young), and Gordon Dunlop of BA (ex-CU).

5 Thatcher, *Downing Street Years*, pp. 757–8, 831–2, 856–7, 861; Anthony Seldon, *Major: A Political Life* (1997), pp. 129ff.; John Major, *The Autobiography* (1999).

6 BRB Minutes, 13 October 1988; BRB Management Brief, 25 November 1988; BRB Policy Unit, briefing for Bob Reid (II) on 'Privatisation: Position Report', 5 February 1990, BRB Secretary's Papers; *Daily Telegraph*, 18 August 1989, p.14; Cecil Parkinson, *Right at the Centre: an autobiography* (1992), pp. 51–4, 272–5, 282–4. Ministry officials claimed that Parkinson's attention-span was often limited: interview with Nichols, 1999.

7 BRB Minutes, 15 February 1990. Parkinson has recalled that he was an enthusiastic supporter of rail privatisation, but had been asked by Thatcher to 'play down the possibility': Parkinson, *Right at the Centre*, p. 287.

8 C. J. F. Brown (Director, BRB Policy Unit)–Fowler and Welsby, 12 September 1990, BRB Secretary's Papers, Box 2053; Thatcher, *Downing Street Years*, pp. 686–7; Parkinson, *Right at the Centre*, p. 288.

9 Rifkind–Reid (II), 13 May 1991, BRB Secretary's Papers, Box 2053; Major, *Autobiography*, p. 248.

10 EC Directive on the Development of the Community's Railways, 91/440/EC, 29 July 1991, and see also Rifkind–Reid (II), 9 October 1991, Secretary's Papers, Box 2049, and Welsby–R. J. Coleman (Director-General for Transport, EC), 29 November 1991, BRB Policy Unit file, AN170/26, PRO.

11 J. Palmer, Memo on 'Privatisation and Access Liberalisation', 9 January 1992, BRB Minutes, 9 January 1992; *Independent on Sunday*, 19 January 1992, p. 12.

12 Conservative Party, *The Best Future for Britain* (March 1992), pp. 35–6; MacGregor–Reid (II), 16 April 1992, Sec Box 2006.

13 On the latter cf. Chris Green (Director NSE)–Myers, Kirby, and Welsby, 24 August 1987, Welsby's Papers, Sec Box 2311.

14 Nigel Pain, 'The UK Economy', *National Institute of Economic Research*, No. 144 (May 1993), p. 12; Christopher Dow, *Major Recessions: Britain and the World, 1920–1995* (Oxford, 1998), pp. 26, 353.

15 BRB, *R&A 1988/9–93/4*. See Appendix D, Table D.1 and D.2.

16 BRB Minutes, 10 June 1993. From 1975 all infrastructure investment had been deleted from BRB's balance sheet, and 'replacement' investment was charged to operating expenditure. The decision to charge all investment to capital account was part of more general pressure by the DTp to introduce modified historic cost accounting, following the recommendations of the Byatt report: see Kirby and Fowler, Memo on 'Objectives for 1992/93', 29 June 1989, Appendix A, BRB Minutes, 6 July 1989; James Jerram,

Memo on 'The Accounting Basis of the Board's Published Accounts', n.d., BRB Minutes, 7 November 1991; *Accounting for Economic Costs and Changing Prices. A Report to HM Treasury by an Advisory Group (Chairman: Ian Byatt)*, Vol. I (1986), pp. 5–6, 12–13.

17 BRB Minutes, 10 June 1993, 9 June 1994; Accounting Standards Board, 'Financial Reporting Standard No 3: Reporting Financial Performance', December 1993. I am grateful to Jo Anson for this reference.

18 Ian Phillips (Director of Finance and Planning), Memo on 'Revenue Budget 1988/9', 26 February 1988, BRB Minutes, 3 March 1988; Derek Fowler, Memo on 'Group Financial Report', 3 March 1989, BRB Minutes, 9 March 1989; MMC, *Provincial*, 1989, paras. 4.8–9. Property sales were ring-fenced at £150 m., ERDF grants at £5 m. Income above these figures would produce a pro rata decrease in the EFL.

19 Derek Fowler, Memos on 'Group Financial Report', 1 December 1989 and 5 January 1990, BRB Minutes, 7 December 1989 and 11 January 1990; BRB, *R&A 1989/90*, p. 11.

20 Reid (II)–Parkinson, 13 July 1990, and reply, 27 July 1990, Reid II's papers, BRB.

21 Welsby–Osmotherly (Dep. Sec., Public Transport & Research, DTp), 4 January 1990 [*sic*: actually 1991], Welsby's Papers, Sec Box 2125; BRB, *R&A 1990/1*, p. 4.

22 BRB Minutes, 10 January, 14 February, and 4 April 1991; Stephen K. Reeves (DTp)–David Allen (Director, Finance, BRB), 27 March 1991, enclosing DTp, Note on 'British Rail's Financial Problems', 27 March 1991, Welsby's Papers, Sec Box 2125.

23 Reid (II)–Rifkind, 24 May 1991, Reid II's Papers, BRB. The letter was sent on Welsby's headed paper.

24 Rifkind–Reid (II), 3 and 24 June 1991, Reid (II)–Rifkind, 19 June 1991, Reid II's papers, BRB.

25 Osmotherly–Welsby, 21 November 1991 and reply, 2 December 1991, Welsby's Papers, Sec Box 2125.

26 Parkinson–Reid (I), 19 December 1989, reproduced in BRB, *R&A 1989/90*, p. 31.

27 J. R. Coates (DTp)–Welsby, 3 January 1990, BRB OfQ Box 65.

28 BRB Minutes, 6 April 1989; Chairman's Group Minutes, 4 May, 30 November, and 14 December 1989; Fowler and Kirby, Memo on 'Objectives for 1992/3', 29 June 1989, BRB Minutes, 6 July and 7 December 1989.

29 Cf. Chairman's Group Minutes, 30 November 1989, BRB Minutes, 7 December 1989.

30 BRB Minutes, 6 July 1989; Jerram, Memo, 1991, cit.

31 Alan J. Nichols (Director, Financial Planning, BRB)–Reid (II), 19 March 1993, MacGregor–Reid (II), draft letter, enclosed in Jane C. Cotton (DTp)–Nichols, 19 March 1993, BRB Minutes, 1 April 1993.

32 BRB, *Towards a Commuter's Charter* (December 1979), appendix; BRB, *The Commuters Charter* (June 1981); BRB Minutes, 6 December 1979, *Modern Railways*, January 1980, p. 54; MMC, *London and SouthEast*, October 1980, paras. 4.10, 4.104–17. Punctuality was defined as arrival within 5 minutes of the booked time. The MMC pointed out that current performance in L&SE was well short of this target, asked for explanations of performance to be made available to the regional Transport Users Consultative Committees (TUCCs), and recommended the monitoring of carriage cleaning. In addition, BRB's 'Policy Options for London & SouthEast Rail Services' of February 1981 highlighted the trade-off between service quality and fare levels. The document was considered by the Commons Transport Committee Report on Transport in London of July 1982. BRB 21-8-32 Pt. 1; Interview with Richard

Edgley, 7 August 2000; *HC Transport Committee Fifth Report on Transportation in London*, 6 July 1982, P.P. 1981–2, xix, HC127.

33 Data on punctuality (percentage of trains arriving within 5 mins of the booked time) for October 1976–7 were revealed in CTCC, *Annual Report for the Year ended 31 December, 1977* (1978), p. 13, and for the three years 1976–8 in *Annual Report 1978* (1979), pp. 12–13. Percentages of trains cancelled first appeared for the years 1978 and 1979 in *Annual Report 1979* (1980), p. 11. For information disclosure after 1981 see CTCC, *Annual Report 1981*, p. 8, *1982*, p. 10, *1983*, pp. 9–10. On DTp interest see Howell–Parker, 10 November 1981, BRB Policy Unit's files on Commuter's Charter, AN170/293, PRO.

34 Ridley–Reid (I), 24 July 1984, reproduced in MMC, *Network SouthEast*, July 1987, Appendix 3.4; BRB, *Code of Practice and Guide to Customer Service* (July 1985); BRB, *Corporate Plan 1984* (October 1984), pp. 14, 16, and *Corporate Plan 1985* (November 1985), pp. 16–17, 27–8. A 90% punctuality objective for L&SE, referred to in the Ridley–Reid letter of July 1984, became an 87.5% objective in the 1984 Corporate Plan. The Code of Practice 'expected' 85% punctuality for InterCity, 90% for other services: *Code*, p. 10.

35 Moore–Reid (I), 21 October 1986, reproduced in MMC, *Network SouthEast*, July 1987, Appendix 3.5, and see paras. 14.1–83 on 'quality of service'.

36 Richard Allan (Director, Policy Unit, BRB), Memo on 'Willingness to Pay for Quality', 28 March 1990, BRB Policy Unit files, AN170/10, PRO.

37 On some of the interpretative problems see MMC, *Network SouthEast*, 1987, paras. 14.17–19, 14.24–6, and MMC, *Provincial*, February 1989, paras. 12.2, 12.10–15, 12.36ff. Interest in train punctuality is of very long vintage: cf. 'Time-Keeping of Southern Railway Trains', *Railway Gazette*, 21 October 1927, p. 477. On the manipulation of train schedules to improve time keeping see Peter Curwen, 'The Citizen's Charter and British Rail', in J. A. Chandler (ed.), *The Citizen's Charter* (Aldershot, 1996), p. 132.

38 CTCC, *Annual Report 1987/8*, pp. 7, 21; Alan Bailey (DTp)–Reid (I), 30 October 1986, Myers's Papers, Sec Box 2240.

39 The dispute between British Rail and the CTCC was resolved after the retirement of the latter's long-serving Secretary Len Dumelow in December 1986, though subsequently more limited information was supplied. CTCC, *Annual Report 1986/7*, pp. 6–8; *1987/8*, p. 21; see Bailey–Reid (I), 20 June and 30 October 1986, Reid–David Mitchell (Minister of State, DTp), 14 August 1986, Myers's Papers, Box 2240; 'Railway Monthly Commentary—June', BRB Minutes, 5 June 1986; MMC, *Network SouthEast*, 1987, para. 14.56.

40 Cabinet Office, *The Citizen's Charter: Raising the Standard*, July 1991, pp. 17, 48, P.P. 1990–1, lv, Cm. 1599. There is a considerable literature on the Charter and the political environment in which it was conceived. See, for example, Seldon, *Major*; Major, *Autobiography*, pp. 246ff.; Sarah Hogg and Jonathan Hill, *Too Close to Call: Power and Politics—John Major in No. 10* (1995), pp. 93ff; and for academic assessments, Ian Bynoe, *Beyond the Citizen's Charter: New Directions for Social Rights* (Institute for Public Policy Research, 1996); Chandler (ed.), *Citizen's Charter*; B. Doern, 'The UK Citizen's Charter: Origins and Implementation in Three Agencies', *Policy and Politics*, 21(1) (1993), 17–30; Keith Faulks, *Citizenship in Modern Britain* (Edinburgh, 1998), Ian Kirkpatrick and Miguel Martinez Lucio (eds.), *The Politics of*

Quality in the Public Sector: the Management of Change (1995); and Chris Willett (ed.), *Public Sector Reform and the Citizen's Charter* (1996).

41 Cf. Major, *Autobiography*, p. 255, Hogg and Hill, *Too Close to Call*, pp. 98–100.

42 For CTCC lobbying on British Rail's conditions of carriage see CTCC, *Annual Report 1981*, p. 4; *Modern Railways*, February 1982, p. 56. New versions of BRB's *Conditions of Carriage of Passengers and their Luggage* had already appeared in January 1983 and June 1986: see BRB Passenger Marketing Services [PMS] Box PMS/F/27.

43 Welsby–Brian Hilton (Director, Citizen's Charter Unit), 27 September 1991, enclosing 'The Citizen's Charter: BR's Response', BRB 95-2-105.

44 Chris Austin (Parliamentary Affairs Manager, BRB)–Reid (II), 1 July 1991, Reid (II)'s Papers, Sec Box 2212.

45 Andrew Turnbull (PM's PPS)–Reid (II), 16 May 1991, BRB Secretary's Papers, Box 2006. Discussions were 'keen and enthusiastic': Major, *Autobiography*, p. 254.

46 Major–Reid (II), 25 February, 22 March, and 9 April 1991, BRB 95-2-105; Board Exec. Minutes, 23 May, 13 June 1991; Welsby, Memo on '"Fair Deal" Leaflet for Customers and Opinion Formers', n.d., Board Exec. Minutes, 27 June 1991; BRB Minutes, 4 July and 1 August 1991.

47 The DTp was one of the departments 'which needed to be led several times to the fence before being ready to jump . . . The Department of Transport seemed to be in thrall to the most blinkered elements within BR management . . . It recoiled from such revolutionary ideas as compensating passengers for poor performance, ensuring that staff could be identified, setting service standards, and giving passengers information on performance line by line': Major, *Autobiography*, p. 255. Cf. also Hogg and Hill, *Too Close to Call*, pp. 98–100.

48 Welsby–Hilton, 27 September 1991, cit.

49 Seldon, *Major*, pp. 190, 360; Hogg and Hill, *Too Close to Call*, pp. 93, 96. 'The schizophrenia of the Treasury when presented with a scheme to improve public services was wonderful to behold': Major, *Autobiography*, p. 253.

50 Board Exec. Minutes, 21 November 1991, BRB Minutes, 5 December 1991, 9 January, 13 February, and 5 March 1992. The Board was challenged by the commitment in the White Paper to produce the Charter 'in the autumn' and the revised conditions of carriage in November 1991. The latter did not appear until May 1993: BRB Minutes, 6 May 1993. There were lengthy negotiations with William Waldegrave, the Minister of Public Service and Science, and the Citizen's Charter Unit over the nature of the Charter and the linkage with revised conditions of carriage, difficulties with the PTEs, who wished to be excluded from the scheme, and with London Transport over Travelcards, and a number of consultation exercises, not least with the passenger businesses and the Central Transport Consultative Committee (CTCC). *Citizen's Charter*, p. 17; Welsby–Hilton, 27 September 1991, Hilton–Welsby, 2 October 1991, BRB 95-2-105; Waldegrave–Reid (II), 9 September 1992 and reply, 17 September 1992, BRB 95-1-20 Pt. 3; BRB Minutes, 5 November and 3 December 1992.

51 BRB, *The British Rail Passenger's Charter* (March 1992), esp. pp. 4–5, 12–15. Discounts of up to 10% (5% for punctuality, 5% for reliability) were promised to holders of monthly or longer-period season tickets, if standards were not met. British Rail was the first public service to provide refunds under a charter: Andrew Pendleton, 'The Emergence and Use of Quality in British Rail', in Kirkpatrick and Martinez Lucio, *The Politics of Quality*, pp. 212, 216.

52 University of Sheffield Statistical Services Unit, 'Survey of British Rail Arrival Times for the Passenger's Charter Audit', 1993 (March 1994) and 1994 (March 1995), BRB PBA Box 154, and correspondence files on 'Passenger's Charter Audit', 1992–6, BRB PBA Box 152. Both surveys concluded that 'there are consistent inaccuracies in recording by BR throughout the system': 1993, p. 13, and 1994, p. 15; see also *Independent on Sunday*, 19 June 1994, p. 1.

53 Cf. data in BRB 95-2-105 and Board Exec. Minutes, 26 November 1992, BRB Minutes, 3 December 1992.

54 Waldegrave, reported in BRB Minutes, 3 December 1992; Major, *Autobiography*, pp. 253–4, 259; BRB Press Release, 23 December 1992. Francis Maude, Major's initial choice for the post, lost his seat in the 1992 election.

55 Andrew Jukes (Director of Business Review, BRB)–Welsby, 28 May 1993; E. V. Gore (Group Performance Adviser, BRB)–Martin Shrubsole (Director, Privatisation Studies, BRB) and David Burton (Director, Quality & Safety, BRB), 27 May 1994, and Note on 'Charter Payments, 1992/93–1995/96', n.d., BRB PBA File on 'Charter Costs', PBA 126. Payments in 1994/5 amounted to £3.5 m., £3.3 m. of which was compensation by voucher.

56 Reid (II)–MacGregor, 22 April 1994, and reply, 9 May 1994, Welsby's Papers, Sec Box 2124; BRB Minutes, 4 November 1993.

57 BRB Minutes, 5 March and 7 May 1992, *Daily Mail*, 5 March 1992, p. 1, *Financial Times*, 5 March 1992, p. 1, *Guardian*, 5 March 1992, p. 16. Particular offence was caused to BR by the *Daily Mail* headline 'BR Cheat on Rail Charter'. See draft letter to Press Complaints Commission, March 1992, BRB 95-2-105. John Prescott apparently called the Charter a 'con trick': *Financial Times*, cit. On the court actions, see *The Times*, 21 December 1990, 1 August and 17 October 1991; on Commons questions see, for example, Simon Burns, *Parl. Deb. (Commons)*, 6th ser. (Session 1990–1), vol. 185, 11 February 1991, cols. 596–7, (Session 1991–2), vol. 201, 13 January 1992, col. 660, vol. 203, 10 February 1992, cols. 644–5.

58 Thirtieth out of 31: *Financial Times*, 26 August 1993, p. 15, cit. in Curwen, 'Citizen's Charter and British Rail', in Chandler, *Citizen's Charter*, p. 137.

59 Curwen, pp. 134–6; CTCC, *Annual Report 1991/2*, pp. 4, 16, 27.

60 The lines were Thameslink (89.5%), Kent Link (85.4%), North London (88.9%), Solent & Wessex (88.1%), Thames (86.4%), Sussex Coast (86.0%), and Kent Coast (83.1%), data for 52 weeks to 29 April 1994, in BRB 95-2-105.

61 The author's experience in travelling from Coventry to London on the evening of 7 February 1991 is still vivid. The locomotive-hauled trains were abandoned, and the efforts of a Class 321 EMU to make the trip at 7 p.m. were frustrated by frozen doors, necessitating long stops at each station. The driver abandoned the train at Bletchley; eventually, another train arrived. However, this encountered frozen points just outside Euston, and remained stationary from midnight to 2 a.m., at which point another train was positioned on an adjoining track, and the passengers were asked to jump from the driver's cab to the driver's cab of the other train.

62 In fact, Worrall was reported thus by the *Evening Standard*, 11 February 1991, p. 1: 'We are having particular problems on this occasion with the type of snow, which is very dry and powdery'. Nevertheless, 'the wrong kind of snow' was the phrase widely reported: cf. *Daily Mail*, 12 February 1991, p. 9, *Sun*, 12 February 1991, p. 2, *Guardian*, 13 February 1991, p. 6, *Rail*, 20 February–5 March 1991, pp. 5–6; Reid (II), unpub-

lished memoir of his period as chairman, BRB. My thanks to Sir Bob for allowing me access to his Mss.

63 BRB Minutes, 14 February 1991.

64 Larry Shore (Director, Traction & Rolling Stock, Network SouthEast), Report on 'Effects of Extreme Weather Conditions on NSE MU Fleet, February 1991', Watson's Papers, Sec Box 2370; 'Report on Railway Response to Snow Conditions Network SouthEast Area 6–13 February 1991: Executive Summary', March 1991, Watson's Papers, Box 2361; Board Exec. Minutes, 28 February 1991; Interview with Dr Peter Watson, 21 June 2000. It should be noted that three-quarters of the traction motor damage occurred with older vehicles. On parliamentary exchanges see *Parl. Deb. (Commons)*, 6th ser. (Session 1990–1), vol. 185, Tony Banks, Malcolm Rifkind, 11 February 1991, cols. 597, 600; Michael Jopling, vol. 187, 11 March 1991, cols. 651–2.

65 BRB Minutes, 7 March and 4 April 1991; Roger Freeman (Minister for Public Transport)–Reid (II), 19 March 1991, Watson's Papers, Box 2370. Freeman, responding to BRB's plans for a press conference on its findings, pointed out: 'it is vitally important that BR should not be seen to be bidding publicly for additional funds ... my view is that we should ask you to avoid volunteering estimates and remove the figures from the Executive Summary'.

66 Cf. *The Times*, 12 November 1980, p. 12; *Guardian*, 26 October 1987, p. 4.

67 Board Exec. Minutes, 14 November 1991; BRB Minutes, 5 December 1991; RMG Minutes, 17 December 1991; *Rail*, 13–26 November 1991, p. 6.

68 As *The Times* noted, 'The Swedish scrubber works with less than Scandinavian efficiency', *The Times*, 19 October 1992, p. 7. See also BRB Minutes, 5 March and 16 July 1992; Trewin–Reid (II) et al., 21 September 1992, enclosing Adrian Shooter (Director of Engineering Performance, BRB), Memo on 'Initiative to Combat Leaf Fall Problems', n.d. Shooter pointed out that there were 75,000 acres of lineside vegetation, an area three times the size of Liverpool. Beech, sycamore, and maple trees provided significant problems. On environmental concern see Reid (II), Memoir, cit.; *The Times*, 29 December 1990, p. 16, *Daily Telegraph*, 8 April 1992, p. 10.

69 Cf. contemporary problems with snow in France, the Netherlands, and Germany reported in *La Vie Du Rail*, 21–7 February 1991, and *Voies Ferrées*, 1991, enclosed in David Maidment (Safety Systems Manager, BRB)–Watson, 7 March 1991, and DTp, *Report of the Review of Arrangements for Dealing with Severe Winter Weather (1990/1991)*, May 1991, Watson's Papers, Box 2361.

70 Prideaux (MD, InterCity), Report on 'InterCity Performance', BRB Minutes, 5 December 1991 (John Prideaux, and Dr Peter Watson); Welsby's Report, BRB Minutes, 1 October 1992.

71 On driver shortages see Network SouthEast Quality Digest, Issue 2, October 1989, BRB Minutes, 11 October 1989; Trevor Toolan, Memo on 'Personnel Objectives', n.d., BRB Minutes, 22 November 1989; Chief Executive's Reports to BRB, December 1989–November 1991.

72 BRB, *R&A 1990/1*, p. 12; Vincent and Green, *InterCity Story*, pp. 38–43; BRB, 'InterCity Strategy Review', November 1987; InterCity, 'West Coast Main Line Strategy Review', December 1989, 'InterCity Strategy', August 1991, and 'InterCity West Coast Main Line Resignalling Strategic Appraisal', February 1992, BRB.

73 BRB, *R&A 1990/1*, p. 14, *1991/2*, p. 14; Mark Lawrence, *Network SouthEast: From Sectorisation to Privatisation* (Sparkford, 1994). John Nelson was Director, NSE, 1992–4.

74 BRB, *R&A 1990/1*, p. 16, *1991/2*, p. 16, *1992/3*, pp. 18–19, *1993/4*, pp. 20–1.

75 Interview with Ivor Warburton, 18 January 2000.

76 Cf. O'Brien, Memo on 'Passenger Pricing 1986', July 1985, BRB Special Meeting Minutes, 30 July 1985; Barry S. Doe, 'BR Fares: the Evolution of Selective Pricing', *Modern Railways*, September 1986, p. 484.

77 Reid (II)–Parkinson, 24 August 1990, Welsby's Papers, Sec Box 2125; Passenger Business Board, Memo on 'Passenger Business Proposals for the January 1991 Fares Increase', n.d., BRB Minutes, 6 September 1990; Welsby, Confidential Memo on 'Proposed Passenger Fares Increase 5 January 1992', n.d., BRB Minutes, 5 September 1991.

78 BRB, Selective Prices Manual No. 22, January 1979, National Fares Manual No. 56, 2 January 1994, AN130/44, 285, PRO. Not all standard fares became more expensive: the Inverness–London single fare increased by only 135%, 1979–94.

79 For example, the cheapest London–Winchester return fare was 238% higher in 1994 than in 1979, while the London–Glasgow Apex (1994) was only 106% higher than the 1979 Day Return: ibid.

80 Conversation with Peter Parker, 19 April 2000. For evidence of informal pressure see BRB Minutes, 4 October 1979, 3 September 1981.

81 Cf. O'Brien, Memo, July 1985, cit.; BRB Minutes, 1 August 1985.

82 British Rail had intended to increase fares by 12.3% for InterCity, 11.6% for L&SE, and 11.0% for Provincial, based on an estimated inflation rate of 8.5% for 1983. In October 1982 intervention by DTp officials revealed that the level of inflation forecast by the Treasury was 'significantly lower' than the BR estimate, and that a double-figure price increase 'would be considerably out of step with present Governmental views'. A deal was struck in which BR agreement to a lower increase was accompanied by the government's agreement to 'transitional funding' support for the PSO. See G. Myers, Confidential Memo on 'Passenger Pricing, 1982', July 1982, BRB Minutes, 5 August and 2 September 1982; G. Myers and P. E. Sellers, Confidential Memo on 'Passenger Fares Increase', 6 October 1982, BRB Minutes, 7 October 1982; *Sunday Telegraph*, 17 October 1982.

83 BRB Minutes, 2 November 1989.

84 Reid–Parkinson, 24 August 1990, cit.; Passenger Business Board, Memo, BRB Minutes, 6 September 1990, cit.

85 BRB Minutes, 7 November 1991; Chris Green (Chairman, Passenger Business Executive), Memo on 'January 1993 Pricing Proposals', September 1992, BRB Minutes, 10 September 1992; BRB Minutes, 19 August, 9 September, 7 October, and 4 November 1993; Trewin–Reid (II) et al., 13 October 1993, Reid (II)–Dr Brian Mawhinney (SoS, DTp), 12 September 1994, BRB Secretary's Papers, Box 2017.

86 Philip S. Bagwell, *The Transport Crisis in Britain* (Nottingham, 1996), pp. 6–9; *Railway Gazette International*, February 1990, p. 77; Interview with Ivor Warburton, 18 January 2000.

87 Cf. BRB Passenger Sales Policy Control Group Minutes, 23 March 1982; Script for Presentations by Ivor Warburton on 'BR—Fares', 19 September 1984, BRB PMS P74/123/3 Pad 3, PMS Box PMS/F/37; BRB Press Releases, 20 October 1980, 22 February

and 22 July 1982, 26 October 1983, 17 March and 14 October 1987, 7 April and 25 October 1988, 16 October 1989, 30 August 1990; Interview with David Rayner, 15 February 2000.

88 BRB Minutes, 4 June and 1 October 1992; BRG Minutes, 1 June and 17 November 1992; InterCity Marketing Initiatives Newsletter, Spring 1993, BRB TRMC Box 8.

89 Jukes, Memo on 'Apex Fares and the Boots Promotion', n.d., InterCity BRG Minutes, 11 May 1993.

90 BRB Minutes, 2 July 1981; Wallace, *Single or Return?*, pp. 460–1; Bagwell, *End of the Line?*, pp. 147–59. On the Law Lords ruling on the October 1981 fare cut, its aftermath, and the political background to the policy see Paul E. Garbutt, *London Transport and the Politicians* (Shepperton, 1985), pp. 71ff.; John Carvel, *Citizen Ken* (1984), pp. 115ff.; Ken Livingstone, *If Voting Changed Anything, They'd Abolish It* (1987), pp. 190ff.

91 Bagwell, *End of the Line?*, p. 151; Livingstone, *Voting*, pp. 191–2.

92 David Rayner (Chief Passenger Marketing Manager), Memo on 'Effect of House of Lords Judgement re G.L.C. "Fares Fair" Policy', 27 January 1982, BRB PMS P104/2, Box PMS/F/23.

93 Ridley–Reid (I), 24 July 1984, cit.; MMC, *Network SouthEast*, 1987, para. 11.2.

94 Bagwell, *End of the Line?*, pp. 147–8. The LT Travelcard and the BRB Capitalcard merged as Travelcard on 8 January 1989: BRB Press Release, 28 October 1988.

95 Bus deregulation and LRT's dissatisfaction with the revenue-apportionment method for Travelcard outside the Greater London boundary provided further pressures. See 'Notes of a Meeting held on 27 April [1990] at 55 Broadway to discuss Travelcard', 14 May 1990; Edward Osmotherley (Dep. Sec, DTp)–David Bayliss (Director of Planning, LRT), 2 May 1990, and Osmotherley–Welsby, 12 July 1990, enclosing Travelcard Working Group, 'Travelcard Review', July 1990, Welsby–Reid (II), 24 July 1990, BRB Secretary's Papers, Box 2125.

96 CTCC, *Annual Report 1981*, p. 11, *1982*, p. 11, *1984/5*, p. 12; *Sunday Times*, 29 November 1981; *Woman*, March 1984; BRB Passenger Marketing Dept., Memo on 'BR Fares Structure: Complexities', 7 September 1983, BRB PMS P74/122 Pt. 12, Box PMS/F/33; Interview with Henry Sanderson, 7 September 1998. Sometimes, complaints worked in the opposite direction. There was quite an outcry when BRB abandoned its 1st Class Day Returns in May 1983.

97 Cyril Bleasdale (Director, InterCity), Memo on 'InterCity Price Structure', 13 February 1984, Marketing Policy Group Minutes, 14 February 1984; O'Brien, Confidential Memo on 'Fares Structure', March 1984, BRB Minutes, 5 April and 7 June 1984; Railcard discounts were also extended and simplified. The expectation was to improve turnover by £18 m. The consultants Transecon International estimated the revenue benefit to be £27.5 m. p.a. by the end of 1986/7: Report on 'The Impact of the New Fare Structure', December 1985, BRB PMS Box PMS/F/41.

98 BRB Public Affairs brief on 'Two-Tier Fare Structure: Norwich Experiment', 7 September 1982, PA File on 'Fares L', PA Box 150; BRB, 'The New Range of Fares from 12 May 1985', in BRB 99-2-1 Pt. 10; J. D. Usher (Passenger Fares Officer, BRB), Memo to BRB Passenger Committee on 'Norwich Fares Experiment: Review', 24 August 1983, BRB PMS P74/122 Pad 12 Box PMS/F/33; Doe, 'BR Fares', p. 484. The Norwich scheme was not an immediate success financially, with divisional revenue falling by 2%, 1982–3: BRB Passenger Pricing Group Minutes, 23 August 1983.

99 Cf. InterCity Marketing Initiatives Newsletter, Spring 1993, cit.; Provincial's marketing tended to be fragmented: see MMC, *Provincial*, February 1989, paras. 8.7ff.

100 InterCity's average 9.3% increase in Jan. 1986 included 7.1% for season tickets in the NSE area, and at least 10.6% for long-distance season tickets. O'Brien, Memo, July 1985, cit.; O'Brien, Confidential Memo on 'Passenger Pricing 1986', 2 October 1985, BRB Minutes, 3 October 1985.

101 BRB InterCity, InterCity Strategy Review, November 1987, pp. 30, 76–7; BRB Minutes, 23 November 1987; O'Brien, Memo On 'Long Distance Season Ticket Pricing', 25 March 1988, BRB Minutes, 31 March 1988.

102 Kirby, Memo on 'Passenger Pricing', 3 August 1988, BRB Minutes, 4 August 1988; C. Gore (Marketing Planning Manager, PMS)–Sector Directors, 13 October 1988, BRB 99-2-1 Pt. 10. There was an even higher increase of 23.8% for London–Gatwick (Express) season tickets. On consumer disquiet about the price rises (although outside its statutory remit) see CTCC, *Annual Report 1988–9*, pp. 5, 14–15.

103 Kirby, Memo on 'Passenger Pricing', n.d., BRB Minutes, 12 October 1989.

104 Cf. Kirby–Prideaux, 22 November 1989, Kirby's Papers, Sec Box 2148.

105 Jukes, Memo on 'Apex Fares', cit. See also BRB InterCity, InterCity Competitive Monitor, January 1992, No. 13. I am indebted to John Prideaux for this reference.

106 Cf. the observation of a senior rail manager that 'there's always a degree of mystique about the freight business, how it's actually managed and the rest. And it actually pays to keep that mystique'. Interview with Colin Driver, 3 August 1999.

107 O'Brien, Memo on 'Freightliner Plan', 24 May 1988, Chairman's Group Minutes, 26 May 1988. A recommendation from the consultants Coopers & Lybrand that Freightliner be reconstituted as a separate business sector was rejected. Coopers & Lybrand, Report on 'The Future Status of Freightliner', January 1987, AN170/46, PRO.

108 BRB Press Release, 6 September 1988; BRB Railfreight Group Executive Minutes, 18 January 1990; Interviews with Colin Driver, 1999, and Ian Brown, 9 May 2000. Leslie Smith became MD Trainload Freight, in September 1989. Colin Driver retired as Director, RailFreight in July 1991.

109 John D. C. A. Prideaux (Director, Policy Unit) and Colin Driver (Director, Freight), 'Summary Report on Railfreight Review. Review of Railfreight Cost and Revenue Determinants. The Ideal Operational Freight Railway Project', July 1985, BPM 21-09-01, PBA Box 112; RE Minutes, 19 June and 19/20 November 1985, BRB Minutes, 6 June 1985. The 1985 Review was undertaken at the DTp's request.

110 Interview with Colin Driver, 1999.

111 The cost of escaping from the Dover–Dunkerque 'Nord Pas de Calais' train ferry obligation—£35.4 m.—was added to the profit and loss account for 1992/3 as an exceptional item. BRB RfD, Profit & Loss Account, 1992/3, Schedule A, Ian Brown's RfD Papers, Box 11; Interview with Ian Brown, 2000.

112 Colin Driver, Memos on 'Freight Review: Progress Report', 3 June, 31 July, and 29 November 1985, BRB Minutes, 6 June and 5 December 1985, 6 August 1987, 15 May 1989.

113 Channel Tunnel Group Ltd., France-Manche S.A., BRB, and SNCF, Usage Contract, 29 July 1987, Clauses 3.1 (i), 3.2.1 (i) (a), and 3.3.1, BRB Reg Doc 15-379. The full text of Clause 3.2.1 (i) (a) was: 'BR shall ensure that, on the first date on which the Railways operate regular commercial services through the Fixed Link both of Trains

carrying Passengers and of Freight Trains, BR has available Railway infrastructure in the United Kingdom which is sufficient in accordance with good railway practice to permit, together with the railway network available for use by BR, the carriage through the Fixed Link during the twelve (12) month period commencing on that date of 17,400,000 Passengers, 5,200,000 Tonnes of Non-Bulk Freight and 2,900,000 Tonnes of Bulk Freight'. The Concession Agreement of 1987 bound the governments to 'use reasonable endeavours' to provide the necessary railway infrastructures. See House of Commons Transport Committee, *Second Report on Preparations for the Opening of the Channel Tunnel*, vol. I, March 1992, P.P. 1991–2, vii, HC12-1, para. 6; RfD Channel Tunnel Strategic Review, February 1990, BRB Special Meeting Minutes, 7 March 1990.

114 BRB Minutes, 14 May 1989, 7 March 1990; Investment Committee Minutes, 3 July 1989; Brown, Memo, n.d., Investment Committee Minutes, 30 April 1990; David Kirby, Memo on 'Reallocation of Channel Tunnel Fixed Toll', August 1989, Chairman's Group Minutes, 10 August 1989.

115 Speedlink losses were £54.8 m. on £88.4 m. turnover in 1985/6, and £46.6 m. loss on £85.2 m. turnover in 1986/7; accumulated losses, including interest, were put at £211 m. for the period 1982–89/90. Richard Allan (Director, Policy Unit), Memo on 'Railfreight Distribution (RfD) Strategy', n.d., BRB Minutes, 7 March, 14 May, 1 November, and 6 December 1990; Ian Brown (MD, RfD)–RfD Terminal Managers, 12 December 1990, BRB RfD 'E' files, Box 58 (P); Brown, 'RfD Progress Report & Key Issues', n.d., BRB Minutes, 7 March 1990; Brown, 'RfD Container Review', n.d., BRB Minutes, 6 June 1991; 11 August 2000; David Allan (Director, Finance, BRB)–Stephen Reeves (DTp), 21 March 1991, RfD Papers, Box IAB8.

116 A review reported in *Rail* revealed that 81% of movements were of distances below 300 miles and 63% of pick-ups were of 5 wagons or fewer. *Rail*, 9–22 January 1991, pp. 26–31.

117 BRB, *R&A 1990/1*, p. 18.

118 Chairman's Group Minutes, 26 April 1990; BRB, 'Railfreight Distribution: Pre-qualification Memorandum', April 1996, pp. 9–10, Appendix III, BRB Secretary's Papers, Box 2133; *Rail*, 18–31 August 1993; Paul Shannon, *Railway Freight Operations* (Shepperton, 1999), pp. 77–95; Interview with Ian Brown, 2000.

119 3.1 m. tonnes in 1998: *Modern Railways*, July 1999, p. 467. There were many reasons for the shortfall, not least RfD's limited terminal spread following the Speedlink closure, British loading-gauge restrictions, the complexity of inter-railway contracting, and competitive weaknesses compared with road haulage. See *Modern Railways*, May 1998, pp. 308–11.

120 About 80% of TLF income came from the CEGB (later National Power, PowerGen, Nuclear Electric), British Coal, British Steel, Foster Yeoman, and ARC (operating as Mendip Rail from October 1993), Blue Circle, BP, and Shell UK. Smith, Presentation on 'Privatisation and Freight on Rail', October 1993, Appendix D, Welsby's Papers, Sec Box 1969. Private-sector investment in railway freight was estimated as £2,844 m. at 1993/4 replacement values: ibid., Appendix J.

121 Leslie Smith (MD, Trainload Freight), 'Trainload Freight Study 14th May 1990', BRB Policy Unit File 636.860 Pt. 2, AN170/104, PRO; BRB Minutes, 14 May 1990; *Modern Railways*, November 1989, pp. 579–87.

122 Interview with Leslie Smith, 1998.

123 Within these sub-sectors, aggregates tonnage fell by 34%, steel by 29%. Leslie Smith (MD, TLF), Confidential Note on 'Freight Company Viability Meeting Marsham Street—8 October 1993', 11 October 1993, BRB Secretary's Papers, Box 2017. Petroleum traffic was also affected by the recession, together with elements created by the oil companies, e.g. the swapping of products to avoid transportation: Interview with Brian Burdsall, 19 June 2000.

124 Smith, Note, cit. and Presentation, October 1993, cit.

125 Private-sector investment in coal was estimated at some £1,079 m. at 1993/4 replacement values, 38% of estimated private investment in freight: Smith, Presentation, October 1993, cit., Appendix J. The business was apparently an example of the railways' best marketing strategy, the '3 Es': Entice; Ensnare; Exploit!

126 Richard Allan (Director, BRB Policy Unit)–Colin Driver (Director, Railfreight), 26 October 1988, enclosing Policy Unit, Confidential Memo on 'The Effects of ESI Privatisation on Railfreight Gross Coal Revenue—Technical Note', 24 October 1988, BRB PU file 636.860 Pt. 1, AN170/105, PRO; Driver, Memo on 'Privatisation of the Electricity Supply Industry (E.S.I.)—Implications for the Rail Transport of Coal to Power Stations', 31 May 1989, Chairman's Group Minutes, 15 June 1989, Appendix I; W. Ashworth, 'British Coal Corporation', *International Directory of Company Histories*, vol. IV (1991), p. 40; British Coal Corporation, *R&A 1994/5*, p. 36; DTI, *Digest of United Kingdom Energy Statistics 1996*, Tables 47, A6.

127 Driver, Memo, 31 July 1987, Policy Unit, Memo, 24 October 1988, cit. The CEGB took the opportunity to use road transport for power stations in Tyneside, Uskmouth, and Didcot, but in fact used rail to a slightly greater extent than that stipulated in the contract: *Modern Railways*, November 1989, p. 579.

128 Driver, Memo, 31 May 1989.

129 £258 m. in 1990/1 prices. BRB and PowerGen, 'Coal Carriage Agreement, 30 March 1990', BRB and National Power, 'Agreement for the Carriage of Coal to Power Stations', 30 March 1990, BRB Reg. Docs 38-18 and 19; Keith McNair (Director of Fuel Management, National Power)–Kim Jordan (Director, Coal), 5 November 1991, BRB Reg. Doc. 38-19, Sec Box Z; Smith, 'Trainload Freight Study', 14 May 1990, cit.

130 BRB Minutes, 5 April and 14 May 1990; Smith, 'Trainload Freight Study', cit..

131 In the event, National Power bought 5 GM Class 59 locomotives and 106 102–tonne wagons for block coal trains operated from November 1995 under the open access arrangements (a sixth locomotive had been acquired earlier for the Tunstead–Drax limestone traffic, but the service was operated from April 1994 for National Power by Transrail). The 'open' service did not last long: in 1997 it was sold to English Welsh & Scottish Railway with effect from April 1998. The other independent operator was British Nuclear Fuels Ltd., via its subsidiary Direct Rail Services (DRS). Ten Class 20 locomotives were acquired for Sellafield services, operating from 1997. See *Modern Railways*, October and December 1995, pp. 621–2, 762–3, January 1996, p. 13, February and October 1997, pp. 76, 622.

132 On the difficulties see Smith–Reid (II) et al., 16 and 23 November 1992, enclosing Memo to HC Employment and Trade & Industry Committees on 'The Employment Consequences for Trainload Freight of the British Coal Pit Closures', 13 November 1992; Patrick Brown (Permanent Secretary, DTp)–Welsby, 11 December 1992; Smith–Jerram and Welsby, 26 January 1993; Smith–Robert Horton (Vice-Chairman,

BRB), 27 January 1993; Kim Jordan–Reid (II) and Welsby, 16 December 1993, Jordan, Confidential Memo on 'Chairman Meeting with Ed Wallis—Chief Executive, Power-Gen—22nd December 1993', 13 December 1993, Welsby's Papers, Sec Box 1969; Mr Freeman's Implementation Group [FIG] Minutes, 17 November 1993. The three freight divisions set up in 1993 were: West; North-East; and South-East.

133 The average length of haul of BRB's coal traffic fell from 73 km in 1979 to 58 km in 1988, then rose to 66 km in 1990/1 and 80 km in 1993/4. DTp, *Transport Statistics*. Environmental regulation embraced coal desulphurisation, producing new limestone, and gypsum traffics to and from power stations at Drax and Ratcliffe. BRB, Information Memo on 'The Sale of British Rail's Trainload Freight Companies', July 1995, Pt.1, BRB Secretary's Papers, Box 2133.

134 The minimum payments were £45.4 m. (Nat. Power) and £25 m. (PowerGen). BRB and Nat. Power, Deed of Variation, 29 March 1993, Reg. Doc 15-528, Sec Box Z117; BRB and PowerGen, Contract, 30 March 1994; BRB Minutes, 1 April 1993.

135 Cf. Ken Glover's 'angle of unreality': Glover, 'Examining Railway Figures', cit. John Prideaux has also referred to British Rail's 'hockey stick' forecasts: Interview with Prideaux, 1998.

136 Jacques César (Mercer Management Consulting)–Jerram, 24 September 1992, Jerram's Papers, Box A7/BM442. About 700,000 tonnes of the 870,000 tonnes cement traffic was lost by April 1993: Smith–Welsby, 30 April 1993, Welsby's Papers, Sec Box 1969. On the somewhat fraught negotiations with Blue Circle see I. S. V. McKenzie (Chief Executive, Blue Circle Cement)–Smith, 19 April 1993 and reply, 13 May 1993, Smith–Reid (II) and Welsby, 14 May 1993, Welsby's Papers, Sec Box 1969.

137 BRB Minutes, 14 May 1990; Smith, Note, 11 October 1993, cit.

138 BR Management Brief, 25 September 1992.

139 DTp, *Transport Statistics Great Britain 1999*, Table 9.3:

	Rail tonneage (m)	Market share (%)	Rail tonne-km (bn)	Market share (%)
1953	294	23.77	37	41.57
1974	176	9.36	22	14.86
1979	169	8.93	20	10.58
1994	97	4.65	13	5.88

140 Reid (I)–Rupert Murdoch (Chairman, News International), 29 January 1986, Michael Connolly (Director, Parcels), Brief for Reid (I), 6 February 1986, Kirby's Papers, Sec Box 2151; BRB Minutes, 13 February–6 November 1986. News International's adoption of road transport was prompted by its dispute with the print unions at Wapping. The out-of-court settlement in 1989 was for £3 m. plus £50,000 interest: Chairman's Group Minutes, 21 December 1989; Interview with Brian Burdsall, 19 June 2000; William Shawcross, *Rupert Murdoch: Ringmaster of the Information Circus* (1992), pp. 334ff.

141 Brian Burdsall (Director, Parcels)–Myers, O'Brien, and Kirby, 8 June 1987, enclosing Robert Maxwell (Mirror Group Newspapers)–Burdsall, 5 June 1987, O'Brien's Papers, Sec Box 2179; BRB Minutes, 2 July 1987, BRB, *R&A 1987/8*, p. 26. The business went to Newsflow, a division of National Carriers.

142 Brian Burdsall (Director, Parcels), Memo on 'Parcels Objective 1989/90', 25 June 1987, BRB Minutes, 2 July 1987; Adrian Shooter (Director, Parcels), Memo on 'Parcels Sector Strategy', n.d., Chairman's Group Minutes, 23 November 1989.

143 BRB, *R&A 1969*, p. 10; Burdsall, Memo, June 1987, cit.; Shooter, Memo *c.*November 1989, cit.; Accent Marketing & Research, 'BR Parcels Group Strategy Review', October 1990, Welsby's Papers, Sec Box 2343; Red Star Information Memorandum, June 1993, BRB Secretary's Papers, Box 2133. The Parcels sector explored the idea of using Parcels TGVs to deliver to Brussels: Charles Brown (Director, Policy Unit)–Welsby, 2 November 1990, Welsby's Papers, Box 2343.

144 MacGregor, Written Answer, *Parl. Deb. (Commons)*, 6th ser. (Session 1992–3), vol. 212, 19 October 1992, *208*; Red Star Information Memorandum, June 1993, cit.

145 Burdsall, Memo, June 1987, cit.; Burdsall–O'Brien, 3 January 1989, Kirby's Papers, Sec Box 2151; Glyn Williams (MD, Parcels Group), Report, incorporated in Welsby, Chief Executive's Report, BRB Minutes, 2 April 1992; Letter Mail Agreement Between British Railways Board and the Post Office 25 October 1984, BRB Reg. Doc. 34–5; Interview with Burdsall, 2000.

146 Board Exec. Minutes, 18 July 1991; Shooter–Welsby et al., 18 January 1990, and Welsby–Shooter, 31 January 1990, Welsby's Papers, Sec Box 2343; BR Management Brief, 24 January 1990; Brown, Memo November 1990, cit.; Coates (DTp)–Welsby, 3 January 1990, cit.

147 Cf. Stan Whittaker (Director of Finance & Planning, BRB)–Derek Fowler, 5 December 1989, Welsby's Papers, Sec Box 2343; Shooter, Memo on 'Parcels Sector Strategy: Post Office Contract', n.d., Chairman's Group Minutes, 13 December 1990.

148 Shooter, Memo *c.*December 1990, cit.; Glyn Williams (MD, Parcels), Memo on 'Royal Mail Contract/Project', 26 October 1993, Board Exec. Minutes, 28 October 1993, BRB Minutes, 4 November 1993; BR Management Brief, 17 December 1993. British Rail's investment was to be £10 m. in vehicles and van modifications. A further investment of £15 m. in infrastructure plus £7 m. in cost effective maintenance was recoverable from Royal Mail.

149 A finding confirmed by the recent, more inventive model of Gathon and Pestieau for the period 1986–8: H.-J. Gathon and P. Pestieau, 'Decomposing efficiency into its managerial and its regulatory components: the case of European railways', *European Journal of Operational Research*, 80 (1995), 500–7.

150 Paul Watkinson, (Group Personnel Director), BRB), Memo on 'Managing Staff Surpluses—1992/93 and Beyond', November 1992, Board Exec. Minutes, 15 October and 12 November 1992 and 28 January 1993; BRB, *R&A 1992/3*, p. 30; *1993/4*, p. 32.

151 See RSNC Minutes, 14 March, 10 and 23 April 1990; 17 February, 18 March, and 14 April 1992; A. Paul Watkinson (BRB)–James Knapp (NUR), Richard Rosser (TSSA) and Derrick Fullick (ASLEF), 24 April 1990, and replies, AN171/311; Watkinson–Unions, 14 April 1992 and replies, AN171/313, PRO.

152 Watkinson–Unions, 24 April 1991, Knapp (RMT)–Watkinson, 29 April 1991 and reply, 2 May 1991, AN171/312, PRO.

153 RSNT, Decision 97, 21 May 1991; Watkinson–Unions, 22 May 1991, Watkinson, Note, 23 May, 1991, AN171/312; BR Management Brief, 23 May 1991. The RSNT consisted of Ian Buchanan (Chairman), John D. Hughes (former Principal, Ruskin College, union nominee), Dr David Grieves (Executive Director, British Steel, BRB nominee). In an extraordinary verdict the recommendation of 7.75% was opposed by

both Hughes and Grieves, who felt the Chairman had been influenced unduly by the RMT strike threat: RSNT, Decision 97, para. 32; Grieves–Watkinson, 24 May 1991, and reply, 13 June 1991, AN171/312. The RSNT's last Decision, No. 98 of 1 September 1992, concerned a TSSA grading claim on behalf of booking office and travel centre staff.

154 BRB Minutes, 10 June, 1 July, and 5 August 1993; Board Exec. Minutes, 17 and 24 June 1993; BR Management Brief, 1 July 1993; Knapp–RMT Members, n.d. [July 1993], copy in AN171/315, PRO; *Financial Times*, 3 August 1993, p. 7. On Knapp's position see Watkinson, Memo 16 March 1994, AN171/708, PRO.

155 BR Management Brief, 27 May 1994; BRB Minutes, 9 June 1994.

156 An example of Horton's unconventional bargaining style was the offer made in public to donate the difference between his and Knapp's salary to charity if talks were resumed. *Guardian*, 4 August 1994, p. 2, 15 August 1994, p. T3.

157 BRB Minutes, 7 July 1994 and 9 March 1995; BRB, *R&A 1994/5*, p. 5. After all elements had been taken into account, the Board's passenger businesses lost *c*.£16 m. Jerram, Memo, 31 March 1995, BRB Minutes, 6 April 1995.

158 Reid (II), quoted in BR Management Brief, 5 July 1994.

159 Cf. Watkinson, Memo on 'Signal Workers Dispute', 9 August 1994, BRB IR94+, Box 4; *Guardian*, 29 September 1994, p. 5, 1 October 1994, p. 3.

160 BRB Minutes, 25 April–7 September 1995; BRB, *R&A 1995/6*, p. 5.

161 Appendix G, Tables G.3 and G.4; *New Earnings Survey, April 1990–4*.

162 BR Council Minutes, 19 November 1992; Gareth Hadley (Employee Relations Manager, BRB)–Unions, 20 November 1992, AN171/712, PRO; Note on 'Special Severance Scheme', 18 February 1993, AN171/708, PRO; *Rail*, 25 November–10 December 1992, p. 6.

163 Watkinson–Knapp, Fullick, and Rosser, 21 January 1993, AN171/712; 'Memo of Meeting held at Paddington on 28 January 1993 between representatives of BRB and RMT, TSSA, ASLE&F, CS&EU, and BTOG', AN171/707, PRO.

164 Fullick, BR Council Minutes, 19 November 1992, cit.

165 ASLEF Emergency [*sic*] Bulletin No. 2, 29 March 1993, Watkinson–Fullick, 2 April 1993 and reply, 7 April 1993, Watkinson–Fullick, 7 April 1993, Fullick–Watkinson, fax letter containing ASLEF EC Resolution 772/380, AN171/712, PRO.

166 Watkinson–Fullick, 8 April 1993, AN171/712, PRO; BRB Minutes, 6 May 1993.

167 'Memo of Meeting held at Euston on 19 February 1993 …', AN171/711; Knapp–Watkinson, 22 February 1993, AN171/712, PRO.

168 Watkinson–Knapp, 24 February 1993, Knapp–Watkinson, 3 March 1993, AN171/712, PRO. The RMT's third demand was that employees wishing to accept voluntary redundancy should have the option of accepting the terms of the special severance scheme or existing contractual entitlements, whichever was the more favourable.

169 Watkinson, Brief on 'April 2nd 1993—RMT & CSEU Strike Action', 27 March 1993, AN171/712, PRO.

170 Watkinson–Knapp et al., 16 April 1993, AN171/712.

171 Knapp–Watkinson, 19 April 1993, 'Memo of Meeting held on 20 April 1994 …', Watkinson–Knapp, 21 April 1993, enclosing note on 'BR position', 20 April 1993, AN171/712; BRB Minutes, 6 May 1993; *Guardian*, 18 May 1993, p. 4.

172 Watkinson–Douglas Smith (Chairman, ACAS), 10 April 1991, AN171/706, PRO; BR Joint Working Party on Machinery of Negotiation and Consultation, proposals

for new procedure agreements tabled by British Rail, 3 December 1991, Hadley–Unions, 13 October 1992, AN171/706; Interview with Paul Watkinson, 14 July 1999.

173 Hadley–Unions, 5 July 1993, 'Memo of meeting held on 15 September 1993 …', BRB IR 80-12-13 Pt. 9; Watkinson, Memo on 'The Employee Relations Scene: October 1995 to March 1995', n.d., Board Exec. Special Meeting Minutes, 4 October 1995; BRB Minutes, 7 March 1996. On the 1994 revisions to the machinery see BRB IR 82-12-13 Pt. 10.

174 Hadley–Reeves (DTp), 3 July 1990, Watkinson–Reeves, 25 July 1990, AN171/164, PRO.

175 Welsby–Knapp, 10 July 1990, AN171/164, PRO; Richard Cook (Executive Remuneration Administrator, BRB), brief for Watkinson, 3 September 1991, Reid (II)–Knapp, 8 April 1991, AN171/164; Board Executive Minutes, 23 January, 6 February, 26 March, and 16 April 1992; Watkinson, Memo, n.d., BRB Minutes, 13 February 1992; Chris Green (MD InterCity)–Knapp, 27 March and 14 April 1992, AN171/1, PRO. The senior conductors' voting in the RMT-organised ballot was: For 50.2%; Against 49.8%.

176 RMG Special Meeting Minutes, 6 August 1991; Board Exec. Minutes, 27 February 1992, BRB Minutes, 11 February 1993; BRB, 'Drivers' Restructuring Initiative: The Presentation of BR's outline proposals to the Unions', 14 January 1992, BRB IR94+ Box 8; Hadley, Note on 'Drivers' Restructuring', n.d. [c.1996], Hadley's Papers, BRB PRI Box 9558; Interview with Watkinson, 1998. The driver's basic rate for a 39-hour week was £10,360 in 1992; with overtime, earnings were c.£18,000.

177 Board Exec. Minutes, 5 and 27 July 1995; Hadley–TOC/FOC Directors, 17 August 1995, BRB IR94+, Box 8; BRB, *R&A 1996/7*, p. 17.

178 BRB Railway Monthly Digest, November 1991; Scotrail, Memo, July 1990, BRB IR 75–2–205/2 Pt. 1.

179 Watkinson, Memo on 'Driver Only Operation Passenger Schemes: Revenue Protection on Train and Penalty Fares', 6 April 1990, Watkinson–Unions on 'Driver Only Operation: Signalmen: Rate of Pay', 6 December 1990, BRB IR 75-2-205; RSNC Minutes, 27 March 1991; BRB Press Release, 26 March 1990; Chris Stokes (Deputy Director, NSE), Memo to NSE Executive Group on 'Driver Only Operation—Current Position', 7 August 1991, BRB SDI CP8; 'Notes of Fact Finding Meeting on 30 December 1991 with Representatives of A.S.L.E.F. on Driver Only Operation, South Central, N.S.E.', 3 January 1992, Terry Worrall (Director of Operations, BRB)–Watkinson, 3 January 1992, BRB IR File on (DOO—NSE).

180 John Nelson (MD, NSE)–Welsby, 23 July 1992, SDI CP8; Jukes and Janet Goodland (Planning and Resources Manager, NSE), Memo on 'NSE: Driver Only Operation Review of Schemes', 6 May 1993, NSE BRG Minutes, 21 May 1993; *Modern Railways*, May 1999, p. 374.

181 NSE, Quality Digest, October 1989, BRB Minutes, 11 October 1989; Nelson, Memo to NSE BRG on 'Review of Driver Only Operation Schemes', n.d., NSE BRG Minutes, 12 May 1993.

182 The investment cost £8.4 m. at Q3/88 prices = £10.6 m. at Q1/92 prices; estimated staff cost savings were at Q1/92 prices. Jukes, Memo on 'Driver-Only Operation—Great Eastern and West Anglia Completion Certificate', 5 March 1992. NSE BRG Minutes, 10 March 1992. The more detailed back-check was provided by Janet

Goodland, Memo on 'Investment Appraisal Backcheck on DOO', 15 July 1992, NSE Investment Panel Minutes, 20 July 1992, BRB SDI CP8.

Chapter 9

1 BRB, *R&A 1992/3*, p. 4.

2 Cf. Jane C. Cotton (DTp)–C. Frank Johnson (Group Chief Accountant, BRB), 30 November 1992, Ian Hodgson (DTp)–John B. Thurgood (Senior Business Analyst, BRB), 18 August 1993, Thurgood, Note, 20 August 1993, Thurgood–Hodgson, 1 November 1993, BRB IA 20-08-05 Pt. 10.

3 Reid (II), Chairman's Statement, 10 June 1993, BRB, *R&A 1992/3*, p. 6; Statement, 9 June 1994, BRB, *R&A 1993/4*, p. 5; Unpublished Minutes of Evidence, HC Transport Committee, 8 February 1995, and BRB, Memorandum to the Transport Select Committee, 31 January 1995, Table 8, BRB PBA Box 167; Jerry Evans (Director, Public Affairs, BRB)–Jerram, 16 September 1993, BRB IA 20-08-05 Pt. 9. Evans wrote: 'if people were to pick up our internal figures, they would get the impression that:—we are going well over the ceiling set by the Department; . . . and we are lying in what we say about problems with this year's levels . . . I see in this such potential confusion and such high risk of very damaging public and political criticism that I would urge you very strongly that we should sort out quickly a reconciliation'.

4 Our data include track renewals, payments in advance, BRPB operating expenditure, and deferred interest. See Appendix B, Tables B.1 and B.2. Our thanks to Alan Nichols for his help with investment.

5 The increase in passenger-mileage was made in spite of transferring 26 km (16 miles) to the Greater Manchester Metro in 1991/2. The route-mileage open to freight only fell from 1,423 to 1,354 miles (2,290 to 2,179 km), 1988/9–93/4, and, as we have seen, the number of freight depots contracted sharply, from 125 in 1988/9 to 60 in 1993/4. DTp, *Transport Statistics Great Britain 1999*, Tables 5.13–14.

6 The proportion made up by traction and rolling stock is understated, since most of the payments in advance movements concerned this element. See Thurgood–J. L. Boon et al., 4 December 1992, BRB IA 20-08-05 Pt. 10.

7 Thurgood–Hodgson, 10 August 1993, BRB IA 20-08-05 Pt. 9.

8 BRB Business Review Group, Memos to BRB Board Executive, 16 September 1993, 31 January 1994, BRD 20-1-67; BRB, *R&A 1989/90*, p. 12, 14; *1990/1*, pp. 14, 16, *1993/4*, p. 20; Vincent and Green, *InterCity Story*, pp. 188–9.

9 Network SouthEast, Press Release, 30 April 1990; BRB, *R&A 1992/3*; David Mackie (Director of Planning & Business Analysis, BRB), Memo, n.d., Board Exec. Minutes, 5 September 1995, BRD 24-4-37 Pt. 5. The figure of £596m. is the cost of the Networker investment in cash terms, and not at base-year prices, as shown in Table 9.4.

10 Note that a tranche of the investment—47 four-car sets—was authorised in March 1992, just before the election, and ordered from ABB in York on 10 April 1992, the day after the election: BRB Press Release, 10 April 1992, BRB.

11 BRB InterCity, Strategy Review, November 1987, paras. 9.3–7, 13.27, 14.1; West Coast Main Line Strategy Review, December 1989, paras. 1.1–7, 11.1–6; BRB Minutes, 23 November 1987, 11 January 1990, BRB; Vincent and Green, *InterCity Story*, pp. 86–9.

12 Investment Commitee Minutes, 5 December 1988, 5 March and 5 November 1990; West Coast Main Line Coach Fleet Replacement: Phase I Appraisal, 25 January 1990;

Stephen K. Reeves (DTp)–Andrew Jukes (Investment Adviser, BRB), 4 October 1990, referring to the view of Roger Ford (editor, *Modern Railways*) that the investment case for the new trains was 'marginal' [!], and reply, 1 November 1990, BRD 28-12-1 Pt. 1; BRB InterCity Press Releases, 21 June 1990, 11 March 1991.

13 Jukes, Memo to BRG, 10 January 1992, enclosing Prideaux, Submission for InterCity 250 Train, 20 December 1991, BRD 28-1-2-1 Pt. 1. Although the case apparently satisfied the 8% test rate, there remained some disquiet about the assumptions made by InterCity.

14 BRB Minutes, 2 July and 1 October 1992, BRB Procurement Committee Minutes, 20 August 1992, BRB; Interview with Dr Peter Watson, 21 June 2000.

15 Chris Green (Managing Director, InterCity)–Welsby, 17 February 1993, BRD 28-12-1 Pt. 1.

16 See Chairman's Group Minutes, 21 December 1989; D. Glyn Williams (Director, Financial Planning, BRB)–John D. C. A. Prideaux (Director, InterCity, BRB), 28 September 1990, and reply, 3 October 1990; Welsby (Chief Executive, BRB)–Prideaux, 17 October 1990 (Welsby as Chief Executive was most concerned about the need to demonstrate an 8% RR); Welsby, Sir Robert Reid lecture to Chartered Institute of Transport (CIT), January 1998, reported in *Modern Railways*, March 1998, p. 160. Chris Green is currently engaged on a further attempt to upgrade the WCML, with Virgin Trains: ibid., February 2000, p. 43.

17 Ian Brown (MD, RfD)–Mackie, 6 July 1994, PIM 26-9-13 Pt. 1; BRB, *R&A 1988/9*, p. 55 [typo]; *1993/4*, p. 63; DTp, *Transport Statistics Great Britain 1995*, p. 115.

18 The Heathrow Express link was first mooted in 1987, and secured ministerial approval in July 1988. BRB held a 30% stake in the joint venture, which was sold to BAA for £20.3m. plus £1.9 m. for liabilities in 1996. See Reid (I)–Channon, 9 November 1987, DTp Press Release, 20 July 1988, GIC 24-10 Pt. 1; InterCity, Memo, n.d., Board Exec. Minutes, 4 August 1993; BRB Minutes, 5 August 1993, 13 January 1994, 6 June and 1 August 1996.

19 BRB, *R&A 1989/90*, p. 12; *1990/1*, p. 16; BRG, Memos to Board Exec., May and August 1993, February 1994, BRD 20-1-67.

20 Centro and West Yorkshire put up the bulk of the Birmingham and Leeds investments, while Greater Manchester provided 45% of the funding for the Manchester Airport link. Investment Committee Minutes, 4 June 1990; Jukes (Investment Adviser), Memo to Board Exec., 19 September 1991, IA 22-3-42 Pt. 2; Jukes (Director of Business Review), Memo 24 August 1993, IA 28-9-3; *Modern Railways*, September 1995, pp. 533–6; Strathclyde PTE, 'Significant Achievements of Strathclyde PTA Up to Present', n.d. [2000] (my thanks to Dr Malcolm Reid for this reference).

21 Board Exec. Minutes, 28 May 1992; David Mackie (Director of Planning & Business Analysis), Memo 25 May 1995, IA 25–30 Pt. 3; InterCity Press Release, 9 February 1994.

22 Jim R. Coates (DTp)–Welsby, 14 December 1990, and reply, 27 February 1991, Coates–Welsby, 4 March 1991 and reply, 8 March 1991, Welsby's Papers, Sec Box 2125; Welsby, Memo on 'Investment Ceiling 1991/92', 30 September 1991, BRB Minutes, 3 October 1991.

23 BRB Minutes, 7 November 1991, Jerram, 'Group Financial Reports', 6 January and 1 May 1992, BRB Minutes, 9 January and 7 May 1992.

24 Gourvish, *British Railways*, p. 527.

25 BRG Minutes, 5 March 1993; Nichols, Memo to BRG, 5 March 1993, BRD 24-0 Pt. 1; Jerram, Memo on 'Leasing of Rolling Stock for Network SouthEast', n.d., BRB Minutes, 2 December 1993.

26 Jim Cornell (MD, Regional Railways)–Welsby, 4 March 1993; John G. Nelson (MD, Network SouthEast), 'Replacement Outer Suburban EMUs for NSE', 29 March 1993; Green–Welsby et al., 23 March 1993; Green–Reid (II) et al., 23 March 1993, and InterCity, 'IC225 for West Coast: The case for leasing new trains', March 1993; Jukes, Memo on 'Rolling Stock Leasing—£150 m (1994/5 & 1995/6)', 1 April 1993, Special Board Exec. Minutes, 2 April 1993; Welsby–Roger Freeman (Minister of State for Public Transport), 2 April 1993, BRD 24-0 Pt. 1; Interview with Dr Peter Watson, 21 June 2000.

27 Welsby, Memos to Board Exec., 21 July and 2 September 1993, BRD 24-0 Pt. 2; BRB Minutes, 9 September 1993.

28 Nichols, Memo on 'Rolling Stock Leasing', n.d., BRD 24-0 Pt. 2; Welsby, Memo, 2 September 1993, cit.; Nelson, Memo on 'Networker Express', 23 September 1993, Board Exec. Minutes, 23 and 30 September 1993; Reid–Freeman, 4 October 1993 and reply, 13 October 1993, BRD 24-0 Pt. 2; Jerram, Memo on 'Leasing of Rolling Stock for Network SouthEast', BRB Minutes, 2 December 1993; Philip Rutnam (Treasury)–Neil MacDonald (DTp), 23 June 1993, Jerram's Papers, 523/BM. The 41 new trains were introduced in October 1996 as Class 365/5s: *Modern Railways*, December 1996, p. 765.

29 BRB, *Future Rail—The Next Decade* (July 1991), and see BRB 23-1-68.

30 Green, address to CIT, reported in *Modern Railways*, July 1989, pp. 351–2, 373–5; Network SouthEast, Confidential Memo on 'Future Rail: The London Agenda', September 1991, BRB Secretary's Papers, Sec Box 2380; Mackie, Memo, September 1995, cit.; Interview with Chris Green, 1 March 2000. The London Agenda had been intended for presentation to the DTp as part of the 1991 financing round, but was quickly abandoned. Cf. Note for Press Office on 'London Agenda', Reid (II)'s Papers, 1990/1.

31 *Modern Railways*, July 2000, p. 35.

32 Cf. the concerns of Reid over the state of the LTS line, and those of John Nelson, MD of NSE: Reid (II)–Rifkind on 'Asset Stewardship: London Tilbury & Southend line', 22 October 1991 and reply, 30 October 1991, Reid (II)'s Papers; 'Chaos reigns again at Fenchurch Street', *Evening Standard*, 29 August 1991; Nelson–Freeman, 1 October 1992, BRB SDI CP10; Interview with John Nelson, 22 August 2000.

33 Board Exec. Minutes, 26 November 1992; Burrage–Nelson, 2 December 1992, Burrage–Welsby et al., 23 December 1992, BRD 21-20-27; Report on 'Signalling Infrastructure Renewals: Prioritization Review' (Hesketh Report), 1992. I am grateful to Ken Burrage for this reference.

34 Jukes, Memo to BRG, 16 December 1993, BRB Network SouthEast Minutes, 17 December 1993, IA 24-3-33 Pt. 2.

35 BRB, 'A Cross-London Rail Link', discussion paper, November 1980, BRB Press Release, 17 November 1980; Interview with John Prideaux, 14 December 1998.

36 DTp, BRB NSE, LRT, and LUL, *Central London Rail Study*, January 1989, copy in BRB Group Investment File, GIC 23-10 Pt. 1; BR Management Brief, 26 January 1989.

37 Green, Memo, 30 January 1990, Investment Committee Minutes, 5 February 1990; Parkinson–Reid (II), 9 October 1990, and reply 17 October 1990, GIC 23-10 Pt. 3; BR Management Brief, 12 October 1990; Network SouthEast Press Release, 12 October 1990.

38 Osmotherly (DTp)–C. W. Newton (Chairman, LRT), 31 July 1991, GLC 23-10 Pt. 3; Osmotherly–Reid (II), 2 January 1992, Reid (II)'s Papers, no ref.; Alan J. Nichols (Director, Financial Planning, BRB), Memo, 3 February 1992, Board Exec. Minutes, 6 February 1992; Nichols–Reid (II) et al., 16 July 1992, GIC 23-10 Pt. 4; BRB Minutes, 13 January, 5 May, and 7 July 1994, 4 April 1996.

39 NSE, Memo on 'Thameslink 2000', BRB Minutes, 5 September 1991; NSE Press Release, 27 November 1991.

40 Rifkind–Reid (II), 26 November 1991, Reid (II)'s Papers, no ref.; Network SouthEast Press Release, 27 November 1991; DTp Press Notice, 27 February 1996; *Modern Railways*, April 1996, pp. 229–30; February 2000, pp. 33–8.

41 David Rayner, Memo on 'Project Management', n.d., RE Minutes, 21 September 1988; D. Glyn Williams (Director, Financial Planning), Memo on 'Investment Management and Forecasting', 4 September 1989, Investment Committee Minutes, 4 September 1989; Williams, Circulation Memo, 6 September 1989, enclosing Touche Ross, 'British Railways Board: Management and Forecasting of Investment Expenditure', September 1989, Williams, Memos on 'Management and Forecasting of Investment Expenditure' (Task Force 1), 17 November 1989 and 10 January 1990, Don L. Heath (Director, Projects), Memo on 'Report of Touche Ross Task Force No 2—Recommendations for Improvements in Project Management', 8 January 1990, RMG Minutes, 16 January and 13 February 1990, BRB New Works File NP/T/7.

42 Ian H. Dudley (Project Director, Investment Forecasting & Control, BRB), Memo on 'Investment Forecasting & Control—The Touche Ross Initiative', 10 August 1990, BRB Financial Planning Files, FP853; Williams and Heath, Memo, 3 July 1990, RMG Minutes, 10 July 1990.

43 Edmonds–Williams and Heath, 15 May 1991, BRB IA 20-2-18-3.

44 Dudley, Memo to Touche Ross Steering Group, 26 June 1991, IA 20-2-18-3; Interview with Roger Hillard, 5 October 2000.

45 BR Management Brief, 16 May 1992, and see Figure 11.1.

46 John Plumb (Business Investment Controller, BRB)–MDs et al., 6 December 1993, BRD 20-1-70.

47 Interviews with John Nelson and Roger Hillard, 2000.

48 Roger S. Peal (DTp)–Jukes, 31 May 1990, reply to Jukes–Peal, 20 April 1990, BRB IA 24-4-38 Pt. 1. British Rail had decided to redeploy the units, thereby shifting the ground from a 'replacement case' to a 'growth build'.

49 Peal–Jukes, 18 June 1990, BRB IA 22-3-41 Pt. 2.

50 Reeves (DTp)–Nichols, 7 February 1992, and reply, 5 March 1992, IA 20-2-51 Pt. 2.

51 Gourvish, *British Railways*, pp. 282–3, 517–18, 521–5.

52 Cf. Hillard–Nichols, 26 February 1993, enclosing draft Memo to Board Exec. on 'Investment Backchecking', dated 1 March 1993, IA 20-2-51 Pt. 2.

53 The seven were: 'Pacer' (Class 141–4) DMUs; 46 Class 321 EMUs for the Great Eastern line; Stansted Airport link; 200 Class 319/321 EMUs; 124 Class 319 EMUs; 400 Class 465 Networkers for NSE; Class 165 DMUs.

54 Andrew W. Sharp (Asst. Investment Manager, BRB), 'Draft Pacer Backcheck', 20 September 1993, GIC 41-6 Pt. 2. No revised report was produced; the draft was sent to the DTp. Interview with Roger Hillard, 2000.

55 Martin Williams (Regional Railways)–John Plumb (Business Investment Controller, BRB), 7 January 1993, enclosing Martin P. Gibbard (Rolling Stock Officer, Regional

Railways), 'Back Check Report on Service Implementation of Class 156 Units', 22 July 1991, BRB IA 24-5-9.

56 Watson, presentation, BRB Procurement Committee Minutes, 10 October 1991; J. D. Milne (Director, Procurement and Materials Management), Memo, April 1994, BRB Procurement Committee Minutes, 15 April 1994.

57 There were 162 variation orders for the Class 158, a number only exceeded by the Class 319 (242) and 321 (206). Roger J. Keeling (Director of Procurement, BRB), Memo to Edmonds and Watson on 'Procurement in BR—a Critical Review', 25 March 1992, enclosed in George W. Buckley (MD, Central Services, BRB)–Trewin, 17 June 1992, BRB Secretary's Papers, Box 2417.

58 Fowler, Memo on 'Supply Committee Stewardship Review', 3 October 1989, BRB Minutes, 12 October 1989; BRB Supply Committee Minutes, 13 April 1989, 12 April, 14 June, and 12 July 1990; Keeling, Memo, 2 May 1991, Procurement Committee Minutes, 16 May 1991, 4 June 1992.

59 Keeling, Memo, June 1992, cit.

60 Keeling, Memo on 'Procurement and Materials Management [P&MM] Strategic Study', 31 January 1992, Procurement Committee Minutes, 13 February 1992.

61 John D. Milne (Acting Director, P&MM, BRB), Memo, June 1992, Procurement Committee Minutes, 4 June 1992; Gerald O'Keene (Director, P&MM, BRB), Memo, 3 February 1993, Procurement Committee Minutes, 11 February 1993. On the tensions between Watson and Buckley see Buckley–Edmonds, 30 March 1992, and Edmonds–Reid (II), 31 March 1992, BRB Secretary's Papers, Box 2417, Buckley–Watson, 13 April 1992, Watson's Papers, Sec Box 2376.

62 Procurement Committee Minutes, 10 October and 5 December 1991; Milne, Memo, June 1992, cit.; Mari Sako, *Prices, Quality and Trust: Inter-firm Relations in Britain and Japan* (Cambridge, 1992).

63 I. A. Todd, Notes on 'Supplier Accreditation Project—Steering Group Meeting 1, 20 May 1992', 21 May 1992; BRB Supplier Accreditation Steering Group Minutes, 15 February 1994, Arthur D. Little, 'Supplier Development Through Accreditation: Biannual Review and Action Plan', 15 February 1994, Watson's Papers, Sec Box 2376; Milne (Director, P&MM), 'P&MM Stewardship Report 1995/6', Procurement Committee Minutes, 16 May 1996; Interview with Watson, 2000.

64 John Nelson, Address to BR Suppliers' Conference, Birmingham 14 July 1993, Watson's Papers, Sec Box 2376; Interview with John Nelson, 2000.

65 National Audit Office, *Major Projects Report 1999*, 6 July 2000, P.P. 1999–2000, HC613; *Guardian*, 6 July 2000, p. 4. See also Committee of Public Accounts, *Ministry of Defence, 33rd Report*, 16 August 2000, P.P. 1999–2000, HC247; Bill Kincaid, *A Dinosaur in Whitehall: The True Cost of Defence Procurement Bureaucracy* (1997).

66 Interviews with Welsby, 2000, David Blake, 16 February 2001, and Roger Ford, 28 February 2001. On the other hand, there were a large number of variations made to the original contract: Keeling, Memo, March 1992, cit.

67 Interviews with Welsby, Watson, Blake, and Ford.

68 Michael Bosworth–Robert Lawrence et al., 14 October 1976, BRB 196-4-1 Pt. 11; T. R. Barron (Director, Planning & Investment, BRB), Memos, 12 May and 28 July 1977, RE Committee Minutes, 16 May and 1 August 1977; BRB, Memo on 'Cross-Channel Rail Link, 10 December 1979, CT Files, Box 82; BRB, *Cross Channel Rail Link* (March 1980); Peter Keen (Director, Channel Tunnel, BRB)–Parker et al., 21 May 1982, Note

on 'Channel Tunnel: 3rd June 1982', n.d., BRB 196-4-1 Pt. 13; Parker, *For Starters*, pp. 222–5, 271.

69 Cf. *Modern Railways*, February 1986, p. 70; March 1986, p. 122.

70 Cf. Derek Fowler, Memo on 'Train Services Through the Channel Tunnel', 26 June 1987, BRB Minutes, 2 July 1987.

71 Usage Contract, July 1987, cit. and see Richard Davies (Principal Investment Adviser, Major Projects, BRB), Note on 'Eurotunnel Usage Contract: An Explanatory Analysis of Rights and Obligations', 22 July 1992, GIC file 28–31; Channel Tunnel Act 1987, c. 53, 23 July 1987, ss.40, 42.

72 Davies, Note, cit.; Roger Hillard (Principal Investment Analyst, BRB)–Jerram, 24 January 1991, GIC 28-3 Pt. 8. The usage agreement provided numerous headaches later on. Eurotunnel pursued a legal claim to renegotiate the terms, and the European Commission, having initially raised no objection to the railways' rights of access under the agreement, changed its mind in December 1994 and sought to impose a more limited access. Both involved lengthy legal battles before being resolved in the Board's favour. See Special Channel Tunnel Committee Minutes, November 1994–November 1996.

73 Fowler, Memo on 'Channel Tunnel Investment', 23 August 1990, BRB Minutes, 6 September 1990.

74 Welsby, Memo on 'Review of Channel Tunnel Project', n.d., BRB Minutes, 31 March 1988.

75 BRB Press Release, 15 December 1989. Welsby had worked under Palmer at the Ministry of Transport in the 1970s: Interview with John Welsby, 29 March 2000.

76 Reid (II)–Parkinson, 2 April 1990, GIC 28-16; Richard Edgley (Director, EPS) and Ian Brown (MD, RfD), Memo, 16 July 1990, Investment Committee Minutes, 19 July 1990; Reid (II)–BRB managers, 28 November 1990, OfQ Box 70.

77 Fowler, Memo, 26 June 1987, cit.; BRB Minutes, 2 July 1987. Ridley–Reid (I), 23 January 1986, GIC 28-3 Pt. 3; Reid–Channon, 14 July 1987, GIC 28-3 Pt. 5.

78 Channon–Reid (I), 10 August 1987, GIC 28-3 Pt. 5; Fowler, Memo on 'Channel Tunnel Project', 25 September 1987, BRB Minutes, 1 October 1987.

79 At constant 1988/9 prices the estimated costs rose from £468m. in January 1986 to £613m. in August 1987 and £1.1bn in October 1989. Fowler, reported in BRB Minutes, 12 October 1989.

80 Channon–Reid (I), 4 May 1989, GIC 28-3 Pt. 6.

81 Reid (I)–Michael Portillo (Minister of State for Public Transport), 13 October 1989, GIC 28-3 Pt. 7; Parkinson–Reid (I), 19 October 1989, GIC 28-36 Pt. 1; Portillo–Reid, 25 October 1989, GIC 28-23.

82 Reid (I)–Portillo, 1 November 1989, Steven K. Reeves (Asst. Sec., DTp) and D. Glyn Williams (Director, Financial Planning, BRB)–John E. Everett (Touche Ross Management Consultants), 28 November 1989, GIC 28-23.

83 M. J. Faulkner, 'Touche Ross—Channel Tunnel Project: Notes of Presentation Meeting 13/12/89', 13 December 1989, 'Notes of Meeting—12 January, 1990', n.d., Portillo–Reid (I), 14 February 1990, GIC 28-23; John Palmer (MD, CT)–Coates, 16 March 1990, GIC 28-16.

84 Fowler–Andrew Jukes (Investment Adviser, BRB) and Roger Keeling (Director of Procurement, BRB), 20 March 1990, GIC 28-16; Jukes, Memo on 'Channel Tunnel Project—Project Direction for 1993 Services', 10 April 1990, and Palmer, Memo, n.d.,

BRB Investment Committee Minutes, 30 April 1990. John Brown fulfilled a similar project management role with London Underground for the refurbishment of the Central Line.

85 Reid (II)–Parkinson, 2 April 1990, GIC 28-16; Fowler, Memo, 23 August 1990, cit.; Palmer–Mrs Charlotte M. Dixon (DTp), 19 December 1990, Andrew Burchell (DTp)–Palmer, 6 March 1991, GIC 28-3 Pt. 8.

86 Base cost in July 1990 at Q3/89 prices; maximum cost including risk provision: £1,382m.: John Brown, Confidential 'Report on Project Definition Channel Tunnel 1993 Services', 2 July 1990, BRB 196-4-1, CT folder.

87 Welsby, Memo, March 1988, cit.; Interview with Welsby, 2000.

88 Hillard–Jerram, 24 January 1991, cit. At the government's request a test discount rate of 8% (instead of 7%) was used by British Rail in investment appraisal from 1989: Williams, Memo on 'Test Discount Rate', 24 July 1989, Investment Committee Minutes, 7 August 1989.

89 Cf. Coates (DTp)–Jukes, 5 April 1990, Fowler–Coates, 4 May 1990, GIC 28-19, PBA Box 14; Reeves (DTp)–Jukes, 10 September 1990, GIC 28-3 Pt. 8.

90 Reid I–Parkinson, 12 February 1990, two letters: Waterloo, GIC 28-7 Pt. 2, North Pole, GIC 28-10 Pt. 1.

91 Fowler–Richard Edgley (Director, EPS), 20 March 1990, and cf. Simon Osborne (Solicitor, BRB)–Jukes, 21 March 1990, GIC 28-7 Pt. 2.

92 £145.15m. in Q3/89/90 prices, cf. the original authorisation of £97.965m. (Q3/89) in May 1990, reauthorised in September 1991 at £131.85 m. (Q3/89/90). Investment Committee Minutes, 2 October 1989; Parkinson–Reid (II), 18 May 1990, Freeman–Reid (II), 2 September 1991, GIC 28-7 Pt. 2; Reid (II)–Rifkind, 26 March 1991, GIC 28-10 Pt. 2; Completion Certificate, 18 May 1994, CTX GEN 008, BRB, *R&A 1992/3*, p. 3 and *1993/4*, pp. 26–7. On the terminal see *New Civil Engineer*, 27 May 1993, pp. 18–23. Some of the gloss of this innovative project has been rubbed off by evident problems with the glazed section of roof (2000).

93 Authorised at £74.056m. (Q2/89 prices), revised authorisation £84.16m. (Q2/89/90), plus a further £4.0m. in changes of scope, final cost £75.89m. in Q2/89 prices, or £96.0m. in current prices. See Reid (I)–Parkinson, 12 February 1990, cit.; Reid (II)–Rifkind, 26 March 1991, cit. The private-sector proposal was from Costain Ventures; environmental concerns included the discovery of a rare species of lizard on the site. R. W. Urie (Infrastructure Project Director, Channel Tunnel Project, BRB)–Dixon (DTp), 28 February 1990, GIC 28-10 Pt. 1; Completion Certificate, 1 October 1993, CTX GEN 008.

94 Estimates at Q1/89 prices. 'Notes of Meeting held at Euston House on Tuesday 11 July 1989', n.d., Edgley–David Allen (Director, Finance), 13 September 1989, Kirby, Memo to Sector Directors on 'Channel Tunnel Advanced Renewals', 2 October 1989, Reeves–Jukes, 12 October 1989, Fowler–Parkinson, 14 September 1990, Parkinson–Fowler, 9 October 1990, GIC 28-36 Pt. 1; Reid (II)–MacGregor, 2 June 1992, and reply, 15 June 1992, GIC 28-36 Pt. 2.

95 BRB Press Release, 18 December 1989, BRB, *International Rail Services for the United Kingdom*, December 1989, p. 9, 'Projects Submitted to Secretary of State for Transport as at 21st December 1989', Investment Committee Minutes, 8 January 1990. The consortium, TransManche Super Train Group, consisted of two Belgian, three French, and two British companies, led by GEC Alsthom and BN.

96 Palmer, 'Note of a Meeting held at the Headquarters of SNCF in Paris on 11th March 1991', 12 March 1991, 'Meeting of Railways' Steering Committee and TMSTG Policy Board—15th October 1991', Watson's Papers, Sec Box 2375; Michael Elland-Goldsmith (Clifford Chance)–Edgley and Terence Jenner (Divisional Solicitor, BRB), 16 June 1992, Watson's Papers, Sec Box 2374; *Rail*, 20 January–2 February 1993, p. 40.

97 E. Fontanel (TMSTG)–Peter Abrey (Project Manager, IPG CTHST), 11 May 1990, CTX GEN005; Palmer–Watson, 18 March 1991, Watson's Papers, Box 2375; Interviews with Watson and Edgley, 2000.

98 Significant failures: one every 380,000 km, cf. one per 2 m. km.; major failures: one every 5.7 km, cf. one every 130 km. Douglas Gadd (GEC Alsthom)–D. Bennett (DTp), 8 February 1994, Watson's Papers, Sec Box 2360; Edgley–Nicholas L. J. Montagu (Deputy Secretary, DTp), 7 February 1994, enclosing Edgley, Memo on 'Eurostar Train Reliability', January 1994. On delivery see BRB Channel Tunnel Project Phases I and II Progress Report No. 43, 12 September–9 October 1993, CTX MREP43; Project Manager's Overview, and BRB Channel Tunnel (1993) Project Rolling Stock Progress Report No. 51, Channel Tunnel High Speed Train Project Report, 1–28 May 1994, CTX MREP46.

99 RfD Channel Tunnel Strategic Review, February 1990, BRB Minutes, 7 March 1990; Channel Tunnel Freight Strategy, October 1990 Review, BRB RfD GM 5-2-0. The February 1990 traffic forecast of 5.5 m tonnes was increased to 6.6 m. tonnes by October.

100 Interview with Ian Brown, 2000.

101 At Q3/89 prices. Parkinson–Reid (II), 18 May 1990, GIC 28-11; Reid–Rifkind, 3 December 1990, Freeman–Reid, 20 December 1990, Rifkind–Reid, 28 June 1991, GIC 28-6 Pt. 2.

102 Rifkind–Reid (II), 24 July 1991, GIC 28-6 Pt. 3; Memo to BRB Channel Tunnel Investment Committee (CTIC) on 'Class 92 Dual-Voltage Electric Locomotives', 1 April 1992, CTIC Minutes, 3 April 1992; Reid–Nicholas Montagu (DTp), 13 April 1992, GIC 28-6 Pt. 3; Hillard–Nichols, 16 March 1993, GIC 28-31 Pt. 2.

103 Nine Class 22200 SNCF locomotives deputised for the Class 92s from June 1994 to October 1995. Brown, Memo to Board Exec., 17 October 1995, GIC 28-6 Pt. 3; *Modern Railways*, August 1995, p. 490, December 1995, p. 757, April 1996, pp. 264–5, August 1996, p. 529, June 1998, pp. 366–7; Interview with Brown, 2000.

104 BRB, Railfreight Distribution Pre-Qualification Memo July 1996, p. 9, Appendix III. Aggregators purchase intermodal rail haulage capacity and sell it in smaller units to other transport companies.

105 BRB, *R&A 1995/6*, p. 61.

106 Jukes–Dixon, 14 May 1990, Dixon–Edgley, 9 August 1990, GIC 28-8 Pt. 1; Jukes, Memo 11 January 1991, CTIC Minutes, 17 January 1991.

107 Reid (II)–Rifkind, 23 January and 25 March 1991, Reeves (DTp)–Williams, 25 March 1991, Rifkind–Reid, 20 May 1991, GIC 28-8 Pt. 2.

108 Freeman–Reid (II), 28 November 1991, and see Reid–Freeman, 5 August 1991, GIC 28-8 Pt. 2.

109 Eurotunnel, *Ashford International Passenger Station* (September 1991), BRB 196-4-1 (folder); *The Times*, and *Daily Telegraph*, 5 October 1991.

110 Reid (II)–Rifkind, enclosing Edgley, Memo on 'Ashford International Passenger Station', March 1992, 11 March 1992, Hillard–Nichols, 13 March 1992, GIC 28-8 Pt. 2.

111 Rifkind–Reid (II), 16 March 1992, MacGregor–Reid (II), 22 March 1993, GIC 28-8 Pt. 2; Hillard, Memo, 28 April 1993, CTIC Minutes, 30 April 1993; *Modern Railways*, January 1996, pp. 53–5; February 1996, p. 72.

112 Vaughan S. Clemow (Principal Investment Adviser, BRB), Memo, 24 May 1989, Investment Committee Minutes, 5 June 1989; Jukes–Jim Coates, 20 July 1989, GIC 28-14 Pt. 1.

113 Fowler, Memo, n.d., BRB Minutes, 30 June 1989, 2 November and 7 December 1989; BRB, *International Rail Services for the United Kingdom*, December 1989, pp. 3, 11. On BR's lengthy consultation process see Transport Geography Study Group and Institute of British Geographers, 'Section 40, 1987 Channel Tunnel Act: Report on Process of Regional Consultation', n.d. [1989], BRB 196-4-1 (folder).

114 Cf. Investment Committee Minutes, 6 August 1990. The traffic forecasts were based on advice from Coopers & Lybrand, and accepted by the DTp.

115 Reid (II)–Parkinson, 22 October 1990, Reid–Rifkind, 27 March and 27 June 1991, Reid–Freeman, 9 August 1991, Rifkind–Reid, 25 November 1991, GIC 28-14 Pt. 2; Rifkind–Lord Weinstock (GEC), 1 July 1991, Kantor's Papers, Sec Box 2234. Problems with the suppliers were also a factor in the decision to abandon splitting trains. Cf. Supply Committee Minutes, 8 November 1990, Edgley, Memo to CTIC, 31 May 1991, GIC 28-14, PBA Box 50, *Financial Times*, 4 October 1991; Interview with Richard Edgley, 7 August 2000.

116 John Palmer (MD, Channel Tunnel, BRB)–Reid (II), 4 March 1991, Reid (II)'s Papers; Davies (Financial Planning Manager, Privatisation, BRB)–Nichols and Hillard, 6 December 1993, GIC 28-14 Pt. 2; Edgley, Memo on 'Channel Tunnel Project: Infrastructure Requirements for the Beyond London Services', 14 January 1994, BRB CTIC Minutes, 21 January 1994; Davies–Jerram, 9 March 1994, enclosing draft letter to Reid (II), GIC 28-14 Pt. 3.

117 Edgley, Memo on 'Night Services Through the Channel Tunnel', 9 November 1990, BRB CTIC Minutes, 15 and 22 November 1990; Reid (II)–Rifkind, 5 and 28 June 1991, Rifkind–Reid, 9 and 25 July 1991, GIC 28-30.

118 David Rowlands (DTp)–Jerram, 1 July 1992, GIC 28-30; Hillard, Memo on 'European Passenger Services Ltd: . . .', 13 September 1993, BRB CTIC Minutes, 17 September 1993.

119 *Modern Railways*, November 1995, pp. 690–4, January 1998, pp. 19–20, August 1999, p. 523, April 2000, pp. 52–4; *Rail*, 12–25 July 2000, p. 47. A report commissioned by the Department of the Environment, Transport and the Regions (DETR) in June 1999 confirmed the view that regional services were neither financially viable nor attractive from a cost–benefit perspective: DETR, *Review of Regional Eurostar Services: Summary Report. Independent Report by Arthur D. Little Ltd.* (February 2000), DETR web site, 2000.

120 DTp/Channel Tunnel Joint Consultative Committee [CTJCC], *Kent Impact Study: Channel Tunnel, a Strategy for Kent* (August 1987); BRB, *Channel Tunnel Train Services: BR Study Report on Long-Term Route and Terminal Capacity* (July 1988); Welsby, Memo on 'Channel Tunnel Phase III Study', n.d., BRB Minutes, 7 July 1988. The four routes were:

1 Sidcup–Longfield–Snodland–Hollingbourne–Charing–North of Ashford.
2 Bromley–Swanley–Longfield, then as 1 (chosen with modifications).
3 Bromley–Swanley–Borough Green–Marden–Pluckley–South of Ashford.
4 Bromley–Orpington–Tonbridge–Marden–Pluckley–South of Ashford.

121 BRB, 'Channel Tunnel Train Services: BR Study Report on Long-Term Route and Terminal Capacity', July 1988, p. 3. The consultants' passenger forecasts for 2003 were: 17.4m. (MVA), 21.4m. (SETEC). The figures were taken to indicate that additional capacity would not be needed until c.2000, on SETEC estimates, or 2005, on MVA estimates: Chairman's Group Minutes, 19 May 1988; Interview with John Welsby, 29 March 2000. A third set of estimates, produced by SNCF, was broadly in agreement with those of SETEC.

122 In 1973 the options were: Victoria, White City, and Surrey Docks, and in 1979–81: Waterloo, Victoria, London Bridge, West Brompton, and Olympia: David McKenna, Memo on 'Channel Tunnel: Choice of London Passenger Terminal', 31 January 1973, BRB Minutes, 8 February 1973; T. R. Barron (Executive Director, Channel Tunnel), Memo on 'London Terminal for Proposed Cross Channel Rail Link Services', 15 April 1981, BRB Railway Directing Group Minutes, 15 April 1981; Greater London Council Planning & Commercial Policy Committee Report, 24 February 1980, BRB 196-4-1 Pt. 12.

123 Welsby, Confidential Memo on 'King's Cross Low Level Station', 30 June 1988, BRB Minutes, 7 July 1988; BRB Press Release, 12 January 1989. On the opposition of Newham and Tony Banks, MP for Newham (North-West) see BRB Minutes, 12 January 1989.

124 A junction at Warwick Gardens (Peckham Rye) was to connect the new line with Waterloo. BRB, *Channel Tunnel Rail Link* (March 1989); BRB Minutes, 20 February, 6 March, and 9 March 1989; BRB Press Release, 8 March 1989.

125 BRB Press Releases, 8 August and 14 September 1989, and see also Gil Howarth (Director, Rail Link Project), Report to BRB on 'Rail Link Project: Comparison of Routes', May 1991, Ch. 7, reproduced in BRB, *Rail Link Project: Comparison of Routes* (June 1991).

126 Interview with Welsby, 2000 and cf. W. S. Atkins, 'Independent Review: Final Report', June 1991, paras. 17–20, in BRB, *Rail Link Project*; Michael Howard (Minister of State, DOE and MP for Folkestone and Hythe)–Welsby, 5 January 1989 and reply, 10 January 1989, BRB PA Box 303; Richard Allan (Director, Policy Unit, BRB), Memo on 'Channel Tunnel Phase III', 15 February 1989, BRB Minutes, 20 February and 6 March 1989, *Modern Railways*, June 1989, pp. 282–3; Professor Sir Frederick Holliday (BRB)–Reid (II), 28 January 1991, Reid (II)'s Papers. On the work of Kent County Council see Howarth, Report, May 1991, cit., pp. 25–6; Kent County Council, *CTJCC Channel Tunnel Impact Monitoring Group: First Annual Report* (April 1989), *Second Monitoring Report* (April 1990); Ian Holliday, Gerard Marcou, and Roger Vickerman, *The Channel Tunnel* (1991).

127 The best-known example of under-resourcing involved the drawing of a map on greaseproof paper placed over an ordnance survey map on a kitchen table: *Independent*, 25 November 1988, p. 4; Interview with Prideaux, 1998, Gil Howarth, 1 August 2000; Andrew Rowe (MP for Mid Kent), *Parl. Deb. (Commons)*, 6th ser. (Session 1988–9), vol. 144, 22 December 1988, col. 640.

128 Portions of the route were put out to engineers: Mott Hay & Anderson (London); Halcrow (West Kent); Scott Wilson Kirkpatrick (Mid Kent); and Alexander Gibb (East Kent). Howarth joined managers such as Bob Urie (initially Infrastructure Project Director, then Project Director, CT) and Cliff Moss (Project Co-ordinator, CTRL); he also appointed Mike Casey to act as the project engineer, 1989–90. Interview with Gil Howarth, 1 August 2000.

129 Investment Committee Minutes, 5 June 1989.

130 Welsby, Confidential Memos on 'Channel Tunnel Progress Report', n.d. [Nov. 1988], 'Channel Tunnel Rail Link: Private Sector Involvement', n.d. [Sep. 1989], and 'Channel Tunnel High Speed Link: Involvement of the Public Sector', 12 October 1989, BRB Minutes, 3 November 1988, 7 September and 17 October 1989; Lazard Brothers, Reports, 30 October 1989, appended to Welsby, Confidential Memo on 'Channel Tunnel Rail Link', 30 October 1989, BRB Minutes, 2 November 1989. The other consortia were: Costain (Taylor Woodrow, Wimpey, etc.), Davy/AMEC, KentRail (Ove Arup, Warburg, etc.), and Laing/Mowlem/GTM.

131 Welsby, Memo 30 October 1989, cit.; Richard Allan (Director, Policy Unit, BRB), Memo on 'Channel Tunnel Rail Link', 1 November 1989, BRB Minutes, 2 November 1989.

132 Welsby–Reid (II), 23 January 1990, Welsby's Papers, Sec Box 2347; Palmer, Memo on 'Joint Venture Company for Channel Tunnel Rail Link', 8 February 1990, Palmer, Confidential Memo on 'Channel Tunnel Joint Venture', 2 March 1990, Fowler, Confidential Memo on 'Channel Tunnel Joint Venture', 6 March 1990, BRB Minutes, 15 February, 8 March, and 27 March 1990; John Fletcher (Trafalgar House and Chairman, Eurorail) and Palmer–Parkinson, 30 March 1990, enclosing Kleinwort Benson, Confidential Memo on 'European Rail Link: Business and Financial Plan Summary', 30 March 1990, Welsby's Papers, Sec Box 2347.

133 Parkinson–Palmer, 14 June 1990, Welsby's Papers, Box 2347, and see also Parkinson's statement, 14 June 1990, *Parl. Deb. (Commons)*, 6th ser. (Session 1989–90), vol. 174, cols. 482–4; BRB Minutes, 5 July 1990. Reid (II) has suggested that he was also persuaded that the joint venture should be terminated: Memoir, cit.

134 BRB Press Release, 14 June 1990; BRB Minutes, 5 July 1990.

135 RACHEL = RAinham to CHannel TunnEL, was published by A. S. T. Hanley in July 1988. TALIS = Thames Alternative Link International System, was devised by T. Bain Smith et al. in January 1989. Rail-Europe chose to promote TALIS after RACHEL had been rejected by British Rail's consultancy, Transmark, in September 1989. See Transmark, Reports on 'Talis', July 1989, and 'Rachel', September 1989, BRB PA Box 156.

136 Newham's proposals were formulated with the help of Colin Buchanan & Partners.

137 Welsby, General Circulation Memo, 15 November 1989, BRB Secretary's Papers, Box 2505; BRB Press Release, 14 June 1990; BRB, Memorandum on 'Rail Link Project: The Consideration by the British Railways Board and Conclusions', June 1991, BRB Minutes, 6 June 1991, paras. 1–37, reproduced in BRB, *Rail Link Project: Comparison of Routes* (June 1991); BRB Rail Link Project Press Release, 24 October 1991.

138 BRB Minutes, 4 April 1991 and Special Meeting Minutes, 25 April and 2 May 1991; Reid (II)–Rifkind, 3 May 1991, Reid (II)'s Papers.

139 Trewin, Briefing for 'Meeting with the Secretary of State 16.30 Hours Wednesday, 17th July, 1991', 16 July 1991, BRB Secretary's Papers, Box 2006; *Independent*, 7

October 1991, p. 1; Reid (II)–Rifkind ('By Hand'), 7 October 1991, Judith Ritchie (Rifkind's Private Secretary, for Rifkind)–Reid (II), 9 October 1991, Reid (II)'s Papers; Interview with Sir Bob Reid, 1 February 2000. See also Andrew Mackinlay (MP for Thurrock), *Parl. Deb. (Commons)*, 6th ser. (Session 1992–3), vol. 222, 2 April 1993, cols. 795–7; Michael Heseltine, *Back to the Jungle: My Autobiography* (2000), p. 399.

140 'If you are in the middle of a pantomime you want to stay with it': *Guardian*, 10 October 1991, p. 24.

141 BRB Press Release, 9 October 1991; Reid (II)–Rifkind, 9 October 1991, Peter Trewin (BRB Secretary, for Reid II)–Rifkind, 11 October 1991 (2 letters), Rifkind–Reid (II), 21 October 1991, Reid II's Papers; Board Exec. Minutes, 10 October 1992; *Rail*, 16–29 October 1991, p. 4. The total figure invested was put at £250 m. to 1991/2: Jerram–Osmotherley, 20 December 1991, Welsby's Papers, Sec Box 2127; G. G. Jones (Group Taxation Accountant, BRB)–Jerram, 11 May 1992, enclosing Price Waterhouse, Report, 6 May 1992, Jerram's Papers, 524/BM.

142 Rifkind, 14 October 1991, *Parl. Deb. (Commons)*, 6th ser. (Session 1990–1), vol. 196, cols. 24–6, and see Palmer–Reid (II), 16 October 1991, Reid (II)'s Papers.

143 Rifkind–Reid (II), 21 October and 12 November 1991, Reid (II)'s Papers.

144 Palmer, Memo on 'Rail Link—Policy Issues', 19 December 1991, BRB Minutes, 9 January 1992.

145 Roger Ford, 'Dr John Prideaux', *Modern Railways*, July 2000, p. 25; Interviews with Prideaux, 1998 and Reid (II), 2000.

146 BRB Minutes, 5 March 1992; BRB Press Release, 8 November 1991; BRB Rail Link Project Press Release, 11 March 1992, BRB PA Box 156; Cliff Moss (Commercial Director, Union Railways)–D. Barnes (Financial Controller, InterCity Great Western), 18 November 1992, BRB GIC 24-10 Pt. 2.

147 BRB Minutes, 6 February and 5 March 1992; Union Railways News Release, 24 July 1992, *Union Railways R&A*, 1992–3, Jerram's Papers, 522/BM.

148 *British Railways Board Report March 1993: Prepared for the Board by Union Railways*, March 1993, para. 2.5, and Annex B. The 42 firms included seven dealing with engineering, 10 with business planning, and 12 with the environment.

149 'Union Railways Limited Report to Government December 1992 [Draft]', and 'The Union Railways Report January 1993', BRB Secretary's Papers; *British Railways Board Report March 1993. Prepared for the Board by Union Railways* (cited as '*Union Railways Report*').

150 Simon Osborne (Solicitor, BRB)–Prideaux, 27 November 1992, Reid (II)'s Papers.

151 See Osborne–David Rowlands (Under-Secretary, DTp), 4 December 1992, Prideaux, Strictly Confidential 'Notes of Meeting held at Department of Transport on Friday, 11 December 1992', 11 December 1992, Reid (II)'s Papers; MacGregor–Reid (II), 23 December 1992, Welsby's Papers, Sec Box 2126.

152 Prideaux (Chairman, Union Railways)–Reid (II), 26 November 1992, re BRB Informal Meeting, Bloomsbury Crest Hotel, 30 November 1992, Reid (II)'s Papers; BRB Minutes, 3 December 1992, 14 January and 22 February 1993; Board Exec. Minutes, 10 December 1992; Reid (II)–MacGregor, 14 January and 24 February 1993, Welsby's Papers, Sec Box 1956; *Rail*, 17–30 March 1993, p. 4.

153 *Union Railways Report*, paras. 2.6, 5.2, 6.1–6.8. A junction with a reinstated Gravesend West branch was to provide a connection via existing lines to Waterloo. There

were also options for additional tunnels to reduce environmental impact, e.g. at Luddesdown, Warren Wood, and Cobham Park.

154 *Union Railways Report*, paras. 14.1–14.4.

155 Ibid., paras. 2.6.5, 7.1–7.5, 8.1–8.4, 9.1–9.8. The Reference case provided for 14 trains an hour (8 international, 6 domestic), the Policy case for 20 (8 + 12): para. 8.2.1. A chapter on Freight concluded that the effect of including freight would be to release capacity elsewhere; however, the investment case was found to be weak: para. 12.7.

156 Norman Lamont, 16 March 1993, John MacGregor, 22 March 1993, *Parl. Deb. (Commons)*, 6th ser. (Session 1992–3), vol. 221, cols. 194, 609–13; MacGregor–Reid (II), 22 March 1993; Prideaux, Memo on 'Union Railways: Announcement', 1 April 1993, Reid (II)'s Papers; Interviews with Prideaux, 1998, Howarth, 2000.

157 Hillard–Jerram, 27 November 1992, GIC 29-1 Pt. 3. The changing treatment of the effects on Waterloo International Terminal is revealing. Cf. 'The current evaluation suggests that concentrating services on King's Cross would be preferable' ('Union Railways December 1992', para. 7.2.2), 'the current evaluation suggests that concentrating a large proportion of services on King's Cross would be preferable' ('Union Railways January 1993', para. 7.2.2), 'The balance of services between Waterloo and King's Cross would need to be reviewed in the light of market experience' (*Union Railways Report*, para. 7.2.2).

158 Richard Tomkins, 'Waterloo terminal may be obsolete in six years', *Financial Times*, 29 March 1993, p. 1; Reid (II)–Prideaux, 31 March 1993, Prideaux–Reid (II), 8 April 1993, Reid II's Papers.

159 Prideaux–Reid (II), 22 July 1993, BRB Secretary's Papers, Box 2147.

160 Reid, 'Note', 7 April 1993, Secretary's Papers, Box 2147. At the same time, Reid, Ken Dixon, James Jerram, and Archie Norman were added to the EPS Board.

161 Howarth–Reid (II), 23 July 1993, Prideaux–Reid (II), 23 July 1993, Secretary's Papers, Box 2147.

162 Reid (II)–Patrick Brown (Permanent Secretary, DTp), 3 August 1993, Trewin–Reid (II), 3 August 1993, Secretary's Papers, Box 2147; John A. Armitt, Memo on 'Situation Report: Union Railways Limited', 1 September 1993, BRB Minutes, 9 September 1993; *Observer*, *Sunday Times*, and *Independent on Sunday*, 22 August 1993. Prideaux was later involved in unsuccessful private-sector bids for the Link. He subsequently became Chairman of Angel Trains, the rolling stock leasing company.

163 Subsequently, Ebbsfleet was chosen as the intermediate station. BRB Minutes, 1 July and 21 October 1993; Union Railways, 'Union Railways Report to Government October 1993'.

164 Jerram–Reid (II), 14 December 1993, enclosing Nichols–Jerram, 14 December 1993, Reid II's Papers.

165 MacGregor, 24 January 1994, *Parl. Deb. (Commons)*, 6th ser. (Session 1993–4), vol. 236, cols. 19–21; DTp Press Notices, 24 January and 28 April 1994; BRB Minutes, 13 January, 10 February, and 14 April 1994. After the abandonment of the King's Cross scheme, the London Regeneration Consortium received £21.5m. in compensation from the Board: BRB Minutes, 7 July 1994.

166 Channel Tunnel Rail Link and European Passenger Services: Information and Pre-qualification Requirements for Prospective Bidders, BRB 196-4-1 (folder); MacGregor, statement, 11 November 1993; DTp Press Releases, 3 March and 10 June 1994; BRB Minutes, 3 March 1994; *Modern Railways*, April 1996, pp. 245–6; July 1998,

p. 433, October 1999, p. 742; DETR, *The Channel Tunnel Rail Link*, HC, 26 March 2001. The other shareholders in London & Continental were the SNCF subsidiary Systra, Halcrow, and S. G. Warburg.

167 *Second Report of HC Transport Committee on Preparations for the Opening of the Channel Tunnel*, 11 March 1992, vol. I, HC12-I, P.P. 1991–2, vii, paras. 76–81.

168 Sir Alastair Morton, Note to Reid (II), 9 October 1991, Reid (II)'s Papers.

Chapter 10

1 The loss of life (35) in the Clapham disaster may be compared with that in the other accidents: Zeebrugge, 193; King's Cross, 31; *Piper Alpha*, 167; M1, 45; Hillsborough, 95; and *Marchioness*, 51.

2 For an in-depth assessment of health and safety in relation to British Rail in the late 1980s see Bridget M. Hutter, *Regulation and Risk: Occupational Health and Safety on the Railways* (Oxford, 2001). For insiders' views see Stanley Hall, *Hidden Dangers: Railway Safety in the Era of Privatisation* (Shepperton, 1999) (Hall was Signalling Officer, BRB, 1977–82), and Edmonds in Freeman, pp. 64–8 (Edmonds was Chief Executive of Railtrack, 1993–7).

3 *Report of the Court of Inquiry into the circumstances attending the collision on the Somerset & Dorset Railway which occurred near Radstock on the 7th August 1876*, 7 September 1876, P.P. 1877, lxxvii; Channon, *Parl. Deb. (Commons)*, 6th ser. (Session 1988–9), vol. 143, col. 647, 12 December 1988. Railway accidents were normally investigated by the Railway Inspectorate without a public inquiry. The Clapham accident was only the fourth railway incident to be investigated publicly under the 1871 legislation following the Radstock inquiry. The others did not involve a collision between trains. They were the Tay Bridge Disaster of 1879, the level crossing accident at Hixon in 1968, and the fire at King's Cross Underground station in 1987. *Report of the Court of Inquiry and Report of Mr. Rothery, upon the Circumstances attending the Fall of a Portion of the Tay Bridge on the 28th December 1879*, 30 June 1880, P.P. 1880, xxxix; DTp, *Report of the Public Inquiry into the Accident at Hixon Level Crossing on Jan. 6, 1968*, 1968, P.P. 1967–8, xvi, Cmnd. 3706; DTp, *Investigation into the King's Cross Underground Fire [by Desmond Fennell, QC]*, November 1988, P.P. 1987–8, lxii, Cm. 499.

4 Incorrect wiring and inadequate inspection and supervision were revealed by the internal inquiry, which reported to the Safety Committee on 22 December. BRB Statement on Internal Inquiry, 16 December 1988, BRB PA 162; *Financial Times*, 17 December 1988; BR Management Brief; 21 December 1988, BRB Minutes, 12 January 1989. The Board also moved quickly in the matter of compensation, offering immediate payments of £2,000 plus funeral expenses.

5 Roger Henderson, QC, 21 February 1989, Clapham Inquiry Transcript, BRB CLAP 150. Henderson's remark was reported widely in the newspapers: cf. 'The White Sheet of Shame . . . ', *Evening Standard*, 21 February 1989, p. 1. Simon Osborne, BRB Solicitor, 1986–93, had been astute in engaging the services of Henderson, who had appeared on behalf of the Court in the King's Cross inquiry. It also meant that the SoS, Channon, was unable to appoint him to head the Clapham inquiry. Interview with Maurice Holmes, 11 November 1998.

6 BRB Minutes, 4 October 1990, 10 January 1991; BRB Safety Committee Minutes, 6 December 1990; Crown Prosecution Service Press Release, 18 May 1990, BRB CLAP 164; BR Management Brief, 13 September 1990.

7 Andrew Sim (Deputy Solicitor, BRB), Memo on 'Clapham Disaster: Health and Safety Prosecution', 30 April 1991, BRB Minutes, 2 May and 4 July 1991; BR Management Brief, 14 and 19 June 1991. The Southern Region's S&T department was found to have responded inadequately to earlier signal failures at Oxted in November 1985 and at Battersea in June 1988, while provision for training in 1982–6 was below the level requested. There had been no formal independent audit of safety practices within S&T at the time of the accident.

8 DTp, *Investigation into the Clapham Junction Railway Accident: Anthony Hidden, QC*, 7 November 1989, P.P. 1988–9, lix, Cm. 820, Chapter 17, and recommendations 1–93, pp. 167–75; BRB Minutes, 7 December 1989.

9 BRB Minutes, 3 December 1987.

10 Parkinson–Reid (I), n.d. [November 1989] and reply, 16 November 1989, copies with Rayner, Memo, 28 November 1989, BRB Minutes, 7 December 1989; Holmes, Memo, n.d., Safety Committee Minutes, 6 December 1990; BRB, 'Clapham Junction Railway Accident: The Implementation of the Recommendations of Sir Anthony Hidden QC', 15 February 1990, Second Report, 20 August 1990, Third Progress Report, 21 February 1991, Reid (II)–Parkinson, 22 August 1990, BRB Secretary's Papers, Box 1564; BRB Press Release, 13 September 1990.

11 Rayner, Memo, cit. The report by Desmond Fennell, QC on the King's Cross fire contained numerous recommendations for London Underground, 113 of which were found to be relevant to British Rail, and 94 of which had been implemented by March 1990: Chairman's Group Minutes, 23 February 1989; Safety Committee Minutes, 3 May 1990; Sir Oscar De Ville (Chairman, Safety Committee), Memo, 26 March 1990, BRB Minutes, 5 April 1990.

12 Cf. Hall, *Hidden Dangers*, p. 32, referring to the retirement of Ken Hodgson, Director S&TE, in March 1989. See Chairman's Group Minutes, 15 September 1988, 23 March 1989.

13 Ken W. Burrage (Director, S&TE), Memo 12 April 1989, Chairman's Group Minutes, 13 April 1989; BRB Minutes, 4 May 1989; Interview with Ken Burrage, 2 November 2000. Burrage succeeded Ken Hodgson, who was Director (in succession to William Whitehouse) from January 1988 to March 1989. Whitehouse and Hodgson had served as Director and Deputy Director from 1981.

14 Rayner, Memo cit.

15 Reid (I)–Fowler, Welsby et al., 21 February 1990, Chairman's Group Minutes, 22 February 1990.

16 Welsby, Memo 13 March 1990, Chairman's Group Minutes, 15 March 1990; Roger Ford, 'Exorcising Hidden Fear: S&T on the Southern', *Modern Railways*, January 1991, pp. 14–16. Welsby's investigation of the problems was assisted by independent advice from Du Pont.

17 Chairman's Group Minutes, 15 March 1990; BR Management Brief, 17 January 1991; BRB, Third Progress Report, February 1991, p. 6; Monitoring Reports, 1992, in BRD 61-3-2 Pt. 2.

18 See Kirby, reported in BRB Minutes, 4 May 1989; Burrage, 'S&T Stewardship Report for 1990/1', April 1991, Appendix A; Burrage, 'BR S&T for the 1990s', Paper to

Institution of Railway Signal Engineers, 12 December 1991; BRB Minutes, 2 April 1992; Interview with Burrage, 2000.

19 Cf. Richard Hope, *Railway Gazette International*, December 1989, p. 851; Hall, *Hidden Dangers*, p. 24.

20 Hidden, *Clapham Accident*, para. 13.3. Cf. also Interview with Stewart Currie, 28 October 1999.

21 Reid (II), Statement, 13 June 1991, *R. v. British Railways Board*, Reid (II)'s Papers. See also Reid, Memoir, cit.

22 Welsby, Memo on 'Safety Management Programme', 12 July 1990, BRB Secretary's Papers, Box 1674. On the consultants' efforts see Holmes, Memo on 'Safety Management on British Rail', n.d., Safety Committee Minutes, 7 December 1989. Robert P. Webber of Du Pont produced 'Safety Management on British Rail—Step 1–3' re the WCML, Dr Bridget Hutter (Oxford University) conducted a study of 'The Perceptions and Practice of Health and Safety at Work on British Railways', and Arthur D. Little undertook an 'Assessment of Safety Management in the Anglia Region'.

23 Safety Committee Minutes, 7 June and 6 September 1990, Chairman's Group Minutes, 19 July 1990; BRB Admin. Instruction No. 141, September 1990; BRB Minutes, 10 January 1991; Reid (II)–Parkinson, 22 August 1990, BRB Secretary's Papers, Box 1564.

24 Holmes, Memo, cit., Safety Committee Minutes, 7 December 1989; De Ville, Memo, March 1990, cit.; Hidden, *Clapham Accident*, para. 13.52; Interviews with Holmes, 1998, and James Cornell, 7 October 1999.

25 Holmes, Memo, cit.; Rayner, Memo n.d., Special Safety Committee Minutes, 11 January 1990.

26 Holmes, Memo, n.d., Safety Committee Minutes, 1 March 1990 and see also 3 May, 7 June, and 6 December 1990; Holmes, Memo 28 March 1990, Production Management Group Minutes, 3 April 1990; Rayner, Memo to Safety Committee, n.d., and Memo to BRB, 5 March 1990, BRB Minutes, 8 March and 5 July 1990.

27 Parkinson–Reid (I), 19 December 1989. This was the first time that safety was included specifically in government objectives for the industry.

28 BRB Special Safety Committee Minutes, 17 October 1990.

29 BRB, *Safety Plan 1991*; BRB Minutes, 6 December 1990; Holmes, General Circulation Memo, 6 February 1991, BRB 145-1-4 Pt. 1. A Technical Appendix to the Plan was produced for the use of BR managers, DTp, and the Railway Inspectorate.

30 BRB, *British Rail Safety 1992* (April 1992), *1993* (June 1993), *1994* (April 1994); BRB Minutes, 2 April 1992, 6 May 1993.

31 Rayner, Memo, 26 February 1990, Safety Committee, 1 March 1990; BRB, Technical Appendix to Safety Plan 1991, December 1990. The corporate safety organisation also had to respond to a series of health and safety measures introduced by the EC, e.g. on manual handling and VDUs.

32 Holmes, Memo, 8 October 1990, Safety Committee Minutes, 6 September and 17 October 1990; Chairman's Group Minutes, 25 October 1990; Board Exec. Minutes, 15 August 1991; Holmes–Reid (II), 25 November 1991, Reid (II)'s Papers; Interview with Holmes, 1998; Hidden, *Clapham Accident*, para. 13.53.

33 Chris Dickinson (Head of Safety Audit), Memo on 'Annual Report Group Safety Audit', 19 August 1993, Board Exec. Minutes, 19 August 1993. BRB Minutes, 2 December 1993. The mean score in the 96 audits was 13.9%.

34 Terry Worrall (Director of Operations, BRB), Memo, n.d., Safety Committee Minutes, 3 May 1990; Steer Davies Gleave, Final Report on 'British Rail Incident Monitoring System', June 1993, and accompanying papers, BRB SDSP Box 4; BRB, *Safety Plan 1993*, p. 10; *1994*, p. 11; Interview with David Rayner, 15 February 2000.

35 BRB Minutes, 6 December 1990; Du Pont Safety Management Services, 'Final Report', October 1991, p. 8; Reid (II)–Business Directors, 18 June 1992, Reid (II)'s Papers.

36 Graham Eccles (Project Director, Trackside Safety), 'An Investigation into the Causes of Fatal Accidents to Railway Staff and Contractors with Recommendations for Improvement', February 1993, BRB SDNW Box 3; Rayner, Memo, 14 June 1993, Board Exec. Minutes, 17 June 1993, and see also 21 January, 18 March, and 1 April 1993. An important contribution was made by the research on the impact of human behaviour on safety commissioned from BR Research and Prof. James Reason of Manchester University.

37 BRB Minutes, 1 December 1994.

38 5 & 6 Vict. c. 55, s.17; BRB Rule Book, 1 October 1972, para. 1.2.2, 2.1(a).

39 Jim Urquhart (ED, Personnel, BRB), Memo to RMG on 'Consumption of Alcohol on Duty', 16 October 1974; RMG Minutes, 22 August and 23 October 1974, 20 August 1975; R. H. Wilcox (Director, Industrial Relations, BRB)–F. D. Pattisson (C.A.O, BRB), 26 May 1982, BRB IR 145-50-12 Pt. 6; Michael J. Andrews (Director, Occupational Health & Safety), General Circulation Memo 18 September 1990, BRB IR 145-50-13 Pt. 1.

40 Wilcox, Memo, 1982, cit.; Memo to BRB Members on 'Alcoholism', October 1982, BRB IR 145-50-12 Pt. 6.

41 Interviews with Trevor Toolan, 10 June 1999, and Rayner, 2000.

42 BRB Policy and Code of Practice: Alcohol and Other Substance Abuse and the Use of Medication on Duty, 13 September 1990, enclosed in Andrews, Memo, cit.; A. Paul Watkinson (Director, Employee Relations), Memo to BR Joint Safety Committee, 17 May 1991, BRB IR 145-50-13 Pt. 1.

43 BRB Minutes, 10 September 1992; HSE, *Report of the collision that occurred on 8 January 1991 at Cannon Street Station* (1992).

44 Rayner–RMG Members, 16 April 1991, DTp Press Notice, 27 August 1992, BRB IR 145-50-13 Pt. 1.

45 Chris Green (MD, InterCity), Memo, 9 December 1992, BRB IR 145-50-13 Pt. 1. See also Board Exec. Minutes, 15 July 1993.

46 Mike Siebert (Director, Safety) and Simon Osborne (Solicitor, BRB), Memo, n.d., Board Exec. Minutes, 17 December 1992; BRB, Draft Alcohol and Drugs Policy, May 1993, Board Exec. Minutes, 20 May and 3 June 1993, 20 January 1994; Rayner, Confidential Memo to Board Exec. Safety Review Group, 20 January 1994. However, we should note that cases of drinking on duty continued to occur: cf. Board Exec. Minutes, 15 September 1994.

47 HSE, *Railway Safety 1990*, p. 20; *1994/5*, p. 26.

48 BRB Minutes, 7 May 1992; BRB, *Safety Plan 1993*, p. 7; *1994/5*, p. 9.

49 HSE, *Railway Safety 1994/5*, p. 26. The number of footpath crossings actually increased due to the downgrading of other crossings, 1989–93/4: in 1989 the figure was 1,957.

50 Chairman's Group Minutes, 19 July 1990; Reid (II)–Parkinson, 1 August 1990, Reid (II)'s Papers.

51 BRB Minutes, 1 November 1990.

52 BRB Safety Committee, 11 January 1990, Chairman's Group Minutes, 19 July 1990; BRB Minutes, 2 August 1990; Reid (II)–Parkinson, 17 August 1990, Reid (II)'s Papers; HSE, *Railway Safety 1994/5*, p. 44.

53 Parkinson–Reid (II), 8 October 1990 and reply, 30 October 1990, Parkinson–Reid (II), 12 November 1990, Reid (II)'s Papers; BRB Minutes, 9 June 1994; HSE, *Railway Safety 1994/5*, p. 44. The figures for over-bridges were much smaller: 129 in 1990, 83 in 1993/4.

54 The precise figures were 587 trespass deaths in 4.25 years (138 p.a.). BRB, *Safety Plan 1993*, p. 7; *1994/5*, p. 77.

55 Note the Roald Dahl campaign, reported in BRB, *R&A 1991/2*, p. 7; *1992/3*, p. 9; BRB Minutes, 14 January 1993.

56 Safety Committee Minutes, 11 January 1990; BRB, *Safety Plan 1991*, p. 23, *1993/4*, p. 9; HSE, *Railway Safety 1994/5*, p. 17.

57 613 suicides, 1990–93/4 = 144 p.a. BRB, *Safety Plan 1994/5*, p. 77.

58 Board Exec. Minutes, 18 November 1993.

59 BRB Minutes, 3 December 1992, Board Exec. Minutes, 21 October 1993; BRB, *Safety Plan 1993*, p. 7; Interview with Lew Adams, 29 July 1998.

60 Pauline Appleby, *A Force on the Move: The Story of the British Transport Police 1825–1995* (Malvern, 1995), pp. 257, 262–3.

61 BRB, *Safety Plan 1992*, p. 32; Reid (II)–Rifkind, 21 February 1991, and reply, 25 February 1991, Reid (II)'s Papers; 'Bomb Threats and Explosions: Security of Stations, Trains and Other Facilities', BRB Group Standards Confidential Instruction MP601, December 1991, revised 16 June 1992; Board Exec. Minutes, 12 March and 26 November 1992, 22 December 1993; John Plumb (for Director of Business Review, BRB), Memo on 'Closed Circuit Television (CCTV) Security Monitoring Systems at London Terminal Stations', 7 February 1994, NSE BRG Minutes, 16 February 1994.

62 Reid (II)–Rifkind, 31 July 1991, Kenneth Clarke–Reid, 1 September 1992, Reid (II)'s Papers; BRB Minutes, 7 November 1991; Reid, Memoir, cit.

63 At any early stage Rayner noted: 'There is almost universal disbelief that the Board means to change its approach to Safety Management from top to bottom': Rayner, Memo on 'Safety Management', n.d., Safety Committee Minutes, 1 March 1990.

64 Safety Committee Minutes, 15 February and 6 September 1990. See also Notes of 'Meeting on Wednesday, 8th November, 1989 to discuss the Hidden Report', included in Holmes, Memo to BRB Safety Committee, 7 December 1989, cit.

65 Adele Biss–Rayner, 20 June 1991, Reid (II)'s Papers. Biss reported that a dominant worry was the transportation of dangerous goods.

66 Burrage–Welsby, 1 August 1991, Reid (II)'s Papers.

67 BRB Minutes, 6 September 1990; ASLEF, *Locomotive Journal Safety Special* (October 1990), Reid (II)'s Papers. Derrick Fullick, General Secretary of ASLEF, who met both Parkinson and Reid in September–October 1990, was particularly angry about the prosecution of the driver in the Purley accident, who was sentenced to 18 months' imprisonment for manslaughter.

68 Cf. Holmes, Memos on 'Safety Management Programme', 30 August 1990 and n.d., Safety Committee Minutes, 6 September and 17 October 1990.

69 David C. T. Eves (Dep. DG, HSE)–Reid (II), 8 October 1991 and reply, 12 December 1991, Reid (II)'s Papers; HSE, *Railway Safety 1991/2*, p. 55; Du Pont Safety Manage-

ment Services, 'Step 3 Report', September 1990, and 'Final Report', October 1991; Holmes–Reid(II), 6 August 1991, enclosing Webber–Holmes, fax, 8 May 1991, Reid (II)'s Papers; BRB Minutes, 5 September 1991. The failure of five managing directors to give priority to meetings to consider Du Pont's final report was taken to be an indication that 'the organisation is not sufficiently committed to the level of change that will be required if we are to alter our safety culture': Bob Poynter (Safety Development Manager, BRB)–Reid (II), 14 November 1991, Reid (II)'s Papers.

70 Rayner, Memo on 'Safety Validation—Follow Up Audit', n.d., Board Exec. Minutes, 17 June 1993.

71 BRB, *Corporate Plan 1989*, p. 6; BRB, *R&A 1990/1*, p. 7; *1991/2*, p. 7; *1992/3*, p. 9.

72 Spending was monitored by the Safety Panel until 1993, but on the basis of departmental function rather than the type of initiative. The 1992 Safety Plan provides a rough indication of the allocation, contending that 20% was being applied to safety management systems (audits, quality, training, and data collection, etc.), 30% to the mitigation of human factors, and 50% to new technology (ATP, data recorders, track warnings, etc.) and fire. BRB, *Safety Plan 1992*, p. 18.

73 BRB, *Corporate Plan 1989* (December 1989), pp. 2, 6; Parkinson, *Parl. Deb. (Commons)*, 6th ser. (Session 1988–9), vol. 159, col. 835, 7 November 1989.

74 Rayner, Memo, 12 February 1990, and BRB, 'Forecasts of Additional Safety Expenditure Beyond Levels Included in 1989 Corporate Plan', 12 February 1990, BRB Minutes, 15 February 1990. The Forecast document, sent to Parkinson with the first Hidden progress report, referred to a figure of £240m. p.a., but this excluded additional *capital* investment. However, all the figures were subject to numerous caveats and approximations.

75 Chairman's Group Minutes, 22 March 1990.

76 Reid (II)–Parkinson, 10 April 1990, Welsby's papers, Sec Box 2125; BRB, *R&A 1990/1*, p. 7.

77 Reid (II)–Rifkind, 24 May 1991, Welsby's Papers, Box 2125. At the time of the Clapham trial Reid reminded Rifkind, 'I shall state categorically that I had a clear agreement with your predecessor and now yourself that any financial proposal which is presented to you on the grounds of safety will be accepted': Reid (II)–Rifkind, 13 June 1991, BRB CLAP 142.

78 Cf. Stephen Reeves (DTp)–David Allen (Director, Finance, BR) on 'Joint Review of British Rail Finances', 27 March 1991, Welsby's Papers, Sec 2125. Tensions between the DTp and BRB on safety expenditure in 1991/2 were carried over into relations between Welsby and his senior managers. Cf. Welsby, Memo to managers on 'Safety Budget', 10 July 1991, Burrage–Welsby, 1 August 1991 and reply, 5 August 1991, Reid (II)'s Papers.

79 Calculated from BRB, *R&A*.

80 Cf. Jukes–Reeves, 21 December 1989, Jukes–Trevor Adams (Project Manager, BRB), 1 February 1990, BRB IA 20-1-41-1 Pt. 1; BRB and DTp, 'Appraisal of Safety Related Projects', 7 February 1991, BRD 61-3-3-1; Reid (II)–Rifkind, 19 December 1991, Welsby's Papers, Box 2125; Coopers & Lybrand, 'British Rail Expenditure Prioritisation System Implementation Plan', December 1992, BRB BRD 61-3-2 Pt. 2.

81 ALARP = As Low As Reasonably Practicable.

82 BRB, *Safety Plan 1993*, pp. 9–10; *1994*, p. 11; David Maidment (Safety Policy Unit, BRB), Paper on 'Cost-Effectiveness of Safety—Railways', Second World Congress of

Safety Science, Budapest, November 1993, in BRB IA 20-1-41 Pt. 2; Rayner–Dr John H. Denning (DTp), 8 November 1993, BRD File, Box 141; Welsby, Memo 17 January 1994, Board Exec. Minutes, 20 January 1994.

83 Siebert (Director of Safety, BRB)–Alan Cooksey (Deputy Chief Inspecting Officer of Railways, HSE), 29 October 1993, BRB Safety Directorate Files [SD], SDI CP11.

84 Cooksey–Siebert, 23 November 1993, ibid. Cooksey agreed to the ending of formal reporting but noted that 'the remaining recommendations are still some way from being "closed out" '. In addition to those identified in the text there was Recommendation 81, which required improvements to BR's communication system in signal boxes.

85 HSE, *First Part of the Report of the Inquiry into the Collision between two passenger trains which occurred at Cowden on 15 October 1994* (May 1995), subsequently published in full as HSE, *Railway Accident at Cowden [Inspector: Major C. B Holden]* (1996); Sim–Welsby, 1 March 1995, BRB SDSM 118; Terry Worrall (Director, Safety), Memo on 'Compliance with Hidden Recommendations', n.d., BRB Minutes, 7 September 1995.

86 Siebert–Cooksey, cit.; Mark Turner (Project Manager, Train Safety Systems, BRB)–Michael Harwood (Privatisation Studies Group, BRB), 6 July 1993, BRB SDSM 80A; Bob Walters, Memo to ATP Steering Group on 'Data Recorders—Background', n.d. [1994], BRB SDI CP4.

87 Holden, *Railway Accident at Cowden*, 1996, para. 148 (Recommendation 15); Health & Safety Commission, *The Southall Rail Accident Inquiry Report: Professor John Uff QC FREng* (2000), Recommendation 15; *Modern Railways*, July 2000, p. 17. Uff has asked for all trains to be fitted within two years.

88 Report of Radio Strategy Working Party, 30 November 1992, BRB SDI CP7.

89 BRB, Third Progress Report, February 1991, cit.; John Plumb (Business Investment Controller, BRB)–Janet Goodland (Head of Business Planning, Railtrack), 4 March 1994, BRB SDI CP11.

90 NSE, Memo to Board Exec., 22 April 1991, BRB SDI CP7. There were a few exceptions, e.g. Bedford–Bletchley, Barking–Gospel Oak, Isle of Wight.

91 Alan Macdonald (Driving Standards Manager, NSE), Memo to BRG, 16 August 1993, BRG Minutes, 19 August 1993; Macdonald, Memo to Network Investment Panel, 8 February 1994, BRB BRD Box 60; Chris Tibbets (Director, Change Management, NSE), at NSE BRG, 21 May 1993, quoted in Plumb–Goodland, 1994, cit.; Clive Kessell (Director, Engineering, BR Telecommunications), 'Minutes of Meeting to discuss implementation of Hidden Recommendation 43...13 July 1994', 19 July 1994, BRB SDI CP2.

92 Holden, *Railway Accident at Cowden*, paras. 142–3.

93 Rayner–Robin Seymour (Chief Inspecting Officer, Railways, HSE), 26 April 1991, enclosing BRB draft report on 'Structural Improvements to Mark I Rolling Stock', 23 April 1991, and Rayner–Seymour, 22 January 1992, enclosing final report, 22 January 1992, BRB GIC 45–3; Rayner–Cooksey, 22 June 1992, Annex I, enclosed in Sim, Memo on 'Hidden 55', n.d., Board Exec. Minutes, 16 March 1995. The BRB report concerned the 1,600 Mark I EMUs reckoned to have a life of 10 years or more.

94 BRB Minutes, 4 July and 1 August 1991, 7 May 1992; Interview with Watson, 2000.

95 Board Exec. Minutes, 21 February–2 March 1995; Stan S. J. Robertson (Chief Inspecting Officer of Railways, HSE)–Reid (II), 14 February 1995, and reply, 13 March 1995,

Robertson–Welsby (Chairman, BRB), 19 May 1995, BRB SDSM 118; BRB, Confidential Interim Report on 'Maintaining a Safe Passenger Network Using Mark I Rolling Stock', August 1995, BRB SDTW 002.

96 Roger Ford, *Modern Railways*, September 1999, p. 634; July 2000, p. 16.

97 Gourvish, *British Railways*, pp. 85–6; Ministry of Transport (MT), *Railway Accidents*; *Report on the Collision which occurred on the 4th December 1957 near St. Johns Station Lewisham . . .* (1958), paras. 91, 95; *Railway Gazette*, 24 October 1930, p. 525, 4 September 1931, p. 316.

98 Gourvish, *British Railways*, p. 512.

99 The route-mileage open to passenger traffic was 8,891 at end of March 1989. An acceleration of the AWS programme in 1988–90 left *c.*500 miles to be installed in October 1990. DTp, *Railway Safety 1988*, p. 47; BRB, *R&A 1988/9*, p. 55; Stanley Hall, 'Safety on BR: is it good enough?', *Modern Railways*, July 1985, p. 362; Holmes (Director, Safety), Memo on 'Board's Safety Plan', n.d., enclosing draft Safety Plan, BRB Safety Committee Minutes, 17 October 1990; Sir David Davies CBE FREng FRS, *Automatic Train Protection for the Railway Network in Britain: A Study* (Royal Academy of Engineering, 2000), paras. 2.1.2–4. There appears to be some confusion about the extent of AWS investment. BRB, in its report to the SoS in March 1994, contended that the AWS programme had been 'substantially completed' by 1968: BRB, 'Automatic Train Protection. Report from British Railways Board to Secretary of State for Transport March 1994', para. 53 Watson's Papers, Sec Box 2364.

100 Stanley Hall (Signalling Officer, BRB)–Regional Signalling Officers, 1 February 1982, BRB Operations File MM/S/104/30; BRB, 'Automatic Train Protection', paras. 6–8; BRB, *Automatic Train Protection* (July 1994), pp. 3–4; Uff, *Southall Accident Report*, para. 12.9. The main weakness of AWS was that it gave the same warning for single yellow, double yellow, and red signals in multiple-aspect colour-light signalling systems.

101 In enhanced systems the driver had to acknowledge the type of signal encountered. After abandonment in 1976 the Southern Region was fitted with the standard system. Ian Campbell (ED, S&O, BRB), Memo, 16 October 1974, RMG Minutes, 23 October 1974; Investment Committee Minutes, 21 September 1976; BRB CS&TE Dept., Technical Report on 'Mark II A.W.S.', May 1977, BRB DM&EE Files, 145-100-154 Pt. 3; 'Memorandum of a Meeting Held in Room 505E at the Paddington Offices on 19 February 1987 for the Purpose of Discussing Enhanced AWS Equipment', n.d., BRB MTN/A/182, SD Box 1; Roger Ford, 'BR Aims to Set New ATP Standards', *Modern Railways*, October 1991, p. 538.

102 Health & Safety Executive (HSE), *Railway Safety 1994/5*, para. 53.

103 Maurice Holmes (Director of Operations, BRB) and Ken Hodgson (Director of S&TE, BRB), Memo on 'Automatic Train Protection: A Strategy for B.R.', October 1988, Holmes, Memo on 'Automatic Train Protection—A Strategy for BR', 27 October 1988, RE Minutes, 16 November 1988. Holmes had been succeeded by Ivor Warburton when the document reached the RE.

104 Holmes–David Rayner, January 1988, cit. in Hidden, *Clapham Accident*, para. 14.21; Interviews with Holmes, 1998, and Rayner, 2000.

105 Train-miles run per SPAD: 576,000 (1979), 390,000 (1985), 318,000 (1988). British Rail Research, 'An Investigation into the Causation of Signals Passed at Danger', January 1990, p. 3, BRB Secretary's Papers, Box 1674; Safety Committee Minutes, 7

December 1989; Terry Worrall (Director of Operations, BRB), Memo on 'Signals Passed at Danger', 21 February 1990, enclosing: BRB Director of Operations Newsletter, 'Up Front: Signals Passed At Danger', February 1990, Safety Committee Minutes, 1 March 1990. Data published by BRB in the 1994 Report give slightly different figures for SPADs, e.g. 638 for 1985 and 814 for 1988: BRB, *Automatic Train Protection*, p. 15.

106 After the Health & Safety at Work &c. Act 1974, the Railway Inspectorate remained in the DTp, conducting inquiries on behalf of the Health & Safety Executive on an agency basis. In December 1990 the Inspectorate was transferred to the Executive.

107 DTp, *Railway Safety 1985*, p. v; *1986*, pp. v–vi, *1988*, p. vi; Ken W. Burrage (Dir. S&TE), Report on 'Automatic Train Protection on British Rail: Present Plans and Future Possibilities', n.d. (*c.*1991), BRB, 'Automatic Train Protection', March 1994, Appendix to Annex 10; Davies, *ATP*, para. 2.1.6; Uff, *Southall Accident Report*, para. 13.1.

108 Maurice Holmes (Director of Operations, BRB) and Ken Hodgson (Director of S&TE, BRB), Memo on 'Automatic Train Protection: A Strategy for B.R.', October 1988, Holmes, Memo on 'Automatic Train Protection—A Strategy for BR', 27 October 1988, RE Minutes, 16 November 1988; Green (Director, Network SouthEast), Memo on 'Automatic Train Protection: a National Strategy', February 1989, Investment Committee Minutes, 6 March 1989; Prideaux (Director, InterCity)–Green, 23 February 1989, BRB IA 24-18-13 Pt. 2.

109 At Q4/90 prices: R. J. Walters (ATP Projects Manager)–Rayner, 31 May 1991, enclosing draft 'Automatic Train Protection National Implementation Strategy', BRB IA 24-18-13 Pt. 3.

110 BRB, 'Automatic Train Protection', March 1994, para. 12.

111 Holmes and Hodgson, Memo, October 1988, cit.; Hidden, *Clapham Accident*, para. 14.29.

112 Investment Committee Minutes, 6 March 1989. At the same time authorisation was given to install, ATP on the BTR1 route to the Channel Tunnel. The SoS Paul Channon revealed the news about the pilot schemes on the day after authorisation: *Parl. Deb. (Commons)*, 6th ser. (Session 1988–9), vol. 148, 7 March 1989, col. 757.

113 Ibid., 5 February and 6 August 1990.

114 Hidden, *Clapham Accident*, paras. 15.16–18.

115 Hall, *Hidden Dangers*, pp. 52–8, 74–82; Uff, *Southall*, para. 13.1. Hall criticised the safety of the single lead junction, a short section of single line used in both directions, which was in use in four accidents in 1989–91, including the accidents at Bellgrove and Newton: *Hidden Dangers*, pp. 46ff.

116 British Rail Research, Investigation, 1990, cit., p. 84; Safety Committee Minutes, 7 December 1989, 1 March and 7 June 1990. The investigation was followed by the appointment of a Project Director, SPADs, J. White, to co-ordinate efforts to reverse the rising trend. White, Memo, November 1990, Safety Committee Minutes, 6 December 1990.

117 Safety Committee Minutes, 1 March 1990 (interventions of Cameron and Davies); Welsby, Memo 27 September 1990, BRB Minutes, 4 October 1990; Rayner, Memo on 'ATP: Strategy for National Implementation', n.d., RMG Minutes, 16 June 1992.

118 Burrage, Report, cit.; Quentin Phillips (Investment Manager, BRB)–Plumb, 26 October 1993, BRB IA 24-18-13 Pt. 4; Richard McClean (Chairman's PA, BRB)–Reid (II), 5 December 1994, enclosing performance analyses for July–November 1994, BRB Secretary's Papers, Box 1845; BRB, 'Automatic Train Protection', pp. 8–9; Hidden Report, paras. 14.30, 15.13; Uff, Southall, paras. 13.4–6; Davies, ATP, para. 2.4.2; Interview with Burrage, 2000. The West Drayton–Paddington section was scheduled to be fitted with ATP with the resignalling/electrification work in 1994–6.

119 Hidden Report, Recommendation 48; BRB, 'Automatic Train Protection', March 1994, paras. 16–17; BRB, *Automatic Train Protection*, p. 6.

120 Sim and Osborne, Note, January 1994, Board Exec. Minutes, 20 January 1994, and see also 27 January and 3 February 1994; BRB Minutes, 10 February 1994.

121 Rayner, Memo on 'Automatic Train Protection: Choices', n.d., Board Exec. Minutes, 27 January 1994; BRB, 'Automatic Train Protection', March 1994, paras. 51–92.

122 BRB, 'Automatic Train Protection', March 1994, cit.; Reid (II)–MacGregor, 31 March 1994, Reid (II)'s Papers, Box 2008; BRB Minutes, 14 April 1994. The 52-page document was supported by 180 pages of annexes.

123 The calculation of ATP-preventable accidents was based on an analysis of accidents, 1968–93, when, it was contended, AWS was fully installed. However, as we have seen, AWS was not fully operative for two decades after 1968, and therefore, the data on ATP-preventable deaths and injuries may well be an over-estimate in that some of them might have been prevented by AWS. See BRB, 'Automatic Train Protection', March 1994, cit., Annex 4. The other area of uncertainty was value of life. The DTp used a figure of £0.715 m. (in June 1992 prices) for road deaths. BR first worked to a figure of £2 m., then accepted the advice of the UEA consultants that since major train crashes could be regarded as catastrophic there was a greater willingness to pay and therefore lives should be valued at a higher figure of £3.2–£4.2 m.

124 Cf. BRB Minutes, 3 February 1994, and minuted views of Christopher Jonas (Member, 1 August 1993), Ken Dixon, Peter Allen (Member, 1 July 1991, tragically killed in the Southall accident in 1997), Jerram, Welsby, Bob Horton (Member, 1 August 1993), and Jeremy Evans (Director, Public Affairs); Rayner–Reid (II) et al., 25 February 1994, BRB Secretary's Papers, Box 1845; Rayner, Memo, n.d., BRB Minutes, 3 March 1994.

125 Cf. BRB Minutes, 4 August, 8 September, and 6 October 1994, 4 May 1995; Board Exec. Minutes, 15 September 1994; Conference on 'Value for Money in Transport Safety', Royal Society of Medicine, 26 July 1994, Executive Summary; Rayner (Director, Safety & Standards, Railtrack)–Christopher Jopling (CBI), 15 September 1994, BRB Secretary's Papers, Box 1845; Railtrack, 'Paper to Joint Meeting of Members of the British Railways Board and Directors of Railtrack Group PLC', 28 September 1994, Trewin, Note on 'Joint Meeting of BRB and Railtrack, 5 October 1994', 3 October 1994, Reid (II)–Bob Horton (Chairman, Railtrack), 20 October 1994, and reply, 24 October 1994; Frank J. Davies (Chairman, HSC)–Brian Mawhinney (SoS, DTp), 23 December 1994; Mawhinney–Horton, 7 January 1995, and reply, 8 February 1995, Reid (II)–Mawhinney, 17 February 1995, Secretary's Papers, Box 2399; HSE, Report to HSC, 21 September 1994, reproduced in Annex F to Railtrack, Paper, cit.; Holden, *Railway Accident at Cowden*, paras. 100–103.

126 Parkinson, *Parl. Deb. (Commons)*, 6th ser. (Session 1988–9), vol. 159, col. 835, 7 November 1989; Portillo (Session 1989–90), vol. 166, 1 February 1990, *249*, vol. 167, 19 February 1990, *591*.

127 BRB ATP Executive Steering Group Minutes, 2 November 1992.

128 Note that the incidence of serious SPADs with driver error (categories 3–8, i.e. excluding those with overruns of up to 200 yards, with no damage) fell from 261 in 1988 to 174 in 1992, BRB, 'Automatic Train Protection', March 1994, Annex 10. However, there were lines with a comparatively high incidence of SPADs, including Paddington–Reading, Liverpool St.–Ingatestone, Victoria–Purley, King's Cross–Peterborough, and Glasgow–Carstairs, and the total number of SPADs rose from 814 in 1988 to 939 in 1991 and 896 in 1992: BRB, 'Automatic Train Protection', Annex 9, Appendices E and F, Annex 10.

129 DTp, *TSGB* 1995, p. 89; Interview with Watson, 2000. See also Prof. Andrew Evans, *Modern Railways*, August 1998, pp. 540–3, December 1999, pp. 887–8, March 2001, pp. 23–7. On the continuing debate see HSC, *Joint Inquiry into Train Protection Systems by Prof. John Uff and Rt Hon Lord Cullen* (2001).

130 BRB Press Desk Brief, 8 March 1991, Malcolm Parsons (Senior Press Officer, BRB)–Paul Sinclair (Principal Asst. Solicitor, BRB) et al., 27 August 1992, BRB PA Box 152; Interview with Watson, 2000.

131 Knight Wendling Consulting, 'Trainside Door Safety Review', February 1991, Watson's Papers, Box 2372. On early union concern cf. Buckton (ASLEF)–Watkinson, 18 February 1987, BRB IR 171-11-9(i).

132 John D. Rimington (DG, HSE)–Rayner, 11, 14, and 19 May 1992, with enclosures, including HSE Press Notice, 20 May 1992, Watson's Papers, Box 2372. The HSE criticised BR for not identifying the problem earlier, and found fault with its installation and maintenance procedures. For BR-commissioned research see also G. E. Curtis (British Rail Research), 'Door Lock Study', 26 July 1991, and Chris Blackman (Business Planning Operations Manager, BRB), 'Statistical Investigation into Incidence of Passengers Falling from Trains', November 1991 and April 1992, Watson's Papers, cit. Work was also carried out by Cambridge University Statistics Laboratory and Imperial College London. BRB Minutes, 2 May, 6 June, and 4 July 1991, 4 June 1992, Board Exec. Minutes, 1 August 1991.

133 HSE, *Report on Passenger Falls from Train Doors* (May 1993); BRB Minutes, 6 May 1993.

134 BRB Minutes, 14 January 1993; Watson, Memo, 17 January 1994, Board Exec. Minutes, 20 January 1994, and see investment authorities and project reports in BRD 24-18-33 Pt. 2 and IA 24-18-33 Pt. 2.

135 Welsby, Memo, 2 June 1993, Board Exec. Minutes, 3 June 1993, 13 December 1994; Tony Roche (BRB Board Member), Memo to Board Exec., 15 June 1995, IA 24-18-33 Pt. 1.

136 Nichols–Denning (DTp), 16 June 1995, BRD 24-18-33 Pt. 1; HSE, *Railway Safety 1994/5*, p. 15, para. 85. A proposal to fit new centrally controlled locks to NSE slamdoor stock presented more of a challenge in terms of returns, and was a matter which passed to the newly formed ROSCOs after 1994. See Plumb–Welsby et al., briefing note, 25 March 1994, BRD 24-18-33 Pt. 1; Roger Ford, 'Mk 1 safety—too much too late?', *Modern Railways*, July 1998, pp. 438–9.

137 A log linear regression for 1974–93/4 yields a growth rate of -3.88%; r2 $= 0.81$. There are too few observations for the period 1988–93/4, but a regression line suggests a rate of -9.32%; r2 $= 0.73$.

138 Cf. Derrick Fullick (General Secretary, ASLEF)–Reid (II), 31 July 1991, Reid (II)'s Papers.

139 Welsby, Memo on 'Safety, Performance', n.d., BRB Minutes, 9 June 1994; BRB, *R&A 1993/4*, pp. 5, 11; Hall, *Hidden Dangers*, p. 124. The number of SPADs, 884 in 1989/90, was 908 in 1993/4.

Chapter 11

1 Privatisations where the net proceeds exceeded £3,000m. See COI, *Britain's Privatisation Policy* (February 1990), p. 4; *Parl. Deb. (Commons)*, 6th ser. (Session 1990–1), vol. 182, John Wakeham, Written Answer, 14 December 1990.

2 Since this chapter was drafted railway privatisation has been the subject of an important monograph, *All Change: British Railway Privatisation* (Maidenhead, Berks., 2000), edited by Roger Freeman, Minister of State for Public Transport (1990–4) and Jon Shaw. The book includes contributions from John Edmonds, John Prideaux, Bill Bradshaw, and the Rail Regulator, John Swift, QC. Shaw is the author of a thesis on privatisation and the passenger market, entitled 'Privatising Britain's Passenger Railway: Expectations and Outcomes of the "Free" Market Approach', University of Plymouth Ph.D. thesis, June 1999.

3 Cf. Kathleen Burk, *The First Privatisation. The Politicians, The City, and the Denationalisation of Steel* (1988); T. R. Gourvish and R. G. Wilson, *The British Brewing Industry, 1830–1980* (Cambridge, 1994), pp. 323–30, 682; Howell, *A New Style of Government* (1970); Paul Salveson, *British Rail: the Radical Alternative to Privatisation* (Centre for Local Economic Strategies, Manchester, 1989), pp. 66–8; Andrew Grantham, 'Privatisation and Reorganisation: Case Studies in Rail Policy Implementation', Ph.D. Thesis, University of East Anglia, 1998.

4 Reid, *R&A 1988/9*, p. 6.

5 Readers are referred to the more detailed accounts in Freeman and Shaw (eds.), *All Change*, and Grantham, thesis (1998).

6 Brown–Sellers, 15 January, 10 August, and 16 October 1981, Sellers–Brown, 20 October 1981, Sellers, Memo on 'Private Capital for Railway Projects', 16 December 1981, BRB Minutes, 5 February 1981; Posner–Parker, 5 January 1981, Sellers–Parker, 29 March 1982, BRB 29–12–1 Pt. 3; Sellers, Memos on 'Private Capital for Railway Projects', 29 March 1982, on 'Private Finance for BRB — Report of the Tripartite Working Group', 24 September 1982, BRB Minutes, 7 October 1982. The NEDC guidelines were: investment to be undertaken in a competitive environment free of government guarantees, etc.; the cost of raising capital to be matched by improved efficiency. The view that joint public-private investment did not represent an escape from the public sector became known as the 'Ryrie rules': see Jon Shaw, 'Designing a Method of Rail Privatisation', in Freeman and Shaw, *All Change*, p. 27, n. 12.

7 Report of Tripartite Working Group on 'Private Finance for BRB', in Sellers, Memo, 24 September 1982, cit.

8 Howell–Parker, 4 October 1982, Parker's Papers; Serpell Committee, *Railway Finances*, para. 8.37; Sellers (Director of Finance and Planning, BRB), Memo on

'Private Capital: Victoria–Gatwick Project', 30 March 1983, BRB Minutes, 7 April 1983.

9 Trewin, 'Note of Meeting with Secretary of State: 21.12.82', 5 January 1983, Chief Executive's files, X81–51; BRB Minutes, 3 February 1983; Rose, Memo on 'Private Ownership/Operation of Specific British Railways Sections', 29 March 1983, BRB Minutes, 7 April 1983; Myers, Memo, 24 May 1983, Board Exec. Minutes, 26 May and 23 June 1983; Prideaux (Director, Policy Unit), Memo, 7 August 1984, Chairman's Group Minutes, 9 August 1984; Confidential Report of Joint BRB/Rail Limited Working Party (Chairman Chris Lewin) on Slough–Windsor, 6 July 1984, Lewin, Note for Chairman's Group on 'Slough–Windsor', 8 August 1984, O'Brien's Papers, Sec Box 2177; Interview with Jim O'Brien, 10 February 1999. In 1985 the Slough–Windsor line was used as a case study to evaluate the merits of agency operation of branch lines. See O'Brien–Osmotherly (DTp), 30 April and 28 June 1985, O'Brien Papers, Sec Box 2177.

10 1983 and 1986 Objectives, in BRB, *R&A 1983*, p. 4, *1986/7*, pp. 4–5.

11 Cf. Radical Rail Policy Group (Jenkins, Heath, Bradshaw, Myers, Trewin, Welsby), Report on 'Radical Rail Policy', 24 September 1982 (the report explored such issues as decentralisation, management buyouts, and the buying in of group services); Conference on 'Private Sector Involvement', Brocket Hall, Welwyn, 28–9 January 1985, O'Brien's Papers, Sec Box 2177; Wood, Memo on 'Private Sector Involvement: the Way Forward', 23 February 1987, Chairman's Group Minutes, 26 February 1987.

12 James Abbott, 'The London, Tilbury & Southend line. Ripe for Privatisation?', *Modern Railways*, January 1984, p. 20; see also pp. 199–201.

13 Malcolm Gylee, 'Alternative Way to Run Railways', *Transport*, 5(1) (January/February 1984), 14–15, David Starkie, 'BR—Privatisation Without Tears', *Economic Affairs*, 5(1) (October/November 1984), 16–19, reproduced as 'British Railways: Opportunities for a Contestable Market', in John Kay, Colin Mayer, and David Thompson (eds.), *Privatisation and Regulation: The UK Experience* (Oxford, 1986), pp. 177–88, and see Salveson, *British Rail*, p. 69, Grantham, thesis, pp. 80–1, and Shaw, thesis, pp. 69ff. Starkie was a transport economist in the University of Adelaide and subsequently Director of TM Economics.

14 ASI, *The Omega Report* (ed. Eamon Butler, Madsen Pirie, and Peter Young, 1985); Kenneth Irvine, *The Right Lines* (ASI, March 1987), and *Track to the Future* (ASI, 1988), pp. 16–23, 38–9, cit. in Salveson, *British Rail*, pp. 65–73, 77–9; *Modern Railways*, May 1987, p. 225. Irvine drew on his contacts with frustrated British Rail managers: Irvine, *File on Four*, BBC Radio 4, 30 November 1999.

15 Andrew Gritten, *Reviving the Railways: A Victorian Future?* (CPS Policy Study No. 97, June 1988), pp. 34–5, cit. in Salveson, *British Rail*, pp. 73–7; Grantham, thesis, pp. 82–3.

16 Gritten, *Reviving the Railways*, pp. 29–32; Irvine, *Track to the Future*, pp. 38–40.

17 Interview with Lord Kelvedon (Paul Channon), 13 September 2000 and cf. John Redwood, *Signals from a Railway Conference* (CPS, November 1988), pp. 15–18.

18 Don Heath (Director, Projects)–David Rayner, 13 March 1989, BRB Privatisation Papers (PRI), File 213.703.

19 Cf. J. R. Castree (Policy Adviser, BRB)–Reid (I), 6 May 1988, Kirby's Papers, Sec Box 2155; *Economist*, 21 May 1988.

20 A sixth option—privatising BR 'as it is'—was also considered. Fowler, Memo on 'Privatisation: Discussions with Department of Transport and No. 10 Policy Unit', n.d. [14 July 1988], Chairman's Group Minutes, 14 July 1988; Channon, speech to Party Conference, 11 October 1988, reported in *Daily Telegraph*, 12 October 1988, and to CPS Conference on 'Reviving the Railways', 28 October 1988, in Redwood, *Signals from a Railway Conference* (1988), pp. 29–39, and *The Times*, 24 October 1988, *Financial Times*, 29 October 1988.

21 Eight papers were discussed informally with the DTp on 5 July 1988: 'The Potential for taking NSE out of Grant', 'Privatisation: Incentives to Maintain Quality Standards', 'Estimates of Inter-Regional Traffic Flows' (BR Policy Unit, all 13 June); DTp, 'Regulation of Privatised Rail Services' (9 June, with BR comments, 27 June), and 'A Track Authority?' (10 June, with BR comments, 1 July); 'Privatisation: Break-up by Region' (BR, 21 June); 'Privatisation: Break-up by Sector', 'Alternatives to Break-up: The "BR plc" Holding Company', (BR, both 30 June 1988), BRB PRI 214.000.

22 Allan–Fowler, 2 and 13 June 1988, Kirby's Papers, Sec Box 2155.

23 Allan–Reid (I), 20 May 1988, Allan–Fowler, 2 June 1988, Kirby–Reid (I), Fowler, and Allan, 7 June 1988, Kirby's Papers, Sec Box 2155; Allan, Memo on 'Privatisation: Meeting with Mr Palmer (DTp), 1st June', 2 June 1988, BR Policy Unit, Discussion Papers on 'Privatisation: Break-Up by Region', 21 June, and 'Alternatives to Break-Up: The "BR plc" Holding Company', 30 June 1988, BRB PRI 214.000.

24 DTp, 'Long Term Options for Railways: Note of Meeting [1 June 1988]', 2 June 1988; DTp, 'A Track Authority?', 10 June 1988, BRB PRI 214.000; Kirby–Allan, 7 June 1988, cit.; Allan–Reid (I), 13 July 1988, BRB PRI 211.200; Fowler, Memo, n.d. [14 July 1988], cit.; Richard Bayly (Policy Adviser, BRB), 'Note of Meeting with Philip Wood Friday, 25th November, 1988', n.d., BRB Secretary's Papers, Box 2385; BRB Policy Unit, Confidential Memo on 'Possible Privatisation: Structural Options', April 1989, BRB Minutes, 26 April 1989; Allan–Fowler, 12 June 1989, BRB PRI 211.500; Interviews with David Kirby, 13 January 1999, Gordon Pettitt, 6 November 2000. The proposal to privatise the Southern Region was advanced by David Hopkinson, Chairman of the Southern Area Board (1983–7) and Chief Executive of M&G Group (1979–87), but it apparently went no further than Bob Reid (I).

25 BRB Minutes, 4 August 1988.

26 Richard Allan (Director, BRB Policy Unit), Memo to Reid (I) on 'Privatisation: Key Points for BR', 12 October 1988. Kirby's Papers, Sec Box 2155; Reid (I), Memo on 'Secretary of State's Speech at Brighton: Future Ownership', 27 October 1988, Annex A, BRB Minutes, 3 November 1988; Fowler, Memo, n.d. [14 July], cit.; Allan–Reid (I), 15 and 22 July 1988, Allan–Charles Brown, 4 August 1988 enclosing (revised) 'Note of an Informal Discussion by Non-Executive Members of the British Railways Board, 25th July 1988', BRB PRI 212.701; Allan–Reid (I), 26 July and 4 August 1988, Kirby's Papers, Sec Box 2155.

27 Lazards (Sir John Nott) were retained as merchant bank advisers, Coopers & Lybrand (Sir Christopher Foster) as accounting and management consulting advisers. The DTp engaged Samuel Montagu and National Economic Research Associates [NERA]. BRB Minutes, 13 October 1988, 12 January 1989; Reid, Memo, 27 October 1988, cit., BRB Minutes, 3 November 1988; Fowler, Memo on 'Privatisation: Advisers' Fees', n.d., Chairman's Group Minutes, 22 February 1990; Policy Unit, Brief for Reid (II) on 'Privatisation: Position Report', 5 February 1990, Welsby's Papers, Sec Box 2341.

28 Deloitte, Haskins & Sell, 'Study of Structural Options for Railway Privatisation', May 1989 (6 vols., *c.*550pp.), BRB PRI Boxes 9494–5; Osmotherly–Fowler, 13 April and reply, 14 April 1989, Allan–Fowler, 16 May 1989, BRB/DTp, Joint Note on 'Study of Structural Options for Privatisation', 15 May 1989, and 'Joint Assessment of Material Presented in Report by Deloitte, Haskins & Sell', 16 May 1989, 'Note of a Meeting between Mr Fowler and Mr Osmotherly to Discuss BR Privatisation—18 May', 22 May 1989, BRB PRI 211.400; Allan, Memo on 'Privatisation: a Radical Decentralisation Option', 1 June 1989, BRB Special Meeting Minutes, 7 June 1989; BRB Minutes, 7 September 1989.

29 DTp/BRB Joint Working Group Report on 'Viability', September 1989, containing Lazards/Coopers & Lybrand, 'Preliminary View of Privatisation and Viability', 1 June 1989, and Samuel Montagu, Report on 'The Feasibility of Privatising British Rail', August 1989, BRB PRI Box 9495.

30 BRB/DTp Draft Report on 'Privatisation of British Rail: Report of the Department of Transport/British Rail Joint Working Group', 20 October 1989, BRB PRI 212.001; Allan, Memo on 'Privatisation: a Radical Decentralisation Option', 1 June 1989, BRB PRI 211.003; Allan–Fowler, 4 September 1989, BRB PRI 212.500; Policy Unit, Brief, 5 February 1990, cit.

31 Vickers and Yarrow, *Privatization*, pp. 384–6; C. D. Foster, *Privatization, Public Ownership and the Regulation of National Monopoly* (Oxford, 1992), p. 133, cit. in Grantham, thesis, p. 85.

32 Parkinson, speech, 12 October 1989, reported, *inter alia*, by *Financial Times*, and *Daily Mail*, 13 October; and Parkinson–Reid (I), 2 November 1989, Allan–Reid (II), 22 January and 14 February 1990, BRB PRI 211.400; BRB Minutes, 15 February 1990; *Railway Gazette International*, October 1990, p. 729.

33 Jim Evans (Director, 1992 Impact Study, BRB), Memo on '1992', 21 April 1989, Richard Allan (Director, Policy Unit), Memo on '1992', 25 April 1989, Chairman's Group Minutes, 27 April 1989; Charles Brown (Director, Policy Unit), Memo on 'European Community Proposals for Community Railways', n.d., Chairman's Group Minutes, 21 June 1990.

34 O'Brien, Memo on 'Overhead Cost Review,' March 1983, BRB Minutes, 31 March 1988; O'Brien, Memo on 'Overhead Cost Review Exercise—Progress Report', 11 July 1988, Chairman's Group Minutes, 14 July 1988; Reid (I), Memo, 6 November 1988, Chairman's Group Minutes, 17 November 1988; Welsby–Edmonds et al., 12 February 1990, Welsby's Papers, Sec Box 2348.

35 Allan–Reid (I), 13 July 1988, BRB PRI 211-200.

36 See BRB Policy Unit, Paper on 'Line of Route Management', 14 April 1989, Allan–Kirby, 13 April 1989, BRB PRI 211.002; John Edmonds, Paper on 'Evolution of BR's Sector-Led Organisation Structure', 23 January 1990, BRB Minutes, 23 January 1990.

37 BRB Policy Unit, Memo on 'Possible Privatisation: Structural Options', April 1989, BRB Special Meeting Minutes, 26 April 1989; Jenkins, Paper on 'Rail Privatisation Options', August 1988, Memo on 'Re Privatisation—Next Steps', 3 May 1989, and Paper on 'Proposal for Line-of-Route Company for the East Coast Main Line', 11 July 1989, BRB PRI 212.701. After his resignation Jenkins ruffled feathers with an article in *The Times* entitled 'How to Run a Railway', in which he castigated BRB for resisting the break-up of its monopoly and once again pressed the regional option: *The Times*, 18 December 1991.

38 Coopers & Lybrand, Report on 'Future Structure for the Railways: A Decentralised Market-Based Structure', June 1989, p. 17, BRB PRI Box 9495; BRB Special Meeting Minutes, 7 June 1989.

39 Initially these were Road Transport, Information Systems & Technology, Architecture & Design, Architectural Services, Transmark, and Projects. BRB Headquarters Admin. Instruction 138, July 1989, BRB 30-2-1 Pt. 4.

40 Edmonds was the classic graduate traffic apprentice. Educated at Trinity College Cambridge, he became a BTC traffic apprentice (management trainee) in 1960. BRB 48-2-66.

41 Allan, Memo on 'Britannia Hotel Discussion, 14 September 1989: Summary of Conclusions', 18 September 1989, BRB PRI 211.600; Edmonds, Memo on 'Organisational Simplification: Progress Report', 30 November 1989, Chairman's Group Minutes, 30 November 1989.

42 Reid–Channon, 8 and 30 June 1989, Reid–Parkinson, 22 September 1989, BRB PRI 211.400; BRB Policy Unit, Note on 'Privatisation and Radical Decentralisation', 25 October 1989, brief for dinner with Parkinson and Portillo, 1 November 1989, BRB 20-100-7 Pt. 2; Parkinson–Reid, 2 November 1989, cit. and reply, 7 November 1989, BRB PRI 211.400; Policy Unit, Briefing Paper for Mr Reid [Bob Reid II] on 'Organisational Simplification', 19 December 1989, Welsby–managers on 'Preparing for the 1990s', 13 December 1979 [sic, i.e. 1989], BRB OfQ Box 65.

43 Reid (II) had gone to see Parkinson over the issue of retail petrol sales, the subject of an MMC inquiry. He was somewhat surprised to be offered the job of Chairman, BRB: Interview with Sir Bob Reid, 2 February 2000; Parkinson, *Right at the Centre*, p. 295; Interview with Lord Parkinson, 19 September 2000.

44 Pronounced 'Oh-eff-Q', but known, more irreverently, as 'Oh-fur-Q'. See Ivor Warburton (General Manager, LMR), 'Organising for Quality: London Midland Region Proposals: Progress Report to Chairman's Group', 16 March 1990, BRB OfQ Box 57; Robin Linsley (Records Officer, BRB), Memo on 'Organising for Quality (OFQ)', July 1992, BRB OfQ Box 65; Interviews with John Edmonds, 7 January 2000, and Ivor Warburton, 18 January 2000.

45 Brian Burdsall, former National Business Manager, Petroleum sub-sector, and Director, Parcels, became Director, Quality Through People, in December 1988. The quality awareness programme embraced a series of courses for managers, referred to as 'Leadership 500' and 'Leadership 5000'. See BRB Minutes, 31 March, 5 May, 13 October 1988, 9 February 1989; Burdsall, Memo March 1989, BR Council Minutes, 21 March 1989; RMG Minutes, 26 September 1989; *Rail*, 27 May–9 June 1992, p. 4.

46 Interview with Reid (II), 2000, and see also his Memoir, cit.

47 The other project team members were Peter Fearnhead (Operations Planning Manager, Operations), Tim Owen (Finance Manager, Anglia), and Malcolm Spiller (Corporate Planning Manager, Finance & Planning), with part-time contributions from Tony Roche (Production Services Director, M&EE), Charles Brown (Policy Adviser [from April 1990 Director], Policy Unit), Chris Kimberley (Passenger Policy Adviser, Passenger Marketing), Alan Deboo (Personnel Manager (Corporate & General), Personnel), and Vivian Chadwick (Project Director, Infrastructure Costs). Edmonds–Sector Directors and RGMs, 30 October 1989, Edmonds's Papers, Sec Box 2217.

48 Some MGR activities involved 'dedicated' locomotives and wagons, routes, and maintenance depots. Goldson was Resource & Development Manager of Railfreight,

1988–9. He had been Assistant Area Manager at Knottingley, 1972–3, and Railfreight Officer (Construction), 1983–6. Edmonds had been Freight Marketing Officer (Coal), 1971–8, and Freight Marketing Manager (Coal), subsequently National Business Manager (Coal), 1982–4.

49 Edmonds, Memos on 'Organisational Simplification: Overview' n.d., 'Organisational Simplification—Summary Paper', 12 January 1990, and supporting papers, BRB Minutes, 23 January 1990; DTp, *Investigation into the Clapham Junction Railway Accident (Anthony Hidden QC)*, November 1989, P.P. 1988–9, lix, Cm. 820.

50 Lindblom, *The Policy-Making Process*. Lindblom asserted that radical change introduced incrementally offers the best chance of success.

51 Cf. DTp, 'Note of a meeting on British Rail Organisation Simplification, 26 April 1990', 4 May 1990, Edmonds–Andrew Whybrow (DTp), 9 May 1990, Edmonds's Papers, Sec Box 2221. Neither the introduction of sector management in 1982, nor the abolition of the divisions in 1984, nor the establishment of Anglia Region in 1988, had required a formal report. However, civil servants remained of the opinion that OfQ *did* fall within the terms of section 45(1), rather than requiring mere consent under section 45(6)(d), and there was an exchange of legal opinion in 1991 before the DTp was minded to order a review in March 1992. See Goldson–Simon Osborne (Solicitor, BRB), 9 December 1991, BRB 48-2-1 Pt. 3; Osborne, Memo, 9 December 1991, Board Exec. Minutes, 12 December 1991; Trewin–Baker (DTp), 24 January 1992, Trewin–Philip Wood (DTp), 9 March 1992, Baker–Trewin, 4 and 12 March 1992, BRB 30-2-1 Pt. 5; Interview with Richard Goldson, 9 February 2000.

52 The six profit centres were: South West, South Central, South East, Great Eastern, West Anglia, and London Tilbury & Southend. Circulation Note on 'Senior Appointments', 16 January 1990, BR Management Brief, 11 May 1990; Edmonds, 'Chairman's OfQ brief', n.d. [July 1990], BRB OfQ Box 70.

53 Reid (II)–Parkinson, 26 June 1990, BRB PRI 211.400; Welsby–Chief Executive's Forum, 7 June 1990, OfQ Box 70; BRB Minutes, 7 June and 5 July 1990; Edmonds, Memo on 'Organisational Simplification', n.d., BRB Chairman's Group Minutes, 22 June 1990; BRB Press Release, 29 June 1990.

54 Established profit centres: June 1991:

> InterCity: ECML, GWML, Anglia/Gatwick Express
> NSE: SW, SC, SE, GE, LTS, West Anglia, Thames & Chiltern
> Regional: ScotRail, South Wales & West, North East
> April 1992:
> InterCity: WCML, MML/Cross Country
> NSE: Thameslink, North
> Regional: Central, North West
> Trainload Freight: Coal, Construction, Metals, Petroleum
> Railfreight Distribution: Europe, UK
> Parcels, reporting to the passenger businesses, had profit centres for Red Star, and Rail Express Systems (trainload parcels).

Goldson, Memo to OfQ Steering Group, n.d., SG Minutes, 6 May 1992, OfQ Box 51.

55 Interview with Goldson, 2000.

56 David Blake (Director, M&EE)–Edmonds, 9 October 1990, George Buckley (Director of Research)–Leslie Smith, John Prideaux, Chris Green, and Gordon Pettit (sector directors), 30 October 1990, Edmonds's Papers, Sec Box 2217; Interview with David Blake, 16 February 2001.

57 George Buckley (Managing Director, Central Services)–Prideaux (Managing Director, InterCity), 29 July 1991, Edmonds's Papers, Sec Box 2217. Buckley added: 'I must express the view frankly that the break-up of DM&EE was long overdue, or at least the injection of real management into a department which was bloated, inefficient, unhelpful, overbearing and overstaffed. Even those smaller numbers now coming to Central Services will need a heavy dose of attitude adjustment. However, the price we have had to pay has been dear, with BR costs inflated dramatically and the skill level asymptotically lower'.

58 Cf. Cornell (Director of Civil Engineering)–Edmonds, 10 October 1991, Edmonds's Papers, Sec Box 2217.

59 Ken Burrage (Director, S&TE)–Edmonds, 1 September 1989, Edmonds's Papers, Sec Box 2217; Burrage–Edmonds, 23 January 1990, Reid–Fowler et al., 21 February 1990, Edmonds's Papers, Sec Box 2221; Interview with Edmonds, 2000.

60 Burrage–Green, Prideaux, and Pettit, 4 July 1990, Burrage–Welsby et al., 3 July 1992, Edmonds's Papers, Sec Box 2217; OfQ Steering Group Minutes, 9 December 1991, 5 February 1992.

61 Peter Rayner–Area managers, LMR, 12 June 1990; *Evening Standard*, 7 August 1990, pp. 1–2; Rayner–Edmonds, 10 August 1990, Welsby–Rayner, 10 August 1990, Welsby, File Note, 13 August 1990, Edmonds's Papers, Sec Box 2218. On Fiennes's maverick behaviour in the 1960s see Gourvish, *British Railways*, pp. 98, 448, 464.

62 Iain King (Area Manager, Manchester, LMR)–Reid (II), 25 February 1991, OfQ Box 27.

63 Peter Rayner (Regional Operations Manager, LMR)–Reid, 18 March 1991, enclosing '"Organising for Quality": A Review after Twelve Months with Suggested Variations to the Original Theme', March 1991, OfQ Box 27; Hidden, *Clapham Accident*, 1989, paras. 14.34–41.

64 See Ivor Warburton (General Manager, LMR)–Rayner, King, and David McKeever, 21 March 1991, BRB Secretary's Papers, Box 2051. Rayner continued to rant against OfQ in his new post as Project Director (Psychometric Testing). After an accident at Newton in Scotland in July 1991 he produced a further diatribe against its evils, precipitating his early retirement in April 1992. See Rayner, 'Why the Decision Came About', March 1992, and Edmonds–Welsby, 16 March 1992, Edmonds's Papers, Box 2218; Peter Rayner, *On and Off the Rails* (Stratford-upon-Avon, 1997), pp. 7–14, 373–6.

65 Hugh Jenkins (Director, Human Resource Development)–Reid (II) on 'Feedback on Perceptions', 22 March 1991, BRB Secretary's Papers, Box 2051; Goldson–Edmonds (commentary on the Yellow Book), 5 April 1991, OfQ Box 27.

66 *Guardian*, 15 April 1991, *Observer*, 19 May 1991, *Independent on Sunday*, 7 July 1991; Les Johnson (District Secretary, District No. 3, ASLEF)–Reid (II), 26 March 1991, Edmonds's Papers, Sec Box 2218; Nigel Spearing (MP, Newham South)–Reid (II), 19 May 1991, Edmonds's Papers, Sec Box 2221; Debate on British Rail (Reorganisation), 7 June 1991, *Parl. Deb. (Commons)*, 6th ser. (Session 1990–1), vol. 192, cols. 575–82. Roger Freeman, Minister for Public Transport, replied for the government. Goldson observed that when the debate was announced 'there was an immediate

exodus from both the chamber and the public gallery! Left in the chamber was what I understand to be the absolute minimum requirement for an Adjournment Debate': Goldson–Welsby et al., 10 June 1991, Sec Box 2221.

67 Cf. Charles Brown (Director, Policy Unit), Note on 'Britannia Hotel Discussion, 18th October 1990: Summary of Conclusions', 5 November 1990, BRB OfQ Box 70; Chris Green (MD, InterCity), quoted in *Rail*, 17 February–2 March 1993, pp. 20–1; *Modern Railways*, February 1997, p. 79; Interview with Edmonds, 2000.

68 Coopers & Lybrand Deloitte, Draft Final Report on 'Organisational Simplification—The Holding Company: Organisation and Management Processes', April 1990, BRB OfQ Box 45, and see synopsis, 18 May 1990, OfQ Box 70. The report cost £462,000. Jackie Rowe (Policy Adviser, BRB)–Edmonds, 29 June 1990, Edmonds's Papers, Sec Box 2216.

69 Heath–Edmonds, 8 May 1990, Edmonds's Papers, Sec Box 2216.

70 Bayly, Paper on 'Business-Led Privatisation', 29 August 1991, BRB PRI Box 9434; Interviews with Prideaux, 1999 and Edmonds, 2000.

71 See Brown–Edmonds, 15 October 1990, Brown, Note, 5 November 1990, OfQ Box 70; Edmonds, Memo on 'Group Headquarters', n.d., Britannia Meeting, 18 October 1990, BRB PRI Box 9564; Reid (II)–BRB managers, 28 November 1990, OfQ Box 70; Reid, Memo on 'Board Organisation and Committee Structure', 9 January 1991, BRB Minutes, 10 January 1991; Interview with Reid (II), 1 February 2000.

72 BRB Headquarters Admin. Instruction No. 100 (revised), April 1992. In addition, there were advisory panels, e.g. for Remuneration, and the BT Police Committee, a statutory body.

73 Edmonds–BRB managers, 9 July 1990, Edmonds, Note on 'Britannia Hotel Discussion: 18th October 1990: Organising for Quality: Central Services', and faxed annexes, n.d., BRB OfQ Box 19; George Buckley (Project Director, Central Services)–Edmonds, 14 October 1990, BRB PRI 9564; Buckley, Memo on 'Central Services', n.d., BRB Minutes, 2 July 1992; BR Management Brief, 16 March 1992. The central services budget for 1992–3 was £562 m.

74 BRB, *R & A 1992/3*, p. 28.

75 Hidden, *Clapham Accident*, paras. 10.12–33.

76 Maurice C. Holmes (Director, Safety)–Business Directors, 2 October 1990, 'OfQ: Safety Validation Checklist', 26 November 1990, BRB PRI Box 9564. Validation was undertaken by a safety panel with the assistance of Bowrings Risk Management Unit; the work of group standards units followed work undertaken by BRB jointly with PA Consulting Group.

77 Rayner and Watson, Memo on 'Group Standards', n.d., OfQ Steering Group Minutes, 13 February 1991; BR Management Brief, 12 February 1992.

78 Edmonds, Memo on 'Ancillary Trading Activities', 18 December 1990, Chairman's Group Minutes, 20 December 1990; BRB Property Working Party, 'British Rail Property Review', November 1991, BRB Minutes, 5 December 1991; Edmonds, Memo on 'Property Review', 2 July 1992; BR Property Board Minutes, 20 May 1992.

79 Edmonds, Memo, 18 December 1990, cit.; BRB Management Brief, 20 March 1991.

80 BR Management Brief, 24 July 1990; BRB, *R&A 1990/1*, p. 28.

81 BRB, *R&A 1990/1*, p. 22. The other remaining Board activities were BT Police, which became a two-tier structure with eight areas (using boundaries based on the five Regional Railways profit centres, London Underground, and NSE North and South),

reporting to Edmonds as Chairman of the Police Committee, and BRML and the Level 5 Maintenance Group, reporting to Watson.

82 There were also 12,000 in Group and Subsidiary activities. Data for 24 March 1990, BRB IR Cassettes, CBTB levels 6 and 9, 13-8890-35 and 36.

83 Some residual regional responsibilities remained after April 1992.

84 There were 9,000 in Subsidiaries, &c. (= EPS, BR Int, BRPB, BRML, Level 5 Depots, BT Police, BRT, and Mega Projects). Data for 25 April 1992, BRB IR Cassettes, MISP level 12 Pt. 3.

85 Excluding Subsidiaries, &c.: data for 2 April 1994, BRB IR Cassettes, MISP level 12 Pt. 5.

86 Edmonds, Memo on 'Organising for Quality', n.d., BRB Minutes, 5 March 1992.

87 Tim Owen–Edmonds, 4 June 1990, Edmonds's Papers, Sec Box 2221; Goldson–Welsby and Edmonds, 15 March 1991, BRB PRI Box 9564; Goldson–Gareth Hadley (Employee Relations Manager, BRB), 10 April 1992, AN171/313, PRO.

88 Spiller, Memo on 'OfQ Trading Relationships: Track Access Guidelines', 28 February 1992, BRB OfQ Box 33, and 'OfQ Trading Relationships: Track Access Q&A Brief', March 1992, OfQ Box 49; Interview with David Rayner, 15 February 2000.

89 This is evident from Reid (II), manuscript Memoir. See also Michael J. Piore and Charles F. Sabel, *The Second Industrial Divide* (New York, 1984); C. K. Prahalad and Gary Hamel, 'The Core Competence of the Corporation', *Harvard Business Review*, 68 (May–June 1990), 79–91; Bennett Harrison, *Lean and Mean: The Changing Landscape of Corporate Power in the Age of Flexibility* (New York, 1994), pp. 3–12; Terry Gourvish, 'Japan's Miracle in Perspective', in Etsuo Abe and Terry Gourvish (eds.), *Japanese Success? British Failure? Comparisons in Business Performance Since 1945* (Oxford, 1997), p. 6.

90 Brown–Fowler and Welsby, 12 September 1990, BRB Secretary's Papers, Box 2053; Brown–E. F. Sanderson (incoming part-time Board member), 13 March 1991, BRB Secretary's Papers, Box 2379; BR Management Brief, 12 October 1990; Parkinson, *Right at the Centre*, p. 288.

91 Putnam Hayes & Bartlett, 'Track Access and Charging Study—Final Report', 5 April 1991 (80pp. plus appendices), BRB PRI Box 9431; Grantham, thesis, p. 87; Interview with Roger Freeman, 15 March 2001.

92 Brown–Reid (II), 4 April 1991, BRB PRI Box 9434; NERA, 'Infrastructure as a Common User Facility', June 1991, and six supporting papers, in BRB PRI Box 9432; Draft remit, 20 March 1991, attached to Brown–Reid (II), 20 March 1991, BRB Secretary's Papers, Box 2379.

93 Rifkind–Reid (II), 13 May 1991, cit.

94 Osmotherly–Reid (II), 15 May 1991, BRB PRI Box 9434.

95 The Leicester University study, undertaken by John Gough was on 'Competitive Track Access: Some Aspects of the 19th Century Experience', 8 July 1991, BRB PRI Box 9433. The report played down the importance of inter-company disputes over running powers, and did not refer to the difficulties which drove the Midland and Manchester Sheffield & Lincolnshire to construct their own routes into London.

96 Brown–Reid (II), 9 August 1991, BRB Secretary's Papers, Box 2379.

97 Baker (DTp)–Brown, 15 July 1991, enclosing DTp, draft report on 'British Rail Privatisation', Jerram's Papers, A2, and see also Brown–Reid (II), 16 July 1991, BRB PRI Box 9431. An internal BRB estimate of the number of separate contractual agreements

required was 15,000–20,000 with separate companies, compared with 3,000 under OfQ: Brown–Reid (II), 4 April 1991, BRB PRI Box 9434.

98 Reid, personal and official letters to Rifkind, both 8 July 1991, BRB PRI Box 9434.

99 Cf. Bayly–Brown, 9 September 1991, BRB PRI Box 9434.

100 BRB Policy Unit, Paper on 'Unitary Privatisation', 30 August 1991, BRB PRI Box 9434.

101 Bayly, Note on 'Board Executive: Britannia, 3 September 1991', 4 September 1991; BRB Policy Unit, Paper on 'Privatisation Through National Railway Authority', 28 August 1991, BRB PRI Box 9434. The NRA might be divided into two bodies, one for NSE, the other for IC/RR.

102 Reid–Rifkind, 27 September 1991, BRB PRI Box 9434.

103 Brown–Reid (II), 24 October 1991, BRB PRI Box 9434; BR Management Brief, 9 October 1991; Seldon, *Major*, pp. 208, 260–1, 268; Interview with Reid (II), 2000. Cf. also *The Times*, 30 December 1991.

104 Brown–Reid (II), 1 October 1991, Judith Ritchie (Rifkind's Private Secretary)–Reid (II), 9 October 1991, BRB PRI Box 9434.

105 Brown–Reid (II), 24 October 1991, cit.; BRB Minutes, 13 February 1992; Welsby, 'CE's Team Briefing 9', 27 January 1992, BRB PRI Box 9391; Palmer–Reid (II), 5 February 1992, Reid (II)–Rifkind, 12 February 1992, BRB Secretary's Papers, Box 2378; Note to BRB CSG on 'Privatisation: Press Indications of Current Ministerial Thinking', 5 March 1992, BRB PRI Box 5470.

106 Reid (II)–Rifkind, 18 November and 6 December 1991, BRB Secretary's Papers, Box 2378.

107 The Chairman's Special Group (CSG), consisting of Reid, Welsby, Jerram, Edmonds, assisted by Palmer and his privatisation team, Jerry Evans, the Director of Public Affairs, and others, held its first meeting on 13 December 1991; Palmer's appointment formally took effect in January 1992. BRB Minutes, 7 November 1991; Bayly–Reid et al., 12 December 1991, BRB PRI Box 7112; Palmer, Memo on 'Privatisation and Access Liberalisation', 13 December 1991, BRB PRI Box 5470; Brown–Reid (II) et al., 22 January 1992, BRB PRI Box 9391; Interview with Reid (II), 2000.

108 Reid (II)–Rifkind, 6 December 1991, BRB Secretary's Papers, Box 2378. Reid repeated his views in a lecture to the Chartered Institute of Transport (CIT) on 13 January 1992: BR Management Brief, 17 January 1992.

109 Cf. Palmer, Memo, n.d., BRB Minutes, 9 January and 13 February 1992.

110 Reid–Rifkind, 17 January 1992, enclosing BRB, Paper on 'A Regional Structure', 17 January 1992, BRB Secretary's Papers, Box 2378. The Paper reiterated the Board's lack of support for the regional option. On Major's support for regional companies see Warwick Smith (Westminster Communications Group)–Chris Austin (Parliamentary Affairs Manager, BRB), 29 January 1992, Secretary's Papers, Box 2379.

111 BRB Policy Unit, Note, 11 December 1991, Philip O'Donnell (Director, Privatisation Studies), Memo to BRB CSG, 20 March 1992, BRB PRI Box 5470; Palmer, Memo on 'Access Liberalisation', n.d., BRB Minutes, 9 January 1992; DTp, White Paper on *New Opportunities for the Railways: The Privatisation of British Rail*, July 1992, P.P. 1992–3, liv, Cm. 2012, paras. 58–61.

112 BRB Railfreight Distribution (RfD) News Release, 24 July 1990. Gisby had been Director of GKN's Industrial Services Development Division. British Rail's stake was 22%. In 1991 Ian Hay Davison, Chairman of Credit Lyonnais Capital Markets

(1988–91) and former Managing Partner of Arthur Andersen (1966–82) and Chief Executive of Lloyd's (1983–6), became involved as an adviser and was then appointed Chairman.

113 *Rail*, 4–17 September 1991, p. 30.

114 Ian Brown (MD, RfD)–Robin Gisby (MD, Charterail), 7 March 1991, Tim Hansford (Director UK, RfD), 'Notes of Meeting with Charterail 1400 Friday 12 July 1991', 15 July 1991, Hay Davison–Welsby, 24 July 1991, and reply, 6 August, Welsby–Roger Freeman (Minister of State for Public Transport), 7 August 1992, Welsby's Papers, Sec Box 1959; *Rail*, 16–29 September 1992, p. 9; HC Transport Ctee, *Second Report on The Future of the Railways in the Light of the Government's White Paper Proposals*, vol. I, 20 April 1993, P.P. 1992–3, xxxix, HC246-I, p. cxli; Interview with Ian Hay Davison (Charterail), 9 February 2000. Tiger Rail also experienced difficulties and went into receivership in February 1992: *Modern Railways*, March 1992, p. 112.

115 Reid (II)–Rifkind, 22 November 1991 and 30 January 1992, Rifkind–Reid (II), 2 January 1992, BRB Secretary's Papers, Box 2378.

116 Other interested parties were Christian Salveson, Sheerness Steel, Hunslet Barclay, and Tiger Rail. See BRB Minutes, 9 January 1992; Stephen Barber (Policy Adviser, BRB), Position Note on 'Short Run, Voluntary Private Sector Access', 17 February 1992, BRB PRI Box 5470.

117 Cf. draft letter from Reid to Rifkind, March 1992, Palmer, Note to BRB CSG, 10 April 1992, BRB PRI Box 5470; Note of 'Private Meeting: Richard Branson: Virgin Atlantic: Tuesday 5th May 1992', 6 May 1992, Welsby's Papers, Sec Box 1959; Welsby, Memo on 'Progress on Response to Virgin', n.d., Board Exec. Minutes, 4 September 1992; Richard Branson, *Losing My Virginity: the Autobiography* (1998), pp. 358–9.

118 Trewin, Note on Stagecoach, 30 December 1991, BRB Secretary's Papers, Box 1856; Green–Welsby, 21 January 1992, Brian Souter (Chairman, Stagecoach Holding)–Welsby, 10 February 1992, Welsby's Papers, Sec Box 1959; BRB Board Exec. Minutes, 19 March 1992; BRB Minutes, 1 October and 5 November 1992; *Rail*, 27 May–9 June 1992, p. 9; Christian Wolmar, *Stagecoach: A Classic Rags-to-Riches Tale from the Frontiers of Capitalism* (1998), pp. 124–5; Queen's Speech, 6 May 1992, *Parl. Deb. (Commons)*, 6th ser. (Session 1992–3), vol. 204, col. 51. Stagecoach continued to book blocks of seats after its initial contract was abandoned.

119 See O'Donnell, Memos to CSG on 'Coopers Access Study', 20 February 1992, and on 'Open Access Study', 5 March 1992, and Note to BRB CSG, 5 March 1992, cit., BRB PRI Box 5470; O'Donnell–Reid (II) et al., 12 March 1992, BRB PRI Box 9214.

120 Conservative Party, *The Best Future for Britain* (1992), pp. 35–6; and see summary in Note for BRB CSG, 20 March 1992, BRB PRI Box 5470.

121 Prescott–Reid (II), 14 January 1991 [*sic*: actually 1992], BRB PRI Box 5470; Labour Party, *It's time to get Britain working again* (April 1992), p. 13.

122 John MacGregor (SoS for Transport)–Reid (II), 16 April 1992, BRB Secretary's Papers, Box 2006.

123 Brown–Reid (II) et al., 27 April 1992, but cf. Board Exec. Minutes, 30 April 1992 (which recorded that the presentation had gone well); Interviews with Reid (II), and David Rayner, 2000. Reid gave some thought to complaining again. A letter was written, but not sent: letter, May 1992, in Palmer–Reid (II), 8 May 1992, BRB Secretary's Papers, Box 2049.

124 MacGregor, Paper to Cabinet Ministerial Committee on Economic and Domestic Policy on 'British Rail Privatisation', 28 May 1992, copy in BRB.

125 Cf. Brown–Reid (II), 13 May 1992, BRB Secretary's Papers, Box 2049; Reid (II), Confidential Note for File, 27 May 1992, Box 2378. Contrary to some assertions, the government's plans were revealed to Reid prior to publication. See Reid's meeting with MacGregor, 20 May 1992, reported in Reid (II), Confidential Note for File, 27 May 1992, BRB Secretary's Papers, Box 2378, and Board Exec. Minutes, 8–9 July 1992.

126 Formal separation of infrastructure from operating had been undertaken in July 1988 to make it possible for the Swedish government to appraise road and rail infrastructure investment and give the track authority socio-economic goals, as was made clear when a joint DTp/BRB group visited Sweden in October 1989. Ian R. Jordan (DTp)–Richard Bloomfield (Policy Unit, BRB), 20 October 1989, and BRB Policy Unit, 'Swedish Railways: Report of DTp/BR visit, October 1989', n.d., John Heath's Papers, and see also Jan-Eric Nilsson, 'Second-best Problems in Railway Infrastructure Pricing and Investment', *Journal of Transport Economics and Policy*, 36(3) (1992), 245–59; Harris and Godward, *Privatisation*, pp. 64–5; Louise S. Thompson and Helene Stephen, 'Infrastructure separation: what have we learned so far?', *Rail Business Report 1998*, pp. 8–10; Chris Nash, 'Privatisation and Deregulation in Railways: An Assessment of the British Approach', in Bill Bradshaw and Helen Lawton Smith (eds.), *Privatization and Deregulation of Transport* (Basingstoke, 2000), pp. 161, 167.

127 Cf. John Dodgson, 'Editorial', and John Welsby and Alan Nichols, 'The Privatisation of Britain's Railways', *Journal of Transport Economics and Policy* 33(1) (January 1999), 1–4, 58–60, and Bill Bradshaw, 'BR at the Crossroads', *Modern Railways*, January 1992, p. 31.

128 Interviews with numerous railwaymen, including Cornell, Rayner, and Reid (II).

Chapter 12

1 MacGregor–Reid (II), 14 July 1992 (public letter), MacGregor–Reid, 14 July 1992 ('personal and strictly confidential letter'), BRB Secretary's Papers, Box 2049; DTp, *New Opportunities for the Railways*, July 1992, paras. 10–18; Welsby and Nichols, 'Privatisation of Britain's Railways', 58–60.

2 BRB Minutes, 29 July 1992; Privatisation Steering Group Minutes, 27 May 1992; Project Management Group Minutes, 11 June 1992. The working groups were for: Access; Franchising; Freight; Parcels; Track Authority; Restructuring; Employee Issues; Safety and Standards; Regulation; International; Network Benefits; and Property.

3 Tim Norman (DTp)–Palmer, 17 August 1992, Roger Peal, Memo, 16 September 1992, BRB Secretary's Papers, Box 2049; BRB Minutes, 1 October 1992.

4 DTp, *The Franchising of Passenger Rail Services* (October 1992), *Railway Privatisation: A Voice for the Passenger* (December 1992), *Ensuring Safety on Britain's Railways: a report submitted to the Secretary of State for Transport by the Health and Safety Commission* (January 1993), *Railway Privatisation: Passenger Rolling Stock* (January 1993), *Railway Pensions after Privatisation: the Government's Proposals* (January 1993), *Gaining Access to the Railway Network: the Government's*

Proposals (February 1993), *Heavier Lorries for Combined Road/Rail Transport* (February 1993).

5 British Coal and British Rail (Transfer Proposals) Act, 19 January 1993, s. 2.

6 DTp, Note on 'Restructuring Group', 12 February 1993, Restructuring Group Minutes, 22 February 1993, Jerram's Papers; Montagu–Reid (II), 11 June 1993, Reid's Papers; Mr Freeman's Implementation Group (FIG) Minutes, 16 June 1993; Interview with Freeman, 2001. FIG replaced a number of the high-level groups, and notably the Privatisation Issues Group (PIG), successor to the Privatisation Steering Group, which met in January–May 1993, and included Brown, Montagu, Reid, and Welsby among its members.

7 HC Transport Ctee, *Second Report on The Future of the Railways in the Light of the Government's White Paper Proposals*, vol. I, 20 April 1993, P.P. 1992–3, xxxix, HC246-I, pp. iv–xvii. See also Grantham, thesis (1998), pp. 95–6.

8 Nick Montagu (DTp)–Reid (II), 11 September 1992, Reid (II)'s Papers; BRB Minutes, 10 September 1992. See also DTp/BRB Restructuring Working Group Minutes, 19 October 1992, BRB Secretary's Papers, Box 2049.

9 *Financial Times*, 27–28 June 1992, p. 6.

10 Reid (II)–Edmonds, 23 March 1993, Edmonds–MacGregor, 23 March 1993, BRB 48-2-66.

11 Reid (II)–MacGregor, 6 November 1992, Reid-MDs and Profit Centre Directors of the Passenger Businesses, 18 November 1992, Secretary's Papers, Box 2049; BRB Board Exec. Minutes, 26 November 1992, BRB Minutes, 3 December 1992; Interviews with Bob Reid (II), 1 February 2000, Brian Burdsall, 19 June 2000, and John MacGregor, 29 March 2001.

12 Chris Green (MD, InterCity)–Tony Baker (DTp), 25 November 1992, Secretary's Papers, Box 2049.

13 DTp, Note on 'Railtrack: Status, Objectives and Tasks', DTp/BRB Track Authority Working Group Minutes, 20 November 1992.

14 DTp Press Notice, 17 December 1992, BRB 48-2-74; MacGregor–Reid (II), 17 December 1992 and reply, 18 December 1992, MacGregor–Reid, 23 December 1992, BRB Secretary's Papers, Box 2379; BRB Minutes, 14 January 1993.

15 Palmer–Reid, enclosing 'Chief Executive Railtrack—Key Points', 9 October 1992, Secretary's Papers, Box 2049; Edmonds–Trewin, 25 November 1992, enclosing Edmonds–Reid (II), 19 November 1992, Secretary's Papers, Box 2380; Interviews with John Edmonds, 7 January 2000, Reid (II), 2000, Richard Goldson, 5 May 2000, and Peter Watson, 21 June 2000.

16 Reid (II)–MacGregor, 21 July 1992, Reid (II)'s papers; BRB Minutes, 29 July 1992; Trewin, Memo on 'Board Member Private Sector Involvement', 9 September 1992, BRB Minutes,10 September 1992; Reid (II)–MacGregor, 29 September 1992, Reid (II)'s Papers.

17 MacGregor–Reid (II), 'by hand', n.d., received 12 October 1992, Reid (II)'s Papers.

18 MacGregor–Christopher Campbell, 28 January 1994, BRB 48-2. The re-marketing of Red Star was undertaken by Campbell on a consultancy basis in January 1994: Trewin–Campbell, 10 January 1994, ibid.

19 MacGregor–Reid (II), 12 and 28 January 1994, Welsby's Papers, Sec Box 2125.

20 Trewin, Memo on 'Appointments to the Board', 5 November 1992, BRB Minutes, 5 November and 3 December 1992; Trewin–Montagu, 9 November 1992, BRB 48-2-67.

The 1976 arrangements for reappointment were reaffirmed in 1990: BRB Minutes, 15 February 1990.

21 Telex Report on 'The World This Weekend', 20 December 1992, Trewin's Papers, Sec Box 2001; 'What the Chairman Said about Privatisation', BRB Privatisation News (Management Brief), 23 December 1992; Reid (II)–MacGregor on 'B.R. Privatisation: Regulation', 11 December 1992, Secretary's Papers, Box 2378; Reid–MacGregor, personal letter, 5 January 1993, marked 'not sent', Box 2379. The HC Transport Committee took Reid's Radio 4 interview to demonstrate 'continuing uncertainty over the unresolved practical issues': HC Transport Ctee, *The Future of the Railways in the Light of the Government's White Paper Proposals: Interim Report*, 20 January 1993, P.P. 1992–3, l, HC375, para. 10.

22 Montagu–Welsby, 6 October 1992, Reid's Papers.

23 Montagu–Edmonds, 17 November 1992, Secretary's Papers, Box 2053, and see also MacGregor–Reid (II), 1 October 1992, Reid's Papers.

24 Philip Wood (DTp)–Reid (II), 18 March 1993, Reid's Papers; Interview with Reid (II), 2000.

25 See, for example, media reactions to the Commons debate on rail privatisation on 12 January 1993, and to the House of Commons Transport Committee's Interim Report, 13 and 20–1 January 1993, and subsequently, e.g. *Financial Times*, 23 January 1993, p. 6, 26 January 1993, p. 17; *Independent on Sunday*, 24 January 1993, p. 7.

26 HC Transport Committee, *Interim Report*, January 1993, para. 8. The other issues concerned the risk of investment blight, the future of railway freight, the regulatory and administrative structure, staff morale, the need to preserve network benefits (through ticketing etc.), and the need to ensure that the private sector did not 'cherry pick' the more modern parts of BR. Adley's personal views were articulated several times in the House. Cf. *Parl. Deb. (Commons)*, 6th ser. (Session 1992–3), vol. 216, 12 January 1993, cols. c. 805–7.

27 This was provided by Prof. Bill Bradshaw (Wolfson College, Oxford), Richard Hope (Consultant Editor, *Railway Gazette International*), Prof. Chris Nash (Leeds University), Tony Taig (SRD Safety Consultants), and Ed Thompson (Tecnecon Consultants). Visits were made to Crewe, and in the London area to Liverpool Street, Stratford, Euston, the LTS line and Borough Market Jnc. HC Transport Cttee, *Future of the Railways*, April 1993, paras. 4–5.

28 Robert Adley, *Parl. Deb. (Commons)*, 6th ser. (Session 1992–3), vol. 216, 12 January 1993, col. 809 and see also *Financial Times*, 26 January 1993, p. 9; Ridley, Young, and Whitelaw, 1992–3, cit. in *Independent on Sunday*, 24 January 1993, p. 7; Christian Wolmar, 'Creating the Passenger Rail Franchises', in Freeman and Shaw, *All Change*, p. 126. On Adley, who died on 13 May 1993, see *Guardian*, 14 May 1993, p. 16, *Independent*, 14 May 1993, pp. 21–2.

29 HC Transport Ctee, *Future of the Railways*, April 1993, paras. 13, 533–47. On outright opposition cf. John Prescott ('We believe there can be a good publicly operated rail system') and Gwyneth Dunwoody ('we need a state railway system…the proposed privatisation of British Rail is an unalloyed disaster'), *Parl. Deb. (Commons)*, 6th ser. (Session 1992–3), vol. 216, 12 January 1993, cols. 772, 797.

30 Freeman and Shaw, *All Change*. See also Grantham, thesis (1998), and Bradshaw, 'The Rail Industry', in Dieter Helm and Tim Jenkinson, *Competition in Regulated Industries* (Oxford, 1998), pp. 175–92.

31 Mrs Gillian Ashmore (seconded to BRB), reporting on the Commons committee stage, Board Exec. Minutes, 18 February 1993.

32 Cf. Railways Bill (Commons), 21 January 1993, Railways Act, 5 November 1993, c. 43, Part II, Sections 84–6; Welsby and Nichols, 'Privatisation of Britain's Railways', 61; Jon Shaw, 'Designing a Method of Rail Privatisation' in Freeman and Shaw, *All Change*, (2000), p. 26.

33 Nick Harvey (MP for North Devon), Commons 2nd reading of Railways Bill, *Parl. Deb. (Commons)*, 6th ser. (Session 1992–3), vol. 218, 2 February 1993, col. 190. cit. in Jon Shaw, 'Rail Privatisation', p. 26. Harvey also argued that 'The Bill is a lawyer's paradise but will prove to be a passenger's hell', col. 191.

34 MacGregor, *Parl. Deb. (Commons)*, 6th ser. (Session 1992–3), vol. 218, 2 February 1993, col. 161.

35 Robert Horton (Vice-Chairman, BRB), Memo on 'Formation of Railtrack Division', 15 March 1993, BRB Committee on Restructuring Minutes, 18 March 1993; Trewin–BRB Members on 'Railtrack Organisation', 24 March 1993, and signed responses of Fred Holliday, 26 March 1993, and Ken Dixon, 29 March 1993, BRB Secretary's Papers, Box 2079; Holliday–Dixon, 25 March 1993, Holliday's Papers, Sec Box 2273. The device of a Railtrack *division* was chosen in order to facilitate the making of designate appointments, and to obviate the need to produce separate accounts. Holliday argued that the decision should have been debated at a Board meeting; Dixon thought it illogical to ask for a signed endorsement when full powers had been delegated to the Board's Restructuring Committee. Formal endorsement by the Board followed on 1 April 1993.

36 Reid (II), Memo, 20 January 1993, BRB Cttee on Restructuring Minutes, 22 January 1993; Horton, Memo on 'Railtrack activities to be undertaken by directly employed staff', n.d., BRB Minutes, 10 June 1993.

37 Horton–Montagu, 25 January 1993, Jerram's Papers, and Horton, reported in BRB Minutes, 10 June 1993.

38 A fact which upset Sheila Masters: see Richard Goldson (BRB), Internal File Note, 8 October 1992, appended to DTp/BRB Restructuring Working Group Minutes, 5 October 1992.

39 Gourvish, *British Railways*, pp. 368–74; McKinsey & Co., 'Building a Commercial Organization for RailTrack: Recommendations to the Board', 26 November 1992, BRB Board Exec. Minutes, 26 November 1992; Gareth Williams (DTp), 'Note of Meeting of [DTp/BRB Track Authority and Restructuring Working Groups] 14 December 1992, 17 December 1992; Goldson, Internal File Note of same meeting, 16 December 1992. The Railtrack zones were described as 'field units' in early papers: DTp, Note on Railtrack, November 1992, cit.

40 McKinsey & Co., 'Building a Commercial Organization for RailTrack', cit.; Interview with Goldson, May 2000.

41 Reid (II)–Freeman, 26 May 1993, Horton–Freeman, 7 June 1993, FIG Minutes, 16 and 30 June 1993; MacGregor–Reid (II), 2 July 1993, Note on 'BR Property', n.d., FIG Minutes, 7 July 1993. An exception was made of North Pole Depot and Waterloo International, which were to be vested in EPS. Palmer regarded Horton's reference to 'retaining value' as 'weasel words for hanging on to as much as possible': Palmer–Reid (II), 15 June 1993, FIG Papers.

42 Railtrack's first accounts revealed that its non-operational property was worth £250m. at year end, 31 March 1995. The increase was largely explained by subsequent

transfers of 'operational' property into the 'non-operational' category. See Board Exec. Minutes, 19 October 1995.

43 The eight London stations were Euston, King's Cross, Liverpool Street, London Bridge, Charing Cross, Waterloo, Victoria, and Paddington, and the provincial stations, Edinburgh Waverley, Glasgow Central, Leeds, Birmingham New Street, and Manchester Piccadilly. Gatwick Airport was added subsequently. Note on 'Stations', n.d., FIG Minutes, 16 and 30 June and 7 July 1993; BRB Privatisation News, 6 October 1993.

44 Railtrack was established as a BRB subsidiary on 28 February 1994. BRB Minutes, 2 December 1993, 10 February and 3 March 1994; BRB, *R&A 1993/4*, p. 6.

45 Montagu–Reid (II), 7 February 1994, Secretary's Papers, Box 2079; Simon Osborne (Solicitor & Secretary, Railtrack), Memo, n.d., BRB Minutes, 10 February 1994.

46 The committee consisted of only those BRB members who would be in office after 1 April 1994 and was designed to avoid conflicts of interest. Trewin, Memo, 2 March 1994, BRB Minutes, 3 March 1994.

47 Cf. remarks of Reid (II)and Horton, BRB Minutes, 3 March 1994.

48 Cf. data on the number of staff per equated track-mile: Interview with Jim Cornell, 7 October 1999.

49 Richard J. Spoors (Director, Privatisation Studies, BRB) and Goldson, Memo on 'A Development Plan to Create Railtrack', n.d., DTp/BRB Joint Track Authority and Restructuring Working Group Minutes, 14 December 1992.

50 Cf. Samuel Montagu, Confidential Draft Report on 'Options for Contracting Out Infrastructure Support Services', 12 January 1992 [*sic*: actually 1993], DTp/BRB Restructuring and Accounting Working Group Minutes, 18 January 1993.

51 BRB Paper on 'Proposals on Future Structure of BR's Infrastructure Services', 18 June 1993, DTp/BRB Restructuring Working Group Minutes, 21 June 1993.

52 BRB Paper on 'BR Infrastructure Services—Development for Privatisation—Progress Report', 12 August 1993, DTp/BRB Restructuring Working Group Minutes, 16 August 1993; McKinsey & Co., 'Defining the BRIS Transition to Privatization', 9 November 1993, annex to Jim Cornell (MD, BRIS), Memo on 'BR Infrastructure Services—Restructuring for Privatisation—Output from Strategic Development Study', n.d., Board Exec. Minutes, 11 November 1993; Freeman–Welsby, 15 December 1993, Reid's Papers. Pairs of ISUs were split into Lead Infrastructure Units (later Infrastructure Maintenance Units [IMUs]) and Permanent Way Production Units (later Track Renewal Units [TRUs]). Two of the latter, SW and SE, merged, leaving six. Cornell has recently claimed that his preference had been to sell the integrated ISUs: Interview with Cornell, 1999.

53 Freeman–Welsby, December 1993, cit.

54 Cornell, Memo on 'BRIS—Contract Negotiations with Railtrack', 19 May 1994, Board Exec. Minutes, 19 May 1994. The main contracts were: RT1 Maintenance (35 contracts); RT1 Renewals (27); Structures (30); Property Maintenance (24); Roll-over (14); and Minor Works (14).

55 Cornell, Memos on 'Pricing Issues for BRIS Contracts', and 'BRIS Contracts to Supply Railtrack: Current Position and Sign Off Process', n.d., BRB 1994 Group Minutes, 24 February and 3 March 1994. The 1994 Group was an informal group of Board members (Reid, Welsby, Jerram, and Watson, later joined by Christopher Campbell), plus Jerry Evans (Public Relations), Paul Watkinson (Industrial Relations), and Peter Trewin

(Secretary), which met weekly from 18 October 1993 to 31 March 1994 to review privatisation issues.

56 Data for 3 February 1996, BRB IR cassettes, MISP level 9, IR Box 8145.

57 Campbell, Memo on 'BRIS—Methods of Sale', Board Exec. Minutes, 19 May 1994, Andrew Sim (Solicitor, BRB), Memo on 'Saleability of BRIS Units', 23 June 1994, enclosing Ashurst Morris Crisp, Report on 'BRIS', 21 June 1994, Board Exec. Minutes, 19 May and 23 June 1994.

58 BRB Minutes, 9 June, 8 August, and 6 October 1994, 12 January 1995; BRIS Directors Group Minutes, 27 October and 27 November 1994; Conversation with Jim Cornell, 27 November 2000.

59 DTp, Note on 'Access Working Group', 22 June 1992, Project Management Group Minutes, 25 June 1992.

60 Philip O'Donnell (Director, Privatisation Studies, BRB), 'Infrastructure Access and Charging: Review Note', 29 June 1992, Jerram's Papers, A/10/BM; Access Working Group (AWG) Minutes, 29 July 1992; Palmer, Memo on 'Implementation of Directive 91/400: Management of and Charging for Access', Board Exec. Minutes, 6 August 1992.

61 Palmer–Wood, 7 August 1992, Jerram–C. J. Hall (DTp), 7 September 1992, Jerram's Papers, A/10/BM; AWG Minutes, 10 September 1992; Jerram, Memo, n.d., Board Exec. Minutes, 17 December 1992.

62 Colin Driver (Consultant, BRB)–Jerram, 29 March 1994, Jerram's Papers, A/10/4/BM.

63 Wood (DTp)–Robson (Treasury), 3 August 1992, AWG correspondence, BRB PRI Box 5440; Interview with James Jerram, 14 December 2000.

64 DTp, Memo on 'Relationship between Franchise and Liberalised Services: Model A', 9 September 1992, AWG Minutes, 10 September 1992.

65 Treasury, Memo on 'Proposal for Stage 2 Charging and Access', n.d., AWG Minutes, 10 September 1992. The Treasury had first argued that operators prepared to take franchises on an unsubsidised basis should have first choice of train-path slots, and that the timetable would have to be completely redesigned, but subsequently made concessions on both points.

66 Robson–Wood, 31 July and 22 September, Wood–Robson, 3 August, Robson–Wood, 5 August, Charles Bridge (DTI)–Wood, 15 September 1992, PRI Box 5440; AWG Minutes, 23 September 1992.

67 Welsby–Jerram and Palmer, 16 September 1992, enclosing 'An Almost Practical Track Charging Regime', AWG correspondence; Palmer, Memo on 'Access: Stage II Principles', 28 September 1992, Jerram, Memo on 'BR Privatisation: Infrastructure Pricing', n.d., Board Exec. Minutes, 29 September and 8 October 1992; N. M. Rothschild & Sons, 'Treasury Proposals for Stage 2 Charging and Access', 13 October 1992, Welsby–Wood, [14] October 1992, enclosing 'Towards a Practical Access Charging and Management Regime', 13 October 1992, AWG correspondence.

68 O'Donnell, Memo on 'Access Working Groups: Latest Government Proposal', 16 October 1992, AWG Minutes, 16 October 1992; Philip Rutnam (Treasury)–Tony Baker (DTp), 21 October 1992, enclosing Treasury paper on 'Rail Access and Charging', 21 October 1992, AWG correspondence; O'Donnell–Jerram, 21 October and 1 November 1992, Jerram's Papers, A/10/BM.

69 Andrew Battarbee (DTp)–O'Donnell et al., 24 November 1992, enclosing AWG Paper to DTp Ministers on 'Access, Charging and Franchising', Jerram's Papers, A/10/BM;

Jerram, Memo on 'Domestic Access: DoT Ministerial Submission and Regulatory Issues', n.d., Board Exec. Minutes, 17 December 1992.

70 Simon Linnett (Rothschild)–Jerram, 5 November 1992, Jerram's Papers, A/10/BM.

71 DTp, *Gaining Access to the Railway Network: the Government's Proposals* (February 1993), pp. 13, 21; Jerram, Memo on 'Access Publication Document', n.d., Board Exec. Minutes, 28 January 1993; MacGregor, 2 February 1993, cit. cols. 156f.

72 O'Donnell (now Railtrack)–Richard Bennett (DTp), 14 April 1993, CIG papers, BRB PRI Box 5463.

73 Hillard, 'Note for File', 28 May 1993, CIG correspondence, BRB PRI Box 5460.

74 Robin Pratt (Coopers & Lybrand)–Andrew Burchell (DTp), 5 May 1993, enclosing 'Railway Infrastructure Access and Charging: Report on Scoping Exercise', May 1993, CIG papers; DTp/BRB/Railtrack Regulation and Access Working Group Minutes, 12 May 1993; 'Notes of [BR] Meeting [on] Infrastructure Access Charging', 7 May 1993, Hillard–Jerram and Palmer, 12 May 1993, Regulation and Access Working Group (RAWG) correspondence, file 3; Wood–Jerram, 14 May 1993, and reply, 18 May, CIG correspondence; PIG Minutes, 25 May 1993; Martin Shrubsole (Director, Privatisation Studies, BRB), Memo to BRB Restructuring Group, 27 May 1993, enclosing Hillard, Memo on 'Infrastructure Access and Charging: Proposals for Infrastructure Costing by Business Unit', 26 May 1993, RAWG correspondence, file 3; Shrubsole–Jerram, 8 June 1993, CIG correspondence.

75 Coopers & Lybrand, 'Railway Infrastructure Access and Charging: Results of first-cut exercise', August 1993, Jerram's Papers, Box 458/BM; CIG, Report on 'Railway Infrastructure and Charging: Results of the "First Cut" Exercise', September 1993, RAWG Minutes, 14 September 1993. The first-cut exercise referred to the LTS, Gatwick Express, and part of the IC Great Western shadow franchises.

76 BRB 1994 Group Minutes, 11 and 18 November and 1 December 1993; Jerram–Wood, 24 November 1993, RAWG correspondence, file 3; FIG Minutes, 1 December 1993; Jerram, Memo, n.d., Board Exec. Minutes, 9 December 1993, 20 January 1994; Wood–Jerram, 24 January 1994, Jerram's Papers, BM/514. On the Rail Regulator's early concerns about exclusion from the initial franchising process, see DTp, Note on 'Initial Access Agreements: Approval by the Regulator', 23 November 1993, RAWG Minutes, 30 November 1993, John Swift (Rail Regulator)–MacGregor, 7 January 1994, DTp/BRB Access Contracts Group correspondence, file 9.

77 John Edmonds, 'Creating Railtrack', in Freeman and Shaw, *All Change*, pp. 68–9; Jerram–Wood, 28 January 1994, CIG correspondence.

78 Contracts were also needed for EPS, RfD, and Rail Express Systems (Parcels).

79 Welsby–Edmonds, 21 March, Edmonds–Welsby, 23 March, Wood–Welsby, 23 March 1994, Jerram–David Moss (Commercial Director, Railtrack), 31 March 1994, Jerram's Papers, A/10/4/BM.

80 BRB Transitional Committee Minutes, 30 March 1994. The total revenue requirement was £2,405 m., including revenue from property, non-franchised businesses, station leases, etc.

81 Coopers & Lybrand, Explanatory Note on 'Summary of first cut franchise access charges', February 1994, CIG papers; BRB Privatisation News, 18 February 1994; Shrubsole–Jerram and Welsby, 15 April 1994, Jerram's Papers, A10/4/BM.

82 Richard Davies (Financial Planning Manager (Privatisation), BRB)–David Redfern (Director of Finance, BRB), 23 March 1994, Jerram's Papers, A10/4/BM.

83 Jerram, Memo on 'Access Charges', n.d., Board Exec. Minutes, 12 May 1994; Freeman and Shaw, *All Change*, pp. 69, 215. Swift was appointed in December 1993.

84 Cf. DTp, Minutes of Meeting on 'Restructuring of the Railways', 28 May 1992. This body was the origin of the joint DTp/BRB Restructuring & Accounting Working Group.

85 DTp, *The Franchising of Passenger Rail Services* (October 1992), and see also Reid (II)–MacGregor, 28 September 1992, Secretary's Papers, Box 2049. The policy was over-turned after an amendment introduced by Lord Peyton in the Lords. However, the resultant revised sections (25 (3) and (4)) in the Railways Act enabled BRB to become a franchisee subject to the agreement of the Franchising Director, and in the event, he decided that BR should not be eligible to bid for the first franchises. John Palmer, Memos on 'BR Participation in Franchises', 28 July 1993, and 'Railways Bill', 3 November 1993, Board Exec. Minutes, 29 July 1993, BRB Minutes, 4 November and 2 December 1993; Lords Peyton and Clinton-Davis, *Parl. Deb. (Lords)*, 5th ser. (Session 1992–3), vol. 547, 5 July 1993, cols. 1068–75; Roger Salmon (Director of Passenger Rail Franchising)–Welsby, 25 April 1995, Trewin's Papers.

86 HC Transport Ctee, *Future of the Railways*, April 1993, vol. I, para. 119, and Mac-Gregor, evidence, 28 October 1992, vol. II, QQ. 42–3. MacGregor's assumptions were included in the *Draft Objectives for the Franchising Director* issued to the Railways Bill Standing Committee in February 1993. The decision about franchise length appears to have emerged from an earlier tussle between the DTp and the Treasury, the former favouring long franchises, the latter favouring short ones. Interview with MacGregor, 2001.

87 The case studies were: Inter City—ECML and Gatwick Express; NSE—LTS, Thames-link, Chiltern, and South Western; Regional Railways—Scotrail and Central. See Welsby, Memo, n.d., Board Exec. Minutes, 6 August 1992 et seq.

88 Joint DTp/BRB Restructuring & Accounting Group Minutes, 16 July and 14 Septem-ber 1992; Board Exec. Minutes, 6 August 1992; MacGregor–Reid (II), 1 October 1992, Reid (II)'s Papers. British Rail contended that until the Paving Bill received the Royal Assent there was a danger of acting *ultra vires* in relation to the infrastructure-owning LTS and Chiltern: DTp Note on 'Timetable for Restructuring', 13 November 1992, Restructuring & Accounting Working Group Minutes, 17 November 1992; Privatisa-tion Steering Group Minutes, 25 November 1992.

89 Board Exec. Minutes, 11 September and 6 October 1992; Samuel Montagu, draft Memo on 'Shadow Running', 1 October 1992, Jerram's Papers; Edmonds, Memo on 'Restructuring of First Five Profit Centres', 29 October 1992, and Montagu, Restruc-turing & Accounting Working Group Minutes, 2 November 1992; Montagu–Edmonds, 17 November 1992, cit.

90 Welsby, cit. Joint meeting of DTp/BRB Restructuring and Franchising Working Groups Minutes, 21 December 1992.

91 Five development directors were appointed in March and April 1993. Privatisation Steering Group Minutes, 26 January 1993; MacGregor, *Parl. Deb. (Commons)*, 6th ser. (Session 1992–3), vol. 218, 2 February 1993, col. 162; BRB Committee on Restructur-ing Minutes, 11 February and 4 March 1993; BR Management Brief, 24 March 1993. The seven franchises were InterCity East Coast, InterCity Great Western, InterCity Gatwick Express, NSE South Western, NSE LTS, NSE Isle of Wight, and Regional Railways Scotrail. (Development directors were not appointed to the smaller Gatwick

and Isle of Wight franchises.) Chiltern and Anglia, selected for the BR case studies, were not included; MacGregor justified this by seeking to counter possible allegations of 'cherry picking': HC Transport Ctee, *Future of the Railways*, April 1993, vol. I, para. 118 and MacGregor, evidence, vol. II, QQ. 2313–23.

92 BRB Minutes, 10 December 1992; file of responses to Consultation Document, BRB PRI Box 5482; Brian Scott (Director, IC GW)–MacGregor, 5 February 1993, Wood–Scott, 24 February 1993, Reid (II)'s Papers.

93 Cf. Board Exec. Minutes, 29 September 1992; Franchising Working Group Minutes, 3 December 1992.

94 BRB Minutes, 7 October 1993; BRB Privatisation News, 17 August 1993; BRB, *R&A 1993/4*, p. 9.

95 *Guardian*, 25 May 1993, p. 3; Freeman and Shaw, *All Change*, p. 42. The LTS contract was subsequently abandoned and re-let after alleged ticketing irregularities. *Modern Railways*, March 1996, p. 137.

96 DTp, *New Opportunities for the Railways*, July 1992, paras. 45–55.

97 HC Transport Ctee, *Future of the Railways*, vol. I, para. 202 and Appendix B; vol. II, QQ. 982–3.

98 Freeman–Reid (II), 23 December 1992, Reid–Freeman, 8 January 1993, Welsby's Papers, Sec Box 2126; Freeman–Reid, 25 January 1993, Jerram's Papers, A7/BM/442.

99 Charles Brown (Director, Privatisation Studies, BRB)–Jerram, 21 August 1992, Wood and Brown–Jacques César (VP, Mercer Management Consulting), 6 August 1992, Graham Pendlebury (DTp), 'Adjudication Document—Freight and Parcels "Stage 2" Consultancy Study', Jerram's Papers, cit.

100 DTp, 'Views on privatisation of existing BR customers and other interested parties: feedback to MERCER from DoT interview programme', 25 November 1992, ibid.

101 Philip Rutnam (Treasury)–Brian Wadsworth (DTp), 18 November 1992, ibid.

102 Rutnam–Wadsworth, 20 November 1992, ibid.

103 Jerram, Memo, n.d., Board Exec. Minutes, 4 and 18 February 1993; Mercer Management Consulting, 'Strategic Options for the Transfer of British Rail's Freight Business into the Private Sector. Stage II Study: Final Report', 5 March 1993, Jerram's Papers, A7/BM/442.

104 MacGregor–Reid (II), 19 April 1993, Jerram's Papers, A7/1/BM; BRB Privatisation News, 20 May 1993; DTp, *Rail freight privatisation. The Government's proposals* (1993). The appointees were: Ian Braybrook (Business Restructuring Director), Nigel Jones (Freight Development Director, Freight Operating Co. 'A'), Chris Harvey ('B') and Robert Watson ('C').

105 Wadsworth–Shrubsole (Director, Privatisation, Freight & Parcels), 10 December 1992, Jerram's Papers, A7/1/BM.

106 Board Exec. Minutes, 18 February 1993; Jerram–Reid (II), 15 March 1993, Jerram's Papers, A7/BM/442; 'Extract from Notes of Meeting between Secretary of State and Chairman held on Thursday, 1 April 1993', Shrubsole–Reid (II), 26 April 1993, Palmer–Reid (II), 30 April 1993, enclosing draft letter Reid–MacGregor (not sent to MacGregor, but passed to Wadsworth), Shrubsole–Wadsworth, 27 April 1993, Jerram's Papers, A7/1/BM. Relations were not improved when Wadsworth complained about British Rail's intention to establish the rump of RfD as a de facto fourth operating company, in order to effect the government's plans for Freightliner and

the Channel Tunnel business: Wadsworth–Jerram, 6 September and reply, 7 September 1993, Welsby's Papers, Box 2126.

107 BRB Minutes, 5 August 1993; Joint DTp/BRB Freight Change Steering Group Minutes, 16 August 1993; Board Exec. Minutes, 2 September 1993. The DTp accepted the force of the argument but pressed on with their encouragement of an entrepreneurial approach. As Wadsworth put it, 'I don't want to raise the Chief Executive's blood pressure, and I do understand the Board's concern that the businesses should not be allowed to behave, while under BRB ownership, in a way which shoots the corporation in the foot . . . Nevertheless I hope that we can err on the side of "letting a hundred flowers bloom" ': Wadsworth–Glyn Williams (MD, Freight Group), 8 April 1994, Jerram's Papers, A10/4/BM.

108 Shrubsole, Memo on 'Freight Companies/Railfreight Distribution/Rail Express Systems: Propositions for Restructuring', n.d., BRB Committee on Restructuring Minutes, 19 August 1993.

109 Freight Change Steering Group Minutes, 8 September 1993.

110 Jerram–Reid (II), 15 March 1993, Jerram's Papers, A7/BM442; Freight Change Steering Group Minutes, 16 August 1993.

111 Welsby–Freeman, 30 September 1993, Welsby's Papers, Box 2126.

112 Freeman–Welsby, 13 September 1993, ibid. The policy was confirmed in Wadsworth–Welsby, 24 November 1993, Jerram's Papers, A7/1/BM.

113 Welsby–Freeman, 30 September 1993, cit.; Welsby–Freeman, 6 October 1993, Smith–Welsby, 30 September 1993, Jerram's Papers, A7/1/BM; Smith–Welsby and Jerram, 7 October 1993, enclosing Freeman, 'Speech for FreightConnection 93 Conference: 5 October 1993', Welsby's Papers, Sec Box 1969; Hugh Bayley (MP for York), *Parl. Deb. (Commons)*, 6th ser. (Session 1992–3), vol. 231, col. 67; *Guardian*, 3 November 1993, p. 2; *Financial Times*, 3 November 1993, p. 10; Julia Clarke, 'Selling the Freight Railway', in Freeman and Shaw, *All Change*, pp. 189–90. The meeting was held on 8 October and not on the 11th as Bayley implied.

114 Lazard Brothers, 'Freight Privatisation: Selling the Freight Companies', 8 October 1993, BRB Minutes, 4 November 1993.

115 BRB Privatisation News, 23 November 1993, 17 January 1994. The companies and their directors were: TLF North East (Ian Braybrook), TLF South East (Kim Jordan), TLF West (Julian Worth), Rail Express Systems (Charles Belcher), and Red Star (Richard Eccles).

116 BRB Transitional Committee Minutes, 30 March 1994; Swift–Horton, 25 March 1994, Jerram's Papers, A10/4/BM.

117 Wadsworth–Williams, 8 April 1994, cit.

118 Board Exec. Minutes, 24 February 1994; Williams–Welsby et al., 25 March 1994, enclosing Williams–Pendlebury, 25 March 1994, Jerram's Papers, A7/2/BM, Wadsworth–Jerram, 21 March 1994, Jerram's Papers, A10/4/BM.

119 £67.1 m. 1974–88/9, c.£17.2 m. in 1989/90–93/4: BRB, *R&A 1988/9*, p. 18, *1989/90*, p. 18, HC Transport Ctee, *Future of the Railways*, vol. I, para. 204 and nn. 3–4.

120 MacGregor, *Parl. Deb. (Commons)*, 2 February 1993, cit.; Railways Act 1993, ss. 137, 139.

121 BRB Minutes, 1 October 1992, Board Exec. Minutes, 18 March, 17 June, 19 August, and 28 October 1993; David Blake (Vendor Unit), Memos on 'Red Star Parcels' and 'Red Star Parcels—Sale', n.d., Board Exec. Minutes, 28 October and 18 November

1993. The MBO bid was non-compliant; the consortium bid asked for a seven-year exclusivity period and a 90% reduction in charges.

122 Board Exec. Minutes, 18 November 1993; Jerram–Wadsworth, 23 November 1993, Jerram's Papers, A6/1, file 5; MacGregor–Reid (II), two letters, 14 December 1993, Reid–MacGregor, 20 December 1993, Reid's Papers; MacGregor–Reid, 12 January 1994, Jerram's Papers, A6/2, file 6.

123 BRB Minutes, 13 January and 10 February 1994; Board Exec. Minutes, 12 May 1994; Reid (II)–Brian Mawhinney (SoS for Transport), 19 December 1994, Reid's Papers, Sec Box 2124; Campbell–Welsby, 2 August 1995, Jerram's Papers, A6/2, file 6; BRB Press Release, 5 September 1995.

124 Sir George Young (SoS, DTp)–Welsby, 21 December 1995, Welsby's Papers, Sec Box 2124; BRB Privatisation News, 11 December 1995, 26 February and 20 May 1996. The consortium, North & South Railways, was renamed English Welsh & Scottish Railway.

125 DTp, *New Opportunities*, para. 33; DTp, Memo on 'Rolling Stock Procurement: A Discussion Paper', 17 November 1992, Joint DTp/BRB Rolling Stock Working Group (RSWG) Minutes, 19 November 1993; DTp, *Railway Privatisation: Passenger Rolling Stock* (January 1993), paras. 11.1–2; National Audit Office (NAO), *Report on Privatisation of the Rolling Stock Leasing Companies*, 3 March 1998, P.P. 1997–8, HC576, para. 1.5. Earlier suggested solutions included an interventionist role for the Franchise Authority.

126 RSWG Minutes, 19 November 1992; Neil K. McDonald (DTp)–Jerram, 22 January 1993, N. J. Lerner (KPMG Peat Marwick)–Wood, 26 February 1993, Jerram's Papers, A13/BM, file 1. The residual value problem might be eased by: longer initial franchises; a guarantee that stock would be used during the second franchise; or by public sector participation in the risk.

127 DTp, Press Notice, 27 January 1993; DTp, *Railway Privatisation: Passenger Rolling Stock* (January 1993), paras. 13–18.

128 Board Exec. Minutes, 18 and 25 March 1993; DTp, Memo on 'British Rail Privatisation: Passenger Rolling Stock', 30 March 1993, Jerram's Papers, A13/BM, file 1.

129 BRB Privatisation News, 30 April 1993.

130 Robert Mills (DTp), Note on 'Rolling Stock "Awayday": 4 May 1993', 14 May 1993, Jerram's Papers, A13/BM, file 2; Board Exec. Minutes, 3 June 1993; BRB Minutes, 10 June 1993.

131 DTp, Press Notice, 3 June 1993; BRB Privatisation News, 18 June 1993.

132 MacDonald–Peter Watson (BRB), 10 September 1993, James A. Stewart (Hambros Bank)–Jerram, 2 March 1994, Jerram's Papers, A13/BM, file 2; Board Exec. Minutes, 23 September, 7 and 14 October, and 18 November 1993. Fleet allocation was decided as follows. The large Class 423 stock was divided into three, the other large classes were divided into two, and the remaining smaller classes allocated to a single ROSCO. The distribution was: Angel 3,753 vehicles (2,099 EMUs, 1,094 DMUs, 539 HSTs); Eversholt 4,050 (2,684 EMUs, 1,366 locos and loco-hauled stock), Porterbrook 3,455 (1,615 EMUs, 681 DMUs, 789 Locos &c., 370 HSTs). John Prideaux, 'Trains: The Rolling-stock Companies', in Freeman and Shaw, *All Change*, p. 99; NAO, *Privatisation of the Rolling Stock Leasing Companies*, March 1998, Figure 3.

133 Board Exec. Minutes, 10 March 1994; Reid (II)–Freeman, 21 March 1994, enclosing Hambros Bank, Report on 'Rolling Stock Companies ("ROSCOs")': Valuation of

the passenger rolling stock and lease pricing', Jerram's Papers, A13/BM, file 2; Freeman–Reid, 11 April 1994, Jerram's Papers, A13/BM, file 3. The valuation and rentals were reduced further before sale: NAO, *Privatisation of the Rolling Stock Leasing Companies*, paras. 9, 218–29; Prideaux, in Freeman and Shaw, *All Change*, pp. 100–1.

134 Watson, Memo, n.d., Board Exec. Minutes, 24 February 1994; Freeman–Reid (II), 7 March 1994, Jerram's Papers, A13/BM, file 2.

135 Board Exec. Minutes, 14 July 1994; Rolling Stock Master Operating Lease Agreement, revised final draft, 15 July 1994, Jerram's Papers, A13/1/BM. The MDs of the new companies were Tony Roche (Eversholt), Sandy Anderson (Porterbrook), and Brian Hassell (Angel Train Contracts). Roche was appointed MD (Central Services) in June 1994 and was succeeded by Andrew Jukes. Staff numbered 146 at 31 March 1995. BRB Privatisation News, 21 April 1994, BRB, *R&A 1993/4*, p. 3, *1994/5*, p. 29. Not all the fleet was transferred. EPS retained the Eurostar fleet, while some stock was retained for charter hire. Clive Charlton, 'The Structure of the New Railway', in Freeman and Shaw, *All Change*, p. 56.

136 Completion was in Jan.–Feb. 1996. Campbell, Note, 9 March 1994, Stewart–Campbell, 11 April, Jerram's Papers, A13/BM, file 2; Jenny Williams (DTp)–Campbell, 14 April 1994, Peter McCarthy (DTp)–Campbell, 26 April 1994, A13/BM/3; BRB Privatisation News, 14 July 1994; Prideaux, in Freeman and Shaw, *All Change*, pp. 99–105.

137 MacGregor–Reid (II), 28 February 1994, MacGregor–P. J. Butler, 28 and 29 February 1994, BRB 48-2; BRB Privatisation News, 21 February 1994; BRB *R&A*, *1993/4*, p. 26; *1994/5*, p. 26. Reid was not happy with the Minister's decision to appoint Butler immediately to the chairmanship of EPS: Reid (II)–MacGregor, 18 February 1994, BRB Secretary's Papers, Box 1860.

138 Edmonds, Memo on 'Privatisation of Central Services', Board Exec. Minutes, 12 November 1992; Watson, Memo on 'Central Services—Stewardship Report', 26 November 1993, BRB Minutes, 2 December 1993; Interview with Watson, 2000; BRB Privatisation News, 14 January and 14 February 1994.

139 Blake, Memo on 'Setting up the Vendor Unit', n.d., Board Exec. Minutes, 21 January 1993; BRB Privatisation News, 8 March 1993, 16 March 1994; BRB Minutes, 10 June and 4 November 1993; Campbell, Memo to 1994 Group on 'Vendor Unit', 9 March 1994; Robert Bolt (Planning Manager, BRB Vendor Unit)–Campbell, 1 July 1994, Christopher Campbell's Papers, Sec Box 2510; BRB, *R&A 1993/4*, p. 10.

140 DTp, *New Opportunities*, para. 98; Board Exec. Minutes, 29 April 1993; BRB Minutes, 1 July and 7 October 1993.

141 BRB Minutes, 4 November 1993. Another element omitted from the Act was the application to private-sector companies of controls on the disposal of 'heritage' artefacts.

142 Andrew Sim (BRB Solicitor), Memo on 'Changes to the Constitution of British Transport Police', n.d., Board Exec. Minutes, 3 February 1994; Desmond O'Brien (Chief Constable, BTP), Memo on 'Jurisdiction of British Transport Police', 20 April 1994, BRB Police Committee Minutes, 13 May 1994; Transport Police (Jurisdiction) Act 1994, 1994 c. 8, 24 March 1994; British Transport Police Force Scheme 1963 (Amendment) Order 1994 (S.I. 1994 No. 609), 8 March 1994; Appleby, *Force on the*

Move, p. 270; *Parl. Deb. (Commons)*, 6th ser. (Session 1993–4), vol. 239, 18 March 1994, col. 1301, vol. 240, 21 March 1994, cols. 52–108; *Lords*, 5th ser. (Session 1993–4), vol. 553, 22 March 1994, col. 622; vol. 553, 24 March 1994, Earl Ferrers, col. 809, Royal Assent, 826.

143 Terry R. Gourvish, 'The Regulation of Britain's Railways: Past, Present and Future', in Lena Andersson-Skog and Olle Krantz (eds.), *Institutions in the Transport and Communications Industries. State and Private Actors in the Making of Institutional Patterns, 1850–1990* (Canton, MA, 1999), pp. 117–32. See also Stephen Glaister et al., *Transport Policy in Britain* (Basingstoke, 1998).

144 BRB, Note on 'Regulation', n.d. (January 1993), Jerram's Papers, A10/2, Reg. file 1; Wolmar, and Swift, 'The Role of the Rail Regulator', in Freeman and Shaw, *All Change*, pp. 122–3, 223.

145 Charles Brown–Palmer, Bayly, et al., 27 May 1992, commenting on DTp paper on 'The Role of the Regulator', n.d., RAWG correspondence, file 3; DTp/Treasury/DOE Restructuring of the Railways Minutes, 29 May 1992 (predecessor of Restructuring & Accounting Working Group); Privatisation Steering Group Minutes, 8 June 1992; DTp, *New Opportunities*, paras. 14–16, 64–75; Swift, in Freeman and Shaw, *All Change*, pp. 206–7.

146 Board Exec. Minutes, 20 August 1992.

147 Patrick Brown (Permanent Secretary, DTp)–Reid, Reid's Papers, 7 January 1993; DTp Press Notice, 7 December 1993; BRB Privatisation News, 10 November and 8 December 1993; *Sunday Telegraph*, 3 April 1994, Business, p. 18; *Financial Times*, 17 October 1994, p. 26; Office of the Rail Regulator (ORR), *Report . . . to the Secretary of State for Transport for the period 1 December 1993 to 31 March 1994*, HCP 662, 19 October 1994, pp. 19–20; Swift, in Freeman and Shaw, *All Change*, p. 207.

148 Reid–MacGregor, 11 December 1992, cit.; Jerram–John Swift (DTp), 1 February 1993, Jerram's Papers, A/10/2, Reg. file 1; HC Transport Ctee, *Future of the Railways*, April 1993, paras. 492–6.

149 Railways Act 1993, 1993 c. 43, ss. 1, 4, 5; ORR, *Report to 31 March 1994*, Appendix 2, pp. 23–4; MacGregor–Salmon, 22 March 1994, reproduced in Office of Passenger Rail Franchising (OPRAF), *Annual Report 1994/5*, Annex, pp. 19–24.

150 ORR, *Report to 31 March 1994*, pp. 6–7, 12–18; CTCC, *Annual Report 1993/4*, p. 8. CRUCC and RUCC meetings were to be held in public.

151 OPRAF, *Annual Report 1994/5*, pp. 4, 20; David Rowlands (Under-Secretary, DTp)–Jerram, 18 March 1993, Jerram's Papers, A14/BM, file 1; OPRAF, *Passenger Rail Industry Overview* (September 1995), p. 35.

152 Cf. Roger Salmon (Special Adviser)–Welsby, 22 January 1993, Secretary's Papers, Box 2126; Wolmar, in Freeman and Shaw, *All Change*, pp. 122–3.

153 Reid (II)–MacGregor, 25 January 1994 and reply, 16 February 1994, Reid (II)'s Papers; Salmon–MacGregor, 3 February 1994, Jerram's Papers, A14/BM, file 2; Swift, in Freeman and Shaw, *All Change*, p. 214.

154 RAWG Minutes, 12 July 1993; Swift, in Freeman and Shaw, *All Change*, pp. 208–9.

155 John Swift, 'Chairman's Comments' , in Michael E. Beesley (ed.), *Regulating Utilities: A Time For Change?* (IEA, 1996), p. 184, also cit. by Swift in Freeman and Shaw, *All Change*, p. 220.

156 ORR, *Competition for Railway Passenger Services: A Policy Statement* (December 1994), p. 2.

157 Cf. John Welsby, 'What Next in Railways?', in Michael E. Beesley (ed.), *Regulating Utilities: Understanding the Issues* (IEA, 1998), cit. by Wolmar in Freeman and Shaw, *All Change*, p. 124.

158 Reid told listeners to 'The World This Weekend': 'I went to the States last week to have a careful look at San Francisco . . . one of the persons I talked to had sent their mother-in-law home and they had to buy seven tickets. Well, that sort of thing we don't want in this country': Telex on 'The World This Weekend', 20 December 1992, cit.

159 Cf. David Gray (DTp), Draft Paper on 'Network Benefits', 7 January 1993, BRB Secretary's Papers, Box 2001; Gray, Paper on 'Railways Bill: Network Benefits', 26 January 1993, enclosed in Welsby, Memo, n.d., Board Exec. Minutes, 13 May 1993.

160 MacGregor, Transcript of BBC Radio 4 'File on Four' programme, 30 November 1999; BRB Privatisation News, 10 December 1993; Interview with Chris Stokes, 16 January 2001.

161 Wood–Welsby, 6 August 1993, Jerram's Papers, A14/BM, file 1.

162 CTCC, *Annual Report 1993/4*, pp. 10, 50; *Guardian*, 5 October 1993, p. 9; *The Times*, 5 October 1993, p. 5, 13 January 1994, p. 2.

163 David Rayner (BRB)–V. Coleman (HSE) and P. McCarthy (DTp), 19 November 1992, Reid (II)–MacGregor, 3 December 1992, Reid's Papers; Board Exec. Minutes, 20 August, 12 and 19 November, and 10 December 1992; BRB Minutes, 10 September 1992; Edmonds, in Freeman and Shaw, *All Change*, p. 65.

164 Board Exec. Minutes, 29 April 1993; Reid (II)–MacGregor, 29 June 1993, Reid's Papers. However, MacGregor was not convinced that *statutory* powers of inspection and audit were required: reply, 30 July 1993.

165 BRB Minutes, 14 January 1993; MacGregor–Reid (II), 12 January 1993, Reid's Papers; DTp Press Notice, 12 January 1993; BRB Press Release, 12 January 1993; HC Transport Ctee, *Future of the Railways*, vol. III, Rayner, evidence, 20 January 1993, QQ. 1822, 1842.

166 HSC, *Ensuring Safety on Britain's Railways* (January 1993), Ch. 12; Rayner, Memo on 'Railtrack: Safety Management Arrangements', 15 March 1993, BRB Ctee on Restructuring Minutes, 18 March 1993; Board Exec. Minutes, 20 May 1993; BRB Privatisation News, 17 August 1993; Rayner, papers in BRB 48-2-63.

167 Reid (II), Memo, 20 January 1993, BRB Ctee on Restructuring Minutes, 22 January 1993.

168 Welsby, Memo, 3 March 1993, BRB Ctee on Restructuring Minutes, 4 March 1993; BRB Privatisation News, 8 March 1993; Interview with Richard Goldson, 5 May 2000.

169 Cf. BRB Transitional Committee Minutes, 30 March 1994, BRB Minutes, 14 April 1994, and Edmonds, in Freeman and Shaw, *All Change*, p. 59.

170 Staffing out-turn for 1 April 1994, BRB Ctee on Restructuring Minutes, 3 March 1994.

171 Allen had been BRB Director of Finance, Ellis Deputy MD, InterCity and Director, TQM, Howarth, MD, Union Railways, Ogilvie Director, Infrastructure, NSE, and Osborne the Board's Solicitor. In addition, Bob Hill, MD, BRPB, became Director, Property, Gerald O'Keane, Director, Procurement, undertook the same role for Railtrack, while David Armstrong, Personnel Director, TLF, became Director, Human Resources. The only outsiders were David Moss, from the DTp's aviation section,

who became Commercial Director, and Roderick Muttram, Director of Electrical Engineering, appointed from Thorn-EMI.

172 Muttram was appointed after a long search in November 1993: BRB Ctee on Restructuring Minutes, 18 November 1993. The five non-engineers had been operating or planning managers. BRB; BRB Minutes, 1 July 1993; Cornell, Memo, n.d., BRB Ctee on Restructuring Minutes, 15 July 1993; Interview with James Jerram, 14 December 2000.

173 Welsby–BRB senior executives, 18 June 1993, BRB Ctee on Restructuring Minutes, 1 July 1993; BRB Privatisation News, 1 July 1993.

174 The Board Executive had initially agreed to 'ring-fence' posts, that is, to offer re-engagement to the top two members of a franchise company if they were not taken on by the successful franchisee. However, this was not implemented, and instead extended notice periods and a special employment protection scheme were introduced. Board Exec. Special Minutes, 11 January 1993; Palmer, Memo on 'Senior Appointments', 20 January 1993, BRB Ctee on Restructuring Minutes, 22 January 1993; Welsby, Memo on 'Appointment of Managing Directors of Shadow Franchises and TOC's', 4 August 1993, BRB Ctee on Restructuring Minutes, 5 August 1993; BRB Remuneration Committee Minutes, 4 August and 8 September 1994, 9 February 1995; BRB Minutes, 8 September and 6 October 1994.

175 Paul Watkinson, Memo on 'Summary of Senior Appointments', n.d., ibid., 3 March 1994. The others were Dominic Booth (IOW), John Buxton (Cardiff), and Richard Parkins (Merseyrail).

176 A policy known as 'Project Thomas'. See Watkinson, Memos on 'Project Thomas', 2 December 1993, and 'Senior Executive Retention', 12 January 1994, BRB Minutes, 2 December 1993 and 12 January 1994.

177 Goldson, Memo on 'Restructuring Progress: Key Issues and Shadow Franchise Propositions', n.d., BRB Ctee on Restructuring Minutes, 15 July 1993.

178 DTp, *New Opportunities*, para. 87.

179 MacGregor–Reid (II), 12 February 1993, Reid's Papers.

180 DTp, *Railway Pensions after Privatisation: The Government's Proposals* (January 1993), paras. 10, 20, 22, 26, 30, 37; Board Exec. Minutes, 25 February 1993; MacGregor–Reid (II), 20 May 1993, Reid's Papers; BRB Privatisation News, 20 May 1993.

181 'Notes of Meeting at Government Actuary's Department 5 July 1993', 6 July 1993, BRB PRI Box 9574; Jerram, Memo on 'BR Privatisation Pensions', 7 July 1993, Board Exec. Minutes, 8 July 1993.

182 Jerram, Memo, cit.; Reid–MacGregor, 8 and 10 June 1993, Reid's Papers.

183 Reid (II)–Brown, 12 July 1993, Reid's Papers; David Adams (Chief Executive, BR Pension Trustee Co.) and Vernon Hince (Chairman, BR Pension Scheme Management Committee), letter to BR Pension Scheme Pensioners, 8 July 1993, BRB PRI Box 9574.

184 BRB Privatisation News, 21 July 1993; Adams–Gareth Hadley (Chairman, BT Police Superannuation Fund Management Committee) and Alex McKinnell (Chairman, BR Superannuation Fund Management Committee), 21 July 1993, BRB PRI Box 9574.

185 David C. Kirk (Director, Privatisation Studies, BRB)–Board Exec. and Restructuring Group, 22 July 1993, BRB PRI Box 9574; Lord Peyton, *Parl. Deb. (Lords)*, 5th ser. (Session 1993–4), vol. 555, 26 May 1994, cols. 864–5; Interview with Lord Peyton, 1 November 1999.

186 Ashmore–Reid (II), 4 August, 5 and 13 October 1993, Reid–MacGregor, 16 August 1993 and reply, 4 October 1993, Reid's Papers; MacGregor, *Parl. Deb. (Commons)*, 6th ser. (Session 1992–3), vol. 231, 2 November 1993, cols. 161–5; Peyton, *Parl. Deb. (Lords)*, 5th ser. (Session 1993–4), vol. 551, 19 January 1994, cols. 606, vol. 554, 19 April 1994, cols. 87–90.

187 See Montagu–Watkinson, 31 March 1994 and Freeman–Frank Dobson MP, 19 May 1994, BRB PRI Box 9574.

188 Railways Pensions Scheme Order 1994; Railway Pensions (Protection and Designation of Schemes) Order 1994; Railways Pension (Transfer and Miscellaneous Provisions) Order 1994. A fourth Order provided for deferral of payments of pensioner benefits preserved under the Transport Act 1980.

189 Reid (II)–MacGregor, 3 December 1992, Reid's Papers.

190 Interview with Allan Leach, 19 January 2001.

191 Freeman–Reid (II), 20 January 1993, Reid's Papers; DTp Press Notice, 20 January 1993.

192 Ashmore–Reid (II), 3 March 1993, Kirk–Reid, 30 June 1993, Reid–Freeman, 11 March, 30 June, and 13 October 1993, Welsby–Freeman, 24 September 1993, Freeman–Reid (II), 2 April, 7 September, and 8 November 1993, Reid's Papers; OIG, in MacGregor–Salmon, 22 March 1994, cit., para. 31; Alan Deboo (Director, Group Personnel Service, BRB), Memo, 1 September 1995, BRB PRI TF4/13, Box 9422.

193 Cf. Wolmar, in Freeman and Shaw, *All Change*, pp. 128–9. By no means all share this assessment: cf. Interview with Sir George Young, 28 March 2001.

194 Swift, 'Chairman's Comments', p. 184.

195 Reid (II)–MacGregor, 31 March 1994, and reply, 27 May 1994, Reid's Papers.

Chapter 13

1 Archie Norman, 'The new railway—serving the customer', Conservative Party News Release, 23 May 2000. It should be pointed out that Norman did not dissent from any decision while a Board member.

2 Sir William Francis–MacGregor, 24 June 1994, BRB 48-2; Sir George Young–Welsby, 2 August 1995, Welsby's Papers, Sec Box 2124. Peter Allen also advised on safety matters. There were 12 Board meetings in 1994, but 24 in 1995, 35 in 1996, and 11 in the first three months of 1997.

3 It had been the intention to sell the Property Board as a single property agency, but after the May 1997 election John Prescott, the Deputy Prime Minister, advised the Board to retain it. BRB Minutes, 6 February, 10 April, and 4 September 1997.

4 Prescott–Welsby, 25 July 1997, Trewin, Memo on 'Role of the Board', 2 September 1997, BRB Minutes, 4 September 1997; DETR, *New Deal for Transport: Better for Everyone* (July 1998); Lord MacDonald (Minister for Transport)–Sir Alastair Morton (Chairman, BRB), 15 February 2000, reproduced in BRB, *R&A 1999–2000*, pp. 6–8; Transport Act 2000, c. 38.

5 Cf. Joy, 'Public and Private Railways' and Welsby and Nichols, 'The Privatisation of Britain's Railways', *Journal of Transport Economics and Policy*, cit.; Freeman and Shaw, *All Change*; Bill Bradshaw, 'The Rail Industry', in Helm and Jenkinson, *Competition in Regulated Industries*; Harris and Godward, *The Privatisation of British Rail*.

6 Campbell, Memo, n.d., BRB Minutes, 10 April 1997.

7 Welsby–Sir George Young (SoS for Transport), 14 December 1995, and reply, 21 December 1995, Welsby's Papers, Sec Box 2124; Joy, 'Public and Private Railways', 41.

8 BRB Minutes, 4 August 1994; Alan Nichols (Director of Planning & Business Analysis, BRB), Memo on 'Passenger Franchise Bids', n.d., BRB Minutes, 7 November 1996; NAO, *Office of Passenger Rail Franchising (OPRAF): the award of the first three passenger rail franchises*, 23 October 1996, P.P. 1995–6, HC701; 'Franchising timetable melt-down', *Modern Railways*, August 1995, p. 462; Clive Charlton, 'The Structure of the New Railway', in Freeman and Shaw, *All Change*, p. 42.

9 BRB Minutes, 8 February 1996; *Modern Railways*, March 1996, p. 137; Grantham, thesis, 1998, pp. 149–50. The LTS franchise was re-let in May 1996.

10 BRB Minutes, 4 May, 21 September, and 7 December 1995; Wolmar, 'Creating the Passenger Rail Franchises' and Wolmar and Ford, 'Selling the Passenger Railway', in Freeman and Shaw, *All Change*, pp. 133–6, 150–2, 156–7; *Rail Privatisation News*, 24 August 1995, p. 3, 14 December 1995, p. 1, 25 January 1996, p. 4; *Modern Railways*, February 1997, p. 68; Grantham, thesis, 1998, pp. 127–30, 139–42, 155–71.

11 Alan Williams, *Modern Railways*, September 1996, p. 606.

12 NAO, *Privatisation of the Rolling Stock Leasing Companies*, 5 March 1998, P.P. 1997–8, HC576, esp. Appendix 3; HC Select Committee on Public Accounts, *65th Report on Privatisation of the Rolling Stock Leasing Companies*, 9 August 1998, P.P. 1997–8, HC782; *Guardian*, 18 December 1997; Paul Foot, 'ROSCO Gold', *Private Eye*, 21 August 1998, p. 26; Christian Wolmar, 'How Labour fed the fattest cat of all', *New Statesman*, 30 October 1998, p. 27.

13 Brian Mawhinney (SoS for Transport), Minute on 'Privatisation of Railtrack', 9 November 1994; Kenneth Clarke (Chancellor of the Exchequer), Note to John Major on 'Privatisation of Railtrack', 15 November 1994, BRB Secretary's Papers, Box 1868. The NAO found that £1.5bn. more might have been raised with a sale in stages: NAO, *The Flotation of Railtrack. Report by the Comptroller and Auditor General*, 16 December 1998, P.P. 1998–9, HC25.

14 BRB, Memo to John Prescott on 'Railway Policy Matters', 6 May 1997, BRB Minutes, 15 May 1997.

15 NAO, *Flotation of Railtrack*, cit.; HC Select Committee on Public Accounts, *24th Report on the Flotation of Railtrack*, 14 July 1999, P.P. 1998–9, HC256; 'Britain's £10 bn rail rip-off', *Evening Standard*, 19 August 1998, p. 37. Recent events have caused Railtrack's share price to slide. On 4 April 2001 the price was only £4.48p.

16 Cf. Christian Wolmar, 'The core question of the rail crisis—what is Railtrack for?', *Rail*, 4–17 April 2001, pp. 26–7.

17 Richard Davies, 'The privatisation of British Rail', and Chris A. Nash, 'Privatisation and deregulation in railways: an assessment of the British approach', in Bill Bradshaw and Helen Lawton Smith (eds.), *Privatization and Deregulation of Transport* (Basingstoke, 2000), pp. 110–16, 170–1. The increase in subsidy was something accepted by the DTp as early as November 1992; DTp, Memo on 'Financing and Subsidy of BR Services', 5 November 1992, FWG Minutes, 11 November 1992. We should also note that Japan's apparently successful privatisation has left the industry with a massive debt burden and no improvement in rail freight: Fumitoshi Mizutani and Kiyoshi Nakamura, 'Privatization of the Japan National Railway: Overview of

Performance Changes', *International Journal of Transport Economics*, 24(1) (February 1997), 95–6, and eid., 'Japan Railways since Privatisation', in Bradshaw and Lawton Smith, *Privatization and Deregulation*, pp. 228–9.

18 NAO, *British Rail Maintenance Limited: Sale of Maintenance Depots*, 19 July 1996, P.P. 1995–6, HC583; *Modern Railways*, July 1996, p. 428, September 1996, p. 552; Bob Linnard (Assistant Secretary, DTp)–Jerram, 19 December 1995, and reply, 21 February 1996, Jerram's Papers, A19/BM, file 2, A19/1/BM, file 3.

19 BRB Minutes, 2 May 1996; NAO, *Department of the Environment, Transport and the Regions: the Sale of Railfreight Distribution*, 26 March 1999, P.P. 1998–9, HC280; BRB, *R&A 1999/2000*, p. 25; Julia Clarke, 'Selling the Freight Railway', in Freeman and Shaw, *All Change*, p. 196.

20 Roger Salmon, quoted by Wolmar and Ford, in Freeman and Shaw, *All Change*, p. 148.

21 Reid (II)–Mawhinney, 24 February 1995 and reply, 8 March 1995, Welsby's Papers, Sec Box 2124; BRB Minutes, 7 September, 5 October, and 2 November 1995; Welsby, Memo on 'BR Bidding for Franchises', 5 June 1996, BRB Minutes, 6 June 1996; Nichols, Memo cit., BRB Minutes, 7 November 1996. Fare capping was announced by the Franchising Director in May 1995, with increases limited to the movement of the RPI for 1996–8, and to the RPI − 1 for 1999–2003.

22 See '*Rail Analysis: Britain's Railways*', *Rail*, 2–15 May 2001, pp. 18–22.

23 Reid (II)–Mawhinney, 15 November 1994, and reply, 19 November 1994, BRB Secretary's Papers, Box 1868.

24 Nichols, Business Performance Report, 2 May 1995, BRB Minutes, 2 May 1995, and cf. Welsby, reported in BRB Minutes, 8 August 1994, 12 January, 9 February, and 3 August 1995. When the effect of distorting elements (strikes, etc.) were eliminated, 25 measures showed reduced performance.

25 CRUCC, *Annual Report 1995/96*, pp. 34–8; *1996/97*, p. 37; *1997/98*, pp. 37–41.

26 MacGregor–Reid (II), 7 July 1994, Welsby–Sir George Young, 1 July 1996, and reply, 3 July 1996, Welsby's Papers, Sec Box 2124.

27 Roger Ford, *Modern Railways*, December 1999, p. 921; Chris Green, 'Phoenix from the Ashes', Sir Robert Reid Lecture, Institute of Logistics and Transport (February 2001).

28 DTp/DETR, *TSGB 1993/4, 2000*.

29 Steer Gleave Davies, *Financing Public Transport: How does Britain compare?* (March 1992), cit. in HC Transport Commitee, *Second Report on the Future of the Railways*, 1993, p. lxxvi.

30 *Independent*, 28 August 2000; Barry Doe, *Rail*, 21 February–6 March 2001, pp. 403–4.

31 Roger Ford, *Modern Railways*, February 2000, p. 4; Interview with Ford, 2001.

32 Strategic Rail Authority, *A Strategic Agenda* (March 2001).

33 See Appendix A, Table A.1; OPRAF, *Annual Report 1997/8*.

34 Cf. Bill Bradshaw, 'New Directions for Britain's Railways', in Freeman and Shaw, *All Change*, p. 231. This figure, derived from a parliamentary answer by Sir George Young on 10 February 1997, is based on an estimate of restructuring, privatisation, franchising, and regulation for the six years since 1990/1. Other costs could also be added: see the discussion in Harris and Godward, *Privatisation of British Rail*, pp. 129ff., and Grantham, thesis, p. 175.

35 Alan Marshall (Information Services Officer, BRB, 1979–84), in *Rail*, 4–17 April 2001, p. 43; Interviews with Burrage, 2000, Ford, 2001.

36 Christopher Campbell, Memo on 'MBO bidders', n.d., BRB Minutes, 3 July 1997.

37 Roger Ford, 'Musical chairs in TOCs', *Modern Railways*, May 1997, p. 264; 'Who runs the railway—2000?', ibid., July 2000, pp. 18–20.

38 Terence R. Gourvish, 'British Rail and the Department of Transport-Treasury Relationship: Social versus Economic Goals', paper to Business History Conference, Miami, April 2001.

39 Dieter Helm, 'A Critique of Rail Regulation', Beesley Lecture, 17 October 2000. I am grateful to Sir Geoffrey Owen for this reference.

40 Welsby and Nichols, 'Privatisation', 76.

Index

Index

Index

Index

Index

Index

Index

Index

Index

Index

Index

Index

Index

Index

Index prepared by Indexing Specialists